W O M E N

and | INTERNATIONAL
HUMAN RIGHTS
LAW

Volume 1
Introduction to Women's
Human Rights Issues

W O M E N

and | # INTERNATIONAL
HUMAN RIGHTS
LAW

Volume 1

Editors | Kelly D. Askin
Dorean M. Koenig

Transnational Publishers, Inc.
Ardsley, New York

Library of Congress Cataloging-in-Publication Data

Women and international human rights law / edited by Kelly D. Askin and
   Dorean M. Koenig.
      v. cm.
      Includes bibliographical references.
      ISBN 1-57105-064-7
      1. Women's rights.   2. Human rights.   3. Women—Legal status,
   laws, etc.   I. Askin, Kelly Dawn.   II. Koenig, Dorean Marguerite
   K644.w64   1998
   341.4'81—dc21   98-20643
                                                                              CIP

Manufactured in the United States of America.

CONTENTS

Section I
Introduction to Legal Discourse

Section II
Women Mobilizing into the Twenty First Century

Section III
Common Abuses of Women Around the World

Section IV
Common Human Rights Issues Affecting Women

ABOUT THE CONTRIBUTORS

Kelly D. Askin has served as Visiting Scholar at the Center for Civil and Human Rights, Notre Dame Law School, since 1995. She has a B.S., J.D., and Ph.D. (Law). Her revised doctoral dissertation, *War Crimes Against Women: Prosecution in International War Crimes Tribunals*, was published in 1997. The primary emphasis of most of Dr. Askin's lectures, research, publications, consultations, and legal practice concerns women's issues in international human rights law, international humanitarian law, and international criminal law, and she has participated in international conferences in these areas. Dr. Askin is the Chair of the 1999 and 2000 Program Committee of the American Branch of the International Law Association's International Law Weekend, an annual conference.

Charlotte Bunch, Founder and Executive Director of the Center for Women's Global Leadership at Douglass College, Rutgers, has been an activist, author, and organizer in the women's and civil rights movements for three decades. She was inducted into the National Women's Hall of Fame in 1996. Professor Bunch has edited seven anthologies, and her latest books are *Passionate Politics: Feminist Theory in Action* and *Demanding Accountability: The Global Campaign and Vienna Tribunal for Women's Human Rights*. She is currently Professor in the Bloustein School of Planning and Public Policy at Rutgers University, and serves on the boards of the Ms. Foundation for Women and the Human Rights Watch Women's Rights Division.

Douglass Cassel, Executive Director of the International Human Rights Institute of DePaul University College of Law, and of its Jeanne and Joseph Sullivan Program for Human Rights in the Americas, received his J.D. from Harvard Law School in 1972. Former legal advisor to the United Nations Truth Commission for El Salvador, he teaches, publishes and advises governments, international organizations and nongovernmental organizations on matters of human rights. Professor Cassel gratefully acknowledges the valuable research assistance of Ms. Rini Gosh, a Dartmouth College undergraduate who served as an intern at the Institute during 1996.

Christina M. Cerna is Senior Specialist in International Human Rights. She has been employed by the Organization of American States since January 1979; most of Ms. Cerna's career has been with the Inter-American Commission on Human Rights. From 1989–1990 she was Visiting Fellow at St. Anthony's College in Oxford, England and from 1992–1994 she was seconded to the UN Centre for Human Rights in Geneva to participate in the organization of the UN World Conference on Human Rights in Vienna.

Hilary Charlesworth is Professor and Director of the Centre for International and Public Law at the Australian National University. She is a recipient of the Frank Knox Memorial Scholarship, the Robert Gordon Menzies Scholarship to Harvard, and a Fulbright Scholarship. Professor Charlesworth holds a B.A. and L.L.B. from the University of Melbourne and an S.J.D. from Harvard Law School. She is Deputy Chair of the National Consultative Committee on the World Summit for Social Development and has been a Hearing Commissioner with the Human Rights and Equal Opportunity Commission. Professor Charlesworth is currently a member of the Foreign Affairs Council of the Minister for Foreign Affairs, Board member of the Diplomacy Training Program and Defense of Children International (Australia), and is President of the Australian and New Zealand Society of International Law.

Lois Chiang, a lawyer, is Director, Special Projects, at the University of Toronto Faculty of Law. She researches trafficking in women as a global phenomenon, focusing on trafficking women in Canada and China. Other areas of research include international human rights, human rights in China, and violence against women. Ms. Chiang was formerly an associate at Stikeman, Elliott in Toronto.

Radhika Coomaraswamy received her B.A. from Yale University, her J.D. from Columbia University, and her LL.M. from Harvard University. She is the author of *Sri Lanka: A Crisis of Legitimacy*, and co-editor of *The Judiciary in Plural Societies, Ethical Dilemmas of Development* and *An Introduction to Social Theory*. She was appointed United Nations Special Rapporteur on Violence Against Women by the United Nations Human Rights Commission.

Leilani Farha received her B.A. and her LL.B. from the University of Toronto. She is the Women's Housing Rights Programme Coordinator and Legal Advisor for the Centre on Housing Rights and Evictions, an international nongovernmental organization based in Geneva, Switzerland. Ms. Farha works with individuals and organizations around the world to promote and protect the right to housing and the right to be free from forced evictions. She would like to thank Lois Chiang for her invaluable editorial comments on this piece and David Wiseman for his tireless support and enthusiasm for her work in this field.

Samantha Frost is Visiting Associate Professor in Women's Studies at the University of California, Santa Cruz. She received her doctoral degree in Political Science from Rutgers University. Professor Frost has been a consultant at the Center for Women's Global Leadership.

Margaret E. Galey holds an M.A. and Ph.D in International Relations and has taught public international law and international organization on faculties of political science. As a member of the professional staff of the then Committee on Foreign Affairs, US House of Representatives, she served as Congressional Staff Advisor to the 1980 and 1985 World Women's Conferences and represented the Commission to Study the Organization of Peace at the 1975 World Conference on IWY. She has authored numerous Committee reports and professional journal articles and has contributed chapters to *Women, Politics and the UN* (Greenwood, 1995), and *Women, Gender and World Politics* (Bergen and Garvey, 1995), and was a US Member of the UN Expert Group on the Beijing Platform of Action.

Isabelle R. Gunning is Professor of Law at Southwestern University School of Law in Los Angeles. She teaches or has taught international human rights, immigration law, women and the law, international dispute resolution, and several clinical or skill oriented classes, especially in the areas of interviewing, counseling, and negotiation. Professor Gunning's research interests have been primarily in the areas of international and transnational law with special concern in the interest of women of color. Her community work includes working with immigrant and refugee women in the United States.

Jill Guzman is an attorney with the Chicago office of Fragomen, Del Ray & Bernsen, P.C. Former Grants Coordinator of DePaul's International Human Rights Law Institute, she earned her J.D. in 1985 from DePaul University College of Law. She has interned in several human rights institutions, including the Inter-American Court of Human Rights.

Berta Esperanza Hernández-Truyol is Professor of Law at St. John's University School of Law. She received her J.D. with honors from Albany Law School of Union University and an LL.M. in International Legal Studies from New York University School of Law. Professor Hernández-Truyol has attended and participated in the Fourth World Conference on Women, the Social Summit, and the International Conference on Population and Development. She has also served on the Commission on Judicial Nomination of the State of New York, the Second Circuit Task Force on Gender, Racial and Ethnic Fairness in the Courts. The St. John's University School of Law Faculty Research Program supported her work. She would like to thank Kimberly Johns (the most terrific research assistant for whom anyone could hope) for her outstanding work.

Courtney W. Howland received her B.A. at Barnard College, Columbia University and her J.D. at Yale University. She is Visiting Scholar in Residence at Georgetown University Law Center where she was Visiting Associate Professor of Law, teaching international and comparative law of the rights of women. Professor Howland is also Scholar in Residence at The George Washington University Law School, and Senior Fellow at the International Rule of Law Center at the same university in Washington, DC. She is pursuing a project that addresses the contemporary rise of religious fundamentalism in major religions and its impact on women's rights. Professor Howland would like to thank Michael Singer who read drafts of this chapter. His extensive comments and invaluable insights are reflected at many points throughout the text.

Dorean M. Koenig is Professor of Law at the Thomas M. Cooley Law School. She is a member of the American Board of the Association Internationale de Droit Penal. She represented the International A.I.D.P. at the Fourth World Conference on Women in Beijing and Huarou, China, in 1995, and the International Criminal Court Treaty Plenipotentiary Conference in Rome in 1998. In addition to her work in the area of women's human rights, Professor Koenig helped draft text for both

Siracusa drafts for an ICC, and published critiques of the Draft Statute for the International Law Association (American Branch) Reports. She has published and lectured on International Human Rights Development on the death penalty and its relationship to the ABA Resolution for a Moratorium. She is the first reporter for the Michigan Standard Criminal Jury Instructions and author of the original commentaries. In 1970, she and her partner, Clarice Jobes, as members of one of the first feminist law firms in the state, Koenig, LeBost and Jobes, successfully litigated the first pregnancy leave case in Michigan.

Lisa M. Kois, B.A., J.D., is a long time advocate for women's rights, previously an advocate for battered women and victim-survivors of rape and presently works as a human rights lawyer specializing in the human rights of women. She is currently living and working—as consultant to the UN Special Rapporteur on Violence Against Women—in Colombo, Sri Lanka, where she also works with local NGOs doing legal, literary and human rights work in the context of Sri Lanka's armed conflict. She has written extensively on issues of human rights and violence against women, recently completing articles on women and torture and on Sri Lanka's Commissions on the 'Disappeared.'

Robin S. Levi is Advocacy Director for the Women's Institute for Leadership Development for Human Rights, a United States women's organization based in San Francisco. She was previously a fellow at the Women's Rights Division of Human Rights Watch and has written and spoken extensively on women's human rights both domestically and internationally. Ms. Levi graduated from Georgetown University's School of Foreign Service and Stanford Law School.

Ann Lucas is Assistant Professor of sociology and criminal justice at the University of Texas, El Paso. She received her J.D. from the Boalt Hall School of Law, University of California, Berkeley, in 1991. She completed her Ph.D. in Jurisprudence and Social Policy also at the University of California, Berkeley, 1997. Professor Lucas is a member of the State Bar of California. For their comments, critical readings, and moral support, she would like to thank Sarah Armstrong, Brooke Bedrick, Jo Doezema, Tom Ginsburg, Kaaryn Gustafson, Mark Harris, Robert Katsura, David Lieberman, Jean Lucas, Kristin Luker, Valerie Margolis, Shelly Messinger, Bronwen Morgan, Bill Nelson, Laura Beth Nielson, Sue Ochi, Tom Scanlon, Marge Schultz, Reva Siegel, and Barbara Sullivan. Thanks especially to Carolyn Patty Blum for her mentioning and sharing of source material.

Valerie L. Oosterveld is Director of the International Human Rights Programme at the Faculty of Law, University of Toronto, and a J.S.D. candidate at Columbia Law School. Prior to this, she practiced labor and employment law at Fasken Campbell Godfrey in Toronto, Canada. In 1997, she co-taught "International Women's Human Rights Law" with Professor Rebecca Cook at the Faculty of Law. She has published and presented in the field of international women's human rights, as well as on Canadian labor rights. Ms. Oosterveld attended the 1995 Fourth World Conference on Women in Beijing, China, as well as interned at the 1993 World Conference on Human Rights in Vienna, Austria.

Dianne Otto B.A., LL.B. (Hons), LL.M. has been a lecturer in international and criminal law at the University of Melbourne since 1994. During 1993 she was the Victorian coordinator of Amnesty International Australia. Prior to this she spent many years working in community development and advocacy with a diversity of grass roots groups including women, young people and consumers of psychiatric services. In addition to her work in the area of women's human rights, Professor Otto has written critically about post-Cold War democratic developments, issues of indigenous peoples' sovereignty, international NGOs, peacekeeping, and on re-thinking the 'universality' of human rights law.

Robin Phillips is Director of the Women's Human Rights Project at Minnesota Advocates for Human Rights. She has investigated human rights violations against women in Romania, Bulgaria, Albania, and Macedonia and has organized international conferences on issues of women's human rights. Ms. Phillips received her law degree from Northwestern University in Chicago, Illinois and practiced law for several years before joining Minnesota Advocates. Her previous law practice included employment discrimination and sexual harassment litigation. She would like to thank Marjorie Allard and Bonnie Kim for their research assistance.

Neil A.F. Popović is an attorney at Heller Ehrman White & McAuliffe in San Francisco, California, and a lecturer at the University of California, Berkeley (Boalt Hall School of Law). He is also Director of Earth Justice Legal Defense Fund (formerly Sierra Club Legal Defense Fund), San Francisco, California—a United Nations Program. Mr. Popović received his A.B. in political science at the University of California, Berkeley in 1983, his J.D. at the University of California, Berkeley (Boalt Hall) in 1987, and his M.A. in international relations at The Fletcher School of Law and Diplomacy, Tufts University in 1992.

Niamh Reilly now lives in Dublin, Ireland, where she teaches courses on human rights and feminist and political theory at Trinity College, Dublin and with the Open University. From 1990 to 1996 she was a Senior Programme Associate with the Center for Women's Global Leadership, Rutgers University, New Jersey. Ms. Reilly is a founding and steering committee member of the Women's Human Rights Campaign, Ireland, and a member of the Joint NGO Department of Foreign Affairs Standing Committee on Human Rights. She holds graduate degrees in economics and politics, and has written extensively on women's human rights. Ms. Reilly is currently completing a Ph.D. on Human Rights and Global Feminism. She is co-author with Charlotte Bunch on *Demanding Accountability: The Global Campaign and Vienna Tribunal for Women's Human Rights*, and the author of *Without Reservation*.

Cheryl Thomas is Adjunct Professor at the University of Minnesota Law School where she teaches Women's International Human Rights. She was Founder and First Director of the Women's Program at Minnesota Advocates for Human Rights. Professor Thomas has traveled extensively in Central and Eastern Europe and in Mexico to work with domestic violence advocates in those regions. She has co-authored three human rights reports on domestic violence in Romania, Bulgaria, and Nepal. In 1995, she coordinated the Minnesota Advocates for Human Rights delegation to the Fourth World Conference on Women in Beijing, China. Professor Thomas would like to thank Mary Schou Viller for her research assistance.

Dorothy Q. Thomas is a consultant with the Shaler Adams Foundation.In 1998 she received a MacArthur Fellowship to continue her work. Ms. Thomas served as Founding Director of the Human Rights Watch, Women's Division from 1990 to 1998. In 1994 she received a Peace Fellowship at the Bunting Institute at Radcliffe College to study the relationship between the international women's human rights movement and work on women's rights in the United States. She has a masters degree in literary theory and women's studies from Georgetown University, which recently awarded her an honorary doctorate. She is the author/editor of several reports and articles including *All Too Familiar: Sexual Abuse of Women in the U.S. State Prisons* and "Advancing Rights Protection in the United States: an Internationalized Advocacy Strategy."

Jennifer C. Wallace has a B.A. in Political Science from the University of Montana. She recently completed work for a Masters in International Politics emphasizing human rights and conflict resolution at the Graduate School of International Studies, University of Denver. Currently, she is working for MINUGUA, the United Nations peacebuilding mission in Guatemala, in the area of strengthening civil society including increasing the participation of women.

FOREWORD

This treatise was first conceived in 1993 as a result of two events: the Vienna World Conference on Human Rights, where a broad range of various women's issues was discussed, and my frustration at the unavailability of adequate resources on some of these same issues while working on a dissertation involving the prosecution of war crimes against women in international tribunals.

The more I searched for information and causation on, and prosecution and redress of, violence against women, the more frustrated I became. Slowly, an outline began emerging—first in my head, and then on paper—on specific issues that affect women in all regions of the world. I became convinced that a work was desperately needed which compiled, explained, analyzed, and presented solutions to most of the major issues affecting women worldwide. Thus, the focus of the work became human rights of women rather than simply violence against women, although violence has remained an important theme of the volumes. It was originally conceived as a reference guide, but it eventually developed into a much more substantive resource. After receiving encouraging responses from publishers to a preliminary outline, I fleshed it out over the next couple of years.

After completing my doctoral thesis, I accepted the position of Visiting Scholar at the Center for Civil and Human Rights, Notre Dame Law School, with the goal of turning the outline into reality. Early on, I sought the advice, and subsequently the assistance, of my law school mentor, Professor Dorean Koenig. After fine-tuning the outline, we surveyed, and eventually solicited, experts in each field to write the pertinent chapters. Dorean and I agreed that it was best to try to get a wide variety of contributors from each region of the world, including scholars, lawyers, judges, activists, government personnel, social scientists, and leaders of nongovernmental organizations. Ideally, we tried to get persons with hands-on expertise. For instance, we got a member of the Committee on the Elimination of Discrimination against Women to write the chapter on that body; for the chapter on women's issues in the World Health Organization, we found a person who worked at the WHO in the field of human rights to write what that organization was doing on behalf of women; we found a human rights lawyer who had worked in environmental law for many years and who was sensitive to gender issues to write about women and the environment. Those we targeted as authors depended in large part on the particular topics at hand.

In working with over 100 contributors from throughout the world, we as editors were dependent on timely submission and continuous commitment by the authors to produce articulate, knowledgeable, and publishable manuscripts. We were rarely disappointed, and consequently express our heartfelt gratitude to those authors who made every effort to honor their commitments in a professional and thoughtful manner. This work, the first volume of what is expected to eventually entail four volumes, is the culmination of hard work and a steadfast commitment from all participants to protect and promote the human rights of women everywhere.

Kelly D. Askin

Although this work has always remained primarily and oftentimes the sole work, as well as the dedicated responsibility, of Kelly Askin, I have been pleased to work in the background with her, my former student and research assistant, and to watch the incredible energy and enthusiasm she has brought to this project. Everyone who knows her knows of Kelly's dedication to the field of human rights and to women everywhere. It was my privilege to attend the Fourth World Conference on Women and to participate in the energy of that time and place, and to bring some of that to this venture.

Dorean M. Koenig

ACKNOWLEDGMENTS

I would like to express my continuing gratitude and love to my parents, Carole and Otis Askin. There are also many others, in addition to my family, to whom I extend my deepest appreciation and affection for all the support, joy, or inspiration they give me (often without their knowing it), either in working on this project or in life in general: Jenny and Graeme Addie, Dot Barbaree, Ann and Larry Bennett, Kitty Butler, Jingle Davis, Bina D{{quotesingle}}Costa, Bonnie and Barry Dubner, Helen Durham, Jane Gronow, Pauline Katshie, Dorean Koenig, Polly Langston, Gayla McSwain, Garth Meintjes, Gabriella Mossi, Carrie Nelle Moye, Faustina Pereira, Judy Potter, Pat Potter, Midori Sasaki, Dinah Shelton, Luma Sherif, Kerry Smith, and Mariela Tenembaum. We also extend our deepest appreciation and respect to those at Transnational who have worked so diligently, professionally, and graciously to making this treatise a reality, most especially Heike Fenton, Adriana Maida, Elizabeth Costello, and Maria Angelini.

Kelly D. Askin

In addition to the gratitude expressed to our many authors and our publishers, I would like to add my personal thanks to them and to the following: My secretaries, Wendy Caudill and Kathy Curtis, and my students, now graduates: Mary Dwyer, Dan Stephaniuk; and Lori Zellers.

Dorean M. Koenig

GENERAL INTRODUCTION

Hilary Charlesworth

A decade ago, a work on women's international human rights would have been one slim book instead of a sizable project consisting of multiple volumes. The idea of women's human rights in international institutions and academic discussion was confined until recently to a limited category of rights. "Women's rights" were generally understood to be a product of those international instruments that dealt specifically with women, including the right to some measures of protection in particular circumstances (e.g., in times of armed conflict), and the right to freedom from discrimination on the basis of sex. The major international instrument on women's rights is the Convention on the Elimination of All Forms of Discrimination Against Women (the Women's Convention), adopted by the United Nations in 1979. As its title indicates, the Women's Convention is concerned with making discrimination against women illegal in international law. The Committee on the Elimination of Discrimination Against Women (CEDAW) and the U.N. Commission on the Status of Women have been regarded as the institutional foci for women's rights at the international level.

In the past few years, however, there has been a fundamental change in the understanding of women's rights, marked by the preference for the term "women's international human rights" which suggests a bold claim to inclusion in the mainstream rather than specialized side waters. The rallying cry, "Women's Rights are Human Rights," captures this claim aphoristically. The change is the product of an extraordinary amount of work by activists and academics, including almost all the contributors to this work. It is also the result of the commitment of some dedicated international and national civil servants who have worked quietly but consistently within bureaucratic structures. We now have documentation of aspects of women's lives that have been ignored in traditional human rights discourse, some of which is included in various chapters of these volumes. We know that women, although a majority of the world's population, receive a small fraction of its economic, social, and political benefits. Women's quality of life, defined by factors such as health, educational and employment status and opportunities, and political rights, is nowhere equal to that of men's.[1] These statistics indicate great disparities between men and women in the enjoyment of human rights. The reasons for this are complex, but one explanation, documented by many chapters in this book, is that the "general" international human rights regime has been developed

---

1.   UNITED NATIONS DEVELOPMENT PROGRAMME, HUMAN DEVELOPMENT REPORT 1995 (1996).

in a way that tends to exclude women. In other words, the apparently non-gender specific principles of human rights law are in fact quite specific in their relevance and application to men's lives. The universality of coverage asserted in international human rights instruments is therefore chimerical. Much feminist energy is now being devoted to finding ways in which human rights law can become less male and more truly human.

This is not to suggest that the women-specific instruments and institutions are no longer important. Indeed, they have supplied an indispensable basis for the developments charted in this work. They have provided almost the only continuous signals that women had a place, albeit on the margins, in the international legal order. They have allowed valuable occasions for networking among women, inspired the creation of non-governmental organizations dealing with women's rights, and made possible the accumulation of knowledge and expertise. The Second World Conference on Human Rights in Vienna in 1993 and the Fourth World Conference on Women in Beijing in 1995, provided the opportunity for reflection on and consolidation of advances in women's human rights. While a feminist utopia might be ''a world in which gender [is] less relevant and the abstractions of humanity more meaningful . . . [rather than] a world in which women have to speak continuously as women—or men are left to speak as men,''[2] it is clear that for the time being the development of women's international human rights law requires both the support of the women-specific institutions and the ''general'' human rights bodies.

The idea of women's international human rights raises important issues at both a theoretical and practical level. For example, how can the notion that there are rights applicable to women everywhere incorporate the fact of diversity among women? Is it useful to develop international or universal understandings of the position of women, or will this necessarily obscure the situation of many particular groups of women? Is human rights law simply the product of the eighteenth century European ''Enlightenment'' and inappropriately extended to non-European societies?

The contributors to this work offer a variety of answers to these questions. One response is to concentrate on rights abuses that appear to be common to women around the world, such as violence against women. Another response is a focus on abuses of women's rights at a regional or national or communal level. Yet another is to examine abuses against certain categories of women, such as indigenous, refugee, or elderly women. The work contains a great range of information, practice, and theoretical approaches that emphasize the point that there cannot be ''one true story'' of women's lives. At the same time, the work is a celebration of the value of collaborative endeavor among women and the richness to be gained from ''world traveling,'' a technique proposed by Maria Lugones and developed by others in different contexts. Isabelle Gunning has defined world traveling as ''multicultural dialogue and a shared search for areas of overlap, shared concerns and

---

2.   ANNE PHILLIPS, ENGENDERING DEMOCRACY 7 (1991).

values."[3] She has developed a tripartite approach to discussion of human rights issues in other cultures: first, being clear about your own historical context; second, understanding how other women might see you, and third, recognizing the complexities of the context of the other women. Rosi Braidotti suggests the image of "multiple literacies" to visualize the global range of feminisms. This entails "being able to engage in conversation in a variety of styles, from a variety of disciplinary angles, if possible in different languages."[4] Unlike Gunning, however, who contemplates the possibility of creating universally shared values, Braidotti insists that feminists must "relinquish the dream of a common language" and resign ourselves to simply "temporary political consensus on specific issues."[5]

Another concern prompted by this project is to clarify the aim of women's human rights. What are the appropriate goals of this development? Are they simply to ensure that women have the same types of protection as men, or are they more radical? The Vienna Declaration presents the aims as "[t]he full and equal participation of women in political, civil, economic, social and cultural life . . . and the eradication of all forms of discrimination on grounds of sex . . ."[6] and this is endorsed in Section I of the Beijing Platform of Action. The ideal of sex equality incorporated in these international instruments appears limited, then, to a notion of equality of access to a world already constituted by men. As Dianne Otto has written, "[u]nderstood in this way, gender equality forecloses contestation of the base-line of men's experience and glosses over the inequalities between men that it reproduces between women."[7] The aim of women's human rights must be more ambitious than simply "adding women and mixing" with respect to the traditional human rights canon. It requires a rethinking of basic notions such as "civil and political," "economic," and "cultural."

Related issues for the development of women's international human rights include the best strategies for promoting this area. Since the Vienna and Beijing Conferences, an accepted international method is that of "mainstreaming" women's human rights. Thus the Vienna Declaration states that "[t]he human rights of women and of the girl-child are an inalienable, integral and indivisible part of universal human rights. . . . The human rights of women should form an integral part of the United Nations human rights activities."[8] Since Vienna, the human rights

---

3.   Isabelle Gunning, *Arrogant Perception, World-Travelling and Multicultural Feminism: The Case of Female Genital Surgeries*, 23 COL. HUM. RTS. L REV. 189, 191 (1991/92).

4.   Rosi Braidotti, *The Exile, the Nomad, and the Migrant Reflections on International Feminism*, 15 WOMEN'S STUDIES INT'L FORUM 7, 9–10 (1992).

5.   *Id.*

6.   World Conference on Human Rights: The Vienna Declaration and Programme of Action, June 25, 1993, U.N. Doc A/CONF.157/23, at Article 18.

7.   Dianne Otto, *Holding Up Half the Sky, But for Whose Benefit?: A Critical Analysis of the Fourth World Conference on Women*, 6 AUST. FEMINIST L. J. 7, 12 (1996).

8.   Vienna Declaration, *supra* note 6, at Article 18. *See also* Fourth World Conference on Women: Beijing Declaration and Beijing Platform for Action, Oct. 17, 1995, U.N. Doc A/CONF/177/20, at paras. 221, 230 31.

treaty bodies, discussed in volume II of this work, have shown some willingness to incorporate a gender analysis in their work. For example, the Human Rights Committee, which monitors the Covenant on Civil and Political Rights, has begun to devote significant space to women's enjoyment of human rights in its concluding observations on states parties reports.[9] "Mainstreaming" is not without its pitfalls, however. Progress has been haphazard, with some treaty bodies evincing a lack of appreciation of what a gender perspective entails.[10] Another strategy to develop women's human rights, discussed in a number of chapters in this work, has been the articulation of women-specific human rights, such as the right to reproductive self-determination. One problem with this approach is that it may allow women-specific human rights to be assigned a lesser status than "general" human rights. The Beijing Platform for Action, for example, draws a distinction between "universal" human rights and women's rights, effectively assigning the latter category to national jurisdiction and removing it from international scrutiny.[11]

The development of women's human rights is significant in many ways, not least because it provides a transformative challenge to the whole human rights canon. It undermines a particular, gendered form of public/private dichotomy that permeates traditional human rights law. Human rights law has long been seen as applicable to state, as opposed to "private" or non-state, activity and this has meant that many harms that women sustain in the "private" spheres of business, home, and family have not been considered true human rights concerns. Women's international human rights activists and scholars have been successful to some extent in expanding human rights protection to aspects of the "private" (e.g., in the 1993 United Nations Declaration on the Elimination of Violence Against Women).[12] This development has positive ramifications for human rights generally, increasing its flexibility and responsiveness, and extending state accountability.

The contributors to this work generally accept, explicitly and implicitly, that women's international human rights are worth pursuing. It is interesting that there are few doubts expressed about the value of the whole enterprise, unlike, for example, the well-known postmodern skepticism about the use of rights discourse to remedy structural disadvantage.[13] Is it better, as Carol Smart once suggested, to be a feminist journalist than a feminist lawyer? The UN Special Rapporteur on Violence against Women, Radhika Coomaraswamy, has written that "the spirit of human rights may be said to be present in all cultural systems and to have universal

---

9.   Christina Brautigam, *Mainstreaming a gender perspective in the work of the United Nations human rights treaty bodies* (paper given at the American Society of International Law Annual Meeting, April 12, 1997).

10.   *Id.*

11.   Otto, *supra* note 7, at 15–19.

12.   Declaration on the Elimination of Violence Against Women, U.N. Doc A/Res/48/104 (1994), *reproduced in* 33 I.L.M. 1049 (1994).

13.   GARY MINDA, POSTMODERN LEGAL MOVEMENTS (1995).

appeal.''[14] This claim may be a controversial one, at least from the perspective of particular states. In any event, while the political power of the idea of human rights is clear in many societies, we must constantly monitor what the language of rights actually delivers for women. The euphoria sometimes prompted by the vocabulary of human rights may occasionally distract us from the deeply entrenched nature of injustice and the many obstacles to change. Many chapters in these volumes reflect on this issue and reach a broad range of conclusions.

Johan Galtung has argued that human rights protect the ''rock bottom of human existence.''[15] The rock bottom of women's existence has had hitherto little impact of the development of legal norms protecting human rights. This work on women's international human rights provides a very broad understanding of many different forms of rock bottom. It will be a valuable introduction and resource for all those interested in world traveling to improve the position of women.

---

14. RADHIKA COOMARASWAMY, REINVENTING INTERNATIONAL LAW: WOMEN'S RIGHTS AS INTERNATIONAL RIGHTS IN THE INTERNATIONAL COMMUNITY 6 (Harvard Law School Human Rights Program, 1997).

15. JOHAN GALTUNG, HUMAN RIGHTS IN ANOTHER KEY 2 (1994).

INTRODUCTION

Kelly D. Askin

The current situation of women globally can be summed up by paraphrasing Charles Dickens: these are the best of times, these are the worst of times. Women are now represented in more international power positions than in any other time in recorded history. Their increasing presence, though severely limited in number, reflects both the historical practice of discriminating against women, and the emerging trend to end this prejudicial practice of excluding women's participation in high level positions within the United Nations and in various other international fora. Thus, while the presence of women is neither equitable nor comparable by any means, unprecedented progress is finally being made nonetheless in reversing systemic hierarchical imbalances. Notwithstanding these advancements, women are also subjected to escalating violence during wartime and peacetime, and women and girls are egregiously oppressed and otherwise abused inside the home and outside the home, in public life and in private life. With increased technology, information, and struggles for equality come, it seems, greater and more frequent demonstrations of cruelty, power, and subjugation, leaving behind a long, wide trail of gender-based poverty, violence, subordination, and persecution.

Until very recently, when women did participate in the international arena in management-level positions, it was most typically limited to stereotypical gendered or social roles in organizations or agencies concerned with women's issues exclusively or predominately, institutions with marginalized power and limited impact. For instance, historically, the presence of women in prominent positions within United Nations agencies or bodies was restricted to those specifically concerned with women's issues, such as the Committee on the Elimination of Discrimination Against Women (CEDAW), the Division of the Advancement of Women (DAW), the U.N. Development Fund for Women (UNIFEM), and the Commission on the Status of Women (CSW). These entities had comparatively little influence in the international scheme until recently, when they began gaining incremental amounts of prominence and influence.

In the 1990s, major progress has been gained in expanding women's presence both in positions of power outside of bodies concerned exclusively or primarily with women, and in increasing the potency of bodies that are devoted predominately to gender issues. This progress has been largely generated as a result of the lobbying, strategizing, coordinating, educating, and unifying efforts of hundreds of women's groups throughout the world (organized chiefly by the Global Fund for Women) in preparation for the 1993 World Conference on Human Rights in Vienna and the 1995 Fourth World Conference on Women in Beijing.

Because of these efforts, in this last decade of the twentieth century unprecedented advances in women's status took place. In 1993, two women, Gabrielle Kirk McDonald (U.S.) and Elisabeth Odio-Benito (Costa Rica) were elected judges of the International Criminal Tribunal for the former Yugoslavia (ICTY) and, in 1995, Judge Navanethem Pillay (South Africa) became the only woman judge of the International Criminal Tribunal for Rwanda (ICTR). Odio-Benito's replacement is Florence Ndepele Mwachande Mumba (Zambia). In 1997, Judge McDonald became the first woman to be elected President of the Tribunal, succeeding the prominent Italian jurist Mr. Antonio Cassese.

In 1996, Justice Louise Arbour (Canada) replaced prosecutor Judge Richard Goldstone (South Africa), and became the Chief Prosecutor of the ICTY and ICTR. Since February 1995, the Registrar of the ICTY has been Dorothee de Sampayo Garrido-Nijgh (Netherlands). Because there were no women in positions of power during the Nuremberg and Tokyo War Crimes Tribunals, the fact that the Chief Prosecutor of the ICTY and ICTR, the ICTY Registrar, and three judges of the two tribunals are women is indeed historic. Further, the ICTY and ICTR established the new position of gender-issues legal officer, held by the ever capable Patricia Viseur-Sellers (U.S.).

In the early 1990s, Rosalyn Higgins (U.K.) became the first woman to have a permanent seat as a judge on the International Court of Justice. Since its establishment by the U.N. General Assembly in 1947, no woman has yet been named to the influential International Law Commission. Denied a presence, women can neither contribute to the commission's work nor preside over their own destiny in relation to pivotal legal decisions made within the commission.

In 1997, Mary Robinson (Ireland) was appointed High Commissioner for Human Rights, the highest human rights office within the United Nations. Of the thirty-six agencies and specialized agencies of the U.N., four have a women as executive director: the United Nations Children's Fund (UNICEF), headed by Carol Bellamy (U.S.); the United Nations Population Fund (UNFPA), led by Dr. Nafis Sadik (Pakistan); the United Nations High Commissioner for Refugees (UNHCR), led by Sadako Ogata (Japan); and the World Food Program, headed by Catherine Bertini (U.S.).

On the European Court of Human Rights, Elisabeth Palm (Sweden) is the sole woman out of forty judges (four seats are vacant). Of the eleven members of the African Commission on Human and Peoples' Rights, two are women: Julienne Ondziel-Gnelenga (Republic of Congo) and Vera Duarte Martins (Cape Verde). At the Inter-American Commission on Human Rights, none of the seven members are women (in previous years, three of the past forty Commissioners have been women); at the Inter-American Court of Human Rights, there has been only one female judge, Sonia Picado Sotela (Costa Rica), who, until her recent retirement, was also the court's vice-president.

Radhika Coomaraswamy (Sri Lanka) is the U.N. Special Rapporteur on violence against women, and her reports have been invaluable tools in recognizing and combating numerous forms of gender-based violence; the Special Rapporteur on the sale of children, child prostitution, and child pornography is Ofelia Calcetas-Santos (Philippines); Gay McDougall (U.S.) is the Special Rapporteur on systematic rape, slavery, and slavery-like practices during wartime (on behalf of the U.N. Sub-Commission, of which she is an alternate member), and, in 1998, was elected to membership in the Committee on Elimination of Racial Discrimination; Elisabeth Rehn (Finland) is the Special Rapporteur on the situation of human rights in the territory of the former Yugoslavia. Of the thirty-seven Members and Alternate Members of the U.N. Sub-Commission on Prevention of Discrimination of Minorities, there are six female members—Judith Sefi Attah (Nigeria), Erica-Irene A. Daes (Greece), Clemencia Forero Ucros (Colombia), Lucy Gwanmesia (Cameroon), Claire Palley (U.K. of Great Britain and Northern Ireland), and Halima Embarek (Morocco)—and three female Alternate Members, namely, Christy Ezim Mbonu (Nigeria), K. Koufa (Greece), and Gay McDougall (U.S.).

The latest Secretary-General of the United Nations, Mr. Kofi Annan (Ghana), has appointed more women than ever before to leadership positions within the U.N., including Louise Fréchette (Canada) as Deputy Secretary-General of the United Nations; Heidi Tagliavini (Switzerland) as Deputy Special Representative of the Secretary-General for the Republic of Georgia; Rafiah Salim (Malaysia) as Assistant Secretary-General for Human Resources Management; Gro Harlem Brundtland (Norway) as the Director-General-Designate of the World Health Organization; and especially, Angela King (Jamaica) as the Secretary-General Special Advisor on Gender Issues and Advancement of Women.

Other women also are making a significant impact both nationally and internationally, whether as judges on the state high courts, as ambassadors to the United Nations, or in high-level governmental or similar positions. For instance, policy or discriminatory practices may be changed by the decisions of women such as Madeleine Albright, the first woman appointed U.S. Secretary of State; Akila Belembaogo (Burkina Faso), Chairwoman of the Committee on the Rights of the Child; or Socorro Flores (Mexico), a member of the Sixth Committee (the legal committee) of the U.N. General Assembly. Nongovernmental organizations, many of which have women in positions of power, have also made a tremendous impact on the international community and in ensuring women's progress both nationally and internationally, as has the increasing influence of women in such areas as academia, science, politics, economics, law, and medicine.

Thus, while the number of women in high-level, decision-making positions is extremely low, some participation is still a major development over the previous practice of completely excluding women from all positions of authority, or of relegating them to marginalized positions concerned solely with issues pertaining to women or children. Women must continue to diligently ensure the promotion of gender parity on behalf of marginalized women, who represent over half of the domestic and global population. Yet it is important to emphasize that numbers or percentages are not as crucial or determinant as are gender sensitivity and aware-ness. Influential women may not promote the interests of women and powerful men may strive to ensure that issues impacting women are carefully weighed and incorporated. Ideally, all persons in positions of influence would take into account the effects any decisions have on both genders in exercising decision-making pow-ers, and women's issues will be mainstreamed within all laws and policies.

It has only in the last few years been acknowledged that human rights and women's rights are not mutually exclusive terms, but rather that women's rights *are* human rights, that ''human'' rights does not and should not simply mean men's rights, because human rights are applicable to all people and all peoples, women and men, girls and boys. The chapters in this volume represent many of the most fundamental human rights issues affecting women. They are intended to provide an introduction to international human rights affecting women by delineating as-sorted issues that favorably or unfavorably impact upon women, examining many of the most common gender-based abuses globally, and providing insight into the international women's movement that endeavors to empower women. Through education, at all levels and venues and in all corners of the world, on international human rights obligations of state and nonstate actors, and on the negative impact all forms of discriminatory treatment have on both the target group and on society, true progress can be achieved.

The first section of this volume provides a brief overview of the historical treatment of women up to the present rights of women under international law, and analyzes the underlying stereotypes, social or cultural values, and power differ-entials that encourage discriminatory treatment and reinforce the subjugation of women. It looks at the development of international law, including the international human rights laws and international humanitarian laws that have particular rele-vance to women.

The second section discusses the global women's movement by reviewing the current trends, principles, and actions in this movement, and provides perhaps some arguments as to limitations of some of the trends, harmful or discriminatory aspects of certain international instruments, and conceptual differences and difficulties inherent in international strategization. It provides a background on the collective participation of women in international fora and suggests reasons as to how and why women have made such dramatic progress in the 1990s.

The third section delves into the most common abuses committed against women in virtually every nation on earth, namely, various forms of violence (physical, mental, and sexual), sexual harassment, sexual discrimination, and trafficking in women and girls. These chapters consider relevant facts, statistics, and practices in certain countries, noting consistent patterns of domestic application of laws and contrasting the laws or practices with international law obligations to prevent, protect against, and provide redress for these gender-based abuses.

The fourth section considers a number of human rights issues of particular relevance to women, and provides a thought-provoking and critical assessment of certain human rights requirements. It discusses guaranteed or limited rights to employment, education, and housing, and further considers some specific issues that have special impact on women, including the environment, religion, and culture. It discusses the widespread practice of prostitution, and analyzes advantages and disadvantages of criminalizing this practice with special emphasis on the positive and negative impacts such action may have on women and girls.

In general, the chapters in this volume are intended to provide the reader with a basic overview of human rights law and its application to women and the girl-child, to provide a framework for examining other issues that impact upon, or disparagingly affect, women, and to provide a foundation for analyzing countless other human rights issues affecting women, many of which will be covered in subsequent volumes of this treatise.

Section I

Introduction to Legal Discourse

HUMAN RIGHTS THROUGH A GENDERED LENS: EMERGENCE, EVOLUTION, REVOLUTION

Berta Esperanza Hernández-Truyol

I can not say that I think you very generous to the Ladies, for whilst you are proclaiming peace and good will to Men, Emancipating all Nations, you insist upon retaining an absolute power over Wives.

Abigail Adams, 1776[1]

INTRODUCTION

As the missive from Abigail Adams to her husband John Adams reveals, it is both imperative and ironic that the first chapter in a comprehensive work on women's international human rights be devoted to a general overview of the origins (emergence), development (evolution), and internationalization (revolution) of human rights law. Ironic, because until very recently the international discourse excluded women in both process and substance. Women, because of their gender, did not participate in the creation or early development of international law, including international human rights law. Women also were excluded from representative positions both in the sphere of the particular states and in the international legal institutions—not only the United Nations system but also intergovernmental organizations and, until relatively recently, even non-governmental organizations. Excluding women from the process inevitably resulted in their invisibility, and hence, also marginalized the issues and concerns central and pivotal to women and their personhood, independence, and development.

Originally, the convenient pretext for this exclusion was that the concern of international affairs was the state, not the individual; women were virtually absent from public matters. However, notwithstanding the emergence of international human rights laws that expanded and transformed the international legal system by affording certain rights to individuals, the category of "individuals" effectively did not include women.

The evolution of international rights belonging to persons is traced to the nineteenth and early twentieth centuries when states concluded that treaties protected

---

1. Letter from Abigail Adams to her husband, John Adams (May 7, 1776), *quoted in* HUMAN RIGHTS IN WESTERN CIVILIZATION 1600–Present 34 (John A. Maxwell & James J. Friedberg eds., 2d ed. 1994) [hereinafter WESTERN CIVILIZATION]. This letter predated the signing of the American Declaration of Independence by a mere two months.

the rights of certain classes (mostly minority populations within a state) and abolished the practice of slavery. Finally, the conventional time line marks as revolutionary the events following the Second World War when, for the first time individuals *in se*, and not only states, were accepted as actors in the global sphere. Post-World War II events rendered individuals both objects and subjects of law and its enforcement.

From a women's perspective, however, the emergence, evolution, and revolution of rights follows a dramatically different time continuum. The most distinct emergence of *women's* human rights occurred after the 1979 United Nations General Assembly's ("U.N.G.A." or "General Assembly") adoption of the Convention on the Elimination of All Forms of Discrimination Against Women ("Women's Convention").[2] For the first time in history, this broad-based, comprehensive document places women's rights at the center of international legal discourse. Nonetheless, the Women's Convention has been criticized by many feminists as being outdated; specific disapproval focuses on its tendency toward advocating equality on a litmus test delineated as "equal to men."[3]

Through a woman-lens, the evolution and internationalization of women's human rights would comprise the time between the adoption of the Women's Convention and the present. In this regard, it is imperative to highlight the significance of the recent four-year span during which six United Nations conferences were convened—on topics as diverse (but interconnected) as environment, population, human rights, social development, women, and housing—all of which recognized the central role of women in, and integrated that role into, the human rights agenda.

From 1993 to 1996, the U.N. conferences also effected a dramatic change in the Western-dominated structure from which the East and the South—much like women from all places—had been effectively excluded from participation. Similarly, states that did not exist when the visionary International Bill of Human Rights was conceived and articulated were present in the last decade of the twentieth century and added their voices to the consensus documents. These documents reiterate some existing norms, as well as expand, develop, and transform those norms to suit a diverse, global society. These expanded norms incorporate the rights to non-discrimination, education, health, welfare, voting, democratic participation, employment, travel, freedom of religion, cultural integrity, economic/social development, political representation, bodily integrity, and free choice on family matters, to name a few.[4]

---

2. Convention on the Elimination of All Forms of Discrimination Against Women, *adopted by* G.A. Res. 180, U.N. GAOR, 34th Sess., Supp. No. 46, at 193, U.N. Doc. A/34/46 (1979), 9 I.L.M. 33 (1980) (entered into force on Sept. 3, 1981)[hereinafter Women's Convention].

3. *See generally* Hilary Charlesworth, Christine Chinkin, & Shelley Wright, *Feminist Approaches to International Law*, 85 AM J. INT'L L 613 (1991); HUMAN RIGHTS OF WOMEN (Rebecca Cook ed., 1994).

4. It is also noteworthy that world events following the fall of the Berlin Wall, the break-up of the Soviet Union, the virtual end of a large sector of Communism, and the destabilizing global consequences of these occurrences, including regional strife, ethnic and religious wars, genocide and ethnic cleansing, and a turn towards nativism, nationalism, and isolationism in politics, governance, and trade, indicate that global society is in a second revolutionary stage, even from a traditionalist human rights perspective.

The conferences that have been the platform from which women's voices have been shared for the first time, also have been the platform in which the North/West domination has begun to cede to global participation; the North and South, East and West—with women at the forefront—have started to conquer the divide and to work side by side with their formerly estranged (ignored/dominated) neighbors to create an inclusive blueprint for the further development of human rights in the twenty-first century.

The consensus documents that comprise this blueprint address issues ranging from the environment to education; from universality of rights to respect for cultural traditions; from population to sustained economic growth and sustainable develop-ment; from gender equity and equality to the empowerment of women; from the role of the family to the role of the government; from health to migration; from equity among generations to the placing of people at the center of development; from the recognition that social development is both a national and international concern to the recognition of the need to integrate economic, cultural, and social policies to achieve desired ends; from education to employment to respect for women to the need for affordable housing so that the health, education, and welfare goals of individuals, of families, of governments, and of the global community can be met. Significantly, women have played a critical role in the drafting, acceptance, and implementation of all of these instruments. Following this time line, from a gendered-lens, the international human rights revolution is only now in the making.

This work, while not engaging in revisionist reconstruction, will nevertheless provide insights into the gendered development of human rights law. The first section of this chapter will present the historical background of human rights law. After providing a definition of human rights, this section discusses the theoretical underpinnings of human rights law; it then provides a general overview of the origins of the protections of the individual in international law.

The next section focuses on the development of human rights law. It first presents the events that conventional wisdom views as the internationalization of human rights and then sets forth the so-called generations of rights. Because the unfolding of international rights jurisprudence presented in these two sections took place during women's exclusion, the final section presents the gendered realities of the developments of the international human rights legal construct and posits an alternative time line for the emergence and evolution of rights from a women's per-spective.

HISTORICAL BACKGROUND

International human rights are those rights vital to individuals' existence—they are fundamental, inviolable, interdependent, indivisible, and inalienable rights and predicates to life as human beings.[5] Human rights are moral, social, religious, legal,

---

5.   *See generally* Berta E. Hernández, *To Bear or Not to Bear: Reproductive Freedom As an Interna-tional Human Right*, 17 BROOK. J. INT'L L. 309 (1991) [hereinafter Hernández, *To Bear*]; *see also* REBECCA M. WALLACE, INTERNATIONAL LAW 175 (1986) ("Human Rights . . . are regarded as those fundamental and inalienable rights which are essential for life as a human being.").

and political rights that concern respect and dignity associated with personhood, with a human being's identity.[6] Human rights' origins are traced to religion, "natural law [and] contemporary moral values."[7] The concept of human rights is a relatively recent, modern concept that is universally applicable at least in principle.[8]

Theoretical Underpinnings of Human Rights Law

The emergence of human rights law is traced to Greece and Rome and has been identified as closely tied to "premodern natural law doctrines of Greek Stoicism (the school of philosophy . . . which held that a universal working force pervades all creation and that human conduct therefore should be judged according to, and brought into harmony with, the law of nature").[9] After the Middle Ages, natural law became associated with theories of natural rights, although in medieval times natural law was viewed as imposing duties upon, as opposed to granting rights to, "man." Intrinsically contradictory to any notion of human rights was the recognition of the legitimacy of slavery and serfdom—concepts anathema to the notion of human rights, liberty, freedom, equality, and dignity that are at the heart of human rights as they are viewed today.[10] From the early days, the view of these rights of "man" as inalienable was reflected in the language in which they were couched. For example, Locke argued that "certain rights *self-evidently* pertain to individuals as human beings . . . that chief among them are the rights to life, liberty (freedom from arbitrary rule), and property" and that individuals in civil society ceded to states the right to enforce these natural rights, not the rights themselves; state failure to safeguard the rights gives "rise to a right to responsible, popular revolution."[11] The underpinnings of natural law are assumptions that there are laws existing in nature—both theological and metaphysical—that confer rights upon individuals as human beings. The two sources for these rights are either in divine will or metaphysical absolutes and they are deemed to constitute a higher law that is identified with all of humankind and requires protections of individual rights. An underlying assumption of natural law is that there is a common human nature that presupposes the equality of all human beings.[12]

The religious foundations of natural law philosophy can be found in the writings of St. Thomas Aquinas who posited that all human laws derive from, and are

---

6. *See generally* Hernández, *To Bear, supra* note 5; *see generally* WALLACE, *supra* note 5.

7. RESTATEMENT (THIRD) OF THE FOREIGN RELATIONS LAW OF THE UNITED STATES § 701 cmt. b (1987).

8. *See infra* notes 168–73 and accompanying text for a discussion of the universality versus relativity debate.

9. Burns H. Weston, *Human Rights, in* 20 ENCYCLOPEDIA BRITANNICA (15th ed. 1985), *reprinted in* INTERNATIONAL LAW ANTHOLOGY 21–22 (Anthony D'Amato ed., 1994).

10. *Id.* at 22.

11. *Id.* (emphasis added).

12. *See* MYRES MCDOUGAL ET AL., HUMAN RIGHTS AND WORLD PUBLIC ORDER: THE BASIC POLICIES OF AN INTERNATIONAL LAW OF HUMAN DIGNITY 68–71, 73–75 (1980) [hereinafter HUMAN DIGNITY], *excerpted in* FRANK NEWMAN & DAVID WEISSBRODT, INTERNATIONAL HUMAN RIGHTS 334–35 (1990).

subordinate to, the law of God. Aquinas thus viewed the law of nature as "a body of permanent principles grounded in the Divine Order, and partly revealed in the Scripture."[13] In his thirteenth-century writings, Aquinas even endorsed the notion that one sovereign can interfere in the internal affairs of another when one sovereign mistreats its subjects.[14] This religious view of the natural law was carried forward by Spanish theologians Francisco deVitoria and Francisco Suárez, both of whom recognized that beyond individual states there existed a community of states that was governed in their interactions with each other by international rules that were established "by rational derivation from basic moral principles of divine origin."[15]

Hugo Grotius, considered the father of the law of nations (international law), is a vitally important international jurist. Although Grotius was guided by natural law, as "a rationalist who derives the principles of the law of nature from universal reason rather than from divine authority,"[16] his natural law concept was secular, based on a person's rationality rather than revelation and deduction of God's will.[17] Indeed, Grotius accepted both positive and natural law.

A principal critique on the inadequacy of natural law principles is presented by McDougal, Lasswell, and Chen, the founders of the Communications Theory of lawmaking, who address the notion that "[w]hen authority is conceived in terms of divine will or metaphysical absolutes, little encouragement is given to that comprehensive and selective inquiry about empirical processes which is indispensable to the management of the variables that in fact affect decision."[18] Grotius himself, while recognizing the notion of a state's sovereignty over its own subjects, wrote that "[if] a tyrant practices atrocities towards his subjects, which no just man can approve, the right of human social connection is not cut off in such case."[19]

---

13.   LOUIS HENKIN ET AL., INTERNATIONAL LAW xxiv (3d ed. 1993).

14.   Michael J. Bayzler, *Reexamining the Doctrine of Humanitarian Intervention in Light of the Atrocities in Kampuchea and Ethiopia*, 23 STAN. J. INT'L L. 547, 570–74 (1987) (*quoting* Fonteyne, *The Customary International Law Doctrine of Humanitarian Intervention: Its Current Validity Under the U.N. Charter*, 4 CAL. W. INT'L L.J. 203, 214 (1974)) *reprinted in* INTERNATIONAL LAW ANTHOLOGY, *supra* note 9, at 19.

15.   COVEY T. OLIVER ET AL., CASES AND MATERIALS ON THE INTERNATIONAL LEGAL SYSTEM 1390–91 (4th ed. 1995); *see also* HENKIN ET AL., *supra* note 13, at xxiv.

16.   HENKIN ET AL., *supra* note 13, at xxiv.

17.   OLIVER ET AL., *supra* note 15, at 1391.

18.   HUMAN DIGNITY, *supra* note 12, *excerpted in* NEWMAN & WEISSBRODT, *supra* note 12, at 334.

19.   Bayzler, *supra* note 14 (*quoting* HUGO GROTIUS, DE JURE BELLI ESTI PACIS 438 (Whewell trans. 1853)) *in* INTERNATIONAL LAW ANTHOLOGY, *supra* note 9, at 20.) *See also* DE VATTEL, LE DROIT DES GENS, OU PRINCIPLES DE LA LOI NATURELLE, APPLIQUÉS A LA CONDUITE ET AUX AFFAIRS DES NATIONS ET DE SOVEREIGNS (1758), *in* OLIVER ET AL., *supra* note 15, at 742. De Vattel articulates in § 71 some of the early notions of human rights law:

> Whoever uses a citizen ill, indirectly offends the state, which is bound to protect this citizen; and the sovereign of the latter should avenge his wrongs, punish the aggressor, and, if possible, oblige him to make full reparation; since otherwise the citizen would not obtain the great end of the civil association, which is, safety.

Grotius provided a bridge to the positivists' theoretical foundations that followed the natural law epoch. Grotius distinguished between natural law and the customary law of nations based on the conduct and will of nations. This latter concern with "the will of nations" became popular and central to the rise of positivism which relied "on the practice of states and the conduct of international relations as evidenced by customs or treaties" for the statement of the law.[20] The shift to positivism signified that the focus of states' conduct would be on what states did in practice rather than what occurred based upon forces existing in nature. The popularity of positivism corresponds to the rise of the nation-state and the view of the state as independent and sovereign.[21]

The value of the positivists' contributions to the development of human rights law lies in their recognition of the importance of organizing rules by established processes of the states. Because of the procedural safeguards, these rules as formulated by states then result in authoritative decision making which protects human rights. Its weakness, however, lies in the fact that the values promoted as human rights become wholly dependent upon the perspective of the governing elite.[22] Under a positivist model, thus, human dignity is what a state makes it.

As will be discussed in the following section, this positivist model parallels the human rights development of the articulation of rights of minorities and the prohibition of slavery by virtue of treaties and agreements between and among nations. This model also led to rules of conduct in times of war such as the League of Nations' condemnation of war. Women were allowed no role in the development of either the positivist or natural law models.

Beyond these traditional theoretical constructs that formed the foundation for the international human rights norms, it is important to describe briefly three contemporary theories that affected, expanded, or transformed the development of

---

Id. Furthermore, § 72 states:

But, on the other hand, the nation or the sovereign, ought not to suffer the citizens to do an injury to the subjects of another state, much less to offend that state itself: and this, not only because no sovereign ought to permit those who are under his command to violate the precepts of the law of nature, which forbids all injuries,—but also because nations ought mutually to respect each other, to abstain from all offense from all injury, from all wrong,—in a word, from every thing that may be of prejudice to others. If a sovereign, who might keep his subject within the rules of justice and peace, suffers them to injure a foreign nation either in its body or its members, he does no less injury to that nation than if he injured it himself. In short, the safety of the state, and that of human society, requires this attention from every sovereign. If you let loose the reigns to your subjects against foreign nations, these will behave in the same manner to you; and instead of that friendly intercourse which nature has established between all men, we shall see nothing but one vast and dreadful scene of plunder between nation and nation.

Id.

20. HENKIN ET AL., *supra* note 13, at xxv.

21. *Id.*

22. *See* HUMAN DIGNITY, *supra* note 12, *excerpted in* NEWMAN & WEISSBRODT, *supra* note 12, at 334.

international human rights law analysis. These three theories are the Communications Theory, the Legitimacy Theory, and the Feminist Theory(ics).

The Communications Theory (also called the New Haven School) views international norms prescription as "a complex process of authoritative and controlling decisions in which rules (and doctrines and principles), are continuously being fashioned and refashioned by a wide variety of global actors to suit the needs of the living."[23] This New Haven School recognizes that communications are at the root of lawmaking yet accepts that the ultimate lawmaking function may be relegated to specialized institutions. Consequently, these institutions, as well as the process of creating, interpreting, and enforcing the laws, must include and integrate the views of those about whom the law is concerned and for whom the law creates expectations as to future behavior. In this view, and in the context of women, such an approach to lawmaking is attractive in that it enables—indeed requires—women's (and others') participation by including women's (as well as various other "outsider") perspectives at all stages of the formal and informal international prescriptive processes: rule-making, rule-interpreting, and rule-rights-enforcing. To achieve this end, it stands to reason that representation of women by women is highly desirable, if not a legal and moral imperative.[24]

Professor Thomas Franck's Legitimacy Theory provides another foundation for a nondiscriminatory analysis of international human rights norms. This theoretical construct is based upon the premise that the legitimacy of a government is dependent upon having the consent of the governed and respect for the opinion of the people.[25] This theory also offers a vehicle for the incorporation of women's (and other outsiders') voices and perspectives into the international human rights construct. Under such analysis, the government, to be legitimate, must ascertain the opinions and desires of the people, including women.

Finally, there is the feminist critique of international law. Given that the United Nations has confessed the marginal status of women globally, including within its own ranks,[26] it is not surprising that critics have noted that sexism is a "pervasive

---

23. Burns H. Weston, *Nuclear Weapons Versus International Law: A Contextual Reassessment,* 28 Revue de Droit de McGill 542, 548 (1983). Communications Theory of lawmaking was developed by Professors Myres McDougal, Harold D. Lasswell, W. Michael Reisman, and Loung-Chu Chen. *See generally* Human Dignity, *supra* note 12; W. Michael Reisman, International Law Making: A Process of Communication, The Harold D. Lasswell Memorial Lecture (April 24, 1981).

24. *See* Berta Esperanza Hernández-Truyol, *Women's Rights As Human Rights—Rules, Realities and the Role of Culture: A Formula for Reform,* 21 Brook. J. Int'l L. 605, 669 (1996) [hereinafter Hernández-Truyol, *Culture*]. The author proposes and develops a theoretical and analytical construct that affects reform by including all women's voices in the human rights process that uses communications theory, legitimacy theory, and critical feminist/race theory and applies the same to international human rights law in a multi-disciplinary, multi-dimensional context. *Id.* at 667–68.

25. *See generally* Thomas M. Franck, The Power of Legitimacy Among Nations (1990); Thomas M. Franck, *The Emerging Right to Democratic Governance,* 86 Am. J. Int'l L. 46 (1992).

26. United Nations Development Programme, Human Development Report 1995 1 (1995) [hereinafter UNHDR 1995].

structural problem'' of international law at the root of which is male dominance and the exclusion of women.[27] The feminist critique has exposed this exclusion and promotes inclusion of women at all levels in the international sphere. Various international feminist legal theories will be covered in other chapters of this work.

Origins of International Law—General Concepts

World War II was the watershed event for the change of the status of individuals in international law. Nazi atrocities resulted in the punishment of war criminals at Nuremberg and Tokyo. The interrelated desire to prevent the recurrence of such crimes against humanity resulted in the development of new standards for the protection of human rights. It is important to note, however, that the individual was recognized in the global setting prior to the Second World War.

History traces the development of rules governing relations between or among different peoples to the end of the Roman Empire when the independent and separate states that emerged needed to develop rules for interaction. The system that emerged was largely founded on the Roman system. In fact, the Roman Empire developed a set of rules—the *jus gentium*—to govern the relations between Roman and non-Roman citizens, in contrasted to the *jus civile,* which applied between or among Roman citizens. The *jus gentium* system, however, incorporated principles of equity in natural law that contemporary scholars analogize to the source of international law called ''General Principles of Law Recognized by Civilized Nations'' contained in Article 38 of the Statute of the Court of International Justice.[28] Thus, one can trace the roots of international law to the need that arose when the formerly unified Roman Empire splintered into diverse nation-states that had to interact on a basis of sovereign equality and mutual respect. Thereafter, increased trade, improvements in navigation, and the discovery of new lands accelerated the development of the new law of nations.[29]

---

27. Hilary Charlesworth et al., *Feminist Approaches to International Law,* 85 AM. J. INT'L L. 613 (1991). For a detailed survey of women's rights literature and identification of three approaches taken by Feminists in seeking to secure women a place in the international human rights framework, *see generally* Karen Engle, *International Human Rights and Feminism: When Discourses Meet,* 13 MICH. J. INT'L L. 517 (1982). *See also generally* Pamela Goldberg & Nancy Kelly, *Recent Developments: International Human Rights and Violence Against Women,* 6 HARV. HUM. RTS. J. 195 (1993) (criticizing that gender-based violence is not recognized as a violation of human rights but rather as a product of cultural or religious practices or as acts of particular isolated individuals; noting the feminist critique that the problem is a gendered (male) conception of right that limits its focus on the public state acts as opposed to private actions; faulting a narrow Western conception of human rights which focuses on civil and political rights and subordinates economic, social, and cultural rights); Charlotte Bunch, *Feminist Visions of Human Rights in the Twenty-First Century, in* HUMAN RIGHTS IN THE TWENTY-FIRST CENTURY: A GLOBAL CHALLENGE 968 (Kathleen E. Mahoney & Paul Mahoney eds., 1993) (noting that feminist visions of human rights transform and add to human rights thought by adding women's experiences to existing human rights classifications and by bringing ''gender consciousness to civil and political as well as social and economic rights''). *Id.*

28. *See* HENKIN ET AL., *supra* note 13, at xxii-xxiii; OLIVER ET AL., *supra* note 15, at 1390.

29. HENKIN ET AL., *supra* note 13, at xxii-xxiii.

The Thirty Years War (1618–1648) in Central Europe is a significant event in the history of rights as it signified the end of one imperial reign over all of Europe. Additionally, it marked the emergence of independent nation-states as the primary actors in the global setting. Such advent of independent sovereigns was key to the evolution of international legal principles as it exposed the need to create norms to govern interactions between and among equals.[30] The diversity of peoples and ideologies required orderly processes for state-to-state communications and interchanges. Indeed, in the seventeenth century, Grotius's visionary statement that "[h]uman rights norms must exist today in a diverse world of immensely varied ideologies and beliefs" effectively predicted the development of a sophisticated human rights system.[31] In its beginnings international law was viewed as applicable only to states. However, this perspective did not impede the emergence of norms—both customary and conventional—that dealt, at the heart, with individuals. The individuals were, for the most part, those in whom the state had an interest, such as diplomatic personnel (diplomatic privileges and immunities), and nationals of foreign sovereigns. To accommodate the latter, treaties of friendship, commerce and navigation, jurisdiction, and laws of war emerged. While in these early stages of providing for individuals the obligations always remained with the state, the benefit redounded to the individual.[32] Other early instances of protections of individuals also existed (e.g., the seventeenth-century negotiations by Catholic princes to ensure appropriate treatment of Catholics by Protestant princes, and vice versa).[33] These protections were precursors of states' later negotiation of protection for ethnic minorities with whom the state identified, even when they were foreign nationals. What is presently known as human rights to life, liberty, and equality were unformulated until the last decades of the eighteenth century. These rights emerged in conjunction with the establishment of democratic forms of government.[34]

In the nineteenth and early twentieth centuries, states entered into an increasing number of treaties with the purpose of protecting the rights of certain classes of persons. At this time, the protection of individuals was limited mostly to minority groups (i.e., persons of a different race, religion, or language from the majority group) within a state. The origins of these treaties can be traced to the period after the First World War when changes in sovereign boundaries required the expansion of rights to minorities because of the rise of nationalistic sentiments that created a real danger of oppression of racial, ethnic, linguistic, and religious minorities. Consequently, the allied and associated powers concluded a number of treaties in which states promised to treat such minority groups justly and equally.

---

30. James Friedberg, *An Historical and Critical Introduction to Human Rights, in* WESTERN CIVILIZATION, *supra* note 1, at 2.

31. *Id. (quoting* HUGO GROTIUS, DE JURE BELLI ESTI PACIS 438 (Whewell trans., 1853) *in* INTERNATIONAL LAW ANTHOLOGY, *supra* note 9, at 20.)

32. HENKIN ET AL., *supra* note 13, at 595–97.

33. *Id.* at 596–97.

34. GERHARD VON GLAHN, LAW AMONG NATIONS 185 (4th ed. 1981).

In 1919, states who participated in the First World War endeavored to establish an international organization, the League of Nations, which would be responsible for the maintenance of world order, resolve disputes between states, and halt aggression.[35] The League of Nations, succeeded by the United Nations in 1946, played an important role in protecting minorities after the redrawing of boundaries following the First World War.[36]

Notwithstanding their treaty obligations, states regularly breached their commitments to equal treatment of minority groups. States considered provisions imposing limitations on how they could treat persons located within their borders as intrusions into their national sovereignty. A noted scholar reported:

> Before the Second World War, scholars and diplomats assumed that international law allowed each equal sovereign an equal right to be monstrous to his subjects. Summary execution, torture, conviction without due process (or any process, for that matter) were legally significant events only if the victim of such official eccentricities were the citizen of another state. In that case, international law treated him as the bearer not of personal rights but of rights belonging to his government, and ultimately to the state for which it temporarily spoke.[37]

This attitude resulted in the Permanent Court of International Justice's reiteration that discrimination against minorities within a state constituted a violation of obligations under the treaties.[38]

In addition to these "minority treaties," other important twentieth-century human rights developments included treaties aimed at abolishing slavery and the slave trade. Conventional views date the recognition of freedom from slavery as a customary international norm to 1915. This norm was reaffirmed in international

---

35.   AHMED M. RIFAAT, INTERNATIONAL AGGRESSION: A STUDY OF THE LEGAL CONCEPT: ITS DEVELOPMENT AND DEFINITION IN INTERNATIONAL LAW 41–42 (1979). *See also* D.W. BOWETT, THE LAW OF INTERNATIONAL INSTITUTIONS 17–18 (4th ed., 1982).

36.   The adjudicative organ of the League of Nations was the Permanent Court of International Justice ("P.C.I.J."), which functioned from 1920 to 1939. *See* RAY AUGUST, PUBLIC INTERNATIONAL LAW 448 (1995). Modeled after the PCIJ, the International Court of Justice (I.C.J.) was created in 1945, as an organ of the United Nations. *Id.*

37.   T. FARER, HUMAN RIGHTS BEFORE THE SECOND WORLD WAR IN INTER-AMERICAN COMMISSION ON HUMAN RIGHTS: TEN YEARS OF ACTIVITIES 1971–1981 v–vi (1982), *reprinted in* RICHARD B. LILLICH, INTERNATIONAL HUMAN RIGHTS 1 (2d ed. 1991).

38.   *See* Advisory Opinion No. 6, German Settlers in Poland, 1923 P.C.I.J. (ser. B) No. 6, at 20; Advisory Opinion No. 44, Treatment of Polish Nationals in Danzig, 1932 P.C.I.J. (ser. A/B) No. 44, at 28; Advisory Opinion No. 64, Minority Schools in Albania, 1935 P.C.I.J. (ser. A/B) No. 64, at 17. The statute of the PCIJ adhered to the traditional view that only states could be parties to international proceedings. Nevertheless, the Court noted that other international instruments, such as the minority treaties, recognized the legal standing of individuals and itself recognized that there was no international principle standing in the way of individuals directly receiving or acquiring rights under a treaty provided that the state parties so intended. *See* Subjects, 1 DIGEST OF INTERNATIONAL LAW (Marjorie Millace Whiteman ed., U.S. Dept. of State, 1963) § 2, at 52 [hereinafter Whiteman DIGEST] (quoting *Survey of International Law in Relation to the Work of Codification of the International Law Commission, Memorandum submitted by the Secretary-General*, U.N. Doc. A/CN.4/1/rev. 1, at 19–21 (1949)).

conventions such as the 1926 Slavery Convention[39] and the 1956 Supplementary Convention on the Abolition of Slavery, the Slave Trade, and Institutions and Practices Similar to Slavery.[40] Subsequent treaties further prohibited the traffic of women and children.[41]

Indeed, early writers recognized the importance of individuals to the Law of Nations because individuals comprise "the personal basis of every State" and, consequently, international law needed to "provide certain rules regarding individuals."[42] Individuals, however, were deemed to be objects, and not subjects, of the Law of Nations.[43] Thus, laws were applicable to individuals but individuals had no standing to enforce infractions.

Notwithstanding these principles, in his early treatise Oppenheim listed the following "rights of mankind" as guaranteed to all individuals by their state of nationality as well as by foreign sovereigns, pursuant to the Law of Nations: "right of existence, the right to protection of honour, life, health, liberty, and property, the right of practicing any religion one likes, the right of emigration and the like."[44] After providing this catalogue of rights, Oppenheim noted that such rights could not be guaranteed by the Law of Nations because individuals cannot be subjects of law that is limited to relations between states. Yet, Oppenheim also recognized the supra-sovereign nature of "human" rights:

> [T]here is no doubt that, should a State venture to treat its own subjects or a part thereof with such cruelty as would stagger humanity, public opinion of the rest of the world would call upon the Powers to exercise intervention for the purpose of compelling such State to establish a legal order of things within its boundaries sufficient to guarantee to its citizens an existence more adequate to the ideas of modern civilization.[45]

---

39. Slavery Convention, 46 Stat. 2183, T.S. No. 778, 60 L.N.T.S. 253 *concluded* Sept. 25, 1926 (entered into force Mar. 9, 1927; entered into force for the U.S., Mar. 1, 1929).

40. Supplementary Convention on the Abolition of Slavery, the Slave Trade, and Institutions and Practices Similar to Slavery, 18 U.S.T. 3201, T.I.A.S. No. 6418, 266 U.N.T.S. 3 *concluded* Sept. 7, 1956 (entered into force Apr. 30, 1957; entered into force for U.S., Dec. 6, 1967). By 1955 it had been affirmed in the General Act of the Berlin Conference on Central Africa that "trading in slaves is forbidden in conformity with the principles of international law." *See* LILLICH, *supra* note 37, at 33–35. Thirty-four years later, the Brussels Conference condemned slave trade and also agreed on measures for the suppression of such practices which included "granting of reciprocal rights of search, and the capture and trial of slave ships." *Id.*

41. *See* International Convention for the Suppression of the Traffic in Women and Children, *opened for signature* Sept. 30, 1921, 60 U.N.T.S. 416, and the Protocol for Suppression, Nov. 12, 1947, 53 U.N.T.S. 13.

42. 1 L. OPPENHEIM, INTERNATIONAL LAW: TREATISE 362–69, § 288 (2d ed. 1912) *reprinted in* LOUIS B. SOHN & THOMAS BUERGENTHAL, INTERNATIONAL PROTECTION OF HUMAN RIGHTS 1 (1973).

43. OPPENHEIM, *supra* note 42, at § 290 *reprinted in* SOHN & BUERGENTHAL, *supra* note 42, at 3.

44. OPPENHEIM, *supra* note 42, at § 292 *reprinted in* SOHN & BUERGENTHAL, *supra* note 42, at 4.

45. *Id.* The evolution of the role of the individual in international law can clearly be seen in Lauterpacht's revision of Oppenheim's work. *See* 1 L. OPPENHEIM, INTERNATIONAL LAW : A TREATISE 632–42 (H. Lauterpacht, 8th ed. 1955) *reprinted in* SOHN & BUERGENTHAL *supra* note 42. For example, in

This statement of limitations on sovereignty proved to be true. During the Second World War, German Nazis were punished for committing atrocities against millions of innocent civilians, including German Jews. Thus, the state was not insulated from sanctions when it committed crimes against its own nationals.[46] Indeed, as a direct response to the German treatment of German Jews and crimes against citizens of other states, the victors in the Second World War established an international war crimes tribunal to punish those most responsible for these crimes.[47]

The establishment of such international war crimes tribunals that occurred as a result of the Second World War marked the real internationalization of individual rights, and gave rise to the International Human Rights Law discipline. This modern view of human rights, with the individual at the center, emerged in 1945 in the wake of the Nuremberg and Tokyo trials with the vivid awareness of the Nazi human rights atrocities and the firm commitment that they would not be repeated.[48] Nuremberg clearly established that rules of international law applied to individuals. In a now oft-quoted phrase, the Nuremberg Tribunal asserted that "[c]rimes against international law are committed by *men*, not by abstract entities and only by punishing individuals who commit such crimes can the provisions of international law be enforced."[49] From origins that recognized and had concern exclusively for relations between states, international law moved towards recognition of the interests and rights of individuals.[50] As such, the law of human rights that provides redress for violations of individual rights is a relatively recent development.

MODERN HUMAN RIGHTS DEVELOPMENTS

The Internationalization of Human Rights Law

It was not until after the signing of the United Nations Charter in 1945[51] that international action concentrated on providing comprehensive protection for all individuals against various forms of injustice. Such protections now exist regardless of whether the abuse or injustice was committed by a foreign sovereign or the

---

revising § 289, Lauterpacht concluded that "[s]tates may, and occasionally do, confer upon individuals . . . international rights *stricto sensu*, i.e., rights which they acquire without the intervention of municipal legislation and which they can enforce in their own name before international tribunals." *Id.* at § 289, *reprinted in* SOHN & BUERGENTHAL, *supra* note 42, at 5.

46. *See generally* WHITNEY R. HARRIS, TYRANNY ON TRIAL, THE EVIDENCE AT NUREMBERG (1954); WERNER MASER, NUREMBERG, A NATION ON TRIAL (1979); BRADLEY F. SMITH, THE ROAD TO NUREMBERG (1981); TELFORD TAYLOR, THE ANATOMY OF THE NUREMBERG TRIALS, A PERSONAL MEMOIR (1992).

47. *See generally* TRIAL OF THE MAJOR WAR CRIMINALS BEFORE THE INTERNATIONAL MILITARY TRIBUNAL, NUREMBERG 14 NOVEMBER 1945–1 OCTOBER 1946 (42 Vols.), (1947).

48. *See* Hernández, *To Bear, supra* note 5, at 320–325; Louis B. Sohn, *The New International Law: Protection of the Rights of Individuals Rather than States*, 32 AM. U. L. REV. 1, 9–10 (1982).

49. *Nuremberg Trial*, 6 F.R.D. 69, 110 (1946) (emphasis added).

50. *See* 1 Whiteman DIGEST, *supra* note 38, at 51 (*quoting* DE VISSCHER, THEORY IN REALITY IN PUBLIC INTERNATIONAL LAW 125, n. 8 (P. E. Corbett trans., 1957)).

51. U. N. CHARTER *amended*, June 26, 1945, 59 Stat. 1031, T.S. No. 993, 3 Bevans 1153 (entered into force Oct. 24, 1945).

individuals' own state of nationality and, for the most part, irrespective of the presence of a war.[52]

The U.N. Charter embraces the natural law notion of these as "rights to which all human beings have been entitled since time immemorial and to which they will continue to be entitled as long as humanity survives."[53] These natural rights differ from positive rights in that they are inalienable and the state can neither give them or take them away. As such, these rights are permanent and universal and are ingrained as one of the purposes of the U.N. Charter to "promot[e] and encourag[e] respect for human rights and for fundamental freedoms for all without distinction as to race, sex, language, or religion. . . . "[54] The universality of rights is founded in Western philosophy and thus open to attack for lacking Eastern and/or African linkages. Such lack of a broad-based ideological foundation makes the international legal structure vulnerable to challenges by states that were not present (or perhaps did not even exist) at the time doctrines of international human rights law were articulated.[55]

It is appropriate to review the U.N. Charter provisions that confirm it as a significant moment in the internationalization of human rights. The preamble provides that members "reaffirm [their] faith in fundamental human rights, in the dignity and worth of the human person, in the equal rights of men and women and of nations large and small" as well as the institution's goal "to promote social progress and better standards of life in larger freedom."[56] In addition, article 55 mandates that the United Nations promote "universal respect for, and observance of, human rights and fundamental freedoms for all without distinction as to race, sex, language, or religion."[57] To achieve this end, state members "pledge themselves to take joint and separate action in cooperation with the Organization for the achievement" of such purposes.[58]

Moreover, the Charter creates and empowers two of the bodies that are central to the development of human rights norms, visions, and protections: the U.N. General Assembly and the U.N. Economic and Social Council ("ECOSOC"). Article 13(1) of the U.N. Charter instructs the General Assembly to initiate studies

---

52. *See* MICHAEL AKEHURST, A MODERN INTRODUCTION TO INTERNATIONAL LAW 75–76 (5th ed. 1984). Two other post-World War II events are noteworthy. First, economic development of states has been polarized. Programs of aid that were envisioned without an understanding of the various cultures and problems in various countries failed and led to schisms in theory and practice. More recently post-Cold War discord and its attendant results of increased nationalism, ethnic strife, civil war, and human rights abuses for which the community of nations was not prepared, have presented a grave challenge to the development of human rights law.

53. Sohn, *supra* note 48, at 17.

54. U.N. CHARTER, *supra* note 51, art. 1, para. 3.

55. *See* OLIVER ET AL., *supra* note 15, at 1390.

56. U.N. CHARTER, *supra* note 51, pmbl.

57. *Id.* at art. 55.

58. *Id.* at art. 56.

and to make recommendations in order to ''assist in the realization of human rights and fundamental freedoms for all without distinction as to race, sex, language, or religion.''[59] Similarly, the Economic and Social Council, established by Chapter 10 of the Charter, is instructed to ''make recommendations for the purpose of promoting respect for, and observance of, human rights and fundamental freedoms for all.''[60] To this end, ECOSOC is instructed to set up a commission ''for the promotion of human rights.''[61]

There exists an ongoing debate as to whether these provisions of the U.N. Charter create binding legal obligations on member states to respect the human rights of persons located within its borders, be they nationals or non-nationals. States have reached different conclusions with respect to the nature of the Charter's human rights obligations. Some view the obligations as binding;[62] others have concluded, particularly in older writings, that they are not binding.[63] Notwithstanding such inconsistent interpretations, the International Court of Justice has referred to the Charter's provisions as ''obligations,'' and to breaches thereof as ''violations of the purposes and principles of the Charter.''[64] The I.C.J. also has stated that ''distinctions, exclusions, restrictions and limitations exclusively based on grounds of race, colour, descent or national or ethnic origin which constitute a denial of fundamental human rights [are] a flagrant violation of the purposes and principles of the Charter.''[65]

Further, many propose that the collective rights in the Charter, together with other documents, have become part of the customary international law of human rights.[66] This analysis legally binds members to the Charter provisions not as treaty

---

59. *Id.* at art. 13, para. 1.

60. *Id.* at art. 62, para. 2.

61. *Id.* at art. 68.

62. *See* Re Drummond Wren (1945), O.R. 778, 4 D.L.R. 647; *see also* Russian Wives Case, G.A. Res. 285 (III), U.N. GAOR, 3d Sess., at 34–35, U.N. Doc. A/900 (1949). (The resolution stated that the measure taken by the U.S.S.R. was thought not to be in conformity with the Charter provisions at §§ 13 & 16).

63. *See* Sei Fujii v. California, 217 P.2d 481. The appellate court opinion held that the Alien Land Law was invalid because of conflicts with Charter human rights provisions, but the California Supreme Court, while invalidating the statute under the 14th Amendment, rejected the status of the Charter as the supreme law of the land and held that the human rights provisions in the Charter were not self-executing. The court stated that the provisions lacked the mandatory nature necessary to show an intent to create enforceable rights. For other cases holding that the human rights provisions of the U.N. Charter are not self-executing, *see* Frolova v. U.S.S.R., 761 F.2d 370, 374 n. 5 (7th Cir. 1985) and cases cited therein. *See also* Oyama v. California, 332 U.S. 633 (1948) (holding that the Alien Land Law is unconstitutional under the 14th Amendment, with four Justices referring to the inconsistency of the law with the U.N. Charter).

64. G.A. Res. 2145 (xxi) U.N. GAOR, 21st Sess., Supp. No. 16, at 2, U.N. Doc. A/6316 (1966) (terminating South Africa's mandate over South West Africa (Namibia)).

65. Legal Consequences for States of the Continued Presence of South Africa in Namibia (South West Africa) notwithstanding Security Council Resolution 276, 1971 I.C.J. 58, 56–57, paras. 129, 130.

66. *See* Egon Schwelb, *The International Court of Justice and the Human Rights Clauses of the*

law, but rather as customary law. Thus, states must obey those human rights obligations that constitute customary international law. Treaty and custom combine to create legally binding obligations.[67]

Other documents that create human rights obligations that are pertinent to women's human rights include the Universal Declaration of Human Rights ("Universal Declaration"),[68] the International Covenant on Civil and Political Rights ("ICCPR"),[69] the International Covenant on Economic, Social, and Cultural Rights ("Economic Covenant"),[70] the Women's Convention,[71] the Convention on the Elimination of All Forms of Racial Discrimination ("Race Convention"),[72] and regional human rights treaties.[73] Furthermore, instruments resulting from U.N. conferences and U.N. declarations and resolutions, while not legally binding, carry moral persuasion and reflect the trend toward customary international law status.

It is instructive to review the historical background of the first three of these documents—the so-called International Bill of Human Rights comprised of the Universal Declaration, the ICCPR, and the Economic Covenant. On February 16, 1946, ECOSOC established the Commission of Human Rights as stipulated in article 68 of the Charter. At its first session, a council resolution mandated that the Commission's work "be directed towards submitting proposals, recommendations

---

Charter, 66 AM. J. INT'L L. 337 (1972); *see generally* Jordan J. Paust, *Customary International Law: Its Nature, Sources and Status as Law of the United States*, 12 MICH. J. INT'L L. 59 (1990).

67.   The four sources of international law, as recognized in the Statute of the International Court of Justice, are (a) international covenants (treaties), (b) customary international law, (c) general principles of law recognized by civilized nations, and (d) teachings of highly qualified publicists. Customary and conventional law are the primary sources of law. *See* Statute of the International Court of Justice, art. 38, *annexed to* U.N. CHARTER. The I.C.J. has recognized custom, which results from a general and consistent state practice followed from a sense of legal obligation, as a source of international human rights law. *See* Barcelona Traction, Light & Power Co., Ltd. (Belgium v. Spain), 1970 I.C.J. 32.

68.   Universal Declaration on Human Rights, G.A. Res. 217, U.N. GAOR, 3rd Sess., Supp. No. 127, U.N. Doc. A/810 (1948)[hereinafter Universal Declaration].

69.   International Covenant on Civil and Political Rights, Dec. 16, 1966, G.A. Res. 2200, U.N. GAOR, 21st Sess., Supp No. 16, at 52, U.N. Doc A/6316 (1966), 999 U.N.T.S. 171 (entered into force Mar. 23, 1976; ratified by the United States June 8, 1992) [hereinafter ICCPR].

70.   International Covenant on Economic, Social, and Cultural Rights, Dec. 16, 1966, G.A. Res. 2200, U.N. GAOR, 21st Sess., Supp No. 16, at 49, U.N. Doc A/6316 (1966), 993 U.N.T.S. 3 (entered into force Jan. 3, 1976) [hereinafter ICESCR or Economic Covenant].

71.   Women's Convention, *supra* note 2.

72.   Convention on the Elimination of All Forms of Racial Discrimination, 660 U.N.T.S. 195, *opened for signature* Mar. 7, 1966 (entered into force Jan. 4, 1969) [hereinafter Race Convention].

73.   African Charter on Human and Peoples' Rights, O.A.U. Doc. CAB/LEG/67/3/Rev.5 (1981), *adopted by* the Organization of African Unity at Nairobi, Kenya, on June 27, 1981, 21 I.L.M. 59 (entered into force on Oct. 21, 1986) [hereinafter African Charter]; American Convention on Human Rights, O.A.S.T.S. No. 36, 9 I.L.M. 673 (1970), *opened for signature* Nov. 22, 1969 (entered into force July 18, 1978) [hereinafter American Convention]; European Convention on Human Rights, 213 U.N.T.S. 222 (1950), *signed at* Rome on Nov. 4, 1950 (entered into force Sept. 3, 1953 and thereafter amended by various protocols) [hereinafter European Convention].

and reports to the Council regarding: (a) An international bill of rights; (b) International declarations or conventions on civil liberties, the status of women, freedom of information. . . ; (c) The protection of minorities; (d) The prevention of discrimination on grounds of race, sex, language or religion."[74] At that time, ECOSOC recognized that the Commission would require special advice with respect to particular concerns relating to women and their status. Consequently, the Council ordered the establishment of a Sub-Commission on the Status of Women that would submit proposals, recommendations, and reports to the Commission with respect to the status of women. Nonetheless, it would be decades before the Commission on the Status of Women ("CSW") became truly active.

At its second session, ECOSOC articulated "provisions for implementation" of the U.N. Charter's purposes to promote and observe human rights. To achieve this end, the Council requested the Commission on Human Rights to provide "suggestions regarding the ways and means for the effective implementation of human rights and fundamental freedoms."[75]

In 1947, with First Lady of the United States, Eleanor Roosevelt (the U.S. representative) as chair, the Commission on Human Rights commenced the drafting process for the International Bill of Rights as mandated by ECOSOC. In December of that year, at the Commission's second session, the Commission decided that the International Bill of Human Rights should consist of a "declaration," a "covenant," and "measures of implementation."[76]

The Universal Declaration of Human Rights was unanimously adopted on November 10, 1948.[77] When the United Nations General Assembly adopted the Universal Declaration it requested that priority be given to preparation of a covenant and measures of implementation.[78] The Universal Declaration is a comprehensive document dealing not only with civil and political rights but also with economic, social, and cultural rights.[79] Included in the Universal Declaration's protections of civil and political rights are the prohibition of slavery, inhuman treatment, arbitrary arrest, and arbitrary interference with privacy, as well as a broad, nondiscrimination provision that mandates equality on the basis of race, color, sex, language, religion, political or other opinion, national or social origin, property, birth, or other status. In addition, the Universal Declaration provides for rights to a fair trial, to freedom

---

74. Human Rights, 13 Whiteman DIGEST, *supra* note 38, at § 11, at 660–61 (quoting ECOSOC Res.1/5, Feb. 16, 1946).

75. *Id.* at 661–62.

76. *Id.* at 663.

77. There were eight abstentions: Byelorussia, Czechoslovakia, Poland, Saudi Arabia, Ukraine, USSR, Union of South Africa, and Yugoslavia. The communist states that had abstained from signing the Declaration accepted the Declaration in the Final Act of the Conference on Security and Co-operation in Europe (CSCE) in Helsinkin 1975.

78. 13 Whiteman DIGEST, *supra* note 38, at 663 (citing G.A. Res. 217 E(III), and Universal Declaration, *supra* note 68).

79. For a discussion of the different types of rights, see *infra* notes 108–122 and accompanying text.

of movement and residence, to political asylum, to have and change nationality, to marry, to own property, to freedom of belief and worship, to freedom of opinion and expression, to freedom of peaceful assembly and association, to free elections, and to equal opportunities for access to public positions. Regarding social, economic, and cultural rights, the Universal Declaration recognizes the rights to social security, full employment, fair working conditions, an adequate standard of living, education, and participation in the cultural life of the community.[80] It is noteworthy that even with the Universal Declaration, while agreement was quickly reached on principles regarding provisions on civil and political rights, difficulty existed with respect to the formulation of social, cultural, and economic rights.[81]

While debate about the legal status of the Universal Declaration is ongoing, many scholars consider the Universal Declaration to be legally binding as a general principle of international law; others consider the Universal Declaration to have the status of *jus cogens*,[82] even though at the time of its adoption the United States representative to the United Nations General Assembly stated: "It is not a treaty; it is not an international agreement. It is not and does not purport to be a statement of law or of legal obligation."[83] Subsequent developments in both domestic and international law, however, generally confirm the Universal Declaration's status as a statement of customary international law.[84] While some argue that the entire document does not reflect customary law, at a minimum, most provisions have clearly achieved customary law status.

For example, two documents reiterating the obligation to "observe faithfully and strictly" the provisions of the Universal Declaration—such as the 1960 U.N.G.A. Declaration on the Granting of Independence to Colonial Countries and Peoples and the 1963 Declaration on the Elimination of All Forms of Racial Discrimination, both of which were unanimously adopted—have led to statements that the Declaration "constitutes an authoritative interpretation of the Charter . . . and has over the years become a part of customary international law."[85] More significantly, the 1968 Declaration of Teheran provides that the "Universal Declaration of Human Rights states a common understanding of the peoples of the world concerning the inalienable and inviolable rights of all members of the human family and constitutes an obligation for the members of the international community."[86] In addition, the Secretary General's 1971 Survey of International Law noted that:

---

80. *See* Universal Declaration, *supra* note 68, *passim*; *see also* SOHN & BUERGENTHAL, *supra* note 42, at 516; Akehurst, *supra* note 52, at 76–77.

81. For history *see* SOHN & BUERGENTHAL, *supra* note 42, at 508–14.

82. CHERIF BASSIOUNI, THE PROTECTION OF HUMAN RIGHTS IN THE ADMINISTRATION OF CRIMINAL JUSTICE xxiv (1994). Essentially, *jus cogens* are peremptory norms so fundamental that contrary treaties or customs are invalidated.

83. 19 DEP'T ST. BULL. 751 (1948).

84. *See* SOHN & BUERGENTHAL, *supra* note 42, at 518–19, 522.

85. Montreal Statement of the Assembly for Human Rights 2 (New York, 1968); *reprinted in* 9 J. INT'L COMM. JURISTS 94, 94–95 (June 1968).

86. Final Act of the International Conference on Human Rights 3, 4, para. 2 (U.N. Doc. A/CONF.32/41; U.N. Publ. E.68.XIV.2)

> [The] Universal Declaration is not in terms a treaty instrument . . . . [However]
> [d]uring the years since its adoption the Declaration has come, through its influence
> in a variety of contexts, to have a marked impact on the pattern and content of
> international law and to acquire a status extending beyond that originally intended for
> it. In general, two elements may be distinguished in this process: first, the use of the
> Declaration as a yardstick by which to measure the content and standard of observance
> of human rights; and second, the reaffirmation of the Declaration and its provisions
> in a series of other instruments. These two elements, often to be found combined,
> have caused the Declaration to gain a cumulative and pervasive effect.[87]

Finally, the Restatement (Third) of Foreign Relations Law provides that "almost all states would agree that some infringements of human rights enumerated in the Declaration are violations of the Charter or of customary international law."[88] More recent commentary has been even more supportive of the Universal Declaration as having achieved binding status as a customary norm.

The finalization of the covenant that was to follow the Universal Declaration presented significantly more difficulties than the drafting and adoption of the Declaration. From 1949 to 1954 the Commission devoted six sessions—the fifth through the tenth—to preparation of the covenant.[89] Difficulties ensued because of disagreements lodged by so-called "developed" states as to whether social, economic, and cultural rights—already articulated in the Declaration—were relevant to, or appropriate as, human rights. Western states maintained that social, economic, and cultural rights were aspirational goals rather than "rights," as the attainment thereof was dependent upon economic resources and economic theory and ideology. Consequently, Western states found such rights inappropriate for framing as binding legal obligations. The different viewpoints resulted in the drafting of two international documents—the ICCPR and the Economic Covenant—as opposed to only one covenant to manifest the rights presented in the Declaration.

Because of these conflicts, in 1950 the General Assembly asked ECOSOC to request the Commission on Human Rights to study the means of securing "the rights of peoples and nations to self-determination" and inclusion in the single covenant envisioned at that time of "a clear expression of economic, social and cultural rights in a manner which relates to the civic and political freedoms proclaimed by the draft Covenant."[90] At ECOSOC's request, in considering the directive to include social, economic, and cultural rights, and in light of the divergent ideological positions held by states, the General Assembly asked the Commission to draft *two* Human Rights Covenants rather than one. These were to be submitted simultaneously for consideration by the General Assembly. One document was to contain civil and political rights and the other social and economic and cultural

---

87. *1971 Survey of International Law, Report of the Secretary-General*, U.N. Doc. A/CN.4/245, at 196.

88. RESTATEMENT (THIRD), *supra* note 7, at § 702, pt. vii.

89. 13 Whiteman DIGEST, *supra* note 38, at 663.

90. *Id.* at 664.

rights. The instruction included a request that, in order to maintain uniformity, both covenants overlap to the greatest extent possible.[91]

The two draft covenants were transmitted to the General Assembly on December 4, 1954. Eight years later, in 1962, the Third Committee of the General Assembly[92] (preparing to consider the articles of implementation of the covenants), recognized that since 1952 the membership of the United Nations had not only doubled but had become dramatically diverse. Thus, it requested that the Secretary General "prepare an explanatory paper bringing his annotations up to date in the light of the developments that have taken place."[93] The new member-states critiqued the structural and inherent inequities of the established norms and rights that predated their participation in the process.[94]

Finally, on December 16, 1966 the General Assembly adopted and opened for signature, ratification, and accession the ICCPR, the Optional Protocol to the ICCPR, and the Economic Covenant.[95] In the two covenants that emerged, the only overlapping provisions were those on non- discrimination (including discrimination based on sex), self-determination, and sovereignty over natural resources.

These two covenants, like the U.N. Charter, reflect the natural law origins of human rights law. For example, the ICCPR's prohibition against the suspension of certain rights by the state, even in the event of public emergencies that threaten the life of the nation, reflect the notion of the inalienability of certain rights. Such rights include the right to life; freedom from torture or cruel, inhuman, or degrading treatment or punishment; freedom from slavery and servitude; non-applicability of retroactive laws; right to recognition as a person before the law; and the right to freedom of thought, conscience, and religion.[96]

---

91. *Id.* at 664–65 (*citing* G.A. Res. 543 (vi), U.N. GAOR, 6th Sess., Supp. No. 20, at 36, U.N. Doc. A/2119 (1952); G.A. Res. 545 (vi), U.N. GAOR, 6th Sess., Supp. No. 20, at 36, U.N. Doc. A/2119 (1952)).

92. The Third Committee is one of the main committees of the General Assembly and is the one concerned with Social, Humanitarian and Cultural Affairs. *See* discussion *infra* following footnote 96.

93. 13 Whiteman DIGEST, *supra* note 38, at 665–66 (*quoting* G.A. Res. 1843(b) (xvii) (1962)).

94. Part of the different ideologies that were brought into the United Nations were related to the Socialist revolutions. For example, Socialist/Marxist doctrine (and the states that followed such ideologies) rejected the notion of customary law because it fostered the interest of the "power elite." *See* OLIVER ET AL., *supra* note 15, at 1390. Although this would indicate that such states rejected the notion of human rights as it had evolved, many scholars note that, to the contrary, such Socialist states have in conduct and practice accepted the conventional rules and principles of human rights law while rejecting those ideologically incompatible with Marxism. *Id.* The basic challenge of the Socialist doctrine to a national state in the legal system is that it exploits the working class and thus is not compatible with the law of nations based upon the national state. This focus changed in the later part of the 20th century with a focus being placed on the social welfare rights of the worker.

95. G.A. Res. 2200, U.N. GAOR, 21st Sess., Supp. No. 16, at 52, U.N. Doc. A/6316 (1966). A Second Optional Protocol to the ICCPR was adopted on Dec. 15, 1989.

96. *See* ICCPR, *supra* note 69, at arts. 6, 7, 8 (1)–8 (2), 15, 16, 18. Aside from the U.N. Charter, the Universal Declaration, the ICCPR, and the Economic Covenant, a rich body of human rights treaties, including regional human rights systems, exists. Other significant treaties (beyond the Women's Conven-

No system is complete without some ability to monitor compliance with, and enforce compliance of, the undertaken obligations. Thus, the newly created human rights system established a complaint procedure. In the system as a whole there are U.N. Charter-based organs and treaty-based organs that deal with human rights. The Charter-based organs that address human rights issues are the U.N. General Assembly, the Security Council, and ECOSOC. Of the General Assembly's six main committees, it is the Third Committee that mainly deals with matters pertaining to human rights. In addition, the U.N.G.A. has subsidiary bodies that are concerned with human rights. As briefly noted above, ECOSOC has directives regarding the investigation and enforcement of human rights. Article 62 empowers the Council to make recommendations "for the purpose of promoting respect for, and observance of, human rights and fundamental freedoms for all." Pursuant to article 64, ECOSOC may request reports from members that reflect their efforts to comply with human rights obligations.

The Commission on Human Rights ("CHR") and the CSW, both established in 1946 by ECOSOC, are charged to investigate violations of, conduct studies on, and make recommendations about human rights. To aid in its functions, the CHR established subcommissions, such as the Sub-Commission on Prevention of Discrimination and Protection of Minorities. The CHR also has various working groups that study particular human rights concerns, such as the working group on children in armed conflict and the working group on the draft Declaration on Indigenous Peoples. ECOSOC also has established procedures to hear complaints of consistent patterns of gross human rights violations worldwide.[97]

Since the 1990s, the Security Council increasingly has addressed human rights violations. The General Assembly has committees that are based upon various thematic or general human rights treaties. For example, it has a committee on the elimination of racial discrimination (CERD, established to monitor compliance with the Race Convention) and a committee against torture (CAT, established to monitor compliance with the Torture Convention).[98]

---

tion) include the Race Convention, *supra* note 72; the Convention against Torture and Other Cruel, Inhuman or Degrading Treatment or Punishment, G.A. Res. 39/46, U.N. GAOR, 39th Sess., Supp. No. 51, at 197, U.N. Doc. A/39/51 (1985), *adopted* Dec.10, 1984, (entered into force June 26, 1987); and the Convention on the Rights of the Child, G.A. Res. 44/25, U.N. GAOR, 44th Sess., Supp. No. 49, at 166, U.N. Doc. A/44/736 (1989), *adopted* Nov. 20, 1989, *reprinted in* 28 I.L.M. 1448 (1989).

97. There are essentially two. First, a public procedure is contemplated in E.S.C. Res. 1235 (XLII), U.N. ESCOR, 42nd Sess., Supp. No. 1, at 17, U.N. Doc. E/4393 (1967). Second, a confidential procedure is allowed by E.S.C. Res. 1503 (XLVIII), U.N. ESCOR, 48th Sess., Supp. No. 1A, at 17, U.N. Doc. E/4832/Add.1 (1970).

98. For a review of the CEDAW, established to monitor compliance with the Women's Convention, *see* Silvia Cartwright, *The Committee on the Elimination of Discrimination Against Women*, in volume II of this work. To illustrate the work of a committee, the work of the Human Rights Committee, monitored by the ECOSOC, will be explained briefly. The committee is established pursuant to article 28 of the ICCPR and its tasks are set out in articles 40–45 of that convention. These tasks include the study of reports on measures parties have adopted to give effect to recognized rights and of progress made in light of such rights; the transmittal of reports and comments to parties, as appropriate; the settlement of disputes between/among states who have recognized the committee's competence to enter-

The Regional Systems

The three regional human rights systems cover the European, Inter-American, and African regions; there is currently no Asian regional human rights system. Some view the European system as the most developed regional system. In 1948, the Hague Congress of the International Committee of the Movements for European Unity resolved that a European Charter of Human Rights be enacted. In 1949, the leaders of post-war Europe created the Council of Europe. European states signed the European Convention for the Protection of Human Rights and Fundamental Freedoms[99] in Rome on November 4, 1950. In this model, everyone, including nationals of nonparties, is assured rights within the jurisdiction of member-states. This European system is distinct because it has a very effective enforcement structure. It is significant that the European Commission on Human Rights, the entity that first receives complaints of violations of the Convention, allows for individual petitions if the member-states agree to abide by the prescribed procedure. Moreover, the European Court of Human Rights may render binding legal decisions. Thus, the European system is essentially composed of the European Convention on Human Rights and Fundamental Freedoms, which sets forth comprehensive human rights guarantees; the European Commission on Human Rights, which monitors compliance with the Convention; and the European Court of Human Rights, which adjudicates disputes within the European Community.

The Inter-American system is comprised of various documents and has two overlapping frameworks. First, the Charter of the Organization of American States ("OAS")[100] established the Inter-American Commission on Human Rights, which was given limited power to promote the human rights embodied in the 1948 American Declaration of the Rights and Duties of Man.[101] In 1970, the OAS Charter was amended by the 1967 Protocol of Buenos Aires which strengthened the Inter-American Commission on Human Rights, and institutionalized the implementation of the Declaration.

---

tain such disputes; and the establishment of conciliation commissions to assist parties with amicable resolution of disputes. Significantly, the First Optional Protocol to the ICCPR provides that individuals who claim their rights (included in the ICCPR) have been violated and who have exhausted their domestic remedies, may submit written communications to the Human Rights Committee for consideration. The committee is limited to communications from state parties to the Protocol. The complaints and investigation procedures under the other treaty-based systems are similar, though not identical to, those under the ICCPR.

99. European Convention for Human Rights and Fundamental Freedoms, *opened for signature* Nov. 4, 1950, 213 U.N.T.S. 221, Europ. T.S. No.5 (entered into force on Sept. 3, 1953).

100. ORGANIZATION OF AMERICAN STATES CHARTER, *signed at* Bogota, Colombia, Apr. 30, 1948, 2 U.S.T. 2394, T.I.A.S. No. 2361, 119 U.N.T.S. 3 (entered into force Dec. 13, 1951). The OAS was established in May 1948 during the ninth Inter-American Conference which was held in Bogota . This conference also adopted the American Declaration of the Rights and Duties of Man.

101. Protocol of Buenos Aires, May 2, 1948, O.A.S. Res. XXX, O.A.S. Off. Rec. OEA/Ser.L/V/II.23/ Doc.21/Rev.6 (English 1979), *reprinted in* 43 AM. J. INT'L L. SUPP. 133 (1949).

Second, in 1969, states of the Inter-American region adopted the American Convention on Human Rights,[102] which was modeled on the European Convention and contained a long list of substantive rights. This framework shares the Inter-American Commission with the OAS system. In 1979, the Commission was reconstituted and charged "to develop an awareness of human rights among the peoples of America."[103] The Commission may receive complaints of violations and issues reports on the status of human rights in the region. The Inter-American Court of Human Rights established by this framework can receive cases only from state parties. In 1988, the Protocol of San Salvador, which covers social and economic rights, was attached to the American Convention.[104]

Finally, the African Charter on Human and Peoples' Rights[105] establishes the most recent and conceptually innovative[106] regional system. The African Charter incorporates not only civil and political rights but also social, economic, and cultural rights, as well as solidarity rights. For example, it provides for duties of the individual towards family, society, the state, local communities, and the international community. The Charter further provides for the establishment of an African Commission on Human Rights to receive complaints and issue reports. Within each region of the world, certain traditions, morals, customs, politics, and religions have influenced the reception, development, application, and indeed, the interpretation, of international human rights. In closing this section of the historical background of international human rights, it should be noted that developments viewed through a woman-lens reveal some tragic intrinsic contradictions. Stratifications of individuals based on certain characteristics or identities is far from achieving the dignity, honor, and respect of those who continue to be marginalized.[107] These differentiations lie at the heart of the disempowerment and invisibility of women. Indeed, as the United Nations has recognized, "[i]n no society today do women enjoy the same opportunities as men."[108]

---

102. American Convention, *supra* note 73.

103. *Id.* at art. 41(a).

104. Significantly, this Protocol (article 19) makes the right to organize trade unions and the right to education subject to the system of individual petition under the Convention. For an extensive treatment of the Inter-American human rights systems, *see generally* THOMAS BUERGENTHAL & DINAH SHELTON, PROTECTING HUMAN RIGHTS IN THE AMERICAS (4th ed. 1995).

105. AFRICAN CHARTER, *supra* note 73.

106. *See generally* Manfred Nowak, *The African Charter on Human and Peoples' Rights*, 7 HUM. RTS. L.J. 399 (1986).

107. *See, e.g.*, Rhoda E. Howard, *Dignity, Community, and Human Rights, in* HUMAN RIGHTS IN CROSS-CULTURAL PERSPECTIVES 81–82 (Abdullahi Ahmed An-Na'im ed., 1992) (differentiating among human rights, dignity, and justice).

108. UNHOR 1995, *supra* note 26, at 29. This report recognizes that quite "a wide-spread pattern of inequality between women and men persists—in their access to education, health and nutrition, and even more in their participation in the economic and political spheres." *Id.* "The reality . . . is that women do not share equally with men in the opportunities, benefits and responsibilities of citizenship and development." *Id.* at 99. The irony of such contradictions, also present in theoretical underpinnings of evolved norms, was captured by Schlesinger in his comment about, among other things, the hierarchical societal structure, that well applies to the religious underpinnings of human rights:

Classification of Specific Human Rights

United Nations documents emphasize the indivisibility and interdependence of all categories of human rights.[109] Nonetheless, although the stratification or classification of human rights is often contested or discounted, different so-called generations of human rights have been asserted, and thus will be covered.[110] This classification of human rights has generally been grouped into civil and political rights (so-called first generation); social, economic, and cultural rights (so-called second generation); and solidarity rights (so-called third generation).

Civil and Political Rights—The First Generation

Civil and political rights comprise the so-called first generation. Ironically called "the rights of *Man*," these rights were in their apogee starting in the eighteenth century. These rights are traced to the "bourgeois" revolutions—particularly the French and American Revolutions in the last quarter of the eighteenth century that gave rise to the declarations that are viewed as the foundation of this group of rights.[111]

As a historian, I confess to a certain amusement when I hear the Judeo-Christian tradition praised as the source of our concern for human rights. In fact, the great religious ages were notable for their indifference to human rights in the contemporary sense. They were notorious not only for acquiescence in poverty, inequality, exploitation and oppression but for enthusiastic justifications of slavery, persecution, abandonment of small children, torture, genocide. Religion enshrined and vindicated hierarchy, authority and inequality. . . .

Arthur Schlesinger, Jr., *The Opening of the American Mind*, N.Y. TIMES, July 23, 1989, at 26 (book review).

109. Significantly, it was based on this notion of indivisibility and interdependence of rights that the United Nations General Assembly had called upon the United Nations Commission on Human Rights to adopt a single convention on human rights. G.A. Res. 421 (V), U.N. GAOR, 5th Sess., Supp. No. 16, at 43, U.N. Doc. A/1775 (1950).

110. It is at best naive to claim that clear distinctions as to the character and nature of rights exist so as to permit inflexible classifications. For example, trade union rights and property rights can be either or both civil and political or social and economic rights. Similarly, the European system considers the right to education and cultural rights as part of the civil rights construct, whereas they appear not in the ICCPR but rather in the Economic Covenant. Notwithstanding the notions of indivisibility and interdependence which argue against "generational" segregation, for convenience of presentation the following sections detail rights within these three classifications.

111. Stephen P. Marks, *Emerging Human Rights: A New Generation for the 1980s?*, 33 RUTGERS L. REV. 435, 437 (1981); *see also* Sohn, *supra* note 48, at 33 (stating that "the commonly recognized starting point for the emergence of international human rights as we know them today is the movement for the 'rights of man' in eighteenth century Europe."). Significantly, notwithstanding these origins, Marks notes that he does not suggest "that the concept of human rights is exclusively or even essentially Western. All cultures and civilizations in one way or another have defined rights and duties of man in society on the basis of certain elementary notions of equality, justice, dignity, and worth of the individual (or of the group)." Marks, *supra*, at 437 (citing UNITED NATIONS EDUCATIONAL, SCIENTIFIC AND CULTURAL ORGANIZATION, BIRTHRIGHT OF MAN (1969) and HUMAN RIGHTS: COMMENTS AND INTERPRETATIONS (1949) for illustrations of universality of rights).

Civil and political rights originally were conceived as negative rights, meaning freedom from governmental interference in the various realms. Rights that fall into this negative construct include rights to freedom of opinion, conscience, religion, expression, the press, assembly, movement; freedom from arbitrary detention or arrest, interference with correspondence; and the right to property.[112] However, such a conception of negative rights is exceedingly (and misleadingly) limiting as civil and political rights also include some rights that can be categorized as positive because they require some state action, such as the right to participate in free elections and the right to a fair trial.

All persons are entitled to first-generation rights on an equal basis. Consequently, nondiscrimination on the basis of race, gender, language, religion, culture, family, ethnicity, national origin, and social origin are basic tenets of civil and political rights.

It is noteworthy that, notwithstanding the broad acceptance of the universality of civil and political rights, these rights as they have developed, and as they exist today, are gendered. For example, women are far from enjoying equal rights to speech, participation, travel, or owning land.[113] Rights of the first generation have been criticized as being ''meant for the majority of the working class and peoples of conquered lands the right to be exploited and colonized. They were regarded as 'formal' freedoms that neglected the material realities of social conditions.''[114]

Social, Economic, and Cultural Rights—The Second Generation

Socialist states posited that the freedoms of the first-generation rights simply permitted the exploitation and subjugation of working and colonized people. The second generation, in contrast, reflects the ideals of the Socialist revolutions of the first two decades of the twentieth century. The ''usher[ing] in [of] the second generation'' was effected and underscored by the post-Socialist revolution Mexican and Russian Constitutions of 1917 as well as by the 1919 Constitution of the International Labour Organisation.[115] Contrasted to the first generations' emphasis on protecting individual rights from governmental tyranny through participation in the political processes, the second-generation rights underscored a rejection of the exploitation of peoples and focused on the intervention of the state in order to effectuate certain claims. These rights emphasize the collective or group, as opposed

---

112. Marks, *supra* note 111, at 438. It appears that the right to property properly belongs as a civil and political right although it can easily be viewed as an economic right. Interestingly, it is often placed under the civil and political rights because property was central to the interest fought for in the French and American Revolutions.

113. In fact, there are states where women cannot travel without their husband's consent. Moreover, the right to travel includes issues of refugees, particularly refugee women who have been documented as suffering particularly harshly and very vulnerable to sexual violence and abuse. *See generally* UNHCR, SEXUAL VIOLENCE AGAINST REFUGEES: GUIDELINES ON PREVENTION AND RESPONSE (1995).

114. Marks, *supra* note 111, at 438.

115. *Id. See also* Sohn, *supra* note 48, at 33.

to the rights of the individual. As distinguished from the "negative" civil and political rights, social, economic, and cultural rights are positive rights—rights that require state action. This second generation includes three different types of rights. First are social rights which consist of, for example, the right to an adequate standard of living, adopting the notion that everyone should enjoy subsistence rights such as adequate food and nutrition, clothing, and housing.[116] Economic rights are also included, ranging from the right to social security to the right to work. Finally, a broad spectrum of cultural rights includes the right to take part in cultural life, the right to enjoy the benefits of scientific progress and its applications, and the right to preserve cultural identity of minority groups.[117] Such protection of cultural traditions is significant because culture contains the basic source of identity and preservation of identity which is important for the well-being and self-respect of a human being (rights that can be called first-generation human rights). Western states in general have resisted the notion of social and economic rights. However, U.S. President Franklin Delano Roosevelt appears to have wholeheartedly embraced them.[118]

---

116. *See generally* Asbjörn Eide & Allan Rosas, *Economic, Social and Cultural Rights: A Universal Challenge*, in ECONOMIC, SOCIAL AND CULTURAL RIGHTS (Asbjörn Eide, Catarina Krause & Allan Rosas eds., 1995) [hereinafter EKR].

117. *See generally id.*; *see also* Asbjörn Eide, *Cultural Rights as Individual Human Rights*, in EKR, *supra* note 116, at 229–30.

118. President Franklin Delano Roosevelt's "Four Freedoms" speech, in which he discussed "four essential human freedoms," established the third freedom as the "'freedom from want, which translated into world terms, means economic understandings which will secure to every nation a healthy peacetime life for its inhabitants everywhere in the world." 87–I CONG. REC. 44, 46–47 (1941), *reprinted in* NEWMAN & WEISBRODT, *supra* note 12, at 362. The four freedoms speech provided:

> In the future days, which we seek to make secure, we look forward to a world founded upon four essential human freedoms. The first is the freedom of speech and expression everywhere in the world. The second is the freedom of every person to worship God in his[/her] own way everywhere in the world. The third is the freedom from want, which translated into world terms, means economic understandings which will secure to every nation a healthy peacetime life for its inhabitants everywhere in the world. The fourth is freedom from fear—which translated into world terms, means a world-wide reduction of armaments to such a point and in such a thorough fashion that no nation will be in a position to commit an act of physical aggression against any neighbor—anywhere in the world.

Id. Later, in his State of the Union message to Congress delivered January 11, 1944, President Roosevelt articulated many of these economic rights as part of his vision for a truly free United States of America. He noted that "true individual freedom cannot exist without economic security and independence", that "[p]eople who are hungry and out of a job are the stuff of which dictatorships are made" and referred to these "economic truths [as being] self-evident." *See* President Roosevelt's State of the Union Message, 90–I CONG. REC. 55, 57 (1944), *reprinted in* NEWMAN & WEISBRODT, *supra* note 12, at 362–63. The President also asked for "the establishment of an American standard of living higher than ever before known" and for "a decent standard of living for all individual men and women and children in all nations" and likened freedom from fear to freedom from want. President Roosevelt presented a long list of rights including the right to a job, to earn enough to provide food, clothing, and recreation, to a decent home for a family, to adequate medical care and the opportunity to achieve and enjoy good health, to adequate protection from the economic fears of old age, sickness, accident, and unemployment, and to a good education. Finally, the President also noted that Americans (presumably meaning U.S. citizens) "cannot be content, no matter how high that general standard of living may be,

It is important to note before closing this section that women's historical exclusion from enjoyment of rights is particularly true and marked when one considers social, economic, and cultural rights. Women have been, and still are, deprived of their rights to such opportunities as work and education sometimes *based upon* the pretext of tradition and culture classifications that should be the *bases* of rights, not the grounds to *deny* rights. Thus, the right to culture has often been applied as the right of men to continue their traditional practice or custom of subordinating women. In a view to the future evolution and transformation of economic, social, and cultural rights it is imperative that the agenda include gender-sensitivity and full participation and inclusion of women at all stages and levels of the process.

Solidarity Rights—The Third Generation

Like the first and second generations of rights, the third generation is also sourced in revolution—the anti-colonialist revolutions that immediately followed the Second World War and, around 1960, resulted in the independence of many nations. Such revolutions influenced the text of human rights instruments by giving importance and context to the rights to self-determination and nondiscrimination—both of which are found in the ICCPR and the Economic Covenant. This movement also emphasized the rejection of foreign domination and occupation, freedom from aggression, and threats against national sovereignty. These rights, too, have been labeled as inalienable rights.[119]

Two distinctive characteristics are attendant to third-generation rights. First, solidarity rights do not belong to the individualistic tradition of the first-generation rights nor to the Socialist tradition of the second-generation rights. Second, while these rights are in an early phase of legislative process, documents reveal that they were in the process of being recognized as international human rights during the 1980s. The rights falling under this third generation category include the right to environment,[120]

---

if some fraction of our people—whether it be one-third or one-fifth or one-tenth—is ill-fed, ill-clothed, ill-housed, and insecure." *Id.*

119. *See* Marks, *supra* note 111, at 439 (citing Declaration on the Establishment of a New International Economic Order, G.A. Res. 3201, U.N. GAOR, 6th Special Sess., Supp. No. 1, at 4, U.N. Doc. A/9559 (1974)).

120. *See* Stockholm Declaration, Report of the United Nations Conference on the Human Environment, June 5–16, 1972, U.N. Doc. A/CONF.48/14, *revised by* U.N. Doc. A/Conf.48/14Corr.1 (1972), 11 I.L.M. 1416, princ. 1 (1972) ("[Wo]Man has the fundamental right . . . to an environment of a quality that permits a life of dignity and well-being, and [s/]he bears a solemn responsibility to protect and improve the environment for present and future generations.") [hereinafter Stockholm Declaration]; Rio Declaration on Environment and Development, U.N. Conference on Environment and Development, Annex, Agenda Item 9, U.N. Doc. A/CONF.151 Rev. 1 (1992), 31 I.L.M. 874 (1992) [hereinafter Rio Declaration]; Report of the United Nations Conference on Environment and Development, Agenda 21: Program of Action for Sustainable Development, U.N. GAOR, 46th Sess., Agenda Item 21, U.N. Doc. A/CONF.151/26 (1992) [hereinafter Agenda 21]; AFRICAN CHARTER, *supra* note 73, at art. 24 ("[a]ll peoples shall have the right to a general satisfactory environment favorable to their development"); Beijing Declaration and Platform for Action, U.N. Fourth World Conference on Women, U.N. Doc. A/CONF.177/20, at ch. IV, sec. K (1995) ("women and the environment") [hereinafter Beijing Declaration]; World Summit for Social Development, Declaration and Programme of Action, U.N. Doc. A/

development,[121] peace,[122] as well as rights to common heritage, communication, and humanitarian assistance.[123]

The notion of interdependence and indivisibility of rights recently was reiterated in the Vienna Declaration which plainly states that ''[a]ll human rights are universal, indivisible and inter-dependent and interrelated.''[124] Moreover, these classifications are disputed by a myriad of significant documents in which the first-, second-, and third-generation rights co-exist, such as in the Children's Convention, the Women's Convention, the Race Convention, and the African Charter. In sum, the concept of human rights is difficult to particularize. To enumerate specific, universally recognized human rights is an onerous task. From a gendered perspective, the unfolding of human rights jurisprudence occurred without women's participation. While women were theoretically included within the nondiscrimination provisions of international documents, in actual practice, women were excluded, invisible, and silenced in the international process.

GENDERED INEQUALITY

Given the overarching gender exclusion that traditional human rights development reveals, it is noteworthy that the formal notion of sex-equality as a core

---

CONF.166/9 (1995) (''[p]eople . . . are entitled to a healthy and productive life in harmony with the environment.'') [hereinafter Social Summit].

121. Report of the International Conference on Population and Development, U.N. Doc. A/CONF. 171/13, princ. 3 (1994) (''[t]he right to development is a universal and inalienable right. . . .'') [hereinafter Cairo Conference]; Report of the World Summit for Social Development, U.N. Doc. A/Conf.166/9, commitment 1(n) (1995) (referring to right to development as ''universal, indivisible, interdependent and interrelated'' human rights) [hereinafter Social Summit Report]; Economic Covenant, *supra* note 70, at art. 1(1); Women's Convention, *supra* note 2, at pmbl.; Declaration on the Right to Development, G.A. Res. 128, U.N. GAOR, 41st Sess., Supp. No. 53, U.N. Doc. A/41/53 (1986) [hereinafter Declaration on Development]; The World Conference on Human Rights: Vienna Declaration and Programme of Action, U.N. Doc. A/CONG.157/23, pt. 1, at para. 10 [hereinafter Vienna Declaration]; Beijing Declaration, *supra* note 120, at para. 220; Declaration on the Elimination of Violence Against Women, U.N. Doc. E/CN.6/WG.2/1992/L.3, at pmbl (approved by the General Assembly) (1993) [hereinafter Declaration Against Violence]; Declaration on Race and Racial Prejudice, *adopted* Nov. 27, 1978, by the General Conference of the United Nations (The right to development has been defined as follows: ''the right of every human being and group to full development . . . implies equal access to the means of personal and collective advancement and fulfillment in a climate of respect for the values of civilizations and cultures, both national and world-wide.'') [hereinafter Race Declaration]; Educational, Scientific and Cultural Organization at its 20th Session, *reprinted in* UNESCO, UNESCO's Standard-Setting Instruments § III.C.1 (1981) (stating that freedom means the supremacy of human rights everywhere) [hereinafter UNESCO].

122. *See generally* Marks, *supra* note 111, at 445–46 and sources cited therein; Sohn, *supra* note 48, at 56–59 and sources cited therein. The 1976 U.N. Commission on Human Rights also said that ''everyone has the right to live in conditions of international peace and security and fully to enjoy economic, social and cultural rights and civil and political rights.'' U.N. Commission on Human Rights, G.A. Res. 5 (XXXII), 60 U.N. ESCOR, 32d Sess., Supp. No. 3, at 62, U.N. Doc. E/5768 [E/CN.4/1213] (1976); AFRICAN CHARTER, *supra* note 73, at art. 23(1) (''[a]ll peoples shall have the right to national and international peace and security'').

123. *See* Marks, *supra* note 111, at 442; Sohn, *supra* note 48, at 59–60; Allan Rosas, *The Right to Development, in* EKR, *supra* note 116, at 247–55.

124. Vienna Declaration, *supra* note 121, at para. 5.

human rights tenet dates to 1945 when the U.N. Charter stated its intention to "reaffirm . . . the equal rights of men and women."[125] The U.N. Charter further stated that one of its purposes was to achieve international cooperation "in promoting and encouraging respect for human rights and for fundamental freedoms for all without distinction as to . . . sex . . . ."[126] Following the U.N. Charter's lead, the Universal Declaration of Human Rights, the ICCPR,[127] and the Economic Covenant[128] all expressly include equality based on "sex." These documents insist that "[e]veryone is entitled to all the rights and freedoms set forth in this Declaration, without distinction of any kind, such as race, colour, *sex*, language, religion, political or other opinion, national or social origin, property, birth or other status."[129]

Moreover, the thematic and regional human rights instruments which have expanded and strengthened the human rights foundations also expressly provide for sex/gender equality. The three regional instruments aimed at the protection of human rights (the European Convention,[130] the American Convention,[131] and the African Charter[132]) all explicitly incorporate sex equality, as do other international human rights instruments. However, notwithstanding the international prohibition against sex-based discrimination as confirmed in human rights documents, women are far from attaining equality. Even in the era predating the so-called internationalization of rights which is viewed as the time when the rights of the individuals were "born," women were excluded from the "rights of *man* revolution." Those who emerged as the true rights-holders were the male elite. As the short history of the human rights jurisprudence has shown, the "trickle-down theory of human rights does not serve any population other than relatively privileged males."[133]

---

125. U.N. CHARTER, *supra* note 51, at pmbl.

126. *Id.* at art. 1(3).

127. ICCPR, *supra* note 69.

128. Economic Covenant, *supra* note 70.

129. Universal Declaration, *supra* note 68, at art. 2 (emphasis added). Similarly, the ICCPR provides that:

> [e]ach State Party to the present Covenant undertakes to respect and to ensure to all individuals within its territory and subject to its jurisdiction the rights recognized in the present Covenant, without distinction of any kind, such as race, colour, *sex*, language, religion, political or other opinion, national or social origin, property, birth or other status.

ICCPR, *supra* note 69, at art. 2 (1) (emphasis added). In addition, in article 26, the ICCPR provides that, with the respect to the nondiscrimination provisions, "the law shall prohibit any discrimination and guarantee to all persons equal and effective protection against discrimination on any ground such as . . . *sex*. . . ." *Id.* at art. 26 (emphasis added). Finally, the Economic Covenant also provides for nondiscrimination on the basis of sex. Economic Covenant, *supra* note 70, at art. 2 (2). In addition, the Economic Covenant provides that parties will "ensure the equal right of men and women to the enjoyment of all economic, social and cultural rights" that are articulated in that treaty. *Id.* at art. 3.

130. European Convention, supra note 73, at art. 14.

131. American Convention, *supra* note 73, at art. 1.

132. AFRICAN CHARTER, *supra* note 73.

133. Marsha A. Freeman & Arvonne S. Fraser, *Women's Human Rights: Making the Theory a Reality,*

Only white men received the rights-privilege; all women, regardless of race, were property, and nonwhite men and women could be slaves.

The notion of human rights that emerged, rather than being universal, was normative; the norm was the white, Anglo-Western/European, Judeo-Christian, educated, propertied, heterosexual able-bodied male. Sociologist Rhoda Howard makes the following observation:

> The easiest and clearest social distinction to make is between men and women; in many societies, as our own language reflects, the male is the standard of humanness and the female is the deviation. As Simone de Beauvoir put it in her classic feminist meditation, to be female is to be the existential "Other". . . . The female possessed of knowledge threatens the orderly acquisition and delimitation of society's cognitive symbols created—in most cultures—by her male status superiors; thus from Eve to medieval wise-woman and beyond, Judeo-Christian culture has punished the woman who exercises the *human* capacity for self-reflection with its attendant threat of making claims upon society.[134]

The emergence, evolution, and revolution of women's human rights dates from 1975, which was proclaimed International Women's Year. The first World Conference on Women, in Mexico City, was also held in 1975. Then followed the United Nations Decade for Women (1976–1985),[135] with the second World Conference on Women held in Copenhagen in the middle of this decade (1980). The U.N. General Assembly adopted the Women's Convention in 1979, and it entered into force in 1981.[136] For the first time in the international human rights discourse, an international instrument was devoted exclusively to protecting and enhancing women's rights. The third World Conference on Women was held in Nairobi in 1985.[137] It was a series of U.N. conferences held in the 1990s, however, in which the women's movement truly gathered momentum and force. Consequently, it was the convening of six gender-marginalization-shattering U.N. conferences which were critical to the inclusion of, participation by, and concern for women in the global agenda.

U.N. Conferences—1990s

Several conferences, starting with the Rio Conference in 1992 ("Earth Summit"),[138] continuing with the 1993 World Conference on Human Rights ("Vienna

---

in HUMAN RIGHTS: AN AGENDA FOR THE NEXT CENTURY 103, 105 (Louis Henkin & John Lawrence Hargrove eds., 1994).

134. Howard, *in* CROSS-CULTURAL, *supra* note 107, at 88.

135. For a thorough discussion of the impact of the U.N. Decade for Women on women's international human rights, see HILKKA PIETILÄ & JEANNE VICKERS, MAKING WOMEN MATTER: THE ROLE OF THE UNITED NATIONS 75–83 (1994). These authors also discuss the women's movement from 1972–1974, which resulted in the Decade for Women.

136. Women's Convention, *supra* note 2.

137. *See generally* PIETILÄ & VICKERS, *supra* note 135, for information on the evolution of the international women's movement, beginning in the early 1970s.

138. United Nations Conference on Environment and Development, Rio De Janeiro, Brazil, U.N. Doc. E/CN.6/1995/5 (endorsing Agenda 21 which extensively incorporates activities for strengthening the

Conference''),[139] the 1994 International Conference on Population and Development ("ICPD" or "Cairo Conference''),[140] the 1995 World Summit for Social Development ("Social Summit" or "Copenhagen Conference''),[141] the 1995 United Nations Fourth World Conference on Women ("Women's Conference" or "Beijing Conference''),[142] and the 1996 United Nations Conference on Human Settlements ("Habitat II''),[143] witnessed the firm inclusion and participation of women at the nucleus of the human rights discourse. From a women's rights perspective, the period following the adoption of the Women's Convention marks the evolutionary period for women's human rights. Thus, it was primarily the Women's Convention, followed some fourteen years later by the Vienna World Conference on Human Rights, which sparked the women's human rights revolution, started by women for women with the goal of inclusion and representation in the global sphere.

The gendered legacy of universal human rights development could not be more evident than in the public/private dichotomy, which is slowly being eviscerated.[144] The sacrosanct distinctions between public and private spheres has greatly attributed to the subordination of women. The private realm, that venue into which the government ought not intrude, is an arena exacerbating women's vulnerability. Indeed, ''the legal concept of privacy can and has shielded the place of battery, marital rape, and women's exploited labor; has prevented the central institutions whereby women are *deprived* of identity, autonomy, control and self-definition; and has protected the primary activity through which male supremacy is expressed and enforced.''[145]

---

role of women in sustainable development and includes a separate chapter on women, Chapter 24, entitled "Global Action For Women Towards Sustainable and Equitable Development," paragraph 24.11 of which provides that all entities involved in the implementation of Agenda 21 "should ensure that gender considerations are fully integrated into all the policies, programmes and activities"); *See* Agenda 21, *supra* note 120.

139. Vienna Declaration, *supra* note 121.

140. Cairo Conference, *supra* note 121.

141. Social Summit Report, *supra* note 121.

142. Beijing Declaration, *supra* note 120.

143. Statement of Principles and Commitments in Global Plan of Action: The Habitat Agenda, U.N. Doc.A/CONF.165/PC.3/4 (1996).

144. For example, it is only now, at the end of the twentieth century, that one of the atrocities of war overwhelming perpetrated against women throughout history, namely rape, is being recognized as a wrong *in se*, rather than as merely a regrettable but unavoidable consequence of war. See Rhonda Copelon, *Women and War Crimes*, 69 ST. JOHN'S L. REV. 61 (1995) (focusing on war crimes against women); Jordan J. Paust, *Applicability of International Criminal Laws to Events in the Former Yugoslavia*, 9 AM. U. J. INT'L L. & POL'Y 499 (1994) (discussing rape as an international war crime).

145. CATHERINE A. MACKINNON, FEMINISM UNMODIFIED 101 (1987) (emphasis in original). Probably the quintessential disempowerment of women based on the public/private dichotomy can be seen in the area of violence. At the World Conference on Human Rights in Vienna, women met unprecedented successes by speaking with one voice in a strategy of making violence against women a focal point of the demands for inclusion of women in the Vienna agenda. Because violence against women is so prevalent worldwide and a common concern for all women from every place and status in the world, this strategy permitted articulation without opposition. *See* Julie Mertus & Pamela Goldberg, *A Perspec-*

The Vienna Declaration for the first time recognized violations of women as violations of human rights laws, incorporating the rights of women as "an inalienable, integral and indivisible part of universal human rights."[146] The Declaration proceeded to condemn "[g]ender based violence and all forms of sexual harassment and exploitation"[147] and instructed the U.N. General Assembly to adopt a draft declaration on violence against women urging states "to combat violence against women" pursuant to U.N. dictates.[148] Such provisions condemning violence against women as a matter of human rights principles are a primary accomplishment of the Vienna Conference.

Subsequent to the Vienna Conference, the General Assembly approved a Declaration on the Elimination of Violence Against Women which, by its terms, breaks down the public/private dichotomy and condemns all violence against women while reiterating women's entitlement to equal enjoyment and protection of all human rights and fundamental freedoms in the political, economic, social, cultural, civil, and other fields.[149] The Declaration on the Elimination of Violence Against Women[150] provides a comprehensive definition of violence that includes both private and public conduct:

(a) Physical, sexual and psychological violence occurring in the family, including battering, sexual abuse of female children in the household, dowry-related violence, marital rape, female genital mutilation and other traditional practices harmful to women, non-spousal violence and violence related to exploitation; (b) Physical, sexual and psychological violence occurring within the general community, including rape, sexual abuse, sexual harassment and intimidation at work, in educational institutions and elsewhere, trafficking in women and forced prostitution; (c) Physical, sexual and psychological violence perpetrated or condoned by the State, wherever it occurs.[151]

This de-polarization of the public/private realms continued at the Cairo Conference on Population and Development where discussions of population policies included reproductive technologies, processes, information, and strategies to ensure not only maternal and infant health but also women's overall well-being. The conference document expressly states that "[t]he human rights of women and the girl-child are an inalienable, integral and indivisible part of universal human rights."[152] The document also emphasizes the importance of eliminating violence against women as a means of eradicating gender inequalities.[153]

---

tive on Women and International Human Rights After the Vienna Declaration: The Inside/Outside Construct, 26 N.Y.U. J. INT'L L. & POL. 201, 213 (1994).

146. Vienna Declaration, *supra* note 121, at para. 11.

147. *Id.* at para. 18.

148. *Id.* at para. 38.

149. *See* Declaration Against Violence, *supra* note 121.

150. *Id.* A declaration does not carry legal force. It is a nonbinding instrument.

151. *Id.* at art. 2.

152. Cairo Conference, *supra* note 121, at princ. 4.

153. *Id.* at para. 4.4(e).

Similarly, the World Summit for Social Development continued to break down the dichotomy by urging the ''[t]aking [of] full measures to eliminate all forms of exploitation, abuse, harassment and violence against women, in particular domestic violence and rape. Special attention should be given to violence resulting from harmful traditional or customary practices and all forms of extremism.''[154]

Finally, the Beijing Declaration and Programme of Action reinforced these developments.[155] These changes in the international human rights paradigm show that, due largely to women's activism, some significant changes have occurred with respect to the private/public schism. In the international legal arena the responsibility of individuals and of states is being redefined and transformed, expanding the states' obligations to reach not only positive acts but also omissions, in a manner that protects women in formerly insulated private spaces.[156]

Women's Enjoyment of Guaranteed Rights

The public/private dichotomy has been a significant cause of women's exclusion. As noted above, the origins of international law reached only states—the public realm. Thus in early stages, the international human rights community focused on the public, and in particular on civil and political rights which primarily have been exercised by men, even if purportedly aspirational for all.

Civil and political rights are meaningless to the population that cannot exercise them. For example, the sacrosanct right to vote means nothing to women who, in entering the twenty-first century, still may not have that right. Although today many more women now have the right to vote and to participate in democratic government, even these political rights have not translated into greater participation by women in high levels of public office. Indeed, women's presence in elected bodies—at all levels of domestic governments and international organizations—is minimal.[157] It has been argued that women's disparate treatment and mistreatment in law and practice

is a direct result of their systematic exclusion, by custom and by law, from access to key elements of empowerment: education, physical and social freedom of movement, and mentorship by those already in power. It is evidence of structural inequality that cannot be addressed effectively by refinement of theoretical concepts or discourse on rights. Structural inequality results in the perpetuation of injustice and ignorance despite all efforts to enact and enforce legal rights. The term 'structural inequality'

---

154. Social Summit Report, *supra* note 121, at para. 79(b).

155. Beijing Declaration, *supra* note 120, *passim*.

156. *See* Airey v. Ireland, 32 Eur. Ct. H. R. (ser. A) 1979) (state responsible for failure to take needed steps to ensure woman's access to court to obtain separation from abusive husband); X and Y v. The Netherlands, 91 Eur. Ct. H. R. (ser. A) (1985) (responsibility for failure to enact adequate laws for providing relief to mentally handicapped victim of rape). For a full discussion of the public/private dichotomy and deconstructions that affect the protection of women in international law, *see* Celina Romany, *State Responsibility Goes Private: A Feminist Critique of the Public/Private Distinction in International Human Rights Law, in* HUMAN RIGHTS OF WOMEN (Rebecca J. Cook ed., 1994).

157. For a documentation of women's exclusion from public life see Charlesworth, *supra* note 27.

refers to the essential power imbalance between women and men, in which men have held most of the power to make decisions that affect women, families, and society. This imbalance results in fundamental injustice.[158]

Significantly, tradition and culture also are often used as explanations or justifications for practices that are harmful to, and discriminatory toward women. Practices such as female genital mutilation, female infanticide, bride burning, foot binding, slavery, face hiding, wife-beating, honor killing, forced pregnancy, forced abortion, and multiple, early, and closely spaced childbearing to name but a few, are regularly inflicted on women under the guise of custom or tradition.[159] Notwithstanding existing "paper rights," women are routinely subject to torture, starvation, terrorism, humiliation, mutilation, rape, multiple births and other maternity-related health risks, economic duress, and sexual exploitation simply because of their sex.[160] Thus, even today, with generally broad acceptance of civil and political rights, and its relative proscription of *de jure* discrimination, *de facto* inequality for women is the norm.

Women's attainment of full enjoyment of social, economic, and cultural rights has not reached the same level of acceptance that civil and political rights have reached, except in socialist or communist societies where women often have access to these rights, but are generally denied full political and civil rights.[161] Unequal access to economic resources, combined with the perceived proper status/role of woman as an actor in the private sector—daughter, wife, or mother—has marginalized women's access to the public sector. Just as women have not participated in the development of public international standards, women are routinely shut out from public and private economic discourse. In the public realm, women comprise a disproportionately small number of actors in international matters, including within the United Nations system. Similarly, very few women are heads of financial institutions or corporations worldwide. Additional economic burdens exist because

---

158. Marsha A. Freeman & Arvonne S. Fraser, *Women's Human Rights: Making the Theory a Reality, in* HUMAN RIGHTS: AN AGENDA FOR THE NEXT CENTURY 105 (Louis Henkin & John L. Hargrove eds., 1994)(footnotes omitted).

159. *See* Hernández-Truyol, *Culture, supra* note 24, at 635–37 and sources cited therein. The author proposes and develops a theoretical and analytical construct that affects reform by including all women's voices in the human rights process that uses communication theory, legitimacy theory, and critical feminist/race theory and applies the same to international human rights law in a multi-disciplinary, multi-dimensional context. *Id.* at 667–68.

160. *Id.* at 634–35 and sources cited therein. The distressing fact is that these are women's realities, notwithstanding the existence of documents that mandate the protection of women's rights to privacy, health, equality and non discrimination, education, religion, travel, family life, decision making regarding the number of children and their spacing, information, life, liberty, security of the person, integrity of the person, freedom from torture, freedom from slavery, political participation, free assembly and association, work, enjoyment of the benefits of scientific progress, development, environment, peace, democracy, self-determination, and solidarity, to name some of the rights pertinent to the protection of women's international status and conditions as human beings. *Id.* at 624–29 and sources cited therein.

161. *See* Katarina Tomasevski, *Women, in* EKR, *supra* note 116, at 273; *see also* Martin Scheinin, *Economic and Social Rights as Legal Rights, in* EKR, *supra* note 116, at 41–62.

equal pay for equal work is not a reality, and in some countries women are precluded from certain professions—e.g., the judiciary—simply because of their sex.

Women also suffer direct economic discrimination by virtue of systems that prohibit them from inheriting and owning property,[162] or that routinely deny them access to education.[163] In some places women are limited as to the education they can receive and the careers they can pursue. In addition, women's progress is often hampered by their direct exclusion from the economic realm, namely their exclusion from certain jobs or professions.[164] In some countries, women need their husband's permission before they can pursue remunerated employment.[165]

As of the mid-1990s, the formal human rights structure has taken a strong stance in favor of ending gender discrimination; this change can be partially attributed to having some women in decision-making positions. General comment number 4 on gender equality by the Human Rights Committee provides that governments have the obligation to "affirmatively design [measures] to insure the positive enjoyment of rights."[166] The measures may consist of laws, policies, or other actions to redress discrimination. In 1989, the Human Rights Committee's general comment number 18 stated that governments are required to ensure spouses equal rights in marriage.[167]

---

162. For example, under Islamic inheritance laws in Kuwait, a Muslim woman may receive only half of what male heirs receive, and under some customary laws in Africa a woman has no rights to exercise ownership over communal or clan property and, in many countries, the husband has exclusive control over marital property. *See, e.g.*, U.S. DEP'T OF STATE, COUNTRY REPORTS ON HUMAN RIGHTS PRACTICES FOR 1995, at 15, 76, 122; *see also* Gwendolyn Mikell, *African Structural Adjustment: Women and Legal Challenges*, 69 ST. JOHN'S L. REV. 7 (1995). For example, in Botswana, Chile, Lesotho, Namibia, and Swaziland, married women are under guardianship of their husbands and have no right to manage property. *See* UNHDR 1995, *supra* note 26, at 43.

163. UNHDR 1995, *supra* note 26, at 34 (noting that there are twice as many illiterate women than men in the world).

164. For example, since the Islamic revolution in Iran:

women have been excluded from 79 out of 159 courses of study in the university; 55 courses out of 84 in technology and mathematics, 7 out of 40 in natural sciences, and 17 out of the remaining 33. . . . Women have been banned from all four fields of agriculture. In faculties of letters and humanities, only 10 of 35 courses are available to women, and women are not allowed to study archeology, the restoration of historic monuments, handicrafts, graphics, visual communications, cinematography. They are banned from central Art Institute. In industrial design, there is the maximum quota of 20 percent women. In most fields, women are denied scholarships and not allowed to leave Iran for postgraduate study.

Akram Mirhosseini, *After the Revolution: Violations of Women's Human Rights in Iran, in* WOMEN'S RIGHTS, HUMAN RIGHTS: INTERNATIONAL FEMINIST PERSPECTIVES 74 (Julie Peters & Andrea Wolper eds., 1995).

165. *See* UNHDR 1995, *supra* note 26, at 43 (noting that "[h]usbands can restrict a wife's employment outside the home in Bolivia, Guatemala and Syria").

166. U.N. Doc. A/34/40.

167. *Id.* at general cmt. no.18, para. 5.

In addition to depicting the overall denial to women of rights based on their gender, these examples underscore the gendered effects of culture and tradition. The gendered nuances of the universality versus relativity debate reveal that women's rights are especially fragile to a claim of "culture." The root of the universality versus relativity debate is the argument that adopting human rights values is tantamount to acceptance of imperialistic, colonizers' Western values and the consequent destruction of social and political independence of non-Western communities. Notwithstanding their impact on women, culturalists may argue that certain practices, including arranged marriage, property inheritance along male lines, and female genital mutilation, are integral to cultural identity and cannot be changed without a harmful impact on the community. There is grave need to reconcile culture and gender; when the two conflict, it must not always be culture that trumps. The opposing rights must be balanced. Cultural, traditional, and religious practices are often converted to justifications for denying women basic civil and political rights, such as the choice of partner in marriage, property ownership, and freedom from torture, without any attempt to determine the overall impact these practices have on women.

Western domination in the development and articulation of law has resulted in challenges to its validity and authenticity. The universality/relativity debate, in part flowing from a critique of Western domination, centers around whether the articulated human rights norms, as evidenced in customary and conventional law, are of universal application. Proclamations of universality frequently meet with resistance from representatives of different cultures, religions, and ideologies.[168] Some Western societies, while embracing the concept of political and civil rights, have rejected the notion of economic and social rights as creating legally binding obligations.[169] China and Cuba, on the other hand, embrace social and economic rights but reject the binding nature of certain civil and political rights. Other cultures reject certain rights for a variety of reasons.[170]

Respect for culture does not require embracing traditions that marginalize and victimize women. For instance, the Women's Convention intends that the rights thereby proclaimed are claimed for all women. Article 5 specifically articulates its aim to "modify the social and cultural patterns of conduct of men and women, with a view to achieving the elimination of prejudices and customs and all other practices which are based on the idea of the inferiority or the superiority of either of the sexes or on stereotyped roles for men and women."[171] Harmful cultural

---

168. *See* Eide & Rosas, *in* EKR, *supra* note 116, at 23.

169. *Id.*; *see also* Philip Alston, *U.S. Ratification of Covenant on Economic, Social and Cultural Rights: The Need for an Entirely New Strategy*, 84 AM. J.INT'L L. 365 (1990).

170. For example, Islamic states resist rights aimed at ensuring equality between men and women including equal access to education, equal pay, and sex-equality in inheritance laws which affect rights to property. In fact, the maintenance of fundamentalist views of Sharia Law presents one of the most often articulated challenges to the universality of human rights. Eide & Rosas, *supra* note 168, at 23.

171. Women's Convention, *supra* note 2, art 5.

practices need to be either rejected, revised, or replaced with positive practices which do not directly or indirectly cause injury to any group or member of society.

Both the universality and the relativity perspectives may present problems when viewed through a woman-lens. The universalists' assumptions, based on Western ideologies of inalienable rights,[172] focus on the public sphere and in so doing often ignores the needs and problems of women in the private sphere, such as constraining cultural views on the "proper" role of women in the home, family, and religion. Relativist doctrine, on the other hand, also incorporates gendered cultural ideas—"traditional practices"—of right and wrong conduct based on gender, regardless of the harm caused. These practices may be contrary to guaranteed and inalienable human rights provisions. For example, with respect to women's rights in China, Sharon Hom has noted that "both the universalist position of the primary human rights documents and relativist position of the Third World developing countries fail to provide a conceptual rights position which either adequately includes women or is responsive to the pervasive injustice of gender inequality."[173]

To address the issues of gendered inequalities and culture-based gender subordination, the next necessary step is to provide jurisprudence with a paradigm that resolves the problem of human rights norms conceptualization as sourced in the normative perspective. A feminist multi-dimensional perspective that considers not only gender, but also race, ethnicity, sexuality, religion, class, ability, and culture is imperative for the inclusion of women in the global community. Thus, in policy discussions and developments, as well as in rule-making, the gender question—are there any gender implications of the proposed lawmaking?—should always be asked.[174] Progressive current feminist debates insist that equality defined as rights

---

172. Inalienability and inviolability of rights is reflected in the language of the American Declaration of Independence proclaiming the *self-evident* truth "that all *men* are created equal, they are endowed by their Creator with certain unalienable Rights, that among these are Life, Liberty and the Pursuit of Happiness." THE DECLARATION OF INDEPENDENCE para. 2 (U.S. 1776)(emphasis added). Similarly, the French Declaration of the Rights of Man and Citizen of August 16, 1789, provided that "men are born and remain free and equal in rights . . . the aim of every political association is the preservation of the natural and imprescriptible rights of man . . . [which are] Liberty, Property, Safety and Resistance to oppression." Liberty is defined to include the right to free speech, freedom of association, religious freedom, and freedom from arbitrary arrest and confinement.

173. Sharon K. Hom, *Female Infanticide in China: The Human Rights Specter and Thoughts Towards (An)Other Vision*, 23 COLUM. HUM. RTS. L. REV. 249, 291 (1991–92).

174. In addition, a second question—the women's question—must be asked: Has the evaluation of the impact of the lawmaking on women been conducted in a non-essentialist, multi-dimensional fashion (considering, for example, national or social origins)? A third culture question also is necessary: What are the implications on the culture of the proposed rule making? As is its corollary: What are the gender-subordination implications of the cultural practice? Such inquiries must continue to include the evaluation of the impact and/or implication of the rule-making on race, ethnicity, language, social origin, sexuality, religion, national origin, political or other opinion, property ownership status, birth, or other status.

This proposed paradigm, in essence, asks the "rights" question: what is the status of the right claimed to exist or to have been violated in the eyes of the claimant of the right and the challenger to the right, or of the violator and of the violated. Of course, the perspective of the governing, as well

equal to those of men is not necessarily the best standard for women, and indeed, this basis for treatment may ultimately impair or deny women's ability to achieve full realization of their human rights and fundamental freedoms.

In conclusion, the development of human rights norms has been relatively recent, full, and rich. It has also been gendered, nationalized, and politicized, to the vast exclusion of women and women's rights. The key to full participation of women in the debate and process is the transformation of the human rights paradigm to one that includes not only women, but women from all races, cultures, religions, ethnicities, colors, national origins, sexualities, *etc.* It must also include women from all aspects of society, such as elderly, widowed, handicapped, and disadvantaged women. The transformation must include a means to implement the reconstructed body of rights which will guarantee women full and positive participation in all levels of the process. Rights-talk must be converted to rights-action.

---

as the governed, needs to be obtained and considered. This paradigm can pave the way to achieve true equality.

WOMEN AND INTERNATIONAL HUMANITARIAN LAW

Kelly D. Askin

INTRODUCTION

International humanitarian law, sometimes referred to as the law of war, is the body of international law that attempts to lessen the horrors of armed conflict on both combatants and noncombatants. It does so through assorted processes and procedures that include setting limits on the means and methods in which war can be waged, regulating the conduct of hostilities on the ground, by air, and at sea, establishing rules for the treatment of combatants rendered *hors de combat* (e.g., the sick, wounded, shipwrecked), mandating minimum standards for the treatment of prisoners of war, and requiring that a distinction be made between combatants and noncombatants (notably civilians, medical personnel, and clergy) and insisting that the latter be spared. The proscriptions intended to reduce wartime suffering are, however, frequently disobeyed in the atmosphere of violence, hatred, chaos, fear, and desperation that is endemic to war. Consequently, armed conflicts are rife with breaches of the laws, customs, and principles comprising this branch of international law. Some of these violations are crimes attributing individual criminal liability to the perpetrator or to others responsible for their commission or omission (usually failure to take the necessary steps to adequately prevent the crime from being committed, to stop the crime once commenced, or to punish the crime once committed), even though applicable treaties may not explicitly pronounce criminal sanctions. Contemporary international law imposes affirmative duties and criminal liabilities not only on states, but increasingly on other entities (e.g., corporations, organizations), including individual and group actors. Many international crimes carry individual criminal responsibility regardless of whether a state or non-state actor is involved.[1]

This chapter will focus on the documents that affect women during periods of armed conflict, the prevalent treatment of women during wartime, and the laws that can be used to prosecute gender-specific war crimes committed against women. The emphasis here will be limited to the rules that govern war once an armed

---

1.   Professor Orentlicher enunciates a broad definition of international crimes that "comprises offenses which conventional or customary law either authorizes or requires states to criminalize, prosecute, and/or punish. Although international law generally establishes rights and duties between and among states, international criminal law imposes obligations on individuals, making them liable to criminal punishment." Diane F. Orentlicher, *Settling Accounts, The Duty to Prosecute Human Rights Violations of a Prior Regime,* 100 YALE L.J. 2537, 2552 (1991).

conflict has begun (the *jus in bello*, such as war crimes, crimes against humanity, and genocide); as such, it will not consider rules governing the right to resort to armed conflict in the first place (the *jus ad bellum*, such as crimes against peace or aggression). There are important works in later volumes of this treatise and elsewhere that address such topics as the rights of women (combatants and noncombatants) during periods of armed conflict, the emotional toll sexual violence takes on victims and other survivors, and the treatment of crimes against women in the Yugoslav and Rwandan war crimes tribunals.

Throughout this chapter, there are continuous references to gender and/or sexual violence. The definitions of these terms, borrowed from the Women's Caucus for Gender Justice in the International Criminal Court, are as follows for purposes of this chapter.[2] "Gender violence" means violence that targets or affects one gender exclusively or disproportionately primarily because of that gender. In this chapter, the focus will be on gender violence affecting—women and girls. Gender violence also includes violence that is based on or perpetuates socially constructed or stereotyped gender roles or the power differentials between men and women. Thus, gender violence will be used when the violence to which women are subjected is directly related to the fact that the victim is female.[3] The term "sexual violence" refers to violence of a sexual nature. Whether directed against women or men,[4] sexual violence is usually a form of gender violence, as an attack on one's gender identity, whether masculine or feminine. For example, women are raped in order to control or subjugate them as women and to signal male ownership over them as property; men are raped to humiliate them through forcing them into the position of women and thereby rendering them, according to the prevailing stereotypes, weak and inferior. In general, throughout this chapter, the term "violence" should be understood to encompass physical, mental (psychological), or sexual violence.

---

2.   The Women's Caucus for Gender Justice in the ICC is the collaboration of women around the world working together to ensure promotion of gender issues in the international criminal court. Professor Rhonda Copelon, CUNY Law School, was a driving force in organizing the Women's Caucus. Please note that the definitions used above are not necessarily identical to the ones proposed by the Women's Caucus, as they have been somewhat modified by the author. For more information on the Women's Caucus, contact iccwomen@igc.org.

3.   As articulated in other chapters of this volume, gender is often but one determinative factor, because other factors such as race, religion, ethnicity, politics, and social status may be intrinsically linked with singling out a woman for violence.

4.   Rape and other forms of sexual violence are increasingly committed against men in wartime, most often as sodomy, rape with foreign objects, by forcing male internees to rape each other, or forcing them to perform oral sex on the guards. *See* U.N. Doc. S/1994/674, 27 May 1994, Annex, Final Report of the Commission of Experts Pursuant to Security Council Resolution 780 (1992), at paras. 230(o), 235, & 250(d) [hereinafter Final Report of the Commission of Experts (Yugoslavia)]; M. Cherif Bassiouni & Marcia McCormick, *Sexual Violence, An Invisible Weapon of War in the Former Yugoslavia* (Occasional Paper No. 1, International Human Rights Law Institute, 1996), at 17–18.

INTERNATIONAL HUMANITARIAN LAW

The principal international treaties that regulate armed conflicts are the 1907 Hague Conventions,[5] the four 1949 Geneva Conventions along with annexes to these conventions,[6] and the two 1977 Additional Protocols to the Geneva Conventions.[7] All or parts of these instruments are now recognized as comprising customary international law. Further, customs of war also play an important role in reinforcing and supplementing the Hague and Geneva Conventions. The charters, judgments, resolutions, and other jurisprudence that emerged from the post-World War II international war crimes tribunals, particularly the Nuremberg and Tokyo trials,[8] have also made a valuable contribution to international humanitarian law. The Yugoslav (ICTY) and Rwandan (ICTR) Tribunals[9] are further expanding this body of law.

---

5.   Convention Concerning the Laws and Customs of War on Land (Hague IV), signed at The Hague Oct. 18, 1907, 3 Martens Nouveau Recueil (3d) 461. Essentially, Hague Law governs the conduct of hostilities and duties of combatants. Additionally, please note that Article 19 of the 1954 Hague Cultural Property Convention "provides for the application of the Convention to non-international conflicts." DOCUMENTS ON THE LAWS OF WAR 448 (Adam Roberts & Richard Guelff eds., 2d ed. 1989). The 1907 Hague Conventions supercede the 1899 conventions. *See* International Convention With Respect to the Laws and Customs of War by Land (Hague II), signed at The Hague July 29, 1899, 2 Martens Nouveau Recueil (2d) 949.

6.   The Conventions signed at Geneva on August 12, 1949, consist of the following: [Geneva] Convention (I) for the Amelioration of the Condition of the Wounded and Sick in Armed Forces in the Field, including Annex I, 75 U.N.T.S. 31; [Geneva] Convention (II) for the Amelioration of the Condition of Wounded, Sick and Shipwrecked Members of Armed Forces at Sea, 75 U.N.T.S. 85; [Geneva] Convention (III) Relative to the Treatment of Prisoners of War, including Annexes I–V, 75 U.N.T.S. 135; [Geneva] Convention (IV) Relative to the Protection of Civilian Persons in Time of War, including Annexes I–III, 75 U.N.T.S. 287 [hereinafter Fourth Geneva Convention]. The 1949 Geneva Conventions supersede the 1864, 1906, and 1929 Geneva Conventions.

7.   Protocol [I] Additional to the Geneva Conventions of 12 August 1949, and Relating to the Protection of Victims of International Armed Conflicts, June 8, 1977, 1125 U.N.T.S. 3, *entered into force* Dec. 7, 1978; Protocol [II] Additional to the Geneva Conventions of 1949, and Relating to the Protection of Victims of Non-International Armed Conflicts, June 8, 1977, 1125 U.N.T.S. 609, *entered into force* Dec. 7, 1978.

8.   The IMT, or the International Military Tribunal, commonly referred to as the Nuremberg Tribunal, was established by the Allies after World War II to prosecute war crimes committed in Europe by the Axis leaders. The IMTFE, or the International Military Tribunal for the Far East, commonly referred to as the Tokyo Tribunal, was established by the Allies after World War II to prosecute war crimes committed in Asia by the Axis leaders.

9.   The International Criminal Tribunal for the former Yugoslavia (ICTY) was established pursuant to S.C. Res. 827 (May 25, 1993) to prosecute "Persons Responsible for Serious Violations of International Humanitarian Law Committed in the Territory of the Former Yugoslavia since 1991." U.N. Doc. S/25704, Annex (1994)[hereinafter ICTY or Yugoslav Statute]. The International Criminal Tribunal for Rwanda (ICTR) was established by S.C. Res. 955 for the "Prosecution of Persons Responsible for Genocide and Other Serious Violations of International Humanitarian Law Committed in the Territory of Rwanda and Rwandan citizens responsible for genocide and other violations committed in the territory of neighbouring States, between 1 January 1994 and 31 December 1994." S.C. Res. 955, Annex [hereinafter ICTR or Rwandan Statute].

International humanitarian law governs international, and increasingly non-international, armed conflicts.[10] The characterization of a conflict as international, internal, mixed, or otherwise poses crucial legal issues. The body of law pertaining to international conflicts is far more developed and codified than that governing internal conflicts.[11] Nonetheless, as the ICTY noted, there is a palpable trend in humanitarian law in which "the distinction between interstate wars and civil wars is losing its value as far as human beings are concerned."[12]

It is also important to emphasize that certain crimes that are prevalent during war, such as genocide, torture, slavery, and crimes against humanity, have achieved *jus cogens* status, and are prohibited in all armed conflicts and even irrespective of the presence of an armed conflict. These peremptory norms supersede any treaty or custom to the contrary. In other words, these crimes do not need a nexus to a war and do not require ratification of a treaty; they are crimes that can be prosecuted by any state on the basis of universal jurisdiction. Crimes of universal jurisdiction are justiciable by any state even if such acts do not violate municipal law in the state in which they were committed, and "even when the prosecuting nation lacks a traditional nexus with either the crime, the alleged offender, or the victim."[13] War crimes have also been recognized as having *jus cogens* status affording universal jurisdiction,[14] but by their very definition, war crimes must be committed in connection with an armed conflict.[15]

The aforementioned categories of crimes have also been recognized as part of customary international law, which differs from *jus cogens*. Customary international law is based on state practice and grounded in the notion of implied agreement, derived from acceptance of or acquiescence to a legal obligation. *Jus cogen*

---

10.   The extension of international humanitarian law to internal armed conflicts has been greatly assisted by the Statutes of the ICTY and ICTR. *See discussion in* Theodor Meron, *International Criminalization of Internal Atrocities*, 89 AM. J. INT'L L. 554 (1995); James O'Brien, *The International Tribunal for Violations of International Humanitarian Law in the Former Yugoslavia*, 87 AM. J. INT'L L. 639 (1993).

11.   *See especially* Richard A. Falk, *Janus Tormented: The International Law of Internal War, in* INTERNATIONAL ASPECTS OF CIVIL STRIFE 185–248 (James N. Rosenau ed., 1964); Rosalyn Higgins, *International Law and Civil Conflict, in* THE INTERNATIONAL REGULATION OF CIVIL WARS 169–186 (Evan Luard ed., 1972); Howard J. Taubenfeld, *The Applicability of the Laws of War in Civil War, in* LAW AND CIVIL WAR IN THE MODERN WORLD 499–517 (John Norton Moore ed., 1974).

12.   ICTY, Prosecutor v. Duško Tadić, Decision on the Defense Motion for Interlocutory Appeal on Jurisdiction, 2 Oct. 1995, IT Doc. IT–94–1–AR72, at para. 97, *reproduced in* 35 ILM 32, 54 (1996).

13.   Kenneth C. Randall, *Universal Jurisdiction Under International Law*, 66 TEX. L. REV. 785, 785 (1988).

14.   Jonathan I. Charney, *Universal International Law*, 87 AM. J. INT'L L. 529, 541 (1993); JORDAN J. PAUST, M. CHERIF BASSIOUNI, SHARON A. WILLIAMS, MICHAEL SCHARF, JIMMY GURULÉ, & BRUCE ZAGARIS, INTERNATIONAL CRIMINAL LAW 12 (1996); Lauri Hannikainen, *Implementation of International Humanitarian Law in Finnish Law, in* IMPLEMENTING HUMANITARIAN LAW APPLICABLE IN ARMED CONFLICT 118 (Hannikainen, Hanski, & Rosas eds., 1992).

15.   Certain intricacies of this distinction become clear when considering the practical application of war crimes. *Jus cogen* status allows war crimes, including rape and murder, to be prosecuted by any

norms constitute principles of international public policy, and serve as rules "so fundamental to the international community of states as a whole that the rule constitutes a basis for the community's legal system. . . . [I]t is a sort of international law that, once ensconced, cannot be displaced by states, either in their treaties or in their practice."[16] Whereas customary international law is derived from state practice based on *opinio juris* (a sense of legal obligation), *jus cogen* norms have their foundation in upholding an international *ordre public*. In the *Siderman* case, Judge Fletcher noted that, while "customary international law derives solely from the consent of states, the fundamental and universal norms constituting *jus cogens* transcend such consent."[17] The fact that torture, genocide, slavery, crimes against humanity, and war crimes, among others, comprise both customary international law and have attained *jus cogens* status evinces that states have condemned these crimes and that the international community supports and endorses the moral and legal functions of preventing and punishing them. General principles of law and determinations of learned scholars[18] may be used to supplement the deficiencies and ambiguities of the laws or customs applicable to armed conflicts.

Disparate Reference to Gender—Specific Crimes in IHL Instruments

International humanitarian law (IHL) instruments regulate everything from the minimum number of cards or letters a prisoner of war can receive each month, to provisions requiring opportunities for internees to participate in outdoor sports, playgrounds for children, and to the maximum number of warships a belligerent may have at any one time in the port of a neutral power.[19] Because many regulations protecting either combatants or civilians are often described in minute and exhaustive detail, it is simultaneously shocking and disturbing, and yet consistent with the standard treatment of women and the silence surrounding women's issues, that very little mention is either specifically or even generally made of war crimes regularly

---

state on the basis of universal jurisdiction. Identical acts, including rape and murder, arguably do not have *jus cogen* status when not committed in connection with war.

16. MARK W. JANIS, AN INTRODUCTION TO INTERNATIONAL LAW 64 (2d ed., 1993).

17. Siderman de Blake v. Republic of Argentina, 965 F.2d 699, 717 (9th Cir. 1992).

18. The Statute of the ICJ enunciates the most widely accepted sources of international law. *See* Statute of the International Court of Justice (27 June 1945), 59 Stat. 1055, 3 Bevans 1179, at art. 38(1). In addition to conventional and customary international law, other sources include general principles of law that comprise the common and fundamental municipal laws of states. Judicial decisions and teachings of the most highly qualified publicists can also be used to assist in interpreting international law.

19. Article 71 of the Third Geneva Convention stipulates that prisoners of war "shall be allowed to send and receive letters and cards . . . [of which] the said number shall not be less than two letters and four cards monthly, exclusive of . . . "; Article 95 of the Fourth Geneva Convention requires that internees be given opportunities to participate in sports and outside games in "sufficient open spaces" and that "[s]pecial playgrounds shall be reserved for children"; Article 14 of 1907 Hague Convention XIII, Convention Concerning the Rights and Duties of Neutral Powers in Naval War of 18 Oct. 1907, provides: "the maximum number of war-ships belonging to a belligerent which may be in one of the ports or roadsteads of that [Neutral] Power simultaneously shall be three."

committed against half the population, most particularly crimes of rape, sexual slavery, and other forms of sexual violence. For example:

— In the entirety of the Hague Conventions, one single article (IV, art. 46) vaguely and indirectly prohibits sexual violence as a violation of "family honour."

— The 42-volume set of transcripts of the Nuremberg Trial contains a 732-page index. Neither "rape," "prostitution," nor even "women" is included in either headings or subheadings in this index, even though crimes of sexual violence were extensively documented in the transcripts.[20]

— In the five indexes added to the 22 volume set documenting the Tokyo Trial, "rape" is included under the subarticle of "atrocities," which might be supportable if afforded representative treatment. Yet a mere four references are briefly cited, representing but a minuscule portion of the number of times rape and other forms of sexual violence were included within the IMTFE documents.[21]

— The four 1949 Geneva Conventions came after the Second World War and the Nuremberg and Tokyo war crimes trials, and the extensive reports of sexual violence documented in these trials. In the entirety of the 1949 Geneva Conventions comprising a total of 429 articles, only one sentence of one article (IV, art. 27) explicitly prohibits "rape" and "enforced prostitution," and only a handful of other provisions can be interpreted as indirectly prohibiting crimes of sexual violence.

— The 1974 Declaration on the Protection of Women and Children in Emergency and Armed Conflict omits any reference to sexual violence.[22]

— In the 1977 Additional Protocols to the Geneva Conventions, which were intended to supplement and clarify the 1949 Conventions, only one sentence

---

20. The official documents of the Nuremberg Trial are contained in TRIAL OF THE MAJOR WAR CRIMINALS BEFORE THE INTERNATIONAL MILITARY TRIBUNAL, 14 Nov. 1945–1 Oct. 1946 (42 vols. 1947) [hereinafter IMT DOCS]. For some examples of documentation of sexual violence by the tribunal, *see e.g.*, Vol. II, transcript at 139; Vol. VI, transcript at 211–214; 404–407; Vol. VII, transcript at 449–467; Vol. XX, transcript at 381.

21. Documents of the Tokyo Trial are reproduced in THE TOKYO WAR CRIMES TRIAL: THE COMPLETE TRANSCRIPTS OF THE PROCEEDINGS OF THE INTERNATIONAL MILITARY TRIBUNAL FOR THE FAR EAST (R. Pritchard & S. Zaide eds., 22 vols. 1981) [hereinafter IMTFE DOCS]. For some examples of documentation of sexual violence by the tribunal, *see, e.g.,* Vol. 2, transcript at 2568–73, 2584, 2593–95, 3904–44, 4463–79, 4496–98, 4501–36, 4544, 4559, 4572–73, 4594, 4602, 4615, 4638, 4642, 4647, 4660; Vol. 6, transcript at 12521–12548, 12995, 13117, 13189, 13641–13642, 13652.

22. Declaration on the Protection of Women and Children in Emergency and Armed Conflict, G.A. Res. 3318 (XXIX) of 14 Dec. 1974. An obvious place for the inclusion of sexual violence prohibitions would have been para. 5, which states: "All forms of repression and cruel and inhuman treatment of women and children, including imprisonment, torture, shooting, mass arrests, collective punishment, destruction of dwellings and forcible eviction, committed by belligerents in the course of military operations or in occupied territories shall be considered criminal."

in each explicitly protects against sexual violence (Protocol I, art. 76; Protocol II, art. 4).

Because of discriminatory norms and patriarchal practices, and the prevailing conviction that war is "man's business," it was overwhelmingly men who were involved in drafting the aforementioned humanitarian law provisions.[23] Women and girls have always been subjected to sexual violence during wartime, yet every document regulating war either inadequately covers, inappropriately characterizes, or even neglects to mention, these crimes. The most obvious conclusion is that the crimes committed primarily against women and girls were considered insignificant by-products or mere accidents of war, unworthy of being addressed.

TREATMENT OF WOMEN AND GIRLS IN ARMED CONFLICT

In 1974, the Declaration on the Protection of Women and Children in Emergency and Armed Conflict expressed its "deep concern over the sufferings of women and children belonging to the civilian population who . . . are too often the victims of inhuman acts and consequently suffer serious harm" and further "deplor[ed] the fact that grave attacks are still being made on fundamental freedoms and the dignity of the human person."[24] In modern wars, the greatest casualties of the conflict are civilians, particularly women, children, and senior citizens.[25]

History is replete with of women being raped, sexually enslaved, and subjected to other forms of sexual violence during periods of armed conflict.[26] For thousands of years, in wars in every region of the world, women have been forced to endure various forms of sexual violence. That situation has not only gone unrectified in twentieth-century wars and legal instruments, it appears to have actually worsened. (However, because researchers, historians, and others generally failed to report or document gender-based war crimes prior to the twentieth century, it is virtually impossible to have a precise comparison on differentiating treatment.) Women continue to be subjected to the same violence to which men are subjected, yet they are also singled out for additional violence—gendered violence—that is commonly

23. Christine M. Chinkin, *Peace and Force in International Law, in* RECONCEIVING REALITY: WOMEN AND INTERNATIONAL LAW 212 (Dorinda G. Dallmeyer ed., ASIL Studies in Transnational Legal Policy, No. 25, 1993) ("Despite the far-reaching consequences of conflict upon women, their voices are silenced in all levels of decision-making about war. . . . The whole area of the use of force is the one from which women's exclusion is most absolute.")

24. Declaration on the Protection of Women and Children in Emergency and Armed Conflict, *supra* note 22, at preamble.

25. THE AMERICAN NATIONAL RED CROSS, HUMANITY IN THE MIDST OF WAR 1–7 (1993).

26. *See generally* THEODOR MERON, HENRY'S WARS AND SHAKESPEARE'S LAW, PERSPECTIVES ON THE LAW OF WAR IN THE LATER MIDDLE AGES (1993); SUSAN BROWNMILLER, AGAINST OUR WILL, MEN, WOMEN AND RAPE (1975); PETER KARSTEN, LAW, SOLDIERS AND COMBAT (1978); M.H. KEEN, THE LAWS OF WAR IN THE LATE MIDDLE AGES (1965); KELLY DAWN ASKIN, WAR CRIMES AGAINST WOMEN: PROSECUTION IN INTERNATIONAL WAR CRIMES TRIBUNALS (1997).

manifested in the form of sexual violence. Recipients of sex crimes are not exclusively, but they are nevertheless overwhelmingly, female.

Rape crime survivors (and those who do not survive) are not the only victims. Sexual violence has a devastating impact on not only those who are assaulted, but also their families, associated groups, local communities, and society at large.[27] These crimes have thrived during wartime for centuries.[28] Although wartime sexual violence, particularly rape and sexual slavery,[29] is prohibited by customary international law, international humanitarian law, international human rights law, international criminal law, and general principles of law (which regularly overlap), this gender-based violence has continued with unabated impunity. It is only now that the international community has recognized the moral, social, economic, and legal importance not only to women, but to all people, of taking adequate measures to prevent these crimes and providing multiple forms of redress when they occur.

Women have always been the primary victims of sexual violence in both wartime and peacetime. Over the centuries, analyses of these crimes demonstrate many innovative attributes, such that the nature of many of the crimes regularly committed against women in times of armed conflict has changed; gender-based crimes have evolved into sophisticated, multifaceted, and quite deliberate tactics aimed at destroying opposing factions mentally as well as or instead of, physically. Hence, while much of the random or widespread nature of the violence remains the same, other forms of violence have emerged and new predicates of destruction have developed. These evolutions are briefly summarized below.

Historical Treatment[30]

Historically, women were considered "property," owned or controlled by men (typically fathers, then husbands). A rape of a woman was a crime against a man's

27. *See, e.g.*, Mary Ann Tétreault, *Justice for All: Wartime Rape and Women's Human Rights*, 3 GLOBAL GOVERNANCE 197, 203 (1997) (Wartime rape destroys nations, families, and community life); Lawrence Weschler, *Inventing Peace*, NEW YORKER, Nov. 20, 1995, at 56, *quoting* Antonio Cassese (recounting story in which a man was beaten and restrained, then forced to watch as soldiers repeatedly raped his wife and daughters, and then killed them. Afterwards, the man begged to die, too, "but his tormentors must have realized that the cruellest thing they could possibly do to him now would simply be to set him free, which they did." After telling his story to U.N. investigators, he then killed himself.); SHATTERED LIVES, SEXUAL VIOLENCE DURING THE RWANDAN GENOCIDE AND ITS AFTERMATH 47 (Human Rights Watch, 1996) (After raping a woman in Rwanda, the older militia members advised the younger ones they needn't bother to kill her since "you've already killed her.")

28. *See especially* Madeline Morris, *By Force of Arms: Rape, War, and Military Culture*, 45 DUKE L.J. 651, 654 (1996); MASS RAPE: THE WAR AGAINST WOMEN IN BOSNIA-HERZEGOVINA (Alexandra Stiglmayer ed., 1994); Rhonda Copelon, *Surfacing Gender: Re-Engraving Crimes Against Women in Humanitarian Law*, 5 HASTINGS WOMEN'S L.J. 243 (1994); Christine Chinkin, *Rape and Sexual Abuse of Women in International Law*, 5 EUR. J. INT'L L. 326 (1994); ASKIN, WAR CRIMES AGAINST WOMEN, *supra* note 26, at 18–33.

29. While "(en)forced prostitution" is usually the term used when women are forced into sexual servitude during wartime, the term "sexual slavery" more accurately identifies the prohibited conduct, and thus will be used in this chapter when appropriate.

30. For more detailed discussion of the concepts covered in the following paragraphs, *see* ASKIN, WAR CRIMES AGAINST WOMEN, *supra* note 26, at 18–33, and references cited therein.

property.[31] In wartime, women were considered part of the booty, the spoils, of war, along with livestock and other chattel. Sexual atrocities against women were deemed mere inevitable consequences of armed conflict. By the late Middle Ages, the rape and slavery of women were inducements to war, such that anticipation of unrestricted sexual access to vanquished women was used as an incentive to capture a town. When customary law began prohibiting rape crimes, sexual violence did not tend to be officially encouraged, but the crimes were merely ignored or tolerated by commanders, many of whom believed sexual violence before a battle increased the soldiers' aggression or power cravings and that rape after a battle was a well-deserved chance to release physical or sexual tensions. Women were again considered incidental or insignificant victims of battles waged by men for men.

Eventually, the far-reaching terrorizing and demoralizing aspects of sexual violence came to be viewed as mighty weapons of war, and thus rape crimes were committed on an organized or systematic basis as part of an integral plan or policy of the war in an effort to defeat the enemy through mental as well as, or in lieu of, physical harm. Tétreault explains:

> Rape in war is intended to convey a set of messages to a target audience. The social and symbolic connection between female chastity and group integrity is a strong motivation for wartime rape. . . . Wartime rape . . . is a political crime against the concept, a means of destroying nations through shame, pollution, and destruction of organized family and community life.[32]

Sexual violence is now commonly perpetrated as a central part of political strategies and military tactics,[33] with the overall objective being to cause serious physical and mental harm to all members of the opposition. Widespread random, isolated, or spontaneous, rape crimes add to the devastating impact of these crimes that are increasingly found to be officially ordered or unofficially encouraged.

IHL PROHIBITIONS OF SEXUAL VIOLENCE

Customs of War Prior to World War II

As Roberts notes, "Up to the mid-nineteenth century the laws of war did exist, but in a form very different from today: in custom, in broad principles, in national

---

31.   There are many publications devoted to this issue. For a recent article, *see* Alexandra Wald, *What's Rightfully Ours: Toward a Property Theory of Rape*, 30 COLUM. J. L. & SOC. PROBS. 459 (1997).

32.   Tétreault, *supra* note 27, at 203. Once the shame, silence, and stigma surrounding sexual violence is properly deconstructed so that the shame and disgrace is not on the victim or her family, but where it belongs—on the perpetrator and superior authorities—much of the power that wartime rape holds will be diminished.

33.   Be aware that this is not always the case. Some nations and some commanders absolutely forbid rape crimes committed by their troops, and take measures to reduce these crimes or to punish them if they occur. *See generally* CORNELIUS RYAN, THE LAST BATTLE (1966); PETER KARSTEN, LAW, SOLDIERS, AND COMBAT (1978). In the Yugoslav conflict, there have been reports of soldiers killed or castrated for refusing to commit rape under direct orders to do so. *See* ASKIN, WAR CRIMES AGAINST WOMEN, *supra* note 26, at 283, 923.

laws and military manuals, and in religious teaching."[34] Long before international humanitarian law was codified, rape crimes were prohibited by the customs of war. Indeed, in the 1300s, Italian lawyer Lucas de Penna urged that wartime rape be punished just as severely as rape committed in peacetime.[35] In the 1474 trial of Sir Peter Hagenbach, an international military court disregarded an invocation of superior orders and sentenced Hagenbach to death for war crimes, including rape, committed by his troops.[36] Eminent jurist Alberico Gentili (1552–1608) provided an historical survey of the literature on colleagues and other scholars who demanded that women not be raped by soldiers. Gentili contended that it was unlawful to rape women in wartime, even if the women were combatants.[37] Hugo Grotius (1583–1645), considered the father of the law of nations, concluded that sexual violence committed in wartime should be punished with the same rigor as sexual assault committed outside the context of war.[38]

In 1863, the United States codified international customary laws of land warfare into the U.S. Army regulations on the laws of land warfare. These regulations, known as the Lieber Code,[39] provided the cornerstone upon which subsequent domestic war codes were based.[40] The Lieber Code listed rape by a belligerent as a war crime. Article 44 of the Lieber Code stated that "all rape[s] . . . [are] prohibited under the penalty of death," and Article 47 dictated that "[c]rimes punishable by all penal codes, such as . . . rape, . . . are not only punishable as at home, but in all cases in which death is not inflicted, the severer punishment shall be preferred." Thus, not only was rape considered a war crime, it was a crime carrying the harshest possible penalty: death.

While customary international law dates back thousands of years, codified international humanitarian law instruments have only been in place for a little over a

---

34.   Adam Roberts, *Land Warfare: From Hague to Nuremberg, in* THE LAWS OF WAR: CONSTRAINTS ON WARFARE IN THE WESTERN WORLD 116, 119 (Michael Howard, George J. Andreopoulos, & Mark R. Shulman eds., 1994).

35.   *See* discussion in RICHARD SHELLY HARTIGAN, THE FORGOTTEN VICTIM: A HISTORY OF THE CIVILIAN 50 (1982).

36.   William Parks, *Command Responsibility for War Crimes*, 61 MIL. L. REV. 4 (1973); M. CHERIF BASSIOUNI, INTERNATIONAL CRIMINAL LAW, A DRAFT INTERNATIONAL CRIMINAL CODE 8 (1980); TELFORD TAYLOR, NUREMBERG AND VIETNAM, AN AMERICAN TRAGEDY 81–82 (1970); LYAL S. SUNGA, INDIVIDUAL RESPONSIBILITY IN INTERNATIONAL LAW FOR SERIOUS HUMAN RIGHTS VIOLATIONS 18–19 (1992); Theodor Meron, *Shakespeare's Henry the Fifth and the Law of War*, 86 AM. J. INT'L L. 1 (1992); M. CHERIF BASSIOUNI & PETER MANIKAS, THE LAW OF THE INTERNATIONAL CRIMINAL TRIBUNAL FOR THE FORMER YUGOSLAVIA 576–79 (1996).

37.   ABERICO GENTILI, DE IURE BELLI LIBRI TRES 258–59 (trans. John C. Rolfe, Vol. II, 1995)(1612).

38.   HUGO GROTIUS, DE JURE BELLI AC PACIS LIBRI TRES 656–57 (trans. Francis W. Kelsey, vol. II, 1995)(1646).

39.   Instructions for the Government of the United States in the Field by Order of the Secretary of War, Washington, D.C., 24 April 1863; Rules of Land Warfare, War Dept. Doc. No. 467, Office of the Chief of Staff, approved 25 April 1914 (G.P.O. 1917) [hereinafter, Lieber Code]. The Lieber Code is also known as General Orders No. 100.

40.   Telford Taylor, *Foreword in* THE LAW OF WAR, A DOCUMENTARY HISTORY xv (Leon Friedman ed., 1972).

century.[41] The sole provision in the Hague Conventions that could be construed as prohibiting sexual violence is the article which insists that "[f]amily honour and rights . . . must be respected."[42] At the turn of the twentieth century, when this provision was drafted, a violation of a family's "honor" commonly meant that a woman had been sexually assaulted.[43] As discussed *infra*, in the 1949 Fourth Geneva Convention, rape and enforced prostitution were again erroneously linked with violations of "honor," although at this date, at least the language identified it as an offense against the woman.[44] It is the person committing the crime who acts dishonorably; the perpetrator violates the victim's body, not her honor.[45]

As a result of gross crimes committed during World War I, the 1919 War Crimes Commission was established by the major Allied powers to investigate and make recommendations regarding methods of punishing suspected Axis war criminals. In its report, the War Crimes Commission listed thirty-two nonexhaustive violations of the laws and customs of war that were determined to have been committed by the Axis powers. "Rape" and "abduction of girls and women for the purpose of forced prostitution" were two of the enumerated offenses, yet again signaling their status as a war crime in the early twentieth century.[46]

Laws and Customs of War After World War II

International War Crimes Tribunals: The IMT and IMTFE

Gender-based crimes were committed against women with a vengeance during World War II. Women were murdered, tortured, enslaved, and otherwise abused, as were men. Yet unlike the treatment of most men, but consistent with the treatment of women in armed conflicts in previous and subsequent wars, hundreds of thousands of women and girls were also raped, forced into sexual slavery, forcibly sterilized and subjected to other reproductive crimes, sexually mutilated, sexually

---

41.   The 1864, 1906, and 1929 Geneva Conventions did not reference crimes against civilians.

42.   Convention Respecting the Laws and Customs of War on Land (Second Hague, IV) of 18 Oct. 1907, 36 Stat. 2277, T.S. No. 539, *entered into force* 26 Jan. 1910, at art. XLVI. The 1899 Convention held a similar provision.

43.   For instance, when Professor J.H. Morgan reported the rape of Belgium women during the First World War, the terminology he used was the "[o]utrages upon the honour of women by German soldiers have been frequent." *As quoted in* BROWNMILLER, *supra* note 26, at 42.

44.   In previous history, rape was a crime against man's property, man's honor. *See* Wald, *supra* note 31, at 459–60. Geneva Convention IV, art. 27, *supra* note 6, protects women against "any attack on their honour, in particular against rape, enforced prostitution, or any form of indecent assault."

45.   The notion that a woman's honor is violated perpetuates the myth that she is partly to blame, that she somehow did something wrong. It also ignores the physical and mental violence involved. *See* discussion in Tétreault, *supra* note 27, at 202–04.

46.   UN WAR CRIMES COMMISSION, XIII LAW REPORTS OF TRIALS OF WAR CRIMINALS 122, 124 (1949); HISTORY OF THE UN WAR CRIMES COMMISSION 34 (1948); "Commission on the Responsibility of the Authors of the War and on Enforcement of Penalties," Report Presented to the Preliminary Peace Conference, March 29, 1919, 14 AM. J. INT'L L. 95, 114 (1920).

humiliated, and forced to endure countless other forms of sexual violence and persecution.[47] Nonetheless, when it came time to hold the perpetrators and other responsible parties accountable for the gender-based crimes, charges were conspicuously absent. In the post-war trials held in Europe (in Nuremberg) by the International Military Tribunal (IMT), although crimes against women were extensively reported and documented, these crimes were omitted from the jurisdiction of the IMT Charter, they were not charged in the indictments, and they were not prosecuted.[48]

In the post-World War II trials held in Asia (in Tokyo) by the International Military Tribunal for the Far East (IMTFE), rape crimes were prosecuted to a limited extent in combination with other crimes. The Tokyo Tribunal charged twenty-eight Japanese Axis defendants with various war crimes.[49] Although, like the Nuremberg Charter, the Tokyo Charter did not specifically list any sex crime, in the Tokyo Indictment, under "Conventional War Crimes," rape of civilian women and medical personnel was alleged as amounting to "inhumane treatment," "mistreatment," "ill-treatment," and "failure to respect family honour and rights."[50]

As a result of these charges, a guilty verdict was rendered against General Iwane Matsui, who was held criminally responsible by the IMTFE for a package of crimes, including rape crimes, committed by persons under his command. Evidence established that Japanese troops in Nanking, China, went on a rampage, committing rape, murder, and other forms of destruction throughout the city (euphemistically known as the "Rape of Nanking"). Matsui was not convicted for committing these crimes himself; he was convicted under the notion of superior authority. The Tribunal held that because of the widespread nature of the crimes, Matsui must have known they were occurring, yet he did nothing effective to "abate these horrors," aside from twice issuing orders urging "propriety of conduct upon his troops." These orders were deemed to be ineffective and inadequate under the circumstances. The Tribunal thus held that Matsui "had the power as he had the duty to control his troops and to protect the unfortunate citizens of Nanking. He must be held criminally responsible for his failure to discharge this duty."[51] In this manner, sexual violence was prosecuted in the IMTFE, albeit not as an independent crime, but as part of a group of or in conjunction with other crimes.[52] It bears mentioning

---

47. See ASKIN, WAR CRIMES AGAINST WOMEN, *supra* note 26, at 49–95. Some offenses, such as sexual mutilation, sterilization, and humiliation, are also commonly committed against men.

48. For arguments on how sex crimes could have been prosecuted in the Nuremberg Trial if there had been the political will to do so, see ASKIN, *id.* at 129–63. In the subsequent CCL10 trials held at Nuremberg, "rape" was listed as a crime against humanity in Control Council Law No. 10.

49. IMTFE DOCS, *supra* note 21, at Vol I.

50. INTERNATIONAL MILITARY TRIBUNAL FOR THE FAR EAST, DISSENTIENT JUDGMENT OF JUSTICE PAL 601–03 (1953).

51. IMTFE DOCS, *supra* note 21, transcript at 49,815–49,816.

52. There were 12 trials held in Nuremberg and conducted by the U.S. subsequent to the "major" Nuremberg Trial. These trials were based on Control Council Law No. 10. Two of these trials of the "lesser" war criminals of the European Axis during WWII concern command responsibility. These

that in war crimes trials held in Batavia after the war, some defendants were convicted of "enforced prostitution."[53]

General Tomoyuki Yamashita,[54] commander of the 14th Area Army of Japan, was charged with failing to exercise adequate control over his troops, who had committed rape, murder, and pillage in Manila with abandon (known as the "Rape of Manila".)[55] Yamashita insisted that he knew nothing of the atrocities because of a complete breakdown of communications; he also alleged that his troops were disorganized and out of control, and thus inferentially, he could not have prevented the crimes even if he had known of them. He also argued that because he was so busy fighting a war and planning military strategies, he could not be held responsible for failing to control all persons under his authority. The Commission concluded, however, that because of the widespread character of the atrocities, Yamashita either did know of the crimes, or that he could and should have known of them if he had made any attempt to do so; indeed, they were common knowledge throughout the military and civilian populations in the territory. Further, the Commission found that the failure to take adequate means to prevent the crimes or to punish the crimes after their commission were also in derelict of his duties. Thus, the crimes did not have to be ordered and there was no requirement of proof that the commander knew of the crimes being committed by persons under his authority, as their widespread commission was enough to impute knowledge to Yamashita, the commander. Yamashita was found guilty of failing his command responsibility and sentenced to death. Although some assert that the Yamashita trial established a strict, or absolute, liability standard, this is incorrect; it was primarily because of

two are No. 7, U.S. vs. List (better known as the Hostage Case) and No. 12, U.S. vs. Wilhelm von Leeb et al. (better known as the High Command Case). These trials are documented in TRIALS OF WAR CRIMINALS BEFORE THE NUREMBERG MILITARY TRIBUNALS UNDER CONTROL COUNCIL LAW No. 10, NUREMBERG, October 1946–April 1949 (15 vols., Washington D.C., U.S. G.P.O., 1949–1953). However, because these trials did not involve gender-specific crimes and because they were based primarily on following illegal orders instead of holding a leader responsible for unauthorized crimes committed by persons under their authority, they will not be further discussed here, other than noting that both trials articulated different, but lesser standards than those enunciated in Yamashita. (The High Command Case rejected the "should have known" standard altogether.)

53. *See discussion in* GEORGE HICKS, THE COMFORT WOMEN 31–34 (1995). The trial of Washio Awochi, who was found guilty of the war crime of enforced prostitution, is reviewed in UNITED NATIONS WAR CRIMES COMMISSION, 8 LAW REPORTS OF TRIALS OF WAR CRIMINALS 122 (1949).

54. Because Yamashita was not charged with "crimes against peace," he was not tried by the IMTFE. *See generally* RICHARD L. LAEL, THE YAMASHITA PRECEDENT, WAR CRIMES AND COMMAND RESPONSIBILITY (1982).

55. The Decision of the United States Military Commission at Manila, December 7, 1945, *reproduced in* THE LAW OF WAR (Friedman ed.), *supra* note 40, at 1596. Although appealed to General Douglas MacArthur and the U.S. Supreme Court, the decision stood and Yamashita was hanged. In re Yamashita, 327 U.S. 1 (1946). *But see* case of Admiral Toyoda, charged with violating the laws and customs of war by tolerating crimes, including rape, committed by his troops. This case articulated a higher threshold for knowledge. Because it was not established conclusively that Toyoda knew the crimes were being committed by his troops, Toyoda was ultimately acquitted. Case described in Gordon Ireland, *Uncommon Law in Martial Courts*, 4 WORLD AFF. Y.B. (1950); William H. Parks, *Command Responsibility for War Crimes*, 62 MIL. L. REV. 1, 69–73 (1973).

the widespread nature of the crimes that he was held to a "knew or should have known" standard. Thus, under the rubric of command responsibility or superior authority, there is clear precedent for holding military and other leaders responsible for crimes, including crimes of sexual violence, committed by persons under their authority.

Particularly as a result of crimes committed against the civilian population during World War II, during which millions of civilians were egregiously abused and systematically exterminated, the Geneva Conventions of 1864, 1906, and 1929 were revised and amended in 1949, resulting in four conventions, the fourth of which was devoted to protecting civilians during wartime.

The 1949 Geneva Conventions

The four 1949 Geneva Conventions are the primary instruments that govern the treatment of certain belligerents (the sick, wounded, and shipwrecked), civilians, and prisoners of war during periods of armed conflict, and they are supplemented by the 1977 Additional Protocols to the 1949 Geneva Conventions. As previously noted, one article of the four 1949 Conventions explicitly prohibits "rape" and "forced prostitution," and one article in each of the two Additional Protocols also prohibit these crimes.[56] Specifically, Article 27 of the Fourth Geneva Convention, Articles 76(1) of Protocol I relating to international armed conflicts, and Article 4(2)(e) of Protocol II relating to internal armed conflicts each prohibit rape crimes. The Fourth Geneva Convention, which applies to the civilian population, mandates the following:

> Art. 27. Protected persons are entitled, in all circumstances, to respect for their persons, their honour, their family rights, their religious convictions and practices, and their manners and customs. They shall at all times be humanely treated, and shall be protected especially against all acts of violence or threats thereof and against insults and public curiosity.
>
> Women shall be especially protected against any attack on their honour, in particular against rape, enforced prostitution, or any form of indecent assault.[57]

---

56. Geneva Convention (IV) Relative to the Protection of Civilian Persons in Time of War, 12 August 1949, 75 U.N.T.S. 287, 6 U.T.S. 3316, TIAS No. 3364; [1977] Protocol Additional to the Geneva Conventions of 12 August 1949, and Relating to the Protection of Victims of International Armed Conflicts, June 8, 1977, 1125 U.N.T.S. 3, *entered into force* Dec. 7, 1978, *reprinted in* 16 ILM 1391 (1977); [1977] Protocol Additional to the Geneva Conventions of 12 August 1949, and Relating to the Protection of Victims of Non-International Armed Conflicts, June 8, 1977, 1125 U.N.T.S. 609, *entered into force* Dec. 7, 1978, *reprinted in* 16 ILM 182 (1977).

57. Fourth Geneva Convention, *id.* at art. 27. The language of Article 27 is primarily gender-neutral, applicable to all protected persons. However, while the coverage of rape, enforced prostitution, and indecent assault is somewhat definitive toward the treatment of women, there is no suggestion that men were not intended to be covered by these provisions. The gendered language may have been used to flag the issue that it is women and girl-children who are primary victims of sexual assault; also during the period it was drafted, most municipal rape provisions defined rape as a crime against women. Under current standards, the fundamental principle of nondiscrimination in human rights law would undoubtedly extend protection from sexual violence to males as well as females. Significantly, the

Article 27 thus enunciates a clear and unequivocal, albeit primitively characterized, prohibition against sexual violence, particularly rape and "enforced prostitution." Similarly, Article 76(1) of Protocol I states: "Women shall be the object of special respect and shall be protected in particular against rape, forced prostitution and any other form of indecent assault."[58] Article 4(2)(e) of Protocol II prohibits "[o]utrages upon personal dignity, in particular humiliating and degrading treatment, rape, enforced prostitution and any form of indecent assault." Again, sex crimes are not treated as crimes of violence; they are associated with moral offenses, violations against "honor" and "dignity." This demarcation grossly mischaracterizes the offense, diminishes the harm, perpetuates detrimental stereotypes, and conceals the nature of the crime. Rape is a crime of extreme physical and mental violence and interminable harm that invades and violates the most sacred, most private parts of a person's body.

There has been concern as to whether violations of the Geneva and Hague Conventions create criminal penalties. Most now agree that when the violations are recognized crimes in international law or in most domestic criminal codes, they can be punished as a war crime. There is no dispute about the fact that grave breaches of the Geneva Conventions do carry criminal liability (although whether they apply in internal conflicts is hotly contested, as discussed *infra*). It was recognized at Nuremberg that it "is not essential that a crime be specifically defined and charged in accordance with a particular ordinance, statute, or treaty if it is made a crime by international convention, recognized customs and usages of war, or the general principles of criminal justice common to civilized nations generally."[59] Explicit and implicit proscriptions against sexual violence in the Hague and Geneva Conventions and Additional Protocols indicate that these are clearly crimes in customary law and under general principles of law. Explicit provisions cited above, and implicit provisions discussed below, therefore do carry criminal penalties for breach.

Common Article 3 of the 1949 Geneva Conventions

Common Article 3 was originally intended to specify minimum standards of conduct during the course of non-international armed conflicts. However, because Common Article 3 is now recognized as part of the body of customary international law, it applies to both internal and international armed conflicts.[60]

---

language of 1977 Additional Protocol II that specifically prohibits rape and enforced prostitution (art. 4(2)(e)), is entirely gender-neutral.

58. Notice that the language in Protocol I is "enforced" prostitution instead of the "forced" prostitution used in Article 27 and Protocol II. Arguments can be made for and against using one over the other. In general, "enforced" connotes a policy or practice; "forced" connotes violence, threats, or coercion.

59. U.S. v. List, 11 TRIALS OF WAR CRIMINALS BEFORE THE INTERNATIONAL MILITARY TRIBUNAL, NUREMBERG, 14 NOVEMBER 1945–1 OCTOBER 1946 1239 (commonly known as the Hostage Case).

60. THEODOR MERON, HUMAN RIGHTS AND HUMANITARIAN NORMS AS CUSTOMARY LAW 35 (1991); Case Concerning Military and Paramilitary Activities in and Against Nicaragua (Nicaragua v. The United States of America) (Merits), 1986 ICJ Reports 4, 114 (June 27, 1986); ICTY, Prosecutor v. Dusko Tadić, Decision on the Defence Motion on Jurisdiction (10 Aug. 1995), at paras. 65–74, *revised and affirmed in part* by the Appeals Chamber (2 Oct. 1995).

According to Common Article 3, certain acts are always prohibited, including: "(a) violence to life and person, in particular . . . mutilation, cruel treatment and torture; . . . (c) outrages upon personal dignity, in particular humiliating and degrading treatment." These prohibitions can be readily understood to encompass and to occur in tandem with crimes of rape, sexual slavery, and other forms of sexual violence.

Whenever possible, rape should be called rape and prosecuted as rape. Other forms of gender violence should likewise be called by whatever term most accurately identifies the nature of the harm, and ideally prosecuted under this identifying language.[61] In exceptional circumstances (e.g., if, for some reason, the act does not fit within more specific language or other categories of crimes), Common Article 3 provisions should be used to prosecute readily identifiable sex crimes. Most often, however, Common Article 3 crimes can and should be used to prosecute indignities commonly suffered in addition to or in conjunction with sexual violence, such as public rapes, rapes with foreign objects, or other forms of mental violence and degradation resulting from or incidental to the assault, whether occurring before, during, or after the commission of the sexual violence. For example, for a public rape, in addition to prosecuting rape, further injury caused by the public nature of the rape could also be prosecuted under the most appropriate Common Article 3 characterization of the crime, with preference given to subarticles depicting crimes of violence (physical or mental) over subarticles depicting crimes of dignity. Nothing prevents developing customary law from using the most accurate terminology possible.

Nonetheless, it must be mentioned that in the ICTY, all indictments for violations of the laws or customs of war for sexual violence have to date been charged exclusively under the vague provisions of Common Article 3, and not under customary international law or as specific violations of Article 27 of the Fourth Geneva Convention or the Additional Protocols.

The First, Second, and Third Geneva Conventions[62]

Women have long been engaged in medical, spiritual, or aid relief work during wartime. The First and Second Geneva Conventions, in addition to protecting wounded, sick, or shipwrecked members of the armed forces, also protect medical personnel and staff exclusively engaged in medical services for the sick or wounded, as well as certain religious personnel and charity aid workers.[63]

---

61. This demonstrates why international law desperately needs to define and codify crimes, in particular various forms of gender or sexual violence, including rape, sexual slavery, enforced prostitution, sexual mutilation, enforced impregnation, enforced maternity, forced sterilization, genocidal rape, and forced marriage. Prosecuting these crimes under vague and ambiguous terms results in confusing and somewhat unconstructive jurisprudence.

62. First and Second Geneva Conventions, *supra* note 6. Geneva Convention (III) Relative to the Treatment of Prisoners of War, 75 U.N.T.S. 135 (12 Aug. 1949), *entered into force* 21 Oct. 1950 [hereinafter Third Geneva Convention].

63. The First Geneva Convention, *supra* note 6, which protects wounded and sick combatants on land,

Women are increasingly taking part in hostilities.[64] Grave breach provisions of the First and Second Geneva Conventions can be interpreted as prohibiting sexual violence against combatants rendered *hors de combat* on land and at sea.[65] Further, the Fourth Geneva Convention forbids the mistreatment of the civilian population, while the Third Geneva Convention prohibits the mistreatment of combatants who are prisoners of war.

The Third Geneva Convention, the convention intended to protect prisoners of war, contains limited provisions requiring distinctive treatment of female prisoners of war, essentially providing that female prisoners of war are not to be in any way mistreated, and if they are subject to punishment, it must be administered by women.[66] The Third Geneva Convention further stipulates that all prisoners of war, men and women alike, "must at all times be humanely treated" and "must at all times be protected, particularly against acts of violence or intimidation and against insults and public curiosity."[67] These provisions would prohibit any sexual violence, including rape or sexual slavery.

The Geneva Conventions are supplemented by the Declaration on Protection of Women and Children in Emergency and Armed Conflict.[68] Article 5 provides that "[a]ll forms of repression and cruel and inhuman treatment of women and children . . . committed by belligerents in the course of military operations or in occupied territories shall be considered criminal."[69] Declarations are not legally binding, but they do reflect the morals of society and the stated intentions of governments. Nonetheless, more specific, legally binding language is needed, criminalizing all forms of wartime sexual violence against any person, including civilians and combatants.[70] Female combatants and other female members of the armed forces remain in serious danger of sexual assault upon capture.[71]

---

also protects "[m]edical personnel exclusively engaged in the search for, or the collection, transport or treatment of the wounded or sick, or in the prevention of disease . . . as well as chaplains attached to the armed forces" (art. 24), and when members of the armed forces are performing certain medical functions for the sick and wounded, they are also protected "if they are carrying out these duties at the time when they come into contact with the enemy or fall into his hands" (art. 25). Red Cross and other Voluntary Aid Society staff members are also protected by the convention (art. 26). The Second Geneva Convention, which protects wounded, sick, or shipwrecked combatants at sea, also protects certain "religious, medical and hospital personnel" (art. 36).

64. *See generally* MIRIAM COOKE, WOMEN AND THE WAR STORY (1996).

65. First and Second Geneva Conventions, *supra* note 6, at art. 50 (First Geneva Convention) and art. 51 (Second Geneva Convention).

66. Third Geneva Convention, *supra* note 62, at arts. 14, 49, 88, 97, and 108. Civilians are not regarded as prisoners of war for purposes of the Third Geneva Convention (art. 4). Imprisoned non-military medical personnel are not considered prisoners of war (arts. 4 and 33).

67. Third Geneva Convention, *id.* at art. 13. *See also* art. 14.

68. Declaration on Protection of Women and Children in Emergency and Armed Conflict, *supra* note 22. *See especially* 4 and 5.

69. *Id.* at art. 5.

70. Ideally, this would be accomplished by means of an optional protocol to the conventions or a separate convention addressing gender issues during armed conflict.

71. Kenneth L. Karst, *The Pursuit of Manhood and the Desegregation of the Armed Forces*, 38 UCLA L. REV. 499, 537–38 (1991).

In conclusion, rape of combatants and noncombatants has been prohibited by customary laws of warfare for centuries, and increasingly this prohibition extends to other forms of sexual violence, including but not limited to sexual slavery, enforced prostitution, enforced impregnation, enforced maternity, forced sterilization, forced marriage, and sexual mutilation.[72] The four 1949 Geneva Conventions, including the interdicts against sexual violence, are not only part of conventional international law, they are also proscribed in customary international law and are binding universally, regardless of whether states are parties to the conventions.[73]

Application of International Human Rights Law to International Humanitarian Law

International human rights law supplements, reinforces, and complements international humanitarian law. As Common Article 2 of the 1949 Geneva Conventions stipulates, the articles of these conventions apply "*[i]n addition to* the provisions which shall be implemented in peacetime."[74] This principle was firmly reinforced in 1968 by the unanimous adoption of the U.N. General Assembly Resolution on Respect for Human Rights in Periods of Armed Conflict, which recognized the importance of minimum standards of conduct and certain fundamental human rights norms applicable in all armed conflicts.[75] Indeed, a driving force behind the establishment of human rights law "grew out of the tragic experience of the Second World War and the horrendous violations of human rights committed in the Holocaust."[76] The Martens Clause provides additional evidence that fundamental human rights norms do not cease to be applicable during armed conflict.[77]

---

72. Jennifer Green, Rhonda Copelon, Patrick Cotter, & Beth Stephens, *Affecting the Rules for the Prosecution of Rape and Other Gender-Based Violence Before the International Criminal Tribunal for the Former Yugoslavia: A Feminist Proposal and Critique*, 5 HASTINGS WOMEN'S L. J. 171, 185 (1994).

73. *See* HILARE McCOUBREY, INTERNATIONAL HUMANITARIAN LAW: THE REGULATION OF ARMED CONFLICT 2 (1990); ROBERT F. DRINAN, CRY OF THE OPPRESSED, THE HISTORY AND HOPE OF THE HUMAN RIGHTS REVOLUTION 170 (1987); Final Report of the Commission of Experts, *supra* note 4, at para. 53; Report of the Secretary-General Pursuant to Paragraph 2 of Security Council Resolution 808 (1993), U.N. Doc. S/25704 of 3 May 1993, at para. 35. *See also* THE LAWS OF ARMED CONFLICT, A COLLECTION OF CONVENTIONS, RESOLUTIONS AND OTHER DOCUMENTS 665, 667, 703 (Dietrich Schindler & Jiri Toman eds., 3d ed. 1988). The Red Cross Fundamental Rules also emphasize that "civilians under the authority of an adverse party are entitled to respect for their lives, dignity, personal rights and convictions. They shall be protected against all acts of violence." ICRC and League of Red Cross Societies, *Fundamental Rules of International Humanitarian Law Applicable in Armed Conflicts* (Geneva, 1979), at para. 4.

74. Geneva Conventions I–IV, *supra* note 6, at art. 2 [emphasis added].

75. Respect for Human Rights in Periods of Armed Conflict, U.N. Doc. GA Res. 2444 (XXIII) of 19 Dec. 1968. See also U.N. Doc. GA Res. 2675 (XXV) of 9 Dec. 1970.

76. Thomas Buergenthal, *The Normative and Institutional Evolution of International Human Rights*, 19 HUM. RTS. Q. 703, 706 (1997).

77. The famous Martens Clause, contained in the preamble of 1899 and 1907 Hague Convention IV, *supra* note 5, and reproduced almost verbatim in art. 1(2) of Additional Protocol I, states: "Until a more complete code of the laws of war is issued, . . . populations and belligerents remain under the protection and empire of the principles of international law, as they result from the usages established between civilized nations, from the laws of humanity and the requirements of the public conscience."

During armed conflicts and public emergencies, some rights may be legitimately suspended, although the core human rights principles are nonderogable. Therefore, in wartime, international humanitarian laws and international human rights laws may both simultaneously apply. The number of human rights treaties,[78] declarations,[79] conference or committee documents,[80] and U.N. resolutions[81] promulgated in the 1990s that condemn, protect against, prohibit, or outright criminalize gender, including sexual violence, is reflective of a common interest in the international community and a political commitment by signatory states, and supports an emerging principle in customary international law to criminalize all forms of physical, mental, or sexual violence against women, irrespective of the presence of an armed conflict.[82]

The Universal Declaration of Human Rights (UDHR)[83] and the International Covenant on Civil and Political Rights (ICCPR)[84] denounce all forms of slavery, torture, and inhuman or degrading treatment, and these rights are explicitly nonderogable (ICCPR, art. 4.2). The Convention on the Rights of the Child obliges states to protect children from sexual assault and torture and to respect rules of

---

78. *E.g.*, Inter-American Convention for the Prevention, Punishment and Eradication of Violence Against Women, *adopted* by the General Assembly of the OAS (9 June 1994), Doc. OEA/Ser.P AG/doc.3115/94 rev.2 (commonly referred to either as the Convention of Belém Do Pará or the Inter-American Convention Against Violence).

79. *E.g.*, Resolution 1992/3 of the Sub-Commission on Prevention of Discrimination and Protection of Minorities (18 Aug. 1992), Contemporary forms of slavery, U.N. Doc. E/CN.4/Sub.2/1992/L.11 (18 Aug. 1992); Declaration on the Elimination of Violence Against Women, GA Res. 104, U.N. Doc. A/Res/48/104 (1994).

80. *E.g.*, Vienna Declaration and Programme of Action, *adopted* by the World Conference on Human Rights in Vienna, U.N. Doc. A/CONF.157/23 (12 July 1993); Beijing Declaration and Platform for Action, Fourth World Conference on Women, A/CONF.177/20 (1995) and A/CONF.177/20/Add.1 (1995)(15 Sept. 1995); Committee on Elimination of Discrimination against Women, General Recommendation 19, U.N. Doc. A/47/38 (Eleventh session, Feb. 1992).

81. *E.g.*, S.C. Res. 798, U.N. Doc. S/798/1992 (18 Dec. 1992) (strongly condemning reports of "massive, organized and systematic detention and rape" in Yugoslav conflict); S.C. Res 820, U.N. Doc. S/820/1993 (17 Apr. 1993) (condemning detention and rape of women and affirming individual responsibility for those responsible for committing or ordering such acts); GA Res. 49/205 U.N. Doc. A/RES/49/205 (23 Dec. 1994) ("Appalled at the continuing and substantiated reports of widespread rape and abuse of women and children in the areas of armed conflict in the former Yugoslavia"); GA Res. 48/143, U.N. Doc. A/RES/48/143 (20 Dec. 1993)(discussing rape and abuse of women in the Yugoslav conflict); Commission on Human Rights resolution 1994/77 (9 March 1994), Rape and abuse of women in the territory of the former Yugoslavia (condemning sexual violence of women during Yugoslav conflict).

82. There are 139 documents on women reproduced, in whole or in part, in UNITED NATIONS, THE UNITED NATIONS AND THE ADVANCEMENT OF WOMEN 1945–1996 (1996). Many of these documents are devoted to protecting women from violence.

83. Universal Declaration of Human Rights, GA Res. 217 A (III), U.N. Doc. A/810, at 71 (1948), at arts. 1, 2, 3, 4, 5, 7, and 12.

84. International Covenant on Civil and Political Rights, 999 U.N.T.S. 171, 6 ILM 368 (1967), *adopted* by the General Assembly on 16 Dec. 1966 (GA Res. 2200 A(XXI)), *entered into force* on 23 March 1976, at arts. 6, 7, and 8.

humanitarian law.[85] The Race Convention prohibits "any distinction, exclusion, restriction or preference based on race, colour, descent, or national or ethnic origin."[86] The Convention Against Torture expressly stipulates that "[n]o exceptional circumstances whatsoever, whether a state of war or a threat of war, internal political instability or any other public emergency, may be invoked as a justification of torture."[87] In this treaty, torture is recognized as a crime "according to the general principles of law recognized by civilized nations" (art. 15(2)).

Enshrined throughout these instruments, and recognized as the most fundamental principle of human rights law, is the principle of nondiscrimination, including discrimination based on "sex".[88] None of these instruments may be interpreted or applied in a manner discriminatory to women. The nondiscrimination principle also requires that rape and other forms of sexual violence be prohibited and punished when committed against men.

The Convention on the Elimination of Discrimination against Women (Women's Convention)[89] prohibits discrimination and disparaging treatment on the basis of gender, including violence against women, as interpreted by the Committee on the Elimination of Discrimination Against Women (CEDAW).[90] The Declaration on Elimination of Violence Against Women [91] and the Inter-American Convention on Violence[92] also urge protection against all forms of violence against women, including sexual violence, whether committed in peacetime or in wartime, in the public sphere or in the private sphere. Significantly, the Declaration Against Violence identifies some of the root causes of violence against women:

[V]iolence against women is a manifestation of historically unequal power relations between men and women, which have led to domination over and discrimination against women by men and to the prevention of the full advancement of women, and [ ] violence against women is one of the crucial social mechanisms by which women are forced into a subordinate position compared with men.[93]

---

85. Convention on the Rights of the Child, GA Res. 44/25 (20 Nov. 1989), U.N. Doc. A/RES/44/25, *entered into force* on 2 Sept. 1990, at arts. 34, 37, and 38.

86. International Convention on the Elimination of All Forms of Racial Discrimination, 660 U.N.T.S. 195, 5 ILM 352 (1966), adopted 21 Dec. 1965, *entered into force* 4 Jan. 1969, at arts. 1, 3.

87. Convention Against Torture and Other Cruel, Inhuman or Degrading Treatment or Punishment, GA Res. 39/46 (10 Dec. 1984), *entered into force* 26 June 1987, at art. 2.

88. *See* Buergenthal, *supra* note 76, at 707–8 ("The only unambiguous provision . . . is the prohibition of discrimination").

89. Convention on the Elimination of all Forms of Discrimination against Women, 1249 U.N.T.S. 13, 19 ILM 33 (1980), *adopted by* GA Res. 180 (XXXIV)(18 Dec. 1979), *entered into force* 3 Sept. 1981.

90. Committee on the Elimination of Discrimination of Violence Against Women, General Recommendation No.19, U.N. Doc A/47/38 (Eleventh session, 1992).

91. Declaration on the Elimination of Violence Against Women, U.N.G.A. Res. 48/104 (23 Feb. 1994).

92. Inter-American Convention on the Prevention, Punishment and Eradication of Violence Against Women, *supra* note 78.

93. Declaration Against Violence, *supra* note 91, at preamble.

In wartime, of course, these conditions are greatly exacerbated and the stigmatizing and destructive nature of sex crimes is intentionally exploited and used as a powerful weapon of the conflict.

The Vienna Declaration & Programme of Action adopted in 1993 at the U.N. World Conference on Human Rights affirms that wartime violence against women violates international human rights and international humanitarian law:

> Violations of the human rights of women in situations of armed conflict are violations of the fundamental principles of international human rights and humanitarian law. All violations of this kind, including in particular murder, systematic rape, sexual slavery, and forced pregnancy, require a particularly effective response.[94]

Although the language in this document refers to "systematic rape," it should be emphasized that systematic rape is understood to mean rape carried out during the course of a systematic attack or as part of the systematic commission of physical, mental, and/or sexual violence. Thus, the rape is not systematic, the attack or the commission of violent acts is systematic.[95]

The Beijing Declaration and Platform for Action adopted at the 1995 Fourth World Conference on Women also recognized that wartime violence against women is pervasive and that women are increasingly targeted for sexual violence as part of a multifarious scheme to harm the opposition:

> While entire communities suffer consequences of armed conflict and terrorism, women and girls are particularly affected because of their status in society and their sex. Parties to a conflict often rape women with impunity, sometimes using systematic rape as a tactic of war and terrorism. . . . [Women and girls] are victims of acts of murder, terrorism, torture, involuntary disappearance, sexual slavery, rape, sexual abuse and forced pregnancy in situations of armed conflict, especially as a result of policies of ethnic cleansing and other new and emerging forms of violence.[96]

These documents reflect an awareness by the international community that wartime violence against civilians (particularly sexual violence) could never be justified by military necessity and is a gross violation of human rights. While

---

94. Vienna Declaration and Programme of Action, *supra* note 80, part II, para. 38. It is regrettable that the term "systematic" was used in front of "rape," because rape does not have to be "systematic" in order to be a crime or in order to be punishable, except, possibly, as prosecuted as a crime against humanity, and that is when an attack is systematic. When this language was adopted, few studies had been conducted on wartime rape, and the tribunal had been established only a month previously. Thus, because Article 5 of the ICTY Statute (established in May 1993), *supra* note 9, listed rape solely as a crime against humanity, perhaps that is the reason for the inclusion of "systematic" in the Vienna document.

95. The standard is not limited to a policy of systematic rape in an organized fashion, or a policy of systematic sexual slavery to sexually service military personnel. The systematic nature of crimes can be found through such means as a policy of ignoring reports of rape or sexual slavery; through an organized plan or policy to cause chaos and terror amongst a population by either encouraging, condoning, or ignoring sexual violence; and even by the prevalence of isolated, individually motivated rape crimes.

96. Beijing Declaration and Platform of Action, *supra* note 80, at para. 136. *See also* paras. 132–34.

international humanitarian laws apply only in the context of an armed conflict, human rights laws, in particular nonderogable rights, apply regardless of the presence of an armed conflict or public emergency. Violations of a convention, however, are seldom criminal offenses without language, recognition, or practice to the contrary.

Neither genocide nor crimes against humanity require the presence of a war in order to be prosecuted, unless required by the applicable statute of the judicial body. (For example, the ICTY Statute requires that crimes against humanity be committed in connection with an armed conflict even though this nexus is not required in customary law.) As noted *supra*, there is general consensus that genocide, slavery, torture, war crimes, and crimes against humanity are violations of *jus cogens,* subject to universal jurisdiction.[97] Many forms of sexual violence may also constitute genocide, slavery, torture, war crimes, and crimes against humanity, making them subject to universal jurisdiction when they meet the constituent elements of these crimes.[98] Gender and sex violence are increasingly becoming independently recognized as international crimes, which is of critical importance as crimes against women should not have to be subsumed under or fit within other categories of crimes, especially when these other categories of crimes are broad and ambiguous and the gender-based or sexual nature of the crimes is not identified. It should be emphasized that civil or tort remedies are also available for these crimes, and that other appropriate forums may be effective means to hold perpetrators or others responsible for serious crimes accountable.[99]

CURRENT EVENTS IN INTERNATIONAL HUMANITARIAN LAW

International War Crimes Tribunals Established—The ICTY and ICTR

As a result of reports in the early 1990s of gross violations of humanitarian law committed in the territory of the former Yugoslavia, the United Nations Security Council established a Commission of Experts to investigate.[100] Based on continued reports and preliminary findings, including reports of widespread or systematic rape to further the policies of "ethnic cleansing," the United Nations Security Council called for the establishment of an *ad hoc* international war crimes tribunal.[101] Consequently, the International Criminal Tribunal for the former Yugoslavia

---

97. *See* Jonathan I. Charney, *Universal International Law*, 87 Am. J. Int'l L. 529, 541(1993); Lauri Hannikainen, *Implementation of International Humanitarian Law in Finnish Law, in* Implementing Humanitarian Law Applicable in Armed Conflict 118 (Hannikainen, Hanski, & Rosas eds., 1992); Jalil Kasto, Jus Cogens and Humanitarian Law (1994); Charlesworth & Chinkin, *The Gender of* Jus Cogens, 15 Hum. Rts. Q. 63 (1993); Askin, War Crimes Against Women, *supra* note 26, at 239–42.

98. Askin, War Crimes Against Women, *id.* at 241–42.

99. *See,* for example, Kadić v. Karadzíć, 70 F.3d 232 (2d Cir. 1995), *reproduced in* 34 ILM 1592 (1995); Beth Stephens & Michael Ratner, International Human Rights Litigation in U.S. Courts (1996); Guide to International Human Rights Practice (Hurst Hannum ed., 2d ed. 1992).

100. S.C. Res. 780 (6 Oct. 1992).

101. S.C. Res. 808 (22 Feb. 1993). S.C. Res. 808, in essence, endorsed the principle of establishing a tribunal.

(ICTY) was established to prosecute "Persons Responsible for Serious Violations of International Humanitarian Law Committed in the Territory of the Former Yugoslavia since 1991."[102]

The Final Report of the Commission of Experts for the former Yugoslavia[103] subsequently described several categories of crimes committed by all sides to the conflict, including five patterns of sexual violence.[104] Briefly, these patterns included:

— individuals or small groups committing sexual assault in conjunction with looting and intimidation of the target ethnic group;

— individuals or small groups committing sexual assault in conjunction with fighting in an area, often including the rape of women in public;

— individuals or groups sexually assaulting people in detention because they had access to the people;

— individuals or groups committing sexual assaults against women for the purpose of terrorizing and humiliating them; [and]

— detention of women in hotels or similar facilities for the sole purpose of sexually entertaining soldiers, rather than causing a reaction in the women. . . .[105]

Some of these crimes were committed through the use of rape camps in which women were detained for illicit purposes and subjected to gang rapes, public rapes, and multiple instances of rape, including rape for furtherance of genocide, forced impregnation, and forced maternity.[106]

As a result of the ensuing conflict in Rwanda, the United Nations appointed a Special Rapporteur for Rwanda in mid-1994,[107] and shortly thereafter the U.N. Security Council established a Commission of Experts to investigate reports and allegations of serious crimes committed during the armed conflict in Rwanda.[108] Subsequently, the Security Council established the International Criminal Tribunal for Rwanda (ICTR) for the "Prosecution of Persons Responsible for Genocide and Other Serious Violations of International Humanitarian Law Committed in the

---

102. S.C. Res. 827 (25 May 1993). The Statute of the ICTY is contained in U.N. Doc. S/25704, Annex (May 3, 1993) which is attached to the "Report on the Secretary-General Pursuant to Paragraph 2 of Security Council Resolution 808."

103. Final Report of the Commission of Experts (Yugoslavia), *supra* note 4.

104. Final Report of the Commission of Experts (Yugoslavia), *id.* at paras. 230–253. The categories have been elaborated on in Bassiouni & McCormick, *Sexual Violence, supra* note 4, at 15–19.

105. Final Report of the Commission of Experts (Yugoslavia), *supra* note 4, at paras. 245–49, respectively.

106. *Id.* at paras. 247, 248, and 250.

107. Commission on Human Rights Resolution S-3/1 (25 May 1994).

108. S.C. Res. 935 (1 July 1994).

Territory of Rwanda and Rwandan citizens responsible for genocide and other violations committed in the territory of neighbouring States, between 1 January 1994 and 31 December 1994.''[109] The Final Report of the Commission of Experts (Rwanda),[110] while documenting very little substantive crimes in any depth, nevertheless noted that ''[d]isturbing reports have been filed with the Commission of Experts that document the abduction and rape of women and girls in Rwanda.''[111] The U.N. Special Rapporteur on Rwanda concluded that ''rape was the rule and its absence the exception,'' adding that many of these rapes resulted in pregnancy.[112]

Development of Gender Issues in IHL in the 1990s

The jurisprudence surrounding the prosecution of crimes committed against women during wartime has made tremendous inroads in this last decade of the twentieth century. In the early 1990s, media reports provided detailed coverage of the war being waged in the territory of the then Yugoslavia, and these reports included continuous references to ''rape,'' ''mass rape,'' ''systematic rape,'' ''rape camps,'' forcing women into ''brothels,'' and other forms of gender-based violence. During this period, the international community began urging the United Nations to take measures to stop and to punish crimes committed during the conflict. Also during this time, legal scholars began searching for legal prohibitions on crimes against women during periods of armed conflict, seeking to analyze criminal responsibility associated with these crimes.[113] The following paragraphs represent a chronology of events that occurred in the 1990s, primarily as a result of the Yugoslav and Rwandan conflicts, which served as the impetus for the development of gender jurisprudence in international humanitarian law.[114]

---

109. S.C. Res. 955 (8 Nov 1994). The Statute of the Rwandan Tribunal is attached to SC Res. 955 as an Annex.

110. U.N. Doc. S/1994/1405, Annex, Final Report of the Commission of Experts on Rwanda.

111. *Id.* at para. 136.

112. Report on the Situation of Human Rights in Rwanda submitted by Mr. René Degni-Segui, Special Rapporteur of the Commission on Human Rights, under paragraph 20 of the resolution S-3/1 of 25 May 1994, E/CN.4/1996/68, at 7, Jan. 29, 1996.

Additionally, while many gender-specific crimes committed against women in the Rwandan conflict are similar to crimes regularly committed against women in armed conflict, there are also indications that some women were forced into marriage. Sexual mutilation also appears to occur in greater frequency in Rwanda than in other wars. *See generally* SHATTERED LIVES, *supra* note 27.

113. In 1975, Susan Brownmiller published *Against Our Will, supra* note 26, a book on rape that dedicated some three chapters to violence against women during various armed conflicts. Never before or after, until the 1990s when the tribunals were established as a result of the Yugoslav and Rwandan conflicts, had a research project on these issues been thoroughly documented and analyzed.

114. Shortly after the tribunal was established, and as a direct result of the reports of gender crimes in the Yugoslav conflict, the author began an advanced degree in law researching the prosecution of war crimes against women in international war crimes tribunals, culminating in a doctoral dissertation on prosecuting war crimes against women in international war crimes tribunals. As a result of both the research and participation in numerous conferences and debates between 1993–1998 on the tribunals, the following paragraphs represent the author's recollections and interpretations of the most significant events that have led to the current status of women in international humanitarian law.

After the U.N. Security Council established a Commission of Experts in October 1992 to investigate reports of war crimes committed during the conflict in Yugoslavia, the preliminary report included instances of widespread gender and sexual violence against women. In December of 1992, the Security Council issued Resolution 798, the first Security Council Resolution in history directly addressing war crimes against women, and this resolution condemned the ''massive, organized and systematic detention and rape of women'' in Bosnia and Herzegovina. When the ICTY was established in May 1993, ''rape'' was included, under article 5 of the statute, as one of the crimes which, when other constituent elements were met, could constitute a crime against humanity.

Many heralded the drafters for including rape as a crime against humanity within the jurisdiction of the statute. With the sole exception of CCL10, this was the first time that a sex crime had been included within the charter or statute of an international war crimes tribunal.[115] A veritable avalanche of articles were being published on crimes committed against women during periods of armed conflicts; many focused on how rape might be prosecuted as a crime against humanity as many of the elements of this crime were unclear (especially as different language was used in enunciating this crime in the IMT, IMTFE, CCL10, ICTY, and eventually ICTR Statutes). Women's groups and certain noted legal scholars, most particularly Professors Meron, Copelon, and Bassiouni, urged that the prosecutions not focus exclusively on ''systematic'' rape, rape which could be prosecuted as a crime against humanity. It was implored that prosecutions must also consist of the most common forms of rape found in every war—isolated, random, or opportunistic rapes—and thus, those responsible for this violence must be charged under other articles of the statute as well, so that the precedent set is not limited solely to crimes against humanity.[116]

However, most members of the tribunal (particularly in the Prosecutor's Office) appeared hesitant to tackle the issue of sexual violence, and some commentators scoffed at suggestions that rape crimes be prosecuted outside of specific language in the statute (e.g., under articles other than Article 5, which specifically listed rape). Fortunately, however, in 1994, Judge Richard Goldstone was appointed Chief Prosecutor of the ICTY.[117] Goldstone, a South African judge with enormous integrity and a leader in South Africa's fight against apartheid, took rape crimes very

---

115. Essentially, rape was not specifically included within the IMT or IMTFE Charters, but it was included within the CCL10, at art. II(1)(c), crimes against humanity. The CCL10 was used to prosecute the ''lesser'' war criminals at Nuremberg, trials held for alleged war criminals in the zones of occupation. *See* Allied Control Council Law No. 10, Punishment of Persons Guilty of War Crimes, Crimes Against Peace and Humanity, 20 Dec. 1945, Official Gazette of the Control Council for Germany, No. 3, Berlin, 31 Jan. 1946. *Reprinted in* 1 FERENCZ 488; 1 FRIEDMAN 908.

116. It would have been disastrous for the precedent set by these tribunals to be that in order for any rape crime to be prosecuted it would have to meet the onerous standard of crimes against humanity. *See* Jennifer Green, Rhonda Copelon, Patrick Cotter, & Beth Stephens, *Affecting the Rules for the Prosecution of Rape and Other Gender-Based Violence Before the International Criminal Tribunal for the Former Yugoslavia: A Feminist Proposal and Critique,* 5 HASTINGS WOMEN'S L.J. 171 (1994); ASKIN, WAR CRIMES AGAINST WOMEN, *supra* note 26, at 344–50, 359–60.

117. S.C. Res. 936, 8 July 1994.

seriously and had no hesitation in denouncing the crimes and pledging to prosecute them.[118]

In November 1994, after reports of rampant violence committed during the Rwandan conflict, including extensive crimes of sexual violence, the ICTR was established. Goldstone and the Prosecutor's Office were charged with prosecuting suspected war criminals in this tribunal, in addition to prosecuting alleged criminals in the Yugoslav Tribunal.

Throughout 1993 and 1994, debates raged on all continents as to whether rape constituted a war crime that could be prosecuted under Article 3 of the ICTY Statute as a violation of the laws or customs of war. Of even greater controversy was whether sexual violence could be incorporated into the grave breach provisions of the Geneva Conventions and prosecuted under Article 2 of the ICTY Statute. Also rigorously contested was whether sexual violence could ever amount to genocide[119] and be justiciable in the tribunals as such.

Of pivotal importance during this period, women's groups around the world were involved in mobilizing, strategizing, and lobbying efforts on behalf of prosecuting gender-based violence, partly as a result of the Vienna World Conference on Human Rights in 1993 and in preparation for the Fourth World Conference on Women's Rights to be held in Beijing in 1995. Lawyers, scholars, reporters, and others were enhancing their awareness of international humanitarian law and grasping the importance of not having the standard of prosecuting rape set at the level of crimes against humanity, as it would be an onerous standard to meet and millions of rape crimes might go unredressed. It was also of profound significance that women became involved in positions of power within the tribunals, an unprecedented event. For instance, two women were elected judges of the ICTY, and one woman was elected judge of the ICTR; these positions[120] resulted in the incorporation of greater gender sensitivity in the rules of procedure and evidence. Crucial to both the prosecution of gender violence and the treatment of women's issues within the tribunals was Patricia Viseur Sellers' status as the gender issues legal officer for the Prosecutor's Office of the ICTY and ICTR. An emminently capable and dynamic woman, Sellers has become the foremost authority on prosecuting war crimes against women and a driving force behind attempting to ensure that crimes against women are afforded given low priority. Her direction has also been vital in other stages of the process, such as witness protection, taking testimony of rape survivors, and training members of the tribunals in enhanced gender issue cognizance.

---

118. In a 1995 facsimile letter to the author, Goldstone pledged to ensure that "rape and other sexual offenses are unequivocally included within the grave breaches of the Geneva Conventions, crimes against humanity and genocide." Letter on file with author.

119. The leader of the genocidal rape campaign has been Catharine MacKinnon, Professor of Law at the University of Michigan. MacKinnon coined the term "genocidal rape" and has been a leading advocate in arguing for the prosecution of rape as genocide, both in the tribunals and in domestic courts.

120. *See also* Kelly Askin, *Introduction*, in this volume for more information on women participating in high-level positions within the tribunals and in international law in general.

Once the research confirmed that rape was indeed a war crime, and had been one for centuries, there was an escalating awareness of the importance of prosecuting other forms of sexual violence and not limiting the prosecution, even under multiple articles of the statutes, exclusively to "rape" or "enforced prostitution." For instance, it is now routinely acknowledged that violence in such forms as sexual slavery, enforced impregnation, enforced maternity, forced sterilization, forced marriage, and sexual mutilation must also be prosecuted.

By late 1995, the majority of scholars, and the Prosecutor's Office of the tribunals, agreed that sexual violence could, and often did, constitute a grave breach of the Geneva Conventions, and that these crimes could additionally be prosecuted under Article 2 of the Yugoslav Statute. (The Rwandan Statute did not allow for grave breaches because, at the time the tribunal was established, the general presumption was that grave breaches applied only to international conflicts, a point which is now contentious). Article 4 of the ICTR Statute, however, did explicitly enumerate rape and enforced prostitution as violations of Common Article 3 to the Geneva Conventions.

In 1996, Goldstone resigned as Chief Prosecutor to return to his seat on the Constitutional Court of South Africa, and Canadian judge Louise Arbour was appointed to replace him. While women's groups were ecstatic that a woman was Chief Prosecutor of an international war crimes tribunal, an historic first, many of these same groups were hesitant in endorsing Arbour, unsure of how she would treat gender-specific war crimes. While Arbour has not demonstrated the enthusiasm shown by her predecessor for prosecuting sexual violence and thus not yet won the confidence regarding gender inclusion and parity that Goldstone achieved, she certainly deserves substantial credit for amending some indictments originated by Goldstone to include gender or sexual violence, and charging them under various articles, including genocide.[121] The new deputy prosecutor at the ICTR, Mr. Bernard Muna (Cameroon), has indicated that the Prosecutor's Office considers sexual violence as evidence of genocide and crimes against humanity.[122]

---

121. For instance, Prosecutor v. Akayesu, ICTR–96–4–I was amended in the ICTR in order to charge Akayesu with gender or sexual violence as constituting genocide, crimes against humanity, and violations of Common Article 3; Prosecutor v. Nyiramasuhuko & Ntahobali, ICTR–97–21–I was amended in the ICTR to charge indictees with gender or sexual violence as constituting genocide, crimes against humanity, and serious violations of Common Article 3.

It should also be noted that prior to her appointment as Chief Prosecutor of the tribunals, Judge Arbour had just completed an extensive inquiry into particular events in which women were subjected to inappropriate and degrading conduct at the hands of male emergency response team members at a women's prison in Canada. Her report showed great sensitivity to and awareness of certain forms of gender-based violence. *See* THE HONOURABLE LOUISE ARBOUR COMMISSIONER, COMMISSION OF INQUIRY INTO CERTAIN EVENTS AT THE PRISON FOR WOMEN IN KINGSTON (1996), especially at 83, 88, 200, 204, 211, 216, and 239.

122. Mr. Muna made these comments during his presentation at the conference "War Crimes Tribunals: The Record and the Prospects" held at the Washington College of Law, American University, March 31–April 4, 1998, under the auspices of the ASIL Regional Meeting, co-sponsored by the Center for Human Rights and Humanitarian Law's War Crimes Research Office of the Washington College of Law. The conference was organized by the Director of the War Crimes Research Office, Professor Diane Orentlicher.

Prosecuting War Crimes Against Women in the ICTY and ICTR

All violations of the Geneva and Hague Conventions are violations of the laws of war. The Yugoslav and Rwandan Tribunals have the authority to prosecute *serious* violations of humanitarian law (thus not merely administrative infractions or relatively minor breaches). More precisely, the tribunals are charged with prosecuting crimes. Rape, sexual slavery, and other forms of gender or sexual violence are widely recognized as serious crimes in domestic laws and in customary international law, and increasingly in international human rights law and international humanitarian law.[123] A rapidly developing field is international criminal law, which has received substantial attention recently because of the adoption of a statute for a permanent international criminal court.[124]

The crimes against women prosecuted in the ICTY and ICTR will likely be used as precedents for future such prosecutions, especially in regional tribunals and in the international criminal court, which will have jurisdiction over a set of core crimes, including war crimes, crimes against humanity, and genocide. As such, this section will briefly explain how crimes of gender or sexual violence can be or have been prosecuted in the ICTY and ICTR and, to a limited extent, outside of these tribunals. Some of the crimes listed within the jurisdiction of the statutes are international crimes in their own right, and may be prosecuted in state courts or in other venues, whether committed in wartime or in peacetime. It should also be emphasized that the Convention on the Non-Applicability of Statutory Limitations to War Crimes and Crimes Against Humanity is still in force.[125] Reparations may also be available for humanitarian law violations.[126]

Violations of the Laws or Customs of War (ICTY, art. 3)

As previously noted, rape has been a war crime for centuries;[127] in codified laws of war, rape and enforced prostitution are explicitly prohibited by the Geneva

---

123. *See* Theodor Meron, *Rape as a Crime under International Humanitarian Law*, 87 AM. J. INT'L L. 424, 425 (1993); M. CHERIF BASSIOUNI & PETER MANIKAS, THE LAW OF THE INTERNATIONAL CRIMINAL TRIBUNAL FOR THE FORMER YUGOSLAVIA 578 (1996); ASKIN, WAR CRIMES AGAINST WOMEN, *supra* note 26, *passim*.

124. See Rome Statute of the International Criminal Court, adopted by the United Nations Diplomatic Conference of Plenipotentiaries on the Establishment of an International Criminal Court on 17 July, 1998, U.N. Doc. A/Conf. 183/9 (1998). For a discussion and analysis of the current status of various issues affecting women in international criminal law, *see* Dorean Koenig & Kelly Askin, *Women and International Criminal Law*, in volume II of this treatise, *forthcoming* 1999.

125. Convention on the Non-Applicability of Statutory Limitations to War Crimes and Crimes Against Humanity, GA Res. 2391 (XXIII) of 26 Nov. 1968, 754 U.N.T.S. 73, *entered into force* 11 Nov. 1970.

126. *See especially* Revised set of basic principles and guidelines on the right to reparation for victims of gross violations of human rights and humanitarian law prepared by Mr. Theo van Boven pursuant to Sub-Commission decision 1995/117, U.N. Doc. E/CN.4/Sub.2/1996/17 (1996); Final Report Prepared by Mr. Joinet, Question of the impunity of perpetrators of human rights violations, U.N. Doc. E/CN.4/Sub.2/1997/20 (1997).

127. *See* Meron, *Rape as a Crime under International Humanitarian Law*, *supra* note 123, at 425;

Conventions (IV, art. 27) and the Additional Protocols (Protocol I, art. 76(1); Protocol II, art. 4(2)(e)), and other provisions implicitly prohibit all forms of sexual or gender violence. At issue is whether violations of the Geneva Conventions outside the grave breach provisions constitute crimes. Article 146 of the Fourth Geneva Convention requires each state to "take measures necessary for the suppression of all acts contrary to the provisions of the . . . [c]onvention other than the grave breaches." Indeed, Meron accurately insists that "[j]ust because the Geneva Conventions created the obligation of *aut dedere aut judicare* only with regard to grave breaches does not mean that other breaches of the Geneva Conventions may not be punished by any state party to the Conventions."[128] Thus, simply because the grave breaches are specifically attributed crime status does not mean that all other provisions are definitively not crimes. Rape is almost universally criminalized in domestic laws and is undisputably regarded as a crime. There is no longer any credible dispute as to the criminality of sexual violence in wartime. It is clear that sexual violence is a criminal offense both in the customs of war and in the laws of war.

Common Article 3 to the Geneva Conventions (ICTR, art. 4)

In each of the four Geneva Conventions, Article 3 contains identical language. Hence, the use of the term "Common Article 3 to the Geneva Conventions."[129] Common Article 3, originally intended to dictate treatment of persons in internal conflicts, is now understood to have become part of customary international law, applicable to internal and international armed conflicts alike. Similar language is used in Protocol II (art. 4(2)), which governs internal conflicts, and which is also included within the jurisdiction of the Rwandan Statute. Common Article 3 prohibits the following acts: "(a) Violence to life and person, in particular murder of all kinds, mutilation, cruel treatment and torture; . . . (c) Outrages upon personal dignity, in particular humiliating and degrading treatment."

The language used in the ICTR Statute is almost identical to that used in Additional Protocol II. Article 4 of the ICTR Statute confers jurisdiction over, in pertinent part: "(a) Violence to life, health and physical or mental well being of persons, in particular murder as well as cruel treatment such as torture, mutilation or any form of corporal punishment; . . . (e) Outrages upon personal dignity, in particular humiliating and degrading treatment, rape, enforced prostitution and any form of indecent assault."[130]

BASSIOUNI & MANIKAS, *supra* note 123, at 578; ASKIN, WAR CRIMES AGAINST WOMEN, *supra* note 26, at 18–48.

128. Meron, *International Criminalization of Internal Atrocities, supra* note 10, at 569. Support is also provided by the Declaration on the Protection of Women and Children in Emergency and Armed Conflict, *supra* note 22, at art. 5 ("[C]ruel and inhuman treatment of women and children . . . shall be considered criminal").

129. Some commentators prefer the term "article 3 common to the Geneva Conventions."

130. ICTR Statute, *supra* note 9, at art. 4, Violations of Article 3 common to the Geneva Conventions and of Additional Protocol II. While most of the language in the ICTR Statute is identical to the language in Protocol II, Article 4(2), there are two significant differences: Subarticles (a)–(e) and (h) are exactly the same in both, and "pillage" is included in both (under differing subarticle letters). But the ICTR

In ICTY indictments charging various forms of sexual violence, Common Article 3 has been charged under Article 2 of the ICTY Statute for violations of the laws or customs of war.[131] Because Common Article 3 is now regarded as applicable to all internal and international armed conflicts and is understood to encompass various forms of sexual violence, and because "rape" and "enforced prostitution" are formally listed within Article 4 of the ICTR Statute, in contemporary analyses sexual violence has received broad acceptance as a crime under Common Article 3 and Protocol II.

Crimes Against Humanity (ICTY, art. 5; ICTR, art. 3)

The notion of crimes against humanity originated as a result of the gross atrocities committed against the civilian population in Europe during the Second World War. The constituent elements of the crime are unclear, because it has been defined differently in the IMT, IMTFE, CCL10, ICTY, ICTR, and ICC. Contemporary general (but not unanimous) consensus suggests that the crime must be part of a widespread or systematic attack against a civilian population.[132] It can consist of crimes committed by a state against its own citizens. Controversy exists as to whether the crime has to be committed on racial, ethnic, religious, national, or political grounds, or whether persecution on these grounds is but one of a number of possible alternate sub-elements. For example, under the Rwandan Statute (art.

Statute adds: "The passing of sentences and the carrying out of executions without previous judgement pronounced by a regularly constituted court, affording all the judicial guarantees which are recognized as indispensable by civilized peoples" (at art. 4(g)), and deletes: "Slavery and the slave trade in all their forms" from Protocol II (at art. 4(2)(f)). It is unclear why slavery was dropped from the language of the ICTR Statute, as sexual slavery could have potentially been charged.

131. *See, e.g.*, ICTY, Karadžić and Mladić, IT–95–5, of 25 July 1995, at Count 4 (outrages upon personal dignity); ICTY, Kikirica and others, IT–95–8, "Seraterm" of 21 July 1995, at Count 19 (cruel treatment); ICTY, Miljkovic and others, IT–95–9, "Bosanski Samac" of 21 July 1995, at Counts 37 and 52 (humiliating and degrading treatment); ICTY, Jelisic and Cesic, IT–95–10, "Brcko" of 21 July 1995, at Count 51 (humiliating and degrading treatment); ICTY, Delalic and others, IT–96–21, "Celebici" of 21 March 1996, at Counts 19 and 22 (torture) or alternatively Counts 20 and 23 (cruel treatment); ICTY, Gagovic and others, IT–96–23, "Foca" of 26 June 1996, at Counts 1–12 (torture), Counts 13–28 (torture), Count 31 (outrages upon personal dignity), Counts 32–35 (torture), Counts 36–55 (torture), Count 59 (outrages upon personal dignity).

132. *See, e.g.*, Diane F. Orentlicher, *Settling Accounts: The Duty to Prosecute Human Rights Violations of a Prior Regime*, 100 YALE L.J. 2537, 2593 (1991); Oren Gross, *The Grave Breaches System and the Armed Conflict in the Former Yugoslavia*, 16 MICH. J. INT'l L. 783, 790 (1995); Joseph L. Falvey, Jr., *United Nations Justice or Military Justice: Which is the Oxymoron? An Analysis of the Rules of Procedure and Evidence of the International Tribunal for the Former Yugoslavia*, 19 FORDHAM INT'; L.J. 475, 523 (1995); Winston P. Nagan, *Strengthening Humanitarian Law: Sovereignty, International Criminal Law and the Ad Hoc Tribunal for the Former Yugoslavia*, 6 DUKE J. COMP. & INT'L L. 127, 164 (1995); James O'Brien, *The International Tribunal for Violations of International Humanitarian Law in the Former Yugoslavia*, 87 AM J. INT'L L. 639, 648–49 (1993); Christopher C. Joyner, *Strengthening Enforcement of Humanitarian Law: Reflections on the International Criminal Tribunal for the Former Yugoslavia*, 6 DUKE J. COMP. & INT'L L. 79, 85 (1995); Theodor Meron, *Rape as a Crime Under International Humanitarian Law*, 87 AM. J. INT'L L. 424, 427 (1993); Matthew Lippman, *The 1948 Convention on the Prevention and Punishment of the Crime of Genocide: Forty-Five Years Later*, 8 TEMP. INT'L & COMP. L.J. 1, 9 (1994).

3), crimes against humanity are justiciable when the following crimes are committed "as part of a widespread or systematic attack against any civilian population on national, political, ethnic, racial or religious grounds: (a) Murder; (b) Extermination; (c) Enslavement; (d) Deportation; (e) Imprisonment; (f) Torture; (g) Rape; (h) Persecutions on political, racial and religious grounds; (i) Other inhumane acts." In the Yugoslav Statute (art. 5), persons can be prosecuted for crimes against humanity "for the following crimes when committed in armed conflict, whether international or internal in character, and directed against any civilian population: (a) murder; (b) extermination; (c) enslavement; (d) deportation; (e) imprisonment; (f) torture; (g) rape; (h) persecutions on political, racial and religious grounds; (i) other inhumane acts." Although the ICTY Statute requires a nexus to an armed conflict, that element is not required under a wide majority of interpretations, so in prosecutions outside the ICTY, the presence of an armed conflict is not a mandatory requirement as a constituent element of the crime. More significantly however, whereas the ICTR Statute requires that the attack be committed on national, political, ethnic, racial, or religious grounds, the ICTY Statute provides that persecutions on political, racial or religious grounds is merely one of nine separate ways in which crimes may be "directed" against a civilian population. Regretfully, however, in the *Tadić* case, the ICTY Tribunal, even after noting the "law in this area is quite mixed" and that the Statute of the ICTY did not impose a discriminatory intent, it nevertheless, in citing wholly unpersuasive reasons, stated: "the Trial Chamber adopts the requirement of discriminatory intent for all crimes against humanity under Article 5."[133] Fortunately, other courts or forums are not similarly bound by restrictive interpretations, and it is important that in future enunciations of the crime, any reference to political, racial, religious, ethnic, or national persecutions should be only alternative requirements, not compulsory elements, of the crime. It makes no sense whatsoever to require that the crime be committed on these five somewhat arbitrarily enunciated grounds, while ignoring persecution on other pertinent grounds such as gender, social group or standing, or sexual orientation.[134]

Genocide (ICTY, art. 4; ICTR, art. 2)

Both the ICTY and the ICTR have reproduced the definition of genocide contained within the Genocide Convention in their respective statutes. According to

---

133. ICTY, Prosecutor v. Tadić, Trial Chamber Opinion and Judgment, IT–94–1–T (7 May 1997), at paras. 650–52. This does not bode well for progressive development of international humanitarian law. Much of humanitarian law is unsettled, so when the tribunal adopts a conservative interpretation instead of a progressive interpretation, the interpretation will carry weight and thus make it more difficult to achieve progress in future cases inside and outside the *ad hoc* tribunals.

134. For instance, the sexual slavery of some 200,000 former "comfort women" during World War II could not be prosecuted as a crime against humanity if the crime required persecution on national, ethnic, racial, religious, or political grounds, because these women were victimized on gender grounds, and under traditional interpretations, those reasons would not be considered sufficient grounds. Also during the war, the Nazis systematically exterminated not only Jews, but also other groups Hitler deemed inferior, such as gypsies, mentally impaired persons, and homosexuals—these were not racial or religious classifications. Targets also regularly include intellectuals.

Article II of the Genocide Convention, genocide is: "any one of the following acts, when committed with an intent to destroy, in whole or in part, a national, ethnical, racial or religious group: (a) killing members of the group; (b) causing serious bodily or mental harm to members of the group; (c) deliberately inflicting on the group conditions of life calculated to bring about its physical destruction in whole or in part; (d) imposing measures intended to prevent births within the group; [or] (e) forcibly transferring children of the group to another group."[135]

Genocide is an international crime[136] imposing individual criminal responsibility upon those committing or assisting in the commission of the crime.[137] It is predominately defined by intent. This intent must be to destroy, wholly or partially, a national, ethnic, racial, or religious group, by any act that fits into the aforementioned list.[138] Genocide is also considered a crime against humanity,[139] although this linkage is falling into disfavor.

The process of destruction of an intended target group is expressly not limited to physical extermination.[140] Genocide can be demonstrated by an intent to destroy, wholly or partially, physically or mentally, any protected group. The possible elements of the crime of genocide are not mutually exclusive, and more than one subelement may apply to any particular crime. Because gender or sexual violence as manifestations of genocide have not been as widely accepted, and have been indicted to a lesser extent in the ICTY and ICTR (particularly as crimes against individuals instead of as part of a grand scheme), the elements of this crime, and how they can be prosecuted, are detailed below.

Under element (a) (killing members of the group), sexual violence can be prosecuted if a determination is made that a defendant was responsible for sex offenses committed with an intent to destroy a member of a protected group, which resulted, intentionally or unintentionally, in the death of that member. This is particularly true when, for instance, a rape is excessively violent, when a sex offense is committed against a particularly young, old, weak, or ill person, when committed by persons who have the HIV/AIDS virus, or when committed against pregnant women. In the latter circumstance, either the death of the woman or the loss of

---

135. Convention on the Prevention and Punishment of the Crimes of Genocide, GA Res. 260 A(III) (9 Dec. 1948), *entered into force* 12 January 1951.

136. Genocide Convention, *id.*, art. 1.

137. Under the terms of the statutes, genocide, conspiracy to commit genocide, direct and public incitement to commit genocide, attempt to commit genocide, and complicity in genocide are all punishable.

138. Genocide Convention, *supra* note 135, at art. II; ICTY Statute, *supra* note 9, at art. 4(2); McCoubrey, *supra* note 73, at 140.

139. For instance, *see* UNGA Res. 2391 (1970), at 3.

140. For discussion of this, *see* Daphna Shraga & Ralph Zacklin, *The International Criminal Tribunal for the Former Yugoslavia,* 5 Eur. J. Int'l L. 360, 368 (1994); M.C. Bassiouni, *Genocide and Racial Discrimination, in* A Treatise on International Criminal Law 530 (M. Cherif Bassiouni & Ved Nanda eds., vol. I. 1973).

the unborn fetus could amount to genocide if the other elements of the crime are satisfied.

Under element (b) (causing serious bodily or mental harm to members of the group), sexual violence can be prosecuted if a determination is made that a defendant was responsible for an intent to destroy a member of a protected group by causing either physical or mental harm to the member of that group through means that include any form of sexual violence. It is well established that sexual violence tends to cause both serious physical and serious mental harm.[141] Any form of sexual violence committed in public, before members of one's family, by multiple persons, with foreign objects, or by anal or oral sex, causes additional physical and mental harm to the victim, and increased mental harm to the family, friends, and community, or other groups with which the victim is associated. Pregnancy resulting from rape would also result in increased mental and physical harm, as would undergoing an abortion or other procedure to abort the fetus of the rapist. Similarly, being prevented from terminating a pregnancy that resulted from rape, or bearing the child of the rapist, would likely cause significant increased mental harm.[142] In general, element (b) is probably the broadest provision and the most accommodating to violence against women; many forms of sexual violence are justiciable under this section.

Under element (c) (deliberately inflicting on the group conditions of life calculated to bring about its physical destruction in whole or in part), crimes include such offenses as forced sterilization, forced abortion, or sexual mutilation. Sexual violence that results in serious physical (including reproductive) harm should suffice. Notice that this element expressly requires physical, not mental, destruction.

Under element (d) (imposing measures intended to prevent births within the group), preventing births could be achieved in many ways.[143] Killing members of the group (especially the women and girls) would prevent births; forced abortion or forced sterilization would prevent births. An order or policy implying that women who become pregnant would face severe punishment prevents births, as demonstrated in Nazi Germany.[144] An intent to destroy a group by forced or coerced sex

---

141. *See, e.g.* KATHRYN QUINA & NANCY L. CARLSON, RAPE, INCEST, & SEXUAL HARASSMENT—A GUIDE FOR HELPING SURVIVORS 86, 143 (1989); P.A. Resick, *The psychological impact of rape,* 8 J. INTERPERSONAL VIOLENCE 223–55 (1993); I.L. Schwartz, *Sexual Violence against women, prevalence, consequences, societal factors, and preventions,* 7 AM. J. PREV. MED. 363-73 (1991), and references cited therein. *See also* Vera Folnegovi-Smalc, *Psychiatric Aspects of the Rapes in the War against the Republics of Croatia and in Bosnia-Herzegovina, in* MASS RAPE: THE WAR AGAINST WOMEN IN BOSNIA-HERZEGOVINA 174 (Alexandra Stiglmayer ed., 1994).

142. *See* Bruno Franceschi, *Shame as rape victims give birth,* AGENCE FRANCE PRESSE, Feb. 15, 1995, *available in* Lexis/Nexis, Newsfile, Arcnws; ASKIN, WAR CRIMES AGAINST WOMEN, *supra* note 26, at 264–67.

143. Kuper states that even prior to the Genocide Convention, "the right of humanitarian intervention on behalf of populations persecuted in a manner shocking to mankind had long been considered part of the law of nations." LEO KUPER, GENOCIDE, ITS POLITICAL USE IN THE TWENTIETH CENTURY 19 (1981).

144. MOSHE PEARLMAN, THE CAPTURE AND TRIAL OF ADOLF EICHMANN 316, 604 (1963); IMT Docs, *supra* note 20, at Vol. VIII, transcript at 133; ILYA EHRENBURG & VASILY GROSSMAN, THE BLACK BOOK 320 (1980).

between different ethnic or racial groups could prevent births of particular blood-lines. Harming the reproductive systems of members of the target group also consti-tutes genocide under this element. Reproductive systems could be harmed through such means as sterilization, venereal disease, and physical damage resulting from sexual violence. Emotional demise resulting from sexual violence, including ruined spousal relationships, women refusing future sex with any man, or men refusing sex with women of the target group incongruously perceived as "damaged goods," would also prevent births within the group.[145] Goldstein appropriately deduces that forced impregnation also prevents certain births; it imposes at least temporary measures preventing births within a group, because "[f]or at least the nine months it takes to carry the rapist's child to term, a woman is incapable of conceiving and bearing a child of her own ethnicity."[146]

Under element (e) (forcibly transferring children of the group to another group), sex crimes could be prosecuted for such acts as forcing women to marry into, and ultimately bear children of, different ethnic groups, as seen in Rwanda, or through forced impregnation and forced maternity, as seen in the former Yugoslavia and in Rwanda.[147] Whether the mother chooses to raise the child born of forced maternity or forced marriage should be irrelevant under element (e) if the biological parents come from different "groups."[148]

Thus, sexual violence is intricately linked to genocide, and genocidal rape results where the social structure is destroyed and the woman becomes unmarriage-able or divorceable if married; where, as a result of repeated rapes, the woman can no longer bear children; or where sexual violence destroys the family or commu-nity.[149] The destruction need not be one of ethnic or racial "purity;"[150] it can

---

145. ASKIN, WAR CRIMES AGAINST WOMEN, *supra* note 26, at 341–42.

146. ANNE TIERNEY GOLDSTEIN, RECOGNIZING FORCED IMPREGNATION AS A WAR CRIME UNDER INTERNA-TIONAL LAW 24 (The Center for Reproductive Law and Policy, 1993).

147. In the former Yugoslavia, many women were reportedly raped with an intention that they become pregnant. In Rwanda and elsewhere, many women were raped and became pregnant as a result of the rape, without the specific intent. Because the violence in Rwanda affected greater numbers of persons than the violence in the former Yugoslavia, more pregnancies likely resulted from rapes in Rwanda than in the former Yugoslavia.

148. This probably means different racial, ethnic, national, or religious groups. For instance, in the Yugoslav conflict, because in Muslim cultures the ethnicity of the father determines the ethnicity of the child, a child borne as a result of a Serbian or Croatian man raping a Muslim woman would result in a Serbian or Croatian child. Adrien Katherine Wing & Sylke Merchán, *Rape, Ethnicity, & Culture: Spirit Injury from Bosnia to Black America*, 25 COLUM. HUM. RTS. L. REV. 1, 18–19 (1993). In the Rwandan conflict "one is considered a Tutsi in Rwanda where the father is Tutsi, regardless of the mother's ethnic background." Final Report of the Commission of Experts (Rwanda), *supra* note 110, at para. 59.

149. Rhonda Copelon, *Women and War Crimes*, 69 ST. JOHN'S L. REV. 61 (1995); ASKIN, WAR CRIMES AGAINST WOMEN, *supra* note 26, at 338–39.

150. MacKinnon passionately argues that many of the rapes committed in the Yugoslav conflict were committed to forcibly impregnate Bosnian Muslim and Croatian women with a Serbian gene. Many women were imprisoned and repeatedly raped until pregnant, then held involuntarily until they were

result from intentional social disenfranchisement, group separatism or relocation, collective emotional trauma, or physical injury of a protected target group. The intent is often to use sexual violence to humiliate, intimidate, or terrorize opposing sides in order to directly cause grave physical, mental, reproductive, or social harms.[151] Sexual violence may, and often does, destroy a group just as completely or effectively as does killing members of a group.[152] Rape of one ethnicity by another ethnicity that causes one group to flee their homes and leave the territory also constitutes genocidal rape, as part of ethnic cleansing. When sex crimes are committed "for the purposes of producing babies of the ethnic class of the rapists, of destroying the family life of the victims and of cleansing the surrounding area of all other ethnic groups rape becomes genocidal."[153]

Various forms of sexual violence, including rape, sexual slavery, and enforced impregnation,[154] may meet the elements of genocide, even when a single member of the protected group is harmed.[155] If the intent of the actor is to seriously harm (i.e., destroy, in whole or in part) a member of the protected group by any of the aforementioned methods, that should constitute genocide, especially when the act is linked to a broader pattern of random or systematic destruction.

It is important to stress that intent can be inferred from all surrounding circumstances. When various methods of violence are employed in order to destroy a group, including the use of sexual violence to devastate lives individually and collectively, that is solid evidence of genocidal intent. This fact has been recognized by the Prosecutor's Office of the ICTY and ICTR.[156]

---

past the point of abortion. *See* Catharine A. MacKinnon, *Crimes of War, Crimes of Peace, in* ON HUMAN RIGHTS: THE OXFORD AMNESTY LECTURES 88–90 (Shute & Hurley eds., 1993); Catharine MacKinnon, *Rape, Genocide and Women's Human Rights*, 17 HARV. WOMEN'S L.J. 5 (1994). This account is supported by the Final Report of the Commission of Experts, *supra* note 4, at para. 248. MacKinnon also seems to argue that all rapes are evidence of genocidal intent, that genocidal rape is not limited to rapes intended to impregnate or rapes perpetrated in rape camps.

151. *See* ASKIN, WAR CRIMES AGAINST WOMEN, *supra* note 26, at 338–42.

152. *See* Siobhán K. Fisher, *Occupation of the Womb: Forced Impregnation as Genocide*, 46 DUKE L.J. 91 (1996) ANNE TIERNEY GOLDSTEIN, *supra*, note 146; Green et al., *supra* note 116, at 188.

153. Christine Chinkin, *Rape and Sexual Abuse of Women in International Law*, 5 EUR. J. INT'L L. 326, 333 (1994).

154. In the Karadžić Rule 61 decision, ICTY, Prosecutor v. Karadžić, Review of Indictment Pursuant to Rule 61 of the Rules of Procedure and Evidence, Case Nos. IT–95–5–R61, IT–95–18–R61 (11 July 1996), at para. 64, there is an obscure suggestion that forced impregnation might be evidence of genocidal intent. Furthermore, Goldstein has written an extensive analysis of how forced impregnation can come within the purview of all elements of the statute, including as genocide. GOLDSTEIN, *supra* note 146, at 24. *See also* Fisher, *supra* note 152.

155. HILARE MCCOUBREY, INTERNATIONAL HUMANITARIAN LAW: THE REGULATION OF ARMED CONFLICT 140 (1990); M. CHERIF BASSIOUNI, A DRAFT INTERNATIONAL CRIMINAL CODE AND DRAFT STATUTE FOR AN INTERNATIONAL CRIMINAL TRIBUNAL 73 (1987); H.H. Jescheck, *International Criminal Law: Its Object and Recent Developments*, H. H. Jescheck, *International Criminal Law: Its Object and Recent Developments, in* A TREATISE ON INTERNATIONAL CRIMINAL LAW 73 (Cherif Bassiouni & Ved Nanda eds., 1973).

156. *See, e.g.*, ICTY, Karadžić and Mladić, IT–95–5, of 25 July 1995, at paras. 19–22, Counts 1–2; ICTY, Kovacevic and Drljaca, IT–97–24, of 13 March 1997, at paras. 11–16, charging indictees with complicity in genocide; ICTR, Akayesu, ICTR–96–4–I, at paras. 10A–12B, at Counts 1–2 (genocide)

'Gender'' should be included within the list of target groups protected from genocidal acts.[157] Women, in particular through their social position and their reproductive capacities, are increasingly the target of genocidal practices. Including "gender" within the list of groups receiving special protections from genocide would appropriately identify gender as a pervasive basis of genocidal persecution, would help enable successful prosecution for violations, and could serve as some deterrence to future gender-based crimes.

Grave Breaches (ICTY, art. 2)

Grave breaches of the 1949 Geneva Conventions are among the most egregious violations of international humanitarian law, and any state has the right to punish these breaches on the basis of universal jurisdiction.[158] The treaties expressly ascribe criminal liability to violations of the grave breaches. The same language regarding criminality of grave breaches is contained in the four conventions in the article immediately preceding the enumeration of grave breaches. Article 146 of the Fourth Geneva Convention provides:

> The High Contracting Parties undertake to enact any legislation necessary to provide effective penal sanctions for persons committing, or ordering to be committed, any of the grave breaches . . .

> Each High Contracting Party shall be under the obligation to search for persons alleged to have committed, or to have ordered to be committed, such grave breaches, and shall bring such persons, regardless of their nationality, before its own courts. . . .

The grave breaches are listed in Article 50 of the First Geneva Convention, Article 51 of the Second Geneva Convention, Article 130 of the Third Geneva Convention, and Article 147 of the Fourth Geneva Convention. Grave breaches are not mentioned in Protocol II, although they are included in Protocol I in Article 11 (para. 4) and in Article 85. While the preceding article to each grave breach imposes criminal penalties for violations in international armed conflicts, there are differing views as to whether criminality extends to non-international conflicts.[159]

---

and Count 4 (incitement to commit genocide); ICTR, Nyiramasuhuko and Ntahobali, ICTR—97–21–I (26 May 1997), at Count 1 (genocide) and Count 2 (complicity in genocide).

157. ASKIN, WAR CRIMES AGAINST WOMEN, *supra* note 26, at 342–43; Green, et al., *supra* note 116, at 189.

158. *See, e.g.*, Final Report of the Commission of Experts (Yugoslavia), *supra* note 4, at para. 45.

159. *See* Prosecutor v. Tadić, Decision on Jurisdiction (Oct. 2, 1995), ICTY Case IT–94–1–AR72, at paras. 84–89 (law not yet developed enough to apply grave breaches to internal armed conflict). Contrarily, *see* Theodor Meron, *The Continuing Role of Custom in the Formation of International Humanitarian Law*, 90 AM. J. INT'L L. 238, 243 (1996) (grave breach provisions may have an "independent existence as a customary norm" and are applicable to Common Article 3, and thus apply also in internal armed conflicts); Jordan Paust, *Applicability of International Criminal Laws to Events in the Former Yugoslavia*, 9 AM. U. J. INT'L L. & POL'Y 499 (1994) (interpreting the grave breaches to apply only to "protected persons" is too restrictive); LAURI HANNIKAINEN, PEREMPTORY NORMS [JUS COGENS] IN INTERNATIONAL LAW: HISTORICAL DEVELOPMENT, CRITERIA, PRESENT STATUS 685 (1988) (grave breaches comprise *jus cogens* and apply to internal or international conflicts); Christopher C. Joyner, *Strengthening Enforcement of Humanitarian Law: Reflections on the International Criminal Tribunal for the*

Under restrictive interpretations of the conventions, the grave breach provisions still apply only to persons or property protected by the conventions. Of particular impact here is the fact that the Fourth Geneva Convention excludes nationals; thus, crimes committed by one nationality or one state against a member of the same nationality or state are not considered within the purview of grave breaches. In international conflicts this would mean, for instance, that a rape committed by a Bosnian Serb against a Bosnian Muslim is not covered. And because many also still consider grave breaches applicable only to international armed conflicts, the provisions could not be used to prosecute the same acts committed in non-international conflicts. In internal conflicts this would mean, for instance, that sexual slavery committed by a Rwandan Hutu against a Rwandan Tutsi would not be a grave breach, because the conflict is considered non-international (and, of course, that the opponents were members of the same nationality would also be determinative). If internal conflicts are determined to fall within the grave breach provisions, the opponents would still presumably need to be members of different nationalities. The better interpretation, however, is that, because the crimes listed as grave breaches are already prohibited by the laws or customs of war, the grave breach provisions should apply to international and internal armed conflicts alike. As Meron observes: "There is no moral justification, and no truly persuasive legal reason, for treating perpetrators of atrocities in internal conflicts more leniently than those engaged in international wars."[160]

As noted previously, no form of sexual violence is specifically listed as a "grave breach."[161] Article 147 of the Fourth Geneva Convention, which protects the civilian population, enumerates the grave breaches:

> Grave breaches to which the preceding Article relates shall be those involving any of the following acts, if committed against persons or property protected by the present Convention: wilful killing, torture or inhuman treatment,[162] including biological experiments, wilfully causing great suffering or serious injury to body or health, unlawful deportation or unlawful confinement of a protected person. . .[163]

Clearly, the language of the conventions is such that sexual violence is subsumed within the grave breach provisions of "torture," "inhuman treatment," "great suffering," and "serious injury to body or health," thus allowing rape, sexual slavery, and other forms of sexual violence to be prosecuted under a variety of the

---

Former Yugoslavia, 6 DUKE J. COMP. & INT'L L. 79, 83 (1995) (Change of "protected persons" to "civilians" in Article 3 of the ICTY Statute extends grave breach provisions to internal conflicts).

160. Meron, *International Criminalization of Internal Atrocities, supra* note 10, at 561.

161. Ideally, the Geneva Conventions should be amended by an additional protocol or annex to specifically enumerate sexual violence as a grave breach. *See* ASKIN, WAR CRIMES AGAINST WOMEN, *supra* note 26, at 313, 322 (arguing, among other reasons, that leaving it up to positive prosecutorial discretion and favorable judicial interpretation is both dangerous and unnecessary).

162. For what constitutes inhuman treatment, *see, e.g.,* Julian J.E. Schutte, *The System of Repression of Breaches of Additional Protocol I, in* THE HUMANITARIAN LAW OF ARMED CONFLICT 184–85 (Asrid J.M. Delissen & Gerard J. Tanja eds., 1991); COMMENTARY: IV GENEVA CONVENTION RELATIVE TO THE PROTECTION OF CIVILIAN PERSONS IN TIME OF WAR 599 (Oscar M. Uhler & Henri Coursier eds., 1958).

163. Fourth Geneva Convention, *supra* note 56, art. 147.

grave breach provisions. This fact has been recognized by legal scholars,[164] by indictments issued in and confirmed by the ICTY,[165] and by regional human rights bodies.[166] Additionally, the Special Rapporteur on Human Rights for the former Yugoslavia, the International Committee of the Red Cross, the U.N. Commission of Experts for the former Yugoslavia, and the Executive Committee of the U.N. High Commissioner for Refugees have each separately determined that rape is included within the grave breach provisions.[167] Furthermore, one of the grave breach

---

164. *See, for instance* Dorean M. Koenig, *Women and Rape in Ethnic Conflict and War,* 5 HASTINGS WOMEN'S L.J. 129, 138 (1994); Kathleen M. Pratt & Laurel E. Fletcher, *Time for Justice: The Case for International Prosecutions of Rape and Gender-Based Violence in the Former Yugoslavia,* 9 BERKELEY WOMEN'S L.J. 77 (1994); Rhonda Copelon, *Surfacing Gender: Reengraving Crimes Against Women in Humanitarian Law,* 5 HASTINGS WOMEN'S L.J. 243 (1994); Mariann Meier Wang, *The International Tribunal for Rwanda: Opportunities for Clarification, Opportunities for Impact,* 27 COLUM. HUM. RTS. L. REV. 177 (1995); Theodor Meron, *Rape as a Crime Under International Humanitarian Law,* 87 AM. J. INT'L L. 424, 426 (1993); Ruth Wedgwood, *War Crimes in the Former Yugoslavia: Comments on the International War Crimes Tribunal,* 34 VA. J. INT'L L. 267, 273 (1994); Rhonda Copelon, *Gendered War Crimes: Reconceptualizing Rape in Time of War, in* WOMEN'S RIGHTS HUMAN RIGHTS 197, 201 (Julie Peters & Andrea Wolper eds., 1995); VIRGINIA MORRIS & MICHAEL P. SCHARF, AN INSIDER'S GUIDE TO THE INTERNATIONAL CRIMINAL TRIBUNAL FOR THE FORMER YUGOSLAVIA 68 (vol. 1, 1995); Oren Gross, *The Grave Breaches System of the Armed Conflict in the Former Yugoslavia,* 16 MICH. J. INT'L L. 783, 821 (1995); M. CHERIF BASSIOUNI & MARCIA MCCORMICK, SEXUAL VIOLENCE: AN INVISIBLE WEAPON OF WAR IN THE FORMER YUGOSLAVIA 32 (Occasional Paper No. 1, Int'l Human Rights Law Institute, DePaul University College of Law, 1996); C.P.M. Cleiren & M.E.M. Tijssen, *Rape and Other Forms of Sexual Assault in the Armed Conflict in the Former Yugoslavia: Legal, Procedural, and Evidentiary Issues,* 5 CRIM. L. F. 471, 491 (1994); Caroline D. Krass, *Bringing the Perpetrators of Rape in the Balkans to Justice: Time for an International Criminal Court,* 27 DENV. J. INT'L L. & POL'Y 317, 341 (1994); Laurel Fletcher, Allyn Taylor, & Joan Fitzpatrick, *Human Rights Violations Against Women,* 15 WHITTIER L. REV. 319, 323 (1994); THE HANDBOOK OF HUMANITARIAN LAW IN ARMED CONFLICTS 216 (Dieter Fleck ed., 1995).

165. For example, *see* ICTY, Miljkovic and others, IT–95–9, ''Bosanski Samac'' of 21 July 1995, at Counts 36 and 51 (inhuman treatment); ICTY, Jelisic and Cesic, IT–95–10, ''Brcko'' of 21 July 1995, at Count 50 (inhuman treatment); ICTY, Delalic and others, IT–96–21, ''Celebici'' of 21 March 1996, at Counts 18 and 21 (torture) and Count 44 (inhuman treatment); ICTY, Gagovic and others, IT–96–23, ''Foca'' of 26 June 1996, at Counts 1–12 (torture), Counts 13–28 (torture), Counts 29–31 (wilfully causing great suffering), Counts 32–35 (torture), Counts 36–55 (torture), and Count 58 (inhuman treatment).

166. In *Cyprus v. Turkey,* the European Commission of Human Rights determined that rape amounted to ''inhuman treatment'' under Article 3 of the European Convention on Human Rights. The European Commission report acknowledged ''wholesale and repeated rapes'' and ''enforced prostitution'' of Cypriot women and girls by Turkish soldiers and officers. Many of the rapes occurred while women were detained in private homes or rooms; women and girls of all ages were sexually assaulted; some rapes were committed publicly or in front of family members; many rapes were exceedingly violent. The Commission found that it had not been established that Turkish authorities took adequate measures to prevent the sexual assaults; further it was not shown that any disciplinary measures had been taken against those responsible following incidents of sexual violence. By a vote of 12 to 1, the Commission concluded the incidents of sexual violence violated protections against ''inhuman treatment.'' Similarly, the Inter-American Commission on Human Rights Report on the Situation of Human Rights in Haiti, Inter-Am. C.H.R. 43, OEA/ser. L./V.II.88, Doc. 10 (1995), considered rape both as ''inhumane treatment'' and torture. *Id.* at 43.

167. *See* Tadeusz Mazowiecki, United Nations Special Rapporteur on Human Rights in the former Yugoslavia, Report on the Situation of Human Rights in the Territory of the Former Yugoslavia Pursuant

provisions prohibits torture and, as it is now widely recognized that sexual violence often constitutes torture, as discussed *infra*, this is yet an additional means in which sex crimes can be prosecuted as grave breaches. Ideally, however, each form of gender and sexual violence should be recognized and identified as a grave breach in its own right, without having to fit within other categories of crimes, especially when the categories are vague, the acts illusory, and the terminology misrepresentative of the nature of the crime.

As the "grave breach" language is intentionally expansive to provide as much protection as possible to persons protected by the conventions, the grave breaches of the Fourth Geneva Convention (the civilian's convention) protect civilians from sexual violence, and the grave breach provisions of the Third Geneva Convention (the p.o.w.'s convention) similarly protect prisoners of war, male and female, from sexual violence; further, grave breach provisions of the First and Second Geneva Conventions provide these same protections to sick, wounded, or shipwrecked combatants.

One of the reasons it is especially important to attribute sexual violence grave breach status is that grave breaches do not carry the additional onerous elements required in crimes against humanity and genocide. (Although, as noted above, at this stage they may arguably require that victim and victimizer be from different states.)

Sexual Violence as Torture

There has been increasing confirmation that sexual violence can, and frequently does, satisfy the elements of torture.[168] Torture is defined in Article 1 of the Convention Against Torture as:

> any act by which severe pain or suffering, whether physical or mental, is intentionally inflicted on a person for such purposes as . . . intimidating or coercing him [or her] or a third person, or for any reason based on discrimination of any kind, when such pain or suffering is inflicted by or at the instigation of or with the consent or acquiescence of a public official or other person acting in an official capacity.[169]

---

to Commission Resolution 1992/S-1/1 of 14 Aug. 1992, U.N. ESCOR, Comm'n on Human Rights, 49th Sess., Annex, Agenda Item 27, U.N. Doc, E/CN.4/1993/59 (1993), at 89; INTERNATIONAL COMMITTEE OF THE RED CROSS, AIDÉ-MÉMOIRE (Dec. 3, 1992), and also COMMENTARY ON THE GENEVA CONVENTIONS OF 12 August 1949: GENEVA CONVENTION RELATIVE TO THE PROTECTION OF CIVILIAN PERSONS IN TIME OF WAR 598 (Oscar M. Uhler & Henri Coursier eds., 1958); Final Report of the Commission of Experts Established Pursuant to Security Council Resolution 780 (1992), U.N. Doc. S/1994/674, 27 May 1994, Annex, at para. 46; United Nations High Commissioner for Refugees General Conclusion 73, 1993, *Refugee Protection and Sexual Violence*, at para. (a), *reprinted in* CENTER FOR THE STUDY OF HUMAN RIGHTS, WOMEN AND HUMAN RIGHTS: THE BASIC DOCUMENTS 221 (Columbia University, 1996).

168. For comprehensive articles arguing that rape constitutes torture, *see generally* Deborah Blatt, *Recognizing Rape as a Method of Torture*, 19 REV. OF L. & SOCIAL CHANGE 821 (1992); Evelyn Mary Aswad, *Torture by Means of Rape*, 84 GEO. L.J. 1913 (1996).

169. Convention Against Torture and Other Cruel, Inhuman or Degrading Treatment or Punishment, 23 ILM 1027 (December 10, 1984), *as modified*, 24 ILM 535 (1985).

Article 2 of the Convention Against Torture provides that "[n]o exceptional circumstances whatsoever, whether a state of war or a threat of war, internal political instability or any other public emergency, may be invoked as a justification of torture. An order from a superior officer or a public authority may not be invoked as a justification of torture."[170] Thus, during both peacetime and wartime, and even when ordered by a superior, torture is forbidden under international law.

Torture is not limited to physical torture. Mental abuse is expressly prohibited. Sexual violence assaults a person in numerous ways, including physically and mentally, a fact well documented and confirmed in contemporary studies.[171] Nigel Rodley, the U.N. Special Rapporteur on Torture, has recognized sexual violence as torture, and further noted that "[i]n addition to being an especially traumatic form of torture for the victim, rape may have insidious correlative consequences."[172] The Special Rapporteur on Torture emphasized that, while men and women could both be subjected to sexual torture, women were affected disproportionately.[173] Significantly, he also acknowledged that in "some instances, the gender of an individual constituted at least part of the very motive for the torture itself, such as in those where women were raped allegedly for their participation in political and social activism."[174]

In a September 1997 decision, *Aydin v. Turkey*, the European Court of Human Rights held that rape constituted torture under Article 3 of the European Convention of Human Rights.[175] In this case, a 17-year-old girl was detained by security forces; while in custody, "she was tortured by being raped and severely ill-treated."[176] The European Commission on Human Rights made the determination that "rape committed by an official or person in authority on a detainee must be regarded as treatment or punishment of an exceptionally severe kind. Such an offence struck at the heart of the victim's physical and moral integrity and had to be characterized as a particularly cruel form of ill-treatment involving acute physical and psychological suffering. . .

---

170. Convention Against Torture, *id.* at arts. 1–3.

171. *See, e.g.*, Coker v. Georgia, 433 US 584, 611–12 (1977) (Burger, C. J., dissenting); Deborah W. Denno, "Why Rape is Different," *in Panel Discussion: Men, Women and Rape*, 63 Fordham L. Rev. 25, 31 (1994); Linda A. Fairstein, Sexual Violence: Our War Against Rape (1993); Elizabeth A. Pendo, *Recognizing Violence Against Women: Gender and the Hate Crimes Statistics Act*, 17 Harv. Women's L.J. 157, 178–79 (1994).

172. U.N. Doc. E/CN.4/1995/34 (12 Jan. 1995), Report of the Special Rapporteur, Mr. Nigel S. Rodley, submitted pursuant to Commission on Human Rights resolution 1992/32, at para. 19. *See also* paras. 15–24.

173. *Id.* at paras. 15 and 18.

174. *Id.* at para. 18. In a report on slavery and slavery-like practices during wartime submitted by Linda Chavez to the Sub-Commission on Prevention of Discrimination and Protection of Minorities, the Special-Rapporteur stated that "systematic rape can also be used as an instrument of torture or as an abhorrent instrument of warfare." U.N. Doc. E/CN.4/Sub.2/1993/44 paras. 1–2, of 7 September 1993, "Contemporary Forms of Slavery, Preparatory document submitted by Mrs. Linda Chavez on the question of systematic rape, sexual slavery and slavery-like practices during wartime."

175. Aydin v. Turkey (57/1996/676/866), European Court of Human Rights, Judgment of 25 September 1997, *available at* http://www.dhcour.coe.fr/eng/AYDIN.E.html.

176. Aydin, *id.* at paras. 64 and 65.

[and thus] the applicant had been the victim of torture.''[177] In agreeing with the Commission's conclusions, the Court held:

> [T]he Court is satisfied that the accumulation of acts of physical and mental violence inflicted on the applicant and the especially cruel act of rape to which she was subjected amounted to torture in breach of Article 3 of the Convention. Indeed the Court would have reached this conclusion on either of these grounds taken separately.[178]

In reaching its decision, the Court recognized both the severe physical and mental violence inflicted by rape, stating: ''[R]ape leaves deep psychological scars on the victim which do not respond to the passage of time as quickly as other forms of physical and mental violence. The applicant also experienced the acute physical pain of forced penetration, which must have left her feeling debased and violated both physically and emotionally.''[179]

In multiple instances, the Inter-American Commission on Human Rights has demonstrated that it considers rape both inhuman treatment[180] and torture, emphasizing that ''rape represents not only inhumane treatment . . . but also a form of torture.''[181]

The International Court of Justice has recognized rape as a form of torture, stating: ''[the] methods of torture reported by Nicaraguan women included . . . rape''[182] Human rights organizations likewise conclude that sexual violence may constitute torture.[183] Legal scholars agree.[184]

---

177. *Id.* at paras. 78–79.

178. *Id.* at para. 86.

179. *Id.* at para. 83.

180. As a side note, "inhuman treatment" is the language usually linked with torture, while "inhumane acts" is the terminology usually linked with crimes against humanity.

181. Inter-American Commission on Human Rights Report on the Situation of Human Rights in Haiti, Inter-Am. C.H.R. 43, OEA/ser. L./V.II.88, Doc 10 (1995), at 43. The Kalin Report, *cited in* the "United Nations Compensation Commission: Recommendations Made by the Panel of Commissioners Concerning Individual Claims for Serious Injury or Death (Category 'B' Claims)," Apr. 14, 1994, 34 ILM 263, 296 (1995), investigated the numerous instances of rape committed during the Gulf War. The Commission determined that "rape was used as a method of torture." *See also* Fernando and Raquel Mejia v. Peru, Inter-American Commission on Human Rights, Report No. 5/96, Case 10,970 (1 March 1996), at 182–88, which determined that sexual violence constituted a form of torture under the American Convention on Human Rights.

182. Nicaragua v. United States (Merits, ICJ 1986), 25 ILM 1337 (1986).

183. U.N. Doc. E/CN.4/1996/NGO/61 (27 Mar. 1996), "Torture and Other Cruel, Inhuman or Degrading Treatment or Punishment," written statement submitted by Human Rights Watch, a nongovernmental organization in consultative status (category II) at para. 2 ("torture [in Peru] has included beatings, use of electric shocks, near-drownings, rape, rape with rifles, . . .); Amnesty International, *Rape and Sexual Abuse: Torture and Ill-Treatment of Women in Detention* 1 (1992) (Sexual assault used by government agents "to coerce, humiliate, punish and intimidate women"); THE HUMAN RIGHTS WATCH GLOBAL REPORT ON WOMEN'S HUMAN RIGHTS 144 (Human Rights Watch, 1995) ("rape and sexual assault in custody amount to a form of torture"). Further, according to the World Health Organization, rape and sexual torture have serious physical, mental, and sexual consequences on the health of the victims. *As reported in WHO Seminar Warns on Violence Against Women*, AGENCE FRANCE-PRESSE, Aug. 1, 1997, *available in* Westlaw, 1997 WL 2163194.

184. Ruth Seifert, *War and Rape: A Preliminary Analysis, in* MASS RAPE 55 (Stiglmayer ed., 1994);

Although not charged in the IMT indictments, rape crimes were documented in the Nuremberg Trial, and the Nuremberg Tribunal implicitly recognized sexual violence as torture:

> Many women and girls in their teens were separated from the rest of the internees . . . and locked in separate cells, where the unfortunate creatures were subjected to particularly outrageous forms of torture. They were raped, their breasts cut off . . .[185]

> [W]omen were subjected to the same treatment as men. To the physical pain, the sadism of the torturers added the moral anguish, especially mortifying for a woman or a young girl, of being stripped nude by her torturers. Pregnancy did not save them from lashes. When brutality brought about a miscarriage, they were left without any care, exposed to all the hazards and complications of these criminal abortions.[186]

Confronted with the realities of sexual violence, even in the 1940s offenses such as rape, sexual mutilation, and forcible miscarriage were considered forms of torture.

In the ICTY and ICTR, sexual torture can be prosecuted under several articles of the statutes, and indictments confirm that the Prosecutor's Office intends to prosecute sexual violence as torture.[187] In the ICTY Statute, torture is explicitly listed as a grave breach (art. 2(b)).[188] Torture is also expressly listed as a crime against humanity (ICTY, art. 5(f); ICTR, art. 3(f)), and as a violation of Common Article 3 to the Geneva Conventions and Additional Protocol II (ICTR, art. 4(a)). It is also independently recognized as an international crime under the Torture Convention and under customary international law.

Nonetheless, in the context of the Yugoslav Tribunal, grave breach status and has been determined to attach only to crimes committed during the course of an international armed conflict, as unfortunately decided by the Appeals Chamber in the *Tadić* jurisdictional decision.[189]

Kathleen M. Pratt & Laurel E. Fletcher, *Time for Justice: The Case for International Prosecutions of Rape and Gender-Based Violence in the Former Yugoslavia*, 9 BERKELEY WOMEN'S L.J. 77, 78 (1994); Copelon, *Women and War Crimes, supra* note 149, at 63; ASKIN, WAR CRIMES AGAINST WOMEN, *supra* note 26, at 314–21; Women in the Law Project of the International Human Rights Law Group, *No Justice, No Peace: Accountability for Rape and Gender-Based Violence in the Former Yugoslavia*, 5 HASTINGS WOMEN'S L.J. 89, 128 n.24 (1994); Green et. al, *supra* note 116, at 171. *See also generally* Blatt, *supra* note 168; Aswad, *supra* note 168.

185. IMT DOCS, *supra* note 20, Vol. VII, transcript at 494.

186. IMT DOCS, *id.*, Vol. VI, transcript at 170.

187. *See especially* ICTY, Gagovic and others, IT–96–23, "Foca," of 26 June 1996, where sex crimes were charged as torture under crimes against humanity, grave breaches, and violations of the laws or customs of war; and ICTY, Delalic and others, IT–96–21, "Celebici," of 21 March 1996, charging sex crimes as torture under grave breaches and violations of laws or customs of war.

188. Once sexual violence is officially given grave breach status, the crimes becomes subject to universal jurisdiction (always in an international conflict, but disputable without an international conflict). *See* Charney, *supra* note 14; Dorothy Q. Thomas & Regan E. Ralph, *Rape in War: Challenging the Tradition of Impunity*, 14 SAIS REV. 81, 95 (1994).

189. Decision on the Defence motion for interlocutory appeal on jurisdiction, Prosecutor v. Tadić, 2 Oct. 1995 (Appeals Chamber), Case No. IT–94–1–AR72, at paras. 80–83. The Appeals Chamber respectfully

Enslavement

Slavery is one of the oldest recognized crimes in international law. Because enslaving persons (whether to perform manual labor or for other reasons) is an international crime, enslaving persons to perform sexual services must also be an international crime, regardless of the presence of a war. The mere unfortunate fact that slavery for sexual labor has not been widely punished nor universally acknowledged does not change the reality that sexual slavery meets the constituent elements of the crime of slavery. It appears that enslavement is the process or practice of making one a slave, and is a slightly broader term than slavery. As noted previously, sexual slavery has most commonly been referred to as "enforced prostitution," although contemporary analyses are beginning to distinguish between these terms.[190] Here, "sexual slavery" or "sexual enslavement" will be used instead of "slavery" or "enslavement" in order to accurately identify and appropriately characterize the sexual nature of the crime.

International treaties, such as the Slavery Convention[191] and the Trafficking Convention,[192] can be used to prosecute certain forms of sexual violence, particularly sexual slavery and rape.[193] The conventions, which prohibit slavery, slavery-like practices, and trafficking in women and children, do not cease to be applicable during periods of armed conflict. Article 1(1) of the 1926 Slavery Convention defines slavery as "the status or condition of a person over whom any or all of the powers attaching to the right of ownership are exercised." During rape, the violator assumes whole or partial ownership rights over the victim, so technically every

---

disagreed with the Trial Chamber on this issue. The Appeals Chamber interpretation of grave breaches as currently requiring an international war nexus has met with both criticism and support.

190. For instance, *see* Report of the Special Rapporteur on violence against women, its causes and consequences, Mr. Radhika Coomaraswamy, submitted in accordance with Commission on Human Rights resolution 1995/85, U.N. Doc. E/CN.4/1996/53 (5 Feb. 1996), at para. 73. *See generally,* Report on the mission of the Special Rapporteur to Poland on the issue of trafficking and forced prostitution of women (24 May to 1 June 1996), submitted by the Special Rapporteur on violence against women, U.N. Doc. E/CN.4/1997/47/Add.1 (10 Dec. 1996).

191. Slavery Convention (25 Sept. 1926) 212 U.N.T.S. 17; 60 L.N.T.S. 253, *as amended by* Protocol amending the Slavery Convention signed at Geneva on 25 September 1926 (23 Oct. 1953), GA Res. 794(VIII); Supplementary Convention on the Abolition of Slavery, the Slave Trade, and Institutions and Practices Similar to Slavery (30 Apr. 1956), ECOSOC Res. 608 (XXI), 266 U.N.T.S. 3, U.N. Doc. E/3822 (1956). A reference to the Slavery Convention will include all the aforecited instruments. Article 6(1) of the Supplementary Convention states that slavery and slavery-like practices are international crimes.

192. Convention for the Suppression of the Traffic in Persons and of the Exploitation of the Prostitution of Others (2 Dec. 1949), GA Res 317 (IV), 96 U.N.T.S. 271. In Article 1 of the Trafficking Convention, state parties to the convention agree to punish violations of the convention, including persons who exploit a prostitute, even "with the consent of that person." This latter provision has been both hailed and condemned by human rights groups.

193. See U.N. Doc. E/CN. 4/Sub. 2/1998/13, 22 June 1998, Contemporary Forms of Slavery, Systematic Rape, Sexual Slavery and Slavery-Like Practices During Armed Conflict, final report submitted by Ms. Gay J. McDougall, Special Rapporteur.

rape could conceivably constitute sexual slavery. In historical instances of slavery, however, as a general rule some sort of work is required to be performed or some form of service is required to be provided. Thus, in analyzing some possible differentiating factors between rape and sexual slavery, as a practical matter, sexual slaves are unlawfully held or detained in a predetermined location to accommodate the victimizer's sexual access (i.e., a service is provided), and the victims are generally subjected to ongoing rapes.

If a person is unlawfully held or detained, and not free to make their own choices or decisions about their bodies, including whether to refuse sexual services or to make decisions as to how the services should be provided (such as requiring a condom, refusing oral or anal sex, insisting on no beatings, etc.), that should satisfy the definition of slavery. While one author unconvincingly argues that "forced prostitution" better describes forcing women into sexual servitude than does slavery, she nevertheless correctly stresses that "during war forced prostitution is relatively easily analogized to historical forms of slavery."[194] Whether held to entertain soldiers or as part of a military strategy, the detention and the multiple nature of the rapes should constitute sexual slavery, although there are instances in which a single instance of rape could constitute sexual enslavement.

It is virtually indisputable that the some 200,000 former so-called "comfort women" of World War II, when subjected to "enforced prostitution" on behalf of the Japanese military, were victims of military sexual slavery.[195] While the purposes of the acts of sexual enslavement in the Yugoslav and Rwandan Tribunals may in many ways be different, the nature of the crime—women forced to endure repeated rapes for weeks, months, or years—has not changed.[196] For example, during the

---

194. Nora V. Demleitner, *Forced Prostitution: Naming an International Offense*, 18 FORDHAM INT'L L.J. 163, 194 (1994).

195. Radhika Coomeraswamy, the U.N. Special Rapporteur on Violence Against Women, issued a report that declared that "military sex slaves" was the more accurate terminology to describe the situation of the former "comfort women." Report on the mission to the Democratic People's Republic of Korea, the Republic of Korea and Japan on the issue of military sexual slavery in wartime: Democratic People's Republic of Korea, submitted by the U.N. Special Rapporteur on Violence Against Women, U.N. Doc. E/CN.4/1996/53/Add.1 (4 Jan. 1996), at paras. 8 and 10. *See also* Ustinia Dolgopol & Snehal Paranjabe, *Comfort Women: An Unfinished Ordeal* (International Commission of Jurists, 1992); Karen Parker & Jennifer F. Chew, *Compensation for Japan's World War II War-Rape Victims*, 17 HASTINGS INT'L & COMP. L. REV. 497, 505–07 (1994); GEORGE HICKS, THE COMFORT WOMEN (1995); Yvonne Park Hsu, *"Comfort Women" from Korea: Japan's World War II Sex Slaves and the Legitimacy of their Claims for Reparations*, 2 PAC. RIM L. & POL. J. 97 (1993); JAN RUFF O'HERNE, 50 YEARS OF SILENCE (1994); YUKI TANAKA, HIDDEN HORRORS, JAPANESE WAR CRIMES IN WORLD WAR II 79–110 (1996); David Boling, *Mass Rape, Enforced Prostitution, and the Japanese Imperial Army: Japan Eschews International Legal Responsibility?*, 32 COLUM. J. TRANS. L. 533 (1995); ASKIN, WAR CRIMES AGAINST WOMEN, *supra* note 26, at 73–87. *But see* "Views of the Government of Japan on the addendum I (E/CN.4/1996/53/Add.1) to the report presented by the Special Rapporteur on violence against women." On file with author.

196. Briefly, during WWII, the Japanese forced some 200,000 Korean and other women into sexual servitude to the military for multiple purposes. The chief objective was to safely and conveniently provide sexual services to the Japanese military. There is no indication that it was used as a strategic weapon of terror by the Japanese—indeed, the Japanese tried to keep the "comfort women" situation secret. In contrast, in the Yugoslav and Rwandan conflicts, sexual violence has been used as a powerful

Rwandan genocide, women were "held in sexual slavery (either collectively or through forced 'marriage')."[197] Ray notes that the concentration camps in the former Yugoslavia frequently served as "brothels" because "[w]omen imprisoned in these camps were raped, and raped, and raped again."[198] The women were not free to leave, not free to refuse sexual services, not free to dictate the terms of the services, not free to make decisions about their bodies—factors that indicate a loss of owner-ship interest in their own bodies. Even if these women had been paid, that would not negate criminality. Payment, or other benefit, is not a required element of sexual slavery. (The notion is perhaps confused because "voluntary" prostitution often involves the exchange of sex for money and, with use of the term "forced prostitu-tion," it is often assumed that the women are compensated.) If you rape someone and then give them money or other compensation, it is still rape. It is the enslave-ment, the loss of ownership rights to one's self, that makes it slavery. Nevertheless, in sexual slavery, someone, not usually the victim but typically a third party, may receive a benefit.[199] In the case of the WWII sex slaves of Japan, persons who ran the "comfort houses" often charged for the services, so money was paid to the brothel owner; additionally, one benefit accruing to the military was convenient, relatively safe sex for the soldiers.

In the Yugoslav conflict, there appear to have been two primary forms of sexual slavery. One is where soldiers or certain others sought sexual release or personal gratification through the use of enslaved women in a brothel-type facility where

---

weapon of war, as an integral part of military strategy, in order to, for instance, terrorize and degrade the enemy, to forcibly impregnate the women, or to cause opposing sides to flee the area. Whether used for sexual gratification and ease or to influence the conflict militarily, the result is women forced to undergo repeated rapes on a daily basis.

197. HUMAN RIGHTS WATCH WORLD REPORT 1997 343 (1996).

198. Amy E. Ray, *The Shame of It: Gender-Based Terrorism in the Former Yugoslavia and the Failure of International Human Rights Law to Comprehend the Injuries,* 46 AM. U. L. REV. 793, 807 (1997).

199. *See generally* ASKIN, WAR CRIMES AGAINST WOMEN, *supra* note 26, at 74–86. In an October 1997 conversation, Ustinia Dolgopol, who has spent several years working on behalf of the former "comfort women," confirmed that situations differed among the various "comfort stations," but that generally the women were rarely ever paid any monies. Some women had been promised that payment would be made to their families when the war ended. Others received small sums. Most received nothing. She agreed that any financial payments would not negate criminal liability for the crimes. According to official documentation, however, the women were supposed to have been paid sizable sums of money. See also Ustinia Dolgopol, *Rape as a War Crime—Mythology and History; in* COMMON GROUNDS: VIOLENCE AGAINST WOMEN IN WAR AND ARMED CONFLICT SITUATIONS 122 (Inda: Lourdes Sajor ed. 1998).

In the situation of women trafficked into sexual slavery outside the context of war, when the women are coerced, tricked, or forced into sexual servitude, there are varied circumstances regarding financial compensation. Usually, the women are subjected to debt bondage: paid minuscule amounts, with monies deducted for their food, toiletries, housing, transportation, etc. Many times the women are paid nothing. Unless the sexual services are truly voluntary, the payment does not exculpate responsible parties from the criminal nature of the repeated rapes and enforced enslavement.

Whether a situation like that of the former "comfort women," non-wartime sex trafficking, or the use of rape facilities, virtually always the women are held in deplorable conditions, subjected to physical violence in addition to the sexual violence, and not allowed to make their own decisions regarding their bodies or their freedom.

women were held primarily for soldiers' sexual use or entertainment; the second is where rape facilities were established, ostensibly to forcibly impregnate women with a different ethnic gene or for some other genocidal, ethnic cleansing, or military or political purpose. In this latter situation, there are strong indications that some soldiers were ordered to rape.[200] Nonetheless these situations frequently overlap. Free rein to kidnap women for usage in a brothel generates just as much terror and destruction as do orders to take women to rape facilities or allowing soldiers to rape women in their homes. It is therefore important to reemphasize that other situations, such as detaining women in their homes and subjecting them to multiple rapes, could also constitute sexual slavery.

Slavery, and thus sexual enslavement, is violative of international criminal law through international treaties and customary international law. It is a universal crime that can be prosecuted by any state, regardless of the connection with a war.[201] In the ICTY and ICTR, "enslavement" is explicitly listed as a crime against humanity (ICTY, art. 5(c); ICTR, art. 3(c)), and it is implicitly included under other articles of the statutes. In the ICTY, "enslavement" has been charged in the "Foca" indictment as a crime against humanity for a variety of sexual offenses, especially sexual entertainment.[202] As alleged in this indictment, detainees were subjected to repeated rapes and other forms of sexual violence during the night and to manual labor (cooking, cleaning, washing) during the day.[203] Further, charges were brought against another indictee for detaining women who were required to perform household chores and to sexually please soldiers. On one occasion, the women were forced to dance naked on a table. At least three of the women were eventually sold to other soldiers.[204]

In another interesting indictment, against Karadzić and Mladić, it appears that acts or omissions constituting sexual slavery have been charged through the combination of grave breaches (unlawful confinement of a civilian) (art. 2(g)) and violations of the laws or customs of war (outrages upon personal dignity) (art. 3, under

---

200. These issues are explored more fully in ASKIN, WAR CRIMES AGAINST WOMEN, *supra* note 26, at 261–97.

201. *See* M. Cherif Bassiouni, *Enslavement as an International Crime*, 23 N.Y.U. J. INT'L L. & POL. 445, 457, 467 (1991). Technically, this is true. Slavery and slavery-like practices are international crimes recognized as having universal jurisdiction and *jus cogen* status. *Id.* at 445. But most slavery prohibitions were established to prevent ownership rights attaching to slaves who were forced into manual labor. In actuality, particularly with regard to sex crimes against women, it is doubtful whether courts or commentators would yet agree that sexual slavery, including forced prostitution in wartime and sex trafficking in women, is a universal crime prosecutable by any state. Because crimes against women are taken less seriously, sexual slavery of women is regularly ignored, and some seemingly cannot understand how forcing women into sexual servitude constitutes slavery. Slavery for sexual servitude should be worse than slavery for manual labor, not considered less onerous.

202. ICTY, Gagovic and others, IT–96–23, "Foca," of 26 June 1996, at paras. 10–12.

203. *Id.* The allegations were charged in Count 56, crimes against humanity (enslavement), Count 57, crimes against humanity (rape), Count 58, grave breach (inhuman treatment), and Count 59, violations of the laws or customs of war (outrages upon personal dignity).

204. *Id.* For these acts, the indictee was charged in Count 61, crimes against humanity (enslavement) and Count 62, crimes against humanity (rape).

Common Article 3).[205] However, because of the illusory language used in both the statute and in the convention, it is difficult to ascertain exactly for which crimes the indictees are charged.

CONCLUSION

Gender and sexual violence constitute serious violations of international human rights laws, international humanitarian laws, and international criminal laws. Sexual violence is increasingly being used for military and political purposes, including as an integral and powerful weapon that serves to devastate the enemy individually and collectively, mentally and physically. There is thus a pogrom of wartime violence against women, and some of these crimes are being indicted and prosecuted in the Yugoslav and Rwandan Tribunals. With these prosecutions comes the hope that the fury man unleashes against women in wartime can be tempered by knowledge that rape crimes can no longer be committed with impunity. With leaders and perpetrators punished for these crimes, this knowledge will hopefully result in a decrease in future sexual violence during periods of armed conflict. Punishment for gender crimes is no longer merely a question of international law, but one of international integrity. The quest for justice for women in the Balkan and Rwandan conflicts is of legal importance and moral significance to all people everywhere.

NOTE

On September 2, 1998, the Rwandan Tribunal Trial Chamber of Judge Laity Kama (Presiding), Judge Lennart Aspegren, and Judge Navanethem Pillay, rendered their Judgement against Akayesu, ICTR-96-4-T, finding him guilty of, amongst other things, rape as a crime against humanity and sexual violence as an integral part of the genocide. In this historic, ground-breaking decision, the Trial Chamber also defined rape and sexual violence, stating: ''The Tribunal defines rape as a physical invasion of a sexual nature, committed on a person under circumstances which are coercive. The Tribunal considers sexual violence, which includes rape, as any act of a sexual nature which is committed on a person under circumstances which are coercive. Sexual violence is not limited to physical invasion of the human body and may include acts that do not involve penetration or even physical contact.'' (para. 690). This judgment is the most important decision on gender-based violence ever rendered.

---

205. ICTY, Prosecutor v. Karadžić & Mladić, IT–95–5, of 25 July 1995, at para. 34.

Section II

Women Mobilizing into the Twenty First Century

MAKING THE GLOBAL LOCAL: INTERNATIONAL NETWORKING FOR WOMEN'S HUMAN RIGHTS

Charlotte Bunch, Samantha Frost, and Niamh Reilly

THE GLOBAL CAMPAIGN FOR WOMEN'S HUMAN RIGHTS

The 1948 United Nations Universal Declaration of Human Rights proclaims that it applies to all human beings unconditionally, "without distinction of any kind such as race, colour, sex, language . . . or other status."[1] Nevertheless, many violations of women's human rights continue to be ignored, condoned, and perpetrated by societies and governments in every region of the world. A particularly clear example is gender-based violence against women, which until quite recently has not been recognized as a human rights issue much less an issue that requires attention from the international human rights community. Over the past decade, a movement around women's human rights has emerged to challenge the gender bias of such limited notions of human rights. It has focused particularly on violence against women as a prime example of the bias against women in human rights practice and theory.

This movement seeks to demonstrate both how traditionally accepted human rights abuses are specifically affected by gender, and how many other violations against women have remained invisible within prevailing approaches to human rights. The international movement for women's human rights crystallized around the second United Nations World Conference on Human Rights held in Vienna in 1993. It emerged in response to numerous concerns, and it reflected women's collaborative efforts in diverse contexts. In particular, many women in different regions believed that the issues they were organizing against—especially various forms of gender-based violence such as battery, rape, female genital mutilation, female infanticide, or trafficking—were human rights crises that were not being taken seriously as human rights violations.

In the decades since the Universal Declaration of Human Rights was adopted, the international human rights community—particularly in the West—has focused primarily on certain aspects of civil and political rights when perpetrated by the state. While this covers many important concerns such as the denial of freedom of expression, arbitrary arrest, torture in detention, and the death penalty, it reflects only a limited sphere of the wide range of human rights addressed in the Universal Declaration. Some nongovernmental initiatives have broadened the focus of human

---

1. United Nations Universal Declaration of Human Rights, art. 2, Dec. 10, 1948, RES217/A/III.

rights in areas such as the right to development, the rights of the child, and issues such as disappearances, racial discrimination, religious intolerance, and contemporary forms of slavery. However, despite such expansions in human rights theory and practice, the U.N. International Covenant on Civil and Political Rights (ICCPR) still receives more resources than other human rights instruments, including the Convention on the Elimination of All Forms of Discrimination Against Women and the International Covenant on Economic, Social, and Cultural Rights (ICESCR), and it has more effective implementation mechanisms.[2] This fairly narrow approach to human rights, which emphasizes the protection of citizens from certain types of direct state coercion, facilitates the perpetuation of male-defined cultural, familial, or religious traditions, often at the expense of the human rights of women. Further, the failure to develop effective measures to monitor violations and secure implementation of human rights in the socio-economic arena has hindered recognition of the gender-specific impact of socio-economic violations which prevail in every region.

The challenge to human rights theory and practice posed by women at the Vienna conference, and later at the International Conference on Population and Development (Cairo, 1994), the World Summit on Social Development (Copenhagen, 1995), and the Fourth World Conference on Women (Beijing, 1995), reflects a movement that has emerged over the past decade. This initiative has its roots in the growth of diverse women's movements globally during and after the U.N. Decade for Women (1976–1985). Since then, women have continually raised the question of why "women's rights" and lives are treated as secondary to the "human rights" and lives of men. By insisting that "women's rights are human rights," women are asserting that gender-based discrimination and abuse is a devastating reality that is as urgently in need of redress as are other human rights violations. Violations of women's human rights committed in the "private sphere" of the home, for example, or in the context of familial or intimate relationships are widespread, but until recently these have not been considered within the purview of a government's human rights obligations.

The Development of the Campaign

While such questions have been raised by some women for a long time, a coordinated effort to change these attitudes using a human rights framework has gained momentum in the 1990s. Various international, regional, and local groups have been crossing the divisions between women's rights and human rights organizations in the effort to make women's human rights perspectives and violations more visible. One of the major expressions of this movement at the international level has been the Global Campaign for Women's Human Rights—a loose coalition of groups and individuals worldwide concerned with women's human

---

2.   International Covenant on Civil and Political Rights, Dec. 16, 1966, U.N. Doc. RES2200/A/XXI; International Covenant on Economic, Social and Cultural Rights, Dec. 16, 1966, U.N. Doc. RES2200/A/XXI; Convention on the Elimination of All Forms of Discrimination Against Women, Dec. 18, 1979, U.N. Doc. RES34/180.

rights—formed in preparation for the U.N. World Conference on Human Rights held in Vienna in 1993.[3] This conference became a natural vehicle for women's groups to highlight emerging visions of human rights concepts and practice. Since the initial call for the conference did not mention women or recognize any gender-specific aspects of human rights in its proposed agenda, this became the starting point for women's human rights activities.

One of the early Global Campaign actions was a petition drive launched in 1991 that aimed to gather 100,000 signatures calling upon the Vienna Conference to "comprehensively address women's human rights at every level of its proceedings" and to recognize "gender violence, a universal phenomenon which takes many forms across culture, race, and class . . . as a violation of human rights requiring immediate action." The petition, initially distributed in English, Spanish, and French by the Center for Women's Global Leadership and the International Women's Tribune Centre, began to circulate through dozens of women's networks and publications. It was taken up by women at the local, national, and regional level to further their organizing efforts in many different ways. It served to inform women that a U.N. World Conference on Human Rights was happening, and later was utilized to spread information on how women could get involved in the conference nationally, regionally, and internationally. More important, it helped to spark discussions about why women's human rights and gender-based violence in particular were left out of human rights considerations.

This initiative was so successful as part of women mobilizing for the Human Rights Conference that the petition was re-issued after Vienna and directed to the Fourth World Conference on Women to be held in Beijing two years later. This time it called for a report from the U.N. on progress toward the implementation of the Vienna Declaration's commitments to women's human rights and for their incorporation into the Beijing Platform for Action.[4] By the time of the Beijing conference in 1995, the petition had well over one million signatures, had circulated in 148 countries, was translated into 26 languages, and had garnered over 1,000 sponsoring organizations.

The petition to the U.N. World Conference in Vienna was launched in 1991 at the first annual campaign of "16 Days of Activism Against Gender Violence," which links November 25 (International Day Against Violence Against Women) to December 10 (International Human Rights Day).[5] Another initiative of the Global

---

3. The Global Campaign for Women's Human Rights was coordinated primarily by the Center for Women's Global Leadership in collaboration with many other organizations and networks around the world. For further information about the Center or the Global Campaign, contact the Center for Women's Global Leadership, Rutgers University, 27 Clifton Avenue, New Brunswick, NJ 08903; phone (908) 932-8782; fax (908) 932-1080; email: cwgl@igc.apc.org.

4. World Conference on Human Rights: The Vienna Declaration and Programme of Action, June 25, 1993, U.N. Doc. A/CONF.157/23; Fourth World Conference on Women: Beijing Declaration and Platform for Action, Oct. 17, 1995, U.N. Doc. A/CONF.177/20.

5. November 25 was declared the International Day Against Violence Against Women by the first Feminist Encuentro for Latin America and the Caribbean in 1981, Bogota, Colombia. The day commemorates the Mirabal sisters who were brutally murdered by the Trujillo dictatorship in the Dominican Republic in 1960. December 10 celebrates the anniversary of the Universal Declaration of Human

Campaign for Women's Human Rights, the 16 Days Campaign aims to provide a global umbrella for local activities that promote public awareness about gender-based violence as a human rights concern and that seek specific commitments to women's human rights at all levels. Groups participating in the campaign select their own particularized objectives and determine their own local activities, but all are done with a sense of being part of this larger global focus. The 16 Days Campaign has grown steadily, involving groups in dozens of countries who have organized hundreds of events from hearings, demonstrations, and panels to media campaigns, cultural festivals, and candlelight vigils. While 16 Days Campaign activities focus on many different issues, a number of the early ones utilized the petition to mobilize women to participate in the preparatory processes of the U.N. World Conferences. Since 1995, many actions have been directed at local and national levels to implement promises made to women in the Vienna, Cairo, Copenhagen, and Beijing documents.

After gathering signatures, many of those involved in the initial petition drive began asking, what next? How do we show more clearly how violence affects women and what it means for women's perspectives to be incorporated into the human rights framework? Following the enthusiastic response to the petition drive of the first 16 Days Campaign, the second 16 Days Campaign called upon participants to hold hearings to give voice to gender-based human rights violations and to document more precisely the spectrum of issues that is covered by the concept of women's human rights. From November 1992 onward, women began to convene public hearings and speakouts to make visible and to document both individual complaints and group cases of violations of women's human rights. Many of these hearings brought media attention to neglected issues, and they were often coordinated with other lobbying efforts by women's human rights advocates. Most of the resulting testimonials were recorded; documentation was then sent to the U.N. Centre for Human Rights in Geneva, thereby providing concrete evidence of the need for human rights mechanisms that are more responsive to women's lives.

At the same time, regional women's groups also began to focus their attention more actively on the forthcoming World Conference on Human Rights and sought to articulate their demands to that global forum. At the U.N. regional preparatory meetings for the Vienna Conference held in Tunis, San José, and Bangkok, women demanded that the human rights of women be discussed. Women in Latin America organized a women's human rights conference called *La Nuestra* prior to the regional meeting in San José.[6] They prepared a 19 Point Agenda to be presented there which women from other regions also utilized. Women were also an active presence at various national preparatory meetings, and likewise held nongovernmental events aimed at influencing the World Conference agenda. For example,

Rights proclaimed in 1948. The period also includes World AIDS Day (December 1), and the anniversary of the Montreal massacre (December 6) when a man gunned down 14 female engineering students for being "feminists."

6.   FIRE (FEMINIST INTERNATIONAL RADIO ENDEAVOR, AT RADIO FOR PEACE INTERNATIONAL), SATELLITE MEETING "LA NUESTRA." (FIRE, 1992).

Women in Law and Development in Africa (WiLDAF) organized a series of sub-regional meetings where women defined their own human rights concerns and drew up a regional women's paper which was presented at preparatory meetings for the World Conference.[7]

As part of this process, the Center for Women's Global Leadership held a Strategic Planning Institute in early 1993 to coordinate plans for how to be most effective in seeking to influence events in Vienna and more specifically how to place violence against women squarely on the conference agenda. The Institute participants were women from around the world who had been active in working for women's human rights regionally. The meeting focused on two levels: 1) developing lobbying strategies for the U.N. Intergovernmental Conference, including further development of a set of recommendations on women's human rights that built on regional activity and that served as the focus for the final international preparatory meeting in Geneva; and 2) planning nongovernmental organization (NGO) activities for Vienna that would highlight women's human rights, and in particular preparing for a Global Tribunal on Violations of Women's Human Rights in order to bring greater visibility to women's demands and organizing. The Global Tribunal in Vienna gave vivid personal expression to the life-and-death consequences of the violation of women's human rights by providing graphic demonstrations of how merely being female can be life threatening, subjecting women to such abuses as torture, terrorism, and slavery. Thirty-three women from all regions of the world testified in the Tribunal about the specific violations they and/or others had experienced in five interconnected areas: Human Rights Abuse in the Family, War Crimes Against Women, Violations of Women's Bodily Integrity, Socio-Economic Violations, and Political Persecution and Discrimination.[8]

Prior to the Vienna conference, the Global Campaign made a strategic decision to emphasize issues of gender-based violence since they illustrate best how traditional human rights concepts and practice are gender-biased and exclude a large spectrum of women's experience of abuse. Because different forms of violence against women clearly parallel other types of human rights violations that the international community has already condemned, such as torture, enslavement, and terrorism, they were a useful starting point for demonstrating a gender perspective on human rights.

The U.N. World Conferences

In Vienna, the message that "violence against women violates human rights" came through loud and clear. It advanced the introduction of new human rights instruments, including the adoption of a U.N. Declaration on the Elimination of

---

7.   FLORENCE BUTEGWA, THE WORLD CONFERENCE ON HUMAN RIGHTS: THE WILDAF EXPERIENCE (Women in Law and Development in Africa, 1993).

8.   For a more detailed account of the Vienna Tribunal, *see* DEMANDING ACCOUNTABILITY: THE GLOBAL CAMPAIGN AND VIENNA TRIBUNAL FOR WOMEN'S HUMAN RIGHTS (Charlotte Bunch & Niamh Reilly eds., 1994).

Violence Against Women and the appointment of a U.N. Special Rapporteur on Violence Against Women.[9] In Vienna, women effectively challenged the public/ private divide in the global human rights arena and exposed violence against women as a human rights violation whether perpetrated by a male relative in the home or by a soldier in a war zone.

The final statement issued by the 171 participating governments at the conference—the Vienna Declaration—devotes several pages to treating the "equal status and human rights of women" as a priority for governments and the United Nations. Further, it sounds an historic call to recognize the elimination of "violence against women in public and private life" as a human rights obligation. This progress on women's human rights was the product of women's organizing and networking nationally, regionally, and globally both before and during the Vienna Conference.

The Women's Caucuses formed at the final Preparatory Committee Meeting in Geneva and during the Vienna Conference proceedings constituted a critical part of this organizing. There was an NGO women's caucus and also a caucus with women from NGOs, governmental delegations, and U.N. agencies. These caucuses were significant and effective because they crossed the traditional governmental/ nongovernmental divide in a concerted effort to make gender visible. The NGO Women's Caucus lobbied governments and kept track of the drafting process. It also provided a space where women could learn about what was happening at the governmental conference and debate what they wanted to achieve in the process as a whole. This caucus provided the emerging women's human rights movement with a place to formulate an identity, which in turn facilitated the networking that has continued to take place among women's human rights activists during the Cairo, Copenhagen, and Beijing World Conferences as well as at the U.N. Human Rights Commission meetings and in other regional and international settings.

Since the Vienna Conference, one of the ongoing tasks of the Global Campaign for Women's Human Rights has been pushing for the implementation of the Vienna Declaration's commitments to women. In addition to continuing the petition campaign, women's human rights activists have coordinated efforts globally to lobby the various human rights mechanisms of the U.N. to fulfill their commitment to the full integration of gender concerns and awareness into their work. Similarly, much effort has gone into working with regional and national bodies, both governmental and nongovernmental, for the full incorporation of gender consciousness and women's human rights into their agendas. However, given the high profile of the U.N. World Conferences on population, social development, and women, and the importance of these to women's human rights, much of the focus of the Global Campaign during 1993–95 continued to be on organizing for these global governmental fora.

---

9.   Resolution on the Special Rapporteur (Resolution Integrating the Rights of Women into the Human Rights Mechanisms of the United Nations), March 2, 1994, U.N. Doc. E/CN.4/1994/L.8/Rev.1; Declaration on the Elimination of Violence Against Women, Dec. 20, 1993, U.N. Doc. A/RES/48/104.

The documentation of female human rights abuse gathered throughout the Global Campaign and at the Vienna Tribunal demonstrated that the prevalence of violence against women in societies everywhere is inseparable from women's lack of socio-economic power and status. Similarly, the routine denial of women's bodily integrity in the implementation of national and international population policies is linked to the same forces that leave women vulnerable to violence. The Vienna Tribunal did feature testimonies on violations of women's socio-economic and cultural human rights, and on gender-based political persecution, but these were largely overlooked by the media. Some women were concerned that the focus on gender-based violence in Vienna detracted attention from other types of human rights issues, especially abuses associated with the actions of non-state actors like international financial institutions and transnational corporations, and in such policy areas as women's health. Since Vienna, the Global Campaign has sought to underscore the indivisibility of women's human rights and to emphasize the interconnectedness of the civil, political, social, economic, and cultural dimensions of all human rights.

To move forward in this direction, participants in the Global Campaign coordinated a series of actions that included workshops, strategic planning meetings, human rights caucuses, and hearings on women's human rights at the 1994 International Conference on Population and Development (ICPD) in Cairo, the 1995 World Summit for Social Development (WSSD) in Copenhagen, and the 1995 Fourth World Conference on Women in Beijing.

The Cairo Hearing on Reproductive Health and Human Rights advanced the message that "women's health is a human right." Women from six regions recounted the human rights abuses they had encountered through involuntary sterilization, forced early marriage and pregnancy, illegal abortion, and the denial of reproductive and sexual health to disabled women and girls. The testimonies demonstrated the multiple forces affecting women's health including the state, population policies, pharmaceutical companies, the medical profession, the family, religion, and culture. The Cairo Hearing further demonstrated that if the international community is serious about women's human rights—as pledged in the Vienna Declaration—then both a gender-aware approach to health as a human right and effective strategies to ensure accountability on the part of diverse non-state actors must be put into place.[10]

The final Programme of Action agreed upon at the ICPD reflected the pivotal role that the women's movement, including women's human rights activists, took place in Cairo.[11] In the guidelines for the formulation and implementation of population and development policies, there were a number of important gains for women. The Programme of Action includes the recognition that women's empowerment,

---

10. For a more detailed account of the Cairo Hearing, *see* THE CAIRO HEARING ON REPRODUCTIVE HEALTH AND HUMAN RIGHTS (Mallika Dutt ed., 1995).

11. International Conference on Population and Development: Programme of Action of the United Nations, Oct. 18, 1994, U.N. Doc. A/CONF.171/13.

the elimination of violence against women, women's education, and the assurance of women's ability to control their fertility need to be cornerstones of development. It recognizes that development is a fundamental human right, and that women's reproductive health and rights, including issues of sexual health, maternal mortality, and the health impact of unsafe abortions, must be addressed. The guidelines for population and development policies also recognize that demographic targets need to be replaced by a focus on the overall reproductive health needs and plans of women.

The Copenhagen Hearing on Economic Justice and Women's Human Rights was co-convened in 1995 by the Center for Women's Global Leadership and DAWN (Development Alternatives with Women for a New Era) in collaboration with others at the World Summit on Social Development. The Summit focused on poverty, unemployment, and social disintegration, and thus was an important venue to make visible violations of women's human rights in the socio-economic arena. The Copenhagen Hearing questioned prevalent understandings of human rights. It also broke new ground in the struggle to ensure human rights accountability by highlighting the United States' complicity in perpetrating socio-economic human rights abuses within the U.S. and internationally. The explicit focus on the United States arose from an acknowledgment of its powerful position in the world economy as well as its self-proclaimed role as a world leader in the protection of human rights. Women from around the world testified about human rights violations resulting from structural adjustment programs (SAPs), budget cuts that target social welfare measures, and trade polices and economic sanctions that are indifferent to human rights, particularly women's human rights. They recounted stories of forced prostitution, the abuse of migrant workers, and environmental destruction—all of which are growing in the face of economic globalization.[12]

While women did not transform the Social Summit's final Programme of Action, there were positive advances toward a gender-aware understanding of human rights as indivisible and toward greater accountability on the part of international financial institutions (IFIs).[13] These advances included an affirmation of the importance of core human rights standards—civil, political, economic, social, and cultural—including the right to development. United Nations member states made a commitment to promote gender equality and to improve the status of women. They recognized the increased burden on women created by poverty, agreed to a broader definition of the family, and made a call for the valuation of women's unremunerated work. The Summit's final Programme of Action contained advancements for the rights of indigenous peoples and workers, including migrant workers. It also acknowledged that SAPs must be reviewed in ways that reduce their negative impact, and that IFIs should give higher priority to social lending.

---

12. For a more detailed account of the Copenhagen Hearing, *see* THE COPENHAGEN HEARING ON ECONOMIC JUSTICE AND WOMEN'S HUMAN RIGHTS (Mallika Dutt, Susana Fried & Deevy Holcomb eds., 1995).

13. World Summit on Social Development: Copenhagen Declaration of Social Development and Programme of Action, Apr. 19, 1995, U.N. Doc. A/CONF.166/9.

The culmination of the hearings campaign was the Global Tribunal on Accountability for Women's Human Rights, which took place September 1, 1995, at the NGO Forum in the city of Huairou, outside of Beijing where the United Nations Fourth World Conference on Women was convened. The Vienna, Cairo, and Copenhagen Hearings and other activities at the World Conferences had achieved greater visibility for violations of women's human rights and advanced a gender-aware understanding of the indivisibility of human rights. The documents emerging from these conferences contained many exemplary commitments to women's human rights. The issue for Beijing was accountability for and implementation of these promises. Women's groups and networks around the world were eager to see the rhetoric of the recent U.N. conferences put into effect in ways that would make a difference in women's daily lives. They wanted governments to be accountable for the realization of their promises, and they wanted governments to be accountable for their complicity in violations of women's human rights, either through direct action or through inexcusable inaction. Further, women wanted governments to hold private individuals and institutions accountable for their perpetration of female human rights abuses.

The Global Tribunal on Accountability for Women's Human Rights therefore sought to move the women's human rights agenda forward from visibility to accountability, from awareness of violations to active implementation of women's human rights. Like previous hearings and tribunals, the Beijing Tribunal set out to provide a high-profile public venue in which to hear women's voices, to document women's human rights violations, and to foster a political climate in which such abuses would no longer be tolerated. In addition, it aimed to build upon the successes of the women's human rights movement in the area of gender-based violence and to further efforts to realize women's human rights in the social, economic, and cultural domains.

This event was also envisioned as an opportunity to demonstrate the ideas and strength of the international movement for women's human rights. Therefore all of the testimonies were developed by organizations actively involved in working to bring change around the issues presented. In addition to presenting accounts of violations, most of the testimonies incorporated recommendations and concrete strategies for achieving accountability in the areas that they addressed. The process of organizing the Beijing Tribunal followed a path similar to that used for previous hearings convened or co-convened by the Center for Women's Global Leadership on behalf of the Global Campaign. An International Coordinating Committee was formed, composed of representatives from regional and national sponsoring organizations who identified and developed potential testimonies for the Tribunal. It was agreed that the focus would be on the interconnected thematic areas of violence against women in the family and in conflict situations, economic discrimination and exploitation, violations of health and bodily integrity, and political persecution. Within this framework, the Tribunal testimonies were selected to reflect the diversity of women's experiences across geo-politics, race, class, sexual orientation, ethnicity, and religion. Where possible, members of the Coordinating Committee worked with testifiers to prepare a "summary of accountability" that identified specific human rights agreements, laws, and standards that had been violated and outlined the political or legal strategies that had either been utilized by advocates or were planned for future action on the violations described.

The Beijing Tribunal was an early and formative event at the NGO Forum and helped to set the tone for many of the activities that followed. This Tribunal, along with the World Public Hearing on Crimes Against Women coordinated by the Asian Women's Human Rights Council, helped to demonstrate the centrality of human rights to many of the critical areas of concern that were being debated in the Platform for Action at the governmental conference. In addition to the tribunals and hearings, hundreds of activities at the Forum consciously addressed women's human rights. The recognition that all women's rights are human rights permeated the atmosphere. Thus, while the distance between the NGO Forum in Huairou and the governmental conference in Beijing made lobbying difficult for many, lobbying efforts were strengthened by the high visibility of women's human rights activities at the NGO Forum. The women's human rights movement that had first become visible in Vienna came of age in Beijing.[14]

A gender-aware human rights perspective permeated debates around the Beijing Platform for Action. Previous U.N. conferences on women had been seen primarily as discussions about "women and development" or "equality." However, the Beijing Conference saw the expansion of human rights to encompass the wider set of concerns women had been organizing around throughout the U.N. Decade for Women as well as at the U.N. world conferences in the 1990s. Thus many people came to understand that the entire conference and Beijing Platform was in fact a referendum on the human rights of women in a whole range of areas.

This shift in consciousness was the result of the many forms of organizing and lobbying that women's human rights activists had been doing at the local, national, regional, and global level since before the Vienna Conference. The function of the Global Campaign for Women's Human Rights was to help give this diverse activity a coherent international expression and visibility. This was achieved through many activities such as the petition campaign and the 16 Days of Activism as well as the hearings and tribunals. In addition, a number of women's organizations networked both regionally and internationally to advance a women's human rights perspective in all the national and regional meetings held in preparation for Beijing. The Fourth World Conference on Women involved a larger number of people working on a wider array of preparatory activities than in any of the previous world conferences. At the final international preparatory meeting in New York and in Beijing itself, the Center for Women's Global Leadership convened a women's human rights caucus as part of the Global Campaign. This caucus worked to incorporate human rights perspectives in many parts of the Platform, and collaborated with other NGO caucuses to prevent the conservative backlash against women's gains that

---

14. For a more detailed account of the Beijing Tribunal, *see* WITHOUT RESERVATION: THE BEIJING TRIBUNAL ON ACCOUNTABILITY FOR WOMEN'S HUMAN RIGHTS (Niamh Reilly ed., 1996). For a discussion of women's human rights in Beijing, *see* Charlotte Bunch, Mallika Dutt & Susana Fried, *Beijing '95: A Global Referendum on the Human Rights of Women*, 16(3) CANADIAN WOMEN'S STUDIES (1996).

threatened to utilize Beijing to undermine the achievements women had made in previous world conferences.[15]

The international and regional networking that women did for Beijing ensured that the Beijing Platform for Action reasserted the universal and holistic nature of women's human rights. Governments agreed to promote and protect women's human rights to freedom from violence, to sexual and reproductive health that is free from discrimination and coercion, and to equal rights to inheritance for women and girls—however, they did not recognize the right to equal inheritance. Further, governments undertook to pursue and punish as war criminals the perpetrators of rape and other forms of sexual violence against women and girls in situations of armed conflict. Universal ratification of the Women's Convention was also called for by the Platform, along with the introduction of an optional protocol to strengthen its implementation. The Platform also calls for the integration of women's human rights throughout the U.N. system. In all of this, commitments to women gained at previous conferences were maintained. In several areas, commitments to women were expanded, such as provisions for the protection of human rights activists, and the acknowledgment that systematic rape during armed conflict is a war crime and, in some cases, a crime against humanity.

Fifty-odd years after World War II, the human rights of people everywhere continue to be disregarded through racism, xenophobia, sexism, homophobia, fundamentalism, the displacement of entire populations through war, and even the genocide that the Universal Declaration of Human Rights sought to make impossible. In addition to the gender-specific human rights violations that all of these entail, there is now also recognition of a wider range of human rights abuses that affect women in particular. Clearly, a human rights framework is needed more than ever, one that moves human rights from rhetoric to reality and that guarantees human rights to all without reservation. The women in every region who are part of the international movement for women's human rights are well-positioned to provide leadership in this direction. Many victories for the ideal of universal human rights have been secured, and many concrete commitments have been made to women's human rights; commitments that, if enacted, will go a long way toward ensuring the reality of human rights for all. A vital piece of the process of realizing this potential is the international networking for women's human rights that has emerged and must continue to grow as global trends and forces increasingly shape local experience.

DIVERSITY, UNIVERSALITY, HUMAN RIGHTS, AND FEMINIST NETWORKING

The extensive mobilization of women around the United Nations Fourth World Conference on Women (Beijing, 1995) reflected the development of new forms of feminist and women's organizing that have emerged over the past decade. The processes of networking around recent United Nations world conferences have

15. Report of the Women's Human Rights Caucus at the Fourth World Conference on Women, Beijing, 1995 (prepared by Susana Fried, with Deevy Holcomb, Center for Women's Global Leadership, 1995).

facilitated women's adaptation and reformulation of the human rights framework. Women are posing challenges that are transforming human rights thinking and making it more responsive to the concerns that women have in their work and their lives. The human rights framework has been a useful educational and mobilizing tool that women have effectively deployed both in local organizing and in challenging governments to recognize and act upon their responsibilities to women's human rights. Human rights approaches used by women have strengthened local mobilization efforts and advanced local objectives, while at the same time linking local agendas to a larger international movement with broad common goals. Indeed, in the past few years, women's use of the human rights framework as a tool for organizing has made the idea of women's human rights sufficiently mainstream that the idea of "women's rights as human rights" was taken up as the overarching theme for the women's conference in Beijing.

Margaret Schuler argues that several decades of disagreement about what constitutes human rights has made the field of human rights amenable to women's challenges and demands. Citing J. Donnelly, Schuler asserts that "[t]he dynamic character of human rights . . . 'allows attention and resources to be shifted to threats that previously were inadequately recognized or insufficiently addressed.' . . . [It] permit[s] women to enter the arena, challenge the current discourse and offer fresh perspectives on both theoretical and practical elements of the debate."[16] Another critical dimension to the adoption of the human rights framework is that women from many different regions around the world are able to use it to articulate diverse demands in relation to a broad array of issues. Human rights language creates a space in which different accounts of women's lives and new ways of demanding change can be developed. It provides overarching principles to frame alternative visions of gender justice without dictating the precise content of those visions. The idea of universal human rights provides a powerful vocabulary for naming gender-based violations and impediments to the exercise of women's full equality and citizenship. Further, the large body of international human rights covenants, agreements, and commitments gives women potential political leverage and concrete points of reference for organizing and lobbying.

The Challenge To Universality

The success and extent of women's human rights networking globally is all the more significant in light of recent critiques that suggest that the effort to find a common articulation of women's concerns or a common basis for women's organizing is seriously flawed. Some argue that to do so is to universalize the category of "woman" and to impose a limited agenda on all women on the basis of the experience of some women—usually white, middle-class, and living in the global North. As women's movements have grown over the past three decades, grassroots

---

16. Margaret Schuler, *Introduction, in* FROM BASIC NEEDS TO BASIC RIGHTS: WOMEN'S CLAIM TO HUMAN RIGHTS 2 (Margaret Schuler ed., 1995). For Donnelly's discussion of this issue, *see* J. DONNELLY, INTERNATIONAL HUMAN RIGHTS THEORY AND PRACTICE 26 (1989).

and professional activists as well as academics have had unprecedented opportunities for dialogue around gender-based oppression. In the course of these important and often contentious debates, women have been pressed to think about the ways in which geography, ethnicity, race, culture, sexuality, class, and tradition shape what it means to be a woman. These issues, combined with specificities of local and national politics, point to the fact that it is difficult to conceive of women or the women's movement as singular and coherent entities.

A major bone of contention among women activists both in the United States and around the world has been the patterns of exclusion and invisibility affecting many women that are reinforced by the uncritical assumption that all women share common and easily identifiable experiences and self-understandings. Women of color in the United States, for example, have leveled powerful critiques at the theory and politics of mainstream feminists, arguing that their analyses and visions for change have tended to be formulated around the concerns of economically privileged, heterosexual, white women-citizens.[17] When this happens, inequality and power differentials among women are not adequately taken into account as key factors that shape women's lives. Consequently, women of color, as well as lesbians and other non-dominant groups, have challenged mainstream feminism to rethink analyses of the social structures and dynamics that affect women. They have questioned who the "we" is that has been invoked in much feminist theory and activism.

In response to such challenges, many feminists have taken steps to critically re-examine their assumptions about the homogeneity of women's experiences, and have sought to analyze whether women's differences from each other preclude the formulation of common political agendas and coalitions for action. These analyses are often framed in terms of identity categories—a move intended to create space for the recognition of specificity in order to counter the effects of generalizations from limited perspectives (white, middle-class, and so on). However, despite some genuine attempts to incorporate "difference" into feminist analysis, an all too common pattern is the listing of factors that differentiate women from one another. Women as a group are still taken as the primary subject of analysis, and "race," "class," "sexual orientation," or "national origin" are brought into the discussion as addenda.[18] Arguably, in order to consider how issues such as class, race, culture, or sexuality actually constitute women as women, such factors must form the very structure of any theory or strategy for action.

Many of the critiques of universal assumptions about the lives and experiences of women are found in the writing and activism of women in post-colonial contexts or in developing regions around the world. Amrita Basu, for example, challenges the idea that there is "a commonality in the forms of women's oppression and

---

17. *See, e.g.,* THIS BRIDGE CALLED MY BACK: WRITINGS BY RADICAL WOMEN OF COLOR (Cherrie Moraga & Gloria Anzaldua eds., Kitchen Table: 1981); BELL HOOKS, FEMINIST THEORY: FROM MARGIN TO CENTER (1984); AUDRE LORDE, SISTER OUTSIDER (1984).

18. For a provocative discussion of this dynamic, *see* ELIZABETH SPELMAN, INESSENTIAL WOMAN: PROBLEMS OF EXCLUSION IN FEMINIST THOUGHT (1990).

activism worldwide,'' and suggests that such an assumption of sameness eludes the multiplicity of women's differences around the world, within different countries, and more specifically in post-colonial and developing countries.[19] Indeed, she argues that ''[w]omen's identities within and across nations are shaped by a complex amalgam of national, racial, religious, ethnic, class, and sexual identities,'' and that these specificities shape and inform the challenges that women face and the work that women do. She claims that in the attempt to create a coherent feminist identity or agenda across national, geographic, cultural, or ethnic boundaries, there is often a failure to appreciate ''the extent to which women's movements are locally situated.''[20] If feminism is defined only in terms of Western conceptions and forms of activism, not only is there a danger of inappropriately imposing Western priorities and goals on women in diverse contexts, but there is a failure to recognize the strength and transformative potential of women's organizing as it exists at local levels around local issues. For Basu, this includes women's participation in ''mainstream'' social and liberation movements and not just within women-specific organizations and campaigns.

The activities and networking of the international movement for women's human rights consciously took into consideration dangers such as those highlighted by Basu. The Global Campaign for Women's Human Rights involved several major regional networks that played leadership roles at both the local and international levels of the Campaign. For example, the various networks organized around the ''16 Days of Activism against Gender Violence'' to strengthen local claims, and they also participated in defining and implementing international lobbying strategies to ensure specific commitments to women's human rights in both the Vienna Declaration and the Beijing Platform for Action. Further, the Campaign included many women who continue to work in the mainstream human rights community to ensure that women's concerns and gender issues are viewed from different angles and form an integral part of the international human rights agenda.

At the same time that women throughout the global South are gaining recognition for their perspectives, analyses, and activism, an other more problematic concept has emerged in the writings of some feminists in the North. As Basu, Chandra Mohanty, Trinh Minh-ha, and other scholars and activists have noted, the category of a singular ''Third World Woman'' is often used to capture the experiences and analyses of hugely diverse populations whose concerns defy singular definition; it reduces the complex situations that women in the global South face to a fictitious common experience.[21] Clearly, any attempt at international feminist networking must acknowledge and affirm the multiple subjective experiences of women, within and across diverse boundaries (including geo-politics, race, ethnicity, class, sexual

19. Amrita Basu, *Introduction, in* THE CHALLENGE OF LOCAL FEMINISMS: WOMEN'S MOVEMENTS IN GLOBAL PERSPECTIVES 2 (Amrita Basu ed., 1995).

20. *Id.* at 4.

21. *See, e.g., Chandra Talpade Mohanty, Under Western Eyes: Feminist Scholarship and Colonial Discourses, in* THIRD WORLD WOMEN AND THE POLITICS OF FEMINISM (Chandra Mohanty, Ann Russo & Lourdes Torres eds., 1991); TRINH T. MINH-HA, WOMAN NATIVE OTHER (1989).

orientation, and so on) and also recognize the necessity of multiple women's movements and feminist analyses. This need to recognize the specificity of local feminisms and women's activism is at the heart of debates about the role of universal
claims in women's organizing: How do we reconcile the recognition of the multiplicity of women's experiences with the assertion that there is a common basis for
women's international networking and collaboration? How can claims be made in
the name of "women" when women around the world face such a broad array of
challenges and experiences?

In thinking about such questions, Mohanty situates third world feminism in the
broader context of international political economy and post-colonialism.[22] While
she emphasizes that third world women are not a monolithic category, she still
asserts that we can identify opportunities for coherent "third world feminist"
struggles that are based on "common differences." That is, even as different
women in the third world experience oppression differently, they do so in relation
to common systems of power and domination that affect all women in the third
world. Power and domination must be seen as omnipresent. Mohanty utilizes feminist sociologist Dorothy Smith's idea of "relations of ruling" to express the myriad
dimensions of power as it is exercised through a "complex of organized practices,
including government, law, business and financial management, professional organization, and educational institutions."[23] Racial, sexual, and class biases pervade
this complex of practices, and women both within and outside the so-called third
world are affected by and experience power differently across such areas as class,
race, and geography.

For example, economic globalization is experienced in the form of SAPs in
Tanzania, where devaluation of currency devastates woman-run cottage enterprises.
Women in other parts of the world, such as Ireland, are facing downward pressure
on their wages and less job security. Women in both situations are affected by the
demands of the global economy. Similarly, violence against women takes different
forms across regions and cultures, from domestic violence and coercive reproductive practices, to dowry deaths and female genital mutilation. Yet there is a common
moment to the use of violence against women which is contained in the idea
of patriarchal domination. Mohanty situates third world feminist struggles at the
"intersection of these relations of ruling," appreciating that women may experience
the oppressive aspects of these relations of ruling differently while also recognizing
the common complex of domination that they face.[24]

Just as Mohanty argues that a coherent third world feminism can be located
despite the multiplicity of locations and identities of third world women, the experience of the women's human rights movement suggests that a global feminism

---

22. Chandra Talpade Mohanty, *Introduction, Cartographies of Struggle: Third World Women and the
Politics of Feminism, in* THIRD WORLD WOMEN AND THE POLITICS OF FEMINISM (Chandra Mohanty, Ann
Russo & Lourdes Torres ed., 1991).

23. *Id.* at 14, *citing* DOROTHY SMITH, THE EVERYDAY WORLD AS PROBLEMATIC: A FEMINIST SOCIOLOGY
3 (1987).

24. *Id.* at 14.

driven by international feminist networking is also possible. Such networking does not require homogeneity of experience or perspective, or even ongoing consensus across a range of issues. Mohanty's metaphor of "cartographies of struggles" is a very useful one for it signals the complexity of the terrain—the structures, institutions, and mores—with which diverse women contend in identifying and ending their oppression, at the same time that it points to the possibility of mapping that complexity and finding common moments at the intersection of diverse paths, or "common differences" as Mohanty calls them.[25]

The question about what can serve as the basis for a global women's movement involves issues echoed in debates about human rights more generally, especially the contentious issue of what universality means in the face of particular claims around culture, national sovereignty, and other forms of group identity. Ironically, just as feminists are exploring the importance of recognizing the diversity of women—including cultural differences—opponents of women's human rights are using similar arguments to deny women's claims to universal human rights. Thus, even as women have worked to recognize, admit, and incorporate diverse perspectives in their thinking and work, they have also struggled to create alliances and to work together in solidarity across differences in the face of conservative and fundamentalist backlashes against feminism occurring in many parts of both the North and the South. Faced with both the need to do justice to the many different ways women experience, articulate, and act upon their concerns and the need to make claims in the name of "women" in order to counter the backlash, what does it mean to say that women's human rights are universal?

As Florence Butegwa points out, on the level of law, human rights are universal in the sense that all extant human rights laws, treaties, and procedures theoretically apply equally to all people, including women.[26] On a more philosophical level, universal human rights and the claims of particular women can be seen as complementary rather than in opposition or in conflict. For example, in articulating what she sees as the basis of third world feminism, Mohanty shifts the focus away from particular experiences to an analysis of the way in which power is exercised in the world.[27] Similarly, through an understanding of the exercise of power as global and interconnected (that is, universally experienced, albeit different in its effects) an argument can be made for universal human rights as a system of accountability required by the way power is exercised. In this way, the idea of universal human rights serves as a regulative principle which informs the articulation of women's local demands and strengthens their resistance to abuses of power. This is very different from a relativist stance which argues that all rights claims must be worked out entirely in relation to the local cultural and political context, a stance in which women's rights can easily be eroded in the name of cultural or religious claims.

---

25. *Id.* at 13.

26. Florence Butegwa, *Limitations of the Human Rights Framework for the Protection of Women, in* CLAIMING OUR PLACE: WORKING THE HUMAN RIGHTS SYSTEM TO WOMEN'S ADVANTAGE (Institute for Women, Law and Development, 1993).

27. Mohanty, *supra* note 22, at 13.

Many critiques of universal human rights coming out of Asia, Africa, and Latin America do not target universality *per se* as the problem.[28] Rather, they challenge false universalization based on the property-based rights of certain individuals against the state. The dominance of the liberal, state-centered model of politics has led to human rights thinking and practice which places too great an emphasis on the civil and political rights that an abstract individual holds *vis à vis* the state, and which suppresses diversity and ignores the economic, social, and cultural dimensions of human rights. As feminists and activists all over the world have recognized, a new approach to human rights, or a new understanding of universality that encompasses the idea of human rights as indivisible, is required. A critical dimension of such a new approach is to shift attention away from the state and to focus on deepening and extending human rights as a broad-based movement that reaches into every dimension of civil society. Radhika Coomaraswamy, the U.N. Special Rapporteur on Violence Against Women, asserts that the human rights framework is greater than the sum of its laws and processes, many of which require fundamental revision as we move toward the realization of universal human rights that include women. She contends that human rights must be rooted in culture rather than simply articulated within the law, the primary tool of the state. For Coomaraswamy, grassroots movements play a pivotal role in this process. She claims that:

> [U]nless human rights values take root in civil society and unless civil institutions and non-governmental organizations take up the cause, then women's rights as human rights will have no resonance in the [public] institutions concerned.[29]

When local women's groups use human rights thinking and practice, especially in the context of international networking, they actively demonstrate the complementary links between universal ideals and local struggles for justice. The Global Campaign for Women's Human Rights can be seen as one example of the kind of mobilization and practice that Coomaraswamy sees as necessary to translate national and international laws into local social and political practice.

Although it is difficult to find a common framework or perspective through which to analyze women's lives and organize for change without falling into the trap of false universalization, the international movement for women's human rights has consciously striven to challenge the idea that we must choose between universality and particularity. The movement began with the central operating principle that its concepts and activities should be developed through a process of networking with women who work and organize at the local, national, and international levels in all regions of the world. Similar types of networking have been taken up as a method of organizing by tens of thousands of women from all over the world, and they have successfully linked together women from diverse backgrounds to work on common projects. It is useful to look at how some of these issues have played

---

28. Rajni Kothari, *Human Rights: A Movement in Search of a Theory, in* RETHINKING HUMAN RIGHTS: CHALLENGES FOR THEORY AND ACTION (Smitu Kothari & Harsh Sethi eds., 1989).

29. Radhika Coomaraswamy, *To Bellow Like a Cow: Women, Ethnicity, and the Discourse of Rights, in* HUMAN RIGHTS OF WOMEN: NATIONAL AND INTERNATIONAL PERSPECTIVES 44 (Rebecca Cook ed., 1994).

themselves out in several of the networks that have been central to the movement for women's human rights as well as in the Global Campaign for Women's Human Rights.

Women's International Networks

In networking, different groups and associations can take into account their organizational strengths and existing commitments and resources, and participate in projects on a flexible basis. Networking allows for non-hierarchical, decentralized, coordinated action around common goals. WiLDAF is one of the major regional networks that has taken a leadership role in the international women's human rights movement.[30] What is important about the development of WiLDAF—and of organizational networks generally—is that the process of planning the network, of formulating its mission and its priorities, and of raising the necessary support, was broadly participatory. Established in 1990, the planning process originally included women from nine African countries, but eventually drew on the ideas, suggestions, and energy of women from more than fifteen African countries and other regional and international networks and organizations. Women attending the Forum on Women, Law and Development held at the U.N. Third World Conference on Women in Nairobi in 1985, found that they were all working on issues arising from the complex relationship between formal and customary law and women's participation in development. WiLDAF grew out of "the realization by the participants that because they all were fighting similar obstacles, combining efforts was an important step towards overcoming those obstacles which women face everywhere."[31] Like many regional and international women's networks, the programmatic goals of WiLDAF are to exchange information, share strategies for women's self-determination, and develop mechanisms for coordinated research and action at national and regional levels. WiLDAF itself identifies legal literacy and rights awareness as its top priorities, and thus the network's main projects include training in legal education, legal analysis, and interprofessional collaboration, setting up a system for information exchange, and the creation of an "emergency response network to mobilize around serious violations of women's rights."[32]

The common training and the exchange of information within the WiLDAF network facilitates systematic rather than piecemeal analyses of the challenges that women encounter, and provides a forum for the development of collaborative action for change. The intergroup connections that the network facilitates at both the national and regional levels lend weight to the analysis and indictment of broad patterns of violence and discrimination that might not otherwise be recognized as

---

30. For further information about WiLDAF, contact WiLDAF, P.O. Box 4622, Harare, Zimbabwe; phone (263-4) 752105; fax (263-4) 733670; email: wildaf@mango.zw.

31. Akua Kuenyehia, *Organizing at the Regional Level: The Case of WiLDAF, in* FROM BASIC NEEDS TO BASIC RIGHTS: WOMEN'S CLAIM TO HUMAN RIGHTS 514 (Margaret Schuler ed., 1994).

32. WOMEN, LAW AND DEVELOPMENT IN AFRICA, WiLDAF: ORIGINS AND ISSUES 10 (1990)[hereinafter WiLDAF].

legitimate concerns by the public. The national and regional coordination of projects or mobilizations provides a context within which local action may seem to be more comprehensible, more acceptable, and hence more effective. The links that WiLDAF establishes at the national and regional levels help "to expand the influence of individual local programs" and thus give much needed support to women working at the grassroots level.[33]

Another network that seeks to create common linkages among diverse women is the International Solidarity Network of Women Living Under Muslim Laws (WLUML).[34] This network is not geographically specific, but rather defines its mission around the needs of women living in Muslim countries and communities all over the world. The WLUML network, established in 1986, has a twofold purpose: to counter or break the myth of the singularly defined "Muslim woman," and to provide a vehicle through which women from different countries, regions, and cultures can work together to challenge and transform practices and traditions harmful to women and justified through fundamentalist versions of Islam.[35] Some of the challenges posed by the coordination of such a diverse and geographically dispersed collection of organizations are met by the highly decentralized and fluid structure of the network. As Farida Shaheed notes:

> [Because] the essence of networks lies in linkages, interactions, and mutual support that bring together different groups of individuals with varying priorities and participation levels, the overall direction and image of the network in a given period will be influenced by which ever groups or individuals are more active at that particular point.[36]

The structure or methodology of networking fosters respect for the diverse "contextual constraints within which women are obliged to live their lives" and for the choices women make.[37]

WLUML gains its strength and critical edge through creating links between diverse women living in a Muslim context, giving women's organizations access both to each other and to information about the sources of law and customary practices. The exchange of information and cross-cultural visits and research provide women in the network with an alternative identity through which they develop political analyses and strategies for change. This is particularly important, for in belonging to the social collectivity that is the WLUML network, women gain an alternative reference group for their experiences and analyses; the network is a

---

33. *Id.* at 5; Kuenyehia, *supra* note 31, at 524.

34. For further information about WLUML, contact Women Living Under Muslim Laws International Solidarity Network, Boite Postale 23, Grabels, France; phone (33-67) 109166; fax (33-67) 109167; email: wluml@mnet.fr.

35. Marie-Aimee Helie-Lucas, *Women Living Under Muslim Laws, in* OURS BY RIGHT: WOMEN'S RIGHTS AS HUMAN RIGHTS 52 (Joanna Kerr ed., 1993).

36. Farida Shaheed, *Linking Dreams: The Network of Women Living Under Muslim Laws, in* FROM BASIC NEEDS TO BASIC RIGHTS: WOMEN'S CLAIM TO HUMAN RIGHTS 322 (Margaret Schuler ed., 1994).

37. *Id.* at 306.

resource for women to reformulate their identities within a Muslim context. Further, in the comparisons that their cultural and national differences make possible, network participants can learn about the ways in which fundamentalist versions of Islam are used to justify culturally or nationally specific social practices and political arrangements. The network gives women living in a Muslim context around the world a way to work towards broadly defined common ends without erasing the richness or diversity of different women's experiences and concerns.

Both WLUML and WiLDAF have been active in the women's human rights movement and were key partners in the Global Campaign's planning for the Vienna World Conference on Human Rights. Both groups have noted that organizing around Vienna was important for their organizations' growth. According to WiL-DAF, it gave network participants an opportunity for self-assessment, fostered attention for their work and for the collaborative aspect of their efforts, and gave them visibility in the international community. WLUML organizers have noted that the world conferences provided key opportunities for the consolidation of the networks, for they allowed face-to-face meetings which fostered discussion and understanding of the rationale for the different strategies undertaken by women.

Several organizations and regional networks worked together to launch the Global Campaign for Women's Human Rights, and they used networking as a primary mode of mobilizing women for the World Conference on Human Rights and the series of conferences leading up to the World Conference on Women in Beijing. The driving force of the Global Campaign is its commitment to action-oriented networking, to building linkages among women across multiple boundaries including class, race, ethnicity, religion, and sexual orientation, both within local-and national-level communities and across geo-political divides. Networking in the Global Campaign is also fostered across professional divisions such as grassroots organizing, service provisions, academia, the medical and legal professions, lobbyists, and governmental or U.N. policy makers. Besides the success afforded by the method of networking, two additional factors were essential to the achievements of the Global Campaign's international mobilization efforts. First, the human rights framework served as an overarching ethical framework with global resonance. A human rights framework operates as a common ethical vision which asserts that each human being has rights that both the state and civil society have a moral obligation to uphold. Even though this idea is best known through its expression in the U.N. Universal Declaration on Human Rights and subsequent treaties and agreements, all of the major religious and philosophical traditions of the world assert similar principles. Thus, the fundamental principles of the human rights framework resonate in different cultural, religious, and social contexts. Also, while there are many disagreements about which human rights are the most important, few governments would reject wholesale the idea that individuals have human rights *per se*. As a broadly expressed ethical vision, therefore, the idea of universal human rights affords a common point of departure for diverse women and activists.

The second factor that contributed to the success of network organizing toward Vienna is the fact that the Campaign built upon a common issue. By the late 1980s, women around the world had begun to identify violence against women as a major obstacle to women's advancement, autonomy, well-being, and health. The reality or threat of violence came into focus as a common factor in women's lives in every region of the world, and a growing body of research demonstrated that it cut across all socio-economic and cultural categories. Thus, despite the many differences among the women organizing for the Vienna Conference, women were able to articulate, develop, and act upon a common agenda that took as its focal point the issue of gender-based violence against women.

Networking, and the important task of exchanging experiences and ideas, can take place on many levels. The Center for Women's Global Leadership, for example, organizes annual residential international leadership Institutes that enhance women's leadership at the local level; it also hosts strategic planning meetings which focus more on jointly achieving specific international objectives. By bringing together women not only from different geographical backgrounds but also with diverse professional experiences as lawyers, policy advocates, organizers, or direct service providers, all participants in the Institutes learn from diversity in the process of planning actions for the future which incorporate a broad spectrum of strategies for local, national, regional, and international networking and organizing. The Institutes also have expanded the emerging women's human rights network by engaging more women in the evolving concept of women's rights as human rights. In fact, the Institutes have fostered leadership among women because they do not simply bring women into activities that have already been defined, but also engage them in making strategies themselves in a concrete context so that they become part of the women's human rights network by helping to create some aspects of it.

The Institutes are an important part of the Global Campaign's networking process for another reason. Creating a time and space in which organizations can make plans together is crucial to building a network in which people actually develop common strategies. Such meetings lay the groundwork for the trust that people need to have in order to work globally, and at such meetings, there must be enough time for people to really learn from each other. For example, while many people had been working together through the 16 Days and Petition Campaigns, often they had never met each other. Face-to-face contact at Institutes, in small meetings, at sessions during the world conferences, or as part of organizing a hearing, was critical to helping the network truly become a network. In this way, women related to each other through their work, but they also began to know each other across their differences. Such encounters prepared women to discuss network strategies in greater depth at the local level and allowed them to formulate local and regional strategies that could contribute to the overall focus of the network.

The worldwide petition drive of the Global Campaign for Women's Human Rights and the annual campaign of 16 Days of Activism Against Gender Violence are other examples of broad-based networking activities that link local initiatives within a framework of international solidarity and purpose. The petition campaign, which was a very concrete activity with very specific goals at the global level, took on a life of its own because of the way that regional networks and local organizations used it as part of their own program work. Similarly, the 16 Days of Activism develops an annual thematic time period around which women organize locally to advance the idea that women's rights are human rights and strengthens local work by participation in a global networking activity.

A defining feature of the 16 Days Campaign is that no one group determines or controls the activities. This allows for local definition of the agenda and of the issues that are important to women in each setting. At the same time, women who participate in the 16 Days Campaign use the fact that they are part of an international action to draw on the international solidarity and to enhance their local organizing. Shaheed highlights similar themes when she discusses networking in the WLUML as a means to "support women in their on-going struggles."[38] She claims that "[l]ocal initiatives need to be strengthened through linkages at the national and international levels. . . . Clearly, positive outcomes are the result of multiple actors working in concert and the [WLUML] network sees itself only as an enabling mechanism for rapidly mobilizing support and activating the right connections as needed."[39] This method of organizing has characterized most of the initiatives of the Global Campaign for Women's Human Rights. Since local and regional organizations have the flexibility to join whichever activities seem appropriate to them, they retain their own autonomy while also cooperating in a larger global endeavor.

In addition to creating opportunities for women to take local, grassroots action in such activities as the 16 Days Campaign or popular hearings, the Global Campaign for Women's Human Rights encourages women to use policy-making processes at the local, national, and international levels to expand and strengthen their networks and to acquire the skills and expertise necessary to influence those processes. The Global Campaign targeted a series of United Nations World Conferences beginning with the World Conference on Human Rights (Vienna, 1993) and culminating with the Fourth World Conference on Women (Beijing, 1995). The Global Campaign utilized these major global fora to promote public awareness, to develop the Campaign, and to seek concrete commitments from the U.N. and governments to women's human rights.

There are now many new and renewed intergovernmental agreements to promote and protect women's human rights. As a result, the focus of the Campaign has shifted to the implementation of these promises, including working to realize the protections that various human rights treaties should provide to women everywhere. This means both pressuring national governments for domestic level implementation of the promises they have made at the international and regional levels, and keeping the momentum of the international networks going so that governments know that they are being monitored worldwide. The experiences that women gained in networking around the U.N. World Conferences have provided the basis of trust

---

38. *Id.* at 306.

39. *Id.* at 318.

from which women can now seek to work on common and diverse projects in collaboration and solidarity on a regular basis. As this work gets translated into local and global expressions, the ability of women's networking to provide a model for affirming the universality of human rights while respecting the diversity of particular experiences grows. This will hopefully lead to more effective action on behalf of all human rights in a time of great challenge, a time in which we need ethical principles that can provide a basis for common action globally.

A POST-BEIJING REFLECTION ON THE LIMITATIONS AND POTENTIAL OF HUMAN RIGHTS DISCOURSE FOR WOMEN

Dianne Otto

INTRODUCTION

There have been many glowing feminist assessments of the official outcomes from the 1995 Fourth World Conference on Women (Beijing Conference).[1] Certainly, it was the largest United Nations (U.N.) conference ever held and it bore a remarkable testament to the strength and vitality of women's movements around the world. Further, some important advances for women resulted, including the commitment by states to recognize and value women's unremunerated work[2] and to encourage women's "empowerment."[3] Also, the parallel nongovernmental (NGO) forum provided an extraordinary opportunity for the development and consolidation of transnational networks of interest among women, which suggests that the future of feminist interventions in international law burgeons with new possibilities.

Without wanting to detract from the advances associated with the Beijing Conference, this author's overall assessment of the Beijing outcomes is considerably less glowing. While the language of equality and human rights, which dominates the Beijing Declaration and Platform For Action (Beijing Platform), proved extremely effective in resisting moves by fundamentalist forces to claw back the advances that women have made since the adoption of the U.N. Charter in 1945, it also functioned to prevent transformative[4] outcomes.

At most, the equality paradigm enables women to argue that we have a right to enjoy the same opportunities and outcomes as similarly situated men. It therefore

---

1. Special Issue, *Beijing and Beyond: Toward the Twenty-First Century of Women,* 24 WOMEN'S STUD. Q. (F. Howe ed., vols. 1–2, 1996); Rhonda Copelon, *Introduction: Bringing Beijing Home,* 21 BROOK. J. INT'L L. 599 (1996); Nicole Streeter, *Beijing and Beyond,* 11 BERKELEY WOMEN'S L.J. 200 (1996).

2. *Report of the Fourth World Conference on Women,* 50th Sess.,16th plen. mtg., Annex 1, Annex 2, U.N. Doc. A/CONF.177/20, 17 (1995) (consisting of the *Beijing Declaration,* Annex 1, para. 1–38 and the *Platform For Action* [hereinafter *Beijing Platform*], Annex 2, para. 39–361) can be found at: <gopher://gopher.undp.org:70/00/unconfs/women/off/a-20.en> (last visited June 13,1997).

3. *Id.,* para. 42. *See also* Chilla Bulbeck, *Less Than Overwhelmed by Beijing: Problems Concerning Women's Commonality and Diversity,* 6 AUSTL. FEMINIST L.J. 31 (1996).

4. *See* DRUCILLA CORNELL, TRANSFORMATIONS: COLLECTIVE IMAGINATION AND SEXUAL DIFFERENCE 1 (1993).

prevents challenges to the underlying masculinist structures of the global economic, political, and legal systems. This is reflected in the strategic objectives spelled out in the Platform which fail to challenge the dominant economic rationalist grip on global economic structures, leave intact the militarized framework for the maintenance of international peace and security, and fall short of naming specific *women's*-rights abuses as human rights violations.

In re-evaluating the emancipatory potential of feminist human rights strategies post-Beijing, the approach here is to situate feminist interventions in the broader context of the liberatory struggles of all non-elite groups. The project of reshaping international law so that it disrupts global regimes of masculinist power is thereby understood as a multidimensional and coalitional project. The common goal is to work towards a system of law that comprehends and promotes multiplicitous and nonhierarchical identities and groupings within an equitable global economic framework. Such a project relies on the development of new conceptions of difference and specificity as an alternative to "cultural relativity," and new paradigms for understanding context and justice as opposed to the imperialism of "universality."

One aspect of this larger project (of transforming international law) involves rejecting the separation that currently exists between, on one hand, feminist strategies which seek to utilize the rubric of "human rights" in an emancipatory way and, on the other hand, strategies of economic justice which contest the canon of capitalist "development." While it must be remembered that *both* the discourses of human rights and development are effects and tools of global elites and therefore treacherous terrain for feminists, nevertheless such powerful knowledge systems also produce resistance from those they subjugate, which is how feminist strategies are generated.

In rejecting approaches that treat the resistant strategies of emancipation (human rights) and economic justice (development) as separate projects, it is proposed that coalitions between the two strategies are necessary to broaden and deepen the international feminist agenda and to enhance our understanding and practice of "solidarity around difference"—a much larger project than either human rights or development, at least as they are currently understood.

This chapter is divided into four parts with the Beijing Conference experience as its focus. The first section outlines how the gendered subject position of the Woman[5] of international legal discourse was produced by the U.N. Charter and its three-tiered progeny of human rights and development instruments during the Cold War.[6] Despite concerted contestation of her identity during the International Decade

---

5. Carol Smart, *The Woman Of Legal Discourse*, 1 Soc. & Legal Stud. 29 (1992) (Smart's theorizing of the role of law in discursively constituting the subject position of Woman, in contradistinction to Man, is also useful in the international legal context).

6. Often referred to as the first, second, and third generations of rights, the Cold War produced the three tiers of civil and political rights; economic, social, and cultural rights; and rights associated with development.

for Women (1975–1985), the Woman produced by international legal discourse tenaciously remained the economically dependent wife and mother.

The second section canvasses three shifts that occurred in the ten-year period between the 1985 Third World Conference on Women (Nairobi Conference) and the 1995 Beijing Conference that influenced the way feminist issues were eventually framed in Beijing: first, the impact of the ascendancy of global capital on mainstream human rights discourse; second, the refocusing of the feminist agenda on human rights in place of women-in-development; and third, the emergent critical international discourse informed by post-colonial, post-structural and queer perspectives.

The third section examines the outcomes from the Beijing Conference with respect to each of the three Cold War categories of rights, with particular attention to the influence of the post-Cold War shifts. It also examines the ways in which issues of women's diversity were contested and contained. This section concludes that the Woman brought into being by the Beijing Platform, in contrast to her Cold War counterpart, faces two additional expectations: that she assume a role in the global free market economy and that she participate in decision-making structures, in addition to her ongoing duties in the family economy as wife and mother.

Finally, the fourth section critically analyzes the main feminist strategy in Beijing of promoting women's rights as human rights. The strategy failed to break through the gendered barricades that defend the masculinist standards regarding the corpus of human rights, except where the violations of women's human rights could be made to fit into "already recognized" human rights norms. Further, the strategy was influenced by the constricted post-Cold War discourse of human rights and equality, and consequently made few links with economic and social rights and no clear connections with Southern issues of economic justice.

In the conclusion, it is suggested that feminist interventions would be more inclusive of the multiplicity of women's identities and issues, and more effective in challenging the underlying masculinist form of international law, if links were forged between an expanded emancipatory human rights framework and a critical development paradigm. This would enable questions of women's diversity to come to the fore and highlight issues of cultural specificity (rather than relativity) which must be addressed. It proposes a coalitional approach whereby feminist practices of "solidarity around difference" could be a powerful means of reconstituting the Woman of international legal discourse as a multiplicitous symbol of women's emancipation and a visionary site of struggle.

THE COLD WAR PRODUCTION OF THE WOMAN OF INTERNATIONAL LEGAL DISCOURSE

The Woman of international legal discourse has her genesis in the 1945 U. N. Charter's assertion of the importance of "the equal rights of men and women" in achieving world peace.[7] She is therefore reliant on the language of equality and

---

7.   U.N. CHARTER pmbl., arts. 1(3), 8, 13(1), 55(c), 56, 62(2), art. 76(c).

rights for her existence, status, and identity. The ensuing Cold War divisions determined the terms of her construction and contestation. In particular, the Woman produced was shaped by the rights and equality discourses of the three major power blocs of the period: the West, East, and Third World.[8]

The masculinist regimes, on both sides of the East/West polarization, ideologically embraced the equality of women. However, the masculinist regimes magnified and entrenched a hierarchical distinction between economic and social equality as promoted by the communist East,[9] and civil and political equality as promoted by the capitalist West.[10] This distinction fragmented women's lives along Cold War divisions, splintering the "socioeconomic web"[11] that is our daily reality. Despite Cold War differences, a shared dominant text was also buttressed. This text unfailingly constructed the subject position of Woman in procreative and heterosexual terms as mother and wife and as inevitably subject to and dependent on "men" in their various forms: individually as fathers and husbands and collectively as the state, the military, and the emergent United Nations.

This dominant text is evident in the protective approach adopted by Cold War women's rights instruments regulating women's employment, international trafficking, and marriage.[12] The measures prescribed in these conventions, such as compulsory maternity leave periods (at lower or no pay) and prohibition of consensual prostitution, effectively limit women's opportunities and assert the primacy of women's role within the family, as homemaker and as dependent spouse, despite the supposed framework of equal rights.[13]

Also shared across the Cold War barricades was a conception of equality as a comparative standard that entitles women to rights, opportunities, and benefits that similarly situated men enjoy. Understood in this way, gender equality forecloses

---

8. The term 'Third World' is used advisedly because it highlights the hierarchical ordering of the United Nations member states during this period which is important to recognize for at least two reasons: first, the term reflects the self-assumed superiority of the First and Second worlds of Europe and, second, Third World categorization was the basis for unity and solidarity for post-colonial states in their struggles to resist European domination.

9. International Covenant on Economic, Social and Cultural Rights, G.A. Res. 2200A, U.N. GAOR, 21st Sess., Supp. No. 16, art. 1, U.N. Doc. A/6316 (1966).

10. International Covenant on Civil and Political Rights, G.A. Res. 2200, U.N. GAOR, 21st Sess., Supp. No.16, art. 1, U.N. Doc. A/6316 (1966).

11. Charlotte Bunch, *Women's Rights As Human Rights: Toward a Re-Vision of Human Rights*, 12 HUM. RTS. Q. 486, 492 (1990).

12. Convention Concerning Maternity Protection, June 28, 1952, 214 U.N.T.S. 322; Convention Concerning Night Work of Women Employed in Industry, July 9, 1948, 81 U.N.T.S. 147; Convention Concerning Discrimination in Respect of Employment and Opportunity, June 25, 1958, 362 U.N.T.S. 31; Convention for the Suppression of the Traffic in Persons and of the Exploitation of the Prostitution of Others, *opened for signature* Mar. 21,1950, 96 U.N.T.S. 271, (*entered into force* July 25, 1951); Convention on the Consent to Marriage, Minimum Age for Marriage, and Registration of Marriages, *opened for signature* Dec. 10, 1962, 521 U.N.T.S. 231(*entered into force* Dec. 9, 1964).

13. Natalie Hevener, *International Law and the Status of Women: An Analysis of International Legal Instruments Related to the Treatment of Women*, 1 HARV. WOMEN'S L. J. 131 (1978).

the possibility of contesting the baseline of men's experience which constitutes the *status quo*, and glosses over the inequalities among men that it reproduces among women. Therefore, the concept of equality ultimately legitimates and endorses existing arrangements of power by advocating for women's participation in them.

A third dimension was added to the international discourse on rights and equality as a result of anti-colonial movements. The Third World's struggle for self-determination and global economic justice, although allied with Marxist thinking, introduced a new liberatory language seeking to replace equality with "equity" and individualism with "solidarity."[14] This altered the contours of the Cold War human rights paradigm by reframing equality as a substantive and redistributive goal benefiting peoples rather than individuals, and asserting the priority of collective over individual rights.[15] The New International Economic Order (N.I.E.O.) was promoted through the General Assembly[16] and many in the Third World believed that all systems of oppression, including sexual discrimination, would end once colonial domination ceased and international economic systems became more equitable.[17]

The Woman created by this discourse was valued for her economic contribution to the nation, and her inequality was countered by strategies aimed at ensuring her integration in the processes of economic, social and political development.[18] Later, in the post-revolutionary environment, the importance of women's reproductive role was emphasized as to nation-building and guardianship of indigenous cultures.[19] Women who had assumed active roles in the struggle for self-determination found themselves excluded from participation in the political institutions of post-colonial states. This effectively reinvented the procreative, dependent Woman of

---

14. MOHAMMED BEDJAOUI, TOWARDS A NEW INTERNATIONAL ECONOMIC ORDER (1979); Surakiart Sathirathai, *An Understanding of the Relationship Between International Legal Discourse and Third World Countries*, 25 HARV. INT'L L. J. 395 (1984).

15. Josiah Cobbah, *African Values and the Human Rights Debate: An African Perspective*, 9 HUM. RTS. Q. 309 (1987); Wil Verway, *The New International Economic Order and the Realization of the Right to Development*, in THIRD WORLD ATTITUDES TOWARD INTERNATIONAL LAW: AN INTRODUCTION 825 (F.E. Snyder & S. Sathirathai eds., 1987).

16. *Declaration on the Establishment of a New International Economic Order*, G.A. Res. 3201 (S–VI), U.N. GAOR, 6th Special Sess., Agenda Item 7, U.N. Doc. A/RES/3201 (S–VI) (1974); Charter of Economic Rights and Duties of States, G.A. Res. 3281 (XXIX), U.N. GAOR, 29th Sess., Agenda Item 48, U.N. Doc. A/RES/3281 (XXIX) (1975).

17. M. Jacqui Alexander, *Not Just (Any) Body Can Be A Citizen: The Politics of Law, Sexuality and Postcoloniality in Trinidad and Tobago and the Bahamas*, 48 FEMINIST REV. 5 (1994).

18. *Integration of Women in the Development Process*, G.A. Res. A/RES/3505 (XXX), U.N. GAOR, 30th Sess., Agenda Item 123 (1976); Rebecca Cook, *The Elimination of Sexual Apartheid: Prospects for the Fourth World Conference on Women*, in ISSUE PAPERS ON WORLD CONFERENCES 22 (American Society of International Law, 1995).

19. *See* African Charter on Human and Peoples' Rights, adopted by the 18th Assembly of Heads of State and Government June, 1981, O.A.U. Doc. CAB/LEG/67/3/Rev.5, 21 I.L.M. 59, art. 18 (*entered into force* Oct. 21, 1986) (printed at United Nations, Geneva GE. 90–16020) (referring to the family as "the custodian of morals and traditional values").

the colonizers, and of international law, in the post-colonial context, albeit with indigenous variations.[20] It left the subjugating global discourse on women, produced by the East/West contestation of equal rights, unchallenged by the Third World's struggle for liberation.

All three approaches to women's equality informed the formulation of the 1979 Convention on the Elimination of All Forms of Discrimination Against Women[21] (Women's Convention), which is widely regarded as taking a more progressive approach than the earlier protective instruments. It covers both Cold War categories of human rights and arguably includes discrimination in the arena of the private, domestic sphere.[22] It also acknowledges Third World perspectives in the preamble[23] by making specific reference to the rights of rural women to participate in and benefit from rural development on a basis of equality with men,[24] which was of particular concern to The Women in Development (W.I.D.) lobby.

These advances should not be under valued, but it must be admitted that the Women's Convention is not a "women's rights" instrument. While it promotes women's equality with men and obligates state parties to implement measures that will counter "discrimination against women," it does not recognize or protect rights that are specific to women's gendered experience and corporeality.[25] For example, the problem of gendered violence is not acknowledged, which has prompted a great deal of feminist activity and a rear guard response from the Convention's Committee (CEDAW).[26] Further, women's access to reproductive information and choice, employment, education, participation in government, and so on, is to be made available "on equal terms with men," which completely ignores the highly gendered form of the institutions involved and the need for structural change.

---

20. Kumari Jayawardena, Feminism and Nationalism in the Third World 9 (1986); Hilary Charlesworth, Christine Chinkin & Shelley Wright, *Feminist Approaches to International Law*, 85 Am. J. Int'l L. 613, 620 (1991).

21. Convention on the Elimination of All Forms of Discrimination Against Women, Dec. 18, 1979, G.A. Res 34/180 (*entered into force* Sept. 3, 1981) [hereinafter Women's Convention].

22. *Id.* Art. 1 (defining the term "discrimination against women" and acknowledging its operation "in the political, economic, social, cultural, civil or *any other* field") [emphasis added].

23. *Id.* pmbl., paras. 9, 10 (referring respectively to the importance of "the new international economic order based on equity and justice" and "the eradication of . . . colonialism [and] neo-colonialism" in achieving the equality of women with men).

24. *Id.* art. 14.

25. *Id.* art. 4(1) (discussing an allowance for temporary special measures to accelerate the attainment of equality between women and men but specifically stating that this "shall in no way entail as a consequence the maintenance of unequal or separate standards").

26. See *Report of the Committee on the Elimination of Discrimination Against Women (Eleventh Session)*, U.N. GAOR, 47th Sess., Supp. No. 38, U.N. Doc. A/47/38 (1992). The Committee on the Elimination of Discrimination Against Women (C.E.D.A.W.) has attempted to ensure that gendered violence does fall within its mandate by adopting General Recommendation 19 which states that "gender discrimination includes gender-based violence."

The Women's Convention also carries a raft of provisions which privilege the homemaker as the primary female subject of international law. It supports protective legislation regulating women's work force participation,[27] emphasizes the paramountcy of the interests of children within the family,[28] refers to family planning information in the context of the health and welfare of "the family,"[29] and assumes a two-parent heterosexual family unit.[30] It makes no explicit reference to discrimination experienced by lesbians, rendering the applicability of its antidiscrimination provisions to lesbians "as women" equivocal.[31] In sum, the Women's Convention illustrates the limited emancipatory scope of a discourse of equal rights, at least as it was understood and shaped during the Cold War era.

Further important contributions to the emergent global gender narrative came from the General Assembly's promotion of the International Decade for Women (1975–1985). Although the Decade had three major themes (equality, development and peace), development assumed prominence, reflecting the decolonization and N.I.E.O. agendas of the General Assembly at the time.[32] This led to many positive outcomes, including the proliferation of women's development groups and linkages between macroeconomic issues and women's equality.[33] However, by the end of the Decade, the idea of women's development "needs" had been appropriated as a goal of economic efficiency and was being promoted by the development establishment as a conservatizing and pragmatic goal.[34] This was to precipitate a re-evaluation of strategies by feminists.

In sum, despite contestation between the three Cold War approaches to gender equality and rights, and the growing influence of political feminist movements in both the North and South, the rubric of equality, as a comparative right, was proving to be an inadequate construct on which to base an emancipatory movement for women. At the end of the Cold War, the family-based normativity of the Woman of international legal discourse appeared to have been bolstered by rights discourse. It was becoming abundantly clear that the modern nation-state of the East and West of Europe depended for its legitimacy on the archetypal heterosexual family

---

27. Women's Convention, *supra* note 21, art. 4(2), art. 11(1)(f), art. 11(2)(d).

28. *Id.* art. 5(b).

29. *Id.* art. 10(h).

30. *Id.* art. 16.

31. Alice Miller, Ann Janette Rosga & Meg Satterthwaite, *Health, Human Rights and Lesbian Existence*, 1 HEALTH & HUM. RTS. 428, 433–34 (1995).

32. Jane Connors, *NGOs and the Human Rights of Women at the United Nations, in* "THE CONSCIENCE OF THE WORLD": THE INFLUENCE OF NON-GOVERNMENTAL ORGANISATIONS IN THE UN SYSTEM 147, 158–60 (P. Willetts ed., 1996).

33. Hilary Charlesworth, *The Public/Private Distinction in International Law and the Right to Development*, 12 AUSTL. Y.B. INT'L L. 190 (1992).

34. Rhoda Howard, *Women's Rights and the Right to Development, in* WOMEN'S RIGHTS, HUMAN RIGHTS: INTERNATIONAL FEMINIST PERSPECTIVES 301, 304 (J. Peters & A. Wolper eds., 1995).

formation and the centrality of women's role within it,[35] and that post-colonial states were following suit.[36] The high stakes involved in contesting women's subjugation were, perhaps, more apparent than ever before.

Post-Cold War Shifts and Challenges

The ten-year period between the Nairobi and Beijing Conferences saw shifts in global relations of power and in the activities and priorities of feminist movements around the world. Three of these shifts were of particular importance in shaping the feminist agenda in Beijing. The first was the unabashed adoption of free-market ideology by global financial institutions and the U.N. in the wake of the Cold War. Second was the reorientation of feminist campaigns to focus on the human rights of women, and third was the emergence of new frameworks for understanding power and difference as a result of post-colonial and post-structural critiques.

The first shift—the rejection of communism in Eastern Europe and the purported "triumph" of capitalism[37]—had the effect of removing issues of class inequality from the global agenda and muffling the platform for women's economic and social rights in human rights discourse. In the former Eastern bloc, the result was that women bore the brunt of the burdens of economic liberalization as unemployment increased and child care and other social services were cut.[38] This was accompanied by a new emphasis on women's domestic role in the home.[39] Women's economic and social rights, promoted so passionately by the East during the Cold War, proved to be easily dispensable in the new world of "freedom" in the form of liberalized economies.

The ascendancy of global capital, and the changed economic policies of Eastern Europe, also served to confirm what many had already claimed as the "failure" of the N.I.E.O. of the South.[40] Development was reframed as best achieved by the operation of free-market forces and a reduced state role in the provision of social services.[41] Structural adjustment programs were implemented in the poorest countries of the South, at the behest of global financial institutions, in response to

---

35. V. Spike Peterson, *Security and Sovereign States: What Is at Stake in Taking Feminism Seriously?*, in GENDERED STATES: FEMINIST (RE)VISIONS OF INTERNATIONAL RELATIONS THEORY 31, 46 (1992).

36. Alexander, *supra* note 17.

37. FRANCIS FUKUYAMA, THE END OF HISTORY AND THE LAST MAN (1992).

38. Dorothy J. Rosenberg, *Shock Therapy: GDR Women in Transition from a Socialist Welfare State to a Social Market Economy*, 17 SIGNS 129, 132–33 (1991); Dianne Otto, *Challenging The "New World Order": International Law, Global Democracy and the Possibilities for Women*, 3 TRANSNAT'L L.& CONTEMP. PROBS. 371, 390 (1993).

39. Maxine Molyneux, *The "Women Question" in the Age of Perestroika*, 183 NEW LEFT REV. 23, 38 (1990); Sally Low, *Polish Women Confront Church and Union*, GREEN LEFT 16 (Melbourne, Australia, June 26, 1991).

40. Thomas Franck, *Lessons of the Failure of the N.I.E.O.*, CAN. CONFED. INT'L. L. ANN. CONF., Oct. 17, 1986.

41. Russel Barsh, *A Special Session of the U.N. General Assembly Rethinks the Economic Rights and Duties of States*, 85 AM. J. INT'L L. 192 (1991).

growing debt burdens and other economic difficulties.[42] These programs have diverted money away from social development and led to a disproportionate increase in the number of women living in poverty.[43] Further, much development assistance has been redirected from the South to the countries of the former Eastern bloc.[44]

The Western prioritization of political and civil rights, increasingly endorsed by the former East, served the new orthodoxy of free-market ideology and neo-imperialist development models, diverting attention from economic rights and social justice. The post-Cold War emphasis on the global promotion of human rights, in fact, reflects a contraction of the discourse of human rights[45] rather than, as often claimed, a new era of cooperation across earlier divisions and a new commitment to the "indivisibility" of human rights.

The second influential shift during this period was devised and promoted by feminists as a result of reassessing strategies after the Nairobi Conference. A global strategy aimed at achieving the recognition of women's "human rights," rather than "needs," was launched.[46] The campaign was not conceived as an assertion of civil and political rights to the exclusion of other categories of rights. Instead, it was hoped that it would provide a new focus for the floundering women-in-development agenda.[47]

The new strategy has been effective in producing many blistering critiques of the masculinist form and content of human rights law.[48] It has also had extraordinary success in placing gendered violence firmly onto the international agenda,[49] including the 1993 adoption by the General Assembly of the Declaration on the Elimination of Violence Against Women (Declaration Against Violence).[50] Many Southern

---

42. Rebecca Cook, *Women's International Human Rights Law: The Way Forward*, 15 HUM. RTS. Q. 230, 242–43 (1993).

43. *Beijing Platform, supra* note 2, paras. 13, 16, 18, 47, and 158; *see also* Christine Chinkin & Shelley Wright, *The Hunger Trap: Women, Food, and Self-Determination*, 14 MICH. J. INT'L L. 262 (1993).

44. Brenda Cossman, *Reform, Revolution or Retrenchment? International Human Rights in the Post-Cold War Era*, 32 HARV. INT'L L.J. 339, 351 (1991).

45. *Id.* at 345.

46. Bunch, *supra* note 11; Elisabeth Friedman, *Women's Human Rights: The Emergence of a Movement, in* WOMEN'S RIGHTS, HUMAN RIGHTS: INTERNATIONAL FEMINIST PERSPECTIVES 18 (J. Peters & A. Wolper eds., 1995); Connors, *supra* note 32, at 163.

47. Connors, *supra* note 32.

48. Rebecca Cook & Valerie Oosterveld, *A Select Bibliography of Women's Human Rights*, 44 AM. U. L. REV. 1429 (1995).

49 Radhika Coomaraswamy, *Commission on Human Rights—Special Rapporteur,* U.N. ESCOR, 50th Sess., Agenda Item 11 (a) of the Provisional Agenda, U.N. Doc. E/CN.4/1995/42 (1994); Hilary Charlesworth & Christine Chinkin, *Violence Against Women: A Global Issue, in* WOMEN, MALE VIOLENCE AND THE LAW 13 (J. Stubbs ed., 1994).

50. Declaration on the Elimination of Violence Against Women, G.A. Res. 48/104, U.N. GAOR, 48th Sess., 85th plen. mtg., Agenda Item 111, U.N. Doc. A/RES/48/104 (1993) [hereinafter Declaration Against Violence].

feminists have also adopted the language of human rights, albeit with some cave-ats,[51] while others have expressed concern about the Eurocentrism of this approach.[52]

Unfortunately, as was later reflected in Beijing, the new women's-rights-are-human-rights strategy lost contact with the women-in-development agenda, and women's economic and social rights were also overshadowed by the issues of sexual violence and legal reform. Although gendered violence, in its many forms, has proven to be a powerful means of uniting women globally, and although the issue of violence traverses the divide between different categories of human rights, its potential to promote an integration of the categories of human rights has not been realized.[53]

Consequently, the global women's human rights strategy has had the unintended effect of endorsing the post-Cold War dominance of civil and political rights. Further, although the campaign against gendered violence was designed with careful attention to women's diverse experiences of violence, more public effort has been directed towards condemning certain non-Western practices, such as genital mutilation, than addressing Western forms of violence against women.[54] This has the effect of privileging the figure of the Western woman as normative and thereby, inadvertently, serving the Eurocentric interests of global capital.

Related developments also saw the emergence of an international sexuality discourse, which mirrored the new feminist strategy by seeking the recognition of sexuality rights as human rights.[55] The new movement literally burst onto the world stage at the 1993 World Conference on Human Rights in Vienna, drawing global attention to lesbian and gay rights issues.[56] The sexuality-rights-are-human-rights strategy has the same problems as the feminist human rights strategy in its isolation

---

51. Radhika Coomaraswamy, *To Bellow Like A Cow: Women, Ethnicity and the Discourse of Rights*, *in* HUMAN RIGHTS OF WOMEN: NATIONAL AND INTERNATIONAL PERSPECTIVES 39 (R. Cook ed., 1994); Sharon Hom, *Female Infanticide in China: The Human Rights Specter and Thoughts Towards (An) Other Vision*, 23 COL. HUM. RTS. L. REV. 249 (1991–92); Takyiwaah Manuh, *The Women, Law and Development Movement in Africa and the Struggle for Customary Law Reform*, *in* THIRD WORLD LEGAL STUDIES 207 (1994–95).

52. Julie Stephens, *Running Interface: An Interview With Gayatri Chakravorty Spivak*, 7/2 AUSTL. WOMEN'S BOOK REV. 19; Isabelle Gunning, *Arrogant Perception, World-Travelling and Multicultural Feminism: The Case of Female Genital Surgeries*, 23 COL. HUM. RTS. L. REV. 189 (1991–92).

53. Declaration Against Violence, *supra* note 50, art. 3 (articulating in a very traditional manner the general human rights entitlements of women).

54. See Isabelle Gunning, *Female Genital Surgeries and Multicultural Feminism: The Ties That Bind; The Differences That Distance*, *in* THIRD WORLD LEGAL STUDIES 17 (1994–95) for a discussion of some of the problems with Western framings of issues associated with female genital surgeries.

55. Julie Dorf & Gloria Careaga Perez, *Discrimination and the Tolerance of Difference: International Lesbian Human Rights*, *in* WOMEN'S RIGHTS, HUMAN RIGHTS 324 (J. Peters & A. Wolper eds., 1995).

56. Douglas Sanders, *Getting Lesbian and Gay Issues on the International Human Rights Agenda*, 18 HUM. RTS. Q. 67, 89 (1996).

from issues of economic rights and social justice.[37] In addition, there is the continuing problem of the tendency for women's sexual diversity to be erased from legal texts by the embodiment of the "homosexual" as a gay man.[58]

The third significant shift in thinking between the Nairobi and Beijing conferences was prompted by post-colonial, post-structural and queer critiques of modernity which exposed claims to "universality" as serving the interests of global elites and drew attention to the importance of understanding the complexities of power and theorizing about difference.[59] These analyses directly raised the issue of which identities are excluded by the Woman of international legal discourse and highlighted the hegemonic effects of Western constructs in constituting international feminist goals and strategies.

Many feminist human rights proponents responded by embracing an incipient new awareness of gender diversities and acknowledged the importance of the intersection of gender with other subordinating structures, such as race and class. The global campaign to eliminate violence against women, despite the shortcomings just referred to, provides a salient example. Notwithstanding the public focus on non-Western forms of violence, the Declaration Against Violence outlines a broadly inclusive, non-exhaustive definition of gendered violence, recognizing that women experience different forms of violence depending on their varying social, economic, political, and cultural contexts.[60]

Further, the new critical perspectives drew attention to the need for increased transparency of the regimes of power served by the dominant formulations of gender and other differences. This was also reflected in the Declaration Against Violence in its use of the potentially transformative language of "power," which stands as a watershed in human rights discourse. By acknowledging that violence against women is a "manifestation of historically unequal power relations between men and women" which has led to "domination over . . . women by men,"[61] the decontextualized "neutrality" of human rights orthodoxy is implicitly rejected. By recognizing that differences in power are the fundamental problem, and that the global systems of male privilege rely on systemic gendered violence, it follows

---

57. Dianne Otto, *Questions of Solidarity and Difference: Towards Transforming the Terms of Lesbian Interventions in International Law, in* SEDUCTIONS OF JUSTICE: LESBIAN LEGAL THEORIES AND PRACTICES (R. Robson & V. Brownworth eds., forthcoming).

58. RUTHANN ROBSON, LESBIAN (OUT)LAW: SURVIVAL UNDER THE RULE OF LAW, ch. 3 (1992) (documenting how lesbianism has been erased from U.S. legal texts by reference to male sexuality).

59. Judith Butler, *Contingent Foundations: Feminism and the Question of "Postmodernism", in* FEMINISTS THEORISE THE POLITICAL 7 (J. Butler & J. Scott eds., 1992); Chandra Mohanty, *Cartographies of Struggle, in* THIRD WORLD WOMEN AND THE POLITICS OF FEMINISM 7 (C. Mohanty, A. Russo & L. Torres eds., 1991); ELIZABETH SPELMAN, INESSENTIAL WOMAN (1988); Linda Alcoff, *Cultural Feminism Versus Poststructuralism: The Identity Crisis in Feminist Theory*, 13/3 SIGNS 405 (1988); Nancy Caraway, *The Cunning of History: Empire, Identity and Feminist Theory in the Flesh*, 12/2 WOMEN & POL. 1 (1992).

60. Declaration Against Violence, *supra* note 50, art.2.

61. *Id.* pmbl., para. 6.

logically that gender-differentiated standards are necessary to redress gendered rights violations.

The shifts in feminist strategy were apparent at the world conferences that preceded the Beijing Conference and served as dynamic forums for the contestation of gender issues and the promotion of the new women's human rights agenda.[62] Most notably, at the 1993 World Conference on Human Rights (W.C.H.R.) held in Vienna, governments declared that "the human rights of women and the girl-child are an inalienable, integral and indivisible part of universal human rights."[63] While there is a widening gap between the rhetoric and reality of these commitments, there is little doubt that the trope of gender came to signify a battleground over citizenship, identity, and power in many global arenas in the lead-up to the Beijing Conference.

In sum, the dramatic shifts in global power in the post-Cold War environment, and the responses from feminists and other critical scholars and activists, shaped both the official and feminist agendas in Beijing. The earlier divisions among the East, West, and Third World were replaced by the competing agendas of North and South, fundamentalists and liberals, cultural relativists and universalists, and anti-feminist and pro-feminist forces. Unfortunately, no coherent alternative voice had emerged to counter the dominant narrative of free-market forces and privatization, and the parallel narrowing of the human rights agenda had been well camouflaged. By 1995, the women's-rights-are-human-rights strategy confronted a complex and multi-faceted set of forces and ideologies in Beijing.

The Beijing Production of the Woman of International Legal Discourse

The debates in Beijing revealed continuing intractable divisions among states over certain fundamental aspects of the global gender narrative, most notably in relation to sexuality, reproductive rights, and families.[64] The final documents announce carefully worded and sometimes ambiguous compromise positions which, in the main, do not retreat from earlier commitments. However, some of the final wording is augmented by a flood of reservations registered by states wishing to distance themselves from the compromises reached, revealing that issues of women's equality and rights continue to be highly controversial.

---

62. *Report of the United Nations Conference on Environment and Development*, U.N. GAOR (UN-CED), at ch. 24, U.N. Doc. A/CONF.151/26 (1992); *Report of the International Conference on Population and Development*, U.N. GAOR, U.N. Doc. A/CONF.171/13 (1994) [hereinafter *I.C.P.D. Report*]; *Report of the World Summit for Social Development*, U.N. GAOR, U.N. Doc. A/CONF.166/9 (1995), commitment 5 [hereinafter *W.S.S.D. Report*].

63. *Report of the World Conference on Human Rights,* U.N. GAOR, para. 18, U.N. Doc. A/CONF.157/24 (1993). *See also* Donna Sullivan, *Women's Human Rights and the 1993 World Conference on Human Rights*, 88 AM. J. INT'L L. 152 (1994).

64. These issues were again subjected to conservative challenge at Habitat II, the second U.N. Conference on Human Settlements, Istanbul, June 1996. See *The Habitat Agenda: Goals and Principles, Commitments and Global Plan of Action. Report of Committee 1. Addendum. Istanbul Declaration on Human Settlement,* U.N. GAOR, Habitat II, U.N. Doc. A/CONF.165/L.6/Add. 10 (1996).

Despite the high levels of disagreement, patterns and consistencies nevertheless emerged that, pieced together, constitute a coherent narrative of the 1990s Woman of international legal discourse who continues to rely on the language of rights and equality. By way of examining this production, this section first examines the treatment of the three main Cold War categories of rights in the Platform. Next, it analyzes the way the Platform manges the issue of women's diversities. It concludes that the Woman who emerges has acquired a new entrepreneurial role in the market-place and expanded access to decision-making opportunities but, at the same time, retains her pivotal functions in the family.

Of three Cold War categories of rights, commitments in the area of civil and political rights constitute the most tangible outcomes from Beijing. In particular, promoting the "full and equal participation"[65] or "increased representation"[66] of women in decision making structures is the dominant action strategy proposed. The Platform calls for women's participation in decision making in most of its twelve priority areas.

While achieving the equal representation of women in domestic and global economic and political institutions would be an important advance for women, reliance on the equality paradigm as the basis for women's civil and political rights forecloses questioning the underlying forms of these institutions which have resolutely functioned to exclude women.[67] In the absence of a recognition that the decision-making structures must themselves change, it is not clear what difference women's equal participation could make. Ultimately, it may merely equally impli-cate women in the perpetuation of the masculinist liberal forms of minimalist representative democracy and capitalist economics.

The second Cold War category of women's economic and social rights was, in general, much more controversial in Beijing than civil and political rights. The section on women's health, which contained almost one-quarter of the bracketed (i.e., contested) text in the draft Platform, was the critical site for contestation of women's reproductive and sexual rights. Despite the long history of feminist strug-gles in this area,[68] the result in Beijing was that reproductive rights continue to be available to women by association with their male partners, on the basis of equality with men in the context of heterosexual family formations, and not as human rights attached specifically to women's bodies and enjoyed independently by women.[69]

---

65. *Beijing Platform, supra* note 2, paras. 58(a)(c), 142(a), 165(d), 190–94, and 239(c).

66. *Id.* paras. 83(f), 108(a), 205(d), and 253(a).

67. CAROLE PATEMAN, THE DISORDER OF WOMEN: DEMOCRACY, FEMINISM AND POLITICAL THEORY (1989); Drucilla Cornell, *Hierarchy, Equality and the Possibility of Democracy, in* CORNELL, *supra* note 4, at 31; Otto, *supra* note 38.

68. Rebecca Cook, *International Protection of Women's Reproductive Rights*, 24 N.Y.U.J. INT'L L. & POL. 645 (1992); Jacqueline Pitanguay, *From Mexico To Beijing: A New Paradigm*, 1 HEALTH & HUM. RTS. 454 (1995).

69. *Beijing Platform, supra* note 2, paras. 95–96, may be read as separating sexuality from reproductive rights, and as recognizing that women's rights in this area exist independently from men's. But in the context of the wording of the rest of the health section, and the many reservations to these two para-graphs, the status of this recognition is very precarious.

More broadly, the Platform conceives of women's economic and social rights in the context of diminished state responsibility and an increased emphasis on the role of the private sector. The outcome is a rearrangement of earlier distinctions between public and private spheres, which reduces the space in the public and increases the reach of the marketplace. This fundamentally reshapes the context within which economic and social rights are understood and highlights the urgent need for feminist analyses of the gendered nature of the "private" sphere that go beyond the domestic economies of the family. In the absence of effective critiques of free-market systems, states' responsibilities have moved from the provision of basic guarantees and safety nets (publicly funded child care does not even rate a mention)[70] to equipping women to compete equally as free enterprise actors by enacting laws and making administrative arrangements that encourage private actors to make credit available to them.[71]

The neglect of economic and social rights is also related to the virtual absence of rights associated with the Third World's earlier radical development agenda.[72] The post-Cold War development paradigm was not seriously in question at the official Conference. Even the World Summit on Social Development's emphasis on the need for social development to accompany economic development was not repeated in the Platform. This stood in dramatic contrast to discussion at the parallel NGO forum where the devastating consequences of structural adjustment programs and economic liberalization for Southern women, were a major concern. It revealed a huge gap between the official agenda and the economic concerns of grassroots women's movements.[73]

The language of rights disappears altogether from the sections in the Platform that address women's poverty and inequality in economic structures. This suggests inadequate links between the feminist human rights agenda in Beijing and issues of global economic and social justice. While the Platform does comprehensively *catalogue* the increased feminization of poverty and other inequitable consequences for women that have resulted from global economic restructuring, this does not lead to a re-evaluation of the capitalist framework of development. Quite the reverse. The Platform assumes, first, that capitalism has the ability to deliver economic equality to the poor women of the world and, second, that the obligation of

---

70. The importance of state provision of child care was referred to in the action programs of all three earlier World Conferences on Women.

71 *Beijing Platform, supra* note 2, paras. 166–68, and 171.

72. See *Id.* para. 5, for a discussion of the inadequacy of the draft Platform's coverage of development and peace issues. It was so extreme that it was agreed to add a new paragraph to the Mission Statement recognizing the importance of these issues, despite the rule that no new wording was to be introduced in Beijing. For further discussion of this issue, see Dianne Otto, *Holding Up Half the Sky, but for Whose Benefit?: A Critical Analysis of the Fourth World Conference on Women*, 6 AUSTL. FEMINIST L. J. 7 (1996).

73. Janet Hunt, *Reflections on Beijing*, 6 AUSTL. FEMINIST L.J. 39, 40–41 (1996) (Such a gap was also apparent with respect to the theme of peace. Women's NGOs were strongly promoting disarmament and demilitarization, which were not seriously debated as part of the official agenda).

states to guarantee certain economic and social rights is made redundant by the more "efficient" processes of free-market forces. Further, the reproduction of gender hierarchies by free-market competition is ignored and there is no attempt to address the global imbalance of wealth and consumption that exists between the North and South. This outcome further highlights the limitations of the equality paradigm, which is blind to the inequitable standards that underpin its formal comparisons.

The issue of women's diversity adds another dimension to evaluating the Beijing outcomes and the "standards" that are enforced by way of the discourse of rights and equality. The tension associated with acknowledging diversities while also seeking to define minimum "universal" standards is, by now, a familiar conundrum for feminists. The issue traverses the three categories of rights, and its "management" is critical to the disciplinary production of the Woman of international legal discourse.

The contestation of women's diversity in Beijing took many forms. Even before the Conference, an eleventh-hour objection to the use of the term "gender" rather than "sex" in the draft Platform was portentous.[74] Although it was eventually decided to retain the word, "gender,"[75] this provides but one example of the way fundamentalist forces aligned to form a powerful lobby in Beijing. This lobby, despite enormous religious and cultural differences, was united in the task of advancing singular and subordinating narratives of womanhood as predetermined by the "self-evidence" of biology.

Another way in which contestation of the limits of women's identities arose was with regard to certain specific contentious identities including lesbians, prostitutes, undocumented migrant workers and internally displaced women. Some "identities" were literally excluded by the denial of accreditation to Tibetan and Taiwanese groups, pro-choice Catholics, and anti-fundamentalist Muslim NGOs.[76] Others, like sex workers, undocumented migrants, and internal refugees, although retaining a presence in the Platform, were less than adequately dealt with. The presence of lesbians was entirely erased by deletion of all references to "sexual orientation."[77]

---

74. This took place at the final preparatory meeting in New York. Objecting states included Guatemala, Honduras, Benin, and Malta. See *NGOs Frustrated by U.N. Preparatory Meeting*, 4 HUM. RTS. DEFENDER 1 (1995). See generally <http://www.igc.apc.org/women/activist/domestic.html> and <http://www. hg.org/women.html> for relevant web sites (last visited June 15,1997).

75. *Report of the Informal Contact Group on Gender. Note by the Secretariat*, U.N. GAOR, U.N. Doc. A/CONF.177/L.2, 1996.

76. Amnesty International, *Report on the Fourth World Conference on Women*, IOR 41/30/95, 22; *Vatican Intervenes on Women's Conference*, THE AGE, Mar. 30, 1995; *U.N. Protest on Tibet Ban*, THE AGE, Mar. 18, 1995; *Protest as Critics Barred from China Conference*, THE AGE, Mar. 30, 1995. See generally <http://www.amnesty.se/women/beijing.html>, for a relevant web site.

77. Dianne Otto, *Lesbians? Not In My Country: Sexual Orientation at the Beijing World Conference on Women*, 6/20 ALT. L. J. 288 (1995); Margot Kingston, *Beijing—Sexual Preference the Stumbling Block*, 4/4 HUM. RTS. DEFENDER 1 (1995).

The final wording of the Platform does recognize that women face many different obstacles to equality including disability, indigeneity, socioeconomic status,
displacement, and gendered violence.[78] This is an important step toward bringing
into being multi-dimensional subject positions for women and is a clear advance
on the 1979 Women's Convention, which refers to only one specific group of
women (rural women). Even so, the expunging of "sexual orientation" indicates
that women's identities continue to be heavily policed and contained within narrow
disciplinary boundaries, and reveals how central the control of women's sexuality
is to the identity of the Woman of international legal discourse and, thereby, to the
maintenance of the existing systems of global power.

Another diversity "powder keg" was the issue of defining the "family," a
central institution in the maintenance of women's inequality. The question was
whether the Platform would acknowledge a *plurality* of family forms, although
states had agreed at earlier world conferences that "various forms of the family
exist."[79] The result, happily, did not capitulate to conservative demands[80] but, again,
many reservations were noted on this issue. A related debate concerned the balance
to be struck between parental rights and those of girl-children. Restrictive language
asserting the primacy of parental rights appeared a total of 23 times in the draft
Platform.[81] The issue was eventually resolved, with many reservations recorded,[82]
by the adoption of wording taken from the Convention on the Rights of the Child.[83]
That the rights of women remain so fundamentally contested from the earliest stages
of our lives suggests that we may need to reinvigorate earlier feminist critiques of
the "family" itself,[84] rather than focusing efforts on widening its meaning.

Finally, women's diversities were also discussed in the context of the "universality" versus "cultural relativity" debates in Beijing. The polarized positions
taken by the main players meant that absolute standpoints were also assumed by
many feminists which was, ultimately, unproductive. The result was an ambiguous
compromise which repeated language adopted at the Vienna Conference, stating
that while states must protect all human rights, "cultural and religious backgrounds
must be borne in mind."[85]

---

78. *Beijing Platform, supra* note 2, paras. 46, 225.

79. *I.C.P.D. Report, supra* note 62, princ. 9, para. 5.1; *W.S.S.D. Report, supra* note 62, commitment
4(k), para. 80.

80. *Beijing Platform, supra* note 2, para. 29.

81. *Proposals for Consideration in the Preparation of a Draft Declaration. Draft Platform for Action.
Note by the Secretary-General,* U.N. GAOR, paras. 93, 106(f),(i),(l),(m), para. 107(e),(g), 108(j),(l),
262, 267, 281(b),(c),(d),(e),(g), and 283(d). U.N. Doc. A/CONF.177/L.1(1995).

82 *Beijing Platform, supra* note 2, (listing reservations by Argentina, Guatemala, Iran, Libya, and Malaysia).

83. *Id.* para. 267.

84. Shiela Cronan, *Marriage, in* RADICAL FEMINISM 213 (A. Koedt, E. Levine & A. Rapone eds, 1973);
MICHELE BARRETT & MARY MCINTOSH, THE ANTI-SOCIAL FAMILY (1982); Ruthann Robson, *Resisting the
Family: Repositioning Lesbians in Legal Theory,* 19 SIGNS 975 (1994).

85. *Beijing Platform, supra* note 2, para. 9.

In sum, at the conclusion of the Beijing deliberations, despite some progress toward recognizing selected diversities among women, these remained ancillary. The Woman of international legal discourse who emerges has a slightly expanded post-Cold War identity as a result of a new alliance between traditional ideas about women as mothers and wives and the current imperative to harness the skills and energies of women to support free-market development. This alliance has produced the Woman who embraces capitalist ideology and entrepreneurial vision and no longer needs social and economic rights to be guaranteed by states. Nor does she need an N.I.E.O. based on notions of collective responsibility, solidarity, and equitable distribution of the world's resources and wealth. Further, she is encouraged to exploit the opportunities that are offered by her putative civil and political rights, particularly to participate more fully in masculinist decision-making structures. And still, she is expected to base her primary identity in the family and continue her functions in relation to maternity and procreative heterosexuality as before, unassisted by guarantees of independent reproductive rights.[86]

A FEMINIST COALITIONAL STRATEGY

The experience of the Beijing Conference suggests that feminists need to reassess the framework within which women's equality and rights in international law are theorized, and reconceive strategies accordingly. The rubric of human rights is, of course, a critical site for feminist struggles to improve women's status and material survival, but it is not the only one and, crucially, it can be used to serve a number of competing agendas. In addition to civil and political rights are the struggles for social and economic rights and global justice which are less likely to be conceived as human rights issues in the post-Cold War environment. One challenge for feminists is to find a way to realize the "indivisibility" of human rights in theory and practice. Further, feminist contestation of the masculinist hold on the identity of the Woman of international legal discourse needs to be informed by post-structural theories of difference and power.

The concluding section critically assesses the contributions of the women's-rights-are-human-rights-strategy in light of the Beijing outcomes and proposes some new directions and strategies which bring together the three discourses of rights and the post-structural discussion of women's diversities. It is suggested that a coalitional approach to the many projects involved in the realization of emancipatory human rights, and in the acknowledgment of women's diversities, can operate in powerful ways toward achieving mutual goals and transforming the Woman of international discourse into a symbol of the diverse and ongoing struggles against women's subordination.

The main goal of the women's-rights-are-human-rights strategy—to have rights that are specific to women recognized as human rights—is still a long way from realization. The affirmation in the Vienna Declaration, that "women's rights are human rights," has proved to be a hollow victory. While the Beijing Declaration

---

86. For another development of this conclusion, see Otto, *supra* note 72.

makes the same assertion,[87] it was not repeated in the section on human rights in the Platform because states had agreed not to recognize any *new* human rights in Beijing. Consequently, the Platform's text is careful to make a distinction between human rights, which are universal, and women's rights, which are not.

This distinction is clearest in the priority areas of health and violence against women, which deal largely with rights that are specific to women. For example, paragraph 95 states that "reproductive rights embrace certain human rights" that are "already recognized" in human rights instruments. Also, violence against women is recognized as "impairing" or "nullifying" women's enjoyment of human rights, *not* as a violation of women's human rights in itself.[88] Even the recognition of women's "human rights" violations during armed conflict is circumscribed. For example, the emphasis on "systematic" rape and ethnic cleansing "as a strategy of war"[89] leaves rape that is not "officially" organized outside the human rights corpus.

The result is that the gendered hierarchy of human rights orthodoxy remains intact. Where the experience of women and men is commensurable, women are granted access to human rights in the same way as men. But female-specific violations, which often result from gendered social practices and institutions, remain outside the heavily policed human rights heartland. Instructively, the language of "power" used in the section on violence against women, in a repeat of language from the Declaration Against Violence, is not used elsewhere in the Platform. The effect is to confine the transformative challenges of the global campaign against gendered violence to a single issue that is firmly positioned outside the human rights mainstream.

While the distinction between human rights and women's rights is carefully drawn throughout the Platform, there *are* inconsistencies. In the section on human rights, violence against women "resulting from harmful traditional or customary practices, cultural prejudices and extremism" is explicitly referred to as a human rights violation,[90] and the two most controversial statements of women's sexual and reproductive rights also allude to at least some of those rights as human rights.[91] Although these inconsistencies create important openings for future feminist interventions, they can hardly be claimed as evidence that women's rights are now officially recognized as human rights.

Missing from the feminist human rights agenda were the important issues of the post-Cold War globalization of capital and the devastating reshaping of the

---

87. *Beijing Platform, supra* note 2, *Beijing Declaration*, para. 14. The Vienna wording is also reaffirmed in *Beijing Platform*, para.2.

88. *Id.* para. 112. *See further* para. 135. Neither does the Declaration Against Violence, *supra* note 50, name gendered violence as a human rights violation in its own right.

89. *Id.* para. 131.

90. *Id.* para. 232(g).

91. *Id.* paras. 95, 96, and 232(f).

development paradigm. Also absent was a class-based awareness of the importance of economic and social rights. Without actively and coherently addressing *all* human rights as indivisible and interdependent, the women's-rights-are-human-right-strategy is in danger of being co-opted by the institutions of global capital, in the same way that the women's development agenda was turned to the service of the development establishment by the end of the Decade for Women.

Further, the impossibility of transformative change while women's issues are contained within the paradigm of equality must now be, if it wasn't before, completely transparent. While gains can still be made for women in the name of equality, and while equality rights have proved a useful tool in resisting fundamentalist attacks, the inequitable structures of the global community remain normalized and unchallenged. Extending to women the rights that men currently enjoy is not enough because it does not contest the underlying social, political, and economic institutions that reproduce gender hierarchies. Further, comparative equality functions to ensure that *women's* rights remain excluded from the category of *human* rights. Also, the concept of equality does not redress the inequitable access to rights that differently situated women (and men) have. And finally, an equality paradigm also serves to silence women's diversities by confining women's rights' entitlements to those who are able to squeeze themselves into the univocal image of the Woman of legal discourse.

The concept of "equity," which until now has been chiefly promoted by the Third World as a basis for redistributive rights,[92] has the potential to extend our understanding and practice of "equality" from a formal, comparative norm to one that has substantive content. Unfortunately, the notion of equity was associated with fundamentalist agendas in Beijing and utilized in an attempt to modify the concept of equality in order to *reduce* women's opportunities.[93] For example, many Islamic countries argued for the recognition of "equitable" (commensurate with different responsibilities) rather than "equal" succession and inheritance rights for girls.[94]

The association of equity with conservative interests weakens the already limited arsenal of shared terminology whereby global redistributive change can be promoted and alternative concepts of substantive equality conceived. The absence of the assertion of equity as a transformative feminist concept not only assisted the fundamentalist co-option of the term, but undoubtedly aided the agenda of Northern governments to evade any commitment of *new* resources toward implementation

---

92. International tribunals and treaties have also invoked the concept of equity as a norm of distributive justice. *See e.g., North Sea Continental Shelf (F.R.G. v. Den.),* 1969 I.C.J. 3 (20 February 1969); *United Nations Convention on the Law of the Sea,* 21 I.L.M. 1261.

93. Women's Linkage Caucus Advocacy Chart, *Take The Brackets Off Women's Lives!,* August 30, 1995, at 17.

94. *Beijing Platform, supra* note 2, para. 274(d). The final text does guarantee "equal" inheritance rights to women and girls, but several states recorded reservations, including Egypt, Iran, Iraq, Libya, Mauritania, Morocco, and Tunisia.

of the Platform,[95] and to ensure there were no other commitments to redressing the enormous North-South disparities in wealth and resources. Feminists could usefully reconceptualize equity as a means of achieving *substantive* redistributive outcomes and of justifying gender-specific standards in certain circumstances. Together with post-structural analyses of "power" and a framework which ensures the indivisibility of human rights, this would transform the discourse of human rights.

Such a re-invention of human rights discourse also has the potential to address some of the issues of women's diversity. For example, the framework of economic and social rights is an important means of acknowledging class and other socioeconomic differences among women, and ensuring that the operation of systems of privilege among women is made both transparent and central in the identification and negotiation of feminist issues. Further, rights associated with transnational solidarity and equity acknowledge that we live in an interdependent world and provide a means of contesting the hierarchies of difference that elites of the global community currently rely upon. This would link feminist interests with emancipatory Southern strategies of post-colonial economic justice and with other critical challenges to the inequitable effects of the globalization of capital and the neo-imperialism which accompanies it.

A feminist integration of the three categories of human rights would provide one means of developing the theory and practice of "solidarity around difference." It would involve developing coalitional strategies both *within* each category of human rights and *across* the terrain of them all, among differently situated women and among women and other non-elite groups. Alliances that do not depend on restrictive notions of commonality, and which refuse to ignore difference, would make transparent the intersections between the emancipation of women and other subjugated groups and, as a result, enable the identification of common interests as a foundation for strategic solidarity.

In addition, post-structural theories of power, particularly of the hegemonic and disciplinary grip of modern Europe, add important dimensions to all three human rights paradigms. This work suggests frameworks for understanding how hierarchies of difference have been a central technique in the global production and legitimation of elite groups.[96] Accepting that difference as an issue of power highlights the importance of recognizing situation and context in the construction and contestation of our social realities. It is important that this not be (mis)understood as a new assertion of individualism but, rather, as a means of understanding how feminists can operate, albeit unwittingly, as servants of the regimes of power that

---

95. *Id.* para. 5. Whether states would commit themselves to making *new* resources available was resolved by reference to "adequate" funds being found by rearranging existing priorities, although it was also recognized that "new and additional resources to the developing countries" would be required. However, most if not all of the Platform's references to *new* resources are merely restatements of earlier commitments. *Id.* para. 59(a).

96. Chandra Mohanty, *Locating the Politics of Experience, in* DESTABILISING THEORY: CONTEMPORARY FEMINIST DEBATES 74 (Michele Barrett and Anne Phillips eds., 1992).

have produced us. Such understanding is critical to realizing the possibility of solidarity across our differences in power.

Post-structuralism must be distinguished from cultural relativity, as well as from individualism. The paradigm of cultural relativity, like that of universality, relies on the hierarchization of difference in relation to a single dominant standard. The contestation in Beijing about cultural differences was, in effect, a contest about which masculinist standard should be recognized as dominant. This bears no resemblance to a post-structural commitment to multiplicity and anti-discipline. Post-structural insights open productive avenues for feminist interventions which could move the discussion away from the rigidly polarized cultural relativity debates of the present toward the development of non-hierarchical conceptions of cultural specificity and diversity. The Beijing outcome that saw the assertion of "universalism" over "relativity" merely reinforced the polarization of the debates, rather than transforming them.

Finally, for feminists, post-structural insights also offer a means of deepening our understanding of a coalitional agenda by insisting that the hegemonic power of privileged Northern women to define and shape "feminist" issues be recognized and resisted. If we can develop ways to appreciate the mobility and multiplicity of women's identities we can, in turn, increase our coalitional possibilities and, ultimately, ensure that women's diversities are reflected by a reconstituted Woman of international legal discourse.

CONCLUSION

Post-Beijing, the difference of gender remains a powerful justification for global inequitable and disciplinary hierarchies of power. Transformative feminist interventions in international law must include an integrated human rights agenda which, in particular, refuses the separation of (emancipatory) human rights and (economically just) development strategies. This involves rejecting the narrow post-Cold War dominant discourse on human rights and equality, and exposing its allegiance to the interests of the West and global capital.

Further, linking the human rights and development agendas of non-elite groups will provide a basis for devising transformative coalitional strategies which recognize women's diversities and enable the development of theories and practices of strategic solidarity around difference, with reference to gender *and* other struggles. This demands moving beyond polarized debates about cultural diversity and universality to a framework that, while insisting on acknowledging difference and specificity, also enables a shared, albeit contingent, language of equity and justice. Finally, post-structural theories of power and difference suggest ways to resist the constrictions of comparative equality and progress toward a better understanding of the elite interests vested in the trope of gender. Together, these strategies enable expansion of an arsenal of transformative theory and practice, and begin to imagine a Woman of international legal discourse who is multiple rather than univocal, resistant rather than compliant, and coalitional rather than universal.

Section III

Common Abuses of Women Around the World

COMMON ABUSES AGAINST WOMEN

Dorothy Q. Thomas and Robin S. Levi

INTRODUCTION

The most common characteristic of human rights abuse against women is its relationship to the belief in and preservation of their subordination. Although the nature of gender-based abuse may change both within and between countries, the underlying function is the same: to construct and maintain women's inferior position. Thus, even as we necessarily distinguish the abuses faced by women in one region or another, as we do in the remainder of this chapter, we must not lose sight of the fact that no one country or region has the monopoly on female subordination.

Most of the abuses against women discussed in this chapter occur in almost every country of the world in patterns that cut across geographical boundaries. For example, women everywhere experience violence in the home, on the street, in custody, and in times of conflict. They confront discrimination in the wording or application of the law that limits their right to equality in the family, in the workplace, and in the political and civil life of their countries.

But even though these violations against women possess certain similarities worldwide, their severity and impact are affected by factors other than gender, including race, class, religion, and sexual orientation. Consequently, the manner in which women experience such mistreatment can differ vastly within and between countries. For example, women of color in the United States who protest domestic and sexual violence must also confront issues of racial discrimination when seeking official redress.[1] Women with sufficient financial resources are better able to access available legal remedies to certain abuses than women with less resources, who may continue to find themselves without legal redress, either because they cannot afford it or are unaware of the relevant remedies.

Despite the prevalence of violence and discrimination against women, the international community until very recently has been silent about such violations. There has been silence by governments, nongovernmental organizations, and the women themselves who, for myriad reasons, are often unable to come forward and speak about the abuses they have experienced. This silence hides problems that can

---

1. See, e.g., Kimberle Crenshaw, Mapping the Margins: Intersectionality, Identity Politics, and Violence Against Women of Color, 43 STAN. L. REV. 1241 (1991); and Jenny Rivera, Domestic Violence Against Latinas by Latino Males: An Analysis of Race, National Origin, and Gender Differentials, 14 B.C. THIRD WORLD L.J. 231 (1994).

destroy, and sometimes end, women's lives. One of the first challenges faced by the women's human rights movement has been to break the silence about discrimination and violence against women. Women's rights advocates worldwide have exposed gender-based abuse and rejected the notion that governments bear no responsibility for such practices, whether committed by their own agents or private actors.

At the 1995 United Nations Fourth World Conference on Women in Beijing, China, the protection and promotion of women's human rights emerged as a central concern of both government and nongovernmental participants. Women's rights activists took the opportunity to demand that governments integrate women's human rights into the U.N.'s system-wide activity, refrain from abusing the human rights of women, and ensure not only that violence and discrimination against women be prohibited, but also that when it occurs, it be denounced and remedied.[2]

Despite the obstacles presented by the host Chinese government and United Nations inaction,[3] nongovernmental participants worked closely with government delegates to produce a Platform for Action that identified the economic, social, and political problems facing women and recommended government action for improving women's status over the next decade. Several official delegations—most notably, the Holy See, Iran, Sudan, Guatemala, and Malta—made concerted efforts to modify or abridge women's human rights in light of religion, culture, or national law. These delegations advanced the concept that women have a "special" role in society and the family as an excuse to deny women their equality, civil liberties, and the right to be free from violence. Thus, although the conference brought many activists together to improve women's human rights, it also highlighted the intense resistance of many governmental and other entities to women's equality and the full realization of their human rights, particularly within the family structure.

Following the Beijing conference, some governments have increased their efforts to protect women's rights: the South African parliament ratified the Convention on the Elimination of All Forms of Discrimination Against Women; the legislature in Nepal introduced legislation to allow women to inherit property; and the governments of Colombia and Ecuador passed laws to protect women in cases of domestic violence. In addition, the impact of the Beijing conference has been reflected in parts of the U.N. that previously overlooked women's concerns. For example, at the June 1996 U.N. Conference on Human Settlements (Habitat), governments vowed to protect women's rights and recognized that discrimination

---

2.   Platform for Action, Section IV.D, Violence Against Women, ¶118 (1995).

3.   The Chinese government seriously undermined the effectiveness of the nongovernmental forum. Some nongovernmental organizations that were critical of Chinese policies, abortion rights groups, and others were denied accreditation by the NGO Forum organizers. Following strong protests that resulted in the reversal of accreditation decisions, the Chinese government denied or delayed entry visas to numerous accredited participants. Then, the NGO site was moved by the Chinese government to Huairou, some sixty kilometers away from the official U.N. conference site in Beijing. Both the United Nations Conference Secretariat and Secretary-General Boutros Boutros-Ghali failed to address these problems adequately. *See* HUMAN RIGHTS WATCH, WORLD REPORT 1996 351–2 (1995).

against women and family violence were causes of women's restricted access to shelter and of homelessness. Governments attending the conference made many pledges to eradicate many of these forms of discrimination against women. The Habitat commitments, however, were not backed up with resources for implementing them. These important steps will have little impact if they are not accompanied by substantive changes in government practice.

Thus, while significant progress has been made in identifying and acknowledging violations of women's human rights, governments now need to take action to prevent and remedy such abuse. This introductory section will provide an overview of the cross-cutting abuses that women face and the evolving understanding of the application of human rights law to them. Each thematic section is illustrated with case studies of human rights abuses against women in specific countries based on investigations conducted by the Human Rights Watch Women's Rights Project. By examining violations of women's human rights that occur throughout the world we can see how such abuses universally function to maintain women's subordinate status. At the same time, the country-specific case studies demonstrate how such abuses can differ depending on the political, economic, and cultural situation within each country and the identity of the victim. The later sections in this chapter will discuss in detail the treaties and legal standards that apply to the different human rights violations.

VIOLENCE AGAINST WOMEN

Women experience violence in virtually all aspects of their daily lives. They experience violence at home, on the street, at work, in prison, and in conflict situations.[4] In some cases, violence is committed by government agents, (e.g., by police officers against women in custody or by members of the military) for political ends. In those situations, the government is directly responsible for the actions of its agents. In other circumstances, governments fail to investigate or punish private actors, either intimate partners or strangers, who beat or sexually assault women.

---

4.   The United Nations Declaration on the Elimination of Violence Against Women defines violence against women as including:

    (a) physical, sexual and psychological violence occurring within the family, including battering, sexual abuse of female children in the household, dowry-related violence, marital rape, female genital mutilation and other traditional practices harmful to women, non-spousal violence and violence related to exploitation;

    (b) physical, sexual and psychological violence occurring within the general community, including rape, sexual abuse, sexual harassment and intimidation at work, in educational institutions and elsewhere, trafficking in women and forced prostitution;

    (c) physical, sexual and psychological violence perpetuated by the State, wherever it occurs.

Declaration on the Elimination of Violence Against Women, G.A. Res. 104, U.N. GAOR, 48th Sess., art. 2, U.N. Doc. A/Res/48/104 (1994). A U.N. declaration is not a treaty that states may ratify and be bound by, but rather it is a non-binding resolution that sets out a common international standard that states should follow.

All too often, violence against women whether committed by state agents or private actors receives less severe punishment and government attention than similar crimes against men. Such a disparity in state response brings all of these acts, whether or not committed by private actors, into the arena of human rights. Where states commit violence against women, they are directly implicated in violating their human rights. When they routinely fail to prosecute such abuses committed by private actors, they are indirectly implicated in human rights violations.

Under international law, governments are obligated to guarantee basic human rights and equality before the law for all of their citizens, without regard to sex.[5] In addition to the right of equal protection, the concept of state responsibility has developed to recognize that states are "obligated to investigate every situation involving a violation of the rights protected by [international law]."[6] For example, the Inter-American Court on Human Rights in the late 1980s interpreted the states' duty under Article 1 of the Inter-American Convention on Human Rights as an obligation "to ensure" the rights within the treaty to all persons within their jurisdiction.[7] The same requirement "to ensure" rights can be found in Article 2 of the International Covenant of Civil and Political Rights (ICCPR), although it has not yet been interpreted. The duty also requires a government to:

> take reasonable steps to prevent human rights violations and to use the means at its disposal to carry out a serious investigation of violations committed within its jurisdiction, to identify those responsible, to impose the appropriate punishment and to ensure the victim adequate compensation.[8]

This includes "ensur[ing] that any violations are considered and treated as illegal acts."[9] Thus, what would otherwise be wholly private conduct can be transformed into a constructive act of the state, "because of the lack of due diligence to prevent the violation or respond to it as required by the [Inter-American Convention]."[10]

Elaborating on the due diligence standard, the court stated that a single violation of a human right or just one investigation with an ineffective result does not establish a state's lack of diligence. Rather, the test is whether the state undertakes its duties seriously. This requirement encompasses the obligation both to provide and enforce sufficient remedies to survivors of private violence. Thus, the existence of a legal system criminalizing and providing sanctions for domestic assault would not be sufficient; the government also would have to perform its functions so as to

---

5. International Covenant on Civil and Political Rights, 993 U.N.T.S. 171 (Dec. 16, 1966), arts. 2 and 26 [hereinafter ICCPR].

6. *Velásquez Rodriguez* (July 29, 1988), Inter-American Court of Human Rights (ser. C) No. 4, ¶176 (specifically discussing rights contained within the Inter-American Convention of Human Rights).

7. *Id.* The court offered this commentary in two cases decided in 1988–89: *Velásquez Rodriguez* and *Godinez Cruz* (Jan. 20, 1989), Inter-American Court of Human Rights (ser. C) No. 5.

8. *Velásquez Rodriguez*, ¶174.

9. *Id.* ¶175.

10. *Id.* ¶172.

"effectively ensure" that incidents of family violence are actually investigated and punished.[11] In the experience of the Human Rights Watch Women's Rights Project, many countries fall far short of this standard; instead they pay limited attention to violence against women and often abdicate their responsibility for its prevention.

Domestic Violence

Women's rights groups have made great strides in documenting and publicizing the level and severity of domestic violence throughout the world. Domestic violence is one of the leading causes of female injuries in almost every country in the world and it accounts in some countries for the largest percentage of hospital visits by women.[12] It operates to diminish women's sense of self-worth and autonomy. For instance, women who experience domestic violence frequently begin to believe that such violence is an acceptable part of their lives and that they are at fault both for provoking the violence and for not preventing it. Often, psychological harm, including verbal abuse and demeaning treatment, precedes physical or sexual abuse, destroying a woman's self confidence. Further, women in battering relationships may be reluctant to make independent decisions because they fear violence if their partner disapproves of a decision.

Police and judicial authorities often dismiss domestic violence as a "private" matter rather than a widespread problem that demands urgent state action. Where law enforcement agencies fail to respond to evidence of murder, rape, or assault of women by their intimate partners, they send the message that such attacks are justified or, at a minimum, will not be punished. In doing so, states fail to take the minimum steps necessary to protect their female citizens' rights to physical integrity and, in extreme cases, to life. State parties to the ICCPR are obligated to combat domestic violence by virtue of having undertaken "to respect and to ensure" the rights recognized in the covenant. In order to live up to their obligations under international human rights law, governments must address domestic violence as a criminal matter, guarantee women equal protection under the law, and take reasonable steps to punish and prevent such violence.

Despite the recent acknowledgment by the international community that unprosecuted domestic violence is a human rights issue, it continues to be endemic in many, if not most, countries of the world. As the case studies below demonstrate, in addition to the lack of a remedy, there are several reasons for the persistently

---

11. *Id.* at 167.

12. A 1993 national survey of domestic violence in Japan by the Domestic Violence Research Group found that 58.7 percent of the sample reported physical abuse by a partner and 59.4 percent reported sexual abuse. In a detailed family planning survey from 1990 in the Kissi district of Kenya, 42 percent of women said they had been beaten by their husbands; in Papua New Guinea, 67 percent of rural women and 56 percent of urban women have been victims of wife abuse, according to a national survey conducted by the Papua New Guinea Law Reform Commission in 1986. Lori L. Heise, VIOLENCE AGAINST WOMEN: THE HIDDEN HEALTH BURDEN 6–9, 14, 18 (1994). "Each of the studies is individually valid, but they are not directly comparable because each uses a different set of questions to probe for abuse." *Id.* at 5.

high levels of domestic violence. First, criminalization alone is insufficient; in order for a government to take "reasonable steps" to prevent domestic violence, it must take additional actions and many governments often do not. In addition, many legal systems allow defenses in domestic violence cases that operate to mitigate sentences for such crimes, and thus reduce the effectiveness of applicable criminal laws. For example, in the United States, some courts have accepted a "cultural defense" and, at times, refused to punish male immigrants who have beaten or even killed their partners.[13] Finally, while some countries may put penalties in place, and may even set forth appropriate civil remedies, they routinely fail to enforce such remedies. For states effectively to meet the international obligation to protect women against domestic violence, they should take a comprehensive approach to the problem, including legal reform, appropriate legal and social services, and efforts which address the need for a clear mechanism for coordination and enforcement of government policy.

Russia: Lack of Remedy

In 1994 and again in 1996, the Women's Rights Project traveled to Russia to investigate the state response to violence against women. The Project visited Moscow, St. Petersburg, Sergiyev Posad, Murmansk, and Nizhni Tagil. Investigators found that the Russian government, and particularly, Russian law enforcement, has denied women's right to equal protection of the law by failing to investigate and prosecute domestic violence.[14] In addition, they failed to put in place the most minimal protections against this abuse. According to victims and activists working on their behalf, local law enforcement officials scoff at reports of violence by domestic partners and refuse to intervene in what they often identify as "family matters."

These stories are familiar the world over, yet neither the federal government nor any of the local governments have taken adequate steps to document and

---

13. There is no formal cultural defense in U.S. law; rather culture usually functions to support a diminished responsibility or mistake of fact defense. The defendant argues that he committed the illegal acts (usually murder or egregious domestic assault) because in the specific factual situation—often alleged adultery—his cultural beliefs permit, or even encourage, such behavior. In addition, culture has also been used to justify a defense of provocation in rape cases. In that situation, the defendant usually asserts that the victim's behavior, interpreted in light of his culture, made him believe that she encouraged or did not object to sexual intercourse. *See, e.g.,* Alice J. Gallin, Note, *The Cultural Defense: Undermining the Policies Against Domestic Violence,* 35 B.C. L.REV. 723 (1994); Melissa Spatz, Note, *A "Lesser" Crime: A Comparative Study of Legal Defenses for Men Who Kill Their Wives,* 24 COLUM. J.L. & SOC. PROBS. 597 (1991); Nilda Rimonte, *A Question of Culture: Cultural Approval of Violence Against Women in the Pacific-Asian Community and the Cultural Defense,* 43 STAN. L. REV. 1311 (1991); Leti Volpp, *(Mis)identifying Culture: Asian Women and the "Cultural Defense,"* 17 HARV. WOMEN'S L.J. 57 (1994); and Catherine Trevison, Note, *Changing Sexual Assault and the Hmong,* 27 IND. L. REV. 393 (1993).

14. This section is based upon information contained in HUMAN RIGHTS WATCH WOMEN RIGHTS PROJECT, NEITHER JOBS NOR JUSTICE: STATE DISCRIMINATION AGAINST WOMEN IN RUSSIA (1995) [hereinafter NEITHER JOBS NOR JUSTICE] and on interviews conducted during a mission to Russia in 1996.

respond to domestic abuse. Not only are criminal sanctions against assault unenforced when the accused is an intimate partner of the victim, but no civil remedy for domestic violence exists. Instead, women must rely solely on the police and prosecutors for help. Unfortunately, police often refuse reports of domestic violence and accord such reports much less importance than reports of other forms of violence. In some cases, police have refused to come to a woman's home unless the woman promised to press charges.[15] Activists told us that when a woman called the police for assistance in preventing her partner from beating her, the police would ask her if she would press charges, and if she either hesitated or said no, the police would refuse to respond to her requests for help. In other cases, the police would arrest the batterer and then release him in the morning without any charges or punishment. Even if women were able to prosecute domestic violence successfully, many women are afraid to report their husbands' violence for fear that criminal charges may result in job loss which, given recent employment discrimination against women, could represent a household's entire income.

Women's rights groups have begun to address the problem by establishing crisis centers to provide psychological counseling and legal advice. But the effectiveness of their efforts is hampered by the Russian government's abdication of its responsibility to prevent and punish domestic violence. Governments must take steps to enforce criminal penalties against domestic abuse and provide civil alternatives to criminal prosecution. Otherwise, most women will not report domestic violence to official law enforcement authorities and will remain without redress and protection.

Brazil: Mitigation of Sentences

A 1991 Human Rights Watch investigation in Brazil revealed that Brazilian women received little or no justice when they reported physical abuse by their husbands or partners to the police.[16] In spite of the approximately 125 specialized police stations (*Delegacias De Defesa De Mulher*) established in Brazil to deal exclusively with violence against women, many women in rural and urban areas found police unresponsive to their claims and encountered open hostility and incredulity when they attempted to report domestic violence. The state's nonresponse to domestic violence has continued. While the government has created shelters for battered women throughout the country, the criminal justice system remains largely unresponsive to women's complaints of domestic abuse except where women have enough money to pursue legal action independently.[17]

---

15. Interviews in Russia (May 1996).

16. The section is based upon AMERICAS WATCH & WOMEN'S RIGHTS PROJECT, CRIMINAL INJUSTICE: VIOLENCE AGAINST WOMEN IN BRAZIL (1991) [hereinafter CRIMINAL INJUSTICE].

17. Telephone interview with Dr. Leila Linhares, Brazil (July 17, 1995).

In some cases, domestic violence culminated in homicide. Defendants in wife-murder cases have successfully employed the "honor defense," whereby the accused states that he acted spontaneously in legitimate self-defense against an imminent attack, albeit the attack was against his honor rather than his physical well-being.[18] For example, in one 1972 case, the couple had been married for sixteen years. When the wife got a job, she began coming home late, and according to testimony from the accused, refused to pay her "conjugal debt." The husband killed her and was acquitted on the grounds that he was legitimately defending his honor. The decision was largely upheld on appeal.[19] In the 1990s, the honor defense has been invoked only erratically in Brazil[20] and is much more likely to be successful in certain regions than in others.[21]

Even when defendants did not use the honor defense, Human Rights Watch found that courts often treated defendants in wife-murder cases more leniently than other murder defendants, largely through the misuse of the "violent emotion" exception to mitigate sentences. For the violent emotion exception to apply, the defendant must, in theory, have responded automatically to an act by the victim.[22] Nonetheless, we found that the violent emotion exception was often applied to defendants in wife-murder cases who had shown substantial premeditation and had not demonstrated "unjust provocation" by the victim. In the wife-murder cases investigated by Human Rights Watch, courts seemed unusually willing to overlook evidence of premeditation on the part of the defendant and focused instead on the behavior of the victim and its alleged provocative effect.[23]

The success of the above defenses highlights fundamental contradictions in government and society. Discriminatory attitudes towards domestic violence render this abuse particularly difficult to eliminate. On the one hand, law enforcement agents may view domestic violence as a crime to be vigorously investigated and prosecuted yet, on the other, they may also view a man's violent actions in response to his partner's perceived disloyalty as acceptable. Consequently, traditional views about protecting a woman's "purity" or "loyalty" becomes a justification for

---

18. For a more detailed discussion of the honor defense, see CRIMINAL INJUSTICE, *supra* note 16, at 20–28.

19. CONSELHO NACIONAL DOS DIREITOS DA MULHER, QUANDO A VITMA E MULHER 126 [WHEN THE VICTIM IS A WOMAN] (1987).

20. *See* HUMAN RIGHTS WATCH, HUMAN RIGHTS WATCH GLOBAL REPORT ON WOMEN'S HUMAN RIGHTS 258–59 (1995). In general, the honor defense is most often used for suspicion of adultery.

21. One prosecutor told Human Rights Watch that the honor defense was successful 80 percent of the time in Brazil's interior.

22. CODIGO PENAL [C.P.] art. 28 (Braz.).

23. On June 3, 1985, Anibal Maciel de Abreu e Silva shot and killed his ex-wife Nicia de Abreu e Silva, from whom he had been separated for three months. In his deposition he said he had waited to see Nicia outside the school where she was studying, and that he was carrying a gun "as usual." The court granted the violent emotion mitigation despite the prosecutor's contention that Anibal had committed the crime out of jealousy by the fact that Nicia had four lovers. For a more detailed analysis of this case and other examples of the violent emotion defense, see CRIMINAL INJUSTICE, *supra* note 16, at 29–36.

battery and even execution. In order to eradicate domestic violence, the underlying stereotypes about male-female relations that fuel these crippling contradictions will have to be eliminated.

South Africa: Non-Enforcement of Civil Remedies[24]

In April 1994, sweeping political changes in South Africa following the first multi-racial general election brought an end to the repressive apartheid policies of the past and ushered in a new government that has pledged to respect human rights and uphold the rule of law.[25] In March 1995, the Women's Rights Project went to South Africa to investigate the post-apartheid government's response to violence against women. We found that despite positive developments in the country overall, female survivors of domestic violence still face a police and judicial system that is unsympathetic and, sometimes, even hostile to women who seek redress. While women's organizations noted that, compared to a decade ago, the response of police and judicial authorities to violence against women has improved, battered women still face an intransigent criminal justice system.

Although the South African government does not prosecute domestic assault as seriously as it does crimes of similar severity, it has taken the important step of providing a civil remedy. In 1993, the Prevention of Family Violence Act improved women's access to protection from domestic violence by simplifying and expediting the procedure for obtaining interdicts (restraining orders) against abusive partners.[26] Under the Act, a battered woman can file for an interdict at the nearest magistrate's court. If the magistrate believes that the woman is in danger of abuse, he or she may grant an interdict, accompanied by a suspended warrant of arrest, to prevent the batterer from further assaulting or threatening the woman.[27] In the event that a woman with an interdict is threatened, the police should immediately arrest the batterer using the suspended warrant of arrest.[28] The penalty is a fine, or imprisonment for up to a year, or both.[29]

While many magistrate courts have used this law effectively, it is limited in several important respects. For example, it only applies to married women, women living with the abusive boyfriend, or women who have lived with the abusive husband or boyfriend.[30] In the South African context, the exclusion of women who have never lived with their abusers is particularly problematic. Under apartheid,

---

24. This section is based upon information contained in HUMAN RIGHTS WATCH/AFRICA & HUMAN RIGHTS WATCH WOMEN'S RIGHTS PROJECT, VIOLENCE AGAINST WOMEN IN SOUTH AFRICA (1995) [hereinafter SOUTH AFRICA].

25. *See id.* at 1–2.

26. Prevention of Family Violence Act (Act No. 133 of 1993).

27. *Id.* art. 2(1).

28. *Id.* art. 3.

29. *Id.* art. 6.

30. *Id.* art. 1.

numerous black families were forced to live apart.[31] Women in these situations may be involved in an abusive relationship, but because they have not lived with their spouses they cannot apply for an interdict. Further, intimate relationships between same-sex partners are not covered. The Act also does not specify what type of abuse qualifies for an interdict. As a result, judges have considerable discretion in determining which abuses entitle a woman to receive an interdict.

Nonetheless, the major impediment to the effective application of this remedy is not the law itself but its implementation by the police and the judiciary. In a July 1994 study conducted in Natal by two South African nongovernmental organizations, paralegals were sent to their area police stations to speak with police officers and establish whether women were using the Act, and if the necessary forms were available at the station.[32] The results indicated that barely 60 percent of the station commanders were even aware of the year-old act and that few stations had the forms available. In only one case had the station commander held informative lectures about the Act for the station's staff. Women living in the townships reported that the Act had only a limited impact on their lives. One woman told us:

> I called [the police] to stop my husband from beating me. I had an interdict so they could arrest him. It took the police one hour to come to my house. By that time, my husband had left. I told the police where my husband had gone. But they were unwilling to go there and arrest him.[33]

Women fleeing abuse have found that the police may not only be unhelpful, but may place them in even greater danger by believing the man's word over their own. In March 1994, a husband followed his daughter and found out that his wife and children were living in a shelter. Upon seeing the husband, the wife—who had an interdict—called the police. The police arrived but refused to take any action against the husband, stating that it was a domestic affair. When they left, the police took the woman's interdict with them, leaving her not only at risk of harm from her abusive spouse, but also without proof of the legal protection to which she was entitled.[34]

The experience of the Family Violence Prevention Act indicates that although civil remedies are extremely useful in reducing the need for the government to take specific action, the effectiveness of such remedies relies on their being given adequate scope and the willingness of law enforcement agencies to execute their responsibilities seriously and to facilitate the survivor's efforts to protect herself.

---

31. JACKLYN COCK, MAIDS AND MADAMS: DOMESTIC WORKERS UNDER APARTHEID 43 (1989).

32. Police stations were visited in the following localities: Chatsworth, Hammersdale, KwaDabeka (Clermont), Kwamashu, Lamontville, Msinini, Nagina, Pinetown, Pungashe, Umlazi, Umsinsini, Umzumber, Vela, and one unnamed location.

33. Interview, in Capetown, South Africa (Feb. 8, 1995).

34. Interview with Debbie Brent, shelter administrator, People Opposing Woman Abuse, in Johannesburg, South Africa (Feb. 17, 1995).

Sexual Assault

Forced or coerced sexual contact, while criminalized in most countries (although marital rape is typically not a crime), is often investigated and punished at a much lower rate than other crimes of similar severity. Prosecution of sexual assault suffers from stereotypes about women and about female sexuality. Law enforcement officials often believe that survivors of sexual violence are complicit in the abuse, either through provocation or by consent that was later revoked. As a result, women often feel ashamed to report rape, and when they do report, rape victims often find their own behavior on trial, rather than their assailants.' The following examples chart the ways in which traditional attitudes about female purity, the intersection of sex discrimination with discrimination based on race, and the general acceptance of these biases based on narrow stereotypes by criminal justice systems operated to reduce survivors' access to justice.

Russia: Rape as an Attack on Purity

In the 1996 Women's Rights Project investigation in Russia discussed previously, we found substantial barriers that prevent women's complaints of sexual violence from being registered by law enforcement and then successfully investigated and prosecuted.[35] While Russian law does not differentiate between being raped by a stranger or by an acquaintance, official practice accords less importance to acquaintance rape. Our interviews indicated that in cases of acquaintance rape, police officers and prosecutors often believe that a woman has in some way provoked the rape or fabricated her report. In many of these cases, women were either turned away by the police or discouraged from filing a complaint. Police officers told women that the investigation would be shameful; they then used investigators to collect information about the women's sexual behavior and past.

If the police accepted the report, the investigative process was extremely grueling because of the frequent interviews and pervasive invasions of privacy. Many survivors told us that defendants and their families harassed and threatened them in an effort to persuade them to drop rape charges. To our knowledge, the police took no steps to protect either survivors or witnesses from this harassment. In one case reported to us by a gynecologist in Moscow, the night after a twenty-three-year old woman reported her gang rape to the police, the accused rapists came to her house and said, "You agreed to go with us on a camping trip. We will make it known to the whole town and college and you will be ashamed." When her mother reported this encounter to the investigators, the investigators told her that they had sent the defendants to her house to settle the case peacefully.[36]

The most troubling aspect of the investigative process for sexual assault in Russia is the focus on "purity" or virginity. Young virgins who were raped by

---

35. This section is based upon information contained in NEITHER JOBS NOR JUSTICE, *supra* note 14, and interviews conducted during a mission to Russia in 1996.

36. Interview with Lola Karimova, gynecologist, Syostri, in Moscow, Russia (Apr. 22, 1996).

strangers were most likely to get redress. Married women or women who were sexually active often were told not to pursue criminal complaints. One activist told us about how the police tried to persuade her to have her client withdraw her report: "[T]hey would say, 'people are murdered on the street, but here it is just rape. And what was so terrible? She was not a virgin, she was not a child.' "[37] Rape is no more or less serious for a woman who is sexually active. It should be prosecuted based upon the actions of the defendants rather than on whether the victim was a virgin.

South Africa: Confronting Race and Gender[38]

During the 1995 Women's Rights Project investigation in South Africa mentioned above, and a subsequent investigation in 1996, we found that the South African legal system is filled with assumptions and biases against women who have been raped.[39] Widespread reports of police mistreatment of rape survivors contributes to the low percentage of reported rapes. Police officers often subscribe to stereotypes of raped women, and women who do not fit those assumptions must convince the police that they have been raped. For example, women face greater difficulty in filing rape charges if they do not resist physically, do not sustain serious injuries, do not appear sufficiently distressed, dated the perpetrator, dressed "provocatively," or are prostitutes. One judge, Mr. Justice Michael Corbett, acting on such assumptions, reduced a convicted rapist's sentence. Justice Corbett stated:

> To my mind, it is a mitigating factor in that the shock and affront to dignity suffered by the rape victim would be ordinarily less in the case where the rapist is a person well-known to the victim and someone moving in the same social milieu as the victim. . . . In my opinion the lack of any serious injury to the complainant and the fact that she was evidently a woman of experience from the sexual point of view, justice would be served by a suspension of half the sentence imposed.[40]

As in other areas of South African life, there are deeply ingrained racial and sexist stereotypes, particularly against black women, which can adversely affect the state's response to sexual violence. Sharon Pratt of Family and Marriage Services of South Africa noted that "If a woman calls from Constantia [a predominately white area], the treatment is fine. But if she calls from one of the black or coloured

---

37. Interview with Zoya Khotkina, Moscow Center for Gender Studies, in Moscow, Russia (Apr. 25, 1996).

38. This section is based upon SOUTH AFRICA, *supra* note 24.

39. Rape is defined in South Africa as intentional, unlawful sexual intercourse with a woman without her consent. Acts of forced oral sex or sodomy, or penetration by foreign objects such as bottles or sticks, are not considered rape, but are criminalized under indecent assault. Kathryn Ross, *An Examination of South African Rape Law, in* WOMEN, RAPE AND VIOLENCE IN SOUTH AFRICA 8 (Community Law Centre ed., 1993).

40. *S v N* 1987 (3) SA 450 Justice Corbett (Viljoen and Nestadt concurring), *quoted in* PEOPLE OPPOSING WOMEN ABUSE, CALLING FOR CHANGE: A DISCUSSION ON SOME ASPECTS OF THE LAWS AND PROCEDURES SURROUNDING SEXUAL VIOLENCE IN SOUTH AFRICA 9 (1994).

townships, there is a breakdown of services.''[41] One police station commander told Human Rights Watch that he believed many of the African women coming to the police station fabricated reports of rape in order to get access to an abortion after becoming pregnant by their boyfriends.[42]

These biases reduce the ability of nonwhite women to receive redress for sexual violence. For instance, rapes of white women were more severely punished than rapes of colored or African women.[43] This disparity also follows for defendants: an analysis of sentencing in 159 rape convictions in the Durban regional courts during 1983 found that white defendants received the least severe sentences.

At the national level, efforts have been made to address these deficiencies through training programs for prospective police officers and by providing more specialized courses to prepare officers for investigating sexual violence cases. There are also more local initiatives that are conducted in connection with local women's rights groups.[44] Nonetheless, the number of prosecutions is minuscule. Less than one-third of reported rapes in South Africa reach the courts.

The experience in South Africa indicates that ingrained stereotypes about women and their behavior restrict the ability of survivors of sexual violence to get redress. Racial prejudice also increases the difficulty black women and women of color have in pursuing criminal charges. That same prejudice further complicates the decision to press charges, because when the survivor and her relatives are aware that the criminal justice system is biased against men of color, sometimes the choice to pursue charges can be perceived as an act against the community.

Documenting Sexual Violence: Forensic Evidence

A major obstacle to successful sexual assault investigations in many countries that we researched is the requirement that survivors be medically examined at a government-run evidence center. Such medical exams are mandated to a greater or lesser degree in Brazil, Haiti, Russia, Peru, and South Africa. This requirement is problematic on a number of scores. For example, for a variety of reasons, the medical evidence frequently is collected incorrectly or incompletely and, at times, valuable evidence has been lost. This is particularly troubling because medical evidence may be the only corroboration of a rape survivor's testimony. In addition, in some countries such an official confirmation of rape is required to obtain a legal abortion.

---

41. Interview with Sharon Pratt, Family and Marriage Services of South Africa, in Cape Town, South Africa (Feb. 9, 1995). Note that "black" refers to persons of purely African descent whereas "coloured" refers to individuals of Asian or mixed backgrounds.

42. Interview with J. Koobair, Major, Sydenham police station, in Sydenham, South Africa (Feb. 2, 1995).

43. Steven Collings, *Rape Sentences—An Empirical Analysis,* 9 S. AFRICAN J. CRIMINAL L. & CRIMINOLOGY (1985).

44. For more detailed information on such training programs, see SOUTH AFRICA, *supra* note 24, at 95–96.

The lack of training for forensic doctors is often reflected in the biased attitudes towards women that affect their investigatory procedures. In many instances, we found that forensic doctors focus on the condition of the hymen and believe the examination of the hymen is the most critical part of the forensic exam.[45] This appears to privilege virginity as evidence of rape and support our finding that—based on doctors' testimony that they rarely examine women not alleged to be virgins prior to the assault—only very young women who are virgins have their reports accepted.

Despite the crucial role of medical evidence, women we interviewed had enormous difficulty getting access to the official centers and receiving sufficient admissible evidence. In Russia, the evidence centers require an official referral from either the police or prosecution, a referral that usually was not provided unless the police first accepted the complaint. In addition, investigators refused in some cases to give women referrals to the evidence center or told women to report to the evidence center days after filing their reports, thereby losing critical medical evidence, such as semen and blood, that disappears quickly. Finally, investigators often failed to inform women of the importance of being examined as soon as possible after the assault, or spoke with the women for several hours, thus intentionally or irresponsibly delaying their examinations and again risking the loss of important forensic evidence. Women were rarely informed to forego washing until after their examination.

In many cases, women in Russia did not report to the police immediately but rather went to a doctor, either state or private, for medical treatment. Unfortunately, this evidence is not admissible without the additional testimony of the examining doctor (if even then) and few doctors are willing to testify in court.[46] As a result of such obstacles, women in Russia often do not have the medical evidence necessary to secure a rape conviction.

In Brazil, within twenty-four hours of a rape, a victim, having already filed a complaint with the police, must proceed to the Medical-Legal Institute (IML), the state medical facility responsible for classifying all crimes of physical and sexual abuse.[47] A National Council on the Rights of Women study in Brazil found that even if a rape survivor goes immediately to the police and then to the IML, there is no guarantee that the treatment she receives will conform to prescribed procedures. For example, often the examination fails to note the signs of physical injuries, recording only the gynecological evidence.[48] As of 1992, the IML made no provision for the training of its staff in the treatment of sexual abuse:

45. Interview with Yuri Sergeevich Solsov, Chief Doctor, Moscow Forensic Evidence Center, in Moscow, Russia (Apr. 25, 1996); and Interview with Larissa Vasilevna Romanova, gynecologist, Moscow Forensic Evidence Center, in Moscow, Russia (Apr. 24, 1996).

46. Interviews with women's rights activists in Moscow and St. Petersburg, Russia (Apr. 1996).

47. Determination by other medical professionals—the victim's personal physician, for example—are not accepted by the government as evidence. Public or private facilities that specialize in violence against women, similar to rape trauma centers in U.S. hospitals, are almost nonexistent in Brazil.

48. QUANDO A VITIMA E MULHER, *supra* note 19, at 21.

Rape victims go to the IML hoping that the report will be honest and correct. She will be examined to be sure she was raped. She may be questioned about her virginity and sexual history. It is enough to discount the charge if the doctor doesn't find sperm. . . . She leaves, sure that she has registered the rape. She finds out the hard way that going to the IML was not enough.[49]

In Brazil we also found that women often wash prior to going to the IML, thereby losing evidence.

In contrast to Russia and Brazil, women in South Africa can receive admissible medical evidence from either a private practitioner or a government district surgeon,[50] but many women are unable to afford the fee for a private practitioner. Although exceptions exist, the reputation of district surgeons among South Africa's women's organizations is, in the word of one counselor, "horrendous."[51] Thus, many women do not want to be examined by them.

Under Haitian law, a woman can go to a private doctor or hospital to certify that forced sexual intercourse had occurred. However, the majority of Haitian women lack the economic resources to pay for a visit to a private doctor. Therefore, it is practically impossible for them to obtain such an exam. According to one Haitian family law attorney, "Material conditions prevent [women] from going to a doctor. A woman who has been raped will probably not be seen at the Port-au-Prince General Hospital, since they tend to treat only grave injuries, and she would be forced to go to a clinic or a private hospital."[52]

The difficulty of accessing and receiving admissible evidence from these government-run evidence centers is compounded by the fact that very few of these centers exist and they are often located in inaccessible sites. For example, in Russia there is only one evidence center per municipality, including Moscow, and the centers are usually open only from approximately 9 a.m. to 5 p.m., six days a week. In Brazil, the IMLs are located in urban areas beyond the reach of the majority of women, who reside in rural areas. We also found that district surgeons in South Africa were often quite far away and heard many reports of women waiting for hours before being examined by a district surgeon.

As stated above, medical evidence may be the only corroboration of rape charges women have. Our findings on medical investigative procedures for sexual assault indicate that clear procedures and accessible, affordable facilities are necessary to facilitate the prosecution of sexual violence. For example, survivors of sexual assault must be aware of and able to access no-fee centers where medical

---

49. Interview with Vilma Lessa, journalist, in Brazil (Apr. 1991).

50. SOUTH AFRICA, *supra* note 24, at 96.

51. Interview with Denise Washansky, counselor at Rape Crisis, in Cape Town, South Africa (Feb. 10, 1995).

52. Telephone interview (Mar. 13, 1994).

evidence can be gathered. Even more important, it is troubling that the inaccessibility of evidence centers and the privileging of virginity means that, at times, such centers perform a gatekeeping function for the criminal justice system.

Custodial Abuse

Incarcerated women in many countries face sexual and physical abuse and pervasive privacy violations. These abuses—forced vaginal, anal, and oral sex; inappropriate sexual touching and fondling; beatings; excessive pat-downs and strip searches; and the use of vulgar, sexualized language by guards toward female prisoners—are facilitated by the power male guards have over the daily lives of female prisoners and by official tolerance of abusive guard behavior. In addition, prison guards and staff often hold over women prisoners the threat of further abuse or retaliation should the women report misconduct or seek redress. As a consequence, incarcerated women are intimidated into silence, and their attackers are rarely held accountable for their crimes.

The abuses listed in the paragraph above, which are committed by state actors (correctional staff), are prohibited under international law and, at times, under domestic law. Nonetheless, governments have not taken action to prevent such abuses. Instead, they have allowed their prison systems to become environments where women prisoners have little privacy, and they have failed to provide male correctional staff with adequate training or supervision. As a consequence of this oversight, some prison systems have permitted male guards to have sexual contact with female prisoners without administrative or criminal punishment. In fact, we found that women fear punishment or retaliation should they report any abuses. The number of incarcerated women is growing worldwide. The following examples demonstrate how violations of women's human rights often occur with impunity. In addition to the case studies below, Human Rights Watch has documented sexual assault against women in the custody of United States border agents[53] and in Egypt.[54]

Pakistan: Role of Discrimination

In Pakistan, a 1992 Human Rights Watch investigation found more than 70 percent of women in custody experienced physical abuse, including sexual abuse, at the hands of their jailers, according to their lawyers.[55] Reported abuses included beating and slapping; suspension in mid-air by hands tied behind the victim's back; the insertion of foreign objects, including police batons and chili peppers, into the vagina and rectum; and gang rape. Yet, despite these alarming reports, police

---

53. *See* HUMAN RIGHTS WATCH/AMERICAS, CROSSING THE LINE: HUMAN RIGHTS ABUSES ALONG THE U.S. BORDER WITH MEXICO PERSIST AMID CLIMATE OF IMPUNITY (1995).

54. *See* HUMAN RIGHTS WATCH/MIDDLE EAST, EGYPT: HOSTAGE-TAKING AND INTIMIDATION BY SECURITY FORCES (1995).

55. This section is based upon information contained in ASIA WATCH & WOMEN'S RIGHTS PROJECT, DOUBLE JEOPARDY: POLICE ABUSE OF WOMEN IN PAKISTAN (1992) [hereinafter DOUBLE JEOPARDY].

officers almost never faced criminal penalties for such abuse, even when incontrovertible evidence of custodial rape existed.

The severity of such assaults was compounded by the fact that many women incarcerated in Pakistan were there as a result of discriminatory laws. Under the *Hudood* ordinances, women have extreme difficulty in proving sexual violence. Their testimony is accorded less value than a man's and, in some situations, several male witnesses are required for a guilty verdict. We found that while courts extend the benefit of the doubt to men accused of rape, they set standards of proof for female rape victims that require extraordinarily conclusive proof that the alleged intercourse was forced. We also found that unless a woman is able to prove extreme resistance or severe bodily injury, the courts tend to disbelieve the woman's testimony and are even likely to presume consent. In addition, sexual contact outside of marriage is strictly forbidden under the ordinances. The result is that women who have reported sexual assault, but were unable to satisfy the onerous, discriminatory evidentiary standards, have themselves been charged with and incarcerated for adultery or promiscuity.

The first crucial step in combating correctional abuse is eliminating laws that discriminate against women, particularly in the prosecution of sexual assault. Such laws result in an increasing female prison population that continues to be vulnerable to sexual assault because they cannot meet the evidentiary standards should a guard sexually assault them.

U.S.: Lack of Clear Rules and Supervision[56]

During a 1994–96 investigation of sexual misconduct in U.S. state prisons, Human Rights Watch found that the rapidly growing population of women incarcerated in the United States face serious and potentially pervasive problems of sexual misconduct by prison officials.[57] Human Rights Watch found that male officers have engaged in rape, sexual violence, inappropriate sexual contact, verbal degradation, and unwarranted visual surveillance of female prisoners in eleven prisons in five states[58] and the District of Columbia. The United States differs from most prison systems in that it employs male staff in positions involving unsupervised contact with female prisoners.[59] It has done so largely to satisfy national labor laws

---

56. This section is based upon information contained in HUMAN RIGHTS WATCH WOMEN'S RIGHTS PROJECT, ALL TOO FAMILIAR: SEXUAL ABUSE OF WOMEN IN U.S. STATE PRISONS (1996).

57. According to the U.S. Department of Justice's Bureau of Justice Statistics, the number of women entering U.S. state and federal prisons between 1984 and 1994 has increased 386 percent. The growth in the number of female prisoners, according to observers, results less from a shift in the nature of crimes women commit than it does from the so-called war on drugs and related changes in legislation, law enforcement practices, and judicial decision making. Drug-related offenses accounted for 55 percent of the increase in the female prison population between 1986 and 1991.

58. California, Georgia, Illinois, Michigan, and New York.

59. The United Nations Standard Minimum Rules for the Treatment of Prisoners prohibit such employment. Standard Minimum Rules for the Treatment of Prisoners, ECOSOC Res 663 C (XXIV) of 31 July 1957 and 2076 (LXII) of 13 May 1977, at Rule 53.

and numerous anti-discrimination suits.[60] Yet, in virtually every prison that we visited, state prison authorities allowed male officers to hold contact positions over female prisoners without the benefit of any clear definition of sexual misconduct, any clear rules and procedures with respect to it, or any meaningful training in how to avoid it. This lack of information applied to both staff and prisoners. The states' failure fully to inform female prisoners about the risks of and remedies for sexual misconduct is particularly negligent given that female prisoners often enter the U.S. correctional system with a prior history of abuse.[61]

In some cases, guards used overt physical force to rape or assault female prisoners. A prisoner in California, Uma M., told us that an officer raped her after a long period of harassment. Uma M. stated that he watched her while she was taking a shower, "cornered" her in a prison laundry room, and hit her on the buttocks and grabbed her breasts as she walked by. Eventually, the officer raped her while her cellmates were at breakfast. Officers have also employed less overt and thus less detectable means of coercion to pressure prisoners into sexual relations. For example, a former corrections employee in New York told us that male staff in women's prisons would threaten to put the female prisoners in segregation or to make their lives a "living hell" by intercepting their packages or stopping their visits if the women did not agree to sexual relations.[62] In many cases that we investigated, the officers used the promise or provision of otherwise unobtainable goods and services to the prisoners to induce them into sexual relations. Of all the abuses we investigated, this form of sexual misconduct was the most common and, in our view, the least addressed by prison authorities.

Human Rights Watch also found that strip searches of female prisoners, while usually conducted by female officers in order to protect the women's privacy, at times took place in the presence of one or more male officers as well. Prisoners also spoke consistently of discomfort caused by inappropriate visual surveillance by male officers, particularly in their living areas. They reported that officers watched them while they were dressing, showering, or using the toilet, and that

---

60. Under Title VII, Civil Rights Act of 1964, 42 U.S.C. §. 2000e *et seq.* an employer may not discriminate on the basis of sex, unless an employee's sex is bona fide occupational qualification (BFOQ), i.e., reasonably necessary to perform the specific job. In the absence of specific circumstances, U.S. federal courts have been unwilling to characterize a person's sex as a BFOQ.

61. Statistics indicate that anywhere from 40 to 88 percent of incarcerated women have been victims of domestic violence and sexual or physical abuse prior to incarceration, either as children or adults. A study of women incarcerated in Oklahoma's state prisons found that 69 percent reported physical and/ or emotional abuse after the age of eighteen. Before eighteen, nearly 40 percent reported being sexually abused—raped or otherwise molested—and 44 percent reported emotional or mental abuse. Sargent et al., *Abuse and the Women Prisoner, in* WOMEN PRISONERS: A FORGOTTEN POPULATION (1993). According to testimony presented in *Jordan v. Gardner*, a case concerning cross-gender pat-frisks, 85 percent of women incarcerated in Washington state have reported a history of abuse, including rapes, molestation, and beatings. 986 F.2d 1525 (9th Cir. 1994).

62. Interview with former corrections employee, New York Department of Corrections, in New York (Jan. 17, 1995).

male officers frequently entered their housing units without first announcing their presence.

All state departments of corrections asserted that sexual misconduct is something they treat as a serious matter and will not tolerate. However, we found little concrete evidence of such commitment. State departments of corrections have repeatedly allowed sexual misconduct to go unremedied. They have taken inadequate efforts to protect women against male officers who have unbridled access to their housing areas. They have failed to institute proper training or adequate rules governing strip searches. In addition, the structure of grievance systems and investigatory procedures makes it extremely difficult for incarcerated women to get redress. For instance, many prison systems require that prisoners first attempt to informally resolve staff misconduct grievances with the guard. Because of legitimate fears of harassment and retaliation, many women prisoners never make it past this requirement. Further, the bias against prisoners means that when it is the prisoner's word against the guard's, which is often the case, the guard is usually believed.

Even in cases where sexual misconduct is proven, the culpable officers are rarely dismissed or criminally sanctioned. To our knowledge, as of December 1996, only twenty-seven states and the District of Columbia expressly criminalize sex in custody, and another five have laws that can be interpreted as prohibiting such conduct.[63] Corrections authorities appear to prefer reassignment, transfer, or voluntary resignation of offenders. Very few cases of custodial sexual intercourse or touching have been prosecuted. The U.S. federal government—which has the ability under 18 U.S.C. sections 241 and 242 to prosecute such cases criminally[64] and under 42 U.S.C. section 1997 to pursue civil suits in cases where a pattern or practice of constitutional violations has emerged[65]—also has taken inadequate measures to prevent and punish sexual misconduct within its state prison systems.

Non-enforcement and lack of effective oversight contributes to the abuses and encourages the misconduct to continue. In situations where governments have male correctional staff guarding female prisoners, they must establish safeguards and adequate training to prevent sexual misconduct. In addition, in order to punish sexual misconduct effectively, they must enforce internal grievance and investigatory procedures without exposing complainants to retaliation or punishment. Without adequate supervision and punishment, male correctional staff will continue to

---

63. In analyzing state laws prohibiting sexual contact in custody between women prisoners and correctional staff, we relied on extensive research done by the National Women's Law Center. For a full text of the report, *see* National Women's Law Center, Fifty-State Survey on State Criminal Laws Prohibiting the Sexual Abuse of Women Prisoners, November 1996. The states that criminalize sex in custody are Alaska, Arizona, Arkansas, California, Colorado, Connecticut, Delaware, Florida, Georgia, Hawaii, Idaho, Indiana, Iowa, Kansas, Louisiana, Maine, Michigan, Missouri, Nevada, New Jersey, New Mexico, New York, North Dakota, Rhode Island, South Dakota, and Wisconsin.

64. 18 U.S.C. §§ 241, 242.

65. 42 U.S.C. § 1997 *et seq.* (Civil Rights of Institutionalized Persons Act).

exploit their authority over female prisoners, forcing these prisoners to have sexual relations with them.

Sexual Violence in Conflict

Widely committed and seldom denounced, instances of rape and other sexual violence in situations of conflict have been viewed more as the spoils of war than as acts that violate humanitarian law. Sexual violence in conflict often is neither seen nor investigated with the same seriousness as other violations of humanitarian law. Although rape during conflict will be specifically discussed elsewhere in this work, it is important to examine the fact that this phenomenon suffers from the same lack of accountability that is found in other forms of violence against women. This neglect similarly has its roots in stereotypes about sexuality and women's role in society, because governments assume that sexual violence is a natural and common occurrence during times of military conflict.

Women and girls are often targeted for sexual abuse in armed conflict purely on the basis of their gender, and irrespective of age, ethnicity, or political affiliation.[66] Rape also has been used as a weapon to terrorize a particular community and to achieve a specific political end. In these situations, gender intersects with other aspects of a woman's identity, such as ethnicity, race, religion, social class, or political affiliation. The humiliation, pain, and terror inflicted by the rapist is meant to degrade not just the individual woman but also the larger group of which she is a part. Through the emphasis placed in every culture on women's sexual virtue as part of the social community, the rape of one woman is translated into an assault upon the community. The shame of rape thus humiliates not only the individual woman, but also the family and all those associated with her. Combatants who rape often explicitly link their acts of sexual violence to this broader social degradation.[67] In the aftermath of such abuse, the harm done to the individual woman is often obscured or even compounded by the perceived harm to the community.

Reports of the widespread use of rape as a tactic of war in the former Yugoslavia have been instrumental in focusing attention on the function of rape in conflict, both in legal circles and among the general public. Moreover, the United Nations International Criminal Tribunal for the Former Yugoslavia has not only specifically taken jurisdiction for the prosecution of rape,[68] it has also handed down indictments for rape. However, that attention has not spread to the practice as it occurs presently in other parts of the world. For example, the Haiti case study examines how rape can be used as a tool for political persecution, but still overlooked as a human

---

66. The legal analysis in this section is drawn from HUMAN RIGHTS WATCH WOMEN'S RIGHTS PROJECT, THE HUMAN RIGHTS WATCH GLOBAL REPORT ON WOMEN'S HUMAN RIGHTS 1–99 (1995).

67. SUSAN BROWNMILLER, AGAINST OUR WILL: MEN, WOMEN AND RAPE 30–31 (1975).

68. Theodor Meron, *Rape as a Crime Under International Humanitarian Law,* 87 A.J.I.L. 424 (1993); and Catherine Niarchos, *Women, War and Rape: Challenges Facing the International Tribunal for the Former Yugoslavia,* 17 HUM. RTS. Q. 649 (1995).

rights abuse. Then we will see how in Rwanda, rape was committed as part of the genocide during the conflict.[69]

Haiti: Rape as a "Private Crime"

Haiti presents an example of rape clearly being used for political repression yet being treated as a random act of a personal nature. The military *coup d'état* against President Jean-Bertrand Aristide on September 30, 1991, plunged Haiti into a maelstrom of state-inflicted, state-sanctioned, and private human rights abuses.[70] Uniformed military personnel and their civilian allies threatened and attacked women's organizations for their work in defense of women's rights and subjected women to a wide range of sex-specific abuse, ranging from bludgeoning women's breasts to rape.[71] Despite the fact that attacks against women were committed by state-sponsored agents, the United States and other governments and international organizations failed to address such abuses as human rights violations until late in the conflict.

Human Rights Watch found that military forces and attachés used rape and sexual violence to punish women for their actual or imputed political beliefs. For instance, F.F., a twenty-six-year-old student, was stopped and sexually assaulted by two attachés on the evening of January 29, 1994. F.F. was an active supporter of President Aristide. She and her fellow students organized demonstrations in support of Aristide's policies while he was in office. F.F. told us:

> They asked me my name, where I lived, and what my political opinions were. When one asked about my political opinions, I thought to myself, "If he is just going to rob me, why is he asking me this?" I said I was not political. Then one said, "In the area where you live, I know you do not have any money, and I do not care what you say, I know everyone in your neighborhood supports Aristide." They proceeded to enquire more about my political beliefs, and they asked if I had a boyfriend, to which I responded, "Yes." Then one said, "I am going to rape you. Tell your boyfriend and your 'Father' [a reference to Aristide] that I am going to rape you."[72]

Both men raped F.F. She did not report the rape to the police, stating that "You really risk your life going to talk to them, because everyone knows they are part of the crime problem." Some women did report rape to the authorities during the

---

69. Besides the case studies below, Human Rights Watch has also documented rape in conflict in Bosnia-Hercegovina, Kashmir, Peru, and Somalia: HELSINKI WATCH, WAR CRIMES IN BOSNIA-HERCEGOVINA, VOLUME II (1993); ASIA WATCH AND PHYSICIANS FOR HUMAN RIGHTS, RAPE IN KASHMIR: A CRIME OF WAR (1993); AMERICAS WATCH AND WOMEN'S RIGHTS PROJECT, UNTOLD TERROR: VIOLENCE AGAINST WOMEN IN PERU'S ARMED CONFLICT; AND HUMAN RIGHTS WATCH/AFRICA, SOMALIA FACES THE FUTURE: HUMAN RIGHTS IN A FRAGMENTED SOCIETY (1995).

70. *See generally* HUMAN RIGHTS WATCH/AMERICAS, TERROR PREVAILS IN HAITI: HUMAN RIGHTS VIOLATIONS AND FAILED DIPLOMACY (1994).

71. This section is based upon information contained in HUMAN RIGHTS WATCH & NATIONAL COALITION FOR HAITIAN REFUGEES, RAPE IN HAITI: A WEAPON OF TERROR (1994) [hereinafter RAPE IN HAITI].

72. Interview with F.F., in Port-au-Prince, Haiti (Feb. 16, 1994).

coup regime but, to our knowledge, the military authorities never publicly denounced these practices or fully disciplined state agents known to have engaged in
them. In addition, the U.S. government failed to acknowledge the use of rape as a
tool of political persecution and hence its legitimacy as the basis for an asylum
claim. In May 1993, the U.S. Board of Immigration Appeals (BIA) granted asylum
to a Haitian woman who alleged that she had been gang-raped by three soldiers
after they broke into her family home and identified her as an Aristide supporter,[73]
but a cable sent by the U.S. Embassy in Haiti in 1994 attempted to down play the
incidence of human rights abuses in Haiti, especially rape.[74] It was not until May
1995 that BIA formally designated the case as binding precedent for future asylum
adjudication and thus formally acknowledged that women may suffer persecution
in the form of rape.

Skepticism that rape can be used for persecution because of real or perceived
political beliefs is a product of society's misperception that rape is solely a sexual
act, and never a violent, premeditated act to punish women for political or other
purposes. The result is that women often find it difficult to access the international
protections available to victims of political persecution. In order to provide women
such protections, governments and international organization must affirmatively
acknowledge that such abuses can qualify as a basis for an asylum or refugee claim.

Rwanda: Impunity

During the 1994 genocide,[75] Rwandan women were subjected to sexual violence
on a massive scale, perpetrated by members of the infamous Hutu militia groups
known as *Interahamwe* (Kinyarwanda for "those who work together"), by civilians, sometimes by soldiers of the Rwandan Armed Forces, and by the Presidential
Guard.[76] Administrative, military, and political leaders at the national and local
levels, as well as heads of militia, directed or permitted this sexual violence to
further their political goals.

---

73. DEBORAH ANKER, LAW OF ASYLUM IN THE UNITED STATES 117 (1996).

74. Cablegram from U.S. Embassy in Haiti to U.S. Secretary of State Warren Christopher, April
12, 1994.

75. During the months of April 1994 to July 1994, between 500,000 and one million Rwandan men,
women, and children were slaughtered in a genocide of the Tutsi minority and in massacres of moderate
Hutu who were willing to work with Tutsi. A circle of political leaders, threatened with loss of power,
organized the killings with the help of the military, Hutu militias, and many other civilians.

On April 6, 1994, the plane of President Juvenal Habyarimana, a Hutu, was shot down as he was
returning from a peace conference in Tanzania. The killing of Habyarimana served as a pretext to
initiate the massive killings that had been planned for months, both of Tutsi and of those Hutu who
were opposed to Habyarimana. For a more detailed discussion of the genocide, see HUMAN RIGHTS
WATCH/AFRICA, GENOCIDE IN RWANDA: APRIL-MAY 1994 (1994).

76. This section is based upon information contained in HUMAN RIGHTS WATCH/ AFRICA & HUMAN
RIGHTS WATCH WOMEN'S RIGHTS PROJECT, SHATTERED LIVES: SEXUAL VIOLENCE DURING THE RWANDAN
GENOCIDE AND ITS AFTERMATH (1996) [hereinafter SHATTERED LIVES].

During the Rwandan genocide, rape and other forms of violence were directed primarily against Tutsi women because of both their gender and their ethnicity. The extremist propaganda that exhorted Hutus to commit the genocide specifically identified the sexuality of Tutsi women as a means through which the Tutsi community would seek to infiltrate and control the Hutu community.[77] Most of the women we interviewed described how their rapists mentioned their ethnicity before or during the rape. A number of women were targeted regardless of ethnicity or political affiliation, and simply on the basis of their gender.

Rape manifested itself in different forms during the genocide. Rapes were sometimes followed by sexual mutilation, including mutilation of the vagina and pelvic area with machetes, knives, sticks, boiling water, and, in one case, acid.[78] Often women were subjected to sexual slavery and held collectively by a militia group for the period of the genocide in order to sexually service the militia group. These forced "marriages," as this form of sexual slavery is commonly known in Rwanda, lasted from a few days to the duration of the genocide, and in some cases longer.

Despite the prevalence and viciousness of these crimes, they have until recently remained invisible and sexual violence in the Rwandan genocide has occurred with virtual impunity. The then Deputy Prosecutor of the International Criminal Tribunal for Rwanda told Human Rights Watch/FIDH that the reason they have not collected rape testimonies is because "African women don't want to talk about rape. . . . We haven't received any real complaints. It's rare in investigations that women refer to rape."[79] Our research indicated that if interviews are conducted in conditions of safety and privacy, and if Rwandan women believe that their testimony will help bring about justice, they will recount their experiences. Further it has taken the Rwandan judicial system years to begin functioning again.[80] Although the lack of

---

77. Beginning in 1990, over a dozen newspapers in Kinyarwanda or French were launched to exploit ethnic hatred. These newspapers, which had a relatively small circulation, included graphic cartoons portraying Tutsi women using their supposed sexual prowess on United Nations peacekeepers (supposed supporters of the Rwandan Patriotic Front, a group based in Uganda and made up mostly of Tutsi refugees, according to the propaganda). RWANDA: LES MEDIAS DU GENOCIDE 45–47 (Jean-Pierre Chrétien ed., 1995). One woman told us, "The propaganda warned Hutu men to beware of Tutsi women;" one Tutsi woman explained "For example, it is said if she gives you a good child, the child is not really for you—the child is really for her Tutsi brothers. 'These women are very sexual, and they sleep with their Tutsi brothers. You will be deceived by them.'" Human Rights Watch/FIDH interview, in Kigali, Rwanda (Mar. 25, 1996).

78. One doctor treated a young woman about twenty-one years old who had been permanently mutilated after acid was thrown on her vagina and who had been sent to Belgium for reconstructive surgery. Interview with Dr. Gladstone Habimana, director, maternity wards, Kigali Central Hospital, in Kigali, Rwanda (Mar. 18, 1996).

79. Interview with Judge Honoré Rakotomanana, deputy prosecutor, International Criminal Tribunal, in Kigali, Rwanda (Mar. 27, 1996). Judge Rakotomanana was dismissed by the U.N. Secretary-General on February 26, 1997.

80. Because the former government fled with virtually all the funds and most of the usable equipment belonging to the state, the new government began this effort with few resources to carry out investigation and prosecutions. In addition, many lawyers, judges, and prosecutors were either killed during the

remedy is not unique to victims of gender-based abuse, it is clear that rape victims face specific obstacles to justice, including that police inspectors documenting genocide crimes for prosecution are predominantly male and rarely collect information on rape.

In addition, little has been done until now to include gender-based violence in the work of the International Criminal Tribunal for Rwanda, created by the United Nations Security Council on November 8, 1994, although it is explicitly empowered to prosecute sexual violence[81] and has done so in the former Yugoslavia, its other jurisdiction.[82] Even among tribunal investigators, who at least have been indirectly exposed through the former Yugoslavia context to the gravity of rape in conflict, there is a widespread impression that rape is somehow a "lesser" crime not worth investigating and that Rwandan women will not come forward to report rape. In July 1996, the Tribunal established a Sexual Assault Committee to coordinate the investigation of gender-based violence.[83] We anticipate that this initiative, if adequately staffed and funded, will lead to the implementation of more appropriate and effective procedures for gathering evidence of such crimes. Nonetheless, it is critical that parties take additional steps to ensure that rape will be investigated and prosecuted to provide redress to the victims and discourage such crimes in the future. Rape in war situations must be prosecuted as diligently as other violent abuse. In addition, rape in war should be prosecuted uniformly, in all the various situations in which it occurs, not just in the one or two cases or countries that receive significant publicity.

GENDER DISCRIMINATION AND SEXUAL HARASSMENT

In many countries governments have imposed or refused to amend legal codes that explicitly discriminate against women. In other situations, governments have applied gender-neutral laws in discriminatory ways or failed to enforce constitutional and other guarantees of nondiscrimination whether in the home, the workplace, or the criminal justice system. Because gender discrimination is not perceived to be as destructive as acts of physical abuse, it often is viewed as being less grave. But discrimination plays a critical role in maintaining women's subordinate position in society, and can often be the motivating factor for grievous physical or psychological harm. Human Rights Watch has investigated such discrimination in two broad areas: family and employment.

Family

Discrimination in many countries is encoded in the laws controlling women's roles in the family. Legal enshrinement of women's subordination in the family

---

genocide, were themselves implicated in the killings, or fled the country. Human Rights Watch/Africa/ FIDH, press release, New Attacks on Judicial Personnel in Rwanda (May 13, 1996).

81. Security Council Resolution 955, arts. 3–4(1994).

82. *See* Meron, *supra* note 68.

83. SHATTERED LIVES, *supra* note 76, at 94.

makes it nearly impossible for women to have the autonomy necessary to realize their full human rights. The condition of never being a full and independent agent can have serious consequences for women. For instance, women and girls may be married without their consent, forced to undergo virginity exams, denied access to divorce and child custody, and left virtually without recourse in situations of domestic violence. Because family law is often based upon assumed cultural norms, this form of discrimination frequently is justified on grounds of cultural necessity and rights to privacy. However, culture is not static. Protecting privacy rights does not require ignoring significant abuse. Rather than existing as one distinct violation of women's human rights, discriminatory family laws often comprise an interrelated system of violations that together can operate to limit women's autonomy. Discriminatory family laws have obliged women to construct innovative approaches in order to create and lead independent lives.

Morocco: Rights in Marriage

Morocco's *Moudawana*, the personal status or family code, renders women effectively minors under the law, regardless of their age.[84] The Moudawana regulates, among other things, legal capacity, marriage, divorce, and inheritance. In each of these areas, the Moudawana grants different rights to women and men, and it consistently renders women's autonomy subject to male guardianship and authority. The Moudawana does so despite the fact that the Moroccan Constitution has been revised to provide that "men and women shall enjoy equal political rights."[85] Thus, although Moroccan women are granted political rights, they are unable to enjoy such rights because of their subordinate role enshrined in the Moudawana. The Moudawana's importance cannot be overestimated. One activist referred to it as "the single most significant obstacle for women."[86]

One of the main beliefs underlying the Moudawana is that women must be controlled by a male. Relations between spouses are based on a set of "reciprocal obligations" that are "under the direction of the husband."[87] For example, the Moudawana requires that a woman obey her husband and submit to his control. Custom condones the husband's use of force in dealing with her recalcitrance. Since the husband will be the primary decision maker in a woman's life, there is a related need to control a woman's selection of spouse. Consequently, Moroccan women have limited ability to select their spouse autonomously. Under the Moudawana, only when her father is dead or legally incapacitated may an adult woman

---

84. This section is based upon information contained in HUMAN RIGHTS WATCH WOMEN'S RIGHTS PROJECT, "WHAT IS MOST SUITED TO THEM": WOMEN'S SECONDARY STATUS UNDER MOROCCAN LAW (forthcoming) [hereinafter SUITED TO THEM].

85. Constitution, art. 10 (Morocco).

86. Interview with Zeinab Miadi, founder and director, Casablanca Centre d'Ecoute et Orientation (Center for Listening and Counseling), in Casablanca, Morocco (Sept. 22, 1995).

87. Moudawana, art. 1 (Morocco).

independently contract her own marriage.[88] In contrast, men over eighteen are not required to seek anyone's permission to marry. Although women have begun to choose their marriage partner with increasing freedom, some interviewees speculated that they would be less likely to do so against the will of their father or a male relative. More important, some officials continue to insist that such permission is necessary. One woman told us:

> On September 20, 1995, . . . the *adouls* (notaries) we went to who administer the marriage certificate refused to do so. Both my husband and I are thirty-four-years old. My father died, and I can marry of my own will. [But], the adouls of my quarter asked for my brothers.[89]

The result of discriminatory family laws, such as the Moudawana, is that even when women are granted certain rights, including the right to vote and seek employment, their ability to enjoy such rights fully is constrained by the limits placed upon them by the legislation's enforcement of male control over their lives.

Botswana: Citizenship and Inheritance Rights[90]

In 1992, the Botswana Court of Appeal held that provisions of the Citizenship Act that prevented Batswana[91] women married to foreign men, but not similarly situated Batswana men, from passing on Botswanan citizenship to their children, were unconstitutional and contrary to international human rights law.[92] Such provisions were found to discriminate on the basis of sex by treating Batswana women differently than men. In August 1995, after a concerted campaign by local and international women's rights activists, the National Assembly of Botswana amended the Citizenship Act to eliminate those discriminatory provisions. The amendment granted citizenship to children, born in or outside of Botswana, whose mother or father is a citizen of Botswana. Although the amendment is not retroactive, it will permit expedited naturalization of minor children who have a parent who is a Botswana citizen. Further, foreign wives and husbands of Botswana citizens now have the same naturalization requirements.

The sex discriminatory provisions of the Citizenship Act were only the tip of the iceberg of statutory and customary law biased against women in Botswana. This is particularly true in the areas of marriage, adoption, inheritance rights, and other matters of personal law, which are exempted from the nondiscrimination requirement of the Constitution.[93] The continuing presence of discriminatory laws

---

88. *Id.* art. 12(4).

89. Interview with A., in Rabat, Morocco (Oct. 26, 1996).

90. This section is based upon information contained in HUMAN RIGHTS WATCH/AFRICA & HUMAN RIGHTS WATCH WOMEN'S RIGHTS PROJECT, SECOND CLASS CITIZENS: DISCRIMINATION AGAINST WOMEN UNDER BOTSWANA'S CITIZENSHIP ACT (1994) [hereinafter SECOND CLASS CITIZENS].

91. Batswana is an adjective that modifies a plural noun, as in "Batswana women."

92. Attorney General v. Unity Dow, Court of Civil Appeal, No. 4/91 (Botswana, 1992).

93. BOTS. CONST. art. 15(4)(c).

in Botswana officially places women in a position subordinate to men. This state-enforced subordination makes it much more difficult for women to establish economic independence and make their own decisions in relation to their careers and financial matters.

For example, under Botswana law a woman is not her husband's customary heir and generally has no rights to any inheritance under customary law, although she is entitled to remain in the family home and be maintained by the male heir until she remarries or dies.[94] The order of inheritance passes through the male children in order of their seniority.

The government has justified such restrictions on the grounds of respect for national customs and tradition. However, by their very nature and function, traditional and customary norms should protect and respect the rights and interests of all members of the community. Tradition and custom are not only constantly evolving and changing in any society, but they are also open to different interpretations at any given point in time. The actions of Batswana women and women's rights organizations in Botswana to protest and circumvent these laws strongly suggest that they should be reexamined in light of the evolving culture and needs of Botswana. Tradition and custom must not be used as an excuse to discriminate against women.

Employment

Women workers around the world face discrimination and sexual and physical violence at the hands of their employers with little or no legal redress. They are often omitted from labor codes and are the first to experience the repercussions of economic decline.[95] Women workers also experience discrimination in retraining programs when they receive training solely in low-skill, low-income occupations. In addition, women increasingly are migrating to other communities or states in order to find work.[96] Migrant women are a particularly vulnerable group because they are often unfamiliar with the laws, language(s), and legal systems of the host country or region.

Sex discrimination in the workplace often is motivated by the perception that women are less reliable, less valuable in terms of household income, less skilled than men, and that women's productive capacity is compromised by their reproductive function. Public and private employers often discriminate with impunity against women, both as women and as mothers or potential mothers. In addition to discrimination in regard to employment decisions, Human Rights Watch investigations have documented violence against women workers that includes rape and other

---

94. SIMON ROBERTS, THE MALETE LAW OF FAMILY RELATIONS 57 (1970).

95. *See* HELSINKI WATCH & WOMEN'S RIGHTS PROJECT, HIDDEN VICTIMS: WOMEN IN POST-COMMUNIST POLAND (1992) and Russia case study in this section.

96. It is estimated that, since the 1980s, the female migrant population has outnumbered the male migrant population, in some cases by wide margins.

forms of sexual violence, and physical abuse such as beating, kicking, slapping, and burning. Numerous women workers, particularly those who are heads of households, remain silent in the face of such abuse by employers. Some fear that by complaining they may lose their jobs in shrinking labor markets. Others do not report abuse because they do not believe that the criminal justice system will respond to gender-related abuses. When women workers do report workplace discrimination or violence, there is a serious lack of accountability for such abuse. The case studies below examine the need for accountability for public employers in Russia, individual private employers in Kuwait, and corporate employers in Mexico.

Russia: Public Sector Employers[97]

Economic and political changes in Russia have left many Russians staggering under the burdens of rising unemployment and disappearing social services.[98] Women in particular have suffered the consequences of such changes: they face widespread employment discrimination that is practiced, condoned and tolerated by the government. Government employers have fired women workers in disproportionate numbers and have refused to employ women because of their sex.[99] According to *Izvestia*, a Moscow newspaper, out of the 2.3 million officially unemployed, more than 70 percent are women.[100]

Women also confront sex discrimination when they seek new employment. Government employers openly express their preference for hiring men. At the request of employers, government employment offices frequently advertise jobs for men only and refuse to refer women to jobs if the employer has indicated a preference for men. In a government employment office in Kaluga, job announcements on the walls describing the salaries and qualifications blatantly included the specification that only men need apply. Female job seekers interviewed by Human Rights Watch identified being a woman, and particularly, a woman with children, as the greatest barrier to finding work. A thirty-four-year-old engineer and mother of two interviewed in a government unemployment office told us:

> I have been unemployed since December 1993 when I lost my job. They reduced the labor force by many. Our plant was mostly women, so most of the fired were women. This is my fifth time in this office. I registered in December, and I have had interviews for jobs as an electrical engineer. But I haven't had any job offers, because they want

---

97. This section is based upon information contained in NEITHER JOBS NOR JUSTICE, *supra* note 14, and interviews conducted during a mission to Russia in 1996.

98. *See generally* ELEANOR RANDOLPH, WAKING THE TEMPEST (1996).

99. Soviet and Russian legislation historically prohibited women from working in jobs perceived as particularly unhealthy or strenuous, such as underground jobs, or in positions that could interfere with their responsibilities as mothers, such as night or weekend jobs. Although these provisions had been erratically enforced, labor legislation passed in 1996 restates these restrictions and the Labor Ministry promises that they shall be enforced.

100. Sergei Strokan, *Russia: NGOs Condemn Sexual Discrimination in the Moscow Workplace*, INTER PRESS OFFICE, Nov. 3, 1995, at 3.

to hire men. This is a man's speciality. When I go for the interviews, they ask me if I have children. Children are often ill, and I would have to take time off to care for them.[101]

Despite the Russian Constitution explicitly stating in Article 19 that women and men have equal rights, the Russian government has made no effort to ensure that women have equal employment opportunities. In fact, far from attacking such discriminatory employment decisions, the government has failed to enforce laws that prohibit sex discrimination. Officials at the Labor Ministry, including the then Labor Minister Gennady Malyikin, have stated explicitly that men should have priority over women in receiving employment.[102]

Human Rights Watch also has received several reports of women in Russia either applying for jobs or who already have jobs being forced to have sex with their supervisors as a requirement for employment.[103] Although this abuse of power was until 1996 specifically prohibited under the Russian criminal code,[104] local women activists told Human Rights Watch that such provision was rarely, if ever, enforced. That provision was omitted from the criminal code adopted in 1996.

Discrimination against women by government employers sends a powerful message to private employers and the citizenry in general. Government must eliminate discriminatory provisions in its labor legislation and ensure that government employers and employment agencies provide equal opportunities to women workers. If the public sector is unable to regulate itself, it cannot be expected to protect women's human rights more generally.

Kuwait: Private Individual Employers

The liberation of Kuwait from Iraqi occupation occurred in March 1991. Thousands of women domestic workers, mainly from Sri Lanka, the Philippines, Bangladesh, and India have fled the homes of abusive Kuwaiti employers and sought

---

101. Interview, in Kaluga, Russia (Mar. 24, 1994).

102. When asked about the problem of women's unemployment in February 1993, Russia's labor minister, Gennady Melikyan, responded, ''Why should we employ women when men are out of work? It's better that men work and women take care of children and do housework. I don't think women should work when men are doing nothing.'' H. Womack, *Why Employ Women When Men Are Out of Work?,''* THE GUARDIAN (London), Mar. 21, 1993, at 11.

103. The Moscow-based Fund for Protection from Sexual Harassment at Work has a list of approximately 300 private businesses where employers regularly abuse or harass their employees. Dmitry Babich, *Workplace Harassment,* MOSCOW TIMES, July 5, 1994. Valery Vikulov, director of the Fund, told the *Moscow Times* that a number of women in Moscow informed him that they were raped by potential or current employers.

104. Russian Criminal Code, Article 118 stated, ''Forcing a woman to engage in sexual intercourse or in the satisfaction of sexual passion in any form by a person on whom the woman is dependent either materially or in terms of employment is punishable by deprivation of freedom for a period of up to three years.''

refuge in their embassies.[105] A Human Rights Watch investigation—based on fact-finding missions in 1992, 1993, 1994 and subsequent updates—found that while most domestic servants in Kuwait do not experience violence at the hands of their employers, the rape, physical assault, and mistreatment of Asian maids, when it does occur, takes place largely with impunity.

Maids face numerous obstacles to reporting abuse or mistreatment by individual employers. For example, in Kuwait, the government explicitly excludes domestic workers from its labor law.[106] The law, which regulates working conditions and arbitration for employment disputes, covers most other private employees, including foreign workers. In addition, female domestic servants have no right to organize.[107] These exemptions make it extremely difficult for domestic workers to access legal remedies for labor law violations and other abusive treatment. Further, in cases of violations of the criminal law, domestic workers again find themselves unable to get redress. Many Asian maids in Kuwait reported being totally or significantly confined by their employers to the premises, and as a result often could not reach the police to report violations. Others who managed to report abuses often confronted police refusal to investigate their complaints, at times because of the influence of their employers.

Only a handful of charges against abusive employers are investigated or prosecuted each year in Kuwait. In an April 1993 letter to Human Rights Watch, the Kuwaiti government stated that between February 1991 and February 1993, only fifteen cases of sexual assault against maids were prosecuted. In our investigation we found evidence of a far higher level of assaults. Many women who had been raped and managed to report their assaults to the police received little or no help. In some cases, women were returned to the employers who allegedly had raped and beaten them.

In some instances, individual Kuwaiti law enforcement officials attempted to provide the abused maids with some assistance. But, in general, the government viewed the maids claims as "exaggerated." In addition, Kuwait has attempted to shift responsibility for the problem to the Asian governments from which the maids emigrated. While sending governments must take responsibility for their citizens' human rights through additional regulation of emigration, they are limited in their ability to do so in the receiving country. As of 1995, the Kuwaiti government had yet to implement the legal and practical reforms necessary, such as including domestic workers in its labor laws and permitting them to organize, to ensure that the pattern

---

105. This section is based upon information contained in MIDDLE EAST WATCH & WOMEN'S RIGHTS PROJECT, PUNISHING THE VICTIM: RAPE AND MISTREATMENT OF ASIAN MAIDS IN KUWAIT (1992) [hereinafter PUNISHING THE VICTIM].

106. Law No. 38 of 1964, Concerning Labor in Private Sector (as amended through 1989), Chapter 1 (Scope of Implementation), Article 2(e) provides that "domestic servants and those having their status . . . [shall] not be subject to the application of this law's provisions."

107. Domestic servants are unable to organize because labor organizations are only authorized under Law No. 38, which excludes domestic servants. Further, Kuwaiti unions can only be established by Kuwaiti employees and, to our knowledge, no Kuwaiti women work as maids.

of rarely punished abuse and mistreatment of Asian maids does not recur. Domestic migrant workers are in a particularly vulnerable position because they work in individual homes. It is unacceptable to compound that invisibility by exempting them from the labor code. Governments that have taken affirmative steps to encourage the migration of female domestic workers to fulfill their employment needs must also take affirmative steps to protect those women's human rights.

Mexico: Corporate Employers

Export processing factories (*maquiladoras*) along the U.S.–Mexico border routinely subject prospective female employees to mandatory urine testing and invasive questions about their contraceptive use, menses schedule, and sexual habits.[108] These companies often refuse to hire pregnant women and mistreat or force those who do become pregnant shortly after being hired to resign because of the high costs of complying with Mexico's maternity benefits law.[109] Despite its international and domestic legal obligations to ensure protection for these workers, the Mexican government has done little to acknowledge or remedy violations of women's rights to nondiscrimination and to privacy by the *maquiladoras*. While Mexico prohibits government employers from practicing such pregnancy discrimination, it has *de facto* exempted corporate employers.

For example, Orfilia is thirty-three years old. She began working for the General Motors-owned plant Delmosa in Reynosa, Mexico, in March 1995. On the day that she applied for a position as a line worker, she and approximately thirty other women applicants had to undergo pregnancy and blood tests.[110] Human Rights Watch spoke to several other women who reported similar experiences; others reported that they were simply asked if they were pregnant or that they were required to provide details of their sex lives.

In addition to pregnancy-testing, no female *maquiladora* worker can be sure that she will keep her job if she becomes pregnant. Human Rights Watch documented several cases of forced resignations. By "forced," we mean that the women tendered their resignations or signed a resignation letter at the insistence, instigation, and urging of *maquiladora* managers. In many of these cases the women were

---

108. This section is based upon information contained in HUMAN RIGHTS WATCH WOMEN'S RIGHTS PROJECT, NO GUARANTEES: SEX DISCRIMINATION IN MEXICO'S MAQUILADORA SECTOR (1996) [hereinafter NO GUARANTEES].

109. According to Mexico's federal labor code, companies are required to protect pregnant women from executing tasks that would cause danger to their health in relation to the fetus; pay pregnant women maternity leave of six weeks before delivery and six weeks after delivery; allow new mothers two paid extra breaks of a half-hour each to breast-feed their infants; and allow pregnant women to take an extra sixty days off while receiving 50 percent of their salary, if they so desire, apart from the twelve weeks of maternity leave, so long as no more than one year after the birth has passed.

110. Interview with Orfilia, in Rio Bravo, Mex. (Mar. 13, 1995).

told there was no work, although, to their knowledge, they were the only persons asked to leave.[111]

Because the ability to bear children is inextricably linked to being female, pregnancy-based discrimination constitutes a form of sex discrimination by targeting a condition only women can experience. When pregnancy-based discrimination has been reviewed in light of international human rights and labor standards, bodies charged with interpreting those standards have consistently recognized it as a form of sex discrimination.[112] The Convention on the Elimination of all Forms of Discrimination Against Women (Women's Convention) explicitly prohibits pregnancy-based employment discrimination. The Women's Convention calls on state parties to take appropriate measures to "prohibit, subject to the imposition of sanctions, dismissal on the grounds of pregnancy or maternity leave."[113]

It is difficult to hold foreign corporations accountable for gender-based discrimination. Not only does it entail more financial and human resources to monitor and reform their actions, but foreign corporations often are the source of valuable financial resources. Further, none of the state-established dispute mechanisms in Mexico are accessible to people who have not been hired; mechanisms to redress post-hire discrimination also function ineffectively.[114] Mexico is consistently failing to take reasonable measures to prevent, investigate, prosecute, or punish sex discrimination, especially when committed by private actors. The women affected by pregnancy discrimination in the *maquiladora* sector are among the poorest, least experienced, and least educated in the workforce. Women's desperation to get or retain *maquiladora* jobs, combined with ignorance of the law, makes them reluctant to contest the discriminatory testing or forced resignations. In many instances women find themselves in the untenable position of choosing between their jobs and their rights.

---

111. For example, Nieves was warned by *maquiladora* managers that she would be administered a pregnancy exam three months after she commenced working there. Nieves realized that she was pregnant before the three-month period had passed. She was sick and her supervisor sent her to see the company doctor, who gave her a pregnancy exam, which came back positive. The supervisor subsequently informed her that he no longer needed her. Interview with Nieves, in Matamoros, Mex. (Mar. 19, 1995).

112. The International Labor Organization's (ILO) Convention 111 on Discrimination in Respect of Employment and Occupation specifically prohibits discrimination based on gender in access to employment. The ILO Committee of Experts has interpreted the scope of the Convention 111 to prohibit pregnancy-based discrimination as a form of sex discrimination. 13 CONDITIONS OF WORK DIGEST 24 (1994). In addition, the European Court of Justice ruled in a 1991 case that pregnancy-based discrimination constitutes impermissible sex discrimination. The court stated that "only women can be refused employment on the grounds of pregnancy and such a refusal therefore constitutes direct discrimination on the grounds of sex." Case C–177/88, Dekker v. Stichting Vormingscentrum voor Jong Volwassenen Plus, E.C.R. 3941 (1991). The court found the company in violation of Directive 76/207/EEC of the European Council on equal treatment.

113. The Convention on the Elimination of all Forms of Discrimination Against Women, GA Res 34/180, Dec. 18 1979, art. 11(1)(b) [hereinafter Women's Convention].

114. *See* NO GUARANTEES, *supra* note 108, at 37–45.

The unfortunate consequence of Mexico's generous maternity benefits has been discrimination against women based upon their reproductive capacity. This discrimination not only unfairly limits women's employment opportunities, but it also unduly influences women's choices on the number and spacing of their children. Government must take action to ensure that the right to enjoy maternity benefits free from pregnancy discrimination is available to all women, including those who work for corporate employers.

ABUSES RELATED TO PROSTITUTION

Within the overall tendency to neglect women's human rights, certain groups of women face particular disregard. Among these are prostitutes. As a result of societies' official contempt for prostitutes, which is often accompanied by legal sanction, many prostitutes experience abuses either committed or tolerated by state agents for which it is extremely difficult to get redress. Human Rights Watch has researched these abuses specifically in relatio.: to women who have been trafficked or migrated to work in prostitution. Many of these women have been abducted, lured, or coerced into situations of prostitution under circumstances where they initially were unaware of the nature of the work. Some women have been offered false promises of marriage or have had family members threatened. Others have been told that they will be working as servants or in factories only to find that they will be compelled to prostitute themselves. In other circumstances, women have been better informed about the nature of the work, but have faced slavery-like working conditions, illegal confinement, beatings, starvation, and psychological abuse.

Domestic criminal and labor statutes, as well as international law, often clearly prohibit such abuse. However, because prostitution is usually illegal and/or the women are in the country illegally, many prostitutes are denied their rights or are extremely reluctant to report their abuse because they have a legitimate fear of being punished themselves. Even in the rare cases where prostitution is not criminalized, prostitutes are perceived by many societies as being of low moral character, which reduces the perceived credibility of their testimony. In addition, prostitutes are often subject to conditions that increase their susceptibility to sexually transmitted diseases, including Acquired Immunodeficiency Syndrome (AIDS), because they are unable to control the number of customers or condom usage.

Many of the women and girls with whom we spoke experienced debt bondage, whereby they are required to work toward the repayment of a so-called debt to their employer, but the value of their services is not reasonably applied toward the liquidation of that debt. In addition, the length of time necessary to repay the debt is not limited and the services required are ill-defined.[115] For most interviewees, their debt appeared to consist of the initial amount their families or companions received from the recruiters, plus transport, protection money or payoffs to police

---

115. Supplementary Convention on the Abolition of Slavery, the Slave Trade, and Institutions and Practices Similar to Slavery, 18 U.S.T. 3201; 266 U.N.T.S.3, Sept. 7, 1956, art. 1(a).

or other officials, and any advances provided for clothing, food, shelter, or other items. These costs are often initially inflated in order to increase the profit to the brothel owner. As a result of this debt inflation and unclear repayment terms, women find it extremely difficult to actually repay their debt and thus their servitude is lengthened. Such slavery-like practice is prohibited by international law.

Rarely did we find governments investigating or prosecuting these abuses. In fact, our research indicates that while governments seldom arrest or prosecute the men responsible for abuses against women involved in prostitution, they often punish prostitutes. Further, in cases where the women are illegally present in the country, governments have imprisoned the women, often in deplorable conditions, for illegal immigration or have deported them summarily, without necessarily giving them an opportunity to testify to the abuses they suffered. Our research in both Thailand and India indicated the lack of accountability that surrounded abuses against prostitutes. In the Thailand case study, we describe the increased susceptibility of prostitutes to Human Immunodeficiency Virus (HIV) and discrimination based upon perceived HIV status. The Nepal case study illustrates how society's perception of sex workers as immoral directly restricts prostitutes' ability to redress abuses against them.

Thailand: Exposure to HIV

In three trips in 1993, Human Rights Watch gathered evidence that Thai government officials were directly involved in trafficking Burmese women and girls into forced prostitution and did not prosecute brothel owners for debt bondage and other human rights violations.[116] Despite international legal protections against debt bondage, every Burmese woman and girl we interviewed reported this abuse. Some women never knew how much they earned, how much they were supposed to earn, or the terms for repayment of the debt.

For example, Tar Tar knew that the going rate in her brothel was 110 baht (US $4.40) per hour. She was told by the other women in the brothel that her share was 30 percent, or 36 baht, plus any tips. Tar Tar figured of the 36 baht, half went toward the payment of her original cash advance, which as 10,000 baht (US $400, doubled to include interest), and half was ostensibly for rent and food, so Tar Tar was never actually able to keep any of it. The owner gave her and the other workers 30 baht a day to buy food, but this amount was deducted from their earnings. She assumed that she and the owner would settle the accounts at the end of the year.

The Thai government had long been aware of the existence of illegal brothels, but had been slow to address the health risks of the women and girls within them despite concern about the transmission of HIV. In fact, this denial continued until at least 1994 as the Thai government's two-fold strategy for combating AIDS—law enforcement and health intervention—was initiated. For the most part this strategy

---

116. This section is based upon information contained in ASIA WATCH & WOMEN'S RIGHTS PROJECT, A MODERN FORM OF SLAVERY: TRAFFICKING OF BURMESE WOMEN AND GIRLS INTO BROTHELS IN THAILAND (1993) [hereinafter MODERN SLAVERY].

targeted Burmese women and girls, considered illegal immigrants and sources of HIV transmission to the general public.

Our 1993 investigation indicated that not only has the Thai government failed to protect Burmese women and girls from human rights violations that render them vulnerable to HIV infection, it has inflicted additional abuses upon them on account of their actual or perceived HIV status. HIV testing frequently was imposed on a mandatory basis, sometimes by public health officials, and without informed consent, on women and girls working in Thai brothels and, for a period in 1992, prostitutes held in detention at Pakkret. Mandatory testing without informed consent is condemned by the U.N. Human Rights Center and the World Health Organization as an unjustifiable interference with an individual's basic right to privacy.[117] Governments may derogate from that right but only if three stringent conditions are met: mandatory testing must be required legally; it must serve a legitimate urgent public purpose; and it must be strictly proportional to the benefit to society.[118] Mandatory testing of the Burmese women and girls failed to meet any of these conditions.[119]

After forcible testing, authorities subjected the Burmese women and girls to the further indignity of withholding their test results, even from those who, aware that they had been tested for HIV, requested to know their status. For instance, Chit Chit was tested four times while in her first brothel in Chaingmai. Then she was tested twice while in another brothel in Bangkok. After her arrest by a plainclothes policeman, she was tested again in Pakkret. She was not given the results of any of those tests. Mandatory testing also resulted in *de facto* discrimination against prostitutes because the customers, pimps, and brothel owners were not subjected to mandatory screening, even though male-to-female transmission is at least three times as efficient as female-to-male transmission.[120]

To our knowledge, not a single brothel owner has been investigated or punished for debt bondage, illegal confinement, forced prostitution, forced labor, or criminal negligence. The Thai government also continued largely to exempt procurers, brothel owners, pimps, and clients from punishment under the law for abuses,

---

117. UNITED NATIONS HUMAN RIGHTS CENTER & WORLD HEALTH ORGANIZATION, REPORT OF AN INTERNATIONAL CONSULTATION ON AIDS AND HUMAN RIGHTS, GENEVA, July 26–28, 1989 55 (1991)[hereinafter AIDS AND HUMAN RIGHTS].

118. *Id.* at 15.

119. Thailand's 1992–1996 National AIDS Plan includes human rights protection guidelines that explicitly rule out testing under any circumstances unless informed consent is given by the individual concerned or by her legal representative. The only exceptions are military and police officials who have to enter combat situations or confront dangerous persons. National Economic and Special Development Board, AIDS Policy and Planning Coordination Bureau, Office of the Prime Minister, Thailand's National AIDS Prevention Plan 23 (1992).

120. AIDS IN THE WORLD Appendix 6.1A (Jonathan Mann et al. eds., 1992). Under the National AIDS Plan, men are tested on an unlinked confidential basis and provided the highest assurance of confidentiality, whereas the women's results frequently are revealed to the government. In unlinked anonymous testing, the blood or saliva sample is identified by a number or other code rather than the name of the patient.

including those that increase the women's susceptibility to HIV infection. Women and girls are unable to negotiate the number of partners or to require that customers use condoms. The Thai government has publicly stated that it will investigate and prosecute these abuses to the fullest extent of the law and they have conducted raids, but rather than prosecuting the brothel owners, the authorities jail the women. Therefore, in addition to the Thai government's inadequate investigation and prosecution of the abusers, it has routinely arrested and punished the abused. This policy not only punishes the women, but feeds into the continued cycle of abuse. Once a woman is arrested, local police frequently allow brothel owners to have access to her in custody. Several of our interviewees had been arrested previously by local police and returned to the brothel after the owner paid their fine. The amount paid by the brothel owner was then added to their debt, thereby prolonging their bondage. This discriminatory arrest pattern constitutes a violation of the Thai government's obligations under the Women's Convention to "accord to women equality with men before the law."[121]

India: Treatment as Social Pariahs

Based on research conducted in Nepal and India in 1994, Human Rights Watch found that many Nepali women working as prostitutes in India were subjected to conditions tantamount to slavery and also to serious physical abuse.[122] In India, police and local officials protect brothel owners from police raids and traffickers, and both policemen and civilian officers patronize the brothels. Meanwhile, Nepali women and girls who complain to the Indian police about rape or abduction, or who are arrested in raids or for vagrancy, are held in detention euphemistically called "protective custody," where the abuse continues.

As in Thailand, debt bondage is prevalent among Nepali prostitutes in India. Every Nepali girl or woman to whom we spoke said that the brothel owner or manager forced her to work by invoking her indebtedness. None of our interviewees knew about the specific monetary arrangements between the brothel owner, the agents, and their families. But all were frequently reminded that they had to work to pay off debts, and many were threatened or beaten for not earning enough. Santhi said she worked in three low-grade brothels and a "bungalow" (a more prestigious brothel). Although Santhi does not know how much she was originally sold for, she was told that each time she was sold it was for a higher price. Santhi had heard there was a rule that the brothel can keep you three years, but after three years they have to give you Rs. 20,000 (US $666), gold, and clothes. After she was there for seven years, her father came to see her, but the owner said she had to stay another two years before she could leave. After two more years, her father came to the brothel and removed her. When she left the brothel she was given Rs. 5,000 (US $166), which she turned over to her father.

---

121. Women's Convention, *supra* note 113, arts. 2 and 15. Thailand ratified the Women's Convention in August 1985.

122. This section is based upon information contained in HUMAN RIGHTS WATCH/ASIA, RAPE FOR PROFIT: TRAFFICKING OF NEPALI GIRLS AND WOMEN TO INDIA'S BROTHEL (1995).

The failure of the criminal justice system to enforce laws against trafficking and related crimes has been a serious problem in both Nepal and India. In India, a lucrative patronage system has developed between corrupt police and brothel owners that ensures unequal law enforcement. Women and girls are reportedly arrested by the thousands under those sections of the law designed to curb public prostitution and solicitation. Their arrests allow the police to promote a public image of vigilance against prostitution while rarely arresting and prosecuting brothel owners and traffickers responsible for the abuses. The owners and traffickers are, in fact, protected from prosecution for some of the most serious offenses by local police who receive regular payment for their services, warn brothel owners of impending raids, and patronize the brothels as customers.

One activist told us that while the police do conduct raids, on the whole women in prostitution are viewed as criminals by the police and not worthy of extra rescue efforts. This same perception is shared by the women themselves. In many cases, they have told officers that they do not want to return home because they are ''violated and spoiled'' and therefore, social pariahs. They also fear their indebtedness and the contempt of family members. Because these women told officers that they did not want to return home, the officers apparently made no effort to free them from the brothel, investigate the conditions, or investigate charges of abuse. Such reports indicate how the perception of prostitutes often makes them unable to receive redress for abuses that clearly violate both human rights law and domestic law.

Regardless of a society's view of prostitutes and sex workers, governments must protect their human rights. Prostitutes must believe that their reports of abuse will be accepted and pursued diligently by law enforcement agents. Further, any raids on brothels must punish those who run the brothels, as well as the employees.

CONCLUSION

Women throughout the world face violence and discrimination either committed by or tolerated by governments. In many cases, these violations of human rights take similar forms such as domestic violence, custodial abuse, and employment discrimination, among others described in this chapter. Often the obstacles to remedying the abuses are also similar. For example, the method of collecting forensic evidence for sexual violence is problematic in every country where we investigated sexual violence; discriminatory family laws are routinely justified by tradition; and prostitutes find that their low social and legal status makes it difficult for them to redress abuse. The result of this commonality is that certain simple actions will go far toward improving protections for women's human rights.

Governments must start by refraining from abusing women themselves. State agents should not rape and assault women in prisons and jails, and they should never use rape or other forms of sexual violence as a tool of war or for political persecution. Moreover, when such acts occur, the governments must act immediately to investigate and punish the perpetrators and not require prohibitive standards of proof. In addition, governments must take concerted action to address common forms of violence against women committed by private actors, such as domestic and sexual violence. The procedures in place for prosecuting sexual and domestic violence should be examined with an eye toward eliminating the impact any bias or underlying stereotypes may have. For example, the beliefs that domestic violence is a private matter and that only virgins should be able to prosecute for rape are based upon stereotypical notions of patriarchal authority and women's sexuality; these stereotypes increase the difficulty of combating such abuses. Discriminatory laws and application of laws based upon derogatory stereotypes about women should be repealed. Finally, the legal status of prostitution and social perceptions about the moral character of sex workers should not prevent law enforcement agents from investigating and prosecuting violations of international and domestic law when committed against prostitutes.

Fighting violence and discrimination against women is an uphill battle. But one of the most powerful weapons is the emergence of a global women's rights movement. Activists have found that a comprehensive strategy is the most useful method for confronting violations of women's human rights. Women's rights activists use political, legal, and social channels to provide redress. Activists also have begun to take action at all levels: international, regional, and local, depending on their goals and the environment in which they work. For example, women's rights activists spearheaded a movement at the 1993 U.N. World Conference on Human Rights in Vienna to put women's human rights on the world agenda. They were largely successful. Russian women's rights activists who had difficulty influencing the federal government have found more success at the local level. In addition, women's rights activists have managed to do this work despite coming from many different backgrounds: racial, ethnic, religious, economic, and sexual preference, to name just a few. To ignore these differences would result in a compounded experience of discrimination for the neglected segment and in the long-run reduce the effectiveness of women's rights groups. Thus, through acknowledging and utilizing these differences, the women's human rights movement has been able to craft more effective remedies for the many abuses that all women face.

VIOLENCE AGAINST WOMEN

Radhika Coomaraswamy and Lisa M. Kois

VIOLENCE AGAINST WOMEN[1]

This chapter aims at setting out the international legal framework and governing issues on violence against women, as well as describing the various manifestations of violence against women and the legal responses to such violence.

The Declaration on the Elimination of Violence Against Women ("The Declaration"), passed unanimously by the United Nations General Assembly in December, 1993, recognizes in its preamble that "violence against women is a manifestation of historically unequal power relations between men and women which have led to domination over and discrimination against women by men. . . ."[2] The Declaration, drafted by leading experts, accepts the fact that structures that perpetuate violence against women are socially constructed and that such violence is a product of a historical process and is not essential or time bound in its manifestations. The recognition that violence against women is a social creation allows the freedom to challenge its use and to suggest alternative plans and programs for its elimination. It grants opportunities to create a new history in which violence against women would be condemned and not recognized as an inevitable and unchangeable consequence of gender relations.

In addition to being historically located, the Declaration affirms that "violence against women both violates and impairs or nullifies the enjoyment by women of human rights and fundamental freedoms."[3] Although violence is a product of historical processes, it violates existing universal norms relating to human rights as found in the instruments of international law. Violence against women is not only a criminal justice issue. It is recognized as a violation of human rights and states are

---

1. This chapter has largely been excerpted from the reports of the U.N. Special Rapporteur on Violence Against Women. *Preliminary Report Submitted by the Special Rapporteur on Violence Against Women, Its Causes and Consequences, in Accordance With Commission on Human Rights Resolution 1994/45,* U.N. Doc. E/CN.4/1995/42 (1994); *Report of the Special Rapporteur on Violence Against Women, Its Causes and Consequences, in Accordance With Commission on Human Rights Resolution 1995/85,* U.N. Doc. E/CN.4/1996/53 (1996); *Report of the Special Rapporteur on Violence Against Women, Its Causes and Consequences, on Violence Against Women in the Community,* U.N. Doc. E/CN.4/1997/47 (1997). Radhika Coomaraswamy is the Special Rapporteur.

2. Declaration on the Elimination of Violence against Women, U.N. GAOR, 3d Comm., 48th Sess., Res. 48/104, U.N. Doc. A/48/629 (1994) [hereinafter Declaration].

3. *Id.* pmbl. ¶ 5.

under a "due diligence" standard to ensure the prevention, investigation, and punishment of perpetrators.[4] While the historical location allows for an understanding of the social, political, and economic forces that have led to violence being enacted upon women, the recognition of the incompatibility of violence against women with fundamental freedoms and human rights ensures a pathway for women's liberation. By empowering women with rights against violence, the Declaration seeks to ensure that women will have redress and recourse to state and civil society machinery to guarantee that violence is not perpetrated against them.

The Declaration, and the principles enunciated therein, are the culmination of an important struggle waged over two decades and calling for the recognition of women's rights as human rights. Common throughout the world, violence against women became a rallying point in this struggle, bringing together a diverse group of women from all regions of the world. Among this group were those working with victims of armed conflict in the former Yugoslavia, Rwanda, and with victims of military sexual slavery during World War II; women from the dynamic movements against domestic violence, rape, and sexual harassment; those struggling against trafficking in women, forced prostitution, and forced labor; women working against female genital mutilation, dowry deaths, Sati, and other traditional practices harmful to the health of women; and representatives from Women Living Under Muslim Laws who drew the link between religious extremism and violence against women. The work of these groups culminated in Vienna at the World Conference on Human Rights of 1993. The women called for international action, including the promulgation of a Declaration on the Elimination of Violence Against Women as well the appointment of a Special Rapporteur on Violence against Women. Within six months of their joint appeal, both international mechanisms were created. The Declaration was passed in December 1993 and the post of Special Rapporteur was created in the spring of 1994 by the U.N. Commission on Human Rights.

Violence against women is a major impediment to the fulfillment and full enjoyment of human rights of women throughout the world. Violence impedes women's participation in the social and public life of the country, and thus women are denied their democratic rights. In addition, the insensitivity of criminal justice systems in many parts of the world results in the denial of women's access to justice and redress for the crimes committed against them. This denial of human rights was one of the main reasons why women around the world united to struggle for a recognition of violence against women as a violation of human rights.

One of the most important factors with regard to the struggle for the elimination of violence against women is the role of the state. The state is an ambiguous locality for women. On the one hand, the state is the site of violence against women. Women in the custody of the state often face torture and demeaning treatment. In addition, during times of armed conflict, state actors are violent toward women and rape and pillage at will at the women's expense. Finally, state inaction with regard

---

4.   *Id.* art. 4.

to violence against women[5] and its refusal to take the violence seriously and to prosecute and punish male perpetrators of the violence results in the victimization of women. On the other hand, it is the state to which women turn to redress their grievances. The criminal justice system in all countries is directly responsible for ensuring women's safety and bodily integrity. It is the state that will enact laws and procedures for the defense of women and for the provision of services for women victims/survivors. For this reason, women are increasingly working with state institutions to sensitize them to the problems faced by women and to ensure the adoption of policies and measures which will be effective in protecting women from crime and assist survivors in seeking redress.

Economic and social factors are increasingly important in the struggle against violence against women. A cross-cultural survey demonstrated the preventative force of economic independence in domestic violence.[6] Economic independence gives women the freedom to walk away from situations of acute crisis as well as the freedom to make important choices. In addition, economic vulnerability in the workplace has been shown to be a causative factor in sexual harassment. Dependent on their employers for a livelihood and vulnerable because of the lack of alternatives, women workers in free trade zones, for example, are often sexually harassed and have little recourse to justice.[7]

Constructions of sexuality play a defining role in the context of violence against women. Rape has been used historically for the subjugation of women and as a means of ensuring that women conform to the behavior patterns required by the community.[8] Fear of women's sexual activity has led to practices such as female genital mutilation. Women who do not conform to traditional sexual expectation, (i.e., sexuality only in the context of a legal, heterosexual marriage), are often the victims of violence in their communities. Compounding such violence are state laws and policies regulating sexuality, many of which result in strictures and violence that compromise women's autonomy and the right to make life choices.

Cultural and religious ideology also contribute to violence against women. Religious extremism in certain societies has led to the complete erasure of women from independent public life. Women are given strictures with regard to clothing and are only allowed to perform limited, if any, public functions.[9] In India, practices such as Sati and dowry have led to violence against women and, despite state attempts to eradicate these practices, some of the customs and traditions remain pervasive. In Western countries, so-called ''Christian Right'' activists have inflicted violence

---

5. For example, see the analysis in HUMAN RIGHTS WATCH/WOMEN'S RIGHTS PROGRAM, CRIMINAL INJUSTICE, VIOLENCE AGAINST WOMEN IN BRAZIL (1991).

6. DAVID LEVINSON, FAMILY VIOLENCE IN CROSS CULTURAL PERSPECTIVE (1989).

7. For example, *see* Carol Aloysius, *Working Women Need Protection from Sexual Harassment*, SRI LANKA SUNDAY OBSERVER, Mar. 23, 1993.

8. *See* SUSAN BROWNMILLER, AGAINST OUR WILL (1975).

9. The Taliban in Afghanistan are an example. *See* AMNESTY INTERNATIONAL, GRAVE ABUSES IN THE NAME OF RELIGION (1996).

against women who seek abortions, thereby restricting women's right to bodily integrity. The failure of states to comply with their international obligations to bring their customary and religious laws in line with international standards has been documented by women from around the world. The Declaration clearly states that the state should not invoke custom, tradition, or religion to justify violence against women.[10] Without strong state measures, it is unlikely that cultural and religious practices of violence against women will be eradicated in the vast majority of countries.

The women's movement has attempted to articulate the problems associated with violence against women in a number of ways. Liberal feminism has historically been concerned with equality and nondiscrimination in the workplace and in family law; issues of violence against women were not initially central to its agenda. It was socialist feminism that first attempted to articulate women's oppression and subordination in the home.[11] Socialist analysis was integrally linked to the dominant modes of production in any given society and the position of women was seen as being derivative of the economic and social forces which determined the contours of women's oppression. This notion that women's position is derivative of other social and economic forces continues to be prevalent among many women thinkers.[12]

In the late 1970s and 1980s, feminists began articulating a radical approach to violence. Seeing constructions of sexuality as central to women's oppression, they argued that women's oppression was not derivative of, but rather central to, patriarchy and the construction of the world along the lines of gender.[13] Working toward androgyny in male/female roles and attempting to protect women's reproductive autonomy, these groups were the main elements of the political movement that made violence against women an item on the international agenda. They saw sexuality, and violence directed against women because of that sexuality, as the major problem that informed the debate on violence against women and strove to create an international consensus aimed at eradicating violence against women in all societies.

The universality and essentialism of the earlier feminist movements are today under question. Although many of these earlier movements created networks of international solidarity and were instrumental in raising awareness and setting international standards, there have emerged schools of feminist thought, drawn from post-modernism, that question the facility with which universal assumptions about women are made. These schools of analysis are sensitive to cultural differences and, while committed to the goals of social justice, prefer to privilege local issues. These post-modernist inspired movements are very active at the grassroots level

---

10. Declaration, *supra* note 2, art. 4.

11. *See* F. ENGELS, THE ORIGIN OF THE FAMILY, PRIVATE PROPERTY AND THE STATE (1978).

12. *See* GAIL OMVEDT, VIOLENCE AGAINST WOMEN (1990).

13. *See* SHULAMITH FIRESTONE, THE DIALECTICS OF SEX (1979).

and are determined to carry out local agendas, leaving behind the era of meta-narratives and global theorization.[14]

At the same time that some feminists were moving toward privileging the local, other groups of feminists were moving in the opposite direction and becoming active players in international civil society. The international women's movement, with its focus on violence against women and women's human rights, created international linkages and sustained international lobbying that led to the creation of new standards on the human rights of women. These global networks continue to be active and continue to push for vigilance with regard to the eradication of violence against women at the national, regional, and international levels.[15]

The international women's movement has succeeded in highlighting interna-tional human rights norms that protect against violence against women as well as creating new norms necessary for the eradication of such violence. According to article 1 of the Universal Declaration of Human Rights, "all human beings are born free and equal in dignity and rights." Additionally all people are entitled to, as set forth in article 2, rights and freedoms without distinction with regard to sex and, according to article 3, "the right to life, liberty and security of person." Article 5 states that "no-one shall be subjected to torture [or] to cruel, inhuman or degrading treatment or punishment." Thus, the Universal Declaration articulates principles that prohibit violence and also provides for the full equality of women in the application of laws, rules, and procedures.[16]

Other international documents also provide for this general protection from arbitrary violence while enshrining the nondiscrimination principle. Articles 2 and 26 of the International Covenant on Civil and Political Rights (ICCPR) proscribe discrimination against women and provide for the equal protection of the law. In addition, article 6 and article 9 provide for the right to life and security of person and article 7 protects persons from torture. Read together, these announce a frame-work for the prohibition of violence against women.[17]

The prohibition on the use of violence against women during times of armed conflict is a principle of the laws of war. Article 27 of the Fourth Geneva Conven-tion states that "[w]omen shall be especially protected against any attack on their honor in particular against rape, enforced prostitution or any form of indecent

---

14. For an interesting approach, see Darini Rajasingham, *On Mediating Multiple Identities: The Shift-ing Field of Women's Sexualities within the Community, State and Nation, in* FROM BASIC NEEDS TO BASIC RIGHTS 233 (Margaret Schuler ed., 1995).

15. Charlotte Bunch, *Women's Rights as Human Rights: Toward a Re-Vision of Human Rights*, 12 HUM. RTS. Q. 486 (1990).

16. The Universal Declaration of Human Rights, *adopted* Dec. 10, 1948, G.A. Res. 217A (III), U.N. Doc. A/810, at 71 (1948).

17. The International Covenant on Civil and Political Rights, G.A. Res. 2200A (XXI), 21 U.N. GAOR Supp. (No. 16) at 52, U.N. Doc. A/6316 (1966).

assault.''[18] Similar principles are enshrined in Common Article 3 of the Geneva Conventions and Protocol II to the Conventions, both of which address internal armed conflicts.

Although the Women's Convention does not have a specific provision on violence against women, the U.N. Committee on the Elimination of Discrimination Against Women (CEDAW), in General Recommendation No. 19, interprets discrimination as encompassing all forms of violence against women. Defining gender-based violence as ''violence directed against a woman because she is a woman or which affects women disproportionately,'' Recommendation 19 requires states, in their reporting to CEDAW, to consider methods to combat and to report on violence against women.[19]

The document that unequivocally articulates standards and principles with regard to violence against women as an item on the agenda of international human rights is the United Nations Declaration on the Elimination of Violence Against Women. Despite its non-binding nature, the Declaration was passed unanimously by the United Nations General Assembly in December 1993, and therefore has the moral force of world consensus. A comprehensive document that identifies causes and suggests remedies for the eradication of violence against women, the Declaration is structured in three parts: a preamble, framing the issues of violence against women; the definition of violence against women and a breakdown of the manifestation of violence against women; and prescriptions for state action with regard to violence against women.

The Declaration also frames the issues of violence against women in terms of development, peace, and equality within United Nations strategies aimed at meeting these goals. With special reference to the Nairobi Forward Looking Strategies, the struggle against violence against women is seen as an integral part of a society's development goals. Violence against women is seen as an obstacle to development and the participation of women in national life. This ''developmental'' frame arises from and gives legitimacy to the issue of violence against women in various parts of the world.[20]

The Declaration is also seen as a culmination of the efforts made by the United Nations system on various aspects of women's equality. Though the Nairobi World Conference of Women is specifically mentioned, there is language in the text that implies that the many world conferences and international seminars sponsored by the United Nations with regard to the advancement of women played an important role in raising issues of violence against women internationally.[21]

---

18. Geneva Convention Relative to the Protection of Civilian Persons in Time of War, Aug. 12, 1949, 6 U.S.T. 3516, 75 U.N.T.S. 287.

19. U.N. Committee on the Elimination of Discrimination Against Women, General Recommendation 19 at 1, U.N. Doc. CEDAW/C/1992/L.1/Add.15 (1992).

20. Declaration, *supra* note 2, ¶¶ 3, 4.

21. *Id.* ¶ 4.

In addition to framing the concern of violence against women in terms of international standards, debates, and policies, the Declaration discusses the cause of violence against women, seeing its roots in the historically unequal power relations between men and women. Using words such as "domination," the Declaration clearly accepts the approach that violence against women is not endemic but is socially constructed and historically justified. This perspective ensures that it is a practice which the drafters feel can be eliminated with concerted intervention by the international community, states, and civil society actors.[22]

The Declaration also highlights certain target groups of women who are particularly susceptible to violence. These include women belonging to minority groups, indigenous women, refugee women, migrant women, women living in rural or remote communities, destitute women, women in detention, female children, women with disabilities, elderly women, and women in situations of armed conflict.[23] However, the Declaration clearly recognizes that violence against women is a pervasive phenomenon cutting across all social categories, including class, ethnicity, income, and culture.[24]

Having set out a general framework for the analysis of violence against women by the international community, the Declaration goes on to define violence against women as a legal phenomenon. The initial definition is broad, covering actual violence and the threat of violence with the emphasis on "coercion" as the litmus test. Most important, the Declaration minimizes the significance of the public/ private distinction traditionally used by states to negate responsibility for acts perpetrated within the "private" sphere. The Declaration defines violence against women as "any act of gender-based violence that results in, or is likely to result in, physical, sexual or psychological harm or suffering to women, including threats of such acts, coercion or arbitrary deprivation of liberty whether occurring in public or private life."[25]

The Declaration, in article 2, breaks violence against women into three categories: violence in the family, violence in the community, and violence perpetrated or condoned by the state. This three-tiered categorization provides activists and scholars with a tool for unpacking the many issues relating to violence against women. Though much of the violence overlaps among the categories, the categorization allows for a comprehensive understanding of the pervasive nature of violence that affects every sector of personal, social, and public life.[26]

After framing the issue and then defining the parameters of violence against women, the Declaration provides specific prescriptions with regard to state action on violence against women. Initially it calls on states to condemn violence and

---

22. *Id.* ¶ 6.

23. *Id.* ¶ 7.

24. *Id.* ¶ 8.

25. *Id.* art. 1.

26. *Id.* art. 2.

prohibits the invocation of custom, tradition, or religious considerations to avoid obligations. It also sets out a standard against which state conduct can be judged and evaluated: "States should pursue by all appropriate means and without delay a policy of eliminating violence against women and, to this end, should . . . exercise due diligence to prevent, investigate and, in accordance with national legislation, punish acts of violence against women, whether those acts are perpetrated by the State or by private persons."[27]

Having set a standard of due diligence to evaluate state competence, the Declaration goes on to outline areas for state activity. Article 4 contains a whole host of policy measures to be taken by the state. These include measures aimed at reforming legislation, restructuring and sensitizing the criminal justice system, setting up social services for women victims, and collecting data and revising educational curriculum to include violence against women. Finally it calls on states to comply with international standards, ratify international human rights instruments, and meet international obligations in their commitments to eliminate the problem of violence against women.

Violence Against Women: The Facts

Violence Against Women in the Family[28]

Violence against women includes:

[p]hysical, sexual and psychological violence occurring in the family, including battering, sexual abuse of female children in the household, dowry-related violence, marital rape, female genital mutilation and other traditional practices harmful to women, non-spousal violence and violence related to exploitation.[29]

According to the myth of family sanctity, in which tranquility and family harmony reign supreme, domestic violence exists as a veritable incongruity—a contradiction in terms. Violence shatters the peaceful image of the home—the safety that

---

27. *Id.* art. 4.

28. Often, as in the Declaration, domestic violence is labeled "family violence," the use of which raises certain conceptual issues. Within any discussion of family violence there must be an accompanying discussion, and ultimately a reconceptualization, of family. This, however, rarely occurs. Discussing domestic violence as family violence, without simultaneously questioning the nature of the family, negates the reality of women when those women or their experiences fail to fit neatly into traditional categories of family. Violence is erased from our consciousness as we allow ourselves to be manipulated by patriarchal systems, acquiescing in the reification of the family and condemning those women who exist outside that paradigm. This is not, however, to suggest that traditional family forms have no utility or to deny the potentiality of the family to serve as a center for care, compassion, support, and community. Rather than relying on the institutionalized definitions of family imputed by the state, however, notions of family should be recognized around expressions of these ideals. There is a need to make room for "difference and plurality" within our understanding of what constitutes family. *See* SUNILA ABEYESEKERA, WOMEN'S HUMAN RIGHTS QUESTIONS OF EQUALITY AND DIFFERENCE (Institute for Social Sciences Working Paper Series No. 186, Feb. 1995) for a discussion of the need to "reconceptualise principles of equality, justice and rights within a framework that is inclusive of difference and plurality."

29. Declaration, *supra* note 2, art. 2(a).

kinship, we are told, provides. Nonetheless, the insidious nature of domestic violence has been documented cross-nationally, cross-culturally, and in all regions of the world. Domestic violence, as one of the ''acts of violence based on gender—like acts of violence based on ethnicity, national origin, religion, and sexual identity—[is] not a random, isolated crime against an individual who happens to be female. Rather, domestic violence is a crime against an individual that is meant to terrorize the larger group or class of people—women.''[30]

At the most basic level, domestic violence is violence that occurs within the province of the domestic or private, generally between individuals who are related through intimacy, blood, or law. Despite the apparent neutrality of the term, domestic violence is invariably a gendered crime perpetrated by men against women. According to the United States Justice Department, women are 11 times more likely to be victims of domestic violence than are men.[31] Increasingly, domestic violence within gay and lesbian relationships is also being exposed.

Domestic violence is a violation of the human rights of women. Policies of the state, manifested by both state action and state inaction, perpetuate, support, and condone violence within the domestic sphere.[32] Domestic violence is utilized by both formal and informal actors to control women by controlling the one space universally dominated by women—the home. States, in their systematic failure to protect women from domestic violence perpetrated by private actors, conspire to deny women their human rights in contravention of international obligations.[33]

---

30. Leslie Wolfe & Lois Copeland, *Violence against Women as Bias-Motivated Hate Crime: Defining the Issues in the USA, in* WOMEN AND VIOLENCE 200, 200 (Miranda Davies ed., 1994). An example of particularly strong anti-hate crime legislation is California's law which defines a hate crime as:

> any act of intimidation, harassment, physical force or threat of physical force directed against any person, or family, or their property or advocate, motivated either in whole or in part by hostility to their real or perceived, ethnic background, national origin, religious belief, sex, age, disability, or sexual orientation, with the intention of causing fear and intimidation.

CAL. PENAL CODE ★ 13519.6(a) (West 1997).

31. Although, admittedly, the reverse does occur—women do strike out against their male partners—such incidents barely put a statistical dent into the gendered nature of domestic violence and most often result when women attempt to physically defend themselves against their abusive partners. Michele Ingrassia & Melinda Beck, *Patterns of Abuse,* NEWSWEEK, July 4, 1994, at 26 (citing Justice Department report of February 1994).

32. According to Rhonda Copelon:

> In the case of intimate violence, male supremacy ideology and conditions, rather than a distinct, consciously coordinated military establishment, confer upon men the sense of entitlement, if not the duty, to chastise their wives. Wife-beating is, therefore, not an individual, isolated, or aberrant act, but a social license, a duty or sign of masculinity, deeply ingrained in culture, widely practiced, denied and completely or largely immune from legal sanction.

RHONDA COPELON, *Intimate Terror: Understanding Domestic Violence as Torture, in* HUMAN RIGHTS OF WOMEN 116 (Rebecca Cook ed., 1994).

33. For a detailed explanation of the impediments to the treatment of domestic violence as a human rights violation, *see* Dorothy Q. Thomas & Michele E. Beasley, *Domestic Violence as a Human Rights Issue,* 15 HUM. RTS. Q. 36 (1993). Although the public-private dichotomy has been conveniently invoked

Corresponding with the stages of a woman's life are various forms of gender-based violence. Most of this violence is domestic violence—occurring within the home, perpetrated by those with whom the woman is closest. Even before birth, women are targeted by the discriminatory practices of sex-selective abortion and female infanticide. Once a girl-child progresses into infancy, violence manifests itself as enforced malnutrition, unequal access to medical care, and physical and emotional abuse. Incest, female genital mutilation, child marriage, the sale of children by their parents for prostitution or bonded labor, and other harmful traditional practices continue to plague girl-children into their adolescence when such violence is then compounded by violence associated with courtship. Throughout their adult lives, women become the victims and survivors of woman battering, marital rape, dowry violence, domestic murder, Sati, forced pregnancy, abortion, sterilization, widow and elder abuse, and violence that accompanies work as domestic servants.

Woman battering, or domestic assault, is the most common form of domestic violence.[34] Such violence is characterized by the use of physical, psychological, or sexual force by the dominant domestic partner (recognizing the overwhelming probability that this partner is male in a heterosexual domestic relationship) for the purpose of intimidating, manipulating, or coercing the subordinate partner (who will most likely be female in a heterosexual relationship).[35] Woman battering often includes various methods of torturous physical, psychological, emotional, financial, and sexual violence. At its most extreme, woman battering leads to domestic murder or femicide.

Marital rape is a particularly pernicious and common form of domestic violence rarely recognized as a ''legal possibility'' by the state. The general belief that marriage provides a husband unlimited sexual access to his wife fuels the difficulties with legal recognition of marital rape as a crime. Increasingly, as a result of work by women's groups, martial rape is being recognized and prohibited by the criminal laws of many countries.

Although batterers justify their violence by any number of actions or omissions undertaken by their partners, batterers, like the purveyors of torture,[36] use an often debilitating combination of physical and psychological violence in a process of

---

by states in order to avoid responsibility for protecting women from violence in their homes, at the same time, states have continued to use their power to regulate the private sphere through statutory and customary laws on marriage, divorce, reproduction, custody, and sexuality as well as other personal laws regarding nationality, property, and inheritance rights. ''The family is indubitably a political unit—guided, promoted, protected and sanctioned by a formal civil or religious authority, or both.'' Seble Dawit, *Culture as a Human Rights Concern: Highlights for Action with the African Charter on Human and Peoples' Rights, in* GENDER VIOLENCE AND WOMEN'S HUMAN RIGHTS IN AFRICA (Center for Women's Global Leadership ed., 1994).

34. LEVINSON, *supra* note 6.

35. This definition attempts to encompass the many manifestations of domestic violence, specifically domestic violence in same-sex relationships, while maintaining the gendered nature of such violence.

36. *See* Rhonda Copelon, *Recognizing the Egregious in the Everyday: Domestic Violence as Torture*, 25 COLUM. HUM. RTS. L. REV 291, 308 (1994) for a discussion of domestic violence as a form of torture.

domination and the exertion of control meant to destabilize and victimize the woman, rendering her powerless.[37] Psychological abuse resulting from the spoken word, limitations on and control of social mobility, and deprivation of economic resources generally accompany physical battering.

Laws

The remedy for victims of domestic violence provided by the criminal law has traditionally been more theoretical than practical. Even without specific statutes on domestic violence, laws against general assault, battery, manslaughter, and murder, among others, should provide remedies for women and girl-children in cases of domestic violence. Except in the case of marital rape, general criminal prohibitions have not explicitly excluded criminal behavior committed within the family. However, because of the "hands-off" approach traditionally assumed by law enforcement agents and the judiciary in cases occurring within the private sphere, such laws have not been invoked to punish perpetrators of domestic violence.[38] Although the myth of high levels of complaint withdrawal among victims of domestic violence has been proven false, the excuse is still commonly used to justify non-prosecution.[39]

Mandatory Arrest

Police, although potentially well positioned to effectively address domestic violence, rarely are well trained. Studies have shown that, when called for domestic violence cases, police throughout the world often try to mediate or counsel the couple rather than treating the incident like a criminal matter.[40] Compounding police inaction are prosecutors, who often refer domestic violence cases to civil courts rather than treating them as criminal matters.

In response to police and prosecutorial failings, some jurisdictions in Canada, Australia, and the United States have adopted mandatory arrest and pro-charging policies that require police and prosecutors to treat domestic violence cases in the same way as any other criminal matter: as a crime perpetrated against the state. Although many advocates support such measures, contending that they appropriately shift responsibility for the violence from the victim to the state, some advocates warn that mandatory arrest and pro-charging policies are contrary to the survivor's best interests and threaten to further weaken her position by taking away her control over the proceedings.[41]

---

37. *See* Peggy Miller & Nancy Biele, *Twenty Years Later: The Unfinished Revolution*, in TRANSFORMING A RAPE CULTURE 47, 49 (Emilie Buchwald et al. eds., 1993); DOMESTIC ABUSE INTERVENTION PROJECT, POWER AND CONTROL WHEEL (visually demonstrates the cycle of power and control).

38. JANE FRANCIS CONNORS, VIOLENCE AGAINST WOMEN IN THE FAMILY 68, U.N. Doc. ST/CSDHA/2 (1989).

39. *Id.* at 56; *see also* Lisa A. Frisch, *Research That Succeeds, Policies That Fail*, 83 J. CRIM. L. & CRIMINOLOGY 209 (1992).

40. CONNORS, *supra* note 38.

41. *See* Kathleen J. Ferraro, *Cops, Courts and Woman Battering*, in VIOLENCE AGAINST WOMEN: THE BLOODY FOOTPRINTS 165 (Pauline B. Bart and Eileen Geil Moran eds., 1993).

Protection Orders

Perhaps the most widely utilized civil remedy for domestic violence is the order of protection or restraining order, which generally forbids abusers from having any contact with the victim/survivor, provides a mechanism for arrest if further contact or violence occurs, furnishes women with protection absent criminal sanctions, and in some cases excludes the abuser from the shared home. These orders, however, are often rendered ineffective when they are introduced absent mechanisms to address practical policy considerations. Issues such as the definition of abuse, the definition of the requisite relationship between the victim and perpetrator, and the costs or legal expertise involved in acquiring a protection order are ones that may serve to undermine the practicality of protection or restraining orders.[42]

Tort and Delict

Tort and delict remedies that provide financial compensation for civil wrongs may also be available to victim/survivors of domestic violence. Survivors of domestic violence, or families of murdered victims, not only may pursue such civil causes of action against the abusive husband but also against law enforcement officials who fail to provide adequate protection to individual victims.[43] In many jurisdictions, however, where marital relationships may exempt husbands from being sued by their wives either directly or effectively because of the woman's status as legal minor, a civil cause of action against the husband is a legal impossibility.

Divorce

Matrimonial relief, or divorce, provides a remedy for victim/survivors of domestic violence in cases in which a marital relationship exists. Laws—including the customary, personal, religious, and secular—on marriage, divorce, property, inheritance, and legal status often undermine married women's autonomy, making them particularly vulnerable to violence and abuse. Uganda and Kenya, for example, have laws forbidding divorce within the first three years of marriage, after which divorce becomes a legal possibility with many practical impediments.[44] The woman seeking divorce has the burden of proving that her husband has committed adultery and has deserted her for a minimum of two years, or the burden of proving he committed adultery and was cruel.[45] Such laws pose particular obstacles for women trafficked for marriage, as they are often kept in prison-like conditions and, thus, unable to gather evidence of adultery, the key to divorce.

---

42.   CONNORS, *supra* note 38, at 69–71.

43.   Douglas D. Scherer, *Tort remedies for victims of domestic abuse* 3 S.C. L. REV. 543 (1992).

44.   MARJAN WIJERS & LIN LAP-CHE, TRAFFICKING IN WOMEN, FORCED LABOR AND SLAVERY-LIKE PRACTICES IN MARRIAGE, DOMESTIC LABOR AND PROSTITUTION 49 (Foundation against Trafficking in Women & Global Alliance Against Traffic in Women eds., preliminary report publicly released April, 1997).

45.   *Id.*

Marital law regimes can be broken down into three groups: general common law based on a European model, customary law as a product of colonialism in which local leaders worked with colonial leaders to codify "custom," and religious laws which are derived from religious texts.[46] General common law systems allow for divorce based on the irretrievable breakdown of the marriage. Within customary law marital regimes, divorce is generally technically possible but strongly discouraged. Such discouragement may intensify in systems in which it is the practice to pay bride price or lobola. In some religiously based marital law regimes, such as those based on Roman Catholic canon law in Ireland and Chile, divorce is prohibited. While women may be able to divorce their husbands because of cruelty, marital law regimes based on Islamic law often greatly restrict a woman's ability to obtain a divorce.[47]

Specific Domestic Violence Legislation

It is argued that comprehensive domestic violence legislation that specifically prohibits domestic violence is by far the most effective legal mechanism in addressing domestic violence. Remedies under this type of legislation include protection from violence and threats of violence, provisions for the safety and security of the victim, her dependents, and property, and assistance in continuing her life without further disruption.

Although the criminal justice system is often utilized only as a last resort, legislation has important normative value in its ability to send a message to the general society, as well as to both victims/survivors and perpetrators, that domestic violence is a serious crime that will not be tolerated. The mere promulgation or existence of legislation, however, can also serve to mask the lack of genuine political will. Weak laws combined with a lack of political will to effectuate such laws can undermine the utility of the laws themselves. It is for this reason that comprehensive laws that include provisions for services, mechanisms of oversight, and financial resources are imperative.

Alternatively, special police stations for violence against women have been effective in giving force to laws on domestic violence and combating traditional police failings in addressing domestic violence. Since the establishment of the first *delegacia da mulher* or women's precinct, a specialized unit that works exclusively with victims of violence against women, in Sao Paulo, Brazil, in 1985, similar units have been established throughout most of the states in Brazil.[48] Brazil's success has inspired the neighboring Colombia and Peru to institute their own versions of the

---

46. Although there is a general lack of uniformity even within each of these three marital law regimes, generalizations have been made regarding the availability of relief in cases of domestic violence. Connors, *supra* note 38, at 66.

47. *Id.*

48. Catherine Tinker & Silvia Pimentel, Violence in the Family: Human Rights, Criminal Law, and the New Constitution in Brazil (unpublished manuscript, on file with office of the U.N. Special Rapporteur on violence against women).

specialized units. The *delegacias* approach domestic violence in a multi-disciplinary fashion, providing comprehensive support to women including social, legal, psychological, housing, health, and day care services.

Traditional Practices of Violence Against Women

In many, if not most societies, women are subjected to violence because of some form of traditional or cultural practice. It could be argued that violence against women *per se* is inherent in patriarchal traditions and culture. The ways in which such violence manifests itself, however, are particularized within the community and generally overtly sanctioned at some level as a product of tradition or culture. Traditiional practices that have been identified internationally as violative of women's human rights include female genital mutilation, son preference, gender difference in nutrition, early childhood marriage, violence related to dowry, widow burning, and virginity testing.

Many traditions and customs harmful to women raise complicated issues of culpability, as it is often female relatives or community members who directly inflict the harm. Human rights law, however, recognizes that it is the state's duty to protect the human rights of its citizens and, thus, irrespective of the private role of the individual perpetrating the violence, shifts legal culpability to the state.

Despite some state's efforts at reviving cultural relativist arguments to defend such practices, the Convention on the Elimination of All Forms of Discrimination against Women, the Convention on the Rights of the Child, the Declaration on the Elimination of Violence against Women, and the Beijing Declaration and Platform for Action all direct states to refrain from invoking custom, tradition, culture, or religious considerations to obviate their international human rights obligations with respect to the elimination of all forms of violence against women.

Female Genital Mutilation

The number of sexually mutilated women and girl-children in Africa and in some parts of Asia had increased to 100 million by 1994. According to the World Health Organization, two million girls are estimated to be at risk of the practices each year—most of them live in 26 African countries, a few in Asian countries, and their numbers are increasing among immigrant populations in Europe, Australia, Canada, and the United States.[49]

Female genital mutilation takes various forms. Clitoridectomy entails the partial or total removal of the clitoris, and excision requires the removal of the clitoris, and the labia minora. Clitoridectomy and excision account for 85 percent of all cases of female genital mutilation. The most extreme form, infibulation, requires the complete removal of the clitoris and the labia minora, as well as the inner surface of the labia majora; the vulva is then stitched together so that only a

---

49. Fran P. Hosken, The Hosken Report: Genital and Sexual Mutilation of Females (4th ed. 1994).

small opening is preserved in the vagina to allow for the passage of urine and menstrual blood.[50]

Violence associated with female genital mutilation has been proven to cause grave physical and psychological damage to women and girls, both in the short and long term. The pain and trauma itself may scar the minds of young women. Sexual intercourse and childbirth may be extremely painful, often resulting in complications. Additionally, other health consequences such as hemorrhage, shock, infection, tetanus, gangrene, urine retention, injury to adjacent tissue, as well as more long-term problems such as bleeding, infertility, incontinence, fistulae and, increasingly, HIV/AIDS, have been recorded.

Some countries, in a response to lobbying by women's groups for the eradication of female genital mutilation, have moved toward the "medicalization" of the practice, undertaking the operations in clinical conditions to reduce the health risks. The World Health Organization, however, is unequivocally opposed to the institutionalization of the practice.[51]

Laws

Increasingly, laws are being promulgated in an attempt to curb the incidence of female genital mutilation. One of the most progressive legal measures undertaken thus far is Ethiopia's constitutionalization of the issue, which states that "women have the right to protection by the State from harmful customs [and that l]aws, customs and practices that oppress women or cause bodily or mental harm to them are prohibited." With the exception of some Northern states where female genital mutilation is practiced by immigrant populations, few countries have legislation prohibiting female genital mutilation.

In Australia, a uniform legislative approach is currently being pursued through the Standing Committee of Attorneys-General. The government has agreed in principle to provide funding for the development of a national education program. The United Kingdom's Prohibition of Female Circumcision Act of 1985 makes it an offense to excise, infibulate, or otherwise mutilate the whole or any part of the labia majora or labia minor or clitoris of another person, or to aid, abet, counsel, or procure the performance by another person of any of those acts on that other person's own body unless such an act is carried out as part of a necessary surgical operation. The Criminal Section of the Court of Cassation in France, in its decision of August 20, 1983, established the principle that the ablation of the clitoris, resulting from willful acts of violence, constitutes mutilation. This decision was based on provisions of the criminal code that penalize assault and battery if the offense has resulted in the "mutilation, amputation or deprivation of the use of a limb, blindness, the loss of an eye or other permanent disability or death without intent."

---

50.   WORLD HEALTH ORGANIZATION, DIVISION OF FAMILY HEALTH, FEMALE GENITAL MUTILATION—THE PRACTICE (1994).

51.   *Id.*

Son Preference

According to the Working Group on Traditional Practices affecting the Health of Women and Children of the U.N. Sub-Commission on the Prevention of Discrimination and the Protection of Minorities, son preference is "the preference of the parents for male children which often manifests itself in neglect, deprivation or discriminatory treatment of girls to the detriment of their mental and physical health." The parental preference for male children, however, is fueled by larger social, cultural, and economic forces.

Indeed, "[t]he persistence in India of cultural practices that discriminate against girls and women means not only the abuse but, finally, the deaths of countless women."[52] In countries such as India and China, where strong cultural and traditional biases in favor of male children already exist, technological advances are used to the detriment of women. For example, the use of amniocentesis and sonograms to detect the sex of a fetus leads to the abortion of thousands of female fetuses. According to a study in one clinic in India, 7,997 out of 8,000 aborted fetuses were female; another survey found that, in one year, 40,000 female fetuses were aborted in Bombay.[53] Within cultures with high levels of son preference, female infanticide provides an alternative for women who do not have access to amniocentesis, sonograms, and abortion.

China's one-child policy demonstrates the interlinkages between state-condoned violence and traditional practices harmful to women. Through China's official one-child policy, the government of China intrudes into the domestic sphere by regulating and restricting the number of children a married couple may have and, at times, by violently enforcing the policy.[54] In a culture where son preference is widespread, the policy encourages and, ultimately, sanctions sex-selective abortions of female fetuses and female infanticide. In 1994, in China, 117 boys were born for every 100 girls, a figure significantly higher than the world average of 106 males to every 100 females. Consequently, approximately 500,000 more male children than female children are born each year in China.[55]

Other Practices

Traditional arranged marriage and related practices still prevail in a number of societies, especially in the Asian and African regions. The consequences of such practices range from death as a result of dowry debts to early marriage, childhood pregnancy, nutritional taboos, and bride and widow burning. In many societies the bride's family must pay dowry to the groom prior to marriage. Additionally, the

---

52. Indira Jaising, *Violence against women: the Indian perspective in women's human rights, in* WOMEN'S RIGHTS, HUMAN RIGHTS: INTERNATIONAL FEMINIST PERSPECTIVES 51 (Julie Peters & Andrea Wolper eds., 1995).

53. *Id.*

54. AMNESTY INTERNATIONAL, WOMEN IN CHINA IMPRISONED AND ABUSED FOR DISSENT (1995).

55. *Id.*

expenses for the marriage are borne by the bride's family. Failure to provide the agreed amount of dowry in many cases leads to violence against the new bride. Such violence manifests itself as verbal abuse, mental and physical torture, and, in certain communities, murder at the hands of the husband and/or his family members.

Child marriage is intended to guarantee a woman's virginity, reduce the number of mouths her family must feed, and ensure a long cycle of fertility to produce many sons. Yet early marriage generally leads to childhood pregnancy which, in turn, lessens the life expectancy of women, adversely affects their health, nutrition, education, and employment opportunities, and lowers their economic participation rates. According to a WHO report, over 50 percent of first births in many developing countries are to women who are under the age of 19.[56]

In many societies, the treatment of widows by the family and community results in grave human rights violations. In India, in certain areas, this treatment has extremely violent overtones, including in some cases the historic practice of Sati, or the immolation of women on their husbands' funeral pyres. Despite a legal ban on the practice, cases of Sati and the religious glorification of Sati shrines has caused renewed concern.

Laws

The governments of India and Bangladesh have sought to criminalize violence related to dowry. The Indian penal code contains provisions that allow for such crimes to be proven by circumstantial evidence and strengthen police powers to investigate suspected dowry violence. Additionally, dowry deaths carry the maximum penalty.[57]

Sati was banned in India by the British in 1825. After the death of Roop Kanwar on her husband's funeral pyre in 1987, renewed calls for state action to restrict such violence were heard. In response, the government of India passed the Sati (Prevention of Glorification) Act. Nonetheless, the state continues to tolerate rituals that glorify the practice.

Child Abuse

While the abuse of children in the form of physical, psychological, and sexual violence is perpetrated against both male and female children, there are gendered dimensions. An estimated 90 percent of victims of child sexual abuse are girl children. More than 90 percent of the perpetrators of child sexual abuse are men.

---

56. World Health Organization, Women, Health and Development (1985).

57. UNICEF, South Asia Regional Office, Working Papers presented to the Second United Nations Regional Seminar on Harmful Traditional Practices affecting the Health of Women and Children, U.N. Doc. E/CN.4/Sub.2/1994/10.

In 85 percent of the cases in the United States, the offender is a member of the child's family or someone with whom the child has a relationship.[58]

There has been a documented link between woman battering and child abuse. In the United States, for example, the rate of child abuse in violent domestic situations is 1,500 percent the national average.[59] Children who live in homes in which their mother is abused risk injury or even death at the hands of their mothers abuser if they intervene in, or inadvertently become involved in, a violent episode. Attempts by children to intervene or to protect their mothers not only have led to injury of the child but also have led children to kill their fathers.

Children from violent homes make up a disproportionately high percentage of street children throughout the world. In Bogota, Colombia, for example, a study by the Metropolitan Police documented that 1,299 children were living on the streets after being forced from homes in which domestic violence occurred. Of these children, a reported 389 children were prostitutes, 32 were beggars, and 122 were drug-addicted.[60]

Violence Against Women in the Community [61]

Violence against women includes:

[p]hysical, sexual and psychological violence occurring within the general community, including rape, sexual abuse, sexual harassment and intimidation at work, in educational institutions and elsewhere, trafficking in women and forced prostitution.[62]

Rape and Sexual Violence

A destructive combination of power, anger, and sex fuels sexual violence against women.[63] Rape and sexual violence occur at many levels of society and in numerous distinct settings. Although all forms are connected as manifestations of sexual

---

58. *Child Sexual Abuse: Why the Silence Must be Broken—Notes from the Pacific Region, in* WOMEN AND VIOLENCE 97, 105 (Miranda Davies ed., 1994).

59. UNITED STATES SENATE COMMITTEE ON THE JUDICIARY, REPORT ON VIOLENCE AGAINST WOMEN ACT 37 (1994).

60. CONNORS, *supra* note 38, at 23 (citing M.I. Plata, case study from Colombia (Bogota Population Center, 1987)).

61. Community is a social space outside the family but not fully under the control of the state. For most women, the community provides the contours for the enjoyment of social space; it determines the nature of their social interactions and the type of values that will condition their lives. The community, however, is also the site of violence against women, often manifesting as restrictions on and regulations of female sexuality. With regard to women's human rights, the term community is, therefore, a Janus-faced concept. On the one hand, the community is often a nurturing space that provides women with social support and solidarity; on the other hand, the community is often the site for the denial of women's rights.

62. Declaration, *supra* note 2, art. 2(b).

63. GAIL ABARBANEL & GLORIA RICHMAN, THE RAPE VICTIM 11 (Rape Treatment Center of Santa Monica Hospital ed., 1989).

violence against women, they are simultaneously distinct in that particularized strategies are necessary in order to provide appropriate remedies. The Indian Forum against the Oppression of Women has enumerated nine distinct forms of rape: 1) communal rape; 2) gang rape; 3) political rape; 4) rape of minors; 5) marital rape; 6) army rape (in situations of war or "peacekeeping"); 7) institutional rape (in hospitals, remand homes, prisons, etc.); 8) rape in economically dependent circumstances; and 9) rape within political organizations.[64]

Sexual violence "is an intrusion into the most private and intimate parts of a woman's body, as well as an assault on the core of her self."[65] Many victims/survivors of rape report experiencing feelings of annihilation as a consequence of being raped. Such feelings arise from the very nature of rape, a direct attack on the self.

The victims/survivor's trauma often is exacerbated after the rape through her interactions with both her community and state structures. Unlike any other crime, women who are raped are blamed for the crimes committed against them; they are publicly chastised, disbelieved, accused of having ulterior motives, and subjected to degrading questions with often pornographic overtones.[66] When women do report the sexual crimes committed against them, prosecution rates are low. Cases that make their way through the criminal justice system run into systemic obstacles and discrimination. Unreasonable evidentiary requirements, the rejection of the victim's uncorroborated testimony, the focus on the woman's character and resistance, the emphasis on the overt use of force, and demands that the victim prove her chastity all serve as obstacles to prosecution and as deterrence for reporting the crime.

A national probability sample of 1,835 women at 95 colleges and universities in Canada found that 23.3 percent of the women had been victims of rape or attempted rape.[67] In Jakarta, Indonesia, city police recorded 2,300 cases of sexual violence against women in 1992; 3,200 cases in 1993; and 3,000 in the first half of 1994.[68] A survey of 2,270 adult women in Seoul, Republic of Korea, found that approximately 22 percent of adult women had been the victim of either attempted

---

64. FORUM AGAINST THE OPPRESSION OF WOMEN, *Women's Organizations against Rape in India: Report of a National Meeting, in* WOMEN AND VIOLENCE 60–62 (Miranda Davies ed., 1994).

65. ABARBANEL & RICHMAN, *supra* note 63, at 1. The best descriptions of the consequences of rape for the rape victims come from survivors themselves. According to one survivor, "[i]t's not just your body that's raped, it's your whole life." *Id.*

66. CENTER FOR CONSTITUTIONAL RIGHTS, A CALL TO ACTION, GOVERNMENTAL FAILURE TO INVESTIGATE AND PROSECUTE RAPE: A VIOLATION OF WOMEN'S HUMAN RIGHTS 1 (1995).

67. LORI L. HEISE ET AL., VIOLENCE AGAINST WOMEN, THE HIDDEN HEALTH BURDEN 10 (World Bank Discussion Paper No. 255) (1994), (*citing* WALTER DEKESEREDY & KATHERINE KELLY, PERSONAL COMMUNICATION, AND PRELIMINARY DATA FROM FIRST NATIONAL STUDY ON DATING VIOLENCE IN CANADA BY THE FAMILY VIOLENCE PREVENTION DIVISION, DEPARTMENT OF HEALTH AND WELFARE, OTTAWA, CANADA (1993)).

68. T. Sima Gunawan & Rita A. Widiadana, *Rape, Violence Rock the Country,* JAKARTA POST, July 30, 1995, at 1.

rape or rape.[69] A 1991 New Zealand study found that 25.3 percent of the respondents reported having been subjected to either an attempted or a completed rape.[70] In 1993 in Poland, 1,313 rape cases were reported to the police; this was a 40 percent increase in the number of rapes reported in 1981.[71] According to Russia's Ministry for Social Protection, out of the 331,815 reported crimes against women in Russia in 1993, 14,000 of them were rapes.[72] In the United Kingdom, a sample survey of 1,476 university and polytechnic women found that 19.4 percent of them had been the victim of sexual violence.[73] One study in the United States estimated that a minimum of 12.1 million American women have been victims of rape at least once in their lifetime.[74]

Traditionally, rape victims have had very little power to impact the legal proceedings in rape prosecutions because, like all criminal cases, the injured party is the state rather than the survivor. The nature of rape, however, is unlike other crimes. In addition to the violence of the act, the loss of power and control over one's own body, which victims/survivors report to be one of the fundamental experiences of rape, is often re-experienced throughout judicial proceedings. During the course of her testimony, the survivor will be forced to dwell on every detail of the attack and to reveal intimate details of her life. Her credibility will be attacked and her reputation challenged. Moreover, some feminist scholars have pointed out the pornographic posturing of many cross-examinations.[75] Even if the state manages to succeed in getting a conviction, judges in rape cases are notorious for giving lenient sentences to rapists.

Laws

Traditionally, rape has been legally categorized as a crime against morality. Although this is changing in many countries as rape is being legally defined as a

---

69. HEISE, *supra* note 67, at 10 (*citing* YOUNG-HEE SHIM, SEXUAL VIOLENCE AGAINST WOMEN IN KOREA: A VICTIMIZATION SURVEY OF SEOUL WOMEN (1992)).

70. *Id.* (*citing Nicola Gavey, Sexual Victimization Prevalence Among New Zealand University Students,* 59 J. CONSULTING & CLINICAL PSYCHOL. 464)).

71. THE SITUATION OF WOMEN IN POLAND, THE REPORT OF THE NGOs' COMMITTEE 50 (1995) (*citing* B. FISZER, PRZEMOC WOBEC KOBIET W POLSCE 28 (Federation for the Advancement of Women and Family Planning ed., 1994)).

72. RUSSIAN ASSOCIATION OF CRISIS CENTERS FOR WOMEN, VIOLENCE AGAINST WOMEN IN RUSSIA: RESEARCH, EDUCATION, AND ADVOCACY PROJECT 1 (1995) (*citing* Boris Dolotin, quoting statistics from the Prosecutor General's Office). Notably, 14,500 women were murdered by their partners or husbands. *Id.*

73. HEISE, *supra* note 67, at 10 (*citing* VALERIE BEATTIE, ANALYSIS OF THE RESULTS OF A SURVEY ON SEXUAL VIOLENCE IN THE UK (1992)).

74. BEVERLY BALOS & MARY LOUISE FELLOWS, LAW AND VIOLENCE AGAINST WOMEN, CASES AND MATERIALS ON SYSTEMS OF OPPRESSION 355 (1994) (citing David Johnston, *Survey Shows Number of Rapes Far Higher Than Official Figures,* N.Y. TIMES, Apr. 24, 1992, at A9).

75. *See* Carol Smart, *Feminism and the Power of Law,* excerpted in BALOS & FELLOWS, *supra* note 74, at 437.

crime against the person or a crime against physical integrity, many countries have retained the legal link between rape and morality. The laws in many Latin American countries, for example, maintain this perspective.[76]

A male standard pervades legal definitions of rape, a crime overwhelmingly committed by men against women.[77] The legal definition of rape in most countries is limited to nonconsensual or forced vaginal penetration. By focusing on penetration, legal definitions emphasize the male perspective of the acceptable boundaries of heterosexual sex rather than the victim's experience of sexualized violence. Some jurisdictions have broadened their definitions of rape to include acts other than penile penetration.

In some countries there have been attempts at reforming laws to adopt a system of gradation with regard to sexual violence. Systems of gradation, whereby the crime is classified, for example, as first degree or second degree sexual assault, are now routinely employed to improve prosecution and conviction rates. Gradation schemes, however, privilege the physical over the sexual violence, and thus undermine the seriousness of sexual violence unaccompanied by physical violence.[78]

Consent has emerged as the legal dividing line between rape and sexual intercourse. In court, the battle over whether the victim did or did not consent often degenerates into a contest of wills and credibility. Not only is it a question of who the judge or jury believes, but it becomes an issue of how, and how forcefully, the victim's non-consent was conveyed. Cases, such as the Mathura judgment in India, have held that the lack of physical injury amounts to consent.[79]

---

76.   In Peru and Bolivia, rape is a crime against good customs whereas in Panama it is a crime against virtue and sexual liberty; Honduras' law frames it in terms of sexual liberty and honesty. Underlying Guatemala's law is the preservation of liberty, sexual security, and virtue. Conversely, Nicaragua, which has the most progressive rape law under Latin America's traditional criminal codes, classifies rape within its crimes against persons. Angela Alvarado, *Rape: The Debate and Limitations of the Social and Legal Dimension, in* WOMEN: WATCHED AND PUNISHED 125, 126 (CLADEM ed., 1993).

77.   Susan Estrich, *Rape*, 95 YALE L.J. 1087 (1986), *excerpted in* BALOS & FELLOWS, *supra* note 74, at 421.

78.   According to the New Zealand Department of Justice and the Institute of Criminology:

The stress upon the violent rather than the sexual component of the offence in determining its seriousness, especially in the New South Wales and Canadian models, is not in keeping with the way in which most victims described their rape experience. . . . They saw it as an act of extreme humiliation and degradation which was qualitatively different from other types of assaults. Victims who had been beaten felt that the act of sexual intercourse rather than the assault was the primary injury. Some felt that the beating and bruising they received assisted them in the criminal justice process, while the rape itself wasn't accorded the centrality it deserved. Any legislation highlighting the violent component of the offence at the expense of the sexual violation involved, would therefore seem to be at odds with the perception of many victims.

DEPARTMENT OF JUSTICE AND THE INSTITUTE OF CRIMINOLOGY, RAPE STUDY, A DISCUSSION OF LAW AND PRACTICE 109 (1983).

79.   FLAVIA, JOURNEY TO JUSTICE, PROCEDURES TO BE FOLLOWED IN A RAPE CASE (1990). A 1958 case asserted the legal position on consent in India:

A mere act of helpless resignation in the face of inevitable compulsion, quiescence, non-

There are two distinct ways in which the issue of consent has been incorporated into rape legislation—either as an element of the crime or as an affirmative defense to the crime. If lack of consent is built into the crime as an element then the prosecution must assume the burden of proving the absence of consent beyond a reasonable doubt. However, if the crime of rape is defined without reference to the issue of consent and consent is instead alleged as an affirmative defense, the burden, to both raise the issue of consent and proof of consent shifts to the accused. Although there is a growing trend toward redefining rape and relocating the issue of consent outside the elements of the crime, it is still overwhelmingly defined in such terms of consent. In the 1983 amendments to the Indian Penal Code, the burden of proving the lack of consent was shifted to the accused in cases of custodial rape.[80]

In many countries, penal codes, criminal procedure, or judicial construction under the common law require that the testimony of the victim be corroborated. Such requirements were challenged, and consequently repealed, in many jurisdictions during the 1980s. Nonetheless, in many cases judges continue to require circumstantial evidence—such as physical injuries, torn clothing, or the presence of semen—to corroborate the victim's story. These requirements fail to account for the fact that, in many cases, the victim's life may depend on her "cooperation" with the rapist, thereby precluding the likelihood that there will be physical evidence of a struggle.

Medical examinations generally are necessary in order to collect evidence for prosecution of rape. Evidentiary requirements vary widely, often dictating how intrusive the process will be. In India, where a woman's virginity becomes an issue for the defense in cases where the victim/survivor is single and perhaps not a virgin, doctors may perform a "finger test." This test determines virginity based on the number of fingers that can be inserted into a woman's vagina.[81]

Such testing derives from and legitimates widespread social perspectives that link virginity with rape-ability, classifying "loose" women (including prostitutes) as "unrape-able." Some laws have gone so far as to formally exclude prostitutes from the protection of rape legislation. More common, however, are laws and evidentiary rules that create a *de facto* exclusion by allowing evidence of the victim's sexual history and making the issue of virginity legally relevant. Such laws

---

resistance or passive giving in, when volitional faculty is either crowded by fear or vitiated by duress, cannot be deemed to be consent as understood in law. Consent on the part of a woman, as a defense to an allegation of rape, requires voluntary participation, not only after the exercise of intelligence based on the knowledge of the significance and moral quality of the act, but after having fully exercised the choice between resistance and assent. *Submission of her body under the influence of fear or terror is no consent. There is a difference between consent and submission.* Every consent involves submission but the converse does not always follow and a mere act of submission does not involve consent.

Rao Harnarain Singh v. State of Punjab, 1958 Cri.LJ 563 (India). (Emphasis added). Twenty years later, however, this position was reversed by the Mathura judgment. FLAVIA, *supra,* at 49.

80. FLAVIA, *supra* note 79, at 47.

81. *Id.* at 29.

generally exist side by side with strict restrictions on the admissibility of the accused rapist's history of sexual violence.

Rape shield laws were designed to protect victims of rape from traditionally discriminatory and abusive cross-examination. Such laws, which have been widely enacted in the United States, limit the admissibility of evidence relating to the victim's past sexual conduct with anyone but the defendant. The scope of protection actually provided by rape shield statutes, however, varies widely.[82]

Statutory rape laws are a mechanism by which the state attempts to define those who are legally incapable of consent. Laws on statutory rape are constructed around age, specifically the age at which a young woman becomes legally "capable" of consensual sex. Generally, what is lacking in statutory rape legislation is a conceptualization in terms of power relationships. Statutory rape laws decontextualize sex, rape, power, and control for those under the age of consent.[83]

Criminal prosecution is not the only legal mechanism for redress for rape victims. Civil suits provide potential remedies as well. The general tort law of most countries provides private causes of action for intentional torts such as assault, battery, and the intentional infliction of emotional distress. The benefit of civil claims is the lower standard of proof. Rather than proving guilt beyond a reasonable doubt—necessary in criminal proceedings—the plaintiff must only prove guilt based on a "preponderance of the evidence." Thus, issues of consent, force, and resistance are less likely to be obstacles in obtaining redress.

Sexual Harassment

Sexual harassment must be understood to exist on the continuum of sexual violence against women. It is akin to rape in the terror that it instills in women. Sexual harassment frequently occurs on the street, in the workplace, in educational institutions, and on public transportation. It is a very personal attack on women's minds and bodies, instilling fear and violating a woman's right to bodily integrity, education, and freedom of movement. According to one advocate, "[s]exual harassment strikes at the heart of women's economic self-sufficiency."[84] Women are nine times more likely than are men to leave their job because of sexual harassment.

---

82. According to Estrich: "[W]hen rape shield laws are needed to protect women in hard cases, the statutes present a very mixed picture. Some are just plain poorly drafted and provide only illusory protections. And even some of the better ones contain loopholes which defense attorneys, in today's environment, may be able to use to swallow the rule." Susan Estrich, *Palm Beach Stories*, 11 LAW & PHIL. 5, 21 (1992).

83. Statutory rape laws treat a fifteen-year-old boy who has consensual intercourse with his fifteen-year-old girlfriend the same, functionally if not legally, as a thirty-year-old man who has intercourse with a fifteen-old-year girl. The power dynamics implicit in the second scenario raise the issue of incapacity to consent in a more profound manner than the first. The law, however, fails to make such distinctions, focusing instead on morality and the preservation of virginity.

84. *Unfriendly Advances*, SOUTH CHINA MORNING POST, Nov. 29, 1994.

In addition to disrupting women's earning capacity by forcing them out of the workplace or school, a link between sexual harassment and severe physical, psychological, and health-related problems has been established. Eating disorders, depression, anxiety, nausea, headaches, insomnia, increased use of alcohol, nicotine or drugs, stomach problems, and weight loss are among the physical and psychological problems that arise for many victims.[85] The United States Merit Systems Protection Board estimates that sexual harassment costs the federal government $267 million over a two-year period.[86] This figure represents costs associated with reduction in productivity, sick leave, and the replacement of employees.

A 1991 survey of sexual harassment in Japan found that 70 percent of the 4,022 respondents had been harassed.[87] In Hungary, sexual harassment has reached epidemic proportions. Although there are no statistics regarding its prevalence, anecdotal evidence is persuasive. According to one commentator, "in a country where I know no one who has been the victim of street crime, I know at least 20 women who have had major incidents of sexual harassment at work, often serious enough for women to leave employment rather than put up with it." [88]

There are numerous disincentives to reporting sexual harassment. Many of those who have come forward have suffered grave consequences including increased harassment, blame for the harassment and/or minimization of its seriousness, public ridicule, job loss, or expulsion from school. A woman who alleges sexual harassment risks being labeled a troublemaker in both her professional and private life. Additionally, in large companies, numerous informal mechanisms have been institutionalized to address employees' complaints. Often such mechanisms are designed around mediation models that seek to "solve" conflicts rather than to address victim's needs and thus fail to hold the perpetrator accountable. Such practices add pressure in the victim's determination of whether or not to pursue a claim against the harasser. With little or no institutional support for reporting, the victim's concerns about her own job status may encourage silence. According to surveys undertaken in the United States and Hong Kong, men, who are more likely to be in positions of authority, are much less inclined to view sexual harassment as a valid complaint.[89]

Laws

Although few states have codified sexual harassment as a criminal offense, recent trends indicate a greater willingness on the part of governments to promulgate legislation to curtail sexual harassment. Such initiatives arise in two forms:

---

85. Jill Earnshaw & Marilyn J. Davidson, *Remedying Sexual Harassment via Industrial Tribunal Claims: An Investigation of the Legal and Psychosocial Process*, 23 PERSONNEL REV. 3 (1994).

86. *Id.*

87. Victor Fic, *Sexual Harassment Still a Fixture in Japanese Office*, TOKYO BUS. TODAY, Dec. 1994, at 24.

88. SHARON LADIN, IWRAW to CEDAW COUNTRY REPORTS, HUNGARY 53 (International Women's Rights Action Watch ed., 1996).

89. *Unfriendly Advances, supra* note 84.

the first is to make sexual harassment a crime under the penal code; the second is to recognize sexual harassment as a violation of women's equality and, therefore, violative of the Constitution and legislation providing for gender equality.

In the United States, sexual harassment has been legally conceptualized in terms of workplace harassment. According to the Equal Employment Opportunity Commission in the United States, sexual harassment is characterized by "repeated demands or continuing behavior of supervisors or co-workers that add a discrimination condition to the terms of employment or create a harmful work environment for men or women."[90] This definition, which is the legal basis for claims brought in the United States, breaks sexual harassment down into two forms. The first is "quid pro quo" harassment in which decisions on hiring, termination, promotion, or pay are made based on the employee's response to sexual advances. The second form of sexual harassment is perpetrated by the creation of a "hostile work environment." A more subtle form of sexual harassment, this behavior includes: 1) discussing sexual activities; 2) touching someone unnecessarily; 3) using demeaning or inappropriate terms (such as "Babe"); 4) using unseemly gestures; 5) granting job favors to those who participate in consensual sexual activity; and 6) using crude or offensive language.[91]

Other legal developments provide a nexus between sexual harassment and certain locations of activity. The European Community has recently introduced a code of practice on sexual harassment in the workplace. According to the code, sexual harassment is "unwanted conduct of a sexual nature, or other conduct based on sex affecting the dignity of women and men at work," including pornography.[92] The code, however, is neither binding nor enforceable. In Australia, the Federal Sex Discrimination Act of 1984 makes sexual harassment unlawful in situations of: 1) employment; 2) education; 3) the provision of goods and services; 4) the provision of accommodation, land transactions, clubs; and 5) the administration of the Commonwealth.[93] In the Philippines, a law has been enacted that criminalizes sexual harassment in the workplace, schools, and training centers.[94] Reportedly, however, the Department of Labor and Employment does not enforce the labor

---

90.   Paul A. Bauer & Brian H. Kleiner, *Understanding and managing sexual harassment, in* 14 EQUAL OPPORTUNITIES INTERNATIONAL (1995). The definition, encoded in Title VII of the Civil Rights Act, is "unwelcome sexual advances, requests for sexual favors, and other verbal or physical conduct of a sexual nature . . . when (1) submission to such conduct is made either explicitly or implicitly a term or condition of an individual's employment, (2) submission to or rejection of such conduct by an individual is used as the basis for employment decisions affecting such individual, or (3) such conduct has the purpose or effect of substantially interfering with an individual's work performance or creating an intimidating, hostile or offensive working environment." *Id.*

91.   *Id.*

92.   Earnshaw & Davidson, *supra* note 85.

93.   Sue Walpole, *Australian Approaches to Sexual Harassment*, MAV/1993/WP.9 (3 October 1993) at 4.

94.   *Ramos Signs Bill Declaring Sexual Harassment Unlawful*, JAPAN ECON. NEWSWIRE, Feb. 14, 1995.

code standards, even in cases of blatant discrimination in job advertisements, hiring practices, and unequal pay.[95]

As is the case for all forms of violence against women, even in the absence of specific legislation relating to sexual harassment, general tort laws may be utilized. In 1993, a woman in Tasmania successfully utilized tort laws on assault and battery to sue her employer for sexual harassment.[96] She was forced to depend on general principles of tort law because Tasmania had no laws governing sexual harassment.

Trafficking in Women

Historically, trafficking was defined as the "trade of women for the purpose of prostitution" generally involving the crossing of international borders.[97] In 1995, the U.N. General Assembly defined trafficking as the:

> illicit and clandestine movement of persons across national and international borders, largely from developing countries and some countries with economies in transition, with the end goal of forcing women and girl children into sexually or economically oppressive and exploitative situations for the profit of recruiters, traffickers and crime syndicates, as well as other illegal activities related to trafficking, such as forced domestic labor, false marriages, clandestine employment and false adoption.[98]

Trafficking in women grows and changes as fast as regional conditions change and potential markets open. Technological advances, such as the railroad, ocean steamer, telegraph, telephone, facsimile, and now the INTERNET, have consistently been employed by traffickers to develop new routes and facilitate international transactions. Currently in the United States, the INTERNET has become an integral component of trafficking in women for the marriage market. It is used not only to advertise marriage brokers but also to display women and girl-children, most of whom are teenagers, for sale as brides.

Trafficking routes replicate migration routes and, as identified by the International Organization of Migration, arise out of situations of poverty, the lack of viable economic opportunities, the disparity in wealth among countries, and the marginalization of women in sending states.[99] The promotion of tourism as a development strategy, promoted by the World Bank and other intergovernmental lending bodies, has contributed to the prevalence of trafficking in women for prostitution.

---

95. SHARON LADIN, IWRAW TO CEDAW COUNTRY REPORTS, PHILIPPINES 67 (International Women's Rights Action Watch ed., 1996).

96. *Australia: Sexual Reeling*, SYDNEY MORNING HERALD, June 1, 1995.

97. Currently, there is no consensus within the international community regarding the definition of trafficking in women. In fact, the issue of trafficking, because of its traditional conceptualization in terms of prostitution, is extremely divisive within the international woman's movement and among states. Roelof Haveman, *Traffic in Persons as a Problem, in* COMBATING TRAFFIC IN PERSONS 137, 139 (Netherlands Institute of Human Rights ed., 1994).

98. G.A. RES 49/166, ¶ 8, U.N. Doc. A/50/369, Aug. 24, 1995.

99. INTERNATIONAL ORGANIZATION OF MIGRATION, TRAFFICKING IN WOMEN TO COUNTRIES OF THE EUROPEAN UNION: CHARACTERISTICS, TRENDS & POLICY ISSUES 6 (1996).

Kenya provides a contemporary example of a country in which a flourishing tourism industry has led to an increase in trafficking in the region. Women from Uganda are lured to Kenya for the purpose of providing prostitutes for the growing tourist population.

Trafficking in women occurs not only from South to North, but also within regions and states. In Colombia, there are prostitution trafficking networks that work solely on internal trafficking of women, networks that traffic women for regional markets (sending women to countries such as Venezuela, Ecuador, and Panama) and traffickers that deal exclusively in global networks, providing Colombian women for markets in Spain, Greece, the Netherlands, Germany, Belgium, and the United States.[100]

In some countries, certain traditional practices give rise to trafficking and slavery-like practices. The Devadasi system in India, for example, entails ritualistic marriages of young girls to gods. Often the Devadasis are later forced into prostitution either out of economic necessity or after being sold by priests to brothels.[101] A similar practice, the Deukis system, is found in Nepal where rich families without daughters increasingly are buying young daughters from impoverished rural families and then offering them to the temple as their own.[102] These girl–children are prohibited from marrying and, thus, become either kept wives or prostitutes. Reportedly, 17,000 girls were endowed as Deukis in 1992.[103]

Traffickers recruit women for prostitution most often through deception. Women rarely know the conditions under which they will be forced to work and often are misinformed about the work they will be forced to do. Armed with "contracts" for waitressing, child care, or domestic labor, many women find themselves in situations of debt bondage and forced into prostitution abroad. Those women who do know they will be working as prostitutes often are deceived about their wages and the conditions of work.

Marriage is another method of recruitment for trafficking in women. Of the 100,000 to 160,000 Nepalese women and girls reportedly working in India's brothels, at least 35 percent have been brought into India under the pretext of marriage or employment.[104] In Kenya, most of the trafficking is accomplished under the guise of marriage, friendly invitations, and offers for employment. Nigerian women known as "madam" or "Mama-Loa" act as the middle-person between the women

---

100. WIJERS & LAP-CHEW, *supra* note 44, at 71 (*citing* FANNY POLANIA MOLINA, PROSTITUTION AND TRAFFICKING IN WOMEN IN COLOMBIA (1996)).

101. *Id.* at 46 (*citing* Meena Poudel, Women Acting Together for Change, Trafficking in Women in Nepal: An Overview, (paper prepared for a conference in Tokyo, Japan, March 15–16, 1994)).

102. Meena Poudel, *Trafficking in Women in Nepal, in* REV. FOR RESEARCH & ACTION 2, 2 (IMADR ed., May 1994).

103. *Id.*

104. WIJERS & LAP-CHEW, *supra* note 44, at 83.

and girls and their traffickers.[105] Parents in Eastern Uganda are deceived into giving their daughters to traffickers who tell them that their daughters will work on farms or as domestic workers in Kenya.[106]

In addition to marriage being used as a recruitment ploy, trafficking in women for the marriage market occurs with increasing frequency. Western Europe, North America, Australia, and Japan all have thriving marriage markets. The women who are sold in these markets are mostly from developing countries, including the Philippines, Colombia, Eastern European countries, and South-east Asian countries.[107] In Taiwan, poor farmers and the elderly constitute a large percentage of the men who pay intermediaries approximately $3,000 for young Vietnamese wives.[108] In Vietnam the traffic in brides is growing as ethnic Chinese women from poor North Vietnamese villages are transported across the border into China to marry rural Chinese men from villages devoid of women.[109] Refugee women from Mozambique are lured across the border into South Africa by traffickers promising work and then sold as concubines or wives to South African men.[110] In China, the incidence of kidnaping and selling women in rural areas has been increasing since the mid-1980s; in some counties and villages, between 30 and 90 percent of the marriages result from trafficking.[111] The shortage of women in rural areas, traditional views on maintaining the family line (which require all sons to marry), and the high expense associated with weddings and betrothal gifts of non-forced marriages all contribute to the situation of trafficking in women for forced marriages in China.[112]

Trafficked women report high levels of state participation in the trafficking. According to a 30-year-old woman from Bangladesh who was trafficked to Pakistan at the age of 27, "[w]e were taken to a secluded place in the jungle before crossing the border to Pakistan under police custody. The border officials kept the girls who were pretty and sexually abused them until the other lots of girls came, then the previous ones were released."[113] Reportedly, both Burmese and Thai officials are involved in trafficking Burmese women to Thailand.

---

105. *Id.*

106. *Id.* at 81.

107. *Id.* at 53 (*citing* Anita Amirrezvani, *Marketing Mail-Order Marriages,* TIMES UNION (Albany), Apr. 16, 1996.

108. *Id.* at 50 (*citing News Report,* FRENCH PRESS AGENCY, Feb. 6, 1996).

109. *Id.* at 51 (*citing* NEWSWEEK, Aug. 28, 1996).

110. *Id.* (*citing* DEBBIE TAYLOR, SERVILE MARRIAGE: A DEFINITION, A SURVEY, AND THE START OF A CAMPAIGN FOR CHANGE 36 (1993)).

111. *Id.* (*citing* Harvard University, Violence Against Women in China (May 1992) (unpublished report)).

112. *Id.* (*citing* Harvard University, *supra* note 111, and Human Rights in China, *Caught between tradition and the state—Violations of the human rights of Chinese Women* (Aug. 1995)).

113. *Id.* at 197 (*citing* LAWYERS FOR HUMAN RIGHTS AND LEGAL AID, THE FLESH TRADE: REPORT ON WOMEN'S AND CHILDREN'S TRAFFICKING IN PAKISTAN (1991)).

Laws

Despite efforts to broaden the definition of trafficking to include other forms of women's economic and sexual exploitation, and efforts to narrow the definition to exclude adult women making knowing, voluntary choices, the nexus between trafficking in women and prostitution remains and thus, definitions of trafficking and the strategies that derive from such definitions must be understood to exist within this context.

There are four identifiable legal paradigms that have been employed to address prostitution: 1) prohibition; 2) abolition; 3) regulation; and 4) decriminalization.[114]

Prohibition seeks to punish, and hence "prohibit," any acts or persons related to prostitution, including the woman herself. Although everyone involved in prostitution—including the women, clients, and third parties—are subject to legal penalties, it is rarely the case that states enforce the laws against men. Countries that employ prohibitionist approaches to prostitution, in which prostitution itself is a criminal offense, include the U.S. (except Nevada), Philippines, Japan, Burma, Sri Lanka, Vietnam, Nepal, Uganda, Namibia, Tanzania, Mali, Iceland, Malta, Slovenia, China, and Romania.

Abolition calls for the elimination of *per se* laws on prostitution. Rather than criminalizing the transaction between the prostitute and the client, the abolitionist strategy targets third parties such as pimps, brothel-keepers, traffickers, and the government. The long term goal is the complete abolition of prostitution. However, with the recognition that many prostitute women are themselves victims, the strategy employed to achieve this end entails decriminalization of the prostitute woman. Although the Trafficking Convention assumes an abolitionist approach, there is no state that follows a purely abolitionist policy.[115] Countries classified as predominantly abolitionist include Thailand, Bangladesh, Hong Kong, India, Ukraine, Poland, Czech Republic, Lithuania, Bulgaria, Finland, Denmark, Italy, Spain, Portugal, France, Belgium, UK, Ireland, Canada, Nigeria, Mali, Cameroon, Dominican Republic, and Colombia.

Regulation is characterized by official state tolerance of what is often understood to be a necessary evil. As a system, regulation seeks to control prostitution through government regulatory schemes. Such schemes can be broken down into two categories: 1) the classic regulated system whereby prostitution is regulated by government authorities primarily through legally permitted brothels; and 2) a neoregulatory system—without legally permitted brothels—whereby regulation is achieved through indirect mechanisms such as taxes or mandatory health examinations. Countries that subject prostitutes to special registration include Bangladesh, Thailand, Australia, Curacao, Peru, Mexico, Ecuador, Dominican Republic, Turkey,

---

114. Although legal paradigms can be broken down into four identifiable groups, in reality, a state rarely employs one pure system.

115. LICIA BRUSSA, SURVEY OF PROSTITUTION, MIGRATION AND TRAFFIC IN WOMEN: HISTORY AND CURRENT SITUATION, EU Doc. EG/PROST (91)2, at 50.

Greece, Austria, and Switzerland. Of these, Australia, Thailand, Turkey, Greece, Switzerland, Curacao, Peru, Ecuador, Mexico, Slovenia, and Belgium have outright prohibitions on prostitution without proper registration.

The decriminalization paradigm views prostitution as work and seeks to decriminalize prostitution and the exploitation of prostitution by third parties. The focus of decriminalization is on coercion and violence rather than on prostitution itself, and it seeks to utilize labor laws to address working conditions and the rights of prostitute women.

Trafficking often involves crossing borders, and third-party assistance in illegal border crossing is proscribed by most Northern countries seeking to protect their borders, including most European Union countries, the United States, and Canada. Such legislation contains provisions on alien smuggling, aiding and abetting, illegal entry, the production of fraudulent documents, hiring illegal workers, transporting illegal aliens, and confiscation and forfeiture of property used in connection with alien smuggling. Migrants entering the country illegally or overstaying their visas are punished with imprisonment varying from six months to two years, fines, and, ultimately, deportation. Some countries, such as Burma and Poland, also have legal proscriptions on leaving the country without permission or valid documentation, thus subjecting undocumented migrant women to punishment both in the destination country and her home country upon return.

There are a few noteworthy strategies being undertaken by states to address trafficking. In 1988 in the Netherlands, largely as a result of a high profile case in which a victim of trafficking brought charges against her traffickers,[116] paragraph B22 was inserted into the Dutch Aliens Law to provide protection to victims of trafficking willing to pursue prosecution. According to B22, "[i]n the presence of the least suspicion of trafficking, a woman should be allowed time to consider pressing charges. When she has done so she should be allowed to stay in the Netherlands until the whole juridical process has been completed."[117] As of 1993, the protection against deportation outlined in B22 was extended to witnesses willing to testify for the prosecution in trafficking cases as well. Belgium has a similar mechanism through which trafficked women willing to participate in the prosecution of their traffickers can stay in the country during the process.

Similar to laws on rape, the elements of consent and force are important factors in the definitional debate. Early definitions, found in the first international agreements on the white slave trade, limited the definition of "traffickable" women to

---

116. The case brought by Lisa M., a Philippine who had been trafficked to the Netherlands in 1981, was instrumental in transforming the law. Lisa played a very active role in the Netherlands by agreeing to address a Dutch parliamentary hearing on trafficking in women and vigorously pursuing her case in criminal court. Although the criminal case in the Netherlands against her Dutch trafficker led to his conviction, the case brought in the Philippines against her Philippine recruiter failed. For a description of the case of Lisa M., *see* SIETSKE ALTINK, STOLEN LIVES, TRADING WOMEN INTO SEX AND SLAVERY 45 (1995); and LIN LAP-CHEW, LISA (Foundation Against Trafficking in Women ed.).

117. LAP-CHEW, *supra* note 44, at 21.

unmarried, chaste women who were trafficked to unlicensed brothels in Europe. Entrenched in the current debates on consent is a similarly dichotomous perspective that attempts to distinguish between women who are and are not worthy of state protection. Notably, those women perceived by laws to be "unrape-able"—e.g. prostitute women—are likewise often perceived to be "untraffickable." Such distinctions highlight the patriarchal posturing of laws on violence against women that are often more concerned with protecting chastity than protecting women.

Violence Against Migrant Women

Because of their double marginalization as women and as migrants, migrant women may easily find themselves in situations in which they are vulnerable to violence and abuse. Women migrants dominate the informal labor market of most countries, working as domestic, industrial, or farm labor, or working within the service industry. The conditions that lead to trafficking in women, as identified above, also stimulate women's migration. In fact, both trafficked women and voluntary migrant women often end up in comparable situations of exploitation, violence, and abuse.

It is not that migrant women experience particularly distinct forms of violence; they, like non-migrant women, are raped, battered, sexually harassed, forced into prostitution, etc. However, the situation of migrant women within most social structures is one of heightened marginalization exacerbated and implicitly condoned by the state. In Saudi Arabia, for example, all domestic workers must surrender their passports upon arrival.[118] This official state policy increases migrant women's vulnerability to exploitation and abuse by institutionalizing complete employer control over domestic workers' freedom of movement.

Domestic labor is one of the primary forms of employment for migrant women.[119] In addition to domestic labor, women migrate primarily for other forms of informal labor. The informal sector, which is largely unregulated, or at best under-regulated, is the site of numerous violations of women's human rights.

More than 2,000 cases of ill-treatment and abuse of migrant domestic workers in the United Kingdom have been documented by NGOs.[120] The abuses include

---

118. SHARON LADIN, IWRAW TO CEDAW COUNTRY REPORTS, PHILIPPINES 54 (International Women's Rights Action Watch ed. 1997).

119. In respect to violence against migrant women, the Special Rapporteur has received a majority of information on migrant domestic workers. In her second report, she identified violence against domestic workers as a form of domestic violence due to the perpetuation of much of that violence in the traditionally defined "private" sphere—the home. However, violence against migrant women also exists as a manifestation of community-based violence because, in many cases, the individuals perpetrating the violence have neither a domestic relationship with the victim nor a formal state function. The blurring of lines between forms of violence against women demonstrates the intersectionality of all forms of violence against women.

120. WIJERS & LAP-CHEW, *supra* note 44, at 61 (*citing* KALAYAAN, Justice for Overseas Domestic Workers 1995 Slavery still alive (1995) (conference paper)).

confiscation of passports, enforced change of contract, withholding of wages, deprivation of food and malnourishment, lack of access to medical and health services,
imprisonment in the home of the employer, prohibition on engaging in social contacts, the interception of letters from home, and physical and sexual violence. The
Anti-Slavery Society, in describing the conditions under which overseas domestic
workers are forced to work in the United Kingdom, labeled the situation as one of
''domestic slavery.'' While their report focused solely on the conditions in the
United Kingdom, they noted that numerous instances of domestic slavery have also
been documented in Middle Eastern states, North America, Hong Kong, and other
EU countries.[121]

According to a 1996 ILO report, approximately 1.5 million Asian women are
working abroad either legally or illegally.[122] Women account for approximately 60
percent of all legal migrants (excluding seafarers) from the Philippines.[123] A survey
conducted at Sri Lanka's international airport found that 84 percent of the migrant
workers leaving the country were women and that 94 percent of the women were
migrating to work as domestic workers.[124]

In Latin America and the Caribbean, domestic labor migration has an extensive
history plagued by reports of violence and abuse. In Asuncion, Paraguay, there are
roughly 15,200 domestic workers between the ages of five and eighteen who have
migrated from rural areas and work for free.[125] Although many of the girls receive
education and accommodations in lieu of a salary, such domestic arrangements
increase their vulnerability to exploitation and violence. In Chile and Colombia,
for example, many rural women migrate internally as seasonal laborers in the fruit
and flower industries, respectively.[126] Numerous violations of human rights have
been reported in these sectors. Illegal prohibitions on women's right to organize
are widespread. Additionally, the women are forced to work twelve to fourteen
hour days in extremely unhealthy conditions during which they are exposed to high
levels of pesticides—many of which have been banned in Northern countries and
then exported to the South. Abnormally high levels of physical illnesses—including
cancer—birth defects, and death have been linked to the exposure to pesticides.[127]

Young Kenyan women are recruited through employment bureaus that charge
thousands of shillings as commission to work as domestic workers in Saudi Arabia.
Women who have returned report numerous instances of sexual and physical abuse,

---

121. *Id.*

122. *Id.* at 34 (*citing* LIN LEAN LIM & NANA OISHI, INTERNATIONAL LABOR MIGRATION OF ASIAN WOMEN,
DISTINCTIVE CHARACTERISTICS AND POLICY CONCERNS (ILO ed., Feb. 1996)).

123. *Id.* at 34.

124. *Id.* at 35 (*citing* LIM & OISHI, *supra* note 122, at n.7).

125. INTERNATIONAL WOMEN'S RIGHTS ACTION WATCH, PARAGUAY, INDEPENDENT INFORMATION SUBMIT-
TED TO THE COMMITTEE ON ECONOMIC, SOCIAL AND CULTURAL RIGHTS 14 (1996).

126. SHARON LADIN, IWRAW TO CEDAW COUNTRY REPORTS, CHILE 18 (International Women's Rights
Action Watch ed., 1995).

127. *Id.* (*citing* Los Plaguicida si Enfermado y Mantando a los Campesinos, *Tierra*, Sept.–Oct. 1993).

harassment, and underpayment.[128] In Morocco, young rural girls are placed with wealthy urban families as domestic servants. Despite promises of education and a better standard of living, the girls are often subjected to inhumane working conditions and forced to live in a state of indentured servitude.[129]

In addition to physical detention, one NGO has identified factors restricting migrant women's ability to leave situations of forced labor including: 1) the lack of alternate employment; 2) the lack of legal literacy, particularly in regard to workers rights; 3) the financial obligations to her family and their dependence on her income; 4) the lack of financial resources, including that which results from wage withholding; 5) the fear of deportation; 6) restrictions on her movement; 7) the lack of identity papers; 8) the fear of arrest; 9) violence by traffickers and employers; 10) debt bondage and the often concurrent fear of retaliation against her family for not paying debts, and; 11) fear of reprisals.[130]

Laws

The unregulated and unprotected nature of informal labor translates into minimal or no legal protection for migrant women. In many cases neither labor codes nor laws providing benefits such as social security extend to migrant workers. The legal status of the migrant worker either as dependent on her employer or as undocumented, and consequently without legal status, undermines her autonomy and limits her power. As the name indicates, dependent visas make migrant women, specifically in regard to their legal status, completely dependent on their employers. The moment she leaves her employer, even if she is fleeing violence or abuse, is the moment she loses her legal residence within the receiving country.

The experiences of women have highlighted internationally the egregious human rights abuses suffered by migrant domestic workers first at the hands of their employers and then at the hands of state penal systems. While such systems for the most part afford little protection to foreign domestics, they provide harsh punishments, including the death penalty, for those who attempt to defend themselves from such violence. For example, domestic workers in Saudi Arabia are required to produce three eyewitnesses in order to maintain a prosecution against their employers for abuse.

Rather than banning the trade altogether, some sending states have established programs to better the position of female domestic workers who go abroad. Some countries have established minimum age limits on migrant domestic workers in an effort to ensure greater agency and, it is hoped, reduce the risk of physical and

---

128. WIJERS & LAP-CHEW, *supra* note 44, at 62 (*citing* BUTEGWA, FLORENCE. PRELIMINARY REPORT, PREPARED FOR STV/GAATW ON TRAFFICKING IN WOMEN IN AFRICA, UGANDA (1996).

129. SHARON LADIN, IWRAW TO CEDAW COUNTRY REPORTS, MOROCCO 24 (International Women's Rights Action Watch ed., 1997) (*citing* UNITED STATES DEPARTMENT OF STATE, COUNTRY REPORTS ON HUMAN RIGHTS PRACTICES FOR 1995).

130. WIJERS & LAP-CHEW, *supra* note 44.

sexual abuse.[131] Indonesian women migrants to the Middle East must be a minimum of 30 years old. Indonesia also has instituted compulsory language and cultural training for domestic workers migrating to the Middle East. In Sri Lanka, the government has taken steps to regulate the deployment of migrant workers through the Overseas Employment Act of 1995. A prospective migrant worker must have an employment contract to obtain a certificate. The Overseas Employment Act also sets forth rules for overseas employers such as requiring the employer to pay the cost of travel and medical benefits for migrants. Oversight of the act, however, is difficult.

Receiving states have implemented a variety of policies to both encourage and discourage the maid trade. Singapore, in 1978, established a formal Foreign Domestic Maid program to encourage educated women to assume formal employment. Malaysia, in an effort to protect domestics against sexual violence, banned the employment of maids by single parents.[132] Singapore levies a substantial tax on the employment of foreign domestics; none of the $146 million per year generated by the tax, however, is used to benefit the workers.[133] Many countries have adopted immigration regimes that reflect xenophobic intentions of keeping immigrants out. The severe penalties attached to illegal migrant workers often makes the illegal immigrants more dependent on their employers and, therefore, more vulnerable to abuse and exploitation.

Violence Perpetrated Or Condoned By The State

Violence against women includes:

Physical, sexual and psychological violence perpetrated or condoned by the State, wherever it occurs.[134]

State inaction in regard to violence against women in the family and violence perpetrated against women by the community may constitute evidence of state complicity and, as such, the above enumerated manifestations of violence against women can be considered violence condoned by the state. States, their actors and agents, however, are also the direct perpetrators of violence against women. Although violence perpetrated by the state against women is in many cases indistinguishable from that which is perpetrated by the state against men, states often use gender-specific forms of violence, most notably rape and other forms of sexual violence, to persecute women.

---

131. Joan Fitzpatrick, Challenging Boundaries: Gendered Aspects of Migration 8 (1996) (unpublished manuscript on file at the Office of the U.N. Special Rapporteur on Violence against Women).

132. *Id.* at 33, n.118. This policy, however, is not only misguided—to the extent that there is no apparent correlation between sexual violence and single parenting—but also flawed in its failure to account for the needs of single working mothers.

133. *Id.* at 21.

134. Declaration, *supra* note 2, art. 2(c).

Custodial Violence Against Women

Violence perpetrated by state actors and agents against women held in state custody is prevalent throughout the world. The at times overzealousness of governments and their agents to apprehend and punish alleged perpetrators, especially those who are perceived as threats to national security, national identity, and national morality, creates a climate of impunity in which detainees are targeted for violence and abuse. The violence committed against women ranges from physical and verbal harassment to physical and sexual torture, including rape. Such violence is perpetrated indiscriminately against female detainees regardless of the alleged offense. The state's protection of government agents is the single most important factor in the perpetuation of violence against women detainees.

Human rights organizations report that thousands of women in custody are routinely raped in police detention centers worldwide; custodial rape not only is perpetrated by prison guards as a crime of opportunity but also is used as a method of torture.[135] Torture is taking increasingly sophisticated, inhumane, and, in many cases, gender-specific forms, ranging from rape with electrically charged metal rods to the refined use of psychotropic drugs.[136] Often the physical and psychological effects of these extreme forms of custodial violence are further compounded by inadequate or unavailable medical treatment. Prolonged illegal detention and deprivation of food, sleep, and water are additional abuses perpetrated by the state against women deprived of their liberty.

Despite provisions for legal counsel in many states, attorneys are routinely withheld from detainees. Rarely are detainees informed of either the alleged offense or the law under which they have been detained. According to a study carried out by Human Rights Watch, "out of 90 women interviewed in a jail in Pakistan, 91 per cent did not know under what law they had been accused, 62 percent had no legal assistance whatsoever, and of those who had lawyers almost half had never met them."[137]

"Disappearances" and extra-judicial killings at the hands of state authorities have been reported in Afghanistan, Brazil, Burundi, Cambodia, Chad, Chile, India, Lebanon, Myanmar, Sri Lanka, and Uganda.[138] The particularly insidious nature of "disappearances" is the official state denial of responsibility. Although relatives or friends are often present when the individual is taken into custody by state actors or agents (albeit rarely self-proclaimed actors or agents), the individual thereafter "disappears." Her existence is wiped from the records, her body is rarely found. "Disappearances" are difficult to unequivocally classify as custodial violence as

---

135. *See* AMNESTY INTERNATIONAL, HUMAN RIGHTS ARE WOMEN'S RIGHTS (1995).

136. 2 TORTURE, 1:92 (IRTC Copenhagen ed., 1992).

137. HUMAN RIGHTS WATCH/WOMEN'S RIGHTS PROJECT, DOUBLE JEOPARDY: POLICE ABUSE OF WOMEN IN PAKISTAN 44 (1992) [hereinafter DOUBLE JEOPARDY].

138. AMNESTY INTERNATIONAL, DISAPPEARANCES AND POLITICAL KILLINGS (1994).

it is nearly impossible to prove the government's responsibility, despite general knowledge of such responsibility.

The emergence of "special laws" in certain countries has led to an increase in custodial abuse of women. According to Pakistan's Hudood Ordinances, for example, all forms of extramarital sex, including rape, constitute non-compoundable, non-bailable crimes punishable by death.[139] The Ordinances allow for women to be arrested without a warrant and detained without being charged for prolonged periods, with no provision requiring attendance by female officers during their arrest or detention. Women detainees have reported systematic sexual torture, including chilies forced into their vaginas in order to coerce confessions of adultery.[140] Gang rape, beatings, molestation, and sexual harassment are common treatment for women accused of sexually deviant behavior.

Laws providing for preventive detention are increasingly becoming legal tools through which impunity is sanctioned. The Terrorist and Disruptive Activities (Prevention) Act in India, the Anti-Subversion Law in Indonesia, the Public Security Law in the Republic of Korea, the Prevention of Terrorism Act in Sri Lanka, to name just a few, are instruments under which police may legally detain persons who "might" commit crimes for prolonged periods without trial. Such legislation, by virtue of the wide and unchecked discretion given to police, enhances police power while minimizing police culpability, thereby creating situations ripe for abuse.

Laws

Violence against, and the abuse of, individuals in state custody present complex enforcement issues. Although such violence is rarely legally sanctioned by the state, it is the very authorities in whom power is vested to enforce and uphold the law that, in turn, abuse detainees.

Many, if not most, countries' codes are formally based on legislation and written codes of conduct, in compliance with the Standard Minimum Rules on the Treatment of Prisoners, adopted in 1955 by the First United Nations Congress on the Prevention of Crime and the Treatment of Offenders. Practice, however, differs greatly and such codes are rarely followed. In the context of violence against women in custody, the Jail Code of Bangladesh stands out as a commendable piece of legislation. According to the Jail Code, male and female prisoners are segregated and male officers are barred from the women's quarters. Women must be chaperoned by a female officer when being questioned or examined by a male officer. Such protective measures are important elements of efforts to curb violence against women in custody.

---

139. A. JAHANGIR & H. JILANI, THE HUDOOD ORDINANCES: A DIVINE SANCTION (1990). Although the Hudood Ordinances apply to both men and women, the largest percentage of those charged are women.

140. DOUBLE JEOPARDY, *supra* note 137. Police in Pakistan systematically refuse to register complaints of rape.

In an effort to increase legal culpability for custodial rape—defined as rape perpetrated in any state-owned institution by a state agent—recent legislation in India requires that the defendant has to prove consent, shifting the evidentiary burden of proof so that the state has the onus of proving that the alleged rape did not take place. This dramatic piece of legislation was a response to the agitation of India's many women's groups.

Rape of Women in Situations of Armed Conflict

Like rape perpetrated in times of relative peace, silence has surrounded rape in wartime. Traditionally viewed as one of the spoils of war, rape has been officially denied and historically minimized. It was only in 1992, when reports were received of the widespread rape and deliberate impregnation of thousands of women in the former Yugoslavia, that rape in wartime became a focus of international attention.

Distinctive patterns of rape have been identified in situations of armed conflict, whether in Korea during the Second World War or in the territories of the former Yugoslavia. Officially, rape has been utilized, prior to military action, as a deterrent for any resistance to the forthcoming military action, to suffocate dissent and to force collaboration. Upon the arrival of the military, women have been raped, sometimes killed, and often deported to detention camps. Both during deportation and in detention camps, women are subjected to physical and sexual abuse. Additionally, there is documentation of women being kept in hotels or similar facilities as sexual slaves for military personnel.[141]

Rape in wartime is a military tactic, a method to terrorize civilian populations through the symbolic rape (i.e. destruction) of the community, culture, or nation.[142] Women thereby become victims in the fight for male honor; the inability to protect women's sexual purity is an act of humiliation.[143] Increasingly, ethnic cleansing through forced pregnancy is an atrocity committed against women during armed conflicts.

On October 6, 1992, the Security Council adopted Resolution 780, establishing a Commission of Experts to investigate and collect evidence in the conflict in the former Yugoslavia.[144] A final report, submitted to the Secretary-General and forwarded to the Security Council on May 24, 1994, stated that the mass rape and/or sexual torture of women in Bosnia and Herzegovina must be considered systematic, ordered acts and an important element of Serbian warfare strategy. The final report of the Commission of Experts identified five patterns of rape and sexual assault

---

141. U.N. Doc. S/1994/672, ¶ 249.

142. Ruth Seifert, *Mass Rapes: Their Logic in Bosnia-Herzegovina and Elsewhere, in* WOMEN'S STUDIES INTERNATIONAL FORUM 2 (1995).

143. Dorothy Q. Thomas and Regan E. Ralph, *Rape in War, Challenging the Tradition of Impunity, in* SAIS REVIEW 89 (1994).

144. S.C. Res. 780, U.N. SCOR, 47th Year, 1992 S.C. Res. & Dec. at 36, para 2, U.N. Doc. S/INF/48 (1992).

and concluded that, in Bosnia and Herzegovina, "these patterns strongly suggest that a systematic rape policy existed in certain areas. . . . [P]ractices of ethnic cleansing, sexual assault and rape were carried out by some parties so systematically that they strongly appear to be the product of a policy."[145]

In March 1994, the United Nations/Organization of American States International Civilian Mission in Haiti issued a press release condemning the use of rape against women as a violation of the rights of Haitian women. Rape and other forms of violence against women have formed an integral component of the political violence and terror, in which armed civilian auxiliaries, attaches, members of the Front for the Advancement and Progress of Haiti, and the armed forces of Haiti have all been implicated.[146]

Most recently, massacres, systematic hunting of survivors, attacks on schools and churches, rapes and abductions of women and girls, and violence against children during the armed conflict in Rwanda have all been described in first-hand testimonies. According to a detailed report on the situation, soldiers and militiamen raided homes, hospitals, and camps for the displaced, looking for women to rape. Girls as young as five have been raped; in some cases women and girls were attacked with machetes and then raped immediately afterwards, while others were allegedly gang raped, sometimes in public places. Some were acquired as concubines or second "wives."[147]

A particularly atrocious form of rape during armed conflict was perpetrated by the Japanese imperial forces during World War II. Between 1932 and 1945, the Japanese imperial forces, through force, pretext, or abduction, enslaved women from colonized or occupied areas as sexual slaves for the soldiers. The "comfort women" or "jugun ianfu" had to endure repeated rapes on a daily basis in the military comfort houses, set up and strictly regulated by the military in such places as China, the Philippines, Korea, the Dutch East Indies, Malaysia, and Indonesia.

Laws

Armed conflict, whether internal or international in nature, is governed by the rules of war articulated through customary international law and largely codified through the four Geneva Conventions on the rules of war. The rape of women and girls in situations of either internal or international armed conflict constitutes a grave breach of international humanitarian law and a serious violation of international human rights law. Rape during wartime, however, has been shrouded in silence, officially denied and discounted. The official failure to condemn or punish rape in wartime has resulted in an international military culture of impunity that

---

145. *Final Report of the Commission of Experts Established Pursuant to Security Resolution 780* (1992), U.N. SCOR, Annex, U.N. Doc. S/1994/674 (May 27, 1994). See web site <http://www.his.com:80/cij/commxyu5.htm#4IV.F.1> [at IV(F)(3)].

146. Press Release, United Nations/Organization of American States International Civilian Mission in Haiti (March 21, 1994).

147. AFRICAN RIGHTS, RWANDA: DEATH, DESPAIR AND DEFIANCE (1994).

allows rape and other forms of sexual torture and ill-treatment to become sanctioned weapons of the military.[148]

Increasingly, mechanisms are being established to prosecute war crimes at the international level. Modeled somewhat on the International Military Tribunal at Nuremberg and the International Military Tribunal for the Far East (Tokyo Tribunal), international war crimes tribunals have been instituted to prosecute atrocities in the territories of the former Yugoslavia and in Rwanda. The tribunal on the former Yugoslavia, in its enumeration of war crimes, has explicitly included rape as a war crime within its mandate for the first time. Additionally, the tribunal has established a specialized unit to investigate and prosecute cases of rape and to work directly with victims/survivors. Indictments charge sexual violence as war crimes, genocide, and crimes against humanity.

Violence Against Women Refugees and Internally Displaced Women

There are an estimated 20 million refugees in the world and 24 million internally displaced persons; women and their dependent children account for 80 percent of the world's refugee population.[149] In addition to the fears and problems that women share with all refugees, women and girls are vulnerable to gender-based discrimination and gender-specific violence and exploitation. The male perpetrators of the exploitation and violence against refugee women include military personnel, immigration personnel, bandit or pirate groups, other male refugees, and rival ethnic groups.

Family structures, which could otherwise be a basis of stability and protection, arc often radically altered in refugee situations. Separation from or loss of members of the family results in female-headed households in which the women are often dependent on external support structures and consequently more vulnerable to exploitation.

The persecution which leads women to seek asylum often takes the form of sexual violence or torture. According to one report, rape was a causative factor in the decision to flee for almost half of the Somali refugee women subsequently raped in Kenyan refugee camps.[150] Likewise, women and girl refugees in flight from the terror of their communities are susceptible to exploitation, rape, abduction, and murder. As the experience of Somali women in Kenyan camps demonstrates, threats of sexual assault and rape do not subside once women reach the refugee camps. The security situation in the camps is generally poor; most camps are not lit, and

---

148. JEANNE VICKERS, WOMEN AND WAR 21 (1993).

149. *See* HUMAN RIGHTS WATCH/AFRICA WATCH, SEEKING REFUGE, FINDING TERROR: WIDESPREAD RAPE OF SOMALI WOMEN IN NORTH EASTERN KENYA (1993) [hereinafter SEEKING REFUGE]; SUSAN FORBES MARTIN, REFUGEE WOMEN (1991).

150. SUSAN FORBES MARTIN, REFUGEE WOMEN (1991).

night patrols to ensure greater protection are infrequent or absent.[151] In fact, some of the attacks in the Somali camps in Kenya have been by police.[152]

Internally displaced women may be more vulnerable to abuse than refugee women because the government that caused the displacement is the same government that is primarily responsible for their safety and access to services. There is no international agency with an explicit mandate to help internally displaced persons, although the International Committee of the Red Cross, some nongovernmental organizations and, increasingly, the United Nations High Commissioner for Refugees, do actively intervene on their behalf.

Laws

Criminal acts of violence against refugee women are punishable under national laws. In part because of extensive international involvement in refugee situations, however, governments have tended either to abdicate responsibility or to act in nominal and ineffective ways. The United Nations High Commissioner for Refugees ("UNHCR") has noted that lack of state protection is at the heart of the problem faced by female refugees.

Both international law and the national law of asylum countries govern the protection of refugee women. The basic international instrument for the protection of refugees is the 1951 Convention relating to the Status of Refugees and its 1967 Protocol. The UNHCR is charged with providing international protection to refugees and with seeking durable solutions to their problems. The Convention defines a refugee as a person who has a well-founded fear of persecution arising from nationality, race, religion, membership in a particular social group, or political opinion.

The Executive Committee of UNHCR has recognized that gender can be a factor in persecution, and moreover, that women can in certain circumstances be considered to constitute a "particular social group." Canada and the United States have reformed immigration policy to include gender-based persecution as a grounds for asylum.

There is no international instrument specifically designed to address the needs of internally displaced persons; human rights instruments, however, do provide general protection against violations of internally displaced peoples' human rights. International humanitarian law, namely the four Geneva Conventions of 1949 and the two Additional Protocols of 1977, often apply to protect internally displaced persons.

CONCLUSION

Although this chapter has been devoted to issues of violence against women through the lenses of both national and international law, legislation alone will

---

151. UNHCR, GUIDELINES FOR THE PROTECTION OF REFUGEE WOMEN (1991).

152. SEEKING REFUGE, *supra*, note 149.

neither lead to the eradication of violence against women nor meet the needs of victims/survivors. While legislation is a necessary component in the fight to eliminate violence against women, such violence is not merely a criminal justice concern. Violence against women is socially constructed and, thus, must be socially deconstructed and, ultimately, defeated.

The most successful programs—whether they address domestic violence, violence in the community, or violence by the state—are those in which there is a genuine partnership between the police and the criminal justice system on the one hand, and nongovernmental women's organizations on the other. Nongovernmental organizations and networks in civil society have a wealth of knowledge and experience in working with female survivors of violence. This expertise is rarely utilized by government. Thus, the need for such partnerships cannot be overestimated. Strategies must be devised with cooperation from all sectors of society and implemented at all levels of society.

DOMESTIC VIOLENCE

Cheryl Thomas

INTRODUCTION

In recent years, the international community has witnessed a dramatic increase of activity in and information on issues surrounding domestic violence. United Nations officials have concluded that domestic violence occurs in every region of the world with devastating effects on the victims, their families, and the community. Wherever domestic violence has been studied, stories emerge of extreme cruelty committed with an impunity rarely found with non-gender based crimes. Activists have recognized a striking global commonality in the experience of domestic violence and have mobilized as a powerful international force. They are committed to ending this violence in their own communities and sharing their knowledge and experience to end domestic violence everywhere. Although domestic violence may encompass many other types of violence and abuse not discussed here, such as violence by in-laws and child-parent violence, the definition of domestic violence offered by the United Nations will be used for purposes of this chapter: "Domestic violence can be defined as the use of force or threats of force by a husband or boyfriend for the purpose of coercing and intimidating a woman into submission. The violence can take the form of pushing, hitting, choking, slapping, kicking, burning or stabbing."[1]

This chapter will focus on the law and activity within the legal community, both international and national. The first section documents criminal justice systems' failure to acknowledge the criminality of wife-assault and to protect women from this offense, and it includes materials that establish domestic violence as a global problem. Police, prosecutors, and judges from every region demonstrate a dangerous unwillingness to understand the causes and consequences of domestic violence and to enforce the laws against it. The attitudes and conduct of these law enforcement officials reflect those of the general community: that domestic violence is not a serious crime but rather a private problem to be dealt with by the woman herself. Many advocates for domestic violence survivors have identified their criminal justice system as an overwhelming obstacle for women seeking to eliminate

---

1.   UNITED NATIONS CENTRE FOR SOCIAL DEVELOPMENT AND HUMANITARIAN AFFAIRS, STRATEGIES FOR CONFRONTING DOMESTIC VIOLENCE: A RESOURCE MANUAL 7 (1993), U.N. Doc. ST/CSDHA/20 (1993) [hereinafter the UNITED NATIONS MANUAL]. This manual, and an earlier United Nations publication entitled "Violence Against Women in the Family" published by the Centre for Social Development and Humanitarian Affairs in 1989, provide an international perspective of the extent and nature of domestic violence and the strategies local activists are using to confront it.

violence from their lives. They have organized efforts at legal reform to improve treatment of domestic violence victims. Some of these efforts focus on changing the laws; some focus on training law enforcement personnel, prosecutors, judges, doctors, and lawyers to more effectively enforce existing laws.

The second part of this chapter describes some of the most dramatic efforts at reform—those which have occurred in international legal standards. In the mid-1990s, the United Nations adopted a resolution strongly condemning domestic violence and appointed a Special Rapporteur to monitor governments' commitments to ending this and other forms of violence against women. At the 1995 U. N. Fourth World Conference on Women, held in Beijing, China, women from every region of the world spoke in unison that ending domestic violence must be a priority in policymaking at every level. Their voices were heard and reflected in the Platform for Action, the official conference document. This section also traces and describes the developments within the United Nations and the lobbying efforts that have led to the creation of these international legal standards.

A significant part of the efforts to improve international legal standards has been the movement to define domestic violence as a human rights violation, thereby invoking the protections offered by human rights treaties and other instruments. New international legal standards on domestic violence specifically requires states to review and reform their criminal justice system's treatment of battered women in order to meet their government's obligations under human rights law. The Beijing Platform for Action, for example, states that domestic violence is a human rights violation and that governments are obligated as member states of the United Nations to effectively address this violence.

These new international legal standards, combined with the scrutiny of the international community, can have a profound effect on the lives of battered women. This internationalization of the problems surrounding domestic violence has given the issue the broadest possible public audience and contributed to the breakdown of the barriers of secrecy that have insulated this violence from public condemnation.

BATTERED WOMEN AND CRIMINAL JUSTICE: AN INTERNATIONAL PERSPECTIVE

In articulation of its laws, a society makes its most powerful statement of what will and will not be tolerated. In its enforcement of those laws, society demonstrates its level of commitment to the values it professes, and begins the process of transforming words into reality. Domestic violence activists around the world have recognized this unique power of the law and its enforcement. They have exposed the legal system's tragic global failure to protect victims of domestic violence, both in word and in act, and they are forcing change.

Evidence from every region of the world indicates that when women turn to their legal systems for recourse from violence in their homes, the treatment they receive is frequently hostile, with authorities failing to acknowledge the crime of wife assault and doing nothing to prevent further violence. This inability to access justice may stem from the law itself; it may result from a failure to enforce laws that are intended to protect women. Jane Connors, who has worked internationally on behalf of battered women, states:

> The criminal law depends for its effectiveness on the actors involved in the penal system—the police, prosecutors and judges—all of whom have notoriously failed to perceive wife abuse as a serious, let alone criminal issue and have thus refused to intervene, arrest, prosecute and convict.[2]

The following section will focus on common worldwide aspects of the criminal justice system's treatment of battered women. First, it will describe mounting evidence demonstrating a consistent global failure by law enforcement officials to treat domestic violence crimes seriously. Then it will delineate efforts to reform the criminal justice system so that it can best address and redress domestic violence.

Evidence of a Global Failure to Protect and Prosecute

The Police

One of the most frequently cited obstacles to battered women's access to criminal justice worldwide is that government officials on the "front line," i.e., the police, do not adequately respond to domestic violence. The importance of the police lies in their unique privilege to use force or removal to stop criminal behavior. One domestic violence advocate has described this fundamental crisis faced by a battered woman, the threat to her life, as one that only the police can redress. In the mid-1970s, faced with a decision as to where to allocate financial resources and advocating that they should be spent training police, this advocate reasoned:

> What was clear to me was that what a battered woman needed most immediately was for someone to come in with a gun in the middle of the night, stop her from being killed and take her violent husband away. Until she could count on that, nothing else mattered.[3]

Evidence from around the world shows that most women cannot count on that. The United Nations has reported:

> Although the role of the police in cases of domestic violence is critical, research indicates that, in general, police response has been significantly different from that observed in other cases of violent behaviour. Police are thought not to offer the victim of domestic violence adequate protection from the perpetrator; they are perceived as

---

2.   Jane Connors, *The Criminal Justice System: A Tool for Domestic Violence Management, in* COMBATTING VIOLENCE AGAINST WOMEN 79, 79 (1993).

3.   Telephone interview with Loretta Frederick, Legal Counsel to the Battered Women's Justice Project in Minnesota, June 21, 1996. In the United States, statistics show that domestic disturbances constitute the largest category of calls to police each year. *See* Joan Zorza, *The Criminal Law of Misdemeanor Violence 1970–1990*, 83 J. CRIM. L. & CRIMINOLOGY 46, 46 (1992).

underestimating the violence and dismissing some appeals for help because they do not think there are sufficient grounds for intervention.[4]

A lack of understanding of the causes and consequences of domestic violence contributes to police unwillingness to effectively respond. Overwhelmingly, police forces are male and have no familiarity with the issues of fear, economic dependency, and lack of control battered women commonly face. In many countries, when called to the scene of a domestic assault, the police attempt to resolve the situation then leave, placing the battered woman more at more risk than ever. For example, in Egypt, women who suffer domestic violence are referred to the social worker at the police station; in Greece, Malaysia, Nigeria, and Thailand, "the police attempt to conciliate between the parties and dissuade victims from taking the matter to court;"[5] police officers in Michigan and California were previously directed to avoid arrests and to mediate domestic violence cases themselves.[6]

An activist from Zimbabwe describes how a male police officer's self-image as fatherly protector in the community can be an obstacle for battered women:

> Another problem is the way that the police view themselves. One result of striving to be a peoples' police force has been that the police are often viewed as elders within a community and asked to intervene in everything from misplaced birth certificates to family disputes. Police in Musasa workshops have enthusiastically embraced the idea of 'counseling' as a solution to domestic violence. As a result, there have been examples of police spending half-an-hour 'counseling' a couple at the station and then sending them home, when in fact the man should have been taken into custody. A connected problem is the possibility that counseling will be aimed only at the woman, telling her to behave.[7]

Police response in some countries fails to even acknowledge that domestic violence is a problem that needs attention. Tracing and comparing the progress of the battered women's movement in Britain and the United States, Dobash and Dobash identified police rejection as one of the most difficult hurdles to overcome. Referring to the origins of the movement in Britain, they report: "[t]he police were strongest in denying the extent or severity of the problem or the need for any change in their service."[8] In the United States, police have been described as "largely indifferent" to domestic violence.[9] The first reported legal case in the United States in which a domestic violence survivor successfully sued police for violating her constitutional rights, involved not only apathy by police, but active disregard of a

---

4. UNITED NATIONS MANUAL, *supra* note 1, at 26.

5. *Id.* at 27.

6. Zorza, *supra* note 3, at 48–49.

7. Sheelagh Stewart, *Working the System: Sensitizing the Police to the Plight of Women in Zimbabwe,* in FREEDOM FROM VIOLENCE: WOMEN'S STRATEGIES FROM AROUND THE WORLD 157, 171 (Margaret Schuler ed., 1992).

8. R. EMERSON DOBASH & RUSSELL P. DOBASH, WOMEN VIOLENCE AND SOCIAL CHANGE 121 (1992).

9. Zorza, *supra* note 3, at 47 (1992). *Also see* Carolyne R. Hathaway, *Comment, Gender Based Discrimination in Police Reluctance to Respond to Domestic Violence Assault Complaints,* 75 GEO. L.J. 667 (1986).

battered woman in the face of immediate danger. In that case, the plaintiff, Tracey Thurman, had been repeatedly attacked by her estranged husband for months. When she obtained a protective order, her assailant continued to violate the order, and police ignored or rejected Tracey's pleas for enforcement.[10] On June 10, 1983, Tracey's husband came to her home and began to stab her repeatedly:

> When police officers arrived on the scene, Charles dropped the bloody knife he was holding and kicked Tracey in the head. He then ran into the house, got their son, and dropped him on Tracey. Charles again kicked Tracey in the head. Several other police officers arrived on the scene and stood by as Charles continued to threaten his wife and wander among the crowd that had gathered. When Charles approached Tracey again as she was lying on a stretcher, he was finally taken into custody.[11]

Evidence of a police failure to take domestic violence claims seriously and investigate them properly exists in many other countries. In Latin America, advocates for battered women have reported that police are at best nonresponsive to the complaints of battered women and often actively hostile to women reporting domestic violence.[12] A researcher working with battered women in Mexico reports:

> In Mexico, the police are notorious for ignoring or violating the rights of women. A woman who appears to file a complaint against a batterer or rapist runs the risk of being ignored, humiliated, threatened, or sexually assaulted by police officers ostensibly there to serve them.[13]

Advocates working with battered women in Chile report:

> Police officers and other legal agents who are required by Chilean law to report all known assault cases fail to prosecute cases brought to their attention by battered women seeking to make complaints.[14]

---

10. Thurman v. City of Torrington, 595 F. Supp. 1521 (D. Conn. 1984). Thurman was the first reported case in which a court held that when police treat victims of domestic violence differently than other assault victims, it is gender discrimination violating the equal protection clause of the United States Constitution. Hathaway, *supra* note 9, at 667.

11. Hathaway, *id.*

12. In Brazil, advocates for battered women reported: "Battery, rape and death threats are routine facts in the lives of many women. . . . Every time women go to the regular *delegacias* (police stations) they suffer another type of violence. This is the violence of refusing to register their complaints, the suspicion cast upon them making them responsible for the crimes they suffered. . . . Such behavior of the authorities reinforces and legitimizes impunity for violence against women and makes them hesitate to fight for their rights." Letter sent to the Secretary of Public Security by the SOS Mulher Chapter in Belo Horizonte, October 1982, *cited in* Crimes Contra A Mulher: A Violecia Denunciada, provisional title, unpublished report written by Maria da Conceicao Marques Rubinger et al., *quoted in* WOMEN'S RIGHTS PROJECT, HUMAN RIGHTS WATCH, CRIMINAL INJUSTICE: VIOLENCE AGAINST WOMEN IN BRAZIL 43 (1991) [hereinafter WOMEN'S RIGHTS PROJECT BRAZIL].

13. Elizabeth Schrader-Cox, *Developing Strategies: Efforts to End Violence Against Women in Mexico, in* FREEDOM FROM VIOLENCE: WOMEN'S STRATEGIES FROM AROUND THE WORLD 175, 182 (Margaret Schuler ed., 1992).

14. Katherine M. Culliton, *Finding a Mechanism to Enforce Women's Right to State Protection from Domestic Violence in the Americas,* 34 HARV. INT'L L.J. 507, 517 (1993), *citing* CECILIA MOLTEDO, ESTUDIO SOBRE VIOLENCIA DOMESTICA EN MUJERES POBLADORAS CHILENAS (1988); and XIMENA AHUMADA & RUTH ALVAREZ, ESTUDIO DE CASO SOBRE LA SITUACION DE LA VIOLENCIA CONYUGAL EN CHILE

Recent investigation in Eastern Europe reveals an alarming failure by police to acknowledge domestic violence as criminal behavior. In Bulgaria, Albania, and Romania, police readily admit their unwillingness to enforce criminal law against domestic batterers.[15] The same police attitude is found in Russia. One domestic violence activist from Moscow reported: "The law doesn't protect women. If a woman goes to police and tells them that she is being beaten by her husband or partner, the police say, 'But he didn't kill you yet.'"[16]

In Russia, the police officers' complete failure to respond to domestic violence appears to have been sanctioned by high-level government officials. The director of the Ministry of the Interior's public relations section agreed that domestic violence is a widespread problem in Russia, but explained police failure to respond to the problem by asserting that women either do not report assaults or that women provoke assaults by "letting themselves go" after marriage.[17]

In its report on violence against women in South Africa, Human Rights Watch documents repeated incidences of a complete failure to respond by police.[18] In one 1994 incident, a battered woman married to a police officer shot herself. She had

---

(1987). In one example, a woman named Maria Luisa filed several complaints of battery with police. None of the complaints were prosecuted except one, held to be a misdemeanor. Later, the husband continued beating Maria Luisa, finally leaving her paralyzed. Culliton, *id.* at 517, citing A. Sabater, *Mi Marido Va A Golpearme*, LA REVISTA FEMININA DE EL MERCURIO, May 27, 1986, at 8.

15. In 1995, a former police officer from Albania explained to human rights investigators that he did not consider domestic violence to be an important issue because it did not involve danger to "society as a whole." MINNESOTA ADVOCATES FOR HUMAN RIGHTS, DOMESTIC VIOLENCE IN ALBANIA 16 (1996) [hereinafter MINNESOTA ADVOCATES ALBANIA]. A representative of the Bulgarian National Police acknowledged that police do not pay much attention to domestic disputes. MINNESOTA ADVOCATES FOR HUMAN RIGHTS, DOMESTIC VIOLENCE IN BULGARIA 15 (1996) [hereinafter MINNESOTA ADVOCATES BULGARIA]. Criminal court records from a 1993 case in Sofia, Bulgaria, document an incident where police were called to stop a continuing barrage of violence over a two-day period by a husband against his wife. Even when the husband acted aggressively toward the police, he was not arrested. *Id.* at 12–13. In Romania, in 1994, Police Academy professors explained to investigators that domestic violence was not a problem in their country because men loved their women so much they would never hurt them. MINNESOTA ADVOCATES FOR HUMAN RIGHTS, LIFTING THE LAST CURTAIN: A REPORT ON DOMESTIC VIOLENCE IN ROMANIA 12 (1995) [hereinafter MINNESOTA ADVOCATES ROMANIA].

16. HUMAN RIGHTS WATCH, THE HUMAN RIGHTS WATCH GLOBAL REPORT ON WOMEN'S HUMAN RIGHTS 373 (1995). A Russian human rights worker reported that a domestic violence victim had complained to the police for a year about assaults by her husband. The police did nothing. *Id.* at 374. Another domestic violence worker reported, "Women don't call the police because they are afraid it will make the situation worse for them and their children. Also, everyone thinks it is shameful to discuss family problems with the police. Some women don't call because they think it's no use. In some cases, they have friends who have contacted the police to no avail." *Id.* at 378.

17. *Id.* at 377. The acting Minister of Social Security in Russia (who is responsible for preparing Russia's report on the status of women to the United Nations) told Human Rights Watch that the police should not be involved in cases of domestic violence.

18. WOMEN'S RIGHTS PROJECT, HUMAN RIGHTS WATCH, VIOLENCE AGAINST WOMEN IN SOUTH AFRICA: STATE RESPONSE TO DOMESTIC VIOLENCE AND RAPE 74–83 (1995) [hereinafter WOMEN'S RIGHTS PROJECT SOUTH AFRICA]. One of the particular problems with the police was a failure to enforce a progressive new law on protective orders or "interdicts." *Id.* at 75–76.

previously reported the violence to a station commander who had reportedly told her simply that "she mustn't worry about it".[19] A South African rape crisis worker reported to Human Rights Watch: "Police culture works against women. . . . [T]he attitudes and assumptions that the police have about women undermine the proper functioning of the law."[20] The growing body of evidence from around the world demonstrates a dangerous police failure to enforce criminal laws to protect battered women.

Institutes of Forensic Medicine

Domestic violence survivors seeking justice worldwide are finding that one of the most difficult hurdles to overcome lies in a procedural or evidentiary requirement common to many legal systems—the medical legal certificate granted by government institutes of forensic medicine. In many countries, battered women are required to obtain this certificate documenting their injuries before they can proceed in court.[21]

In some jurisdictions the medical legal certificate is a prerequisite to any kind of criminal court proceeding. Other jurisdictions may allow some other medical evidence of injury to support a victim's claim. In either case, the system is fraught with difficulties for domestic violence survivors. Foremost of these difficulties is the tendency of the forensic physicians to dismiss a domestic violence claim before it ever reaches the criminal court system, thereby acting as "gatekeepers" to the system. The prejudice and lack of information held by forensic physicians as they evaluate a woman's injuries often denies a domestic violence survivor access to justice.

The general procedure involves an examination of the injured woman by a doctor, usually one trained in the law. The physician then completes a medical legal form or certificate recording his or her evaluation of the case. Often the form calls for an evaluation of the injuries and their cause. Frequently, the certificate calls for the physician's categorization of the injury according to the criminal law.[22] Evidence from several countries indicates that the physician may stray from an objective categorization of an injury to one that includes a personal evaluation of the circumstances surrounding the assault—such as whether a woman provoked an assault by her husband. In Chile, research reveals that the Instituto Medico-Legal "routinely fails to report battered women's injuries as serious enough for criminal prosecution."[23] In Mexico, the "medico legista" may play an even more adversarial role

---

19. *Id.* at 78.

20. *Id.*

21. This practice has been identified in Latin America (Schrader-Cox, *supra* note 13, at 183, and Culliton, *supra* note 14, at 517); South Africa (WOMEN'S RIGHTS PROJECT SOUTH AFRICA, *supra* note 18, at 96–98); and Eastern Europe (MINNESOTA ADVOCATES, *supra* note 15, at 17 (Albania), 11 (Bulgaria), and 13 (Romania)).

22. MINNESOTA ADVOCATES, *supra* note 15, at 11 (Bulgaria), and 13 (Romania).

23. Culliton, *supra* note 14, at 517.

towards a woman seeking the certificate; in cases of rape, "the expressed purpose of the physical examination is to discredit a woman's account of the attack."[24] More specifically, "[t]he medico legista is instructed to consider that the woman has not been raped and to look for inconsistency in her story or evidence that contradicts her allegations."[25]

In one criminal case occurring in Bucharest, Romania, which was reviewed by Minnesota Advocates for Human Rights in 1994, the forensic physician categorized an injury in a less serious class of criminal assault than the injury dictated according to the express language of the criminal code.[26] Asked about the discrepancy, the presiding judge explained that the categorization certified by the doctor may be affected by what he or she views as mitigating circumstances, such as the complainant's state of intoxication or whether the doctor feels the abuser was provoked.[27] This case highlights the inherent injustice in such a system; before a woman ever reaches a courtroom, her assault claim may be adjudicated by a physician who acts as investigator and arbitrator of her claim.

Procedures at the institutions also present practical problems to domestic violence victims and may often hinder the goal of providing accurate court documentation of injuries. For example, a domestic violence survivor in rural Romania described how, after an incident of battery, she went to the forensic institution repeatedly to find it closed. By the time she was able to see a doctor her injuries had healed somewhat and her bruises had faded.[28] Women have reported a similar problem in Chile:

> [B]ecause the Institute is generally backlogged, appointments often cannot be made immediately after an attack and often are put off for a week or more. Wounds are thus less apparent, the victim's proof often lost, and cases dropped.[29]

Forensic institutions present other problems to domestic violence survivors. As institutions existing for the purpose of providing documentation for court proceedings, their primary focus may not be the best medical care and treatment of domestic violence survivors, a goal which is lost in these legal requirements.[30] Women seeking

---

24.   Schrader-Cox, *supra* note 13, at 183.

25.   *Id.*

26.   In the Bulgarian criminal code, injuries are classified according to necessary healing times. [MINNE-SOTA ADVOCATES ROMANIA *supra* note 15 at 13.]

27.   *Id.*

28.   Interview with advocate working with domestic violence survivors in rural Romania, May 1995.

29.   Culliton, *supra* note 14, at 518 (*citing* Vivian Bustos, Address at the Coegio de Abogados de Chile y Consejo Nacional de orientacion Familiar (July 13, 1988)).

30.   In South Africa, where doctors with duties similar to that of forensic physicians are referred to as district surgeons: "The district surgeon system has been criticized by health professionals for providing a sub-standard service for the state. District surgeons are badly paid by comparison with private practice, and there is no incentive to come out in the middle of the night to examine a rape victim or to provide any medical care beyond the collection of medical evidence. The Department of Health does not provide district surgeons with appropriate training in assisting rape victims. The department also has not expanded the responsibility of district surgeons to include the provision of basic medical treatment to rape

treatment for their injuries may be confused and misled by the process and end up never receiving adequate medical care.

Advocates from some regions have begun to identify the problems presented by forensic institutions. They have clarified the need to determine the appropriate role of forensic institutions and to provide training where necessary on issues surrounding domestic violence survivors, their injuries, and their right to criminal justice.[31]

Prosecution

If a domestic violence victim manages to reach the stage in the criminal justice process where she either seeks or requires the assistance or authority of the prosecutor's office, she frequently encounters a lack of enthusiasm or even hostility parallel to that which she found with the police. The United Nations reports:

> The decision to prosecute cases of domestic violence rests, in most jurisdictions, with the prosecutors' office which represents the State. These offices have not prosecuted most cases of domestic violence referred to them. Nor have they treated these cases in the same manner as cases involving violence between strangers.[32]

Prosecutorial failure to pursue domestic violence offenses may be grounded in the language of the law. For example, according to Bulgarian law, in the case of medium-level injuries, the law distinguishes between an assault by a stranger and one by a relative.[33] Those injured by a relative are not entitled to involvement by the state prosecutor's office. They may prosecute their cases but must do so alone; they must locate and call their own witnesses and present their own evidence in court.[34] A prosecutor from Sofia, Bulgaria, explained in 1995: "A woman must decide for herself whether she wants to harm the family relationship through prosecution; the state will not damage the family by assisting her."[35]

---

victims; although in many cases the district surgeons will be the only doctor that a raped woman will see—ever." WOMEN'S RIGHTS PROJECT SOUTH AFRICA, *supra* note 18, at 97.

31. For example, in April 1996, a group of medical and legal experts from Latin American and the United States convened to discuss "gatekeepers" to the legal system and other hurdles facing battered women in the region. The conference was sponsored by the Women and International Law Program at American University's Washington College of Law and the Pan American Health Organization's Women Health and Development Policy Project.

32. UNITED NATIONS MANUAL, *supra* note 1, at 38. The report of the U. N. Secretary-General on domestic violence in 1990 included a similar conclusion. Noting the limited research available, the report stated: "the available findings on the prosecution of family violence cases as compared with crimes of violence between strangers tends to support the contention of differential prosecution policy, linked primarily to differences, or perceived differences in victim/witness co-operation, and only secondarily, to the quality and quantity of the physical evidence available." Domestic Violence, Report of the Secretary General, U.N. Doc. A/CONF.144/17 (July 1990), at 15.

33. Bulgarian Criminal Code, Crimes Against the Person, art. 161.

34. MINNESOTA ADVOCATES BULGARIA, *supra* note 15, at 10. Although there is a provision in the law that grants discretion to government prosecutors to take on domestic violence cases, the prevailing negative attitude towards battered women makes it highly unlikely that would happen.

35. *Id.* at 11.

The opinion among prosecutors that domestic violence victims have no place seeking criminal sanctions against their batterers prevails in many parts of Eastern Europe. In Albania, where procedure dictates that a woman bring her case to the prosecutor if she seeks criminal sanctions, it is standard policy for the prosecutor to try to convince her to drop the case.[36] In Poland, a battered woman reported that the prosecutor's response to her request for assistance was essentially, "Unless they took you out in a plastic bag, the public prosecutors' office would not be interested."[37]

A general failure to prosecute domestic violence cases persists in other regions of the world. In South Africa, prosecutors with wide discretion encourage battered women to drop their cases.[38] In Mexico City, prosecutors' attitude that battered women should not bring criminal complaints against their abusers is entrenched.[39] For example, to encourage battered women to reconcile with their batterers, a public official called the "Conciliator" maintains an office in the Ministerio Publico, the office charged with criminal prosecution in Mexico City. One of the most common ways prosecutors handle domestic violence claims is to send a woman to the Conciliator to encourage dismissal of the criminal charges.[40]

In Brazil, despite an increased police response to domestic violence in recent years, cases are rarely prosecuted.[41] Human Rights Watch attributed this in part to huge backlogs in the courts. The group also noted a persistent failure among law enforcement officials to recognize the criminality of the act.

Resolution and Sentencing

Of the few battered women in the world who actually have claims against their batterers adjudicated, even fewer receive real justice. The conduct of many judges reveals a shocking willingness to ignore criminal conduct by men against their wives or partners, or dismiss it as unimportant. Many countries provide judges with wide discretion in imposing sentences in cases of domestic violence, which has been used to both the benefit and detriment of domestic violence victims. Stiff sentences, including imprisonment, dispel the belief that domestic violence is a second class crime. As the United Nations concluded:

> Courts usually order incarceration only in the most serious cases of domestic violence. It may be the only appropriate option where the offender is a threat to the safety of

---

36. MINNESOTA ADVOCATES ALBANIA, *supra* note 15, at 17.

37. Letter to author from Polish woman (June 20, 1996).

38. WOMEN'S RIGHTS PROJECT SOUTH AFRICA, *supra* note 18, at 85.

39. Schrader-Cox, *supra* note 13, at 182.

40. Interview with official at Centro de Atencion a la Violencia Antrafamilia (CAVI), a government office in Mexico City serving battered women (March 20, 1996). One of these Conciliators in Mexico City is open about his opinion that it is a husband's right to beat his wife and thus state prosecution of these crimes is inappropriate.

41. WOMEN'S RIGHTS PROJECT BRAZIL, *supra* note 12, at 49.

the victim or the community. When offenders have continued to threaten or use violence despite sanctions, the court may have little choice. The existence of incarceration as a sentencing option helps create equivalency with other violent crimes.[42]

The priority of elevating the crime of wife assault, however, must be balanced against the needs and concerns of the victim herself. As one advocate has pointed out, ''What most women want is for the violence to stop, not for their husbands to be sent to jail.''[43]

In many parts of the world, judicial decisions reflect that wife-assault or even wife-murder is simply irrelevant in the face of preservation of either the family itself or the family ''honor.'' Judicial decisions in Pakistan reveal this attitude in its most extreme form. Hina Jilani, a lawyer and human rights advocate from Pakistan, reported in 1992:

> In cases where a woman has been murdered by a male member of her own family, sentences have been extremely lenient. Most cases of grave and sudden provocation involve a man who is accused of killing his wife due to her marital infidelity. However, courts have been willing to apply the grave and sudden provocation exception even where the man has not caught his wife in the act. Moreover, the courts generally accept the defense on very little evidence and then drastically reduce the sentence given to the man.[44]

Jilani notes that the more violent the crime, the more willing the court is to accept a provocation defense, because ''[t]he assumption is that for a husband to kill his wife in such a brutal manner, she must have given some provocation.''[45]

Research from Eastern Europe reveals that the criminality of an act of domestic violence is of little concern and low priority to judges in the region. Consistent with the attitude of some prosecutors, judges see penalizing a batterer as an assault on the family as an institution. Indeed, one judge justified his decision by indicating that he would ''feel responsible for destroying the family if he sentenced an abusive husband to serve time in prison. This judge explained that he believes that domestic violence is not a serious problem.''[46]

A judicial reluctance to convict and punish domestic violence offenders has also been found in Bulgaria. After a review of forty-three criminal case files from the Sofia Regional Court involving domestic violence, Minnesota Advocates for Human Rights concluded:

---

42.   UNITED NATIONS MANUAL, *supra* note 1, at 44.

43.   Margaret Schuler, *Violence Against Women: An International Perspective, in* FREEDOM FROM VIOLENCE: WOMEN'S STRATEGIES FROM AROUND THE WORLD 33 (Margaret Schuler ed., 1992).

44.   Hina Jilani, *Whose Laws?: Human Rights and Violence Against Women in Pakistan in* FREEDOM FROM VIOLENCE: WOMEN'S STRATEGIES FROM AROUND THE WORLD 63, 69 (Margaret Schuler ed. 1992).

45.   *Id.*

46.   MINNESOTA ADVOCATES ALBANIA, *supra* note 15, at 16.

Many of the cases were startling in their brutality and in the courts' reluctance to punish the violent conduct. No matter what the facts or the injuries, the courts were often satisfied if the parties agreed to reconcile.[47]

This attitude has also been reflected in judicial decisions in Latin America.[48] Similarly, in the United States case of State of Maryland v. Peacock, Judge Robert E. Cahill imposed an inappropriately lenient sentence on defendant Kenneth Peacock, who had killed his wife after finding her in bed with another man. In reaching his decision, the judge stated:

> I seriously wonder how many married men . . . would have the strength to walk away . . . without inflicting some corporal punishment, whatever that punishment might be. I shudder to think what I would do.[49]

Improvement and Reform of Criminal Justice Systems

Recognizing the law as a potent tool for changing attitudes and, ultimately, behavior, many activists around the world are focusing their efforts on rewriting laws and improving their enforcement to more effectively confront domestic violence crimes. One obvious advantage to improved laws is that they can clearly articulate standards of behavior not only for batterers but also for law enforcement officials and the community. A specific law criminalizing domestic violence, for example, is a direct and authoritative response to the batterer who continues to see it as his duty or right to admonish his wife, and the police officer who agrees with him. Effective enforcement of that law powerfully confirms the moral and legal culpability.

Feminist scholars also articulate the disadvantage of focusing energy and effort on legal reform. Some argue that the law reflects a structure of female subordination and that continued efforts at reform will not significantly improve women's condition.[50] The argument that the law, with its patriarchal underpinnings and structure, cannot be effective in addressing injustice in women's lives has particular merit

---

47. MINNESOTA ADVOCATES BULGARIA, *supra* note 15, at 12.

48. Schrader-Cox, *supra* note 13, at 182.

49. Case Number 94–CRO943 Baltimore County Court (October 1994). Peacock received the minimum sentence allowable under Maryland guidelines: three years. All but eighteen months of the sentence was suspended, during which time Peacock was allowed a work release.

50. One scholar describes the law as foreign to women's experience: "Many feminists have pointed out that law is part of the structure of male domination. Its hierarchical organization, its adversarial format, and its aim of the abstract resolution of competing rights make the law an intensely patriarchal institution. Law represents a very limited aspect of human experience. The language and imagery of the law underscore its maleness: it lays claim to rationality, objectivity, and abstraction, characteristics traditionally associated with men, and is defined in contrast to emotion, subjectivity, and contextualized thinking, the province of women." Hilary Charlesworth, *What are "Women's International Human Rights"?*, in HUMAN RIGHTS OF WOMEN 58, 65 (Rebecca Cook ed., 1994). For further discussion, *see* Frances Olsen, *Feminism and Critical Legal Theory: An American Perspective*, INT'L. J. SOC. L. 18 (1990); and CATHARINE MACKINNON, FEMINISM UNMODIFIED: DISCOURSES ON LIFE AND LAW (1987).

when viewed in the context of domestic violence.[51] In addition, many domestic violence advocates and survivors point to the problems in women's personal lives posed by enforcement of the criminal law against batterers. Seeking redress in the criminal justice system may isolate a woman from her extended family or result in acts of revenge against her by the husband's family.[52] Incarceration of a batterer does not permanently ensure a woman's safety and, in fact, may result in increased violence upon his release. A woman is likely to experience serious economic hardship if her husband is put in jail, and if he is fined, payment will probably come out of the family budget. One writer describes the clash between criminal law and family intimacy:

> When domestic violence takes place, the criminal law intrudes into the domain of family relationships. This unhappy incursion lends crimes between intimates a unique and complex quality, importing concomitant difficulties around the offense and appropriate sentencing. Domestic abuse in fact raises the question whether law is at all suited to traverse the divides, the conflicts and contradictions of human intimacy.[53]

The ineffectiveness of, and potential harm presented to battered women by the criminal justice system has caused some activists to instead focus efforts on establishing services for domestic violence survivors. Such services may include health care, financial maintenance, and, most important, shelters or safe homes.[54]

However, the urgent global need to protect women's safety, and the belief that domestic violence will never be eliminated without the effective intervention of the

---

51. Dobash and Dobash discuss and compare the domestic violence movements in England and the United States. They examine the criminal justice system response and point out, "What is important here is that activists have been left with the dilemma that leaving the concerns about violent men to the criminal justice system alone has not been effective in meeting the movement goals of protecting women from male violence." DOBASH & DOBASH, *supra* note 8, at 45.

52. Connors, *The Criminal Justice System, supra* note 2, at 80.

53. Joanne Fedler, *Lawyering Domestic Violence Through the Prevention of Family Violence Act 1993–An Evaluation After a Year in Operation*, 112 S. AFR. L.J. 231, 233 (May 1995).

54. Dobash and Dobash describe the origins of the shelter movement in Britain and the United States in the early 1970s. The first recognized shelter in the world, Chiswick Women's Aid, was established in Britain in 1972. DOBASH & DOBASH, *supra* note 8, at 63.

Jane Connors writes: "Shelter provision has proven to be the most important service for victims of domestic violence. Shelters, which were originally conceived as advice centers for women at risk and ultimately developed to provide residential accommodation for them and their children exist in such varied countries as Trinidad and Tobago, Egypt, Malaysia, Zimbabwe and India. Although many are now government staffed and funded, most were initiated by volunteer women who themselves had been victims of violence. In many countries where the government has adopted the shelter model, shelters are established for specific groups of women, such as immigrant women, women with disabilities, and aboriginal women. Unfortunately, even countries that have introduced shelters generally do not provide sufficient funding and shelters are overcrowded and understaffed. Other services that exist for victims of domestic assault include toll-free advice lines, counselling services and advice centers." Jane Connors, *Government Measures to Confront Violence Against Women, in* COMBATTING VIOLENCE AGAINST WOMEN 21, 24 (1993). In some regions, such as Central and Eastern Europe, shelters have only recently been opened and, in Hungary for example, establishments meant to provide services for the general population have become *de facto* battered women's shelters because of the great need.

criminal justice system, continues to drive many activists to focus efforts on legal reform. As a beginning point, for example, advocates are committed to prompt reform of criminal laws that explicitly relegate domestic violence to less serious categories of crime, such as the Bulgarian Criminal Procedure Code, or that of Nigeria, which eliminated wife-battery from the penal code.[55] Activists recognize that discriminatory legal practices, such as the use of the honor defense, must be directly confronted and ultimately eliminated.[56]

The following are some of the areas on which advocates have focused legal reform efforts specifically within the criminal justice system.

Efforts to Improve Police Response

A variety of reform strategies have developed with the goal of improving police response to domestic violence. Among the most important efforts at reform are probable cause and mandatory arrest policies. In cases involving simple or minor injuries, probable cause arrest policies allow police officers to make arrests based on the presence of evidence (such as damaged property, visible injuries, or a frightened woman) that would lead to the conclusion that an assault occurred. Police may make the arrest without witnessing the crime, as in felony assaults.[57] Mandatory arrest policies take this one step further and require the police to make an arrest at the scene of a domestic assault.[58] These ''pro-arrest'' policies are seen as necessary to combat the long- standing and globally prevalent police attitude that domestic violence is not a crime. These policies are reinforced by research that indicates that arrest is the most effective method of reducing domestic violence.[59] Such policies can, however, be problematic in countries with a history of government oppression. As a women's advocate from Bolivia explained:

---

55. Pat Mahmoud, *Patterns of Violence Against Women in Nigeria with Specific Focus on Domestic Violence, in* COMBATTING VIOLENCE AGAINST WOMEN 1, 6 (1993) (*citing* THE PENAL CODE LAW, LAWS OF NORTHERN NIGERIA (1963)).

56. The honor defense, though directly contradicting the express language of the penal code, has been used successfully for many years in Brazil to obtain acquittal of defendants accused of killing their spouses. Usually the assailant is the husband and the victim is the wife. WOMEN'S RIGHTS PROJECT BRAZIL, *supra* note 12, at 20–30 (*citing* Brazilian Penal Code, art. 28).

57. In the United States: ''Most states now allow arrest without a warrant for misdemeanor assault and/or domestic violence where the arresting officer has probable cause to believe that an offense has occurred. Arrest is permissive in forty-three states and mandatory in seven. The remaining five states either mandate that an officer use all reasonable means, including arrest, to prevent further abuse or leave it to the local police departments to develop a policy compatible with statutory guidelines.'' Nancy James, *Domestic Violence: A History of Arrest Policies and a Survey of Modern Laws*, 28 FAM. L.Q. 509, 513 (1994).

58. As of 1994, seven states in the United States had mandatory arrest policies. *Id.* at 513. Other countries have instituted mandatory arrest policies. Israel, for example, implemented police guidelines that require an arrest at the scene of domestic violence. UNITED NATIONS MANUAL, *supra* note 1, at 29.

59. Lawrence W. Sherman & Richard A. Berk, *The Specific Deterrent Effects of Arrest for Domestic Assault*, 49 AM. SOC. REV. 261 (1984). This article describes a study conducted in conjunction with the police department in Minneapolis, Minnesota, in which the authors followed the behavior of domestic

In times when the state and its instruments have penetrated the bedroom only to repress and pillage, such as during the dictatorships which coerced the law to legitimize their authoritarian regimes, it is quite difficult to publicly debate the problem of domestic violence without appearing to endorse the misuse of power.[60]

These policies can also have the unintended and undesired result of the arrest of a victim and, according to other research, may contribute to increased violence.[61]

One of the most dramatic efforts to improve police response has been the opening of women's police stations. Beginning in Brazil, these "delegacias" were established to deal exclusively with violence against women.[62] Luiza Nagib Eluf describes the background of this effort, its successes, and lessons learned in her article on women's police stations in Brazil.[63] In essence, a growing community perception that violence against women in Brazil had reached crisis proportions and that the police were the "most immediate solution since their role was to fight crime," resulted in the first women's police station in São Paulo in 1985.[64] The establishment of many other women's police stations followed, resulting in a huge increase in reports of violence against women, including domestic violence.[65] Although there were many positive results from the women's police stations, such as altering the attitude that domestic violence is acceptable, conviction rates did not improve.[66]

A strategy undertaken in the United States in the 1970s was class action lawsuits against the police for a failure to protect women from domestic violence. Activists saw this litigation as necessary in view of the refusal by police to change practices

---

violence offenders who had been arrested. Referring to the results of the study, the authors concluded that, "arrest and initial incarceration alone may produce a deterrent effect, regardless of how the courts treat such cases, and that arrest makes an independent contribution to the deterrent potential of the criminal justice system." *Id.* at 270.

60. Sonia Montana, *Long Live the Differences, with Equal Rights: A Campaign to End Violence Against Women in Bolivia, in* FREEDOM FROM VIOLENCE: WOMEN'S STRATEGIES FROM AROUND THE WORLD 213, 225 (Margaret Schuler ed., 1992).

61. Studies from Nebraska, North Carolina, and Milwaukee concluded that arrest resulted in increased violence. *Legal Responses to Domestic Violence,* 106 HARV. L. REV. 1498, 1539 (1993). (*But see* Zorza, *supra* note 3, at 65–72 for a discussion of the flaws in these studies.)

62. Argentina and Peru have also established women's police stations. UNITED NATIONS MANUAL, *supra* note 1, at 31. Colombia, Malaysia, Spain, and Pakistan have similar police stations. Report of the Special Rapporteur on Violence Against Women, U.N. ESCOR 52nd Sess. at para. 137, U.N. Doc. E/CN.4/1996/53.

63. Luiza Nagib Eluf, *A New Approach to Law Enforcement: The Special Women's Police Stations in Brazil, in* FREEDOM FROM VIOLENCE: WOMEN'S STRATEGIES FROM AROUND THE WORLD 199 (Margaret Schuler ed., 1992).

64. *Id.* at 204.

65. *Id.* at 205. Further, "[a] 1987 study of over 2,000 battery cases registered at the Sao Paulo delegacia from August to December 1985, found that over 70 percent of all reported crimes of violence against women occurred in the home." WOMEN'S RIGHTS PROJECT BRAZIL, *supra* note 12, at 44.

66. WOMEN'S RIGHTS PROJECT BRAZIL, *id.* at 49 and 55.

and policies with regard to domestic violence victims.[67] The first class action suit was filed against the Oakland, California, city police in 1976.[68] Two months later, activists filed suit against the New York City Police, for failure to comply with state laws. Both lawsuits were settled with both police departments agreeing to change their practices in domestic violence cases.[69] In this effort:

> Within this context of resistance, lawsuits were extremely important; they raised public awareness of the problem, publicized institutional forms of injustice, led to changes in State laws and set a precedent for police response all over the country.[70]

These lawsuits were followed by a ''flurry of activity'' in the United States to improve police and law enforcement response to battered women.[71]

Many jurisdictions have also attempted to improve police response through legislation requiring police officers to take specific steps in assisting domestic violence victims. This may include ensuring that a victim receives any necessary medical treatment and providing for her safety. Laws from Puerto Rico and Malaysia contain such provisions.[72] Other legislation, such as that from Guyana, gives police authority to enter premises where they suspect an assault is taking place.[73]

Reform efforts from every region recognize the importance of improved police response. Though contact with the police is only one phase of the battered woman's journey through the criminal justice system, it is then that she faces the most imminent danger. An effective police response can have the dual effect of ensuring a woman's safety and demonstrating to the batterer and the community that her safety is an important priority. Equally as important, the effective operation of the law, beginning with the police, can have an empowering effect on the victim. As one activist articulated: ''The woman who manages to get the police to remove her husband until the violence stops, to acquire a peace order, and to have her maintenance assured, is a woman who has learned that she can affect change.''[74]

---

67. DOBASH & DOBASH, *supra* note 8, at 165.

68. Complaint for Declaratory and Injunctive Relief and Petition for Writ of Mandate, Scott v. Hart No. C–76–2395 (N.D. Cal. filed Oct. 28, 1976).

69. Bruno v. Codd, 90 Misc.2d 1047, 396 N.Y.S.2d 974 (Sup. Ct. Special Term 1977), *rev'd in part, appeal dismissed in part,* 64 A.D.2d 582, 407 N.Y.S.2d 165 (1978), *aff'd,* 47 N.Y.2d 582, 393 N.E.2d 976, 419 N.Y.S.2d 901 (1979). This case was brought by the Litigation Coalition for Battered Women in New York on behalf of twelve women, all of whom had received no response from police when they were assaulted by their intimate partners. The complaint charged police and courts with gross failure to comply with New York state laws. One of the plaintiffs described an incident where police witnessed her husband's attempt to strangle her, yet still did not arrest him.

70. DOBASH & DOBASH, *supra* note 8, at 166.

71. *Id.* at 167.

72. WOMEN, LAW AND DEVELOPMENT INTERNATIONAL, STATE RESPONSES TO DOMESTIC VIOLENCE 82 (1996).

73. *Id.* at 82. *See also* UNITED NATIONS MANUAL, *supra* note 1, at 28.

74. Stewart, *supra* note 7, at 164.

Protective Orders

Protective orders, issued by a judge upon application and prohibiting batterers from coming near the applicant, have been a major focus of global legal reform. The purpose of such orders is not to punish the behavior of a batterer, but to protect a woman from further injury.

In the United States, the law regarding protective orders was a primary focus of reform in the initial stages of the battered women's movement. These orders, though obtained through civil procedures, can be an important tool for protecting survivors of domestic violence.[75] Nonetheless, protection orders are not without problems. They are frequently violated and often do not result in arrest for their violation.[76] Early on, efforts to improve the effectiveness of protective orders resulted in laws that granted police the power of arrest within the enforcement mechanisms of such orders.[77] Thus, a breach of the protective order might qualify as a misdemeanor, criminal offense, or criminal contempt and result in arrest. Another power given to police in some states was the ability to obtain a protective order by telephoning a judge during hours when the court was closed. In this way, police were able to serve a batterer with an order at the scene of an assault. In recent years, United States courts have imposed criminal liability for violations of protective orders.[78]

In 1993, the British Commonwealth Secretariat published model legislation on family violence that focused entirely on protection orders. The model law provides that application could be made to the court prohibiting the respondent from entering the applicant's home, place of work, or other area described in the order. According to this model legislation, application for such orders could be issued *ex parte* and enforced with criminal sanctions.[79]

---

75. Catherine F. Klein & Leslye E. Orloff, *Providing Legal Protection for Battered Women: An Analysis of State Statutes and Case Law*, 21 HOFSTRA L. REV. 801 (1993). This article provides a comprehensive and detailed description of civil protection order laws and court decisions on domestic violence from all fifty states of the United States, the District of Columbia, and Puerto Rico.

76. *Legal Responses to Domestic Violence, supra* note 61, at 1510. The article also notes criticism that protection orders are a "soft" approach to domestic violence that fails to treat wife-assault as a serious crime. *Id.* at 1511 (*citing* Peter Finn, *Civil Protection Orders: A Flawed Opportunity for Intervention, in* WOMAN BATTERING: POLICY RESPONSES 129, 155 (Michael Steinman ed., 1991)).

77. DOBASH & DOBASH, *supra* note 8, at 168.

78. State v. Steed, 665 A.2d 1072 (N.H. 1995) (New Hampshire Supreme Court affirmed lower court's conviction of defendant who violated domestic violence restraining order when he drove to victim's home with a gun in his car); Commonwealth v. Beckwith, 674 A.2d 276 (Pa. Super. Ct. 1996) (Superior Court of Pennsylvania upheld criminal conviction for violation of a Protection From Abuse Order obtained by 16–year-old victim.)

79. *Commonwealth Secretariat, Commonwealth Fund for Technical Cooperation, CARICOM Secretariat, Model Legislation with Respect to Family Violence, in* COMBATTING VIOLENCE AGAINST WOMEN, *supra* note 2, at 109.

In a recent international survey of twenty-one countries' specific domestic violence legislation, almost all had provisions for protective orders.[80]

Efforts to Improve Prosecution

Several strategies have developed around the world to improve prosecution of domestic violence offenders. Experience has shown that the most successful prosecutorial policies have been those which reflect the priorities of victim safety and ending the violence, and which recognize the critical role prosecutors play in reaching those goals.[81] Thus, efforts to improve prosecution frequently focus on supporting the victim through the criminal justice process and on prosecutor-initiated proceedings.[82]

One of the first coordinated criminal justice reform efforts in the United States, the Domestic Abuse Intervention Project (DAIP), initiated in Duluth, Minnesota, included the goal of improving prosecution of batterers as a central element.[83] To support a battered woman through the prosecution and trial of the case, DAIP assigned an advocate to work with the survivor beginning with her first contact with the city attorney's office:[84]

> The role of the advocate is to assist victims in making the determination whether to press charges, to prepare the victim for the court process, to provide the prosecuting attorney with information concerning the case and assistance in evidence gathering and to assist the prosecutor in making decisions regarding the case (i.e. providing factual information to determine whether a subpoena should be issued and giving sentencing recommendations.)[85]

While DAIP did not institute a strict "no drop," or absolute prosecution, policy, the previous practice of automatically dropping charges against the assailant upon the survivor's request was eliminated.[86] In addition to focusing on and coordinating

---

80. State Responses to Domestic Violence, *supra* note 72, at 83.

81. In one manual for prosecutors published in the United States, prosecutors are advised that they have the ability to "dramatically increase the safety of victims" and that as they proceed with a case they should develop a victim safety plan. Sarah Buel, *Family Violence, Manual for Prosecutors* (Texas District and County Attorneys Association, 1994).

82. Domestic Violence, Report of the Secretary General, *supra* note 32, at 15. The recent United Nations Manual includes a section outlining strategies used to improve prosecution of domestic violence cases. United Nations Manual, *supra* note 1, at 39–45.

83. Domestic Abuse Intervention Project, Coordinated Community Response to Domestic Assault Cases: A Guide for Policy Development (Duluth, Minnesota rev. ed., 1996). *See also* Ellen Pence, *The Duluth Domestic Intervention Project*, 6 Hamline L. Rev. 247 (1983).

84. See the discussion of Quincy Court Model Domestic Abuse Program in *Legal Responses to Domestic Violence, supra* note 61, at 1516. This approach also trained advocates to accompany domestic violence survivors through the criminal justice system.

85. Pence, *supra* note 83, at 260.

86. *Id.* Absolute prosecution policies prohibit charges from being dropped after they are initiated, even at the request of the battered woman. This has been instituted in other jurisdictions in the United States with mixed results. In one extreme case in a jurisdiction with a strict no-drop policy, a domestic violence

reform with the police, prosecutors, and judges, DAIP enlisted the involvement of supportive agencies such as shelters, and counseling, rehabilitative, and education services that help ensure the success of criminal justice reform. The project resulted in increased numbers of arrests of batterers, reduced numbers of repeat calls to police, increased numbers of criminal sanctions against batterers, and a large increase in the number of women filing for protective orders. Most important, the project ''shift[ed] the focus of intervention from the victim to the assailant.''[87] As advocate Ellen Pence described: ''Criminal justice and human service providers now consider ending the violence as the primary intervention goal.''[88]

Jurisdictions in other regions have created specialized prosecution units that solely address family violence cases. In Canada, these specialized law enforcement officials prosecute cases aggressively, often without victim participation. In Manitoba, professionals working in a special criminal Family Violence Court are knowledgeable not only about domestic violence law but also about the unique problems that face battered women in the legal system.[89] The Family Violence Court,

> addresses the unique requirements of domestic violence cases by having staff (a) process cases as quickly as possible to reduce trauma and encourage victims to continue to participate in the criminal justice process; and (b) provide victims and offenders with information on other support services. After sentencing, they refer offenders to treatment programmes.[90]

To respond to a general failure to treat domestic violence claims seriously, Mexico City established a special unit within the attorney general's office to work with domestic violence survivors. Although important progress has been made within this unit, prosecution rates have not substantially improved.[91]

Law enforcement officials in San Diego, California, have initiated a policy that assumes the survivor will not participate at all in the prosecution of her case.[92] This

---

survivor was jailed for contempt when she refused to testify against her batterer. *Legal Responses to Domestic Violence, supra* note 61, at 1540–41.

87.   Pence, *supra* note 83, at 269. Dobash and Dobash described the success of DAIP: ''The Duluth project has made significant progress in shifting the focus of criminal justice intervention from the victim to the assailant, establishing meaningful consequences for violent abusers and reducing the frustrations and dissatisfactions of members of the criminal justice system.... Rather than seeing violence in the family as merely a 'domestic' problem arising from pathological individuals or dysfunctional families, battering is now seen as a criminal offense.'' DOBASH & DOBASH, *supra* note 8, at 183.

88.   Pence, *supra* note 83, at 269.

89.   UNITED NATIONS MANUAL, *supra* note 1, at 40.

90.   *Id.*

91.   Interview with official at Centro de Atencion a la Violencia Antrafamilia (CAVI), a government office in Mexico City serving battered women (March 20, 1996).

92.   As noted by the United Nations Secretary-General, ''The fact that in many jurisdictions the legal procedures employed in the prosecution of family assaults categorized as misdemeanors require the victim to be the plaintiff, and not just a witness, can create special problems for the victim who, in addition to an understandable reluctance to play an active prosecution role, may also become more vulnerable to threats and retaliation from the assailant.'' Domestic Violence, Report of the Secretary General, *supra* note 32, at 15.

policy has been labeled "victimless prosecution."[93] Police investigation is also conducted with the assumption that the battered woman will not testify. This results in more thorough gathering and preserving of evidence at the initial stages of the case.[94] The San Diego City Attorney has explained this policy as the best way to ensure the safety of the woman: "If you require a victim to press charges or prosecute, you've just drawn a target on her chest."[95] The "victimless prosecution" policy has resulted in increased convictions and a reduced number of homicides.[96]

Efforts to Improve Judicial Resolution

Efforts to improve judicial treatment of domestic violence cases involve primarily educating and training the judiciary in the causes and consequences of domestic violence and in the impact of the law on domestic violence survivors. Many efforts are underway around the world to train judges and other law enforcement personnel. For example, a program to train judges and other legal professionals has been developed by The International Centre for Criminal Law Reform in Vancouver, B.C., Canada.[97] This center developed a core curriculum for judges and justice officials in requesting countries. The curriculum was then translated and adapted for use by its sister institutes in Europe and Latin America.[98] The U. N.'s Resource Manual describes several other programs aimed at improving resolution of domestic violence cases.[99]

Specific Domestic Violence Legislation

In the 1980s and 1990s, many countries passed specific domestic violence legislation. These national and state laws represent an effort to address the myriad of social obstacles battered women face as they attempt to escape domestic violence. Such legislation aims to integrate a government's response to battered women that will most effectively terminate the violent behavior. Many activists view this specific legislation as highly preferable to piecemeal changes in generally applicable criminal and civil laws: "Domestic violence legislation serves as a useful tool for

---

93. In an international survey soliciting recommendations for improvements in the laws, respondents advocated for victimless prosecution. STATE RESPONSES TO DOMESTIC VIOLENCE, *supra* note 72, at 97–98.

94. Joan Zorza, *Battered Women Behave Like Other Threatened Victims,* I (6) DOMESTIC VIOLENCE REPORT 5 (Aug./Sept. 1996).

95. Stephanie Goldberg, *Nobody's Victim,* AM. BAR ASSN. J. 48, 50 (July 1996).

96. *Id.*

97. 1 (2) International Centre for Criminal Law Reform and Criminal Justice Policy Newsletter (Spring 1996).

98. The sister institutes are: The European Institute for Crime Prevention and Control (HEUNI) in Helsinki, Finland, the United Nations Interregional Crime and Justice Research Institute (UNICRI) in Rome, Italy, and the Instituto Latino Americano de Naciones Unidas Par la Prevencion del Delito y Tratamiento del Delincuente (ILANUD) in San Jose, Costa Rica.

99. UNITED NATIONS MANUAL, *supra* note 1, at 72.

packaging and integrating the remedies necessary to women who have been subjected to violence while still criminalizing the act of domestic violence.''[100]

In addition to providing a more effective government response to battered women, specific domestic violence legislation sends a forceful message to society that domestic violence will henceforth not be tolerated. The risk of specific domestic violence legislation is that it will not be supported by adequate training of law enforcement officials and the social services necessary to make it effective. For instance, referring to the South Africa Prevention of Family Violence Act of 1993, Joanne Fedler writes:

> [The] enactment [of domestic violence legislation] was not accompanied by government funding for support structures or by programmes to address gender bias in the police and court system or by initiatives to put an end to the inadequacies of the maintenance court system. . . . In the absence of support structures to make it workable, the Act offers a potentially empty remedy.[101]

The book, ''State Responses to Domestic Violence,'' summarizes the results of a survey of domestic violence laws around the world. The authors reviewed specific domestic violence legislation from twenty-one countries, as well as non-specific civil and criminal laws.[102] Some specific domestic laws provide for distinct criminalization of domestic violence. Many activists have stressed the need to emphasize the criminal nature of wife–assault in the letter of the law. They report the lack of knowledge that domestic violence is a crime as one of the primary obstacles to ending domestic violence.[103]

Often, specific domestic violence legislation focuses heavily on the safety of the victim and her ability to live independently of the batterer. As mentioned earlier, almost all of the specific domestic violence laws surveyed had provisions for protective orders. Other common features of specific domestic violence legislation include definitions of domestic violence, complaint mechanisms and procedures, special powers of police to enter premises and make arrests, and counseling provisions.[104]

---

100. STATE RESPONSES TO DOMESTIC VIOLENCE, *supra* note 72, at 71.

101. Fedler, *supra* note 53, at 234.

102. STATE RESPONSES TO DOMESTIC VIOLENCE, *supra* note 72. The book reviews specific domestic violence laws from the following countries and describes particular features of the laws in: Argentina, Australia, Barbados, Bahamas, Belize, Cayman Islands, Chile, Cyprus, United Kingdom (proposed law), Ecuador, Guyana (pending), Hong Kong, Israel, Malaysia (draft law), New Zealand, Peru, Puerto Rico, Trinidad and Tobago, South Africa, St. Vincent and the Grenadines, and the United States. *Id.* at 72.

103. *Id.* at 83.

104. STATE RESPONSES TO DOMESTIC VIOLENCE provides a description of features. *Id.* at 71–90. While some of these laws provide that courts may order either or both parties to undergo counseling, it is important to note that such provisions can be very harmful to domestic violence victims. To require that a victim of domestic violence undergo counseling or mediation can send the message that she shares responsibility for the batterer's violent behavior. An order to undergo counseling may also send a message that reuniting the family is more important than the woman's safety. As one writer states, ''Battery in the family is symptomatic of power monopolies in the family unit in which one person is the abuser, the other the abused. It is not a relationship of equals. Violence is not a subject for compro-

In her 1996 report, the United Nations Special Rapporteur on Violence Against Women included a recommendation urging governments to enact specific domestic violence legislation:

> States are urged to enact comprehensive domestic violence legislation which integrates criminal and civil remedies rather than making marginal amendments to existing penal and civil laws.[105]

Included as an addendum to her 1996 report is a framework for model legislation. The framework includes provisions for definitions of domestic violence, relationships to be regulated, duties of law enforcement officials, criminal complaint mechanisms, protective orders, civil proceedings, and service provisions for battered women.[106]

INTERNATIONAL LEGAL STANDARDS

International legal standards and enforcement mechanisms provide a means to hold accountable those responsible for the public safety where a government systematically ignores widespread deaths and injuries from wife-assaults. As Meron writes:

> With regard to peace-time violence against women, the role of international human rights law assumes critical importance in light of the failure of national legal systems to protect women from the violence that occurs with terrifying frequency. Whatever the case for restricting the role of international law in intimate and interfamilial relations, a strong case can be made for establishing international obligations of states where the state tolerates, acquiesces in, or fails to punish gender-specific violence.[107]

With the adoption of the Universal Declaration of Human Rights in 1948, the international community declared certain individual rights inviolable. Since then an entire body of international laws and legal standards on human rights has developed, primarily through the mechanisms of the United Nations and other intergovernmental regional organizations. Until quite recently, this human rights law and its enforcers completely failed to redress or even explicitly acknowledge violence against women in their homes. In the 1990s, increased state accountability for private violations of human rights emerged, along with an acceptance that women's rights were included within the realm of human rights. These changes have the potential to dramatically affect the lives of battered women.

---

mise, because parties are not on an equal footing to be able to negotiate the terms of the relationship.'' Fedler, *supra* note 53, at 238.

105. Report of the Special Rapporteur on Violence Against Women, U.N. ESCOR 52nd Sess., at para. 4, U.N. Doc. E/CN.4/1996/53/add.2.

106. *Id.*

107. Theodor Meron, *State Responsibility and Violence Against Women, in* COMBATTING VIOLENCE AGAINST WOMEN, *supra* note 2, at 48–49.

This section will begin with a background discussion on domestic violence as a human rights violation. It will then trace the international legal standards specifically on domestic violence, developed through the United Nations and other governmental institutions since 1975, which now clearly articulate that domestic violence is a violation of international human rights laws. Finally, it will describe one international advocacy method—human rights fact finding and reporting—that has been used to extend protections to and increase awareness of domestic violence victims.

Background on International Human Rights and Domestic Violence

The effort to identify domestic violence as a violation of international human rights has in many ways defined international activism and lobbying on domestic violence in recent years. At the center of human rights law is what is known as the International Bill of Human Rights, consisting of three documents: the Universal Declaration of Human Rights,[108] the International Covenant on Civil and Political Rights,[109] and the International Covenant on Economic, Social and Cultural Rights.[110] In addition to the International Bill of Human Rights, other human rights instruments also provide protections of particular significance to women.[111] One such treaty is the Convention on the Elimination of All Forms of Discrimination Against Women (Women's Convention).[112] Unfortunately, the Women's Convention does not refer specifically to domestic violence or other forms of violence against women. In fact, none of these human rights instruments directly address domestic violence. However, they do articulate fundamental human rights that are commonly violated in domestic violence cases, such as the right to life, the right to physical and mental integrity, the right to equal protection of the laws, and the right to be free from discrimination. Violence against women is now recognized as a violation of human rights.

---

108. Universal Declaration of Human Rights, G.A. Res. 217 A(III) Dec. 10, 1948, U.N. Doc. A/810 (1948).

109. International Covenant on Civil and Political Rights, G.A. Res. 2200 A(XXI), December 16, 1966, 21 U.N. GAOR Supp. (No. 16) at 52, U.N. Doc A/6316 (1966), 999 U.N.T.S. 171, *entered into force* March 23, 1976.

110. International Covenant on Economic, Social and Cultural Rights, G.A. Res. 2200 A(XXI), December 16, 1966, 21 U.N. GAOR Supp. (No. 16), U.N. Doc A/6316 (1966), 999 U.N.T.S. 171, *entered into force* March 23, 1976.

111. Convention Against Torture and other Cruel, Inhuman or Degrading Treatment or Punishment, 23 I.L.M. 1027 (1984). The regional human rights conventions are: American Convention on Human Rights, Nov. 22, 1969 O.A.S. T. S. No. 36, O.E. A/ser S/II.23 (1979); African Charter on Human and Peoples' Rights, O.A.U. Doc. CAB/LEG/67/3, Rev.5, (1982); and European Convention on the Protection of Human Rights and Fundamental Freedoms, Nov. 4, 1950, *entered into force* Sept. 3 1953, 213 U.N.T.S. 222 (1953).

112. The Convention on the Elimination of All Forms of Discrimination Against Women, G.A. Res. 34/180, U.N. GAOR Supp. (No. 46), U.N. Doc. A/Res/34/180, *entered into force* Sept. 3, 1981. This convention is sometimes referred to as an international bill of rights for women.

At the core of the movement to force the inclusion of violence, including domestic violence, into the rubric of international human rights law was the sense that fundamental human rights principles have a unique power that transcends national boundaries. Consequently:

> Human rights discourse is a powerful tool within international law to condemn those state acts and omissions that infringe core and basic notions of civility and citizenship. 'To assert that a particular social claim is a human right is to vest it emotionally and morally with an especially high order of legitimacy'. Violence is an egregious form of such an infringement of the core and basic notions of civility and citizenship. Violence assaults life, dignity, and personal integrity. It transgresses basic norms of peaceful coexistence.[113]

In the early 1990s, there was a growing awareness that omitting domestic violence from human rights dialogue and advocacy diminishes the most basic concept of human rights:

> International human rights law is facing the challenge of being relevant and credible in improving the circumstances in which the vast majority of the world's women live their lives. The blight of many women's lives exposes the shortcomings that have beset international law, both in its origins and in its more modern developments.[114]

One of the most significant hurdles to addressing domestic violence as a human rights violation was the sense that the domain of international law governed only the relationship between nation states or the treatment of individuals by government or public officials. Because states were reluctant to involve themselves in what was considered private matters within the home, including domestic violence, there was serious reluctance to invoke international law to apply to conduct between private actors. This dichotomy between public and private issues[115] allowed the exclusion of domestic violence from the domain of international law by defining it as a private issue outside the scope of international law. Indeed, "[n]owhere is the effect on international human rights practice of the public/private split more evident than in the case of domestic violence—which literally happens 'in private'."[116]

---

113. Celina Romany, *State Responsibility Goes Private: A Feminist Critique of the Public/Private Distinction in International Human Rights Law, in* HUMAN RIGHTS OF WOMEN: NATIONAL AND INTERNATIONAL PERSPECTIVES 85, 85 (Rebecca Cook ed., 1994) (*citing* Richard Bilder, *Rethinking International Human Rights Law; Some Basic Questions,* WIS. L. REV. 171 (1969)). *Also see* Charlotte Bunch, *Women's Rights as Human Rights: Toward a Re-Vision of Human Rights,* 12 HUM. RTS. Q. 486, 487 (1990); and Florence Butegwa, *International Human Rights Law and Practice: Implications for Women, in* FROM BASIC NEEDS TO BASIC RIGHTS 27 (Margaret Schuler ed., 1995).

114. S. Picado Sotela, *Foreword, in* HUMAN RIGHTS OF WOMEN: NATIONAL AND INTERNATIONAL PERSPECTIVES ix, ix (Rebecca Cook ed., 1994).

115. For a discussion of the public/private distinction in international law, *see* Hilary Charlesworth, Christine Chinkin, & Shelley Wright, *Feminist Approaches to International Law,* 85 AM. J. INT'L. L. 613 (1991); Dorothy Thomas & Michele Beasley, *Domestic Violence as a Human Rights Issue,* 15 HUM. RTS. Q. 36–62 (1993); and Romany, *supra* note 113.

116. Thomas & Beasley, *id.* at 40.

However, an examination of "mainstream" human rights law reveals that it does provide a basis for protecting domestic violence victims.[117] Human rights law clearly articulates a state's responsibility to protect its citizens even against acts of private individuals.[118] Thus, state inaction in the face of pervasive domestic violence, prevalent in criminal justice systems worldwide, is a violation of international human rights law. As one activist and scholar writes:

> The necessary theory of accountability can be found in the traditional human rights movement's gradual acceptance of the argument that the state can be held responsible under international human rights law for its inaction as well as its action. . . . When the state makes little or no effort to stop a certain form of private violence, it tacitly condones that violence. This complicity transforms what would otherwise be wholly private conduct into a constructive act of the state.[119]

A state also has an obligation under human rights law to apply its laws without discriminating against women and to provide an adequate remedy for acts violating fundamental rights:[120]

> [O]nce a state moves beyond the stage of obvious complicity, a discrimination-based theory of state responsibility permits an additional argument: a state can be said to condone a particular form of violence because it pays inadequate attention to prevent it in relation to comparable forms of violence.[121]

In summary, an analytical shift has occurred in the international community, allowing domestic violence to be identified and addressed as a human rights violation. This shift underlies the development of specific international legal obligations directly addressing domestic violence, as outlined below.

---

117. *See* Kenneth Roth, *Domestic Violence as an International Human Rights Issue, in* HUMAN RIGHTS OF WOMEN 326 (Rebecca Cook ed., 1994); and Rebecca Cook, *The Way Forward, in* HUMAN RIGHTS OF WOMEN 326 (Rebecca Cook ed., 1994).

118. Velasquez Rodriguez v. Honduras, Judgement of 29 July 1988, Inter-Am. C.H.R., OAS/ser.L./V./III.19, doc.13 (1988) (government was held responsible for not using the organs of state to address disappearances of individuals committed by private actors); Herrera Rubio v. Colombia, Comm. No. 161/1983 U.N. Doc. CCPR/C/OP/2. 192 (government was held responsible for inaction in regard to disappearances and deaths). *See also* Romany, *supra* note 113, for further discussion of state responsibility for private acts of violence.

119. Roth, *supra* note 117, at 329–30.

120. International Covenant on Civil and Political Rights, *supra* note 109. (Article 26 of the covenant articulates an independent duty on states to not discriminate based on gender. Article 8 of the Universal Declaration of Human Rights and Article 2 of the International Covenant on Civil and Political Rights guarantee that states shall provide an effective and adequate remedy for acts violating fundamental rights guaranteed by law.)

121. Roth, *supra* note 117, at 334. For a discussion of how domestic violence can be seen as a human rights violation under an equal treatment "paradigm," *see* Joan Fitzpatrick, *The Use of International Human Rights Norms to Combat Violence Against Women, in* HUMAN RIGHTS OF WOMEN 532 (Rebecca Cook ed., 1994). Fitzpatrick makes the important point that an equal treatment approach for battered women leaves important issues unaddressed. She emphasizes that domestic violence survivors "operate under pressures not felt by other crime victims." *Id.* at 539. They may not be able to sever ties to their assailants in a way that accommodates the application of general criminal laws. Instead domestic violence survivors may require additional services to truly achieve equal treatment.

Intergovernmental Legal Standards on Domestic Violence: The United Nations and the Organization of American States

Over the last twenty years, intergovernmental institutions such as the United Nations, have increasingly adopted new legal standards that address and condemn domestic violence. This section tracks developments within the United Nations concerning domestic violence, and discusses the use of the Inter-American Convention to Prevent, Eradicate and Eliminate Violence Against Women to combat domestic violence.[122]

The United Nations

The Decade on Women 1976–85

Activity during the United Nations Decade on Women (1976–1985) provided a foundation for the creation of an international domestic violence movement that would blossom at the end of the Decade. During the Decade, the U.N. sponsored two world conferences on women, adopted a treaty specifically concerning women, and began to set up an infrastructure within its own agencies to address women's issues. The conferences, the monitoring committee for the Women's Convention, and the new U.N. agencies were new forums for international dialogue and action on domestic violence. Through these forums, and others within the United Nations, it became increasingly clear that when women came together to discuss global women's issues, domestic violence was a priority around the world.

In 1975, the United Nations sponsored the first world conference on women in Mexico City, Mexico. Delegates to the Mexico conference recommended that the period 1976–1985 be declared the United Nations Decade on Women. The final conference document, the World Plan of Action, mentioned the issue of family conflict, but did not specifically address domestic violence.[123] Rather, the World

---

122. O.A.S. Doc. OEA/Ser.L/II.7.4, CIM/Doc.1/91, *reprinted in* 33 I.L.M. 1534 (1994). Other intergovernmental organizations or conferences that have focused and acted on domestic violence within the last ten years are the Council of Europe, the Commonwealth Secretariat, the European Forum on Urban Security, and the 85th Inter-Parliamentary Conference held in Pyongyang in 1991. UNITED NATIONS MANUAL, *supra* note 1, at 2.

123. World Plan of Action, Mexico City, E/Conf.66/34 (1976) (76.IV.1). Though not reflected in the Mexico conference document, international communication between domestic violence groups was occurring in the early 1970s. This communication corresponded with the initiation of the shelter movement in Britain and the United States. For example, in 1976 the First International Tribune on Crimes Against Women was held in Brussels, with some two thousand women from over thirty countries coming together to testify, hold workshops, and share information. SUSAN SCHECTER, WOMEN AND MALE VIOLENCE THE VISIONS AND STRUGGLES OF THE BATTERED WOMEN'S MOVEMENT 150 (1982). That conference produced a resolution that stated: "The women of Japan, Netherlands, France, Wales, England, Scotland, Ireland, Australia, USA, and Germany have begun the fight for the rights of battered women and their children. We call for urgent action by all countries to combat the crime of woman-battering. We demand that governments recognize the existence and extent of this problem and accept the need for refuges, financial aid and effective legal protection for these women." *Id.* (*citing* Diana E. H. Russell, *Introduction, in* BATTERED WIVES (1976)). During this period, international conferences

Plan drew attention to the need for dignity, equality, and security of family members in conflict.[124]

In 1979, the middle of the United Nations Decade on Women, the U.N. General Assembly adopted the Convention on the Elimination of All Forms of Discrimination Against Women.[125] The Women's Convention was a groundbreaking instrument and represented major progress for women. As noted previously, it does not expressly mention any form of violence against women. The Women's Convention does however address inequality within the family and refers to a limited number of specific acts of gender-based violence, such as trafficking, exploitation, and prostitution of women. Since the creation of the convention, the U.N. committee that monitors it, CEDAW, has recognized the serious global impact of domestic violence. Through the committee's recommendations and other activities, CEDAW has worked to focus attention on all forms of violence against women, including domestic violence.[126]

In 1980, the United Nations sponsored the Second World Conference on Women, held in Copenhagen. Domestic violence activists were particularly effective during this conference and influenced the official focus of the conference.[127] The conference marked the first time domestic violence was explicitly referred to in an official document of the United Nations.[128] The final report of the conference referred directly to domestic violence in several sections. For example, the Programme of Action outlined a series of measures to be taken at the national level. The "Legislative measures" section states:

> Legislation should also be enacted and implemented in order to prevent domestic and sexual violence against women. All appropriate measures, including legislative ones, should be taken to allow victims to be fairly treated in all criminal procedures.[129]

The conference also produced a resolution entitled "Battered Women and Violence in the Family," which emphasized that "domestic violence was a complex problem and constituted an intolerable offense to the dignity of human beings."[130]

---

organized by nongovernmental groups which focused on domestic violence were held again in 1978 and 1981.

124. World Plan of Action, *supra* note 123, at paras. 124 and 131.

125. Women's Convention, *supra* note 112.

126. General Recommendation No. 19, Jan. 29, 1992, U.N. Doc. CEDAW/C/1992/L.1/Ass.15.

127. Arvonne Fraser, founder of the non-profit group International Women's Rights Action Watch, attributed the official focus on domestic violence at Copenhagen to the commitment and work of the NGOs and activists in the domestic violence movement. ARVONNE FRASER, THE U.N. DECADE FOR WOMEN: DOCUMENTS AND DIALOGUE 87 (1987) (book now out of print, copies of manuscript may be obtained from Arvonne Fraser, IWRAW, Hubert Humphrey Institute of Public Affairs, University of Minnesota, 301–19th Ave. South, Minneapolis, MN 55455, USA, ph (718) 575–4300, fax (612) 625–6351).

128. Report of the World Conference of the United Nations Decade for Women: Equality, Development and Peace, Copenhagen, July 1980, U.N. Doc. A/CONF.94/35 (80.IV.3).

129. *Id.* at para. 65.

130. Jane Chapman, *Violence Against Women as a Violation of Human Rights*, 17 (2) SOCIAL JUSTICE 57 (1990).

After the Copenhagen Conference, agencies within the United Nations began to address violence against women in the home. At the 1982 and 1984 sessions of the Commission on the Status of Women (CSW) and the Committee on Crime Prevention and Control, domestic violence was a priority item.[131] Discussion within these agencies led to the adoption by the Economic and Social Council (ECOSOC) of Resolutions 1982/22 on abuses against women and children, and 1984/14 on violence in the family and women as victims.

In 1985, the end of the Decade on Women, significant advances on domestic violence were achieved within the United Nations. First, the Seventh United Nations Conference on the Prevention of Crime and Treatment of Offenders adopted a resolution on domestic violence.[132] The U. N. General Assembly then followed up by issuing Resolution 40/36 of November 29, 1985. This was the General Assembly's first resolution on domestic violence. It called for criminological research on domestic violence and requested that United Nations member states implement specific measures to address domestic violence.[133]

At the Third World Conference on Women, held in 1985 in Nairobi, violence against women in the home was a major focus. Throughout the final conference report, Nairobi Forward Looking Strategies, violence against women was referred to and identified as a major obstacle in women's lives.[134] The report identified violence against women as a serious impediment to the objectives of the Decade on Women, and as an "area of special concern."[135] The Nairobi Forward Looking Strategies stated:

> Special attention should be given in criminology training to the particular situation of women as victims of violent crimes. . . . Guidance should be given to law enforcement and other authorities on the need to deal sensibly and sensitively with the victims of such crimes.[136]

The conference document called on governments to,

> undertake effective measures, including mobilizing community resources to identify, prevent and eliminate all violence, including family violence, against women and

---

131. UNITED NATIONS CENTRE FOR SOCIAL DEVELOPMENT AND HUMANITARIAN AFFAIRS, VIOLENCE AGAINST WOMEN IN THE FAMILY 4 (1989) (E.89.IV.5).

132. *Id.* (*citing* Seventh United Nations Congress on the Prevention of Crime and the Treatment of Offenders, Milan 25 Aug.–Sept. 1985, at chap. IV, sec. C, para. 229 (E.86.IV.1)).

133. UNITED NATIONS MANUAL, *supra* note 1, at 3. *Also see* VIOLENCE AGAINST WOMEN IN THE FAMILY, *supra* note 131, at 4.

134. Report of the World Conference to Review and Appraise the Achievements of the United Nations Decade for Women: Equality, Development and Peace, held in Nairobi, July 1985, including Nairobi Forward-Looking Strategies for the Advancement of Women, U.N. Doc. A/CONF.116/28/Rev.1 (85.IV.10) [hereinafter Nairobi Forward-Looking Strategies].

135. *Id.* sec. IV, para. 288.

136. *Id.* sec. I, para. 76.

children and to provide shelter, support and reorientation services for abused women and children.[137]

Although United Nation conference documents are not binding legal obligations in the same manner as are treaties and conventions, their strength lies in their representation of the general consensus of the international community regarding fundamental human rights standards.[138] By the end of the Decade on Women in 1985, the United Nations, through its conference statements and various agencies, had identified domestic violence as a major obstacle to development and peace and had begun to establish mechanisms to address this violence.

Post-Nairobi to Vienna

The period from Nairobi in 1985 to the World Conference on Human Rights in Vienna in 1993 witnessed specific efforts within United Nations agencies to address domestic violence. In 1986, pursuant to a resolution by the Economic and Social Council, the United Nations convened in Vienna an "Expert Group Meeting on Violence in the Family with Special Emphasis on its Effects on Women."[139] The meeting brought together domestic violence experts from every region of the world to examine the nature of domestic violence, its causes, current methods of intervention, and services available to victims of family violence.[140] The meeting produced recommendations for action to confront domestic violence and to ensure more effective responses from criminal and civil justice systems. The U. N. Secretary-General, acting on recommendations by the Economic and Social Council, issued a report in 1990 on criminal justice policy options and other measures to prevent and mitigate the effects of domestic violence.[141]

In 1990, the General Assembly adopted its second resolution directly addressing domestic violence. It urged member states to "develop and implement, policies, measures and strategies, within and outside the criminal justice system, to respond to the problem of domestic violence."[142]

---

137. *Id.* sec. II, para. 231.

138. Conference documents are "signposts of the direction in which international human rights law is developing and should influence states that have accepted a commitment of progressive development toward enhanced respect for human rights in their international conduct and domestic law." Rebecca J. Cook, *The Elimination of Sexual Apartheid: Prospects for the Fourth World Conference on Women* 29 (Am. Society Intl Law, 1995).

139. UNITED NATIONS MANUAL, *supra* note 1, at 3.

140. The expert meeting was organized by two United Nations branches—the Division for the Advancement of Women and the Crime Prevention and Criminal Justice Branch. VIOLENCE AGAINST WOMEN IN THE FAMILY, *supra* note 131, at 4.

141. Domestic Violence, Report of the Secretary General, *supra* note 32.

142. G.A. Res. 45/114 (1990). *See also* UNITED NATIONS MANUAL, *supra* note 1, at 3. In this resolution, the General Assembly requested the Secretary-General to convene another working group of experts to formulate guidelines or publish a manual for advocates working to eliminate domestic violence. STRATEGIES FOR CONFRONTING DOMESTIC VIOLENCE: A RESOURCE MANUAL was published as a result. UNITED NATIONS MANUAL, *supra* note 1, at 3.

In 1992, in response to mounting international concern about violence against women and domestic violence, CEDAW adopted General Recommendation Number 19.[143] As an official interpretation of the Women's Convention, the General Recommendation defines gender-based violence as "violence directed against a woman because she is a woman or which affects women disproportionately," including "acts which inflict physical, mental or sexual harm or suffering, threats of such acts and other deprivations of liberty."[144] General Recommendation 19 marked the first time a human rights treaty or convention was officially interpreted to explicitly prohibit violence against women.[145] It made clear that this prohibition included domestic violence:

> Under general international law and specific human rights covenants, States may also be responsible for private acts if they fail to act with due diligence to prevent violations of rights or to investigate and punish acts of violence and for providing compensation.[146]

In providing that the Women's Convention applies to acts committed by both public figures and private actors, General Recommendation No. 19 solidified the international law community's stance regarding increased state responsibility for private acts.[147]

The Vienna Conference and Beyond

By the arrival of Second World Conference on Human Rights, held in Vienna in 1993, nongovernmental women's advocacy groups had organized themselves in an effort to permanently change international discourse and United Nations policy on the issue of violence against women, including domestic violence.[148] One powerful international effort, known as the "Global Campaign for Women's Human Rights," eventually had participation from over 1,000 women's groups from every corner of the world. As the Vienna Conference approached, the Global Campaign

---

143. General Recommendation No. 19, Committee on the Elimination of Discrimination Against Women, U.N. Doc A/47/38 (1992). General Recommendation 19, as an official interpretation of the Women's Convention, addresses the convention's silence on violence.

144. *Id.* at para. 7.

145. Anthony P. Ewing, *Establishing State Responsibility for Private Acts of Violence Against Women Under the American Convention on Human Rights,* Colum. Hum. Rts. L. Rev. 751, 759 (1995). Despite its strong and clear language, General Recommendation No. 19 is not formally binding on the party states and, arguably, does not diminish the strength of their reservations. There are a huge number of formal state reservations to the Women's Convention and they deeply affect the effectiveness of the convention.

146. General Recommendation 19, *supra* note 143, at para. 9.

147. Work has been done within the United Nations to approve an Optional Protocol to the Women's Convention. This mechanism would allow individuals to present justiciable charges of states' non-compliance with the Women's Convention and would provide an enforcement mechanism to strengthen the effect of the convention.

148. Lori Heise, *Violence Against Women: Translating International Advocacy into Concrete Change,* 44 Am. U. L. Rev. 1207, 1208 (1995).

defined its focus as the integration of gender into all facets of United Nations human rights machinery. One of its major initiatives was to redefine human rights to include rape and domestic violence, independent of the perpetrator's status as a state or private actor.[149]

At the Vienna Conference, women of the Global Campaign presented official conference delegates with nearly 500,000 signatures from 128 nations demanding that the United Nations recognize violence against women as a violation of international human rights.[150] The final conference document, the Vienna Declaration and Programme of Action, stated:

> In particular, the World Conference on Human Rights stresses the importance of working towards the elimination of violence against women in the public and private life[,] . . . the elimination of gender bias in the administration of justice and the eradication of any conflicts which may arise between the rights of women and the harmful effects of certain traditional or customary practices. . .[151]

In the wake of Vienna, the General Assembly adopted the U. N. Declaration on the Elimination of Violence Against Women (DEVAW) in 1993. A result of efforts within the United Nations Commission on the Status of Women (CSW) and the Economic and Social Council (ECOSOC), DEVAW makes important advances with respect to domestic violence.[152] It identifies the subordination of women as a principal cause of domestic violence, stating: ''violence against women is a manifestation of historically unequal power relations between men and women, which have led to domination over and discrimination against women by men.''[153] It also condemns the ''crucial social mechanisms by which women are forced into a subordinate position as compared with men.''[154] DEVAW also defines violence against women in a broad and sophisticated manner, including violence occurring in both ''private or public life,''[155] and provides explicit directions to member

---

149. *Id.* at 1209.

150. Nongovernmental groups organized an international tribunal at which women presented well-documented cases of gender-based abuse. *See* CENTER FOR WOMEN'S GLOBAL LEADERSHIP, TESTIMONIES OF THE GLOBAL TRIBUNAL ON VIOLATIONS OF WOMEN'S HUMAN RIGHTS (1994) (presenting the testimony of 33 women who spoke at the Global Tribunal on Violations of Women's Human Rights during the Vienna Conference).

151. Vienna Declaration and Programme of Action, sec. II, B para. 38, U.N. Doc. A/Conf.157/24 (Oct. 1993).

152. Declaration on the Elimination of Violence Against Women, G.A. Res. 48/104 (1993) [hereinafter DEVAW]. In 1991, the Economic and Social Council had called for a meeting of experts to discuss the preparation of an international instrument on violence against women. The U.N. Division on the Advancement of Women convened such a meeting in November 1991 in Vienna and prepared a draft declaration on violence against women. ECOSOC later approved an intersessional working group of the CSW to further develop this declaration. Rebecca Cook, *The 1991 U.N. Expert Meeting on Violence Against Women and the Draft Declaration on Violence Against Women, in* COMBATTING VIOLENCE AGAINST WOMEN, *supra* note 2, at 40–42.

153. DEVAW, *id.* at pmbl. para. 6.

154. *Id.*

155. *Id.* at arts. 1 and 4.

states not to "invoke any custom, tradition or religious consideration to avoid their obligations with respect to its elimination." Importantly, DEVAW sets forth specific steps a member state should take in combatting domestic violence. These steps include directives to national criminal justice systems, including investigating and punishing acts of domestic violence; developing comprehensive legal, political, administrative, and cultural programs to prevent violence against women; providing training to law enforcement officials; and promoting research and collecting statistics relating to the prevalence of domestic violence.

While DEVAW does not have the binding legal effect of a convention, it does represent "the first international instrument to express international political consensus that states have human rights obligations to prevent gender-based violence and to redress the harm caused."[156] Some have critized the declaration, however, asserting it merely implies that domestic violence is a human rights violation. Although violence against women is defined in Articles 2 and 3, there is no explicit link made between such violence and human rights.[157]

In response to concerted lobbying at the Vienna Conference, and the consistent, continuing expression of the need for international accountability to domestic violence victims, the U. N. Commission on Human Rights appointed a Special Rapporteur on Violence Against Women to investigate and report on the causes and consequences of global violence against women and to make recommendations for its remedy.[158] Thematic Rapporteurs are seen as one of the most effective tools within the United Nations to monitor human rights violations. In 1994, Radhika Coomaraswamy of Sri Lanka was appointed as the first Special Rapporteur on Violence Against Women. In her preliminary report, she emphasized that states have a duty under international human rights law to protect women from violence in their homes.[159] Her report stated:

> All States are not only responsible for their own conduct or the conduct of their agents, but are now also responsible for their failure to take necessary steps to prosecute private citizens for their behaviour, in compliance with international standards.[160]

---

156. Donna Sullivan, *The Public/Private Distinction in International Human Rights Law, in* WOMEN'S RIGHTS HUMAN RIGHTS 126, 131 (Julie Peters & Andrea Wolper eds., 1995).

157. Although the preamble states that "violence against women constitutes a violation of the rights and fundamental freedoms," express language in the operative language of DEVAW is lacking. DEVAW, *supra* note 152, at pmbl. para 5. For a more detailed discussion of the declaration, *see* Christine Chinkin & Hilary Charlesworth, *Violence Against Women: A Global Issue, in* WOMEN, MALE VIOLENCE AND THE LAW (Julie Stubbs ed., 1994).

158. U.N. C.H.R. Res. 1994/45 (ESCOR 1994), paras. 6 and 7. The mandate of the Special Rapporteur, as articulated by the Commission is to "seek and receive information on violence against women, its causes and consequences, from Governments, treaty bodies, specialized agencies, other special rapporteurs . . . [and] recommend measures, ways and means, at the national, regional and international level to eliminate violence against women and its causes, and to remedy its consequences. . . ." Paras. 7 (a) and (b).

159. Preliminary Report of the Special Rapporteur on Violence against Women to the Commission on Human Rights E/CN.4/1995/42 (1994), paras. 99–107.

160. *Id.* at para. 107.

The appointment of the Special Rapporteur was further representation of the international community's strong commitment to address violence against women in all its forms.

The Fourth World Conference on Women

At the 1995 Fourth World Conference on Women, held in Beijing, China, significant progress was made on the issue of domestic violence at both the NGO forum and the government conference. The Beijing Platform for Action[161] identifies domestic violence as a human rights violation. The Platform for Action affirms that violence against women, whether it occurs in the private sphere or in the public sphere, is a violation of human rights.[162] The Platform asserts: "Violence against women both violates and impairs or nullifies the enjoyment by women of their human rights and fundamental freedoms."[163] It addresses violence against women as a separate "Critical Area of Concern"[164] and specifically includes it under the "Human Rights" section. The Platform firmly articulates the need to confront global violence against women. It acknowledges the longstanding failure of governments to promote and protect a woman's human right to be free of violence.

The language of the Platform tracks the strong language of the Declaration on the Elimination of Violence Against Women and outlines many specific actions governments, nongovernmental groups, and others should take to confront and combat the problem.[165] Recommended actions include strengthening legal systems' response to all forms of violence against women, including domestic violence. The Platform states that governments should:

(c) Enact and/or reinforce penal, civil, labour and administrative sanctions in domestic legislation to punish and redress the wrongs done to women and girls who are subjected to any form of violence, whether in the home, the workplace, the community or society . . .

(d) Adopt and/or implement and periodically review and analyze legislation to ensure its effectiveness in eliminating violence against women, emphasizing the prevention of violence and the prosecution of offenders; take measures to ensure the protection of women subjected to violence, access to just and effective remedies, including compensation and indemnification and healing of victims, and rehabilitation of perpetrators . . .

(n) Create, improve or develop as appropriate, and fund the training programmes for judicial, legal, medical, social, educational and police and immigrant personnel, in order to avoid the abuse of power leading to violence against women

---

161. U.N. Doc. A/Conf.177/20 (1995).

162. Beijing Platform for Action, paras. 113–15.

163. *Id.* at para. 113.

164. *Id.* at paras. 46 and 113–31.

165. *Id.* at paras. 125–31.

and sensitize such personnel to the nature of gender-based acts and threats of violence so that fair treatment of female victims can be assured . . .[166]

Again, much of the progress at Beijing was due to the intensive focus and lobbying efforts of nongovernmental groups on the issue of domestic violence. At the nongovernmental forum, domestic violence was a highly visible issue that dominated many forums of discussion. Numerous workshops, presented by women from every region of the world, were dedicated to the issue. In particular, several groups presented information on the criminal justice system's hostile or inadequate treatment of domestic violence survivors. These presentations compared and contrasted obstacles and reform efforts from different regions.

The two and one half year period that included the Vienna Conference, the Declaration on the Elimination of Violence Against Women, the appointment of a Special Rapporteur on Violence Against Women, and the Beijing Conference was extremely important for domestic violence survivors. With these developments, which occurred between 1993 and 1995, the United Nations ended any debate on whether domestic violence could be classified as a human rights violation. This violence was clearly identified as a violation of international law and named a top national and international priority.

The Inter-American Convention to Prevent, Eradicate and Eliminate Violence Against Women

One of the strongest intergovernmental instruments addressing domestic violence is a regional convention of the Organization of American States (OAS). In 1994, the General Assembly of the OAS approved the Inter-American Convention to Prevent, Eradicate and Eliminate Violence Against Women.[167] Created by the Inter-American Commission for Women (CIM) acting under the directive of the O.A.S. General Assembly, this convention provides a specific model for an institutional, regional mechanism dedicated to investigating and ruling on violence against women, including domestic violence. Clarifying that the convention applies to violence in public or private life, it states that "violence against women constitutes a violation of their human rights and fundamental freedoms" and calls on governments to eradicate this violence.[168] Importantly, the Inter-American Convention

---

166. *Id.* at para. 125.

167. Inter-American Convention to Prevent, Eradicate and Eliminate Violence Against Women, *adopted by* acclamation, twenty-fourth session of the General Assembly of the OAS, 9 June 1994. This convention is also known as the Convention of Belém do Para.

168. The convention states: "The States Parties condemn all forms of violence against women and agree to pursue, by all appropriate means and without delay, policies to prevent, punish and eradicate such violence and undertake to: . . . b. apply due diligence to prevent, investigate and impose penalties for violence against women; c. include in their domestic legislation penal, civil, administrative and any other type of provisions that may be needed to prevent, punish and eradicate violence against women and to adopt appropriate administrative measures where necessary; d. adopt legal measures to require the perpetrator to refrain from harassing, intimidating or threatening the woman or using any method that harms or endangers her life or integrity, or damages her property; e. take all appropriate measures, including legislative measures, to amend or repeal existing laws and regulations or to modify legal or customary practices which sustain the persistence and tolerance of violence against women; f. establish

includes an individual complaint procedure, which allows individual petitioners and NGOs to file complaints against states with the Inter-American Commission on Human Rights.[169] The convention allows lawsuits against states to compel government authorities to, at a minimum, investigate, prosecute, and punish domestic violence.[170] The OAS Convention reflects the work of Latin American women who have been particularly active in working to confront domestic violence and to identify it as a human rights violation.

Human Rights Advocacy and Enforcement Efforts

The identification of domestic violence as a human rights violation has naturally led to new efforts to enforce international law on behalf of domestic violence victims. One established human rights enforcement mechanism is the human rights fact-finding and reporting model. For several decades, human rights groups have used this tool to pressure governments to adhere to international human rights standards. Advocates who use this model document violations of human rights and expose them to the international community. One author describes such fact-finding and reporting as "the persuasive force of public embarrassment [which is] the major tool of nongovernmental human rights organizations."[171] Another scholar describes how international fora can be used to improve women's situation:

> International standards and procedures can be used to improve women's position as follows. The first is by 'going international', that is taking one's concerns and allegations of rights violations to an international forum in order to place pressure on the state concerned to respond (or even to move international actors to address systemic problems or the situation in individual states.)[172]

In the domestic violence context, advocates can refer to the now clearly established international human rights standards, which condemn this violence and expose systematic failure by states to protect women from wife-assault.[173]

---

fair and effective legal procedures for women who have been subjected to violence which include, among other, protective measures, a timely hearing and effective access to such procedures; . . ." (art. 7).

169. *Id.* art. 12.

170. Culliton, *supra* note 14, at 535. In her article (published before the adoption of the OAS Convention on violence) Culliton describes a serious and widespread problem of domestic violence in the United States, Latin America, and the Caribbean. She outlines criminal justice systems in the region and their failure to effectively address this violence and establishes their obligations under international human rights law to remedy this failure. She proposes several options to enforce countries human rights obligations including litigation in national and international courts. She concludes that the Inter-American system provides the most practical means for enforcement of country obligations to domestic violence victims under international human rights law.

171. Thomas & Beasley, *supra* note 115, at 56.

172. Andrew Byrnes, *Strategies for Using International Human Rights Law and Procedures to Advance Women's Human Rights, in* CLAIMING OUR PLACE: WORKING THE HUMAN RIGHTS SYSTEM TO WOMEN'S ADVANTAGE 51, 52 (1993).

173. Before human rights fact-finding and reporting was used in the domestic violence context, it was applied to other forms of gender violence. Hina Jilani described how international attention to cases of violence against women in Pakistan redefined the importance of the problem within the country. To

The fact-finding and reporting model has required some new techniques when used in the domestic violence context. On the positive side, sources (either the victims themselves, witnesses, or the professionals who were able to describe stories of victims) are frequently very willing to talk and express no fear of government retaliation that may be common in traditional human rights fact-finding and reporting. Sources are often demanding to be heard in order to focus government attention on this secret problem that is ignored by most officials. Thus, witness interviews may be easier to obtain and not as risky.

Fact-finding and reporting in the domestic violence context is also different from the traditional model because the ''direct'' perpetrators are private actors. The goal of the report is more than to expose the individual act (as in the case of torture by a government agent for example) but rather to demonstrate the governments' failure to protect women from violence in their homes and to prosecute offenders. Thus, the interviews must be extensive, exploring patterns of government inaction in the face of widespread violence in the home. The interviews may also focus on establishing discriminatory treatment by government officials in the making of and enforcing of laws.[174] Conversations with survivors may be corroborated by consistent and repeated testimony from government officials that domestic violence is simply not a priority for government action.

Only recently have fact-finding and reporting been used to address domestic violence. Dorothy Thomas and Michele Beasley elaborate on the significance of this movement by noting the harm caused in failing to criticize governments for their neglect of domestic violence issues:

> By failing to focus on the sex-discriminatory practices of governments, human rights organizations have neither challenged the broadest form of sex discrimination that relegates women and what happens to them to the 'private' sphere, nor denounced one of its immediate effects: governments devaluation of women and their resulting failure to prosecute violence against women equally with other similar crimes. Instead, human rights organizations have allowed a pattern of discriminatory non-prosecution of such violence to flourish unchecked. . . . [I]n the case of domestic violence, the widespread failure by states to prosecute such violence and to fulfill their international

---

''internationalize'' the issue was to elevate it in a way that focused government attention on the issue. Referring to the issue of violence against women in custody, she reported, ''One example of a positive experience of collaboration between national and international NGO's was on the issue of violence against women in custody. The local NGO's were able to place the issue in the proper perspective, provide the facilities, recommend the modalities of investigation and provide documented case studies. An independent investigation by an NGO lent the report objectivity on the one hand, and on the other emphasized the issue as that of international concern. This added to the pressure on the state authorities to respond and measures were announced for dealing with this form of violation. . .'' Hina Jilani, *Diversity in Human Rights NGO's, in* CLAIMING OUR PLACE, *id.* at 107, 111. Jilani notes also how the women's human rights advocacy effort affected the general human rights movement: ''Another significant contribution of the women's rights movement to the human rights movement in Pakistan was the internationalization of human rights issues. As a deliberate strategy, these issues were projected as a concern for the international community, rather than of domestic or local relevance only.'' *Id.* at 112.

174. *See* Thomas & Beasley, *supra* note 115, for further discussion of using human rights fact-finding and reporting methodology to document domestic violence.

obligations to guarantee women equal protection of the law has gone largely unde-nounced.[175]

In 1991, the first human rights report on domestic violence was published. In their report on violence against women in Brazil, Human Rights Watch examined the criminal justice system's treatment of battered women and analyzed its failure to effectively prosecute batterers as human rights violators.[176] The report concluded that Brazil had failed to meet its obligations under international human rights law to protect domestic violence victims and had discriminated against women by failing to prosecute domestic violence.

In 1994 and 1995, Minnesota Advocates for Human Rights published reports on domestic violence in Romania, Albania, and Bulgaria.[177] The fact-finding and reporting model was a particularly useful tool for women seeking change in the Balkan region. A primary goal was to focus government and public attention on domestic violence. Little documentation of the problem existed, which made this effort extremely difficult. In this region with severe economic difficulties, high unemployment, and increasing crime, domestic violence was largely ignored. The human rights reports provided a focal point for dialogue on domestic violence. Where local advocates were struggling to be heard, the reports demonstrated that the international community was concerned about the problem and watching.[178]

Additionally, the reports served to "bring the international back home." By clearly identifying applicable international human rights standards and outlining how government failure to address and redress domestic violence violated these standards, the reports served as a tool for advocates in the region.

In addition to producing human rights reports for general distribution, advocates can use other human rights enforcement mechanisms in the domestic violence context. For example, most of the major human rights instruments have a treaty body with supervisory duties over countries that are parties. Reports of human rights violations can be made to these entities. An individual complaint procedure is also available under some of the human rights instruments.[179]

---

175. *Id.* at 48.

176. WOMEN'S RIGHTS PROJECT BRAZIL, *supra* note 12.

177. MINNESOTA ADVOCATES FOR HUMAN RIGHTS, *supra* note 15.

178. The international partnership that developed between Minnesota Advocates and women's groups in the Balkans bolstered advocacy efforts. Nongovernmental groups committed to social change, such as women's rights groups, were new in these countries, which had recently transitioned from communism. There were no shelters, hotlines, or advocacy groups specifically devoted to domestic violence in the region. The partnership enabled Balkan advocates to access resources and information from women in Minnesota who had worked on domestic violence for twenty years.

179. For a further discussion of human rights advocacy efforts in the context of women's human rights, *see* Andrew Byrnes, *Toward More Effective Enforcement of Women's Human Rights Through the Use of International Human Rights Law and Procedures, in* HUMAN RIGHTS OF WOMEN 189 (Rebecca Cook ed., 1994).

CONCLUSION

Within the last ten years, women working to confront domestic violence have successfully internationalized the issue. They have communicated across national borders to garner information, resources, and support for their work. More important, they have joined together to create a new force in the movement to eliminate domestic violence: international scrutiny. By recognizing a woman's right to be free from violence and demanding that governments acknowledge and enforce that right, activists have transformed a secret personal horror into an issue of government failure and embarrassment. By their communication and lobbying efforts, activists have succeeded in codifying a woman's right to be free from domestic violence in intergovernmental agreements. These agreements can be used to hold public officials accountable. Now, when officials ignore domestic violence, they ignore their concrete obligations as members of the international community.

The creation of international standards condemning domestic violence must now be followed by implementation and enforcement, issues uniquely difficult in the context of international law. It is critical that new international standards not follow the path of national and state laws to protect battered women, which have not been enforced. Enforcement mechanisms such as the individual complaint procedure articulated in the Draft Optional Protocol to the Women's Convention and the procedures used by the Special Rapporteur on Violence Against Women will give strength to the new international standards if they are made a priority by governments and international institutions.

The international movement to end domestic violence has the advantage of years of experience and lessons learned by local activists. The movement also has the momentum, and now the tools, to make significant progress toward the permanent elimination of this violence. This movement is a new promise to end the worldwide crisis of battered women.

VIOLENCE IN THE WORKPLACE: SEXUAL HARASSMENT

Robin Phillips

After enduring months of unwanted touching and sexual attention, a young woman in Korea was dismissed from her position as a lab assistant for refusing the sexual advances of her professor.[1]

In Russia, many employment advertisements now openly seek young, attractive women "without complexes," a code word meaning a willingness to provide sexual favors.[2]

In the United States, as part of the training for a sales position with an international company, women were expected to engage in social activities that involved dancing and drinking with the company's top executives. The encounters often included unwelcome touching, kissing and requests for sex.[3]

In Australia, female staff members were repeatedly subjected to unwelcome touching, hugging and kissing by their boss, a high ranking government official in Parliament.[4]

In Bulgaria, a young woman desperately in need of permanent employment was told that she would not be offered an administrative position unless she agreed to also act as a "mistress" to her boss.[5]

INTRODUCTION

Sexual harassment, an insidious form of violence against women, is common to all cultures. The stories are strikingly similar from country to country; only the names and the places change. Sexual harassment can take a variety of forms. It includes both physical violence and more subtle forms of violence such as coercion or the creation of a hostile work environment.[6]

---

1.   *South Korean Professor Sued for Sexual Harassment,* REUTER LIBRARY REP., Nov. 23, 1993, *available in* LEXIS, News Library, Reuwld File.

2.   Martina Vandenberg, *New Feminist Backlash*, THE MOSCOW TIMES, Mar. 8, 1996, *available in* LEXIS, News Library, Mostms File.

3.   Mark Maremont & Jane Sasseen, *Abuse of Power,* BUS. WEEK, May 13, 1996, at 86.

4.   *Australia: Sexual Reeling*, SYDNEY MORNING HERALD, June 1, 1995, *available in* LEXIS, World Library, Allwld File.

5.   Interview May 18, 1995, Sofia, Bulgaria.

6.   The United Nations has defined violence against women broadly to include both physical and nonphysical violence. In the Declaration on the Elimination of Violence Against Women, the term "violence against women" is defined as "any act of gender-based violence that results in, or is likely to result in, physical, sexual or psychological harm or suffering to women, including threats of such acts, coercion or arbitrary deprivation of liberty, whether occurring in public or private life." Declaration on the Elimination of Violence Against Women, art. 1, G.A. Res. 48/104 (1993). Article 2(b) of the

Women in workplaces around the world are routinely subjected to hostile and demeaning work conditions and are forced to endure discrimination, humiliation, sexual assault, sexual blackmail, and, in the most extreme cases, rape. Research indicates that sexual harassment is a serious and pervasive problem in countries around the world.[7] For example, in a survey conducted by Bonn's Ministry for Women's Affairs in 1991, 93% of the almost 2,000 women surveyed reported that they had been sexually harassed at work.[8] In the United Kingdom, 73% of 46,000 women interviewed reported being sexually harassed at work.[9] In a 1994 survey by the Tokyo city government, approximately one-third of the women workers surveyed reported having had some unpleasant sex-related experience on the job.[10] In a research study conducted by the Tanzanian Media Women's Association in 1994, almost 90% of 200 women surveyed said that sexual harassment was a threat to their jobs and economic survival.[11] More than 68% of executives surveyed in ten countries and territories in Asia view sexual harassment as a problem in the Asian workplace.[12]

In many countries, a woman has no legal recourse for injuries caused by sexual harassment. Like other forms of violence, sexual harassment is a demonstration of power and control and can cause physical, psychological, emotional, economic, and professional injuries to those who experience it. In response, women's advocates in countries around the world are beginning to fight back.[13]

Declaration specifically includes sexual harassment as a form of violence against women. For a discussion of the necessity of an expanded definition of violence, *see* Berta Esperanza Hernandez-Truyol, *Sex, Culture, and Rights: A Re/Conceptualization of Violence for the Twenty- First Century*, 60 ALB. L. REV. 607 (1997).

7.   Survey studies vary greatly within countries depending on the types of questions, number surveyed, and the level of awareness of sexual harassment in the country. The most accurate surveys are those that seek to determine whether people have experienced specific conduct that has been defined as sexual harassment rather than ask respondents to identify whether they have been sexually harassed. International Labour Office, *Combating Sexual Harassment at Work,* 11 CONDITIONS OF WORK DIGEST 160 (1992) [hereinafter CONDITIONS OF WORK DIGEST]. CONDITIONS OF WORK DIGEST is a comprehensive review of the problem of sexual harassment in the workplace and the measures taken to address the problem in twenty-three industrialized countries. For a review of this publication, *see* Tariq Mundiya, *Conditions of Work Digest: Combating Sexual Harassment At Work*, 15 COMP. LAB. L. J. 119 (1993).

8.   *German Survey Shows Nine in 10 Working Women Sexually Harassed*, REUTER LIBRARY REP., Oct. 16, 1991, *available in* LEXIS, News Library, Reuwld File.

9.   Jimmy Burns, *Managers Seen As Arrogant*, FIN. TIMES, Dec. 22, 1987, at 8.

10.   Andrew Pollack, *It's See No Evil, Have No Harassment in Japan*, N.Y. TIMES, May 7, 1996, at D6.

11.   Shehnilla Mohamed, *Zimbabwe: Sexual Harassment Under the Spotlight*, INTER PRESS SERVICE, Feb. 18, 1994, *available in* LEXIS, World Library, Allwld File. Approximately 8% of the women surveyed in the Tanzanian study said that they had no alternative but to comply with the demands of the perpetrator of sexual harassment.

12.   *Asia: Asian Execs Say Sexual Harassment Widespread at Work*, BANGKOK POST, June 29, 1996, at 14.

13.   Although laws and policies should be drafted in a gender neutral fashion to reflect the reality that men also experience sexual harassment, women are far more likely to suffer from sexual harassment in the workplace. While the principles are generally applicable to sexual harassment by women against

Legal protection against sexual harassment is a relatively new development. The United States and Great Britain first recognized a cause of action for sexual harassment in the mid-1970s.[14] Other countries that currently provide legal protection against sexual harassment generally did not do so until the 1980s and early 1990s.[15]

The United States first recognized a cause of action for sexual harassment in the workplace, and also prohibits sexual harassment in educational institutions.[16] Other countries have subsequently provided legal protection against sexual harassment and have taken various approaches to addressing the problem. In the United States and other countries such as Great Britain and Australia, sexual harassment is treated as an unlawful form of discrimination based on sex. Other countries have addressed sexual harassment in their labor codes or in tort law. Still others treat sexual harassment as criminal conduct, a form of sexual blackmail or extortion.

The international community has also recognized violence against women generally, and sexual harassment specifically, as violations of international human rights standards. The United Nations has strongly condemned sexual harassment and has called on governments to develop policies to combat it.[17] The European Union and the Organization of American States have also condemned sexual harassment and have called on member states to work to eliminate the problem.[18]

In countries that provide legal protection against sexual harassment, two types of conduct in the workplace have generally been prohibited. In the United States, this conduct has been identified as *quid pro quo* sexual harassment and harassment that creates a hostile work environment.[19] *Quid pro quo* sexual harassment occurs when an employer or supervisor threatens negative employment consequences if an employee refuses requests for sexual favors, or conditions a benefit of employment on the granting of a sexual favor. Some countries also prohibit sexual harassment resulting from a hostile work environment. These laws protect an employee from being forced to endure a workplace made hostile by unwelcome requests for sexual favors, inappropriate jokes of a sexual nature, sexual comments, stories, innuendos, or sexually explicit or pornographic pictures or other materials.

---

men and to same-sex harassment, this chapter focuses on the sexual harassment of women by men. CONDITIONS OF WORK DIGEST, *supra* note 7, at 8.

14. *See* Williams v. Saxbe, 413 F. Supp. 654 (D.D.C. 1976), *rev'd* 587 F.2d 1240 (D.C. Cir. 1978).

15. CONDITIONS OF WORK DIGEST, *supra* note 7, at 49.

16. This chapter will focus on sexual harassment in the workplace. For information about sexual harassment of students by teachers in educational institutions, *see* Neera Rellan Stacy, *Seeking a Superior Institutional Liability Standard Under Title IX for Teacher-Student Sexual Harassment*, 71 N.Y.U. L. REV. 1338 (1996); David S. Doty and Susan Strauss, *Prompt and Equitable: The Importance of Student Sexual Harassment Policies in the Public Schools*, 113 ED. LAW REP 1 (1996). For information about student to student sexual harassment, *see* Daniel B. Tukel, *Student Versus Student: School District Liability for Peer Sexual Harassment*, 75 MICH. B. J. 1154 (1996).

17. *See infra* text accompanying notes 74–78.

18. *See infra* text accompanying notes 143–161.

19. *See infra* text accompanying notes 20–64.

Governments and employers are faced with many difficulties in trying to eliminate sexual harassment. Women often fear retaliation if they report inappropriate conduct and, as a result, rarely report sexual harassment. They are sometimes ashamed or embarrassed about their experiences or do not feel that their claims will be taken seriously. Even if a woman does report sexual harassment, it is often difficult to prove because there are not always witnesses willing to provide information. Either the conduct occurs when the two parties are alone or other employees are afraid that they will jeopardize their own jobs if they testify or provide any evidence of offensive conduct. In addition, many employers misunderstand the causes and consequences of sexual harassment and fail to treat the problem seriously or respond appropriately to it. Often, companies do not learn about sexually offensive conduct until it becomes unbearable for some of their female employees or another crisis arises because of the inappropriate conduct.

This chapter focuses on the most common form of sexual harassment—harassment of females by males in the workplace; note, however, that cases have been successfully brought by males against females, and that same-sex sexual harassment cases are increasingly litigated. This chapter provides a general overview of the problem of sexual harassment and the different legal approaches that have been implemented to solve it. The first section outlines in detail the law prohibiting sexual harassment in the United States. Because it has the richest litigative or legislative history regarding sexual harassment, the development of the law relating to sexual harassment in the United States is used here to illustrate the complicated issues that must be addressed in attempting to protect people from discrimination based on sex.

The second section provides examples of the laws relating to sexual harassment in other countries around the world. Many of the countries that have adopted statutes, either civil or criminal, to prohibit sexual harassment have not yet decided any cases under these statutes. Therefore, the implementation and enforcement of the laws are still unclear.

The third section describes how international organizations have addressed sexual harassment. Although many of the international instruments condemning sexual harassment are not technically binding, the standards set by the international community provide strong support for advocacy groups lobbying their governments for national legislative change. In addition, the treaties that are binding can be used in individual countries to challenge specific discriminatory laws, policies, and practices that violate the terms of the treaties.

THE DEVELOPMENT OF SEXUAL HARASSMENT LAW IN THE UNITED STATES

Under federal law in the United States,[20] a cause of action for sexual harassment arises out of the provisions prohibiting discrimination in employment under Title VII of the 1964 Civil Rights Act.[21] This section provides:

---

20. Most states in the United States also provide for a state cause of action for sexual harassment. This chapter will only focus on the federal law.

21. 42 U.S.C. § 2000e–2, *et. seq.*

It shall be an unlawful employment practice for an employer 1) to fail or refuse to hire or to discharge any individual, or otherwise to discriminate against any individual with respect to his compensation, terms, conditions or privileges of employment because of such individual's race, color, religion, sex or national origin; or 2) to limit, segregate or classify his employees or applicants for employment in any way which would deprive or tend to deprive any individual of employment opportunities or otherwise adversely affect his status as an employee, because of such individual's race, color, religion, sex or national origin. [22]

In 1976, the federal courts first recognized sexual harassment as a form of sex discrimination prohibited under Title VII.[23] The early cases decided under Title VII involved blatant examples of *quid pro quo* sexual harassment in which employers used the terms and conditions of employment as a means to extort sexual favors.[24]

In 1980, the Equal Employment Opportunity Commission (EEOC)[25] published guidelines on sexual harassment. The guidelines recognized harassment on the basis of sex as a violation of Title VII and identified two separate forms of sexual harassment: *quid pro quo* sexual harassment and hostile environment sexual harassment.[26] The guidelines defined sexual harassment as ''[u]nwelcome sexual advances, requests for sexual favors, and other verbal or physical conduct of a sexual nature,''[27] where:

1) submission to such conduct is made either explicitly or implicitly a term or condition of an individual's employment;

2) submission to or rejection of such conduct by an individual is used as the basis for employment decisions affecting such individual; or

3) such conduct has the purpose or effect of unreasonably interfering with an individual's work performance or creating an intimidating, hostile or offensive working environment.[28]

This definition has been applied by federal courts in the United States to cases of sexual harassment brought under Title VII.[29]

---

22. 42 U.S.C. § 2000e–2(a)(1) (1994).

23. *See* Williams v. Saxbe, 413 F. Supp. 654 (D.D.C. 1976), *rev'd* 587 F.2d 1240 (D.C. Cir. 1978). In *Williams*, the Court found that the retaliatory actions of a male supervisor, taken because a female employee declined his sexual advances, constitute sex discrimination under Title VII of the Civil Rights Act of 1964.

24. *See, e.g.*, Williams v. Civiletti, 487 F. Supp. 1387 (D.D.C. 1980). *See also* Susan Estrich, *Sex at Work*, 43 STAN L. REV. 813, 822 (1991).

25. The EEOC was created by the United States Congress to enforce the Civil Rights Act of 1964, 42 U.S.C. § 2000e–2, *et. seq.*

26. *See* 29 C.F.R. § 1604.11(a) (1990).

27. *Id.*

28. *Id.*

29. *See, e.g.*, Henson v. City of Dundee, 682 F.2d 897, 903 (11th Cir. 1982); Bundy v. Jackson, 641 F.2d 934, 947 (D.C. Cir. 1980).

Federal courts in the United States have applied a similar analysis to sexual harassment in educational institutions.[30] Sexual harassment in educational institutions that receive public money is prohibited as improper discrimination based on sex under Title IX of the 1964 Civil Rights Act.[31]

Quid Pro Quo Sexual Harassment

Quid pro quo sexual harassment is the most commonly recognized form of sexual harassment. It generally involves an employer, supervisor, or manager who conditions a benefit or term of employment, such as continued employment, promotion, or increased compensation on participation in some sexual activity.[32] *Quid pro quo* sexual harassment occurs when submission to or rejection of such conduct by an individual is used as the basis for employment decisions affecting that individual.[33]

To establish a *prima facie* case of *quid pro quo* sexual harassment, a plaintiff must show that:

1. the employee belongs to a protected class; [34]

2. the employer subjected the employee to unwelcome conduct in the form of sexual advances or requests for sexual favors;

3. the harassment was based upon sex; and

4. the employee's acceptance or rejection of the harassment was an express or implied condition to the receipt of a job benefit or the cause of a tangible job detriment.[35]

If a plaintiff in a sexual harassment case is able to establish each of the above elements, the burden of proof then shifts to the employer to articulate a legitimate nondiscriminatory reason for the adverse employment action.[36] If the employer is able to provide a legitimate reason for its actions, the employee must then establish

---

30. *See* Alexander v. Yale Univ., 459 F. Supp. 1 (D. Conn. 1977), *aff'd*, 631 F.2d 178 (2d Cir. 1980); Moire v. Temple Univ., 800 F.2d 1136 (3d Cir. 1986).

31. 20 U.S.C. § 1681(a).

32. *See, e.g.*, Highlander v. K.F.C. Nat'l Management Co., 805 F.2d 644, 648 (6th Cir. 1986).

33. EEOC Policy Guidance on Current Issues of Sexual Harassment, Daily Lab. Rep. (BNA) No. 61, at E-1 (March 28, 1990).

34. Title VII sets forth the classes that are protected from discrimination. It prohibits discrimination based on race, color, religion, sex, or national origin. 42 U.S.C. § 2000e(a)(1) (1994). For sexual harassment, as in other cases of sex discrimination, a plaintiff establishes that he or she is in a protected class through a simple stipulation that the employee is a man or a woman. *See* Henson v. City of Dundee, 682 F.2d 897, 903 (11th Cir. 1982).

35. *See* Sparks v. Pilot Freight Carriers, Inc., 830 F.2d 1554, 1564 (11th Cir. 1987); Jones v. Flagship, Int'l, 793 F.2d 714, 721–722 (5th Cir. 1986), *cert. denied* 479 U.S. 1065 (1987).

36. *Id.*

that the reasons provided by the employer are not the real reasons for the employment decision and are merely a pretext for unlawful discrimination.[37]

Hostile Work Environment Sexual Harassment

Sexual harassment also occurs when an individual experiences unwelcome sexual advances, requests for sexual favors, or other verbal or physical conduct of a sexual nature where such conduct has the purpose or effect of unreasonably interfering with that individual's work performance or creating an intimidating, hostile, or offensive working environment.[38] To establish a *prima facie* case of sexual harassment based on a hostile work environment, a plaintiff must show that:

1) the plaintiff belongs to a protected class;[39]

2) the plaintiff was subjected to unwelcome sexual harassment;

3) the harassment was based on sex;

4) the harassment affected a term, condition, or privilege of employment; and

5) the employer knew or should have known the conduct was occurring.[40]

Much of the litigation in the United States has centered around whether conduct was "unwelcome"[41] and whether the harassment was sufficiently severe and pervasive that it affected a term, condition, or privilege of employment.

In 1986, the United States Supreme Court addressed the issue of hostile environment sexual harassment under Title VII for the first time in *Meritor Savings Bank v. Vinson.*[42] In *Meritor,* the Supreme Court held that a plaintiff may establish a violation of Title VII by proving that discrimination based on sex created a hostile work environment.[43] The Court also addressed the standard for determining whether sexual advances are "unwelcome."

---

37. *Id.*

38. 29 C.F.R. § 1604.11(a).

39 *See supra* note 34.

40. *See* Cram v. Lamson & Sessions Co., 49 F.3d 466, 473 (8th Cir. 1995).

41. For an article devoted exclusively to the requirement that harassing behavior be "unwelcome," *see* Joan S. Weiner, *Understanding Unwelcomeness in Sexual Harassment Law: Its History and a Proposal for Reform,* 72 NOTRE DAME L. REV. 621 (1997).

42. Meritor Savings Bank v. Vinson, 477 U.S. 57 (1986).

43. For an analysis of the United States' Supreme Court decision in Meritor, *see* Ronald Turner, *Employer Liability Under Title VII for Hostile Environment Sexual Harassment by Supervisory Personnel: The Impact and Aftermath of Meritor Savings Bank,* 33 How. L.J. 1 (1990); Marlisa Vinciguerra, *The Aftermath of Meritor: A Search for Standards in the Law of Sexual Harassment,* 98 YALE L.J. 1717 (1989); Katherine S. Anderson, *Employer Liability Under Title VII for Sexual harassment After Meritor Savings Bank v. Vinson,* 87 COLUM. L. REV. 1258 (1987); Grace M. Dodier, *Meritor Savings Bank v. Vinson: Sexual Harassment at Work,* HARV. WOMEN'S L.J. 203 (1987).

The plaintiff in *Meritor,* Mechelle Vinson, worked in a bank and rose through the ranks from teller-trainee to assistant branch manager.[44] Shortly after her probationary period as a teller-trainee, Vinson's supervisor invited her to dinner and asked her to have sexual relations with him at a motel. Initially, Vinson refused his advances but eventually agreed because she was afraid she would lose her job. Over the next three years, the supervisor demanded sexual relations numerous times. He touched and fondled Vinson in front of other employees, followed her into the women's restroom, exposed himself to her, and forcibly raped her on several occasions.[45] Vinson notified the supervisor that she was taking sick leave for an indefinite period of time. The bank eventually fired her. Vinson sued both the bank and the supervisor claiming that she had "constantly been subjected to sexual harassment" by the supervisor during her four years of employment.[46]

The Court determined that the fact that Vinson had voluntarily engaged in a sexual act does not preclude a finding that the supervisor's conduct was "unwelcome" and thus, sexual harassment. Rather, the Court stated, "[t]he correct inquiry is whether [Vinson] by her conduct indicated that the alleged sexual advances were unwelcome, not whether her actual participation in sexual intercourse was voluntary."[47] By distinguishing between voluntary actions and submission to unwelcome conduct, the Court acknowledged the power differential in most relationships between employees and employers or supervisors. Because of this power differential, employees may feel forced or coerced to engage in conduct in which they would otherwise not participate.

Although the standard set by the Supreme Court in *Meritor* appears to be a victory for women, it also creates a problem by shifting the focus from the offensive conduct of the harasser to the woman's behavior.[48] The Court explained that a plaintiff's sexually provocative speech or dress is "obviously relevant" to the hostile environment sexual harassment case.[49] The result is that the litigation may focus on the woman's personal life,[50] her dress, her speech, and even her choice of lunch companions—rather than the perpetrator's inappropriate conduct.

In 1993, the United States Supreme Court established standards for determining whether a harasser's conduct is so severe as to affect a term, condition, or privilege

---

44. According to the Court, Vinson's advancement was undisputedly based on merit alone. *Meritor,* 477 U.S. at 60.

45. *Id.* at 60–61.

46. *Id.* at 60.

47. *Id.*

48. *See* Susan Estrich, *Sex at Work,* 43 STAN L. REV. 813, 827–28 (1991) (criticizing the welcomeness standard set by the Supreme Court in sexual harassment cases, comparing it to the rape standards of consent and resistance).

49. *Meritor,* 477 U.S. at 69.

50. *See* Sonja A. Soehnel, *Discoverability and Admissibility of Plaintiff's Past Sexual Behavior in Title VII Sexual Harassment Action,* 73 A.L.R. FED. 748 (1996).

of employment.[51] In *Harris v. Forklift Systems, Inc.,* the Supreme Court held that the offensive conduct need not have caused serious physical or emotional injury to the plaintiff.[52] Therefore, evidence of psychological injury is not necessary to establish a claim for sexual harassment based on a hostile and abusive work environment.[53] In this case, the plaintiff, Harris, sued her former employer, alleging that the president of the company created a hostile work environment by questioning her about her sex life, insulting her, and subjecting her to sexual innuendos. The president suggested to Harris, in front of other employees, that she accompany him to a local hotel to negotiate her raise. He asked Harris and other female employees to retrieve coins from his pockets. On other occasions, he threw objects on the ground in front of Harris and other female employees and asked them to pick up the objects.[54] The Court stated:

> Title VII comes into play before harassing conduct leads to a nervous breakdown. A discriminatorily abusive work environment, even one that does not seriously affect employees' psychological well-being, can and often will detract from employees' job performance, discourage employees from remaining on the job, or keep them from advancing in their careers. . . .

The Court in *Harris* outlined various factors to be considered in determining whether conduct creates a hostile work environment:

> This is not, and by its nature cannot be, a mathematically precise test. . . . [W]hether an environment is "hostile" or "abusive" can be determined only by looking at all the circumstances. These may include the frequency of the discriminatory conduct; its severity; whether it is physically threatening or humiliating, or a mere offensive utterance; and whether it unreasonably interferes with an employee's work performance. The effect on the employee's psychological well-being is, of course, relevant to determining whether the plaintiff actually found the environment abusive. But while psychological harm, like any other relevant factor, may be taken into account, no single factor is required.[55]

The Court determined that whether conduct is sufficiently severe to create a hostile environment must be evaluated both from the standpoint of an objective or "reasonable person" and from a subjective standpoint. Objectively, the conduct must be so offensive that a reasonable person would have been offended under the

---

51. Harris v. Forklift Systems, Inc., 114 S. Ct. 367 (1993).

52. For more information about the United States' Supreme Court decision in Harris v. Forklift Systems, *see* Kerry A. Colson, *Harris v. Forklift Systems, Inc.: The Supreme Court Moves One Step Closer to Establishing a Workable Definition for Hostile Work Environment Sexual Harassment Claims,* 30 New Eng. L. Rev. 441 (1996); Stuart L. Bass and Eugene T. Maccarrone, *Supreme Court Reaffirms Meritor and Refines Requirements for Hostile Work Environment in Sexual Harassment Suits: The Impact of Harris v. Forklift Systems, Inc.,* 16 Women's Rts. L. Rep. 53 (1994); Susan Collins, *Harris v. Forklift Systems: A Modest Clarification of the Inquiry in Hostile Environment Sexual Harassment Cases,* 1994 Wisc. L. Rev. 1515 (1994); Mary C. Gomez, *Sexual Harassment After Harris v. Forklift Systems, Inc.—Is It Really Easier to Prove,* 18 Nova L. Rev. 1889 (1994).

53. *Harris,* 114 Ct. at 371.

54. *Id.* at 369.

55. *Id.* at 371.

circumstances. Subjectively, the individual plaintiff bringing the claim must have, in fact, been offended by the conduct. The Court stated:

> Conduct that is not severe or pervasive enough to create an objectively hostile or abusive work environment—an environment that a reasonable person would find hostile or abusive—is beyond Title VII's purview. Likewise, if the victim does not subjectively perceive the environment to be abusive, the conduct has not actually altered the conditions of the victim's employment, and there is no Title VII violation.[56]

An individual plaintiff can usually establish that she perceived her work environment to be hostile from a subjective point of view through direct evidence of her reaction to the situation.[57] If, however, the evidence establishes that an individual plaintiff did not perceive the alleged harasser's behavior as offensive, she will not have a claim for sexual harassment regardless of how offensive the perpetrator's conduct was from an objective perspective.[58]

A plaintiff may have more difficulty establishing that the harasser's conduct created a hostile and abusive work environment from an objective point of view. In tort law, courts generally analyze conduct from the perspective of the ostensibly gender-neutral "reasonable man" or "reasonable person" standard. The definition of "reasonable man" has been the focus of numerous lawsuits in the United States. Some courts have recognized that the average man and the average woman may respond differently to certain behavior and have adopted a "reasonable woman" standard to evaluate whether a work environment is hostile or abusive for a female plaintiff in a sexual harassment case.

For example, in *Ellison v. Brady,* the Ninth Circuit Court of Appeals rejected the reasonable man standard and adopted a reasonable woman standard for sexual harassment cases, stating that "a sex-blind reasonable person standard tends to be male-biased and tends to systematically ignore the experiences of women."[59] The Court in *Ellison* recognized that the average woman may be offended by conduct that the average man does not find objectionable. The court explained its reasoning as follows:

---

56. *Id.* at 370.

57. *See, e.g.*, Dey v. Colt Const. & Development Co., 28 F.3d 1446, 1455–56 (7th Cir. 1994). In *Dey*, the Court held that the plaintiff was not required to show that she could not complete her job responsibilities in a timely fashion or that she completely disassociated with the alleged harasser to establish that she perceived her work environment to be hostile. Evidence that the plaintiff was upset and embarrassed and that she complained to her supervisor, told the alleged harasser she was uncomfortable with his behavior, and reported that she was going to start keeping a log of offensive conduct was sufficient to maintain a cause of action for hostile environment sexual harassment.

58. *See* Sauers v. Salt Lake County, 1 F.3d 1122, 1127 (10th Cir. 1993). In *Sauers*, the Court dismissed a claim for hostile environment sexual harassment despite significant evidence of harassment. The Court found that the plaintiff had willingly engaged in sexual banter in the office, including the exchange of off-color stories with the alleged harasser. In addition, the plaintiff had never objected to the atmosphere in the office and had denied that the alleged harasser had done anything inappropriate in response to a sexual harassment claim by another employee.

59. Ellison v. Brady, 924 F.2d 872, 879 (9th Cir. 1991).

We realize that there is a broad range of viewpoints among women as a group, but we believe that many women share common concerns which men do not necessarily share. For example, because women are disproportionately victims of rape and sexual assault, women have a stronger incentive to be concerned with sexual behavior. Women who are victims of mild forms of sexual harassment may understandably worry whether a harasser's conduct is merely a prelude to violent sexual assault. Men, who are rarely victims of sexual assault, may view sexual conduct in a vacuum without a full appreciation of the social setting or the underlying threat of violence that a woman may perceive. . . .

In order to shield the employers from having to accommodate the idiosyncratic concerns of the rare hypersensitive employee, we hold that a female plaintiff states a *prima facie* case of hostile environment sexual harassment when she alleges conduct which a reasonable woman would consider sufficiently severe or pervasive to alter the conditions of employment and create an abusive working environment.[60]

Although other courts have recognized the difficulty of applying a gender-neutral standard to behavior in a sexual harassment case and have adopted the "reasonable woman standard,"[61] it has not ᵇeen universally accepted by federal courts in the United States.[62]

The frequency of the objectionable conduct is also relevant to establishing a claim for hostile environment sexual harassment. Generally, isolated or relatively innocuous incidents do not support a finding of sexual harassment.[63] A series of seemingly isolated incidents, however, may establish a pattern that creates a hostile work environment when considered as a whole. Courts must evaluate isolated incidents cumulatively to obtain a realistic view of the work environment.[64]

Employer Liability for Acts of Its Employees

Under federal law in the United States, the general rule is that an employer is *strictly liable* for *quid pro quo* sexual harassment when the perpetrator is a manager

---

60. *Id.* at 878–79.

61. *See, e.g.,* Burns v. McGregor Elec. Indus., Inc., 989 F.2d 959, 962 (8th Cir.1993) (appropriate standard in hostile environment litigation under Title VII is that of a reasonable woman under similar circumstances); *see also,* Andrews v. City of Philadelphia, 895 F.2d 1469, 1482 (3d Cir. 1990) (the Court determined that successful plaintiff in a hostile environment sexual harassment case must establish, *inter alia,* that the discrimination would detrimentally affect a reasonable person of the same sex).

62. *See, e.g.,* DeAngelis v. El Paso Mun. Police Officer's Ass'n, 51 F.3d 591, 594 (5th Cir. 1995), *cert. denied* 116 S. Ct. 473 (1995); Simon v. Morehouse School of Medicine, 908 F. Supp. 959, 969 (N.D. Ga. 1995).

Feminist scholars disagree on whether the "reasonable woman" standard should be applied in sexual harassment cases. For a discussion of different feminist theories, *see* Naomi R. Cahn, *The Looseness of Legal Language: The Reasonable Woman Standard in Theory and Practice,* 77 CORNELL L. REV. 1398 (1992).

63. *See* Koelsch v. Beltone Electronics Corp., 46 F.3d 705, 708 (7th Cir. 1995) (two isolated incidents of unwelcome physical contact and isolated crude jokes that were not related to the unwelcome physical contact did not create a hostile environment).

64. *See* Harris v. Forklift Systems, Inc., 510 U.S. 17 (1993); Doe v. R. R. Donnelley & Sons, Co., 42 F.3d 439, 444 (7th Cir. 1994).

or supervisor; the courts will therefore impose liability on the employer regardless of whether the employer had knowledge of the harasser's conduct.[65]

In a case of hostile environment sexual harassment, perpetrated by a supervisor or manager, the employer is liable if the employer knew or should have known that the offensive conduct was occurring and failed to take prompt remedial action.[66] Similarly, an employer is liable for sexual harassment created by a plaintiff's peers or colleagues if the employer knew or should have known about the offensive conduct and did not take steps to stop it.[67]

Remedies

A victim who brings a successful claim for sexual harassment under Title VII of the Civil Rights Act may have access to a variety of remedies including the recovery of compensatory damages such as future economic loss, loss of enjoyment of life, and back pay.[68] Successful plaintiffs may also recover punitive damages, attorneys' fees, and expert fees.[69] To recover punitive damages, a plaintiff must establish that the employer acted with malice or reckless indifference to her rights.[70]

SEXUAL HARASSMENT AROUND THE WORLD

Many countries still do not provide legal protection against sexual harassment in the workplace. Generally, countries that provide legal protection for sexual harassment, except for the U.S. and Great Britain, developed the laws in the 1980s or early 1990s.[71] Legal protections against sexual harassment can take the form of laws prohibiting discrimination, labor laws, or criminal laws.[72] In addition, some courts have also applied traditional tort laws to obtain redress for sexual harassment in the workplace.[73] There are advantages and disadvantages to each approach. This section will provide examples of the laws in different countries to illustrate the issues that should be considered when attempting to draft legislation to prohibit sexual harassment.

---

65. *See* Nichols v. Frank, 42 F.3d 503, 513 (9th Cir. 1994); Horn v. Duke Homes, Inc., 755 F.2d 599, 604–6 (7th Cir. 1985); Henson v. City of Dundee, 682 F.2d 897, 903 (11th Cir. 1982).

66. *See, e.g.,* Karibian v. Columbia Univ., 14 F.3d 773, *cert. denied* 114 S. Ct. 2693; Kaufman v. Allied Signal, Inc, 970 F.2d 178 (6th Cir. 1992), *cert. denied* 113 S. Ct. 831.

67. *See, e.g.,* Barrett v. Omaha Nat'l Bank, 726 F.2d 424 (8th Cir. 1984); Katz v. Dole, 709 F.2d 251 (4th Cir. 1983).

68. 42 U.S.C. 1981(a) (1994).

69. *Id.*

70. *Id.*

71. *See* CONDITIONS OF WORK DIGEST, *supra* note 7, at 49.

72. *See generally id.* for a detailed survey of sexual harassment laws in 23 industrialized countries.

73. For example, tort law has been applied to sexual harassment claims in Japan, Switzerland and the United States. CONDITIONS OF WORK DIGEST, *supra* note 7, at 56.

Laws Prohibiting Discrimination

As discussed previously, the United States addresses sexual harassment under the law prohibiting discrimination in employment. Several other countries, including Great Britain[74] and Australia,[75] have taken a similar approach. One benefit of treating sexual harassment as unlawful discrimination is that antidiscrimination laws recognize the gender dynamics often involved in sexual harassment cases. Specifically, treating sexual harassment as improper discrimination acknowledges that women are sometimes forced to endure inappropriate and offensive conduct simply because they are women. In addition, under discrimination laws, employers can be held liable for the conduct of their employees, managers, and supervisors under many circumstances.[76] This increases the likelihood that victims of sexual harassment can recover money damages for the injuries they sustain as a result of the harassment.

There are some potential disadvantages to this legal framework. For example, when a cause of action arises out of sex discrimination, blatantly offensive conduct of a sexual nature may not be actionable where both the victim and the perpetrator of the harassment are the same sex.[77] Also, in theory, a defendant who creates an abusive and hostile environment may not be liable for sexual harassment if he can

---

74. Sexual harassment is prohibited under the Sex Discrimination Act 1975, dated 12 November 1975 (General Acts and Measures, Vol. 2, Chapter 65, 1975), as amended up to 7 November 1986 (General Acts and Measures, Vol. 3, Chapter 59, 1986). For a comparison of sexual harassment law in the United States and Great Britain, *see* Toni P. Lester, *A Yankee Women in King Arthur's Court—What the United States and the United Kingdom Can Learn from Each Other about Sexual Harassment,* 17 B.C. INT'L & COMP. L. REV. 233 (1994).

75. In Australia, sexual harassment is prohibited under the Federal Sex Discrimination Act of 1984, section 106. Several states in Australia also have individual laws prohibiting sexual harassment as an improper form of sex discrimination. *See, e.g.,* Queensland's Anti-Discrimination Act of 1991, section 133.

76. *See* discussion of United States' law *supra; see also* CONDITIONS OF WORK DIGEST, *supra* note 7, at 58–59.

77. In the United States, the courts disagree as to whether sexual harassment involving people of the same gender is actionable.

See, e.g., Hopkins v. Baltimore Gas & Elec. Co., 871 F. Supp. 822, 834 (D. Md. 1994) (court held that Title VII does not provide a cause of action for employee who claims to have been the victim of sexual harassment by supervisor or co-worker of the same gender); Garcia v. Elf Atochem North America, 28 F.3d 446, 451–52 (5th Cir 1994) (harassment by a male supervisor of a male subordinate does not state a claim under Title VII even though the harassment has sexual overtones); *cf.* Quick v. Donaldson Company, Inc., 90 F.3d 1372 (8th Cir. 1996), *reh'g en banc denied,* 1996 U.S. App. LEXIS 24919 (1996) (court reinstated Title VII claim of a male who alleged he was the target of sexual harassment by male co-workers.) For a thorough discussion of issues related to same-gender sexual harassment, *see* Cullen P. Cowley, *Same Gender Harassment and Homosexuality in Title VII Sexual Harassment Litigation,* 50 WASH. U. J. URB. & CONTEMP. L. 443 (1996); Pamela J. Papish, *Homosexual Harassment or Heterosexual Horseplay? The False Dichotomy of Same-Sex Sexual Harassment Law,* 28 COLUM. HUM. RTS. L. REV. 201 (1996); Susan Perissinotto Woodhouse, *Same-Gender Sexual Harassment: Is it Sex Discrimination Under Title VII?,* 36 SANTA CLARA L. REV. 1147 (1996).

establish that he does not discriminate against women because his behavior offends men and women equally.[78] Offensive sexual conduct can be used as a form of intimidation or control regardless of the gender of the victim and perpetrator.

Criminal Law

Certain criminal conduct, such as rape and other forms of sexual assault, may also be classified as sexual harassment when it occurs in the workplace. Some countries have expressly codified sexual harassment as a separate criminal offense. For example, in the Philippines, both conduct that can be classified as *quid pro quo* sexual harassment and conduct that can be classified as hostile environment sexual harassment are punished as criminal acts.[79] This law, passed in February 1995,[80] makes it illegal for an employer, a superior, or an instructor to demand sexual favors as a condition of employment or advancement, or of attaining a passing grade. Inappropriate conduct resulting in an intimidating, hostile, or offensive environment for an employee, trainee, apprentice, or student is also considered sexual harassment.

In Russia, *quid pro quo* sexual harassment is treated as a criminal offense. The Russian Penal Code provides:

> **Forcing a Woman to Engage in Sexual Intercourse.** Forcing a woman to engage in sexual intercourse or in the satisfaction of sexual passion in any form by a person on whom the woman is dependent either materially or in terms of employment—is punishable by deprivation of freedom for a period of up to three years.[81]

The law in Russia does not specifically prohibit hostile work environment sexual harassment.[82]

France also has a provision in its Penal Code that prohibits sexual harassment.[83] The law provides that "[t]he act, by anyone abusing authority that is conferred by his or her position to pressure [someone] with the intention of obtaining sexual

---

78. This same analysis can be applied to cases where a woman is the perpetrator.

79. An Act Declaring Sexual Harassment Unlawful in the Employment, Education or Training Environment, and for Other Purposes, Republic Act No. 7877 (1995).

80. *Philippines Passes Law Making Sexual Harassment Illegal*, DEUTSCHE PRESSE-AGENTUR, Feb. 14, 1995, *available in* LEXIS, World Library, Allwld File.

81. Russian Penal Code, art. 118.

82. Journalists have reported appalling conditions for women in the workplace in Russia during the time of transition to democracy and a free market economy. One report described a "job fair" that was operated like a beauty pageant. Women seeking positions in office administration were paraded across the stage and asked to respond to personal questions, including how they would respond to certain behavior by their supervisors or clients. Stephanie Simon, *Finding a Job in Russia is a Wild Free-for-All,* STAR TRIB. (Minneapolis-St. Paul), Jan. 14, 1996, at 5A.

83. *See* French Penal Code, art. 222–32–1.

favors, is punishable.''[84] Like the Russian statute, the French statute does not address hostile work environment sexual harassment nor does it specifically define the term "sexual harassment."

Criminalizing sexual harassment may have unintended negative consequences. Criminal conduct generally requires a higher standard of proof for conviction. As a result, a woman may have no effective recourse even when harassment is severe because she cannot meet this higher standard of proof. Sexual harassment cases are often difficult to prove even using the lower standards of proof applied in civil cases. Potential criminal penalties may also be an additional deterrent for women to report sexual harassment. Many women hesitate to report sexual harassment because they do not want to harm the harasser's career, they simply want the behavior to stop. The threat of criminal penalties may provide an additional barrier to a woman's willingness to report sexual harassment.

Under criminal law, the alleged harasser alone is prosecuted for the conduct constituting sexual harassment.[85] Normally, the employer would not be liable for the alleged harasser's criminal conduct.[86] Therefore, a victim of sexual harassment may not be able to recover money damages as a result of her injuries.[87]

Tort Laws

A victim of sexual harassment may also bring a tort claim in some situations. In the United States, a tort is a private or civil wrong or injury for which the court will provide a remedy in the form of an action for damages.[88] In many countries, tort law is defined in civil codes as the general responsibility to exercise due care towards others and the obligation to pay for damages caused by injury which results from the failure to exercise due care.[89] Much of the behavior that gives rise to a claim for sexual harassment also amounts to a tort claim. For example, in a highly publicized case in Japan, a woman alleged that she was forced to leave her job because her supervisor was spreading rumors in the workplace about her personal life and sexual behavior.[90] The Court, in finding for the plaintiff, recognized a violation of the plaintiff's right to privacy as well as hostile environment sexual harassment.[91] In the United States, many cases alleging sexual harassment also

---

84. French Penal Code, art. 222–32–1.

85. CONDITIONS OF WORK DIGEST, *supra* note 7, at 60.

86. *Id.*

87. Although criminal laws may allow for compensation of the victim, a convicted harasser may not have the resources to pay a judgment.

88. *See* BLACK'S LAW DICTIONARY 1489 (6th ed. 1990).

89. CONDITIONS OF WORK DIGEST, *supra* note 7, at 56.

90. *See* Nancy Patterson, *No More Naki-Neiri? The State of Japanese Sexual Harassment Law: Judgment of April 16, 1992, Fukuoka Chiho Saibansho, Heisei Gannen (1989) (SA) No. 1872, Songai Baisho Jiken (Japan),* 34 HARV. INT'L L. J. 206 (1993).

91. *Id.*

include claims for other torts such as negligent retention of an employee, intentional infliction of emotional distress, and assault and battery.

Traditional tort law is seldom the most effective approach to remedy sexual harassment. Many forms of sexual harassment cannot be easily defined in tort law. Tort law is appropriate to address behavior such as unwelcome touching and other conduct so outrageous that it would rise to the level of a tort regardless of whether it occurred in the workplace. Tort law, however, also generally requires evidence of injury. Complainants should not be required to wait until the sexual harassment is so severe that they experience the level of injury necessary to maintain a cause of action in tort before bringing an action to stop the harassing behavior.

In addition, as with criminal law, tort law may limit the ability of a person injured by sexual harassment to recover monetary damages for her injuries.[92] Employers are not always liable for the torts of their employees, managers, and supervisors.[93] Generally, an employer is only responsible for the acts of employees committed within the scope of employment.[94] Therefore, unless a tort claim such as negligent retention of an employee is brought directly against the employer, a plaintiff's potential recovery may be limited to the harrasser's ability to pay a judgment.

Labor and Contract Law

Some countries have provisions in their labor codes that prohibit sexual harassment. For example, in Spain, sexual harassment is prohibited under the Worker's Charter. The Charter provides that "all workers shall enjoy [the right] to respect for his privacy and proper consideration for his dignity, including the protection against verbal or physical offense of a sexual nature."[95]

New Zealand has a much more detailed statutory framework prohibiting sexual harassment in its Labor Code.[96] According to the definition of sexual harassment in the Employee Contracts Act:

> [A]n employee is sexually harassed . . . if that employee's employer or a representative of that employer (a) makes a request of that employee for sexual intercourse, sexual contact, or other form of sexual activity which contains (i) an implied or overt promise of preferential treatment in that employee's employment; or (ii) an implied or overt threat of detrimental treatment in that employee's employment; or (iii) an implied or overt threat about the present or future employment status of that employee; or (b) by (i) the use of words (whether written or spoken) of a sexual nature; or (ii) physical behavior of a sexual nature, subjects the employee to behavior which is unwelcome or offensive to that employee (whether or not that is conveyed to the employer or representative) and which is either repeated or of such a significant nature that it has

---

92. CONDITIONS OF WORK DIGEST, *supra* note 7, at 59.

93. *Id.*

94. *Id.*

95. Worker's Charter, Article 4(2)(e) (Spain).

96. Employment Contracts Act 1991, Act No. 22, May 7, 1991 (New Zealand).

a detrimental effect on that employee's employment, job performance, or job satisfaction.[97]

This statute prohibits essentially the same conduct as do the EEOC guidelines in the United States, but does not require a showing of discrimination based on sex to maintain a cause of action. Because the statute focuses on specifically identified offensive conduct, it may apply to a broader range of behaviors.

Victims of sexual harassment may also bring claims under general labor law or contract principles. For example, a woman who loses her job for refusing the sexual advances of her supervisor may bring an action for unfair dismissal under general labor laws.[98] Other potential causes of action may arise under provisions of individual labor contracts or agreements that guarantee specific work conditions, discipline standards, or grievance procedures.

Labor codes and contract provisions specifically prohibiting sexual harassment or guaranteeing just and favorable conditions of work may be the most effective method of holding employers and harassers accountable for sexual harassment. Although the specific provisions may become complicated to cover a broad range of conduct, they do not have the same conceptual problems that can arise under theories of discrimination. Laws that directly prohibit specific conduct allow an individual to bring a claim regardless of whether she can show that offensive conduct of a sexual nature was directed at her because of her sex. In addition, a carefully constructed statute can clearly define the liability of employers and employees for sexual harassment in the workplace.

General Considerations

There are many ways to approach the problem of sexual harassment. The main goals of any legal effort should be to prevent harassing conduct from occurring, to halt and punish it when it does occur, and to provide redress to victims of sexual harassment. Sexual harassment can take many forms; therefore, a combination of laws may be necessary to fully address the problem. Some forms of sexual harassment are best addressed in civil courts under labor laws or antidiscrimination laws. Other forms rise to the level of sexual assault, including rape, and should be prosecuted as criminal conduct.

Legal approaches should be combined with efforts by individual employers to eliminate sexual harassment through employment policies, education, and training. Employment policies should clearly identify the behavior that is prohibited and provide a procedure to report violations of the policy to managers or supervisors within the company. Employers should ensure that all employees understand the sexual harassment policies they adopt, and that the policies are consistently applied and enforced. Employers should also provide a detailed mechanism for addressing the problem in a confidential and sensitive manner after a grievance has been

---

97. *Id.* Section 29(1).

98. *See* Conditions of Work Digest, *supra* note 7, at 49.

filed. A well-constructed and well-implemented plan within a company may stop inappropriate conduct before it creates a problem for individual employees or the company.

SEXUAL HARASSMENT IN INTERNATIONAL LAW

Sexual harassment violates the most basic principles of international human rights law. It undermines the inherent dignity of the person and violates the right of every human being to physical and mental integrity. Sexual harassment is an insidious form of discrimination and violates the antidiscrimination provisions of all the major human rights treaties.[99] Sexual harassment also violates the right to just and favorable conditions of work recognized in the Universal Declaration of Human Rights (UDHR),[100] the International Covenant on Economic Social and Cultural Rights (ICESCR)[101] and the Convention on the Elimination of All Forms of Discrimination Against Women (Women's Convention).[102] In addition, a government's failure to provide an effective remedy to victims of sexual harassment violates the right to an effective remedy for the violation of fundamental human rights guaranteed by the ICCPR[103] and the UDHR.[104]

The United Nations and other international organizations have recently recognized that women's rights are human rights, and that violence against women is a violation of the human rights of women.[105] These organizations have specifically condemned sexual harassment in a series of international instruments as a prohibited form of violence against women. The United Nations has emphasized the responsibility of member states to create conditions that protect the human rights of individuals in both public and private life,[106] and has acknowledged that governments may be responsible for inaction in the face of human rights abuses by

---

99. International Covenant on Civil and Political Rights, art. 2(1), G.A. Res. 2200 A(XXI), Dec. 16, 1966, 21 U.N. GAOR Supp. (No. 16) at 52, U.N. Doc A/6316 (1966), 999 U.N.T.S. 171, *entered into force* Mar. 223, 1976 [hereinafter ICCPR]; International Covenant on Economic, Social and Cultural Rights, art. 2(2), G.A. Res. 2200A (XXI), 21 U.N. GAOR Supp. (No. 16) at 49, U.N. Doc. A/6316 (1966), 993 U.N.T.S. 3, *entered into force* Jan. 3, 1976 [hereinafter ICESCR]; Convention on the Elimination of All Forms of Discrimination Against Women, art. 11, G.A. Res. 34/180, U.N. GAOR Supp. (No. 46), U.N. Doc. A/Res/34/180, *entered into force* Sept. 3, 1981 [hereinafter the Women's Convention].

100. Universal Declaration of Human Rights, art. 23(1), G.A. Res. 217A (III), U.N. Doc A/810 at 71 (1948) [hereinafter UDHR].

101. ICESCR, *supra* note 99, art. 7.

102. The Women's Convention, *supra* note 99, art. 11(f). Article 11(f) provides for the right to protection of health and to safety in working conditions.

103. ICCPR, *supra* note 99, art. 2(3)(a).

104. UDHR, *supra* note 100, art. 8.

105. *See infra* text accompanying notes 126–42 and 143–47.

106. Vienna Declaration and Programme of Action, U.N. DOC. A/CONF. 157/24 (1993) [hereinafter VDPA].

private actors just as they are for abuses committed by state actors.[107] This express condemnation of human rights violations commonly experienced by women reflects a growing recognition in the international community that the traditional human rights work of international organizations and nongovernmental organizations, by focusing mainly on violations of civil and political rights, largely ignored the experiences of women.[108]

In spite of this growing recognition of violence against women as a human rights abuse, the language in many of the international instruments is vague with respect to sexual harassment. With limited exceptions, there are no enforcement mechanisms for violations of human rights instruments. Notwithstanding the serious limitations of these documents, the strong international condemnation of sexual harassment may provide the necessary legitimacy to women's advocates working to adopt national legislation to prohibit sexual harassment in countries that have not yet addressed the problem.

The United Nations

Convention on the Elimination of All Forms of Discrimination Against Women

The Women's Convention, adopted by the United Nations in 1979, does not expressly mention violence against women or sexual harassment. It does, however, prohibit discrimination in employment.[109] Specifically, the Women's Convention provides:

> States Parties shall take all appropriate measures to eliminate discrimination against women in the field of employment in order to ensure, on a basis of equality of men and women, the same rights, in particular:
>
> a) The right to work as an inalienable right of human beings:
>
> b) The right to the same employment opportunities, . . .
>
> f) The right to protection of health and to safety in working conditions,[110] . . .

The Women's Convention created the Committee on the Elimination of Discrimination Against Women (CEDAW) to monitor states parties' implementation

---

107. For an in-depth discussion of the distinction between public and private actions, *see* Donna Sullivan, *The Public/Private Distinction in International Human Rights Law, in* WOMEN'S RIGHTS HUMAN RIGHTS: INTERNATIONAL FEMINIST PERSPECTIVES 126 (Julie Peters & Andrea Wolper eds., 1995); Celina Romany, *State Responsibility Goes Private: A Feminist Critique of the Public/Private Distinction in International Human Rights Law, in* HUMAN RIGHTS OF WOMEN 85 (Rebecca Cook ed., 1994).

108. *See* Hillary Charlesworth, *What are "Women's International Human Rights?" in* HUMAN RIGHTS OF WOMEN 58 (Rebecca Cook ed., 1994); Charlotte Bunch, *Women's Rights as Human Rights: Toward a Revision of Human Rights,* 12 HUM RTS. Q. 486 (1990).

109. The Women's Convention, *supra* note 99, art. 11.

110. *Id.*

of the Convention.[111] States parties to the Convention are required to submit a report to CEDAW within a year of ratifying the Women's Convention[112] and, thereafter, they must submit additional reports every four years and when specifically requested by CEDAW.[113]

In 1992, CEDAW issued General Recommendation 19,[114] which addresses violence against women and sexual harassment in employment. It notes that "equality in employment can be seriously impaired when women are subjected to gender specific violence, such as sexual harassment in the workplace."[115] General Recommendation 19 recognizes both *quid pro quo* sexual harassment and hostile environment sexual harassment as forms of discrimination. Sexual harassment is defined to include "such unwelcome sexually determined behavior as physical contacts and advances, sexually colored remarks, showing pornography, and sexual demands, whether by words or actions."[116] This conduct is identified as discriminatory when a woman has reasonable grounds to believe that her objection would result in adverse employment action or when it creates a hostile working environment.[117]

General Recommendation 19 also recognizes that sexual harassment may constitute a health and safety problem.[118] It calls on states parties to implement effective procedures for filing complaints and remedies, including compensation, for sexual harassment.[119] States parties are also encouraged to include information about sexual harassment and measures to protect women from sexual harassment in the workplace in their reports to CEDAW.[120]

General Recommendation 19 recognizes that gender-based violence, "violence which is directed against a woman because she is a woman or which affects women disproportionately," includes acts that inflict physical, mental, or sexual harm or suffering as well as threats of such acts or coercion.[121] CEDAW recommends that states parties take all legal and other measures necessary, including preventive measures, penal sanctions, and compensatory provisions to protect women against sexual harassment in the workplace.[122] General Recommendation 19, although not

---

111. *Id.* art. 17.

112. *Id.* art. 18(1)(a).

113. The Women's Convention, *supra* note 99, art. 18 (1)(b).

114. United Nations Committee on the Elimination of Discrimination Against Women: *General Recommendation 19: Violence Against Women* (Eleventh Session, New York, January 1992), document no. CEDAW/1992/L.1/Add.15.

115. *Id.* para. 22.

116. *Id.* para. 23.

117. *Id.*

118. *Id.* para. 23.

119. *Id.*

120. *Id.* para. 24.

121. *Id.* para. 7.

122. *Id.*

technically binding, is important because it represents a consensus opinion of CEDAW that sexual harassment is an impediment to equality in the workplace and that it is the obligation of states parties to take actions to eliminate it.

Sexual harassment is an egregious form of employment discrimination. It compromises the health and safety of women workers. States parties to the Women's Convention that do not have laws protecting women against sexual harassment are in violation of their obligations under the Convention to prohibit discrimination in employment, to provide equal opportunity, and to protect the health and safety of women workers. Unfortunately, although the Women's Convention is a binding treaty and states parties must report their progress in implementing it, there are currently no mechanisms for filing individual complaints for violations of the Convention.[123] Advocacy groups, however, can use the provisions of the Convention to advocate for new laws or to challenge existing laws, policies, or practices that contravene the terms of the Convention.

The Nairobi Forward Looking Strategies for the Advancement of Women

The first United Nations' document to directly address sexual harassment was the Nairobi Forward Looking Strategies for the Advancement of Women,[124] adopted in July 1985 at the Third World Conference on Women in Nairobi, Kenya. This document states:

> The working conditions of women should be improved. . . . Appropriate measures should be taken to prevent sexual harassment on the job and sexual exploitation in specific jobs.[125]

This provision is significant because most of the countries attending the Conference in Nairobi did not provide any legal protections against sexual harassment in their national legislation at the time of the Conference. This document focused international attention on the prevention of sexual harassment for the first time. For many countries attending the Conference, it also constituted their first formal commitment to address the problem. The Forward Looking Strategies do not, however, identify sexual harassment as a human rights violation or as a form of discrimination or violence against women.

The Vienna Declaration and Programme of Action

At the World Conference on Human Rights in Vienna in 1993, great advances were made in the recognition of women's human rights with the adoption of the

---

123. The Special Rapporteur on Violence Against Women, Radhika Coomeraswamy, recommended that the United Nations adopt an Optional Protocol to provide a mechanism for filing individual complaints under CEDAW in her second report to the Commission on Human Rights. E/CN.4/1996/53, Feb. 5, 1996.

124. A/CONF. 116/28/Rev.1(85.IV.10), 1986.

125. *Id.* para. 139.

Vienna Declaration and Programme of Action.[126] The Programme of Action recognizes that the "human rights of women and of the girl-child are an inalienable, integral and indivisible part of universal human rights."[127] This document articulates that the "full and equal participation of women in political, civil, economic, social and cultural life, at the national, regional and international levels, and the eradication of all forms of discrimination on grounds of sex," are priorities of the international community.[128]

The Vienna Declaration recognizes that sexual harassment is a practice incompatible with human dignity.[129] It stresses the importance of working toward the elimination of violence against women in "public and private life."[130] The Programme of Action includes specific provisions condemning sexual harassment:

> Gender-based violence and all forms of sexual harassment and exploitation, including those resulting from cultural prejudice and international trafficking, are incompatible with the dignity and worth of the human person, and must be eliminated. This can be achieved by legal measures and through national action and international cooperation in such fields as economic and social development, education, safe maternity and health care, and social support.[131]

The Vienna Declaration marks the beginning of the United Nations' recognition of women's rights as an integral part of universal human rights. It reflects a new understanding that violence against women, including sexual harassment, is a violation of women's human rights and that this violence should be examined within the context of human rights standards and gender discrimination.[132] This document also recognizes that many violations of women's human rights occur in the private sphere or by private actors, and acknowledges the responsibility of governments to eliminate these violations.[133]

Declaration on the Elimination of Violence Against Women

The Vienna Declaration called for the adoption of the draft declaration on violence against women and urged governments to combat violence against women in accordance with its provisions.[134] Subsequently, the General Assembly adopted

---

126. VDPA, *supra* note 106.

127. *Id.* para. 18.

128. *Id.*

129. *Id.* para. 7.

130. *Id.* para. 38.

131. *Id.* para. 18.

132. Donna Sullivan, *Women's Human Rights and the 1993 World Conference on Human Rights*, 88 AM. J. INT'L L. 152 (1994).

133. VDPA, *supra* note 106, para. 38.

134. *Id.*

the Declaration on the Elimination of Violence Against Women (DEVAW).[135] DE-VAW condemns violence against women, including sexual harassment, as a violation of the fundamental human rights of women.[136] Violence against women is defined broadly to include all forms of private and public violence. The Declaration enumerates the human rights and fundamental freedoms to which women are entitled, including:

    d. The right to equal protection under the law;

    e. The right to be free from all forms of discrimination;

    f. The right to the highest standard attainable of physical and mental health;

    g. The right to just and favorable conditions of work;

    h. The right not to be subjected to torture, or other cruel, inhuman or degrading treatment or punishment.[137]

The Declaration calls on member states of the United Nations to:

    c. Exercise due diligence to prevent, investigate and, in accordance with national legislation, punish acts of violence against women, whether those acts are perpetrated by the State or by private persons;

    d. Develop penal, civil, labor and administrative sanctions in domestic legislation to punish and redress wrongs caused to women who are subjected to violence; women who are subjected to violence should be provided with access to the mechanisms of justice and, as provided for by national legislation, to just and effective remedies for the harm that they have suffered; States should also inform women of their rights in seeking redress through such mechanisms; [138]

At the time it was adopted, DEVAW contained the strongest language ever used by the General Assembly to condemn violence against women, including sexual harassment. It outlines specific actions that governments should take to combat violence against women. DEVAW does not, however, contain a definition of sexual harassment or provide specific recommendations for addressing this problem.

Beijing Declaration and Platform for Action

The Beijing Declaration and Platform for Action,[139] adopted in 1995 at the United Nations Fourth World Conference on Women, also contain a strong condemnation of sexual harassment and situate it as a form of violence against women and

---

135. Declaration on the Elimination of Violence Against Women, G.A. Res. 48/104 (1993).

136. *Id.*

137. *Id.* art. 3.

138. *Id.* art. 4.

139. U.N. Doc. A/CONF.177/20 (1995).

a violation of human rights. The section relating to violence against women contains much of the same language as does the Declaration on the Elimination of Violence Against Women. The Platform for Action reflects a greater understanding that sexual harassment negatively impacts many aspects of women's lives and that it is an obstacle to enjoyment of a variety of rights. In addition to condemning sexual harassment as an unacceptable form of violence against women and a violation of women's human rights, the Platform for Action recognizes sexual harassment as an obstacle to full access to education,[140] and to access to and enjoyment of economic opportunity.[141] Sexual harassment is also recognized as an impediment to full implementation of the Platform for Action by organizations and institutions.[142] Unfortunately, as with previous United Nations documents, it does not provide a detailed definition of sexual harassment or a mechanism to address the problem. It does, however, create a minimum acceptable standard for states to achieve in protecting women against sexual harassment in the workplace.

Regional Organizations

European Union

The European Union[143] has been the most active international organization in defining the specific obligations of its member countries to provide legal protections against sexual harassment.[144] Through a series of recommendations and resolutions, the Council of Ministers, the European Parliament, and the European Commission have developed a comprehensive definition of sexual harassment and enumerated specific steps member states can take to work toward its elimination.

In December 1984, the Council of Ministers of the European Union adopted the Recommendation on the Promotion of Positive Action for Women.[145] In the Recommendation, the Council recommends that member states adopt a policy designed to eliminate existing inequalities affecting women in the workplace and to promote a better balance between the sexes in employment. It encourages member states to take positive action to increase the respect for the dignity of women in the workplace.[146] The Recommendation also encourages employers to promote positive action within their own organizations by suggesting guidelines, principles, or codes of conduct.[147]

In June 1986, the European Parliament adopted the Resolution on Violence Against Women. In this Resolution, the Parliament calls on the Council of Europe

---

140. *Id.* para. 73.

141. *Id.* paras. 163 and 180.

142. *Id.* para. 290.

143. The European Union was formerly called the European Communities.

144. CONDITIONS OF WORK DIGEST, *supra* note 7, at 23.

145. *Official Journal of the European Communities,* Vol. 27, No. L.331, Dec. 19, 1984, at 34–35.

146. *Id.*

147. *Id.* para. 7.

to encourage national governments to conduct studies and gather statistics relating to violence against women.[148] The Resolution calls for the organization of public education campaigns to increase public awareness of the existence and extent of violence against women, publicize the resources available to assist victims, and encourage victims to report violence.[149] The Resolution on Violence Against Women calls on the European Commission to conduct a study estimating the costs incurred by member states' social security bodies for illness or absence from work because of sexual blackmail at work (psychosomatic disease, neuroses, etc.),[150] and evaluating the relation between drops in productivity in public or private companies and sexual blackmail in the workplace.[151]

The Resolution on Violence Against Women also sets forth detailed recommendations for member states to address the problem of sexual harassment.[152] The Parliament calls on the Commission to review national labor and antidiscrimination legislation to determine their applicability to cases of sexual harassment and to propose additional legislation to address any inadequacies in these laws.[153] The Parliament also calls on the national governments, equal opportunities commissions, and trade unions to educate the labor force about individual rights of workers and remedies available to victims of sexual harassment and to include education about sexual harassment in school curriculums.[154]

In 1990, the Council of Ministers adopted the Resolution on the Protection of the Dignity of Women and Men at Work.[155] The Council recognizes both *quid pro quo* and hostile environment sexual harassment as an "intolerable violation of the dignity of workers and trainees."[156] In this Resolution, the Council calls on member

---

148. *Official Journal of the European Communities*, Vol. 29, No. C.176, July 14, 1986, at para. 1.

149. *Id.* para. 2.

150. *Id.* para. 37(a).

151. *Id.* para. 37(b).

152. *Id.* paras. 38–43.

153. *Id.* para. 38.

154. *Id.* para. 40.

155. *Official Journal of the European Communities*, Vol. 33, No. C.157, June 27, 1990, at 3–4.

156. *Id.* para. 1. Paragraph 1 of the Resolution:

Affirms that conduct of a sexual nature, or other conduct based on sex affecting the dignity of women and men at work, including conduct of superiors and colleagues, constitutes an intolerable violation of the dignity of workers or trainees and is unacceptable if:

(a) such conduct is unwanted, unreasonable and offensive to the recipient;

(b) a person's rejection of, or submission to, such conduct on the part of employers or workers (including superiors or colleagues) is used explicitly or implicitly as a basis for a decision which affects that person's access to vocational training, access to employment, continued employment, promotion, salary or any other employment decision; and/or

(c) such conduct creates an intimidating, hostile or humiliating working environment for the recipient.

states to develop training and education for employers and employees to combat sexual harassment and to emphasize that sexual harassment may be contrary to the principle of equal treatment.

The European Commission also developed a detailed Code of Practice on Measures to Combat Sexual Harassment.[157] The Code of Practice focuses on sexual harassment as a form of employment discrimination and defines sexual harassment as follows:

> Sexual harassment means unwanted conduct of a sexual nature, or other conduct based on sex affecting the dignity of women and men at work. This can include unwelcome physical, verbal or nonverbal conduct.
>
> Thus, a range of behavior may be considered to constitute sexual harassment. It is unacceptable if such conduct is unwanted, unreasonable and offensive to the recipient; a person's rejection of or submission to such conduct on the part of employers or workers (including superiors or colleagues) is used explicitly or implicitly as a basis for a decision which affects that person's access to vocational training or to employment, continued employment, promotion, salary or any other employment decisions; and/or such conduct creates an intimidating, hostile or humiliating working environment for the recipient.
>
> The essential characteristic of sexual harassment is that it is unwanted by the recipient, that it is for each individual to determine what behavior is acceptable to them and what they regard as offensive. Sexual attention becomes sexual harassment if it is persisted in once it has been made that it is regarded by the recipient as offensive, although one incident of harassment may constitute sexual harassment if sufficiently serious. It is the unwanted nature of the conduct which distinguishes sexual harassment from friendly behavior, which is welcome and mutual.[158]

The Code of Practice sets out recommendations to employers on how to deal effectively with the problem of sexual harassment and how to prevent its occurrence.

As with many of the United Nations documents, the measures taken by the European Union relating to sexual harassment are not binding on its member states. These measures, however, provide a more detailed recommendation for addressing the problem than previous international documents have provided. They also reflect an understanding that sexual harassment is a serious and widespread problem requiring government action.

Organization of American States

In June 1994, the Organization of American States (OAS) adopted the Inter-American Convention on the Prevention, Punishment and Eradication of Violence Against Women.[159] This Convention is the first binding regional instrument to directly address violence against women. The Convention requires states parties to

---

157. *Official Journal of the European Communities,* Vol. 35, No. L.49, Feb. 24, 1992.

158. *Id.* para. 3.

159. Inter-American Convention on the Prevention, Punishment and Eradication of Violence Against Women, 33 I.L.M. 1534 (1994).

the Convention to include in their national reports to the Inter-American Commission on Women information on measures adopted to prevent and prohibit violence against women and to assist women affected by violence. States parties are also required to report any difficulties they observe in applying those measures and the factors that contribute to violence against women.[160] The Convention is also significant because it provides a mechanism for individuals or groups to file petitions or complaints with the Inter-American Commission on Human Rights against state parties that have violated the Convention.[161]

The Convention provides that "[e]very woman has the right to be free from violence in both the public and private spheres."[162] It recognizes that violence against women is a serious human rights violation regardless of the perpetrator of the violence. Sexual harassment is explicitly enumerated as a form of violence against women. The Convention defines violence against women to include:

> ... physical, sexual and psychological violence [t]hat occurs in the community and is perpetrated by any person, including, among others, rape, sexual abuse, torture, trafficking in persons, forced prostitution, kidnapping and sexual harassment in the workplace, as well as educational institutions, health facilities or any other place; ...[163]

The Convention declares that the right to be free from violence includes the right to be free from all forms of discrimination and the right to be valued and educated "free of the stereotyped patterns of behavior and social and cultural practices based on concepts of inferiority or subordination."[164] States parties have agreed to pursue policies to prevent, punish, and eradicate violence against women.[165] They have also agreed to provide legal remedies for women victims of violence and to undertake measures to:

f. Establish fair and effective legal procedures for women who have been subjected to violence which include, among others, protective measures, a timely hearing and effective access to such procedures;

g. Establish the necessary legal and administrative mechanisms to ensure that women subjected to violence have effective access to restitution, reparations or other just and effective remedies; and

---

160. *Id.* art. 10

161. *Id.* art. 12. Article 12 provides:

Any person or group of persons, or any nongovernmental entity legally recognized in one or more member states of the Organization, may lodge petitions with the Inter-American Commission on Human Rights containing denunciations or complaints of violations of Article 7 of this Convention by a State Party, and the Commission shall consider such claims in accordance with the norms and procedures established by the American Convention on Human Rights and the Statutes and Regulations of the Inter-American Commission on Human Rights for lodging and considering petitions.

162. *Id.* art. 3.

163. *Id.* art. 2.

164. *Id.* art. 6.

165. *Id.* art. 7.

   h. Adopt such legislative or other measures as may be necessary to give effect
to this Convention.[166]

   The commitment of states to provide a legal remedy to women victims of
violence is especially significant for victims of sexual harassment. Often, a perpetrator's conduct is outrageous and has debilitating consequences for women victims
but does not constitute physical assault or some other commonly recognized form
of unlawful conduct.

   States parties have also agreed to undertake measures to educate the public
about a woman's right to be free from all forms of violence, including in the
workplace, and to undertake measures to modify social and cultural practices that
legitimize or exacerbate violence against women.[167] They have committed to provide
social services to women victims of violence and to conduct research and gather
statistics related to the causes and consequences of violence against women.[168]
Because sexual harassment is deeply ingrained in the culture and social practices
of many countries, public education, research, and specific programs targeted at
modifying these practices are critical prerequisites in eliminating the problem.

CONCLUSION

   Women's human rights are being systematically violated in workplaces around
the world. While some countries recognize the problem and work toward its reduction or elimination, many countries provide no protection whatsoever. Even in
countries that have laws prohibiting sexual harassment, many people misunderstand
both the problem and its consequences. Sexual harassment is a form of violence
used to intimidate and control women in the workplace and is often unrelated to
sexual attraction. It can have devastating consequences both on the physical and
mental health of victims and on the productivity of the workplace as a whole. One
report from the United States estimated that overall costs associated with sexual
harassment amount to approximately 6.7 million U.S. dollars annually for the average Fortune 500 company.[169]

   In addition to the direct costs to the company, employers may face large legal
fees and potentially high judgments in sexual harassment cases. For example, in a
highly publicized case in the United States, a jury awarded a plaintiff over seven
million U.S. dollars in a hostile environment sexual harassment case against an
international law firm.[170]

---

166. *Id.*

167. *Id.* art. 8

168. *Id.*

169. Susan Crawford, *A Wink Here, a Leer There: It's Costly*, N.Y. TIMES, Mar. 28, 1993, at F17,
citing a 1988 study by Freada Klein of 160 Fortune 500 companies. The study calculated losses linked
to absenteeism, low productivity, and turnover; it did not include hard-to-measure costs of legal defense,
time lost, and tarnished public image.

170. *The High Cost of Sex Harassment*, The N. Y. TIMES, Sept. 12, 1994, at A14. The Court later
reduced the award to 3.8 million dollars. *Sex Harassment Award Reduced*, N. Y. TIMES, Nov. 29, 1994,
at A22.

International organizations should provide more detailed guidance on ways of addressing violence in the workplace, including a comprehensive definition of the term "sexual harassment." A strong, detailed statement from the United Nations would assist in dispelling the myths and misconceptions about sexual harassment that may be impeding the enactment of national legislation by member countries. The United Nations should also ensure that a forum exists for the adjudication of individual complaints relating to violence against women.

Individual countries should recognize sexual harassment as a form of violence against women and provide various avenues of legal redress. The legal remedies should be accompanied by policies promoting awareness and public education to assist in preventing the occurrence of the problem.[171]

Prevention strategies for sexual harassment implemented by individual employers are essential to effective elimination of the problem. The remedy most women prefer is simply for the unwelcome, offensive conduct in the workplace to stop. A well–constructed and well-implemented plan within a company may prevent sexual harassment or stop potentially offensive conduct before it rises to the level of actionable sexual harassment. By treating the problem fairly and directly, a company may avoid costly, destructive litigation and maintain a healthier, more productive work environment.

Sexual harassment is a widespread violation of the fundamental human rights of women. Governments, private industry, and organizations must work together to implement strategies to protect the victims, punish the perpetrators, and ultimately prevent the problem.

---

171. For information about preventing sexual harassment, *see* Mark I. Schickman, *Sexual Harassment: The Employer's Role in Prevention,* 13 No. COMPLEAT LAW. 24 (Winter 1996); Rebecca J. Wilson, *How to Prevent Sexual Harassment in Your Own Backyard,* 63 DEF. COUNS. J. 237 (April 1996); Fran Sepler, *Sexual Harassment: From Protective Response to Proactive Prevention,* 11 HAMLINE J. PUB. L. & POL'Y 61 (Spring 1991).

THE LAW AND REALITY OF DISCRIMINATION AGAINST WOMEN

Douglass Cassel and Jill Guzman

Never has the global gap between noble laws and ignoble realities of discrimination against women been wider. Not that today's realities are worse than those of the past; rather, the gap has grown because international law against gender discrimination has never been stronger. The first part of this chapter reviews the current state of international law, and the second part describes the realities. Recommendations and concluding observations then follow.

INTERNATIONAL LAW AGAINST GENDER DISCRIMINATION[1]

The Prohibition of Gender Discrimination

A strong case can be made that discrimination against women is now prohibited worldwide by all three main sources of international law: treaties, customary law, and general principles of international law.[2] This section develops that case. It also considers a partial exception for predominantly Islamic states. It then discusses the definition of "discrimination," followed by issues of interpretation, including the relatively limited role played by a ban on gender discrimination in securing women's rights.

---

1. Most international instruments refer to discrimination on the basis of "sex." This chapter uses "gender" and "sex" interchangeably to differentiate men and women. This is consistent with the "ordinary, generally accepted usage" of the word "gender," as used in the *United Nations Fourth World Conference on Women: Declaration and Platform for Action*, Sept. 15, 1995, at 1, U.N. Doc. A/CONF.177/20 (1995) and U.N. Doc. A/CONF.177/20/Add.1 (1995) [hereinafter *"Beijing Declaration"*], *reprinted in* 35 I.L.M. 401, at 482 (1996). This is not to dispute that "sex" refers to biological differences, whereas "gender" may encompass social stereotypes as well. *E.g.*, Rebecca J. Cook, *State Responsibility for Violations of Women's Human Rights*, 7 HARV. HUM.RTS. J. 125, 133 (1994).

   As used in the International Covenant on Civil and Political Rights, U.N. G.A. Res. 2200 (XXI), 21 U.N. GAOR, Supp. (No. 16) 52, U.N. Doc. A/6316 (1966), Dec. 19, 1966 [hereinafter "Civil and Political Covenant"], the term "sex" has also been held by the Human Rights Committee to include "sexual orientation." Toonen v. Australia, No. 488/1992, at 12 para. 8.7 (1994). However, discrimination on the basis of sexual orientation, a substantial topic in itself, is beyond the scope of this chapter.

2. The Statute of the International Court of Justice, June 26, 1945, 59 Stat. 1031, U.N.T.S. 993, art. 38(1), directs the Court to apply "(a) international conventions, . . .; (b) international custom, as evidence of a general practice accepted as law; [and] (c) the general principles of law recognized by civilized nations; . . ."

Broad prohibitions of sex discrimination have been incorporated in treaty law for half a century. Since 1945, the Charter of the United Nations[3] has bound the now 185 member states to take action to achieve human rights for all "without distinction as to . . . sex."[4] This prohibition was elaborated in the International Bill of Human Rights, which includes the Universal Declaration of Human Rights, the International Covenant on Civil and Political Rights, and the International Covenant on Economic, Social, and Cultural Rights, as discussed below.

The Universal Declaration of Human Rights, adopted in 1948,[5] proclaims that all persons are entitled to human rights without distinction as to sex,[6] and "are equal before the law and are entitled without any discrimination to equal protection of the law."[7] The International Covenant on Civil and Political Rights ("Civil and Political Covenant"), adopted in 1966,[8] prohibits gender discrimination not only as it affects civil and political rights, but also in all national laws and their administration, including laws concerning economic, social, and cultural rights.[9] The International Covenant on Economic, Social and Cultural Rights ("Economic Rights

---

3.   U.N. CHARTER, June 26, 1945, 59 Stat. 1031, U.N.T.S. 993. For the legally binding nature of Charter provisions on human rights, *see* United States v. Iran, 1980 I.C.J. 3, 42 (1980) (wrongful deprivation of liberty in hardship conditions is "manifestly incompatible with the principles of the Charter of the United Nations"); Legal Consequences for States of the Continued Presence of South Africa in Namibia (South West Africa), 1971 I.C.J. 16, 57 (1971) (South African apartheid in Namibia was a "flagrant violation of the purposes and principles of the Charter"); *see generally* Egon Schwelb, *The International Court of Justice and the Human Rights Clauses of the Charter*, 66 AM.J.INT'L L. 337 (1972).

4.   Art. 56 pledges member states "to take joint and separate action in cooperation with the Organization for the achievement of the purposes set forth in Article 55." Among the purposes in art. 55 are "c. universal respect for, and observance of, human rights and fundamental freedoms for all without distinction as to . . . sex . . . ."

In addition, art. 1.3 lists among the U.N.'s purposes "[t]o achieve international co-operation . . . in promoting and encouraging respect for human rights and for fundamental freedoms for all without distinction as to . . . sex . . . ."

All of these provisions may be read in light of the Preamble's reaffirmation of faith "in the equal rights of men and women. . ."

5.   U.N. G.A. Res. 217A (III), U.N. Doc. A/810, at 71 (1948).

6.   Art. 2 provides, "Everyone is entitled to all the rights and freedoms set forth in this Declaration, without distinction of any kind, such as . . . sex . . . ."

The theme of equality, especially gender equality, pervades the Declaration. In addition to Articles 2 and 7 referred to in the text above, art. 1 declares, "All human beings are born free and equal in dignity and rights. . . ." Art. 16.1 provides, "Men and women . . . are entitled to equal rights as to marriage, during marriage and at its dissolution." The Preamble reaffirms faith in the "equal rights of men and women."

7.   *Id.* art. 7, which adds: "All are entitled to equal protection against any discrimination in violation of this Declaration . . ."

8.   Civil and Political Covenant, *supra* note 1. This Covenant is also known as the ICCPR.

9.   *E.g.*, Civil and Political Covenant, *supra* note 1, at arts. 2.1, 3 and 26; Broeks v. The Netherlands, *Report of the Human Rights Committee*, U.N. GAOR, 42nd Sess., Supp. No. 40, at 139, 148–49, paras. 12.1 to 12.5, U.N. Doc. A/42/40 (1987); *see infra* notes 66–70 and 90–92 and accompanying text.

Covenant''), also adopted in 1966,[10] commits states parties to undertake to guarantee exercise of its rights ''without discrimination of any kind as to . . . sex . . .,'' (art. 2.2), and ''to ensure the equal right of men and women'' to enjoy its rights (art. 3), including equal opportunity in employment (art. 7) and equal access to higher education (art. 13).[11]

These prohibitions, in turn, have been further amplified and elaborated by the Convention on the Elimination of All Forms of Discrimination Against Women (the ''Women's Convention''), adopted in 1979,[12] which binds states to a policy of eliminating discrimination against women that impairs their ''human rights and fundamental freedoms in the political, economic, social, cultural, civil or any other field.''[13] The Women's Convention moved beyond the earlier instruments, which had been understood to cover only discrimination by states, to reach also the private realms of family and workplace where most discrimination against women is experienced.[14]

Treaty Law

The combined result of the United Nations Charter, the International Bill of Human Rights, and the Women's Convention is that treaties outlawing discrimination

---

10. Dec. 19, 1966, U.N. G.A. Res. 2200 (XXI), 21 U.N. GAOR, Supp. (No. 16) 49, U.N. Doc. A/6316 (1966). This Covenant is also known as the ICESCR.

11. *See generally* MATTHEW C. R. CRAVEN, THE INTERNATIONAL ECONOMIC, SOCIAL AND CULTURAL RIGHTS: A PERSPECTIVE ON ITS DEVELOPMENT 153–81 (1995). Despite the general rule of progressive implementation of rights under art. 2.1 of the Covenant, the Committee's General Comment 3 (1990) states that its prohibition of discrimination is ''of immediate effect.'' *See, e.g., International Human Rights Instruments: Compilation of General Comments and General Recommendations Adopted by Human Rights Treaty Bodies*, at 43, U.N. Doc. HRI/GEN/1 (1992) [hereinafter *''General Comments''*].

In practical terms, however, while important to include in analyses and to reinforce nondiscrimination principles, the nondiscrimination provisions of the Economic Rights Covenant do not have a substantial effect on women's rights. Because they are limited to rights within the scope of the treaty, or to matters affecting them, the Committee monitoring the treaty ''will not concern itself with matters that do not fall within the general scope of economic, social and cultural rights.'' CRAVEN, *supra*, at 180. Yet these matters are already covered by the requirements of equality before the law and equal protection of the law in art. 26 of the Civil and Political Covenant, *Broeks, supra* note 9, and by the broad provisions of art. 2 of the Women's Convention.

Further, of the 137 states parties to the Economic Rights Covenant, only one—the Solomon Islands—is not also party to either the Women's Convention or the Civil and Political Covenant. UNESCO, HUMAN RIGHTS: MAJOR INTERNATIONAL INSTRUMENTS STATUS AS AT 31 MAY 1996 (1996) [hereinafter ''UNESCO''], at 19 and 20.

12. U.N. G.A. Res. 34/180, 34 U.N. GAOR Supp. (No. 46) 193, U.N. Doc. A/RES/34/180 (1980), Dec. 18, 1979.

13. *Id.* at arts. 1 and 2.

14. *See generally* RADHIKA COOMARASWAMY, REINVENTING INTERNATIONAL LAW: WOMEN'S RIGHTS AS HUMAN RIGHTS IN THE INTERNATIONAL COMMUNITY (Harvard Law School Human Rights Program 1997); *see, e.g.,* Women's Convention, *supra* note 12, arts. 2(e) and (f), 5(a) and (b), and 6.

against women now bind most states and, in theory, protect the overwhelming majority of the world's women. As of September 1998, the most far-reaching of these treaties, the Women's Convention, has been ratified by 162 states.[15] The Civil and Political Covenant has been ratified by 137 states, including several not parties to the Women's Convention, and the Economic Rights Covenant by 140 states, including one not a party to either the Women's Convention or the Civil and Political Covenant.[16]

Thus, some 171 states are now bound by one or more of these treaties to adopt wide-ranging bans on discrimination against women. The combined coverage of even the first two treaties alone is impressively global. Only 13 non-Islamic states are not party to either the Women's Convention or the Civil and Political Covenant.[17] Girl-children are even more widely protected by treaties against discrimination. Nearly all states (i.e., 191 states) are now parties to the Convention on the Rights of the Child,[18] which guarantees rights to all children under age eighteen "irrespective of the child's . . . sex . . ."[19] In short, on the basis of treaty law alone, outside the Islamic world, and subject to continuing litigation and debate over the scope of the prohibition, most women and girls are now protected by international instruments prohibiting sex-based discrimination.

---

15.   UNESCO, *supra* note 11, at 20 (through May 1996). By August 15, 1997, seven more states had ratified or acceded to the Women's Convention, bringing the total to 161 states. These include: Andorra, Jan. 1997; Botswana, Aug. 1996; Lebanon, Apr. 1997; Mozambique, Apr. 1997; Myanmar, July 1997; Switzerland, Mar. 1997; and Turkmenistan, May 1997. *See* Multilateral Treaties Deposited with the Secretary-General, United Nations, New York ST.LEG/SER.E, as available on http://www.un.org/ Dept/Treaty (last accessed September 2, 1998) [hereinafter Multilateral Treaties on Web].

16.   UNESCO, *supra* note 11, at 14–20 (through May 1996). By August 15, 1997, four more states had ratified or acceded to the Civil and Political Covenant, bringing the total to 138 states. These include: Belize, June 1996; Monaco, June 1997; Sierra Leone, Aug. 1996; and Turkmenistan, May 1997. Multilateral Treaties on Web, *supra* note 15. States party to the Civil and Political Covenant, but not the Women's Convention, are Afghanistan, Democratic Republic of Korea, Iran, Kyrgyzstan, Niger, San Marino, Somalia, Sudan, Syria, and the United States. By August 15, 1997, three more states had ratified or acceded to the Economic Covenant, bringing the total to 137 states. These include: Monaco, June 1997; Sierra Leone, Aug. 1996; and Turkmenistan, May 1997. Multilateral Treaties on Web, *id.* The one state party to the Economic Rights Covenant that is not a party to either of the other two treaties is the Solomon Islands. UNESCO, *supra* note 11, at 19. The United States is a party to the Civil and Political Covenant, but not to the Women's Convention or the Economic Covenant.

17.   The 13 states include ten Pacific Island states, each with relatively small populations: Cook Islands, Federated States of Micronesia, Kiribati, Marshall Islands, Nauru, Niue, Palau, Solomon Islands, Tonga, and Tuvalu. UNESCO, *supra* note 11, at 14–20. The Solomon Islands have ratified the Economic Rights Covenant. *Id.* at 19. Of course, the fact that the populations of these countries are comparatively small does not make protection of the rights of the women who live in them any less important.

      They also include three other states with small populations: the Holy See, Sao Tome and Principe, and Swaziland. UNESCO, *supra* note 11, at 14–20, with Multilateral Treaties on Web updates, *supra* note 15. Two of these three, however, are subject to legal prohibitions of gender discrimination. Sao Tome and Principe and Swaziland are parties to the African Charter on Human and Peoples' Rights. UNESCO, *id.* at 26, 29. In addition, the constitution of Sao Tome and Principe prohibits gender discrimination. *Infra* notes 35 and 36.

18.   Nov. 20, 1989, G.A. Res. 44/25, annex, 44 U.N. GAOR Supp. (No. 49) at 167, U.N. Doc. A/44/ 49 (1989).

19.   Arts. 1 and 2.1.

Customary Law

Widespread participation in these treaties also evidences the recent maturing[20] of a customary international law rule against gender discrimination. Customary international law, i.e., "international custom, as evidence of a general practice accepted as law,"[21] consists of a "settled practice" of states "carried out in such a way, as to be evidence of a belief that this practice is rendered obligatory by the existence of a rule of law requiring it."[22] In other words, customary law has two elements: the objective element of a general practice of states and, second, the subjective element of *opinio juris*, or state recognition that the practice is legally binding.[23]

State adherence to human rights treaties may provide persuasive evidence of both elements.[24] Thus, by itself, the extensive state participation in the United Nations Charter, the Civil and Political and Economic Rights Covenants, and the Women's Convention, supports the existence of a customary rule accepted by the ratifying states.[25]

---

20.   *See generally* Shirley C. Wang, *The Maturation of Gender Equality Into Customary International Law*, 27 N.Y.U. J. INT'L L. & POL. 899 (1995). In 1987 the RESTATEMENT (THIRD) OF THE FOREIGN RELATIONS LAW OF THE UNITED STATES, section 702, opined that customary international law prohibits states, as a matter of state policy, from practicing, encouraging, or condoning seven categories of human rights violations. These included "systematic racial discrimination," but not gender discrimination. However, Comment (l) observed that while sex discrimination "is still practiced in many states in varying degrees, . . . freedom from gender discrimination as state policy, in many matters, may already be a principle of customary international law." Comment (a) added that the list in section 702 included only those rights "whose status as customary law is generally accepted (as of 1987). . . . The list is not necessarily complete, and is not closed. . . ." Comment (a) ended: "See Comments j, k, and l ['Gender discrimination']."

Since 1987, the case for a customary law rule against gender discrimination has become much stronger. As of 1987, only 91 states had ratified the Women's Convention, Comment (l) to section 702, compared to 160 states by August 1997. UNESCO, *supra* note 11, at 20, with Multilateral Treaties on Web updates, *supra* note 15. In the decade since the Restatement, nearly all states have joined in the 1993 Vienna Declaration, the 1993 Declaration on the Elimination of all Forms of Violence Against Women, and the 1995 Beijing Declaration, discussed *infra* notes 28–32 and 97 and accompanying text.

Even under the Restatement, gender discrimination violates customary law when it is part of "a consistent pattern of gross violations of internationally recognized human rights." RESTATEMENT section 702(g). Most gender discrimination fits a consistent pattern, and much of it is gross (e.g., domestic violence). *See generally*, *infra* notes 117–44 and accompanying text. And most of it now violates internationally recognized standards. *See* discussion of the definition of gender "discrimination" *infra* notes 90–97 and accompanying text.

21.   Statute of the International Court of Justice, *supra* note 2, art. 38(1)(b).

22.   North Sea Continental Shelf Cases, 1969 I.C.J. 3, 44 (Judgment of Feb. 20).

23.   *E.g.*, Hurst Hannum, *The Status of the Universal Declaration of Human Rights in National and International Law*, 25 GA. J. INT'L & COMP. L. 287, 319 (1995/96).

24.   AMERICAN LAW INSTITUTE, RESTATEMENT (THIRD) OF THE FOREIGN RELATIONS LAW OF THE UNITED STATES section 701, n. 2 (1987).

25.   *But see* Arthur M. Weisburd, *The Significance and Determination of Customary International Human Rights Law: The Effect of Treaties and Other Formal International Acts on the Customary Law of Human Rights*, 25 GA. J. INT'L & COMP. L. 99 (1995–96). Citing weak enforcement provisions of the Civil and Political Covenant and Women's Convention (*id.* at 112–19), the many nonparties to the

The rule is further evidenced by at least three other widely supported United Nations declarations or General Assembly resolutions, the very kinds of instruments to which the International Court of Justice, in ascertaining customary international human rights law, attributes "central normative significance."[26] The first is the Universal Declaration of Human Rights. Its basic civil and political rights are now widely regarded as binding, either as interpretations of the U.N. Charter or as customary international law, or both.[27]

Second is the Vienna Declaration of the 1993 World Conference on Human Rights.[28] Adopted by acclamation by 171 states, it asserts that respect for human rights "without distinction of any kind is a fundamental rule of international human rights law" and calls eradication of sex discrimination a "priority objective."[29] The affirmation that non-discrimination is a "fundamental rule of international human rights law," without limiting the rule to particular treaties or states parties, is evidence that states regard the rule as binding customary law.

Covenant and reservations to the Convention (*id.* at 124–28), and state failures to comply (*id.* at 129–34), Professor Weisburd concludes that these treaties fail an "obey or be sanctioned" test for customary law. *Id.* at 134–35. He acknowledges however, "numerous authorities disagree" with his proposed test. *Id.* at 104. *E.g.*, RESTATEMENT, *supra* note 20, section 701 n. 2; Hannum, *supra* note 23, 25 GA. J. INT'L & COMP. L. at 319–22; Jordan J. Paust, *The Complex Nature, Sources and Evidences of Customary Human Rights*, 25 GA. J. INT'L & COMP.L. 99 (1995–96).

Moreover, applied to gender discrimination, his test proves too much. As noted *infra* notes 35 and 36, the constitutions or laws of most states prohibit gender discrimination, yet they practice it. His test would then prove that state laws, too, are not laws. In reality, the rampant violations of the treaties reflect a more generalized absence of the rule of law in most states. The answer is not to deny their character as laws—whether national or international—but to strengthen institutions for enforcing them.

26. The International Court of Justice "accords limited significance to state practice, especially to inconsistent or contrary practice, and attributes central normative significance to resolutions both of the United Nations General Assembly and of other international organizations. . . . The burden of proof to be discharged in establishing custom in the field of human or humanitarian rights is thus less onerous than in other fields of international law." THEODOR MERON, HUMAN RIGHTS AND HUMANITARIAN NORMS AS CUSTOMARY LAW 108 (1989). Likewise the RESTATEMENT (THIRD), *supra* note 20, section 701 n 2, treats state support for United Nations human rights resolutions and declarations as persuasive evidence of customary international law.

27. For a summary of opinions to that effect by states, scholars, and others, *see* Hannum, *supra* note 23, at 317–39. With respect to the right of nondiscrimination set forth in arts. 1, 2, 6, and 7 of the Declaration, Hannum finds it "difficult to deny the widespread acceptance of such a right to equal treatment under the law," subject to certain caveats. *Id.* at 342. One caveat, in his view, is that "state practice does not support a conclusion that there is full compliance with the principle of equality. Women are prevented from exercising their human rights on an equal footing with men in many states; . . ." *Id.* at 343. While true, it does not negate the customary status of the Declaration's right to non-discrimination, at least outside the Islamic world. *See supra* notes 25–26.

28. *United Nations World Conference on Human Rights, Vienna Declaration and Programme of Action*, June 25, 1993, at 1, U.N. Doc. A/CONF.157/24 (Part I)(1993), *reprinted in* 32 I.L.M. 1661 (1993) [hereinafter "*Vienna Declaration*"].

29. Ch. I, para. 15, 18. Para. 18 states: "The human rights of women and of the girl-child are an inalienable, integral and indivisible part of universal human rights. The full and equal participation of women in political, civil, economic, social and cultural life, . . ., and the eradication of all forms of discrimination on grounds of sex are priority objectives of the international community." Para. 39 "urges the eradication of all forms of discrimination against women, both hidden and overt."

Third, the Beijing Declaration of the 1995 World Conference on Women,[30] adopted by 189 states (albeit subject to numerous reservations, mainly by Islamic states, or on issues other than direct gender discrimination),[31] reaffirms states commitment to "equal rights . . . of women and men" as enshrined in the U.N. Charter, the Universal Declaration, the Women's Convention, and other instruments.[32]

Outside the Islamic world, then, the case for a customary international law rule against gender discrimination, based on its repeated expression in treaties ratified and declarations adopted by the overwhelming majority of non-Islamic states, is now solid.

General Principles of Law

General principles of law, as reflected in the major legal systems of the world[33] with the partial exception of Islamic law, also prohibit gender discrimination. As of 1995, according to the U.S. State Department Country Reports on Human Rights,[34] at least 158 states have laws broadly prohibiting gender discrimination;[35]

---

30. *Beijing Declaration, supra* note 1.

31. Fifty-eight states expressed reservations or made interpretative declarations. *Beijing Declaration, supra* note 1, 35 I.L.M. at 472–82. Most relate to issues such as abortion, sexual activities outside marriage, and sexual orientation, which, despite their discriminatory overtones, are beyond the scope of this chapter. With respect to the reservations of Islamic states, *see infra* notes 43–47 and accompanying text.

32. In para. 8, governments "reaffirm their commitment to: . . . 8. The equal rights and inherent human dignity of women and men and other purposes and principles enshrined in the Charter of the United Nations, to the Universal Declaration of Human Rights and other international human rights instruments, in particular the Convention on the Elimination of all Forms of Discrimination Against Women . . ., as well as the Declaration on the Elimination of Violence Against Women. . . ."

33. *See generally* M. Cherif Bassiouni, *A Functional Approach to 'General Principles of International Law,'* 11 Mich. J. Int'l L. 768 (1990); Bruno Simma & Philip Alston, *The Sources of Human Rights Law: Custom, Jus Cogens, and General Principles,* 12 Austl. Y.B. Int'l L. 82 (1992). Professor Bassiouni argues for deriving "general principles" from principles common to the "the world's major legal systems," Bassiouni, *id.* at 809, which as of 1990 he identified as the Romanist-Civilist-Germanic, Common Law, Marxist-Socialist, Islamic and Asian "families" of legal systems. *Id.* at 812.

34. Country Reports on Human Rights Practices for 1995, U.S. Dept. of State Report to Comm. on Int'l Rels., U.S. House of Reps., and Comm. on Foreign Relations, U.S. Senate, 104th Cong., 2nd Sess., Joint Committee Print April 1996 [hereinafter "Country Reports"].

35. In addition to the 118 states with constitutional prohibitions listed *infra* note 36, the following 40 states have legal prohibitions according to the indicated pages of the Country Reports, *supra* note 34:

   Africa (3 states): Cote D'Ivoire at 70, Eritrea at 85, and Ethiopia at 93.

   Americas (7 states): Argentina at 317–18, Chile at 359–60 (by domestic incorporation of Women's Convention as prevailing over local laws), Costa Rica at 378, Dominican Republic at 396, Saint Lucia at 520–21, Suriname at 528, and United States (not listed in Country Reports; *see* Craig v. Boren, 429 U.S. 190 (1976)).

   Asia and Pacific (7 states): Australia at 550–51, Indonesia at 623, Iraq at 1170, Israel at 1176, Singapore at 715, Solomon Islands at 719 and Sri Lanka at 1359–60.

   Europe (23 states): Albania at 757, Austria at 770, Belarus at 785–86, Belgium at 789, Cyprus at

118 of those include such laws in their constitutions.[36] Three more states have policies against gender discrimination.[37] Only 30 states do not have laws or official policies prohibiting gender discrimination; of these, 22 are predominantly Muslim.[38]

835, Czech Republic at 842–43, Denmark at 847, Finland at 856–57, France at 860, Germany at 872, Hungary at 890–91, Iceland at 894, Ireland at 900, Italy at 905–06, Kyrgyz Republic at 920, Luxembourg at 938, Monaco at 957, Netherlands at 959, San Marino at 1008 (not comprehensive), Serbia-Montenegro at 1019, Slovak Republic at 1025, Sweden at 1043, and the United Kingdom at 1100–01.

36.   Constitutional prohibitions are reported in the following 118 countries at the indicated page numbers of the Country Reports, *supra* note 34:

Africa (41 states): Algeria at 1126, Angola at 6, Benin at 11, Burkina Faso at 21, Burundi at 29, Cameroon at 39, Cape Verde at 44, Central African Republic at 48, Chad at 55, Comoros at 60, Congo at 63, Djibouti at 76, Egypt at 1149, Equatorial Guinea at 81, Gabon at 99, The Gambia at 104, Ghana at 111, Guinea at 118, Guinea-Bissau at 121, Lesotho at 138, Liberia at 147, Libya at 1226, Madagascar at 154, Malawi at 164, Mali at 164, Mauritania at 170, Mauritius at 175, Mozambique at 183, Namibia at 188, Niger at 194, Nigeria at 207, Rwanda at 214, Sao Tome and Principe at 218, Senegal at 222, Sierra Leone at 233, South Africa at 246, Togo at 277, Uganda at 285, Zaire at 293, Zambia at 299, and Zimbabwe at 307.

Americas (27 states): Antigua and Barbuda at 312, Bahamas at 322, Barbados at 326, Belize at 331, Bolivia at 337, Brazil at 348, Canada at 816, Colombia at 371, Cuba at 388, Dominica at 391, Ecuador at 403, El Salvador at 411, Grenada at 417, Guatemala at 430, Guyana at 438, Honduras at 455, Jamaica at 461, Mexico at 471, Nicaragua at 485, Panama at 493, Paraguay at 500, Peru at 512, St. Kitts and Nevis at 517, Saint Vincent and Grenadines at 523, Trinidad and Tobago at 533, Uruguay at 537, and Venezuela at 544.

Asia and Pacific (23 states): Cambodia at 572, China at 588, Taiwan at 602, Fiji at 610, Japan at 633, Kiribati at 638, Democratic Rep. Korea at 644, Rep. of Korea at 650, Laos at 658, Marshall Islands at 674, Fed. States Micronesia at 677, Mongolia at 681, Nauru at 684, Nepal at 1331, New Zealand at 687, Palau at 690, Papua New Guinea at 696, The Philippines at 704, Thailand at 726, Tuvalu at 734, Vanuatu at 737, Vietnam at 745, and Western Samoa at 749.

Europe (27 states): Andorra at 760, Armenia at 767, Azerbaijan at 778, Bosnia and Herzegovina at 804, Bulgaria at 811, Croatia at 829, Estonia at 853, Georgia at 867, Greece at 882–83, Kazakstan at 914, Latvia at 927, Liechtenstein at 931, Lithuania at 935, Macedonia at 944, Malta at 947, Moldova at 953, Norway at 964, Poland at 970, Portugal at 976, Romania at 986, Russia at 1004, Spain at 1036–37, Switzerland at 1048, Tajikistan at 1057, Turkmenistan at 1083, Ukraine at 1091 and Uzbekistan at 1116.

37.   *Id.* at 227 (Seychelles), 271 (Tanzania), and 1031 (Slovenia).

38.   The eight non-Islamic states whose national laws do not expressly prohibit or, in some cases, allow gender discrimination are Botswana, Kenya, Swaziland, Haiti, Burma (Myanmar), Tonga, Bhutan, and India. COUNTRY REPORTS, *supra* note 34, at 15 (Botswana), 132 (Kenya), 263 (Swaziland), 448 (Haiti), 564 (Burma), 732 (Tonga), 1307–08 (Bhutan), and 1318 (India). However, even they fall short of an unqualified endorsement of gender discrimination. Five have ratified treaties prohibiting gender discrimination: Botswana and Burma (Myanmar) are parties to the Women's Convention, *see supra* note 15, and Botswana, Kenya and Swaziland are parties to the African Charter on Human and Peoples' Rights, June 27, 1981, OAU Doc. CAB/LEG/67/3 Rev.5 (1981) [hereinafter "African Charter"], while Haiti is a party to the American Convention on Human Rights, Nov. 22, 1969, OAS T.S. No. 36, at 1, OAS Off.Rec. OEA/Ser. L/V/II.23 doc. rev. 2 [hereinafter "American Convention"]. UNESCO, *supra* note 11, at 28–29. Swaziland law prohibits gender discrimination in employment; Haiti's constitution requires equal working conditions regardless of sex; and India has an equal remuneration law. COUNTRY REPORTS, *supra* note 34, at 263, 448, 1318. The Islamic States are discussed *infra* notes 40–55 and accompanying text.

Even though broad constitutional bans on discrimination are not always consistently reflected in national laws,[39] the legal acceptance by states of the principle that gender discrimination is impermissible is now so nearly universal as to qualify as a "general principle of law."

Applicability in Predominantly Islamic States

The predominantly Islamic states[40] constitute a partial gap in this international legal consensus. Nine Islamic states are not parties to either the Women's Convention or the Civil and Political Covenant.[41] Although at least 23 have ratified one or both treaties,[42] at least eight did so only with substantial reservations to women's rights.[43] Moreover, 16 of the states parties, plus six additional Islamic states, have constitutions and laws that do not expressly prohibit gender discrimination.[44] And, at the Fourth

---

39. As noted in note 36 *supra*, Egypt's constitution, for example, prohibits gender discrimination. Yet "[b]y law, women need their husbands' or fathers' permission to obtain a passport or travel abroad. . . . Only males can confer citizenship. . . . Muslim female heirs receive half the amount of a male heir's inheritance, while Christian widows of Muslims have no inheritance rights. . . . Male Muslim heirs have the duty to provide for all family members who need assistance." COUNTRY REPORTS, *supra* note 34, at 1149.

40. "Islamic states" herein refers to states with predominantly Muslim populations, regardless of whether they are formally "Islamic republics" or otherwise governed by Islamic law. There are, of course, borderline cases, such as Uzbekistan, not here counted as an Islamic state.

41. Bahrain, Brunei, Djibouti, Kazakhstan, Mauritania, Oman, Qatar, Saudi Arabia, and the United Arab Emirates. UNESCO, *supra* note 11, at 14–20, with updates from Multilateral Treaties on Web, *supra* note 15.

42. At least eleven predominantly Islamic states—Algeria, Egypt, Iraq, Jordan, Kuwait, Lebanon, Morocco, Senegal, Tunisia, Turkmenistan and Yemen—are parties to both treaties. UNESCO, *supra* note 11, at 14–20. Six more—Bangladesh, Indonesia, Malaysia, Maldives, Pakistan, and Turkey—have ratified the Women's Convention, and six—Afghanistan, Iran, Niger, Somalia, Sudan, Syria—are parties to the Civil and Political Covenant. *Id.*

43. For example, the reservation of Bangladesh to the Women's Convention states that it "does not consider as binding upon itself the provisions of articles 2, 13(a) and 16(1)(c) and (f) as they conflict with Shariah law based on Holy Koran and Sunna." *Multilateral Treaties Deposited with the Secretary-General, Status as at 31 Dec. 1992*, at 163, U.N. Doc. ST/LEG/SER.E/11 (1993) [hereinafter "*Status*"]. For similar reservations, see *id.* at 164 (Egypt), 165 (Iraq), 166 (Libya), and 167 (Tunisia). Somewhat narrower reservations were made by Jordan and Turkey. *Id.* at 166, 168. For Morocco's reservations to Articles 2 and 16 based on the Islamic Shariah, *see Convention on the Elimination of all Forms of Discrimination Against Women: Report of the Secretary-General*, U.N. GAOR, 48th Sess., Provisional Agenda Item 112, at 8–9, U.N. Doc. A/48/354 (1993) [hereinafter "*Secretary-General Report*"].

Several Islamic states similarly made general reservations to the Convention on the Rights of the Child to the extent it conflicts with Islamic law. *E.g., Status, supra*, at 188 (Afghanistan), 190 (Djibouti), 192 (Iran, Kuwait, Mauritania), and 193 (Pakistan, Qatar, Tunisia). Others, such as Egypt, *id.* at 190, limited their religious law reservations to the Convention's provisions on adoptions. Only Tunisia's reservation expressly mentions Convention art. 2 (which prohibits gender discrimination) as inconsistent with national law "concerning personal status, particularly in relation to marriage and inheritance rights." *Id.* at 193.

44. These states and pertinent page numbers in the COUNTRY REPORTS, *supra* note 34, are as follows: Afghanistan at 1292, Bahrain at 1134, Bangladesh at 1300, Brunei at 555–56, Iran at 1158, Jordan at 1202, Kuwait at 1209, Lebanon at 1220, Malaysia at 668, Maldives at 1325, Morocco at 1234, Oman

World Conference on Women in 1995, at least 23 Islamic states made "interpretative statements or expressed reservations" on the Beijing Declaration and Platform of Action.[45]

With respect to treaty obligations, it has been argued that the reservations of Islamic states parties to the Women's Convention are invalid, because they are incompatible with the object and purpose of the treaty.[46] As objected by Mexico, for example, such reservations, "if implemented, would inevitably result in discrimination against women on the basis of sex, which is contrary to all the articles of the convention."[47]

With respect to customary law, there are two primary ways to view the partial non-participation of Islamic states.[48] One would treat most Islamic states as "persistent objectors," that is, states which so clearly and consistently express their refusal

---

at 1243, Pakistan at 1346–47, Qatar at 1247, Saudi Arabia at 1256, Somalia at 240, Sudan at 257, Syria at 1264–65, Tunisia at 1272–73, Turkey at 1075, United Arab Emirates at 1278, and Yemen at 1284–85.

45. *Beijing Declaration, supra* note 1, 35 I.L.M. at 472–82. Ten Islamic states—Egypt, Indonesia, Iran, Iraq, Kuwait, Libya, Malaysia, Mauritania, Morocco, and Tunisia—put their reservations in writing for inclusion in the record of the Conference. *Id.*

46. Objections to various reservations of Islamic states, for incompatibility with the object and purpose of the treaty, or for invalid reliance on internal law as justification for failure to perform a treaty, have been made by Denmark, Finland, Germany, Mexico, The Netherlands, Norway, and Sweden. *Status, supra* note 43, at 170–72. *See generally, e.g.*, Rebecca J. Cook, *Reservations to the Convention on the Elimination of All Forms of Discrimination Against Women*, 30 Va. J. Int'l L. 643 (1990); *see also* Belinda Clark, *The Vienna Convention Reservations Regime and the Convention on Discrimination Against Women*, 85 Am. J. Int'l L. 281 (1991).

47. *Status, supra* note 43, at 171.

48. A third, inadvisable approach would be to carve out a "religious exception," or at least an "Islamic religious exception," to the customary prohibition on gender discrimination. This would reflect the fact that both the laws and treaty reservations of Islamic states contemplate gender discrimination only to the extent compelled by Islamic law. For example, broad prohibitions on gender discrimination can be found even among predominantly Muslim, albeit secular, states: in the constitutions of Algeria, Egypt, and Libya, and in the laws of Iraq. Country Reports, *supra* note 34, at 1126 (Algeria), 1149 (Egypt), 1170 (Iraq), and 1226 (Libya). As to treaty reservations, *see Status, supra* note 43, at 163–170 (reservations to Women's Convention); *Beijing Declaration, supra* note 1, 35 I.L.M. at 472–82 (reservations to Beijing Declaration).

The vague contours of such an exception, however, could expand to swallow the rule. Different schools of Islam and different Islamic states have varying interpretations of Islamic law. *See generally, e.g.*, Bharathi Anandhi Venkatraman, Comment, *Islamic States and the United Nations Convention on the Elimination of all Forms of Discrimination Against Women: Are the Shari'a and the Convention Compatible?*, 44 Am. U. L. Rev. 1949 (1995). As stated in Norway's objections, "A reservation by which a State Party limits its responsibilities under the Convention by invoking religious law (Shariah), . . . is subject to interpretation, modification, and selective application in different states adhering to Islamic principles, ..." *Status, supra* note 43, at 172. Better to maintain a clear rule, even at the risk of leaving out Islamic states, than subject it to dilution.

And if a "religious exception" were to be allowed for Islam, why not also for other religions as well? India, for example, reserved to the Convention's principle of compulsory registration of marriages, as "not practical in a vast country like India with its variety of customs, religions and levels of literacy." *Status, supra* note 43, at 165.

to be bound by a customary rule that they are therefore exempted from it.[49] Treating Islamic states as persistent objectors to the rule against gender discrimination, to the extent it is considered inconsistent with Islamic law, would help maintain the integrity of the customary rule for other states.

If Islamic non-participation were deemed so substantial as to call into question the existence of a global customary rule against gender discrimination,[50] a second approach would rest on "regional custom."[51] There exists strong evidence of regional customary prohibitions of gender discrimination in Europe,[52] the Americas,[53]

Also, Israel reserved the right to exclude women as religious court judges "where this is prohibited by the laws of any of the religious communities in Israel," and reserved to art. 16 on nondiscrimination in marriage "to the extent that the laws on personal status which are binding on the various religious communities in Israel do not conform. . . ." *Id.* at 166. In any case, the practical benefit of watering down the *customary* rule in order to bring Islamic states within it would be limited; all but nine are already parties to *treaties* barring gender discrimination. *See* note 42 *supra.* (The combined estimated population of these nine states in the year 2000 is about 48 million, as follows: Saudi Arabia, 21.3 million; Kazakhstan, 17.7 million; Mauritania, 2.6 million; Oman, 2.6 million; United Arab Emirates, 2.1 million; Bahrain, 0.6 million; Djibouti, 0.6 million; Qatar, 0.6 million; and Brunei, 0.3 million. U.N. DEVELOPMENT PROGRAMME, HUMAN DEVELOPMENT REPORT 1995 186–87, 208 (1995).)

49. *E.g.*, IAN BROWNLIE, PRINCIPLES OF PUBLIC INTERNATIONAL LAW 10–11 (3d ed. 1979).

50. To constitute a rule of customary international law, state practice must be "general" but need not be "universal." BROWNLIE, *supra* note 49, at 4–6. The partial nonparticipation of Islamic states deprives the rule against gender discrimination of universality. Views may differ, however, on whether the nearly universal participation of non-Islamic states, detailed *supra*, suffices to achieve the requisite "generality."

51. *E.g.*, The Asylum Case, 1950 I.C.J. 266 (1950). The Court there in principle permitted Colombia to invoke "an alleged regional or local custom peculiar to Latin-American States" under Article 38 of the Court's Statute, so long as the custom reflected "a constant and uniform usage practised by the States in question." There, however, it did not. *Id.* at 276–77.

In accommodating local custom, however, a regional approach to human rights cannot deny their universality. Para. 5 of the 1993 Vienna Declaration, for example, insists on the universality of human rights, although it adds that "the significance of national and regional particularities and various historical, cultural and religious backgrounds must be borne in mind, ..."

52. All European states have ratified either the Women's Convention or the Civil and Political Covenant, except for the Holy See. UNESCO, *supra* note 11, at 14–20, with Multilateral Treaties on Web updates, *supra* note 15. In addition, 33 European states have ratified the European Convention on Human Rights, Article 14 of which requires states to secure the rights and freedoms of the Convention "without any discrimination on any ground such as . . . sex." European Convention for the Protection of Human Rights and Fundamental Freedoms, Nov. 4, 1950, 213 U.N.T.S. 221, art. 14 [hereinafter "European Convention"]. UNESCO, *supra* note 11, at 26. European Union member states are also subject to the requirement of "equal pay for equal work" by women and men in Article 119 of the European Union Treaty, as well as requirements of equal treatment for women and men in social security, Council Directive (EEC) 79/7 of 19 Dec. 1978, OJ L6 10.1.79 p. 24, and in occupational social security schemes, Council Directive (EEC) 86/378 of 24 July 1986, OJ L225 12.8.86 p.40. *See generally* Walter van Gerven, Wouter Devroe and Jan Wouters, *Current Issues of Community Law Concerning Equality of Treatment Between Women and Men in Social Security, in* EQUALITY OF TREATMENT BETWEEN WOMEN AND MEN IN SOCIAL SECURITY 7–8 (Christopher McCrudden ed., 1994) [hereinafter EQUALITY OF TREATMENT] In addition, as noted in notes 35 and 36 *supra*, all 50 European states ban gender discrimination either in their constitutions (27 states) or laws (23 states).

53. All states of the Americas have ratified either the Women's Convention or the Civil and Political Covenant. UNESCO, *supra* note 11, at 14–20. They are also bound by regional instruments. Twenty-

and, except for Islamic states, in Africa[54] and in the Asia and Pacific region.[55] A (nearly) global customary ban on gender discrimination would then result from the sum total of regional rules.

---

five states have ratified the American Convention, *supra* note 38. UNESCO, *supra* note 11, at 32. They thereby undertake to ensure the free and full exercise of a range of rights "without any discrimination for reasons of . . . sex . . ." (art. 1.1); "to ensure the equality of rights and the adequate balancing of responsibilities of the spouses" (art. 17.4); and to recognize that all persons are "equal before the law" and "entitled, without discrimination, to equal protection of the law" (art. 24). As discussed *infra* note 104, the Inter-American Court of Human Rights has defined these non-discrimination provisions by the same test used for the Civil and Political Covenant.

Furthermore, all member states are bound by the Charter of the Organization of American States, April 30, 1948, 119 U.N.T.S. 3, *am'd* Feb. 27, 1967, 21 U.S.T. 607, *am'd* Dec. 5, 1985, OAS T.S. No. 1–E. In art. 3(k), "The American States proclaim the fundamental rights of the individual without distinction as to . . . sex." Interpretation of Charter rights is guided by the American Declaration of the Rights and Duties of Man, May 2, 1948, OAS Res. XXX, OAS Off. Rec. OEA/Ser.L/V/I.4 Rev. (1965); *see generally* Adv. Op. OC-10/89, "Interpretation of the American Declaration of the Rights and Duties of Man," 1989 ANN. REP. INT-AM. CT. H. RTS. 109, 119–21 at paras. 39–43 (1989). Art. II of the Declaration provides, "All persons are equal before the law and have the rights and duties established in this declaration, without distinction as to . . . sex. . . ."

In addition, in para. 14 of the *Final Declaration of the Regional Meeting for Latin America and the Caribbean of the World Conference on Human Rights*, or "*San José Declaration*," of Jan. 22, 1993, these states "reaffirm that Government must emphasize the implementation of actions to recognize the rights of women, to promote their participation in national life with equality of opportunity, [and] to eradicate all forms of hidden or overt discrimination on grounds of sex. . . ." 14 H. RTS. L. J. 368, 369 (1993).

Finally, all but one of the American states prohibit gender discrimination in their constitutions (27 states) or laws (7 states); only Haiti lacks an express, comprehensive ban on gender discrimination in its domestic law. Notes 35, 36, and 38 *supra*.

54. All non-Islamic African states are parties to the Women's Convention or the Civil and Political Covenant, except for two, Sao Tome and Principe and Swaziland. Note 17 *supra*. In addition, 49 African states, including these two, are parties to the parallel prohibitions of gender discrimination in the African Charter, *supra* note 38. UNESCO, *supra* note 11, at 28–29. Following a Preamble in which African states recognize their duty to dismantle "all forms of discrimination, particularly those based on . . . sex - . . .," art. 2 declares every individual entitled to enjoy the rights and freedoms in the Charter "without distinction of any kind such as . . . sex . . .," and art. 3 declares every individual "equal before the law" and "entitled to equal protection of the law." *But see, e.g.*, Hilary Charlesworth, Christine Chinkin and Shelley Wright, *Feminist Approaches to International Law*, 85 AM. J. INT'L L. 613, 636–37 (1991), noting that art. 17(3) "states that '[t]he promotion and protection of morals and traditional values recognized by the community shall be the duty of the State.'. . . [T]he conjunction of the notion of equality with the protection of family and 'traditional' values poses serious problems."

Although *The Final Declaration of the regional meeting for Africa of the World Conference on Human Rights*, or "*Tunis Declaration*," of Nov. 6, 1992, does not refer to gender discrimination, in its para. 1, "The African States reaffirm their commitment to the principles set forth" in the Universal Declaration, the Civil and Political Covenant, the Economic Rights Covenant and the African Charter. 14 HUM. RTS. L. J. 367 (1993).

Finally, as noted *supra* notes 35 and 36, 41 African states prohibit gender discrimination in their constitutions and three more in their laws. Among non-Islamic African states, only Botswana, Kenya, and Swaziland lack general prohibitions of gender discrimination in their domestic laws, although Swaziland bars gender discrimination in employment. Note 38 *supra*. Botswana acceded to the Women's Convention in August 1996. Multilateral Treaties on Web, *supra* note 15.

55. All non-Islamic Asian and Pacific states, excluding ten small Oceanic states, are parties either to

The Definition of Gender Discrimination

Outside the Islamic states, both conventional and customary international law[56] appear to define the prohibition against gender discrimination in a consistent manner. The definitions (discussed below) in the Women's Convention and in United Nations Human Rights Committee interpretations of the Civil and Political Covenant guide states parties to those treaties.[57]

There is also a strong case that these treaty definitions constitute a customary international law definition of gender discrimination, except perhaps in the Islamic states. As noted earlier, some 171 states are parties to the Women's Convention or the Civil and Political Covenant (and in most cases both), and the non-parties are mostly Islamic. While parties to the Women's Convention have made an inordinate number of reservations,[58] only a few (mainly from Islamic nations and of dubious validity) reach the definition of discrimination.[59]

---

the Women's Convention or the Civil and Political Covenant. Note 17 *supra.* But substantive reservations were made by India, Korea, and Thailand. *Status, supra* note 43, at 165, 167.

There is currently no Asian or Pacific regional human rights treaty. However, in para. 22 of the *Final Declaration of the regional meeting for Asia of the World Conference on Human Rights*, or *"Bangkok Declaration,"* of April 2, 1993, the Asian states reaffirm "their strong commitment to the promotion and protection of the rights of women through the guarantee of equal participation in the political, social, economic and cultural concerns of society, and the eradication of all forms of discrimination and of gender-based violence against women; . . ." 14 H. Rts. L. J. 370, 371 (1993).

Finally, as noted in notes 35 and 36 *supra,* thirty Asian and Pacific states prohibit gender discrimination in their constitutions (23 states) or laws (7 states). The only non-Islamic Asian or Pacific states that lack such domestic laws are Burma (Myanmar), Tonga, Bhutan, and India. Note 38 *supra.* Note that Myanmar acceded to the Women's Convention in July 1997. Multilateral Treaties on Web, *supra* note 15.

56. Gender "discrimination" is not generally defined in national constitutions. To the extent "general principles" derive from common elements in the world's major legal systems, *e.g.*, Bassiouni, *supra* note 33, extensive research into the statutes and jurisprudence of diverse and representative states would be needed to ascertain whether there exists a "general principle" of law defining gender discrimination.

57. The Economic Rights Covenant does not define "discrimination" and its monitoring Committee has not given a general definition. The "only definition" in the Committee's work, explains Craven, is in its guidelines for state reporting on employment discrimination. Consistent with the Civil and Political Rights Covenant definition, the Committee requests information on "any distinctions, exclusions, restrictions or preferences, be it in law or in administrative practices or in practical relationships, between persons or groups of persons, made on the basis of . . . sex . . . which have the effect of nullifying or impairing the recognition, enjoyment or exercise of equality of opportunity or treatment in employment or occupation." Craven, *supra* note 11, at 163–64, *quoting Reporting Guidelines*, at 91, para. 3, U.N. Doc. E/1991/23, Annex IV, U.N. ESCOR, Supp. (No. 3) (1991).

58. In General Recommendation No. 4, *General Comments, supra* note 11, at 63, the Committee on the Elimination of Discrimination Against Women "[e]xpressed concern in relation to the significant number of reservations that appeared to be incompatible with the object and purpose of the Convention." *Accord, Vienna Declaration, supra* note 28, at para. 39 ("States are urged to withdraw reservations that are contrary to the object and purpose of the Convention . . ."); *see generally* Clark, *supra* note 46.

59. *See* notes 43, 46, and 47 *supra.* At least two Islamic states argue for a test of marital "equilibrium and complementarity" instead of equal rights and responsibilities. *E.g., Secretary-General Report, supra* note 43, at 9 (Morocco). Egypt's reservation to art. 16 of the Women's Convention elaborates that the Sharia accords women "rights equivalent to those of their spouses so as to ensure a just balance between

If there is, then, a customary international law definition of gender discrimination, what is it? The Women's Convention, in Article 1, defines discrimination as follows:

> For the purposes of the present Convention, the term "discrimination against women" shall mean any distinction, exclusion or restriction made on the basis of sex which has the effect or purpose of impairing or nullifying the recognition, enjoyment or exercise by women, irrespective of their marital status, on a basis of equality of men and women, of human rights and fundamental freedoms in the political, economic, social, cultural, civil or any other field.

This definition has been adopted in slightly modified form by the Human Rights Committee for purposes of interpreting the Civil and Political Covenant. The modifications reflect the Covenant's protection of men as well as women,[60] and its prohibition of discrimination on any one of numerous grounds, including but not limited to sex. The Committee's General Comment 18 (1989) accordingly provides:

> [T]he term "discrimination" as used in the Covenant should be understood to imply any distinction, exclusion, restriction or preference which is based on any ground such as . . . sex, . . ., and which has the purpose or effect of nullifying or impairing the recognition, enjoyment or exercise by all persons, on an equal footing, of all rights and freedoms.[61]

---

them. . . . [O]ne of the most important bases of these [marital] relations is an equivalency of rights and duties so as to ensure complementarity which guarantees true equality between the spouses." More specifically: "The provisions of the Sharia lay down that the husband shall pay bridal money to the wife and maintain her fully and shall also make a payment to her upon divorce, whereas the wife retains full rights over her property and is not obliged to spend anything on her keep. The Sharia therefore restricts the wife's rights to divorce. . . ." *Status, supra* note 43, at 164.

Such "equivalency" falls short of the treaty's mandate: instead of equality, it would substitute a balance of inequalities.

The United States "understanding" of "non-discrimination and equal protection" in the Civil and Political Covenant is not necessarily inconsistent with the treaty. It states in part that the U.S. "understands distinctions based upon . . . sex . . . as those terms are used in Article 2, paragraph 1 and Article 26—to be permitted when such distinctions are, at minimum, rationally related to a legitimate governmental objective. The United States further understands the prohibition in paragraph 1 of Article 4 upon discrimination, in time of public emergency, based 'solely' on the status of . . . sex . . . not to bar distinctions that may have a disproportionate effect upon persons of a particular status." SENATE COMM. ON FOREIGN RELATIONS, INTERNATIONAL COVENANT ON CIVIL AND POLITICAL RIGHTS, S. EXEC. REP. No. 23, 102d Cong., 2d Sess. (1992), at 14–15, *reprinted in* 31 I.L.M. 645 (1992). In any event, the U.S. explanation of this understanding expresses concerns only as to other grounds of distinction (age and citizenship), not gender. *Id.*

60. For example, states parties to the Covenant undertake to "respect and to ensure to all . . . the rights recognized in the present Covenant, without distinction of any kind, such as . . . sex . . . ." (art. 2.1); and to "ensure the equal rights of men and women to the enjoyment of all civil and political rights set forth in the present Covenant" (art. 3). See discussion *infra* notes 72–89 and accompanying text.

61. *General Comments, supra* note 11, at 26, para. 7. The Committee's addition of "preference" and substitution of "on an equal footing" for "on a basis of equality of men and women," follow the definition of discrimination in the International Convention on the Elimination of all Forms of Racial Discrimination, Mar. 7, 1966, 660 U.N.T.S. 195, quoted by the Committee, along with the definition in the Women's Convention, in the preceding paragraph of its General Comment.

Similar definitions have been adopted in other global human rights treaties,[62] as well as in jurisprudence under regional treaties,[63] thereby reinforcing the customary law status of the Women's Convention and Civil and Political Covenant definitions. For several reasons, however, neither is suitable for literal adoption. First, the Women's Convention definition, protecting only women, is too narrow,[64] whereas the Civil and Political Covenant definition, covering discrimination on numerous grounds, is broader than necessary for purposes of gender discrimination.

Second, neither definition achieves sufficient clarity in prohibiting distinctions made not "on the basis of sex" (Women's Convention), but on some other ground which indirectly discriminates against women or men. For example, the extensive jurisprudence of the European Court of Justice on such "indirect discrimination" has dealt with differences in compensation between full-time and part-time (disproportionately female) workers, as well as social security and pension payments that vary depending on whether the recipient has a dependent spouse.[65]

---

62. *E.g.*, the ILO Convention Concerning Discrimination in Respect of Employment and Occupation (ILO No. 111), June 25, 1958, 362 U.N.T.S. 32, art. 1(1) defines "discrimination" as "any distinction, exclusion or preference made on the basis of . . . sex . . . which has the effect of nullifying or impairing equality of opportunity or treatment in employment or occupation." Similarly, the UNESCO Convention Against Discrimination in Education, Dec. 14, 1960, 429 U.N.T.S. 93, art. 1(1), defines "discrimination" as "any distinction, exclusion, limitation or preference which, being based on . . . sex . . . has the purpose or effect of nullifying or impairing equality of treatment in education."

As of May 1996, there are 120 states parties to ILO Convention No. 111, and 85 to the UNESCO Convention. UNESCO, *supra* note 11, at 20.

63. *E.g.*, The Belgian Linguistics Case, 1968 Y.B. Eur. Conv. H. Rts. 832 (Eur. Ct. H. Rts. 1968) (discrimination generally); Abdulaziz et al. v. U.K., 7 E.H.H.R. 471 (Eur.Ct.H.Rts. 1985) (gender discrimination); Adv.Op. OC-4/84, "Proposed Amendments to the Naturalization Provisions of the Constitution of Costa Rica," 1984 Ann. Rep. Int.-Am. Ct. H. Rts. 43, 59–64 (1984) (gender discrimination). These and other European cases are discussed *infra* notes 72–89 and accompanying text. A comparable definition can be inferred from European Union Council Directives and judicial interpretations thereof. *See* Van Gerven *et al.*, *supra* note 52, at 12–13.

64. See discussion *infra* notes 72–89 and accompanying text.

65. *See generally* Francis Herbert, *Social Security and Indirect Discrimination*, and Christopher McCrudden, *Issues from the Discussion*, in Equality of Treatment *supra* note 52, at 117–36 and 217–18, respectively. Through October 1993 the European Court of Justice had rendered 13 judgments on indirect discrimination between the sexes. *Id.* at 117 and n. 2. They include, for example, *id.* at 120–22, Bilka, Case 170/84 [1986] ECR 1607 (only 2.7% of men but 27.7% of women worked part-time); and Teuling, Case 30/85 [1987] ECR 2497 ("significantly greater number of married men than women" receive a supplement linked to family responsibilities).

In general, whether such distinctions are discriminatory turns on whether their adverse gender impacts are disproportionate to their legitimate benefits. *See infra* notes 101–02 and 106–07 and accompanying text.

The classic case on disparate impact of facially neutral measures is a 1935 advisory opinion of the Permanent Court of International Justice. Adv. Op. No. 64, Minority Schools in Albania, 1935 P.C.I.J. (ser. A/B) No. 64 (1935). There Albania, having abolished private schools, defended the abolition as nondiscriminatory because it applied to both majority and minority private schools. However, because state schools remained under majority (ethnic Albanian) control, the real effect was to close ethnic Greek minority schools. The Court advised that this violated the right to "true equality." It

Third, both definitions, if taken outside the context of their treaties, might be read to refer only to discrimination affecting internationally protected human rights.[66] Neither definition, by itself, unambiguously reaches discrimination in national laws that does not affect internationally protected human rights. Yet both do so when read in the context of their treaties. For example, the mandate of both treaties that men and women be "equal before the law"[67] means that national laws must be administered without discrimination,[68] while their guarantee of "equal protection of the law"[69] bars national legislatures from enacting discriminatory laws.[70] To avoid potential confusion, such discrimination in national laws and their administration should be expressly covered.

Fourth, neither definition takes account of the fact, recognized by the Human Rights Committee, that not all distinctions based on sex are prohibited, but only those not justified on "reasonable and objective" grounds, discussed *infra*.

Finally, both definitions are burdened by needless verbiage, and could benefit from streamlining. A synthesis of the two definitions, distilling their common elements in light of the foregoing observations, might then yield the following customary law definition:

---

explained, "Equality in law precludes discrimination of any kind; whereas equality in fact may involve the necessity of different treatment in order to attain a result which establishes an equilibrium between different situations. It is easy to imagine situations in which equality of treatment of the majority and minority, whose situations and requirements are different, would result in inequality in fact; . . . ." *Id.* at 17, 19.

66. The reference in the Women's Convention definition to "human rights and fundamental freedoms in the political, economic, social, cultural, civil *or any other field*" [emphasis added] evidences an intent to not limit protections to only those provided by the Civil and Political Covenant or the Economic Covenant.

67. Art. 26 of the Civil and Political Covenant provides, "All persons are equal before the law . . ." Art. 15 of the Women's Convention requires states "to accord women equality with men before the law."

68. MANFRED NOWAK, U.N. COVENANT ON CIVIL AND POLITICAL RIGHTS: CCPR COMMENTARY 462, 466–67 (1992) [hereinafter NOWAK]. Nowak contends that the right to equality before the law "does not give rise to a claim of whatever nature to substantive equality but instead solely to a formal claim that existing laws be applied in the same manner to all those subject to it. The right to equality before the law thus is not directed at legislation but rather exclusively at its *enforcement*. It essentially means that judges and administrative officials must not act *arbitrarily* in enforcing laws." *Id.* at 466 (Italics in original.)

69. Art. 26 of the Civil and Political Covenant provides, "All persons . . . are entitled without any discrimination to the equal protection of the law." Although the Women's Convention does not use the phrase "equal protection of the law" in art. 2, states undertake "a. To embody the principle of the equality of men and women in their national constitutions or other appropriate legislation . . . . [and] c. To establish legal protection of the rights of women on an equal basis with men. . . ."

70. NOWAK, *supra* note 68, at 467–69. The distinction between "equal protection of the law" and "equality before the law" is neither transparent nor universally accepted. See *id.* at 468 and n. 53, 469 and n. 57. Nowak suggests that "equal protection of the law" also imposes a positive duty on the legislature to pass laws against discrimination. But this portion of his argument relies in part on the express imposition of such a duty in the second sentence of Article 26 of the Civil and Political Covenant, discussed below. *Id.* at 468.

Sex-based discrimination is any distinction made on the basis of sex or which affects men and women differently, whose purpose or effect is to impair the exercise, on a basis of equality of women and men, of internationally protected human rights, or of rights under national laws, and which is not reasonably and objectively justified as a proportionate means to achieve a legitimate aim.[71]

Analysis of the Definitions

Nondiscrimination: A Comparative Standard?

This section focuses mainly on a single aspect of the broader issues of gender equality: the international law duty not to discriminate.[72] Moreover, it attempts to

---

71. This definition derives from the Women's Convention definition, modified as follows:

1.   "Distinction, exclusion or restriction" is reduced to "distinction," because exclusions and restrictions are distinctions.

2.   "Or which affects men and women differently" is added to cover distinctions made on some other basis (e.g., height) that have disparate gender impacts. (See *supra* note 65.)

3.   "Impairing or nullifying" is reduced to "impairing," because whatever nullifies necessarily impairs.

4.   "Recognition, enjoyment or exercise" is reduced to "exercise," because the exercise of rights implies their recognition and enjoyment.

5.   "By women, irrespective of their marital status," is omitted. "By women" is unnecessary to prohibit discrimination against either gender. (This point is not devoid of controversy; *see* notes *infra* 72–89 and accompanying text.) "Marital status" is not necessary to define sex discrimination.

6.   "Human rights and fundamental freedoms" in various fields is reduced to "internationally protected human rights," which covers all of them.

7.   "Or of rights under national laws" is added, because gender discrimination in national law or its administration is also prohibited by the two treaties, as discussed *infra* notes 92 and 95 and accompanying text.

8.   "And which is not justified as a proportionate means to achieve a reasonable and objective aim" is added to reflect the jurisprudence discussed infra notes 98–107 and accompanying text.

It should be noted that the phrase "on a basis of equality of women and men", taken from the Women's Convention definition and included in the customary law definition in the text above, is a subject of heated debate. *See generally infra* notes 72–89 and accompanying text.

An alternative synthesis, adhering more closely to the treaty verbiage, might read:

Any distinction, exclusion or restriction made on the basis of sex or which affects men and women differently, which has the effect or purpose of impairing or nullifying the recognition, enjoyment or exercise, on a basis of equality of men and women, of human rights and fundamental freedoms in the political, economic, social, cultural, civil or any other field, or of rights under national law, and which is not reasonably and objectively justified as a proportionate means to achieve a legitimate aim.

The derivation is the same as for the previous definition, except that the only modifications made to the Women's Convention definition are those in steps 2, 5, 7, and 8.

72. For a recent, general discussion of various concepts of equality, including nondiscrimination, *see* CRAVEN, *supra* note 11, at 154–57.

articulate that law as developed to date by international human rights bodies, without reaching policy arguments advanced elsewhere for radically different approaches.[73]

A heated debate concerns whether the yardstick for measuring discrimination against women should be their treatment as compared to men, or some other measure that takes into account the unique realities faced by women. On this point, it has been argued that the definition of discrimination in the Civil and Political Covenant differs markedly from that in the Women's Convention. The Civil and Political Covenant definition, according to Professor Cook, is based upon the "similarity and difference" model of discrimination.[74] This model has been criticized, she notes,

> because it uses a male standard to determine equality and assesses women as inherent copies of their male counterparts. Under this model, women are forced to argue either that they are the same as men and therefore should be treated alike, that they are different but should be treated as if they were the same, or that they are different and should be accorded special treatment. The model does not allow for any exploration of ways in which laws, cultures, or religious traditions have constructed and maintained the secondary status of women, or the extent to which institutions are male-defined and built upon male norms.[75]

While the Women's Convention also uses language based on equality with men, "read as a whole, the concept of equality in the Women's Convention clearly extends beyond formal equality."[76] The Women's Convention, continues Professor Cook,

> develops the legal norm of nondiscrimination from a women's perspective. The Convention moves from a sex-neutral norm that requires equal treatment of men and women, usually measured by how men are treated, to a norm that acknowledges that the particular nature of discrimination against women is worthy of a legal response. The Women's Convention progresses beyond the earlier human rights conventions by addressing the pervasive and systemic nature of discrimination against women, and

---

73. *See generally, e.g.*, Charlesworth, Chinkin and Wright, *supra* note 54, at 644 ("a fundamental restructuring of traditional international law discourse and methodology to accommodate alternative world views"); Berta Esperanza Hernández-Truyol, *Women's Rights as Human Rights—Rules, Realities and the Role of Culture: A Formula for Reform*, 21 Brook. J. Int'l L. 605, 667–68 (1996), (proposing a "theoretical construct that uses communication theory, legitimacy theory, and critical feminist/race theory" to pose three inquiries at each stage of international human rights lawmaking: first, the "gender question," second, the "women's question," and third, the "culture question") (footnotes omitted).

74. Cook, *supra* note 1, at 155.

75. *Id.* (footnotes omitted).

76. Kathleen Mahoney, *Theoretical Perspectives on Women's Human Rights and Strategies for Their Implementation*, 21 Brook. J. Int'l L. 799, 839 (1996). In support, Sullivan states: "The object of the basic guarantee of gender equality articulated in the Women's Convention is not to ensure that women receive treatment identical to that of men, nor that laws and practices will impact women and men in the same way. Rather, the aim is to ensure that gender does not impede women's ability to exercise rights protected by international human rights law. . . ." Donna Sullivan, *Gender Equality and Religious Freedom: Toward a Framework for Conflict Resolution*, 24 N.Y.U. J. Int'l L. & Pol. 795, 800 (1992).

identifies the need to confront the social causes of women's inequality by addressing "all forms" of discrimination that women suffer.[77]

To remedy the shortcomings of the Civil and Political Covenant definition, and borrowing from Canadian jurisprudence, Professor Cook proposes a "disadvantage" test to define discrimination:

> The standard should focus on powerlessness, exclusion, and disadvantage of women, rather than on sameness and difference. . . . A law or policy that maintains or aggravates the disadvantages of a persistently disadvantaged group is discriminatory. A test of "disadvantage," as opposed to a test of "similarity and difference," requires judges to look at women as they function in the real world to determine whether women's abuse or deprivation of power is due to their place in a sexual or gender hierarchy. No comparator, male or otherwise, is needed.[78]

Other scholars, perceiving similar inadequacies in the "equal to men" standard, respond with different formulations. For example, Liesbeskind urges that the right to human dignity should be included, because "by omitting dignity from the definition, the definition leaves open the possibility for interpreting acts which literally comply with the equality dictates, yet violate a woman's integrity."[79]

Perhaps international law should and will move toward a more encompassing definition of discrimination that takes into account women's traditional powerlessness and recognizes one's right to dignity. At present, however, both the Civil and Political Covenant and the Women's Convention, as well as subsequent instruments, tend to define "discrimination" by a comparative test: distinctions are forbidden if they impair the exercise of rights, in the terms of the Women's Convention, "on a basis of equality of men and women."[80] International human rights bodies to date, as discussed *infra*, have consistently used a comparative standard to determine sex discrimination in adjudicative and quasi-adjudicative proceedings.[81]

---

77. Cook, *supra* note 1, at 155 (footnote omitted).

78. *Id.* at 156. Similarly, other authors note that "equality is not freedom to be treated without regard to sex but freedom from systematic subordination because of sex." Charlesworth, Chinkin & Wright, *supra* note 54, at 632.

79. Michelle Lewis Liesbeskind, *Preventing Gender-Based Violence: From Marginalization to Mainstream in International Human Rights*, 63 Rev. Jur. U.P.R. 645 (1994) (publication page not available, p. 32 in Westlaw).

80. Women's Convention, *supra* note 12, art. 1. For a discussion on equal treatment proponent's arguments, *see* Mai Chen, *Protective Laws and the Convention of the Elimination of All Forms of Discrimination Against Women*, 15 Women's Rts. L. Rep. 1, 4–6 (1993).

81. Even while allowing a partial exception for a matter unique to women—maternity leave—the European Court of Justice recently reiterated the comparative standard. Ruling that women are not entitled to receive full pay during maternity leave but are entitled to pay increases awarded during their leave, the Court explained, "It is well settled that discrimination involves the application of different rules to comparable situations or the application of the same rule to different situations [citation omitted]. The present case is concerned with women taking maternity leave provided for by national legislation. They are in a special position which requires them to be afforded special protection, but which is not comparable either with that of a man or with that of a woman actually at work." Gillespie and Others V. Northern Health and Social Services Board and Others, Case C-342/93 [1996] All ER (EC) 284, [1996] 2 CMLR 969 (Eur.Ct.J. Feb. 13, 1996), *available in* LEXIS, Intlaw Library, Eccase File, at 19–20.

To the extent present international law, however inadequately, addresses systemic and underlying cultural inequalities, it does so primarily in two ways. First, the ban on "discrimination" is not asked to carry the entire load. The Women's Convention, for example, goes well beyond merely prohibiting discrimination. It also imposes a series of positive duties on states to root out discrimination.[82] Second, even the bare ban on "discrimination," i.e., prohibiting unequal treatment of men and women absent sufficient case-by-case justification, often erodes underlying gender stereotypes. For example, when the Human Rights Committee ruled discriminatory a Peruvian law allowing husbands but not wives to sue, it undermined the patriarchal stereotype that women are not competent in legal and financial matters;[83] when the European Court of Human Rights ruled that women resident aliens are equally entitled as men to bring in their spouses, and rebuffed an argument that men would be more likely to burden domestic employment markets, it weakened images of women as presumptive homemakers and men as breadwinners; [84] when the European Court ruled discriminatory a denial of disability payments to mothers (but not fathers) of young children, it rejected an assumption that mothers, even if healthy, would be less likely to work outside the home;[85] and when the European Court granted husbands the same right as wives to hyphenate their last names, traditional surname customs were updated.[86]

In some cases, the direct impact of shielding men from discrimination may seem at odds with the goal of lifting women out of oppression. Immediate benefits may be conferred only on men,[87] or burdens imposed only on women.[88] Even in such cases, however, the indirect impact is to blur the boundaries of traditional sex roles. For example, when the European Court found women equally obliged as men to pay a tax in lieu of volunteer fire service, the direct impact may have cost women money, but the indirect impact challenged the myth that the frail creatures cannot serve as firefighters.[89]

---

82. *See generally infra* notes 109–16 and accompanying text.

83. Ato del Avellanal v. Peru, no. 202/1986, *Report of the Human Rights Committee*, U.N. GAOR, 44th Sess., Supp. No. 40, at 196, 198–99 at para. 10.2, U.N. Doc. A/44/40 (1989).

84. Abdulaziz et al. v. U.K., 7 E.H.H.R. 471, 499–503 (1985).

85. Schuler-Zgraggen v. Switzerland, 16 E.H.H.R. 405, 435 (1993).

86. Burghartz v. Switzerland, 18 E.H.H.R. 101, 116 (1994).

87. *E.g.*, Pauger v. Austria, *Report of the Human Rights Committee*, U.N. GAOR, 47th Sess., Supp. No. 40, at 333, U.N. Doc. A/47/40 (1992). There, pensions were awarded to widows regardless of income, but to widowers only if they had no other income. *Id.* at 333, para. 2.1. The Committee's view was that "men and women, whose social circumstances are similar, are being treated differently, merely on the basis of sex. Such a differentiation is not reasonable, ..." *Id.* at 335–36, para. 7.4.

88. Schmidt v. Germany, 18 E.H.H.R. 513 (1994) (exemption of women from tax in lieu of firefighting service discriminates against men). One judge, although concurring, expressed discomfort on the ground that human rights instruments are "principally aimed at protecting women, . . ."

89. *Id.* In *Schmidt*, the Court did not have to decide whether excluding women from firefighting was discriminatory, because in practice volunteers were never called; it found discrimination on the narrower ground that men but not women had to pay a fire levy in lieu of service. 18 E.H.H.R. at 528, para. 28.

Scope of Application

The ban on discrimination covers a spectrum of at least five degrees of state involvement, ranging from state discrimination in protection of internationally guaranteed rights, to private discrimination in matters governed by domestic law. First, states must respect and ensure all internationally protected human rights—whether civil, political, economic, social, cultural, or other—without gender discrimination.[90] Second, states must avoid discrimination in national laws—such as nationalization criteria—that do not directly regulate internationally protected rights, but which may affect such rights.[91] Third, states must avoid gender discrimination in all national laws and their administration. This obligation stems from their commitments to treat men and women as "equal before the law" and to provide them "equal protection of the law."[92]

Even so, the case provoked debate over gender roles. Two dissenters argued the tax was "not a difference of treatment founded exclusively on sex, but a difference based on fitness to carry out . . . fire brigade duty. The legislature could legitimately consider that men are ordinarily better suited . . . We believe that such a difference of treatment has an objective and reasonable justification. . . ." *Id.* at 529.

The majority, on the other hand, noting "that some German *Lander* do not impose different obligations . . . and that even in Baden-Wurttemberg women are accepted for voluntary service in the fire brigade." It left open "whether or not there can nowadays exist any justification for treating men and women differently as regards compulsory service in the fire brigade. . . ." *Id.* at 528, para. 28.

90. Art. 1 of the Women's Convention defines discrimination against women to prohibit distinctions that impair the equal exercise by women "of human rights and fundamental freedoms in the political, economic, social, cultural, civil or any other field."

States parties undertake to ensure "the equal rights of men and women to the enjoyment of all civil and political rights set forth in the present Covenant" (art. 3 of the Civil and Political Covenant), as well as "the equal rights of men and women to the enjoyment of all economic, social and cultural rights set forth in the present Covenant" (art. 3 of the Economic Rights Covenant).

In Broeks v. The Netherlands, *Report of the Human Rights Committee*, U.N. GAOR, 42nd Sess., Supp. No. 40, at 139, 148–49, paras. 12.1 to 12.5, U.N. Doc. A/42/40 (1987), the Committee adopted the view that art. 26 of the Civil and Political Covenant prohibits discrimination in state legislation on economic and social rights, and may be enforced by individual complaints under the Optional Protocol to the Covenant, even though such discrimination is also prohibited by the Economic Rights Covenant.

91. The Human Rights Committee's General Comment 4 (1981) on Article 3 of the Civil and Political Covenant states, at para. 3, that the state's positive duty to ensure nondiscriminatory enjoyment of Covenant rights "may itself have an inevitable impact on legislation or administrative measures specifically designed to regulate matters other than those dealt with in the Covenant but which may adversely affect rights recognized in the Covenant. One example, among others, is the degree to which immigration laws which distinguish between a male and a female citizen may or may not adversely affect the scope of the right of the woman to marriage to non-citizens or to hold public office." *General Comments, supra* note 11, at 4.

92. See notes 67–70 *supra*. Art. 26 of the Civil and Political Covenant provides: "All persons are equal before the law and are entitled without any discrimination to the equal protection of the law. In this respect the law shall prohibit any discrimination and guarantee to all persons equal and effective protection against discrimination on any ground such as . . . sex . . ."

The Human Rights Committee, in its General Comment 18 on Non-discrimination (1989), elaborates in para. 12: "While article 2 limits the scope of the rights to be protected against discrimination to those provided for in the Covenant, article 26 does not specify such limitations. That is to say, article 26 provides that all persons are equal before the law and are entitled to equal protection of the law

Once past these realms of state action, a fourth level requires states to take reasonable measures to prevent and punish unlawful gender discrimination even by private persons. General human rights treaties like the Civil and Political Covenant are now interpreted to impose such a duty on states; to the extent states fail, and tolerate or acquiesce in private discrimination, they become responsible for it.[93] The result is a partial breach of the oft-criticized barrier of the "public-private" distinction, by which traditional human rights law directed itself almost exclusively at oppressive conduct by states, even though much oppression of women is inflicted by such non-state actors as husbands, fathers, and employers.[94]

Fifth, most states now also have more specific, treaty-based obligations to prohibit purely private gender discrimination. States parties to the Women's Convention must take reasonable measures to prevent and punish private discrimination in many matters.[95] For instance, domestic violence—acts that may be purely

without discrimination, and that the law shall guarantee to all persons equal and effective protection against discrimination on any of the enumerated grounds. In the view of the Committee, article 26 does not merely duplicate the right already provided for in article 2 but provides in itself an autonomous right. It prohibits discrimination in law or in fact in any field regulated and protected by public authorities. Article 26 is therefore concerned with the obligations imposed on States parties in regard to their legislation and the application thereof. Thus, when legislation is adopted by a State party, it must comply with the requirement of article 26 that its content should not be discriminatory. In other words, the application of the principle of non-discrimination contained in article 26 is not limited to those rights which are provided for in the Covenant." *General Comments, supra* note 11, at 27.

In Broeks v. The Netherlands, *supra* note 90, at p. 149 para. 12.3, the Committee adopted the same broad interpretation of art. 26, explaining that it derives from art. 7 of the Universal Declaration of Human Rights, "which prohibits discrimination in law or in practice in any field regulated and protected by public authorities."

93. The Women's Committee, in para. 9 of its General Recommendation No. 19 (1992) asserts: "Under general international law and specific human rights covenants, States may also be responsible for private acts if they fail to act with due diligence to prevent violations of rights or to investigate and punish acts of violence, and for providing compensation." *General Comments, supra* note 11, at 75; *see generally* Cook, *supra* note 1, at 150–52.

The leading modern case is *Velásquez-Rodriguez, 1988* ANN. REP. INT.-AM. CT. H. RTS. 35, 71 paras. 172 and 173 (1988). There the Inter-American Court of Human Rights stated, "An illegal act which violates human rights and which is initially not directly imputable to a State (for example, because it is the act of a private person . . .) can lead to international responsibility of the State, not because of the act itself, but because of the lack of due diligence to prevent the violation or to respond to it as required by the [American] Convention. . . . What is decisive is whether a violation . . . has occurred with the support or acquiescence of the government, or whether the State has allowed the act to take place without taking measures to prevent it or to punish those responsible." The Human Rights Committee takes a similar view under the Civil and Political Covenant. Mojica v. Dominican Republic, No. 449/s1991, July 15, 1994.

94. *See generally* Charlesworth, Chinkin & Wright, *supra* note 54, at 626–28, 638–43.

95. *See infra* notes 109–16 and accompanying text. In its General Recommendation 19 (1992), para. 9, the Women's Committee emphasizes "that discrimination under the Convention is not restricted to action by or on behalf of Governments. . . . For example, under article 2(e) the Convention calls on States parties to take all appropriate measures to eliminate discrimination against women by any person, organization or enterprise." *General Comments, supra* note 11, at 75.

In addition, art. 5(a) of the Convention commits states to take all appropriate measures to "modify the social and cultural patterns of conduct of men and women, with a view to achieving the elimination

private—constitutes "discrimination" under the Women's Convention.[96] Indeed, this and other instruments evidence a developing customary international rule against all forms of violence against women, including purely private and domestic violence.[97]

Justification

Not all distinctions based on gender are discriminatory. The general rule is "that not every differentiation of treatment will constitute discrimination, if the criteria for such differentiation are reasonable and objective and if the aim is to achieve a purpose which is legitimate. . . ."[98] The "reasonable and objective" test for permissible distinctions originated by the European Court of Human Rights in

---

of prejudices and customary and all other practices which are based on the idea of the inferiority or the superiority of either of the sexes or on stereotyped roles for men and women."

96.   General Recommendation 19 (1992) of the Committee on the Elimination of all forms of Discrimination Against Women, *General Comments, supra* note 11, at 74–75, states: "6. . . . The definition of discrimination includes gender-based violence, that is, violence that is directed against a woman because she is a woman or that affects women disproportionately. It includes acts that inflict physical, mental or sexual harm or suffering, threats of such acts, coercion and other deprivations of liberty. . . . 7. Gender-based violence, which impairs or nullifies the enjoyment by women of human rights and fundamental freedoms under general international law or under human rights conventions, is discrimination within the meaning of article 1. . . ."

97.   The *Vienna Declaration, supra* note 28, at para. 18, states, "Gender-based violence and all forms of sexual harassment and exploitation, including those resulting from cultural prejudice and international trafficking, are incompatible with the dignity and worth of the human person, and must be eliminated."

The Declaration on the Elimination of Violence against Women, U.N. G.A. res. A/RES/48/104 (1993) is endorsed in para. 38 of the *Vienna Declaration* and in para. 8 of the *Beijing Declaration, supra* note 1. Its preamble affirms that violence against women "constitutes a violation of the rights and fundamental freedoms of women and impairs or nullifies their enjoyment of those rights and freedoms." This language fits squarely within the definitions of "discrimination" quoted previously. The preamble further recognizes that violence against women "is a manifestation of historically unequal power relations between men and women, which have led to domination over and discrimination against women by men. . . ." Art. 1 then defines "violence against women" to mean "any act of gender-based violence that results in, or is likely to result in, physical, sexual, or psychological harm or suffering to women, including threats of such acts, coercion or arbitrary deprivation of liberty, whether occurring in public or private life."

The *Beijing Declaration,* at para. 112, repeats, "Violence against women both violates and impairs or nullifies the enjoyment by women of their human rights and fundamental freedoms. . . ." And at para. 113 it reiterates the definition of "violence against women" from the Declaration on Violence.

In addition, through May 1996, 21 states have ratified and four more have signed the Inter-American Convention on the Prevention, Punishment and Eradication of Violence Against Women, June 9, 1994. ORGANIZATION OF AMERICAN STATES, INTER-AMERICAN COMMISSION ON HUMAN RIGHTS, BASIC DOCUMENTS PERTAINING TO HUMAN RIGHTS IN THE INTER-AMERICAN SYSTEM 119–20 (1996). Art. 1 defines violence against women as "based on gender," and art. 6(a) declares that women's right to be free from violence includes their right "to be free from all forms of discrimination. . . ."

98.   General Comment No. 18 (1989) of the Human Rights Committee on Non-discrimination, para. 13, *General Comments, supra* note 11, at 27.

its 1968 *Belgian Linguistics* decision.[99] In that case involving discrimination between French- and Dutch-speaking Belgians, the European Court explained:

> [T]he Court, following the principles which may be extracted from the legal practice
> of a large number of democratic States, holds that the principle of equality of treatment
> is violated if the distinction has no objective and reasonable justification.[100]

In applying the test of "objective and reasonable," the Court looks both to the
"aim and effects," as well as to the ends and means, of the distinction. The purpose
must be legitimate, and the means "proportional" to the purpose:

> The existence of such a justification must be assessed in relation to the aim and effects
> of the measure under consideration, regard being had to the principles which normally
> prevail in democratic societies. A difference of treatment in the exercise of a right
> laid down in the Convention must not only pursue a legitimate aim: Article 14 [of
> the European Convention] is likewise violated when it is clearly established that there
> is no reasonable relationship of proportionality between the means employed and the
> aim sought to be realised.[101]

Proportionality, in turn, depends on a balancing test:

> Article 14 does not prohibit distinctions in treatment which are founded on an objective
> assessment of essentially different factual circumstances and which, being based on
> the public interest, strike a fair balance between the protection of the interests of the
> community and respect for the rights and freedoms safeguarded by the Convention.[102]

The test of "reasonable and objective" justification has since been adopted by the
Human Rights Committee,[103] by the Inter-American Court of Human Rights,[104] and,

---

99.   1968 Y.B. EUR. CONV. H. RTS. 832 (1968).

100.   *Id*. at 864–66.

101.   *Id*.

102.   *Id*. at 884.

103.   *See* note 98 *supra*. The Human Rights Committee has generally applied the test in cases under
the Optional Protocol. *Reports of the Human Rights Committee*, U.N. GAOR: 42nd Sess., Supp. No.
40, U.N. Doc. A/42/40 (1987), Broeks v. The Netherlands, at 139, 150 para. 13; Danning v. The
Netherlands, at 151, 159 para. 13; Zwaan-de Vries v. The Netherlands, at 160, 168 para. 13; 44th Sess.,
Supp. No. 40, U.N. Doc. A/44/40 (1989), Vos v. The Netherlands, at 232, 237–38 para. 11.3; 47th
Sess., Supp. No. 40, U.N. Doc. A/47/40 (1992), Pauger v. Austria, at 333, 335 para. 7.3.

   But see id., 36th Sess., Supp. No. 40, U.N. Doc. A/36/40 (1981), Mauritian Women v. Mauritius,
at 134, 141 para. 9.2(b)2(I)8 ("[n]o sufficient justification"); 44th Sess., Supp. No. 40, U.N. Doc. A/
44/40 (1989), Ato del Avellanal v. Peru, at 196, 198–99 para. 10.2 (no standard given).

   More recently, in Simunek v. The Czech Republic, no. 516/1992, July 31, 1995, at p. 8 para. 11.5,
and Pons v. Spain, no. 454/1991, Nov. 8, 1995, at p. 4 para. 9.4, the Committee used a different form
of words: "A differentiation which is compatible with the provisions of the Covenant and is based on
reasonable grounds does not amount to prohibited discrimination. . . ." However, this variation does
not appear to imply a different test. In these cases the Committee cited *Zwaan-de Vries, supra*, and said
that it "reiterates its jurisprudence." *Id*.

104.   Adv.Op. OC-4/84, "Proposed Amendments to the Naturalization Provisions of the Constitution
of Costa Rica," 1984 ANN.REP.INT.-AM. CT. H. RTS. 43, 60 (1984). The Inter-American Court expressly
cited, with approval, the European Court's "objective and reasonable" test in *Belgian Linguistics*. *Id*.
at 60 para. 56. It then elaborated, "Accordingly, no discrimination exists if the difference in treatment
has a legitimate purpose and if it does not lead to situations which are contrary to justice, to reason or

in substance, by the European Court of Justice.[105] No international body appears to have adopted a contrary test, and no state appears to object. Hence it may fairly be said that the "reasonable and objective" standard constitutes the customary international law test for discrimination generally.

In the case of gender discrimination, the European Court of Human Rights has modified the test to make it stricter: not only must all state-imposed distinctions be "reasonable and objective," but distinctions based on gender must also be justified by "very weighty reasons."[106] The European Court explained:

> [I]t can be said that the advancement of the equality of the sexes is today a major goal in the member-States of the Council of Europe. This means that very weighty reasons would have to be advanced before a difference of treatment on the ground of sex could be regarded as compatible with the Convention.[107]

The same is true at the global level. Elimination of discrimination against women was described in the *Vienna Declaration* as a "priority objective," as reflected also in such instruments as the Women's Convention and the *Beijing*

---

to the nature of things. It follows that there would be no discrimination in differences in treatment of individuals by a state when the classifications selected are based on substantial factual differences and there exists a reasonable relationship of proportionality between these differences and the aims of the legal rule. . . . These aims may not be unjust or unreasonable, that is, they may not be arbitrary, capricious, despotic or in conflict with the essential oneness and dignity of humankind." Echoing the European Court's language, the Inter-American Court added that a state is permitted "to establish certain reasonable differentiations based on factual differences . . . , viewed objectively, . . ." *Id.* at 61 para. 59. It then upheld a number of distinctions based on nationality, but found that a distinction based on gender "cannot be justified." *Id.* at 63 para. 67.

105. The test used by the European Court of Justice in cases involving indirect gender discrimination in employment, social security, and pensions is whether the distinction rests on "objective justification." Herbert, *supra* note 65, at 129, citing Bilka, Case 170/84 [1986] ECR 1607. In operation this test appears similar to the "reasonable and objective justification" test of the European Court of Human Rights. According to Herbert, the "objective justification" test requires that the distinction rest on a lawful and valid objective of sufficient importance to justify an infringement of the fundamental principle of equality, and that the means used to achieve it be proportional, i.e., adequate and necessary to achieve the objective. *Id.* However, he notes that its application to governmental classifications affecting social security and other benefits seems more lenient than its application to private employers, because of the Court's practice of allowing governments a "reasonable margin of discretion" in selecting measures and means. *Id.* at 131; *see also* Professor McCrudden's comments, *id.* at 217–18.

Writing in the same 1994 volume, Professor McCrudden notes that the Commission has taken the position before the European Court of Justice that direct gender discrimination may likewise be justified, but that the Court as of that date had not yet addressed the issue. *Id.* at 215–17.

106. Abdulaziz et al. v. U.K., 7 E.H.H.R. 471, 501 para. 78 (1985). There the Court was "not convinced that the difference . . . between the respective impact of men and women on the domestic labour market is sufficiently important to justify the difference of treatment" in allowing immigrant husbands but not wives to bring their spouses into the country. *Id.* at 502 para. 79.

The European Court has consistently followed the "very weighty reasons" test in subsequent gender discrimination cases. Rasmussen v. Denmark, 7 E.H.H.R. 371, 381 (1984); Schuler-Zgraggen v. Switzerland, 16 E.H.H.R. 405, 435 para. 67 (1993); Schmidt v. Germany, 18 E.H.H.R. 513, 527 para. 24 (1994); Burghartz v. Switzerland, 18 E.H.H.R. 101, 116 para. 27 (1994).

107. *Abdulaziz, supra* note 106, at 501 para. 78.

Declaration.[108] Just as international law has accepted the European Court of Human Rights "reasonable and objective" test for discrimination generally, so too it should accept the Court's requirement of "very weighty reasons" for gender discrimination.

Positive Duties of the State

States parties to the Women's Convention or the Civil and Political Covenant have wide-ranging positive duties with regard to gender discrimination. They must ensure that women and men equally enjoy internationally protected human rights,[109] and must prohibit and provide effective protection against gender discrimination in national laws and their administration.[110] They must act to modify discriminatory "social and cultural patterns," prejudices, and stereotypes,[111] and to ensure women equal rights with men in education, employment, health, and financial credit, among other fields.[112] And they must take steps to ensure equality of rights and responsibilities of spouses,[113] including steps to eliminate domestic violence.[114]

States' positive duties extend not merely to ensuring nondiscrimination, but also to temporary discrimination in favor of women where necessary to overcome the continuing effects of past discrimination (i.e.,"affirmative action" in the

---

108. *See supra* notes 3–32 and accompanying text.

109. Art. 2.1 of the Civil and Political Covenant provides that states parties undertake "to ensure to all . . . the rights recognized in the present Covenant, without distinction of any kind, such as . . . - sex. . . ." Art. 3 adds that they undertake "to ensure the equal rights of men and women to the enjoyment of all civil and political rights set forth in the present Covenant."

In parallel fashion, art. 2.2 of the Economic Rights Covenant provides that states parties "undertake to guarantee that the rights enunciated in the present Covenant will be exercised without discrimination of any kind as to . . . sex . . . ," while art. 3 adds that they "undertake to ensure the equal rights of men and women to the enjoyment of all economic, social and cultural rights set forth in the present Covenant."

110. Art. 26 of the Civil and Political Covenant provides, "All persons are equal before the law and are entitled without any discrimination to the equal protection of the law. In this respect the law shall prohibit any discrimination and guarantee to all persons equal and effective protection against discrimination on any ground such as . . . sex. . . ."

111. Art. 5(a) of the Women's Convention requires states to take all appropriate measures to "modify the social and cultural patterns of conduct of men and women, with a view to achieving the elimination of prejudices and customary and all other practices which are based on the idea of the inferiority or the superiority of either of the sexes or on stereotyped roles for men and women."

112. Arts. 10, 11, 12, and 13(b).

113. Art. 23.4 of the Civil and Political Covenant provides that states parties "shall take appropriate steps to ensure equality of rights and responsibilities of spouses as to marriage, during marriage and at its dissolution. . . ."

114. *See* notes 96–97 *supra.*

U.S.),[115] so long as the measures adopted do not go too far by imposing rigid quotas.[116]

THE FACTS OF GENDER DISCRIMINATION

Despite advances in international and national laws on gender equality, and marked global progress in women's health and education between 1970 and 1990,

---

115. Art. 4(1) of the Women's Convention expresses the principle in a cautiously permissive sense. It states that temporary affirmative action measures are not discriminatory: "Adoption by States Parties of temporary special measures aimed at accelerating de facto equality between men and women shall not be considered discrimination . . . , but shall in no way entail as a consequence the maintenance of unequal or separate standards; these measures shall be discontinued when the objectives of equality of opportunity and treatment have been achieved.''

In its General Comment 18 on Non-discrimination (1989), the Human Rights Committee goes further, stating that affirmative action is sometimes obligatory: "The Committee also wishes to point out that the principle of equality sometimes requires States to take affirmative action in order to diminish or eliminate conditions which cause or help to perpetuate discrimination. . . .'' *General Comments, supra* note 11, at 27 para. 10.

116. In Kalanke v. Freie Hansestadt Bremen, ECJ case no. C-450/93 (1995), *reprinted in* 35 I.L.M. 265 (1996), the European Court of Justice found discriminatory a German law granting automatic priority for employment to equally qualified female applicants, whenever women did not make up at least 50% of the staff in the personnel category. European Union directives prohibited gender discrimination in employment "directly or indirectly,'' but "without prejudice to measures to promote equal opportunity for men and women, in particular by removing existing inequalities which affect women's opportunities.'' *Id.* at 272. The Court reasoned, "National rules which guarantee women absolute and unconditional priority . . . go beyond promoting equal opportunities and overstep the limits. . . . Furthermore, in so far as it seeks to achieve equal representation of men and women in all grades and levels within a department, such a system substitutes for equality of opportunity . . . the result which is only to be arrived at by providing such equality of opportunity.'' *Id.* at 272–73.

The decision was met by sharp criticism from women's groups, and a European Commission spokeswoman announced that amendments to EU directives would be considered. *EU affirmative action ruling blasted,* U.P.I., Oct. 17, 1995, *available in* LEXIS, News Library, Curnews File. In March 1996, the European Commission reportedly amended its directives to clarify that "only rigid quota systems, which do not leave open any possibility to take account of individual circumstances are illegal.'' Member states and employers could pursue "all other forms of positive action, and including flexible quotas.'' European Commission Clarifies Affirmative Action Law, IMMIGRATION ADVISOR, April 1996, *available in* LEXIS, News Library, Curnews File.

However, in April 1997, the Social Affairs Council, disappointing the Commission, reportedly "shelved indefinitely'' the Commission's proposed clarification, explaining that EU governments wanted to await the outcome of talks on EU treaty reforms, as well as further case law on quotas. *EU Suspends Work on Clearer Jobs Quotas Law,* REUTERS EUROPEAN COMMUNITY REPORT, April 17, 1997, *available in* LEXIS, News Library, Curnews File. On May 15, 1997, the Advocate General of the European Court of Justice, in the case of Marschall v. Land Nordrhein-Westfalen, case C-409/95, advised the Court, contrary to the view of the European Commission, that a German rule giving priority to women for high-level posts fell afoul of *Kalenke,* even though the rule incorporated flexibility through a proviso allowing reasons specific to a male candidate to predominate. *German sex bias rules 'unlawful,'* FINANCIAL TIMES, May 27, 1997, *available in* LEXIS, News Library, Curnews File. As of this writing, the case is pending before the Court.

Meanwhile, EU leaders at the June 1997 Summit in Amsterdam reportedly agreed on EU treaty revisions by which art. 119 (*supra* note 52) "will include scope for the introduction of positive measures

the United Nations Development Program ("UNDP") recently reported that a "widespread pattern of inequality between women and men persists—in their access to education, health and nutrition, and even more in their participation in the economic and political spheres."[117]

The depth and details of these patterns of gender inequality have been documented elsewhere[118] and need not be repeated here. The purpose of this brief summary is merely to place the foregoing discussion of laws against gender discrimination in realistic perspective.

If health and education are indicia of women's physical and mental *capabilities*, and if their economic and political participation reflect their *opportunities*, then, as the UNDP concluded:

> The progress of the past two decades can be summarized in simple terms: expanding capabilities and limited opportunities. It is still an unequal world, reflecting both the past deficit in women's human development and the current institutional, legal and socioeconomic constraints to their access to opportunities.[119]

With respect to the lag in overcoming effects of past inequalities, the UNDP explained that "even when legal discrimination is removed, it can take generations for practice to catch up with the revised law."[120]

The following sections provide illustrative highlights of the UNDP findings of discriminatory practices in countries throughout the world.

Health

More girls than boys die at a young age; especially in Asia, abortions of baby girls and female infanticide are so prevalent that, as a result, an estimated 100 million women are "missing" from the world's population.[121] More women suffer than men from malnutrition.[122] Further, their special health needs suffer considerable neglect.[123] For example, half a million women die each year in childbirth in Asia and Africa, even though maternal deaths are now rare in the industrialized world.[124]

---

in favour of women (response to the *Kalanke* ruling . . .)". European Information Services, EUROPEAN REPORT, June 18, 1997, *available in* LEXIS, News Library, Curnews File.

117. U.N. DEVELOPMENT PROGRAMME, HUMAN DEVELOPMENT REPORT 1995, 29 (1995) [hereinafter "HDR"].

118. For example, on the occasion of the Fourth World Conference on Women, much of the 1995 HDR was devoted to a comprehensive analysis of the facts of gender inequality. *See generally id.* at 1–10, 29–116; and UNITED NATIONS, THE WORLD'S WOMEN 1995: TRENDS AND STATISTICS, U.N. Doc. ST/ESA/STAT/SER.K/12, U.N. Sales no. E.95.XVII.2 (1995).

119. HDR, *supra* note 117, at 34.

120. *Id.* at 42–43.

121. *Id.* at 35.

122. *Id.*

123. *Id.* at 4.

124. *Id.* at 36.

In addition, violence against women is a "universal issue, crossing boundaries of culture, geography, race, ethnicity, class and religion."[125] On the other hand, between 1970 and 1990, women's life expectancy in developing countries increased by nine years—20% more than the increase for men—while their fertility rates fell by a third.[126] Women's life expectancy now exceeds men's in nearly all nations.[127]

However, these gains are not necessarily durable. Rapid and relatively equal health and education improvements for women and men, achieved by some socialist states in the 1970s and 1980s, are being undermined during transitions to market economies. An important policy issue for these countries is "[t]he extent to which the transition weighs more heavily on women than on men."[128]

Education

Women's literacy rates are lower than men's in countries at all levels of development, but especially in developing nations where they are less than three quarters those of men.[129] Among the world's 900 million illiterate people, women outnumber men two to one.[130] School enrollment rates of women and girls are also well below those of males at all levels of education in the developing world.[131] Girls are the majority of the 130 million children without access to primary school.[132] But here too there has been progress. Gender gaps in developing countries were halved between 1970 and 1990. Women's literacy rose from 54% to 74% of the male rate, and their combined primary and secondary school enrollment increased from 67% to 86% of the male rate. At the tertiary level, their enrollment rose from under 50% to 70% of the male rate and, in 32 countries, exceeds the male rate.[133] There are questions, however, about whether existing levels of progress can be maintained, let alone further progress achieved.[134]

Economic Opportunities

More than 70% of the world's 1.3 billion people living in poverty are female. And the trends are ominous: "Increasingly, poverty has a woman's face."

Even in the industrialized United States, women rose from comprising 40% of the poor in 1940 to 62% in 1980.[135] The reasons are not hard to find. Women's

---

125. *Id.* at 44.

126. *Id.* at 29.

127. *Id.* at 66–68.

128. *Id.* at 32.

129. *Id.* at 66–68.

130. *Id.* at 34.

131. *Id.* at 66–68.

132. *Id.* at 34.

133. *Id.* at 33–34.

134. *Id.* at 32.

135. *Id.* at 36.

participation in the paid labor force rose only four points between 1970 and 1990, from 36% to 40%, compared to 58% for men. And when they do join the paid labor force, women's average wages are considerably lower than men's; where data are available, women earn about 75% of the male wage outside agriculture.[136]

Moreover, women are overrepresented in the informal sector where jobs pay below minimum wage, are less secure, and working conditions are generally poor.[137] Women also have more difficulty obtaining credit; most banks require that borrowers be wage-earners or property owners with acceptable collateral.[138] Finally, women are hit harder by economic adjustment programs: they are generally responsible for feeding the family and are more likely to eat last when food subsidies are cut, while they are also more directly affected by cuts in health and child care services, and are often forced to enter the paid work force or informal sector to make up shortfalls.[139]

Political Participation

Women constitute half the electorate but hold only 10% of the seats in the world's parliaments and 6% in national cabinets. Yet studies suggest that in order for women to exert meaningful influence on policies, a 30% participation in political institutions is the critical mass.[140] Throughout history until early 1995, only 21 women have served as heads of state or government. As of early 1995, ten were in office.[141]

Discrimination in Laws

Despite developments in international and national laws described *supra*, legalized inequalities persist. In 1995, the UNDP gave the following "small sample:"

Right to nationality. In much of West Asia and North Africa, women married to foreigners cannot transfer citizenship to their husbands, though men in similar situations can.

Right to manage property. Married women are under the permanent guardianship of their husbands and have no right to manage property in Botswana, Chile, Lesotho, Namibia, and Swaziland.

Right to income-earning opportunities. Husbands can restrict a wife's employment outside the home in Bolivia, Guatemala, and Syria.

Right to travel. In some Arab countries, a husband's consent is necessary for a wife to obtain a passport, but not vice versa.[142]

---

136. *Id.* at 36–37.

137. *Id.* at 39.

138. *Id.*

139. *Id.* at 40–41.

140. *Id.* at 41.

141. *Id.* at 42.

142. *Id.* at 43.

Cultural and Attitudinal Discrimination

Women continue to be victims of cultural and attitudinal discrimination that ranges from sexual harassment in North America and machismo in Latin America to female genital mutilation in Africa, dowry deaths in India, and female infanticide in China.[143]

In short, as the UNDP concluded in 1995, "In no society today do women enjoy the same opportunities as men."[144]

RECOMMENDATIONS

The following recommendations concern international law prohibitions of gender discrimination.

Customary International Law

1. The maturing of a customary international law rule against gender discrimination should be recognized and reflected in the next revision of the Restatement of Foreign Relations Law.[145]

2. The definition of gender discrimination under customary international law should reflect the common elements of the definitions in the Women's Convention and the Civil and Political Covenant, as well as the jurisprudence of international courts and treaty enforcement bodies.[146]

3. The practice of Islamic states does not fully conform to the customary rule; this reality must be taken into account, perhaps by treating certain Islamic states as persistent objectors.[147]

4. The recent emergence of a customary international law rule against gender-based violence should also be recognized.[148]

5. An exception to the customary international rule against gender discrimination has to be developed, to permit temporary preferences for women in order to overcome the effects of past discrimination, so long as they do not amount to rigid quotas.[149]

Treaties Against Gender Discrimination

1. The jurisprudence of the European Court of Human Rights, which permits gender discrimination only where reasonably and objectively justified by

---

143. *See generally, e.g.*, Hernández-Truyol, *supra* note 73, at 630–38.

144. HDR, *supra* note 117, at 29.

145. Notes 20–32 *supra*, particularly note 20, and accompanying text.

146. Notes 56–116 *supra*, particularly note 71, and accompanying text.

147. Notes 40–55 *supra* and accompanying text.

148. Notes 96 and 97 *supra*.

149. Notes 115 and 116 *supra*.

"very weighty reasons," should be adopted by the United Nations Human Rights Committee, the Inter-American Court of Human Rights, the European Court of Justice, and other international bodies responsible for interpreting human rights treaties.[150]

2. Reservations to treaties prohibiting gender discrimination based on religious objections must, at minimum, be narrowly and precisely drawn; blanket reservations against all treaty provisions which may conflict with religious law should be withdrawn or, at a minimum, reformulated, and should be deemed void as contrary to the object and purpose of the Women's Convention and other human rights treaties prohibiting gender discrimination.[151]

General Principles of Law

1. The prohibition of gender discrimination by states is now so well-established in most domestic laws that it should be regarded as constituting a "general principle of law."[152]

CONCLUDING OBSERVATIONS

Radhika Coomaraswamy, United Nations special rapporteur on violence against women recently observed that, "A revolution has taken place in the last decade. Women's rights have been catapulted onto the human rights agenda with a speed and determination that has rarely been matched in international law."[153]

Part of this revolution has been an expanding acceptance of the prohibition of discrimination against women in treaty and customary international law and in general principles of international law. A decade ago, only half the U.N. member states were parties to human rights treaties broadly banning sex-based discrimination; today, over 170 states are parties,[154] and nearly all have ratified the children's rights treaty prohibiting gender discrimination against the girl-child.[155] A decade ago, while the rule against sex discrimination "may already" have attained the status of customary law, it was not yet "generally accepted" as such;[156] today, thanks largely to energetic work by nongovernmental organizations in the women's rights movement,[157] the case for a customary law prohibition of discrimination against women, outside the Muslim world, is compelling.[158] And in the last decade the number of states whose constitutions or laws prohibit sex discrimination has

---

150. Notes 98–108 *supra* and accompanying text.

151. Notes 43–47 *supra* and accompanying text.

152. Notes 33–39 *supra* and accompanying text.

153. COOMARASWAMY, *supra* note 14, at 9.

154. *See supra* notes 15–17.

155. Notes 18–19 *supra*.

156. Note 20 *supra*.

157. *See generally* COOMARASWAMY, *supra* note 14, at 10–16.

158. *See supra* notes 20–32 and 50–55 and accompanying text.

grown large enough that the prohibition may now also be regarded as a ''general principle of law.''[159]

This advance has not gone unchallenged. Predominantly Muslim states have rejected it in part,[160] and treaty provisions addressing women's rights have attracted unusually high numbers of reservations.[161]

Moreover, reality lags far behind the normative expansion of domestic and international prohibitions on sex-based discrimination. Despite progress in women's health and education in the decades of the 1970s and 1980s, women still struggle behind men in these fields, and even more so in economic and public life.[162] The daily subjection of women to violence and discrimination in the home and workplace, their systematic exclusion from or gross underrepresentation in political life, and their special victimization by war and poverty, mock international law norms against discrimination.

The next decade, warns Ms. Coomaraswamy, will witness a struggle over whether this gap between noble laws and ignoble reality can be overcome: ''Although international civil society has been active in the field of women's rights, at the national level, when it comes to family and community in many countries, civil society is far more conservative. . . . This national struggle is the difficult fight, not the international one. Unless human rights discourse finds legitimacy in these areas of a country's national life, women's rights and human rights will remain mere words on paper.''[163]

---

159. *See supra* notes 33–39 and accompanying text.

160. Notes 40–49 *supra* and accompanying text.

161. Notes 43 and 46–47 *supra* and accompanying text.

162. *See generally supra* notes 117–44 and accompanying text.

163. COOMARASWAMY, *supra* note 14, at 27.

TRAFFICKING IN WOMEN

Lois Chiang

Trafficking in women. The flesh trade. The child sex trade. Sex tourism. Sexual slavery. Forced prostitution. Terms designed to capture the reader's attention and imagination as well as frame a particular issue. These terms are seen with increasing frequency in the media as well as in human rights documents. What precisely is meant by each of these terms is likely foggy to the casual reader and may even be somewhat unclear for the human rights activist. And for good reason. These terms are linked, they overlap, and at times may even be synonymous. The decision to use one term over another is strategic, often governed by the precedents laid down in international human rights law and the moral authority one hopes to harness by adopting a particular characterization. This strategy is not uncommon when tackling the human rights of women, as the post-World War II international human rights instruments were drafted without a full appreciation of the range of abuses perpetrated against women. Consequently, the human rights of women have not been adequately recognized or protected under international instruments and mechanisms.[1] Activists attempt to "fit" abuses against women within the definitions of human rights designed to address the concerns of men.[2] With respect to trafficking in women, activists have had to latch onto recognized human rights violations such

---

1.   *See generally* Charlotte Bunch, *Women's Rights as Human Rights: Towards a Re-Vision of Human Rights*, 12 HUM. RTS. Q. 486 (1990); Hilary Charlesworth, *Human Rights as Men's Rights*, in WOMEN'S RIGHTS, HUMAN RIGHTS: INTERNATIONAL FEMINIST PERSPECTIVES 103 (Julie Peters & Andrea Wolper eds., 1995); Hilary Charlesworth & Christine Chinkin, *The Gender of Jus Cogens*, 15 HUM. RTS. Q. 63, 69–76 (1993); Celina Romany, *State Responsibility Goes Private: A Feminist Critique of the Public/Private Distinction in International Human Rights Law*, in HUMAN RIGHTS OF WOMEN: NATIONAL AND INTERNATIONAL PERSPECTIVES 85 (Rebecca J. Cook ed., 1994) [hereinafter HUMAN RIGHTS OF WOMEN]; FROM BASIC NEEDS TO BASIC RIGHTS (Margaret A. Schuler ed., 1995); OURS BY RIGHT, WOMEN'S RIGHTS AS HUMAN RIGHTS (Joanna Kerr ed., 1993); WOMEN'S RIGHTS, HUMAN RIGHTS (Julie Peters & Andrea Wolper eds., 1995).

2.   One example of the lack of recognition of human rights abuses against women is domestic violence. Domestic violence was not specifically captured by any of the pre-1990 international human rights instruments and only became an international issue after 1990. While it has been one of the most pressing, prevalent, and persistent forms of physical abuse against women worldwide, it remains unstated in all but one of the existing human rights conventions (*E.g.,* the Inter-American Convention on the Prevention, Punishment and Eradication of Violence Against Women (Convention Against Violence). Aside from incidences that are covered by the Convention Against Violence, attempts to have domestic violence recognized as a serious human rights abuse must typically be accomplished by fitting it into an existing category. For example, *see* Rhonda Copelon, *Intimate Torture: Understanding Domestic Violence as Torture,* in HUMAN RIGHTS OF WOMEN, *supra* note 1, at 116.

as slavery and child prostitution in order to find some, albeit limited, recognition, legitimacy, and redress for the abuses that arise from trafficking in women.

Without a doubt, all options within the existing international human rights system must be explored and exhausted. There must also be precision and rigor in the use and application of the term "trafficking in women." By failing to precisely define what is meant by "trafficking in women," many instances of trafficking in women will remain unseen, unexposed, and unaddressed. Further, without a clear definition of what trafficking in women entails, implementation of legislation and strategies aimed at preventing and addressing trafficking in women will remain haphazard and of limited utility.

This chapter aims to clarify the issue of trafficking in women. While related concerns such as slavery, the girl-child, prostitution, migrant workers, mail-order brides, and trafficking in women during armed conflict will be referred to, a detailed development of the factual and legal arguments and issues surrounding such topics are left to other chapters in this work.[3] The first section of this chapter considers the issue of a definition of "trafficking in women." The second section discusses the factual background of trafficking in women as it is known today. The third section sets out the framework for addressing the human rights violations arising from trafficking in women through international human rights law and mechanisms. The fourth section returns to the issues around defining "trafficking in women," and highlights the importance of establishing a clear, authoritative definition of "trafficking in women" as a precursor to any concerted international action to fight, prevent, and eradicate this practice.

TRAFFICKING IN WOMEN: A DEFINITION

A number of related problems have plagued the issue of trafficking in women, making it difficult to address this phenomenon in an effective manner. First, as with many gender-specific human rights violations, it has taken a long time to recognize the fact that trafficking in women is even a human rights issue.[4] Second, the very nature of trafficking has contributed to the invisibility of this practice. Trafficking in women is accomplished through a variety of methods that lead to a wide range of human rights abuses. In turn, trafficking in women has been dealt

---

3. In this chapter, references to women who are trafficked will often include girls. However, a detailed discussion of the human rights issues around trafficking solely in children is beyond the scope of this chapter.

4. *See generally* KATHLEEN BARRY, FEMALE SEXUAL SLAVERY (1979) [hereinafter FEMALE SEXUAL SLAVERY]; Bunch, *supra* note 1; Romany, *supra* note 1. Indeed, the literature suggests that trafficking in women was a phenomenon that only arose in the nineteenth century, as that was when the issue was identified and the term first used. However, in closely examining the experiences of women throughout time, trafficking in women has in fact been an integral part of our world history. For historical examples, *see* SIETSKE ALTINK, STOLEN LIVES: TRADING WOMEN INTO SEX AND SLAVERY 8–40 (1995); MAUDE E. MINER, SLAVERY OF PROSTITUTION: A PLEA FOR EMANCIPATION (1916); BENSON TONG, UNSUBMISSIVE WOMEN: CHINESE PROSTITUTES IN NINETEENTH-CENTURY SAN FRANCISCO (1994).

with by focusing on these human rights abuses and concerns.[5] As a result, there has been no consistent approach to addressing trafficking in women. Rather, focusing on the multitude of human rights abuses arising from trafficking in women has resulted in a piecemeal approach to this practice. Thus, in spite of the existence of an international treaty on the suppression of trafficking in women, there has yet to be an authoritative definition of trafficking in women in international human rights law. Consequently, it is necessary to construct a definition that captures the targeted activity. A dictionary definition of trafficking describes it as "an illegal trade in a commodity;" in this case, that commodity is women. Next, a definition is needed that articulates and sets out the activities that result in the trade of women. The definition that appears to be gaining authority is the following:

> All acts involved in the recruitment and/or transportation of a woman within and across national borders for work or services by means of violence or threat of violence, abuse of authority or dominant position, debt-bondage, deception or other forms of coercion.[6]

There are three key elements involved in this definition. First, trafficking requires the recruitment and/or transportation of a woman. Applying the plain meaning of these words, "recruitment" refers to the acts of hiring or otherwise obtaining women for the performance of services, and "transportation" involves moving or causing a woman to move from her habitual place of residence. Recruitment and/or transportation may take place within or across national borders; that is, trafficking in women does not require crossing a national border. Second, the purpose of the recruitment and/or transportation of women is to engage them in some form of work or services. Defined broadly, "work" or "services" include both paid and unpaid work, sexual services, as well as domestic services and general labor.

---

5.   Information regarding trafficking in women may be found under various headings, including but not limited to: child prostitution, child sex trade, forced marriage, forced prostitution, mail order brides, migrant workers, prostitution, sexual slavery, sex tourism, sex trade, and slavery. However, simply reviewing the literature under those topics will not yield a full view of the topic. For example, trafficking, as defined here, does not include voluntary prostitution, while some writers treat voluntary prostitution as synonymous with involuntary prostitution. Other writers are less clear. In addition, some of the literature focuses only on the actual working and living conditions of the sexually exploited, that is, the manifestations of trafficking rather than the process of trafficking. For example, some writers on child prostitution do not analyze the process through which a child is forced into prostitution, but rather focus on overcoming the obstacles that prevent a child from escaping prostitution. Finally, many instances of trafficking in women are not yet recognized, either by society or the literature.

6.   This definition was a proposed working definition articulated by the Foundation Against Trafficking in Women (STV) in Holland for use in a report on trafficking in women for the Special Rapporteur on Violence Against Women, Its Causes and Consequences. The United Nations General Assembly has defined trafficking as the "illicit and clandestine movement of persons across national and international borders, largely from developing countries and some countries with economies in transition, with the end goal of forcing women and girl-children into sexually or economically oppressive and exploitative situations for the profit of recruiters, traffickers and crime syndicates, as well as other illegal activities related to trafficking, such as forced domestic labour, false marriages, clandestine employment and false adoption." *See* Report of the Special Rapporteur on violence against women, its causes and consequences, Ms. Radhika Coomaraswamy, U.N. Document E/CN.4/1997/47, at 14 [hereinafter COMMUNITY VIOLENCE REPORT].

However, it would appear that these two elements are necessary but not suffi-cient. A woman can be recruited and/or transported for work or services and the process will not necessarily raise human rights concerns. What attracts attention then is the third element: coercion. Coercion lies at the heart of trafficking. The limits of what constitutes (or should constitute) coercion in trafficking in women remain undefined. How coercion is defined will determine the scope of the activity captured by any international definition of trafficking in women.

There are two forms of coercion that must be examined. First, coercion may take the form of actual or direct actions. Such coercion is typically more visible and includes the use of physical force or threats of physical force to compel someone to act against their will. This form of coercion is easily recognized. More problem-atic is the second form of coercion, which is less visible and is typically made up of implied or indirect acts. While indirect, such acts in effect limit one's alternative courses of action to such a degree that one party is subjugated to the will of another party. Such coercion is often referred to as economic, psychological, cultural, or social coercion. Whether any or all of these sources of pressure constitute or should constitute coercion is unsettled and hotly debated. For example, some argue that women have no real choice but to turn to prostitution for economic survival. There-fore, any prostitution is coercive. Others argue that women can voluntarily choose to enter the sex trade. Similarly, in places where there are strong family and commu-nity pressures on women to submit to arranged marriages, an argument can be made that these women are somewhat coerced to enter into these arranged marriages, even though actual force or threats are not used. Others contest this characterization and argue that women are still able to resist pressures and choose to enter into such arrangements.

A major dilemma is whether to include all forms of coercion within the defini-tion of trafficking. The aforementioned definition does not clarify whether all forms of coercion are included or intended. Moreover, coercion may take various forms, including actual violence, the threat of violence, abuse of authority, debt bondage,[7] and deception. The inclusion of deception as a form of coercion is not without problems, as it would potentially broaden the scope of trafficking in women to include a situation in which an employer recruited a woman for work or services and deceived the woman in terms of issues such as her working hours, salary, or bonus. In those cases, deception alone would not raise human rights concerns related to trafficking, although other issues such as employment rights may arise.

The point of raising this definition and the issues around the meaning of coercion is to highlight the fact that no definition is yet satisfactory. (The issue of a definition of trafficking in women will be discussed more fully later in this chapter.) For the moment, it is helpful to use the definition set out above as a reference point, as it

---

7.   Debt bondage is another form of coercion that is specific to cases where women are trafficked into forced prostitution or labor (as discussed *infra*). It involves the imposition of a debt upon a woman that she must repay by engaging in forced prostitution or forced labor. The debt may flow from money paid to her family in the form of a loan or it may simply consist of the brothel owner's expenses in acquiring, housing, or feeding her.

does generally set out the activities that must be covered in order to address trafficking in women. However, closer examination of the factual background to trafficking in women is required to establish more precisely the range of activities to be captured. Any mention of trafficking in women will conjure up a few stereotypical situations in the minds of many readers, the most common perhaps being the image of a straightforward economic transaction involving the sale of a woman or girl to a brothel in return for a money payment. Thereafter, the woman or girl is condemned to a lifetime of forced prostitution. While that situation is certainly common, it is only one facet of trafficking in women. The following section outlines the factual background to trafficking in women in order to demonstrate the complexity of the problems faced in eradicating this practice and to clarify the essential elements required for an international legal definition of trafficking in women.

TRAFFICKING IN WOMEN: THE FACTS

In spite of the fact that trafficking in women is often discussed as a "regional" issue, it is in fact a global phenomenon.[8] It does, however, have fairly clear regional characteristics and routes. Regional characteristics aside, certain components are common to all trafficking. First, trafficking requires supply and demand. The supply consists of vulnerable women and the demand is made up of men who purchase women for various purposes including sexual gratification, reproduction and/or for labor. Once supply and demand exists, targeted women will be recruited and/or transported to meet the demand. The following discussion outlines the process of trafficking, beginning with how women and girls are targeted, how they are trafficked, and what type of living and working conditions they are forced to endure. Generally, women are trafficked in two ways: either they are lured by a ploy or they are forcibly abducted. Such women are forced into one of three situations: forced prostitution, forced marriage, or forced labor.[9] At the outset, it should be noted that the following facts are of a general nature. There will be differences in the nature and degree of human rights abuses experienced by women who are trafficked. Because many trafficking situations have not yet been uncovered or even recognized, there may be experiences and circumstances not addressed in this

---

8.   ALTINK, *supra* note 4, at 15–40; COALITION AGAINST TRAFFICKING IN WOMEN-ASIA PACIFIC, TRAFFICKING IN WOMEN AND PROSTITUTION IN THE ASIA PACIFIC 24–27 (1995) [hereinafter CATW]; INTERPOL REPORT, *Traffic in Women: Recent Trends*, in FEMALE SEXUAL SLAVERY, *supra* note 4, at 238–48.

9.   Forced prostitution has traditionally been seen as the only consequence of trafficking in women. Now, trafficking in women is recognized as leading to other consequences. The *Beijing Declaration and Platform for Action* includes forced marriages and forced labor in its concept of trafficking. U.N. Doc. A/CONF.177/20, at para. 130(b). This is also the position adopted by the Secretary-General of the United Nations in his report, Report of the Secretary General on Traffic in Women and Girls, U.N. Doc. A/51/309, at para. 5 [hereinafter Traffic in Women]. While it is recognized that trafficking in women leads to forced labor, in this chapter, forced labor has been incorporated into forced prostitution and forced marriage. Data documenting trafficking in women leading to forced labor remains sparse and typically is an important collateral reason women are trafficked into forced prostitution and forced marriages. *See* CATW, *supra* note 8, at 31; *Four Executed in China for Abduction, Sale of Women and Children*, AGENCE FRANCE PRESSE, Feb. 25, 1995, available in LEXIS, Nexis Library, World File, Topnws.

chapter. The purpose of the factual discussion below is to impart to the reader a set of facts that will flag the issues that generally arise when women are trafficked.

The Women

In most recognized cases of trafficking, the targeted women[10] are from the poorer regions of their country, typically rural areas where the level of education and sophistication is quite low. As Human Rights Watch has reported:

> On the supply side, adverse socioeconomic conditions in many regions increase the likelihood that women and girls will be lured into forced prostitution or involuntary marriage. In most parts of the world, most notably in rural areas, women and girls have fewer educational and economic opportunities than males. The attraction of a big city, better-paying jobs, and a better life cause women and girls who have few options at home to accept alleged job or marriage offers far away. Moreover, even if the woman or girl herself is not tempted, the preference for sons in many societies . . . and the promise of immediate payments often lead families to sell their daughters.[11]

However, victims are not always rural women or girls. University students have been trafficked in China,[12] and women have been abducted in urban centers such as Paris[13] and Montreal.[14] In cases leading to forced marriages, some victims have been adolescent girls raised in urban areas of the United States,[15] Scotland,[16] and

---

10.   Young boys are also victims of trafficking, either for purposes of prostitution or as sons for couples in China who cannot have a son. However, the issue of trafficking in boys is beyond the scope of this chapter. *See* Rahul Bedi, *Call for New Law as Paedophiles Turn to Sub-Continent*, THE DAILY TELE-GRAPH, Mar. 25, 1996; *China Convicts 35 Farmers for Kidnapping Babies*, REUTERS, Mar. 3, 1995, *available in* LEXIS, Nexis Library, News File, Curnws.

11.   HUMAN RIGHTS WATCH, THE HUMAN RIGHTS WATCH GLOBAL REPORT ON WOMEN'S HUMAN RIGHTS 196 (1995) [hereinafter GLOBAL REPORT].

12.   *People Pedlars: Trade in Women is Widespread in Rural Areas*, FAR EASTERN ECONOMIC REVIEW, Feb. 23, 1989, at 41; *Three Executed in China for Abducting Women*, REUTERS, Aug. 26, 1993, *available in* LEXIS, Nexis Library, World File, Topnws.

13.   FEMALE SEXUAL SLAVERY, *supra* note 4, at 47.

14.   *Montreal Torture Case Likely to Snowball*, THE GLOBE AND MAIL, Oct. 29, 1996.

15.   Gerard Aziakou, *Islam, US Law Clash Over Alleged Forced Marriages of Iraqi Girls*, AGENCE FRANCE PRESSE, Dec. 28, 1996; Dave McIntyre, *Old-world Wedding Lands Iraqis in New World Court*, DEUTSCHE PRESSE-AGENTUR, Dec. 3, 1996; Don Terry, *Cultural Tradition and Law Collide in Middle America*, N. Y. Times, Dec. 2, 1996, *available in* LEXIS, Nexis Library, World File, Allnws.

16.   Audrey Gillian, *Kidnap Girls Fly Home*, SCOTLAND ON SUNDAY, Mar. 31, 1996; Audrey Gillian, *A Marriage Made in Hell*, THE GUARDIAN, Apr. 4, 1996; Chris Starrs, *'Abduction' Father to Sue Labour Hopeful; Man Disputes Claims that He Forced His Daughters into Illegal Marriages*, THE HERALD (GLASGOW), Dec. 9, 1996; Chris Starrs, *Sarwar Flies Out Today Kidnap Four Reunited in Safe Refuge*, THE HERALD (GLASGOW), Mar. 26, 1996; Ken Symon, *'Kidnap' Inquiry Father to Return*, SUNDAY TIMES, Dec. 1, 1996; Sarah Urquhart, *Father Raises Damages Claim on Sarwar*, THE HERALD (GLASGOW), Dec. 23, 1996; Craig Watson, *Glasgow Councilor Tells of Efforts to Let Woman and Daughters Leave Pakistan*, THE HERALD (GLASGOW), Apr. 1, 1996; *Councilor Suffers Backlash After High-Profile Mission to Rescue Abducted Sisters; Pakistani Group Attacks Sarwar*, THE HERALD (GLASGOW), Apr. 16, 1996, *available in* LEXIS, Nexis Library, World File, Allnws.

England.[17] What all victims share is vulnerability that stems from their status as women[18] as well as from other factors such as youth, a low level of education, a lack of sophistication, mental retardation,[19] family coercion, poverty,[20] sheer desperation, or a combination of these factors. Some may have merely been in the wrong place at the wrong time.

Contrary to the media's emphasis on trafficking in women from Southern countries, Northern countries are not immune to this practice.[21] Aspects of trafficking in women occur in nearly every country, whether it is a receiving country, sending country, transit country, or simply a country within which trafficking takes place. The more notorious and well-known trafficking routes include: the Caribbean, Thailand, Philippines, Ghana, Columbia, and Eastern Europe to Western Europe;[22] Thailand and the Philippines to Japan;[23] Burma to Thailand;[24] Nepal to India;[25] and Bangladesh to Pakistan.[26] Lesser-known routes include trafficking from Southeast

---

17. *See generally* MIRIAM ALI WITH JANA WAIN, WITHOUT MERCY: A WOMAN'S STRUGGLE AGAINST MODERN SLAVERY (1995) [hereinafter WITHOUT MERCY]; EILEEN MacDONALD, BRIDES FOR SALE? HUMAN TRADE IN NORTH YEMEN (1988) [hereinafter BRIDES FOR SALE].

18. One stark example is that of brothers who sell their unmarried sisters after the death of their parents simply because they find their sisters to be a burden. *See* K.K. MUKHERJEE, FLESH TRADE: A REPORT 71 (1989).

19. Lan Cao, *Illegal Traffic in Women: A Civil RICO Proposal*, 96 YALE L.J. 1297, 1299 (1987); Yojana Sharma, *China: Keeping Social Problems Within the Family*, INTER PRESS SERVICE, May 31, 1991, *available in* LEXIS, Nexis Library, World File, Topnws; NICHOLAS D. KRISTOF & SHERYL WuDUNN, CHINA WAKES: THE STRUGGLE FOR THE SOUL OF A RISING POWER 212 (1994) [hereinafter CHINA WAKES].

20. As an example, Shanta Bai, a prostitute in Bombay was sold at age 11. She was orphaned quite young and raised by an elderly village woman who eventually could not afford to feed her. So the woman sold Bai to a trafficker. *See* Molly Moore, *Even If I Run Away, Where Would I Go?*, WASH. POST, Feb. 16, 1993, *available in* LEXIS, Nexis Library, World File, Allnws.

21. For example, *see* Margot Hornblower, *The Skin Trade: Poverty, chaos and porous borders have turned prostitution into a global growth industry, debasing the women and children of the world*, TIME, Jun. 21, 1993, *available in* LEXIS, Nexis Library, News File, Curnws; KATHLEEN BARRY, THE PROSTITUTION OF SEXUALITY 190–195 (1995) [hereinafter PROSTITUTION OF SEXUALITY].

22. Hornblower, *id*; Fanny P. Molina, *Sex Trafficking from Colombia to Europe: Marta's Story*, in WITHOUT RESERVATION: THE BEIJING TRIBUNAL ON ACCOUNTABILITY FOR WOMEN'S HUMAN RIGHTS 69 (Niamh Reilly ed., 1996) [hereinafter WITHOUT RESERVATION]; Report on the mission of the Special Rapporteur to Poland on the issue of trafficking and forced prostitution of women (24 May to 1 June 1996), U.N. Document E/CN.4/1997/47/Add.1, at para. 44 [hereinafter POLAND REPORT].

23. CATW, *supra* note 8, at 20; William Chapman, *Flesh Supermarkets of the Third World: For Some, Life on the 'Sex Tour' is the Only Escape From Hunger in the Village*, WASH. POST, Mar. 3, 1985, *available in* LEXIS, Nexis Library, News File, Curnws; JAPAN FEDERATION OF BAR ASSOCIATIONS, REPORT ON THE NATIONAL REPORT FOR THE FOURTH WORLD CONFERENCE ON WOMEN (1995) [hereinafter JAPAN FEDERATION].

24. HUMAN RIGHTS WATCH, A MODERN FORM OF SLAVERY: TRAFFICKING OF BURMESE WOMEN AND GIRLS INTO BROTHELS IN THAILAND (1993) [hereinafter MODERN FORM OF SLAVERY].

25. HUMAN RRIGHTS WATCH/ASIA, RAPE FOR PROFIT: TRAFFICKING OF NEPALI GIRLS AND WOMEN TO INDIA'S BROTHELS (1995) [hereinafter RAPE FOR PROFIT].

26. GLOBAL REPORT, *supra* note 11, at 257–273.

Asia to Australia; Vietnam to China;[27] Southeast Asia and France to the Middle East;[28] United States to Japan;[29] England to Yemen;[30] and Russia to Israel, Macau, and Western Europe.[31] Finally, the least recognized trafficking occurs within national borders. To name a few documented examples, internal trafficking occurs in places such as Algeria,[32] Brazil,[33] Canada,[34] China,[35] Taiwan,[36] and the United States.[37] These examples represent only a portion of the trafficking that occurs worldwide.[38]

The political and economic backgrounds of the countries implicated often exacerbate the vulnerability of women. For example, one well-known trafficking route runs from Nepal to India. In addition to the conditions of extreme poverty and

---

27. CATW, *supra* note 8; *Three Arrested for Trafficking Across Vietnam Border*, BBC SUMMARY OF WORLD BROADCASTS, Nov. 1, 1994, *available in* LEXIS, Nexis Library, Asia PC File, Allnws.

28. CATW, *supra* note 8, at 19; FEMALE SEXUAL SLAVERY, *supra* note 4, at 47.

29. Cao, *supra* note 19; Hornblower, *supra* note 21.

30. ALI, *supra* note 17; MACDONALD, *supra* note 17.

31. Hornblower, *supra* note 21.

32. Zazi Sadou, *The Martyrdom of Girls Raped by Islamic Armed Groups*, *in* WITHOUT RESERVATION, *supra* note 22, at 28; *Two Sisters, Allegedly Kidnapped for Forced Marriage, Found Dead*, BBC Summary of World Broadcasts, Nov. 9, 1994; *Mother of Two Sisters Beheaded by "Terrorists" Also Killed*, BBC SUMMARY OF WORLD BROADCASTS, Nov. 28, 1994, *available in* LEXIS, Nexis Library, World File, Allnws.

33. ANTI-SLAVERY INTERNATIONAL, SLAVERY IN BRAZIL-A LINK IN THE CHAIN OF MODERNIZATION 94–103 (1993); Christina Lbel, *Teenagers Sold as Sex Slaves in Midst of Amazon Jungle*, SUNDAY TIMES, Apr. 26, 1992; Julia Preston, *Brazil Frees Minors in Brothels; Police Raid Amazon Saloons Said to Enslave 22 Girls*, WASH. POST, Feb. 27, 1992; *Brazilian Girls Forced into Prostitution in the Amazon*, REUTERS, Mar. 27, 1992, *all available in* LEXIS, Nexis Library, News File, Allnws.

34. *Hints of Crackdown Cool Under-Age Sex Trade*, GLOBE AND MAIL, Feb. 5, 1997, at A1; and *Montreal Torture*, *supra* note 14.

35. *See generally* HE LIANGCHEN, GUANYU YANJIN MAIYIN PAIOCHANG DE JUEDING, GUANYU YANCHENG GUAIMAI BANGJIA FUNU ERTONG DE FANZUI FENDZI DE JUEDING: JIEYI (1992); XIE ZHIHONG & JIA LUSHENG, GUAIMAI FUNU SHILU (1989); *China Convicts*, *supra* note 10; CHINA WAKES, *supra* note 19, at 211–21; EMILY HONIG & GAIL HERSHATTER, PERSONAL VOICES: CHINESE WOMEN IN THE 1980s 286–91(1988) [hereinafter PERSONAL VOICES]; Huang Wei, *Crackdown on Abduction of Women and Children*, BEIJING REVIEW, Jul. 29–Aug. 4, 1991, at 25; HUMAN RIGHTS IN CHINA, CAUGHT BETWEEN TRADITION AND THE STATE: VIOLATIONS OF THE HUMAN RIGHTS OF CHINESE WOMEN, A REPORT WITH RECOMMENDATIONS MARKING THE FOURTH WORLD CONFERENCE ON WOMEN 8–17 (1995) [hereinafter HUMAN RIGHTS IN CHINA].

36. CATW, *supra* note 8, at 28–29.

37. Cao, *supra* note 19; Neal Kumar Katyal, *Men Who Own Women: A Thirteenth Amendment Critique of Forced Prostitution*, 103 YALE L.J. 791 (1993).

38. There are less well-known trafficking cases from Southern country to Southern country, such as Colombia, China, Burma, Yugoslavia, and Latin America to Thailand. *See* Aphaluck Bhatiasevi, *China: Thailand Fills Central Role on Sex Markets*, Sept. 2, 1995; *Thai Police Save Colombian Women from Forced Prostitution*, REUTERS, Feb. 8, 1990, *available in* LEXIS, Nexis Library, World File, Allnws. *See generally* ALTINK, *supra* note 4, at 8–40; LICIA BRUSSA, SURVEY ON PROSTITUTION, MIGRATION AND TRAFFIC IN WOMEN: HISTORY AND CURRENT SITUATION (1991); Hornblower, *supra* note 21; PROSTITUTION OF SEXUALITY, *supra* note 21, at 165–97.

subsistence agriculture that most rural Nepalis live under, Nepal is economically dependent on India. A 1950 treaty providing for an open border policy between the two countries eliminates the need for immigration checks for Nepalis crossing the border, therefore traffickers need not obtain visas or other documentation for the women they are transporting. Because of its economic independence on India, Nepal cannot afford to end the treaty and India does not want to lose the privileges attached to such a policy.[39]

The combination of the deteriorating economic and political situation in Burma spurs an outflow of trafficked women into Thailand. This flow is facilitated by Thai officials eager for cheap labor or personal profit.[40] The transition from communism to capitalism in Eastern Europe has altered the trafficking of women into Western Europe. In the past, women were trafficked into Western Europe from Southern countries such as Colombia, the Dominican Republic, Ghana, Thailand, Zaire, and the Philippines.[41] Now, the trade has turned to Eastern Europe as the primary source of women.[42] This shift basically stems from increased opportunities for traffickers in the form of lower transportation costs, less onerous or no visa requirements, and the fact that these women are much more difficult to detect.[43]

Economic and political factors can encourage trafficking in women within countries as well. While women are trafficked into and out of the Philippines, trafficking of Filipino women occurs internally. As one commentator noted, the imminent collapse of the Philippines sugar industry would provide more rural girls for the Manila prostitution market.[44] In China, the flourishing urban areas have become a beacon for the surplus rural labor force, a surplus due to increased rural efficiency. Substantially increased mobility has made it easy for the surplus rural labor to flock to urban centers where women are recruited and/or abducted and transported to remote areas of China.[45] The political decentralization of China has resulted in

---

39.   RAPE FOR PROFIT, *supra* note 25, at 9, 11–12.

40.   MODERN FORMS OF SLAVERY, *supra* note 24, at 10–20.

41.   Galina Vromen, *Dutch Seek to Curb Forced Prostitution of Foreign Women*, REUTERS, Feb. 16, 1988, *available in* LEXIS, Nexis Library, News File, Curnws.

42.   POLAND REPORT, *supra* note 22; *The Trade in Women Must be Stopped*, speech given by Commissioner Anita Gradin at the Annual Meeting of the Social Democratic Women's Association, held on Aug. 26, 1995 in Goteborg, Commission of the European Communities, Press Release; Marlise Simons, *Red-Light Express: East European Job Seekers Shanghaied by West's Sex Mills*, CHINA. TRIB., Aug. 15, 1993, *available in* LEXIS, Nexis Library, News File, Curnws.

43.   Such women can also be easily rotated through various European countries when their visas have expired. Simons, *id.* Also, as the Special Rapporteur has reported, as the physical appearance of women from Eastern Europe tend to be more European, these women are less likely to arouse the suspicion of border guards. *See* POLAND REPORT, *id. See generally* Gillian Sharpe, *On the Trail of Slave Traders*, SCOTLAND ON SUNDAY, Jan. 7, 1996; David Crossland, *Brothel Murder Spotlights Eastern Europe Prostitution*, REUTERS, Aug. 16, 1994, *available in* LEXIS, Nexis Library, News File, Curnws.

44.   Chapman, *supra* note 23.

45.   He notes that following the economic development in China in the late 1980s, abductors and traffickers have moved to urban areas, following the movements of female peasants who form part of the labor surplus in rural areas. He, *supra* note 35, at 92. *See also* CHINA WAKES, *supra* note 19, at 219; PERSONAL VOICES, *supra* note 35, at 290; Wei, *supra* note 35.

situations where village leaders are powerful enough to actively prevent trafficked women from escaping or to obstruct outside authorities from rescuing abducted women.[46]

Traffickers and the Process

As illustrated by the transit routes set out above, trafficking in women typically involves the transportation of women over substantial distances. As a practical matter, the transportation of a person is not easily accomplished. Traffickers in women are successful for a number of reasons. First, many traffickers have some connection to the trafficked women. Many gangs of traffickers are compatriots of the trafficked women.[47] As members of gangs, they may either be small-time opportunists or participants in large procuring networks that traffic in women to supply organized crime's prostitution activities.[48] Some are locals who know local girls, women, and their families.[49] In addition, traffickers may be returned prostitutes who now are either brothel keepers, managers, or owners themselves, or who were released on the condition that they find substitute prostitutes.[50] The connection between traffickers and their victims may be much more intimate, involving immediate family members who knowingly force or sell their female relatives (typically daughters) to recruiters, brothel owners, or ''husbands,'' or who are willfully blind to the fate of these women and girls.[51] In one case in China, one man was convicted of selling eighteen women, including his wife, three-year-old daughter, and mother.[52] In cases of forced marriages between a young woman and a distant relative or family friend, those responsible for the transportation of women and girls are often the father and/or other male relative.[53] However, a connection to a woman or girl is not essential. Some traffickers use advertisements for jobs and brides as a lure. Reports show that, in some cases, the abduction of girls has been conducted by soldiers under governmental orders.[54]

---

46.   CHINA WAKES, *supra* note 19, at 219; HUMAN RIGHTS IN CHINA, *supra* note 35, at 8–17.

47.   Crossland, *supra* note 43.

48.   Cao, *supra* note 19, at 1299; Hornblower, *supra* note 21; Simons, *supra* note 42.

49.   RAPE FOR PROFIT, *supra* note 25, at 22.

50.   Bhatiasevi, *supra* note 38; MODERN FORM OF SLAVERY, *supra* note 24, at 48; RAPE FOR PROFIT, *supra* note 25, at 22–23.

51.   Maria Jaschok & Suzanne Miers, *Traditionalism, Continuity and Change, in* WOMEN AND CHINESE PATRIARCHY: SUBMISSION, SERVITUDE AND ESCAPE 264, 265 (Maria Jaschok & Suzanne Miers eds., 1994); Katyal, *supra* note 37, at 795; MODERN FORM OF SLAVERY, *supra* note 24, at 47–48; RAPE FOR PROFIT, *supra* note 25, at 21. In one well-known practice in India, women and girls are offered to a temple through a religious ceremony, after which they are forced to become prostitutes out of economic necessity or after being sold by priests to brothels (devadasis). *See* COMMUNITY VIOLENCE REPORT, *supra* note 6, at 15. The Community Violence Report also notes the existence of a similar practice in Nepal called the Deukis system. *See* COMMUNITY VIOLENCE REPORT, *id.*

52.   Robert Benjamin, *Women and Children are Sold by Relatives in Age-Old 'Flesh Trade'*, MONTREAL GAZETTE, Jun. 14, 1991 *available in* LEXIS, Nexis Library, World File, Allnws.

53.   *See generally* BRIDES FOR SALE?, *supra* note 17; WITHOUT MERCY, *supra* note 17.

54.   Barry reports that ''[i]n Sep. 1970 a truckload of soldiers under governmental orders went to the

Second, traffickers use two main techniques for trafficking women, namely deception and/or outright force. Where deception is used, the motivating factor for many women and girls is often the chance to escape poverty, combined with the opportunity to relieve the economic pressure on their families.[55] Fictitious offers of employment or marriage are two common lures. Employment offers range from jobs as a factory worker, a domestic worker, receptionist, or nanny, to a job as a hostess, waitress, singer, or model.[56] Fraudulent marriage offers may be either wholly fictitious or traffickers may actually go through with the marriage process.[57] In Pakistan, pimps actually marry a woman then abandon her in a crowd. At that point, an accomplice offers to help her find her "lost" husband or outright forces her into prostitution.[58]

However, lures are not limited to job offers or marriage proposals. Basically, any story that will work is used. Where young girls are forced by their fathers to marry strangers, the girls are often told that they are going on a family trip. When they arrive at the groom's hometown, the girls are then informed that they are going to be married. Lures may even be as inventive as proposing to go to the countryside to buy antique silver coins, which could be sold for a profit.[59] That lure led one woman in China to be trafficked into a forced marriage with a farmer. In Russia, a Russian student of German literature was lured by an invitation to complete her education in Germany. Upon arrival in Germany, she was forced into prostitution.[60]

---

homes of four Persian girls in Zanzibar and held their families at gunpoint as the girls were dragged off screaming. They were taken before the Revolutionary Council, where they were forced into Muslim marriages with high-ranking government officials, most of whom had other wives. The abduction, forced marriage and enslavement of these girls were carried out under the direction of Vice-President Karume, then dictator of the island, in accordance with the post-revolutionary policy of compulsory racial integration through intermarriage." FEMALE SEXUAL SLAVERY, *supra* note 4, at 47. *See also* Robin McDowell, *Cambodia's sex-for-sale will stay despite new law, say women*, DEUTSCHE PRESSE-AGENTUR, Jan. 25, 1996 *available in* LEXIS, Nexis Library, News File, Curnws.

55. GLOBAL REPORT, *supra* note 11, at 257; Jaschok & Miers, *supra* note 51, at 265; Lbel, *supra* note 33; MODERN FORM OF SLAVERY, *supra* note 24, at 46; RAPE FOR PROFIT, *supra* note 25, at 15, 21; Sharpe, *supra* note 43.

56. Cao, *supra* note 19, at 1299–1301; Commission, *supra* note 42; GLOBAL REPORT, *supra* note 11, at 262; Eileen Guererro, *Philippines Keeps Maids Home after Harassment Reports*, REUTERS, Jan. 20, 1988 *available in* LEXIS, Nexis Library, News File, Curnws; HUMAN RIGHTS IN CHINA, *supra* note 35, at 14; JAPAN FEDERATION, *supra* note 23; Katyal, *supra* note 37, at 808; Samia Nakhoul, *Asians Plead for end to Trafficking in Workers*, REUTERS, Sep. 8, 1994, *available in* LEXIS, Nexis Library, News File, Curnws; POLAND REPORT, *supra* note 22, at para. 60; RAPE FOR PROFIT, *supra* note 25, at 28; Sharpe, *supra* note 43; Thai Police, *supra* note 38.

57. Trirat Petchsingh, *Thai Girls Tricked into Prostitution*, REUTERS NORTH EUROPEAN SERVICE, May 22, 1985, *available in* LEXIS, Nexis Library, News File, Curnws.

58. Hornblower, *supra* note 21; Petchsingh, *supra* note 57; RAPE FOR PROFIT, *supra* note 25, at 29; Simons, *supra* note 42.

59. *People Pedlars, supra* note 12, at 41.

60. Hornblower, *supra* note 21.

In cases where lures are not used or do not succeed, traffickers resort to outright abduction.[61] Such abduction often involves the use of drugs to sedate the women and girls,[62] or the use of violence to control them.[63] As with lures, traffickers will use whatever means are most likely to succeed in abducting a woman and will exploit whatever opportunities arise. For example, two Burmese sisters hired a motorcycle driver to take them to the market only to be abducted and sold to a brothel. Similarly, a 10-year-old girl looking after the family's water buffalo was abducted and sold to a brothel.[64]

Once the lure is set or the woman is forcibly abducted, the transportation begins. Transporting a person is not necessarily a quick or easy process. It requires establishing routes as well as contacts and housing along the way. A trafficker may take a woman directly to the place of sale—the brothel, market, or residence of the wife-purchaser. Or a trafficker may take a woman only as far as the national border, at which point another trafficker (or series of traffickers) will take her to the first point of sale and sell her to a brothel or wife-purchaser. However, in some cases, traffickers do not need to be actively involved in the transportation. A woman who is responding to a false offer of employment may travel to the traffickers, unaware of her fate. Similarly, where a family member has made arrangements to force a girl or woman into an unwanted marriage, the girl or woman often travels willingly to the residence of the "groom" under the erroneous belief that she is merely taking a vacation.

Trafficking is often carried out at particular points in the year when women and girls are most vulnerable. Thus, in Nepal, recruiters return to participate in local festivals in June, late August, or early September. These months, known as the "hungry months," precede the harvest so poverty is most acute.[65] In China, traffickers look for women who have spent all their money and are stranded in an unfamiliar urban center far from home.[66] In the Philippines, fierce typhoons may ruin farmers who then send a wage-earner to the big city, most commonly, a daughter.[67] Traffickers are well aware of the vulnerable situations girls and women face. As one Hungarian pimp in Romania revealed, he "took the kind of girl no one would miss if she disappeared. Girls who were having trouble with their parents

---

61. GLOBAL REPORT, *supra* note 11, at 258; MODERN FORM OF SLAVERY, *supra* note 24, at 52; RAPE FOR PROFIT, *supra* note 25, at 30–31.

62. GLOBAL REPORT, *supra* note 11, at 258; Jaschok & Miers, *supra* note 51, at 265.

63. Jaschok & Miers, *supra* note 51, at 265.

64. MODERN FORM OF SLAVERY, *supra* note 24, at 52.

65. ABC/NEPAL, A NEPALI WOMEN'S NGO WORKING AGAINST GIRL TRAFFICKING AND AIDS, RED LIGHT TRAFFIC: THE TRADE IN NEPALI GIRLS 36 (1992); RAPE FOR PROFIT, *supra* note 25, at 21. This occurs in Thailand and Burma as well. Trafficking of girls is at a prime during the "green rice season" when farmers are short of money while the rice grows. CATW, *supra* note 8, at 12.

66. CHINA WAKES, *supra* note 19, at 221.

67. Chapman, *supra* note 23.

or who lived alone. So when they were resold, no one would look for them.''[68] In cases of trafficking leading to forced marriage, women or girls are not informed that they are being sent away to marry a stranger. Rather, they are typically sent on holidays to an unfamiliar land where an unfamiliar language is spoken. Once miles away from any support and anything familiar, she is forced into a marriage that had been pre-arranged by a relative.

Trafficked women serve two main purposes. They are either sold to brothels, massage parlors, bars, and other entertainment centers and forced into prostitution, or they may be sold or given to men as wives or mistresses. Their initial destination is rarely final.[69] They are often sold from one brothel to another,[70] or sold to a number of different husbands, one after the other.[71]

The next two subsections will outline what happens to women when they are either sold into prostitution, or sold or forced into marriages.[72] While the human rights abuses experienced by these women are similar, the two situations are distinct because the issues, considerations, and obstacles facing these women require different strategies.

Forced Prostitution

Women who are trafficked into forced prostitution may either be sold outright to a brothel owner or sold at an auction.[73] After being sold, many women undergo what is known as a ''breaking- in'' period. Breaking-in may be done either through physical means alone or in tandem with psychological means.[74] In all of these cases, women or girls are detained against their will. Where physical means are used, the breaking-in period is typically marked by repeated rapes, gang rapes, cigarette burns, electric shocks, and beatings by brothel guards.[75] (In certain cases, rape is

---

68. Hornblower, *supra* note 21.

69. MODERN FORM OF SLAVERY, *supra* note 24, at 51.

70. JAPAN FEDERATION, *supra* note 23, at 65; RAPE FOR PROFIT, *supra* note 25, at 15–16; Simons, *supra* note 42.

71. Xie, *supra* note 35, at 290.

72. There is more fluidity between the different consequences of trafficking in women than suggested here. Women can be trafficked into forced marriage and then sold into forced prostitution or, when a woman is not successful as a prostitute, she may be turned over to a family as a domestic slave. STV has on file three reports of domestic workers who were trained to be prostitutes at the same time. *See* ALTINK, *supra* note 4, at 144. Because of the paucity of information on this aspect, it is not discussed here.

73. GLOBAL REPORT, *supra* note 11, at 258; The Poland Report by the Special Rapporteur focuses on trafficking leading to forced prostitution in Poland. *See* POLAND REPORT, *supra* note 22.

74. Cao, *supra* note 19, at 1302.

75. Ray Moseley, *Conference hears of horrors against women*, CHI. TRIB., Jun. 17, 1993 *available in* LEXIS, Nexis Library, News File, Curnws; RAPE FOR PROFIT *supra* note 25, at 28, 35; Simons, *supra* note 41; *Thai Police*, *supra* note 38; Paul Watson, *Thousands Sold into Brothels*, TORONTO STAR, Aug. 3, 1996, at A16.

not used to "break-in" girls so that they may be purchased as virgins.)[76] One common tactic in India involves both physical and psychological means. Certain brothel staff treat the victim abusively, telling her repeatedly that she is dirty or defiled, while another staff member (often the brothel manager) consoles her and tells her she is among family.[77]

Once a woman or girl has been "broken in," she is forced to work in the brothel. She cannot negotiate any terms of the sexual transaction. She typically has no control over who she services, how many men she must service,[78] or how she must service them. She is often forced to work seven days a week, in spite of illness or menstruation.[79] Even when recuperating from an abortion, she receives little time off.[80] Refusal to service a customer tends to result in beatings or other abuse.[81] Some women have even reported a daily quota of men they must service or solicit which, if not reached, results in further beatings.[82] Moreover, she often has little or no access to birth control. Even when she does have access to condoms, she has no power to ensure that a customer wears one.[83] This has lead to a prevalence of sexually transmitted diseases in trafficked women, particularly the fatal HIV virus.[84] As a result, for many women, being trafficked is essentially a death warrant.

In many cases, her confinement is near total and she is kept under strict surveillance. She is not allowed to leave the brothel or its immediate surroundings without escorts. And even then, threats are used to ensure that she does not attempt to escape. Because of the controlled environment that she lives under, she has to rely on her captors for access to food and clothing. As she often does not see much of the money paid by her customers, the cost of her survival must be supplemented by any tips she receives directly from customers. She may live under situations where food and other necessities are brought into the brothels by vendors who may overcharge these captive women.[85] Her confinement is usually relaxed only once her captors feel that she will not attempt to escape.[86]

---

76. RAPE FOR PROFIT, *supra* note 25, at 35.

77. *Id.*

78. Numbers vary, most commonly according to age. Very young girls may be required to service 2–3 men a day at the beginning of their captivity while older women may be forced to service anywhere from 10–100 men a day, depending on the brothel-owner. *See* Nicholas Kristof, *Child Prostitution Unabated in Asia*, GLOBE AND MAIL, Apr. 15, 1995, at A12.

79. Hornblower, *supra* note 21; Agnieszka Swiecka, *Prostitution Prevention Program: Giving Lost Women a Road Back Home*, THE WARSAW VOICE, Dec. 17, 1995 *available in* LEXIS, Nexis Library, News File, Curnws.

80. Swiecka, *id.*

81. RAPE FOR PROFIT, *supra* note 25, at 43.

82. Moseley, *supra* note 75; Petchsingh, *supra* note 57; Preston, *supra* note 33; Sharpe, *supra* note 43.

83. Swiecka, *supra* note 79.

84. For a thorough discussion on this issue, *see* MODERN FORM OF SLAVERY, *supra* note 24, at 125–147.

85. RAPE FOR PROFIT, *supra* note 25, at 40–41; POLAND REPORT, *supra* note 22, at para. 66.

86. Paul Watson, *supra* note 75.

Brothel owners and pimps utilize a number of control mechanisms in combination to ensure that these women and girls remain compliant, obedient, and do not attempt to escape. Most of all, they know that these women are vulnerable and they ensure that these women are constantly reminded of their extreme vulnerability and of the brothel owner's or pimps' power. The vulnerability stems from a number of factors including isolation in the brothel and the community, constant surveillance, and near total confinement. They face unrestricted beatings, rapes, or other forms of violence at the hands of their captors. Threats of violence are also used. In addition, the captors may threaten to sell a woman to another brothel,[87] to reveal that she is a prostitute to her family,[88] or to harm her family.[89]

Often, women are trafficked into places that are geographically unfamiliar, linguistically different, and quite remote.[90] Thus, they do not know where to seek assistance or refuge and cannot communicate with the people around them. Even in cases of internal trafficking in places like China, language barriers and even cultural barriers place trafficked women in positions of extreme vulnerability. In addition, a woman's identification papers and money are always taken away.[91] Without money, she cannot venture far from where she is being kept. And without proper identification papers, she is susceptible to arrest and/or immediate deportation.[92] As discussed above, these women were originally targeted for existing vulnerabilities, which are only compounded by their unfamiliarity with the area, the language barrier, and the lack of money and identification papers.

Aside from violence and threats of violence, one of the main means of control is through the invocation of debt bondage. Essentially, brothel owners will tell a trafficked woman that she has been purchased from a recruiter or her family, and that she will have to work until she pays off the purchase price (the "debt.") Once she pays off that amount, she is purportedly "free to go." The debt includes all of the brothel owner's expenses. Thus, not only is her actual purchase price included,

---

87.   JAPAN FEDERATION, *supra* note 23, at 65; RAPE FOR PROFIT, *supra* note 25, at 34.

88.   One Polish woman trafficked to Germany was photographed while being raped and later threatened with exposure of those photos to her family. *See* Moseley, *supra* note 75.

89.   Sharpe, *supra* note 43.

90.   For Brazilian girls trafficked into the Amazon jungles, towns are so remote that trying to escape into the jungle means certain death. Lbel, *supra* note 33.

91.   JAPAN FEDERATION, *supra* note 23, at 63; Simons, *supra* note at 42; Swiecka, *supra* note 79; *Thai Police, supra* note 38.

92.   Nao Nakanishi, *Trade in Women Flourishing in Germany*, REUTERS, Oct. 26, 1992, LEXIS, Nexis Library, World File, Allnws; Simons, *supra* note 42. While it may appear that deportation would at least mean an end to a woman's trafficking ordeal, that is not necessarily the case. For example, Burmese women who have been trafficked into Thailand and deported back to Burma face either the possibility of arrest, fines, and/or detention for leaving the country illegally, or the possibility of charges and incarceration if they are suspected of being a prostitute as prostitution is illegal in Burma. *See* MODERN FORM OF SLAVERY, *supra* note 24, at 111–12. Even if a woman does not face arrest or deportation upon return to her country of origin, she often experiences continuing abuse, violence, and denial of basic legal rights during the arrest and deportation process in the receiving country. In addition, there is rarely an attempt to provide redress for the crimes committed against her person.

but protection money paid to the police, shelter, clothing, food, medical care (including abortions), travel expenses, cost of travel papers and passports, bail, and even taxes are included. In addition to the calculation of expenses, interest is added.[93] In many cases, women do not know any of the terms of repayment, the amount they earned, or the state of their account.[94] A high proportion of these trafficked women see only a portion, if any, of the money paid by customers. Some are given approximately one-third of what customers paid for their services while others get substantially less, or no money at all, except for tips from customers.[95]

For some women, debt bondage is a concept that they are familiar with, as it is a common or known practice in their home country. For women who have never heard of this concept, debt bondage works as a means of control because it offers the illusion of escape. It is the traffickers' incentive structure, their means of making these women comply with the trafficker's demands. In reality, it is the means through which many of these women are kept in a vicious cycle of debt.[96] For some women, the existence of this debt further increases their health risks because they will try to service as many men as possible, perform whatever services are requested, and avoid any extra expenses—such as health care costs—in order to pay off their debt as soon as possible.[97]

In addition to these control mechanisms, brothel owners often have state authorities on their side, which further ensures continued compliance and obedience. Numerous investigations reveal that local authorities turn a blind eye to trafficking in women.[98] In many places, local authorities and police are customers and are clearly complicit with the brothel owners in keeping these women under control.[99] One survivor in Cambodia was raped by a student in her embroidery class before men clad in military uniforms took her to a brothel in Battambang. During her eight

---

93. Cao, *supra* note 19, at 1306; CATW, *supra* note 8, at 13; JAPAN FEDERATION, *supra* note 23, at 63; Lbel, *supra* note 33; MODERN FORM OF SLAVERY, *supra* note 24, at 54; Preston, *supra* note 33; RAPE FOR PROFIT, *supra* note 25, at 36; Simons, *supra* note 42.

94. According to an in-depth investigation by Human Rights Watch, two women trafficked into Thailand were told that their families had borrowed more money, which was added to the girl's account. The girls had no way of verifying that their families had actually borrowed the money. In addition, Human Rights Watch found that some girls had arranged for money to be sent to their families but had no idea whether that money constituted a new debt or was part of what the girls had already earned. *See* MODERN FORM OF SLAVERY, *supra* note 24, at 56.

95. CATW, *supra* note 8, at 13; JAPAN FEDERATION, *supra* note 23, at 64; MODERN FORM OF SLAVERY, *supra* note 24, at 53–59; RAPE FOR PROFIT, *supra* note 25, at 36–40; Simons, *supra* note 42; Swiecka, *supra* note 79.

96. As some reports indicate, brothel networks have a system of rotation whereby a woman is sold to another brothel just before her debt with her current brothel-owner is paid. Once sold to another brothel, she is forced to begin all over again, paying off the purchase price paid by the next brothel owner. CATW, *supra* note 8, at 13; JAPAN FEDERATION, *supra* note 23, at 65.

97. MODERN FORM OF SLAVERY, *supra* note 24, at 57.

98. Lbel, *supra* note 33; Preston, *supra* note 33.

99. MODERN FORM OF SLAVERY, *supra* note 24, at 76–78; Molina, *supra* note 22.

months in the brothel, she was routinely forced to have sex with policemen and soldiers.[100] In other cases, police have actually returned women to their abusers.[101] Even where police are not overtly complicit with particular brothel owners, women are often the subject of crackdowns on prostitution, while the brothel owners, pimps, and male customers are ignored. While in police custody, women are subject not only to physical and sexual abuse, but their rights to due process are typically ignored. Furthermore, in cases where the illegal status of these women is discovered, many are deported without any investigation into how they were forced into trafficking and without any attempt to obtain their testimony for any possible police investigations. Such treatment at the hands of authorities lead women to believe that police are at best an ineffective force against brothel owners, and at worst, allies of brothel owners.

Brothel owners can also use legislation to threaten trafficked women and girls. In Thailand, brothel owners can threaten women and girls with the Immigration Act of Thailand. Under this act, illegal entry into Thailand is criminalized and punishable by detention of up to two years or the payment of substantial fines. Moreover, this legislation grants the authorities powers of summary arrest and deportation.[102] Burmese women trafficked into Thailand not only face abuse throughout the deportation process, they then face the possibility of charges on return to Burma for leaving the country illegally and engaging in prostitution, which is illegal in Burma.[103] In Pakistan, brothel owners use threats of exposing women as illegal immigrants. In addition, pimps are now resorting to marrying the women they traffick or marrying them off to other pimps.[104] Consequently, pimps can control these women by threatening to denounce them under the Hudood laws, which penalize sex outside of marriage through long prison terms and severe corporal punishment.[105]

Finally, where families are complicit in the sale of their daughters or wives, the control by brothel owners over these women and girls is reinforced by cooperation between the brothel owner or pimp and the trafficked girl's family. In India, if there are several women in Bombay brothels, a prominent member of the village may be appointed to travel to India, collect the money earned by these trafficked women, and bring it back to their parents. For such women and girls, this means that not only are they under pressure to pay off their debt to the brothel owner, but they are expected to help support their families out of whatever earnings they do

---

100. McDowell, *supra* note 54.

101. Hornblower, *supra* note 21.

102. MODERN FORM OF SLAVERY, *supra* note 24, at 17–18.

103. MODERN FORM OF SLAVERY, *supra* note 24, at 19, 111–12.

104. GLOBAL REPORT, *supra* note 11, at 260.

105. PROSTITUTION OF SEXUALITY, *supra* note 21, at 170–71; GLOBAL REPORT, *supra* note 11, at 259. The Hudood Ordinance (1979) imposed the punishments of death by stoning, 10 years imprisonment, whipping up to 30 stripes, and fines. LAWYERS FOR HUMAN RIGHTS AND LEGAL AID, THE FLESH TRADE: THE TRAFFICKING OF WOMEN AND CHILDREN IN PAKISTAN 16 (1993).

receive in the form of tips[106] and cannot expect any assistance or support from their families for escape or rescue.

Forced Marriage

At first glance, it appears that there is not as much uniformity in trafficking that leads to forced marriages as there is in trafficking that leads to forced prostitution. Generally, there appear to be three different circumstances in which trafficking in women leads to forced marriage. First, women are trafficked into forced marriages for economic gain. Second, women are trafficked and forced into marriage under the banner of religion. Third, girls are trafficked into forced marriages under the guise that it is in "the best interest of the girls." Closer examination reveals that, while the motivation behind each of these three circumstances ostensibly differs, the objective conditions of the women and girls caught in such circumstances do *not* differ significantly from those of women who are trafficked into prostitution. The significance of this similarity is that, regardless of the motivation behind those responsible, trafficking women into forced marriages should be recognized simply as trafficking in women. Motivation must be recognized when examining root causes and designing strategies to address trafficking in women, but should in no way excuse the fact that such forced marriages are a form of trafficking in women. It will be clear from the factual background that such women and girls are subject to grave human rights abuses. For women and girls trafficked into forced marriages purely for profit and under the banner of religion, the abuses during the trafficking process are virtually identical to the abuses experienced by women forced into prostitution. Violence, threats of violence, and coercion are used to control the woman. For women trafficked into forced marriages by close family members, deception remains the primary means through which a woman is transported. As the girl or woman is unaware of her fate, there is no coercion or violence until she has arrived at the destination and must be forced to participate in the wedding and thereafter in the marriage. Because trafficking leading to forced marriage is less familiar than trafficking leading to forced prostitution, each of these three circumstances will be briefly described before examining the working and living conditions that these women endure.

Women can be trafficked into forced marriages almost exclusively for reasons of profit.[107] This situation is analogous to women who are trafficked into forced prostitution. The experiences of women trafficked into forced marriage during the recruitment and transportation phase mirror those of the women forced into prostitution. Such trafficking in women is rampant in China[108] and is also found in places

---

106. RAPE FOR PROFIT, *supra* note 25, at 40.

107. Note that this form of forced marriage is often quite different from circumstances of "mail- order" brides. *See* Nora Demleitner, *International Obligation to Protect Mail-Order Brides, in* WOMEN AND INTERNATIONAL HUMAN RIGHTS LAW (Kelly Askin & Dorean Koenig eds., vol. II, forthcoming 1999).

108. According to a Chinese newspaper report, 50,000 traffickers were arrested in the two years between 1993–1995. *Dalu liangnian lai gongdai renkou fanzi jin wuwan,* SHIJIE RIBAO, Mar. 31, 1995, at A19. Translation is that of the author.

such as Pakistan and Bangladesh.[109] The purchasers of many of these women are typically farmers from poorer regions who require women to cook, clean, and bear children (preferably sons). Because trafficked women cost only a portion of what a dowry and wedding costs, the demand for such women remains high.[110] In China, this demand is compounded by the decreasing number of women in the country.[111] The poor and uneducated or unsophisticated are not the only purchasers of women and girls. There are wealthy men from the Gulf region who purchase wives from countries in South Asia in this manner.[112] Girls are often sold to be temporary wives while these men work in South Asia; in some cases, they may be taken back to the Middle East with the purchaser. Typically, a young girl is sold to a much older man; the age difference in one case was 72 years.

Trafficking under the banner of religion refers to situations where radical religious sect leaders recruit and/or abduct women into their sects and "marry" them in the name of religion. The Algerian experience with such practice was raised at the Beijing Tribunal on Accountability for Women's Human Rights at the 1995 United Nations Fourth World Conference on Women. Men who belong to fundamentalist organizations abduct and rape young girls. The rationale for these abductions (often committed during or after armed conflict) was described by one woman as follows:

[D]ozens of young girls and women continue to be abducted and raped on a daily basis by groups of fundamentalist terrorists who consider females to be the spoils of war to which they are entitled. These self-proclaimed emirs would assert that Islam authorizes them to take any woman they desire as a "temporary wife". This practice from the dark ages has now become "legal" and was generalized by a "fatwa."[113] In this way, barbaric acts such as rape, mutilation, and decapitation are trivialized

---

109. CATW, *supra* note 8, at 19, 31; Uli Schmetzer, *Slavery a Way of Life on Indian Subcontinent*, CHI. TRIB., Nov. 19, 1991, *available in* LEXIS, Nexis Library, World File, Allnws. One report indicates that young women in high school are being abducted in Ethiopia for the purpose of forced marriage. See *Ethiopian Female Students Victims of Abduction*, REUTERS NORTH AMERICAN WIRE, Oct. 31, 1995, *available in* LEXIS, Nexis Library, World File, Allnws.

110. CATW, *supra* note 8, at 19; PERSONAL VOICES, *supra* note 35, at 291.

111. CHINA WAKES, *supra* note 19, at 232; PERSONAL VOICES, *supra* note 35, at 291.

112. In return, families receive money and gold. In many cases, these young girls are abandoned after a few days of sex. However, families do not always sell their daughters purely for personal economic gain. As one father explained, when authorities intervened in the marriage of his 12-year-old daughter to a 60-year-old Saudi man, he claimed that they spoiled his daughter's chances for a good life. If taken at face value, this man's comment reflects the complexity of the reasons for trafficking in women. See CATW, *supra* note 8, at 22; M. RITA ROZARIO, TRAFFICKING IN WOMEN AND CHILDREN IN INDIA: SEXUAL EXPLOITATION AND SALE 71 (1986); Ernest Kamau, *Kenya: Forced Marriages on the Increase*, INTER PRESS SERVICE, Mar. 17, 1993; Judith Matloff, *In Africa, Money Isn't the Only Reason Young Girls are Sexually Exploited*, THE CHRISTIAN SCIENCE MONITOR, Sep. 12, 1996; Molly Moore, *India's Bazar for Cheap Muslim Brides*, INTERNATIONAL HERALD TRIBUNE, Jun. 22, 1994, *available in* LEXIS, Nexis Library, World File, Allnws.

113. For a thorough discussion of fatwas, or religious decrees, *see* Faustina Pereira, *Fatwa in Bangladesh: Patriarchy's Latest Sport*, forthcoming in a later volume of this work.

and justified as retaliation and appropriate punishment for women who refuse to submit to the dictates of a theocratic and fascist ideology.[114]

A similar practice also occurs in Turkey, where radical segments of an organized group have abducted and coerced young women into religious "marriages."[115]

Trafficking women and girls into forced marriage in the "best interest of the girls" occurs when family members (typically male members) force or outright sell their daughters or female relatives into arranged marriages. The instances referred to here clearly involve physical coercion, such as the case of two teenage girls from Britain whose father sent them to Yemen (his country of origin) on the pretext of a family vacation. Upon their arrival, they were taken to a backward village in the remote bandit territory in North Yemen and forced into marriages arranged and sanctioned by their father.[116]

That these arranged marriages are a form of trafficking in women remains, for the most part, unacknowledged in our society. Such marriages are often justified by the motivations of those responsible, that is, that they are in the best interest of girls. That motivation is often combined with the "cultural defense," the defense that some variations in cultural practices cannot be legitimately criticized by outsiders to that culture. This has been a large critique of international human rights law because it has been historically developed, for the most part, without the direct contribution of many developing countries. The cultural defense is raised when a "non-Western" cultural practice is captured by international human rights law as a human rights violation. The problem with such arguments is not that they are made insincerely or are deliberate subterfuges to mask the oppression of women and girls; the problem stems from the fact that such arguments wholly ignore the conditions and experiences of girls and women and treat them as human beings unworthy of consideration.

In order to respect the dignity and worth of women and girls as human beings, at a minimum, the "woman question" must be asked. The woman question demands that the objective conditions, experiences, needs, and risks that women face be examined and addressed. In examining what happens to women and girls forced

---

114. Sadou, *supra* note 32, at 29.

115. Oral report of the Government of Turkey to the Committee on the Elimination of All Forms of Discrimination Against Women, given on Jan. 17, 1997, at the United Nations. Because the PKK is considered an opponent of the government, there are potential political issues involved. The Turkish government's comment on this practice was confirmed by a woman representing a Turkish nongovernment organization. Notes on file with the author. Information on this specific incidence of trafficking in women remains sparse.

116. This case is reported on in two books, BRIDES FOR SALE?, *supra* note 17 and WITHOUT MERCY, *supra* note 17. In a similar case, a man in Scotland organized the abduction and forced marriages of two of his daughters, aged 22 and 15, upon their arrival in Pakistan on a supposed holiday in June 1995, *supra* note 16. Finally, in another case, a 15-year-old girl was reported missing by her father and husband a few days after her marriage ceremony. She had run away with her boyfriend and on being found, she and her sister told authorities that they had been forced to marry and have sexual intercourse against their will, *supra* note 15.

into marriages in this manner, the elements of trafficking are present, most compellingly in the human rights abuses that arise in their daily lives (for example, violations of the right to life, liberty, and security of the person; right to health; right to marry and found a family; right to be free from slavery, forced labor, and torture; and the right to be free from violence). The only difference is that the institution of marriage legitimizes such transactions, transactions which for the most part involve an exchange of money, property, or other benefit between the families. Arguments may be made to counter the significance of the exchange of money (or dowry) in such transactions. However, even if no exchange of money or other benefit is evident, these women and girls are still being recruited and transported by means of coercion, in the same fashion as women trafficked by strangers, and the human rights abuses against them remain almost identical to those suffered by women trafficked by strangers. Families that engage in these types of arranged marriages are no different from families who sell their daughters into prostitution to meet familial economic obligations. In these types of forced marriages, however, women and girls are used to meet not only economic obligations but social, community, domestic service, and procreative obligations as well.

There is considerably less information on the details of the living and working conditions of these women. In particular, we are only now beginning to hear of the forced marriages that take place under the banner of religion. This lack of information in general stems, in part, from the fact that many instances of forced marriage are unrecognized as involving human rights abuses. However, there is sufficient information to paint a picture of what generally happens to these women. From the time she knows of the plan to force her into marriage, she will be detained and confined by her captors. Often physical force and/or the use of drugs are used to detain and confine her.[117] Where a woman is being sold purely for profit or abducted in the name of religion, she will likely be raped and/or subject to other forms of physical and sexual violence.[118] Sexual violence, though not restricted to situations where a woman is sold purely for profit, is less common during the period prior to the marriage forced upon a girl ''in her best interest.'' After marriage, the husband may legally force or require any services whatsoever from the woman or girl; her wishes are irrelevant.

Even if she is not confined indoors continuously, in many cases, she is trafficked to a village so remote that she virtually has no chance of escaping.[119] In addition, the village is typically in a region geographically unfamiliar and linguistically different from her homeland. Any identification papers she has will be taken away.[120] The complicity of the villagers, the village officials, and her own family (where her family is responsible for forcing her into marriage), virtually seals her fate, barring outside assistance.

---

117. Gillian, *supra* note 16.

118. Sadou, *supra* note 32, at 28.

119. Lbel, *supra* note 33.

120. Gillian, *supra* note 16.

After the wedding ceremony and/or sale transaction, she will be raped by her "husband." As procreation is usually one of the reasons for which she is purchased, she will be repeatedly raped until she is pregnant.[121] Such rapes will continue throughout the duration of her ordeal. She may be subjected to extreme violence if she has daughters instead of sons. In addition, she will be forced to take on the physical labor required of married women in that region. In Mokbana, a remote bandit region in Yemen to which many young girls are sold into marriages, such physical labor involves rising at four o'clock in the morning to work in the fields and gather water, which may be miles away.[122]

Those trafficked into forced marriage are controlled through any combination of the following means: beatings, rapes, other forms of violence, threats of violence, confinement, and complicity of the community, officials, and family members. As discussed above, these methods are also used to control women trafficked into forced prostitution. One means of control uniquely available to captors of women trafficked into forced marriage involves the children born as a result of the repeated rapes. Once pregnant, it becomes physically more difficult for some women to escape. For others, escape becomes psychologically more difficult; many women refuse to leave their children behind.[123]

Escape or Rescue of Women Trafficked into Forced Prostitution and Forced Marriage

Few trafficked women ever manage to escape or be rescued. Some are killed in the process of escaping, while others simply have no way to escape.[124] For those who do attempt to escape and are unsuccessful, the consequences are harsh and even fatal. The violence to which she has already been subjected, in the form of beatings, rapes, and other forms of violence, is intensified, and sometimes leads to death.[125] Any confinement and/or surveillance is increased. Upon return, often the owner will horribly beat and mutilate her in front of other women and girls as an example of what will happen to them if they too try to escape. Moreover, women

---

121. Gillian, *id.* Procreation does not appear to be one of the motivating factors in marriages between wealthy men from the Gulf Region and the girls that they purchase from South Asia because "wives" are often abandoned after a few days of sex or deserted, with any children, much later in time.

122. BRIDES FOR SALE?, *supra* note 17, at 16.

123. As one husband stated, he wanted the children as compensation if his wife was allowed to leave Yemen. *See* WITHOUT MERCY, *supra* note 17, at 189.

124. Lbel, *supra* note 33; PERSONAL VOICES, *supra* note 35, at 290; *Two Sisters, Allegedly Kidnapped for Forced Marriage, Found Dead*, BBC SUMMARY OF WORLD BROADCASTS, Nov. 9, 1994; *Mother of Two Sisters Beheaded by "Terrorists" Also Killed*, BBC SUMMARY OF WORLD BROADCASTS, Nov. 28, 1994, *available in* LEXIS, Nexis Library, World File, Allnws.

125. Here are just a few examples: One victim of trafficking has reported that women who tried to escape from the remote Amazon town have been tied to tree trunks and lynched. Preston, *supra* note 33. Another victim in Algeria reported that a girl was shot in the head and killed on her first attempt to escape from the Algerian fundamentalists who had abducted her. Sadou, *supra* note 32, at 32. Another girl in Cambodia witnessed the murder of a fellow prostitute who was trying to escape the brothel. Paul Watson, *Stolen Innocence*, TORONTO STAR, Aug. 4, 1996, at E6.

trafficked into forced prostitution or forced marriage face the possibility of being resold to another purchaser as a result of attempted escapes.[126] Repeated attempts at escape are dealt with severely.[127] One investigative reporter in China related a meeting he had with a forced marriage survivor who had attempted to escape:

> I saw her in the hospital in Shandong. . . . [She was] a woman who had been sold as a wife to an uneducated Shaanxi peasant. The first time she tried to flee, the peasant tied her to the bedpost. The second time she tried, he beat her. The third time, he gouged out her eyes. When I saw her in the hospital, she had white gauze covering the top of her head. The only thing you could see left of her eyes were two deep holes.[128]

For those fortunate enough to escape or be rescued, the ordeal does not end. Generally speaking, upon rescue a woman is confronted with two scenarios. She is either immediately deported without consideration for how or why she ended up in her situation, or she is detained for an indeterminate period of time because no one wants to take responsibility for her or assist her. In the first situation, it is her illegal status in the country that officials consider, so she is deported without a statement being taken from her and without any attempt to investigate her case and find her traffickers. In the second situation, there is often no established procedure to assist such women, so women tend to be ignored while they are in detention. As a stark example, in Japan, when a trafficked woman becomes ill, brokers take her to the embassy of her country (most commonly Thailand) and leave her there. As embassies do not have custodial facilities and the Japanese Immigration Bureau refuses to take charge of the women even if they are considered to be in the country illegally, Thai embassy officials contact an NGO, which eventually arranges for a shelter to care for the victim. It is through the NGO that survivors make arrangements to return home.[129] The delays and egregious treatment these women endure in the hands of authorities are often so unbearable that many women return to the brothels of their own accord.[130] Moreover, detention in the receiving country may be followed by detention and even arrest in the country of origin, as happens to Burmese women who have been trafficked to other countries. [131]

Aside from these issues, survivors of trafficking must then attempt to face their families, friends, and society as a whole. It is a rare occasion when a woman is

---

126. Preston, *supra* note 33; XIE & JIA, *supra* note 35, at 290–91 (woman who escaped her first "husband" only to be caught by her abductors and sold to another "husband"). Translation is that of the author.

127. After repeated attempts at escape, another woman had her legs broken with a bat by her "father-in-law." *Inner Mongolia: Campaign Against Organized Abduction and Trafficking in People*, BBC SUMMARY OF WORLD BROADCASTS, Apr. 28, 1994, *available in* LEXIS, Nexis Library, World File, Allnws.

128. CHINA WAKES, *supra* note 19, at 217.

129. JAPAN FEDERATION, *supra* note 23, at 65. A similar situation arises for pregnant Bangladeshi women trafficked to Karachi. CATW, *supra* note 8, at 40.

130. Trafficked women who turn to prostitution after being rescued is not limited to women who were forced into prostitution. For instance, one report states that many prostitutes in Ethiopia were victims of forced marriages who had escaped their abductors. See *Ethiopian Female Students, supra* note 109.

131. MODERN FORM OF SLAVERY, *supra* note 24, at 111–12.

welcomed back into her family and community with open arms. Oftentimes, women are rudely confronted with the fact that they are now ostracized, stigmatized, and considered "spoiled" or "damaged" goods.[132] Not only are women shunned, any children they have as a result of being raped are similarly stigmatized. Some women realize this cruel reality fairly early on. For example, upon being rescued, one woman decided to stay with her new "husband" because she was scared that her real husband would kill her for having "been" with another man.[133] When asked about leaving a brothel, another girl replied, "Where would I go? If I tried to go home, my family would cut my throat."[134] Other women find out they have been rejected when their families do not come to take them home, or when they are publicly scorned and ridiculed upon their return to their villages. The stigmatization, coupled with the lack of opportunities for these women, results in many of those trafficked (particularly those trafficked into prostitution) returning to the brothels.[135]

INTERNATIONAL HUMAN RIGHTS LAW

From the factual record, the issues that need to be addressed in order to combat and eradicate this practice can be determined. The focus here will be on international human rights law. However, it should be emphasized that international human rights law provides only one possible weapon in the war against trafficking. Many other tools, both legal and nonlegal, can and should be used to end trafficking in women. Before embarking on any discussion of using international human rights law to address these issues, a brief synopsis of state responsibility is provided below, because state responsibility gives rise to legal liability for a breach of an international legal obligation, which is currently one of the main means of recourse under international law.[136]

State Responsibility

Simply put, a state is legally liable for any breaches of its international law obligations. International law obligations may stem from treaty law or customary

---

132. HUMAN RIGHTS IN CHINA, *supra* note 35, at 19–20; POLAND REPORT, *supra* note 22, at para. 69; Paul Watson, *supra* note 75; John Stackhouse, *Aids Fears Prompt Brothel Raids*, GLOBE AND MAIL, Aug. 29, 1996, at A12.

133. XIE & JIA, *supra* note 35, at 284.

134. Moore, *supra* note 20.

135. As one rescue organization in Bombay discovered, of the 1,000 young women they rescued, approximately 98 percent are back at work as prostitutes because their families would not accept them or because they could not adapt to other ways of life, even after being taught skills. Seeing other women escape and return one year later to the life of prostitution because they cannot do anything else impacts on women who are still in the brothels. *Id.*

136. *See generally* IAN BROWNLIE, SYSTEM OF THE LAW OF NATIONS, STATE RESPONSIBILITY (PART I, 1983). For state responsibility with respect to women's human rights, *see generally* Rebecca J. Cook, *State Responsibility for Violations of Women's Human Rights,* 7 HARV. HUM. RTS. J. 125 (1995) for how developments in the international law of state responsibility can be applied to ensure more effective protection of women's rights [hereinafter Cook (1995)]; Rebecca J. Cook, *State Accountability Under*

international law. For international obligations flowing from treaty law, one must look to the written document signed and ratified by that state. Only states that sign and ratify such documents are committed to upholding the obligations within those treaties and/or conventions, unless those obligations are part of customary international law. Customary international law is international law that has been formed through the general practice of states and *opinio juris*; there is no written document to turn to as evidence of customary international law unless a treaty has codified the practice. The lack of written instruments makes it difficult to determine whether obligations fall under the rubric of customary international law. Generally speaking, two elements are required to establish customary international law. First, evidence of consistent state practice (what states say and do) is required. Second, evidence that states act in a particular way because they feel that international law demands they do so (sense of legal obligation or *opinio juris*) is required. As a general rule, once there is evidence of customary international law, then all states are committed to upholding these obligations.[137]

In order to find a state to be legally liable, one must find an international obligation owed by that state. Among the rights potentially violated by trafficking in women that are guaranteed by states through either treaty or customary international law are: the right to life, liberty, and security of the person; the right to equality; the right to be free from discrimination;[138] the right to be free from slavery or servitude; the right to be free from torture or cruel, inhuman, or degrading treatment; the right to be free from forced labor; the right not to be subject to arbitrary arrest and detention; the right to marry and found a family; and the right to health. There is also a newly recognized right to be free from certain forms of violence, including sexual violence. In addition, states parties to the Trafficking Convention and the Women's Convention (discussed below), are obligated to punish those who traffic women and exploit prostitutes, and to suppress all forms of traffic in women and exploitation of the prostitution of women.[139]

After determining that a state owes an international legal obligation, a breach of that obligation, through either an act or omission, must be established in order to find a state legally liable. Such liability has traditionally been incurred through the acts or omissions of a state actor or an agent of the state. However, states are under increasing and evolving obligations to prevent violations by private actors.

---

the Convention on the Elimination of All Forms of Discrimination Against Women, in HUMAN RIGHTS OF WOMEN, *supra* note 1, at 228 [hereinafter Cook (1994)].

137. A detailed discussion of customary international law has been omitted. For a detailed analysis of customary international law, *see* MICHAEL AKEHURST, A MODERN INTRODUCTION TO INTERNATIONAL LAW 25–34 (6th ed. 1987); IAN BROWNLIE, PRINCIPLES OF PUBLIC INTERNATIONAL LAW 4–11 (3rd ed. 1979).

138. While there is an argument to be made in some states that the lack of state action in prosecuting and punishing those trafficking in women constitutes discrimination on the grounds that crimes committed against men are investigated and pursued more vigorously, this argument will not be developed here.

139. The reader should be alert to the fact that all international human rights obligations, whether stemming from treaty law or customary international law, have specific meanings that limit their applicability. However, it is beyond the scope of this chapter to discuss the meanings of all international human rights obligations that are possibly relevant to issues arising from trafficking in women.

Thus, in recent years, the doctrine of state responsibility has been broadened, requiring governments to take preventive steps to protect the exercise and enjoyment of human rights, to investigate alleged violations, to punish proven violations, and to provide effective remedies.[140] Therefore, even if a state (through its organs or agents) does not traffick in women, if there are pervasive, persistent patterns of trafficking in women within its borders and no state action is taken to investigate and punish traffickers or to prevent trafficking in women, then a state can potentially be found legally responsible for its lack of due diligence in protecting these women and girls.

Examples of state breaches of international legal obligations related to trafficking in women are abundant whether considered through the traditional or the expanded concept of state responsibility.[141] Reports have clearly shown that state agents, functioning primarily in the roles of border guards, immigration officials, police officers, soldiers, and village officials, actively participate in trafficking in women by transporting trafficked women,[142] selling women to brothels, and forcing trafficked women who have escaped to return to brothels.[143] In addition, the staggering numbers of women trafficked in certain jurisdictions and the lack of prosecution of those responsible for either recruitment, transportation, purchase, and/or exploitation of these women is evidence of the lack of due diligence on the part of some states, which triggers the expanded, modern version of state responsibility. In these cases, states are complicit in trafficking in women through their acts or omissions, such as ignoring trafficking at borders, preventing women from escaping from or leaving the "husbands" who purchased them, preventing outside authorities from rescuing such women, and deporting trafficked women immediately without investigating any of their cases. [144]

---

140. Cook (1994), *supra* note 136, at 151.

141. For the purposes of this section, the definition of trafficking as set out in text accompanying note 6 will be used to define what acts will constitute trafficking.

142. Here, the taking of bribes by border officials in exchange for allowing traffickers to take women across national borders is included as an act that constitutes trafficking in women. While the state has likely not authorized such action, it is responsible for the acts of its officials who are on duty.

143. Hornblower, *supra* note 21.

144. While there is no report that compiles global figures for the number of women trafficked, there are reports, even quasi-official, that point to the widespread nature of the problem. The starkest example is perhaps the 1991 finding of the Human Rights Commission of Pakistan where not a single trafficker was known to have been apprehended, while 1,400 Bengali women languished in different jails of Pakistan, all brought in from their country by deception. *See* Moore, *supra* note 20. The *People's Daily*, a Chinese newspaper reported that 10,000 women and children who had been abducted were rescued by authorities in 1989–90. *See Dalu Liangnian, supra* note 108. The former ambassador of the Federal Republic of Germany to Thailand, Mr. Edgar Schmidt-Daul, has been quoted as stating that, "a terrifyingly high number of marriages of German men in Thailand who appear there as tourists aim only at bringing young Thai women to the Federal Republic in order to force them into prostitution there." *See* ULLA OHSE, FORCED PROSTITUTION AND TRAFFIC IN WOMEN IN WEST GERMANY 12 (1994). The Special Rapporteur has described the role of police in Poland in combating and contributing to trafficking in women. *See* POLAND REPORT, *supra* note 22, at paras. 90–96.

International Instruments

There are a variety of sources of state obligations in international human rights law that potentially address the numerous human rights violations that accompany trafficking in women. This section will discuss the four conventions that directly include trafficking in women and girls, followed by a brief discussion of other sources of international human rights obligations and the mechanisms of the Working Group on Slavery and the Special Rapporteur on Violence Against Women, Its Causes and Consequences.

The main convention relating to trafficking in women is the Convention for the Suppression of the Traffic in Persons and the Exploitation of the Prostitution of Others[145] (Trafficking Convention). The Trafficking Convention is significant as it represents the first time that an international instrument declared that prostitution and the traffic in persons is "incompatible with the dignity and worth of the human person and endanger[s] the welfare of the individual, the family and the community."[146] The primary purpose of the Trafficking Convention is to punish the trafficking and the procurement of women *for the purposes of prostitution* and to punish the exploitation of prostitutes, regardless of the victim's age or consent.[147] In addition to punishing traffickers, procurers, and exploiters of prostitutes, states parties are required to abolish any form of registration or supervision of prostitutes,[148] take measures to prevent prostitution and rehabilitate victims of prostitution,[149] take measures in connection with immigration and emigration procedures to deal with trafficking in persons,[150] repatriate victims of international traffic,[151] and supervise employment agencies to prevent those seeking employment from being exposed to the dangers of prostitution.[152]

---

145. Convention for the Suppression of the Traffic in Persons and the Exploitation of the Prostitution of Others, 96 U.N.T.S. 271, G.A. Res. 317 (IV) of 2 Dec. 1949, *entered into force* Jul. 25, 1951. As of 1996, only 71 states were signatories to the convention. Traffic in Women, *supra* note 9, at para. 24. For background of this convention, *see generally* Nora V. Demleitner, *Forced Prostitution: Naming an International Offense,* 18 FORDHAM INT'L L.J. 163 (1994); Nina Lassen, *Slavery and Slavery-Like Practices: United Nations Standards and Implementation,* 57 NORD. J. INT'L L. 197 (1988); Laura Reanda, *Prostitution as a Human Rights Question: Problems and Prospects of United Nations Act,* 13 HUM. RTS. Q. 207–11 (1991); Susan Jeanne Toepfer & Bryan Stuart Wells, *The Worldwide Market for Sex: A Review of International and Regional Legal Prohibitions Regarding Trafficking in Women,* 2 MICH. J. GENDER & L. 83, 96–100 (1994).

146. Trafficking Convention, *supra* note 145, Preamble; *see also* Reanda, *supra* note 145, at 209.

147. Trafficking Convention, *supra* note 145, art. 1 and 2. *See generally* Brussa, *supra* note 38; Reanda, *supra* note 145; Toepfer & Wells, *supra* note 145.

148. *Id.* at art. 6.

149. *Id.* at art. 16.

150. *Id.* at art. 17.

151. *Id.* at art. 19.

152. *Id.* at art. 20.

Under the Trafficking Convention, states parties are required only to annually communicate to the Secretary-General any laws, regulations, and measures relating to the traffic of persons. This information is to be published periodically by the Secretary-General to all members and non-members of the United Nations.[153] In spite of the fact that the Trafficking Convention came into force in 1951, the mechanism for receiving such information was not established until the mid-1970s.[154] One of the reasons for the inefficiency in setting up a mechanism to review these reports is the fact that there is no established body to monitor states parties' compliance with this convention. Without such a body, there will be few resources available and scant political will to ensure adherence to the Trafficking Convention.

Another international convention that directly addresses trafficking in women is the Convention on the Elimination of All Forms of Discrimination Against Women (Women's Convention).[155] Article 6 of the Women's Convention requires that states parties shall take all appropriate measures, including legislation, to suppress all forms of traffic in women and the exploitation of prostitution of women.[156] This obligation goes beyond that in the Trafficking Convention by requiring states parties to address the root causes of trafficking and the exploitation of prostitution, not simply to punish trafficking in women after the fact.[157]

Unlike the Trafficking Convention, the Women's Convention sets up a Committee (CEDAW) for compliance monitoring purposes.[158] As part of its monitoring

---

153. *Id.* at art. 21.

154. Reanda, *supra* note 145, at 210. According to a report by the Secretary-General, 48 states had already signed and ratified the Trafficking Convention by 1980. *See* Traffic in Women, *supra* note 9, at para. 24.

155. Convention on the Elimination of All Forms of Discrimination Against Women, 1249 U.N.T.S. 14, *entered into force* Sept. 3, 1981. *See generally* Andrew Byrnes, *The 'Other' Human Rights Treaty Body: The Work of the Committee on the Elimination of Discrimination Against Women,* 14 YALE J. INT'L. L 1 (1989); Cook (1994), *supra* note 136; INTERNATIONAL WOMEN'S RIGHTS ACTION WATCH (IWRAW) USA AND COMMONWEALTH SECRETARIAT, WOMEN'S AND YOUTH AFFAIRS DIVISION (prepared by JANE CONNORS, ANDREW BYRNES, & CHALOKA BEYANI), ASSESSING THE STATUS OF WOMEN: A GUIDE TO REPORTING UNDER THE CONVENTION ON THE ELIMINATION OF ALL FORMS OF DISCRIMINATION AGAINST WOMEN (2nd ed. 1996) [hereinafter IWRAW]; Catherine Tinker, *Human Rights for Women: The Convention on the Elimination of All Forms of Discrimination Against Women,* 3 HUM. RTS. Q. 31 (1981); Shelley Wright, *Human Rights and Women's Rights: An Analysis of the United Nations Convention on the Elimination of All Forms of Discrimination Against Women, in* HUMAN RIGHTS IN THE TWENTY-FIRST CENTURY: A GLOBAL CHALLENGE 75 (Kathleen Mahoney & Paul Mahoney eds., 1993).

156. There are other relevant provisions in the Women's Convention that will not be discussed here. One example is article 16, which requires states parties to take all appropriate measures to eliminate discrimination in all matters relating to marriage. In particular, states parties are required to ensure equality in the right to freely choose a spouse and to enter into marriage only with free and full consent, and the right to decide the number and spacing of children. Moreover, article 16(2) of the Women's Convention specifically requires a state party to institute a minimum age for marriage and to nullify betrothals and marriages of children.

157. IWRAW, *supra* note 155, at 19.

158. CEDAW was established by article 17 of the Women's Convention to consider "progress made in the implementation" of the Women's Convention.

task, CEDAW has elaborated slightly on the meaning of this article in its General Recommendation No. 19 on Violence Against Women.[159] In that General Recommendation, CEDAW has noted that poverty, unemployment, wars, armed conflicts, and the occupation of territories have led to increased opportunities for trafficking in women. In addition, CEDAW has recognized that there are new forms of trafficking, such as the "recruitment of domestic labour from developing countries to work in developed countries, and organised marriages between women from developing countries and foreign nationals." Finally, CEDAW reaffirmed that these practices are incompatible with the equal enjoyment of rights by women and with the respect for their rights and dignity.

As of the sixteenth session of CEDAW, there were 154 signatories to the Women's Convention.[160] Under article 18, states parties must submit country reports to CEDAW on the legislative, judicial, administrative, or other measures adopted to give effect to this convention. Reports are due within a year after entry into force for the state concerned and at least every four years thereafter or whenever CEDAW so requests.[161] During these sessions, CEDAW members question reporting states on the contents of their country reports and formulate "Concluding Comments" at the end of each session on each country report presented. Such comments include recommendations and suggestions, which are to be acted upon and then reported on in that country's next country report.

CEDAW's enforcement powers are limited. Up until January 1997, CEDAW could only meet annually for two weeks. Now, CEDAW is allotted two three-week sessions per year. CEDAW cannot demand reports, or impose sanctions on countries that do not submit reports or submit reports so late as to be of limited utility for CEDAW to properly formulate questions and assess the situation for women in that particular country. The Committee's concluding comments are submitted to the General Assembly; however, CEDAW cannot demand specific action by states.[162]

One promising development related to the Women's Convention is the proposed Optional Protocol. The discussion of such a mechanism is currently before members of the United Nations. If adopted, the Optional Protocol would potentially allow individuals to bring complaints about human rights violations before CEDAW. Moreover, if an inquiry procedure is established under such Optional Protocol, CEDAW would be granted the power to make investigations into complaints of women's human rights violations. The outcome of any successful complaint or

---

159. General Recommendation No. 19, U.N. Document A/47/38. In addition, in its General Recommendation No. 12, the Committee recommends that states parties include information specific to violations against women, including legislation, other measures, support services, and statistical data. U.N. Doc. A/44/38.

160. United Nations Department of Public Information, Women's Anti-Discrimination Committee to hold its sixteenth Session in New York from Jan. 13–31, 1997 (Dec. 1996).

161. Women's Convention, art. 18(1)(b).

162. Reanda, *supra* note 145, at 219.

inquiry could potentially be as meaningful as an individual remedy or a systemic recommendation, both of which would be binding upon states parties.

One of the potential sources of international law are the regional human rights instruments. At present, the relevant ones are the European Convention on Human Rights,[163] the American Convention on Human Rights,[164] the African Charter on Human and Peoples' Rights,[165] and the Inter-American Convention on the Prevention, Punishment and Eradication of Violence Against Women (Convention Against Violence).[166] The focus here will be on the Convention Against Violence.[167] The purpose of the Convention Against Violence is to prevent, punish, and eradicate all forms of violence against women. It defines violence against women as "any act or conduct, based on gender, which causes death or physical, sexual or psychological harm or suffering to women, whether in the public or private sphere."[168] Such violence is understood to fall into three categories: violence occurring in the family or domestic unit, violence occurring in the community, and violence that is perpetrated or condoned by the state or its agents.[169] Trafficking in women and forced prostitution are explicitly recognized as violence against women occurring in the community.[170] However, as with the other existing conventions relevant to the protection of women's rights, the Convention Against Violence does not adequately define trafficking or outline specific state actions that would trigger the Conventions protections.

There are three aspects to the enforcement mechanism of the Convention Against Violence. First, there is an obligation on states parties to include information in their national reports to the Inter-American Commission of Women on: (i) measures adopted to prevent and prohibit violence against women; (ii) measures adopted to assist women affected by violence; (iii) any difficulties states have observed in applying those measures; and (iv) factors that contribute to violence against women.[171] Second, states parties to the Convention Against Violence and the Inter-American Commission of Women may request advisory opinions on the

---

163. European Convention for the Protection of Human Rights and Fundamental Freedoms, 213 U.N.T.S. 221, *signed* in Rome on 4 November 1950, *entered into force* on 3 September 1953.

164. American Convention on Human Rights, 9 I.L.M. 673 (1970), *signed* on 22 November 1969.

165. African Charter on Human and Peoples' Rights, *adopted by* the 18th Assembly of the Heads of State and Government of the Organization of African Unity, Nairobi, Kenya, June 27, 1981.

166. Inter-American Convention on the Prevention, Punishment and Eradication of Violence Against Women, *adopted by acclamation by the twenty-fourth regular session of the General Assembly of the Organization of American States, 9 June 1994.*

167. More detailed examinations of the general protection of women's human rights can be found in other parts of this work. The discussion here on the Convention Against Violence will accordingly be brief.

168. Convention Against Violence, *supra* note 166, art. 1.

169. *Id.* art. 2.

170. *Id.*

171. *Id* art. 10.

interpretation of the convention from the Inter-American Court of Human Rights.[172] Third, there is a complaints procedure that provides ''any person or group of persons, or any non-governmental entity legally recognized in one of more member states of the Organization'' with recourse to lodge a petition with the Inter-American Commission on Human Rights. Any such petitions must be based upon a violation of article 7 of the Convention Against Violence.[173] Article 7 outlines the duties that states parties are obligated to undertake, which include refraining from engaging in any act or practice of violence against women, ensuring that their authorities and agents act in conformity with this obligation, being duly diligent in preventing, investigating, and imposing penalties for violence against women, and establishing fair and effective legal procedures for women who have been subjected to violence.[174] While the enforcement provisions of this convention grant the widest range of remedies, it is still too early to assess its overall effectiveness in addressing the issue of trafficking in women.

Finally, there is the Convention on the Rights of the Child[175] (Children's Convention), which deals directly with trafficking in girl-children. Generally, this convention will apply to any individual under the age of 18, unless majority is attained at an earlier age under domestic laws.[176] There are a number of provisions relevant to the issue of trafficking in girls. In particular, states parties have an obligation to take measures to combat the illicit transfer and non-return of children abroad;[177] to take all appropriate measures to protect children from all forms of physical or mental violence, injury or abuse, neglect or negligent treatment, maltreatment or exploitation, including sexual abuse, while in the care of parent(s), legal guardian(s), or any other person who has care of the child;[178] to protect children from economic exploitation;[179] to protect children from all forms of sexual exploitation and sexual abuse;[180] to take all appropriate measures to prevent the abduction of, the sale of, or traffic in children for any purpose or in any form;[181] and to take all appropriate measures to promote the physical and psychological recovery and social reintegration of a child victim of any form of exploitation, abuse, torture, or any other form of cruel, inhuman, or degrading treatment or punishment.[182] In addition, the

---

172. *Id.* art. 11.

173. *Id.* art. 12.

174. *Id.* art. 7.

175. Convention on the Rights of the Child, U.N. Doc. A/RES/44/25, *entered into force* Sept. 2, 1990.

176. Children's Convention, *supra* note 175, art. 1.

177. *Id.* art. 11.

178. *Id.* art. 19.

179. *Id.* art. 32.

180. *Id.* art. 34.

181. *Id.* art. 35.

182. *Id.* art. 39.

Children's Convention provides for the right to health;[183] the obligation of a state party to ensure that a child is not separated from his or her parents against their will except in cases where it is determined that such separation is necessary for the best interests of the child;[184] the right, where a child resides in a different state from his or her parent, to leave and enter any country;[185] and the obligation of a state party to protect children from the illicit use of narcotic drugs and psychotropic substances.[186]

Enforcement of the obligations set out in the Children's Convention is mainly conducted through a reporting mechanism, similar to that for the Women's Convention. In the case of the Children's Convention, states parties report to the Committee on the Rights of the Child (CRC). A state party must present a report within two years of entry into force of the convention for that state party and every five years thereafter. The Children's Convention broadens the possible scope of international cooperation on this convention. The specialized agencies, particularly the United Nations Children's Fund and other United Nations organs, may be represented at the consideration of the implementation of provisions of the Children's Convention that fall within these organizations' mandates, or they may submit reports on such implementation. In addition, the CRC may invite these organizations or any other competent body to provide expert advice on the implementation of the Children's Convention.[187] Furthermore, the CRC may make a recommendation to the General Assembly to request the Secretary-General to undertake studies on specific issues relating to the rights of the child.[188]

International legal obligations related to issues arising from trafficking in women and girls are not limited to these treaties. For example, the Slavery Convention[189] and the Supplementary Convention on the Abolition of Slavery, the Slave Trade, and Institutions and Practices Similar to Slavery[190] (collectively, the Slavery Convention), have provisions that are relevant to slavery, debt bondage, and forced marriage. Under the Slavery Convention, states parties undertake to prevent and suppress the slave trade and to bring about, progressively and as soon as possible, the complete abolition of slavery in all its forms.[191] In addition, states parties are obliged to "take all practicable and necessary legislative and other measures to

---

183. *Id.* art. 24.

184. *Id.* art. 9.

185. *Id.* art. 10(2).

186. *Id.* art. 33.

187. *Id.* art. 45.

188. *Id.* art. 45(c).

189. Slavery Convention, 212 U.N.T.S. 17, *entered into force* Mar. 9, 1927, *amended* convention *entered into force on* Jul. 7, 1955.

190. Supplementary Convention on the Abolition of Slavery, the Slavery Trade, and Institutions and Practices Similar to Slavery, 266 U.N.T.S. 40, *entered into force* Apr. 30, 1957.

191. Art. 2 of the Slavery Convention.

bring about progressively and as soon as possible the complete abolition or the abandonment of the following institutions and practices,'' including:

(a) Debt bondage . . .

(c) Any institution or practice whereby:

    (i)   A woman, without the right to refuse, is promised or given in marriage on payment of a consideration in money or in kind to her parents, guardian, family or any other person or group; or

    (ii) The husband of a woman, his family, or his clan, has the right to transfer her to another person for value received or otherwise; or . . .

(d) Any institution or practice whereby a child or young person under the age of 18 years, is delivered by his [or her] natural parents or by his [or her] guardian to another person, whether for reward or not, with a view to the exploitation of the child or young person of his [or her] labour.[192]

Other treaties, such as the International Covenant on Civil and Political Rights, the International Covenant on Economic, Social and Cultural Rights, regional human rights instruments, and the Forced Labor Conventions (Nos. 29 and 105) adopted by the International Labor Organization,[193] are also relevant. As noted above, international law obligations may also stem from customary international law. Strong arguments can be made that the prohibition against slavery is recognized as *jus cogens*, as well as a human rights norm under customary international law. Similar arguments can be formulated with respect to the rights of children.

Other International Mechanisms

There are also international mechanisms that can address the issue of trafficking in women. Only two will be discussed here. First, there is the Working Group on Contemporary Forms of Slavery (Working Group).[194] It has provided a more effective way of addressing the issue of trafficking in women than have some of the treaty-bodies discussed above. It was set up by the United Nations Economic and Social Council as a working group that sits under the Sub-Commission on Prevention of Discrimination and Protection of Minorities (Sub-Commission), which, in turn, sits under the Commission on Human Rights (Commission). It is composed of five expert members of the Sub-Commission and sits annually for five days.[195] The Working Group was established with the threefold mandate to review developments in the areas covered by the Slavery and Trafficking Conventions, to consider

---

192. Art. 1 of the Supplementary Convention.

193. Convention (No. 29) Concerning Forced Labour, *adopted* on Jun. 28, 1930, by the General Conference of the International Labour Organization, *entered into force* May 1, 1932, and Convention (No. 105) concerning the Abolition of Forced Labour, *adopted* on Jun. 25, 1957, by the General Conference of the International Labour Organization, *entered into force,* Jan. 17, 1959.

194. For a general discussion on the Working Group, *see* Lassen, *supra* note 145; Reanda, *supra* note 145, at 213–16.

195. Reanda, *supra* note 145, at 213.

and examine information received from credible sources, and to make recommendations to the Economic and Social Council (through the Sub-Commission and the Commission) for action.[196] However, it is well recognized that this Working Group is not a mechanism to monitor compliance with these two conventions.

In spite of its limited mandate, the Working Group has in many ways acted as a quasi treaty-monitoring body. Moreover, the work accomplished by this Working Group has been highly regarded. As one commentator has noted:

> [T]he Working Group has approached its mandate rather boldly and imaginatively. . . . Its success is due in part to its relationship with NGOs and providing them with a forum for the submission and review of information on specific situations. Through its flexibility, the group has been able not only to act as a kind of fact-finding mechanism, but also to identify and address practices not covered by the Conventions and which would not otherwise be dealt with by the international system. It is now established practice for government representatives to participate in meetings of the group at which NGO country-specific reports are considered and to respond to the information given.[197]

The Working Group's ability to operate flexibly addresses the limits of the Trafficking Convention and provides an international forum for the discussion and investigation of contemporary forms of trafficking in women. The NGO relationship that has developed is critical to making progress on eradicating trafficking in women, as the Working Group and other U.N. bodies are generally limited in the resources and information available to them. Written and oral submissions from NGOs provide the Working Group with much needed information and data. Moreover, the practice now established by the Working Group engages governments, which are otherwise not required by existing international law to cooperate with the Working Group, in the issues around trafficking in persons and brings them together in a cooperative relationship with NGOs.

Second, the mechanism of the Special Rapporteur on Violence Against Women, Its Causes and Consequences (Special Rapporteur) warrants mention. The Special Rapporteur on Violence Against Women was created in 1993 as a result of the lobbying of women's groups at the Vienna Conference on Human Rights. The Special Rapporteur, Ms. Radhika Coomaraswamy, was given a three-year mandate (subsequently extended three more years), which includes (i) setting out elements of the problems, the international legal standards and a general survey of incidents and issues as they relate to many problem areas, and (ii) identifying and investigating factual situations, as well as allegations that may be forwarded to the Special Rapporteur by concerned parties.[198]

The Special Rapporteur fulfills her mandate in four main ways:[199]

---

196. ECOSOC decision 16 (LVI) of May 17, 1974.

197. Reanda, *supra* note 145, at 214.

198. Preliminary Report Submitted by the Special Rapporteur on Violence Against Women, Its Causes and Consequences, Nov. 22, 1994, U.N. Document E/CN.4/1995/42.

199. *See* the United Nations High Commission for Human Rights website from which most of this information was taken, at http://www.unhchr.ch/html/menu2/7/b/women/a__main.htm.

1. *Communications:* The Special Rapporteur has prepared a standard form for reporting alleged cases of gender-based violence against women. She has established procedures to seek clarification and information from governments on specific cases of alleged violence (based on these communications) in order to identify and investigate specific situations and allegations of violence against women. The Special Rapporteur may also request that governments take further steps, such as investigation, prosecution, imposition of sanctions, or provision of redress for issues of a general nature with the view to preventing the recurrence of certain violations of women's human rights.

2. *Urgent Action Communications:* Communications involving situations of imminent threat or fear of threat to the right to life of the person may be sent to the Special Rapporteur. Based on such communications, the Special Rapporteur may urge the relevant national authorities to (i) provide full information on the case alleged; (ii) conduct an independent and impartial investigation; and (iii) take immediate action to ensure no further violations of the human rights of women are committed.

3. *Field Missions:* The Special Rapporteur conducts fact-finding missions to specific countries at the invitation of governments. The objective of such missions is to obtain first-hand information on the situation of violence against women in a particular country, through meetings with both government and nongovernment representatives. During any visit, the Special Rapporteur will focus on a specific theme or aspect of violence against women.

4. *Reports to the Commission on Human Rights:* On an annual basis, the Special Rapporteur reports to the Commission. This annual report covers communications sent to the governments by the Special Rapporteur, the replies received by her, and the state of violence against women globally.

The Special Rapporteur has already touched upon the issue of trafficking in women in her Preliminary Report, noting that trafficked women and prostitutes are subject to economic exploitation, enormous legal and moral isolation, custodial rape and abuse, health hazards, and violence.[200] In addition, the Special Rapporteur conducted a fact-finding mission to Poland in mid-1996, and has provided an overview of the issue of trafficking in women internationally in her report on violence against women in the community, which was distributed in February 1997.[201] Both of the Special Rapporteur's aforementioned reports provide factual background on trafficking in women, identify relevant national and international laws, discuss strategies and initiatives currently in place to combat and prevent trafficking in women, and finally, provide recommendations for action at both the international

---

200. Prelininary Report, *supra* note 198, at paras. 205–19.

201. There is an international report project to assist the Special Rapporteur, undertaken by Global Alliance Against Trafficking in Women (GAATW) and coordinated by the Foundation Against Trafficking in Women (STV).

and national levels. As discussed above, the reports of the Special Rapporteur are submitted to the Commission and, ultimately, to the Economic and Social Council.

ISSUES AND RECOMMENDATIONS

As the discussion above illustrates, there are serious and complicated issues that arise from trafficking in women. The focus in this section will return to the issue of the definition of trafficking in women, as the definition will determine the scope and success or failure of any concerted international action on preventing, combating, and eradicating trafficking in women and in punishing the traffickers and other persons or states who, through their acts or omissions, are responsible for trafficking in women and girls.

It is perhaps at this point in time, when the issue of trafficking in women is gaining international attention, that the articulation of a precise definition of what constitutes trafficking in women is most critical. There needs to be a general consensus on an international definition that can be applied clearly and consistently. The necessity for a consistent and rigorous approach is not motivated by academic reasons; rather, it is required for very practical considerations. First, recognition as a survivor of trafficking is critical for many women because it is their only source of legal protection. As described above, many women are trafficked into forced prostitution. As prostitutes, they are vulnerable to arrest and mistreatment if prostitution is illegal in the receiving country or in their home country (when and if they return there). Moreover, many of these women are trafficked across national borders and have illegal status in the receiving country. As such, they are susceptible to arrest and deportation. Women trafficked into forced marriages are confronted with the same problem that survivors of domestic violence face—the lack of recognition for the abuses against them arising from the perception of authorities (and often the broader community) that issues related to marriage are ''private matters'' to be resolved without outside interference. Also, for women and girls trafficked ''in their best interest'' into forced marriages, being recognized as a victim of trafficking will provide a potential source of protection where such women are trafficked to countries where a ''husband's'' consent is required by domestic law in order to leave the country to which they were trafficked.

Second, a clear and unambiguous definition of trafficking in women is needed in order to begin to clarify state obligations under international human rights law. Until then, it is unrealistic to expect to hold states legally responsible for trafficking in women. We already see the results of the lack of a definition of trafficking in women from the experiences of this century. The potentially conflicting approaches to addressing the issues around trafficking in women and prostitution have had a significant impact on the ratification of the Trafficking Convention.[202] There are

---

202. There are three basic models of prostitution policies: regulation, abolition, and prohibition. Simply put, in a regulation system, prostitutes can be officially registered but brothels cannot. Under such a model, registration and medical checks are compulsory. Under an abolition system, it is not prostitution that is abolished but control of prostitution by public authorities that is prohibited. Thus, it is the exploitation of prostitutes by third parties and public soliciting that should be forbidden and punished.

only 71 signatories to the Trafficking Convention, a low figure for an international human rights treaty. Even if the number of signatories increased, universal ratification will never be achieved based on the Trafficking Convention as currently worded. One obstacle to universal ratification is article 6, which prohibits any regulation or supervision of prostitution. For some states, such as Australia, this requirement conflicts with domestic laws that legalize and regulate prostitution.[203] In its reply to the Secretary-General, the government of Australia articulated its position on the Trafficking Convention:

> On the suppression of the traffic in persons and of the exploitation of the prostitution of others, although this Convention does not require that acts of prostitution be criminalized, several of its provisions have the indirect effect of making the practice of prostitution illegal. Such provisions run counter to the legislation in some States and territories. In its views, these provisions also blur the distinction between voluntary and coerced prostitution. To consider voluntary sex work and coercive prostitution as the same issue, and therefore demand the outlaw of prostitution per se, is to view prostitution as a moral issue and to consider sex workers as people unable to make informed decisions on their life. Such a view is paternalistic and raises serious human rights implications. Further, criminalization of the voluntary sex industry fosters conditions of violence against women sex workers. It facilitates the underground sex industry, leaving women with little or no legal redress for abuse experienced during work and militates against such workers seeking police intervention in abusive situations. In terms of industrial matters, criminalization of voluntary prostitution also creates the conditions for women to be exploited in terms of pay and conditions by employers as industrial regulation is prohibited. This is particularly critical in relation to occupational health and safety laws, particularly given the danger of sexually transmitted diseases.[204]

For other states, such as Germany, the confusion in the relationship between trafficking in women and prostitution has led to the position that no ratification of the Trafficking Convention is required because their existing legislation is sufficient to protect women from being forced into prostitution or from being exploited as prostitutes.[205]

Even when ratification is not an issue, the lack of a definition of trafficking in women has clearly impacted on what actions a state feels obliged to take to fulfill its international obligations. For example, while the Women's Convention does not, on its face, pose the same conflicts with domestic prostitution legislation and policies, the undefined terminology has lead to a vague understanding of the nature of state obligations under article 6.[206] Thus, it remains unclear what constitutes

---

Finally, in a prohibition system, prostitution itself is criminalized along with all exploitation of prostitutes.

203. It is precisely for this reason that the Netherlands has refused to ratify the Trafficking Convention. Altink, *supra* note 4, at 157.

204. Traffic in Women, *supra* note 9, at para. 26.

205. OHSE, *supra* note 144, at 5.

206. This was recognized in the Secretary-General's report, Traffic in Women and Girls, U.N. Doc. UN/9/50/369, para. 23.

trafficking in women and what constitutes the exploitation of prostitutes. In addition, it remains ambiguous whether any measures that punish the victims of trafficking through imprisonment, fines, and other means are inappropriate measures under this provision.[207] The lack of clarity has lead to vagueness in country reports submitted to CEDAW. As the Secretary-General has noted:

> During the period 1991–1996, 63 periodic reports were submitted by 58 States. Of the 63 reports, 80 per cent provided information on elements of article 6. However, slightly less than half of the reports mentioned trafficking at all and less than a quarter provided information on measures taken to address trafficking. A larger number of reports mentioned prostitution without reference to trafficking.[208]

If, as evidenced by the record of reports submitted by states parties under the Women's Convention, very few states even recognize trafficking as an issue in their jurisdictions, then most probably very little, if any, action is being taken to address this practice.

While the intimate connection between trafficking and prostitution is critical, it is often blurred by the debate on whether entering the prostitution trade can truly be voluntary. The emphasis on that debate has hindered the quest to find a clear definition of trafficking and, in turn, an effective policy. As Brussa notes:

> The problem of definition is still with us, due not only to ideological differences and differences of opinion and culture, but also to different policies on prostitution. Until a standard international definition is agreed on, active intervention policies will inevitably be limited.[209]

As a practical issue, it is difficult to separate trafficking from domestic prostitution.[210] Those charged with enforcing anti-trafficking laws are often unclear as to how to differentiate prostitutes who have been trafficked from those who have not.[211] Authorities often do not question how a woman has ended up in prostitution. As a matter of course, authorities subject trafficked women to any prostitution laws and treat trafficked women poorly. One commentator has noted:

---

207. Toepfer and Wells argue: "because trafficking is a crime which violates women's equality rights, legislation designed to 'suppress' trafficking must end [the trafficking], and not simply reshape, sex trafficking. Also any measures which punish the victims of trafficking . . . are inappropriate remedies under the Convention." Toepfer & Wells, *supra* note 145, at 102.

208. Traffic in Women, *supra* note 9, at para. 30.

209. BRUSSA, *supra* note 38, at 17.

210. This was noted as early as 1927 in a report conducted by the League of Nations. Report of the Special Body of Experts on Traffic in Women and Children, League of Nations Docs. C.52.M.52.1927.IV (1927) and C.52(2)M.52(1)1927.IV (1927).

211. Indeed, one police officer assigned to finding victims of traffickers admits that he still grapples with a definition of what precisely "trafficking in women" means: "They have no grip on how many women are subjected to 'a high degree of coercion, financial dependence or deception', as [the police officer] defines trafficking. 'I wasn't there when deals were made in Warsaw or Manila.'" Guido de Bruin, *Netherlands: Trafficking in Women Shifts to Eastern Europe,* INTER PRESS SERVICE, June 2, 1992, *available in* LEXIS, Nexis Library, News File, Curnws.

[I]n those countries where prostitution is legal, abuses surrounding prostitution are difficult to document because legalization has created an atmosphere that sanctions prostitution and ignores any problems associated with prostitution.[212]

These problems are further compounded by the fact that many who are charged with enforcing prostitution policies, "see the abuse but accept sexual exploitation and violence as normal for those engaging in prostitution."[213]

Any international definition of trafficking in women must focus on the trafficking process and not solely on the manifestations of trafficking in women typically seen in the media, i.e., the stories of young girls being sold to brothels at a very tender age and forced to service 10–30 men per day. A focus on the process is critical for two main reasons. As a preventive measure, national and international legislation and action should be directed at the process of trafficking. Unless and until the acts involved in the process of trafficking in women are identified, it will continue unabated. The preventive approach is particularly compelling when one looks at the problems that arise if one waits until trafficking manifests itself in the form of forced prostitution or forced marriage. By this time, the woman has endured severe human rights abuses. Moreover, as the factual discussion illustrates, once trafficked for a long period of time, it becomes increasingly difficult for women to extricate themselves from the sex trade because it becomes their primary source of income for survival, or, in the case of those trafficked into forced marriages, it becomes increasingly difficult to leave as they usually bear children who are not allowed to leave with them.

While the definition provided in the first section is the best existing definition, it is by no means perfect. This chapter has adopted a reading of the definition that requires three essential elements to establish trafficking in women: (i) recruitment and/or transportation of a woman; (ii) for work or services; (iii) through the use of coercion. However, certain issues require further consideration and clarification.

Closer examination of the word "recruitment" raises the question of whether or not there is an element of transportation in the phrase "obtaining women." If so, is transportation in fact a distinct and essential component of trafficking in women? Would it be more precise to limit the definition to "all acts of recruitment" and include acts of transportation in the definition of recruitment? If not, on what basis do we then distinguish between obtaining women through abduction and transporting women? Moreover, to ensure there is a precise definition encapsulating the activity intended to be captured, it is necessary to decide when the process of trafficking in women ends. So, for example, if trafficking in women is defined as "all acts in the recruitment and/or transportation," does trafficking then end once she is no longer being recruited or transported? That will depend on how recruitment and transportation are defined. But based on the facts, it appears that trafficking does not clearly end once a woman is no longer being recruited or transported,

---

212. FEMALE SEXUAL SLAVERY, *supra* note 4, at 65.

213. *Id.* at 7.

because trafficked women are subject to the possibility of being transported (and resold) to another brothel or wife-purchaser at random points in time, at times even years from when she was initially sold. Are they to be considered trafficked only at that time? What happens in between the initial recruitment and/or transportation and the next incident? One possible approach is to state that a woman retains the status of a trafficked woman until the coercion is lifted. Contemplation of the merits of this approach should include consideration of cases where a woman trafficked into prostitution has resigned herself to her fate and there is no visible coercion, yet she is resold to another brothel at a later date.

Obviously, the definition of what constitutes coercion will determine what activity is covered. However, as discussed briefly *supra*, the definition of coercion remains unarticulated. What is to be included in "other forms of coercion"? How broadly should coercion be defined? Is deception, in fact, meant to be included as a form of coercion? While deception is certainly one of the methods through which traffickers lure women, recruitment of women for the purposes of work or services by means of deception also captures situations that do not involve sexual trafficking in women, but involve solely unfair employment practices. On the other hand, deception for the purposes of trafficking in women should be captured by any definition established because waiting until "coercion" is used is too late for many women. One possibility is to analogize to the drug trafficking situation and criminalize recruitment (which would include deception as one of the acts) for the purposes of trafficking.

However, if coercion is limited to the visible forms of coercion, the resale of trafficked women must be considered. Intuitively, it would seem that the resale of a woman should be characterized as trafficking.[214] Whatever an international definition of trafficking in women may state with respect to the issue of coercion, a fair amount of discretion will likely be left to domestic laws with respect to how coercion (or the lack of consent) will be recognized and/or measured. Given how poorly many domestic courts deal with the issue of consent in rape cases,[215] care should be taken to structure an international definition of trafficking in women to avoid, to the extent possible, problems that arise when proving coercion or the lack of consent in trafficking in women.

Articulating a clear definition is not merely an exercise in finding the right words. As illustrated in the discussion on the problems that have resulted as a consequence of a lack of a definition of trafficking in women, some accommodations to the various existing policies on prostitution must be made. The definition set out

---

214. On a related issue, the criminal responsibility of the client of a trafficked woman should be clarified. An analogy to the drug trafficking situation suggests that a consumer of a trafficked product is not necessarily a trafficker. As a general rule, this seems to be appropriate except in situations where a client also undertakes activities involving the actual recruitment, transportation, sale, or other acts such as the "breaking in" of a girl. One clear situation is where men purchase wives from traffickers or purchase wives from families directly. Such activity would seem to clearly fall under any definition of trafficking.

215. Community Violence Report, *supra* note 6, at 7.

previously does not require states to adopt any particular policy on prostitution. However, as in the case of article 6 of the Women's Convention, even if there is no obvious conflict between trafficking and prostitution policies, states are not necessarily clear themselves on what the relationship is between these two issues. This potentially leads to a situation where states will not be held legally responsible because there is no clear international legal standard against which their actions can be measured.

Similarly, the differences, if any, between trafficking in women and other related concerns must be contemplated. For example, many Filipino women are lured into marriages with men abroad through mail-order bride agencies. Some mail-order bride agencies are mere fronts for trafficking networks. Such agencies are used only as a lure to attract women who will be forced into prostitution, marriage, or labor. However, there are other situations where women sign up with agencies and their photos and background information are forwarded to prospective "grooms." A client pays a fee and can arrange to meet a woman, oftentimes by having her flown to his country. If the client does not like the woman, he can send her back to the agency. To be "sent back" does not necessarily mean that she is physically sent back to her home country. Rather, she is often abandoned in the country she traveled to, without any money for survival, the flight home, or a work permit. It is at this point that she is often forced or lured into prostitution or domestic slavery.[216] Given this set of facts, mail-order bride services in and of themselves are not necessarily engaging in trafficking in women as these women may have voluntarily, without coercion, signed up to participate in such services and the clients are ostensibly prospective husbands, which these women are seeking. Thus, considerable analysis must be undertaken in determining to which of these various circumstances legal responsibility for trafficking in women should be attributed.

Another issue requiring further thought is arranged marriages that do not involve any overt coercion. The examples raised previously clearly include overt coercion in the form of physical detention, violence, and threats of violence. An example of a less clear situation is an arranged marriage flowing from omiai (arranged meetings for the purposes of marriage) in Japan. Thirty percent of all Japanese marriages are formed in this manner.[217] In these cases, families involve a matchmaker who finds a "suitable" match for the woman. While there may be some family and community pressure, there is no overt physical coercion or threat of physical coercion or even overt psychological pressure.[218] As contrary to the notion of equality

---

216. David Jones, *Filipino Women Said to be Forced into European Prostitution,* REUTERS, May 22, 1987, LEXIS, Nexis Library News. This situation is not limited to Filipino women. Latin American women and East European women also commonly find themselves in this situation. *See* Nakanishi, *supra* note 92.

217. SUSAN ORPETT LONG, FAMILY CHANGE AND THE LIFE COURSE IN JAPAN 43–44 (1987).

218. A similar case occurred in India where a woman had written to the Supreme Court Chief Justice complaining that her father and brothers were forcing her to marry a police constable. The Delhi High Court took up the letter as a petition and ordered her brother not to force his sister into marriage. See *Indian Court Rescues Woman from Forced Marriage,* REUTERS, Feb. 14, 1996, *available in* LEXIS, Nexis Library, World File, Allnws.

as any form of arranged marriage may be to some, a distinction could arguably be made between these marriages and trafficking in women.

Numerous causes of trafficking in women have been proposed, such as the presence of military bases, sex industry multinationals, and sex tourism. The definition of trafficking must be revisited to ensure that the appropriate activity is captured, keeping in mind that using the services of a trafficked woman does not necessarily constitute trafficking in women. Similarly, creating a market for the sex trade may not necessarily constitute trafficking in women. Consider the analogy to jurisdictions where prostitution is legalized. While such legalization may create a market for women who are trafficked, all forms of prostitution would not likely be captured within trafficking in women.

There are a few practical considerations to take into account when determining the definition of trafficking, the limits of coercion, or other definitional issues in international law. As decision-making in international fora is achieved through consensus, the broader the definition, the less likely it is that consensus will be reached. Whether economic coercion alone could or should constitute trafficking is among the most contested issues. Even if consensus is reached on a broad definition of coercion, there will be less political will to ratify or enforce any treaty containing a broad definition. States, for the most part, will voice the sentiment that they will only ratify treaties that they can fulfill in good faith. Moreover, if cultural practices are defined as a source of coercion, states implicated in those cultural practices will present resistance to such a definition. However, as a practical matter, a very narrow definition should be avoided. Once an international legal definition is established and agreed upon, it will be extremely difficult to change it to adapt to changing circumstances.[219]

A clear definition of trafficking in women is also crucial for proper data collection, documentation, and research. As stated above, information on trafficking in women is currently found under a variety of different subject headings. The variety of ways to categorize trafficking in women reflects the multitude of human rights abuses that occur as a result of trafficking and the numerous strategies that have been adopted to try to address the problems that arise. However, this ad hoc characterization of the issue may obscure situations that constitute trafficking in women. For example, conceptualizing trafficking in women as forced prostitution excludes discussion and recognition that trafficking in women also leads to forced marriages. As an evidentiary matter, there are currently no comprehensive statistics on the number of women and girls who are trafficked and from where and to where they are trafficked. One reason for the lack of statistics is that trafficking in women is not reported as a category in crime statistics collected by the U.N. or many countries.[220] The difficulties of addressing the problem without adequate information has

219. For example, consider the 1951 Convention Relating to the Status of Refugees and its definition of ''refugee.'' While many activists feel that the definition needs to be expanded, the fear is that any re-examination of the definition will provide states with an opportunity to narrow the definition.

220. Traffic in Women, *supra* note 9, at para. 15.

been noted by governments.[221] Certainly, the lack of a clear, authoritative definition is a preliminary obstacle to collecting such statistics.

By working from an authoritative definition, more in-depth research on trafficking in women and its causes and consequences can be conducted. As noted above, there is still scant information on the daily lives of women trafficked into forced marriage. Even where it appears that there is an abundance of information, as in some of the cases involving trafficking leading to forced prostitution, the vast majority of cases remain invisible. In order to consider what forms of coercion are involved in trafficking in women and what types of evidence will be available to demonstrate such coercion in domestic or international courts, more detailed information is required. Moreover, a significant portion of information on trafficking in women is found in sources such as newspapers and magazines, sources which are limited by the nature of the medium in terms of the amount of information that can be provided. Reliable information must be collected to establish the factual record upon which to base any claim of human rights violations arising from trafficking in women. Even with an internationally accepted definition of trafficking in women, the underreporting of violence faced by women who have been trafficked will have to be addressed. The Special Rapporteur has noted the following as some of the obstacles to reporting the violations faced by trafficked women: lack of legal literacy and of confidence in the legal system, fear of arrest or legal sanctions, the need to maintain financial support for their families, outstanding debts, fear of reprisals by the trafficking network and of deportation, and language barriers.

Undeniably, the fundamental root cause of trafficking in women lies in the unequal status of women in society, which makes women vulnerable to such practices. Women's fundamental inequality is rooted in an intricate, complex web of historical, economic, biological, social, and cultural reasons (to name a few). Consequently, there is no one strategy or even set of strategies that will eradicate trafficking in women in the near future. There are resources that have set out recommendations for international action on trafficking in women that should be accessed before designing any new internationally based strategies. Some of the best sources include the reports of the Special Rapporteur, the Working Group on Slavery, the Secretary-General Reports to the General Assembly on the Traffic of Women and Girls, and the Beijing Platform for Action. Particular attention should be paid to the developments in the Programme of Action for the Prevention of Traffic in Persons and the Exploitation of the Prostitution of Others, which has already been approved by the Commission on Human Rights.[222] Perhaps the Committee on the Elimination of All Forms of Discrimination Against Women will begin to articulate the state obligations under article 6 of the Women's Convention, either through a General Recommendation on the issue, through established questions to reporting states parties on the issues of trafficking, or both. Since trafficking in women fits into the broader issue of violence against women, which is intimately

---

221. *Id.* at para. 18.

222. U.N. Doc. E/CN.4/Sub.2/1995/28/Add.1.

tied to women's persisting inequality, sources under these categories should be accessed for possible recommendations and strategies.

In the end, the actions undertaken will be determined by the particular resources, skills, and expertise available in conjunction with the goals, objectives, and entry points for intervention that have been identified. However, future work on trafficking in women should be guided by precision and rigor, first by establishing a viable definition of trafficking in women, followed by a consistently uncompromising application.

Section IV

Common Human Rights
Issues Affecting Women

WOMEN AND EMPLOYMENT

Valerie L. Oosterveld

Traditionally, women's social and economic rights have been articulated through labor- and employment-related rights.[1] It is therefore important to examine how women's employment rights have been articulated in international law, as well as whether these rights are being respected or implemented at the national level. International labor standards relating to women are mainly found in the conventions and recommendations formulated by the International Labor Organization, discussed *infra*. However, important rights are also located in other documents, such as the Convention on the Elimination of All Forms of Discrimination Against Women (the "Women's Convention"), and in the General Recommendations of the Committee to that Convention, referred to as the "CEDAW Committee." The labor standards set out in these documents tend to either fall within the "protective" realm or follow the nondiscrimination norm. The protective standards are often considered to be occupational health and safety related; some have been attacked in recent years as overprotective and antithetical to nondiscrimination legislation. The nondiscrimination standards relate to equal pay for work of equal value and equal access for women to vocational training, employment, and occupational advancement. Maternity rights may be considered to contain both protective and nondiscriminatory elements by acknowledging both women's reproductive capacity and the fact that this reproductive ability should not disadvantage women's equality in the workplace.

Despite the development of women's labor standards internationally, a disturbing trend of labor deregulation has developed in many export-driven economies seeking new investment. This chapter presents three case studies to contrast the reality of working women in these economies with their internationally recognized rights. This divergence between the law and economic reality is nowhere more apparent than in statistics regarding women's employment. Between 1970 and 1990, women's average share in the formal labor force increased significantly in all regions except sub-Saharan Africa, where there was a slight decline, and eastern Asia, where the increase was only one percentage point.[2] Women's share of the

---

1. Rebecca P. Sewall, *Reconstructing Social and Economic Rights in Transitional Economies*, *in* FROM BASIC NEEDS TO BASIC RIGHTS 155, 155 (Margaret A. Schuler ed., 1995).

2. The World's Women 1995: Trends and Statistics, U.N. Doc. ST/ESA/STAT/SER.K/12 109 (1995) [hereinafter "The World's Women"].

labor force now averages 40 percent or more in Europe, North America and Australia, the Caribbean, and eastern, central, and southeastern Asia.[3]

Three trends emerge from these facts. First, this increase in labor force participation is not reflected in wage rates: women's wage rates average approximately 60 to 70 percent of men's rates, although in many countries women earn less than half of what men earn.[4] In addition, women often work longer hours than do men in their formal employment: studies show women working at least two—and often five to ten—hours per week more than do men in 13 countries.[5] Second, unpaid household work dominates women's time in virtually every country, while paid work accounts for the greater proportion of men's work everywhere. This means that, in most countries, women work approximately twice the unpaid time men do—and in some countries, this rises to nine times.[6] Third, the daily time men spend on work and household activities tends to be the same over their working life, while women's working time fluctuates widely and at times is extremely heavy, as a result of combining work, household, and child-care responsibilities.[7]

Besides the differences revealed by the statistics on income and time spent in unpaid housework, women often work in different economic sectors than men do. Labor force distribution surveys show a heavy concentration of women in one particular area, usually the service sector, but in some cases, manufacturing. In the developed regions outside Eastern Europe, and in Latin America and the Caribbean, around 75 percent of women in the labor force are in service industries.[8] In the informal sector, women appear to provide up to 75 percent of services in selected African countries.[9] In southern Asia, 25 percent of women work in the industrial sector, as compared to 14 percent of men.[10] In contrast to the female labor force, the male labor force is more equally distributed between the industrial and service sectors.[11] Even when women comprise the majority of workers in a particular sector, closer study reveals that these jobs tend to be of a more unskilled, lower-paying, and less secure nature than jobs in sectors where men predominate.

Women's work is also undervalued in economic calculations. While the United Nations System of National Accounts has been revised in recent years to include many productive activities usually done by women that had not been counted earlier,

---

3.   *Id.* at 109.

4.   SUSAN BULLOCK, WOMEN AND WORK 29 (1994) citing International Labour Organization General Survey of the Committee of Experts on Equal Remuneration (1986).

5.   The study mainly examined developed countries from 1984–1992. The World's Women, *supra* note 2, at 105.

6.   *Id.* at 106, especially noting Japan for disparity between women and men for hours of unpaid work.

7.   *Id.*

8.   *Id.* at 113.

9.   *Id.* at 117.

10.   *Id.* at 113.

11.   *Id.*

there are some serious concerns about the fact that unpaid housework and certain work in the informal sector is still excluded from accounting. This renders much of women's daily output invisible to government policymakers and statisticians; this omission may seriously harm development projects and planning.

The first section of this chapter will examine the international and regional labor standards currently in place. Using three case studies of women in the export sector, the second section will contrast the labor standards with women's actual working conditions. The economic valuation of women's work is discussed in the third section, followed by conclusions and recommendations for action.

INTERNATIONAL STANDARDS AND THE "RIGHT TO WORK"

The International Labour Organization

The earliest international labor standards directly applicable to women were adopted by the International Labour Organization ("ILO")[12] at its first session in 1919. At that session, the ILO considered Convention No. 3, Maternity Protection ("1919 Maternity Protection Convention"), and Convention No. 4, Night Work (Women) ("1919 Night Work Convention"). The adoption of these two conventions reflected the outlook of the international community at the time with respect to working women: these initial standards were designed to protect and safeguard women's family and social roles, ensure pregnancy protection, and restrict women from employment in certain sectors of production considered incompatible with society's image of women.[13]

The adoption of these two conventions set the tone for the type of labor legislation that has followed: the ILO conventions and recommendations generally either fall within the "protective" realm or address nondiscrimination norms. For the first half of the century, "protective" regulation was more common, especially in matters concerning occupational health and safety. As the equality principle has moved from the periphery to the center of human rights discourse during the last forty years,[14] nondiscriminatory labor laws have grown in importance. This change of focus has led to what Compa describes as an "inherent conflict" between

---

12. The ILO was established in 1919 by the Treaty of Versailles, which followed the end of World War I. The ILO's overriding objective is to promote social justice and contribute to maintaining peace. The ILO is a specialized agency of the United Nations ("U.N.") system. As of January 1, 1996, the ILO had 173 member states. The ILO is responsible for the body of international labor standards made up of conventions and recommendations dealing with human rights, employment policy, conditions of work, industrial relations, occupational health and safety, social security, and other related questions. The ILO is unique in the U.N. system in that its governing bodies are made up not only of representatives of governments, but also of employers' and employees' organizations. Tripartism characterizes all of the decision-making bodies of the ILO: from the introduction to ILOLEX, the ILO CD-ROM Database of International Labour Standards (1997 release).

13. MA. DEL MAR SERNA CALVO, LEGISLATION ON WOMEN'S EMPLOYMENT IN LATIN AMERICA: A COMPARATIVE STUDY 2 (1996).

14. Sara Hossain, *Equality in the Home: Women's Rights and Personal Laws in South Asia, in* HUMAN RIGHTS OF WOMEN: NATIONAL AND INTERNATIONAL PERSPECTIVES 465, 468 (Rebecca J. Cook ed., 1994).

international standards that protect women and standards that promote equality between women and men.[15]

"Protective" ILO Standards

Occupational Health and Safety

Apart from the 1919 Night Work Convention discussed above,[16] the ILO has promulgated several conventions and recommendations with the goal of protecting women workers from unsafe or unhealthy work situations. Some of these standards refer to potentially hazardous chemical compounds. Recommendation No. 4 of 1919 regarding Lead Poisoning (Women and Children) advised states to prohibit women from working in various manufacturing and industrial cleaning jobs that would expose them to high levels of lead, "in view of the danger involved to the function of maternity and to the physical development of children."[17] However, women were permitted to work in processes involving the use of lead compounds, subject to the existence of certain conditions, such as locally applied exhaust ventilation.[18] Convention No. 13 of 1921, White Lead (Painting), prohibited all women from using white lead paint in work of an industrial character.[19] However, only men under eighteen years of age were similarly prohibited.[20]

Later conventions follow a less restrictive route and prohibit pregnant women and nursing mothers, rather than all women, from working with certain substances. The 1971 Benzene Convention, No. 136, states that women "certified as pregnant, and nursing mothers, shall not be employed in work processes involving exposure to benzene or products containing benzene."[21] Similarly, the Chemicals Recommendation of 1990, No. 177, formulated to be applied in conjunction with the 1990 Chemicals Convention, No. 170, states that "[w]omen workers should have the right, in the case of pregnancy or lactation, to alternative work not involving the use of, or exposure to, chemicals hazardous to the health of the unborn or nursing child, where such work is available, and the right to return to their previous jobs at the appropriate time."[22] Radiation Protection Recommendation 114 of 1960 is also less restrictive insofar as it does not create a prohibition. Rather, it recommends that "[i]n view of the special medical problems involved in the employment of

---

15. Lance Compa, *International Labour Standards and Instruments of Recourse for Working Women*, 17 YALE J. INT'L L. 151, 151 (1992).

16. The 1919 Night Work Convention is discussed in more detail *infra* at note 32–52 and accompanying text.

17. Recommendation No. 4 of 1919, Lead Poisoning (Women and Children), para. 1.

18. *Id.* at para. 2.

19. Convention No. 13 of 1921, White Lead (Painting), Article 3(1).

20. *Id.* at Article 3(1).

21. 1971 Benzene Convention, No. 136, Article 11(1).

22. Chemicals Recommendation of 1990, No. 177, para. 25(4).

women of child-bearing age in radiation work[,] every care should be taken to ensure that they are not exposed to high radiation risks."[23]

Other health and safety standards govern the working environment or employment tasks. Convention No. 45 of 1935, Underground Work (Women) (''1935 Underground Work Convention''), prohibited the employment of women[24] in underground work in any mine, regardless of age. This convention was adopted amidst discussion of the arduous nature of underground work and the abuse women often faced in mining employment.[25] Under Convention No. 127 of 1967, Maximum Weight, women must be limited to manually transporting only light loads.[26] The maximum weight of these loads must be ''substantially less than that permitted for adult male workers.''[27] The corresponding 1967 Maximum Weight Recommendation, No. 128, reflects this wording[28] and elaborates on other protective measures for women workers. Paragraph 16 states that, ''as far as possible, adult women workers should not be assigned to regular manual transport of loads.'' Paragraph 17 of the Recommendation addresses limitations for women who are assigned to carry loads: the time spent by a woman on actual lifting and carrying should be reduced, and women should be prohibited from being assigned to jobs which require ''especially arduous'' manual transport of loads. Finally, Paragraph 18 deals with pregnant women: ''No woman should be assigned to manual transport of loads during a pregnancy which has been medically determined or during the ten weeks following confinement if in the opinion of a qualified physician such work is likely to impair her health or that of her child.'' Note that the Maximum Weight Convention has relatively few ratifications (23),[29] compared with over 100 for each of the two main nondiscrimination conventions discussed below.

Another protective recommendation related to the working environment and employment tasks is No. 102, Welfare Facilities, under which rooms for rest should be provided to meet the needs of women workers.[30] Paragraph 16 of the Recommendation states that ''[i]n undertakings where any workers, especially women and young workers, have in the course of their work reasonable opportunities for sitting

---

23. Radiation Protection Recommendation of 1960, No. 114, para. 16.

24. ''National laws or regulations may exempt . . . (a) females holding positions of management who do not perform manual work; (b) females employed in health and welfare services; (c) females who, in the course of their studies, spend a period of training in the underground parts of a mine; and (d) any other females who may occasionally have to enter the underground parts of the mine for the purpose of a non-manual occupation.'' Convention No. 45 of 1935, Underground Work (Women), at Article 3.

25. NICOLAS VALTICOS & GERALDO W. VON POTOBSKY, INTERNATIONAL LABOUR LAW 209 (1995).

26. Convention No. 127 of 1967, Maximum Weight, Article 7(1).

27. *Id.* at Article 7(2).

28. 1967 Maximum Weight Recommendation, No. 128, para. 15.

29. INTERNATIONAL LABOUR ORGANIZATION, LISTS OF RATIFICATIONS BY CONVENTION AND BY COUNTRY (as at 31 December 1993) (with update to June 1, 1994) 169 (1994) [hereinafter ''LISTS OF RATIFICATIONS''].

30. Convention No. 102, Welfare Facilities, para. 19.

without detriment to their work, seats should be provided and maintained for their use." This is separate from Paragraph 17(1), which recommends that "[i]n undertakings where a substantial portion of any work can be properly done seated, seats should be provided and maintained for the workers concerned."

The Shift from Protective Standards: Night and Underground Work

In recent years, these ILO standards of protection have come under attack as too rigid and counter to the developing ILO standards of nondiscrimination, with states either demanding greater flexibility to the protective conventions, or actually denouncing the conventions. In addition, other United Nations agencies have publicized their opinions of the protectionist standards. For example, the World Bank has recently concluded that "women as a group gain much more from better access to modern sector jobs than from special standards" to protect those who already have stable employment.[31]

An example of the shift from prohibitions to flexibility can be found in the history of the Night Work Conventions. The 1919 Night Work Convention prohibited the employment at night of women of any age in any public or private industrial undertaking, including mining, manufacturing, and construction, except in cases of extreme necessity.[32] "Night" was defined as "a period of at least eleven consecutive hours, including the interval between ten o'clock in the evening and five o'clock in the morning."[33] The question of whether the Night Work Convention applied to women in supervisory or management positions was taken to the Permanent Court of International Justice in 1932, and was answered in the affirmative.[34] This decision led to a revision of the Convention in 1934: Convention No. 41, Night Work (Women) (Revised), excluded from the scope of the convention "women holding responsible positions of management who are not ordinarily engaged in manual work."[35] In addition, the period in which women were prohibited from working

---

31. WORLD BANK, WORLD DEVELOPMENT REPORT 1995: WORKERS IN AN INTEGRATING WORLD 73 (1995).

32. Convention No. 4 of 1919, Night Work (Women): Extreme necessity was defined in Article 4 as in cases of *force majeure* which was impossible to foresee and not of a recurring nature, and in cases where the work had to do with raw materials or materials in the course of treatment which were subject to rapid deterioration, when night work was necessary to preserve these materials from certain loss.

33. *Id.* at Article 2(1).

34. VALTICOS & VON POTOBSKY, *supra* note 25, at 206–7. The case was that of *Advisory Opinion on the Interpretation of the Convention of 1919 Concerning Employment of Women During the Night*, Permanent Court of International Justice, P.C.I.J. Series A/B, 1932, No. 50, at 365; OB Vol. XVII No. 5, 1935, at 129–97; 3 WORLD CT. RPTS. 99 (1932–1935). Interestingly, at that time, there was a parallel trend in international standards regulating the night work of young persons. However, the standards governing young workers have developed in a different direction than that of women's night work. While the standards relating to night work of young persons were subsequently revised with a view to raising their level, the standards on night work for women have faced some controversy, as described *infra*, and have had to be revised several times in order to be made more flexible.

35. Convention No. 41, Night Work (Women) (Revised), Article 8.

was made more flexible in that the interval between eleven p.m. and six a.m. could be substituted for the interval of ten p.m. to five a.m.[36]

The 1919 Night Work Convention was revised again in 1948[37] to provide greater freedom in the determination of the interval defined as "night," and in the women included in the prohibition. However, since that time, doubts have been expressed by several states, as well as by nongovernmental organizations, as to the suitability of maintaining the prohibition on women's night work when similar rules do not apply to men.[38] It was agreed in discussions at the ILO that this prohibition might have an adverse impact on women's access to employment, especially higher-waged employment, and on equal remuneration.[39] Specifically, if women are excluded from night work, they are also excluded from earning wages at a premium rate, as most night work shifts pay extra for those willing to work them. In 1985, the International Labor Conference adopted a resolution on equality of opportunity and treatment of men and women which called for regular examination of ILO instruments containing special protection for women, including the 1948 Night Work Convention, to determine their continuing appropriateness.[40] Two years later, the ILO's Governing Body put the issue on the agenda of the annual ILO Conference,[41] and in 1990 the Conference adopted a Protocol to the 1948 revised Night Work Convention, as well as a new convention and recommendation—Convention No. 171, Night Work, and Recommendation No. 178 on Night Work.

Convention No. 171 of 1990 is different from the previous Night Work Conventions in many ways: it applies to both men and women,[42] it changes the definition of night work to an interval between midnight and five a.m.,[43] and it contains a more flexible interpretation of the kinds of employees falling under this convention.[44] This convention takes into account the provisions of the 1952 Maternity Protection Convention (Revised), and allows for pregnant women to ask for an alternative to

---

36. *Id.* at Article 2(2).

37. Convention No. 89 of 1948, Night Work (Women) Convention (Revised). Under this Convention, "night" was defined as "a period of at least eleven consecutive hours, including an interval prescribed by the competent authority of at least seven consecutive hours falling between ten o'clock in the evening and seven o'clock in the morning: the competent authority may prescribe different intervals for different areas, industries, undertakings or branches of industries or undertakings, but shall consult the employers' and workers' organizations concerned before prescribing an interval beginning after eleven o'clock in the evening." Article 2. This convention also states, in Article 8, that women holding responsible positions of a managerial or technical character, and women employed in health and welfare services who are not ordinarily engaged in manual work, are excluded. The addition of health and welfare workers was an expansion of the exception first codified in Article 8 of the 1934 revision.

38. VALTICOS & VON POTOBSKY, *supra* note 25, at 207.

39. *Id.*

40. *Id.* at 208.

41. *Id.*

42. Convention No. 171 of 1990, Night Work, Article 1(b).

43. *Id.* at Article 1(a)

44. *Id.* at Article 2.

night work eight weeks prior to childbirth, as well as during a period following delivery.[45] Recommendation 178 accompanies Convention No. 171, and further elaborates on financial compensation and rest periods for night workers. Protocol 89 also makes the 1948 Night Work Convention more flexible, in an attempt to gain more ratifications. For example, Article 1(a) allows national laws or regulations to vary the definition of "night" from that provided for in the 1948 Convention, although pregnant women are exempted from this variation for a period of 16 weeks before and after childbirth.[46]

Despite the efforts of the ILO to "modernize" the 1919, 1934, and 1948 Night Work Conventions, there is a definite trend away from what these conventions represent. The 1948 revision, Convention No. 89, has 65 ratifications, but of these, 15 states have denounced their ratifications.[47] The Protocol has only one ratification to date.[48] Only one country, the Dominican Republic, has ratified the 1990 Convention No. 171.

Commentators have argued that the trend away from protective ILO standards is reflective of a recognition of the paternal[49] or patriarchal aspects of these standards, coupled with a general move to more balanced equality standards. Polson illustrates the discriminatory aspects of the night work standards by observing that, practically speaking, if a working day had three "shifts," and if women are excluded from working at least seven hours between 10 p.m. and 7 a.m. as they are under Convention No. 89, women would necessarily be excluded from working anything except the day shift.[50] The effect of this is to exclude women from higher-paying night shifts and to reduce the available workforce substantially. In addition, Polson argues that if a job is so dangerous that a certain segment of society should not be doing it, the criteria for deciding who does it should be skill, choice, age, or number of dependents—each of which is a more rational criteria than gender.[51] According to Polson, this view is best summarized by a decision of the United States Court of Appeals for the Fifth Circuit, in which the Court commented on a company's

---

45. *Id.* at Article 7.

46. 1990 Protocol to Convention No. 89, Night Work (Women) Convention (Revised), Article 2.

47. Lists of Ratifications, *supra* note 29, at 116–17. Even though countries may denounce the Night Work Conventions, there may still be problems implementing access to night work for women. The March 1997 issue of the ILO publication World of Work reported: "Swiss voters rejected a bill on "night work" in a December [1996] referendum. The law would have authorized night work for women, allowed shops to open six Sundays a year without prior authorization, reduced the time slot entitling workers to higher pay for night work, and permitted employers to compensate such workers either by more pay or time off. This bill resulted from the decision taken by the Government in 1992 to revoke the ILO Night Work (Women) (Revised) Convention, 1948 (No. 89)." International Labour Office, *Working World*, World of Work, March 1997, at 26.

48. The Czech Republic, *id.*

49. World Bank, *supra* note 31, at 444 refers to "paternalistic night work" restrictions.

50. Terry Ellen Polson, *The Rights of Working Women: An International Perspective*, 14 Vir. J. Int'l L. 729, 738 (1973–74).

51. *Id.* at 739.

contention that women could not work alone during late-night hours or be hired on a job requiring strenuous physical activity:

> ... Title VII [of the Civil Rights Act of 1964] rejects just this type of romantic paternalism as unduly Victorian and instead vests individual women with the power to decide whether or not to take on unromantic tasks. Men have always had the right to decide whether the incremental increase in remuneration for strenuous, dangerous, obnoxious, boring or unromantic tasks is worth the candle. The promise of Title VII is that women are now to be on an equal footing.[52]

The night work standards governing women clearly appear to be contradictory to nondiscrimination norms, eliminating women's choice of working hours unnecessarily and resulting in the over-protection of one gender.

The 1935 Underground Work Convention has suffered a similar reappraisal, as more states wish to employ women in mines and as mining safety standards have improved. Therefore, even though 95 states have ratified the convention, eight have since denounced it.[53]

The Debate Regarding Protective Standards

Compa notes that the ILO has historically opted for protective measures for women, and has moved only with great care to reconsider and scale back these protective provisions to expand employment opportunities for women.[54] He observes that even when the Night Work Convention was revised in 1991, the ILO still chose to limit night shift work done by pregnant women.[55] The fact that the ILO retains protective measures that, in many places, are viewed as outdated and are essentially ignored causes two problems that may undermine the effectiveness of international labor rights generally. The first is that the protective standards often conflict with national equality and nondiscrimination legislation. This may force labor advocates to support ILO standards in one context and not in another, making them appear contradictory.[56] Second, "this conflict in turn allows countries violating international labour standards in ways that do not serve the goal of equality between men and women to claim that all international labour standards may be violated at will if the violations serve national purposes."[57] In order to rectify this, Compa

---

52. *Id.* quoting *Weeks v. Southern Bell Telephone and Telegraph Co.*, 408 F.2d 228, 236 (5th Cir. 1969), rev'g 277 F. Supp. 117 (S.D. Ga. 1967).

53. Denunciations from Australia, Canada, Ireland, Luxembourg, New Zealand, Sweden, the United Kingdom, and Uruguay: Lists of Ratifications, *supra* note 29, at 67–68.

54. Compa, *supra* note 15, at 157.

55. *Id.* at 158.

56. *Id.*

57. *Id.* at 161. Human Rights Watch has also commented on this problem with respect to employers: "The existence of sex discrimination sometimes exacerbates the problem of sex discrimination. Protective legislation is intended to shield women from hazardous work or to enable women to balance their responsibilities at work and at home. Employers often use it, however, as an excuse to discriminate with impunity against women workers on the grounds that they are too expensive or their rate of

recommends that labor advocates lobby for modifications in international labor standards to favor the norm of equality over the norm of protection, both internationally and nationally.[58]

ILO Standards of Nondiscrimination

Equal Pay and Nondiscrimination Standards

As in the 1919 Maternity Convention discussed above, the ILO has addressed certain nondiscrimination issues in its conventions and recommendations. These ILO standards have a double aim: to eliminate inequality of treatment and to promote equality of opportunity.[59] Foremost among these are Convention No. 100 of 1951, Equal Remuneration ("Equal Remuneration Convention"), and Convention No. 111 of 1958, Discrimination (Employment and Occupation) ("Nondiscrimination Convention").

The principle that women and men should receive equal pay for work of equal value is mentioned in the General Principles found in the initial text of the ILO Constitution.[60] When the Constitution was amended in 1946, this principle was integrated into the preamble of the new text.[61] However, it was not until 1951 that the Equal Remuneration Convention was adopted. The Equal Remuneration Convention provides for equal pay for men and women for work of equal value, without discrimination on the basis of sex.[62] This principle is to apply to all aspects of an employee's remuneration, and therefore not only includes basic or minimum wages or salaries, but also any additional emoluments whatsoever, whether paid directly or indirectly, or in cash or in kind.[63] This wide definition of remuneration attempts to catch discriminatory pay differentials in cases where men and women are paid the same basic salary, but men receive certain benefits or bonuses that women do not.

The Equal Remuneration Convention, and its supplementary Recommendation No. 90, take a purposive view by adopting standards governing equal pay for work of equal value. The Universal Declaration of Human Rights (UDHR) only refers

---

absenteeism is too high relative to male workers." HUMAN RIGHTS WATCH, THE HUMAN RIGHTS WATCH GLOBAL REPORT ON WOMEN'S HUMAN RIGHTS 277 (1995).

58. Compa, *supra* note 15 at 161.

59. VALTICOS & VON POTOBSKY, *supra* note 25, at 118.

60. *Id.* at 209.

61. *Id.*

62. The word "sex" is used in the convention, although it may more properly be referred to as a "gender" issue, as social attitudes play a large part in pay differentials between men and women. In this chapter, "gender" will generally be used, except where referring to a convention or recommendation that uses the term "sex" in its text.

63. Convention No. 100 of 1951, Equal Remuneration, Article 1(a): "The term "remuneration" includes the ordinary, basic or minimum wage or salary and any additional emoluments whatsoever payable directly or indirectly, whether in cash or in kind, by the employer to the worker and arising out of the worker's employment."

to "equal pay for equal work" in Article 23(2).[64] According to a formalist reading of the UDHR's definition, a woman doing the exact same job as a man must be paid at the same rate. This interpretation is narrow, and fails to address women who are doing jobs that are comparable to, or that involve the same skills as, jobs held primarily by men. In other words, this definition does not address the question of what a woman is to be paid who is not in a job that has a male comparator. The Equal Remuneration Convention's reference to "equal pay for work of equal value" seems to address this concern, as does Article 7 of the International Covenant of Economic, Social and Cultural Rights.[65] The notion of "work of equal value" as opposed to "equal work" aims, in particular, at avoiding indirect limitations in the implementation of the pay equity principle[66] by allowing for "work" to be evaluated based on, for example, the tasks and duties involved and energy expended. Although determining "work of equal value" may raise difficult questions as to how to compare different types of work,[67] the Convention and Recommendation recommend that each state party adopt an objective job appraisal system on the basis of work to be performed.[68]

The Equal Remuneration Convention is one of the most widely ratified ILO instruments,[69] even though some states have criticized it as too overreaching. States that have not ratified it argue that the government cannot interfere directly in the determination of wages in the private sector, and that therefore the convention asks them to do something that they cannot do.[70] However, the convention did anticipate this problem and imposes an obligation on governments to ensure equal remuneration only when this is compatible with the wage-fixing methods in the country, and otherwise provides that the principle may be promoted by means of national laws or regulations, legally established or recognized machinery for wage determination, collective agreements, or a combination of these means.[71] Recommendation No. 90

---

64. Universal Declaration of Human Rights, *adopted* 10 December 1948, G.A. Res. 217A (III), 3 U.N. GAOR (Resolutions, part 1) at 71, U.N. Doc. A/810 (1948), Article 23(2).

65. International Covenant on Economic, Social and Cultural Rights, *adopted* 16 December 1966 and *entered into force* 3 January 1976, 993 U.N.T.S. 3, G.A. Res. 2200 (XXI), 21 U.N. GAOR Supp. (No. 16), at 49, U.N. Doc. A/6316 (1966), Article 7. However, note that Article 7 curiously refers to both equal pay for equal work and equal pay for work of equal value: "The States Parties to the present Covenant recognize the right of everyone to the enjoyment of just and favourable conditions of work which ensure, in particular: (a) Remuneration which provides all workers, at a minimum, with: (i) Fair wages and equal remuneration for work of equal value without distinction of any kind, in particular women being guaranteed conditions of work not inferior to those enjoyed by men, with equal pay for equal work."

66. VALTICOS & VON POTOBSKY, *supra* note 25, at 210.

67. *Id.*

68. Convention No. 100 of 1951, Equal Remuneration, Article 3(1), and para. 5 of its Recommendation No. 90 of 1951.

69. As of June 1, 1994, the Equal Remuneration Convention had 120 ratifications. LISTS OF RATIFICATIONS, *supra* note 29, at 100.

70. VALTICOS & VON POTOBSKY, *supra* note 25, at 210.

71. Convention No. 100 of 1951, Equal Remuneration, Article 2.

gives more detailed guidance on the means of application of pay equity, pointing out that progress can be realized through such methods as job analysis, vocational guidance, employment counselling, job placement, welfare and social services, promoting public understanding, and investigations.[72]

The aim of the Nondiscrimination Convention is to promote equality of opportunity and treatment in respect to employment and occupation. Discrimination is defined as "[a]ny distinction, exclusion or preference made on the basis of race, colour, sex, religion, political opinion, national extraction or social origin, which has the effect of nullifying or impairing equality of opportunity or treatment in employment or occupation."[73] Additionally, a state (with appropriate consultations) may add any other distinction, exclusion or preference which has the effect of nullifying or impairing equality of opportunity or treatment.[74] Some states have identified language, age, disability, and membership or nonmembership in a trade union as relevant grounds.[75] Similarly, other ILO instruments refer to grounds of discrimination not included in the list, such as older workers, workers with family responsibilities, and marital status.[76] The Nondiscrimination Convention prohibits discrimination in access to vocational training, access to employment and to particular occupations, and in terms and conditions of employment.[77] However, Article 5 provides that special measures, protection, or assistance, such as affirmative action programs, provided for in other ILO conventions or recommendations shall not be deemed to be discrimination.[78] As well, any distinction, exclusion, or preference

---

72. Recommendation No. 90 of 1951, paras. 6 and 7.

73. Discrimination (Employment and Occupation) Convention No. 111 of 1958, Article 1(a).

74. *Id.* at Article 1(b).

75. VALTICOS & VON POTOBSKY, *supra* note 25, at 121.

76. Recommendation 162 of 1980, Older Workers; Convention No. 156 of 1981, Workers with Family Responsibilities; and Convention No. 158 of 1982, Termination of Employment.

77. Discrimination (Employment and Occupation) Convention No. 111 of 1958, Article 1(3).

78. *Id.* at Article 5(2). A strict reading of Article 5 could actually reinforce the outdated "protective" measures described *supra*. Article 5(1) states: "Special measures of protection or assistance provided in other Conventions or Recommendations adopted by the International Labour Conference shall not be deemed to be discrimination." Article 5(2) states: "Any Member may, after consultation with representative employers' and workers' organizations, where such exist, determine that other special measures designed to meet the particular requirements of persons who, for reasons such as sex, age, disablement, family responsibilities or social or cultural status, are generally recognized to require special protection or assistance, shall not be deemed to be discrimination." In other words, this appears to preserve aspects of other conventions and recommendations that appear to be discriminatory on their face, such as Convention No. 45 of 1935, Underground Work (Women). Section 15 of the Canadian Charter of Rights and Freedoms (Schedule B to the *Canada Act* 1982, (U.K.) 1982, c. 11) avoids this possibility by allowing for affirmative action programs in the following manner: "(1) Every individual is equal before and under the law and has the right to the equal protection and equal benefit of the law without discrimination and, in particular, without discrimination based on race, national or ethnic origin, colour, religion, sex, age or mental or physical disability. (2) Subsection (1) does not preclude any law, program or activity *that has as its object the amelioration of conditions of disadvantaged individuals or groups* including those that are disadvantaged because of race, national or ethnic origin, colour, religion, sex, age or mental or physical disability." [emphasis added].

in respect of a particular job based on its inherent requirements is not discrimination, nor are measures relating to activities prejudicial to the security of the state.[79] As is the Equal Remuneration Convention, this convention is widely ratified.[80] Valticos and von Potobsky observe that the inclusion of discrimination on the grounds of sex seems to be the most frequent obstacle cited by countries in connection with the ratification of the convention: the difficulties relate both to access by women to employment and to conditions of employment.[81]

Balancing Work and Family

Key to the issue of women balancing work and family are maternity rights. The 1919 Maternity Protection Convention applied to industrial and commercial undertakings, including mining, manufacturing, construction, and transportation,[82] and provided for twelve weeks of maternity leave for women in these industries: six weeks prior to the expected date of birth and six weeks after birth.[83] The Maternity Protection Convention also stated that a woman absent from work on maternity leave shall be paid benefits sufficient for the full and healthy maintenance of herself and her child, to be provided out of public funds or insurance.[84] In addition, women were to be provided access to free attendance by a doctor or certified midwife, and were to have half an hour, twice a day, during working hours to nurse a child.[85] Finally, this convention also prohibited the dismissal of a woman absent on maternity leave,[86] a development that was arguably quite progressive at that time.

The 1919 Maternity Protection Convention was revised in 1952 by Convention No. 103. Convention No. 103 applies to women working in a wide variety of settings: those in industrial undertakings, in nonindustrial occupations, and in agriculture, including female wage earners working at home.[87] The scope of this convention is wider than its predecessor, because the 1919 Convention did not include women wage earners employed at home or in domestic work in private households. Twelve weeks of maternity leave are provided for under Convention No. 103 and, unlike the 1919 Convention, the entire leave may be taken after the birth of the child.[88] A six-week period of compulsory leave is provided for after birth.[89]

---

79. *Id.* at Articles 1(2) and 4 respectively.

80. Lists of Ratifications, *supra* note 29, at 148–49. It had 118 ratifications as of June 1, 1994.

81. Valticos & von Potobsky, *supra* note 25, at 120.

82. Convention No. 3 of 1919, Maternity Protection, Articles 1 and 2. This convention does not apply to women working in family undertakings.

83. *Id.* at Articles 3(a) and (b).

84. *Id.* at Article 3(c).

85. *Id.* at Articles 3(c) and (d).

86. *Id.* at Article 4.

87. Convention No. 103 of 1952, Maternity Protection, Article 1(1).

88. *Id.* at Articles 3(2) and (3).

89. *Id.* at Article 3(3).

Convention No. 156 of 1981, Workers with Family Responsibilities, recognizes in its preamble that the Nondiscrimination Convention does not expressly cover distinctions made on the basis of family responsibilities, and states that the goal of Convention No. 156 is to provide supplementary standards in this respect. Specifically, it aims to create effective equality of opportunity and treatment for men and women workers with family responsibilities where such responsibilities restrict the possibilities of participating or advancing in economic activity.[90] This convention updates a Recommendation made in 1956 that focused on women with family responsibilities and encouraged states to enable women to "fulfil their various responsibilities at home and at work harmoniously" without explicitly recognizing that both parents (if possible) should share the family responsibilities.[91] The Workers with Family Responsibilities Convention not only applies to women and men with child-care responsibilities, but also to workers with "responsibilities in relation to other members of their immediate family who clearly need their care or support."[92]

Under the Workers with Family Responsibilities Convention, the state is to make it an aim of national policy to enable persons with family responsibilities to engage in employment without being subject to discrimination and, to the extent possible, without conflict between their employment and family responsibilities.[93] States are obligated to take all measures compatible with national conditions: to enable workers with family responsibilities to exercise their right to free choice of employment; to take account of their needs in terms and conditions of employment and in social security; to take account of the needs of these workers in community planning; and to develop and promote community services, public or private, such as child-care and family services and facilities.[94] One of the methods mentioned by the convention is for the state to promote community services, such as child-care facilities. Another important advance in nondiscrimination is found in Article 8, under which family responsibilities shall not, as such, constitute a valid reason for termination of employment.[95]

Termination of Employment

The goal of Convention No. 158 of 1982, Termination of Employment, is to protect against termination of employment by an employer without reason. The employment of a worker, must not be terminated unless there is a valid reason connected with the capacity or conduct of the worker or based on the operational requirements of the undertaking or service. Specifically, termination based on the

---

90. Convention No. 156 of 1981, Workers with Family Responsibilities, Article 1(1).

91. Recommendation 123 of 1965, Employment (Women with Family Responsibilities), para. 1(b).

92. Convention No. 156 of 1981, Workers with Family Responsibilities, Article 1(2).

93. *Id.* at Article 3(1).

94. *Id.* at Articles 4(a), 4(b), 5(a), and 5(b) respectively.

95. As of June 1, 1994, only 21 countries had ratified this convention. LISTS OF RATIFICATIONS, *supra* note 29, at 200.

sex of the employee, and termination based on pregnancy, family responsibilities, or absence from work during maternity leave are prohibited.[96]

Other ILO Nondiscrimination Standards

Other nondiscrimination standards adopted by the ILO include: Convention No. 122 of 1964, Social Policy, which specifically prohibits sex discrimination in social policy[97] and Convention No. 142 of 1975, Human Resources Development, which promotes equality of men and women in the provision of vocational guidance and training linked to employment, in particular through public employment services.[98] Convention No. 142 is supplemented by the 1975 Human Resources Development Recommendation No. 150, which contains a detailed listing of policies and programs for the promotion of equality and opportunity for women and men in vocational guidance, training, and employment.

Sexual Harassment

Sexual harassment in the workplace is a clear violation of the right to protection against sex discrimination, and is closely linked to the inequality that women encounter in the labor market.[99] The ILO does not have a convention or recommendation concerning the issue of sexual harassment.[100] However, the 1985 ILO Resolution on Equality of Opportunities and Treatment of Men and Women Workers in Employment addressed the issue, stating that "sexual harassment at the workplace is detrimental to employees' working conditions and to employment and promotion prospects."[101] Thus, "[p]olicies for the advancement of sexual equality should therefore include measures to combat and prevent sexual harassment."[102]

The issue of sexual harassment in employment is dealt with in the U.N. General Assembly's Declaration on the Elimination of Violence Against Women ("Declaration Against Violence"), adopted in 1993.[103] In the Declaration Against Violence,

---

96. Convention No. 158 of 1982, Termination of Employment, Articles 5(d) and (e).

97. Convention No. 122 of 1964, Social Policy, Article 1(2)(c).

98. Convention No. 142 of 1975, Human Resources Development, Article 1(1).

99. DEL MAR SERNA CALVO, *supra* note 13, at 41.

100. The ILO does not have a convention dealing specifically with sexual harassment, except in the case of sexual harassment of indigenous women [Convention No. 169 of 1989, Indigenous and Tribal Peoples in Independent Countries, Article 20(3)(d)]. The ILO's view is that sexual harassment is covered by the Discrimination (Employment and Occupation) Convention No. 111 of 1958: International Labour Office, *Unwelcome, Unwanted and Increasingly Illegal: Sexual Harassment in the Workplace*, WORLD OF WORK, March 1997, at 7, 8.

101. DEL MAR SERNA CALVO, *supra* note 13, at 41.

102. Para. 5 of the Resolution adopted on June 27, 1985, cited in *id.*

103. Declaration on the Elimination of Violence Against Women, G.A. Res. 48/104, 48 U.N. GAOR Supp. (No. 49) at 217, U.N. Doc. A/48/49 (1993).

violence against women is understood to encompass physical, sexual, and psychological violence (including rape, sexual abuse, sexual harassment, and intimidation) occurring at work.[104] States are asked to pursue several strategies to eliminate violence against women, including sexual harassment at work, such as developing penal, civil, labor, and administrative sanctions in domestic legislation to punish and redress the wrongs caused to women who are subjected to violence.[105] The 1994 Inter-American Convention on the Prevention, Punishment, and Eradication of Violence Against Women (Convention of Belém do Pará) (''Inter-American Convention Against Violence'')[106] elaborates on the issue of workplace sexual harassment. Under this convention, ''violence against women'' is defined as ''any act or conduct, based on gender, which causes death or physical, sexual or psychological harm or suffering to women, whether in the public or private sphere.''[107] Sexual harassment may be perpetrated by any person in the workplace,[108] including co-workers, and is not limited to harassment by a superior. Importantly, women and nongovernmental organizations can lodge petitions with the Inter-American Commission on Human Rights containing denunciations or complaints of violations of a state's duty under the convention,[109] providing a regional avenue of redress.

Sexual harassment in the workplace is clearly prohibited by the U.N. Convention on the Elimination of All Forms of Discrimination Against Women (Women's Convention),[110] as interpreted by the Committee on the Elimination of Discrimination Against Women (CEDAW Committee). The CEDAW Committee states in General Recommendation 19 of 1992:

> 7. Gender-based violence, which impairs or nullifies the enjoyment by women of human rights and fundamental freedoms under general international law or under human rights conventions, is discrimination within the meaning of article 1 of the Convention. The rights and freedoms include: (h) The right to just and favourable conditions of work.[111]

The Committee comments more specifically that ''[e]quality in employment can be seriously impaired when women are subjected to gender-specific violence, such as sexual harassment in the workplace.''[112] Unlike the Declaration Against

---

104. *Id.* at Article 2(b).

105. *Id.* at Article 4(d).

106. Inter-American Convention on the Prevention, Punishment, and Eradication of Violence Against Women (Convention of Belém do Pará), *signed* 9 June 1994, *entered into force* 3 March 1995, *reprinted in* 3 I.L.M. 1534 (1994).

107. Inter-American Convention Against Violence, Article 1.

108. *Id.* at Article 2(b).

109. *Id.* at Article 12.

110. Convention on the Elimination of All Forms of Discrimination Against Women, G.A. Res. 34/180, U.N. GAOR, 34th Sess., Supp. No. 46 at 193, U.N. Doc. A/34/46 (1979), *adopted* 3 September 1981.

111. General Recommendation 19 of the Committee on the Elimination of Discrimination Against Women, (11th session, 1992), Violence Against Women, U.N. Doc. HRI/Gen/1/Rev. 1 (1994).

112. General Recommendation 19, para. 17.

Violence and the Women's Convention, the CEDAW Committee defines sexual harassment: "Sexual harassment includes such unwelcome sexually determined behaviour as physical contact and advances, sexually coloured remarks, showing pornography and sexual demand, whether by words or actions."[113] The Committee notes that sexual harassment "can be humiliating and may constitute a health and safety problem; it is discriminatory when the woman has reasonable grounds to believe that her objection would disadvantage her in connection with her employment, including recruitment and promotion, or when it creates a hostile working environment."[114]

The issue of sexual harassment in job recruitment is of particular concern to human rights and labor activists, because recruitment falls outside of the formal employment relationship. Del Mar Serno Calvo notes that sexual harassment occurs most frequently in the employment context when women are at their most vulnerable, i.e., when entering a new job or when an employment contract is being renewed.[115] Clearly, the latter would fall within the definitions outlined in the Declaration Against Violence and the Inter-American Convention Against Violence, unless the original employment contract had already expired. The former situation is of concern because women may face sexual harassment in the hiring process, while they are not technically employees. While the Committee on the Elimination of Discrimination Against Women recognizes that sexual harassment in hiring falls within Article 11 of the Women's Convention, further clarification as to how far the employment link extends may have to be sought in domestic legislation. For example, Canadian law clearly addresses this concern by prohibiting sexual solicitations or advances by a person in a position to confer, grant, or deny a benefit (which includes those who make hiring decisions), as well as prohibiting reprisals or threats of reprisals from such a person.[116]

Other United Nations Conventions and Instruments

One of the most important international documents for women workers, apart from the ILO documents mentioned above, is the 1979 Convention on the Elimination of All Forms of Discrimination Against Women.[117] The Women's Convention contains several articles of importance to working women. Article 2 obliges states to take active steps to embody the principle of equality between women and men

---

113. *Id.* at para. 18.

114. *Id.*

115. DEL MAR SERNA CALVO, *supra* note 13, at 41.

116. See the *Canadian Human Rightss Act*, R.S.C. 1985, c. H-6, section 14(1) and the Ontario *Human Right Code*, R.S.O. 1990, c. H.19, section 7(3). Section 7(3) of the Ontario *Human Rights Code* states: "Every person has a right to be free from, (a) a sexual solicitation or advance made by a person in a position to confer, grant or deny a benefit or advancement to the person where the person making the solicitation or advance knows or ought reasonably to know that it is unwelcome; or (b) a reprisal or a threat of reprisal is made or threatened by a person in a position to confer, grant or deny a benefit or advancement to the person."

117. Women's Convention, *supra* note 110.

in national constitutions and other relevant legislation, and to take other appropriate measures to eliminate discrimination against women. Under Article 3, states undertake to take all appropriate measures to ensure the full development and advancement of women on a basis of equality with men. Article 4 allows states to adopt temporary special measures to combat discrimination, which would include affirmative action programs in the workplace.

Article 11 of the Women's Convention deals specifically with equality in employment and labor rights. Article 11 builds upon and consolidates many of the rights of women set out by the ILO, and states clearly that women shall enjoy the basic human right to work.[118] Under this article, states are obligated to take all appropriate measures to eliminate discrimination against women in employment in order to ensure an equal right to work, the right to equal employment opportunities, the right to free choice of profession and employment (and the correlating right not to be automatically channeled into "women's work"[119]), the right to equal remuneration (including benefits),[120] the right to social security, and the right to protection of health and safety. This last right is seen to encompass the right to be free from sexual harassment by co-workers or employers.[121] In General Recommendations 12 and 19 on violence against women, the CEDAW Committee calls upon states to include in their reports to the Committee information on laws prohibiting sexual harassment in the workplace.[122]

Under Article 11(2) of the Women's Convention, states shall take appropriate measures to prohibit dismissal on the grounds of pregnancy or maternity leave, and to prohibit discrimination on the basis of marital status. States must also introduce maternity leave with pay or comparable social benefits without loss of employment, seniority, or social allowances. States are bound to encourage the provision of necessary supporting social services to enable parents to combine family obligations with work responsibilities and participation in public life, in particular through promoting the establishment and development of a network of child-care facilities. Finally, Article 11(2) obliges states to take all appropriate measures to make available special protection to women during pregnancy in types of work proven to be

---

118. UNITED NATIONS CENTRE FOR HUMAN RIGHTS, DISCRIMINATION AGAINST WOMEN: THE CONVENTION AND THE COMMITTEE 20 (1994).

119. *Id.* For example, as secretaries, child-care workers, housekeepers, etc.

120. Note that the right to equal remuneration set out in Article 11 of the Women's Convention is directly linked to the right to equal remuneration set out in ILO Convention No. 100, Equal Remuneration for Men and Women Workers for Work of Equal Value through General Recommendation 13 of the Committee on the Elimination of Discrimination Against Women, (8th Session), Equal Remuneration for Work of Equal Value, U.N. Doc. HRI/Gen/1/Rev. 1 at 78 (1994). In General Recommendation 13, states are encouraged to ratify ILO Convention No. 100 in order to implement fully the Women's Convention.

121. UNITED NATIONS CENTRE FOR HUMAN RIGHTS, *supra* note 118, at 20.

122. General Recommendation 19, *supra* note 111, at para. 24(j). General Recommendation 12 of the Committee on the Elimination of Discrimination Against Women, (11th session, 1992), Violence Against Women, U.N. Doc. HRI/Gen/1/Rev. 1 at 78 (1994), para. 24(j).

harmful to them. Article 11(3) reflects a cautious attitude toward protective measures. It provides that protective legislation relating to matters covered by Article 11 shall be reviewed periodically in light of scientific and technological knowledge and shall be revised, repealed, or extended as necessary.

Other international documents also govern women in the workplace. The 1948 Universal Declaration of Human Rights embodies the equality/protection dichotomy referred to above. Article 23(2) states that "Everyone, without any discrimination, has the right to equal pay for equal work," while Article 25(2) states that "Motherhood and childhood are entitled to special care and assistance," albeit in a manner that can be reconciled.[123] The International Covenant on Economic, Social and Cultural Rights provides in Article 7(a)(i) for "[f]air wages and equal remuneration for work of equal value without distinction of any kind, in particular women being guaranteed conditions of work not inferior to those enjoyed by men, with equal pay for equal work." Like the Universal Declaration, the Covenant also states in Article 10(2) that: "[s]pecial protection should be accorded to mothers during a reasonable period before and after childbirth. During such period working mothers should be accorded paid leave or leave with adequate social security benefits."

Regional Application of International Standards

The European Convention on Human Rights[124] contains a nondiscrimination clause: under Article 14, the enjoyment of the rights and freedoms set forth in the convention—including the prohibition of forced labor and the right to form and join trade unions—shall be secured without discrimination on any ground such as sex, race, color, language, religion, political or other opinion, national or social origin, association with a national minority, property, birth, or other status.

The European Social Charter, which entered into force in 1965, deals in a more direct fashion with women's labor rights. Part I, para. 8 states: "[e]mployed women, in case of maternity, and other employed women as appropriate, have the right to special protection in their work." Under Article 4(3), the right of men and women workers to equal pay for work of equal value is noted, mirroring the wording of the Equal Remuneration Convention and the International Covenant on Economic, Social and Cultural Rights. Article 8 deals specifically with the rights of employed women. Under this section, states undertake to provide at least 12 weeks of maternity leave,[125] as described in the ILO Maternity Conventions. However, the European Social Charter differs from the ILO standards when it states that such leave should be provided either by paid leave, by adequate social security benefits, or by

---

123. Discussed in the Summary of International Standards, *infra.*

124. European Convention for the Protection of Human Rights and Fundamental Freedoms, opened for signature 4 November 1950 and *entered into force* 3 September 1953, 213 U.N.T.S. 221, ETS 5.

125. European Social Charter, signed 18 October 1961, entered into force 26 February 1965, 529 U.N.T.S. 89, ETS 35, Article 8(1).

benefits from public funds.[126] The ILO Maternity Conventions only authorize the latter two methods of financing, and prohibits the employer from being made liable for the cost of maternity benefits, in order to prevent employers from discriminating against women of child-bearing age, and to avoid any difficulties by women in obtaining payment. The Consultative Assembly voted by a large majority to amend this provision to delete the reference to paid leave, but the Social Committee of the Council of Europe chose to keep it.[127]

Under Article 8(2) of the European Social Charter, it is unlawful for an employer to give a woman notice of dismissal during her absence on maternity leave. Article 8(3) provides that mothers shall be entitled to sufficient time off to nurse. Article 8(4) allows for the regulation of the employment of women night workers in industrial employment, and prohibits the employment of women workers in underground mining, and, as appropriate, on all other work which is unsuitable for them by reason of its dangerous, unhealthy, or arduous nature. This text does not go as far as do the ILO Night Work and Underground Work Conventions, but it has led certain Scandinavian delegations to express their opposition to the principle of protection of women workers generally, except for pregnant or nursing women.[128] However, the Scandinavian proposal to attenuate the terms prohibiting employment of women in mining and dangerous, unhealthy, or arduous work was rejected by the Consultative Assembly.[129] The Social Charter provides only implicitly for nondiscrimination in employment. Article 1(2) relates to the "right of the worker to earn his [or her] living in an occupation freely entered upon." However, in 1988, an Additional Protocol to the Social Charter was adopted.[130] Under Part I of the Additional Protocol, states should pursue, by all appropriate means, conditions where "[a]ll workers have the right to equal opportunities and equal treatment in matters of employment and occupation without discrimination on the grounds of sex."[131] In addition, Article 1 of Part II provides for equal access, without discrimination on grounds of sex, to employment, protection against dismissal, occupational resettlement, vocational guidance, training, retraining, rehabilitation, terms of employment, working conditions including remuneration, and career development including promotion.[132] Specific measures to create a situation of de facto equality are allowed,[133] and provisions regarding pregnancy, confinement, and the post-natal

---

126. *Id.* at Article 8(1).

127. VALTICOS & VON POTOBSKY, *supra* note 25, at 213.

128. *Id.* The ILO Night Work Conventions prohibit night work of women generally, with some exceptions, while the Social Charter provides merely for the regulation of women in industry. However, the Social Charter prohibits underground work as the ILO Underground Work Convention does, and also prohibits certain unhealthy, dangerous, or arduous work.

129. *Id.*

130. Note, however, that it has not yet entered into force. Additional Protocol to the European Social Charter, *adopted* 5 May 1988, not in force, ETS 128.

131. Additional Protocol to the European Social Charter, Part I, para. 1.

132. *Id.* at Part II, Article 1(1).

133. *Id.* at Part II, Article 1(3).

period are not to be considered discriminatory.[134] On the other hand, "[o]ccupational activities which, by reason of their nature or the context in which they are carried out, can be entrusted only to persons of a particular sex" may be excluded from any special protection,[135] leaving an opening for discrimination that may possibly be abused.

The American Convention on Human Rights[136] contains a general guarantee against acts of discrimination (not specifically linked to the labor context). However, its 1988 Additional Protocol in the Area of Economic, Cultural and Social Rights obliges states to guarantee the exercise of the rights set forth in the instrument without discrimination of any kind for reasons related to, inter alia, sex.[137] Under Article 6(2) of the convention, states undertake to implement and strengthen programs to help ensure suitable family care, so that women may enjoy a real opportunity to exercise the right to work. Article 15(a) of the convention obliges states to provide special care and assistance to mothers during a reasonable period before and after childbirth.

Article 2 of the African Charter on Human and Peoples' Rights[138] guarantees the enjoyment of rights set out in the Charter without distinction of any kind such as, inter alia, sex. Under Article 15, "each individual shall have the right to work under equitable and satisfactory conditions, and shall receive equal pay for equal work." Under Article 18(3), "the State shall ensure the elimination of every discrimination against women and also ensure the protection of the rights of the woman and the child as stipulated in international declarations and conventions."

Summary of International Standards

ILO standards found in conventions and recommendations have created a wide-ranging and fairly comprehensive network of women's labor rights. These rights may be divided between those rights that can be seen as "protective," and those which follow the nondiscrimination norm. Some of the earliest protective rights, namely those prohibiting women from night work and from working underground, have recently been challenged as overprotective and antithetical to nondiscrimination legislation.

There are certain rights that are reflected in almost all of the international and regional documents—namely, maternity rights. Although maternity rights may be

---

134. *Id.* at Part II, Article 1(2).

135. *Id.* at Part II, Article 1(4).

136. American Convention on Human Rights, *opened for signature* 22 November 1969 and *entered into force* 18 July 1978, OASTS No. 36, *reprinted in* 9 I.L.M. 673 (1970).

137. Additional Protocol to the American Convention on Human Rights in the Area of Economic, Cultural and Social Rights (Protocol of San Salvador), *adopted* 17 November 1988, not in force, OASTS 69, *reprinted in* 28 I.L.M. 156 (1989), *corrections at* 28 I.L.M. 573 and 1341 (1989), Article 3.

138. African Charter on Human and Peoples' Rights, *adopted* 27 June 1981 and *entered into force* 21 October 1986, OAU Doc. CAB/LEG/67/3/Rev. 5 (1981).

seen as "protective" in some sense, they do not draw criticism as the night and underground work standards do because they are essentially nondiscriminatory in nature. Maternity rights reflect the fact that some women carry and bear children, and in this situation will require a period of leave from employment. On the other hand, maternity rights prohibit women from being dismissed from their employment because of the biological reason that they either may or do become pregnant and have children. In other words, women should not be punished because of their reproductive capacity, and if they do become pregnant, they should still be able to compete in the workplace in a situation of equality with men.

THE LINK BETWEEN TRADE AND WOMEN'S LABOR RIGHTS: CASE STUDIES

Many states have changed their development focus over the past few decades from accepting that social and economic rights may further develope, to the view that these very same rights are impediments to a country's economic growth.[139] This has led to what may be termed "labor deregulation,"[140] whereby employers and governments attempt to circumvent implementing the employees' rights described in the previous section. Countries with a high premium on export-led production, and those reliant on attracting foreign and private investment for the success of their structural adjustment strategy, must offer certain incentives to encourage both investment and exports.[141] These incentives include tax holidays, subsidized credits, customs exemptions, unrestricted remittances of profits, and the waiver or lowering of wage and labor[142] legislation. In some countries, labor costs are artificially low because they are competing against other countries with even lower labor costs to attract investment.[143] Many countries have instituted Export Processing Zones (EPZs), to geographically define the area within which the tax, investment, wage, and labor deregulation is valid. In other countries, companies have bargained with the government to create EPZ-like conditions for their particular factory or factories.

Green refers to the proliferation of EPZs as the "world market factory," promoting globally dispersed production units for the "outsourcing" of manufactured production for export to developed country markets.[144] EPZs are usually foreign subsidiaries or local contracting firms engaged exclusively in the assembly, subassembly, or finishing of manufactured products for a predetermined export market.[145]

---

139. Sewall, *supra* note 1, at 158.

140. *Id.*

141. *Id.* at 159.

142. *Id.*

143. *Id.*

144. Cecilia Green, *At the Junction of the Global and the Local: Transnational Industry and Women Workers in the Caribbean, in* HUMAN RIGHTS, LABOR RIGHTS, AND INTERNATIONAL TRADE 118, 118 (Lance A. Compa & Stephen F. Diamond eds.,1996).

145. *Id.*

Green describes the typical EPZ in the Caribbean: a foreign company, usually American, German, Japanese, Hong Kong Chinese, South Korean, or Taiwanese, sets up an offshore facility for the assembly or subassembly of goods. These operations are usually low-cost, labor-intensive methods using precut or prefabricated components supplied by the parent company. The finished or semi-finished products are then exported back to the foreign company's country (or transferred to another EPZ subsidiary for further finishing) where customs duty fees are paid only on the value added by the foreign operations.[146] This description also accurately describes EPZ and EPZ-like industries in other areas of the world.

Typically, the EPZ industries are light, labor-intensive manufacturing operations employing mainly female assembly-line workers at low levels of skill and pay.[147] Common examples include garment and semiconductor electronics assembly enterprises.[148] The requirements and characteristics of garment and electronics assembly are highly compatible with the conditions offered by the EPZ facilities, as they require relatively light capital investment, a high labor and low skill intensity ratio, and easy product transportability.[149] Electronic components, in particular, are well-suited to EPZ assembly because they have a high value in relation to their volume and weight, and therefore transport costs are relatively low.[150] Other products produced in EPZs include "footwear, leather products, plastics, toys, optical goods, sporting goods, furniture, car parts, housewares, artificial flowers, and minor transport equipment."[151]

EPZs provide an opportunity to study women's labor rights in a microcosm. With the shift to EPZs and EPZ-like manufacturing has come an increasing demand for female labor. As governments remove, waive, or weaken wage legislation and other labor safeguards in EPZ areas, a proliferation of low-wage jobs paying individual, rather than family, wages typically ensues.[152] Employers also tend to hire casual and short-term laborers, rather than full-time salaried workers, in order to reduce fixed labor costs.[153] However, this has also meant reduced income and security for workers.[154] As minimum wages are eroded, employers substitute lower-cost female labor for high-cost male labor: in virtually all countries that have established successful export-led production, there has been both an absolute as well as relative

---

146. *Id.*

147. *Id.* at 119.

148. *Id.*

149. *Id.*

150. *Id.* citing INTERNATIONAL CONFEDERATION OF FREE TRADE UNIONS, NEW TECHNOLOGY AND WOMEN'S EMPLOYMENT 46 (1983).

151. Green, *supra* note 144, at 119, *citing* CORNELIA H. ALDANA, A CONTRACT FOR UNDERDEVELOPMENT: SUBCONTRACTING FOR MULTINATIONALS IN THE PHILIPPINE SEMICONDUCTOR AND GARMENT INDUSTRIES 17 (1989).

152. Sewall, *supra* note 1, at 160.

153. *Id.* at 160.

154. *Id.* at 160.

growth in the use of female labor.[155] The sum of these trends leaves women with lower-paying, less-secure, casual, short-term, or contract positions, even while their labor force participation is increasing. Most often, these are dull, repetitive jobs with little room for advancement, despite a generally high turnover.[156]

There are complex reasons as to why women form the vast majority of the cheap labor force for EPZs. Sewall summarizes them in this way:

> [W]omen are one of the cheapest sources of labour (next to children) because patriarchal, socio-cultural factors outside of the labour force make them temporary and adjunct members of the labour force and secondary wage earners in the family. Women's primary role as wife and mother means families are less likely to invest in their education and skill training. With little education and few marketable skills, women are more likely to resort to [and be given] low-skilled and low-paying jobs. Since women in most countries are viewed as only secondary wage earners, they are more likely than men to accept jobs paying individual rather than family wages. Employers are also more likely to hire women for jobs paying low wages, because they believe that when men are paid individual wages, they respond by reducing their effort.[157]

In addition to this analysis, employers hire women for jobs stereotypically viewed as "women's work" because of the need for "nimble fingers and near-divine patience."[158] This reason is most often given for hiring women to do the minute or meticulous work required in sewing, especially hand sewing, and in assembly of electronics. However, while it provides a convenient excuse for hiring women to do these tedious and extremely repetitive jobs, it does not mean that women are compensated when they develop repetitive strain injuries or related health problems. Often, women are forced to leave their jobs due to debilitating health conditions caused by the factory work, usually at a time when they would otherwise be commanding higher wages based on their experience.[159]

In most situations, employment in the EPZs has done little to help integrate women into their national economies in a meaningful way.[160] In fact, these jobs often entrench further degradation of women's labor rights. Sewall notes that perhaps more disturbing is the fact that, because a nation's prospect for development has become reliant upon the low-wage work of women, female workers have been

---

155. *Id.*

156. *Id.*

157. *Id.*

158. *Id.* at 161. *See also* LOURDES BENERIA & MARTHA ROLDÁN, THE CROSSROADS OF CLASS AND GENDER: INDUSTRIAL HOMEWORK, SUBCONTRACTING, AND HOUSEHOLD DYNAMICS IN MEXICO CITY 46 (1987), in which the authors explain that, when asked, managers preferred to hire women for assembly work because of women's perceived "greater dexterity" and "manual ability." However, these characteristics, while recognized as skills, were not seen as deserving of the same financial reward as were physical strength and mechanical ability. The authors call this problem "the artificiality of skill definition."

159. Sewall, *supra* note at 161.

160. *Id.*

increasingly subjected to repressive national policies to preserve their compliance.[161] In many countries, union formation is prohibited for a specific period of time, usually from 12–24 months,[162] or outlawed altogether.[163] Even where union activity remains legal, severe "informal" pressure serves as a deterrent to union formation and participation.[164] For example, the presence of foreign staff specifically to "union-bust" acts as a deterrent. The use of state guards and paramilitary forces to enforce compliance is commonplace in many countries.[165]

Three case-studies will shed light on conditions for women in export-driven economies. The first is that of Caribbean EPZ workers; the second looks at Colombian flower-workers in an EPZ-like situation. Finally, *maquiladoras* situated on or near the United States-Mexico border provide a glimpse of how EPZ and EPZ-like practices affect women's labor rights.

Caribbean Garment Workers

The first case study is of a factory, St. Vincent Children's Wear, located on the Eastern Caribbean island of St. Vincent.[166] St. Vincent Children's Wear was owned by Bayliss Brothers of Cincinnati, Ohio, and is now a subdivision of Hanson Trust, a large conglomerate. Bayliss Brothers marketed an upscale line of children's apparel with the brand name "Polly Flinders," which was sold in major chain stores. The factory in St. Vincent produced hand-smocked children's dresses. Hand-smocking increases durability, and is considered to provide a higher quality garment than machine-smocking. This fact is reflected in the final price of the dresses produced in St. Vincent.

The factory employed 230 in-factory workers and 1,500 home smockers. The company operated on a system of subcontracting to meet orders from its large retail customers. Thousands of stenciled, pre-cut, dress fronts were smocked in rural homes every week by "self-employed"[167] smockers, and then collected by area supervisors for shipment back to the factory, where they were assembled into whole dresses by the workers. Although an immense amount of value was actually added to the final product by the hand-smocking, the home smockers earned very low piece-rate wages. One study found that the income of the St. Vincent smockers

---

161. *Id.*

162. GREEN, *supra* note 144, at 126–27, knowing full well that this gives foreign companies the time they need to develop anti-union strategies among their workforces.

163. Sewall, *supra* note 1, at 161.

164. *Id.*

165. *Id.*, citing Cynthia Enloe, *Women Textile Workers in the Militarization of Southeast Asia, in* WOMEN, MEN AND THE INTERNATIONAL DIVISION OF LABOUR 70, 89 (J. Nash ed., 1989).

166. This case study, including all accompanying facts, is set out in Green, *supra* note 144, at 131–32.

167. Although the 230 in-factory workers were unionized, the 1,500 home-workers were considered independent contractors, sparing the company overhead expenses and labor "troubles" for the majority of its workers. *Id.* at 131.

rarely exceeded $27 per month.[168] The designing, styling, cutting, and distributing was all done at company headquarters in Cincinnati in an automated plant employing mostly women. When Green asked about the company's motive for locating in St. Vincent, the American manager replied bluntly, "No American woman would sit home and smock."

St. Vincent's Children's Wear enjoyed special tariff privileges: when the finished goods re-entered the U.S. market, duty was paid only on the value added in St. Vincent, and was based only on the low wages paid to the home smockers and not on the painstaking labor and time expended.

Colombian Flower Workers

Flower workers in Colombia face difficulties similar to those of the Caribbean home smockers: low pay, little job security, and occupational health hazards.[169] There are currently about 450 companies in the Colombian flower industry; most are located in the Bogotá Savannah. The flower industry creates approximately 80,000 jobs directly, and another 60,000 in spin-off employment. Seventy percent of these 80,000 direct workers are female. The flower industry also produces high revenues: of the top 100 exporting companies in Bogota, 22 are in the flower industry. According to the Colombian Association of Flower Exporters, ASOCOL-FLORES, the annual growth rate of the industry in the 1990s hovers around 16 percent. The main market for the flowers is North America; the United States receives approximately 80 percent of the flower exports.

Women are overwhelmingly recruited into the lower-paying flower jobs, usually those in the production process and the preparation of flowers for air transport. Women are selected because the employers believe that they will have the necessary high level of discipline and skill for delicate handling. Many flower workers come from urban Bogotá, and are transported by bus or truck to the fields. The workforce is chosen from two main groups: young, single women who have not had children and who have little or no professional experience, and women who are at least 35 years old and are not interested in having more children. Through these hiring policies, employers attempt to reduce their liability for maternity leave and avoid the need to accommodate pregnant workers by changing job assignments.

Usually, women are employed through either fixed-term or piecework contracts. These varied contractual arrangements make it more difficult for unions to organize the flower workers. In addition, the flower industry rotates its workers frequently, which makes it difficult for workers to form stable relationships and further discourages unionization: less than 20 percent of the flower industry workers are unionized.[170] Because of layers of subcontracting, many flower companies are not directly

---

168. *Id.* at 131–32, *citing* BURGHARD CLAUD ET AL., YOUTH AND EMPLOYMENT IN THE LESSER ANTILLES 82 (1982).

169. Gladys Acosta Vargas, *Flowers That Kill: The Case of the Colombian Flower Workers, in* FROM BASIC NEEDS TO BASIC RIGHTS 169, 171–79 (Margaret A. Schuler ed., 1995). All facts and descriptions in this case study come from Vargas, *id.* at 171–79.

170. *Id.* at 177, noting that of the existing unions, many are sponsored by the employers.

responsible for layoffs or contract termination. Workers interviewed by Acosta Vargas said that some companies who send representatives to recruit workers in the working class areas of Bogotá ask women to take a pregnancy test before they will be considered for hiring. Many women begin work without any formalization of their position—even, at times, without having to show identification. Only later, when they are immersed in their jobs, are they asked to sign a complicated contract, which they often do without any direction or guidance. In several cases, women thought that they were signing a contract to continue work, when in fact they had signed a form agreeing to their dismissal.

Women plant and weed on their knees. Other tasks women perform include irrigation in high humidity, flower harvesting, and preparation for storage. Most tasks require the workers to stand all day. There are very few women in supervisory or management roles. Men perform most of the jobs requiring heavy physical strength, such as the opening of water channels and fumigation, and they are better paid than are women.

The production of flowers is chemical-intensive—about 95 different chemicals are used in the flower industry, including fertilizers, dyes, pesticides, fungicides, and insecticides. The chemicals are used to produce flowers of export quality that are entirely free of insects or disease (to satisfy both customs and customers). Workers in the field suffer from many health problems attributable to the chemicals, such as severe respiratory afflictions, headaches, dizziness, cramps, weakness, and fainting. In addition, those in the flower industry refer to a condition called "intoxication," which occurs when recently fumigated flowers are placed against the body or when fumigation dust is inhaled once the product dries out. Sometimes "intoxication" of the intestines, ovaries, and eyes leads to hospitalization. The most serious threats to health are from insecticides that affect the nervous system and can cause paralysis.

These working conditions are the norm despite the Constitution of Colombia, which provides for maternity benefits and expressly prohibits discrimination, and the fact that Colombia has signed many of the major human rights and ILO treaties that protect women workers.

Maquiladora Workers

The *maquiladora* sector provides the third and final case study. *Maquiladoras* are Mexican factories, mainly assembly plants, established along the border of the United States and Mexico to produce goods for export to the developed world. *Maquiladoras* have been used by the Mexican government to integrate that country's economy with that of the rest of the continent.[171] The number of *maquiladoras* has increased since their inception in 1966; 2,158 plants employing approximately

---

171. Kathryn Kopniak, *Household, Gender and Migration in Mexican Maquiladoras: The Case of Nogales, in* INTERNATIONAL MIGRATION, REFUGEE FLOWS AND HUMAN RIGHTS IN NORTH AMERICA: THE IMPACT OF FREE TRADE AND RESTRUCTURING 214, 215 (Alan B. Simmons ed., 1996).

546,000 people.[172] These plants account for over $29 billion (USD) in export earnings for Mexico.[173]

At least half of the Mexicans employed in the *maquiladora* sector are women, and the income they earn supports them and their families at wages higher than they could earn in any other employment sector in northern Mexico,[174] even though real wages had decreased between 1982 and 1990 in the *maquiladora* plants studied by Kopniak.[175]

Women employed in *maquiladoras* routinely suffer gender discrimination. Many plants require them to undergo pregnancy testing as a condition of employment. These exams are administered by doctors or nurses employed at individual *maquiladoras* or by private clinics contracted by the companies. The female applicants are denied work if the tests show them to be pregnant. If a woman becomes pregnant soon after gaining employment at a *maquiladora,* she may be mistreated or forced to resign. For example, the pregnant worker may be assigned to more physically demanding work, or may be continually asked to work extensive overtime.

Many of the female *maquiladora* employees have not finished primary school and have very little work experience outside of the manufacturing sector. As a consequence, as in the flower industry in Colombia,[176] many women view domestic service as their only other employment alternative, an alternative that generally pays poorly, allows them little control over their schedules and working conditions, and provides no health insurance or social security. Given the stark choice between work as a domestic or work in the *maquiladoras,* and the fact that many women are their families' chief or sole breadwinners, women are unwilling to challenge discriminatory practices in the *maquiladoras.*

Maquiladora employers discriminate against pregnant female employees and women of childbearing age largely to keep overhead costs low. Hiring or employing pregnant women entails higher costs because Mexico's federal labor laws contain explicit maternity provisions. According to the federal labor code, companies are required to: protect pregnant women from executing tasks that could cause danger to their health in relation to the fetus; pay pregnant women maternity leave of six weeks before and six weeks after delivery; allow new mothers two paid extra breaks of a half-hour each to breast-feed their infants; and allow pregnant women to take an extra sixty days off while receiving 50 percent of their salary, if they so desire, apart from the twelve weeks of maternity leave. Thus, while many *maquiladoras*

---

172. As of May, 1993. *Id.* at 214.

173. HUMAN RIGHTS WATCH WOMEN'S RIGHTS PROJECT, NO GUARANTEES: SEX DISCRIMINATION IN MEXICO'S MAQUILADORA SECTOR 2 (1996).

174. *Id.* at 2. Unless otherwise noted, all facts and descriptions are from *id.* at 2–5.

175. Kopniak, *supra* note 171, at 216.

176. Vargas, *supra* note 169, at 173.

seek to hire women because they are considered more diligent workers and emotionally and anatomically better able to execute the work than men, employers attempt to weed out potentially costly women workers from the applicant pool.

Women are consciously targeted to fill the least-skilled jobs within the *maquiladoras*.[177] Kopniak found that newspaper advertisements for *maquiladora* jobs often specify gender, and women are overwhelmingly recruited as unskilled production workers.[178] In the workplace, women receive much less training than do men and do not move from unskilled to skilled jobs after acquiring seniority.[179] Because the government has set a minimum wage that has been interpreted as a maximum wage by employers, most female *maquiladora* workers in unskilled positions earn no more than the minimum.[180] Thus, there is little hope of advancing through the ranks to a higher paying job. Finally, women not only fail to gain seniority if they are dismissed or are forced to leave when pregnant, but they also lose seniority because of the fact that they are often migrants.

Companies do not allow for the fact that the migration process is not usually completed in one move, and may take the worker away from the plant for extended periods.[181] Kopniak gives the example of one 19–year-old woman from Guasave who worked in another town on an assembly line putting connectors onto circuits.[182] When she had to return to Guasave, a sixteen hour bus ride away, to help her mother and her younger brother move to join her, she asked for a leave of absence. The plant would not give her permission for a leave of absence, so she had to quit and be rehired, and lost all of her seniority in the process. She may have therefore lost the opportunity to do different jobs or learn new skills, as seniority is sometimes used to determine the kind of work a worker can do in the *maquiladora*.[183]

Lessons of the Case Studies

There are similarities in women's working conditions in all three case studies: low wages, exploitative working conditions, and a disregard for women's reproductive capacity. The low wages attract the export-based businesses as they represent a lower overhead. Women hired on a contract basis (such as the flower workers) or paid piece rates (such as the garment workers) usually do not receive social insurance benefits, as their employer is not required to make contributions to the government on their behalf. Labor deregulation also means that employers can ignore the occupational health and safety of women and view them as part of an unskilled, expendable workforce that can be dismissed once disabled by repetitive

177. Kopniak, *supra* note 171, at 216.

178. *Id.*

179. *Id.*

180. *Id.* at 219.

181. *Id.* at 222.

182. *Id.*

183. *Id.* at 222–23.

strain injuries or exposure to chemicals. Labor deregulation also leads to avoidance of maternity costs. The ILO tried to avoid just such a result by putting the burden of maternity protection on the government in its Maternity Protection Conventions; however, it appears that in practice, many employers in export industries refuse to pay either direct or related maternity costs (such as hiring another person for the duration of the maternity leave) and they therefore avoid hiring women who are or may become pregnant. This is not such a problem in the Caribbean garment worker example, as they work from the home and likely are not entitled to maternity leave. However, the flower and *maquiladora* industries overtly attempt to reduce overhead costs by manipulating the workforce's reproductive capacity.[184] The reality of the labor deregulation surrounding export-based industries is that women's international and regional labor rights are often sidestepped in order to advance the economy.

EXPANDING THE DEFINITION OF PRODUCTIVE ENTERPRISE: THE DEBATE ON WOMEN'S WORTH

Besides the inevitable results of labor deregulation outlined above, women's work is also undervalued in another way: the value of women's production in domestic and agricultural work is usually ignored when a country calculates its Gross Domestic[185] or Gross National Product.[186] It is important that women be included in GDP and GNP calculations for several reasons. First, unless women who work at home in informal labor or in agriculture are included, the tasks that fill the majority of women's time are accordingly devalued and made "invisible" within the national and international economic system, even though the work actually forms an important part of the economic production process. Second, in omitting women from the calculation, fundamental aspects of women's work are ignored by planners, policymakers, and statisticians, which can have serious effects on development projects. Third, GNP and GDP calculations that do not include women's work are accordingly skewed and therefore incorrect: calculations that report women's contributions reflect the true health of the nation and the actual status of women in the nation.

Current national economic policies and practices remain gender-blind because of certain fundamental misperceptions. The first is that the participation of women

---

184. Either through demographically choosing women least likely to become pregnant or by demanding proof of birth control.

185. Gross Domestic Product, "GDP," is a measure of the market value of all goods and services produced within the boundaries of a nation, regardless of asset ownership. Unlike Gross National Product, GDP excludes receipts from that nation's business operations in foreign countries, as well as the share of reinvested earnings in foreign affiliates of domestic corporations. JOHN J. CAPELA & STEPHEN W. HARTMAN, DICTIONARY OF INTERNATIONAL BUSINESS TERMS 230 (1996).

186. Gross National Product, "GNP," is a measure of the market value of all goods and services produced by labor and property of a nation, regardless of asset ownership. GNP includes receipts from that nation's business operation in foreign countries, as well as the share of reinvested earnings in foreign affiliates of domestic corporations. *Id.* at 230.

in the labor force is a recent phenomenon.[187] This assumption reveals a focus on only formal work, such as that one in offices or factories, where it is true that women are recent additions. States thereby fail to count a fundamental portion of production; that is, unpaid work done in the home or in agriculture, or "cottage industry" work done from the home. According to Amato, "work" is traditionally defined by states as jobs held primarily by men, "production" is defined as what men do in the labor force, and GNP is computed according to these traditionally single-sex inputs.[188] Thus, tasks that women have been assigned biologically and culturally, such as reproducing, cooking, sewing, nurturing, supervising, shopping, carrying, and gathering, have not been defined or counted as "work."[189] To describe this in economic terms, the work that many women do in or near the home is not seen as being of as much use-value as work done in the formal economy.[190]

The fact that certain elemental aspects of women's work are not counted in GDP and GNP calculations also renders women's reality invisible to national statisticians, planners, and policymakers.[191] This is problematic, as the underreporting of women's contributions has serious consequences for development policies and strategies, and for the value systems that form the basis of socioeconomic decisions.[192] For example, development policies that fail to understand that women play a particularly important role in the agricultural sector—contributing up to 80 percent of the agricultural labor in African countries south of the Sahara[193]—may be misconceived and actually harm, rather than improve, the economy.

These omissions have been addressed to some extent at the international level. The United Nations Systems of National Accounts (UNSNA)[194] broadly counts the production of goods and services for sale or barter in the market, and the production of goods for personal consumption. Activities included that are relevant to women are: growing or gathering field crops, fruits, and vegetables; producing eggs, milk, and other food; cutting firewood; carrying water; threshing and milling grain; curing hides and skins; preserving meat and fish; making beer, wine, and spirits; crushing oil seeds; weaving baskets and mats; weaving textiles; dressmaking and tailoring;

---

187. Theresa A. Amato, *Women at Work, Rights at Risk—Toward the Empowerment of Working Women,* 17 YALE J. INT'L L. 139, 141 (1992).

188. *Id.*

189. *Id.*

190. BULLOCK, *supra* note 4, at 12.

191. *Id.*

192. SHIRLEY NUSS ETTORE DENTI & DAVID VIRY, WOMEN IN THE WORLD OF WORK: STATISTICAL ANALYSIS AND PROJECTIONS TO THE YEAR 2000 2 (1989).

193. *Id.* at 15, *citing* UNITED NATIONS WORLD SURVEY ON THE ROLE OF WOMEN IN DEVELOPMENT 15 (1986).

194. The UNSNA was revised in 1993, and at that time recommended for the first time that all production of goods in households for their own consumption be included in the measurement of economic output, although it continues to exclude own-account production of services. The World's Women, *supra* note 2, at 107.

and making handicrafts from nonprimary products.[195] In essence, the UNSNA recognizes subsistence and nonmarket activities, as well as household enterprises producing for the market. The United Nations Statistical Commission has stated that national planners adopting a similar valuation model will ultimately be provided with a better picture of production in the household and informal sectors and of important activities in households outside the production boundary, thereby improving the understanding of women's roles in the economy and providing a more accurate and comprehensive basis for social and economic planning.[196]

Note, however, that workers who only render services for personal consumption are not counted by the UNSNA. Cleaning, decorating, and maintaining a dwelling; cleaning and repairing household durables, vehicles, or other goods; preparing and serving meals; caring for, training, and instructing children; caring for the sick, infirm, or elderly; and transporting household members or their goods, for example, are not counted in the UNSNA.[197]

It is important to realize how much weight the UNSNA carries nationally and internationally. Not only do the annual reports of the World Bank, International Monetary Fund, and U.N. agencies rely upon the UNSNA statistics, but the U.N. uses national accounts to assess national contributions and to appraise the success of regional development programs.[198] In addition, aid donors use the UNSNA to identify deserving countries, determining "need" by per capita GDP.[199] The World Bank uses the figures to identify nations that urgently need economic assistance; multinational corporations use the same figures to locate sites for overseas investment; and companies rely on them to project markets for their goods and plan their investment, personnel, and other internal policies.[200] The end result is that many of the core activities that allow society to continue to function, such as child-care and preparation of meals, are not valued as input into production, either at the domestic, regional, or international levels. The true value and breadth of a nation's economy are therefore underestimated, and women's work, knowledge, and experience in the area of personal consumption is ignored in planning economic assistance, overseas investment, and corporate policies, personnel, and spending.[201]

One commentator states that the economic borderline between production occurring in the workplace and consumption occurring in the household is only a conventional line convenient for distinguishing between relatively easy-to-measure

---

195. INTERNATIONAL LABOUR ORGANIZATION, WORLD LABOUR REPORT 1995 14 (1995) [hereinafter "WORLD LABOUR REPORT"].

196. Official Records of the Economic and Social Council, 1989, Supplement No. 3 (E/1989/25), par. 139 cited in The World's Women, supra note 2, at 107.

197. WORLD LABOUR REPORT, supra note 195, at 14.

198. MARILYN WARING, COUNTING FOR NOTHING: WHAT MEN VALUE AND WHAT WOMEN ARE WORTH 2 (1988).

199. Id. at 2.

200. Id.

201. The effect of this invisibility on development programs is noted at notes 192 and 193, supra.

monetary transactions on the one hand, and harder-to-measure non-monetary production for exchange or self-consumption on the other.[202] Whether or not to move
this ''borderline'' to include child-care and preparing meals, for example, is at the
core of a debate centered around three main issues: 1) the extent to which unpaid
household work should be considered ''economic activity'' 2) how this ''economic
activity'' should be identified and measured in surveys and censuses; and 3) what
monetary value should be attached to the measurement of economic activity for
statistical and other assessments.[203]

This ongoing debate was discussed at the United Nations Fourth World Conference on Women, and was described in the resulting Beijing Declaration and Platform for Action:[204]

> 156. . . . Women contribute to development not only through remunerated work but
> also through a great deal of unremunerated work. On the one hand, women participate
> in the production of goods and services for the market and household consumption,
> in agriculture, food production or family enterprises. Though included in the United
> Nations System of National Accounts and therefore in international standards for
> labour statistics, this unremunerated work—particularly that related to agriculture—is
> often undervalued and under–recorded. On the other hand, women still also perform
> the great majority of unremunerated domestic work and community work, such as
> caring for children and older persons, preparing food for the family, protecting the
> environment and providing voluntary assistance to vulnerable and disadvantaged indi-
> viduals and groups. This work is often not measured in quantitative terms and is not
> valued in national accounts. . . .

This paragraph of the Platform for Action highlights the progress that has been
made with the inclusion of agricultural and food production and work in family
enterprises in the UNSNA and identifies the continuing omission of a large portion
of women's everyday domestic, environmental, and volunteer work.

Countries still raise arguments against the inclusion in the GNP and GDP of
production stemming from the informal sector—as long as it is to their advantage.
One main argument for excluding intra-household services from the count of economic activity has been the problem of directly comparing them with marketed
services.[205] However, this argument becomes weaker as economies become more
service-oriented: as the service sector becomes broader, market prices are increasingly being set for services that were once considered to exist only within the

---

202. LUISELLA GOLDSCHMIDT-CLERMONT, UNPAID WORK IN THE HOUSEHOLD: A REVIEW OF ECONOMIC
EVALUATION METHODS 1 (1982).

203. NUSS ET AL., *supra* note 192, at 16, *citing* F. Mehran, *Measurement of Women's Work, in* WOMEN
AT WORK 12 (1983).

204. Report of the Fourth World Conference on Women (Beijing, 4–15 September 1995), A/CONF.177/
20 (17 October 1995).

205. The World's Women, *supra* note 2, at 107. Interestingly, Marilyn Waring comments on countries
that argue that there is a conceptual problem with how to assign value to women's worth: ''It does not
deem to occur to them that if you have a conceptual problem about the activity of half of the human
species, you then have a conceptual problem about the whole.'' Waring, *supra* note 198, at 65.

unpaid household sector.[206] For example, in developed countries, services such as the provision of child-care, elder-care, preparation of meals, housecleaning, transport, and leisure services are now supplied from within the household, through the market, and by the government.[207] Food processing, meal preparation, and provision of water and fuel are also increasingly marketed in developing regions.[208] In addition, time-use accounts and household production accounts may provide a reliable method for measuring outputs. Time-use accounts measure, over a fixed period of time, the actual time a woman spends on each of her tasks. Household production accounts tally what is actually produced when a woman does each of her daily tasks. Each method is detailed and has the advantage of being easily linked to national accounts through the measurement and distribution of labor inputs and outputs of goods and services.[209]

Besides the argument that it is too difficult to measure the economic production of the informal sector, some have argued that inclusion of this production will artificially "inflate" the GDP or GNP of a country, perhaps to the country's disadvantage. However, Waring points out that this "inflation" and concomitant "deflation" already go on; she refers to this as "shifting boundaries" when valuing GNP and GDP. She notes that the boundary is often shifted when an undeveloped country recognizes "black market activities" or work by rural women as economically productive but then realizes that the boosted GDP may jeopardize the country's "undeveloped" status under the definition of the World Bank, which may consequently jeopardize the country's ability to access concessionary loans.[210] The reverse scenario occurs when countries like Thailand seek additional World Bank loans, and therefore shift the boundary of production to include revenues created by prostitution, trafficking in women, and related work, to demonstrate that it has the ability to repay the loan.[211] This argument may be answered by looking to the recommendation of the ILO for a consistent worldwide method of valuing women's work.[212]

A third argument, which is actually a fear of severe political consequences, is that a proper classification of economic activity could reveal massive underemployment, as well as hidden unemployment, of women who would prefer jobs in the formal sector to unpaid family work in the informal sector.[213] However, this fear

---

206. The World's Women, *supra* note 2, at 107.

207. *Id.*

208. *Id.*

209. *Id.*

210. Marilyn Waring, *The Exclusion of Women from "Work" and Opportunity, in* HUMAN RIGHTS IN THE TWENTY-FIRST CENTURY 109, 111 (Kathleen E. Mahoney & Paul Mahoney eds., 1993).

211. *Id.*

212. BULLOCK, *supra* note 4, at 13, *citing* the ILO Convention on Labour Statistics (1985), revisions to the International Standard Classification of Occupations, and efforts by the United Nations Food and Agricultural Organization to change the guidelines for the World Programme of Agricultural Censuses.

213. NUSS ET AL., *supra* note 192, at 16.

does not recognize the importance to governments, planners, statisticians, and policymakers of knowing and understanding the true state of affairs of the country.

The Committee on the Elimination of Discrimination Against Women, (CEDAW Committee), has addressed the issue of valuing women's unpaid work, recognizing that valuation is not possible without the collection of gender-specific data. In 1989, the CEDAW Committee adopted General Recommendation 9 on "Statistical data concerning the situation of women,"[214] requesting that states parties make every effort to ensure that their national statistical services responsible for planning national censuses and other social and economic surveys formulate their questionnaires in such a way that data can be disaggregated according to gender. In 1991, the Committee formulated General Recommendation 17 on "The measurement and quantification of the unremunerated domestic activities of women and their recognition in the gross national product," which requests that states take steps to quantify and include the unremunerated domestic activities of women in the GNP, as well as to report on efforts to measure and value unremunerated domestic work.[215] In addition, the CEDAW Committee formulated General Recommendation 16 that same year on "Unpaid women workers in rural and urban family enterprises." This General Recommendation asks states parties to: include in their reports to the Committee information on the legal and social situation of unpaid women working in family enterprises; collect statistical data on women who work without payment, social security, and social benefits in enterprises owned by a family member, and include these data in their report to the Committee; and take all necessary steps to guarantee payment, social security, and social benefits for women who work without such benefits in enterprises owned by a family member.[216]

CONCLUSIONS

International labor standards, whether found in ILO conventions and recommendations, in the Women's Convention and the CEDAW Committee's General Recommendations, or elsewhere create a fairly comprehensive web of protective and nondiscrimination rights for women. This does not mean that women's labor interests are completely addressed, however. There is much room for development of labor laws in areas such as women homeworkers and sexual harassment in the workplace. The issue of whether and how labor standards can be used to protect women working mainly in the informal sector should be pursued. Labor rights for

---

214. General Recommendation 9 of the Committee on the Elimination of Discrimination Against Women, (8th session, 1989), Statistical Data Concerning the Situation of Women, U.N. Doc. HRI/Gen/1/Rev. 1 (1994).

215. General Recommendation 17 of the Committee on the Elimination of Discrimination Against Women, (10th session, 1991), Measurement and Quantification of the Unremunerated Domestic Activities of Women and Their Recognition in the Gross Domestic Product, U.N. Doc. HRI/Gen/1/Rev. 1 at 82 (1994), paras. (b) and (c).

216. General Recommendation 16 of the Committee on the Elimination of Discrimination Against Women, (10th session, 1991), Unpaid Women Workers in Rural and Urban Family Enterprises, U.N. Doc. HRI/Gen/1/Rev. 1 at 82 (1994).

women who are self-employed, or who are part-time, contract, or piece workers also require detailed study and resolution. Additionally, work needs to be done by advocates to reject or reconcile protective standards, such as night and underground work by women, and nondiscrimination norms.

One of the most difficult challenges for advocates working in labor issues is comparing the existing labor standards, whether international or national, with practical consideration of working women. In some cases, existing national laws are being ignored, and in others international laws which have been ratified have not been implemented domestically. In some cases, national labor standards have been waived in order to attract export industries, and no political will exists to counter this labor deregulation. Advocates are countering these alarming trends by bringing complaints to the ILO and other international bodies, including unions, as well as protesting nationally.

Finally, although the United Nations System of National Accounts has been revised to include many tasks mainly performed by women, advocates must lobby national governments to follow the lead of the United Nations to include women's work in economic indicators. One step is to lobby states to redesign census questionnaires to reflect time-use of women's unpaid work. Another strategy is to contribute to the discussions assigning value to previously unvalued activities. A longer-term goal may be to revise the UNSNA again to include those activities presently excluded that represent a large portion of women's unpaid work. Once these economic questions begin to be asked from the vantage point of women's work, it will be possible to discern some of the outlines of the radical transformation in our political and economic structures that will be demanded when women's experience is taken seriously.[217]

---

217. BULLOCK, *supra* note 4, at 4, *citing* Maria Riley, *Women and Work: Linking Faith and Justice, in* WORLD COUNCIL OF CHURCHES REPORT 7 (1988).

WOMEN AND EDUCATION

Margaret E. Galey

INTRODUCTION

Several international instruments set forth the international right to education for all people. One instrument specifically (though not exclusively) addresses the right to education for women and girls. Together, these instruments define the international right to education for all women and girls and delineate state responsibility for providing it. But, despite this, the staggering number of illiterates in the world, estimated to be 905 million (65% of them women and girls), illustrate that the international right to education is being neglected.[1]

A major proposition of this chapter is that the international right to education for women and girls, and state responsibility for giving effect to this right, has been adequately defined in these instruments. A corollary is that although ratifying states have consented to provide education for everyone, including women and girls, they have not yet fulfilled their obligations for political and institutional reasons. Women who have become a political force in the world have not yet succeeded in influencing governments to provide, improve, or expand education. Discriminatory attitudes against educating women and girls persist. Political leaders often give higher priority to other pressing issues, whether they be restoring war-torn societies, building infrastructure for civil societies, or attempting to cope with rapid population growth. The latter is outpacing the expansion of educational facilities.

Institutional problems also impede the enjoyment of education by women and girls. The relevant international instruments have created a decentralized arrangement for giving effect to education at national and international levels. Coordination at both levels among major entities is essential but is not always effective. In addition, technical assistance programs of U.N. Agencies and Programs have not fully incorporated gender perspectives into their programs and policies.

In considering these propositions, it is useful first to describe briefly the international right to education and its scope as set forth in the various instruments, and then to analyze the institutional framework for implementing the right to education.

---

1. UNITED NATIONS, FROM NAIROBI TO BEIJING 225–234 (1995) [hereinafter FROM NAIROBI TO BEIJING].

FORMULATING THE INTERNATIONAL RIGHT TO EDUCATION FOR WOMEN, 1945–1997

It was not until the U.N. Commission on the Status of Women recommended, and the U.N. General Assembly approved, the 1979 Convention on the Elimination of All Forms of Discrimination Against Women (Women's Convention) that the right to education for women and girls was first explicitly specified in a legally binding international instrument. Prior to this time, however, two major international conferences in the immediate post-World War II period helped pave the way for governments to formulate an international right to education.

The first conference, in 1945, was the San Francisco Conference on International Organization. Delegations did not define the right to education, but they gave human rights and fundamental freedoms without distinction as to race, sex, nationality, or religion a new international legal status, thus preparing the way for development of the right. They also pledged in U.N. Charter Article 55 to achieve friendly relations among states and, to this end, promote international cultural and educational cooperation. In Article 57, delegations agreed to create a specialized agency in the fields of education and culture.[2]

The second conference, the Conference of Inter-Allied Ministers of Education (CAME), which was initiated in 1942, led to the establishment of the Educational, Scientific and Cultural Organization of the United Nations (UNESCO) in November 1945.[3] The UNESCO Constitution, in its preamble, refers to "full and equal opportunities for education for all" and states that "the education of humanity for justice and liberty and peace are indispensable . . . and constitute a sacred duty which all the nations must fulfill in a spirit of mutual assistance and concern." UNESCO's purposes included contributing to "peace and security by promoting collaboration among nations through education, science and culture" and giving "fresh impulse to popular education." To these ends, members are "to collaborate in developing educational activities and to advance the ideal of equality of educational opportunity without regard to race, sex, or any distinctions, economic or social."[4]

Subsequently, two U.N. policy bodies—the U.N. Commission on Human Rights and the Commission on the Status of Women—and one U.N. Specialized Agency—UNESCO—have prepared several major international instruments that incorporate the right to education and define state responsibility for it.

---

2. In 1941, U.S. President Roosevelt articulated the four freedoms in his 1944 State of the Union Address. Notably, the "right to a good education" was one of the points included in what Roosevelt called a "second bill of rights." The American Law Institute proposed that in addition to listing the rights contained in the U.S. Bill of Rights, the draft international Bill of Rights include a range of rights, notably, that the state has a duty to require that every child within its jurisdiction receive primary education. HENRY STEINER & PHILIP ALSTON, INTERNATIONAL HUMAN RIGHTS IN CONTEXT 258–259 (1996). *See also* LELAND GOODRICH & EDVARD HAMBRO, CHARTER OF THE UNITED NATIONS: COMMENTARY AND DOCUMENTS (3rd ed. 1969); and RUTH RUSSELL, HISTORY OF THE UNITED NATIONS CHARTER (1958).

3. C. Mildred Thompson, *United Nations Plans for Post-War Education,* 20 FOREIGN POL'Y REP. 310–19, March 1, 1945.

4. UNESCO Constitution, Nov. 16, 1945, 52 U.N.T.S. 275–302.

— The U.N. Commission on Human Rights (CHR): Established at the first session of the Economic and Social Council (ECOSOC) in 1946, the CHR prepared the Universal Declaration on Human Rights, the Convention on the Elimination of Race Discrimination, the International Covenant on Economic, Social and Cultural Rights, and the Convention on the Rights of the Child, all of which assert rights to education.[5] CHR also prepared the International Covenant on Civil and Political Rights, which does not explicitly refer to the right to education.[6]

— The U.N. Commission on the Status of Women (CSW): CSW's amended terms of reference stated its aim to prepare recommendations and report to ECOSOC on promoting women's rights in political, economic, civil, social, and educational fields. Based on responses to a comprehensive questionnaire sent to governments, CSW urged them to affirm women's access to all levels of education and recommended to UNESCO that it draft a Convention Against Discrimination in Education.[7] Subsequently, after preparing several conventions (on Political Rights, Nationality and Consent to Marriage and Registration of Marriages), CSW recommended the 1967 Declaration and the 1979 Convention on the Elimination of All Forms of Discrimination Against Women.[8]

— UNESCO: The General Conference adopted the Convention Against Discrimination in Education in 1960 upon recommendations from CSW and CHR's Sub-Commission on Prevention of Discrimination and Protection of Minorities.[9] In

---

5.   UNITED NATIONS CENTRE FOR HUMAN RIGHTS, UN ACTION IN THE FIELD OF HUMAN RIGHTS 134–139, U.N. Doc. ST/HR/2/REV.4(1994) [hereinafter UN ACTION 1994]. The texts of the international instruments are to be found as follows: The Universal Declaration of Human Rights, UNGA Resolution 217(III)A of 10 Dec. 1948, *reprinted in* 43 ASIL (Supp.) 127(1949) [hereinafter Universal Declaration]. The Convention on the Elimination of All Forms of Racial Discrimination, *adopted* March 7, 1996, 660 U.N.T.S. 195 (*in force* January 4, 1969) [hereinafter Race Convention]. The International Covenant on Economic, Social and Cultural Rights, *adopted* Dec. 16, 1966, 993 U.N.T.S. 3 (*in force* Jan. 3, 1976) [hereinafter ICESCR]. The Convention on the Rights of the Child, *adopted* Nov. 20, 1989, U.N. Doc. A/RES/44/25 (*in force* Sept. 2, 1990), *reprinted in* 28 ILM 1448–90 (1989) [hereinafter Child Convention].

6.   The International Covenant on Civil and Political Rights, *adopted* Dec. 16, 1966, 999 U.N.T.S. 171 (*in force* March 23 1976) [hereinafter ICCPR]. Article 18(4) refers to the ''liberty of parents, and when applicable, legal guardians to ensure the religious and moral education of their children in conformity with their own convictions.''

7.   THE UNITED NATIONS AND THE ADVANCEMENT OF WOMEN 1945–1995, 135–144, 169–171 (U.N. Blue Book Series VI, 1995); M.E. Galey, *Women Find a Place, in* WOMEN, POLITICS AND THE UNITED NATIONS 11, 27 (Anne Winslow ed., 1995).

8.   The Convention on the Elimination of All Forms of Discrimination Against Women, *adopted* Dec. 18, 1979, 1249 U.N.T.S. 13 (*in force* Sept. 3 1981) [hereinafter Women's Convention]. The Declaration on the Elimination of All Forms of Discrimination Against Women, *adopted* Nov. 7, 1967, UNGA Res. 2263(XXII), *in* YEARBOOK OF THE UNITED NATIONS 518–520 (1967). The Convention on the Political Rights of Women, 193 U.N.T.S. 135 (*in force* March 31, 1953). The Convention on the Nationality of Married Women, 309 U.N.T.S. 65 (*in force* Aug. 11, 1958). The Convention on the Consent to Marriage, Minimum Age for Marriage and the Registration of Marriages, 521 U.N.T.S. 231 (*in force* Dec. 9, 1964).

9.   UNESCO Convention Against Discrimination in Education [hereinafter UNESCO Convention], December 14, 1960, 429 U.N.T.S. 93 (*entered into force* May 22, 1962) [hereinafter UNESCO Convention]. See discussion in LOUIS B. SOHN & THOMAS BUERGENTHAL, INTERNATIONAL PROTECTION OF HUMAN

1990, UNESCO, along with the World Bank, the U.N. International Children's Fund, and the U.N. Development Program, prepared the World Declaration on Education.[10]

In addition, several regional organizations have developed instruments that assert the right to education: the OAS Charter as amended by the Protocol of Buenos Aires,[11] the Additional Protocol to the American Convention on Human Rights in the Area of Economic, Social and Cultural Rights,[12] the First Protocol to the European Convention on the Protection of Human Rights and Fundamental Freedoms,[13] and the African Charter on Human Rights and Peoples' Rights.[14]

In this chapter, the following major U.N.-sponsored instruments which articulate state responsibility for education for women and girls are discussed:

— The Universal Declaration on Human Rights (Universal Declaration)

— UNESCO Convention Against Discrimination in Education (UNESCO Convention)

— Convention on the Elimination of All Forms of Racial Discrimination (Race Convention)

— International Covenant on Economic, Social, and Cultural Rights (ICESCR)

— Convention on the Elimination of Discrimination Against Women (Women's Convention)

— Convention on the Rights of the Child (Child Convention)

— Declaration on Education (Education Declaration)

RIGHTS 533–535 (1973). UNESCO has also adopted several regional conventions on the Recognition of Studies, Diplomas and Degrees in Higher Education in Latin America and in the Caribbean; in the Arab and European States Bordering on the Mediterranean; in the Arab States; in the Europe Region, and in the African States. For texts of UNESCO's Conventions and other documents, *see* UNESCO's STANDARD-SETTING INSTRUMENTS I.A.1 I.A.8 (1992).

10.   MEETING BASIC LEARNING NEEDS: BACKGROUND DOCUMENT OF THE WORLD CONFERENCE ON EDUCATION FOR ALL 152, 164 (United Nations, WCEFA, 1990).

11.   The OAS Charter as amended by the Protocol of Buenos Aires, *reprinted in* 33 ILM 1994, 987–1004. The OAS Charter as amended by the Protocol of Washington urges "eradication of illiteracy and expansion of educational opportunities for all" (art. 33(h)). Signed in Bogota in 1948 and amended by the Protocol of Buenos Aires in 1967 and by the Protocol of Cartagena de Indias in 1985, *in force* Nov. 16, 1988.

12.   The Additional Protocol to the American Convention on Human Rights, in the Area of Economic, Social and Cultural Rights, *reprinted in* 28 ILM, 160–169 (1989), at art. 13. This Protocol is also known as the "Protocol of San Salvador" (not yet in force, *see* art. 21).

13.   Protocol No. 1 to the European Convention on the Protection of Human Rights and Fundamental Freedoms, Council of Europe (20 March 1954), at art. 2; 1 EUROPEAN CONVENTIONS AND AGREEMENTS 39–47 (1971).

14.   The Organization of African Unity's African Charter on Human and Peoples' Rights, *reprinted in* 21 ILM 59–68 (1982) [hereinafter African Charter], at art. 17.

NATURE OF THE RIGHT AND SCOPE OF STATE RESPONSIBILITY FOR EDUCATION

It is necessary to define the nature and scope of state responsibility with respect to who is to be educated, the purposes of education, the conditions of education, the types of education, and achieving the right to education.

Who Is To Be Educated?

The following major international instruments refer to the right of all people to education:

The Universal Declaration states "everyone has the right to education." (art. 26)

The UNESCO Convention, in its preamble, affirms Article 26 of the Universal Declaration. It further provides that "everyone" regardless of race, color, sex, language, religion, political, national or social groups, or any person or group of persons is entitled to education. It also refers to the right of members of national minorities to carry on their own educational activities. (art. 1)

The Race Convention provides for the right of "everyone" to enjoy the right to education and training. (art. 5(e)(v))

The Child Convention refers to the right of the "child" to education. (art. 28)

The ICESCR refers to "the right of everyone to education". (art. 13)

The Women's Convention refers to ensuring women equal rights with men in the field of education. (art. 10)

The Declaration on Education "recalls that education is a fundamental right for all people, women and men, of all ages" (preamble); holds that "every person-child, youth, and adult-shall be able to benefit from educational opportunities designed to meet their basic learning needs". (art 1)

Thus, only the Women's Convention and the Declaration on Education explicitly refer to the right of women and girls to education. The gender-neutral terms "everyone," "all" and "child" may, however, be assumed to include both females and males.[15] Collectively, these instruments establish the international right of everyone, women and men, girls and boys, to education.

---

15. Gender neutral terms appear in several regional instruments. Protocol No. 1 to the European Convention, *supra* note 13, provides that "[n]o person shall be denied the right to education." (art. 2). The African Charter, *supra* note 14, provides that "[e]very individual shall have the right to education." (art. 17). The Additional Protocol to the American Convention on Human Rights, *supra* note 12, provides that "[e]veryone has the right to education." (art. 13(1)).

Purposes of Education

None of the major instruments define the meaning of education, but they do identify several purposes, types, and conditions of education.[16] The principle purpose of education is the full development of the human personality. The Universal Declaration, the UNESCO Convention, and ICESCR all assert this purpose.[17] The Child Convention, referring to both girls and boys, emphasizes the development of the child's personality, talents, and mental and physical abilities to their fullest potential.[18] The Women's Convention provides that all ratifying states are to take "all appropriate measures to ensure the full development and advancement of women" and "all appropriate measures to eliminate discrimination against women in order to ensure to them equal rights with men in the field of education."[19]

Subsidiary purposes of education include: strengthening respect for human rights and fundamental freedoms;[20] promoting understanding, tolerance, and friendship of all nations, racial or religious groups;[21] furthering the activities of the United Nations for maintaining peace;[22] and promoting respect for parents.[23] Uniquely, the

---

16. The European Court of Human Rights defined education as distinct from instruction. Education refers to the process in society in which adults seek to transmit their beliefs, culture, and other values to the young. Teaching or instruction refers to the transmission of knowledge and to intellectual development. The word "education" in international instruments refers to the more formal types of instruction given in institutions. GERALDINE VAN BUEREN, THE INTERNATIONAL LAW ON THE RIGHTS OF THE CHILD 233 (1994).

17. Universal Declaration, *supra* note 5, art. 26(2); UNESCO Convention, *supra* note 9, art. 5(1)(a); ICESCR, *supra* note 5, art. 13(1).

18. Child Convention, *supra* note 5, art. 29(1)(a).

19. Women's Convention, *supra* note 8, arts. 3 and 10.

20. The major instruments all assert this purpose. *See* Universal Declaration, *supra* note 5, at preamble and art. 26(2); ICESCR, *supra* note 5, art. 13(1); UNESCO Convention, *supra* note 9, art. 5(1)(a); and the Child Convention, *supra* note 5, art. 19(1)(b). The Women's Convention, *supra* note 8, does not specify it in Article 10 (education), but does stipulate that states are to ensure the full development of women to guarantee their exercise and enjoyment of human rights and fundamental freedoms (art. 3).

21. The major instruments all assert this purpose, except the Women's Convention. *See* Universal Declaration, *supra* note 5, art. 26(2); UNESCO Convention, *supra* note 9, art. 5(1)(a); ICESCR, *supra* note 5, art. 13(1); Child Convention, *supra* note 5, art. 29(1)(d). The Women's Convention, *supra* note 8, instead enjoins states parties to take all appropriate measures to modify social and cultural patterns of conduct of men and women to achieve elimination of prejudices and customary and discriminatory practices (art. 5(a)).

22. The Universal Declaration, the UNESCO Convention, and ICESCR each provide this in art. 26(2), art. 5(1)(a), and art. 13(1) respectively. The Child Convention implies it by its reference to promoting human rights and fundamental freedoms and the preparation of the child for life in society in the spirit of understanding, peace, and tolerance. The 12th preambular paragraph of the Women's Convention states that full and complete development of a country, the welfare of the world, and the cause of peace require maximum participation of women on equal terms with men.

23. The ICCPR, *supra* note 6, enjoins states parties to have respect for the liberty of parents and, where applicable, legal guardians to ensure the religious and moral education of their children in conformity with their own convictions (art. 18). The Child Convention, *supra* note 5, asserts the "development of respect for the child's parents" to be an aim of education along with his or her own cultural identity, language, and values, for the national values of the country in which the child is living, the

Child Convention provides for the development of respect for the natural environment.[24]

Regarding the role of parents, the Universal Declaration, ICCPR, ICESCR, and the UNESCO Convention call on ratifying governments to respect the liberty of parents to choose schools for their children and ensure their moral and religious education in conformity with their convictions.[25] The Women's Convention contains no similar reference but calls on states to ensure the recognition of the common responsibility of men and women in the upbringing and development of children.[26]

Conditions of Education

Collectively, these major instruments set forth three principal conditions of education that ratifying states must provide. The first condition, free and compulsory education, is defined in the Universal Declaration, ICESCR, and Child Convention.[27] The UNESCO Convention calls on states parties to make primary education free and compulsory by formulating, developing, and applying a national policy.[28] The Women's Convention does not refer to free and compulsory education but does address all types of education, including primary education.

The second condition is non-discrimination and equal educational opportunity for all. The Universal Declaration, the ICCPR, the ICESCR, and the Race Convention all affirm this condition. The UNESCO Convention, the Women's Convention, and the Child Convention are more specific. Each condemns and prohibits discrimination. In the 1960 UNESCO Convention, "discrimination" includes any distinction of any kind, such as race, color, sex, language, religion, political or other opinion, national or social origin, property, birth or other status, or exclusion, limitation, or preference which has the effect of nullifying or impairing equality of treatment in education.[29] The UNESCO Convention specifies the meaning of impaired treatment and three situations deemed to be non-discriminatory and it also

---

country from which he or she originates, and for civilizations different from his or her own. (art. 29(1)(c)). Neither the Universal Declaration, UNESCO Convention, ICESCR, nor the Women's Convention refer to this.

24. Child Convention, *supra* note 5, art.29(1)(e).

25. Universal Declaration, *supra* note 5, art. 26(3); UNESCO Convention, *supra* note 9, art. 5(1)(b); ICESCR, *supra* note 5, art. 18(4); ICCPR, *supra* note 6, art. 18(4).

26. Women's Convention, *supra* note 8, art. 5(2).

27. Universal Declaration, *supra* note 5, art. 26(1); ICESCR, *supra* note 5, art. 13(2)(b) and art. 14; Child Convention, *supra* note 5, art. 28(1)(d). Importantly, the ICESCR obliges states to immediately establish primary free and compulsory education for all and if a state party has not satisfied this obligation, to take very precise measures toward this goal in two years. This immediacy contrasts with the principle of the "progressive introduction" of all other types of education identified in the ICESCR. Philip Alston, *The International Covenant on Economic, Social and Cultural Rights, in* MANUAL ON HUMAN RIGHTS REPORTING 67–68 (1991).

28. UNESCO Convention, *supra* note 9, art. 4(a).

29. Vernon Van Dyke, *Equality and Discrimination in Education: A Comparative and International Analysis*, 17 INT'L STUDIES Q. 375–404 (1973).

calls on states parties to pay the greatest attention to any recommendations adopted by subsequent UNESCO Conferences that define measures to be taken against different forms of discrimination and to ensure equality of opportunity and treatment in education.[30]

The Child Convention reiterates the non-discrimination provision of the Universal Declaration and the two Covenants (ICCPR and ICESCR) in its preamble. It then prohibits sex-discrimination and enjoins states to take all appropriate measures to ensure that children are protected against all forms of discrimination.[31]

The Women's Convention definition of discrimination is similar to that in the UNESCO Convention, but it specifically emphasizes discrimination against women. Article 1 defines this as "any distinction, exclusion or restriction . . . which has the effect or purpose of impairing or nullifying the recognition, enjoyment or exercise by women, irrespective of their marital status, on a basis of equality of men and women, of human rights and fundamental freedoms in the political, economic, social, cultural, civil or any other field." Article 2 of the Women's Convention condemns discrimination and calls on states parties to persue by "all appropriate means" to eliminate it "without delay." Article 10 of the Women's Convention calls on states parties to "take all appropriate measures to eliminate discrimination against women in order to ensure them equal rights with men in the field of education," and, on a basis of equality of men and women, to ensure the same educational conditions and opportunities. In Article 4, the Women's Convention provides that states parties may adopt temporary special measures to accelerate *de facto* equality between men and women. These are not to be considered discriminatory and in no way are they to maintain unequal or separate standards, but shall be discontinued when the objectives of equality of opportunity and treatment have been achieved.

---

30. UNESCO Convention, *supra* note 9, art. 1(1) and art. 2. The four examples of impaired treatment comprise: 1) depriving or limiting any person or group of persons of access to education of any type or any level; 2) limiting any person or group of persons to education of an inferior standard; 3) establishing or maintaining separate educational systems or institutions for persons or groups of persons subject to Article 2; or 4) inflicting on any person or groups of persons conditions incompatible with the dignity of human beings. The three situations defined as non-discriminatory are: 1) separate educational systems for pupils of the two genders, if they offer equivalent access to education, teaching staff and equipment, and equivalent courses; 2) establishment for religious or linguistic reasons, of separate educational systems that offer education in keeping with the wishes of parents or legal guardians, if participation or attendance is optional and if it conforms to standards set forth by competent authorities; 3) establishment or maintenance of private educational institutions if the object is not to exclude any group but provide facilities in addition to those provided by public authorities. Burrows notes that the UNESCO Convention does not define the term "equivalent" in the phrase "equivalent access to education" and this omission enables the state to define the term and its use. The UNESCO Convention in this respect does not address the problem of sex-role stereotyping in education. Noreen Burrows, *The 1979 Convention on the Elimination of All Forms of Discrimination Against Women*, 32 NETHERLANDS INT'L L. REV. 435 (1985).

UNESCO'S General Conference has adopted numerous subsequent recommendations in this regard. *See* UNESCO'S STANDARD-SETTING INSTRUMENTS, *supra* note 9; Stephen Marks, *UNESCO and Human Rights*, 13 TEX. J. INT'L L 35–67 (1977).

31. Child Convention, *supra* note 5, art. 2(1)(2) and art. 28(1). *See* Frances Olsen, *Feminist Approaches to Children's Rights, in* CHILDREN, RIGHTS AND THE LAW 197 (Philip Alston, Stephen Parker & John Seymour eds., 1992).

Λ third condition reflected in these instruments is minimum state standards. The UNESCO Convention, ICESCR, and the Child Convention call for educational institutions to conform to minimum standards established by the state.[32] The UNESCO Convention provides that the standard of education must not be lower than the general standard approved by the competent authorities.[33] The Women's Convention does not refer to such standards. Rather, it calls on states parties to take all appropriate measures to eliminate discrimination against women and to ensure the same conditions for various types of education.[34]

These conditions and the non-discriminatory principle of education strengthen the interpretation of the gender neutral terms "everyone" and "all" and "every person" to mean girls and women and boys and men.

Types of Education

The conditions of non-discrimination and equal opportunity, as well as minimum standards, are to apply to various types of education, including free and compulsory primary education, as illustrated in Table I, infra. The UNESCO Convention and the Women's Convention offer the most comprehensive coverage. The

TABLE I

Type of Education	UDHR	UNESCO	ICCPR	ICESCR	Child Conv.	Women's Conv.
Fundamental/Primary	X	X			X	X
Secondary		X	X		X	X
Higher Education	X	X	X		X	X
Technical/Vocational		X			X	X
Continuing		X				X
Functional Literacy Programs for School Leavers					X	X
Sports/Physical Ed.		X				X
Family Planning Information						X
Teacher Training		X				X
Scholarships/Study Grants		X			X	X
School Discipline			X		X	

SOURCE: Compendium of International Conventions Concerning the Status of Women (1988).

32.   ICESCR, *supra* note 5, art. 13(4); Child Convention, *supra* note 5, art. 29(2); UNESCO Convention, *supra* note 9, art. 5(1)(c)(ii).

33.   UNESCO Convention, *id.* art.5(1)(c)(ii).

34.   Women's Convention, *supra* note 8, art. 10.

UNESCO Convention refers to all types and levels of education. The Women's Convention specifies all categories of education from pre-school and general through higher education.

Achieving the Right to Education

State responsibility to provide education differs in each treaty. The ICESCR and the Child Convention call for the progressive realization of the right, but state that primary education shall have immediate effect. The UNESCO Convention and the Women's Convention do not refer to progressive realization, but both offer strong formulations for achieving the right.

"All appropriate measures," as defined in Article 2 of the Women's Convention, are the most comprehensive of any of the international instruments considered here, requiring ratifying states:

(a) To embody the principle of equality of men and women in national constitutions or other appropriate legislation . . . and to ensure, through law and other appropriate means, the practical realization of this principle;

(b) To adopt appropriate legislative and other measures, including sanctions where appropriate, prohibiting discrimination against women;

(c) To establish legal protection of the rights of women on an equal basis with men and to ensure through competent national tribunals and other public institutions the effective protection of women against any act of discrimination;

(d) To refrain from engaging in any act or practice of discrimination against women and to ensure that public authorities and institutions shall act in conformity with this obligation;

(e) To take all appropriate measures to eliminate discrimination against women by any person, organization or enterprise;

(f) To take all appropriate measures, including legislation, to modify or abolish existing laws, regulations, customs and practices which constitute discrimination against women; [and],

(g) To repeal all national penal provisions which constitute discrimination against women.[35]

Besides providing for achieving the right to education, each of these conventions also defines the procedure by which governments consent to fulfill their obligations. Each prescribes how ratification is to be achieved, under what conditions, when the treaty will enter into force, the permissibility of reservations, and where the instruments of ratification are to be deposited. Ratifying states also undertake obligations to implement the respective conventions through international efforts, discussed below.

---

35. Women's Convention, *id.* at art 2. Article 4 of the Women's Convention provides that states may also adopt temporary measures to achieve de facto equality; Article 5, requires measures to modify social and cultural patterns of the conduct of men and women with a view to eliminating prejudice and customary and other discriminatory practices.

In sum, these eight major international instruments: the Universal Declaration, the ICCPR, the ICESCR, the Race Convention, the Child Convention, the UNESCO Convention, the Women's Convention, and the Declaration on Education, together articulate a comprehensive state responsibility to provide all people, women and men, girls and boys, education of all categories and types. The Women's Convention's emphasis on women and girls strengthens this assertion. These instruments also identify the purposes of education and the conditions of education. In the latter respect, free and compulsory primary education, non-discrimination and equal access to all forms of education, and minimum standards are to be achieved.

The international right to education for women and girls is indisputable. But, despite its existence in international human rights law, education is but one of many rights enumerated in these instruments. With the exception of the UNESCO Convention, whose exclusive focus is education, all refer to other human rights such as life, liberty, and the security of the person; the right to thought, conscience, and religion; the right of peaceful assembly; the right to stand for election and hold public office; the right to employment, and the right to health. The incorporation of several human rights within individual instruments raises the question of the priority governments accord rights to be achieved.[36] Undoubtedly, the right to education is interrelated with other human rights.[37] The typology of rights developed by Donnelly and Howard elucidates the fundamental importance of education. They define survival rights (rights to life), membership rights (those pertaining to belonging to a community), protection rights (those regarding protection from sexual abuse and exploitation), and empowerment rights (the right to education). Education is considered an empowerment right because it is concerned with personal autonomy and efficacy and enables the individual to shape the direction of his or her life by providing the basic intellectual capacity to think seriously about the good life, assess actions, institutions and ideas, and choose a course of action.[38] Education is necessary for full enjoyment of the other sets of rights.

GIVING EFFECT TO THE INTERNATIONAL RIGHT TO EDUCATION

To apply the right to education, governments must give effect to the provisions of these instruments through national and international action. National action is essential. It may be supplemented by international action, but the latter cannot substitute for it. Action at both national and international levels has fostered a complex decentralized institutional structure to promote compliance with the right to education; yet, this very structure may impede full implementation.

---

36. Dinah L. Shelton, *Women and the Right to Education,* VII RENUE DES DROITS DE L'HOMME 51–70 (1975).

37. Shelton, *id. See also* Manfred Nowak, *The Right to Education, in* ECONOMIC, SOCIAL, AND CULTURAL RIGHTS 193 (Asbjorn Eide et al. eds., 1995) who refers to the first generation political and civil rights; second generation economic, social, and cultural rights and third generation group rights.

38. Jack Donnelly & Rhoda Howard, *Assessing National Human Rights Performance: A Theoretical Framework,* 10 HUM. RTS Q. 214–248 (1988); LAWRENCE J. LEBLANC, CONVENTION ON THE RIGHTS OF THE CHILD 175 (1996).

After discussing national action, this chapter considers the following aspects of international implementation: 1) reporting procedures of U.N. policy bodies; 2) reporting and complaint procedures of treaty bodies; 3) recommendations of international conferences; 4) technical assistance measures; and 5) the activities of nongovernmental organizations (NGOs).

National Action

Governments must ratify or accede to the instruments and then enact implementing legislation or other measures to give effect to the rights embodied in the instruments in municipal law and practice. All of these conventions have been ratified by the required number of states and have entered into force.[39] In ratifying, states may make reservations, declarations, or understandings to a convention if the treaty permits it.[40] The UNESCO Convention prohibits reservations. However, several states have reserved on Article 13 (Education) of the ICESCR[41] and on Article 10 (Education) of the Women's Convention.[42] Several governments have made general

---

39. The UNESCO Convention entered into force on 22 May 1960, and has 75 states parties. *Supra* note 9. The ICESCR entered into force 3 January 1976 and has 133 states parties; the ICCPR entered into force on 3 January 1976 and has 132 states parties; the Women's Convention entered into force on 3 September 1981 and has 151 states parties; the Child Convention entered into force on 2 September 1990 and has 185 states parties. MULTILATERAL TREATIES DEPOSITED WITH THE SECRETARY-GENERAL, Status as at 31 December 1995, U.N. Doc. ST EG/ SER.E/14 111, 121, 167, 185 (1996)[hereinafter MULTILATERAL TREATIES].

40. In ratifying, acceding, or succeeding to a treaty, states parties are permitted to make reservations. A reservation is defined by Article 2(d) of the Vienna Convention on the Law of Treaties as "a unilateral statement, however phrased or named, made by a State, when signing, ratifying, accepting, approving or acceding to a treaty, whereby it purports to exclude or to modify the legal effects of certain provisions of the treaty in their application to that State." A recent CEDAW study identified three categories of reservations: 1) general reservations, which are usually directed at the scope of the whole convention; 2) reservations made to "core articles," namely the articles considered to be the heart of each treaty; 3) reservations made to substantive articles, namely those articles relating to different areas and sub-areas of human rights that concern the exercise of certain duties and the provision of different means of achieving the convention's goals. Articles concerning the right to education are substantive articles, but they may be affected by reservations of a general nature or those on core articles. Report of the Secretariat on Ways and Means of Expediting the Work of the Committee on the Elimination of Discrimination Against Women, 14th session, 7, 8–9, U.N. Doc. CEDAW/C/1995/6 (1994).

41. Algeria and the Congo reserved on Article 13(3)(4). Algeria stated that the article cannot impair its right to organize its education system; the Congo similarly stated that the Covenant's provisions are inconsistent with nationalized education and its monopoly in this area. Several other states: Barbados, Madagascar, Japan, Zambia, and the United Kingdom on behalf of the Gilbert Islands, Solomon Islands, and Tuvalu have reserved on Article 13(2). Barbados, Madagascar, and Zambia stated that the financial implications relating to primary education are such that full application of the principles cannot be guaranteed at this stage. Japan said it could not be bound by "the progressive introduction of free education." Ireland and Malta also reserved on the Article. Ireland reserved the right to permit parents to provide for education of children in their homes provided that it met minimum standards. Malta's concern focused on the religious and moral education of children. Since it is predominately Roman Catholic, Malta found that limited financial and human resources made difficult providing religious and moral education in accordance with the particular religious or moral belief of small groups. ICESCR, MULTILATERAL TREATIES, *supra* note 39, at 108–112.

42. Thailand reserved its right to apply the provisions of arts. 7 and 10, only within the limits estab-

declarations as well as substantive reservations to t ̳onvention's Articles 28 and 29 on education.[43] The number of rese. ̳tions to ̳hese articles, however, is not large and is therefore not considered a major impediment to implementation.

Governments enact legislation or issue executive orders to incorporate treaty provisions in domestic law; they are then obliged by the enabling statute to promote the right in practice. In this respect, the UNESCO Convention calls on its member states to formulate, develop, and apply a national policy that will promote equality of opportunity and of treatment in education.[44] Many governments have done so and have created Ministries or Departments of Education to monitor and implement such policies.[45]

Besides Ministries of Education, a number of governments have established "national machinery" either by legislation or executive decree to monitor day-to-day observance of rights and propose measures to improve observance of those rights, including the right to education.

Examples include national human rights institutions to strengthen the promotion and protection of human rights at the national level to advise governments on

---

lished by national laws, regulations, and practices. The U.K. accepted the obligations under art. 10(c) within the limits of the statutory powers of the central government. It noted that teaching curriculum, the provision of textbooks, and teaching methods are reserved for local control and are not subject to central government direction. The U.K. accepted t⊦ of encouraging coeducation without prejudice to the right of the U.K. to encourage other ' ̳pes of education. Several states have maintained reservations. The United Kingdom reserved on art. 1 and art. 2(f)(g). Bangladesh, Egypt, Libya, Maldives, Morocco, and Singapore have reserved on art. 2. The Bahamas has reserved on art. 2(a); Lesotho on art. 2(e); Malaysia and New Zealand on art. 2(f); and Iraq on arts. 2(f) and (g). Report of the Ninth Meeting of States Parties of the Committee on the Elimination of Discrimination Against Women, U.N. CEDAW, 9th session, 14, 16, 24, 25, 27, 30, 33–38, U.N. DOC. CEDAW/SP/1996/2 (1996).

Six states entered eight reservations to Articles 1 through 3, the core articles and twenty-seven states have lodged seventy-seven reservations on substantive articles. However, due to the observations, recommendations, and comments made by several U.N. policy organs and treaty bodies, one state has withdrawn its general reservation, thirteen states have withdrawn reservations to substantive articles, and eight states have withdrawn reservations to Article 29. Report by the Secretariat on Ways and Means of Expediting the Work of CEDAW, *supra* note 40, at 9, 27.

43.   Four states entered reservations to core articles of the Child Convention and thirty states entered sixty-three reservations to substantive articles. Of these, the following reserved on arts. 28 or 29: Algeria stated its intent to interpret the article in compliance with the Family Code which stipulates that education is to be in accord with the religion of the father; Djibouti said it would not be bound by any provisions that were incompatible with its religious and traditional values; Tunisia stated it would not adopt any legislative or statutory decisions that conflicted with its constitution and implementation would be limited by the means at its disposal; India declared certain rights of the child could only be progressively implemented in developing countries, subject to available resources; Iran, Mauritania, and Pakistan reserved the right not to apply any provision that is incompatible with Islamic Laws; Indonesia, Thailand, and Turkey reserved on art. 29, stating that it must be in accord with national law or the constitution; the Holy See interpreted the articles in a way which safeguards the primary and inalienable rights of parents, insofar as these rights concern education. MULTILATERAL TREATIES, *supra* note 39, at 199–211. Report of the Committee on the Rights of the Child, 9th session, 196, 198–199, U.N. DOC. CRC/C/ 43 (1995).

44.   UNESCO Convention, *supra* note 9, art. 4.

45.   Ministries of Education, UNESCO Education CD-ROM (1996).

human rights matters, and to investigate and resolve complaints of violations committed by public and private entities. They are called Human Rights Commissions or Civil Rights Commissions. Some have established the Office of Ombudsman. In addition, U.N. members have endorsed a set of principles to combat all forms of discrimination to govern these human rights institutions.[46] Little is known about the degree to which these entities address women's rights. However, governments agreed in a 1995 CHR International Workshop that the concerns of women were fundamental human rights issues to be addressed by national institutions and all other bodies involved in promoting and protecting human rights.[47]

Governments have also created national commissions for women. The United States was the first to do so, in 1964.[48] Subsequently, many other governments created women's commissions to help commemorate International Women's Year in 1975. As the World Women's Conferences endorsed the idea, over one hundred governments have now established Women's Ministries or alternative bureaus or offices within existing departments of education, culture, youth, law, or social affairs. In some instances, non-governmental organizations have established them.[49] However, insufficient data exists about the extent to which these entities have successfully promoted women's rights, including the right to education, or the extent to which they cooperate with national human rights institutions (or Commissions on the Child in a number of countries), or with Ministries or Departments of Education.[50]

Besides these human rights entities, UNESCO's Constitution mandates national cooperating bodies or national commissions to affiliate principal bodies interested in educational, scientific, and cultural matters with the work of the organization and to advise national delegations and governments. They were intended to be "the crown, the living expressions in each Member States of its commitment to free intellectual life."[51] Most UNESCO member states have a national commission, most are currently headed by women, and all include women's issues on their agendas. In addition, the movement of UNESCO Clubs, Centres, and Associations in more than 110 countries, many actively headed by women, also can promote public awareness about the need to improve women's status, including their status in education.[52]

---

46. UNITED NATIONS CENTRE FOR HUMAN RIGHTS, NATIONAL HUMAN RIGHTS INSTITUTIONS 3–38 (1995).

47. Report of the Third International Workshop on National Institutions for the Promotion and Protection of Human Rights, U.N. CHR, 52nd sess. U.N. DOC. E/CN.4/1996/8 10–11 (August 1995).

48. U.S. Executive Order No. 10980 of Dec. 14, 1961; THE PRESIDENT'S COMMISSION ON THE STATUS OF WOMEN, AMERICAN WOMEN (1963). See also Report of Commission on the Status of Women at its 26th session, U.N. ECOR, 62nd Supp. 3, 13, U.N. DOC E/5909 (1977).

49. Report of the Third International Workshop, supra note 47, at 10–11; FROM NAIROBI TO BEIJING, supra note 1, at 225–234.

50. Report of the Secretariat on Technical Assistance and Women: From Mainstreaming to Institutional Accountability, U.N. CSW, 39th sess., at 34, U.N. DOC. E/CN.6/1995/6 (1994); VAN BUEREN, supra note 16, at 408–410.

51. RICHARD HOGGART, AN IDEA AND ITS SERVANTS: UNESCO FROM WITHIN 83–84, 210 (1978).

52. For reports provided by the Specialized Agencies of the U.N. on the implementation of the

The role of universities and colleges in promoting the aims of education at all levels through training of teachers and professors is important and deserves particular mention. An example is the National Center on Adult Literacy (NCAL) established in 1990 in the University of Pennsylvania's Graduate School of Education with support from the U.S. Department of Education, federal, state, and local agencies, private foundations, and corporations with aims to enhance the quality of literacy work. Its goals are to improve understanding of adult learners, to foster innovation and increase effectiveness in adult basic education and literacy, and to expand access to information and build capacity for adult literacy services on a nationwide scale. The Center conducts applied research and development, and disseminates results to achieve these aims. It publishes a newsletter, convenes forums, roundtables, and video conferences on topics of interest to the adult literacy community, and disseminates reports, policy papers, practice guides, and books through its Website on the Internet.[53]

National policies and institutions, whether human rights commissions, women's bureaus, child rights commissions, UNESCO national commissions, Departments of Education, or Schools of Education within Universities, may participate in promoting the right to education within countries; so may entities responsible for administering technical assistance programs for women and girls. Yet, where several entities exist, each seeking to promote the same or similar objective, the authority for promoting and enforcing the right may be diffused, rather than centralized within a government department. Clear responsibility for administration and enforcement needs to be assigned to one authority and the supplemental role of related entities defined. Otherwise, promoting and enforcing a right such as education may fall victim to well-intended, but uncoordinated, efforts.

National policies and their administering authorities have been criticized in general for their lack of gender-sensitivity. Recommendations of a 1995 CSW expert group urge that national authorities incorporate gender approaches and remove stereotypes that prevent women and men from fully realizing their capacities, skills, and aspirations.[54]

International Action

International action can supplement national action, but should not substitute for it. Such action may include: reporting by states to international policy and treaty bodies; complaints and communications procedures; measures approved by international conferences; technical assistance activities; and the work of NGOs.

---

convention in areas falling within the scope of their activities, *see* UNESCO, UN CEDAW, 14th sess., at 21–34 U.N. DOC. CEDAW/C/1995/3/Add.3(1994). When the US withdrew from UNESCO in 1984, the U.S. National Commission was terminated due to lack of funds.

53. National Center on Adult Literacy, Mission Statement, Dec. 6, 1996 (Mimeo).

54. Report of the Secretariat on promotion of literacy, education and training, including technological skills, U.N. CSW, 39th Sess. 12–14, U.N. DOC. E/CN.6/1995/11 (1995).

Reporting Practices

U.N. policy bodies and U.N. treaty bodies are intended to influence states' practice by requiring reports on their efforts to implement the recommendations and treaty obligations respectively to fulfill the right to education for women and girls.[55]

U.N. Policy Bodies

Three U.N. policy bodies have competence to discuss educational rights: the Commission on the Status of Women, the Commission on Human Rights, and the Sub-Commission on the Prevention of Discrimination and Protection of Minorities.

Commission on the Status of Women (CSW)

CSW's reporting system has been revised as its activities have expanded. In connection with its agenda item on education, in its early years, members reviewed educational practices of reporting governments and recommended through ECO-SOC the preparation of a Convention Against Discrimination in Education. Later, members reviewed periodic reports submitted under the 1967 Declaration on the Elimination of Discrimination Against Women. More recently, CSW has appraised reports of governments on progress in achieving the goals of the World Women's Conferences, specifically the World Plan of Action (Mexico, 1975), the World Program of Action (Copenhagen, 1980), the Forward Looking Strategies for the Advancement of Women (Nairobi, 1985), and the Platform of Action (Beijing, 1995). In its first appraisal of the Forward Looking Strategies for the Advancement of Women, CSW highlighted education. In its second review of the period between Nairobi and Beijing, CSW determined several critical areas of concern among global social and economic spheres; one was the "inequality in access to education."[56] Education became one of the twelve critical areas of concern addressed at the 1995 Beijing World Conference on Women. Education for women and girls is considered within CSW's priority theme, development. At its 1997 session, literacy, education, and training for women and girls was on the CSW agenda.[57]

Commission on Human Rights (CHR)

Having prepared ICESCR, the Commission has, in Alston's view, played an "inconsistent and rather ineffectual role" in developing the concept of economic and social rights. Prior to 1981, CHR received periodic reports on civil and political

---

55. JACK DONNELLY, UNIVERSAL HUMAN RIGHTS IN THEORY AND PRACTICE 269 (1989).

56. FROM NAIROBI TO BEIJING, *supra* note 1, at 81–107.

57. Report of the Secretariat on promotion of literacy, education and training, *supra* note 54; Report of the Secretariat on the Implications for the Work of the Committee of the Priority Themes of the CSW, CEDAW, 14th sess. U.N. DOC. CEDAW/C/1995/5 4–6 (1994).

rights, then economic and social rights, and the freedom of information. As governments increasingly failed to report, CHR began to defer the agenda item and in 1981, abolished these reports.[58] Meanwhile, in 1975, CHR appointed a Special Rapporteur, Manouchehr Ganji, to prepare a study of economic, social and cultural rights and subsequently endorsed action by the Sub-Commission on the Prevention of Discrimination and Protection of Minorities on the subject. On the Sub-Commission's recommendation, CHR has adopted a number of resolutions on the realization of economic, social and cultural rights.[59]

The Sub-Commission on the Prevention of Discrimination and Protection of Minorities

Notably, the Sub-Commission has addressed discrimination in education in several resolutions entitled "Realization of economic, social and cultural rights" and in several studies prepared by Special Rapporteurs.[60] It has also proposed a minimum content of each economic, social, and cultural right and defined the right

---

58. Philip Alston, *The Commission on Human Rights, in* THE UNITED NATIONS AND HUMAN RIGHTS 183–184 (Philip Alston ed., 1992).

59. *Id.* at 190–191. For instance, *see* Res. 1990/16 at 39–40 in U.N. DOC. E/CN.4/1991/2(1990); Res. 1991/27 at 61–62 in U.N. DOC. E/CN.4/1992/2(1991); Res. 1992/29 at 72–75 in U.N. DOC. E/CN.4/1993/2(1992).

60. *Id.* At its 1993 session, the Sub-Commission articulated several aspects of economic, social, and cultural rights in resolutions on human rights and population transfers, adequate housing, human rights and extreme poverty, and human rights and income distribution. Report of the Sub-Commission on the Prevention of Discrimination and Protection of Minorities at its 45th session, at 76–77, 79–80, 77–78, 85–86, U.N. DOC. E/CN.4/Sub.2/1993/45(1993). In Res. 1994/37 the Sub-Commission requested the Secretary-General, inter alia, to consider convening expert seminars focused on special economic, social, and cultural rights, including the right to work, social security, housing, food, health, education, and culture and to elaborate universally relevant policy guidelines for each of these rights based on international human rights law. Report of the Sub-Commission on the Prevention of Discrimination and Protection of Minorities at its 46th session, at 87–91, U.N. DOC. E/CN.4/Sub.2 1994/56 (1994). The Sub-Commission recommended, and the Commission on Human Rights endorsed, the appointment of a Special Rapporteur to report on the relation of human rights and income distribution and to pay particular attention to the impact of the right to education. Report of the Sub-Commission at its 47th session, U.N. DOC. E/EN.4/Sub.2/1995/14 (1995).

Preliminary Report by Special Rapporteur, Danilo Turk, on the Realization of Economic, Social and Cultural Rights to the Sub-Commission at its 41st session, U.N. DOC. E/CN.4/Sub.2/1989/19 (1989). Progress report by Danilo Turk to the Sub-Commission at its 42nd session, U.N. DOC. E/CN.4/Sub.2/1990/19 (1990); Second Progress Report by Danilo Turk to the Sub-Commission at its 43rd session, U.N. DOC. E/CN.4/Sub.2/1991/17 (1991); Final report by Danilo Turk to the Sub-Commission at its 44th session, U.N. DOC. E/CN.4/Sub.2/1992/16 (1992). *See also* Preliminary Report on the Right to Adequate Housing by Mr. Rajindar Sachar to the Sub- Commission at its 45th session, U.N. DOC. E/CN.4/Sub.2/1993/15 (1993); his Second Progress Report to the Sub-Commission at its 46th session, U.N. DOC. E/CN.4/Sub.2/1994/20(1994); and his Final Report to the Sub-Commission at its 47th session, U.N. DOC. ECN.4/Sub.2/1995/12 (1995). Report on Human Rights and Extreme Poverty by the Special Rapporteur, Mr. Leandro Despouy, to the Sub-Commission at its 45th session, U.N. DOC. E/CN.4/Sub.2/1993/16 (1993); and Interim Report on Human Rights and Extreme Poverty by Leandro Despouy to the Sub-Commission at its 46th session, U.N. DOC. E/CN.4/Sub.2/1994/19 (1994).

to education as requiring at a minimum access to reading, writing, and the main symbolic codes, which are necessary for individuals to exercise civil and political rights.[61]

Subsequently, the CHR's Secretariat prepared a preliminary set of basic policy guidelines on structural adjustment programs and economic, social, and cultural rights. These referred to education in several instances and urged states to provide free compulsory primary education to all, to provide progressively free secondary and higher education, to achieve universal access to quality primary and technical education, to promote job training and literacy, and to eliminate gender disparities.[62]

U.N. Treaty Bodies

Various international instruments call for the creation of treaty bodies to help promote compliance by states parties with their respective provisions. Upon entry into force of the treaty, ratifying governments meet to elect members of the respective committees, develop guidelines for preparing reports, and convene sessions to review and comment on reports at regular intervals.

The committees to be considered are: the Committee on Economic, Social and Cultural Rights (CESCR); the Committee on the Elimination of Discrimination Against Women (CEDAW); and the Committee on the Rights of the Child (CRC). In addition, the UNESCO Convention provides that UNESCO's General Conference consider reports.

Each treaty body initially developed its own reporting guidelines and rules of procedure. Then, due to overlapping and frequent reporting requirements, the heads of treaty bodies met in the early 1990s to consolidate reporting guidelines for all reporting governments.[63]

Each treaty body considers reports from ratifying governments on measures taken to implement education as well as other human rights enumerated in the respective conventions. In reviewing reports, members of the treaty body make general or specific comments to the reporting state on ways to improve national practice and call attention to particular problems. At the conclusion of each session, the treaty body prepares a report for submission to the U.N. General Assembly.

---

61. Preliminary Report by Mr. Jose Bengoa to the Sub-Commission on the Prevention of Discrimination and Protection of Minorities, 47th sess. at 9–10, 14, U.N. DOC. E/CN.4 Sub.2/1995/14 (1995). The Special Rapporteur has proposed a further study on the relation between income distribution and equality of access to education.

62. Report on a preliminary set of basic policy guidelines on structural adjustment programmes and economic, social and cultural rights, U.N. ECOR, 1995, at 21–22, U.N. DOC. E/CN.4/Sub.2/1995/10 (1995).

63. UN CENTRE FOR HUMAN RIGHTS AND UNITAR, MANUAL ON HUMAN RIGHTS REPORTING (1991). An earlier assessment of reporting appears in A. GLENN MOWRER, INTERNATIONAL COOPERATION FOR SOCIAL JUSTICE 47–65 (1985).

Committee on Economic, Social and Cultural Rights (CESCR)

Article 2(1) of the ICESCR calls on ratifying governments to take steps, individually and through international assistance and cooperation, to the maximum of available resources to achieve progressively and without discrimination the full realization of the rights recognized in the ICESCR by all appropriate means.[64] Articles 16 through 25 address international implementation. Ratifying governments agree to report through the Secretary-General to ECOSOC and the appropriate specialized agencies that may report on provisions within their jurisdiction. ECOSOC may send to the CHR for study and general recommendation information from state reports. ECOSOC in turn reports to the General Assembly and brings to the attention of other U.N. organs matters to assist them in deciding on international measures to implement the ICESCR.[65]

To these ends, ECOSOC initially convened a "Sessional Working Group" (1979–1982) and a "Sessional Working Group of Governmental Experts" (1983–1986) before creating the Committee on Economic, Social and Cultural Rights (CESCR). At its first session in 1987, CESCR elected 18 experts. Between 1987 and 1994, the CESCR considered first reports on Articles 1 to 3, second on Articles 4 to 11; and third on Articles 12 to 15. The third report included discussion of education along with the right to health (art. 12) and the right to participate in cultural life (art. 15).[66]

A revised reporting cycle approved in 1994 requires a single comprehensive report covering all provisions of the ICESCR. Thus, the right to education continues to be only one of numerous economic, social, and cultural rights to be reported upon.[67] Shortly before the Beijing Conference in 1995, the CESCR issued a statement, based on reports it had reviewed, in which it indicated that women continue

---

64. ICESCR, *supra* note 5, art. 2(1). Drafters understood that developing countries did not have the resources to achieve them at once and provided for ECOSOC to alert international institutions concerned with providing technical assistance so that such institutions could assist countries whose reports reflected the need for assistance. L.B. Sohn, *The New International Law: Protection of the Rights of Individuals Rather Than States*, 32 Am. U. L. Rev. 39–41 (1982).

65. ICESCR, *supra* note 5, arts. 20–23. In art. 23, ratifying governments agree that international action to achieve the rights set forth include concluding conventions, adopting recommendations, providing technical assistance, and holding regional and technical meetings.

66. ECOSOC Res. 1985/17b. *See* Philip Alston, *The Committee on Economic, Social and Cultural Rights*, in THE UNITED NATIONS AND HUMAN RIGHTS 473–508 (Philip Alston ed., 1992); Scott Leckie, *An Overview and Appraisal of the Fifth Session of the UN Committee on Economic, Social and Cultural Rights*, 13 HUM. RTS. Q. 546 (1991); MATTHEW C.R. CRAVEN, INTERNATIONAL COVENANT ON ECONOMIC, SOCIAL AND CULTURAL RIGHTS 42–45 (1995).

67. Report of the Committee on Economic, Social, and Cultural Rights of its Eighth and Ninth Sessions, U.N. ECOR, 1994 sess., Supp. 3, 14–17, U.N. DOC. E/1994/23 (1994). The revised guidelines for the content of reporting on Article 13, Education, are found in the Report of the Committee on Economic, Social and Cultural Rights of its fifth session, U.N. ECOR, 1991 sess., Supp. 3, 106–107, U.N. DOC. E/1991/23 (1991).

to suffer the effects of discrimination in education.[68] It proposed that governments ensure women equal opportunity especially in relation to the right to work and the right to education. It also recommended that governments take steps to overcome the negative influence of tradition and custom and adopt measures to accord greater priority to the education of women, including the eradication of female illiteracy.[69]

The CESCR devotes "days of discussion" to particular topics and then adopts comments and recommendations. In 1995, following a "day of discussion" on the elderly, CESCR approved General Comment No. 6 on the "Economic, Social and Cultural Rights of Older Persons." This refers to the right of elderly persons to benefit from, among other opportunities, educational programs, and to the importance of making their knowledge and experience available to younger generations.[70] It illustrates the linkages between topics of current concern and education and how the issue of women and girls may be submerged within them.

The CESCR has invited ratifying governments to give the situation of women special consideration in their reports and has requested the U.N. specialized agencies, U.N. programs, and NGOs that participate in its annual sessions to provide gender-specific information.[71]

The Committee on the Rights of the Child (CRC)

Articles 42 through 45 of the Child Convention provide for implementation of a committee. Ratifying governments first met in March 1990 to elect ten members of the Committee on the Rights of the Child (CRC) to review reports of governments.[72] The CRC has discussed about six government reports at each session; at its ninth session it also began hearing views of the specialized agencies, the Children's Fund, and other U.N. organs.[73]

In developing its rules of procedures, CRC gained insight from the other treaty bodies. In view of the overwhelming number of reports received and its need to discuss technical assistance measures, CRC members agreed on two annual sessions

---

68. Report of CESCR of its 12th and 13th sessions, U.N. ECOR, 1996 sess., Supp. No. 2, Annex VI, 133–135, U.N. DOC. E/1996/22 (1996). Reports also indicated that women continue to suffer discrimination in employment, inequalities in health care, sex harassment, abuse and exploitation, and lack of access to economic opportunities, social security, and housing.

60. *Id.* at 134.

70. *Id.* at 97–105.

70. *Id.* at 135.

72. Child Convention, *supra* note 5. Assessments of the CRC's reporting procedure are found in LeBlanc, *supra* note 38, at 227–272, and in Van Bueren, *supra* note 16, at 378–421. Current Guidelines appear in Report of the Committee on the Rights of the Child, U.N. GAOR, 47th sess., Supp. 41, at 14–19, U.N. DOC. CRC/C/58(1996).

73. Report of the Committee on the Rights of the Child at its 9th session, 34–37, 58–60, U.N. DOC. CRC/C/43(1995). The Child Convention, *supra* note 5, art. 45, provides for the participation of the UNICEF and other U.N. organs and specialized agencies in CRC when considering the implementation of provisions within their mandate. CRC provides for this in Rule 34 of its Rules of Procedures.

rather than one. They called for ratifying governments to submit initial reports within two years after the entry into force of the convention and then every five years thereafter. The Committee also agreed to a thematic rather than an article-by-article approach to reporting. As a result, education is discussed within Theme VII: Education, Leisure and Cultural Activities. Ratifying governments must report on principal legislative, judicial, administrative, or other measures and any difficulties in implementation regarding: a) education, including vocational training and guidance; b) the aims of education; and c) leisure, recreation, and cultural activities.[74]

From the start, CRC has considered gender issues in relation to various rights, including education. In assessing reports, CRC uses gender-specific information and statistics on inequality and discrimination in education, health, and employment, changes in the image of women in the media, and in school textbooks.[75] CRC, in focusing on the problem of the girl–child, including the denial of educational opportunities, cooperated with the preparatory committee for the Beijing Conference and has sought to participate in reviewing the implementation of the provisions for the girl–child in the Platform of Action.[76]

Committee on the Elimination of Discrimination Against Women (CEDAW)

Articles 17 through 23 of the Women's Convention call for establishing a committee to review reports of states parties on legislative, judicial, administrative, or other measures that give effect to the provisions of the convention.[77]

After its first meeting in 1981 to elect members and adopt guidelines for reporting by states parties, the Committee on the Elimination of Discrimination Against Women (CEDAW) began reviewing reports in 1982. As the sole comprehensive convention on women's rights, CEDAW is the major treaty-body concerned with the human rights of women, including education. Ratifying governments normally report on education in their second report.[78] In the early

---

74. Other themes include: Civil Rights and Freedoms, Family Environment and Alternative Care, Basic Health and Welfare, and Special Protection Measures. Current Guidelines, *supra* note 72, at 16–19.

75. In its general principles for reporting, CRC agreed that states parties should provide relevant information in regard to non-discrimination and relevant statistical information and indicators relating to children. Report of the Committee on the Rights of the Child, U.N. GAOR, 47th sess. Supp. 41, 16, 18, U.N. DOC. CRC/C/43 (1993).

76. *Id. See also* Report of the Secretary-General on the extent to which violations of women's human rights have been addressed by human rights mechanisms, U.N. ECOR, 1996, Supp. 6. at 4–5, U.N. DOC. E/CN.6/1996/9 (1996).

77. Women's Convention, *supra* note 8, art. 18.

78. Andrew C. Byrnes, *The Other Human Rights Treaty Body: The Work of the Committee on the Elimination of Discrimination Against Women*, 14 YALE J. INT'L L 1–68 (1989); Roberta Jacobson, *The Committee on the Elimination of Discrimination Against Women, in* THE UNITED NATIONS AND HUMAN RIGHTS 466–468 (Philip Alston ed., 1992); Arvonne Fraser, *The Committee on the Elimination of Discrimination Against Women, in* WOMEN, POLITICS AND THE UNITED NATIONS (Anne Winslow ed., 1995); M.E. Galey,*Women and Human Rights, in* 3 WOMEN AND INTERNATIONAL DEVELOPMENT ANNUAL 115–143 (Rita Gallin, Anne Ferguson, & Janice Harper eds., 1993).

1990s, overwhelmed with the backlog of reports and the length of time needed to question individual reporting states, CEDAW called for two sessions each year beginning in 1997.

CEDAW has monitored: 1) women's and girl's equal access to education; 2) whether education provided is of the same type and quality; 3) government policies, programs, and specific action aimed at achieving the goals of equality in education; and 4) specific action to provide for special groups of women, such as rural women. CEDAW has urged governments to collect and present extensive statistical data on the overall educational situation. Specifically, they request ratifying governments to report on literacy rates, percentage at preschool, primary, secondary, tertiary, technical, professional, and higher technical education and in vocational training, as well as the percent of females graduating from any educational establishment as compared with males. CEDAW has also sought information on the number of women teachers, their positions in government and educational establishments, and on persistent inequality in access to education.

CEDAW's Secretariat prepared, prior to the 1995 Fourth World Conference on Women, a comprehensive study on progress in implementing the Women's Convention. It reported that Article 10 is unequivocal on the nature of females' equal right to education with males and encompasses equality of access to the same type and quality of education and equal educational opportunity. CEDAW attributes unequal educational opportunity for women to persisting customs and traditions, economic circumstances, lack of equal access to the same type of education for women and girls, as well as a lack of understanding of the importance of education for women and girls. Inequalities in education in turn affect inequalities for women in the labor force, in decision-making, and in public and private life.[79]

U.N. Educational, Scientific and Cultural Organization (UNESCO)

The UNESCO Convention Against Discrimination in Education (UNESCO Convention) is the primary convention against discrimination in education. Article 7 of the UNESCO Convention calls on ratifying governments to report periodically to the General Conference on legislative and administrative provisions and related legal action. At its 13th session, the General Conference invited the Executive Board of UNESCO to establish by 1965 a procedure for submission and examination of such reports. The Board decided that the reports should be prepared on the basis of a questionnaire and presented at regular intervals. It also decided that a special Committee of the Board, the Committee on Conventions and Recommendations in Education, should consider reports and transmit them with comments from the Executive Board to the General Conference.[80]

As a result, reports by ratifying governments are prepared on the basis of detailed questionnaires, analyzed by the Secretariat and reviewed by the Committee.

---

79. Report of the CEDAW on Progress Achieved in Implementing the Convention and its Contributions to International Conferences, 14th sess., 89–93, U.N. DOC. CEDAW/C/1995/7 (1994).

80. UN ACTION 1994, *supra* note 5, at 308–309.

Afterwards, the Committee prepares a report for discussion by the Executive Board and the General Conference. One result of the reporting efforts has been UNESCO's assistance to the Committee on the Elimination of Discrimination Against Women (CEDAW) on education of women and girls. In a 1995 Report, UNESCO described its efforts to eliminate stereotyped concepts of the role of men and women in education and initiate a regional project to train educators in seven Asian countries to develop and implement curricula on basic education. The 1995 Report also referred to increasing public awareness and support of women's education through a Pan-African Conference on the Education of Girls, another similar conference in Asia, and to the 1994 session of the International Conference on Education (ICE).[81]

In its early years, the Committee on Conventions and Recommendations of UNESCO's Executive Board dealt solely with questions of discrimination in education. However, in 1978, its responsibilities expanded to include general questions on human rights violations as well as cases by individuals or associations, discussed below.[82]

Inter-Committee Coordination and Optional Protocols

The four treaty committees discussed here, CESCR, CRC, CEDAW, and UNESCO, each have international responsibilities for promoting implementation of the right to education. As a result, the heads of treaty bodies meet to coordinate information in their respective reports and establish fair standards to assess achievement and the need for further implementation. The sheer volume of material presented in reports by state parties requires efficient processing of information, storage, and retrieval by the secretariats of the respective committees and committee members in order to chart progress or lack of progress in various areas, including education for women and girls. In this respect, proposals for computerization of information in government reports could, if implemented, promote greater efficiency.[83]

To strengthen compliance with each convention, three treaty committees have been considering the adoption of a complaint procedure in the form of an Optional Protocol. Complaint procedures permit aggrieved individuals or groups to petition

---

81. Reports provided by the Specialized Agencies of the U.N. on the implementation of the convention in areas falling within the scope of their activities to CEDAW, *supra* note 52.

82. Stephen Marks, *The Complaint Procedure of the United Nations Educational, Scientific and Cultural Organization, in* GUIDE TO INTERNATIONAL HUMAN RIGHTS PRACTICE 86–98 (Hurst Hannum ed., 1992); Georges-Henri Dumont, *A Behind-the-Scenes Struggle for Human Rights*, UNESCO COURIER, June 1990, at 43–44. Dumont writes that more than 200 cases have been submitted to the Committee since 1978. Of this number, 30 were settled between 1978 and 1981; 85 were settled between 1982 and 1985; and 86 were settled between 1986 and 1989. In certain cases, the Director-General may intervene personally, either confidentially or publicly. *See also* Francine Fournier, *The Rights of All*, UNESCO COURIER, March 1994, at 37.

83. Cynthia Price Cohen, Stuart N. Hart & Susan M. Kosloske, *The UN Convention on the Rights of the Child: Developing an Information Model to Computerize the Monitoring of Treaty Compliance*, 14 HUM. RTS Q. 216–231 (1992).

an international body to allege violations of human rights.[84] The international body may hear the petitioners, investigate their allegations, and determine whether allegations can be substantiated in fact. If substantiated, the international body may recommend an appropriate response, including remedies. The Optional Protocol to the International Covenant on Civil and Political Rights permits individuals from ratifying governments to petition the Human Rights Committee to seek redress for violations of rights set forth in the Covenant.[85] UNESCO developed a complaint procedure in 1978.[86]

Three treaty committees, CESCR, CEDAW, and CRC, are each contemplating the adoption of an Optional Protocol. CRC's proposed drafts would address child prostitution and armed conflict.[87] The proposals before CESCR would permit individuals or groups to petition for, among other violations, those concerning educational rights. The proposed protocol to the Women's Convention would provide a clear benchmark of the international community's commitment to the enforcement of gender-specific human rights.[88]

CESCR's decision to propose an Optional Protocol to the ICESCR resulted from a reported conflict of interpretation over the right to education.[89] Members agreed that a complaint procedure would publicize the Committee and the ICESCR, promote greater interest in reporting by states, and increase the Committee's effectiveness. But they disagreed on the justiciability of economic, social, and cultural

---

84. Complaint procedures are to be distinguished from communication procedures. In the latter regard, the Commission on Human Rights (CHR) and the Commission on the Status of Women (CSW) each receive communications. CHR's procedure evolved in 1970 to enable it to deal with "gross and persistent violations of human rights." CSW's authority remains relatively weak. *See* UN Action 1994, *supra* note 5, at 309–318; Laura Reanda, *The Commission on the Status of Women, in* THE UNITED NATIONS AND HUMAN RIGHTS 296 (Philip Alston ed., 1992); M.E. Galey, *International Enforcement of Women's Rights*, 6 HUM. RTS Q. 463–490 (1984). At its 1996 session, CSW's Communications Working Group emphasized the insufficiency and ineffectiveness of the procedure and recommended that it be improved. Report of the CSW, U.N. CSW, 40th sess., Supp. 6 at 87–88, U.N. DOC. E/1996/26 (1996); Howard Tolley, *The UN Commission on Human Rights' Response to Confidential Communications*, 6 HUM. RTS. Q. 420–462 (1984); Philip Alston, *The Commission on Human Rights*, *supra* note 66, at 138–181.

85. UN ACTION 1994, *supra* note 5, at 314–316.

86. *Id.* at para. 269.

87. VAN BUEREN, *supra* note 16, at 410–411.

88. Introductory Statement by Angela E.V. King to the Commission on the Status of Women, March 10, 1997 at 2 (mimeo).

89. A state party introduced tuition fees for full-time university students. The National Students Association challenged the decision and sought views of the national Human Rights Commission. The latter concluded that the fees would violate art. 13(2)(c). The Government rejected the Commission's interpretation and insisted that its approach was consistent with art. 13(2)(c). Committee members found this case raised questions of "considerable importance in terms of interpretation," namely the nature of the undertaking in art. 13(2)(c); the meaning of "progressive realization"; the basis for determining what resources are "available" for purposes of the covenant; and the extent to which existing levels of the enjoyment of economic rights can be intentionally reduced on the grounds of economic necessity. Report of CESCR at its 7th Session, U.N. ECOR, 1993 sess. Supp. 2, 87, 91–92, U.N. DOC. E/1993/22 (1993).

rights. Some members said such rights were non-justiciable, that is, not able to be adjudicated because of their imprecision and generality. Others believe that the rights and obligations identified by the CESCR as requiring immediate implementation are justiciable. Such rights include free and compulsory education (art. 13(2)(a)), respect for parental choice in education (art. 13(3)), and the right to establish and direct educational institutions (art. 13(4)).[90] The Committee's General Comment No. 3 on the nature of state's obligations under Article 2(1) refers to "minimum essential levels of each of the rights" as incumbent on every state party.[91] This means, in Alston's view, that a state party in whose territory any significant number of individuals are deprived of essential foodstuffs, essential primary health care, basic shelter and housing, or *the most basic forms of education,* is, *prima facie,* failing to discharge its obligations under the ICESCR.[92]

Within CEDAW, the idea of an optional protocol or protocols was initially raised in 1991 in connection with domestic violence and to place the Women's Convention on the same footing with ICCPR. The 1993 World Conference on Human Rights and the 1995 Fourth World Women's Conference endorsed CEDAW's proposal for a draft optional protocol.[93] CSW created an Open-Ended Working Group to discuss such a protocol and requested the Secretary-General to submit a comprehensive report containing views of governments, intergovernmental organizations, and NGOs to its 1996 session.[94] Two members of CEDAW are participating in the CSW Working Group.[95]

UNESCO already has two procedures for complaints, one for inter-state complaints and another for individual complaints. The former was created in 1962 when

90. CRAVEN, *supra* note 66, at 98–101. Report of CESCR at its 4th session, U.N. ECOR, 1990, Supp. 2, Annex III at 84, U.N. DOC. E/1990/23 (1990).

91. *Id.* CESCR also requested governments to inform the Committee as to whether they have adopted specific policies aimed directly at the realization of rights recognized by the covenant, whether constitutions recognize such rights or whether governments have incorporated provisions of the covenant into national law, and whether such laws create any right of action on behalf of the individuals or groups who feel their rights are not being fully recognized. Such rights include the right to education. CRAVEN, *supra* note 66, at 98–101; STEINER & ALSTON, *supra* note 2, at 298–310; Martin Scheinin, *Economic and Social Rights as Legal Rights, in* ECONOMIC, SOCIAL, AND CULTURAL RIGHTS 41–62 (Asjborn Eide et al. eds., 1995).

92. Alston, *supra* note 66, at 495. Eide points to the Limburg Principle 8 as the best guide to state obligations under CESCR. It provides that full realization of the rights recognized in the covenant is to be attained progressively and the application of some rights can be made justiciable immediately, while other rights become justiciable over time. Asjborn Eide, *Economic, Social and Cultural Rights as Human Rights, in* ECONOMIC, SOCIAL AND CULTURAL RIGHTS 21–40 (Asjborn Eide et al. eds., 1995).

93. Report of the CSW at its 39th session, U.N. ECOR, 1995, Supp. 6 at 5–7, U.N. DOC. E/CN.6/1995/14.

94. Report of CSW at its 40th session, U.N. ECOR, 1996, Supp. 6, at 30–31, 89–90, 106–123, U.N. DOC. E/1996/26 (1996). *See also* Report of the Secretary-General to CSW at its 41st session on Comparative Summary of Existing Communications and Inquiry Procedures and Practices Under International Human Rights Instruments and Under the Charter of the United Nations, U.N. ECOR, 1997, U.N. DOC. E/CN.6/1997/4 (1997).

95. Report of the CEDAW of its 15th session, U.N. GAOR, 51st sess., Supp. 38 at 2–3, U.N. DOC. A/51/38 (1996).

the General Conference approved a Protocol for a Conciliation and Good Offices Commission to settle any dispute between governments that had ratified its Convention Against Discrimination in Education.[96] Its members, elected by the General Conference, discuss communications from states alleging that another party has not fulfilled provisions of the Convention. Members ascertain the facts and provide good offices to disputants. Their decisions are binding.[97]

UNESCO's Executive Board in 1967 initiated a procedure for individual communications on alleged violations of individual human rights within UNESCO's competence. To make the procedure more effective, the General Conference requested a study which led in 1978 to a procedure whereby individuals may submit communications on violations of human rights within UNESCO's fields of competence—education, science, and culture—to the Executive Board's Committee on Conventions and Recommendations.[98] This procedure could be used to deal with questions relating to violations of women's educational rights specifically and UNESCO has advised CEDAW of that opportunity.[99]

Policy and Consciousness-Raising for Education

Publicity, consciousness-raising, and the adoption of international policy measures by U.N.- sponsored commemorative days, years, and decades, and by conferences of the U.N. and UNESCO have contributed to implementing human rights, including the right to education for women and girls.

U.N. General Assembly-Sponsored Years and Decades

Education has been an important theme of Human Rights Day, International Literacy Day, the International Day for Eliminating Racial Discrimination, International Women's Year (1975), the International Year for Human Rights (1968), the International Year of the Child (1979) and International Literacy Year (1990).[100] These along with various U.N. Decades, such as the U.N. Decade for Women (1976–1985) and the current U.N. Decade for Human Rights Education, have helped raise awareness of and publicity for the need to improve education for women and girls.

---

96. UNESCO Convention, *supra* note 9. *See also* UNESCO'S STANDARD SETTING INSTRUMENTS I.A.1 (1992).

97. *Id. See also* UN ACTION 1994, *supra* note 5, at 321–322.

98. UN ACTION 1994, *supra* note 5, at 322; UNESCO 104 EX/Dec. 3.3(1978).

99. *Supra* note 52, at 25. This report notes that only three women have alleged human rights violations.

100. Message of UNESCO Director-General for Int'l Literacy Day, UNESCO/2319, Sept. 7, 1978, at 1–3. The U.N. General Assembly proclaimed 1990 as International Literacy Year in A/RES/42/104 of Dec. 7, 1987 and invited UNESCO to assume the role of lead organization for the preparation and observance of the Year. *1990: International Literacy Year (ILY),* WOMEN'S INTERNATIONAL NETWORK NEWS, Spring, 1990, at 5–6. UNGA Res. 31/169 proclaimed 1979 as the International Year of the Child.

U.N. General Assembly-Sponsored Conferences

Numerous world conferences convened by the U.N. General Assembly have addressed women's and girls' access to education within their respective platforms or programs of action. Several examples are illustrative.

World Conference on Education for All

This conference, convened by UNESCO, UNDP, UNICEF, and the World Bank, in Jomtien, Thailand from March 3–5, 1990, approved a World Declaration on Education for All and a Framework for Action to Meet Basic Learning Needs. The Framework called on states to reorder spending priorities to meet three principal goals: basic education for at least 80% of the world's children by the year 2000; a 50% reduction in the 1990 rate of adult illiteracy; and equality of educational opportunity for girls and boys.[11] The Declaration and the Framework reflect worldwide consensus on an expanded vision of basic education and a renewed commitment to ensure that the basic learning needs of all children, youth and adults are met effectively in all countries.[102] In December 1993, nine high-population countries held an Education for All Summit and approved the Delhi Declaration, reaffirming the goals of the 1990 Conference.[103]

The Women's Conferences

Each of the four U.N. World Women's conferences has identified education of women and girls as necessary to advancing women's status and promoting economic and social development. The 1975 World Plan of Action identified education and training as a specific area for national action and Conference Resolution 24 emphasized women's access to education.[104] The 1980 Program of Action reiterated the importance of education and training for women and girls as did Conference Resolution 30, promoting equality in education and training for women and girls.[105]

The 1985 Forward Looking Strategies for the Advancement of Women (FLS) addressed education as the "basic tool that should be given to women in order to

---

101. U.N. Centre for Human Rights and UNICEF, *Education: Convention on the Rights of the Child*, May 1993 (mimeo).

102. World Declaration on Education for All and Framework for Action to Meet Basic Learning Needs, *supra* note 10. *See also* Frank P. Dall, *Children's Right to Education: Reaching the Unreached, in* IMPLEMENTING THE CONVENTION ON THE RIGHTS OF THE CHILD 143–182 (James R. Himes ed., 1995).

103. EDUCATION FOR ALL SUMMIT OF NINE HIGH POPULATION COUNTRIES, FINAL REPORT, UNESCO Doc. (1994). The countries were Bangladesh, Brazil, China, Egypt, India, Indonesia, Mexico, Nigeria and Pakistan.

104. Report of the World Conference on International Women's Year, including the World Plan of Action, Resolutions, and Regional Plans of Action, U.N. DOC. E/CONF.66/34 (1976). The Regional Plans of Action acknowledge the importance of women's access to education and in turn the educated woman's contribution to economic and social development. *Id.* at 23–24, 33–37, and 91–93.

105. Report of the World Conference of the Mid-Decade for Women: Equality, Development and Peace, 23–24; 33–37; 91–93, U.N. DOC. A/CONF/94/35 (1980).

fulfill their role as full members of society.'' The FLS reiterated recommendations of previous conferences and also referred to women's role in education for peace.[106] The 1995 Platform of Action acknowledged that education is a human right and an essential tool for achieving the goals of equality, development, and peace. One of the twelve areas of critical concern that it defined was the lack of access by the girl–child to education and vocational training. The usual explanations for failure to provide education were also recited, as were recommendations to eliminate them.[107]

The World Human Rights Conference

The 1993 World Plan of Action in Vienna mandated mainstreaming women's rights within the U.N. human rights program and called on CSW and CEDAW to strengthen their reporting procedures and to consider how best to deal with violations of women's rights.[108]

The International Conference on Population and Development

Building on the earlier conferences on World Population, Women, Environment, Human Rights, and the Children's Summit, this conference approved the 1994 Program of Action.[109] It acknowledged that education is one of the most important means of empowering women with the knowledge, skills, and self-confidence necessary to participate fully in the development process. It urged governments to ensure that women and men have the education necessary to meet their basic human needs and to exercise their human rights.[110] It urged governments to provide universal access to quality education and to promote non-formal education.[111]

The World Social Summit for Social Development

In the 1995 Copenhagen Declaration, governments pledged to promote and attain the goals of ''universal and equitable access to quality education.'' They also emphasized universal access to basic education and completion of primary education by at least 80% of school-age children by the year 2000, closing the gender gap in primary and secondary school education by 2005, and implementing universal primary education before 2015.[112]

---

106. Report of the World Conference to Review and Appraise the U.N. Decade for Women, U.N. DOC. A/CONF.116/28/Rev.1 (1985).

107. UNITED NATIONS, THE BEIJING DECLARATION AND PLATFORM OF ACTION, Fourth World Conference on Women, A/CONF.177/20 (1995), paras. 26, 33, 71, 73, 81–90 (1996).

108. UNITED NATIONS, WORLD CONFERENCE ON HUMAN RIGHTS: THE VIENNA DECLARATION AND PROGRAM OF ACTION 53–57 (1993).

109. Report of the International Conference on Population and Development, U.N. DOC. A/CONF. 171/13/Rev. 1 (1994), at 14.

110. *Id.* at 23–24.

111. *Id.* at 82–83.

112. WORLD SUMMIT FOR SOCIAL DEVELOPMENT, THE COPENHAGEN DECLARATION AND PROGRAM OF ACTION 22–26, 71 (1995).

UNESCO Conferences

The UNESCO General Conference addresses all types of education and issues of gender and race discrimination in education.[113] In addition, UNESCO and the International Bureau of Education (IBE) have jointly convened the International Conference on Education. The latter offers a forum for dialogue among ministers of education on specific themes. Recent themes have been the improvement of secondary education, diversification of post-secondary education, and the struggle against illiteracy through universal primary education and adult education.[114]

UNESCO also sponsors a number of international congresses to promote education about the Universal Declaration of Human Rights in schools, among adult populations, and through the press, radio and cinema. Such congresses, focusing on teaching human rights, met in Vienna in 1978, Malta in 1987, and Montreal in 1993. The Montreal Congress adopted a "World Plan of Action on Education for Human Rights and Democracy" aimed at all who teach human rights, in or outside the education system, in conflict situations and during the transition from authoritarian to democratic polities.[115]

Each of the U.N. World Conferences, as well as UNESCO's conferences and congresses, has highlighted the problem of the lack of access by women and girls to education of all types, particularly primary education. Each has called on governments, affiliated international organizations, and NGOs to implement recommendations including those on education of women and girls. Yet, despite increased awareness of the problem, these conferences have not yet afforded adequate education to women and girls.

Technical Assistance

A complex array of institutions authorize, provide, or administer technical assistance for women's and girls' education. The international instruments discussed here specify or imply its use. ICESCR calls on governments to take steps individually and through international assistance and cooperation, technical and economic, to the maximum of available resources to achieve the full realization of the rights enumerated. The phrase "all available resources" in the Child Convention encompasses such assistance.[116] CEDAW's references to "all appropriate measures" and "all necessary measures" to eliminate discrimination against women in education encompasses these rights as does the UNESCO Convention's call to ratifying governments to take "all necessary measures" to ensure the application of the principles of Article 5(1), the purposes of education.

---

113. UNESCO'S STANDARD-SETTING INSTRUMENTS, *supra* note 9. *See also* Records of the General Conference of UNESCO, UNESCO DOC. I 28C/Res. 1.13 (1995).

114. National Reports Submitted to the Sessions of I.C.E., UNESCO's Education CD-Rom (1996).

115. Fournier, *supra* note 82, at 37.

116. Note by the Secretary-General to the Committee on the Rights of the Child, U.N. GAOR, 1–9, CRC/C/40/Rev.3 (1996).

The U.N. policy bodies, especially the CSW and CHR, have prepared and discussed reports on technical assistance or called for technical assistance programs to aid members in promoting human rights measures.[117]

But treaty and policy bodies are not responsible for authorizing or administering assistance; that responsibility belongs to technical assistance bodies such as the United Nations Children's Fund (UNICEF), the U.N. Development Program (UNDP), the U.N. Fund for Population (UNFPA), the U.N. Development Fund for Women (UNIFEM), and the U.N. Program of Advisory Services and Technical Assistance in Human Rights.[118] UNESCO administers technical assistance for education provided by UNDP, UNFPA, and UNIFEM. The International Bank for Reconstruction and Development (World Bank) and the Regional Banks also fund education, including education for women and girls. In addition, NGOs may help deliver such assistance.

To highlight the importance of technical assistance programs for women, UNI-FEM was established following the 1975 World Women's Conference. Several technical assistance programs created Women and Development Offices (WID) in the 1970s. But such offices were insulated from the mainstream of agency effort and a gender approach began to replace WID in the 1980s and was incorporated into planning assistance programs.[119] Several programs renamed their WIDs to reflect this. UNDP's Office of Women and Development became the Gender and Development Program. The gender approach aims to put people at the center of development and differentiates between men and women.[120] It views women and men in terms of the roles they play in society, roles which change as societies change. By comparing women and men, rather than focusing exclusively on women as a group in isolation, gender analysis illuminates a key aspect of the structure of society and facilitates identifying obstacles to overcome problems.[121]

---

117. UN ACTION 1994, *supra* note 5, at 134–139; Report of the Commission on Human Rights on Technical Cooperation in the field of human rights, U.N. ECOR, U.N. DOC. E/CN.4/1996/90 (1996); Note by the Secretary-General to the Committee on the Rights of the Child, CRC/C/40/Rev.1 (1986); Report on Technical Assistance and Women, *supra* note 50. For a discussion of resources, *see* Thomas Hammarburg, *Children, in* ECONOMIC, SOCIAL, AND CULTURAL RIGHTS 299–302 (Asbjorn Eide et al. eds., 1995); James R. Himes, *Introduction, in* IMPLEMENTING THE CONVENTION ON THE RIGHTS OF THE CHILD 4–7 (James R. Himes ed., 1995).

118. Report of the High Commissioner for Human Rights, U.N. GAOR, 50th sess., Supp. 36, at 11–17, U.N. DOC. A/50/36 (1995); Report of the Executive Board of UNICEF, U.N. ECOR, 1995, Supp. 13, at 52–54, U.N. DOC. E/1995/33/Rev.1 (1995); UNICEF AND WOMEN: THE LONG VOYAGE: A HISTORICAL PERSPECTIVE (1987).

119. Hilkka Pietila & Ingrid Eide, *UNDP: Women in Development as a Priority, in* THE UN AND THE ADVANCEMENT OF WOMEN: THE ROLE OF THE NORDIC COUNTRIES 41–53 (1990)(A study Commissioned by the Nordic UN Project).

120. FROM NAIROBI TO BEIJING, *supra* note 1, at 295–350; Margaret Snyder, *The Politics of Women and Development, in* WOMEN, POLITICS AND THE UNITED NATIONS 95–116 (Anne Winslow ed., 1995); Report on Technical Assistance and Women, *supra* note 50, at 1–54.

121. THE UNITED NATIONS AND THE ADVANCEMENT OF WOMEN, *supra* note 7, at 468.

In preparation for the 1995 World Women's Conference, the Commission on the Status of Women invited the Secretary-General to report on technical and financial cooperation for women in order to develop ways to overcome major obstacles, including education for women and girls. The resulting report emphasized the need for organizational accountability at national and international levels. This meant that existing organizations had to incorporate the gender approach into planning programs sensitive to women and girls. It also meant that constructive dialogue among and between representatives of technical assistance missions and governments, international agencies, and NGOs (particularly women's groups), had to be initiated to foster accountability in government donors as well as recipients of assistance.[122]

The 1995 Platform of Action reiterated these themes and called on governments to provide necessary budgetary resources for education. It also requested international organizations, particularly UNESCO and the multilateral banks, to provide technical assistance upon request to developing countries to strengthen their capacity to close the gap between men and women in basic education and training and research and in the elimination of illiteracy.[123]

PUBLIC EXPENDITURE ON EDUCATION

The UNESCO "World Education Report of 1995" indicates that the level of public expenditure for education has virtually doubled between 1980 and 1992 from $526.7 billion to $1196.8 billion worldwide. As a percentage of GNP, expenditure increased from 4.9% (1980) to 5.1% (1992) worldwide. Table II illustrates this increase in developing and developed countries and as a percentage of GNP.

TABLE II
Growth of Public Expenditure and Percent of GNP On Education[124]

Developing Countries		Developed Countries*	
1980	*1992*	*1980*	*1992*
$102.2 b.	$209.5 b.	$425.5b.	$987.3b.
3.8%	4.2%	5.1%	5.7%

*excluding the former Soviet Union.[125]

---

122. Report on Technical Assistance and Women, *supra* note 50, at 34.

123. THE BEIJING DECLARATION & PLATFORM FOR ACTION, *supra* note 107, at 49, 54–55.

124. UNESCO, WORLD EDUCATION REPORT 109 (1995).

125. *Id.*

In adult literacy and school enrollment, the gaps between women and men were halved between 1970 and 1990 in developing countries. Women's literacy increased from 54% of the male rate in 1970 to 74% in 1990, and combined female primary and secondary enrollment increased from 67% of the male rate to 86%.

Despite these gains, women outnumber men two-to-one among the world's 905 million illiterates, and 65% of the 130 million children without access to primary education are girls.[126] The problem in part is due to the fact that in some societies, population has been growing faster than women's education has expanded. In India and China, for instance, population growth increased annually from 2.7 percent to 3.4 percent on average between 1975 and 1987.[127] In addition, the education gender gap is widest in the poorest countries where a mix of economic and cultural factors inhibit education of girls and women. Education costs, such as tuition and school supplies, opportunity costs of lost work by daughters at home or in the marketplace, and cultural costs of going against society's norms regarding female behavior, each act to prevent or hinder girls' education. In poor countries, many children, especially girls, also lack basic health and nutrition from infancy, which can cripple their learning ability. The laws of many countries do not provide women the same protection and rights as men; domestic laws in some countries do not provide for compulsory education, or prohibit child labor, or both.[128]

As a result, technical assistance agencies and programs, as well as government participants in, for instance, the World Conference for Education for All, have sought ways to improve educational efficiency and reduce educational costs, to provide basic health and nutrition to small children as well as adults, and to find ways to alter national labor and education policies.[129] As there is a close relationship between advances in women's education and lower fertility rates, unless ways and means can be found to educate girls and boys at primary school levels and reduce fertility, increases in illiteracy are likely to occur.[130]

A change in attitudes regarding incorporating gender perspectives and acknowledging the important roles that girls and women play in national development will be necessary to solve widespread illiteracy.

Activities of International Non-Governmental Organizations

Non-governmental organizations (NGOs), both national and international, have helped influence the formulation and implementation of international human rights

---

126. FROM NAIROBI TO BEIJING, *supra* note 1, at 225; UNITED NATIONS DEVELOPMENT PROGRAM, HUMAN DEVELOPMENT REPORT 3–5, 29–30 (1995); UNITED NATIONS, THE WORLD'S WOMEN 1995, 89–103 (1995).

127. WORLD CONFERENCE ON EDUCATION, BACKGROUND DOCUMENT 30 (1990).

128. Myron Weiner, *The Child and the State in India, in* INTERNATIONAL HUMAN RIGHTS IN CONTEXT 287–289 (Henry Steiner & Philip Alston eds., 1996).

129. INTERNATIONAL HUMAN RIGHTS IN CONTEXT 1–98 (Steiner & Alston eds., 1996).

130. UN DEVELOPMENT PROGRAM, HUMAN DEVELOPMENT REPORT 3–5; 29–30 (1995); UNITED NATIONS, THE WORLD'S WOMEN 1995 89–103 (1995).

of women, including the right to education. U.N. Charter Article 71 enables NGOs with global or regional memberships to have consultative status with the Economic and Social Council (ECOSOC) and its subsidiary bodies, a status that permits oral and written statements. NGOs with consultative status with ECOSOC, and particularly with CSW, CHR, and UNESCO, have helped publicize decisions of these bodies within their memberships and, in turn, influenced governments to give effect to the obligations of international conventions that they have ratified. NGOs may also encourage governments that have not yet ratified particular instruments to do so and to take steps to give effect to treaty provisions, such as the right to education.[131]

NGOs have become indispensable partners in the development of international human rights law within the U.N. policy bodies. Regrettably, only two of the three U.N. treaty bodies—CRC and CESCR—permit the official participation of NGOs. Accredited NGOs may have consultative status with UNESCO. Within the Child Committee, NGOs have been instrumental both in preparing the Convention and in its implementation.[132] In 1988, CESCR permitted NGOs, including those not in consultative status with ECOSOC, to submit written statements "that might contribute to full and universal recognition and realization of the rights in the Covenant."[133] They may also participate in general discussions and give oral presentations to CESCR's pre-sessional working group. At this writing, very few NGOs have availed themselves of this opportunity.[134]

In CEDAW, NGOs have no official role, although members of various NGOs frequently attend meetings of states parties and the Committee itself. One such participating NGO is the International Women's Rights Action Watch (IWRAW). It has served as a clearinghouse of information for the implementation of CEDAW through its newsletter. IWRAW advises major NGOs in states scheduled to report to CEDAW, gathering information from them on the condition of women before CEDAW meets. After compiling information on each state, IWRAW sends this information to individual members of CEDAW. Such information has the potential to improve the quality of questions from Committee members and to let governments know that NGOs are monitoring their performance.[135]

---

131. THOMAS G. WEISS & LEON GORDENKER, NGOS, THE UN AND GLOBAL GOVERNANCE (1996); David Weisbrodt, *Contributions of International Non-Governmental Organizations to the Protection of Human Rights, in* HUMAN RIGHTS IN INTERNATIONAL LAW 403–430 (Theodore Meron ed., 1995); WOMEN, POLITICS AND THE UN (Anne Winslow ed., 1995); Alston, *The Commission on Human Rights, supra* note 58, at 202–204.

132. Cynthia Price Cohen, *The Role of NGOs in the Drafting of the Convention on the Rights of the Child,* 12 HUM. RTS. Q. 137–47 (1990); Per Miljeteig-Olssen, *Advocacy of Children's Rights—The Convention as More than a Legal Document,* 12 HUM. RTS Q 145–155 (1990). VAN BUEREN, *supra* note 16, at 405–408 identifies the NGOs participating in the Child Network. *See also* LEBLANC, *supra* note 38, at 258–272.

133. Alston, *The Committee on Economic, Social and Cultural Rights, supra* note 66, at 473–508; CRAVEN, *supra* note 66, at 80–81.

134. Alston, *id.,* at 501–502. CRAVEN, *id.,* at 80–82. The International Women's Rights Action Watch has begun to monitor CESCR sessions. IWRAW Newsletter, June 1996, at 2.

135. Jacobson, *Committee on the Elimination of Discrimination Against Women, in* THE UNITED NATIONS

NGOs have held consultative status with UNESCO since its establishment, thanks to Julian Huxley, the first Director-General. UNESCO even offered modest financial support to strengthen existing organizations and/or stimulate the birth of new ones.[136] Among NGOs enjoying consultative status with UNESCO has been the International Council of Women (ICW). ICW's Standing Committee on Education has emphasized access of women to education at all levels, family influence on education, the status of women in teaching, the impartial teaching of history, problems of vocational and technical training of girls, the extension of compulsory schooling, education for citizenship, and the eradication of illiteracy. It has been a source of initiatives for the UNESCO General Conference.[137]

In addition, NGO Forums have been organized at virtually all of the U.N. General Assembly-sponsored conferences.[138] These unofficial forums have sponsored seminars, lectures, and meetings on a wide range of topics related to the conference's themes. They have facilitated networking among participants, generated newsletters and bulletins, and fostered new associations. For instance, following the World Conference on IWY, the International Women's Tribune Center began to prepare and circulate materials to all registered participants, including "how to" bulletins. Following the 1990 World Conference on Education for All, UNESCO, with support from the Government of Italy, began publishing "EFA 2000" for the Secretariat of the International Consultative Forum on Education for All. Issues of "EFA 2000" publicize book notes, notices of upcoming government and NGO meetings, and articles on the work of NGOs, for instance, in basic education.[139] After the 1990 World Conference, the Coalition for Education for All was established to promote the global Framework for Action in response to the conference's call for new and revitalized partnerships. The Coalition aims to unite diverse groups that share a commitment to identifying barriers that impede achievement of education and help coordinate efforts to provide it. Members include individuals as well as groups, U.N.-accredited NGOs, and representatives of international programs such as UNICEF and UNDP.[140] Another notable NGO, the Women's Environment and Development Organization (WEDO), after the Beijing Conference, translated the key demands in the Platform of Action into a 12 point Contract with Women of the United States. Point 7 of the Contract with Women

---

AND HUMAN RIGHTS 466–468 (Philip Alston ed., 1992); Fraser, in WOMEN, POLITICS AND THE UNITED NATIONS (Anne Winslow ed., 1995).

136. HOGGART, *supra* note 51, at 85. Current rules regarding NGO relations with UNESCO are in Revision of the Directives Concerning UNESCO'S Relations with International Non-governmental Organizations Recommended by the Executive Board to the General Conference, UNESCO, 28th session, UNESCO DOC. 28C/43 (1995).

137. INTERNATIONAL COUNCIL OF WOMEN, WOMEN IN A CHANGING WORLD 168–170 (1966).

138. Sophie Bessis, *NGOs: the Fight to be Heard*, UNESCO COURIER, March 1994, at 12–14; Martha A. Chen, *Engendering World Conferences: The International Women's Movement and the UN*, in NGOS, THE UN AND GLOBAL GOVERNANCE 139–55 (Weiss & Gordenker eds., 1996).

139. *NGOs in Basic Education: A Force to Reckon With!*, EFA 2000, Jan.-March 1996, at 2–4.

140. U.S. COALITION FOR EDUCATION FOR ALL, CONFERENCE REPORT (1991); CENTER FOR POLICY ALTERNATIVES, A MATTER OF SIMPLE JUSTICE (1996).

addresses educational equity. WEDO President Bella Abzug urged all women in-volved in the Beijing Conference to use the model WEDO Contract to develop contracts in their own countries as a means of meeting educational goals.[141]

CONCLUSIONS

This chapter has explored two major propositions. It first asserted that the international right to education is adequately formulated for women and girls in several major international instruments. It then asserted that ratifying states have not implemented the responsibilities undertaken in consenting to these instruments for institutional and political reasons. As a result, widespread illiteracy exists.

With respect to the first proposition, the provisions of six major international instruments have been compared to assess the adequacy of the formulation of the right to education: the Universal Declaration on Human Rights, the UNESCO Convention Against Discrimination in Education, the International Covenant on Economic, Social and Cultural Rights, the Child Convention, the Convention on Eliminating Race Discrimination, and the Convention on the Elimination on All Forms of Discrimination Against Women.

Only one of these, the UNESCO Convention Against Discrimination in Educa-tion, addresses the right to education exclusively. The right, as it applies to women and girls, is only explicitly and exclusively defined in the Women's Convention. All of the other instruments refer to gender neutral "everyone" or "every child" as those who are to be educated. Yet, the non-discrimination provisions of these instruments and the Women's Convention's emphasis on the right to education for women and girls, confirm that "everyone" can be interpreted as expressly encompassing women and girls as well as men and boys.

Collectively, these instruments elucidate state responsibility to provide various types of education, ensure certain conditions of education, honor the role of parents, and cooperate to promote education for women and girls. This is not to say that further formulation is not desirable, but that further legal development (whether general comments, recommendations, declarations or protocols) is not necessary to define the right to education for women and girls. In sum, the provisions of these instruments offer a sufficient international legal basis for governments and other appropriate institutions to act to educate women and girls.

A second purpose of this chapter has been to explore the reasons for the lack of fulfillment of the international right to education. In this respect, the implementa-tion of the right to education at national and international levels has been assessed. Treaty bodies established by the instruments discussed here are only a part of the complex, decision-making structure in which governments, NGOs, or Secretariat officials act (or fail to act) to promote the right to education for women and girls.

---

141. Women's Environment and Development Organization, 9 NEWS AND VIEWS, June-July 1996, at 1, 3–4, 6–7.

U.N. treaty bodies, U.N. policy bodies, Specialized Agencies, particularly UN-ESCO, the World Bank, the regional economic and political organizations, governments, and grassroots activities of national and international non-governmental organizations (INGOs) all play a role in implementing the right to education.

At the national level, many governments have ratified relevant instruments, enacted national legislation, and adopted national educational policies. Except for the UNESCO Convention, which has less than one hundred ratifications, the other principal instruments (except for the Universal Declaration) claim one hundred or more ratifications or accessions. Though, in consenting, a few governments have reserved on education provisions, the vast majority have not done so. Reservations, therefore, do not account for the lack of implementation of the right to education for women and girls.

National governments have also created official entities to administer educational law and policy for women and girls. They may be in the form of national executive departments of education, UNESCO Commissions, human rights, women's rights, or child rights offices or bureaus, or ombudspersons.

Despite these considerable and complex organizational arrangements in which the right to education is to be promoted at national and international levels, statistics on widespread illiteracy demonstrate that organizations are not fulfilling responsibilities to provide education, particularly education of girls and women. Coordination among disparate entities at inter-agency and intergovernmental levels could and should no doubt be improved and greater funding should be allocated for technical assistance projects for education. However, improved organizational arrangements alone will not solve this problem. Underlying priorities of officialdom impede implementation, as do perspectives or stereotypes of, for instance, women's education as the basis for competition with men for scarce employment opportunities and the concomitant reduction in the number of women in the home.

Traditional attitudes toward the education of girls and women have begun to change, as increased government funding for education for women and girls in developing and developed states reflects. But change occurs slowly. In many parts of the world, the lack of gender-sensitivity on the part of political leaders, government civil servants, clergy, labor leaders, mission directors, or even governing elites has been found to discriminate against educating women and girls. Those responsible for treaty interpretation and application and for authorizing and administering assistance, whether intergovernmental or governmental entities, must become accountable to the requirements of the international right to education by acquiring necessary gender sensitivity and awareness.

The global U.N. Conferences have for more than two decades raised consciousness among international and government officials and interested publics about the right to education for women and girls and affirmed the need for organizational accountability for women's education. Importantly, such conferences have spurred policy cooperation and coordination among disparate entities charged with formulating strategies to implement educational and other programs. In preparation for the 1995 World Women's Conference, for instance, ICESCR, CRC, and UNESCO all reported to CEDAW on measures they had taken to advance education for women and girls. But absent the stimulus of global conferences to spur special studies, measures, and coordination, and to prod government consciences, organizational entities must develop not only a habit or policy of coordination, but a sensitivity to gender issues that supports sustained, if not increased, levels of funding for education of women and girls to enable educational institutions to expand ahead of rapid population growth.

Political perspectives and attitudes influence the priorities of governments and intergovernmental bodies. Government agendas, crowded with priorities that compete for attention and funding, often give top priority to security, defense, and economic development. Human rights issues usually receive low priority in domestic and international affairs. Women's issues fall below general human rights issues. Further, if and when governments act to promote human rights, they may emphasize political, civil, economic, social, and cultural rights rather than the right to education for women and girls. Clearly, governments must begin to acknowledge the important interrelation among education for women and girls, national security, and economic development.

NGOs, particularly women's organizations and those committed to solving this problem, have a key political role to play. Women have made considerable progress in recent decades and have become a political force to influence change and increase awareness of the need to combat illiteracy and the lack of education. Nonetheless, these pressing problems persist. Women's efforts in cooperation with men must continue. Ongoing discussions with U.N. treaty bodies offer women, as representatives of NGOs, the possibility of developing the content of existing treaties by promoting agreement of states parties on treaty interpretation, whether recommendations, comments, treaty amendments, protocols, complaint procedures, and other declarations or conventions.[142] Although women's official energies internationally have tended to focus on CEDAW, they need to find ways to influence the interpretation of the right to education in other treaty bodies, such as CESCR and CRC, and in UNESCO. In doing so, they must work cooperatively to achieve those efforts. They must also continue to work in policy bodies and agencies at national and international levels, and at the grassroots, to influence government action to fulfill the right to education for women and girls.

---

142. Rebecca J. Cook, *Introduction: The Way Forward, in* HUMAN RIGHTS OF WOMEN 10–25 (Rebecca J. Cook ed., 1994).

WOMEN AND THE ENVIRONMENT

Neil A.F. Popović

The continuing environmental degradation that affects all human lives has often a more direct impact on women. Women's health and their livelihood are threatened by pollution and toxic wastes, large-scale deforestation, desertification, drought and depletion of the soil and of coastal and marine resources, with a rising incidence of environmentally related health problems and even death reported among women and girls. Those most affected are rural and indigenous women, whose livelihood and daily subsistence depends directly on sustainable ecosystems.[1]

Women have a vital role in environmental management and development. Their full participation is therefore essential to achieve sustainable development.[2]

INTRODUCTION

For largely social and to a lesser extent biological reasons, women are affected by environmental conditions in ways that differ from their effects on men. Because women and men have different life experiences, they bring different perspectives to the consideration of the relationship between people and nature.[3] Those differences, in experience and perspective, have significant implications for the ways in which environmental factors affect women's and men's human rights. Those implications form the basis of this chapter, which addresses the intersection of women, the environment, and human rights. That intersection includes factual aspects of women's relationship to the natural environment, as well as the legal implications of that relationship.

In many, if not most, societies, custom and practice have placed women in positions of increased vulnerability to environmental stresses. Social considerations have also put women in positions where they *should* be able to make special contributions to environmental protection, with benefits for themselves and for society. In practice, however, women often find themselves excluded from meaningful participation in the decision-making processes that determine how a society deals with environmental issues. But even in the face of such marginalization, women make extraordinary contributions to environmental problem solving.

---

1. Platform for Action, *in* Report of the Fourth World Conference on Women, U.N. Doc. A/CONF.177/20, ann. II, ¶ 34 (1995) [hereinafter Platform for Action].

2. United Nations Conference on Environment and Development; Rio Declaration on Environment and Development, princ. 20, U.N. Doc. A/CONF.151/PC/WG.III/L.33/Rev. 1 (1992) [hereinafter Rio Declaration].

3. *See* JANICE JIGGINS, CHANGING THE BOUNDARIES 7 (1994).

As discussed below, women have internationally recognized legal rights that should protect them against human rights violations that result from degradation. Women also have rights that should guarantee them equal access to participation in environmental decision making, and full recognition for their contributions to environmental management.

The chapter will first address how women's human rights are affected by environmental problems. The next section will discuss ways in which women are particularly vulnerable to human rights violations from environmental degradation, the key role of women in protecting human rights and the environment, and the necessity of ensuring effective participation by women in that protection. Then, the heart of the chapter will address the array of legal considerations that bear on women's environmental human rights.[4] This will include discussion of the substantive content and procedural significance of the rights at issue, as well as examination of sources of law that support and give meaning to women's environmental human rights. Finally, the chapter will consider some institutional strategies for enhancing the protection of women's environmental human rights. The power imbalances, stereotypes, and social or cultural factors that attribute household responsibility/maintenance to women are addressed elsewhere in this volume.

FACTUAL PARAMETERS

Substantive Burdens

All over the world, women are the primary users of natural resources.[5] Women have been given exclusive or primary responsibility for childbearing, child rearing, providing food, processing and preparing food, gathering water, gathering fuelwood, providing childhood education, providing health care, and providing shelter.[6] Because those responsibilities share a close connection with environmental conditions, when the environment degrades, women feel it first and they feel it worst,[7] environmental degradation making many of these responsibilities more difficult to fulfill.[8]

---

4.   The expression environmental human rights is meant to encompass the environmental dimension of recognized human rights. *See* Neil A. F. Popović, *In Pursuit of Environmental Human Rights: Commentary on the Draft Declaration of Principles on Human Rights and the Environment*, 28 COLUM. HUM. RTS. L. REV. 487 (1996).

5.   JIGGINS, *supra* note 3, at 5; Pietronella van den Oever, *Women's Roles, Population Issues, Poverty and Environmental Degradation, in* WOMEN AND CHILDREN FIRST 111, 112 (Filomina Chioma Steady ed., 1993) [hereinafter WOMEN AND CHILDREN FIRST]; Bella Abzug, *Women and the Environment*, FOCUS ON WOMEN 1, UN Doc. DPI/1692/Wom—95–12521–Apr. 1995–30M (1995) (U.N. International Author Series); Carol Bellamy, *Women and the Environment*, 7:4 OUR PLANET 7, 7 (1995); Irene Dankelman, *Women, Children, and Environment, in* WOMEN AND CHILDREN FIRST 131, 132, *supra*.

6.   Jodi L. Jacobson, *Gender Bias: Roadblock to Sustainable Development*, Worldwatch Paper 110, at 6 (1992).

7.   UNITED NATIONS ENVIRONMENT PROGRAMME, POVERTY AND THE ENVIRONMENT 94 (1995) [hereinafter POVERTY AND THE ENVIRONMENT].

8.   Jacobson, *supra* note 6, at 13.

Even where women do not experience increased exposure or closer proximity to environmental hazards, women may suffer health consequences unique to their gender, such as breast cancer danger or damage to unborn children.[9] Women face increased vulnerability to environmental hazards in connection with childbearing and child rearing because those functions are particularly vulnerable to environmental factors.[10] Women need a healthy environment to carry out childbearing and child rearing.[11] Environmental contamination endangers maternal and fetal health.[12] Child rearing becomes more difficult when the resources necessary to nurture a growing child become more difficult to obtain.[13] Critical parenting resources affected by environmental conditions include everything from leisure time (reduced, for example, when women have to work longer hours to coax productivity from degraded land) to sufficient quantities of nutritious food.

But even with respect to environmental hazards that do not necessarily have greater adverse effects on women, women still face disproportionately greater exposure and they therefore face a correspondingly disproportionate share of human suffering as well.[14] Diminishing quantities and quality of water mean women have to search longer and harder for safe and adequate water and/or they have to settle for unsafe water.[15] Transportation of large amounts of water can cause falls and injuries, while water scarcity forces women to carry water even longer distances and therefore makes accidents more likely.[16]

Deforestation decreases the availability of biomass for household fuel, which forces women to take longer and work harder to gather fuel.[17] In some cases, women end up contributing to the very deforestation that renders fuelwood scarcer in the first place because they are forced to cut wood from live trees rather than gather fuel from fallen limbs.[18] Tree cover reduction also reduces the availability of other forest resources for handicrafts, food, animal fodder, and medicines.[19] Disruption

---

9. Marie-Thérèse Danielson, *Problems in Paradise: The case of Tahiti*, 19 INSTRAW NEWS 47, (1993).

10. UN Focus: Women and the Environment, U.N. Doc. DPI/1050–40178–Feb. 1990–3M, at 2 (1990) [hereinafter UN Focus]; *see also* Robert F. Housman, *The Muted Voice: The Role of Women in Sustainable Development*, 4 GEO. INT'L ENVTL. L. REV. 361, 366 (1992) (pesticides can make breast-feeding dangerous).

11. van den Oever, *supra* note 5, at 113.

12. *See, e.g.*, ANNABEL RODDA, WOMEN AND THE ENVIRONMENT 92 (1993) (describing prenatal problems and birth defects associated with working at Moruroa nuclear test site); Housman, *supra* note 10, at 366 (breast-feeding can be dangerous where mother has been exposed to pesticides).

13. van den Oever, *supra* note 5, at 113.

14. JIGGINS, *supra* note 3, at 26.

15. Dankelman, *supra* note 5, at 139.

16. Soon-Young Yoon, *Water for Life, in* WOMEN AND CHILDREN FIRST, *supra* note 5, at 199, 201.

17. Dankelman, *supra* note 5, at 141.

18. POVERTY AND THE ENVIRONMENT, *supra* note 7, at 94.

19. Paula J. Williams, *Women, Children, and Forest Resources in Africa, in* WOMEN AND CHILDREN FIRST, *supra* note 5, at 171, 178.

of forest ecosystems has wide-ranging ecological effects and it has equally wide-ranging social consequences, affecting food production, economic activities, and cultural practices. As primary food preparers, women also face health risks from fumes they inhale from indoor cooking stoves that lack proper ventilation.[20] And when the food is prepared, women tend to get less of it than men.[21] When food becomes scarce, women are the first to fall below the level of nutrition everyone requires. To compound the problem, food scarcity may also result in additional work responsibilities for women because environmental degradation makes food cultivation more difficult.

Women who spend more time gathering water and fuel and cultivating and preparing food for household consumption have less time to spend educating their children. They also have less time to provide health care for the young and the old, all of whom require increasing health care as environmental conditions deteriorate.[22] Providing food and providing shelter similarly become increasingly difficult as productive land gives way to desertification, and increasing privatization and corporatization of land resources decrease the availability of agricultural land and shelter for domestic use. The increasing difficulty of meeting a family's basic needs affects everyone, but women remain the ones who have to work harder to meet their families' needs because their responsibilities continue, even when food or water becomes more difficult to obtain.[23]

The disproportionate burden women bear from environmental degradation is evident in a wide range of issues. For example, purposeful deforestation, for industrial logging and for land development, decreases the availability of fuelwood. Extra efforts required to overcome such decreased availability fall primarily on women because women are largely responsible for providing fuelwood for the family.[24] The loss of agricultural land to agribusiness and other commercial enterprises makes subsistence farming more difficult because the lands left for domestic farming require more effort to produce sufficient food to meet a household's needs.[25] Because of their responsibility for household food production, women bear the brunt of this increased burden. Commercial fishing makes it harder to find sufficient

---

20. *E.g.*, JIGGINS, *supra* note 3, at 93; Honorine Kiplagat, *Who makes the decisions?*, 7:4 Our Planet 17, 17 (1995).

21. *See* Women: Challenges to the Year 2000 23 (United Nations, 1991).

22. *See* Danielson, *supra* note 9, at 47 (nuclear testing); Rosina Wiltshire, *Problems of Environmental Degradation and Poverty With Particular Emphasis on Women and Children of Island Nations*, in WOMEN AND CHILDREN FIRST, *supra* note 5, 69, 77 (mining).

23. Jacobson, *supra* note 6, at 19.

24. *E.g.*, Bellamy, *supra* note 5, at 7; Alicia Bárcena, Rebeckah Johnson & Lydia Alpizar, *Victims, Managers and Healers*, 7:4 OUR PLANET 14, 15 (1993); JIGGINS, *supra* note 3, at 93; Abzug, *supra* note 5, at 2; Jacobson, *supra* note 6, at 19; Housman, *supra* note 10, at 365–66; van den Oever, *supra* note 5, at 112; Dankelman, *supra* note 5, at 141; Williams, *supra* note 19, at 173, 178.

25. Bárcena, Johnson & Alpizar, *supra* note 24, at 15 (Greece, Cote d'Ivoire); Michael M. Horowitz and Muneera Salem-Murdock, *River Basin Development Policy, Women, and Children: A Case Study from the Senegal River Valley in* WOMEN AND CHILDREN FIRST, *supra* note 5, at 317, 318–19 (Senegal).

food as stocks that might otherwise be available for domestic consumption are diverted to the commercial market instead.[26] Degradation of water from pesticide runoff and other contaminants associated with commercial enterprises makes it harder to find enough safe water.[27] As access to clean water diminishes, women must re-use water, travel farther to fetch clean water and, in some cases, use unsafe water, all of which may increase their exposure and vulnerability to diseases.[28]

Women's imposed labor roles, including their imputed responsibility for providing food, water, and fuelwood, put them face to face with these and other environmental problems,[29] while men reap a disproportionate share of the economic benefits offered to justify the environmental destruction. Cash-cropping, commercial fishing, and other commercial activities that exploit natural resources and damage the environment primarily provide economic opportunities for men, not women.[30]

Other types of environmental problems adversely affect women without producing any countervailing benefits for men or for society at large that might even arguably make them socially justifiable. For instance, exposure to nuclear radiation from weapons testing and nuclear power generation causes radiation-related health problems in women, including reproductive irregularities, which add to the burden of their duty to care for the sick, compounded by increasingly difficult searches for food due to radiation effects on food-producing natural systems such as coral reefs and agricultural land.[31]

The heightened physical and psychological burdens women bear have direct effects on their health and lives, subjecting them to increased physical exertion and exposing them to environmental hazards.[32] Women also encounter psychological burdens because they must figure out how to overcome environmental crises such as fuel, water, and food scarcity, in order to meet their families' daily needs.[33] Each

---

26. *See* Abzug, *supra* note 5, at 1.

27. Bárcena, Johnson & Alpizar, *supra* note 24, at 15; Abzug, *supra* note 5, at 2. *See* Housman, *supra* note 10, at 365.

28. Bellamy, *supra* note 5, at 7; Abzug, *supra* note 5, at 2; Women: Challenges to the Year 2000, *supra* note 21, at 1; Jacobson, *supra* note 6, at 13, 19, 38; Housman, *supra* note 10, at 365; JIGGINS, *supra* note 3, at 39; Filomina Chioma Steady, *Women and Children: Managers Protectors and Victims of their Environment in* WOMEN AND CHILDREN FIRST *supra* note 5, at 17, 26 [hereinafter Steady, *Women and Children*]; Dankelman, *supra* note 5, at 139, 142; Yoon, *supra* note 16, at 201; WORLD HEALTH ORGANIZATION COMMISSION ON HEALTH AND ENVIRONMENT, OUR PLANET, OUR HEALTH xvi [hereinafter OUR PLANET, OUR HEALTH] (1992).

29. Bárcena, Johnson & Alpizar, *supra* note 24, at 15; Dolores Huerta, *The Impact of Poverty and Environmental Degradation on Women Migrant Workers, in* WOMEN AND CHILDREN FIRST, *supra* note 5, at 223.

30. *See* Jacobson, *supra* note 6, at 7, 27–28; RODDA, *supra* note 12, at 59, 84, 108, 118.

31. Danielson, *supra* note 9, at 47.

32. JIGGINS, *supra* note 3, at 93; Lalla Racine Sanou, *Beating Back the Desert: The case of Burkina Faso* 19 INSTRAW NEWS 40–41 (1993); Jacobson, *supra* note 6, at 33.

33. JIGGINS, *supra* note 3, at 205.

and every day countless women face the stress of wondering whether they will be able to provide sufficient fuel, water, and food to keep their families going.

Unsafe water contributes to some 80 percent of diseases in the world.[34] Because women have been charged with primary responsibility for providing water, maintaining household sanitation, and bathing children, women must expend the extra time and effort needed to search for safe water when environmental conditions render water increasingly scarce. They must handle and otherwise deal with waste water contaminated by household uses, and they must immerse themselves in the often dirty water in which they bathe their children. All of these activities pose threats to women's health.[35] Measures to improve water conditions, while critically important, also place disproportionate burdens on women. For example, as cleanup efforts inflate the price of water, women who bear family responsibility for obtaining water must work harder and longer to earn the necessary money.[36] Along similar lines, measures to reduce waste, such as using cloth diapers instead of disposable ones, requires additional work and more handling of dirty water for women, who typically end up doing the increased washing.[37]

To make things worse, environmental degradation that makes farming more difficult and less profitable often leads to migration by men to search for employment, which further increases the burden on women to perform the tasks necessary for the day-to-day sustenance of the family.[38] Women's vulnerability is also intensified by their disproportionate representation among the poor.[39] Women make up a high proportion of those in poverty, and even among the poor they suffer more than men because they look after children affected by poverty, they manage resource-strapped households, they suffer from diseases related to lack of clean water and sanitation deficiencies, and they care for the sick.[40] Damage to the environment makes each of these problems worse and in each case imposes added burdens on women.[41]

Women, along with children, also make up the majority (70 to 80 percent) of the world's refugees and displaced persons.[42] With environmental factors playing an increasing role in the generation of refugee flows, the already disproportionate

---

34. Women: Challenges to the Year 2000, *supra* note 21, at 17.

35. *Id.* at 17.

36. JIGGINS, *supra* note 3, at 39.

37. *Id.*

38. Noeleen Heyzer, *The view through a triple lens*, 7:4 OUR PLANET 9, 10 (1995); Bárcena, Johnson & Alpizar, *supra* note 24, at 15.

39. Kiplagat, *supra* note 20, at 17.

40. OUR PLANET, OUR HEALTH, *supra* note 28, at xvi.

41. *Id.*

42. Steady, *Women and Children, supra* note 28, at 17, 23; Filomina Chioma Steady, *Gender, Shelter and Sustainable Development, in* WOMEN AND CHILDREN FIRST, *supra* note 5, at 301, 308 [hereinafter Steady, *Gender, Shelter, and Sustainable Development*].

suffering women experience because of environmental problems seems likely to rise.[43] Women refugees face a double dose of environmental woes—the environmental problems that force them to flee their homes and the often difficult environmental conditions they face in their place of refuge.[44]

Procedural Burdens

Given women's imputed responsibility for family sustenance and their associated vulnerability to environmental degradation, it would make sense for women to have equal or even enhanced access to land, education, and opportunities to participate in environmental decision making. Reality is quite the contrary. Women have been denied access to land, education, information, and political power.[45] Women are deprived of meaningful roles in decision making regarding the environment, while at the same time suffering the most immediate and severe consequences from those very decisions.[46]

Although many aspects of women's environmental burdens relate to their relationship to land, in many countries women do not even have equal or any rights to ownership or use of land.[47] As a result, female-headed households are more likely to be located in environmentally marginalized areas, which in turn puts added stress on the land and endangers the life and health of women and their families.[48] Women lack control over other crucial natural resources as well. For example, in some societies, trees are men's property.[49] Certain development programs may only make things worse. Programs that promote cash crops for export shift control over natural resources away from women, who traditionally control food cultivation for household use, and towards men, who usually control commercial food cultivation.[50] Land reform efforts in many cases have a similar anti-female effect because development agencies invariably give land title to men, eroding traditional land use rights of women and undermining their ability to feed their families.[51] Dissolution

---

43. Steady, *Gender, Shelter, and Sustainable Development, supra* note 42, at 308.

44. *Id.; see also* the U.N. Sub-Commission on Prevention of Discrimination and Protection of Minorities, Human Rights and Environment, Final Report Prepared by Ms. Fatma Zohra Ksentini, Special Rapporteur, U.N. DOC. E/CN.4/Sub. 2/1994/9 & Corr. 1, at 40–41 (1994) [hereinafter Ksentini Final Report].

45. POVERTY AND THE ENVIRONMENT, *supra* note 7, at 93.

46. Housman, *supra* note 10, at 363.

47. *E.g.*, Committee on the Elimination of Discrimination Against Women, Consideration of Reports Submitted by States Parties Under Article 18 of the Convention on the Elimination of Discrimination Against Woman, U.N. Doc. CEDAW/C/ETH/1–3/Add.1, at 26–27 (1995) (Ethiopia) [hereinafter 1995 Ethiopia Report].

48. POVERTY AND THE ENVIRONMENT, *supra* note 7, at 94.

49. Dankelman, *supra* note 5, at 136.

50. Jacobson, *supra* note 6, at 13.

51. *Id.* at 26; Vandana Shiva, *Women and Children Last, in* WOMEN AND CHILDREN FIRST, *supra* note 5, at 48.

of customary land tenure reduces the amount of land available to cultivate sustenance crops, which leads to more work for women, to increased stress on the land,
and to increased soil degradation.[52] In some places, such as India, land reform
programs that change the title to what had been communal land affect fuel gathering
as well, by precluding women from gathering fuel on the newly privatized or
government-owned land, forcing them to work harder and longer to gather sufficient fuel.[53]

Along with formal title comes an array of land rights, including the right to
decide what to plant. In the hands of men, that right gets exercised according to
men's prerogatives which tend toward commercial rather than sustenance crops.[54]
In some countries, the legal system expressly permits title and control of land to
rest in the hands of men.[55] But even where the law guarantees gender equity in
land resources, the guarantee is often in word only.[56] In reality, women often lack
credit, capital, and other prerequisites to the meaningful exercise of land rights.[57]
Moreover, government agencies, aid administrators, and even courts do not apply
or enforce the relevant laws in an equal or equitable fashion.[58]

Women's lack of land rights stems from and contributes to a self-perpetuating
pattern of exclusion from decisions that affect the environment.[59] Men almost universally have decision-making power over natural resource use.[60] Women lack equal
access to information, education, and other empowerment tools that enable effective
participation.[61] Women's inability to participate in decisions that affect the environment invites decisions that fail adequately to account for women's needs and perspectives.

For example, women's lack of participation in the formulation and implementation of development policies leads to development projects that fail to take adequate
account of the projects' impact on women and the environment. Development
strategies that focus on economic growth may stimulate the expansion of industrial
agriculture and the displacement of small-scale cultivation and other subsistence
activities, without giving adequate attention to the social and environmental consequences of those changes.[62] For example, in Ghana, communal land given to men

---

52. Jacobson, *supra* note 6, at 7, 27–28.

53. *Id.* at 36.

54. Heyzer, *supra* note 38, at 10.

55. *See* Annie Foster, *Development and Women's Political Leadership: The Missing Link in Sub-
Saharan Africa*, 17 FLETCHER FORUM OF WORLD AFFAIRS 106, 110 (1995); JIGGINS, *supra* note 3, at 198.

56. *See, e.g.,* Jacobson, *supra* note 6, at 26.

57. Dankelman, *supra* note 5, at 132.

58. Jacobson, *supra* note 6, at 48.

59. Kiplagat, *supra* note 20, at 17.

60. Steady, *Women and Children, supra* note 28, at 28–29.

61. Heyzer, *supra* note 38, at 10; 1995 Ethiopia report, *supra* note 47, at 11.

62. Bárcena, Johnson & Alpizar, *supra* note 24, at 15.

to farm is taken out of the hands of women for food cultivation.[63] Left with reduced plots on poorer soil, Ghanaian women must resort to increasingly inferior farming methods that lead to soil erosion and loss of the land's fertility, which in turn leads to reduced food production and increased malnutrition.[64]

In a similar vein, countless programs to reverse deforestation have failed because their planners did not think to consult the village women who are the primary managers and harvesters of forest products in their communities.[65] Such projects, in many cases, exacerbate environmental problems and make it harder for women to carry out their socially prescribed responsibilities,[66] marginalizing women even further and dooming the programs to failure.[67]

The problem of gender-insensitive development policies is part of a self-reinforcing cycle that occurs when men predominate at every level of the decision-making process—from the development agencies that formulate plans to the officials who are consulted and charged with implementing development programs at the local level. Environmental issues that affect women most, such as domestic water supply and the availability of land for food cultivation, tend not to receive adequate consideration if women are not part of the planning process,[68] and the programs installed to address such issues tend not to account for relevant social and environmental factors if women are not part of the implementation process.

Women also face systematic exclusion from educational opportunities. That exclusion hampers women's ability to deal with environmental difficulties and it impedes any improvements in the situation. Less than one-half of all girls in Africa are enrolled in school.[69] In Uttar Pradesh, India, girls older than eight cannot attend school because they must help their mothers gather fuel.[70] In Bangladesh, women's education receives only 44 percent of spending at the primary education level, 32 percent at the secondary level, and a mere 13 percent at the university level.[71]

Women and girls systematically receive far less education—i.e., formal education and training—than males.[72] Lack of access to education and the tools of literacy

---

63. Jacobson, *supra* note 6, at 7.

64. *Id.* at 7–8.

65. *Id.* at 8.

66. *Id.* at 38–39.

67. Housman, *supra* note 10, at 381; Foster, *supra* note 55 at 101; POVERTY AND THE ENVIRONMENT, *supra* note 7, at 94.

68. Yoon, *supra* note 16, at 205. In a similar vein, major forestry programs scarcely consider the role of women in forest conservation and utilization. Williams, *supra* note 19, at 173.

69. Foster, *supra* note 55, at 102.

70. JIGGINS, *supra* note 3, at 142.

71. Nilufar Ahmad, *Stresses and Storms: The case of Bangladesh*, 19 INSTRAW NEWS 27 (1993) (Bangladesh); *see also* Rodda, *supra* note 12, at 101.

72. Ahmad, *supra* note 71, at 23, 27; Jacobson, *supra* note 6, at 6 (in general).

perpetuates women's subordination and hampers their ability to practice and promote sustainable resource use.[73] Women's exclusion from educational opportunities not only impedes their ability to overcome economic difficulties; it may also pose affirmative threats to their health. Lack of training, for example, in the use of pesticides and fertilizers, can lead to increased exposure to environmental hazards for women agricultural workers.[74] Lack of education deprives women of opportunities to advance intellectually, economically, and politically. These deprivations in turn affect women's ability to participate in public affairs,[75] including their representation in positions of authority.[76]

Women suffer further marginalization because of their depressed economic position.[77] Women's lack of money may in turn lead to environmental problems, for example, where the high price of alternative fuel sources compels women to harvest wood instead.[78] Not only do women tend to make less money than men for similar work, much of the environment-related work they perform, such as gathering water, gathering fuel, and preparing food, goes unrewarded and unrecognized altogether as economic activity.[79] Moreover, as environmental degradation makes women's tasks more difficult, women do not receive additional compensation (indeed, they may not receive any compensation).[80] This lack of recognition is cruelly ironic given the indispensability of women in maintaining families and in preserving the environment.

Women's Special Contributions

Notwithstanding the persistent and powerful obstacles they face, "women of every class, colour and culture have emerged as a powerful organized force for positive change around the world,"[81] including change that helps prevent environmental damage. Women's social roles—as land managers, forest users, water and fuel gatherers, food producers and preparers, childbearers, and child-raisers—often render them most directly affected by environmental problems. Because these roles bring women in close and continuing contact with the environment, women are typically the first to recognize the existence of environmentally induced health

---

73. Foster, *supra* note 55, at 102; Jacobson, *supra* note 6, at 10.

74. Dankelman, *supra* note 5, at 140; *see also* Hamid Farabi, *Industrial Pollution and Its Effects on Women and Children, in* WOMEN AND CHILDREN FIRST, *supra* note 5, at 266 (lack of access to information heightens women's vulnerability to environmental hazards); Huerta, *supra* note 29, at 228–30.

75. Sanou, *supra* note 32, at 40–41; Jacobson, *supra* note 6, at 10; Foster, *supra* note 55, at 111.

76. Foster, *supra* note 55, at 11; *see also* Wiltshire, *supra* note 22, at 88 (women are poorly represented in planning and policy making positions regarding environment and development).

77. *See* OUR PLANET, OUR HEALTH, *supra* note 28, at xvi.

78. Wiltshire, *supra* note 22, at 69–70 (describing situation in Jamaica).

79. Jacobson, *supra* note 6, at 6 (food cultivation not considered "economic activity").

80. Horowitz & Salem-Murdock, *supra* note 25, at 318–19, 324.

81. Abzug, *supra* note 5, at 1.

problems and the need for preventative and corrective measures.[82] As primary users of natural resources, many women depend on healthy and sustainable ecosystems for their and their families' existence.[83]

As managers of natural resources, women often have extensive knowledge of local ecosystems, such as where to find food, water, and fuel, or which land is most productive for which crops, and the need to use natural resources in sustainable ways.[84] For example, rural women in India are careful in conserving forests because they rely on them; they consequently favor the collection of dead branches from the ground over the harvesting of living trees.[85] It is no accident that women harvest fuel sustainably; they depend on ecosystem replenishment for their and their families' subsistence.[86] Where women are primary users of forests and their resources, "women are well aware of their value, and of the need to limit the rate of exploitation below regeneration capacity."[87]

Born of generations of experience, women's indigenous knowledge can provide the key to solving problems of agriculture and animal husbandry in fragile ecosystems—this in spite of disproportionately high levels of illiteracy among indigenous women.[88] In societies where women supply water, they have acquired specialized knowledge about local water management and use,[89] such as where to find clean water, and the need to conserve other resources, such as forest land, that are necessary for the replenishment of water resources.[90] Because many of the activities women perform require water, women have determined that certain uses require the cleanest water, while other things can be done with second-, and even third-use water.[91] Because of their social roles, such as the responsibility for getting food on the table year in and year out, women have distinctive knowledge of agricultural practices such as crop rotation and plant species that allow them to provide continuing food security in light of limited land resources.[92]

Women also have an enhanced physical and psychological link to ecological considerations because of their role in bearing and raising children.[93] For example,

82. *Id.*; UN Focus, *supra* note 10, at 2.

83. van den Oever, *supra* note 5, at 113; Jacobson, *supra* note 6, at 14; Steady, *Women and Children, supra* note 28, at 18.

84. Steady, *Women and Children, supra* note 28, at 18; Abzug, *supra* note 5, at 2; UN Focus, *supra* note 10, at 2.

85. Abzug, *supra* note 5, at 2; UN Focus, *supra* note 10, at 1; Jacobson, *supra* note 6, at 22.

86. Jacobson, *supra* note 6, at 22.

87. UN Focus, *supra* note 10, at 1.

88. Rosemary Berewa Jommo, *African Women's Indigenous Knowledge in the Management of Natural Resources, in* WOMEN AND CHILDREN FIRST, *supra* note 5, at 157, 161.

89. Dankelman, *supra* note 5, at 131.

90. *See* Jacobson, *supra* note 6, at 22.

91. *Id.* at 134.

92. JIGGINS, *supra* note 3, at 209; UN Focus, *supra* note 10, at 1.

93. *See* Shiva, *supra* note 51, at 61 ("Because women bring forth and nurture future generations,

mothers of children threatened by death and disease first raised the alarm about chemical poisoning in Love Canal, a New York community built on top of buried chemical waste.[94] Mothers at Love Canal persisted in their activism until relevant authorities took steps to address the toxic contamination in their community. Contributions like those of the women of Love Canal have positive effects on society as a whole.[95]

Two of the best-known examples of women's contributions to the protection of the environment and human rights are the Chipko Movement in the Indian Himalayas and the Green Belt Movement in Kenya. The Chipko Movement began in 1973 in the Chamoli District of Uttar Pradesh, India, where women joined hands around trees and prevented commercial logging of the area's forest.[96] The group's efforts forced the government to ban logging in the Himalayan ecosystem.[97] Over the next ten years, women's groups in the Chamoli district planted more than two million trees and inspired similar movements in other parts of India.[98]

In Kenya, the National Council of Women identified tree loss as a major factor in the problem of desertification.[99] Observing also that poor women fed their children easy-to-cook but not very nutritious foods because they lacked cooking fuel, Dr. Wangari Maathai recognized the need to replenish trees, water, and other natural resources that go hand-in-hand with healthy forests.[100] Under her direction, women's groups in Navasha began a Green Belt Movement which involved tree planting efforts, including a comprehensive program of education, distribution of seeds and seedlings, monitoring, coordinating and evaluating the cultivation of trees.[101]

The Green Belt Movement is a shining example of women using limited resources and unlimited resourcefulness to formulate and implement a sustainable solution to a serious environmental problem. As Green Belt spearhead Dr Maathai put it:

---

they have an inherent ecological ethic based on the integrity of creation and the need to maintain that integrity.'').

94. *Id.* at 57.

95. By the same token, contributions *to* women, such as providing education, tend to have a positive effect on women's income, women's and children's health, life expectancy, and nutrition, while decreasing infant mortality and decreasing fertility. Foster, *supra* note 55, at 102.

96. *E.g.*, Jacobson, *supra* note 6, at 14; Shiva, *supra* note 51, at 60; JIGGINS, *supra* note 3, at 98; RODDA, *supra* note 12, at 110.

97. Shiva, *supra* note 51, at 60; RODDA, *supra* note 12, at 110.

98. JIGGINS, *supra* note 3, at 98. According to Worldwatch Institute researcher Jodi Jacobson, the Chipko movement became a ''full-fledged ecological movement.'' Jacobson, *supra* note 6, at 14; *see also* RODDA, *supra* note 12, at 111.

99. *See* Housman, *supra* note 10, at 370–71; RODDA, *supra* note 12, at 111.

100. JIGGINS, *supra* note 3, at 97.

101. *Id.*; RODDA, *supra* note 12, at 111.

We needed to do something within our reach. We didn't have a lot of money, but we had a lot of hands, so we decided to start with what we could do and that was to plant trees.[102]

The Green Belt Movement grew into a major tree nursery program, involving more than 50,000 women and scores of nurseries, planting more than ten million trees.[103]

Other examples of women's noteworthy contributions to protection of people and the environment are in evidence all over the world.[104] A small sampling follows:

— The Women's Environment Network in the United Kingdom educated the public about dangers associated with chlorine bleach, leading to unbleached paper, diapers, tea bags, and other products.[105]

— The Women's Environment and Development Organization (WEDO), based in the U.S., organized hearings on links between environmental pollutants and reproductive diseases such as breast cancer.[106]

— In Kenya, women's groups initiated a water-for-health program.[107]

— In Malawi, women's groups initiated a handpump maintenance program.[108]

— The Bambi movement in the former Soviet Union works to increase children's awareness of environmental issues.[109]

— The League of Women Voters in the U.S. has had and continues to have an active and pioneering role in water pollution issues.[110]

— WorldWIDE (World Women Dedicated to the Environment), based in the U.S., works to make women more involved and enhance their influence in environmental issues.[111]

— Women in Australia, Canada, New Zealand, and the U.S. used their role as food shoppers to boycott tuna caught with purse seine nets, providing an

---

102. Interview with Dr. Wangari Maathai, *reported in* DEVELOPMENT FORUM, Oct. 1986, at 15, *cited in* JIGGINS, *supra* note 3, at 98.

103. JIGGINS, *supra* note 3, at 98; Housman, *supra* note 10, at 371; RODDA, *supra* note 12, at 111.

104. *See generally* RODDA, *supra* note 12, chs. 5 & 6 (compiling examples of women as agents of environmental improvement); UN Focus, *supra* note 10, at 3 (listing women and environment success stories).

105. Abzug, *supra* note 5, at 2.

106. *Id.*

107. UN Focus, *supra* note 10, at 2.

108. *Id.*

109. *Id.* at 3.

110. *Id.*

111. *Id.*

important boost to the development of international environmental law and public awareness about fishing activities that endanger dolphins.[112]

— In Senegal, a women's fish drying project provides benefits for the environment and for families.[113]

— In Somalia, women trained in nursery management and horticulture operate tree nurseries that support fuel gathering, honey production, and vegetable growing.[114]

— Women in Quito, Ecuador, organized to fight chemical pollution.[115]

— In Guyana, the Women's Revolutionary Socialist movement started a biogas program to save fuel, restore fertility to the land, and reduce women's drudgery.[116]

— In southern Honduras, women have used land exhausted from cotton cultivation to grow vegetables.[117]

— In San Miguel, the Philippines, women living in degraded environmental conditions started a program to green the city and to diversify their own economic activities beyond the use of natural resources.[118]

— Women have organized to prevent pollution and to clean up waste sites in many places, including Bamako, Mali; the Pacific Islands, where they cleaned up beaches; Karachi, Pakistan, where they established sanitation and latrine projects; and Dhaka, Bangladesh, where they also established sanitation and latrine projects.[119]

— Women have organized protests to stop the building of dams in India, Malaysia, Kenya, and the Philippines.[120]

— Women have organized protests in, among other places, the Pacific Islands, the United Kingdom, and the U.S. to oppose nuclear testing.[121]

— Women in New Mexico build ecologically sustainable adobe houses based on oral tradition.[122]

---

112. *See* Marilyn Waring, *Gender and International Law: Women and the Right to Development*, 12 AUSTL. Y.B. INT'L L. 177, 181 (1992).

113. *See* Housman, *supra* note 10, at 369.

114. *See id.*

115. Dankelman, *supra* note 5, at 146.

116. *Id.*

117. *Id.*

118. *Id.*

119. *Id.*

120. *Id.* at 147.

121. *Id.*

122. Steady, *Gender, Shelter and Sustainable Development*, *supra* note 42, at 301, 310.

The list could continue, and the foregoing examples are not necessarily the most impressive ones available, but they do make the point: Women's presence at the forefront of significant environmental initiatives is not coincidental; it has everything to do with the fact that women see and face the ecological and the human consequences of environmental problems most directly and most often.[123]

LEGAL PARAMETERS

The substantial environment-related deprivations borne by women, as well as the remarkable contributions they have made to protecting human rights and the environment, have both occurred alongside major developments in international human rights and international environmental law. As progressive as they are in some respects, instruments of international human rights and international environmental law have typically employed sexist phraseology and perpetuated a male-oriented approach to law and to protecting human rights and the environment. Notwithstanding their sexist language, however, human rights instruments and environmental instruments embody substantial protections for women's environmental human rights, protections that, if honored, could make significant changes in the conditions of women and the environment throughout the world.

Environmental Human Rights

Overview

With some notable exceptions (discussed below), international human rights instruments contain relatively few explicit references to the interconnectedness between human rights and the environment. At the same time, the manifold connections between human rights and the environment are inescapable, and those connections implicate a wide array of established human rights principles.[124] Irrespective of formal recognition of an explicit "right to environment," environmental problems that impair people's quality of life raise human rights concerns under other human rights principles. Conversely, human rights violations that have adverse environmental effects raise issues that implicate principles of international environmental law. Both situations substantiate the depth and breadth of the connections between human rights and the environment, and the need to develop a framework for dealing with the underlying problems.

One such framework that has begun to be developed is the concept of environmental human rights. Environmental human rights represent the environmental dimension of recognized human rights principles, such as the right to life, to health, to housing, the rights of future generations, the right to information, to popular participation, to adequate remedies, and the right to non-discrimination.[125] Environmental human rights encompass the particular types of human rights violations that result from or contribute to environmental degradation.

---

123. Abzug, *supra* note 5, at 3; UN Focus, *supra* note 10, at 2; Jacobson, *supra* note 6, at 22.

124. *See generally* Ksentini Final Report, *supra* note 44; Popović *supra* note 4.

125. *See generally* Popović, *supra* note 4.

Although no binding global human rights instrument yet includes specific protection of the right to a secure, healthy, and ecologically sound environment, several come close. Article 24 of the African Charter of Human and Peoples' Rights (African Charter), which covers the members of the Organization of African Unity (and thus is regional rather than global), provides: "All peoples shall have the right to a generally satisfactory environment favourable to their development."[126] The Additional Protocol to the American Convention on Human Rights in the area of Economic, Social and Cultural Rights (Protocol of San Salvador), though not yet ratified (and also regional in scope), recognizes for everyone "the right to live in a healthy environment."[127] These instruments put a fine point on the environmental coverage of human rights principles but, as discussed below, the principles are already substantively encompassed by widely ratified and well-recognized human rights treaties.

Various human rights institutions have also contributed to the recognition and refinement of the environmental dimension of human rights. In *Lopez Ostra v. Spain*, for example, the European Court of Human Rights construed the right to privacy and personal security (recognized in Article 8 of the European Convention for the Protection of Human Rights and Fundamental Freedoms (European Convention))[128] to include protection against the placement of an environmentally disruptive waste facility near the applicant's home.[129]

In addition, the United Nations Sub-Commission on Prevention of Discrimination and Protection of Minorities oversaw a four-year study on the connections between human rights and the environment.[130] The study was carried out by Sub-Commission Special Rapporteur Fatma Zohra Ksentini and culminated in the presentation of Ksentini's final report to the Sub-Commission in 1994.[131]

Ksentini's final report on human rights and the environment includes a section devoted to women and the Draft Declaration of Principles on Human Rights and the Environment (Draft Declaration).[132] The section on women addresses the decisive role of women in preserving the environment, the discrimination women face,

---

126. Organization for African Unity, African Charter on Human and Peoples' Rights, arts. 2, 18, O.A.U. Doc. CAB/LEG/67/3/Rev.5, art. 24, 21 I.L.M. 58 (1982) [hereinafter African Charter].

127. Additional Protocol to the American Convention on Human Rights in the Area of Economic, Social and Cultural Rights, art. 11(1), *opened for signature* Nov. 17, 1988, O.A.S.T.S. No. 69, 28 I.L.M. 161 (1989) [hereinafter Protocol of San Salvador].

128. European Convention for the Protection of Human Rights and Fundamental Freedoms, art. 14, *done* Nov. 4, 1950, 213 U.N.T.S. 222 [hereinafter European Convention] (general non-discrimination clause).

129. Lopez Ostra v. Spain, Eur. Ct. Hum. Rts. Case No. 41/1993/436/515 (Judgment of 9 Dec. 1994).

130. *See* Ksentini Final Report, *supra* note 44, at 3–6; Adriana Fabra Aguilar & Neil A.F. Popović, *Lawmaking in the United Nations: The UN Study on Human Rights and the Environment*, 3 Rev. Eur. Com. & Int'l Envtl. L. 197 (1994).

131. Ksentini Final Report, *supra* note 44.

132. *Id.* at 37 (section on women), annex I (Draft Principles on Human Rights and the Environment) [hereinafter Draft Declaration].

and the suffering they bear because of environmental degradation.[133] The section notes also the linkage between the deprivation of women's civil, political, and cultural rights and their ability to participate effectively in public life.[134]

The Draft Declaration is the product of a May 1994 meeting of experts convened by the Sierra Club Legal Defense Fund (a U.S.-based nongovernmental organization) at the United Nations in Geneva.[135] The Draft Declaration is the first-ever international instrument that brings together and spells out the environmental coverage of the entire spectrum of human rights—civil, cultural, economic, political, and social; substantive and procedural—that are involved when environmental problems affect people's lives. The Draft Declaration's 27 principles specify the environmental human rights of individuals and groups, including women, as well as the duties that correspond to those rights.[136] The Draft Declaration covers the right to nondiscrimination in matters that affect the environment, the rights of future generations, the right to health, the right to safe and healthy food and water, the right to safe and healthy working conditions, the right to housing, the right to humanitarian assistance, the rights of indigenous peoples, the right to information about the environment, the right to freedom of opinion and expression, the right to political participation, and the right to a remedy.[137]

In contrast to many human rights and environmental instruments, the Draft Declaration employs gender-neutral language throughout and incorporates a comprehensive anti-discrimination provision.[138] The Draft Declaration also calls for special attention to "vulnerable persons and groups."[139] The Draft Declaration speaks to many of the environment-related problems that women face.

Whether or not the Draft Declaration develops into a binding legal instrument, however, women's environmental human rights merit legal recognition already because of the environmental implications of so many human rights principles—especially the nondiscrimination principle, which expressly includes prohibition of discrimination based on "sex." The basic instruments of international human rights, each of which encompasses environmental rights, as discussed below, uniformly proclaim the equal human rights of men and women and prohibit discrimination based on gender. The preamble to the U.N. Charter proclaims the determination of "the peoples of the United Nations . . . to reaffirm faith in fundamental human rights, in the dignity and worth of the human person, in the equal rights of men

---

133. Ksentini Final Report, *supra* note 44, at 37.

134. *Id.*

135. Ksentini Final Report, *supra* note 44, annex II; Fabra & Popović, *supra* note 130, at 200–01; Popović, *supra* note 4, at 492.

136. *See* Draft Declaration, *supra* note 132.

137. *Id.*

138. *Id.*, princ. 3 ("All persons shall be free from any form of discrimination in regard to actions and decisions that affect the environment.").

139. *Id.* princ. 25; *see also* Popović, *supra* note 4, at 592–93.

and women. . . .''[140] Article one of the Charter includes among the U.N.'s purposes: "promoting and encouraging respect for human rights and for fundamental freedoms for all without distinction as to race, sex, language, or religion.''[141]

All of the primary global and regional human rights instruments, including the Universal Declaration of Human Rights (UDHR),[142] the International Covenant on Economic, Social and Cultural Rights (ICESCR),[143] the International Covenant on Civil and Political Rights (ICCPR),[144] the European Convention for the Protection of Human Rights and Fundamental Freedoms (European Convention),[145] the American Declaration of the Rights and Duties of Man (American Declaration),[146] the American Convention on Human Rights (American Convention),[147] and the African Charter,[148] recognize the equal right of men and women to enjoy all human rights.[149]

The human rights instruments that explicitly safeguard environmental human rights also prohibit sex discrimination. Thus, the African Charter's prescription in Article 2 that "[e]very individual shall be entitled to the enjoyment of the rights and freedoms recognized and guaranteed in the present Charter without distinction of any kind,'' includes distinctions based on gender, and it combines with Article 24's recognition of environmental rights to provide affirmative legal protection for the environmental human rights of women. In the same way, the Protocol of San Salvador's requirement that parties guarantee the rights set forth therein without

---

140. UN Charter, pmbl. ¶ 2.

141. UN Charter, art. 1(3).

142. Universal Declaration of Human Rights, art. 2, U.N. G.A. Res. 217A (III), U.N. Doc. A/810, (10 Dec. 1948) [hereinafter UDHR] (general nondiscrimination clause).

143. International Covenant on Economic, Social and Cultural Rights, arts. 2, 3, U.N. G.A. Res. 2200A (XXI), 21 U.N. GAOR Supp. (No. 16) 52, U.N. Doc. A/6316 (1966), 993 U.N.T.S. 3 (Dec. 16, 1966) [hereinafter ICESCR] (art. 2: general nondiscrimination provision; art. 3: requiring parties to ensure equal right of men and women to rights in the covenant).

144. International Covenant on Civil and Political Rights, arts. 2, 3, U.N. G.A. Res. 2200A (XXI), 21 U.N. GAOR Supp. (No. 16) 52, U.N. Doc. A/6316 (1966), 999 U.N.T.S. 717, [hereinafter ICCPR] (art. 2: general nondiscrimination provision; art. 3: requiring parties to ensure equal right of men and women to rights in the covenant).

145. European Convention, *supra* note 128, art. 14.

146. American Declaration of the Rights and Duties of Man, art. 2, *signed* May 2, 1948, O.A.S. Off. Rec. OEA/Ser.L/V/II.23, doc. 21, rev. 6, adopted by the Ninth International Conference of American States, Bogota (1948) [hereinafter American Declaration] (general nondiscrimination clause).

147. American Convention on Human Rights, art. 1, *done* at San Jose, 22 Nov. 1969, O.A.S.T.S. No. 36, O.A.S. Off. Rec. O.E.A./Ser.L/V/II.23 doc. 21 rev. 6, 9 I.L.M. 673 (1970) [hereinafter American Convention] (general nondiscrimination clause).

148. African Charter, *supra* note 126, (art. 2: general nondiscrimination clause; art. 18: state duty to ensure elimination of discrimination against women).

149. Ironically, many of the very instruments that prohibit sex discrimination themselves use gendered language. For example, UDHR Article 25(1) provides: "Everyone has the right to a standard of living adequate for the health and well-being of *him*self and of *his* family, including food, clothing, housing and medical care. . . .'' UDHR, *supra* note 142, art. 25(1) (emphasis supplied).

discrimination based on sex combines with the protocol's guarantee of the right to a healthy environment to guarantee *women's* right to a healthy environment.[150]

Like the African Charter and the Protocol of San Salvador, the European Convention, under which the *Lopez Ostra* case was decided, also guarantees the equal rights of women.[151] That means the environmental application of the right to privacy and personal security recognized by the European Court of Human Rights in the *Lopez Ostra* case must protect women on an equal basis with men.[152]

Although other human rights instruments may not explicitly protect women's environmental rights as human rights, those instruments contain all the requisite elements of an effective regime to guarantee such rights. As explained below, each of the instruments addresses substantive and procedural rights that should apply to environmental situations, and each also includes an equal protection element that includes women. Together, each of the basic human rights instruments should encompass women's equal right to protectic.1 from human rights violations that flow from environmental degradation.

The International Covenant on Economic, Social and Cultural Rights provides a useful illustration. Article 12 of the ICESCR recites the right to health and includes among the steps required to achieve full realization of that right, "the improvement of all aspects of environmental and industrial hygiene."[153] Thus, Article 12 makes clear that the right to health includes an environmental component. Article 3 of ICESCR, by which the parties "undertake to ensure the equal right of men and women to the enjoyment of all economic, social and cultural rights," means that women, as well as men, have the right to improved environmental hygiene.[154] That combination provides a straightforward path to the recognition of women's environmental human rights within the scope of numerous existing human rights instruments.

The ICESCR example provides a basic formula for widespread protection of women's environmental human rights. A substantive human rights principle, such as the right to health, encompasses environmental problems that threaten or impair the right to health; application of the relevant instrument's nondiscrimination principle guarantees equal availability of the right to women. The same formula should apply for the entire catalog of human rights principles implicated by environmental problems.[155] In this way, every human rights principle and thus every environmental

---

150. Protocol of San Salvador, *supra* note 127, art. 3.

151. European Convention, *supra* note 128, art. 14.

152. The claimant in *Lopez Ostra* was a woman. Lopez Ostra v. Spain Eur. Ct. Hum. Rts. Case No. 41/1993/436/515 (Judgment of 9 Dec. 1994).

153. ICESCR, *supra* note 143, art. 12.

154. *Id.*, art. 3.

155. For a relatively comprehensive edition of that catalog, see the Draft Declaration, *supra* note 132.

human rights principle has embedded within it a gender element. Whatever the right, women and men are entitled to its realization on an equal basis.

Substantive Human Rights Affected by Environmental Factors

The Right To Life

The right to life represents the essential and nonderogable prerequisite to the enjoyment of all other rights.[156] Everyone has the right to life, the right must be protected by law and no one may be arbitrarily deprived of life.[157] The right to life is implicated whenever environmental problems endanger human life[158]—either directly, as when an industrial accident releases lethal chemicals into the air, as occurred in Bhopal, India, or indirectly, as when timber-cutting disrupts the forest ecosystem upon which people rely for their sustenance, as has occurred in many parts of Latin America.

The Draft Declaration of Principles on Human Rights and the Environment specifically recognizes "the right to freedom from pollution, environmental degradation and activities that adversely affect the environment, threaten life, health, livelihood, well-being or sustainable development . . . ."[159] To the extent such environmental problems affect women more than men, as they often do, then they implicate the human rights principle of nondiscrimination as well. For example, the release of large amounts of radiation into the air at Chernobyl, Ukraine, in 1986 initially produced death and destruction without regard to gender. But longer-term effects, including disruption of food cultivation, reproductive problems among exposed women, and the need to provide care for affected people, have fallen harder on women. The relevant governments' failure to prevent or ameliorate this disproportionate impact makes it an issue of women's human rights because women have the right to equal protection from life-threatening environmental hazards.

The Right to Health

The right to health, already mentioned because of ICESCR Article 12's explicit reference to "environmental hygiene," protects everyone's right to the "highest

---

156. See, e.g., Ksentini Final Report, supra note 44, ¶¶ 172–174.

157. UDHR, supra note 142, art. 3; ICCPR, supra note 144, art. 6; African Charter, supra note 126, art. 4; American Declaration, supra note 146, art. 1; American Convention, supra note 147, art. 4; European Convention, supra note 128, art. 2.

158. See B.G. RAMCHARAN, THE RIGHT TO LIFE IN INTERNATIONAL LAW 310–11 (1985) ("Threats to the environment or serious environmental hazards may threaten the lives of large groups of people directly; the connection between the right to life and the environment is an obvious one."); Human Rights Case (Environment Pollution in Baluchistan), P.L.D. 1994 (S.C.) 102 (Pakistan) (dumping of nuclear waste in coastal areas of Pakistan could violate Pakistani constitutional right to life, which right includes the right to a clean environment); Subhash Kumar v. State of Bihar, 1991 A.I.R. (S.C.) 420, 424 (India) (declaring that Indian constitutional right to life "includes the right to enjoyment of pollution free water and air for full enjoyment of life.").

159. Draft Declaration, supra note 132, princ. 5.

attainable standard'' of health.[160] Like the right to life, the right to health is a prerequisite for the enjoyment of other rights, including (ironically) the right to life. The environmental dimension of the right to health is spelled out in the Draft Declaration as ''the right to the highest attainable standard of health free from environmental harm.''[161]

Environmental degradation of many types, particularly pollution, impinges on the enjoyment of this right because it endangers and detracts from human health.[162] The environmental content of the right to health is inherent in general statements of the right to health as well. Human rights principles that prohibit discrimination against women should apply the right to protection from health-threatening environmental problems to women on an equal basis. The combination of the right to health and the right to nondiscrimination thus means that women should be protected from environmental problems that threaten everyone's health, and that women should be protected from environmental problems that may threaten their health in ways that are more serious than or different from the ways in which those problems affect men. Moreover, because the antidiscrimination norm includes discriminatory effects as well as discriminatory purposes,[163] women should have the right to equal enjoyment of the right to health no matter whether the disproportionate impact they suffer stems from conscious discrimination, social circumstances, or human physiology.

The Right to Food and Water

The right to food and water is an essential right for human survival. The UDHR and ICESCR address it as an element of the right to an adequate standard of living.[164] The right to food encompasses the right to be free from hunger,[165] the explicit right to food,[166] and aspects of the right to health.[167] The Draft Declaration

---

160. ICESCR, *supra* note 143, art. 12; *see also* African Charter, *supra* note 126, art. 16; American Declaration, *supra* note 146, art. 11; Protocol of San Salvador, *supra* note 127, art. 10; European Social Charter, art. 11, 529 UNTS 89 (1961).

161. Draft Declaration, *supra* note 132, princ. 7.

162. For example, in the *Yanomami Case*, the Inter-American Commission on Human Rights determined that negative environmental effects connected with deforestation violate the right to health and well-being of affected indigenous peoples. Decision of 5 March 1985, Case No. 7615, Inter-Amer. C.H.R. 24, O.A.S. Doc. OEA/Ser.L.V/II/66, doc. 10, rev. 1 (1985).

163. Convention on the Elimination of all Forms of Discrimination Against Women, U.N. G.A. Res. 34/180 (1979) [hereinafter Women's Convention] art. 1 (discrimination against women means distinction, exclusion or restriction based on sex that ''has the effect or purpose of impairing or nullifying'' women's equal enjoyment or exercise of human rights).

164. UDHR, *supra* note 142, art. 25; ICESCR, *supra* note 143, art. 11.

165. ICESCR, *supra* note 143, art. 11.

166. Protocol of San Salvador, *supra* note 127, art. 12.

167. American Declaration, *supra* note 146, art. 11.

recognizes "the right to safe and healthy food and water adequate to . . . well-being,"[168] implying, without explicitly stating, that access to food and water is part and parcel of environmental human rights.

Harmful environmental conditions can frustrate realization of the right to food because food safety and food production depend on environmental factors, and because food scarcity undermines environmental conditions by forcing people (largely women) to overutilize the natural resources at their disposal.[169] Application of the nondiscrimination principle to the right to food means that women should be protected against the special hardships they endure in connection with environmental factors that affect food availability, food production, and food preparation.

The right to water is an essential requisite of the right to food, the right to an adequate standard of living, and the right to health.[170] It is also dependent on environmental factors and has special significance for women. The right to water includes the right to clean drinking water, water for sanitation purposes, agriculture, navigation, industrial processes, and other human uses.[171] Degradation of fresh water sources, by pollution, deforestation, and other environmentally harmful activities, reduces the quality and quantity of accessible water that is safe and usable.

Because women bear primary responsibility for gathering water, and because their daily activities require them to handle water, any problem with water quality or quantity affects women disproportionately. Degradation of water quality and reduction of water quantity in many cases may lead to, or constitute, a failure to realize the right to water, especially where the problem results from government action or neglect. The disproportionate impact these problems have on women indicates potential violations of women's equal protection rights as well.

The right to food and water is closely connected to environmental conditions and has profound significance for many women because of their role (discussed above) in producing and preparing food and in gathering and using water. To provide sustenance for their families, women must provide potable water and nutritious food in sufficient quantities to satisfy their families' needs.

The Right to Housing

Like the right to food and water, the right to housing is an element of the right to an adequate standard of living.[172] According to the U.N. Committee on Economic,

---

168. Draft Declaration, *supra* note 132, princ. 8.

169. *See* Asbjørn Eide, *Right to Adequate Food as a Human Right*, Study Ser. No. 1, U.N. Pub. Sales No. E.89.XIV.2 (1989); United Nations, Committee on Economic, Social and Cultural Rights, *Debate on the Right to Food*, U.N. Doc. E/C.12/1989/SR.20, at 2–12 (1989).

170. *See, e.g.*, Convention on the Rights of the Child, U.N. G.A. Res. 25, U.N. GAOR, 44th Sess., Supp. No. 49, at 166, 170, U.N. Doc A/RES/44/25 (1990), art. 24(2)(c) (right to health includes "provision of adequate nutritious foods and clean drinking-water, taking into consideration the dangers and risks of environmental pollution").

171. *See generally* Stephen C. McCaffrey, *A Human Right to Water: Domestic and International Implications*, 5 Geo. INT'L ENVTL. L. REV. 1 (1992).

172. *See* UDHR, *supra* note 142, art. 25; ICESCR, *supra* note 143, art. 11.

Social and Cultural Rights, which oversees implementation of the ICESCR, the right to adequate housing includes the requirement that "housing should not be built on polluted sites nor in immediate proximity to pollution sources that threaten the right to health of the inhabitants."[173] The environmental dimension of the right to housing also includes the right not to be evicted because of environmental decisions, the right to participate in resettlement decisions, and the right to compensation.[174]

Conversion of land previously used for subsistence farming into commercial farmland, or the exploration for oil, gas, and minerals on indigenous peoples' lands all threaten the right to housing by polluting the surrounding environment, depriving the land of its productive capacity, and by displacing the local peoples. Even efforts to create nature preserves in areas where people have learned to live in harmony with their surroundings (as has occurred in South Africa and Burma), may violate the right to housing. Because of women's special responsibility for locating and maintaining housing for their families, as well as their responsibility for cultivation and preparation of food, the environmental difficulties associated with deprivations of the right to housing fall hardest on women. That disproportionate impact, even if driven by ostensibly neutral policies, may violate nondiscrimination principles and thus may violate women's human rights.

The Right to Safe and Healthy Working Conditions

The right to just and favorable working conditions includes the right to safe and healthy working conditions.[175] The right includes the right to be free from environmental hazards in the workplace, such as exposure to dangerous chemicals and pesticides.[176] The International Labour Organisation has generated a substantial body of binding legal instruments that address this right in the context of particular workplace hazards, many of which affect women.[177] Environmental hazards visited

---

173. United Nations, Committee on Economic, Social and Cultural Rights, General Comment No. 4, U.N. Doc. E/C.12/1991/4, at 114–20; *see also* Draft Declaration, *supra* note 132, princ. 10 (right to adequate housing, land tenure and living conditions in secure, healthy, ecologically sound environment); United Nations, Sub-Commission on Prevention of Discrimination and Protection of Minorities, The right to adequate housing; Second progress report submitted by Mr. Rajindar Sachar, Special Rapporteur, U.N. Doc. E/CN.4/Sub.2/1994/20; Draft International Convention on Housing Rights, art. 11(2), *in* U.N. Doc. E/CN.4/Sub.2/1994/20, at 27–35 ("Occupants of housing built on or near to sources of pollution shall have the right to claim compensation from public authorities, who shall have the legal duty to de-contaminate the area and/or to reduce pollution sources to levels which do not in any way threaten public health.").

174. Draft Declaration, *supra* note 132, princ. 11; *see also* Popović, *supra* note 4, at 533–35.

175. *See* ICESCR, *supra* note 143, art. 7; African Charter, *supra* note 126, art. 15; American Declaration, *supra*, note 146, art. 14; Protocol of San Salvador, *supra* note 127, art. 7; European Social Charter, *supra* note 160, art. 3; Draft Declaration, *supra* note 132, princ. 9.

176. *See* Ksentini Final Report, *supra* note 44, at 48–49, ¶ 1930.

177. *See* ILO Chemicals Convention (No. 170, 1990); ILO Convention (No. 169) Concerning Indigenous and Tribal Peoples in Independent Countries, 28 I.L.M. 1382 (1989) [hereinafter ILO Convention No. 169]; ILO Safety and Health in Construction Convention (No. 167, 1988); ILO Asbestos Convention

uniquely or disproportionately on women workers, or that pose special hazards for women, may violate women's environmental human rights.[178] Disproportionate impact may result from unequal enforcement of workplace safety rules or because of women's subordinate social status, which tends to place them in less desirable, more hazardous jobs. Such situations may violate the right to safe and healthy working conditions and the nondiscrimination principle.

The Right to Humanitarian Assistance

Although not specified in the principal human rights instruments, the right to humanitarian assistance nonetheless commands recognition as a moral and social imperative.[179] In 1992, the International Institute of Humanitarian Law concluded that "victims of emergency situations should have the right to demand and to receive humanitarian assistance, in particular if their life, health or physical integrity are endangered."[180] The Draft Declaration proclaims this right to include the right to humanitarian assistance "in the event of natural or technological or other human-caused catastrophes."[181]

As with other elements of women's environmental human rights, the right to humanitarian assistance is covered by the nondiscrimination principle. Accordingly, women have the right to seek and obtain humanitarian assistance on an equal basis with men. Moreover, because the nondiscrimination principle addresses discriminatory effects as well as discriminatory purposes, women have the right to receive assistance that meets their needs. For example, women faced with environmental disasters may have special needs for childcare, and they may be subject to unwanted sexual advances from aid workers and others.[182] Protection of women's rights requires attention to those types of concerns. Recognition of women's right to humanitarian assistance requires gender sensitivity on the part of those who

---

(No. 162, 1986); ILO Convention on Occupational Safety and Health (No. 155, 1981); ILO Working Environment (Air Pollution, Noise and Vibration) Convention (No. 148, 1977); ILO Occupational Cancer Convention (No. 139, 1974); ILO Benzene Convention (No. 136, 1971); ILO Hygiene (Commerce and Offices) Convention (No. 120, 1964); ILO Radiation Protection Convention (No. 115, 1960). (All ILO Conventions, with the exception of ILO Convention No. 169, *reprinted in* INTERNATIONAL LABOUR CONVENTIONS AND RECOMMENDATIONS 1919–1991 (International Labour Organisation ed., 1992)).

178. Restricting women's employment opportunities to protect them from hazards that might interfere with healthy childbearing, however, raises its own array of equal protection concerns. *See generally* Hannah Arterian Furnish, *Beyond Protection: Relevant Difference and Equality in the Toxic Work Environment*, 21 U.C. DAVIS L. REV. 1 (1987).

179. Humanitarian assistance refers to the provision of assistance to victims of natural and anthropogenic disasters to help those victims meet their basic needs, such as food and shelter. Humanitarian assistance encompasses a broader spectrum of emergencies than is covered by traditional humanitarian law, which deals with armed conflict situations.

180. XVIIth Round Table of the International Institute of Humanitarian Law (San Remo, 2–4 Sept. 1992), closing statement, *reprinted in* 291 INT'L REV. RED CROSS 592, 601 (1992).

181. Draft Declaration, *supra* note 132, princ. 12.

182. *See* Sadako Ogata, *Refugee women: the forgotten half*, 7:4 OUR PLANET 19, 21 (1995).

distribute aid, those who determine whether it is needed, and those who determine how much and what type of aid is provided. Bias at any of these levels may violate women's environmental human rights.

The Rights of Indigenous Peoples

Many of the specific rights addressed in this chapter are particularly important in the context of indigenous peoples, whose lifestyles and cultures in many cases incorporate a strong connection to nature and natural resources.[183] The environmental needs and rights of indigenous peoples are specifically addressed in the U.N. Draft Declaration on the Rights of Indigenous Peoples (Indigenous Peoples Declaration);[184] and in International Labour Organisation Convention Concerning Indigenous and Tribal Peoples in Independent Countries (ILO Convention No. 169).[185] The Indigenous Peoples Declaration and ILO Convention No. 169 incorporate the right to sovereignty over natural resources, the right to manage and conserve traditional lands and other natural resources, the right to protection against destruction of indigenous peoples' environments,[186] and the right of indigenous peoples to participate in decisions that affect their environment.[187] The role of women in indigenous societies, particularly their involvement with the use and maintenance of natural resources, makes these rights especially important to indigenous women. Decisions that affect the availability and use of land, water, and other resources may have profound effects on the day-to-day lives of indigenous women. Where those effects result in special hardships for women, they may violate the antidiscrimination principle that guarantees indigenous women's equal right to realization of their environmental human rights.

Procedural Rights Relevant to the Environment

Women's enjoyment of the substantive environmental human rights discussed above depends considerably on their enjoyment of procedural rights. Procedural

183. *See, e.g.*, Peter Whitely, *Paavahu and Paanagawu*, CULTURAL SURVIVAL Q. 40 (Winter 1996) (discussing role of water in Hopi culture and life).

184. Draft Declaration on the Rights of Indigenous Peoples, U.N. Doc. E/CN.4/Sub.2/1995/2 (1995), 34 I.L.M. 541 (1995) [(hereinafter Indigenous Peoples Declaration].

185. ILO Convention No. 169, *supra* note 177.

186. Indigenous Peoples Declaration, *supra* note 184, art. 10 (right to protection against relocation), art. 21 (right to self-determination and means of subsistence), art. 27 (right to protection against damage to or loss of lands), art. 28 (right to protection of the environment), art. 30 (right to exploitation of natural resources), art. 31 (right to "own, develop, control and use" traditionally relied upon environment and natural resources); ILO Convention No. 169, *supra* note 177, art. 4(1) (right to protection of indigenous peoples' environment), art. 15(1) (right to "participate in the use, management and conservation" of natural resources); *see also* Draft Declaration, *supra* note 132, princ. 14 (right to control lands, territories, natural resources, right to protection against degradation, destruction of territories).

187. *See* ILO Convention No. 169, *supra* note 177, art. 2(1) (overall obligation to protect indigenous peoples, including "participation of the peoples concerned"); art. 4 (duty to adopt special measures to safeguard indigenous peoples environment, among other things, "not . . . contrary to the freely-expressed wishes of the peoples concerned."); art. 7(4) (measures "in co-operation with the peoples concerned" to protect environment).

rights relevant to the environment include the right to information, the right to freedom of opinion and expression, the right to freedom of association and assembly, the right to education, the right to participation, and the right to a remedy. Recognition and protection of procedural rights can make a marked difference in the way women interact with the environment and in their ability to protect both the environment and their substantive human rights.

The Right to Information

The right to information includes the right to seek, receive, and impart information.[188] And it includes the right to seek, receive, and impart information about the environment, that is, the right to environmental information.[189] The right to environmental information includes the right to obtain information about environmental conditions and environmentally significant activities on request from government sources.[190] It also includes the "right to know," which means the right to be kept informed of environmental hazards irrespective of specific requests.[191] Environmental information provides an important tool for effective participation in environmental decision making.

Women's lack of access to environmental information results from and contributes to women's underrepresentation in positions of power. Male control of the flow of environmental information makes it all the more difficult for women to realize their substantive environmental human rights because it deprives them of the factual foundation for effective participation and sound decision making.

Recent developments in international environmental law reflect increasing recognition of the importance of information and the necessity of making it available.[192] Accordingly, women's equal right to seek, receive, and impart environmental information is a crucial factor in enabling women to achieve equality and to enhance protection of their own (and others') environmental human rights. Violations of

---

188. UDHR, *supra* note 142, art. 19; ICCPR, *supra* note 144, art. 19; African Charter, *supra* note 126, art. 9; American Convention, *supra* note 147, art. 13; European Convention, *supra* note 128, art. 10.

189. Draft Declaration, *supra* note 132, princ. 15; *see also* Rio Declaration, *supra* note 2, princ. 10, ("each individual shall have appropriate access to information concerning the environment"); *see also* Popović, *supra* note 4, at 544–48.

190. *See* Neil A. F. Popović, *The Right to Participate in Decisions that Affect the Environment*, 10 PACE ENVTL. L. REV. 683, 695 (1993).

191. *Id.* at 697; *see* Emergency Planning and Community Right-to-Know Act, 42 U.S.C. §§ 11001–50; Popović, *supra* note 4, at 547.

192. *See, e.g.*, Rio Declaration, *supra* note 2, princ. 10; Convention Concerning the Protection of the World Cultural and Natural Heritage, art. 27(2), Nov. 15, 1972, 27 U.S.T. 37, 11 I.L.M. 1358 (1972); Antarctic Protocol on Environmental Protection, art. 6(1)(c), Oct. 4, 1991, 30 I.L.M. 1455 (1991); Council Directive 90/313 on the Freedom of Access to Information on the Environment, 1990 O.J. (L 158/56) 33; UN Economic Commission for Europe, Draft Convention on Access to Environmental Information and Public Participation in Environmental Decision-Making; Popović, *supra* note 190, at 694–98.

women's right to environmental information have grave and far-reaching consequences for women, for the environment, and for society.

The Right to Freedom of Opinion and Expression

Another important procedural right, closely connected to the right to information, is the right to freedom of opinion and expression, which is recognized in global and regional human rights instruments.[193] This right includes the right to hold and express opinions about a broad range of topics, including environmental issues.[194] Women's right to freedom of expression and opinion about environmental matters safeguards an important social function—communication—which in turn facilitates constructive and informed political action on environmental issues. Freedom of expression and opinion is especially important for women because of their continued underrepresentation in positions of authority and their corresponding lack of access to official channels of communication that influence environmental decisions. What women lack in official means of communication they must make up for in informal communication. Women's right to freedom from discrimination furnishes an equal protection overlay that should bolster women's ability to hold and express opinions about matters related to the environment.

The Right to Freedom of Association & Assembly

The right to freedom of association and assembly, like the right to freedom of opinion and expression, contributes to effective participation and enjoys widespread recognition in human rights instruments.[195] The right includes the right to associate and assemble to protect the environment.[196] Group protests, community education, and forms of collective action can play significant roles in women's ability to participate in environmental decision-making and to improve environmental conditions, particularly where women lack access to formal means of influencing environmental decisions. Thus groups like the Chipko Movement in India, the Green Belt Movement in Kenya, and many others have used association and assembly to build solidarity and enhance protection of their environmental human rights by accomplishing in concert what they could not achieve individually. Application of the nondiscrimination norm to women's right to freedom of association and assembly should guarantee that women can continue to join forces to enhance protection of human rights and the environment.

---

193. UDHR, *supra* note 142, art. 19; ICCPR, *supra* note 144, art. 19; African Charter, *supra* note 126, art. 9; American Declaration, *supra* note 146, art. 4; American Convention, *supra* note 147, art. 13; European Convention, *supra* note 128, art. 10.

194. Draft Declaration, *supra* note 132, princ. 16.

195. *See* UDHR, *supra* note 142, art. 20; ICCPR, *supra* note 144, arts. 21, 22; African Charter, *supra* note 126, arts. 10, 11; American Declaration, *supra* note 146, arts. 21, 22; American Convention, *supra* note 147, arts. 15, 16; European Convention, *supra* note 128, art. 11.

196. Draft Declaration, *supra* note 132, princ. 19.

The Right to Education

The right to education is another keystone of effective participation and a widely recognized human right.[197] The right to education includes education about human rights, about the environment (including how to protect it) and about the existence of environmental human rights.[198]

As discussed above, exclusion of girls and women from formal and informal education and training—in general and in environmental matters—perpetuates their marginalization from generation to generation. Although women contribute mightily to the protection of human rights and the environment in spite of their exclusion from educational opportunities, education remains a crucial stepping stone to the echelons of power in government, industry, and other fields that largely determine the fate of the environment and the fate of women who deal with the environment day in and day out.

Education holds the key to literacy and the promise of teaching women how to educate themselves—about how to protect themselves, how to protect the environment, and about the existence and content of their human rights. The equal right of women and girls to environmental and human rights education should be guaranteed by the combination of principles of nondiscrimination, and the inherent environmental dimension of the right to education.[199] Women should have the right, on an equal basis with men, to receive education about how to protect the environment and how to protect their environmental human rights.

The Right to Participation

The right to information, the right to freedom of opinion and expression, the right to freedom of association and assembly, and the right to education are the building blocks of participation in public affairs, the hallmark of democracy. The right to participate in government is incorporated into global and regional human rights instruments,[200] and it includes the right to participate in environmental decision making.[201]

---

197. *See* UDHR, *supra* note 142, art. 26; ICESCR, *supra* note 143, arts. 13, 14; African Charter, *supra* note 126, art. 17; American Declaration, *supra* note 146, art. 12; Protocol of San Salvador, *supra* note 127, art. 13; European Convention, *supra* note 128, Protocol No. 1, art. 2.

198. UDHR, *supra* note 142, art. 26; Draft Declaration, *supra* note 132, princ. 17; ICESCR, *supra* note 143, art. 13.

199. *See* Popović, *supra* note 4, at 551–54.

200. *See* Popović, *supra* note 190, at 684–86. UDHR, *supra* note 142, art. 21; ICCPR, *supra* note 144, art. 25; African Charter, *supra* note 126, art. 13; American Declaration, *supra* note 146, art. 20; American Convention, *supra* note 147, art. 23.

201. Draft Declaration, *supra* note 132, princ. 18; World Charter for Nature, U.N. GAOR, 37th Sess., Supp. No. 51, at 23, U.N. Doc. A/RES/37/7 (1973); *see generally* Popović, *supra* note 189.

Where decisions are made by vote, participation includes the right to vote and to have one's vote counted equally with others, regardless of gender. Where decisions are taken by government agencies, participation must include the ability to express one's views and to have those views meaningfully considered in the decision-making process.[202] For women and the environment, participation is all too often the missing link that results in decisions that fail adequately to account for women's needs and interests *vis-à-vis* the environment. Many of the problems women face in connection with the environment, as discussed earlier in this chapter, can be linked to deprivations of women's right to participate. Decisions about crop selection, land use, housing location, and other elements of daily life have ramifications for women and for the environment. The antidiscrimination provisions of global and regional human rights instruments guarantee that women should have equal rights to participate in decisions that affect the environment.

The Right to a Remedy

As a reinforcement for all the environmental human rights principles discussed above, all states that participate in human rights regimes must provide access to adequate remedies in the event of violations.[203] The right to a remedy includes the right to effective legal or administrative remedies and redress for the entire spectrum of human rights violations, including those associated with environmental harm.[204] That means women adversely affected by environmental degradation should be able to go to court or to an administrative agency and secure compensation, remediation, preventive measures, or whatever other remedy is appropriate under the circumstances. Under these principles, women forced to bear a disproportionate share of the burden of environmental problems should have recourse to the power of the state to protect them and to set things right. That means women should have access to justice—the opportunity to institute proceedings and effective means of enforcement.

The nondiscrimination principle includes the right to equality before the law.[205] It should guarantee women's equal right to accessible and meaningful remedies for environment-related human rights deprivations.

The Right to a Just World Order

Finally (although the foregoing list by no means exhausts the linkage points among human rights, the environment, and women), the right to a social and international order in which all human rights and fundamental freedoms can be

---

202. *See* Popović, *supra* note 190, at 698–99.

203. UDHR, *supra* note 142, art. 8; ICCPR, *supra* note 144, art. 2; African Charter, *supra* note 126, art. 7; European Convention, *supra* note 128, art. 13.

204. *See* Draft Declaration, *supra* note 132, princ. 20; UDHR, *supra* note 142, art. 8, ICCPR, *supra* note 144, art. 2(3).

205. *E.g.*, UDHR, *supra* note 142, art. 7; ICCPR, *supra* note 144, art. 14; American Declaration *supra* note 146, art. 2; American Convention, *supra* note 147, art. 24.

realized provides a holistic context for all environmental human rights. The right to a social and international order conducive to human rights is explicitly recognized in the UDHR, and implicit in any comprehensive scheme of human rights.[206] The concept includes the right to a social and international order in which environmental human rights can be fully realized.[207]

A system in which women's environmental human rights can be fully realized is a system that guarantees women's environmental human rights are protected and that they are protected no less than are men's rights. That, in turn, means a system that maintains the rule of law, controls the voracious environmental appetites of transnational corporations, and ensures that economic forces, such as international trade, do not overwhelm environmental and social considerations. And it means governments must establish and maintain such systems in ways that guarantee the equal enjoyment of human rights for women.

The Convention on the Elimination of Discrimination Against Women

The foregoing rights should also be protected through the Convention on the Elimination of All Forms of Discrimination Against Women (Women's Convention). The Women's Convention, discussed extensively in other chapters, provides an encompassing framework that links the substantive and procedural elements of basic human rights with the elemental principle that women are entitled to recognition, enjoyment, and exercise, "irrespective of their marital status, on a basis of equality of men and women, of human rights and fundamental freedoms in the political, economic, social, cultural, civil or any other field."[208] That guarantee is more than broad enough to encompass environmental human rights—rights that come easily within the scope of the Women's Convention's enumerated fields. The Women's Convention makes explicit the gender component of the nondiscrimination norm that is included in all of the major global and regional human rights instruments. The convention prohibits sex discrimination with respect to all human rights and it guarantees women equality before the law.[209]

The human rights principles set forth in the Women's Convention have widespread relevance to women's environmental human rights. For example, Article 7 of the Women's Convention protects women's equal rights to vote and be elected, to participate in decision making, and to participate in nongovernmental organizations and associations.[210] Each of these rights protects an element of women's right to participate in public affairs, including matters that affect the environment. Article

---

206. UDHR, *supra* note 142, art. 28.

207. Draft Declaration, *supra* note 132, princ. 27.

208. Women's Convention, *supra* note 163, art. 1.

209. *Id.*, art. 15.

210. *Id.*, art. 7; *see also* Committee on the Elimination of Discrimination against Women, Consideration of Reports Submitted by States Parties, Second Periodic Report of Australia, U.N. Doc. CEDAW/C/AUL/2, at 179 (1992) (describing women's participation in community environment organizations and their lack of representation in decision making positions) [hereinafter 1992 Australia Report].

10 of the Women's Convention guarantees women's equal right to education, including access to studies, access to curricula and school infrastructure, elimination of gender stereotyping in education, access to financial assistance, access to continuing education programs and programs for women and girls who have left school prematurely, access to sports and physical education, and access to educational information on health and family planning.[211] Education and training can provide women with critical skills, knowledge, and social status to help them formulate long-term solutions to environmental issues and to increase their ability to influence environmental decision making.[212] Education can also help women break the cycle of illiteracy, poverty, and repression that exacerbates environmental problems for present and future generations.

Article 11 of the Women's Convention protects women's equal employment rights, including the right to work, the right to equal employment opportunities, the right to free choice of profession and employment, the right to equal compensation, the right to social security, and the right to protection of health and safety in the work environment.[213] The Women's Convention's employment rights provisions encompass many of the environment-related hardships women face, such as exposure to dangerous substances and cultivation of marginal land. Laws and customs that allocate to women the jobs most vulnerable to environmental stress, such as water gathering, fuel gathering, and household food production, violate women's right to equal employment opportunities and their right to free choice of profession. The failure to guarantee the safety of women's work—whether by forcing them to transport large quantities of water or by permitting them to be exposed to dangerous pesticides—violates their right to safe and healthy working conditions. And social structures and accounting models that ignore or undervalue the economic importance of women's work (work that women in many instances have to perform because of social conditions),[214] such as water and fuel gathering and food production, violate women's right to equal compensation.[215]

Article 14 of the Women's Convention focuses on rural women and addresses important environment-related topics. Under Article 14, women in rural areas have equal rights to participate in development planning, to access health care (including information on family planning) to benefit *directly* from social security programs, to training, including literacy and technical training, to organize and get equal access to employment, to participate in community activities, and

---

211. Women's Convention, *supra* note 163, art. 10.

212. *See* Committee on the Elimination of Discrimination Against Women, Consideration of Reports Submitted by States Parties, Initial, Second and Third Periodic Reports of Ethiopia, U.N. Doc. CEDAW/C/ETH/1–3, at 20 (1993) (noting women's access to training as a factor in agricultural crisis and the "worsened" situation of women) [hereinafter 1993 Ethiopia Report].

213. Women's Convention, *supra* note 163, art. 11.

214. *See* 1993 Ethiopia Report, *supra* note 212, at 21 (men feel embarrassed to help their wives with "women's" chores).

215. *See* 1995 Ethiopia Report, *supra* note 47 (noting undercounting of women's participation in the labor force).

to have access to agricultural credit and loans, marketing facilities, appropriate technology and equal treatment in land and agrarian reform as well as in land resettlement schemes.[216]

Many of the elements of the Women's Convention Article 14 relate directly to the lack of land rights suffered by many women, and the environmental human rights deprivations that result from that lack. For example, in its consideration of country reports submitted by Ethiopia, the Committee on the Elimination of all Forms of Discrimination Against Women (CEDAW) noted a substantial lack of access to piped water and pointed out the resulting health effects on women, including the high demand on women's energy, that results from the arduousness of fetching water.[217]

Article 14 of the Women's Convention also guarantees women the equal right to adequate living conditions with respect to housing, sanitation, electricity, water supply, transportation, and communications.[218] Environmental conditions bear on each of these elements. Inadequate housing may be the result of environmental problems, as when housing is located near environmental hazards, and it may contribute to environmental problems, as when housing is so dense that available land cannot produce sufficient food and is degraded as a result. Levels of sanitation, access to electricity, water, transportation, and communications are also sensitive to environmental conditions. Improvements in these areas should relieve stress on the environment, and improvements in environmental conditions should make these elements easier to achieve.

The rights set forth in the Women's Convention include many, if not all, of the human rights most affected by women's relationship to the natural environment. The Women's Convention draws out the gender equity element inherent in all those rights and has the potential to illuminate the environmental content in those rights. For that to happen, however, country reports must include environmental considerations, and the CEDAW must evaluate states parties' performance with reference to environmental considerations. That process has begun, but not yet in a systematic way.[219]

International Action to Protect Women's Environmental Human Rights

Several important international conferences have also contributed to the recognition of women's environmental human rights.

---

216. Women's Convention, *supra* note 163, art. 14.

217. 1995 Ethiopia Report, *supra* note 47, at 31. Women are already nutritionally vulnerable, especially during pregnancy. *Id.*

218. Women's Convention, *supra* note 163, art. 14.

219. *See* the following reports of the Committee on the Elimination of Discrimination against Women: U.N. Doc. CEDAW/C/AUL/3, at 48–49 (1995) (Australia) [hereinafter 1995 Australia Report]; 1992 Australia Report, *supra* note 210, at 178–80; 1995 Ethiopia Report, *supra* note 47; at 6–8, 24–26 (Ethiopia); 1993 Ethiopia Report, *supra* note 212; at 20–22 (Ethiopia).

The 1972 Stockholm Conference on the Human Environment

The 1972 U.N. Conference on the Human Environment held in Stockholm, Sweden, provided a singularly powerful boost to the development of modern international environmental law and helped pave the way for formal consideration of the human rights impact of environmental problems. Although remarkably progressive in many respects, the Stockholm Declaration on the Human Environment employs much of the gendered—and thus sexist—language of the times. Principle 1 of the Stockholm Declaration provides:

> Man has the fundamental right to freedom, equality and adequate conditions of life, in an environment of a quality that permits a life of dignity and well-being, and he bears a solemn responsibility to protect and improve the environment for present and future generations. In this respect, policies promoting or perpetuating apartheid, racial segregation, discrimination, colonial and other forms of oppression and foreign domination stand condemned and must be eliminated.[220]

Stockholm principle 1 uses rights language and it gives eloquent expression to the premise that environmental quality is a key determinant of quality of life. However, taken at face value, the Stockholm Declaration's recognition of the right to a healthful environment applies only to men and its nondiscrimination provision focuses on race, with no mention of gender. While it is safe to assume that the Stockholm drafters used the term "man" in its generic sense, as subsuming women, the failure expressly to include women is nonetheless a glaring omission.

The sexist pattern continues in Stockholm principle 8, which provides: "Economic and social development is essential for ensuring a favorable living and working environment for man and for creating conditions on earth that are necessary for the improvement of the quality of life."[221] Principle 8 draws the connection between environmental conditions and the human condition, but it leaves out half of humanity. The same can be said for Stockholm principle 19, which states that environmental education is essential for all, and justifies it as a means "to enable man to develop in every respect."[222] Environmental education is of course essential for women to develop in every respect as well.

The Stockholm Declaration might not have been consciously sexist, but even the casual or inadvertent exclusion of women indicates the marginalization of women's concerns and perspectives in the formulation of the Stockholm Declaration. The gender insensitivity of the Stockholm Declaration is symptomatic of the exclusion of women from positions of power in government and in environmental organizations—a problem that persists in the environmental movement.[223] That an international conference, sponsored by the U.N., and addressing an issue of overriding

---

220. United Nations Conference on the Human Environment, Declaration on the Human Environment, U.N. Doc. A/CONF.48/14/Rev.1, at 3 (1973) [hereinafter Stockholm Declaration].

221. *Id.* princ. 8.

222. *Id.* princ. 19.

223. *See* Diane Valantine, Joy Belsky & Sally Cross, *A New Challenge: Overcoming Green Sexism*, EARTH ISLAND JOURNAL 34 (Spring 1996).

social and political significance, could overlook (or dismiss) women's issues speaks volumes about the state of women's environmental human rights at the time.

The 1992 U.N. Conference on Environment and Development

Twenty years after the Stockholm Conference, the U.N. convened another environmental conference in Rio de Janeiro, Brazil, on the subject of environment and development. The Rio Conference produced a very different picture. Several important instruments came out of the Rio Conference, including the Rio Declaration on Environment and Development; Agenda 21: Program of Action; and the Convention on Biological Diversity.[224] The Rio Declaration, agreed to by more than 178 governments, sets forth an extensive list of the elements of sustainable development, that is, development that meets the needs of present generations without sacrificing the needs of future generations.[225]

The Rio Declaration embodies many principles that encompass women's environmental human rights. In addition to principle 20 (quoted at the beginning of this chapter), which recognizes the importance of women's participation, the Rio Declaration also recognizes the need to eradicate poverty to achieve sustainable development, the special situation and needs of developing countries, the need to eliminate unsustainable patterns of consumption and production, the importance of participation and the related need for environmental information, the need for environmental impact assessment, the vital role of indigenous peoples, and the adverse effects of warfare, all of which have special relevance for women.[226] Although the Rio Declaration hedges in many areas, such as trade,[227] it is unequivocal in its recognition that sustainable development and protection of the environment are women's issues.

Agenda 21 is the Rio Conference's agenda for international action to achieve sustainable development. Agenda 21 devotes an entire chapter to "global action for women towards sustainable and equitable development."[228] Chapter 24 of Agenda 21 emphasizes participation by women in national and international ecosystem management and cites the Women's Convention, conventions entered into

---

224. Rio Declaration, *supra* note 2; Earth Summit Agenda 21: The United Nations Programme of Action From Rio, ch. 24, U.N. Sales No. E.93.I.11 (1993) [hereinafter Agenda 21]; Convention on Biological Diversity, pmbl. ¶ 13, 31 I.L.M. 818 (1992), *done* at Rio de Janeiro, 5 June 1992, *entered into force* 29 December 1993 [hereinafter Biodiversity Convention]. The Biodiversity Convention was opened for signature at the UNCED in Rio in 1992.

225. Rio Declaration, *supra* note 2, princ. 3; Stockholm Declaration, *supra* note 220, princ. 2 ("The natural resources of the earth including the air, water, land, flora and fauna and especially representative samples of natural ecosystems must be safeguarded for the benefit of present and future generations through careful planning or management, as appropriate.")

226. Rio Declaration, *supra* note 2, princs. 5, 6, 8, 10, 17, 22, 24.

227. *See* Rio Declaration, *supra* note 2, princs. 12, 16.

228. Agenda 21, *supra* note 224.

under the auspices of the International Labour Organisation, and conventions entered into under the auspices of the United Nations Educational and Scientific Organization (UNESCO) as pertinent instruments for ending gender discrimination and ensuring women access to land, natural resources, education, and safe and equal employment.[229]

Agenda 21 establishes several objectives relevant to the realization of women's environmental human rights. The objectives include: women's participation in ecosystem management and control of environmental degradation; increased numbers of women decision makers in environmental and development fields; elimination of obstacles to women's participation in sustainable development and public life; and equality in all aspects of society, including literacy, education, training, nutrition, health, and participation in a decision-making capacity in management of the environment.[230] Agenda 21 further directs governments to take active steps to:

— increase the proportion of women decision makers, planners, managers, scientists, and technicians involved in sustainable development plans;

— strengthen and empower women's nongovernmental organizations and groups in connection with capacity-building for sustainable development;

— eliminate illiteracy and increase and expand the enrollment of women in education, and promote full access for girls to primary and secondary education, especially including science and technology;

— reduce the workload of women and girls, increase the availability of affordable child-minding, promote sharing of household tasks, promote environmentally sustainable technologies developed with women's participation, and promote accessible clean water, efficient fuel supplies, and adequate sanitation facilities;

— support and strengthen equal employment opportunities and equitable remuneration in formal and informal sectors, as well as equal access to land, credit, and other natural resources;

— establish rural banking and increase women's access to credit; and

— review progress made in these areas.[231]

Agenda 21 also calls on parties to the Women's Convention to review the convention and to suggest amendments with a view to strengthening elements related to environment and development, especially regarding access to natural resources, technology, banking, and low-cost housing, and control of pollution and toxicity at home and in the workplace.[232] Agenda 21 further calls on the Women's

---

229. *Id.* ¶ 24.1.

230. *Id.* ¶ 24.2.

231. *Id.* ¶ 24.3.

232. *Id.*, ¶ 24.5. Country reports submitted by Ethiopia have already illustrated how environmental problems may interfere with access to land, technology, credit, housing, and health. *See* 1995 Ethiopia Report, *supra* note 47.

Convention parties to clarify the scope of the convention and to request the CEDAW to develop guidelines on reporting on environment and development issues under particular provisions of the Women's Convention.[233] The CEDAW has not yet issued such guidelines, but some governments have already begun to address environmental issues in their country reports.[234]

Agenda 21 also directs countries to take urgent measures to avert environmental degradation in developing countries in areas suffering from drought, desertification, deforestation, armed conflict, natural disasters, toxic waste, and the after-effects of agricultural products.[235] Each of those problems has direct effects on women's lives, effects that may violate women's rights to health, to life, to an adequate standard of living, to humanitarian assistance, to housing, to satisfactory working conditions, and to political participation.

Agenda 21 further provides that women should be fully involved in decision making and implementation of sustainable development activities.[236] Agenda 21's chapter on women represents a relatively comprehensive enumeration of what women need to realize their environmental human rights. Chapter 24 is but one of forty chapters in Agenda 21, though, and it remains to be seen how much attention women's rights will receive in the implementation and monitoring to be carried out by the responsible institutions: individual governments and the Commission on Sustainable Development (CSD).[237]

Like the Rio Declaration and Agenda 21, the United Nations Framework Convention on Biological Diversity explicitly recognizes the vital role women play in conservation and sustainable use of natural resources and affirms the need for full participation of women in policy making and implementation with respect to the protection of biological diversity.[238] That recognition informs the operative provisions of the Biodiversity Convention, which call for the parties to develop strategies, plans, and programs for conservation and sustainable use of biodiversity, including research and training, public education and awareness, and exchange of information.[239] All of those issues must be addressed with reference to women's role and the need for their participation.

---

233. *Id.*, ¶ 24.5.

234. *See* the following reports of the Committee on the Elimination of Discrimination against Women: 1995 Australia Report, *supra* note 219; 1992 Australia Report, *supra* note 210, at 178–80; 1995 Ethiopia Report, *supra* note 47, at 6–8, 24–26; 1993 Ethiopia Report, *supra* note 212, at 20–22.

235. Agenda 21, *supra* note 224, ¶ 24.6.

236. *Id.* ¶ 24.7.

237. The U.N. established the Commission on Sustainable Development (CSD) in the wake of the 1992 Rio Conference and gave the CSD the mandate of implementing Agenda 21. *See* Agenda 21, *supra* note 224, ch. 38; Resolution on Institutional Arrangement to Follow Up the United Nations Conference on Environment and Development, U.N. Doc. A/47/191, 32 I.L.M. 238 (1993).

238. Biodiversity Convention, *supra* note 224, pmbl. ¶ 13. Biodiversity means "the variability among living organisms from all sources including, *inter alia,* terrestrial, marine and other aquatic ecosystems and the ecological complexes of which they are a part; this includes diversity within species, between species and in ecosystems." *Id.*, art. 2.

239. *Id.* arts. 6, 12, 13, 17.

The Rio Conference produced a wealth of progressive thinking and progressive instruments with the potential to advance protection of women's environmental human rights. However, none of the Rio instruments are framed in human rights terms, and the CSD is not a human rights body, so women who suffer violations of human rights as the result of environmental problems will still have to turn to traditional human rights institutions and other relevant forums for relief, even when the activities that lead to their deprivations run afoul of one of the Rio instruments.

The 1995 Beijing Conference on Women

Three years after Rio, at the Fourth United Nations Conference on Women in Beijing, China, the relationship among women, environment, and human rights again received international attention. The more than 190 governments that participated in the Beijing conference produced a manifesto on women's rights, known as the Beijing Declaration. Among the many subjects it covers, the Beijing Declaration recites the conference participants' conviction that women's equal rights, opportunities, and access to resources are among the critical factors in the well-being of the family and the consolidation of democracy.[240] The Beijing parties further recognized that eradication of poverty based on sustained economic growth, social development, environmental protection, and social justice requires "the full and equal participation of women and men."[241] These provisions demonstrate recognition that women's equal rights, including their right to resources, is a key to everyone's quality of life and that effective environmental protection requires participation by women.

The Beijing parties also memorialized their determination to: promote people-centered sustainable development, including provision of education, literacy and training, and primary health care for girls and women; ensure equal access to and equal treatment of women and men in education and health care; develop the fullest potential of girls and women and ensure their full and equal participation in building a better world for all; ensure women's equal access to credit and land; and empower poor women to use environmental resources sustainably as a necessary foundation for sustainable development.[242]

The Beijing Conference also produced a Platform for Action, described in the document as "an agenda for women's empowerment." The Platform for Action addresses societal problems and social factors that impede equality between men and women and lays out "strategic objectives" to deal with and overcome those problems.[243] The Platform for Action notes the need to emphasize the social dimension of development, including growth, gender equality, social justice, conservation and protection of the environment, sustainability, solidarity, participation, peace,

---

240. Beijing Declaration, *in* Report of the Fourth World Conference on Women, U.N. Doc. A/ CONF.177/20, ann. I, ¶ 15 (1995).

241. *Id.* ¶ 16.

242. *Id.* ¶¶ 27, 30, 34, 35, 36.

243. Platform for Action, *supra* note 1, ann. II ¶ 34.

and respect for human rights.[244] To that end, the Platform for Action calls upon governments, the international community, and civil society to take strategic action to address gender inequalities in the management of natural resources and in the safeguarding of the environment.[245]

The Platform for Action also includes a separate section on women and the environment. The introductory portions of the section summarize many of the problems described in the introduction to this chapter, such as the adverse effects of environmental degradation on women's health, employment roles, and ability to provide sustenance for their families.[246] The section describes women's prominent role in the use and management of natural resources, as well as their virtual absence from positions that involve policy formation and decision making regarding natural resources and environmental management.[247] The Platform for Action concludes that sustainable development programs that do not involve women are doomed to failure.[248]

The Platform for Action includes three strategic objectives on women and the environment:

1. Involve women in environmental decision making at all levels;

2. Integrate gender concerns and perspectives in policies and programs for sustainable development; and

3. Activate mechanisms at all levels to assess the impact of development and environmental policies on women.[249]

To achieve the first strategic objective, governments must:

— ensure opportunities for women, including indigenous women, to participate in environmental decision making;

— facilitate and increase women's access to information and education;

— encourage protection and use of knowledge, innovations, and practices of women of indigenous and local communities (while safeguarding their intellectual property rights);

— reduce risks to women from environmental hazards at home, at work, and in other environments;

— integrate gender perspectives in the design and implementation of environmentally sound and sustainable resource management, production techniques, and infrastructure development;

---

244. *Id.* ¶ 14.

245. *Id.* ¶ 44.

246. *Id.* ¶¶ 246, 247.

247. *Id.* ¶¶ 248, 249.

248. *Id.* ¶ 251.

249. *Id.* at 108 (strategic objective K.1), 110 (strategic objective K.2), 111 (strategic objective K.3).

— empower women as producers and consumers so they can take effective environmental actions; and

— promote participation of women in urban planning.[250]

Each of these government commitments would advance women's environmental human rights. Some would accomplish this by reducing the extent and severity of environmental hazards women face, while others would work by providing the tools to enhance women's participation in decisions that affect the environment.

In addition, the Platform for Action provides that international organizations, governments, and the private sector should consider the gender impact of the work of the Commission on Sustainable Development; promote women's involvement, gender perspective, and projects that benefit women in the Global Environment Facility;[251] increase the proportion of women involved as decision makers, planners, managers, scientists, technical advisers, and beneficiaries; and address environmental degradation and its impact on women.[252] The Platform for Action also directs nongovernmental and private sector entities to take up issues of concern to women and to facilitate women's access to knowledge, skills, marketing services, and environmentally sound technologies to strengthen women's roles in management of natural resources and biodiversity.[253]

To meet the second strategic objective—integration of gender concerns and perspectives into policies and programs for sustainable development—the Platform for Action prescribes a similar array of actions. Governments, for example, should:

— integrate women and their perspectives into decision making regarding natural resource management;

— evaluate policies and programs regarding their impact on the environment and on women's equal access to natural resources;

— ensure adequate resources to assess women's particular susceptibility to environmental hazards;

— integrate rural women's traditional knowledge and sustainable resource use and management information into environmental management programs;

— integrate gender-sensitive research into mainstream policies;

— promote knowledge of and sponsor research on the role of women in food gathering and production, soil conservation, irrigation, watershed management, sanitation, coastal zone management, land-use planning, forest conservation and community forestry, fisheries, natural disaster prevention, and new and renewable energy sources;

---

250. *Id.* ¶ 253.

251. The Global Environment Facility, established in 1990, is an umbrella institution affiliated with the U.N. that administers several trust funds to finance projects on global warming, pollution of international waters, biodiversity and depletion of the ozone layer. *See* Agenda 21, *supra* note 224, ch. 33.

252. Platform for Action, *supra* note 1, ¶ 254.

253. *Id.* ¶ 258.

— eliminate obstacles to women's full and equal participation in sustainable development and equal access to control over natural resources;

— promote education of girls and women in science, technology, economics and other areas relevant to the natural environment;

— develop programs to involve female professionals and to train women and girls in environmental management;

— identify and promote environmentally sound technologies designed, developed and improved in consultation with women;

— support women's access to housing infrastructure, safe water, sustainable and affordable energy technologies; and

— ensure the availability of clean drinking water to all by the year 2000.[254]

As with Beijing's first strategic objective, the second involves women's environmental human rights in many respects, including women's right to participate in environmental decisions, their equal right to natural resources, their right to environmental education, their right to environmentally sound housing, and their right to water.

International organizations, nongovernmental organizations, and the private sector are to take action to involve women from the communications industry in consciousness-raising; encourage consumers to use their purchasing power to promote environmentally safe products; and support women's consumer initiatives on organic products and recycling.[255] This type of plan uses women's social role (as primary shoppers) as a tool of empowerment for environmental protection.

To achieve the Platform's third environmental strategic objective—activation of mechanisms to assess impacts on women—governments, international organizations, and nongovernmental organizations need to: provide technological assistance to women; develop gender-sensitive research tools; ensure full compliance with relevant obligations, including those required by the Basel Convention on Hazardous Wastes[256] and the Code of Practices of the International Atomic Energy Administration; and promote coordination within and among institutions to implement the Platform for Action and Chapter 24 of Agenda 21.[257]

The Platform for Action and Agenda 21 together provide a blueprint for the advancement of women's environmental human rights. Both instruments address the procedural building blocks of women's environmental human rights—education, information, and participation—as important means to enhance the related substantive rights, including health, housing, and working conditions. The Platform

---

254. *Id.* ¶ 256.

255. *Id.* ¶ 257.

256. Basel Convention on the Control of Transboundary Movements of Hazardous Wastes and Their Disposal, *done* at Basel, 22 Mar. 1989, 28 I.L.M. 657 (1989).

257. Platform for Action, *supra* note 1, ¶ 253.

for Action's suggested activities and Agenda 21's areas for action also support and recognize the often unacknowledged role women already play as environmental managers. The Beijing and Rio instruments represent important collections and expressions of women's environmental human rights. However, they are not legally binding in and of themselves, and they are not self-activating. To the contrary, they require activism by governments and by nongovernmental actors.

CONCLUSION

The relationship among women, the environment, and human rights embodies some consistent and critically important themes. Women's role as resource managers and sustenance providers renders them particularly vulnerable to environmental stresses and provides them with special insight into the need to manage natural resources sustainably. Nonetheless, women remain excluded from information, education, policy making and decision making, and other elements of participation in matters that affect the environment and their human rights. In both respects, women's roles are largely defined by social convention, not by biological predisposition.

The international community has recognized the imperative to address women's environmental needs and to facilitate women's participation in relevant processes, most notably in Agenda 21 and the Beijing Declaration and Platform for Action. Women, as individuals and acting collectively, have made enormous contributions to the protection of environmental human rights, in many cases facing opposition from powerful social and governmental forces.

Instruments such as Agenda 21 and the Beijing Platform for Action provide a framework for using international human rights instruments and international environmental instruments together to enhance women's environmental human rights. Relevant institutions, including the Commission on Sustainable Development, the Committee on the Elimination of All Forms of Discrimination Against Women, the U.N. Environment Programme, the U.N. Development Program, international financial institutions, regional human rights bodies, and national institutions (including courts, administrative agencies, and legislative bodies), must be sensitized to women's environmental human rights. The international community has spelled out the relevant obligations; it remains for the stakeholders (*i.e.*, individuals, nongovernmental organizations, private sector entities, governments, and international organizations) to give formal recognition to women's environmental human rights and to bring those rights to life.

WOMEN AND HOUSING

Leilani Farha

The right to housing affirms the complex interplay between individuals and groups including both personal space and collective neighbourhood, and security of both the individual and the community. It will be claimed in a variety of political spaces, from a plurality of struggles. It not only includes housing provision but also addresses inequities in tenure and in distribution of existing resources; violence and inequity within the household; design and production; urban and rural issues; home and community; freedom to move or to stay put; access to knowledge and resources; and land and technology. It is claimed by a woman in her relationship[s][,] . . . by young mothers, by neighbourhoods under attack, by squatters, by indigenous people, by people with a disability, by people of colour, by residents and former residents of psychiatric institutions, by single persons and families. . .

. . . What will be shared within the movement as a whole is a common determination that none will be silenced, that each will be heard in his or her own voice and language.[1]

INTRODUCTION

Over the past few years, the right to housing has generated more discussion, debates, legal opinions, and comments than any other right contained in the International Covenant on Economic, Social and Cultural Rights (ICESCR).[2] Although there remains some opposition, the right to adequate housing[3] is now widely recognized as a fundamental international human right with a solid legal foundation comprised of United Nations covenants, conventions, resolutions, declarations, recommendations, comments, and reports. Most recently and despite a U.S. backlash, global support for the right to adequate housing was confirmed at the U.N. World Conference, *Habitat II: The City Summit.*[4] This broad-based documentary recognition of the right to adequate housing is mirrored on the ground with the rise of housing rights movements in many regions throughout the world, including India, Japan, Palestine, the Philippines, the Dominican Republic, and Tibet. The right to

---

1.   Bruce Porter, *Human Rights and the Right to Housing,* NOW MAGAZINE, 1990, Power Plant Insert at 11.

2.   Adopted by U.N.G.A. Res. 2200A(XXI), of December 16, 1966, and *entered into force* Jan. 3, 1976 [hereinafter ICESCR].

3.   In this chapter, the terms "right to housing" and "right to adequate housing" are used interchangeably. However, technically speaking, it is the "right to *adequate* housing" that is codified and defined by international law.

4.   Istanbul, Turkey, June 1–14, 1996 [hereinafter *Habitat II*].

housing derives its richness and strength from the fact that it can be and is used by both nongovernmental and community-based organizations (hereinafter, NGOs and CBOs) in housing rights movements to address broader political, economic, and social crises.

Although the establishment of the right to housing as a fundamental human right is important for us all, there nevertheless remains the need to reassess the right to housing from the perspective of women. Once this perspective is introduced, it becomes clear that for the right to housing to have tangible, practical significance for women, it must be understood and articulated as a woman's human right, particularly given women's relation to housing. Further, this approach is an effective strategy to simultaneously address women's immediate housing concerns and the broader struggle against women's oppression.

This chapter commences with a defense of a *rights*–based approach to *women's* housing conditions. It then introduces the right to adequate housing by providing an overview of some of the international instruments that codify and define the right. Relevant documents are reviewed (all of which contribute to the development of the right) to determine whether they contemplate a ''women's human right to housing.'' This review exposes that, at the international level, there is a dearth of information that details in a substantial or substantive manner the meaning of the international right to housing for women; at the same time, however, the definition of the international right to adequate housing in no way forecloses the possibility of articulating a women's right to housing.

The subsequent section explores some of the women and human settlements/ shelter literature (which focuses on the housing and living conditions of women globally),[5] and begins to paint a picture of women's global primary housing concerns. Though it is recognized that the right to housing will not mean the same thing for all women, three housing issues that affect women in both the North and the South are highlighted. These three issues support an argument that an understanding of women's actual housing experiences must inform a definition of women's right to housing.

The final section reviews the international and NGO literature that adopts a rights approach to housing to assess whether it adequately addresses any or all of women's housing issues. The conclusion reached is that, while some literature ensures that women's concerns are included in discussions of housing rights, there is still not enough literature that sufficiently defines or describes women's human right to housing. The chapter closes with recommendations that might move us in the direction of putting a women's right to housing on the international human rights agenda. This chapter is only one small step toward developing a women's

---

5.   The human settlement literature refers mainly to the literature published by the United Nations Centre for Human Settlements [hereinafter UNCHS]. The women and shelter literature refers, for example, to the work of Caroline Moser and Watson and Austerberry (1986). For a literature review of these two bodies of work, *see* H. Dandekar, *Women and Housing: Concerns of the Past, Future Directions in* HOUSING QUESTION OF THE OTHERS (Emine M. Komut ed., 1996).

right to housing and is by no means exhaustive. The goal of this chapter is to provide the reader with enough information and incentive to continue the struggle to better define, and hence defend, women's right to adequate housing.

HOUSING AND WOMEN'S HUMAN RIGHTS: A NECESSARY CONNECTION

Surarith captures the sentiments of many involved in women's struggle for an international right to adequate housing by stating:

> I am not a trained academic on housing and urban affairs. However, I have become involved in the fight for housing rights for the poor to a large extent because I am a woman and know the attachment we women have to the home—how important it is to us to have a secure place for our children. I believe that women feel this much more strongly than men as we women spend more of our time in the home and with our children. Our house is not simply a place where we go to sleep at night, but it represents our home, which means everything to our lives.[6]

There is an enormous scarcity of published and accessible literature specifically regarding women and the *right* to housing. Perhaps one reason for this omission is that women have not wanted to continue women's ongoing global oppression by either highlighting or focusing greater attention on the close relationship between women and housing. Canadian researcher and academic Sylvia Novac expresses a similar sentiment when she writes:

> Men dominate housing policy and planning decision-making, not only in their persons, but in a way of thinking about housing that is profoundly shaped by the ideological foundations of traditional patriarchal thought: women are sequestered at home, there is a gendered division of labour, household equals family, and the family is male-dominant. *From this flows the strong association between "home" and women, an association that reinforces the secondary status of women's public role."*[7]

While Novac heeds an important warning—that the close association between women and the home can serve (and has served) to reinforce women's oppression both within and outside the home—she appears to neglect the practical consequences of ignoring the fact that housing plays a fundamental role in women's lives and that without adequate housing, women may not be able to make progress in attaining other rights, including rights associated with both the public and private spheres. Thus, while some feminist activists strive to disassociate women from the home and lure them from their kitchens and onto the "public playing fields," perhaps a preferable strategy to attacking the association between women and housing is to deconstruct and then reconstruct the ideological foundations upon which this association is built. In other words, it may not be the association *per se* that is problematic; rather, it may be the ideological framework that defines this association that constitutes the real problem.

---

6. Somporn Surarith, *Women's Struggle for Housing Rights in Thailand,* 11(2) CDN. WOMEN STDS 15, 15 (1990).

7. Sylvia Novac, *Seeking Shelter: Feminist Home Truths,* in CHANGE OF PLANS, TOWARDS A NON-SEXIST SUSTAINABLE CITY 51, 58 (Margrit Eichler ed., 1995)(emphasis added).

Despite the fact that, worldwide, women are the primary users of housing and are therefore the most affected by housing, women have been excluded from virtually every aspect of the housing process, be it policy development, planning and design, ownership, construction, and even housing movements. And so, though the house is considered a "woman's place," in most communities she is not permitted to control it.

While the home can be the site of women's oppression, it can also be one of central importance to women. In many cultures and societies, rightly or wrongly, the home is the only sphere in which a woman can exist. Further, many women in both the North and the South choose to stay at home. Beyond basic shelter, it is a place to care for children; it provides respite from the fighting on the streets; and for some it is the place of employment, where income is generated. The home may be the one location where woman can participate in social activities.[8]

Given the interconnectedness of some women with housing, to call for the disassociation of all women from the home may be a culturally insensitive move, the practical effects of which might prove more devastating than helpful for women and their families. Rather than regarding the home necessarily as a site of oppression—which might be regarded as a distinctly Western feminist approach—given the right ideological framework, one where women are no longer viewed as members of men's households and thus under male control, the home might in fact become the potential site of women's autonomy, independence, and freedom. And so, instead of disassociating women from housing perhaps women should move to reconstruct or continue to build upon that association.

Some of the women and human settlement/shelter literature complements this suggestion. Caroline Moser, for example, argues that social relations are constructed within the household and that this results in differential experiences of housing for men and women.[9] Hence, to assist women, it is first necessary to understand women's particular housing needs. Moser defines these particular needs—distinct from men's—as both "practical" and "strategic." She argues that practical needs are those that arise from the concrete conditions of women's positioning, by virtue of their gender, within the sexual division of labor. Within these positions, needs are formulated by women themselves in response to the living conditions that they face daily. For example, clean water supply, adequate food, or community day care facilities are identified as the practical gender needs of low-income women. In other words, practical needs are those that arise out of women's everyday realities and, if addressed, do not necessarily alter the structure of social relations between men and women.[10]

---

8. This is not to gloss over the fact that for many women the home is the site of violence. This issue is addressed later in this chapter where it is argued that women's right to housing must include the right to be free from domestic violence.

9. Caroline Moser, *Women, human settlements, and housing: a conceptual framework for analysis and policy-making, in* WOMEN, HUMAN SETTLEMENTS, AND HOUSING 12, 12 (Caroline Moser and Linda Peake eds., 1987).

10. *Id.* at 29.

By contrast, Moser asserts that strategic gender needs are those identified from the analysis of women's subordination. To adequately answer those needs requires the development of an alternative social organization that transforms the current structure and nature of relationships between men and women. Depending on the particular socio-political context, strategic gender needs may include the abolition of the sexual division of labor, the alleviation of the burden of domestic labor and child care, and the removal of institutional forms of discrimination by creating equal right to land ownership or to access to credit. Strategic gender needs are those that result from systemic disparities and must be answered through structural change.[11]

Moser's distinction between practical and strategic housing needs suggests that an improvement in women's relationship to housing requires a two-pronged approach whereby activists must attempt to satisfy women's practical or immediate housing needs while concurrently working to erode the structural framework that has caused the sexual division of labor and women's oppression within the home. As such, Moser's work clarifies that, while women's everyday lives within the home and their general relationship to housing is undoubtedly experienced as oppressive, at the root of this oppression is the structural framework that defines the association between women and housing, and not the association *per se*. This rights-based approach to housing can take up Moser's challenge to address women's everyday practical housing needs while simultaneously deconstructing the framework that has led to women's subordinate status in and outside of the home.

It should be recognized that adopting rights discourse to challenge patriarchy (the ideological framework that most informs women's relationship to the home) in its various dimensions is not without problems. There are two particularly persuasive arguments against the use of rights discourse.[12] First, critics argue that rights discourse is steeped in traditional liberalism. As such, rights have been held by the privileged in society and "selectively invoked to draw boundaries, to isolate and to limit" and ultimately to protect privilege.[13] As Bruce Porter says, liberal rights are oriented toward loss (rather than lack) so that "where rights are infringed, the remedy is to restore one's lost property. It is assumed that we all have property to lose."[14]

Second, critics argue that not only have rights served to protect the privileged and isolate the disadvantaged, but that traditional rights approaches are gender biased. Porter articulates this point eloquently:

---

11. *Id.* at 29–30.

12. There are, of course, other arguments against the use of rights discourse. For example, related to the understanding that rights come out of traditional liberalism is the argument that human rights discourse—as it exists today—is in fact a form of cultural imperialism. For interesting insights into this issue, see the following excellent collection of essays, HUMAN RIGHTS IN CROSS-CULTURAL PERSPECTIVES: A QUEST FOR CONSENSUS (Abdullahi An-Na'im ed., 1992).

13. Patricia Williams, *Alchemical Notes: Reconstructing Ideals from Deconstructed Rights*, HARV. CIV. RTS-CIV. LIB. L. REV. 401, 405 (1987).

14. Porter, *supra* note 1, at 10.

Liberal rights are conceived as idealized appendages vulnerable to castration, pieces of property which must be contractually protected from encroachment. They are discreet abstract entities, mysteriously attached to persons yet not quite part of them, vulnerable attributes which men guard with our lives as we warily enter into any social arrangement. These rights do not include material comfort, nurture, or envelopment, themes which Carol Gilligan found to be recurrent among women articulating of rights "in a different voice." They are by and large articulations of the violence *men* fear, with very little inclination to protect women from the violence of men, or to articulate infringement in a manner that is meaningful to women.[15]

Feminist critics also note that the granting of rights does not inevitably spell progress for women, particularly in the case of competing rights. For example, the right of women and children not to be subjected to violence in the home may lose out against the property rights of men in the home or men's right to family life.[16] That is, rights relating to the protection of the family contained in human rights instruments often ignore that, to many women, the family is a unit for abuse and violence and that protection of the family preserves the power structure within the family, which can lead to subjugation and dominance by men over women.[17]

Despite these pitfalls, strong arguments can be made to support a rights approach to women and housing and the establishment of housing as a women's right. As an economic and social right, the right to housing confronts traditional liberalism head-on, it is progressive and forward-looking rather than nostalgic and restorative.[18] Whereby civil and political rights are claimed to restore to the claimant something they have lost or were forced to give away, economic and social rights are claimed not only to restore but also to provide. Moreover, instead of drawing protective boundaries that isolate individuals from the collective, the right to housing embraces the connection between individuals and groups. Not only does the right to housing address the provision of accommodation to an individual, it is a social right that recognizes the group nature of disadvantage and discrimination and, as such, it has the potential to support social movements initiated by disadvantaged groups such as pavement dwellers, indigenous populations, and women.[19] Feminist scholars and activists working in the area of international law have argued persuasively that "the major forms of oppression of women operate within the

---

15. Bruce Porter, Materializing Rights: The Right to Adequate Housing, text presented at Strategies of Critique IV the Shape of the Earth/Visions of the World 1, 5 (1990) (unpublished). While Porter critiques traditional liberal rights approaches, he offers an alternative rights approach where rights discourse addresses "lack" and not just loss.

16. H. Charlesworth, C. Chinkin and S. Wright, *Feminist Approaches to International Law*, 85 Am. J. Int'l L. 613, 635 (1991).

17. *Id.* at 636–37.

18. Porter, *Materializing Rights, supra* note 15, at 13. *See also* Havi Echenberg and Bruce Porter, *Poverty Stops Equality: Equality Stops Poverty, The Case for Social and Economic Rights, in* Human Rights in Canada: Into the 1990s and Beyond (Ryszard Cholewinski ed., 1990).

19. Porter, *supra* note 1, at 11.

economic, social and cultural realms''[20] and hence they have particular relevance to women.

Nevertheless, whether liberal rights are regarded as phallic appendages threatened with castration as Bruce Porter suggests, or an attempt to placate propertied men's fears of violence as Charlotte Bunch proffers,[21] it is clear that civil and political rights have been constructed *by* privileged men *for* privileged men. The International Covenant on Economic, Social and Cultural Rights, on the other hand, could be used as a basis for promoting structural economic and social reform to reduce some of the causes of women's disadvantage and abuse.[22] To begin, housing rights discourse explicitly includes the very individuals who are so often excluded by liberal notions of rights—the propertyless. In other words, housing rights claimants are precisely those without "appendages" (i.e., property), such as women and, more specifically, poor women. Furthermore, an essentialist might argue that the home, and by implication the right to housing, is actually gender-biased in favor of women as it embodies those values or principles that are particular to women. That is, the home can be a place of nurture, representing security, warmth, safety, and community—terms that Carol Gilligan found women often use to describe rights.[23]

To date, women's housing conditions and experiences have largely been described in terms of their "needs" as opposed to their "rights." Drawing on the work of Philip Alston, Scott Leckie, a leading housing rights activist, argues that rights discourse enhances the level of importance of a social demand, noting that the characterization of a specific goal as a human right "elevates it above the rank and file of competing societal goals, gives it a degree of immunity from challenge, and generally endows it with an aura of timelessness, absoluteness and universal validity."[24] In other words, and practically speaking, when needs are translated into rights they have the force of law behind them. It is more difficult for a government to ignore *legal* obligations than it is to ignore a campaign promise or policy objective.[25]

Rights discourse and its societal acceptance also offers a ready and powerful means of self-definition, a means that disadvantaged groups find alluring:

> To say that blacks never fully believed in rights is true; yet it is also true that blacks believed in them so much and so hard that we gave them life where there was none before. We held onto them, put the hope of them into our wombs, and mothered them—not just the notion of them. We nurtured rights and gave rights life. . . . But if

---

20. Charlesworth, Chinkin, and Wright, *supra* note 16, at 635.

21. Charlotte Bunch, *Transforming Human Rights from a Feminist Perspective, in* WOMEN'S RIGHTS HUMAN RIGHTS: INTERNATIONAL FEMINIST PERSPECTIVES 11, 13 (Julie Peters and Andrea Wolper eds., 1995).

22. Charlesworth, Chinkin and Wright, *supra* note 16, at 645.

23. CAROL GILLIGAN, IN A DIFFERENT VOICE: PSYCHOLOGICAL THEORY AND WOMEN'S DEVELOPMENT (1982).

24. Scott Leckie, *Housing as a Human Right* 1(2) ENV'L. AND URBNZTN 90, 95 (1989).

25. *Id.* at 96.

it took this long to breathe life into a form whose shape had already been forged by society and which is therefore idealistically if not ideologically accessible, imagine how long would be the struggle without that sense of definition without the power of that familiar vision.[26]

The symbolic power of rights discourse for women living under adverse housing conditions was evident at *Habitat II*. At a public hearing on global housing rights violations, Kurdish, Indian, Tibetan, Brazilian, Mexican, American, and Japanese women testified to their housing experiences and each woman, in her own way, employed rights language in telling her story. These are some of their stories:[27]

The witness from Japan, a woman from Kobe, described her experiences in securing accommodation after the Great Hanshin Earthquake of 1995. She was compelled to live in temporary shelter in a community centre, with many other families. This ''evacuation center'' was located at some distance from her original residence. At the public hearing, she complained that in being located far away from her prior residence, her *right* to live in her place of choice, that is, close to her friends and family had been violated. She also stated that her *right to privacy* had been violated in the evacuation center as there were no walls separating her living space from that of others.

A Kurdish woman, having been forced to migrate from her village to the mega-city, Istanbul, after her house and village were completely destroyed by fire, stated that she has a *right* to return to her original home and land.

An African-American woman from Atlanta, Georgia, stated that many black residents of Atlanta, particularly the poor, had suffered *housing rights* violations as they had been evicted from their homes to accommodate the summer Olympics.

After listening to these women's testimonies, there was little doubt that women from around the world—even those without legal knowledge or training—often find rights discourse comfortable and appropriate as a means of articulating what they experience as injustice and as a means of seeking redress for their individual and collective housing experiences.

If it is possible and appropriate to articulate women's housing concerns in the language of rights, it is but a short step to the idea that the right to housing must itself be articulated from the perspective of women. Simply put, the right to housing and its attached protections are particularly relevant for women, especially in light of the fact that over recent years there has been a dramatic increase in the number of women-headed households globally, which of course has resulted in a close relationship between women and housing, where a woman's survival is integrally linked to the state of her housing.

While the claims of women to the right to housing are burgeoning, the dimensions of the right to housing are rapidly evolving at the international level with very little input directly from women. As such, the international right to housing, though crucial to women, does not take full account of women's insights, experiences, and lives. When women are excluded from housing policy, so too are their

---

26. Williams, *supra* note 13, at 422.

27. Based on personal notes taken by the author during a public hearing at *Habitat II*.

interests. It is because of this exclusion that the right to housing must be articulated as a women's human right.[28]

For instance, policymakers, planners, architects, and designers within governments and international agencies may believe that they are "planning for people," but there is an almost universal tendency by these professionals to assume that the household is nuclear in structure and that within the family there is a clear sexual division of labor in which the man of the family is the breadwinner and is engaged in productive work outside the home, while the woman takes overall responsibility for the child rearing and domestic work within the household. Implicit in this may be the erroneous assumption that within the household there is equal control over resources and power of decision-making between the man and the woman in matters affecting the household livelihood.[29] Hence, unless the right to housing is regarded as a women's human right, there is no reason to believe that these same assumptions will not be used to define and implement the right to housing. If these assumptions remain unchallenged, structural change that rectifies the fundamental inequality and power imbalance between men and women will never be realized.

It is clear that to exclude women from the struggle to define the right to housing—a right in which they have a very large stake—may keep society further away from the solutions that are actually needed in the area of the human right to housing.[30] Simply put, it is only appropriate that those most affected by housing should actively participate in the construction of the meaning of the right to housing.

Once the right to housing is fully and adequately defined by women, it will not have the same meaning for all women globally. Housing rights, like all human rights, are neither temporally static nor geographically specific. As Adetoun O. Ilumoka argues, women should use rights discourse as a means of naming a legal claim and acquiring public, political space to advance certain goals, and as a means of empowerment in the struggle for social justice. The goals of the struggle, however, must be defined within and by a specific society and, once formed, these goals must be the reference point for the definition and assessment of the right to housing.[31]

Having reviewed the theoretical and practical reasons for advancing women's housing concerns from a "women's rights" perspective, the rest of this chapter is aimed at articulating what a women's right to housing might include. To this end,

---

28. *See* REPORT OF THE FOURTH WORLD CONFERENCE ON WOMEN, A/CONF. 177/20 at para. 222 (1995), which asserts: "If the goal of full realization of human rights for all is to be achieved, international human rights instruments must be applied in such a way as to take more clearly into consideration the systematic and systemic nature of discrimination against women that gender analysis has clearly indicated" [hereinafter Platform for Action].

29. Moser, *supra* note 9, at 13.

30. Bunch, *supra* note 21, at 11.

31. Adetoun O. Ilumoka, *African Women's Economic, Social, and Cultural Rights—Towards a Relevant Theory and Practice, in* HUMAN RIGHTS OF WOMEN, NATIONAL AND INTERNATIONAL PERSPECTIVES 307, 320 (Rebecca Cook ed., 1994).

it will begin with an overview of the current status and definition of the right to adequate housing in international law, for it is this definition that must be utilized to advance the claim for women's housing rights at the international level.

THE INTERNATIONAL RIGHT TO ADEQUATE HOUSING

The Law

The United States' recent unsuccessful challenge to the existence of the right to housing at *Habitat II* confirms what housing rights activists have known for years: the right to housing is a widely accepted, fundamental human right. Its existence as such is a result of the explicit recognition of the right to housing in a plethora of international legal instruments. Each of the following declarations articulates the concept of a right to housing: The Universal Declaration of Human Rights,[32] the Declaration of the Rights of the Child,[33] the Vancouver Declaration on Human Settlements,[34] and the Istanbul Declaration on Human Settlements.[35]

The right to housing also appears in several conventions, ratified by hundreds of nations globally, such as the International Convention on the Elimination of All Forms of Racial Discrimination,[36] the International Convention on the Rights of

---

32. *Adopted and proclaimed by* U.N. GA Res. 217 A (III) of December 10, 1948. Article 25.1 states in part:

> Everyone has the right to a standard of living adequate for the health and well being of himself and his family, including food, clothing, housing and medical care and necessary social service . . .

33. *Adopted and proclaimed by* U.N. GA Res. 1386 (XIV) of November 29, 1959. Paragraph 4 provides:

> The child shall enjoy the benefits of social security. He shall be entitled to grow and develop in health; to this end special care and protection shall be provided both to him and his mother, including adequate prenatal and postnatal care. The child shall have the right to adequate nutrition, housing, sanitation, electricity and water supply, transport and communications.

34. *Adopted by* the U.N. Conference on Human Settlements of 1976. Section III (8) states:

> Adequate shelter and services are a basic human right which places an obligation on governments to ensure their attainment by all people, beginning with direct assistance to the least advantaged through guided programmes of self-help and community action.

35. *Adopted by* the U.N. Conference on Human Settlements, of June 14, 1996. Paragraph 8 provides:

> We reaffirm our commitment to the full and progressive realization of the right to adequate housing as provided for in international instruments. To that end, we shall seek the active participation of our public, private and non-governmental partners at all levels to ensure legal security of tenure, protection from discrimination and equal access to affordable, adequate housing for all persons and their families.

36. *Adopted by* U.N. GA Res. 2106 A (XX), of Jan. 4, 1969. Article 5(e)(iii) provides:

> In compliance with the fundamental obligations laid down in article 2 of this Convention, States Parties undertake to prohibit and to eliminate racial discrimination in all of its forms and to guarantee the right to everyone, without distinction as to race, colour, or national or ethnic origin, or equality before the law, notably in the enjoyment of the following rights: . . . (e) economic, social and cultural rights, in particular . . . (iii) the right to housing.

the Child,[37] and the Convention on the Elimination of All Forms of Discrimination Against Women in which rural women's right to housing is explicitly codified:

States Parties shall take all appropriate measures to eliminate discrimination against women in rural areas in order to ensure, on a basis of equality of men and women, that they participate in and benefit from rural development and, in particular, shall ensure to such women the right . . . (h) *to enjoy adequate living conditions, particularly in relation to housing,* sanitation, electricity and water supply, transport and communications.[38]

At the international level, the most significant articulation of the right to housing is the ICESCR which provides that:

The States Parties to the present Covenant recognize *the right of everyone to an adequate standard of living for himself [or herself] and his [or her] family, including adequate food, clothing and housing and to the continuous improvement of living conditions.* The States Parties will take appropriate steps to ensure the realization of this right, recognizing to this effect the essential importance of international cooperation based on free consent.[39]

This articulation of the right to housing is particularly significant because the ICESCR falls under the responsibility and jurisdiction of the United Nations Committee on Economic, Social and Cultural Rights (hereinafter, the Committee). The Committee is legally responsible for examining the degree to which countries that have ratified the ICESCR have undertaken the necessary steps towards the full enjoyment of the rights found in the ICESCR for all citizens. To adequately undertake this task, the Committee has attempted to articulate the substantive meaning of particular rights protected by the Covenant and, in this vein, the right to housing has received a significant amount of attention. For this reason, the Committee's work is essential to an understanding of the right to housing.

Legal Standards

Initially, the Committee was concerned to elaborate a definition of the right to housing that required an appreciation of the fact that, unlike some civil and political rights, broadly speaking, economic and social rights such as the right to housing are difficult to define. This is not because, as critics might suggest, social and economic rights are not genuine or legitimate rights, rather it is attributable to the

---

37. *Adopted by* U.N. GA Res. 44/25, of Nov. 20, 1989 and *entered into force* Sept. 2, 1990. Article 27(3) states:

States Parties in accordance with national conditions and within their means shall take appropriate measures to assist parents and others responsible for the child to implement this right and shall in the case of need provide material assistance and support programmes, particularly with regard to nutrition, clothing and housing.

38. *Adopted by* U.N. GA Res. 34/180, of Dec. 18, 1979 and *entered into force* Sept. 3, 1981, at art. 14(2)(h)(emphasis added)[hereinafter the Women's Convention].

39. ICESCR, *supra* note 2, at art. 11(1)(emphasis added).

fact that economic and social rights recognize that social and economic disadvantage is the result of a complex interplay of factors (political, economic, social, cultural, individual, and group) that renders tidy definitions difficult.[40] For example, it is now understood that housing disadvantage goes beyond homelessness (which might be construed narrowly as the "right to have a roof over one's head") and is related to issues such as poverty, the availability of services, security of tenure, cultural adequacy of housing structures, and democratic participation in housing processes.

The definition of the right to housing is also somewhat cumbersome and deliberately broad, for although it is a self-standing right, the right to housing must also be regarded as a component of the other human rights contained in both the ICESCR and the International Covenant on Civil and Political Rights.[41] The right to adequate housing provides a place for every individual to live in peace and dignity and includes the following core elements, discussed *infra*: legal security of tenure; availability of services, materials, facilities, and infrastructure; affordability; habitability; accessibility; location; and cultural adequacy.

Article 11(1) of the ICESCR asserts that the right to housing is part of the broader right to an adequate standard of living. Beyond this, the Committee's leading interpretation of the meaning of the right to housing under Article 11(1) of the ICESCR[42] also states that the full enjoyment of other rights such as the right to freedom of expression, the right to freedom of association, the right to freedom to choose one's residence, and the right to participate in public decision making are each indispensable if the right to adequate housing is to be realized by all members of society.[43] Additionally, the Committee suggests that the rights not to be subjected to arbitrary interference with one's privacy, family, home, or correspondence constitute very important dimensions in defining the right to housing.[44] The final report of the past United Nations Special Rapporteur on the right to housing, Justice Rajindar Sachar, also emphasized the interdependence of housing rights with other rights, particularly, the rights of women, children, land rights, the right to food, and the right to health.[45]

---

40. *See, e.g.,* Porter, *supra* note 1; and Scott Leckie, *Housing Rights: Some Central Themes,* text presented at Sustainable Habitat on an Urbanized Planet Conference, Berlin, Germany, 1990.

41. *Adopted by* U.N. GA Res. 2200 A (XXI) of Dec. 16, 1966 and *entered into force* on Mar. 23, 1976 [hereinafter ICCPR].

42. General Comment No. 4 on the Right to Adequate Housing, *adopted by* the U.N. Committee on Economic, Social and Cultural Rights, U.N. Doc. E/C.12/1991/4 (1991) at para.9 [hereinafter General Comment No. 4].

43. *Id.*

44. *Id.*

45. Justice Rajindar Sachar, The Right to Adequate Housing: Report of the Special Rapporteur, UN Commission on Human Rights, Subcommission on Prevention of Discrimination and Protection of Minorities, 47th Sess., U.N. Doc. E/CN.4/Sub.2/1995/12, (1995) [hereinafter Report of the Special Rapporteur].

It is vitally important to recognize the interdependence and indivisibility of housing rights with other human rights. This is particularly true for those countries whose constitutions do not explicitly recognize the right to housing but recognize other rights of which the right to adequate housing is an essential component, such as liberty, security of the person, and equality.[46]

Despite the complexity that results from the fact that the right to housing appears to incorporate and invoke other fundamental human rights, the Committee has developed a working definition of the right to housing in General Comment No. 4,[47] which is the most authoritative international legal interpretation of the right to adequate housing to date. Beyond delineating seven core principles that attach to the right to housing, the Committee stipulates that the right to housing should not be construed narrowly to mean merely the right to have a roof over one's head. Instead, the Committee suggests that the right to live somewhere in "security, peace and dignity" constitutes one of the fundamental pillars of the right to housing. Recognizing that disadvantaged groups are more likely to be subject to housing rights violations, the Committee also stresses that the focus of the right to adequate housing must be on those social groups living in unfavorable conditions.[48]

In General Comment No. 4, the Committee highlights the following aspects as necessary for the realization of the right to *adequate* housing:

a) *Legal security of tenure*: Tenure takes a variety of forms, including rental (public and private) accommodation, cooperative housing, lease, owner-occupation, emergency housing and informal settlements, including occupation of land or property. Notwithstanding the type of tenure, all persons should possess a degree of security of tenure that guarantees legal protection against forced eviction, harassment, and other threats. States parties should consequently take immediate measures aimed at conferring legal security of tenure upon those persons and households currently lacking such protection, in genuine consultation with affected persons and groups;

b) *Availability of services, materials, facilities and infrastructure*: An adequate house must contain certain facilities essential for health, security, comfort and nutrition. All beneficiaries of the right to adequate housing should have sustainable access to natural and common resources, potable drinking water, energy for cooking, heating and lighting, sanitation and washing facilities, food storage, refuse disposal, site drainage and emergency services;

c) *Affordable*: Personal or household financial cost associated with housing should be at such a level that the attainment and satisfaction of other basic needs are not threatened or compromised. . .;

---

46. Human Rights Caucus, Amendments to Bracketed Text in the Habitat II Agenda, (1996) (unpublished).

47. General Comment No. 4, *supra* note 43.

48. *Id.* at para. 11. The Committee's definition of "disadvantaged groups" can be found under the principle of "accessibility." Women are conspicuously absent. As we shall see later in this chapter, very strong arguments can be made to have women considered a disadvantaged group or a "social group living in unfavourable conditions."

d) *Habitable*: Adequate housing must . . . [provide] inhabitants with adequate space and [protect] them from cold, damp, heat, rain, wind or other threats to health, structural hazards and disease vectors. The physical safety of occupants must be guaranteed as well. . .

e) *Accessibility*: Adequate housing must be accessible to those entitled to it. Disadvantaged groups must be accorded full and sustainable access to adequate housing resources. Thus, such disadvantaged groups as the elderly, children, the physically disabled, the terminally ill, HIV-positive individuals, persons with persistent medical problems, the mentally ill, victims of natural disasters, people living in disaster-prone areas, other groups [including women] should be ensured some degree of priority consideration in the housing sphere. Both housing law and policy should take fully into account the special housing needs of these groups. . . . [I]ncreasing access to land by landless or impoverished segments of the society should constitute a central policy goal . . .

f) *Location*: Adequate housing must be in a location which allows access to employment options, health care services, schools, child care centres and other social facilities . . . ,[and]

g) *Culturally adequate*: The way housing is constructed, the building materials used and the policies supporting these must appropriately enable the expression of cultural identity and diversity of housing. . .[49]

State Obligations

Despite the difficulties, the Committee has laid down a relatively clear and coherent interpretation of the right to adequate housing. However, its success in this respect has perhaps merely cleared the way for controversy concerning the extent and nature of state party obligations that attach to the right. This controversy stems from the general argument that social and economic rights suffer from a lack of precision with respect to obligations that attach to the state party. This argument has been answered eloquently by Patrick Macklem and Craig Scott, who argue that the United Nations has invested considerable energy in developing a fairly precise, layered structure of state party obligations that imposes on state parties the duty to respect, protect, and fulfill social and economic rights.[50] Each term is defined as follows:

> *Duty to Respect:* State parties are obligated to refrain from infringing a social right directly. In other words, the state is prohibited from interfering with the normal means by which a person claims the right. For example, they argue, the right to housing would be violated if the government destroyed homes or evicted a squatter without providing alternative and comparable housing.[51]

---

49. *Id.* at para. 8.

50. Patrick Macklem and Craig Scott, *Constitutional Ropes of Sand or Justiciable Guarantees? Social Rights in a New South African Constitution*, 141 UNIV. PENN. L. REV. 1, 73 (1992).

51. *See id.* at 74.

Duty to Protect: The state is under a positive duty to prevent a right from being infringed by private actors. A state's obligation to protect the right to housing would be violated if the "government's policy . . . allowed the hovels of poor people to be torn down and replaced by luxury [private market] housing which the original inhabitants could not afford and without providing them with access to alternative housing on reasonable terms."[52]

Duty to Fulfill: This translates into the state's duty to provide housing *to those in society without the means to provide for themselves.* The authors stipulate, however, that the obligation to fulfill does not mandate universal entitlement to housing, for example, according to which the government would be obliged to provide benefits to all free of charge.[53]

Despite this clear delineation of the scope of a state party's duty to fulfill social and economic rights, it remains the most misunderstood component of state obligations with respect to the right to housing. For example, at *Habitat II*, several government delegations including that of the United States were under the impression that the right to housing requires governments who have ratified the ICESCR to provide housing free of charge for the *entire* population.[54]

Not only does this obligation not appear in any of the international legal instruments or literature pertaining to the right to housing, activists argue that such state provision of housing is in fact undesirable. Placing all of the emphasis on state provision of housing severs social and economic rights from civil and political rights in a manner that serves only to deprive poor people and other vulnerable groups of things like neighborhood, control, choice, autonomy, and esteem.[55] Experience has shown that state provision of housing results in the social control of poor people, women, ethno-racial minorities, native people, and others which, in turn, means that oppressed groups and individuals are denied the opportunity to affirm their own entitlement, control their own lives, create their own type of housing, and develop their own communities, all of which are acts protected by civil and political rights.[56]

Additionally, to believe that populations want governments to provide them with housing ignores inherent realities. In most parts of the world, housing is a community or neighborhood concern. If there are problems, those affected usually seek solutions either on their own or together as a community, but usually without government assistance.[57] Anywhere between 50 and 80 percent of all housing built in the Third World is built by the dwellers themselves. And so, while state-built

---

52. *See id.* at 75; and G.J.H. van Hoof, *The Legal Nature of Economic, Social and Cultural Rights: A Rebuttal of Some Traditional Views, in* The Right to Food (Philip Alston & Katarina Tomasevski eds., 1984) *cited in* Macklem and Scott, *supra* note , at 75.

53. Macklem and Scott, *supra* note 50, at 75–76, in particular n. 252.

54. At the time of writing, the U.S. is one of five countries that has not ratified the ICESCR.

55. Porter, *supra* note 15, at 2.

56. *Id.*

57. Scott Leckie, *The Justiciability of Housing Rights*, 18 SIM Special 35, 44 (1996).

housing may assist in the realization of a population's right to housing, it is by no means a required or even desired component of the right.[58]

Underlying the duty to respect, protect, and fulfill social and economic rights, the right to housing also imposes legal obligations on governments consisting primarily of the duties found in the ICESCR, which states:

> Each State Party to the present Covenant undertakes to take steps, individually and through international assistance and co-operation, especially economic and technical, to the maximum of its available resources, with a view to achieving progressively the full realization of the rights recognized in the present Covenant by all appropriate means, including particularly the adoption of legislative measures.[59]

Article 2(1) has been interpreted to impose both immediate and long-term obligations on state parties.[60] The obligation to "undertake to take steps" is immediate. Upon ratification, the ICESCR requires state parties to review all relevant national legislation to ensure that it complies with its international legal obligations. State parties are also required to take steps "by all appropriate means," indicating that, in addition to legislative measures, administrative, judicial, economic, social, and educational steps must be taken.[61] The Committee has determined that the adoption of legislation mirroring the nondiscrimination clauses of the ICESCR, protection against discrimination in all aspects of housing, monitoring the status of the rights in question, and the protection of security of tenure must occur immediately following ratification.[62]

The phrase, "to achieve progressively," has been interpreted as less immediate and imposes an obligation on state parties to move as quickly and effectively as possible toward the goal of realizing fully each of the rights found in the ICESCR. At a minimum, state parties are obliged to demonstrate that every effort has been made to use all resources at its disposal (within a state and those provided by other states or the international community) in an effort to satisfy the rights found in the ICESCR. The unavailability of resources is, however, a valid excuse for escaping legal obligations under the ICESCR and one that the Committee considers when reviewing state compliance.[63] Thus, the Committee acknowledges that the provision of adequate and affordable housing to those in need through subsidies or through

---

58. Leckie, *supra* note 40, at 3.

59. ICESCR, *supra* note 2, at art. 2(1).

60. *See, e.g.,* General Comment No. 3, The Nature of State Parties' Obligations (Article 2(1) of the Covenant), U.N. Doc. E/C.12/1990/8 (1990).

61. Centre for Human Rights, The Human Right to Adequate Housing (Fact Sheet No. 21), at 11.

62. *Id.* at 13. *See also* Leckie, *supra* note 57, at 49–52. Obligations of immediate effect flowing from the right to adequate housing are also recognized in many resolutions of U.N. bodies, including the U.N. Sub-Commission on Prevention of Discrimination and Protection of Minorities resolutions 1994/39 and 1991/12, U.N. Centre for Human Settlements (Habitat) resolution 14/6, and U.N. Commission on Human Rights resolution 1993/77.

63. Leckie, *supra* note 40, at 5.

housing programs may be limited by availability of resources and therefore subject in some countries to progressive rather than immediate realization.

Violations of State Obligations

The right to housing is subject to violation or infringement just as is any other human right. The Committee's General Comment No. 4 provides two particular circumstances in which a state parties' actions would be deemed "inconsistent" with the ICESCR, namely, where there has been a general decline in living and housing conditions attributable to policy and legislative decisions by state parties and in the absence of accompanying compensatory measures (para. 11), and in instances of forced evictions (para. 18).

At the present time, there is no formal, judicial complaint procedure at the international level where victims of housing rights can have their cases heard. The Committee does, however, accept oral and written submissions, or "parallel reports," from NGOs. These submissions can have a substantial influence on the realization of housing rights for disadvantaged peoples. For example, depending on the gravity of the situation, the Committee may conduct its own investigation of the housing and living conditions at issue and, where appropriate, the Committee may declare a country to be in violation of the right to housing. The Committee can also use its power to pressure governments into complying with the Covenant. For example, at its fourteenth session (April 29–May 17 1996), after the Committee received oral and written submissions from Palestinian NGOs regarding the housing and living conditions of Palestinians in East Jerusalem and those living in Israel proper, the Committee officially informed the government of Israel that if the Palestinian NGOs' allegations were found by the Committee to be true, then the Committee would be compelled to find the State of Israel in violation of the ICESCR. The Committee then urged the Israeli government to submit its now overdue state report so that the issues raised by the Palestinian NGOs could be fully resolved.

Thus, though the international right to housing can be violated, and evidence of violations can be taken from NGOs, these violations are not justiciable at the international level. Activists, however, are currently lobbying the United Nations to adopt an Optional Protocol for the ICESCR that would include a complaints procedure where housing rights and other petitions regarding violations of economic and social rights could be heard. Housing rights activists acknowledge, however, that any efforts at the international level to further legitimize the right to housing and to render it justiciable are only effective and worthwhile if, simultaneously, housing rights movements are initiated and sustained at the grassroots level by communities directly affected by and subject to housing rights violations.

Women and the Right to Adequate Housing

The most obvious and yet insightful measure of the current extent of women's inclusion in the right to housing is found in the very wording that establishes the right. Recall that the ICESCR, adopted in 1966, recognizes "the right of everyone to an adequate standard of living for *himself* and *his family.*"[64] This male-specific language is an antiquity that in modern times must be read to include women. Further, the term "everyone" in that same sentence suggests that women are included within the ambit of the right. Women, particularly poor women, recognize and live the social limitations that male-biased language conveys. Thus, according to the language of article 11(1) of the Covenant, women's housing rights are invisible, subsumed under men's. Pamela Sayne articulates this point:

> In the limited patriarchal legal imagination of "covenants," all women are invisible but assumed to cohabit with "himself and his family"—which would come as a great surprise to most lesbians. . . . In 1987, the UN International Year for Shelter for the Homeless, Riane Eisler summed up the continual conflict between language and experience as follows:
>
>> Human rights have traditionally been defined as "men's inalienable right to life, liberty and property." The term "men" has sometimes been said to include women. But this has not been reflected in human rights theory or in its application. . .
>>
>> Modern theories of "human rights" have historically developed in two separate theoretical strains. Leading philosophers writing on the "rights of man" . . . specifically articulated a double standard of thought. . . . Women, on the other hand, were defined not as individuals but as members of men's households and thus, along with their offspring, under male control. [65]

If women's housing rights are founded on the notion that women are members of men's households (fathers or husbands) and that as such their housing rights are adequately protected and ensured if and when men's right to housing is protected, then on its language, the right to housing delegitimizes women's specific housing needs and realities. After all, there are many instances where this perception of women's housing rights would in fact assist in propagating housing conditions that might otherwise be regarded as a violation of women's right to housing. For example, if women's housing rights are subsumed under men's, then domestic violence and the unavailability of shelters for battered women may not be regarded as pertinent issues. In turn, with nowhere to go, women are forced to remain in abusive relationships and thus suffer a number of human rights violations, including the right to housing.

The Committee has explicitly addressed and attempted to remedy the ICESCR's under-inclusive language. Although at paragraph 1 in General Comment No. 4 the male-specific language of article 11(1) of the ICESCR is quoted without amendment, at paragraph 6 the Committee adopts a position similar to that articulated by Sayne and Eisler:

---

64. ICESCR, Art. 11(1), *supra* note 2, (emphasis added).

65. Pamela Sayne, *Ideology as Law: Is There Room for Difference in the Right to Housing?, in* Shelter Women and Development First and Third World Perspectives 97, 99–100 (Hemalata Dandekar ed., 1992). See also Pamela Sayne, *Housing Language, Housing Reality?* 11(2) Cdn. Women Stds. (1990).

The right to adequate housing applies to everyone. While reference to ''himself and his family'' reflects assumptions as to gender roles and economic activity patterns commonly accepted in 1966 when the Covenant was adopted, the phrase cannot be read today as implying any limitation upon the applicability of the right to individuals or to female-headed households, or other such groups. Thus, the concept of ''family'' must be understood in a wide sense. Further, individuals, as well as families, are entitled to adequate housing regardless of age, economic status, group or other affiliation or status and other such factors.[66]

As expected, the language used to set out the right to housing contained in the Women's Convention is woman specific. The Women's Convention stipulates that ''States Parties shall take all appropriate measures to eliminate discrimination against *women in rural areas* in order to ensure . . . to such women the right . . . [t]o enjoy adequate living conditions, particularly in relation to housing.''[67] This codification of the right to housing also has limitations as it only protects *rural* women's housing rights. Although traditionally rural women have been neglected by human settlements and human rights literature and instruments, it is a mistake to exclude women citydwellers from the right to housing. Given that rural migration to the cities is on the rise globally, and that women who reside in cities are equally affected by male-centered housing policies, women citydwellers must be explicitly included within the scope of housing rights.

The concept of women's right to housing was marginally advanced as a result of the Fourth World Conference on Women in Beijing. The Platform for Action[68] identifies several pertinent substantive issues regarding women's living and housing conditions, including: women's systemic disadvantage and oppression, poverty, lack of access to inheritance and property, exclusion from power and decisionmaking, and constant threat of physical, sexual, and psychological violence within the home.[69] Despite these insights into women's living and housing conditions, the Platform for Action fails to note the significant role that the *right* to housing might play in addressing many of these issues. As a result of this absence, the Platform for Action cannot be relied upon to support or argue for women's right to housing. At best, activists and lawyers can either extract the right to housing through references to women's economic, social, and cultural rights or, more tenuously and where appropriate, the right to housing might be interpreted as incorporated in the existing Platform for Action.[70] As these options are somewhat onerous, the Platform

---

66. General Comment No. 4, *supra* note 43.

67. The Women's Convention, *supra* note 38, at art. 14(2)(h).

68. PLATFORM FOR ACTION, *supra* note 28.

69. At the NGO Forum at the Fourth World Conference on Women, female grassroots activists from all over the world built a house to demonstrate that shelter is a women's issue. This was done as a reaction to the fact that so little space in the Platform for Action was devoted to issues relating to women and shelter. *See* Ihsan Bouabid, *Women-Housing: Next Stop Istanbul*, INTERPRESS SERVICE, Sept. 9, 1995, at 3.

70. For example, the right to housing might be read into Chapter IV, Section A, para. 61(b) of the Platform for Action so that governments are urged to ''undertake legislative and administrative reforms to give women full and equal access to economic resources, including the right [to housing], to inheri-

for Action is best used, with respect to women's housing issues, as a resource on women's living and housing conditions globally but not as evidence of women's right to housing.[71]

The *Habitat Agenda*,[72] which emerged from *Habitat II,* on the other hand, moves toward developing—at least theoretically—the constituent elements of a women's right to housing. The document begins by calling attention to women's disadvantage in the human settlement sphere, stating:

> Women have an important role to play in the attainment of sustainable human settlements. Nevertheless, as a result of a number of factors, including the persistent and increasing burden of poverty on women and discrimination against women, women face particular constraints in obtaining adequate shelter and in fully participating in decision-making related to sustainable human settlements. The empowerment of women and their full and equal participation in political, social and economic life, the improvement of health and the eradication of poverty are essential to achieving sustainable human settlements.[73]

Broadly speaking, the *Habitat Agenda* goes on to reaffirm a commitment to the full and progressive realization of the right to adequate housing.[74] At the same time, it addresses several housing issues that are pertinent to women. The *Habitat Agenda* is particularly articulate on the issue of women's right to land and property ownership and on the incompatibility of domestic violence and adequate shelter. For example, immediately following the commitment to the right to adequate housing, the document commits governments to:

> 40. (b) Providing legal security of tenure and equal access to land to all people, including women and those living in poverty; and undertaking legislative and administrative reforms to give women full and equal access to economic resources, including the right to inheritance and to ownership of land and other property, credit, natural resources and appropriate technologies. . . .
>
> (l) Promoting shelter and supporting basic services and facilities for education and health for the homeless, displaced persons, indigenous people, women and children who are survivors of family violence, persons with disabilities, older persons, victims

---

tance and to ownership of land and other property, credit, natural resources and appropriate technologies.''

71.   Chapter IV, Section I, of the Platform for Action entitled, ''Women's Human Rights,'' is predominantly a broad call for the recognition that the human rights of women and the girl–child are an inalienable, integral, and an indivisible part of universal human rights, the promotion and protection of which must be considered a priority objective of the United Nations (paras. 212, 213). Several particular rights are mentioned, such as women's reproductive rights, women's right to be free from violence, and the rights of refugee women, but the right to housing is only mentioned indirectly by calling for the protection of women's economic, social, and cultural rights.

72.   As found in the Report of the United Nations Conference on Human Settlements Habitat II, *supra* note 4.

73.   *Id.* at para.15.

74.   *Id.* at para. 39.

of natural and man-made disasters and people belonging to vulnerable and disadvantaged groups, including temporary shelter and basic services for refugees.[75]

Later, the document complements these objectives with corresponding strategies for implementation, recommending the eradication of legal and social barriers to women's equal and equitable access to land and, more specifically, calling for the promotion of mechanisms for the protection of women who risk losing their homes and properties when their husbands die.[76] Although the *Habitat Agenda* does not articulate these as "women's housing rights," they are placed in the context of a document that is at least partially aimed at protecting and promoting the right to adequate shelter for all. In this way, the *Habitat Agenda* may be regarded as the first, preliminary U.N. document that promotes women's right to housing.[77]

As a first step, women's housing rights will be secured only if inclusive language and rights language is clearly, consistently, and repeatedly articulated and employed in both instruments and literature that address the right to housing.[78] While the efforts of the women's coalition at *Habitat II* have undoubtedly moved in this direction, more work must be done. As it is extremely unlikely that the language of the ICESCR or the Women's Convention will be amended, the onus rests on activists, advocates, academics, U.N. officials, and any others working in the area of housing rights to adopt inclusive language that renders women visible and clearly establishes a relationship between women and the right to housing.

The International Actors and Women and the Right to Adequate Housing

Scott Leckie is one of the leading activists and most prolific writers on the international right to adequate housing. In his early work, Leckie specifically identifies the housing needs of women as particularly pertinent to the right to housing. In a 1989 article aimed at developing an "appropriate approach" to housing rights for the Committee, Leckie includes women as a group that must be protected against all forms of discrimination with respect to all aspects of housing. In this piece, Leckie specifically cites women's right to refuge housing as worthy of legal codification.[79] Further, in a 1990 paper, Leckie notes that the housing needs of Third

---

75. *Id.* at para. 40(a)(1).

76. *Id.* at paras. 78, 78(g).

77. Arguments could be made for and against this claim. The sometimes vague wording and awkward structure of the *Habitat Agenda* make it difficult to determine which commitments are constituent elements of the reaffirmed right to adequate housing and which remain "needs" that ought to be addressed by governments. On one hand, the document contains rights language, such as the right to adequate housing, and women's right to land, property, and inheritance. On the other hand, terms such as "shelter," "shelter policies," and "shelter delivery systems," not commonly used in housing rights discourse, are also found throughout the document.

78. PLATFORM FOR ACTION, *supra* note 28, at paras 212–213.

79. Scott Leckie, *The UN Committee on Economic, Social and Cultural Rights and the Right to Adequate Housing: Towards an Appropriate Approach*, 11 HUM. RTS. Q. 522, 551–52 (1989).

World women are far too frequently ignored with respect to housing or land legislation and the planning and management of human settlements.[80]

Unfortunately, Leckie's more recent work does not give the same emphasis to women's housing rights. For example, in an article that attempts to push the boundaries of the right to housing by demonstrating that, like other rights, the right to housing is justiciable, Leckie outlines the evolution of housing rights. In this overview he notes that the right to housing goes beyond housing provision for the homeless and includes addressing the housing needs of distinct disadvantaged groups within society. His list mirrors that articulated the Committee's General Comment No. 4, consisting of: "the disabled, the chronically ill, persons with HIV/ AIDS, migrant workers, the elderly and other groups."[81] The omission of women from this list (or their implied status as "other"), coupled with the fact that women's particular housing concerns are not mentioned at any other point in the paper, suggests that women's housing rights are either unimportant or have been put on the back burner.[82]

Women's right to housing has been recognized both formally and substantively by the former Special Rapporteur on the Right to Housing, Justice Rajindar Sachar. In his final report, the Special Rapporteur identifies women as a group that requires increasing focus throughout the United Nations system. In this vein, he devotes several paragraphs to a discussion on the right to housing and women's rights.[83] In the opening paragraph, he states:

> From all information available to the Special Rapporteur it is abundantly clear that women across the world continue to suffer from discrimination in the attainment of all aspects of the right to housing: land security and inheritance of right to land and property; access to credit facilities; access to information essential for participation in housing activities and in contributing to the improvement of the living environment;

---

80. Leckie, *supra* note 40, at 3.

81. Leckie, *supra* note 57, at 45.

82. This is not to suggest that Leckie is no longer concerned with women's housing rights. Indeed, he assisted in the preparation of this chapter and he insisted that our fact-finding mission report on the Kobe earthquake include documentation regarding the housing rights violations experienced by the women of Kobe. The point here is that Leckie has neglected to maintain this interest in his own literature. This unsatisfactory position is confirmed in a paper Leckie presented at *Habitat II* regarding human development and shelter where he suggests that priority, attention, and targeted strategies be adopted to satisfy the housing needs of certain disadvantaged groups. Again, women failed to make his list. As a result, we are left to wonder, where have all the women gone? The recent absence of women from Leckie's later work is troubling. As it stands, women's voices are barely heard in the international human rights world and a strong voice like that of Scott Leckie, who is very much part of the international human rights system, would greatly assist in women's struggle to have their housing rights realized—at least at the international level.

83. REPORT OF THE SPECIAL RAPPORTEUR, *supra* note 45, at paras. 45–49. To assist with this final report the Special Rapporteur put out a request for information from various countries regarding particular issues and distinct groups such as the poor and women. Interestingly, only one government explicitly mentioned its efforts to create wider opportunities for women to participate in housing development (at para. 128).

availability of essential housing services and resources including potable water, sanitation, fuel and fodder and access to appropriate housing projects, upgrading schemes and resettlement areas.[84]

The Special Rapporteur then briefly touches on three housing issues that he has determined are particularly significant for women: land ownership/security of tenure (para. 46), evictions/resettlement (para. 47), and the recent energy crisis (para. 48). He concludes that gaining and securing the right to housing can lead women to attain other rights and create possibilities for the improvement of the environment in which women live.[85]

Women also appear in the portion of the Special Rapporteur's report dedicated to "indicators" developed to assist in the assessment of state compliance with the provisions of the right to adequate housing. Drawing extensively on the work of Miloon Kothari[86] (a leading activist on the right to housing at both the international and grass roots level), under the heading "Gender equality" the Special Rapporteur notes that women bear the primary responsibility for sustaining and maintaining homes, that women are the most affected by crisis situations in their country's resource base, and that a significant portion of women—particularly in developing countries—are essentially homeless with no rights to natal or marital homes. To address these issues, the Rapporteur states that it is necessary to alter the unjust and exploitive social and cultural practices and processes against women and to ensure that these issues are explicitly considered in all aspects of housing policy, programs, and legislation. To determine whether states have complied with women's right to housing, the following approach is recommended:

> . . . Given the high level of participation of women in all matters concerning housing and the particular need to recognize the critical role that they play in these matters, it is crucial that all core indicators and elements, from security of tenure to local participation to economic parity of women and so forth, take into account both the particularly adverse impact that violations of the right to housing have on women and the contribution that women make in gaining and retaining the right to housing.[87]

Maintaining this momentum, the report proceeds to recommend that states should guarantee women full equality of treatment regarding any and all aspects of the human right to adequate housing, with particular attention paid to rights to land and/or property ownership and inheritance, that influence decision-making processes.[88]

The only weakness in Justice Sachar's report is that it fails to provide any examples of housing rights violations actually experienced by women. For example,

---

84.   *Id.* at para. 45.

85.   *Id.* at para. 49.

86.   *See* Miloon Kothari, *The Human Right to Adequate Housing: Towards Ideal Indicators and Realistic World Views*, HR/Geneva/1993/SEM/BP.16 (1993).

87.   REPORT OF THE SPECIAL RAPPORTEUR, *supra* note 45, at para. 118.

88.   *Id.* at 169.

though the report provides an overview of the housing conditions in Thailand, Malaysia, and Palestine, the report fails to discuss any specific housing rights violations experienced by women in these particular areas. Moreover, in its discussion of the prominent housing problems in these regions (eviction, house demolition, land confiscation), the report neglects to include any information on the impact these housing rights violations have on women—despite the fact that it is now accepted in housing rights literature and practice that women bear the primary burden of forced evictions.[89]

Despite this weakness, the Special Rapporteur's final report and its explicit references to women's housing rights mark an important step toward the development of women's international right to adequate housing. It is significant because it recognizes three fundamental factors. First, it overtly acknowledges that women, as a group, suffer from discrimination in the attainment of the right to housing. Second, the report acknowledges the particular relevance of the right to housing for women, given the critical role that women play in all matters concerning housing. Last, the report stipulates that women suffer from systemic oppression in the housing field and, therefore, for the right to housing to be meaningful to women, systemic discrimination in housing policy, programs, and legislation, must be addressed head-on.

The recognition of these three factors underscores the necessity to develop women's right to housing. As seen in the following section, it is not necessary to alter the framework of the right to housing to accommodate these concerns, rather it is merely a matter of having these concerns recognized and then accommodated within the existing framework.

UNDERSTANDING WOMEN'S GLOBAL HOUSING CONDITIONS

To properly develop a women's right to housing, it is essential to have at least a basic understanding of women's housing and living conditions globally. If the substance of a right is at least in part a function of the needs of the right's holder, then a full understanding of women's housing needs is imperative to any definition of women's right to housing. At the same time, as Moser's work has shown, to dismantle the structural framework that is the root cause of women's oppression within (and outside) the home, it is essential to understand and address women's practical and strategic needs. The women and human settlement/shelter literature, and the recent work in the area of women, land, and property rights (which springs from the women and human settlement work), provides a good preliminary picture of some of the central housing concerns with which women are faced globally. Because the focus of this chapter is women and the right to housing, an expansive review of these various bodies of literature is not to be provided, though seminal texts were consulted to assist in the development of a realistic, if broad, picture of

---

89. *See* CENTRE FOR HUMAN RIGHTS, FORCED EVICTIONS AND HUMAN RIGHTS (FACT SHEET No. 25) at 9; REPORT OF THE SECRETARY-GENERAL TO THE COMMISSION ON THE STATUS OF WOMEN, at para. 5, U.N. Doc. E/CN.6/1994/3 (1994).

women's primary housing concerns globally. Each of the issues highlighted affect women in both Northern and Southern countries, though in what manner and to what degree depends on many factors, including the region in which the women are located.

For the purposes of this chapter the aforementioned seminal texts are not regarded as *housing rights* literature *per se*, as the women and human settlement/shelter literature does not consistently approach women's housing issues from a rights perspective and often regards housing as merely one component of the broader human settlements sphere.[90] This is reflected in the fact that this literature uses the terms "shelter" and "human settlements," rather than "housing," on the basis that the term "housing" relates only to four walls and a roof whereas "human settlements" and "shelter" include not only the actual house but also the wider area in which it is located (i.e., infrastructure and other neighborhood and community level facilities). As noted earlier, however, according to international law, the right to adequate housing goes beyond the simple notion of the right to a roof over one's head and includes such things as access to basic amenities, services, cultural adequacy, and security of tenure. In turn, from a housing rights perspective, "housing" is a suitable term to cover a broad range of issues and, because the term "housing" or "house" is now closely associated with a rights perspective, it is the term used throughout this section.

The literature regarding women, land, and property rights also is not considered housing rights literature because it does not explicitly connect land and property rights with the right to housing as articulated in international legal instruments such as the ICESCR.[91] Also, this literature is primarily concerned with women's economic well-being and, as such, it commonly refers to women's right to economic resources and/or agricultural land as opposed to women's right to housing or land associated more directly with housing.[92] The right to housing, on the other hand, includes the right to land and property—in respect of housing—within its definition.

At the same time, however, the importance of the women and human settlements/shelter literature and the women, land, and property rights literature cannot

---

90. There are, of course, exceptions. The literature accessed regarding the National Housing Rights Campaign in India provides both an overview of women's housing conditions while utilizing a rights framework. Additionally, one aspect of the work undertaken by the Habitat International Coalition, Women and Shelter Network headquartered in Colombia does address women's housing conditions from a rights perspective. Unfortunately, the author was unable to obtain any literature beyond newsletters and flyers that demonstrate this commitment to housing as a woman's human right.

91. This is not to say that all literature on land and property rights does not include the right to housing. The two issues are so integrally linked—particularly for women—that dealing with land/property rights and housing rights as distinct issues is an artificial construction. For an example of the interconnectedness of women's property or land rights and women's right to housing, *see* Lydia Kompe and Janet Small, *Demanding a Place Under the Kgotla Tree: Rural Women's Access to Land and Power in* THIRD WORLD LEGAL STUD. 137 (1991).

92. See Hemalata Dandekar, *Introduction, in* Shelter WOMEN AND DEVELOPMENT: FIRST AND THIRD WORLD PERSPECTIVES, *supra* note 65, at 3; Moser, *supra* note 9, at 1.

be overemphasized, because it provides pertinent information and insight into women's housing needs, information that is only scantily available in the housing rights literature. And so, while this literature cannot be regarded as a substitute for housing rights literature or a housing rights approach to women and housing, it can (and must) be used to implement a construction of women's right to housing.

Women and Housing: Facts and Issues

General Overview

There are two facts repeated throughout the literature regarding women's housing and living conditions: women constitute one of the poorest segments of society globally and the number of woman-headed households is increasing at an exponential rate around the world.[93] The actual manifestation of these two facts indicates that women are a disadvantaged "social group" living in unfavorable conditions, and as such ought to be a group on which the right to adequate housing focuses.[94]

The housing conditions of many people worldwide can be regarded as health and/or life threatening. Poverty is at the root of many of these inadequate living and housing conditions.[95] As a result of women's relationship to both housing and poverty, women find themselves in a particularly deprived position. As women and children spend the most time at home, they are the most severely affected by inadequacies in their housing situation. For example, an estimated 70 million women and children worldwide suffer from severe indoor pollution from cooking fires that causes respiratory and other health problems. Moreover, every day some 50,000 persons, mostly women and children, die as a result of poor shelter, polluted water and inadequate sanitation.[96] Furthermore, the dramatic increase in the number of *de facto* or *de jure* female-headed households exacerbates women's poverty because it forces women to undertake greater responsibilities without greater access to resources.[97] It is now estimated that approximately one-fourth of the world's households are headed by women. In urban areas, especially in Latin America and parts of Africa, the figure exceeds 50 percent. Female-headed households represent a high proportion of households in informal settlements, and are among the poorest; they are generally much poorer than those headed by men and they face many

---

93. See UNCHS, WOMEN IN HUMAN SETTLEMENTS DEVELOPMENT: GETTING THE ISSUES RIGHT (Wandia Seaforth ed., 1995).

94. *See* General Comment No. 4, *supra* note 43, at para. 11, which states that in recognition of the fact that disadvantaged groups are more likely to be subject to housing rights violations, the Committee stresses that the focus of the right must be on those social groups living in unfavorable conditions.

95. This is not to say that poverty is the sole cause of women's inadequate living and housing conditions. Patriarchal laws, for example, are also a contributing factor.

96. UNCHS, *supra* note 93, at 5.

97. Moser, *supra* note 9, at 14. *De facto* female-headed households are those where, for example, a woman's male partner is absent because of economic or political reasons, often not communicating with his family for a long period of time. *De jure* female-headed households are those where a woman is living with her children and does not have a male partner.

problems in their attempts to secure a place to live, as well as in their daily fight for survival.[98] As reported at the *Fourth World Conference on Women*, while poverty affects households as a whole, because of the gender division of labor and responsibilities for household welfare, women bear a disproportionate burden, attempting to manage household consumption and production under conditions of increasing scarcity.[99]

In response to their situation of inadequate provision of housing and basic services in conjunction with the global recession and massive economic restructuring, women have had no alternative but to respond to this economic crisis by expanding their own family and household responsibilities even further, performing what some commentators have called the "triple role of women."[100] In most low-income households, "women's work" includes not only reproductive work (childbearing and rearing), but also productive work as primary or secondary income earners (agricultural, informal, or formal sector enterprises). Additionally, as a means of survival, women are increasingly involved in community management, that is, organizing at the community level in relation to the provision of items of collective consumption.[101] This multiple role exacts a heavy toll on women's relation to housing:

> Because the triple role of women is not recognized, so neither is the fact that women, unlike men, are severely constrained by the burden of simultaneously balancing the three roles of *productive, reproductive and community-managing work.* In addition only productive work, because it has an exchange value, is recognized as work. Reproductive and managing work, because they are both seen as 'natural' and nonproductive, are not valued. This has serious consequences for women. It means that most of their work fails to be recognized as such, either by men in the community or by those planners whose responsibility it is to assess different needs within low-income communities. While the tendency is to see the needs of women and men as similar, the reality of women's lives is very different.[102]

Much of the women and human settlement/shelter empowerment literature is based on the premise that housing policy has not considered gender differences in its definition of housing needs. Instead, housing needs have been defined as "gender neutral" and ideas of the nuclear family or the nuclear and extended family as the universal norm have permeated all aspects of the shelter-provision system.[103] In contrast, the women and shelter literature offers a gender-sensitive approach to

---

98. UNCHS, *supra* note 93, at 1. It is easy to see how this process of the "feminization of poverty" might lead to women's absolute poverty and how it likely contributes to the rapidly increasing number of homeless women worldwide. On this point, *see* Vinitha Aliyer and Sujata Shetty, *A Policy Overview, in* SHELTER WOMEN AND DEVELOPMENT: FIRST AND THIRD WORLD PERSPECTIVES, *supra* note 65, at 16.

99. PLATFORM FOR ACTION, *supra* note 28, at para. 50.

100. *See* Moser, *supra* note 9; Sylvia Chant, *Women, Shelter and Survival Strategies: Issues for Consideration in Developing Countries, in* HOUSING QUESTION OF THE OTHERS, *supra* note 5, at 117.

101. Moser, *supra* note 9, at 13.

102. *Id.* at 14 (emphasis added).

103. Hemalata Dandekar, *supra* note 92, at 7.

planning and housing that incorporates theoretical feminist concerns. Rather than attempting to merely slot women into existing planning paradigms, Moser and others have attempted to restructure the paradigm to ensure the accommodation of women's realities. Every aspect of housing affects women directly, be it the construction of housing, its interior design, access to basic amenities and services, or the ability to access and maintain housing. For the purposes of clarity and to ensure a basic understanding of women's relationship to housing globally, the next section identifies and details, with examples, three distinct housing issues that are of particular importance to women.[104]

SPECIFIC HOUSING ISSUES

Inheritance, Land, and Property Rights[105]

As noted previously, security of tenure for "all persons" is one of the seven core principles of the definition of adequate housing as articulated by the Committee on Economic, Social and Cultural Rights in General Comment No. 4.[106] With respect to land and property ownership, women's security of tenure needs are distinct from those of men and as such must be specifically considered and addressed in the protection and promotion of women's housing rights.

The issue of women's access and rights to land and property ownership and inheritance is currently receiving more attention than any other single issue related to women and housing. Not only is it discussed in the human settlement and women and shelter literature, but it has also found public, oral exposure at two recent conferences, the first in Sweden hosted by the United Nations Centre for Human Settlements (UNCHS/Habitat) (October, 1995), and most recently at *Habitat II* (June, 1996) in an UNCHS-NGO co-sponsored event.

One of the most critical issues for women in both developed and developing countries with respect to housing is security of tenure. As Moser points out, women's lack of rights to tenure or ownership has grave implications because, without rights to land, women are often unable to protect themselves and their children from unstable or violent domestic situations.[107] Without land rights, women are often unable to provide collateral to gain access to credit. Where women have no title to land, they may end up homeless or without capital savings (land value appreciates over time) in the event of marital separation, and property rights tend to reinforce the control that the man already has over the household and its dependants.[108]

---

104. While the author has attempted to be regionally representative, many constraints were faced (language, public access) in obtaining information from particular regions.

105. The following section deals with the issue of women, land, and property rights in the context of the right to housing. For essential reading on women's property rights, *see* BINA AGARWAL, A FIELD OF ONE'S OWN: GENDER AND LAND RIGHTS IN SOUTH ASIA (1994).

106. General Comment No. 4, *supra* note 43, at para. 8.

107. On this point, *see also* Kompe and Small, *supra* note 91, at 148.

108. Moser, *supra* note 9, at 17.

More often than not, men—presumed to bc heads of households—are afforded security of tenure to the exclusion of women. This arises as a result of three predominant factors: 1) gender-biased laws that exclude women; 2) custom and tradition, which posit women as subordinate to men and in some cases as men's property, and which has the force of law, rendering women incapable of land or property ownership; and 3) economic barriers. The following are instructive examples.

Gender-Biased Laws

In many instances, a woman's marital status determines her legal ability to own property or land. For example, in Swaziland, legislation forbids women from possessing land or property or engaging in contractual agreements. This stands in stark contrast with the fact that in Swazi society women have been responsible for producing and maintaining their own shelter.[109]

Similarly, in Cameroon, women do not enjoy legal access to property. Because women are not actually mentioned in the law relating to legal ownership of property, a gap is created, leaving it to the discretion of judges to make exceptional decisions in favor of women. Not surprisingly, this lacuna does not work to the advantage of women, as judges often base their judgments on traditional practices that bar women's right to use or own land without the intermediacy of men. Common practice is such that women cannot inherit land or property from their fathers because it is assumed that they will be married outside the communities in which their parents owned land, and a widow cannot inherit land from her husband because land goes back to his family upon his death.[110]

Gender-Biased Custom, Religion, and Tradition

In many regions, it is custom rather than law that prohibits women from land or property ownership. A woman may have the legal right to inherit property, but this may remain merely a documentary right if the law is not enforced, or if the claim is not socially recognized as legitimate and family members pressure the woman to forfeit her share in favor of a male family member.[111]

For example, in India, women have considerable legal rights to own and inherit property, yet few women are able to lay claim to these legal rights. Although India has a fairly gender-progressive legal framework, it is rooted in a social framework that denies women the legitimacy of such legal claims and of being able to exercise "control" over their land in the cases where they do own land.[112] Laws relating to

---

109. UNCHS, Towards a Strategy for the Full Participation of Women in All Phases of the UN Global Strategy for Shelter to the Year 2000 12 (1990).

110. UNCHS, Women And Human Settlements Development 1, 38 (1989).

111. Agarwal, *supra* note 105, at 19.

112. *See* Gayatri A. Menon, Women's Access, Control and Tenure of Land and Settlement in India, text presented at the International Workshop on Women's Access, Control and Tenure of Land, Property and Settlement (Istanbul, Turkey)(1995)(unpublished). *See also* Agarwal, *supra* note 105.

inheritance or property are based primarily on religious law and tradition. For example, in Hindu law, daughters and sons do not have equal rights to joint family property. A daughter is not a member of the coparcenary (an institution that holds ancestral property in the male line for three generations), and therefore has no right to claim partition of ancestral property.[113]

Similarly, in Nigeria, the *Land Use Act* which codifies the system of land ownership, does not exclude women; however, women's socio-economic position within Nigeria bars them from claiming land ownership.[114] Women in Nigeria are prime subjects of patriarchy. Once married, to the outside world a woman loses her identity as it is subsumed under that of her husband. Therefore, only her husband's name is expected to appear in land titles. Most married women, who understand and accept this "cultural trap," lose interest in the acquisition of property. Where they maintain their initiative they register the property in their husband's name.

In rural Muslim communities in Palestine, despite the fact that Islamic law entitles women to inherit a limited percentage of land and property, custom is such that women commonly renounce their inheritance rights.[115] For example, upon the death of her father, a woman with brothers is likely to renounce her right to inheritance in favor of her male siblings because demanding her share would disrupt her kinship ties with her brothers and render their support and assistance unavailable. As the position of a woman in her husband's house often depends on the support she can count on from her own kin, this would simultaneously undermine her position with her husband and her in-laws. Brotherless women tend to take their share relatively more often, although this too is by law less than a male's share.[116]

In Kenya, current land reform laws, unlike customary land tenure rules, allow women to inherit land from their fathers and husbands. Whether women actually do inherit and acquire the capability to exercise the rights that go with individual ownership, however, depends largely on the goodwill of their fathers and husbands.[117] Additionally, customary practices, which are still highly respected despite land reform laws, continue to preclude a daughter's right to inherit land. To pass such land to a daughter would "threaten the territorial integrity of the clan upon [the daughter's] marriage," which would be regarded as socially unacceptable.[118]

---

113. Indira Jaising, *Violence Against Women: The Indian Perspective, in* WOMEN'S RIGHTS AS HUMAN RIGHTS: INTERNATIONAL PERSPECTIVES 51, 52 (Julie Peters and Andrea Wolper eds., 1995).

114. Jadesola Akande, untitled paper presented at the International Workshop on Women's Access, Control and Tenure of Land, Property and Settlement (Gavle, Sweden).

115. ANNELIES MOORS, WOMEN, PROPERTY AND ISLAM: PALESTINIAN EXPERIENCES, 1920–1990 48 (1995). Moors notes that while women have the right to inherit under Islamic law, these rights are generally more limited than those of men, where male preference is given with respect to the shares of widows and daughters.

116. *Id.* at 55.

117. Perpetua W. Karanja, *Women's Land Ownership Rights in Kenya,* THIRD WORLD LEGAL STUD. 109, 127 (1991).

118. *Id.* at 128.

In the Transvaal province of South Africa, when a married woman's husband dies, the land and household become the responsibility of his family. While in most cases the wife is allowed to stay on the homestead, theoretically his family can take over the house, land, household possessions, and even the children. In practice, the widow occupies her homestead only with the goodwill of her husband's family. If a woman decides to remarry after her husband's death, she is expected to leave her home and land.[119]

Gender-Biased Economic Policies

Even in those countries where custom and law permit a woman to own land or a house, she is often prevented from doing so for a variety of economic reasons. This is not simply a result of women's overwhelming poverty, but is also because of gender-biased policies regarding financial assistance for housing.

The economic and financial policies, the priorities of financial institutions, and the rules and procedures commonly employed for loans, mortgages, and other forms of credit in both the formal and informal sectors have put women at a significant disadvantage in acquiring credit for housing, as well as for other types of investment in the housing sector.[120] The constraints on women in obtaining housing finance are societal and operational, and arise from social prejudices and institutional practices. For example, loans taken to finance dwelling units are often large (as small loans are not "good business"), entail long-term repayment, often require legal-tenure documentation, and cover only a percentage of the price. On the basis of having to safeguard their capital, conventional lending institutions require proof of an adequate and dependable income (i.e., formal employment) as well as ownership of the property. Thus, these requirements, directly and constructively, preclude many women from obtaining such loans.

Down payments are also often required in order to receive a loan and secure property. Normally a down payment of approximately 25–40 percent of the cost of the dwelling unit is required. Experience shows that many low-income applicants, especially women (who have nominal savings at best), have difficulty in raising even 10 percent. Additionally, in some countries, women are classified as minors and, as such, they cannot acquire credit or can only acquire credit on a husband's or male relative's guarantee.[121]

As a result of these economic barriers, credit programs for women's housing projects have begun to emerge in many countries. For example, in Egypt, the Principal Bank for Development and Credit started a program that provides loans, credit facilities, and other services to enable women to participate more adequately in land management and to encourage them to keep or purchase land.[122]

---

119. Kompe and Small, *supra* note 91, at 149.

120. UNCHS, *supra* note 109, at 18.

121. *Id.*

122. Personal notes taken by the author at the International Workshop on Women's Access, Control and Tenure of Land, Property and Settlement, (Istanbul Turkey), 1996 [hereinafter International Workshop].

Similarly, the Masese Women's Self-Help Project in Uganda provides a unique credit/loan scheme for women. In Uganda, under customary traditional laws or practices; women are considered inferior to men and, as a result of this perceived inferiority, are not permitted to own property. Masese was one of the poorest and most rapidly deteriorating informal settlements in the Jinja Municipality where communities squatted on public land. Many destitute single mothers, widows, and orphans were living under appalling conditions. Housing structures, most of which were made of mud and wattle wall with grass thatched roofs, had extremely poor sanitation and were in deplorable condition. To address the housing and living problems in Masese, the Self-Help project originally provided women with loans to secure land tenure and to build their own houses. These same women were then offered employment in commercial materials production to generate income to assist them in paying off their housing and community facility loans.[123]

The project has proven hugely successful. It currently is predicted that all of the participants (700) will receive title deeds after repayment of their loans (whereas, prior to the scheme, 80% of the population were squatters). Houses that were built of mud have been replaced with permanent units, potable water is now more accessible, all houses have access to motorable roads, and, where houses were predominantly rented prior to the project (80%), houses are now predominantly owned (70%). In implementing the right to housing, it is these realities that we must account for if we hope to vindicate women's right to housing.

Domestic Violence

The right to live somewhere in "security, peace and dignity" is one of the fundamental pillars of the right to housing and, according to the Committee, housing is only adequate if it guarantees the safety of its occupants.[124] These provisions take on particular significance when considered in the context of domestic violence.

> Domestic violence or family violence . . . primarily affects women and operates to diminish women's autonomy and sense of self-worth. Domestic violence usually involves the infliction of bodily injury accompanied by verbal threats and harassment, emotional abuse or the destruction of property as a means of coercion, control, revenge or punishment, on a person with whom the abuser is involved in an intimate relationship. The assailant frequently blames the attacks on the victim and her behaviour. He may also use the attacks to control his partner's actions. A battered woman may become isolated with little community or family support and be afraid to leave her home.[125]

---

123. Hilda Musubira, Gendered Best Practice—Women's Land/Property Rights: A Case of the Masese Women's Self-Help Project Jinja-Uganda (unpublished) text presented at International Workshop, *supra* note 122.

124. General Comment No. 4, *supra* note 43 at para. 11 and para. 8. Although this section addresses violence within the home, the right to safety of its occupants is more often construed as requiring both safety standards within the home (e.g. meeting fire/earthquake regulations, etc.) and also outside the home (safe neighborhood/community, etc.).

125. HUMAN RIGHTS WATCH, THE HUMAN RIGHTS WATCH GLOBAL REPORT ON WOMEN'S HUMAN RIGHTS 341 (1995).

All the available research evidence suggests that violence against women in the home is a universal problem.[126] A large percentage of the violence women suffer occurs in the home. For example, Human Rights Watch reports that, in Brazil, over 70 percent of all reported incidents of violence against women takes place in the home;[127] in Russia, spousal abuse is widespread and largely accepted;[128] and the levels of domestic violence against women in South Africa are "staggering."[129] In India, 80 percent of wives are victims of violence, domestic abuse, dowry abuse, or murder;[130] in Austria, domestic violence against the wife was given as a factor in the breakdown of marriage in 59 percent of 1,500 divorce cases;[131] in Australia, a study indicated that one in five men believed it acceptable for men to beat their wives;[132] and, in Papua New Guinea, the Law Reform Commission found that up to 67 percent of wives had suffered marital violence.[133] Human Rights Watch reports that domestic violence is one of the leading causes of female injuries in almost every country in the world, and it accounts in some countries for the largest percentage of hospital visits by women.[134] The Beijing Platform for Action declares violence against women an obstacle to the achievement of the objectives of equality for women[135] and provides the following instructive commentary:

> Acts or threats of violence, whether occurring within the home or in the community, or perpetrated or condoned by the State, instill fear and insecurity in women's lives. . . . Violence against women is one of the crucial social mechanisms by which women are forced into a subordinate position compared with men. In many cases, violence against women and girls occurs in the family or within the home, where violence is often tolerated. The neglect, physical and sexual abuse, and rape of girl children and women by family members and other members of the household, as well as incidences of spousal and non-spousal abuse, often go unreported and are thus difficult to detect.[136]

Not surprisingly, in much of the literature regarding women and housing, violence against women and domestic violence in particular, is discussed as one of the most serious issues affecting women. The connection between domestic violence and housing, though somewhat obvious, bears elucidation.

---

126. United Nations, The World's Women: Trends and Statistics 158 (2nd ed. 1995).

127. Human Rights Watch, *supra* note 125, at 351.

128. *Id.* at 373.

129. *Id.* at 386.

130. Charlotte Bunch, *Women's Rights as Human Rights: Towards a Re-Vision of Human Rights*, 12 Hum. Rts. Q. 486, 490 (1990) *as cited in* Hilary Charlesworth and Christine Chinkin, *The Gender of Jus Cogens*, 15 Hum. Rts. Q. 63, 72–73 (1993).

131. United Nations, The World's Women, 1970–1990: Trends and Statistics 19 (1991).

132. Australian Government, Office of the Status of Women, Community Attitudes Towards Domestic Violence in Australia 2 (1988).

133. United Nations, Violence Against Women in the Family 20 (1989).

134. Human Rights Watch, *supra* note 125, at 341.

135. Platform for Action, *supra* note 28, at para. 112.

136. *Id.* at 117.

Because the home continues to be constructed as a "private" realm, a place within which "family matters" should remain, and because women's housing needs and rights continue to be ignored, domestic violence is able to flourish. The relationship between poverty, housing, and domestic violence is captured in the words of an Ecuadorean woman living in the urban settlement of El Guasmo. She explained:

> I live in a half-shack, half-built house, dusty in the winter, muddy in the summer. The rubbish collectors do not come when they are supposed to so there are heaps of garbage on the road. It is difficult to get enough water to do the housework. Transport is always difficult. Buses are crowded and full of gangs that try to steal everything from you. Where can I leave my children if I go to work? There is no children's centre nearby.
>
> It is important for my husband to find his lunch ready for him when he gets back from work and enough water to have his shower. Yes, he beats me when something is lacking. He comes home drunk in the evening and he sometimes beats me again.[137]

Housing is an extremely important issue with respect to domestic violence, for a woman's housing situation can encourage domestic violence. Take, for example, the case of Chinese women who often endure physical and emotional abuse by their husbands rather than leave the relationship and face homelessness. Because of direct discrimination, divorced women in China experience extreme difficulties in accessing and securing accommodation, a predicament in which divorced men do not find themselves. As a result of housing allocation practices, most married couples live in housing assigned by the husband's work unit. Upon divorce, it is therefore often the woman who has to leave the home and find somewhere else to live. Most often, she has no choice but to return to her natal home. If she has brothers who have settled their families in the parents' home, the abused woman has nowhere to live and faces homelessness.[138]

In many societies, land, house, or property ownership is not a right extended to women and rental accommodation is difficult to access in light of legal discrimination against women or customary/traditional practices, which have the same effect. Laws, policies, culture and/or custom often make it difficult or impossible for a woman to live in either a rental unit or in a house that is neither her father's nor her husband's. Thus a woman subject to domestic violence has nowhere to go to escape the abusive relationship.[139] Even temporary or emergency relief may be difficult to access, given that in developing nations battered women's shelters are not commonplace and, in developed nations such as Canada, "cut backs" to social services have resulted in a decrease in the number of shelters and the number of spaces available in shelters. This combination of factors means that, with nowhere to go, women victims of domestic violence are forced to either endure physical/psychological abuse for long periods of time, or accept homelessness and its risks.

---

137. Valli F.K. Yanni, *Women with self-esteem are healthy women: community development in an urban settlement of Guayaquil, in* WOMEN AND URBAN SETTLEMENT (Caroline Sweetman ed., 1996).

138. EMILY HONIG AND GAYLE HERSHATTER, PERSONAL VOICES: CHINESE WOMEN IN THE 1980s, 226 (1988).

139. Moser, *supra* note 9, at 17.

Some housing situations also help to create a social context in which domestic violence is likely to occur. For example, in many regions throughout the world, such as the Philippines, occupied Tibet, and Palestine, families are subjected to house demolition. Once these people are forcibly evicted from their homes, the difficulty in finding alternative accommodation compels them to reside with their extended family. Living arrangements are thus cramped and overcrowded. A woman in these circumstances becomes responsible for the care of not just one man, but perhaps for two or three others, as well as for the care of her children. Overcrowded living conditions coupled with other frustrating factors such as unemployment or extreme poverty can cause tempers to flare, can lead to increased levels of alcohol consumption, and can ultimately result in situations of domestic violence.[140]

Sylvia Novac identifies women's poverty as another condition that contributes to women's experience of domestic violence.[141] Novac notes that the home is often regarded as a place of security from external violence, and yet ironically, women are at even greater risk of physical and sexual violence in the home than outside it. One of the forms of male dominance within the home that affects women's housing security (at least in Northern, developed countries such as Canada) is sexual harassment, particularly by landlords and their agents. When housing is treated as a market commodity, the ability to pay rent or buy determines housing security.[142] When women (especially sole support parents or female heads of households) in developed countries face even higher levels of poverty as governments reduce welfare entitlements and enforce other "deficit reducing" policies based on economic restraint, already vulnerable women become even more vulnerable. Housing activists fear that women, unable to pay their rent or unable to pay rent in a timely fashion, may fall prey to those male persons in positions of power within the housing market—landlords and property managers.

Feminist legal scholars and activists have attempted to address the issue of domestic violence from a human rights perspective in a number of ways. For instance, domestic violence has been framed as a violation of the right to life. This approach has met with disapproval on the basis that the international legal system addresses "public" actors, that is, actions of the state as opposed to the acts of private individuals. Similarly, attempts to frame violence against women as inconsistent with the right to be free from torture has met resistance because, according to the international legal definition, torture only takes place in the public

---

140. *See* The World Bank, Confronting Crisis: A Summary of Household Responses to Poverty and Vulnerability in Four Poor Urban Communities 16 (ESD Monograph Series No. 7)(1996). In this piece Moser notes that in all research communities in this study (Chawama in Lusaka, Zambia; Cisne Dos in Guayaquil, Ecuador; Commonwealth, in Metro Manila, the Philippines; and Angyalfold, in Budapest, Hungary) women reported that domestic violence was prevalent, and they identified a direct link between declining male earnings and increasing domestic violence, often associated with alcohol abuse.

141. Novac, *Seeking Shelter, supra* note 7, at 68.

142. Novac, *Boundary Violations: Sexual Harassment within Tenancy Relations, in* Shelter Women and Development: First and Third World Perspectives 68, 69–70, *supra* note 65.

realm. To address this resistance, scholars and activists have argued that what happens "behind closed doors"—the actions of men that harm their spouses within the private sphere—must be subject to human rights standards and must be recognized as private–realm human rights violations. Others argue that the private sphere and an act such as spouse abuse is a result of the relationships between men and women that are structured on power, domination, and privilege of men over women, and that this structure is supported and upheld by the patriarchal hierarchy of the nation state. Therefore, what goes on in private is inextricably linked with the public and the state is accountable for the actions of individuals and as such, acts such as spousal abuse *do* fall within the purview of international human rights law.[143]

Most of these arguments are aimed at recognizing violence against women as within the protections of the ICCPR. As discussed *supra*, however, domestic violence also falls under the protections afforded by the ICESCR, particularly the right to housing. The international right to housing offers a useful approach to domestic violence. If cases of domestic violence were brought before the Committee, for example, it might be persuaded to work toward recognizing that the actions of private actors do fall within the jurisdiction of the ICESCR and can be reviewed by the Committee. The housing rights approach to domestic violence is also unique as it allows the issue of domestic violence to be dealt with at the very site where it occurs most often: in the home.[144] And so, for women victims of domestic violence, the right to live in "peace, security and dignity" means more specifically, the right to live in a space devoid of domestic violence.

Women's Participation in the Housing Process

According to General Comment No. 4, the right to adequate housing extends to everyone (men, women, and children alike), the enjoyment of the right must not be subject to any form of discrimination, and the right to participate in public decision making is "indispensable" if the right to adequate housing is to be realized and maintained by all groups in society.[145]

These assertions may combine to guarantee women the right to participate in the housing process in two ways. First, they support the notion that women's discriminatory exclusion from the constituent elements of what might be referred to as "the housing process" (e.g., planning, design, construction) is itself a violation

---

143. Gayle Binion, *Human Rights: A Feminist Perspective,* 17 HUM. RTS. Q. 509, 520 (1995). *See also* Charlotte Bunch, *Organizing for Women's Human Rights Globally, in* OURS BY RIGHT: WOMEN'S RIGHTS AS HUMAN RIGHTS 141 (Joanna Kerr ed., 1993); SUSAN OKIN, JUSTICE, GENDER AND THE FAMILY (1989).

144. This is not intended to imply or suggest that a housing rights approach is the sole route that feminist activists and academics should pursue to address domestic violence.

145. General Comment No. 4, *supra* note 43, at para. 6. See also Article 2(2) of the ICESCR, *supra* note 2, which states that: "The State Parties to the present Covenant undertake to guarantee that the rights enunciated in the present Covenant will be exercised without discrimination of any kind as to race, colour, *sex*, language, religion, political or other opinion, national or social origin, property, birth or other status" (emphasis added).

of the right to housing, regardless of the consequences of that exclusion. Alternatively, these assertions support the notion that when women's exclusion from the housing process results in a discriminatory outcome, though only the outcome may be regarded as a violation of her right to housing, the fact that it was precipitated by a discriminatory exclusion from the housing process gives rise to a derivative right for women to participate in the process. In either case, the legal interpretation of the right to housing contains language that affirms women's right to participate in the housing process as part of their broader right to housing.

The women and human settlement/shelter literature is replete with examples of women's exclusion from the design and planning stages of housing projects, particularly those that emerge in the modern, formal construction sector. For instance, in many low-income housing projects in Africa, Asia, and Latin America, future residents are not consulted in the planning or design of their new units. The UNCHS reports that this inevitably leads to inadequate housing and that as soon as residents assume ownership of the new project houses, they start to make changes: knocking down walls to make bigger rooms, constructing partitions to enclose certain areas, and building extensions to accommodate more people. In other words, the new houses are modified to meet their actual needs. As one woman who moved into a new housing project in Kenya aptly said, "'[i]nstead of putting in two bathrooms in the house, they should have provided a place to store charcoal.'"[146]

Planners, builders, and women themselves do not always recognize the crucial role that women can and do play in the building of housing in communities.[147] Women living in traditional societies pose a good example as they are principally involved in the construction and maintenance of their homes; they may plaster walls, mold bricks, pack down new mud floors, or help repair a roof. For instance, the Maasai, pastoralists in Kenya and Tanzania, give women complete control over housing. When a Maasai woman marries, her first task is to build her own house with help from other women in the homestead; throughout her life she will build a new house approximately every ten years. Once built, the house belongs to her and no one may enter without her permission. Unfortunately, as in many traditional societies, the Maasai women's role in building housing is being eroded as technology and development forces them to alter their traditional ways.[148]

The participation of women within the formal construction sector is remarkably low worldwide. High technology and imported materials in urban formal construction have removed women from a sector in which they have traditionally had a significant role.[149] The participation of women in construction is particularly low

146. UNCHS, Women in Human Settlements Development, *supra* note 93, at 25.

147. Caroline Moser, *Introduction, in* Women and Human Settlement Development, *supra* note 9, at 8.

148. Nick Hall, *Smoke Gets in Your Throat,* The New Internationalist, Feb., 1996, at 17.

149. UNCHS, Towards a Strategy, *supra* note 109, at 14.

in African countries.[150] One of the most limiting constraints on the greater participation of women in housing construction is, of course, lack of proper training, although women's construction training programs are beginning to emerge in many regions. Significantly, housing projects for women are increasingly including women's participation at the planning and implementation phases.[151]

Beyond being excluded from the planning and construction stages of the housing process, women as a group are also excluded from actively participating in community decision-making bodies (the decisions of which often have a direct impact on housing) and in housing movements. For example, in South African Transvaal rural communities, the decision-making body, the *kgotla*, is responsible for such matters as allocating land, resolving disputes, and meting out punishment for wrongdoings. Not surprisingly, women are generally excluded from regular meetings. Women are only relied upon when the community is faced with a crisis such as when apartheid government officials attempted to forcibly remove the entire Driefontein and Mogopa communities from their land. Women, threatened with eviction, fearful but angry, were often the first line of confrontation with government authorities. The pivotal role women played in such crises has made it difficult for the *kgotla* to continue to exclude women from discussions regarding the community's well-being. In fact, in Mogopa, the *kgotla* has gone so far as to accept women into its structure.[152]

Women are similarly excluded from housing rights movements. During a fact-finding mission to Kobe, Japan, in October, 1995, to assess, from a rights perspective, the housing situation of the citizens of Kobe approximately six months after the Great Hanshin Earthquake,[153] the fact-finding team visited a host of community groups as well as municipal, prefectural, and federal government officials. Overall, women's voices, experiences, and housing needs were inaudible above the roar of male community leaders and government officials. When women's voices were heard, it was either arranged by or at the request of the fact-finding mission.[154] Two years later, the citizens of Kobe had a housing rights movement that is gaining momentum. The women of Kobe are very much involved in this movement, but some of the women housing activists within the movement stated that it is a continual battle to ensure that their housing needs and rights are consistently and adequately promoted and protected.

---

150. In Korea, Singapore, Sri Lanka, and Thailand, the rate of women in construction remains relatively high.

151. *See* Irene Vance in WOMEN, HUMAN SETTLEMENTS AND HOUSING, *supra* note 9. She describes women's participation in the San Judas self-building housing project, which started as a ''bottom-up'' initiative generated largely by the women and then received government recognition of its participatory approach to house construction.

152. Kompe and Small, *supra* note 91, at 145–46.

153. The author was a participant in this fact-finding mission. *See* HABITAT INTERNATIONAL COALITION, STILL WAITING: HOUSING RIGHTS VIOLATIONS IN A LAND OF PLENTY: THE KOBE EARTHQUAKE AND BEYOND (1996).

154. At the NGO forum at *Habitat II*, women were very much included in the Kobe presentations and workshops. A woman from Kobe also testified at a public hearing on housing rights violations, which was hosted by Habitat International Coalition.

Women in Palestine have experienced similar exclusion from the growing housing rights movement in East Jerusalem. This movement is part of a larger struggle
to maintain a Palestinian presence in Jerusalem. In turn, nationalism has conquered
feminism and women's specific housing needs and rights have been trumped by
the housing rights of Palestinians as a people.

If the proponents of the right to housing take seriously the standard of nondiscrimination required by Article 2(2) of the ICESCR and paragraph 6 of General
Comment No. 4, women will move from the periphery onto center stage so that they
can participate in every aspect of the housing process, including the development of
the meaning of women's right to housing.

The Literature

Because women are often associated with "home" and "housing," a significant
amount of literature specifically on women's right to housing might be expected.
Such is not the case. Little published literature on women and the right to adequate
housing exists, and the literature developed by nongovernmental organizations is
difficult to access. Despite the lack of literature in this area, the admittedly narrow
definition of what constitutes "housing rights" literature has been adopted here,
for the purposes of this review, by limiting it to those works that explicitly refer
to the international right to housing. In turn, this literature review refers to just a
few journal publications, U.N. documents, and NGO publications from regions
with housing rights movements (Israel, East Jerusalem, Nigeria, and India (Asia)).[155]

International Literature

The international literature on the right to housing along with the NGO literature
reviewed below, has not yet adopted a gender perspective on the right to housing,
save for some of the work of the past Special Rapporteur on the right to adequate
housing, Justice Rajindar Sachar.

As demonstrated above, the issue of land and property rights is an extremely
important issue for women globally and is inextricably linked with housing rights.
Despite the fundamental importance of this issue, only one international housing

---

155. To assess the literature, the yardstick used here is the extent to which women's housing concerns,
and in particular the three housing issues just highlighted, are considered and understood in the literature.
The premise of this assessment is the understanding that women's housing experiences are largely
informed by the social construction of gender roles, and therefore, that in order for the right to housing
to be meaningful for women, the literature pertaining to the right must be capable of addressing the
structural position of women to the extent that they are subordinated. Where the review determines that
a piece fails to consider women and their constructed position within society, the author has attempted
to provide insight into how this literature might be expanded upon such that a meaningful understanding
of women's right to adequate housing emerges. For clarity's sake, this review is divided into two
sections; it begins with an assessment of what will be called the "international literature" (journal
articles by activists working at the international level and U.N. documents); it then moves on to review
the various NGO publications on the right to housing.

rights article is specifically concerned with women's land security issues: the Special Rapporteur's final report.[156]

Drawing on the work of the National Campaign for Housing Rights in India (reviewed below), the Special Rapporteur notes that in most countries women have neither a right to the home in which they were born nor to the home they live in after marriage and that this "essential homelessness" dramatically affects women's ability to participate in the housing process. The Rapporteur also notes that even in countries where inheritance laws and laws governing the right to home ownership and security of tenure have progressed, women are seldom able to exercise these rights. In turn, recognizing the broader implications of his findings regarding women and land or property rights, the Rapporteur concludes that "the most critical factor in the perpetuation of gender inequality and poverty is the continued discrimination faced by women in all matters of land and property."[157] Unfortunately, within the international literature, the Special Rapporteur's conclusion is a sole voice amidst a sea of others. Perhaps over time, his knowledge and understanding of women's housing rights will be recognized in greater depth.

The international literature is even more sparse with respect to the issue of domestic violence and housing. Although the empirical evidence about violence against women is strong and has been documented by the United Nations, it has only recently reflected in the development of international law.[158]

Despite the fact that much of the literature on women and housing discusses domestic violence as one of the most serious issues affecting women, as it stands, the only literature that directly adopts a housing rights approach to domestic violence is that from the National Campaign for Housing Rights (reviewed below).[159] This general neglect does not mean, however, that such an approach is impossible or without merit.

The international literature does not fare much better on the issue of women's participation in the housing process. It is true that much of the right to housing literature stipulates the importance of democratic participation in the realization of the right to housing. For example, General Comment No.4 paragraph 9, emphasizes that the right to participate in public decision-making is "indispensable" if the right to adequate housing is to be realized and maintained by all groups in society.[160]

---

156. Although there is a rapidly growing amount of literature on women, land, and property rights, it is rarely framed in a housing rights perspective.

157. REPORT OF THE SPECIAL RAPPORTEUR, *supra* note 45, at para. 46.

158. Charlesworth and Chinkin, *supra* note 130, at 71–72. *See also* Bunch, *supra* note 130, at 486.

159. General Comment No. 4, *supra* note 43, does not mention domestic violence, however, it does include the following troubling statement at para. 9: "Similarly, the right not to be subjected to arbitrary interference with one's privacy, family, home or correspondence constitutes a very important dimension in defining the right to housing." This could, arguably, be used by governments and individuals to defend the position that domestic situations whether they include violence or not, should remain "private" and behind closed doors.

160. General Comment No. 4, *supra* note 42, at para. 9.

Scott Leckie identifies democratic participation as central to the right. Quoting John Turner he writes:

> ... When dwellers control the major decisions and are free to make their own contributions to the design, construction or management of their housing, both the process and the environment produced stimulate individual and social well-being. When people have no control over nor responsibility for key decisions in the housing process, dwelling environments may instead become a barrier to personal fulfilment and a burden on the economy.[161]

Similarly, in a discussion pertaining to the development of an International Convention on Housing Rights, Leckie suggests that for this process to be meaningful the full participation of all sectors of all societies is required.[162]

None of the above-mentioned literature specifically calls for women's participation in the housing process. This may be because those who call for democratic participation in the housing process assume this call includes men and women alike. At this point, such reasoning should sound familiar and inadequate because it directly parallels the argument that the term ''man'' refers to both men and women, an argument already deconstructed. Given the extreme disadvantage women experience in almost every aspect of housing, gender-neutral language regarding democratic participation in the housing process is simply inappropriate. In many ''democratic'' societies, democratic participation means men's participation. For example, in Kobe, Japan, during our fact-finding mission, women were sometimes present at site visits; however, they were not always given an opportunity by their community leaders (who were always men) to speak and participate in discussions. When one community leader was asked whether women were being included in a meaningful way in the housing movement, he gave assurances that they were. Later, at the home of a feminist woman activist, it was learned that women's specific housing concerns were not being considered by the community leaders. For example, the issue of increased incidents of violence against women (a direct consequence of overcrowded housing caused by the earthquake) was being completely ignored. Apparently, the men of Kobe believed women's presence alone constituted ''participation.''

In turn, in most ''democratic'' societies, patriarchal notions of appropriate roles for women will have to be challenged at all levels—within families, communities, institutions, and government bodies—if women are to actively participate and engage in housing construction, design, policy, law, advocacy, etc. The silencing of women must end. If women's right to housing is to be realized, individual men, male-dominated communities, male-dominated governments, and male-biased housing rights advocates will have to learn that women's participation in the housing process must mean being seen, listened to, and heard. Ana Basurto, a housing rights activist in Mexico who also works at the international level, articulates

---

161. JOHN TURNER, HOUSING BY PEOPLE: TOWARDS AUTONOMY IN BUILDING ENVIRONMENTS *as cited in* Leckie, *supra* note 50, at 6.

162. SCOTT LECKIE, HOUSING RIGHTS IN THE 1990s CITIES 33, 35 (1991).

this very point by arguing that governments must ensure that women's abilities, leadership, concerns, interests, and needs arc integrated equally with those of men into all participatory processes. In this vein, Basurto states that "the democratic management of housing" is one of the key principles of the right to housing and notes that for this aspect of the right to be fully realized and meaningful, "special measures" that guarantee women equal access and full participation in the structures of power and decision making must be adopted.[163]

NGO Literature

With the exception of one book regarding evictions from Asia and one document from India, the other available NGO publications fail to recognize that women have distinct housing needs/rights and that women's specific housing issues are obscured or rendered invisible. In turn, the structural disadvantage women experience in society generally and in the home more specifically, is largely ignored. And so, rather than an assesssment of these women-deficient works in terms of the three particular housing concerns of women identified earlier, a short overview of each publication and a brief critique on the omission of women's housing experiences in these works has been provided.

Israel, East Jerusalem, and Nigeria

In 1996, three NGO reports on the right to adequate housing emerged. *Housing For All? Implementation of the Right to Adequate Housing for the Arab Palestinian Minority in Israel*,[164] prepared for and submitted to the Committee in May, 1996, provides a thorough overview of the housing, living, health, and environmental conditions of the Palestinian minority living inside Israel, including those living in "mixed" cities (where Arabs and Jews live together), unrecognized Arab villages, and Arab Bedouin townships. *Living in Jerusalem: An Assessment of Planning Policy, Housing and Living Conditions in Light of the Palestinians' Right to Adequate Housing*,[165] also submitted to the Committee for consideration in May, 1996, documents the implementation of Israeli planning policy and the state of housing and living conditions of Palestinians living in East Jerusalem. The most recent publication comes from the Shelter Rights Initiative in Lagos, Nigeria, and is entitled, *Study on the Right to Adequate Housing in Nigeria*.[166] This booklet argues that civil and political rights will remain inadequate unless they are supported by socio-economic rights that define the concrete living conditions of most Nigerians. The booklet is an attempt to begin to develop basic materials that explain, in a

---

163. ANA BASURTO, THE RIGHT TO SHELTER: PRINCIPLES, POLICIES AND INSTRUMENTS 69, 77 (1996). *See also* DECLARATION AND PROGRAM OF ACTION OF THE WORLD SUMMIT ON SOCIAL DEVELOPMENT, Chapter IV, Social Integration, para. 70(1)–(11).

164. The Arab Coordinating Committee on Housing Rights (ACCHRI)(1996)[hereinafter *Housing for All*].

165. Palestine Housing Rights Movement (PHRM)(1996)[hereinafter *Living in Jerusalem*].

166. Shelter Rights Initiative (1996)(Nigeria).

user-friendly manner, economic rights. To this end, the author focuses on the right to housing, tracing its origins in Nigeria from the colonial to the post-colonial period and compares the sources of Nigerian law with international legal standards. The piece then concludes with recommendations on how to better protect the right to housing.

There is no doubt that each of these works is an important contribution to the development of the international right to housing and will be used by these NGOs in their national or regional housing rights movements. *Housing for All,* for example, is an important work in that it offers unique information and insights into the housing and living conditions of a minority population in Israel often forgotten or overlooked: Palestinian Arabs. *Housing in Nigeria* is also a important work in the area of economic and social rights and the right to housing as it provides a concise but cogent guide to the history of Nigeria's housing rights legislation, some of the fundamental tenets of the international right to adequate housing as it exists today, and the status of Nigerian housing law in relation to international legal standards.

The central weakness in these reports is their unanimous failure to identify, discuss, or make recommendations with respect to the housing needs and rights of women, even when it would seem logical or natural to do so. For example, in a section of *Housing for All* entitled, "Internal Environment of the Home,"[167] while the young and elderly are identified as groups that are particularly vulnerable to housing inadequacies, the authors neglect to mention the impact that these same conditions have on women's everyday lives. Similarly, in its overview on health in the Arab sector, health is regarded as a gender-neutral concept and women's specific health concerns and issues, including their experiences of domestic violence, for example, are not mentioned.[168] In *Living in Jerusalem*, the demolition of Palestinian homes is reported as one of the primary housing rights violations suffered by this population. Though the report includes a section on the social and economic consequences of house demolition, women's experiences of this violation are not mentioned. This is surprising, given that activists generally regard house demolition as a housing rights violation that is particularly detrimental to women who must cope with the practical, economic, social, and psychological implications of this type of forced eviction.[169]

The complete omission of women's housing experiences from each of these reports is most disappointing when viewed in light of the fact that, in claiming the

---

167. *Housing for All, supra* note 164, at 74.

168. *Id.* at 66–73.

169. *Living in Jerusalem, supra* note 165, at 44. The report does include one case study where a girl who was living in a tent because her family home had been demolished was the victim of an attempted rape. While this case study is an important acknowledgment, the structural, gender-biased context within which such incidents occur is not discussed. For the effects of house demolition on women, *see* NASREEN CONTRACTOR AND MILOON KOTHARI, PLANNED SEGREGATION: RIOTS, EVICTIONS AND DISPOSSESSION IN JOGESHWARI EAST, MUMBAI/BOMBAY, INDIA (1996); DENIS MURPHY (Urban Poor Associates); MINAR PIMPLE (Asian Coalition for Housing Rights), EVICTION WATCH ASIA: FORCED EVICTIONS AND HOUSING RIGHTS ABUSES IN ASIA (1995)(reviewed).

right to housing for its people, each report relies (disingenuously) upon the Women's Convention (which secures the right to housing for rural women) as an example of an international convention that imposes legal obligations on states to uphold the right to housing.[170] Therefore, these reports simply utilize the Women's Convention instrumentally, that is, simply for its codification of the right to housing rather than to support *women's* right to housing.[171]

The *Jerusalem Declaration, A Draft Charter of the Palestine Housing Rights Movement,*[172] is annexed to *Living in Jerusalem.* The Declaration adopts a clear gender perspective, stating at the outset that the right to housing means the "right of every *woman,* man and child to a place to live in dignity and security".[173] Additionally, under its "Plan of Action," the Declaration goes on to stipulate that one of its four guiding principles is to empower all Palestinians by promoting democratic processes that enable all people, "especially women," to participate fully and actively in decisions affecting their housing and community.[174] Similarly, *Housing in Nigeria* includes as an appendix the *Draft International Convention on Housing Rights,* an example of a convention that, if adopted, would enrich the essence of the right to housing and lead to a better articulation of the legal force

---

170. Shelter Rights Initiative, *supra* note 166, at 1(fn); *Living in Jerusalem, supra* note 165, at 5; *Housing for All, supra* note 164, at 7.

171. Why does this contradiction arise? Is it because when first claiming the right to housing within a region, the actual content of the documents relied upon is less important than the symbolic value of the document? Is it because none of these regions are culturally or politically ripe to admit that women's human rights are as important as those of men? The real answer to this question is difficult to determine. Probably the fact that each report refers to and relies upon at least one document that codifies the right to housing for women indicates that these three regions are, in fact, not very far from adopting a gender-perspective on the right to housing. This "hunch" is supported by the fact that as the ACCHRI's work develops in Israel, Palestinian women's needs and rights are being considered in a serious manner. Having made its submissions to the Committee on Economic, Social and Cultural Rights and the Minority Rights Working Group at the U.N. and having actively participated at *Habitat II,* the ACCHRI has now turned its attention to the human rights of Palestinian women living in Israel, launching the Women's Human Rights Project for 1997. Additionally, it seems that a number of women are actively involved in the East Jerusalem housing rights movement, and they made significant contributions at the NGO Forum at *Habitat II.* Similarly, Shelter Rights Initiative recently released a report entitled, Update on Women's Socio-Economic Rights In Nigeria (Housing, Labour, Education and Violence Against Women) (unpublished, 1997) that details the status of women's economic, social, and cultural rights in Nigeria. This report adopts a critical perspective on women's position in Nigerian society and includes a general overview of women's housing conditions. In particular, this report identifies the following housing issues as being of particular concern to Nigerian women: access to child care services, availability of services, materials, facilities, and infrastructure, access to housing for single women and female-headed households, ownership and inheritance of land, and access to credit and participation in decision-making processes that shape the development of human settlements. The findings of this report will be submitted as part of an NGO parallel report to the Committee; Nigeria will be reviewed by the Committee at its 18th session in May 1998. For further information on women's living and housing conditions in Nigeria, please contact Shelter Rights Initiative, Gender Action Project, Bank Chambers, Anambra House, 27/29 Martins Street (3rd Fl.), Lagos; Telefax: 266.1947.

172. *Living in Jerusalem, supra* note 165, at Annex I, p. 52 [hereinafter the Declaration].

173. *Id.* (emphasis added).

174. *Id.* at 54.

of this right. Notably, the draft convention stipulates at Article 3 on gender equality, that "[t]he housing rights of men and women shall, in every respect, be equal in law and in practice."[175]

Asia and India

Although this chapter has not discussed the issue of forced evictions as a gross violation of women's right to housing, a brief review of *Eviction Watch Asia: Forced Evictions and Housing Rights Abuses in Asia*[176] is instructive; it is one of only two publications on the right to housing that genuinely incorporates women and their housing experiences within its text.

Eviction Watch Asia is an initial report of the Asian Coalition for Housing Rights that documents the numbers as well as the social and economic repercussions of evictions across Asia.[177] From a women's rights perspective, this report is both refreshing and groundbreaking for, unlike other texts, it includes several case studies on female victims of eviction, photographs of women and their living conditions post-eviction, and references to the particularly harmful effects of eviction and the threat of eviction on women. Moreover, rather than risk marginalizing women's experiences by confining them to an obscure part of the text or relegating them to the appendix, *Eviction Watch Asia* incorporates women's experiences into the body of the text throughout the various regional reviews. Obviously, the experiences of women are most prominent in those sections of the report pertaining to regions where women are particularly active in the area of housing rights (e.g., the Philippines and India).

The only troubling aspect of *Eviction Watch Asia* is that it is unclear upon what theoretical framework, beyond international law, the Coalition bases its understanding and acceptance of women's right to housing and their complementary right to be free from forced evictions. For example, on a number of occasions the report states that forced evictions cause suffering particularly to women or that evictions hurt women most of all. Without a clearly articulated theoretical framework, it is difficult to determine *why* eviction affects women more severely than men. A theoretical framework would help determine why women are most affected by eviction and this answer would, in turn, determine how to adequately protect women's right to housing and their right to be free from forced evictions. Given the current focus on women within the Coalition's work, perhaps as it develops and grows, a more solid theoretical framework will emerge.

The literature from the National Campaign for Housing Rights (NCHR) in India addresses women's right to housing both theoretically and practically and, at this

---

175. Shelter Rights Initiative, *supra* note 166, at 49.

176. EVICTION WATCH ASIA: FORCED EVICTIONS AND HOUSING RIGHTS ABUSES IN ASIA (1995)(*see book review*)[hereinafter EVICTION WATCH ASIA].

177. The report examines practices in: Bangladesh, Burma, Cambodia, China, Hong Kong, Indonesia, India, South Korea, Malaysia, Nepal, Pakistan, Papua New Guinea, Philippines, and Thailand.

point, certainly stands as a model as to how women's housing rights can be included in a broader housing rights movement.

The NCHR, an independent coalition of organizations and individuals from several states in India, is a nationally oriented campaign that recognizes that housing is a basic right for all—a right to a secure place to live in peace and dignity.[178] The campaign compiled a long list of conditions that are essential to the realization of the right to adequate housing. Among these conditions were several that directly address women's housing conditions such as: democratically constituted organizations of dwellers for creating appropriate conditions for equal or majority participation by women; free and safe movement in public spaces at any time of the day or night, especially for women; and special meeting places for women.[179] In its attempts to develop a "People's Bill of Housing Rights" in the 1980s, the NCHR also produced four approach papers and one, entitled *Humanising Housing in India Today: Report of the NCHR National Workshop on Gender and Housing*,[180] focused on women and housing. The workshop on which the approach paper was based identified four categories particularly pertinent to women and housing: 1) basic building design, technology, planning, zoning, and essential conditions of housing; 2) domestic violence, security, peace, dignity, and status of women in patriarchal society; 3) property rights, ownership, and power relations between men and women; and 4) production of life, child care, women and work, environment, and ecology.

The frank manner in which the NCHR reports that women's intolerable living conditions are directly related to patriarchy is refreshing and provides a useful framework and perspective that may assist in the full realization of women's housing rights. The report notes the relationship between patriarchy, capitalism, class, and religion as central impediments to women's housing rights:

> It is important to understand that the struggle for women's right to housing cannot successfully be waged without acknowledging that the deterioration of the housing situation under capitalism is shaped not only by property relations expressed in class but also property and social relations expressed in patriarchy. The power relationship of patriarchy up to a point precedes class and is reinforced and strengthened by class, caste and religious forces throughout history. . . . Patriarchy . . . curtails women's access to property[,] . . . curtails women's legal rights and their access to self expression and self-organization by cultural controls like education, media ideologies, religion, health system and other institutions. In fact, women's class allegiance has to be redefined by not subsuming women under the class of their male relatives automatically but by placing women themselves, in their access to property, their position in the production process and access to cultural self expression. [181]

---

178. NCHR, THE HOUSING RIGHTS BILL 1 (1992).

179. Scott Leckie, *The UN Committee on Economic, Social and Cultural Rights and the Right to Adequate Housing: Towards an Appropriate Approach*, 11 HUM. RTS. Q. 522, 528–29 (1989).

180. NCHR (1987) (unpublished).

181. *Id.* at 18.

Although the participants in the workshop did not explicitly discuss the right to adequate housing as codified in the ICESCR, they clearly adopt a rights approach to the issue of housing for women. The women participants demonstrate sophisticated insight into the systemic and structural discrimination that women in Indian society now face and how that discrimination is at the foundation of women's relationship to housing and land. The workshop participants were clear that patriarchal capitalism contributes to women's essential homelessness and is the means by which women are denied the basic human right to housing.

Beyond the theoretical, the NCHR includes insightful discussions on the practical issues that face women in their relationship with housing. Like the Special Rapporteur's report, the NCHR report concludes that for women to have genuine housing security, capitalistic and patriarchal power relations must be dismantled and, for this to occur, women must be granted full ownership rights because traditional legal security of tenure and joint ownership would not meet this goal. As the NCHR sees it, this means that women's land security must be regarded as distinct from men's and that laws, policies, and actions that specifically address women's "essential homelessness" must be undertaken.

The NCHR then goes even further with its analysis of women's lack of security, linking women's essential homelessness with the issue of domestic violence. According to its report, the NCHR regards the relationship between domestic violence and housing rights as two-pronged. First, domestic violence is an infringement of women's right to security (of tenure) within the home, and second, domestic violence is caused or exacerbated by adverse housing and living conditions. In other words, domestic violence is itself a violation of women's right to housing and at the same time other housing rights violations, such as women's essential homelessness, subject women to domestic violence. Developing a relationship between domestic violence and housing rights is both a unique and progressive approach to this fundamental form of oppression experienced by women.

The efforts of the NCHR working group have proved very effective and their success is reflected not only in the continued active involvement of women in the housing rights movement but also in The Preamble of the *Final Draft of the Housing Rights Bill* that emerged from the NCHR in 1992, which states:

> [I]t is the essential obligation of the state to guarantee conditions for women to adequately house themselves under all circumstances and to devise housing programmes to meet the specific needs of disadvantaged women, in terms of exclusive use of home, access to credit, home based employment, maternal and child welfare. . .[182]

While the literature on women's right to housing is sparse, with women in India and other parts of Asia exposing women's housing conditions and highlighting the connection between these conditions and patriarchal social structures that oppress

---

182. NCHR, *supra* note 178, at 1.

women, in conjunction with the strengths of the *Habitat Agenda*, it may be that an international right to housing for women is emerging.

CONCLUDING REMARKS AND VISIONS

At this point, there should be little doubt that, if the international right to housing is to be meaningful for women, it is not only appropriate but also necessary that the right be based on women's actual experiences and perspectives.

Though there is a paucity of literature in the area of women's housing rights, the existing texts, used in conjunction with the work being done to improve the living and housing conditions of women globally, lay a solid foundation on which to build. This chapter has attempted to outline this foundation by exposing that, in most societies, the relationship between men and women is structured so that women are subordinate to men. The practical consequences of this imbalanced and oppressive structure is seldom more apparent than in women's housing and living conditions. It is this structure that is at the root of women's worldwide poverty and women's disadvantage in respect of the ownership of land or property, domestic violence, and women's exclusion from active participation in the housing process. In turn, to develop a meaningful women's right to housing, the overarching goal must be to eradicate women's structural or systemic oppression. For instance:

> In those regions of the world with existent or burgeoning housing rights movements such as Palestine, Tibet, Japan, Thailand, the Philippines, India, Mexico, or Nigeria, activists must ensure that women's specific interests, needs and rights are protected and promoted. In many of these places women already play the central role in fighting for housing rights (particularly in resisting evictions and house demolition); [183] it is time that this role is recognized, legitimized, and reflected with the inclusion of women in every aspect of the housing process at the grassroots, national and international levels.

There are two ways in which a women's perspective can be included in a housing movement: women can be included within the housing movement as a whole (as a disadvantaged group that requires particular attention), or a separate but parallel women's housing movement can be established alongside that of the men. The former option may only be an effective strategy if the relationship between men and women within the housing movement does not mirror that of the broader society where women are in fact subordinate to men. Because it is difficult to ensure that the dominant social structure worldwide that defines women as men's subjects does not rear its head within the social housing rights movement, it may be more effective to adopt the latter alternative where women initiate their own parallel housing rights movement. This segregation of men and women may not be ideal; however, women's political and social aims in a housing rights movement may be very different from those of men or other groups. Women have a vested

---

183. *See* Somporn Surarith, *supra* note 6, at 15–16 (Thailand); EVICTIONS WATCH ASIA, *supra* note 169, at 84 (Philippines).

interest in altering social relationships and relieving their own housing disadvantage, an interest that is not shared (and is in fact actively resisted) by many men.

Activists and academics must continue to document and record women's experiences at all stages of the housing process. Where resources permit, women's stories must be recorded in women's voices and statistically sound data must be collected, summarized, and written in report form so that it is accessible to the public, the media, and United Nations officials.

NGOs and CBOs that work with women in those regions of the world with existing or burgeoning housing rights movements must learn more about the U.N. system and how it can work to protect women's right to housing. More particularly, women's NGOs and CBOs and those that work with women must be encouraged to submit reports, and representative women must make oral submissions to the Committee on Economic, Social and Cultural Rights regarding the violations of the right to housing as experienced by women.

These same women and those who work closely with U.N. bodies must lobby the Committee to ensure that women's economic rights, including the right to housing, are actually enforceable because unenforceable rights are illusory rights. Energies must be focused on establishing effective enforcement mechanisms for economic, social, and cultural rights. This can be achieved, at least in part, by lobbying the Committee to adopt an optional protocol. National or domestic litigation efforts that demonstrate the justiciability of economic rights may help to influence the Committee in this direction. And so, lawyers litigating in the area of economic rights worldwide must network, exchange, and make public information regarding novel litigation in the area of economic and social rights, effective legal strategies, claimants' experiences before and during the litigation process, and any innovative or creative means used to enforce economic rights.

In this same vein, at the domestic or national level, lawyers and activists must continue or begin to litigate cases pertaining to the protection and enforcement of all economic rights, including women's right to housing. Although a legal victory does not always result in a social victory, that is, an actual change on-the-ground, it may in fact be one small but formidable step toward changing social reality.

Housing rights activists worldwide must publish articles in international human rights journals and periodicals that expose the housing rights violations experienced by women. Activists who are familiar and affiliated with the U.N. system must also use their experience and influence to ensure that the Committee is devoted to the development of a clear definition and relevant indicators of housing rights violations against women.

As a result of activist lobbying, the Committee recently issued a General Comment on Forced Evictions. With similar lobbying efforts, over time, the Committee may be persuaded to issue a General Comment regarding women and their social and economic rights, including the right to housing.

Lastly, in order that a rich and thoughtful definition of women's right to housing emerges, women's housing concerns, needs, and problems must be fully recognized and understood. Beyond receiving reports from housing rights activists from different regions throughout the world in this regard, this understanding can also be reached if housing rights activists and those working in the area of women and human settlements/shelter work cooperatively, develop a network, and regularly exchange and disseminate information and insights.

Clearly these are just some of the steps that could be taken at the international and domestic levels to immediately actualize women's right to housing and to begin to solve women's global oppression where it most often occurs: in the home.

NOTE

At its 50th session the United Nations Sub-Commission on the Prevention of Discrimination and Protection of Minorities, a UN human rights body, adopted its second resolution on women and the right to land, property and adequate housing. Resolution 1998/15 is an important achievement in the area of women's rights because women's relationship to land, property and housing is placed unequivocally in a human and equality rights framework. Moreover, the Resolution offers a broad definition of the types of remedies that might be required to address violations of women's rights to land, property and housing, recognizing that, in some instances, formal equality (treating men and women the same) may not be sufficient and that there may be situations that require the adoption and enforcement of laws and policies designed to address women's specific situation.

Beyond the employment of a human rights framework, this resolution is significant as it draws a link between land, property and housing and women's economic disadvantage by recognizing women's central position in the informal economy and thus the fundamental role that land, property and housing play in women's economic livelihood. Resolution 1998/15 is also important for noting that women's inadequate housing and living conditions can contribute to, cause and are often the result of violence against women. In so doing, the Sub-Commission acknowledges that women's social and economic rights (not just civil and political rights) may be implicated in violence against women.

WOMEN AND RELIGIOUS FUNDAMENTALISM*

Courtney W. Howland

INTRODUCTION

Religions have traditionally promoted, or even required, differentiated roles for women and men. It may well be argued that any separation of gender spheres is detrimental to women's equality. However, there is no need to address this broad question in the context of religious fundamentalism, whose rise in all major religions has been accompanied by a vigorous promotion and enforcement of gender roles whose explicit intent entails the subordination and disempowerment of women.

Religious fundamentalism poses the most acute problems for women's equality, but many conservative religious groups share substantial areas of doctrine with the fundamentalists. The two groups are often differentiated solely by the political activism of fundamentalists rather than by significantly different religious beliefs. This political activism throws into sharp relief the conflicts between rights of religious freedom and women's rights of liberty and equality.

The first section of this chapter defines "religious fundamentalism" and discusses the contemporary rise of religious fundamentalism in Buddhism, Christianity, Hinduism, Islam, and Judaism. A common goal of these movements is to pass state laws that reflect religious laws. There is a special concern with family laws and personal status laws, which have a particularly strong impact on women.

The second section focuses on a particular doctrine of fundamentalists common to the five religions that well illustrates their goal of subordinating women: a wife is required to submit to the authority of her husband. This doctrine requires, either explicitly or implicitly, that a wife is to be obedient to her husband. The obedience rule legitimates the husband's discipline of his wife and thus makes women vulnerable to physical abuse. Fundamentalist modesty codes help to reinforce the oppressive aspect of the obedience law. Moreover, the obedience law, subordinating in and of itself, also serves as a basic norm justifying a variety of religion-specific discriminatory rules.

---

*   A slightly different version of this chapter first appeared as an article, entitled "The Challenge of Religious Fundamentalism to the Liberty and Equality Rights of Women: An Analysis under the United Nations Charter," in the Columbia Journal of Transnational Law, 35 COLUM. J. TRANSNAT'L L. 271 (1997).

The third section analyzes religious fundamentalist laws under the United Nations Charter (Charter)[1] and The Universal Declaration of Human Rights (Universal Declaration).[2] The Charter is the foundational treaty for international law and provides a paradigm for the analysis of the conflicts within international human rights laws raised by religious fundamentalist laws. This chapter argues that the text of the Charter itself makes clear that the entitlement to human rights is not to be determined by any religious law and that race, sex, and religious discrimination must be treated equally. It further demonstrates that the international community has already resolved the conflict between racial discrimination and religious freedom under the Charter, and also under the Universal Declaration, and that the same standard must apply to the conflict between sex discrimination and religious freedom. In addition, these assertions are applied to a completely new area through arguments that states violate the Charter by asserting religious fundamentalist doctrine as a basis for entering general reservations to provisions in human rights treaties that uphold women's rights. It concludes that a state that enacts into its legal system religious laws that subordinate women, or that creates under state law a zone of autonomy for religion to impose such religious laws upon women, is in violation of the Charter. Suggestions are made as to how the international community should treat states in violation of the Charter.

CONTEMPORARY RELIGIOUS FUNDAMENTALISM

The use of the term "fundamentalism" to describe a religious movement evokes high emotion.[3] Whatever the preferred term, however, the movement thus identified is an important reality recognized by women from many diverse backgrounds and religions throughout the world. The term "religious fundamentalism" is particularly meaningful for many religious women as representing a movement within religion that they understand to be oppressive of women.[4] Women have recognized

---

1.   United Nations Charter, June 16, 1945, 59 Stat. 1031, T.S. No. 993, 3 Bevans 1153 [hereinafter U.N. Charter].

2.   The Universal Declaration of Human Rights, G.A. Res. 217A (III), U.N. GAOR, 3rd Sess., pt. 1, at 71, U.N. Doc. A/810 (1948) [hereinafter Universal Declaration].

3.   The term has sometimes been used pejoratively to describe religious activism by some religious group other than the writer's group. *See* John S. Hawley & Wayne Proudfoot, *Introduction, in* FUNDAMENTALISM & GENDER, 1, 18, 19 (John S. Hawley ed., 1994). It has particularly been used to fuel anti-Muslim sentiments. *See* Gita Sahgal & Nira Yuval-Davis, *Introduction: Fundamentalism, Multiculturalism and Women in Britain, in* REFUSING HOLY ORDERS 1, 3 (Gita Sahgal & Nira Yuval-Davis eds., 1992).

4.   Religious women fighting fundamentalism come from a wide variety of religions and races and many of them lay stress on their cultural origins and attachments. Although an outsider's critique of a religion and culture may well be as valid as that of an insider, most of these religious women generally confine their critique to their own respective religion and culture and so do not raise the issue of outsider critique. Religious women may analyze fundamentalist groups as violating their own religious norms of dignity and respect as well as Western norms. Thus, it is improper to dismiss them—as some fundamentalists are wont to do—as representing only a Western, white, or Christian perspective. *See infra* notes 5, 6, 23, 25, and accompanying text. Indeed, a number of the women find themselves in the dilemma of wanting to fight both the West and fundamentalism. *See infra* notes 6, 23. The fact that women from different religions, perspectives, and a great variety of cultures recognize these religious

the phenomenon and movement of fundamentalism and have formed groups around the world specifically to fight fundamentalism.[5] For example, Women Against Fundamentalism is a group composed of Catholics, Protestants, Hindus, Sikhs, Muslims, and Jews, all of various origins (Afro-Caribbean, English, Asian, Indian, Iranian, Irish, and others) whose activities are aimed at curbing fundamentalism across a wide range of religions and countries.[6]

Acting in a quite different context, academic scholars too have observed the modern phenomenon defined as religious fundamentalism. Some scholars have expressed concern or given apologias about defining the phenomenon of fundamentalism cross-culturally or using the term "fundamentalism" itself (instead preferring other terms[7]). Nonetheless, there has developed an extensive academic discipline that uses the term, even if uneasily, because these scholars have "felt the cumulative force of a series of 'family resemblances' as [they] move from one militantly antimodern religious group to another, tradition by tradition, and culture by culture."[8] These family resemblances have prompted scholars to endeavor to set out

movements as detrimental to women demonstrates that this recognition is cross-cultural and supports the cross-cultural legitimacy of defining and critiquing fundamentalism.

5. *See* Sahgal & Yuval-Davis, *supra* note 3, at 8–9, 16–25 (discussing strong link between fundamentalist movements and women's oppression which has caused women to establish organizations in many countries to fight fundamentalism).

6. The women who write for Women Against Fundamentalism include not only scholars but a school teacher, journalist, novelist, filmmaker, activist, and political exiles. *See* REFUSING HOLY ORDERS, *supra* note 3, at 16–25, 236–37. The group also includes many other women with whom these women have worked, and whom they include in their writings. Other such groups include Women Living Under Muslim Laws (WLUML), which is an international network linking women in different Muslim countries to exchange information and to fight against women's discrimination that has increased under fundamentalism, *see* Marie A. Hélie-Lucas, *Women Living Under Muslim Laws, in* OURS BY RIGHT 52–64 (Joanna Kerr ed., 1993), and Jyoti Mhapasekara's group of drama activists in India which takes a strong stand against religious fundamentalism, *see* Katherine K. Young, *Women in Hinduism, in* TODAY'S WOMAN IN WORLD RELIGIONS 77, 91 (Arvind Sharma ed., 1994).

7. Some scholars and political leaders, from various religions, have proposed other terms, but these have their own drawbacks. Other terms that have been suggested include "obscurantism," "extremism," "renaissance," and "revivalism." "Obscurantism" and "extremism" seem inherently more pejorative than "fundamentalism," and are less exact ("obscurantism" does not suggest the militant antimodern religious *activism* characteristic of fundamentalism and "extremism" acknowledges the activism but not the religious ideology and political theory underpinning it). "Renaissance," on the other hand, aims to be an unqualified approving term of fundamentalism and its usage usually demonstrates a desire to avoid any critical analysis. "Revivalism" fails to capture the substantive nature of *how* the religion is being "revived" in this contemporary phenomenon: by a backward historical glance to "fundamentals" expressed in simplified, easy-to-understand, easy-to-relate to, easy-to-emote about terms. Thus, as the editors of The Fundamentalism Project conclude, "[n]o other coordinating term was found to be as intelligible or serviceable. And attempts of particular essayists to provide distinctive but in the end confusing accurate alternatives led to the conclusion that they were describing something similar to what are here called fundamentalisms." Martin E. Marty & R. Scott Appleby, *Introduction: The Fundamentalism Project: A User's Guide, in* 1 THE FUNDAMENTALISM PROJECT: FUNDAMENTALISMS OBSERVED vii, viii (Martin E. Marty & R. Scott Appleby eds., paperback ed. 1994) (1991) [hereinafter *Introduction*, FUNDAMENTALISMS OBSERVED]. For all these reasons, "fundamentalism" remains a preferable, if problematic, choice.

8. Hawley & Proudfoot, *supra* note 3, at 5; *see Introduction*, FUNDAMENTALISMS OBSERVED, *supra* note 7, at ix (discussing apologias of scholars and "family resemblances" of fundamentalisms).

definitional criteria[9] and determine the various sociological causes and effects of the phenomenon.[10] These scholars come from a variety of religions, races, and nations[11] and work in various disciplines.[12]

Although these two groups (religious women engaged in political struggle and academic scholars) are not always explicit or precise in defining fundamentalism, an analysis of their work shows plainly that the two groups generally agree on the broad criteria that define a religious group as fundamentalist. These are that the group: believes that the group and society need to be rescued from the secular state;[13] rejects Enlightenment norms, particularly individual rights and secularism;[14] is committed to the authority of ancient scripture;[15] holds a total worldview such that

9.   Scholarly definitions derive from the first use of the term by a branch of American Protestantism that emerged at the turn of the century to defend militantly the strict maintenance of traditional, orthodox beliefs against liberalizing trends. The group members referred to themselves as "fundamentalists" by virtue of their commitment to what they termed the "five fundamentals" of their religion. See Hawley & Proudfoot, *supra* note 3, at 11–15; MARGARET L. BEDROTH, FUNDAMENTALISM AND GENDER: 1875 TO THE PRESENT 3–4 (1993); Sahgal & Yuval-Davis, *supra* note 3, at 3. For a discussion of the criteria used by scholars to define religious fundamentalism, see *infra* notes 13–21 and accompanying text.

10.   For examples, see Hawley & Proudfoot, *supra* note 3, at 19–35; *Introduction*, FUNDAMENTALISMS OBSERVED, *supra* note 7, at vii–x; Martin E. Marty & R. Scott Appleby, *Conclusion: An Interim Report on a Hypothetical Family, in* 1 THE FUNDAMENTALISM PROJECT: FUNDAMENTALISMS OBSERVED, *supra* note 7, at 814, 816 [hereinafter *Conclusion,* FUNDAMENTALISMS OBSERVED]; BRUCE B. LAWRENCE, DEFENDERS OF GOD: THE FUNDAMENTALIST REVOLT AGAINST THE MODERN AGE 106–19 (1989); STUDIES IN RELIGIOUS FUNDAMENTALISM 14–20 (Lionel Caplan ed.,1987). Also, the individual essays and articles that comprise THE FUNDAMENTALISM PROJECT, and which are cited in this chapter, discuss how the definition of fundamentalism is applied to specific religious groups.

11.   For example, in most cases in the several volumes of THE FUNDAMENTALISM PROJECT, the author is from the nation or religious tradition about which he (or in a few cases, she) is writing, and some are in sympathy with fundamentalism. See Martin E. Marty & R. Scott Appleby, *Introduction, in* 3 THE FUNDAMENTALISM PROJECT: FUNDAMENTALISM AND THE STATE 1, 5 (Martin E. Marty & R. Scott Appleby eds., 1993) [hereinafter *Introduction,* FUNDAMENTALISM AND THE STATE]. The scholar may not be a fundamentalist, but that does not necessarily mean that the scholar's critique is wholly Western. Marty and Appleby thus have no basis for regarding the participants in THE FUNDAMENTALIST PROJECT as "resolutely of the Western Academy," *see id.* at 5 & n.7. Possibly they are, incorrectly, assuming either that only the Western Academy is capable of tolerance or that any capacity within a culture for critique of its own norms must derive from Western Enlightenment thought.

12.   The disciplines of the scholars writing for THE FUNDAMENTALISM PROJECT include, *inter alia,* anthropology, economics, history, philosophy, political science, sociology of religion, and theology.

13.   For this criterion as part of religious women's definition, see Sahgal & Yuval-Davis, *supra* note 3, at 7–8, and as part of academic definition, see Hawley & Proudfoot, *supra* note 3, at 16–17, 19.

14.   For this criterion as part of religious women's definition, see Sahgal & Yuval-Davis, *supra* note 3, at 7–8, and as part of academic definition, see Hawley & Proudfoot, *supra* note 3, at 16; *Introduction,* FUNDAMENTALISMS OBSERVED, *supra* note 7, at vii.

15.   This criterion is of course applicable only within religious traditions based on scripture. For this criterion as part of religious women's definition, see Sahgal & Yuval-Davis, *supra* note 3, at 3–5, and as part of academic definition, see Hawley & Proudfoot, *supra* note 3, at 13, 14, 20–21; *Conclusion,* FUNDAMENTALISMS OBSERVED, *supra* note 10, at 820; Lionel Caplan, *Introduction, in* STUDIES IN RELIGIOUS FUNDAMENTALISM, *supra* note 10, at 14–20; Gideon Aran, *Jewish Zionist Fundamentalism, The Bloc of the Faithful in Israel (Gush Emunim), in* 1 THE FUNDAMENTALISM PROJECT: FUNDAMENTALISMS OBSERVED, *supra* note 7, at 265, 305.

religious beliefs are inseparable from politics, law, and culture;[16] relies on an ideal-ized past;[17] is selective in drawing from the past for religious traditions and orthodox practice;[18] centers that idealized past in a patriarchal framework mandating separate gender spheres and a "pristine morality";[19] rejects outsiders and the concept of pluralism;[20] and is committed to activism and fighting for changed social, political, and legal order.[21]

Fundamentalism thus defined exists within many religions, ethnic groups, and countries, and takes different forms within these various contexts.[22] Nevertheless,

---

16. For this criterion as part of religious women's definition, see Sahgal & Yuval-Davis, *supra* note 3, at 4, 7; Hélie-Lucas, *supra* note 6, at 53, and as part of academic definition, see *Introduction,* FUNDAMENTALISMS OBSERVED, *supra* note 7, at ix; Rhys H. Williams, *Movement Dynamics and Social Change: Transforming Fundamentalist Ideology and Organizations, in* 4 THE FUNDAMENTALISM PROJECT: ACCOUNTING FOR FUNDAMENTALISMS 785, 793, 802 (Martin E. Marty & R. Scott Appleby eds., 1994); *see also* John H. Garvey, *Fundamentalism and American Law, in* 3 THE FUNDAMENTALISM PROJECT: FUNDAMENTALISMS AND THE STATE, *supra* note 11, at 28, 38, 39.

17. This criterion falls within religious women's criteria of selectivity and reliance on the patriarchal framework. *See infra* notes 18, 19. For this criterion as part of academic definition, see Martin E. Marty & R. Scott Appleby, *Introduction, in* 4 THE FUNDAMENTALISM PROJECT: ACCOUNTING FOR FUNDA-MENTALISMS, *supra* note 16, at 1 [hereinafter *Introduction,* ACCOUNTING FOR FUNDAMENTALISMS]; Haw-ley & Proudfoot, *supra* note 3, at 16; *Introduction,* FUNDAMENTALISMS OBSERVED, *supra* note 7, at ix; *see also* Lawrence, *supra* note 10, at 106–19; Robert E. Frykenberg, *Accounting for Fundamentalisms in South Asia: Ideologies and Institutions in Historical Perspective, in* 4 THE FUNDAMENTALISM PROJECT: ACCOUNTING FOR FUNDAMENTALISMS, *supra* note 16, at 591, 594 [hereinafter Frykenberg, *Accounting for Fundamentalisms*].

18. For this criterion as part of religious women's definition, see Sahgal & Yuval-Davis, *supra* note 3, at 3–4; Hélie-Lucas, *supra* note 6, at 53; and as part of academic definition, see Hawley & Proudfoot, *supra* note 17, at 13; *Introduction,* ACCOUNTING FOR FUNDAMENTALISMS, *supra* note 17, at 1; *Introduction,* FUNDAMENTALISMS OBSERVED, *supra* note 7, at ix.

19. For this criterion as part of religious women's definition, see Sahgal & Yuval-Davis, *supra* note 3, at 8, and as part of academic definition, see Hawley & Proudfoot, *supra* note 3, at 25–35; Caplan, *supra* note 15, at 14–20; Hava Lazarus-Yafeh, *Contemporary Fundamentalism—Judaism, Christianity, Islam,* 47 JERUSALEM Q. 27, 37 (1988). For noting fundamentalist endorsement of "pristine morality," see Hawley & Proudfoot, *supra* note 3, at 20, 26–35; *Introduction,* FUNDAMENTALISMS OBSERVED, *supra* note 7, at ix; Caplan, *supra* note 15, at 14–20.

20. For this criterion as part of religious women's definition, see Sahgal & Yuval-Davis, *supra* note 3, at 4, and as part of academic definition, see Hawley & Proudfoot, *supra* note 3, at 13, 19–20; *see also Introduction,* FUNDAMENTALISMS OBSERVED, *supra* note 7, at x; Frykenberg, *Accounting for Fundamentalisms, supra* note 17, at 594, 596; *Introduction,* ACCOUNTING FOR FUNDAMENTALISMS, *supra* note 17, at 1–2; Jay M. Harris, *"Fundamentalism": Objections from a Modern Jewish Historian, in* FUNDAMENTALISM & GENDER, *supra* note 3, at 137, 138–40 (arguing against use of term "fundamental-ism" while acknowledging that a criterion of scholars' definition of term is rejection of pluralism).

21. For this criterion as part of religious women's definition, see Sahgal & Yuval-Davis, *supra* note 3, at 4, and as part of academic definition, see Hawley & Proudfoot, *supra* note 3, at 16, 20–21, 30; *Introduction,* FUNDAMENTALISM AND THE STATE, *supra* note 11, at 2; *Introduction,* FUNDAMENTALISMS OBSERVED, *supra* note 7, at ix; Frykenberg, *Accounting for Fundamentalisms, supra* note 17, at 594. The aim is "to replace existing structures with a comprehensive system emanating from religious principles and embracing law, polity, society, economy and culture . . . [and] contains within it a totalitar-ian impulse." *Conclusion,* FUNDAMENTALISMS OBSERVED, *supra* note 10, at 824. Scholars may list additional criteria, but those criteria listed in text are regarded as the most critical.

22. Thus, it is not claimed that the existence of some "pure" form of fundamentalism "totally

these fundamentalist movements share in common the feature that they are effecting political, legal, and social changes that are highly detrimental to women's rights. For most academic writers, this is merely one aspect of the general political activism that characterizes the movement. However, women, and especially religious women, engaged in political struggle against the movement emphasize that the central aim of its social and political activism is to restrict women to a narrowly defined role and exercise control over them within the patriarchal family structure.[23] They also see fundamentalism's militant activism in changing social and legal structures of society as inextricably linked with its appeal to selected traditional beliefs encompassing separate-spheres ideology for men and women.

It might be argued that a definition of fundamentalism that focuses on the group's reliance on historical patriarchal doctrine fails to distinguish fundamentalism from "conservative" religion, and even from religion in general. The major religions emerged and developed in patriarchally structured societies, and their texts and traditions are imbued with patriarchy and with treating women unequally in various contexts.[24] Although this argument has intuitive and logical appeal, it

---

differentiated from other forms of culture and independent of all social institutions." *Conclusion,* FUNDA-
MENTALISMS OBSERVED, *supra* note 10, at 817.

23.   *See supra* notes 4, 5, 21 and accompanying text; Lazarus-Yafeh, *supra* note 19, at 37 (arguing that factors in definition of "fundamentalism" are fundamentalist attitudes about gender roles and fundamentalists' rejection of legal changes that would ensure equality of women); Sahgal & Yuval-Davis, *supra* note 3, at 8; *see also* Hélie-Lucas, *supra* note 6, at 52–56. In Buddhism, *see* Helen Hardacre, *Japanese New Religions: Profiles in Gender, in* FUNDAMENTALISM & GENDER, *supra* note 3, at 111, 113, 129 [hereinafter Hardacre, *Japanese New Religions*] (discussing how Japanese new religions hold traditional patriarchal family as sacred and under attack). In Christianity, *see* DAPHNE HAMPSON, THEOLOGY AND FEMINISM 6, 9–11 (1990) (discussing how Christianity and Judaism are rooted in patriarchal historical past). In Hinduism, *see* Gita Sahgal, *Secular Spaces: The Experience of Asian Women Organizing, in* REFUSING HOLY ORDERS, *supra* note 3, at 163, 176–77, 180, 187–90 (discussing how Hindu fundamentalism draws nostalgically on historic epics of patriarchy). In Islam, *see* Hélie-Lucas, *supra* note 6, at 54 (discussing how fundamentalist Islam is promoting version of Islam based on a centuries-old way of life that subordinates women). An Iranian woman in exile states "Fundamentalism is about absolute control over the female body and mind. It is about segregation and exclusion of women. The regime in Iran is founded on sexual apartheid . . . ." Maryam Poya, *Double Exile: Iranian Women and Islamic Fundamentalism, in* REFUSING HOLY ORDERS, *supra* note 3, at 141, 159 (quoting Alma Gharehdaghi). Iranian women are one of the largest group of political exiles living in Britain. These women worked against the regime of the Shah, but then needed to escape Iran after the fundamentalist regime attacked women's rights. See Sahgal & Yuval-Davis, *supra* note 3, at 1–4, 8–11, 18–25; Hélie-Lucas, *supra* note 6, at 52–54. In Judaism, *see* Pnina N. Levinson, *Women and Sexuality: Traditions and Progress, in* WOMEN, RELIGION AND SEXUALITY 45, 46, 60 (Jeanne Becher ed., First Trinity Press Int'l 1991) (1990) (discussing that for fundamentalist Jews religious values are based on historical tradition which upholds separate-spheres gender ideologies).

24.   *See* Harris, *supra* note 20, at 163–64 (rejects concept of fundamentalism in Judaism by implicitly arguing that women have always been subordinate in Judaism and so there is no difference between so-called fundamentalist Judaism and religious Judaism); Mary E. Becker, *The Politics of Women's Wrongs and the Bill of Rights: A Bicentennial Perspective,* 59 U. CHI. L. REV. 453, 458–79 (1992) (arguing that sexism and patriarchy pervade Christianity and Judaism, such that Freedom of Religion clause as currently interpreted subordinates women); Nira Yuval-Davis, *Jewish Fundamentalism and Women's Empowerment, in* REFUSING HOLY ORDERS, *supra* note 3, at 198, 223 (discussing Jewish feminist theologians, Judith Plaskow and Gail Chester, who argue that removing patriarchal bias from Judaism is impossible and feminism is inherently incompatible with religion); Hampson, *supra* note 23,

igiiores the experience of many religious women who have suffered under fundamentalism and fought to resist it. Fundamentalism is real and has meaning for numbers of religious women from different religions and countries who experience it as a very real threat to their freedom and often their lives. These women perceive themselves to be religious despite their resistance to fundamentalist trends within their religion, and may perceive themselves to be feminists despite the intensity of their religious belief.[25]

Scholars generally rely on the militant activism of fundamentalism to distinguish it from "conservative" or "traditional" religion. Fundamentalists fight in and against society for political, social, and legal changes, through the legal and political system or by means of violence, whereas traditional conservative groups appear more passive in accepting the political and legal structures of society.[26] Indeed, fundamentalists have often critiqued the traditional conservatives of their respective religions for not being sufficiently involved in activist political ideology and militant action.[27] Nonetheless, there will be groups that are difficult to characterize clearly

---

at 6, 9–11 (arguing that equality of women is incompatible with Christianity because Christianity is rooted in patriarchal historical past, and since Christianity and Judaism share history it is also incompatible with Judaism). Thus, no matter how much the religion is "reformed" it will retain its patriarchal bias as part of its defining ethos. *See also* HAMPSON, *supra* note 23, *passim.*

25. *See* HAMPSON, *supra* note 23, at 32–41 (arguing that feminist Christian theologians' struggle for critical feminist re-readings of scriptures operate as apologetics and the only justification must be that they want to remain and be named Christians); *see, e.g.,* REFUSING HOLY ORDERS, *supra* note 3, *passim* (discussing how majority of authors continue to be Catholic, Hindi, Jewish, Muslim, Protestant and are opposed to fundamentalism within their religions); Deniz Kandiyoti, *Women and Islam: What are the Missing Terms?, in* WOMEN LIVING UNDER MUSLIM LAWS, *DOSSIER* 5/6, at 5, 8 (Dec. 1988–May 1989) (arguing that critique of inherent patriarchal nature of Islam is no longer a useful analytical tool when Islam varies so much, but aim should rather be to fight Islamic laws that subordinate women); Rajni Kothari, *Fundamentalism is Not Essence of Hinduism,* ILLUSTRATED WEEKLY OF INDIA, Dec. 7–13, 1986, at 16 (arguing that Hinduism was complex network of interrelated groups and notion of majoritarian fundamentalist group is alien to Hinduism); THE JEWISH WOMAN: NEW PERSPECTIVES, *passim* (Elizabeth Koltun ed., 1976) (all contributors to this work are religious and are attempting to reform Judaism to incorporate feminist principles); *see also* Becker, *supra* note 24, at 469–74 (discussing why women are attracted to Christianity and Judaism despite sexism of both religious doctrines).

26. *See* Hawley & Proudfoot, *supra* note 3, at 12; *Introduction,* FUNDAMENTALISMS OBSERVED, *supra* note 7, at ix–x.

27. For examples of fundamentalists taking this position, see Mumtaz Ahmad, *Islamic Fundamentalism in South Asia: The Jamaat-i-Islami and the Tablighi Jamaat of South Asia, in* 1 THE FUNDAMENTALISM PROJECT: FUNDAMENTALISMS OBSERVED, *supra* note 7, at 457, 463 (discussing Jama'at-i-Islami's criticisms of conservative *ulama*); Aran, *supra* note 15, at 265, 314 (describing Gush Emunim's criticism of religious establishment for not being sufficiently political activist); William D. Dinges, *Roman Catholic Traditionalism and Activist Conservatism in the United States: 1. Roman Catholic Traditionalism, in* 1 THE FUNDAMENTALISM PROJECT: FUNDAMENTALISMS OBSERVED, *supra* note 7, at 66, 67, 72, 74–75 (describing Catholic fundamentalist movements and political actions of CTM, ORCM and Society of St. Pius X in their critique of Roman Catholicism's Second Vatican Council, which they perceive as promoting a loss of Catholic hegemony in social and political sphere); James Hitchcock, *Roman Catholic Traditionalism and Activist Conservatism in the United States: 2. Catholic Activist Conservatism in the United States, in* 1 THE FUNDAMENTALISM PROJECT: FUNDAMENTALISMS OBSERVED, *supra* note 7, at 101, 103–09 (discussing how conservative Catholic activism—his term for fundamentalism—rejects supreme legislative authority of Second Vatican Council).

as fundamentalist or conservative.[28] To avoid this problem groups in each religion that are generally agreed to be fundamentalist rather than merely conservative. However, the fact that the groups are clearly fundamentalist does not prevent their legal doctrine overlapping with the doctrine of conservative groups.

Throughout this chapter fundamentalist doctrine and the legal and political acts that fundamentalists perform are discussed. No attempt is made to interpret or rely on any of the primary religious texts, revelatory texts, or sacred myths of the religions as religious theology.[29] Nonfundamentalist religious groups may argue that fundamentalism misinterprets the religious texts or doctrines, or even that it wrongly asserts nonreligious views as religious doctrine, but these internal theological disputations are irrelevant to this analysis. The point is that religious fundamentalists believe in and assert their interpretations as religious doctrine, and raise claims of religious freedom for their actions based upon these doctrines.

RELIGIOUS FUNDAMENTALIST LAWS REQUIRING THE OBEDIENCE OF WOMEN

In this section, the focus is on a particular religious fundamentalist legal norm that will be called the "obedience rule." This states that a wife is required to submit to the authority of her husband—to be obedient to her husband. In addition to being subordinating in and of itself, this rule serves as a basic general norm justifying a variety of religious rules that limit women's independence and autonomy, and ensure women's subordinate position to men.

Attention is focused on this rule of obedience for two main reasons: first, the rule is such a gross manifestation of the subordination of women that there can be little good faith argument that the rule promotes the equality of women; and second, the effect of the rule on women's lives is profound because it ramifies into laws regarding education and employment. Thus, the obedience rule serves as a clear example of a rule designed to maintain women in a subordinate position, and as

---

28. A group may shift from one category to the other. Scholars have noted how a conservative group may experience a sense of besetment and beleaguerment that propels it into political militant action, transforming it into a fundamentalist group. See Hawley & Proudfoot, *supra* note 3, at 21–23; *Introduction*, FUNDAMENTALISMS OBSERVED, *supra* note 7, at ix; *cf.* Harris, *supra* note 20, at 160–61. However, the group may still rely on conservative religious legal norms as the base for its political and social activism.

29. The sources for this are: first, the writings of fundamentalists; second, the writings of scholars who have studied fundamentalisms from different disciplinary perspectives including anthropology, economics, history, philosophy, political science, and sociology; third, religious women fighting fundamentalism who have experienced fundamentalism firsthand; and fourth, religious conservatives and reformers who are cognizant of fundamentalist positions on certain matters. Unfortunately, much fundamentalist writing is not available in translation or is difficult to obtain, forcing reliance on secondary sources. Despite this obstacle, such an overall survey is important in order to highlight the structural similarities of oppression between movements despite their very different contexts.

such it brings the conflict between rights of religious freedom and women's rights of equality and liberty into sharp relief.

The first part of this section discusses in general the subordinating aspect of a relationship founded on obedience. The second part is divided into five sections discussing fundamentalism within five major religions: Buddhism, Christianity, Hinduism, Islam, and Judaism.

Women's Religious Duty of Submission and Obedience to Men

Religious fundamentalist legal structures regard women's sexuality as potentially evil and destructive of men.[30] The legal structures of fundamentalist marriage and divorce and modesty codes[31] serve as enforcement mechanisms to maintain women's chastity and control their sexuality. The principle underlying these structures is that women are to be submissive to men in general, and in particular that a wife must submit and be obedient to her husband.

In a fundamentalist regime, girls first learn obedience to their fathers[32] and marriages may be arranged for them at a young age in order to protect their chastity.[33] The marriage ceremony or marriage contract gives the husband the right to his wife's submission and obedience.[34] Moreover, her obligation to submit and obey is also regarded as her own duty of religious practice and worship. If she disobeys her husband, she is thus guilty of a double violation: of her husband's right to her obedience and of her own religious duties.

The obedience rule means that a husband has the right of sexual access to his wife at any time, the final say in reproductive decisions, the right to forbid his wife to work, and the right to forbid his wife to continue her education. A wife's submission to her husband has no time limit, but continues through the rest of her life. Moreover, it is generally legitimate for men to enforce the obedience rule

---

30. *See infra* notes 48 (Buddhism); 75 (Christianity); 121 (Hinduism); 158–60 (Islam); 207, 224 (Judaism).

31. Modesty codes require the segregation of women from men in general, and demand that women stay primarily in their homes, act modestly, and dress with their entire body covered. *See infra* notes 133 (Hinduism); 170, 178, 195–201 (Islam); 224–30 (Judaism); *see also infra* notes 54 (Buddhism); 87 (Christianity).

32. *See infra* notes 50 (Buddhism); 82 (Christianity); 123 (Hinduism); 166, 179 (Islam); 210 (Judaism) and accompanying text.

33. *See infra* notes 49 (Buddhism); 125 (Hinduism); 158 (Islam); 208 (Judaism) and accompanying text; *see also* UNITED NATIONS, HARMFUL TRADITIONAL PRACTICES AFFECTING THE HEALTH OF WOMEN AND CHILDREN, FACT SHEET No. 23, at 17 (Aug. 1995).

34. *See infra* notes 50–51, 55, (Buddhism); 81–86, 88–90 (Christianity); 129–32, 134 (Hinduism); 164–69, 178–85 (Islam); 215–20 (Judaism) and accompanying text.

through physical punishment. As a result, women may be subject to beatings and physical violence for disobedience. The obedience rule places a crippling physical burden on women. Under religious fundamentalist doctrine there is general insistence on the hierarchical relations between women and men, with men having a divine mandate to exercise authority over women with little restriction.

Fundamentalists do not deny that women have fewer rights than do men under the obedience rule. Some argue that this structure is appropriate because women are inferior.[35] Others, often in response to international disapproval of a doctrine of inferiority of women and to claims of religious women that religious fundamentalism is not treating them equally, have argued that women and men are equal before the deity but have natural and different—rather than unequal—rights and duties under religious law.[36] According to this latter argument, the entire religious fundamentalist social structure justifies women having fewer rights in certain areas, including the obedience rule. Thus, fundamentalists claim that a wife's duty of submission and obedience is an equal exchange for the duty of "protection" that her husband owes to her, in the form of an obligation to provide basic material and financial support—food, shelter, and clothing.[37] Wives are assigned the role of having children and caring for them in the private sphere of home, while the public sphere of employment and government belongs to men.

This "protection," however, does not alleviate the wife's subordination, but rather enhances it by increasing her financial dependence on her husband, making her more vulnerable in the event of divorce or widowhood. This is particularly dangerous in this fundamentalist context, where it is generally much easier for a husband than a wife to obtain a divorce.[38] In addition, the wife may lose her right to maintenance during marriage or be divorced if she is disobedient or "rebellious."[39] Thus, if women do not obey their husbands' wishes, their very survival is

---

35. *See, e.g., infra* notes 53 (Buddhism); 80 (Christianity); 148–49 (Hinduism) 164 (Islam) and accompanying text.

36. *See infra* notes 81 (Christianity); 164 (Islam) accompanying text; KHURSHID AHMAD, FAMILY LIFE IN ISLAM 17, 34–35 (6th prtg. 1993) (1974) (Islam); SAFIA IQBAL, WOMAN AND ISLAM LAW i–ii, viii, xi, 17–18, 98–134 (rev. ed. 1991) (Islam); Yuval-Davis, *supra* note 24, at 213, 217 (Judaism); Frances Raday, *Israel—The Incorporation of Religious Patriarchy in a Modern State, in* 4 INT'L REV. OF COMP. PUB. POL'Y 209, 211 (1992) (Judaism); Paula Hyman, *The Other Half: Women in the Jewish Tradition, in* THE JEWISH WOMAN, *supra* note 25, at 105, 108–09 (Judaism).

37. *See infra* notes 57–61 (Buddhism); 78, 85–86 (Christianity); 112 (Hinduism); 184–85 (Islam); 211–12 (Judaism) and accompanying text.

38. *See infra* notes 61–62 (Buddhism); 93 (Christianity); 151–53 (Hinduism); 191 (Islam); 215–20 (Judaism) and accompanying text. In some fundamentalist regimes, divorce is simply not permitted. *See infra* notes 99–100 (some Christian groups) and accompanying text.

39. *See infra* notes 88 (Christianity); 181–90 (Islam); 215, 218–20 (Judaism); *see also* notes 61 (Buddhism); 134–38 (Hinduism) and accompanying text.

in danger.[40] The wife is particularly vulnerable in the event of the husband's death, as she is unlikely to have accumulated any property during her child-bearing years because of her dependence upon her husband, and is also unlikely to have any training to be able to earn wages. Some fundamentalist structures will not permit her to work in any event. If she is lucky, she may become dependent upon a son or other male relative, to whom she now owes her duty of submission.

Fundamentalists' substantive arguments fail to provide a credible defense for the obedience rule, and fail to demonstrate that the obedience rule supports women's equality or is necessary for women's equality. It is thus difficult to credit these *ad hoc* different–but-equal arguments with good faith because they support the same hierarchy of relations between genders as is supported by traditional fundamentalist (and conservative) religious doctrines that, in turn, are explicitly based on the natural inferiority of women.[41]

Five Major Religions

The following five subsections deal with the respective religious contexts of Buddhism, Christianity, Hinduism, Islam, and Judaism. In each subsection, the first part identifies the fundamentalist religious-legal doctrine concerning the obedience rule and the second part reviews the success of the political activity of fundamentalists in conforming the law in their respective states to their religious-legal doctrine.

Buddhism

Buddhist fundamentalism is found in several parts of the Buddhist world.[42] This

---

40.   *See* Shahla Haeri, *Obedience versus Autonomy: Women and Fundamentalism in Iran and Pakistan, in* 2 The Fundamentalism Project: Fundamentalisms and Society 181, 187 (Martin E. Marty & R. Scott Appleby eds., 1993).

41.   For example, in Christianity, Thomas Aquinas, who is regarded by many as the normative theologian of the Roman Catholic Church, viewed women as inferior. *See* Rosemary R. Ruether, *Catholicism, Women, Body and Sexuality: A Response, in* Women, Religion and Sexuality, *supra* note 23, at 221, 222; Uta Ranke-Heinemann, Eunuchs for the Kingdom of Heaven: Women, Sexuality, and the Catholic Church 157, 183–84, 188–90 (Peter Heinegg trans., 1990). Aquinas taught that women were defective human beings, morally, mentally and physically, supporting their subordination to men. Hampson, *supra* note 23, at 16–17; Ruether, *supra*, at 222–23; Ranke-Heinemann, *supra*, at 183–200. His clear doctrine of women's inferiority would now meet with international disapproval, but "present Catholic teaching attempts to retain the conclusions of Thomas's thought without his premises." Ruether, *supra*, at 224; *see infra* notes 72, 81. In Islam, traditional fundamentalist rhetoric found women to be inferior due to their mental and physical inferiority, *see infra* notes 162–67 and accompanying text, and recent arguments that support the same roles for women as equal but different are also founded on women's physical and mental inferiority. *See, e.g.,* Iqbal, *supra* note 36, at 98–134. In Judaism, *see infra* note 209.

42.   Fundamentalist groups exist in Theravada Buddhism, Mahayana Buddhism, and the New Religions of Japan. The primary sources for Buddhist fundamentalism are generally limited, particularly because of the paucity of translations available. Further links need to be established with women fighting Buddhist fundamentalism in order to publicize fundamentalist policies.

subsection deals primarily with fundamentalist movements in Theravada Buddhism[43] in Sri Lanka[44] and Thailand,[45] and in the New Religions of Japan.[46]

The Religious-Legal Doctrine

Various fundamentalist groups support notions of a traditional family and morality that, in turn, serve as the basis for separate roles and spheres of activities for women and men.[47] A central doctrine underlying separate-spheres ideology is that

43. Theravada Buddhism takes different forms in various countries, but relies heavily on traditional conservative Buddhist doctrine. Modern Theravada groups in Thailand and Sri Lanka share characteristics that have led to the characterization of movements within those countries as fundamentalist. Donald K. Swearer, *Fundamentalistic Movements in Theravada Buddhism, in* 1 THE FUNDAMENTALISM PROJECT: FUNDAMENTALISMS OBSERVED, *supra* note 7, at 628, 633; *see generally* RICHARD H. ROBINSON & WILLARD L. JOHNSON, THE BUDDHIST RELIGION: A HISTORICAL INTRODUCTION 3 (Wadsworth, Inc., 3d. ed. 1982) (1970)(discussing traditional Theravada Buddhism).

44. Sri Lanka's contemporary Buddhist fundamentalism finds its roots in an early twentieth-century revival movement in reaction against British colonialism. Stanley J. Tambiah, *Buddhism, Politics, and Violence in Sri Lanka, in* 3 THE FUNDAMENTALISM PROJECT: FUNDAMENTALISMS AND THE STATE, *supra* note 11, at 589, 590, 603–04; Swearer, *supra* note 43, at 636. The person mainly responsible for this movement, Dharmapala, reinterpreted Buddhist spiritual ideas into a program designed to restore Sinhalese pride and to emphasize a puritanical sexual morality and etiquette of family life. *See* Tambiah, *supra*, at 590; Swearer, *supra* note 43, at 637, 649; *see* RETURN TO RIGHTEOUSNESS: A COLLECTION OF SPEECHES, ESSAYS AND LETTERS OF ANAGARIKA DHARMAPALA 108–110, 227, 234, 317–22 (Ananda Guruge ed., 1965) [hereinafter RETURN TO RIGHTEOUSNESS]. He appealed selectively to the Pali Chronicles, which portray Sri Lanka as an island sanctified by Buddha himself and ruled by just kings who defended Buddhism against evil forces, particularly the Tamils. Swearer, *supra* note 43, at 647; Tambiah, *supra*, at 590; James Manor, *Organizational Weakness and the Rise of Sinhalese Buddhist Extremism, in* 4 THE FUNDAMENTALISM PROJECT: ACCOUNTING FOR FUNDAMENTALISMS, *supra* note 16, at 770, 772. His support for a Sinhalese Buddhist state led him to reject the idea of a secular state or a pluralist state tolerating Christianity, Hinduism, and Islam. Dharmapala's ideas and rhetoric continue to form a major part of the foundation of Buddhist fundamentalism.

Buddhist fundamentalism in Sri Lanka is evident in the political activist group, Janata Vimukti Peramuna (JVP), a Buddhist revival movement involved in the killings and violent conflicts with Tamil Hindus. Swearer, *supra* note 43, at 645. The JVP was banned in Sri Lanka in 1983, but it continues to operate under the cover of other organizations and includes members of political parties, members of the *sangha* (Buddhist monks), and individual lay Buddhist activists. *See* Tambiah, *supra*, at 608, 611–12, 615.

45. An example of a Buddhist fundamentalist group in Thailand is the Thai Theravada Buddhist group of Wat Dhammakaya ("Dhammakaya"). *See* Swearer, *supra* note 43, at 666, 667; Charles F. Keyes, *Buddhist Economics and Buddhist Fundamentalism in Burma and Thailand, in* 3 THE FUNDAMENTALISM PROJECT: FUNDAMENTALISMS AND THE STATE, *supra* note 11, at 367, 394. Dhammakaya is estimated to have more than a million adherents and continues to grow rapidly. Keyes, *supra*, at 394. Dhammakaya intends to create a new unity between national, religious and personal identity, thus renewing Thailand as a Buddhist state. Swearer, *supra* note 43, at 658, 660, 665–66; Keyes, *supra*, at 394. The group manifests intolerance to other perspectives on Buddhism, *see* Keyes, *supra*, at 395, and has been associated with the "militant, reactionary political group," the Red Guards, who justify the killing of communists because they are "less than human." *See* Swearer, *supra* note 43, at 666; Keyes, *supra*, at 393.

46. The New Religions of Japan are derived primarily from Buddhism and Shintoism and are estimated to include one-fourth to one-third of the Japanese people. Hardacre, *Japanese New Religions, supra* note 23, at 113–14. There are over 3,000 New Religions, but this section relies primarily on three

women are unable to control their dangerous sexuality which is potentially destructive of men.[48] To deal with this problem, marriages are arranged for women at young ages before their chastity is in danger,[49] at which point they enter the realm of their husband's authority. According to traditional doctrine, embraced in Theravada movements, every woman must bear three kinds of subordination: "to her father when young, to her husband while married, and to her son when old."[50] In the New Religions of Japan, "[w]omen are urged to be meek and submissive and to build up the husband's ego by performing elaborate gestures of deference and respect, simultaneously indicating self-effacement and humility on their part."[51] Thus, being a good wife and mother is not only the proper role for women, but is imbued with religious significance.[52] The New Religions unabashedly assert men's superiority over women: "[i]t's men who are superior, and the women who are behind all the trouble in the world."[53] Modesty codes also require that a woman have humility in all things, particularly in relation to men.[54]

The doctrine of a woman's submission and obedience to her husband goes beyond rhetoric; it is enforced by the threat and reality of sanctions. A woman who does not conform to this approved role may experience stigmatization and

---

particularly successful fundamentalist groups that have roots in Buddhism: Soka Gakkai, Seicho no Ie, and Reiyukai Kyodan. *See* Hardacre, *Japanese New Religions, supra* note 23, at 113–14; Winston Davis, *Fundamentalism in Japan: Religious and Political, in* 1 THE FUNDAMENTALISM PROJECT: FUNDAMENTALISMS OBSERVED, *supra* note 7, at 782, 797, 799, 801; *see also* EDWIN O. REISCHAUER, JAPAN: THE STORY OF A NATION 309 (1970); William Dawkins, *Anti-Religious crusade holds political message,* FIN. TIMES, Sept. 23/24, 1995, at 3. The religions are significantly entwined with political parties and emphasize the convergence between national identity and religion. *See* Hardacre, *Japanese New Religions, supra* note 23, at 127–32.

47. *See* RETURN TO RIGHTEOUSNESS, *supra* note 44, at 32, 180–81, 345, 346; Hardacre, *Japanese New Religions, supra* note 23, at 118–22, 127.

48. Traditional Buddhism, as followed by fundamentalists, regards women as temptresses. *See* DIANE Y. PAUL, WOMEN IN BUDDHISM: IMAGES OF THE FEMININE IN MAHAYANA TRADITION 3–5, 51 n.8, 52 (2d. ed. 1985).

49. The New Religions of Japan "tend to favor arranged marriages." HELEN HARDACRE, KUROZUMIKYO AND THE NEW RELIGIONS OF JAPAN 190 (1986) [hereinafter HARDACRE, KUROZUMIKYO]; *see* Hardacre, *Japanese New Religions, supra* note 23, at 111, 123–24 (finding that New Religions encourage women to marry at young age and have numerous children). In the new religion of Reiyukai, 69% of families are from arranged marriages. HELEN HARDACRE, LAY BUDDHISM IN CONTEMPORARY JAPAN 60 (1984) [hereinafter HARDACRE, LAY BUDDHISM].

50. RITA M. GROSS, BUDDHISM AFTER PATRIARCHY: A FEMINIST HISTORY, ANALYSIS, AND RECONSTRUCTION OF BUDDHISM, 42 & n.* (1993); Women's Information Centre, *Shelter for Battered Women in Thailand, in* THIRD WORLD/SECOND SEX (vol. 2) 205, 208 (Miranda Davies ed., 1987).

51. HARDACRE, LAY BUDDHISM, *supra* note 49, at 47; *see* HARDACRE, KUROZUMIKYO, *supra* note 49, at 190 (noting that women are required, subject to censure, to defer to men).

52. Hardacre, *Japanese New Religions, supra* note 23, at 119.

53. *See id.* at 111 (quoting sermon of religious leader).

54. *See id.* at 119. Even in the few Buddhist sects that allow for nuns, the nuns must wear fivefold robes, while monks wear only three robes. Nancy J. Barnes, *Women in Buddhism, in* TODAY'S WOMAN IN WORLD RELIGIONS, *supra* note 6, at 137, 141.

devaluation. Moreover, violence to enforce obedience to the husband is also a constant threat. In Thailand, for example, where many people consider that "a husband is entitled to 'discipline' his wife," battered women often believe that their situation is due to bad "karma," in accordance with the Buddhist belief that the accumulation of good or bad deeds in the past may influence one's present life.[55] Fundamentalists are also concerned that as a woman's economic independence increases, she will be less committed to the patriarchal family.[56] Consequently, they regard employment outside the home as interfering with her role as wife and mother. Thus, the requirement that wives submit to husbands has the additional impact of limiting a woman's earning possibilities.

Political Activity to Conform State Law to Religious-Legal Doctrine

A great deal of fundamentalist political activity is devoted to maintaining and enlarging the requirement of women's submission. A number of the Japanese New Religions are lobbying to bring back the *ie* model of patriarchal family life by reinstating the relevant parts of the prewar Meiji Civil Code.[57] The *ie* model of family consisted of the "househead, wife-of-househead, successor, successor's wife, and the unmarried children of the successor generation."[58] The eldest male was the head of the family, and normally he was succeeded by his eldest son. The househead had authority over all *ie* property.[59] Women could not own real property other than in very exceptional circumstances, and any other property a woman brought to the marriage belonged to her husband for him to dispose of without her consent.[60] Men could divorce women for, among other reasons, adultery or failure to produce a male child and the divorced wife had no automatic entitlement to financial assistance.[61] Women could only initiate divorce under rare circumstances (not including adultery).[62] The husband obtained custody of children as members of his *ie*.[63] The Meiji Civil Code also strictly forbade contraception and education about contraception.[64] The repeal of the Meiji Civil Code brought many legal reforms for women in the areas of marriage, divorce, and property, and consequently increased their power in postwar Japan.[65] A number of the New Religions desire to reverse these reforms.[66]

---

55. Women's Information Centre, *supra* note 50, at 206–07. A random sampling of Bangkok women in 1985 found that half of them had experienced physical violence and abuse. *Id.* at 207.

56. *See* Hardacre, *Japanese New Religions, supra* note 23, at 124.

57. *Id.* at 118–19, 131; Davis, *supra* note 46, at 794, 803.

58. Hardacre, *Japanese New Religions, supra* note 23, at 121.

59. *Id.* at 120.

60. *Id.* at 121.

61. *Id.*

62. *Id.*

63. *Id.*

64. *See id.* at 121, 129.

65. *Id.* at 119–22.

66. *Id.* at 118–19, 131.

Christianity

Fundamentalisms in Christianity exist in traditional branches such as the Roman Catholic Church (RCC), the Orthodox Church, and Protestantism, and have also developed in other Christian sects or off-shoots.[67] The vast array of Christian fundamentalist groups is spread over strikingly diverse geographic locations: from the United States to Latin and Central America, and from Britain to India.[68] Examples are drawn from this wide range of Christian fundamentalist groups with particular emphasis on fundamentalist groups within American Protestantism,[69] such as sect fundamentalists[70] and

---

67. For a discussion of Mormon fundamentalism, see D. Michael Quinn, *Plural Marriage and Mormon Fundamentalism*, in 2 THE FUNDAMENTALISM PROJECT: FUNDAMENTALISMS AND SOCIETY, *supra* note 40, at 240. For a discussion of Pentecostals and Rastafarians, see Diane J. Austin-Broos, *Pentecostals and Rastafarians: Cultural, Political, and Gender Relations of Two Religious Movements*, 36 SOC. & ECON. STUD. (no.4) 1 (1987).

68. *See, e.g.*, David Stoll, *"Jesus is Lord of Guatemala": Evangelical Reform in a Death-Squad State*, in 4 THE FUNDAMENTALISM PROJECT: ACCOUNTING FOR FUNDAMENTALISMS, *supra* note 16, at 99; Jorge E. Maldonado, *Building "Fundamentalism" from the Family in Latin America*, in 2 THE FUNDAMENTALISM PROJECT: FUNDAMENTALISMS AND SOCIETY, *supra* note 40, at 214; Elaine Foster, *Women and the Inverted Pyramid of Black Churches in Britain*, in REFUSING HOLY ORDERS, *supra* note 3, at 45; Steve Bruce, *Fundamentalism, Ethnicity, and Enclave*, in 3 THE FUNDAMENTALISM PROJECT: FUNDAMENTALISMS AND THE STATE, *supra* note 11, at 50 (Northern Ireland); Susan Bayly, *Christians and Competing Fundamentalisms in South Indian Society*, in 4 THE FUNDAMENTALISM PROJECT: ACCOUNTING FOR FUNDAMENTALISMS, *supra* note 16, at 726.

69. Protestant fundamentalism has its roots in American Protestant groups that emerged at the turn of the century and identified themselves as fundamentalists. *See supra* note 9.

70. In the 1940s and 1950s American Protestant fundamentalism split, with one segment, led by Billy Graham, thereafter describing itself as "evangelical." The rest, led by such individuals as Carl McIntire and Bob Jones, continued to describe themselves as "fundamentalists." *See* Laurence R. Iannaccone, *Heirs to the Protestant Ethic? The Economics of American Fundamentalists*, in 3 THE FUNDAMENTALISM PROJECT: FUNDAMENTALISMS AND THE STATE, *supra* note 11, at 342, 345; Nancy T. Ammerman, *North American Protestant Fundamentalism*, in 1 THE FUNDAMENTALISM PROJECT: FUNDAMENTALISMS OBSERVED, *supra* note 7, at 1, 4 [hereinafter Ammerman, *North American Protestant*]. The term "sect fundamentalism" is used here to describe groups of Christians who define themselves as fundamentalists after the split, and follow the doctrine and beliefs (as evolved) of the original fundamentalists. (Correspondingly, the term "sect evangelical" describes groups that have evolved from evangelicals after the split.) The term "fundamentalism" without qualification is used as elsewhere in this chapter, and subsumes the fundamentalisms of both sect evangelicals and sect fundamentalists. *See* Iannaccone, *supra*, at 343, 344 & n.7; Robert Wuthnow & Matthew P. Lawson, *Sources of Christian Fundamentalism in the United States*, in 4 THE FUNDAMENTALISM PROJECT: ACCOUNTING FOR FUNDAMENTALISM, *supra* note 16, at 18, 24.

An example of a sect fundamentalist group is Jerry Falwell's ministry and Moral Majority, Inc. organization. *See* JERRY FALWELL, LISTEN AMERICA! 258 (1980); Ammerman, *North American Protestant, supra*, at 43. Although Falwell officially disbanded the Moral Majority in 1989, it was absorbed into his Liberty Federation group. *See* Iannaccone, *supra*, at 346 n.19. Falwell identifies himself as a sect fundamentalist, and his groups and associated organizations all meet the definition of fundamentalism. *See* Iannaccone, *supra*, at 344, 346; Ammerman, *North American Protestant, supra*, at 43–49; Wuthnow & Lawson, *supra*, at 26; Garvey, *supra* note 16, at 28, 29, 32. These organizations (with other Christian fundamentalist groups too numerous to mention) are collectively referred to as the New Christian Right (NCR) of which Falwell is a major spokesman. *See* Ammerman, *North American Protestant, supra*, at 43, 44; Iannaccone, *supra*, at 346; *see also* Garvey, *supra* note 16, at 32.

Reconstructionists,[71] and from fundamentalist groups within the RCC.[72] The RCC groups rely heavily on traditional conservative doctrine, with some groups fully endorsing RCC interpretations of doctrine.[73]

The Religious-Legal Doctrine

Many of these various Christian fundamentalist groups perceive Western culture to be in a desperate state because of the decline of what they perceive to be the basic unit of society, the "traditional family."[74] They regard women's sexuality as potentially dangerous and destructive of men.[75] Fundamentalists look back with

71. Reconstructionists clearly meet the definition of fundamentalism. *See* Ammerman, *North American Protestant, supra* note 70, at 53–55; Iannaccone, *supra* note 70, at 349; Wuthnow & Lawson, *supra* note 70, at 46. The two main Reconstructionist leaders are Rousas Rushdoony and his son-in-law, Gary North. *See* Ammerman, *North American Protestant, supra* note 70, at 49–50; Iannaccone, *supra* note 70, at 348. Their theological foundation is Calvinist, Ammerman, *North American Protestant, supra* note 70, at 50, and their central ideological claim is that "Christians are called by God to exercise dominion," and to spread their gospel to all nations. *See* GARY NORTH, THE THEOLOGY OF CHRISTIAN RESISTANCE 60 (1983); ROUSAS JOHN RUSHDOONY, THE INSTITUTE OF BIBLICAL LAW 9 (1973) [hereinafter RUSHDOONY, BIBLICAL LAW]. Reconstructionist "dominion" theory is filtering into the mainstream of the NCR, Pentecostal traditions and sect fundamentalists, although these groups do not always want to be openly associated with Reconstructionists. *See* Ammerman, *North American Protestant, supra* note 70, at 53–55; Iannaccone, *supra* note 70, at 349; Wuthnow & Lawson, *supra* note 70, at 46.

72. The Vatican remains very politically active throughout the world to institute Roman Catholicism as state religion and to promote Roman Catholic laws and principles within secular societies. Because the Vatican has done exactly this for centuries, scholars are reluctant to call it "fundamentalist," although this conclusion is often hinted at or implied. *See* Hawley & Proudfoot, *supra* note 31, at 24–25 (noting how Vatican expressed solidarity with Muslim fundamentalists in the Salman Rushdie affair in the context of how fundamentalists engage in mutual support); Frances Kissling, *The Challenge of Christianity*, 44 AM. U. L. REV. 1345, 1345–46 (1995) (discussing fundamentalist tendencies within all religions with particular emphasis on Vatican). Vatican fundamentalist tendencies are particularly manifest in groups to which it gives support. A representative such group, which meets the definition of fundamentalism, is the Comunione e Liberazione (CL). *See* Dario Zadra, *Comunione e Liberazione: A Fundamentalist Idea of Power, in* 4 THE FUNDAMENTALISM PROJECT: ACCOUNTING FOR FUNDAMENTALISMS, *supra* note 16, at 124, 124–45. The CL, an organization founded in Italy, claims divine authority for the RCC and aims to bring back the "expelled Church" and papal state to Italy and reassert "Catholic hegemony." *Id.* at 124, 126–28, 142. The CL rejects Enlightenment norms, particularly the notion of the secular state and freedom of the individual. *Id.* at 126, 129, 130. The CL regards itself as speaking "for the Church and for its rights. . . . CL can point to approval from the hierarchy and significant support from the Vatican in backing that claim." *Id.* at 126, 143. CL's political arm has been connected to the Christian Democrat Party in Italy and became increasingly influential during the early 1990s. *See id.* at 134, 141. The CL has produced an "echo effect" in the RCC world, legitimating RCC condemnations of Enlightenment theory as the traditional enemy, along with Humanism and Protestantism. *See id.* at 143, 144. For discussions of other Catholic fundamentalist groups, see Dinges, *supra* note 27, at 66–101; Hitchcock, *supra* note 27, at 101–39.

73. *See supra* notes 27, 72.

74. *See* Zadra, *supra* note 72, at 131, 141 (discussing CL views of fall of Italian society as directly linked to modern "undermining" of traditional family life); *see, e.g.*, FALWELL, *supra* note 70, at 121–37 (discussing idea as sect fundamentalist); JAMES D. HUNTER, EVANGELICALISM: THE COMING GENERATION 76–109 (1987) (discussing idea as sect evangelical).

75. *See* BEDROTH, *supra* note 9, at 69 (discussing that fundamentalist Protestants viewed women as having the matches to light the dynamite in men, and thus women must contain their sexuality and not

nostalgia to the nineteenth-century construct of a middle-class family[76] or even to a seventeenth-century construct.[77] Fundamentalists define "traditional" family as a legally married man and woman with children, where the man is the head of the family and preferably is the sole financial supporter of the group.[78] They strongly support a separate–spheres gender ideology,[79] which they base on a religious requirement that women be submissive and subordinate to men. Some read the scriptures as calling for the headship of man and the subordination of woman.[80] Others, steeped in the belief that the Bible is infallible and that it condones women's subordination, come to view the hierarchy of men over women as somehow "natural."[81] All agree that a girl grows up subject to the authority of her father, who then delivers her in marriage to her husband's authority.[82] The father, as leader of the family,[83] exercises discipline with absolute authority over his wife and children.[84] He is the chief, if not sole, breadwinner, and the protector of and provider for his wife and family.[85] In return, the wife is to submit to her husband and serve the

cause men to fall morally); *see also* GEORGE H. TAVARD, WOMEN IN CHRISTIAN TRADITION 183 (1973) (finding that in Protestant tradition, woman was viewed as far more sexual than man).

76.   *See* Helen Hardacre, *The Impact of Fundamentalism on Women, The Family, and Interpersonal Relations, in* 2 THE FUNDAMENTALISM PROJECT: FUNDAMENTALISMS AND SOCIETY, *supra* note 40, at 129, 133 [hereinafter Hardacre, *Impact*].

77.   *See* Ammerman, *North American Protestant, supra* note 70, at 50 (discussing Reconstructionists' nostalgia for 17th century); *see, e.g.*, GARY NORTH, POLITICAL POLYTHEISM: THE MYTH OF PLURALISM 242–45 (1989) [hereinafter NORTH, POLYTHEISM].

78.   *See* Ammerman, *North American Protestant, supra* note 70, at 68; Garvey, *supra* note 16, at 30; Hardacre, *Impact, supra* note 76, at 131–32.

79.   *See* Ammerman, *North American Protestant, supra* note 70, at 8, 40; Garvey, *supra* note 16, at 30; Hardacre, *Impact, supra* note 76, at 132, 139; *see, e.g.*, FALWELL, *supra* note 70, at 150; RUSHDOONY, BIBLICAL LAW, *supra* note 71, at 344.

80.   *See* HAMPSON, *supra* note 23, at 14; TAVARD, *supra* note 75, at 181; Susan D. Rose, *Women Warriors: the Negotiation of Gender in a Charismatic Community*, 48 SOC. ANALYSIS 245, 245 (1987). Sects of the Orthodox Church also require women to be submissive, and because of their general inability and weakness therefore to be ruled by men. Anca-Lucia Manolache, *Orthodoxy and Women: A Romanian Perspective, in* WOMEN, RELIGION AND SEXUALITY, *supra* note 23, at 172, 180.

81.   With respect to Protestants, see BEDROTH, *supra* note 9, at 98, 124; HAMPSON, *supra* note 23, at 14. With respect to the RCC, see *The Vatican's Summary of "Evangelium Vitae," reprinted in* CNS DOCUMENTARY SERVICE, 24 ORIGINS, Apr. 6, 1995, at 730 (no. 42) ("A very special task is entrusted to women, who are particularly close to the mystery of life, who are called to be its guardians and to reveal its fruitfulness when that task matures into relationships marked by unselfish giving and *willing service . . . free from individualism*.") (emphasis supplied); John Paul II, *On the Dignity and Vocation of Women, reprinted in* CNS DOCUMENTARY SERVICE, 18 ORIGINS (no. 17), Oct. 6, 1988, at 281.

82.   *See* NORTH, POLYTHEISM, *supra* note 77, at 601.

83.   *See* FALWELL, *supra* note 70, at 128, 151; Hunter, *supra* note 74, at 79; GARY NORTH, VICTIM'S RIGHTS: THE BIBLICAL VIEW OF JUSTICE 45 (1990); Rose, *supra* note 80, at 246.

84.   *See* BEDROTH, *supra* note 9, at 103–04; TAVARD, *supra* note 75, at 181; Nancy T. Ammerman, *Accounting for Christian Fundamentalisms: Social Dynamics and Rhetorical Strategies, in* 4 THE FUNDAMENTALISM PROJECT: ACCOUNTING FOR FUNDAMENTALISMS, *supra* note 16, at 149, 154 [hereinafter Ammerman, *Accounting for Christian Fundamentalisms*]; *see, e.g.*, FALWELL, *supra* note 70, at 128–29, 151; HUNTER, *supra* note 74, at 79.

85.   *See* FALWELL, *supra* note 70, at 128–29; HUNTER, *supra* note 74, at 79.

needs of her husband and children.[86] She is also subject to a modesty code in matters of behavior and dress.[87]

Fundamentalist Protestants' model for marriage is thus based on an exchange of protection for obedience and submission. A wife who does not obey is termed "rebellious," and she is admonished to treat her husband as a "high priest and prophet of God."[88] This is particularly oppressive because modern studies show a high incidence of spousal abuse in fundamentalist Christian homes.[89] "[W]here wives are taught to submit blindly to their husbands' every word and deed, . . . such teachings provide a good covering for abuse under the guise of bringing one's wife 'into subjection.' Thus the batterer does not consider his actions abusive; he is simply fulfilling his God-given responsibilities."[90] Many women whose husbands enforce obedience through physical violence are counseled by Christian religious advisors to stay in these battering relationships, and convinced that they themselves are in the wrong.[91]

The requirement of submission and obedience detracts from the possibility of a woman achieving any economic independence or autonomy, because her husband may exercise his authority by limiting or forbidding her from working outside the

---

86. FALWELL, *supra* note 70, at 128–29, 151; HUNTER, *supra* note 74, at RUSHDOONY, BIBLICAL LAW, *supra* note 71, at 347–53; *see* BEDROTH, *supra* note 9, at 109 (quoting Protestant evangelical who states that Christian wife is to be obedient in all things); Randall Balmer, *American Fundamentalism: The Ideal of Femininity, in* FUNDAMENTALISM & GENDER, *supra* note 3, at 47, 52–55 (discussing fundamentalist religious requirement of feminine submission and obedience); *see also* Ammerman, *Accounting for Christian Fundamentalisms, supra* note 84, at 154, 159; Ammerman, *North American Protestant, supra* note 70, at 8, 40–41; Garvey, *supra* note 16, at 30; Rose, *supra* note 80, at 245; *see, e.g.,* MARABEL MORGAN, THE TOTAL WOMAN 55 (1973) ("A Total [Christian fundamentalist] Woman caters to her man's special quirks, whether it be salads, sex or sports.").

87. *See* BEDROTH, *supra* note 9, at 69, 82, 114 (explaining that fundamentalist Christian women must adopt modest dress, properly covered, with no display of themselves that may cause Christian men to sin); Foster, *supra* note 68, at 45, 49, 65 (noting that in fundamentalist English Christian Black churches, maintenance of moral and modest dress codes are important).

88. BEDROTH, *supra* note 9, at 103.

89. *See* BEDROTH, *supra* note 9, at 116; JAMES ALSDURF & PHYLLIS ALSDURF, BATTERED INTO SUBMISSION: THE TRAGEDY OF WIFE ABUSE IN THE CHRISTIAN HOME 10, 16–17 (1989). Christian fundamentalist (Protestant and Catholic) emphasis on women's self-sacrifice and the glorification of their suffering and victimization make women particularly vulnerable to accepting battering relationships. *See* Becker, *supra* note 24, at 465. Generally, such abuse is common in families with rigid sex roles and gross inequities in power distribution. *See* ALSDURF & ALSDURF, *supra*, at 17; David Finkelhor, *Common Features of Family Abuse, in* THE DARK SIDE OF FAMILIES: CURRENT FAMILY VIOLENCE RESEARCH 17, 19 (David Finkelhor et al. eds., 1983).

90. ALSDURF & ALSDURF, *supra* note 89, at 18.

91. Becker, *supra* note 24, at 465; BEDROTH, *supra* note 9, at 116; ALSDURF & ALSDURF, *supra* note 89, at 16, 18, 23. Under traditional religious law of the Orthodox Church a husband had a right to beat his wife, but if a wife raised her hand against her husband she could be divorced. Manolache, *supra* note 80, at 179–80. Although civil law rather than religious law now applies, the religious attitudes are unchanged. *See id.* at 180.

home. Fundamentalists regard a woman's economic independence as undesirable because it will reduce her commitment to patriarchy.[92]

Political Activity to Conform State Law to Religious-Legal Doctrine

Christian fundamentalists are increasingly active in the political arena to enact their vision of Christian society into law.[93] For example, in the United States, they hope to pose a direct threat to the secular state and to establish the United States as a Christian country.[94] Not surprisingly, their particular goal is to establish the

---

92. *See* FALWELL, *supra* note 70, at 124–25.

93. Since the 1970s, there has been a surge in Protestant fundamentalist activism. *See* Ammerman, *North American Protestant, supra* note 70, at 38; *see generally* Jeffrey K. Hadden, *Televangelism and Political Mobilization, in* AMERICAN EVANGELICALS AND THE MASS MEDIA 215–29 (1990). In Catholicism, CL's political actions are often aimed at lobbying for legislation affecting the family and bringing back Catholic hegemony. *See* Zadra, *supra* note 72, at 131, 140.

Fundamentalists have also fought to retain unequal laws in the face of reform. For example, the Indian Christian community has its own marriage and divorce laws under the Indian Divorce Act of 1869 and the Indian Christian Marriage Act of 1872. LESLIE J. CALMAN, TOWARD EMPOWERMENT: WOMEN AND MOVEMENT POLITICS IN INDIA 150, 152 & n.17 (1992); *see also supra* notes 152, 415 (discussing family laws in India that are divided along religious lines, with Hindus covered by the civil Hindu laws and Muslims covered by their own respective religious laws). Fundamentalists fought to retain these laws, under which a Christian husband may obtain divorce if his wife commits adultery, but a "husband's adultery, however, is not sufficient grounds for a wife to seek divorce." *Id.* at 152. This law was challenged, and the Kerala High Court in India held in 1995 that Christian women may now seek dissolution on grounds of desertion, cruelty, and adultery. *See* 9 IWRAW, THE WOMEN'S WATCH 6 (no. 3) 6–7 (Jan. 1996). It remains to be seen if standards of proof are enforced equally.

94. Falwell's groups fight against secular or liberal humanism for the return of "Christian civilization" in the United States. *See* FALWELL, *supra* note 70, at 17–18; Ammerman, *North American Protestant, supra* note 70, at 46–47. The political party of these groups is the Republican party. Falwell has endorsed the "civil disobedience" of another fundamentalist group, Operation Rescue, which has engaged in violent direct action against abortion clinics and doctors, justifying its violence as being based on divine law rather than secular laws. *See* Faye Ginsburg, *Saving America's Souls: Operation Rescue's Crusade against Abortion, in* 3 THE FUNDAMENTALISM PROJECT: FUNDAMENTALISMS AND THE STATE, *supra* note 11, at 557, 563, 567, 569, 573 (noting that it is disingenuous for Operation Rescue to distinguish its "direct action" from "violent activities," because its activities are designed to create "an atmosphere of chronic fear of physical and emotional assault for both personnel and clients" by verbally and physically accosting women entering the clinics, blocking access to the clinics, following women and tracing their license plates in order to harass them at home, picketing the homes of clinic's personnel and physicians who in addition receive threatening letters and phone calls); Ammerman, *North American Protestant, supra* note 70, at 45; Garvey, *supra* note 16, at 32; Sara Maitland, *Biblicism: A Radical Rhetoric?, in* REFUSING HOLY ORDERS, *supra* note 3, at 26, 34–35; *see, e.g.,* RANDALL TERRY, OPERATION RESCUE 175 (1988) (explaining that Operation Rescue's fight against abortion is to establish a nation whose politics and judicial system are founded on Judeo-Christian "Higher Laws"). Reconstructionists also hope to establish a Christian nation. *See* NORTH, POLYTHEISM, *supra* note 77, at 4, 15, 28, 35, 84–85; Rousas J. Rushdoony, *Biblical Law and Western Civilization,* 2 J. CHRISTIAN RECONSTRUCTION 2, 5 (1975); Ammerman, *North American Protestant, supra* note 70, at 50, 51. Rushdoony has proposed a legal system based on the law of Hebrew Scripture. *See* RUSHDOONY, BIBLICAL LAW, *supra* note 71, *passim;* Ammerman, *North American Protestant, supra* note 70, at 52. Some of his suggestions for implementing Mosaic laws have met with controversy, particularly that habitually rebellious children be put to death. *See, e.g.,* RUSHDOONY, BIBLICAL LAW, *supra* note 71, 185–92. *See* Ammerman, *North American Protestant, supra* note 70, at 52.

legal structure of the patriarchal family and women's subordinate role in it. Thus, Christian fundamentalists strongly opposed the Equal Rights Amendment to the U.S. Constitution[95] as preventing women from serving in their proper submissive role as wives and mothers,[96] and are credited with its defeat.[97] They have also worked to prevent passage of statutes or to repeal already-enacted statutes that protect abused children and abused wives because the statutes interfere with the husband's disciplinary rights to enforce obedience.[98]

Catholic fundamentalist groups have also politically supported "traditional" family laws and opposed laws that did not fit the patriarchal family model.[99] The RCC itself is always heavily involved in political activity, including the political lobbying of individual states.[100] A recent Vatican success was lobbying China to ban reformist Catholic groups from the 1995 United Nations Conference on Women's Rights in Beijing.[101] Thus, these groups, which have long fought for women's equality, were excluded from the debate on formulating international legal policy on women's equality, whereas the Vatican, which has historically and consistently opposed women's equality, even women's fight for suffrage, participated in the debate.[102]

Hinduism

There are several Hindu fundamentalist movements; the main movements are located in India and focused on making India a Hindu state.[103] The most important

---

95. *See* REBECCA E. KLATCH, WOMEN OF THE NEW RIGHT 136–39 (1987); Garvey, *supra* note 16, at 30; *see, e.g.*, FALWELL, *supra* note 70, at 150–51.

96. *See* Ammerman, *North American Protestant, supra* note 70, at 40–41; Garvey, *supra* note 70, at 30, 37; *see, e.g.*, FALWELL, *supra* note 70, at 19, 150–64.

97. *See* Ammerman, *North American Protestant, supra* note 70, at 44–45.

98. *See* Ammerman, *North American Protestant, supra* note 70, at 45; *see also* THE ALAN GUTTMACHER INSTITUTE, *Supremacy of Parental Authority New Battlecry For Conservative Activists*, WASHINGTON MEMO, Dec. 21, 1995, at 4 (discussing introduction of bill "Parental Rights and Responsibilities Act" which would prohibit any federal, state, or local government to usurp right of parent to, *inter alia*, discipline child and would have a "chilling" effect on intervention in child abuse cases).

99. *See* Zadra, *supra* note 72, at 131, 140, 141 (discussing CL's promotion of traditional family legal structures and its lobbying against divorce and abortion); Dinges, *supra* note 27, at 91; Hitchcock, *supra* note 27, at 110.

100. For example, the Vatican recently negotiated with ex-President Walesa a concordat with Poland concerning contraception, abortion, and divorce, and giving the RCC the right to teach religion in the state schools and special tax concessions to its clergy. However, the governing coalition declined to ratify the concordat until a new constitution was in place. Christopher Bobinski, *Walesa in threat to resign over abortion reform*, FIN. TIMES, Jul. 6, 1994, at 2. Walesa lost the elections in November 1995, and the RCC may well see its power in Poland checked as a result.

101. *See* Julia Preston, *U.N. Summit on Women Bars Groups: China, Vatican Block Opponents' Admission*, WASH. POST, Mar. 17, 1995, at A36.

102. *See* Ruether, *supra* note 41, at 223. For discussion on the Vatican's historic opposition to women's equality, see generally MARY DALY, THE CHURCH AND THE SECOND SEX: WITH THE FEMINIST POSTCHRISTIAN INTRODUCTION AND NEW ARCHAIC AFTERWORDS (1985).

103. Hindu fundamentalism began at the turn of the century with Dayananda Sarasvati, the primary

is Rashtriya Swayamsevak Sangh (RSS),[104] a combined religious and cultural organization whose political manifestation is the Bharatiya Janata Party (BJP) (The Indian People's Party)[105] and whose affiliate Vishva Hindu Parishad (VHP) (World Hindu Society) is responsible for promoting religious and cultural aspects of Hindu fundamentalism.[106]

---

leader of the group Arya Samaj, which aimed to revive Hinduism in India through the establishment of a self-conscious Hindu identity with Hindu collective goals. Daniel Gold, *Organized Hinduisms: From Vedic Truth to Hindu Nation, in* 1 THE FUNDAMENTALISM PROJECT: FUNDAMENTALISMS OBSERVED, *supra* note 7, at 531, 538–39; *cf.* Krishna Kumar, *Hindu Revivalism and Education in North-Central India, in* 2 The Fundamentalism Project: Fundamentalisms and Society, *supra* note 40, at 536, 539 (discussing importance of Arya Samaj in Hindu "revivalism"). Arya Samaj started the first religio-political group of Hindu communalism, which eventually became known as the Hindu Mahasabha. Gold, *supra,* at 539. By the 1930s, Hindu Mahasabha was led by the author Vinayak Damodar Savarkar who wrote one of the most influential works of Hindu fundamentalism, *Hindutva,* defining what it means to be Hindu and calling for Hindu unity. *See* VINAYAK DAMODAR SAVARKAR, HINDUTVA 1 (Bombay: Veer Savarkar Prakashan ed. 1969) (1923/24). Hindu Mahasabha provides the link between Arya Samaj tradition and the Rashtriya Swayamsevak Sangh (RSS), *see infra* note 104, which the Hindu Mahasabha nurtured as a youth group. Gold, *supra,* at 539.

104. RSS's founder and first leader, Kesnav Baliram Hedgewar, devoted his life to restoring the sought-after unity of *Hindutva, see supra* note 103. He regarded the Muslim and Christian invaders as the enemies of the Hindu nation. *See* Ainslie T. Embree, *The Function of the Rashtriya Swayamsevak Sangh: To Define the Hindu Nation, in* 4 THE FUNDAMENTALISM PROJECT: ACCOUNTING FOR FUNDAMENTALISMS, *supra* note 16, at 617, 624. Hedgewar developed the RSS as an organization for training cadres of young men in the Sanskritic ideals of the warrior. Robert E. Frykenberg, *Hindu Fundamentalism and the Structural Stability of India, in* 3 THE FUNDAMENTALISM PROJECT: FUNDAMENTALISMS AND THE STATE, *supra* note 11, at 233, 241 [hereinafter Frykenberg, *Hindu Fundamentalism*]. RSS's next leader, M. S. Golwalkar, gave the RSS a systematic ideology of extreme intolerance of other modes of life and religion that has been compared to Hitler fascism. Embree, *supra,* at 627; Gold, *supra* note 103, at 566; *see* Frykenberg, *Hindu Fundamentalism, supra,* at 240–41; *see, e.g.,* M.S. GOLWALKAR, WE OR OUR NATIONHOOD DEFINED 47–48 (Nagpur: Bharat, 1939).

The RSS has political and cultural affiliate organizations, but retains its religious base. Embree, *supra,* at 619, 629. Although RSS was ostensibly banned in January 1993 after the destruction of the mosque at Ayodhya, *see infra* note 106, the organization and its network of two and a half million dedicated members continue to operate effectively, Embree, *supra,* at 649, as evidenced by the large political gains made by its political party the BJP, *see infra* note 105.

105. RSS formed its first political party in 1951, the Bharatiya Jana Sangh, which drew on members of Arya Samaj, Hindu Mahasabha, and RSS itself. The Jana Sangh broke apart and the new party became the Bharatiya Janata Party (BJP) in 1980. Frykenberg, *Hindu Fundamentalism, supra* note 104, at 244–45; Gold, *supra* note 103, at 572; Embree, *supra* note 104, at 638; Deepak Lal, *The Economic Impact of Hindu Revivalism, in* 3 THE FUNDAMENTALISM PROJECT: FUNDAMENTALISMS AND THE STATE, *supra* note 11, at 410, 411–12. The BJP opposes the current relatively secular Indian government and fights to make India a Hindu state. Frykenberg, *Hindu Fundamentalism, supra* note 104, at 248–51. The RSS and BJP made large gains in the 1996 elections and the BJP emerged as the biggest group in parliament. *See* Mark Nicholson, *Indian PM to resign after poll rebuff,* FIN. TIMES, May 10, 1996, at 1.

106. *See* Gold, *supra* note 103, at 567, 572, 574; Frykenberg, *Hindu Fundamentalism, supra* note 104, at 242–48; Peter van der Veer, *Hindu Nationalism and the Discourse of Modernity: The Vishva Hindu Parishad, in* 4 THE FUNDAMENTALISM PROJECT: ACCOUNTING FOR FUNDAMENTALISMS, *supra* note 16, at 653, 653; Embree, *supra* note 104, at 632, 637–38. VHP was started by Golwalkar in 1964 for the purpose of creating a permanent Hindu religious establishment for all of India. Frykenberg, *Hindu Fundamentalism, supra* note 104, at 245; van der Veer, *supra,* at 655. The VHP is primarily led by

The Religious-Legal Doctrine

The RSS-VHP-BJP ideology embraces selected traditional and conservative practices of Hinduism that correspond to its view of an idealized past, particularly the glory of India and the glorification of male warriors.[107] Its rhetoric centers on certain mythological epics of Hinduism that it seeks to make relevant to contemporary times.[108] It vigorously promotes the epic *Ramayana* as grounded in historical fact, representative of Hindu truths and providing a moral foundation for contemporary India.[109] The epic is the story of Lord Rama, the human incarnation of the god Vishnu, and his wife, Sita.[110] Sita sacrifices her life to prove her chastity to her doubting husband and thereby uphold his honor.[111] Throughout Hindu fundamentalism in India, Rama is considered admirable and represents the ideal Hindu man, a warrior, while Sita is considered to be the ideal wife, chaste, obedient, and self-

---

religious leaders, and its goal is to impose Hinduism as the national religion of India. *See* van der Veer, *supra*, at 653, 656. It has been particularly successful in staging mass events of religious-political ritual. The most famous of these campaigns involved destruction of the Muslim mosque at Ayodhya (argued to be the birthplace of the god-hero Rama, *see infra* notes 109–111 and accompanying text), which resulted in the deaths of thousands of people, mostly Muslims. *See* van der Veer, *supra*, at 656, 662; John S. Hawley, *Hinduism: Sati and Its Defenders, in* FUNDAMENTALISM & GENDER, *supra* note 3, at 79, 79–80; Embree, *supra* note 104, at 646–48; Sahgal, *supra* note 23, at 172. The RSS and VHP also operate abroad. *See* Sahgal, *supra* note 23, at 163–97.

107. *See* Kumar, *supra* note 103, at 550–56; Lal, *supra* note 105, at 412; Frykenberg, *Hindu Fundamentalism, supra* note 104, at 251–53; Embree, *supra* note 104, at 628–33; *see also* Gold, *supra* note 103, at 551, 553–55.

108. *See* Kumar, *supra* note 103, at 550–56; Frykenberg, *Hindu Fundamentalism, supra* note 104, at 234, 253.

109. *See* Embree, *supra* note 104, at 632; Kumar, *supra* note 103, at 554; Frykenberg, *Hindu Fundamentalism, supra* note 104, at 246–47; van der Veer, *supra* note 106, at 662–63; Sahgal, *supra* note 23, at 189–90.

110. Hindu fundamentalists have promoted Lord Rama as an historical rather than mythological figure. They claim his birth place to be a real northern Indian town, Ayodhya, *see* Sahgal, *supra* note 23, at 171, where VHP's *Ramayana* campaign resulted in the destruction of the mosque and widespread rioting and killing, *see supra* note 106.

111. In the *Ramayana*, a demon abducts Sita, but refrains from raping her. Rama wages war and rescues Sita, but doubts her chastity (for which she, although abducted, is plainly responsible) and publicly disowns her. Sita defends her virtue by a test of fire, and the god of fire rescues her and testifies to her virtue and chastity. Rama and Sita return home and live in peace until further rumors surface, questioning Sita's chastity during the abduction. As a result, Rama banishes the pregnant Sita who soon thereafter gives birth to two sons. Rama then recalls her and requires her to undergo a second test of fire for his people. Sita chooses to defend her virtue by dying, announcing publicly that she will thereby remove Rama's grief, shame, and dishonor, and asserts her loyalty to him by stating that she hopes he will be her husband in her next rebirth. For an account of this epic as related here, see LEIGH MINTURN, SITA'S DAUGHTERS: COMING OUT OF PURDAH 170–73 (1993); Gerald J. Larson, *Hinduism in India and in America, in* WORLD RELIGIONS IN AMERICA: AN INTRODUCTION 177, 186 (Jacob Neusner ed., 1994).

sacrificing.[112] These role models reinforce strong gender ideologies that require separate and distinct roles for each sex.[113]

Hindu fundamentalism reaffirms these divine role models in another epic myth that constitutes important rhetoric for the movement: the story of the god Siva and his consort, the goddess Sati, whose name means chastity or virginity.[114] Like Sita, Sati sacrifices herself to save the honor of her husband.[115] Along with Sita, Sati represents the Hindu ideal woman,[116] whose devotion to her husband constitutes "the fire of her inner truth (sat) . . . [that] bursts forth in flames" and consumes her.[117] *Sati* is thus the name given to a woman who is burned to death on her husband's funeral pyre, with this ultimate sacrifice for her husband's honor representing the ideal of virtuous and honorable womanhood.[118] The RSS holds strongly to the view that women are best able to serve the Hindu nation by following this deepest tradition of the role of women in Hindu society as manifested by Sita and Sati.[119]

Thus, the primary religious role for Hindu women as promoted by the RSS family of organizations is to be a devoted wife and mother.[120] However, Hinduism

112. MINTURN, *supra* note 111, at 173; Sahgal, *supra* note 23, at 189; Vasudha Narayanan, *Hindu Perceptions of Auspiciousness and Sexuality, in* WOMEN, RELIGION AND SEXUALITY, *supra* note 23, at 64, 67. *Ramayana's* powerful effect on role models is particularly apparent during the marriage ceremony where the groom is regarded as representing Lord Rama, and the bride, Sita. *See* LINA M. FRUZZETTI, THE GIFT OF A VIRGIN: WOMEN, MARRIAGE AND RITUAL IN BENGALI SOCIETY 13 (1982).

113. Thus, the women's organization of the RSS, *see infra* note 120, finds that "the basic principles and philosophy of women's life in India are quite different from those of men." Embree, *supra* note 104, at 641.

114. In the myth, Sati becomes an ascetic like Siva and thereby wins him in marriage. Sati's father, disapproving of Siva as an unkempt ascetic hermit, holds an important sacrifice to which he invites all the top divinities except Siva. Sati confronts her father about this insult, but is ignored, and so she kills herself to protest the insult to her husband. For an account of this epic as related here, see MINTURN, *supra* note 111, at 168.

115. *See* Narayanan, *supra* note 112, at 67.

116. *See id.* at 65–67.

117. *See* Hawley, *supra* note 106, at 82 (paragraph break suppressed, footnote omitted).

118. *See id.* at 81; MINTURN, *supra* note 111, at 168–69. In European languages, the word *sati* is generally used to denote the religious practice of widow immolation rather than the woman herself, as it is used in Hindi.

119. *See* Embree, *supra* note 104, at 641; *seealso* SWAMI DAYANANDA SARASWATI, OM LIGHT OF TRUTH OR ENGLISH TRANSLATION OF THE SATYARTH PRAKESH 124–25 (Chiranjiva Bharadwaja trans. ed., 1975) [hereinafter DAYANANDA, OM] (asserting that a wife should be subject to her husband's control). Fundamentalists argue that Hinduism is not based on individual rights and personal freedoms, but on community responsibilities. MINTURN, *supra* note 111, at 169; Young, *supra* note 6, at 121–22. Thus, women who follow in Sita's or Sati's steps are oriented to the community, not selfishly concerned with their independent freedoms. However, Hindu fundamentalists consistently require self-sacrifice and selflessness primarily from women for the benefit of men, and not the other way around. In this way, even the attractive concept of community responsibility is mustered in support of subordinating women.

120. *See* Embree, *supra* note 104, at 641. Accordingly, women cannot join the RSS because the Hindu tradition of segregating the sexes prohibits joint activities in this context. *See id.*; Gold, *supra* note 103, at 568. However, there is a separate women's organization related to the RSS, the Rashtra Sevika

views women as possessed of a dangerous sexuality that constantly threatens to destroy their virtue, and that they cannot themselves control.[121] Consequently, women must be subject to external controls to maintain their virtue.[122] The girl or young woman is first controlled by her father or male guardian.[123] If, despite this control, she loses, or is perceived to have lost, her virtue, she disgraces her family and her male relatives are therefore ''obliged to execute her.''[124]

The woman's marriage reduces her potential to disgrace her family.[125] Consequently, a family is always anxious to marry off daughters, and will pay for the privilege in the form of dowry.[126] Dowry as practiced in Hinduism reinforces the view of women as objects that men control and dispose of like chattels,[127] and this is sufficient reason to justify the Indian government's prohibition of dowry.[128]

Samiti. It promotes the realization of true Hindu womanhood, emphasizing ''woman's chastity, purity, boldness, affection and alertness.'' *See* Embree, *supra* note 104, at 641. The group rejects equal rights and economic independence for women because ''this unnatural change in the attitude of women might have led to the disintegration of the family.'' *See id.* (*quoting* RASHTRA SEVIKA SAMITI: AN ORGANIZATION OF HINDU WOMEN 13 (Nagpur: Sevika Prakashan, n.d.)).

121. Hinduism regards women as being more sexual than men, and although women's sexuality has some positive aspects it is nonetheless viewed as a source of temptation. Hindu belief is that women have stronger sex drives and psychic power (*shakti*) than men. *See* MINTURN, *supra* note 111, at 201–08 (noting that husbands must satisfy women's sex drive or wives will be unfaithful, and women's sex drive drains men such that ''women are an incurable disease and a barrier to a man's virtue''); Julia Leslie, *Sri and Jyestha: Ambivalent Role Models for Women, in* ROLES AND RITUALS FOR HINDU WOMEN 107, 126 (Julia Leslie ed., 1991) (''In general terms, all women [in certain Hindu myths] are portrayed as inherently impure, innately weak and wicked.''); DAYANANDA, OM, *supra* note 119, at 27, 48 (explaining that men by avoiding looking at women—which promotes male lust—gain in strength); *see also* Narayanan, *supra* note 112, at 73–78.

122. *See* MINTURN, *supra* note 111, at 221.

123. *See* Sanjukta Gupta, *Women in the Saiva/Sakta Ethos, in* ROLES AND RITUALS FOR HINDU WOMEN, *supra* note 121, at 193, 194–95.

124. MINTURN, *supra* note 111, at 202 (''[N]othing is punished more severely than dishonor in women.'').

125. Marriages are arranged for daughters at young ages, preferably before menstruation, to prevent premarital affairs. *See* MINTURN, *supra* note 111, at 46–47, 203, 230; *see also* DAYANANDA, OM, *supra* note 119, at 90–92 (referring to Laws of Manu as his source for ages of marriage). The Hindu Marriage Act 1955 and Hindu Minority and Guardianship Act 1956, which raised minimum marriage ages to 18 for women and 21 for men, have generally been ignored. CALMAN, *supra* note 93, at 152. As recently as 1986, the Health Minister of the state of Uttar Pradesh in India admitted that there were a number of villages in Uttar Pradesh where all the girls over age 8 were married. *See id.*

126. Dowry is a gift of property from the bride's family. Although ostensibly made to the bride, it is in reality a payment to the groom and groom's family as a condition for performance of the marriage. Young, *supra* note 6, at 118. The amount of dowry depends upon the relative value (or, rather, lack of value) placed upon the girl, with detriments in her looks, education, and age ''outweighed by an unusually high dowry.'' *See* FRUZZETTI, *supra* note 112, at 35. Dowry was originally a Brahmanical religious practice. With the spread of fundamentalism and reaffirmation of Hindu values through ''Sanskritization'' and Brahmanical values, dowry has been reinforced as an appropriate religious practice, Young, *supra* note 6, at 115–18, and has expanded into more communities and castes. CALMAN, *supra* note 93, at 128.

127. *See* CALMAN, *supra* note 93, at 126.

128. The Dowry Prohibition Act of 1961 was amended in 1984 and made giving or receiving dowry a

Marriage transfers the woman from the control of her father to the control of her husband. "After her marriage, her husband is for her in the position of god. . . . The husband of a married woman is her 'lord' and master. . . ."[129] The highest religious duty of a woman is to be "devotional and conjugal" to this her personal god.[130] This role requires her absolute obedience,[131] and indeed the RSS describes the duty of absolute obedience that RSS members owe to the leader as that found in an "ideal Hindu family."[132]

Hindu fundamentalists prescribe or legitimate a number of social mechanisms for ensuring the wife's obedience and maintaining the husband's control. The religious modesty laws of *purdah* require a woman to stay indoors and segregated from men, effectively keeping women isolated and submissive.[133]

It is also accepted practice that the husband may enforce his wife's duty of obedience by beatings and other violence.[134] Because he is the sole judge of whether she is obedient, this further condones his being violent if she displeases him in any way. His displeasure commonly finds expression in complaints of inadequate dowry that escalate into beatings, torture, and murder. Such murders are known as "dowry deaths" or "bride-burnings" and, despite their illegality, they occur frequently and regularly in Hindu society in India, and are on the increase.[135] Most dowry deaths

---

substantive offense. Young, *supra* note 6, at 118; Kirti Singh, *Obstacles to Women's Rights in India, in* HUMAN RIGHTS OF WOMEN 375, 392 (Rebecca J. Cook ed., 1994); Madhu Kishwar, *Towards More Just Norms for Marriage: Continuing the Dowry Debate*, 53 MANUSHI 2–9 (1989).

129. Gupta, *supra* note 123, at 194–95; *see* FRUZZETTI, *supra* note 112, at 13; *seealso* CALMAN, *supra* note 93, at 124 n.13 (observing that traditional Hindu family structure concentrates unchecked power in hands of men, particularly husbands and male elders).

130. *See* FRUZZETTI, *supra* note 112, at 13. There is no apparent exception for the wife, as devotee, to refuse sex. Some authors argue that wives should agree with husbands in sexuality, but they acknowledge that, in practice, if a wife refuses sexual relations her husband may beat her or elder woman of house may make sure the wife becomes more obedient and accessible to her husband. MINTURN, *supra* note 111, at 209–11; RENUKA SINGH, THE WOMB OF THE MIND 198–99, 201–02 (1990) (stating that Hindu women have marital duty to submit to husbands sexually and may be beaten if they do not).

131. *See* MINTURN, *supra* note 111, at 221.

132. Embree, *supra* note 104, at 625–26; *see* Gold, *supra* note 103, at 560–61.

133. *Purdah* is the cloistering of women by high-caste Hindus, with some aspects now popularized among other classes by "Sanskritization" and fundamentalism. *See* MINTURN, *supra* note 111, at 73–93. Strict *purdah* requires a woman to cover her face in front of her husband and older men. *Purdah* also restricts a woman's travel alone which otherwise would "contaminate" her character. *See* DAYANANDA, OM, *supra* note 119, at 128–29.

134. *See* SINGH, *supra* note 130, at 198–99, 201–02; *see also supra* note 124.

135. CALMAN, *supra* note 93, at 124, 127; Govind Kelkar, *Violence Against Women: An Understanding of Responsibility for their Lives, in* THIRD WORLD/SECOND SEX (vol. 2), *supra* note 50, at 179, 184. The Dowry Prohibition Act of 1961 was amended in 1984 and 1986 to make dowry death illegal. Indian Penal Code 304B; *see* Singh, *supra* note 128, at 392. But dowry deaths continue to increase year by year. CALMAN, *supra* note 93, at 127–28; *see* Kelkar, *supra*, at 181–82. A typical week's newspaper reports about eight deaths of women that the authorities have evidence to link with dowry. Three typical examples that Calman reprints are:

"Haryana official victim of dowry": Mrs. . . Dala, a senior officer of the Haryana Government, died of burns in her in-laws' house on Tuesday night. . . . Her husband . . . was arrested

take the form of the husband setting the wife on fire and then claiming that the burning was a kitchen accident or that the wife committed suicide in a good derivation of the *sati* tradition.[136] As a result, the police often classify dowry deaths as accident or suicide, and consequently there are few prosecutions.[137] Some wives, in the Sita and Sati tradition, do commit suicide, often as a result of great harassment, beatings, and torture from their husbands.[138]

The greatest and most spectacular demonstration of loyalty, obedience, and submission is made by the wife who becomes a *sati* for her husband's benefit.[139] The religious practice of becoming a *sati* was outlawed by the British in 1829 and has remained illegal, although it has continued to occur.[140] However, it was not until Roop Kanwar became a *sati* in 1987 that the religious practice created a furor in India.[141] The eighteen-year-old Roop Kanwar had been married eight months to a twenty-four-year-old man when he died.[142] Some eyewitnesses said that she mounted his funeral pyre voluntarily, whereas others claimed that she was drugged by her in-laws, tried nevertheless to escape, and was pushed back on to the pyre to burn.[143]

---

on a charge of abetment to suicide. In her dying declaration, she stated she had been tortured by her husband and in-laws for not bringing enough dowry. (Statesman, 6 June 1986)."

"Commits Suicide": A 28–year-old woman allegedly burnt herself to death because she could not stand the harassment by her husband. . . . The police have registered a case of abetment to suicide against the husband, an employee of the New Delhi government. (Times of India, 6 June 1986)."

"Burnt for a Refrigerator": A young life was lost because of the rapacity of the in-laws. It began when the newly married Nirmal (24 years old) was unable to bring a refrigerator as part of her dowry. Nirmal was burnt to death. (Statesman, 11 June 1986).

CALMAN, *supra* note 93, at 123. The government now estimates that in the decade since Calman's report dowry deaths have increased 170 percent, with 6,200 recorded last year. Molly Moore, *Consumerism Fuels Dowry-Death Wave*, WASH. POST, Mar. 17, 1995, at A35.

136. CALMAN, *supra* note 93, at 123, 127–28; Kelkar, *supra* note 135, at 184.

137. Kelkar, *supra* note 135, at 181–82. One researcher in the Greater Bombay area examined all the Coroner's death and post-mortem certificates for these accidental deaths due to burns and concluded that authorities were reluctant to call dowry deaths murder and that not one certificate gave a "hint" as to how these "accidents" could have occurred. CALMAN, *supra* note 93, at 127 (quoting Malini Karkal, *How the Other Half Dies in Bombay*, EPW, 24 Aug. 1985).

138. CALMAN, *supra* note 93, at 124, 127.

139. *See supra* notes 116–19 and accompanying text.

140. Hawley, *supra* note 106, at 81. It is not known how widespread the practice is because not all *satis* are reported, given that the practice is illegal.

141. *Id.*

142. *Id.*

143. *Id.* at 81–85.

This *sati* prompted Hindu fundamentalists, including the Hindu religious political parties such as the BJP, to rally to support the institution and practice of becoming a *sati*, particularly against the government law.[144] All the major actors in this movement were men: men served in the religious roles of the *sati sthal*, men ran the Committee for defending the *sati*, men organized the rallies to support the *sati*, men gave the speeches to support the *sati*, and men have been combing the religious and historical texts to justify the *sati*.[145] However, these fundamentalist men ignored the fact that not every *sati* acts voluntarily: many are pushed onto the pyre.[146] Even absent immediate physical coercion, a widow in Indian Hindu society is regarded as so inauspicious and burdensome and faces such a bleak prospect that she may well yield to social pressure to become a *sati* as the path of least resistance.[147]

In 1974 the Indian government Committee on the Status of Women issued a report, *Towards Equality*, which concluded that Hinduism was one of the critical determinants in women's inferior status in India.[148] The report observed that a

---

144. *Id.* at 87–91; Young, *supra* note 6, at 119–23.

145. Hawley, *supra* note 106, at 100; *see also* Young, *supra* note 6, at 121 (discussing Hindu scholars re-examining the history of *sati* in order to legitimate the practice).

146. Hawley, *supra* note 106, at 83; *see* MARY DALY, GYN/ECOLOGY: THE METAPHYSICS OF RADICAL FEMINISM 113–33 (1978). There are economic reasons why a family might want its widowed daughter-in-law to become a *sati*. This prevents her from inheriting her husband's property, which used to be prohibited under religious law, but is now allowed under civil law. Young, *supra* note 6, at 122. Also, families make money from visitors to *sati* shrines. Hawley, *supra* note 106, at 84.

147. A widow's lack of virtue is regarded as responsible for her husband's death, but she may expiate this bad karma by becoming a *sati*. MINTURN, *supra* note 111, at 230; Narayanan, *supra* note 112, at 81–85. A widow who does not become a *sati* (most women) is perceived as having no further role in life because when her husband dies, her reproductive power, sexuality, and femaleness are regarded as being permanently removed because she gave them irrevocably to him upon marriage. *See* MINTURN, *supra* note 111, at 229; Narayanan, *supra* note 112, at 81–85; FRUZZETTI, *supra* note 112, at 103. Her in-laws's greatest fear is that she may become unchaste and "pregnant, *casting a possible shadow on the legitimacy of any previous children.*" MINTURN, *supra* note 111, at 229 (citing D.K. Stein, *Women to burn: Suttee as a normative institution*, 4, (2) SIGNS: J. WOMEN IN CULTURE AND SOC. 253–68 (1978)) (emphasis added). For this reason, widows were forbidden to remarry and were to shave their heads in order to make them ugly so that they would remain chaste. Narayanan, *supra* note 112, at 81, 85. Widow remarriage was made legal in India, but it is rare for widows to remarry because remarriage is still regarded as highly dubious. *See* FRUZZETTI, *supra* note 112, at 103; Narayanan, *supra* note 112, at 83, 85; Vinaya Saijwani, *The Personal Laws of Divorce in India with a comment on Chaudry v. Chaudry*, 11 WOMEN'S RTS. L. REP. 41, 49 (1989). Ironically, this religious prohibition against remarriage to protect the woman's chastity and dead husband's honor has encouraged young widows into prostitution as their only economic source of survival. Narayanan, *supra* note 112, at 83. Despite legal reforms concerning remarriage, widows' position in society has actually worsened in recent times. *See* Young, *supra* note 6, at 114; MINTURN, *supra* note 111, at 221–22. Widowers, however, suffer no detriment from their status and have always been expected to remarry. There is not even a Hindi word for a widowed man. FRUZZETTI, *supra* note 112, at 104.

148. *See generally* GOVERNMENT OF INDIA, MINISTRY OF EDUCATION AND SOCIAL WELFARE, TOWARDS EQUALITY: REPORT OF THE COMMITTEE ON THE STATUS OF WOMEN IN INDIA (1974). The rhetoric of traditional Hinduism offers no apologetics for its derogatory images of women and its regard for women as inferior. "[I]n many important respects orthodox [Hindu] religious law . . . equated women with the lowest class of men." Frederick M. Smith, *Indra's Curse, Varuna's Noose, and the Suppression of*

woman in orthodox Hinduism "is called fickle-minded, sensual, seducer of men; given to falsehood, trickery, folly, greed, impurity and thoughtless action; root of all evil; inconsistent and cruel. . . . In childhood a woman must be subject to her father, in youth to her husband, and when her lord is dead to her sons. A woman must never be independent."[149] But despite legal reforms in the last twenty years since *Towards Equality*, the rise of Hindu fundamentalism has brought an increase in dowry deaths, an increased acceptance of *purdah*, *sati*, and the general dependency of women.[150]

Political Activity to Conform State Law to Religious-Legal Doctrine

The RSS-VHP-BJP family, flush with power from its 1996 electoral gains, continues its intense political activity, pushing for legal reforms that correspond to its notion of a Hindu state. In furtherance of this goal, Hindu fundamentalists call for repeal of the Hindu Marriage Act of 1955 and the Hindu Succession Act of 1956[151] that reformed Hindu religious practices by giving women more rights in marriage, banning polygamy, allowing for widow remarriage, giving women statutory bases for divorce, and giving women some rights in inheritance where they formerly had none.[152] Their nationalist aim for a Hindu state is enhanced by cutting back on women's rights, as was already clear at the time of the passage of the Hindu Marriage Act and Hindu Succession Act when fundamentalist opponents of the bills called them "anti-Hindu and anti-Indian" and declared that they would put "religion in danger."[153]

Women in the Vedic Strauta Ritual, *in* ROLES AND RITUALS FOR HINDU WOMEN, *supra* note 121, at 17, 18–19.

149. GOVERNMENT OF INDIA, *supra* note 148, at 40–41.

150. *See* Young, *supra* note 6, at 115.

151. Young, *supra* note 6, at 114, 125.

152. *See* Singh, *supra* note 128, at 375, 380–82; Saijwani, *supra* note 147, at 41. Family laws in India are divided along religious lines, with Hindus covered by the civil Hindu laws, and Muslims and Christians each covered by their own respective religious laws. *See supra* note 93; Singh, *supra* note 128, at 378–79.

153. *See* Young, *supra* note 6, at 114; Singh, *supra* note 128, at 380–81.

Islam

In Islam, fundamentalist groups are found among both the Sunni and Shi'ite Muslims in a broad range of geographic locations. Examples here are drawn from a wide variety of groups with particular emphasis on three representative groups: the Muslim Brotherhood;[154] the Jama'a-t-i-Islami;[155] and the Ayatollah Khomeini's

---

154. In the Sunni Arab world, The Muslim Brotherhood, founded in Egypt in 1928 by Hasan al-Banna, is one of the largest and most widespread of Muslim fundamentalist groups. *See* John O. Voll, *Fundamentalism in the Sunni Arab World: Egypt and the Sudan, in* 1 THE FUNDAMENTALISM PROJECT: FUNDAMENTALISMS OBSERVED, *supra* note 7, at 345, 360. It has member groups in Egypt, Jordan, Syria, Sudan, Palestine, Saudi Arabia, Kuwait, Qatar, and the United Arab Emirates. Voll, *supra*, at 359, 366, 390; Gehad Auda, *The Normalization of the Islamic Movement in Egypt from the 1970s to the Early 1990s, in* 4 THE FUNDAMENTALISM PROJECT: ACCOUNTING FOR FUNDAMENTALISMS, *supra* note 16, at 374, 380. The Brotherhood meets the definition of fundamentalism. *See* Auda, *supra*, at 375, 379–81, 382–83, 386–89; James Piscatori, *Accounting for Islamic Fundamentalisms, in* 4 THE FUNDAMENTALISM PROJECT: ACCOUNTING FOR FUNDAMENTALISMS, *supra* note 16, at 361, 363–64; Abdel Azim Ramadan, *Fundamentalist Influence in Egypt: The Strategies of the Muslim Brotherhood and the Takfir Groups, in* 3 THE FUNDAMENTALISM PROJECT: FUNDAMENTALISMS AND THE STATE, *supra* note 11, at 152, 152; Voll, *supra*, at 366. Al-Banna rejected Enlightenment principles of individual and intellectual freedom and any division between religion and politics. *See* Voll, *supra*, at 360; *see, e.g.*, HASAN AL-BANNA, FIVE TRACTS OF HASAN AL-BANNA (1906–1949) 28–29, 75 (Charles Wendell trans., 1978) [hereinafter "AL-BANNA, FIVE TRACTS"]; MEMOIRS OF HASAN AL-BANNA (M.N. Shaikh trans., 1981). He demanded that Egyptian law be reformed according to the Shari'ah (body of Islamic law derived primarily from the Qur'an) and that militaries be strengthened for Islamic *jihads* against non-believers. Auda, *supra*, at 386.

In the early 1960s, Sayyid Qutb gave The Brotherhood new inspiration. *See* Voll, *supra*, at 370–71. His ideology aims to "re-create" Islamic life in totality such that divine sovereignty is paramount and the Shari'ah is followed; thus, prevailing social orders and political regimes must be overturned in the name of true Islam, violently if necessary. *See* SAYYID QUTB, MILESTONES 15–17, 23, 34–35, 43–62, 80–84 (trans. unnamed, AM. TRUST PUB. 1990) (1964); Auda, *supra*, at 377–78; Voll, *supra*, at 372; *see also* AL-BANNA, FIVE TRACTS, *supra*, at 80, 82, 133–61. Qutb drew many of his ideas from the Islamic Pakistani fundamentalist, Abul A'la Maududi, *see* Ramadan, *supra*, at 156, who is discussed in detail below, *see infra* note 155. Qutb was tried and executed under the Nasser government, but his ideology continues to provide a base for Islamic fundamentalist movements. *See* Voll, *supra*, at 370, 372.

The Muslim Brotherhood has had various connections to violent *jihad* movements including the Jihad Organization, *see* Auda, *supra*, at 382; Voll, *supra*, at 383, 388, 389; Courtney W. Howland, *Scepticism over brotherhood's protestations*, Letter, FIN. TIMES, Dec. 8, 1995, which is regarded as responsible for the assassination of President Sadat in 1981. Auda, *supra*, at 379. Such militant groups manifest particularly strong anti-semitism and very limited, if any, tolerance for Christians, *see* Andrea B. Rugh, *Reshaping Personal Relations in Egypt, in* 2 THE FUNDAMENTALISM PROJECT: FUNDAMENTALISMS AND SOCIETY, *supra* note 40, at 151, 166–67; Auda, *supra*, at 387, 389, and are involved in violent activities, including the bombing of Christian churches. *See* Voll, *supra*, at 389; Rugh, *supra*, at 153. The Brotherhood fully entered legal organized politics in the 1980s and joined forces with the New Wafd party with whom it won a number of seats in parliament. *See* Auda, *supra*, at 387. Although certain factions of the Brotherhood have been viewed in recent times as less extreme than other Islamic fundamentalist groups, the Brotherhood is still strongly campaigning against the government and engaging in extremist tactics triggering arrests and reprisals. *See* James Whittington, *Mubarak cracks down on Islamists*, FIN. TIMES, Nov. 24, 1995, at 8; John Lancaster, *Fundamentalists Jailed Before Egypt's Election*, WASH. POST, Nov. 24, 1995, at A31–A32; *Egypt Releases Islamic Activist*, WASH. POST, Nov. 2, 1995, at A26.

155. The Jama'at-i-Islami is a major group clearly meeting the definition of fundamentalism. *See* Rafi-

Islamic movement in Iran and its related groups.[156] Despite great diversity within Muslim fundamentalism and with regard to the interpretation of orthodox practices, the movements are strikingly similar in certain doctrines and goals.[157]

The Religious-Legal Doctrine

A central doctrine throughout Muslim fundamentalism is that women harbor the seeds of destruction of all society and that, to avoid this, they and their sexuality

---

uddin Ahmed, *Redefining Muslim Identity in South Asia: The Transformation of the Jama'at-i-Islami, in* 4 THE FUNDAMENTALISM PROJECT: ACCOUNTING FOR FUNDAMENTALISMS, *supra* note 16, at 669, 669; Ahmad, *supra* note 27, at 462; Sajeda Amin & Sara Hossain, *Women's Reproductive Rights and the Politics of Fundamentalism: A View From Bangladesh,* 44 AM. UNIV. L. REV. 1319, 1336 (1995). The group was founded by Abul A'la Maududi whose extensive writings, translated into many languages, provide excellent examples of fundamentalist rhetoric and theory and are central to Islamic fundamentalism today. *See* Ahmad, *supra* note 27, at 464; *see, e.g.,* Riffat Hassan, *An Islamic Perspective, in* WOMEN, RELIGION AND SEXUALITY, *supra* note 23, at 93, 107–10; Hugh Roberts, *From Radical Mission to Equivocal Ambition: The Expansion and Manipulation of Algerian Islamism,* 1979–1992, *in* 4 THE FUNDAMENTALISM PROJECT: ACCOUNTING FOR FUNDAMENTALISMS, *supra* note 16, at 428, 440 (noting that Algerian fundamentalism relies upon doctrines of Maududi and Qutb). Maududi founded Jama'at to give institutional support to his ideas for constructing an Islamic society where all civil institutions and state authority would be subordinate to divine law of the Qur'an and the Shari'ah. *See* Ahmed, *supra,* at 674; Ahmad, *supra* note 27, at 470. Religious scholars would exercise authority over all legislation to ensure that laws and practices were in accordance with the Qur'an and the Sunnah. *See* Ahmad, *supra* note 27, at 459, 463, 469; ANN E. MAYER, ISLAM AND HUMAN RIGHTS: TRADITION AND POLITICS 26 (1991).

The Jama'at launched strong political campaigns to found Pakistan as an Islamic state. In the 1960s, it campaigned against reforms in family law, birth control, and the "modernizing" of Islam through acceptance of Western practices and Western sexual permissiveness. *See* Haeri, *supra* note 40, at 201–02; Ahmad, *supra* note 27, at 474. The Jama'at continues its drive today for further "Islamization" in Pakistan, Bangladesh, and India. *See* Ahmed, *supra,* at 688–95; Ahmad, *supra* note 27, at 501–07; Amin & Hossain, *supra,* at 1336–40. Although Jama'at's own constitution forswears violence, it has been involved in a number of violent activities, and Maududi believed that *jihad* could be used to wage war against the infidels, including apostates and reformers. *See* Ahmed, *supra,* at 678–95.

156. Fundamentalism in the Shi'ite Muslim world is represented by various movements from Ayatollah Khomeini's Islamic movement in Iran to The Islamic Call and Islamic Fighters in Iraq and Battalions of Lebanese Resistance (AMAL). *See* Abdulaziz A. Sachedina, *Activist Shi'ism in Iran, Iraq, and Lebanon, in* 1 THE FUNDAMENTALISM PROJECT: FUNDAMENTALISMS OBSERVED, *supra* note 7, at 403, 403–04, 442, 446.

The Iranian post-revolutionary regime is considered a fundamentalist government. *See* Mahnaz Afkhami, *Women in Post-Revolutionary Iran: a feminist perspective, in* IN THE EYE OF THE STORM: WOMEN IN POST-REVOLUTIONARY IRAN 5, 12 (Mahnaz Afkhami & Erika Friedl eds., 1994); Haeri, *supra* note 40, at 187–89; Poya, *supra* note 23, at 141, 141–62; Sachedina, *supra,* at 403–07, 429. Khomeini's and subsequent post-revolutionary governments incorporate a strong reaction against modernization, particularly in the form of Western secularism based on Enlightenment principles which they see as responsible for displacing the Qur'an and the Sunnah as the proper framework for societal institutions and laws. *See* Sachedina, *supra,* at 411. Khomeini regarded the Shah's policies, particularly those aimed at reforms in family law and women's rights, as inimical to an Islamic society and thus they were first on his agenda for repeal. *See infra* notes 158, 178; Haeri, *supra* note 40, at 188, 190–93.

157. Indeed, many of the various fundamentalist groups maintain contact with each other. For example, the Jama'at-i-Islami of Bangladesh, India, and Pakistan, *see supra* note 155, the groups Dar-ul-Islam in

must be carefully controlled.[158] Fundamentalists blame women's uncontrolled sexuality for the modern Western "sensate culture" represented by selfishness, greed, and immorality.[159] Unless women adhere strongly to their "natural" role as childbearers, they will become unchaste and immoral and bring down the rest of society.[160] To avoid these consequences, Muslim fundamentalists support traditional notions of morality with emphasis on separate gender spheres.[161] Their separate-spheres ideology requires segregation of the sexes so that women's alluring sexuality does not morally undermine men. Under this ideology, the place for the woman is confined at home caring for her family, of which the man is indisputably head.[162] A man must be head of the family in order to maintain control over the dangerous sexuality of the women in the family, and because women are considered unsuited to any role of authority by virtue of their submissive nature and periodic instability.[163]

Indeed, a number of Islamic fundamentalists explicitly declare men to be superior to women,[164] which places men in control of women and requires that women

Indonesia and Parti Islam Se-Malaysia in Malaysia, *see* Ahmad, *supra* note 27, at 458–59, and the groups Hizb-i-Islami of Afghanistan, the Islamic Movement of Algeria, the Jamiyat-al-Islah of Bahrain, the Islamic Tendency Society of Tunis and the Rafah party of Turkey have all met together for conferences. *Id.* at 457.

158. *See* ABUL A'LA MAUDUDI, PURDAH AND THE STATUS OF WOMAN IN ISLAM 2 (Al-Ash 'ari trans. ed., 1972) (1939) [hereinafter MAUDUDI, PURDAH] ("'[When] woman is raised to prominence . . . a storm of immorality and licentiousness follows in her wake. . . . She is actually reduced to the position of the Devil's agent, and . . . starts the degeneration of Mankind in general.'"); *see also* AL-BANNA, FIVE TRACTS, *supra* note 154, at 26. Marriages are arranged for girls at young ages in order to protect their chastity and honor. In a number of Islamic-law states, the minimum age for girls for marriage is on average about 15. JAMIL J. NASIR, THE STATUS OF WOMEN UNDER ISLAMIC LAW AND UNDER MODERN ISLAMIC LEGISLATION 7–10 (2d. ed., 1994) [hereinafter NASIR, STATUS OF WOMEN]. One of the first acts of the post-Revolutionary Iranian government was lowering the age for marriage for girls in the aim of protecting their chastity. *See* MAYER, *supra* note 155, at 130; Jane I. Smith, *Women In Islam, in* TODAY'S WOMAN IN WORLD RELIGIONS, *supra* note 6, at 303, 314. In rural areas the average age of brides is between 13 and 15, but in certain parts of Iran 80% of wives had been married between the ages of 9 and 16. NASIR, STATUS OF WOMEN. *supra*, at 9.

159. *See* SYED ABUL A'LA MAUDUDI, BIRTH CONTROL 16 (Khurshid Ahmad & Misbahul Islam Faruqi trans. ed., 1st ed. reprtg. 1987) (1943) [hereinafter MAUDUDI, BIRTH CONTROL]; MAUDUDI, PURDAH, *supra* note 158, at 39–72; QUTB, *supra* note 154, at 83; Hassan, *supra* note 155, at 103, 108–09.

160. *See* QUTB, *supra* note 154, at 83, 119; S. ABUL A'LA MAUDUDI, THE MEANING OF THE QUR'AN (VOL. IV) 16 (1976) (n.d.); *see also* MAUDUDI, BIRTH CONTROL, *supra* note 159, at 18.

161. *See* Rugh, *supra* note 154, at 158, 169–73 (discussing The Muslim Brotherhood); Haeri, *supra* note 40, at 183, 186, 188–95, 199, 201–04 (discussing Jama'at-i-Islami and post-revolutionary Iran); Ahmad, *supra* note 27, at 471–74 (discussing Jama'at-i-Islami); Amin & Hossain, *supra* note 155, at 1336–42 (discussing Jama'at-i-Islami).

162. MAUDUDI, PURDAH, *supra* note 158, at 121; AHMAD, *supra* note 36, at 34 (Khurshid Ahmad has been a translator of Maududi's and is a contemporary follower in Maududi's tradition.); *cf.* IQBAL, *supra* note 36, at 102–05 (noting that a woman may not be head of family, much less the leader of a state because this is inconsistent with her duties to care for children and home).

163. MAUDUDI, PURDAH, *supra* note 158, at 121–23 (noting that women are naturally "submissive and impressionable" and that "[i]n order to maintain the family system and save it from confusion some one must be entrusted with necessary authority. . . . Such a one can only be the man. For the member whose mental and physical state becomes unstable time and again during menstruation and pregnancy

be obedient to men.[165] The requirement of obedience to the male head of household extends through every woman's entire life,[166] but is particularly compelling for a married woman in respect of her husband.[167] Obedience requires submission to her husband in all things, including sexual and social matters.[168] Furthermore, fundamentalist doctrine allows men to enforce this duty of obedience through violence. If a wife is disobedient, a proper husband is first to ''appeal to her good sense, and if she does not improve, then he may abandon her in her marital bed. Thereafter, it is permissible for him to give her a good, but gentle, beating.''[169]

---

cannot be expected to use such authority with wisdom and discretion. . . . To maintain this division [of labor between husband and wife] there must be some safeguards provided in the social system. . . .''); *see also* Azizah Y. al-Hibri, *A Comparative Study of Certain Egyptian, Syrian, Moroccan and Tunisian Marriage Laws*, 4 INT'L REV. OF COMP. PUB. POL'Y 227, 231 (1992).

164. MAUDUDI, PURDAH, *supra* note 158, at 148; S. ABUL A'LA MAUDUDI, THE MEANING OF THE QUR'AN (VOL. II) 325 n.57 (1971) [hereinafter MAUDUDI, THE MEANING OF THE QUR'AN (VOL. II)]; Hassan, *supra* note 155, at 110, 114; *see also* MAYER, *supra* note 155, at 131–32 (discussing examples of inferior status assigned to women under Iranian regime of Khomeini). Contemporary writers try to avoid this rhetoric and instead declare that the issue of equality is not relevant to the Islamic context. *See* AHMAD, *supra* note 36, at 34–35.

165. *See* MAUDUDI, THE MEANING OF THE QUR'AN (VOL. II), *supra* note 164, at 321, 325 nn.56–59 (''Men are the managers of the affairs of women because Allah has made the one superior to the other. . . . Virtuous women are, therefore, obedient; they guard their rights carefully in their absence under the care and watch of Allah.''); MAUDUDI, PURDAH, *supra* note 158, at 148–49; *see* AHMAD, *supra* note 36, at 34.

166. *See* MAUDUDI, PURDAH, *supra* note 158, at 153 (''[J]ust as a married woman has to obey and be looked after by her husband, so an unmarried woman has to obey and be looked after by the responsible men of her family.'').

167. *See* IQBAL, *supra* note 36, at 100 (''If he orders, she obeys him.''); HUDA KHATTAB, THE MUSLIM WOMAN'S HAND BOOK 40–41 (1993); JOHN L. ESPOSITO, WOMEN IN MUSLIM FAMILY LAW 23 (1982); MAUDUDI, PURDAH, *supra* note 158, at 153; Wael B. Hallaq, Islamic Response to Contraception-Fact Pattern VI.B., *Symposium on Religious Law: Roman Catholic, Islamic, and Jewish Treatment of Familial Issues, Including Education, Abortion,* In Vitro *Fertilization, Prenuptial Agreements, Contraception, and Marital Fraud,* 16 LOY. L.A. INT'L & COMP. L.J. 9, 79 (1993) (''[I]n matters as relate to family life, the husband's wishes override those of the wife.'').

168. *See* KHATTAB, *supra* note 167, at 40–41; ESPOSITO, *supra* note 167, at 23; Hallaq, *supra* note 167, at 79. According to Rugh, a study of correspondence to Egyptian *Islamic Banner* demonstrates fundamentalist views ''that husbands have indisputable right to sex in the marriage relation. A writer explained to a reader that the Qur'an says women are a tilth for you to cultivate, so go to your tilth as ye will; in sum it is forbidden for a man to copulate with his wife during menstruation, but apart from that it is his right and privilege to penetrate her as long as it occurs through the proper channel.'' Rugh, *supra* note 154, at 171. For example, during any fast a woman must refuse her husband's sexual advances. KHATTAB, *supra* note 167, at 5. Therefore, a married woman may not observe any of Islam's optional fasts without her husband's permission, because he may prefer to safeguard his right of sexual access to his wife and refuse her permission to fast. MAUDUDI, PURDAH, *supra* note 158, at 146–47; KHATTAB, *supra* note 167, at 5, 40–41.

169. Rugh, *supra* note 154, at 170; MAUDUDI, THE MEANING OF THE QUR'AN (VOL. II), *supra* note 164, at 321 (footnotes omitted) (''As for those women whose defiance you have cause to fear, admonish them and keep them apart from your beds and beat them.''). Maududi explains that ''there are some women who do not mend their ways without a beating.'' MAUDUDI, THE MEANING OF THE QUR'AN (VOL. II), *supra* note 164, at 325 n.59.

Muslim fundamentalists also utilize the modesty doctrine of *hejab* for ensuring the wife's obedience and reinforcing the husband's control, particularly his economic control. *Hejab* (as interpreted by fundamentalists) requires segregation of women and men and dictates that women are not to leave their houses unless absolutely necessary, and if they do go out, they should be fully covered, often including veiling the face.[170] *Hejab* sets up barriers against a woman working outside the home, and makes it very difficult for her to achieve economic independence. This accords with fundamentalist doctrine disallowing a woman to earn money like a man[171] and forbidding her to work without her husband's permission.[172] Fundamentalists disfavor any economic independence for a woman because it would "ma[k]e her free of the authority of the father and husband."[173] A woman's inheritance rights are also very limited.[174] A woman who nevertheless succeeds in living outside male control is regarded as a threat to the good morality of society, and as such is in constant mortal danger.[175]

---

170. *See* MAUDUDI, PURDAH, *supra* note 158, at 163–216. (Maududi's book is translated from Urdu into English and Arabic. The Arabic term for *purdah* is *hejab*. *Purdah*, in fact, is the term for the segregation of women in Hinduism.) *Hejab* is justified as a "wide-ranging system which protects the family and closes those avenues that lead towards illicit sex or even indiscriminate contact between the sexes in society." AHMAD, *supra* note 36, at 35. *Hejab* restricts women far more severely than men, on the ground that women's sexuality presents the danger and must be controlled. *See* Hassan, *supra* note 155, at 118–22. Some Egyptian fundamentalists state that unattractive women need not cover themselves because they will not cause men immoral thoughts, whereas other Egyptian fundamentalists find that "[t]he whole of a woman's body is a pudendum except her face and hands." Rugh, *supra* note 154, at 172; *see* KHATTAB, *supra* note 167, at 14–16 (noting that "External" *hejab* requires that woman's dress cover whole head and body, including neck, forearms, ears, legs; clothing should be loose, thick enough to conceal skin, not perfumed, not resemble men's clothing, not bright colors, not similar to clothing of non-Muslims, not dress of vanity, not be an adornment that would attract men's attention); IQBAL, *supra* note 36, at 52–59 (*Hejab* requires total segregation of sexes and requires that woman is completely covered and concealed if she leaves her house so as to deter anti-social elements and not to attract attention).

171. *See* MAUDUDI, PURDAH, *supra* note 158, at 25, 120–22, 154, 161; Haleh Esfandiari, *The Majles and Women's Issues in the Islamic Republic of Iran, in* IN THE EYE OF THE STORM: WOMEN IN POST-REVOLUTIONARY IRAN, *supra* note 156, at 61, 71.

172. *See* IQBAL, *supra* note 36, at 25; NASIR, STATUS OF WOMEN, *supra* note 158, at 66–67 (discussing Iraqi law that woman loses right to maintenance if she works without her husband's permission); Sima Pakzad, *Appendix I: The Legal Status of Women in the Family in Iran, in* IN THE EYE OF THE STORM: WOMEN IN POST-REVOLUTIONARY IRAN, *supra* note 156, at 169, 174 (noting that under Iranian Islamic law husband may prevent wife from working if he can prove that occupation is against family interests).

173. MAUDUDI, PURDAH, *supra* note 158, at 14–15, 68. "Why should a woman who wins her own bread, supports herself economically and does not depend on anyone for security and maintenance, remain faithfully attached to one man only for the sake of satisfying sexual desires? Why should she be prepared to subject herself to so many moral and legal curbs to shoulder the responsibilities of family life?" *Id.* at 14. For a similar attitude in Buddhist and Christian fundamentalism, see *supra* notes 56 (Buddhism) and 92 (Christianity) and accompanying text.

174. For example, a daughter inherits half the share of a son. MAUDUDI, PURDAH, *supra* note 158, at 154 n.1; Ahmad, *supra* note 36, at 35.

175. *See* Khalida Messaoudi, *for "Oum Ali," Algeria, in* CENTER FOR WOMEN'S GLOBAL LEADERSHIP, TESTIMONIES OF THE GLOBAL TRIBUNAL ON VIOLATIONS OF WOMEN'S HUMAN RIGHTS AT THE UNITED NATIONS WORLD CONFERENCE ON HUMAN RIGHTS, VIENNA, JUNE 1993, 76 (1994). Messaoudi, an Algerian, testified

Political Activity to Conform State Law to Religious-Legal Doctrine

Fundamentalist political activity has pressed for enactment of family and personal status laws as part of state legal systems, and this has succeeded in a number of states.[176] In most cases, fundamentalists owe this success not to any vote of confidence in their viewpoint but rather to their use of violence to intimidate people into silent compliance with their actions, which is especially effective where the populace is already intimidated by corrupt, oppressive, and undemocratic government.[177] Fundamentalist success is reflected in the enactment of state laws requiring the obedience of women: marriage and divorce laws, and *hejab*.[178] The marriage

---

to the case of Oum Ali, who was too terrorized to testify in Vienna. Oum Ali was divorced, abandoned by her husband, and living with seven children in an Algerian town. The fundamentalists regarded her as a menace to the morality of the town, and came into her home, threw heating oil on the bed, and set fire to it in order to purify the house. The house was burned down and one child was burned to death. Twelve men were arrested, prompting demonstrations by fundamentalists demanding their release. They did not deny the crime, but "[i]n their minds . . . ,they have the right to persecute any person—particularly women who are alone, who they believe are representatives of Satan, representatives of danger and immorality." *Id.* at 77.

176. Fundamentalist interpretations of the Shari'ah are being increasingly imposed and enforced in a number of countries: Algeria, *see* Marie-Aimée Hélie-Lucas, *Bound and Gagged by the Family Code*, *in* THIRD WORLD-SECOND SEX (vol. 2), *supra* note 50, at 3, 3–15; Bangladesh, *see supra* note 155; Egypt, *see supra* note 154; Iran, *see supra* note 156; Iraq, *see* Hélie-Lucas, *supra* note 6, at 55, 61; Pakistan, *see supra* note 155; Rashida Patel, *Challenges Facing Women in Pakistan*, *in* OURS BY RIGHT, *supra* note 6, at 32, 32–39; Sudan, *see* Asma Mohamed Abdel Halim, *Challenges to the Application of International Women's Human Rights in the Sudan*, *in* HUMAN RIGHTS OF WOMEN, *supra* note 128, at 397, 399–405. *See also* Ann E. Mayer, *The Fundamentalist Impact on Law, Politics, and Constitutions in Iran, Pakistan, and the Sudan*, *in* 3 THE FUNDAMENTALISM PROJECT: FUNDAMENTALISMS AND THE STATE, *supra* note 11, at 110, 110–52; Hélie-Lucas, *supra* note 6, at 54–59 (discussing Islamization in several countries). This has been accomplished by either passing state laws or enforcing state laws through incorporation of fundamentalist interpretation of the Shari'ah. These interpretations may well echo conservative Islamic codes, *see* Ahmad, *supra* note 27, at 463; al-Hibri, *supra* note 163, at 239, which are difficult to reform due to fundamentalist pressure.

177. Violent activity ranges from Islamic fundamentalist groups smuggling "surface-to-air missiles, 80mm mortars, hand-held rocket launchers and M-16 rifles" into the Philippines from Pakistan for military raids on Christian towns in the south of the country, *see* Edward Luce, *Pakistan, Philippines to combat terrorism*, FIN. TIMES, Apr. 29/30 1995, at 3, to violently harassing Muslim women who do not conform to their "natural" roles, *see supra* note 175 (burning down single woman's house). Fundamentalist activity in Egypt is having a general intimidating effect. *See* Raymond Stock, *How Islamist Militants put Egypt on Trial*, FIN. TIMES, Mar. 4/5, 1995, at III (discussing fundamentalist violence in Egypt including stabbing of Nobel-prize-winning author, Naguib Mahfouz). At least 29 women have been killed in Algeria for protesting laws placing limitations on women. 8 IWRAW, THE WOMEN'S WATCH 2 (no. 1) (June 1994). Individual protests continue in Iran. Dr. Darabi was dismissed from her job as physician for refusing to wear a veil, and continued to be harassed when she attempted to set up in private practice. Her husband refused to allow her to leave Iran. She set herself on fire in a public square in Teheran to protest oppression of women in Iran. *Id.*

178. *See supra* notes 170–72 and accompanying text. In the context of obedience laws, fundamentalist doctrine overlaps with conservative doctrine. However, fundamentalists fight to prevent reform of conservative obedience laws, to strengthen such laws, or to repeal laws in conflict with the obedience laws. For example, in Iran, one of Khomeini's first acts was to nullify the Iranian Family Protection Act, which had been a reform to improve women's status and rights during marriage and divorce. MAYER, *supra* note 155, at 130.

laws of various Islamic states provide that marriage transfers a woman from the control of her father to the protection and control of her husband.[179] As a wife, her duty of obedience to her husband may be statutorily explicit[180] or implicit through the concept of *nashiz* . A *nashiz* is a disobedient or rebellious wife,[181] and this may include a woman who acts superior to her husband, disobeys his orders, leaves her marital home without legitimate reason or her husband's permission, works outside the home without his permission, or uses contraception without permission.[182] For example, Shi'ite Muslim fundamentalists specifically define a *nashiz* to include a wife who denies her husband his conjugal rights, even temporarily, and a wife who borrows money without the permission of a judge or of her husband.[183]

A *nashiz* loses her right to protection under the marriage contract for as long as she is disobedient.[184] This protection is the right to maintenance—food, clothing and housing—as long as "she places or offers to place herself in the husband's power so as to allow him free access to herself at all lawful times . . . and . . . obeys all his lawful commands for the duration of the marriage."[185] This is a serious threat to a woman who is made financially dependent on the husband and may not

---

179. The extent of the father's control is particularly clear in his role as marriage guardian (*wali*). If the father is dead, another male relative, or, if there is none, a judge (who is male) becomes marriage guardian. Under guardianship laws, a woman cannot contract her own marriage, even if she possesses full legal capacity. NASIR, STATUS OF WOMEN, *supra* note 158, at 10–12 (discussing laws of Morocco, Algeria, Iraq, Jordan, and Syria); Halim, *supra* note 176, at 400–02 (discussing Sudan's Islamization and subsequent passage of Personal Law for Muslims Act of 1991 requiring *wali* for women).

180. *See, e.g.,* Moroccan Code, Bk. 1, Title 6, art. 36, clause 2; Algerian Code, Bk. 1, title 1, Ch. 4, art. 39, Clause 1; Tunisian Code, art. 23; Jordanian Code, art. 32; Sudan Personal Law for Muslims Act of 1991, *in* Halim, *supra* note 176, at 402; *see* al-Hibri, *supra* note 163, at 238–39. Laws of obedience also apply in Iran and Pakistan. *See* Haeri, *supra* note 40, at 181, 185–86.

181. This concept of "rebellious" wife is similar to the Christian concept, *see supra* note and accompanying text, and the Jewish concept, *see infra* notes 215, 218–20. However, there are greater legal ramifications and punishments for women based on the concept of a "rebellious" wife in present-day Islam and Judaism.

182. *See, e.g.,* NASIR, STATUS OF WOMEN, *supra* note 158, at 66–70 (discussing laws of Iraq, Jordan, Syria, Egypt, Kuwait); JAMIL J. NASIR, THE ISLAMIC LAW OF PERSONAL STATUS 129–30 (1990) [hereinafter NASIR, ISLAMIC LAW OF PERSONAL STATUS]; Sudan Personal Law for Muslims Act of 1991, *in* Halim, *supra* note 176, at 402; Hallaq, *supra* note 167, at 80. A wife loses her right to maintenance if she travels unaccompanied by her husband, and conversely is bound to travel with her husband to wherever he wishes as long as it is safe—otherwise she loses her maintenance. NASIR, STATUS OF WOMEN, *supra* note 158, at 68 (citing Jordan art. 37; Iraq art. 2(3); Syria art.70; Kuwait art. 90).

183. *See* Pakzad, *supra* note 158, at 172; NASIR, STATUS OF WOMEN, *supra* note 158, at 67.

184. *See* NASIR, STATUS OF WOMEN, *supra* note 158, at 68; NASIR, ISLAMIC LAW OF PERSONAL STATUS, *supra* note 182, at 129–30.

185. *See* NASIR, STATUS OF WOMEN, *supra* note 158, at 64–65, 66 (footnote omitted); Sudan Personal Law for Muslims Act of 1991, *in* Halim, *supra* note 176, at 402. This is the law in countries that adopt Shari'ah by incorporation, such as Saudi Arabia, as in countries which have enacted the provision as statute, such as Egypt, Jordan, Iraq, Kuwait, and Syria. *See, e.g.,* NASIR, STATUS OF WOMEN, *supra* note 158, at 65 (citing Egypt 25/1920, art.1; Jordan art. 67; Iraq art. 23; Kuwait art. 74; and Syria art. 72/1); Sudan Personal Law for Muslims Act of 1991, *in* Halim, *supra* note 176, at 402.

work without his permission.[186] Moreover, a husband may obtain an obedience order from a court against his wife, and "[i]f she still persists, he is entitled to divorce her and, because she has violated his rights, he is under no obligation whatsoever to provide maintenance for her."[187]

The ultimate act of disobedience by a wife is adultery.[188] In 1990, Iraq decreed that, according to its fundamentalist ideology, men were allowed to kill their womenfolk for adultery.[189] Because the killing is based on the husband's (not a court's) assessment of the situation, it may easily occur if the adultery is merely feared or suspected rather than real. Kurdistan has recently passed a law absolving a man for murder of his wife if he can prove she was morally disobedient.[190]

A further threat is that a man may divorce his wife at will or whim.[191] After a divorce an ex-wife is entitled to maintenance in some circumstances during the

---

186. See NASIR, STATUS OF WOMEN, supra note 158, at 66–67.

187. Hallaq, supra note 167, at 80. For example, a wife who disobeys her husband by using contraceptives violates his right to her obedience and he may "legally enjoin" her from using contraceptives. Id. Happily, in Kuwait "no obedience order obtained by the husband against her shall be implemented using force, the only penalty of noncompliance thereto being the loss of her maintenance." NASIR, STATUS OF WOMEN, supra note 158, at 68 (citing Kuwait art. 88).

188. Women's chastity is so important to men that some states even provide by statute the husband's "right" that the wife shall guard her chastity. See NASIR, STATUS OF WOMEN, supra note 158, at 41 (discussing Moroccan law).

189. Hélie-Lucas, supra note 6, at 55. Stoning to death is a punishment for women's adultery under fundamentalist interpretation of the Hudd punishments. See, e.g., Patel, supra note 176, at 32–33, 36–37 (discussing application of Hudd punishments for adultery in Pakistan); see also Hélie-Lucas, supra note 6, at 58–59. In Iran there is a law that regulates the size of the stone with which the woman is to be killed. Messaoudi, supra note 175, at 76, 78–79. It should not be too large because then she would be killed too quickly, nor too small because then she would not be killed. Id. at 79. Amnesty International reported on the stoning of Saraya in Iran: "Saraya was buried up to her shoulders. . . . The stones were flying, her head and her chest were reduced to raw flesh. Using all of his strength, the man hits her skull many times, her brain is scattered on the ground, and a big cry of joy arises, 'Allah o Akbar.' " Id. at 78.

190. See 8 IWRAW, THE WOMEN'S WATCH 4 (no. 3) (Dec. 1994) (noting that this law was passed by the "autonomous Kurdistan government" and that "550 women have been murdered since the establishment of the new government.").

191. In general, husbands may divorce their wives at will and without court order (the right of talaq). See NASIR, STATUS OF WOMEN, supra note 158, at 74–76; Hélie-Lucas, supra note 6, at 59. Talaq is the unilateral declaration of a husband divorcing and repudiating his wife and can be performed by word of mouth or in writing. It is legally binding. For statutory enactment of talaq, see, e.g., Syria art. 87/2, Morocco art. 44, Jordan art. 87, Iraq art. 34, and Kuwait art. 104; Sudan Personal Law for Muslims Act of 1991, in Halim, supra note 176, at 403. Other Muslim states incorporate Shari'ah law with its provisions of talaq. Fundamentalists have interpreted these to allow the husband to make an unwitnessed declaration of repudiation, with no evidence that he has repudiated other than his own word. See NASIR, STATUS OF WOMEN, supra note 158, at 79 n.7. If the woman divorced by unwitnessed repudiation now remarries, her ex-husband, either for revenge or financial reasons, may later deny he pronounced talaq, at which point the woman can be tried for adultery (with the new husband) for which she risks being stoned to death. See Hélie-Lucas, supra note 6, at 59. For example, in Pakistan, the state allows the ex-husband to retain control over his ex-wife by granting him the sole responsibility of filing a divorce

three-month period of *iddat* which is intended to determine whether she is pregnant.[192] After this she is not entitled to maintenance regardless of the number of years of marriage and her financial dependence on her husband. The fear of unilateral divorce and no financial support strongly encourages obedience. It is also important to note that, during the period of *iddat*, the husband may unilaterally revoke the divorce,[193] and is thereupon entitled to "resume the conjugal relationship with the wife without her consent."[194]

Finally, fundamentalists have succeeded in enforcing their interpretation of *hejab* by public laws specifically requiring the dress of *hejab*. In Sudan, the fundamentalist military regime has required that "women should dress in loose long dresses and cover their heads,"[195] and, when their dress is inappropriate, they are now subject to amputation of hands and feet, hanging, stoning to death, or hanging followed by crucifixion of the body.[196] Khomeini's Islamic regime quickly passed a law making it mandatory for women to wear the "Islamic veil" in public.[197] Violation brings a woman seventy-four lashes and internment for rehabilitation,

---

notice of *talaq* with the state. In a case where the husband had pronounced *talaq*, failed—allegedly purposefully—to file the divorce notice, and subsequently notified the police of his wife's remarriage, the court found the ex-wife and her new husband guilty of adultery and fornication and ordered them flogged and imprisoned for 7 years. *See* Shera v. State, P.L.D. 1982 F.S.C. 229 (1982); *see generally* Mark C. Hulbert, *Islamization of the Law in Pakistan: Developments in Criminal Law and the Regulation of Banking* (unpublished paper on file with author).

A wife may be able to get a divorce if she can get her husband's consent by giving him consideration (*khula*) for her freedom. *See* NASIR, STATUS OF WOMEN, *supra* note 158, at 84–87. Often this amounts to the wife forfeiting the dowry due to her on marriage. *See also id.* at 87. Otherwise, the grounds of divorce for a wife are very narrow and limited. *See* NASIR, STATUS OF WOMEN, *supra* note 158, at 92–101; Sudan Personal Law for Muslims Act of 1991, *in* Halim, *supra* note 176, at 403.

192. NASIR, STATUS OF WOMEN, *supra* note 158, at 108–11, 113. The wife is generally not entitled to maintenance at all if she is divorced for disobedience. *Id.*

193. The husband may make the *talaq* irrevocable by making his pronouncement of repudiation three times with three *iddat* periods. *See* NASIR, STATUS OF WOMEN, *supra* note 158, at 82–84 (citing Egypt Act No. 25/1929 art. 3; Sudan Sharia Circular no. 41/1935 art. 3; Syria art. 92; Morocco art. 51; Iraq art. 37/2; Jordan 85; Kuwaiti art. 109.)

194. NASIR, STATUS OF WOMEN, *supra* note 158, at 112.

195. Halim, *supra* note 176, at 401. The Muslim Brotherhood members of the Egyptian Parliament also demand the legal and universal imposition of fundamentalist Islamic dress on women. *See* Auda, *supra* note 154, at 387–88.

196. Amnesty International USA, *Sudan*, AMNESTY ACTION (Winter 1995) at 1, 3.

197. *See* Haeri, *supra* note 40, at 188. Veiling in Iran should be understood in the context of its political significance. Some Iranian middle-class women donned the veil during the Revolution to show solidarity with working class women, *see* Nayereh Tohidi, *Gender and Islamic Fundamentalism: Feminist Politics in Iran*, *in* THIRD WORLD WOMEN AND THE POLITICS OF FEMINISM 251, 251–52 (Chandra Mohanty et al. eds., 1991), as a reaction against Shah Reza Pahlavi's repressive regime, which had prohibited veiling. But recognizing the political and historical context of voluntary veiling should not obfuscate the structural oppression of women manifested by fundamentalist interpretations of *hejab* requiring mandatory veiling. *See generally* Afkhami, *supra* note 156, at 17–18 ("Western feminists . . . appear as self-deprecating defenders of atrociously anti-feminist conditions, when they explain away oppressive behavior in the developing world on grounds of cultural relativism.").

with her family being compelled to pay her internment expenses.[198] In Iran, police may now beat women on the streets and otherwise harass them if they are not veiled,[199] and women have been tried and even executed for failure to observe *hejab*.[200] *Hejab*, also serves to justify other limitations on women. For example, in Iran and Saudi Arabia, women are not allowed to drive; in Kuwait, women do not have the right to vote; and in Algeria, fundamentalist law has now delegated women's right to vote to men.[201]

This treatment of women under state laws is designed to make them submissive and obedient. The violence inflicted by husbands, religious men in the streets, and Shari'ate jurists is designed to keep women in their subordinate place, obedient and dependent. Indeed, the success of Islamization throughout the Muslim world has primarily been measured in terms of either the repeal of laws that granted women more rights or the codification of fundamentalist interpretation of Shari'ah personal status and family laws that support the institution of the patriarchal family.[202]

Judaism

Examples of Jewish fundamentalism are drawn from a wide variety of groups, with particular emphasis on groups known as *haredim* (Ultra-Orthodox Jews)[203]

---

198. *See* Haeri, *supra* note 40, at 190. The "veil" is defined differently by different Muslim fundamentalist groups, but Khomeini's regime interpreted it to mean at least a long overcoat, pants, and a dark-colored scarf. *See id.* at 188 n.44.

199. *See Baha'is Calm in Centre of Storm*, TORONTO STAR, Jan. 22, 1994, at L15; U.S. STATE DEPARTMENT, COUNTRY REPORTS ON HUMAN RIGHTS PRACTICES FOR 1992 1001 (1993); UNITED NATIONS ECONOMIC AND SOCIAL COUNCIL, COMMISSION ON HUMAN RIGHTS, 48TH SESS., QUESTION OF THE VIOLATION OF HUMAN RIGHTS AND FUNDAMENTAL FREEDOMS IN ANY PART OF THE WORLD, WITH PARTICULAR REFERENCE TO COLONIAL AND OTHER DEPENDENT COUNTRIES AND TERRITORIES: REPORT ON THE HUMAN RIGHTS SITUATION IN THE ISLAMIC REPUBLIC OF IRAN BY THE SPECIAL REPRESENTATIVE OF THE COMMISSION ON HUMAN RIGHTS, MR. REYNALDO GALINDO POHL, PURSUANT TO COMMISSION RESOLUTION 1991/82, U.N. Doc. E/CN. 4/1992/34, 2 Jan. 1992, ¶190, at 34; U.S. STATE DEPARTMENT, COUNTRY REPORTS ON HUMAN RIGHTS PRACTICES FOR 1990 1454, 1457 (1991); U.S. STATE DEPARTMENT, COUNTRY REPORTS ON HUMAN RIGHTS PRACTICES FOR 1987 1168 (1988); *see, e.g.,* Fisher v. I.N.S., 37 F.3d 1371 (9th Cir. 1994) (involving Iranian woman stopped by police for some strands of her hair outside her veil). An Iranian woman fled to Canada as a refugee after being fired from her job and being punished with 35 lashes for not wearing a veil within the privacy of her own home. Joanna Kerr, *The Context and the Goal, in* OURS BY RIGHT, *supra* note 6, at 3, 5.

200. Hélie-Lucas, *supra* note 6, at 59.

201. *Id.*

202. *See* Ann E. Mayer, *Islam and the State*, 12 CARDOZO L. REV. 1015, 1027 (1991); *see also* al-Hibri, *supra* note 163, at 241.

203. The term *haredim* has come to denote essentially the radical segment of Orthodox Jews (Ultra-Orthodox), where "Orthodox" denotes Jews who observe the Torah and its commandments, and interpret those commandments to require a traditional way of life punctiliously attached to ritual. Samuel C. Heilman & Menachem Friedman, *Religious Fundamentalism and Religious Jews: The Case of the Haredim, in* 1 THE FUNDAMENTALISM PROJECT: FUNDAMENTALISMS OBSERVED, *supra* note 7, at 197–99; *see* Avishai Margalit, *Israel: The Rise of the Ultra-Orthodox, in* N.Y. REV. BOOKS, Nov. 9, 1989, at 38.

who are primarily anti-Zionist,[204] and the Zionist group, Gush Emunim (GE).[205] Each group follows its own interpretation of Jewish religious laws (*halakhah*), but their interpretations are quite similar in certain doctrines because they share many Ultra-Orthodox norms.

Orthodoxy primarily divides into two groups, Hasidim and Misnagdim. Heilman & Friedman, *supra*, at 208. The Hasidim began as followers of a spiritual and mystical movement in Eastern Europe that emphasized the legal authority of particular rabbis. Heilman & Friedman, *supra*, at 206–07; Jacob Neusner, *Judaism in the World and in America*, in WORLD RELIGIONS IN AMERICA: AN INTRODUCTION, *supra* note 111, at 151, 168. The Misnagdim (Hebrew "opponents") emphasized rabbinic law and Talmudic learning and opposed Hasidic practices and mysticism. Heilman & Friedman, *supra*, at 209. However, the two groups developed in ways that now make them quite similar with respect to the outside world: they measure their religious commitment in terms of fidelity to Jewish law, *id.* at 217; they share "an animosity to the culture of the non-observant and assimilation-oriented Jews," *id.* at 211; and they believe that "Jewish life and tradition was a superior alternative to anything that non-Jewish contemporary culture could offer," *id.* at 213; *see* Margalit, *supra*, at 38 (discussing "halakhic fundamentalists").

204. The Hasidim and Misnagdim oppose Zionism, the notion of a secular Jewish state. *See* Heilman & Friedman, *supra* note 203, at 234; Izhak Englard, *The Relationship Between Religion and State in Israel*, in JEWISH LAW IN ANCIENT AND MODERN ISRAEL 168, 172, 174–75 (1971). These anti-Zionist *haredim* include such groups as the Lubovitch Hasidim (existing in Brooklyn and Israel) and other Hasidic and Misnagdim groups which meet the definition of fundamentalism. *See* Heilman & Friedman, *supra* note 203, at 204–05, 212, 216–18, 226, 232, 257; Yuval-Davis, *supra* note 24, at 206, 209–10; Charles S. Liebman, *Jewish Fundamentalism and the Israeli Polity*, in 3 THE FUNDAMENTALISM PROJECT: FUNDA-MENTALISMS AND THE STATE, *supra* note 11, at 68, 68–69; Ehud Sprinzak, *Three Models of Religious Violence: The Case of Jewish Fundamentalism in Israel*, in 3 THE FUNDAMENTALISM PROJECT: FUNDAMEN-TALISMS AND THE STATE, *supra* note 11, at 462, 469, 463–69; Michael Rosenak, *Jewish Fundamentalism in Israeli Education*, in 2 THE FUNDAMENTALISM PROJECT: FUNDAMENTALISMS AND SOCIETY, *supra* note 40, at 374, 380–81; IAN LUSTICK, FOR THE LAND AND THE LORD: JEWISH FUNDAMENTALISM IN ISRAEL (1988); LAWRENCE, *supra* note 10, at 120–52; Margalit, *supra* note 203, at 38; *cf.* Harris, *supra* note 20, at 142–66 (arguing that fundamentalist term is inappropriate for these Jewish groups because they have always had these characteristics). Some *haredim* have more recently developed Zionist concerns, and have served as a basis for yet more extreme groups, such as those associated with Rabin's assassination. *See Raised in a Pious Family, Rabin's Killer Was Soldier, Scholar*, WASH. POST, Nov. 12, 1995, at A.30; Avi Machlis & Julian Ozanne, *Act spotlights growing culture of extremism*, FIN. TIMES, Nov. 6, 1995, at 2.

205. Gush Emunim (GE) meets the definition of fundamentalism. *See* Samuel C. Heilman, *Quiescent and Active Fundamentalisms: The Jewish Cases*, in 4 THE FUNDAMENTALISM PROJECT: ACCOUNTING FOR FUNDAMENTALISMS, *supra* note 16, at 173, 174–75; Liebman, *supra* note 204, at 69, 82; Aran, *supra* note 15, at 265–344; Yuval-Davis, *supra* note 24, at 207–08; Sprinzak, *supra* note 204, at 469–77; *but see* Rosenak, *supra* note 204, at 402 (arguing that although GE has strong fundamentalist tendencies, it is "questionable" to identify it as fundamentalist within Judaism). Zvi Yehuda Kook (Kook the Younger) was the founding religious ideologue for the movement, which in more recent times has been headed by Moshe Levinger. Aran, *supra* note 15, at 266, 268; Yuval-Davis, *supra* note 24, at 207; *see* Sprinzak, *supra* note 204, at 470. In contrast with the *haredim*, GE is Zionist, *see* Sprinzak, *supra* note 204, at 470; Aran, *supra* note 15, at 268; Yuval-Davis, *supra* note 24, at 207, and supports the Israeli militia as a vital religious and spiritual obligation. Aran, *supra* note 15, at 268 (citing to Rabbi Zvi Yehuda Kook, *Psalm XIX to the State of Israel*, in A. BEN-AMI, EVERYTHING: THE BOOK OF THE WHOLE LAND OF ISRAEL (1977) (Hebrew)). GE's goal is to increase Israeli sovereignty over all the "Land of Israel within its maximum biblical boundaries (from the Euphrates River in Iraq to the Brook of Egypt)." Aran, *supra* note 15, at 268; *see* Sprinzak, *supra* note 204, at 469–70. GE is notorious for its lawless activism, especially: its illegal activities in settlement in the occupied territories, *see* Sprinzak, *supra*

The Religious-Legal Doctrine

Jewish fundamentalists reject modernity, which for them means decadent contemporary Western culture.[206] They see the sexual licentiousness of modernity as a consequence of women straying from their proper role as wife and mother, and their ideology strongly endorses separate gender spheres and segregation of the sexes.[207] All of the groups require a degree of submissiveness and obedience of women to men, most particularly in marriage.[208]

Although fundamentalist Judaism does not explicitly declare that a wife must be submissive and obedient to her husband, the overall structure of marriage and divorce laws delegates such a degree of authority and power to the husband as to allow him effectively to coerce his wife's obedience.[209] The assumption is "that authority over her was transferred from her father to her husband."[210] Fundamentalist norms of marriage oblige the husband to provide for the wife's basic physical needs, and normally impose on him a financial obligation in the event of divorce.[211]

---

note 204, at 469–71; Yuval-Davis, *supra* note 24, at 207–08; Aran, *supra* note 15, at 267–68; its acts of vandalism and harassment of the Arab population; *see* Sprinzak, *supra* note 204, at 472–73; Aran, *supra* note 15, at 267 & n.26; its killing of a significant number of Palestinians, *see* Aran, *supra* note 15, at 285; and its resisting any peace accord with Arabs. Aran, *supra* note 15, at 287 & n.27. For an account of GE's violent activities, see Sprinzak, *supra* note 204, at 473–77.

206. *See* Rosenak, *supra* note 204, at 381, 389, 406; Heilman & Friedman, *supra* note 203, at 198. With respect to GE, see Aran, *supra* note 15, at 277 & n.19, 281, 336.

207. *See* Heilman & Friedman, *supra* note 203, at 216–17 (discussing *haredim*); *see also* Rosenak, *supra* note 204, at 387–88. For GE, preventing moral decay requires segregating the sexes in education and entertainment from early childhood. *See* Aran, *supra* note 15, at 306, 313. Fundamentalists have justified their attempts to block participation by women in local religious councils and in the electoral college (which designates the Ashkenazic Chief Rabbi) on the basis of the threat to their morality if they had "to sit in the same room and discuss things at the same table with females who were not their wives." Levinson, *supra* note 23, at 60.

208. Although doctrine formally requires a woman's consent to marriage, *see* HAIM H. COHN, HUMAN RIGHTS IN JEWISH LAW 170 (1984); Blu Greenberg, *Female Sexuality and Bodily Functions in the Jewish Tradition, in* WOMEN, RELIGION AND SEXUALITY, *supra* note 23, at 1, 8, in practice most girls in fundamentalist communities have their marriages arranged at an early age. *See* Yuval-Davis, *supra* note 24, at 199, 217. Early arranged marriages help protect a girl's chastity. This concern is reflected in marriage contracts, which normally provide for higher alimony for a virgin bride than for a non-virgin bride. Greenberg, *supra*, at 36.

209. Fundamentalists tend to obfuscate the subordinate position of women in the fundamentalist legal system, *see* Yuval-Davis, *supra* note 24, at 213–20; *see also* Saul Berman, *The Status of Women in Halakhic Judaism, in* THE JEWISH WOMAN: NEW PERSPECTIVES, *supra* note 25, at 114, 116 (describing "attempt through homiletics and scholasticism to transform problems into solutions and to reinterpret discrimination to be beneficial."), but the underlying rhetoric stresses the "natural" differences between the sexes and insinuates that women are inferior. *See* Yuval-Davis, *supra* note 24, at 211–14, 217; Becker, *supra* note 24, at 464; Levinson, *supra* note 23, at 50; Berman, *supra*, 115–17.

210. Greenberg, *supra* note 208, at 1, 9; *see* Harris, *supra* note 20, at 163–64.

211. *See* IRWIN H. HAUT, DIVORCE IN JEWISH LAW AND LIFE 6 (1984); MOSHE MEISELMAN, JEWISH WOMAN IN JEWISH LAW 83 (1978); Greenberg, *supra* note 208, at 9 n.33. His obligations are spelled out in a marriage contract (*ketubah*). *See* HAUT, *supra*, at 7; MEISELMAN, *supra*, at 88. These fundamentalist norms of marriage and divorce and property rights are based on "traditional" Jewish law. *See* Harris, *supra* note 20, at 163–64.

In return, the wife is obliged to care for the home and children.[212] In this context, the husband's coercive power is established by three fundamentalist *halakhah* norms: first, during the life of the marriage, the husband has rights to his wife's earnings, the produce of all property she owned prior to the marriage, and inheritance of her property upon her death;[213] second, the husband retains the exclusive power of divorce;[214] and third, the husband may obtain a divorce on the ground of the wife being "rebellious."[215]

Under fundamentalist law, no divorce may take place unless the husband consents and gives his wife a divorce writ (*get*).[216] Until he does so, the marriage

---

212. *See* Yuval-Davis, *supra* note 24, at 199–200, 214; Greenberg, *supra* note 208, at 9 n.33. In practice, the Jewish Israeli marriage pattern across cultural and social lines conforms to the religious one as childcare is almost exclusively the wife's concern, except for discipline of children which is left to the husband, and the husband, as head of the family, controls the family budget. *See* LESLEY HAZLETON, ISRAELI WOMEN 174 (1977).

213. HAUT, *supra* note 211, at 6; *see* COHN, *supra* note 208, at 169 (noting that all property of wife vests in her husband during marriage). Meiselman argues that as a wife may waive certain benefits in order to be financially independent, criticism of inequality in this context is unwarranted. MEISELMAN, *supra* note 211, at 82. However, this ignores the power of the structural norm that the wife would have to opt out of, a norm based on her being financially dependent. Evidence of the strength of the structural norm is that the rabbinical courts in Israel continue to adjudicate certain matters in accordance with Jewish law, such as enforcing the husband's right to income from his wife's property during marriage, even though the High Court of Justice opines that the matters are no longer the law of Israel. *See* Ariel Rosen-Zvi, *Forum Shopping Between Religious and Secular Courts (and its Impact on the Legal System)*, 9 TEL AVIV UNIV. STUD. L. 347, 356 & n.28 (1989).

214. *See infra* notes 216–17 and accompanying text.

215. *See infra* notes 218–20 and accompanying text.

216. COHN, *supra* note 208, at 171–72; *see* Philippa Strum, *Women and the Politics of Religion in Israel*, 11 HUM. RTS. Q. 483, 492 (1989); Raday, *supra* note 36, at 211–12; *see also* HAUT, *supra* note 211, at 17–21. Divorce requires a proceeding in a rabbinical court which either party may initiate. *See* Greenberg, *supra* note 208, at 10. If the court finds an appropriate ground for divorce it will recommend that the marriage be terminated, and this gives the husband a right to give his wife a *get*. *See* Asher Maoz, *Enforcement of Rabbinical Court Judgments in Israel*, XIII-XIV DINÉ ISRAEL 7, 22 (1986–88). However, he has no obligation to give a *get*, even if the court recommended the divorce on one of the few grounds available for the wife. The husband generally has more grounds than does his wife for divorce. For example, "[a] married woman commits adultery when she has sexual relations with any other man than her husband, while a married man is legally an adulterer only when he becomes sexually involved with another man's wife." Hyman, *supra* note 36, at 110; *see* COHN, *supra* note 208, at 173; Greenberg, *supra* note 208, at 33–34. If a woman's marriage is dissolved because of her adultery, she is not allowed to be married either to her former partner or her partner in adultery, whereas a man may divorce his wife and marry his adulterous partner or remarry his wife. COHN, *supra* note 208, at 173; *see* Greenberg, *supra* note 208, at 34. Occasionally, rabbinical courts in Israel have ordered a husband to give a *get*, and on rare occasions his failure then to do so has triggered civil penalties, even imprisonment. However, current practice in Israeli rabbinical courts declines to issue such orders, on the ground that a *get* that a husband issues against his free will is of doubtful validity. *See* Raday, *supra* note 36, at 211–12; MOSHEH CHIGIER, HUSBAND AND WIFE IN ISRAELI LAW 271 (1985) (noting that from 1953 to 1977 rabbinical courts issued only 12 compulsion orders). For certain Ashkenazic communities, a wife's consent to divorce is now theoretically needed, but a rebellious wife's consent is not necessary. *See* Raday, *supra* note 36, at 212. "Rebellious" may be defined so broadly in this context as to eviscerate any requirement of the wife's consent. A husband may remarry despite not having his wife's consent to divorce, and his remarriage is not defined as bigamous. COHN, *supra* note 208, at 172 (citations

continues in existence and he continues to exercise control over her earnings and income from her property. Thus, she remains economically dependent on the marriage and without financial resources to leave. His price for agreeing to end the marriage may be a beneficial financial settlement.[217] The husband's unilateral power with respect to divorce is further enhanced by the concept of the rebellious wife (*moredet*), which may serve him as a ground for divorce.[218] If a wife refuses sexual relations or fails to do housework without valid reason, her husband may deem her rebellious and divorce her, whereupon she forfeits her divorce settlement.[219] In Israel, there have been cases of women being declared "rebellious" for refusing to sew buttons on their husband's shirts or perform other domestic chores, and in consequence, being denied maintenance in the divorce.[220]

By vesting these powers in the husband, fundamentalist Judaism gives him coercive force to ensure that his wife is submissive and obedient and behaves as he wishes. Jewish fundamentalists, however, are not clear as to whether a husband may beat his wife. Some rabbis interpret the *halakhah* as giving the wife grounds for divorce if she is beaten, although, of course, the divorce still requires her husband's consent.[221] Under other interpretations of the *halakhah* a wife who leaves her husband because of a beating may be termed rebellious and thereby made to

---

omitted). However, if a wife fails to obtain a *get*, she may not remarry without committing bigamy. *See* Greenberg, *supra* note 208, at 12.

217. Greenberg, *supra* note 208, at 12. In the United States, civil courts have just begun to penalize husbands for withholding the religious divorce writ in order to obtain financial concessions from the wife. *See* Ronald Sullivan, *Refusing to Agree to a Religious Divorce Proves Costly*, N.Y. TIMES, Oct. 5, 1994, at B3. For example, New York statutes require that if a marriage is solemnized by a religious leader, then an individual must take all steps to remove barriers to remarriage, *see* N.Y. Dom. Rel. Law §253 (McKinney 1986); Friedenberg v. Friedenberg, 523 N.Y.S. 2d 578 (App. Div. 1988), and that effective barriers to remarriage must be taken into account in equitable distribution of property and maintenance, *see* N.Y. Dom. Rel. Law §236B (5)(h), (6)(d) (McKinney supp. 1993); *see also* Avitzur v. Avitzur, 58 N.Y.2d 108 (1983) (forcing husband to appear before rabbinical courts with respect to dispute concerning a *get*).

218. Raday, *supra* note 36, at 213. There is a concept of a rebellious husband (*mored*), but this is narrowly construed in terms of failure to fulfill basic marital obligations, whereas *moredet* is more widely defined. Moreover, the sanctions imposed on a *moredet* are much stricter and more onerous. *Id.* This concept of "rebellious wife" in fundamentalist Judaism is similar to the concept in Christianity and Islam, particularly in that it is founded on an underlying concept of obedience of the wife to the husband. *See supra* notes 88 (Christianity), 181–90 (Islam) and accompanying text.

219. *See* DAVID M. FELDMAN, BIRTH CONTROL IN JEWISH LAW 63 (1968); Greenberg, *supra* note 208, at 22. A wife who is "rebellious" for denying sexual relations suffers greater financial detriment in this context than does a man who fails in his duty to have conjugal relations. *See* FELDMAN, *supra*, at 63 n.23; *see generally* Hardacre, *Impact, supra* note 76, at 132.

220. Yuval-Davis, *supra* note 24, at 219. It was not a sufficient defense to failure to do domestic chores that the husband was living with another woman at the time. For discussion of this and other such cases, see Yuval-Davis, *supra* note 24, at 219 (*citing* S. ALONI, NASHIM KIVNEH ADAM [WOMEN AS HUMANS] (Mabat Publication 1976) (Hebrew)).

221. *See* Yuval-Davis, *supra* note 24, at 219; Greenberg, *supra* note 208, at 12; Raday, *supra* note 36, at 211.

forfeit the divorce settlement.[222] In any event, physical abuse of the wife in fundamentalist families, by her sons as well as her husband, is a serious problem.[223]

The *halakhah* norms of modesty reinforce a woman's dependency on men, particularly her husband. The purpose of the modesty laws is to guard women's chastity and to prevent women from "tempting" men into adultery.[224] The modesty laws require segregation of the sexes in all public areas: at the synagogue, at school, in government, and in entertainment.[225] The rules restrict women's dress, movement, employment, and independence.[226] Modesty laws also require women to be generally quiet because a woman's voice is regarded as seductive.[227] They further require that a woman should stay in her home if possible and, in any event, within the confines of her fundamentalist community.[228] Some sects do not allow women to drive.[229]

The modesty laws operate as gate-keepers. By confining women to their homes, performing housework and childcare, these laws generally aid in legitimating women's submission to the authority of their husbands. By confining women to their community, these laws ensure that women do not hear new ideas that might allow them to reevaluate their subordinate position. By preventing women from working outside the house, these laws ensure women's economic dependency.[230] In sum, under fundamentalist legal structures, the modesty, marriage, and divorce laws ensure women's obedience to their husbands and confine them to the role of wife and mother.

---

222. HAZLETON, *supra* note 212, at 177–78.

223. Denise L. Carmody, *Today's Jewish Women*, in TODAY'S WOMAN IN WORLD RELIGIONS, *supra* note 6, at 245, 252 (*quoting* Galia Golan, *Movement toward Equality for Women in Israel*, 2 TIKKUN (no. 1) 19–20 (1987)).

224. Greenberg, *supra* note 208, at 36–37; *see also* Levinson, *supra* note 23, at 45–46. After their extensive study of the *haredim*, Heilman & Friedman concluded that this was the primary reason for the modesty laws. *See* Heilman & Friedman, *supra* note 203, at 217.

225. *See* Heilman & Friedman, *supra* note 203, at 214–15, 226, 233, 237, 239; Aran, *supra* note 15, at 306; Levinson, *supra* note 23, at 57, 60; *cf.* Neusner, *supra* note 203, at 170.

226. "[F]rom their beginnings the *haredim* stressed 'modesty' in women's dress. . . . To this day, the neighborhoods of the *haredim* are plastered with signs warning visitors, particularly the women among them, to be 'modest' in their dress." Heilman & Friedman, *supra* note 203, at 217; *see also* Greenberg, *supra* note 208, at 36–37. The rules regarding a woman's dress are strict. Her body must be substantially covered if she goes out in public. *See* Heilman & Friedman, *supra* note 203, at 217; Yuval-Davis, *supra* note 24, at 212; Aran, *supra* note 15, at 306, 312–13. Upon marriage, a woman must cover her hair or shave her head and cover it with a wig, *see* Heilman & Friedman, *supra* note 203, at 217; Yuval-Davis, *supra* note 24, at 212; Aran, *supra* note 15, at 306, and "there continue to be calls to do away with wigs in favor of shaved heads and kerchiefs" in an effort for women to show more virtue. Heilman & Friedman, *supra* note 203, at 218.

227. *See* Levinson, *supra* note 23, at 51, 60.

228. *See* Heilman & Friedman, *supra* note 203, at 218; *see also* Berman, *supra* note 209, at 122.

229. Yuval-Davis, *supra* note 24, at 212.

230. *See* Heilman & Friedman, *supra* note 203, at 218 (noting how computers and modems may be important to *haredi* women who wish to be employed without needing to leave their homes).

Political Activity to Conform State Law to Religious-Legal Doctrine

Jewish fundamentalists are politically active in Israel. Many a fundamentalist group has its own political party, while other fundamentalist groups join together for political representation.[231] The resulting small parties wield great influence in Israel because neither of the two major political parties is generally able to form a government without forming an alliance with these religious parties.[232] As a result, these religious parties have a history of being able to extract concessions and financial benefits from the Israeli government. Some fundamentalist political effort is directed at maintaining and extending the force of their doctrine within their own communities.[233] Other political efforts are aimed at replacing the secular state with a religious state that acknowledges the *halakhah* as its exclusive law.[234] For example, GE has a "Proposed Torah Constitution for the State of Israel," and seeks to "institute the ancient system of law and justice" of the *halakhah*.[235]

Fundamentalists have succeeded in making *halakhah* norms part of state law in several crucial areas. The religious courts have exclusive jurisdiction in marriage, divorce, and ancillary matters,[236] and concurrent jurisdiction (with consent of the

---

231. For a discussion of the various political parties associated with fundamentalist groups, see Heilman & Friedman, *supra* note 203, at 225, 246–50; Aran, *supra* note 15, at 326; *see also* Liebman, *supra* note 204, at 70–71 (discussing religious party groups).

232. This is particularly true in the recent 1996 elections, which the right-wing Likud party won by such a slim majority that the small parties of the Ultra-Orthodox effectively hold the balance of power. *See* Julian Ozanne, *Israel braces for retreat from secularization: The orthodox right is making the formation of a government a religious issue*, FIN. TIMES, June 13, 1996, at 4; Julian Ozanne, *Netanyahu would look to smaller parties*, FIN. TIMES, May 31, 1996, at 4; Liebman, *supra* note 204, at 70–71, 82–84 (discussing power of religious parties in 1990 elections); Carmody, *supra* note 223, at 250–51.

233. *See* England, *supra* note 204, at 178–79. For example, state financial support of religious schools (which for most sects are only open to boys) has increased enormously because of the religious groups' political power. Yuval-Davis, *supra* note 24, at 206–07; Heilman & Friedman, *supra* note 203, at 236–37, 240, 249, 251. *Haredim* have also fought against universal army service for women (religious girls did not belong in licentious unsegregated environment of army) and complete Sabbath observance in areas near *haredi* neighborhoods (no driving, etc.). Heilman & Friedman, *supra* note 203, at 240.

234. *See* Heilman & Friedman, *supra* note 203, at 219, 235, 248, 250–51 (discussing *haredim*); Liebman, *supra* note 204, at 74 (discussing *haredim*); Sprinzak, *supra* note 204, at 486 (discussing GE); Aran, *supra* note 15, at 319 (discussing GE). The *halakhah* "sees itself as applying to everybody, gentile as well as Jew, everywhere, at everytime." England, *supra* note 204, at 171 (footnote omitted).

235. Aran, *supra* note 15, at 319. The drafter of the Constitution was imprisoned for participating in a plot to blow up the Muslim mosque on the Temple Mount. *Id.* GE has established an institute whose stated purpose is "to promote the full application of ancient Hebrew law in the modern national state." *Id.* This includes not only the complete details of biblical worship, "but also the institution of the Bible as the standard of conduct of public systems normally regulated by the state." *Id.*

236. The Rabbinical Courts Jurisdiction (Marriage and Divorce) Law 210, 7 L.S.I. 139 (1952–53), placed marriage and divorce of Jews under the exclusive jurisdiction of the Rabbinical Courts. *See* Raday, *supra* note 36, at 209; Amnon Rubinstein, *Law and Religion in Israel, in* JEWISH LAW IN ANCIENT AND MODERN ISRAEL, *supra* note 204, at 194–98; Strum, *supra* note 216, at 491. The King's Order in Council, 1922–1947; s. 52, also placed jurisdiction of marriage and divorce in Shari'ah courts for Muslims and in Christian denominational courts for Christians. *See* Raday, *supra* note 36, at 209.

parties) in personal status and property disputes between spouses.[237] Other religious norms have been enacted as Israeli law.[238] Moreover, fundamentalists fight to broaden Rabbinate jurisdiction in general,[239] and specifically to empower the religious courts to nullify marriage or divorce proceedings outside Israel.[240] The fundamentalist focus on marriage and divorce and modesty laws is of particular concern to women because of the disproportionately negative impact that these laws have on them. Jewish fundamentalists are engaged in political activity aimed to ensure that the laws of the state implement their vision of woman's proper role as wife and mother, and to make sure that women occupy no legitimate place in the public life of the polity.[241]

THE INTERNATIONAL LEGAL FRAMEWORK

The previous section demonstrated that religious fundamentalist laws systematically treat women differently from men. The marriage and divorce laws and modesty codes require women to submit to the authority of their husbands and obey them, resulting in a great disparity of power between men and women. This disparity subjects women to physical abuse and economic dependence, and limits their educational and employment opportunities. Fundamentalists are trying to make these religious laws part of state legal systems and have already succeeded in a number of instances. Such laws discriminate on their face and deny women the rights to equality and liberty provided under international human rights treaties.

---

237. There is civil law governing issues of matrimonial property, and this may be superimposed on the personal law systems. However, it is in practice overridden because the husband's bargaining power deriving from his unilateral ability to grant a divorce. *See* Raday, *supra* note 36, at 216; *see also* Rosen-Zvi, *supra* note 213, at 347–96.

238. *See* Heilman & Friedman, *supra* note 203, at 235: State funding of religious education and a network of state religious schools, see State Education Law, 5713–1953, 7 L.S.I. 113 (1952–53); State Education Regulations (Religious State Education Council), 5713–1953, K.T. 5723, 1423; Jewish Sabbath and Holidays are prescribed days of rest in the state, on which no Jew may be employed, see Days of Rest Ordinance, 1948; 1 L.S.I. 18 (1948); Hours of Work and Rest Law, 5708–1951, 5 L.S.I. 125 (1950–51) §18A; Jewish dietary laws enforced for a variety of public institutions, see Pig-Raising Prohibition Law, 5722–1962, 16 L.S.I. 93 (1961–62); Kosher Food for Soldiers Ordinance, 5709–1949, 2 L.S.I. 37 (1948–49); military-service exemptions for yeshivah-kollel students, *supra* note 233; *see* Heilman & Friedman, *supra* note 203, at 240.

239. Aran, *supra* note 15, at 319 (GE wants to expand religious courts' jurisdiction to cover everything, not just marriage and divorce). "Despite the fact that many Israeli citizens do not consider themselves religious . . . , The Hasidim have worked with other Orthodox Jews to make the precept of the religious law (halakah [sic]) binding in Israeli civil life." Carmody, *supra* note 223, at 251; *Cf.* Aran, *supra* note 15, at 319; 7 IWRAW, WOMEN'S WATCH (no.1) 3 (1993) (noting new proposed Israeli Constitution states that sex discrimination prohibitions do not apply to marriage and divorce which remain with religious courts).

240. Carmody, *supra* note 223, at 251 (*quoting* Galia Golan, *Movement toward Equality for Women in Israel*, 2 TIKKUN (no. 1) 19–20 (1987)). Secular Israelis have avoided the exclusive jurisdiction of the religious courts by marrying or divorcing outside the state. Until now, the state has recognized the foreign civil marriage or divorce, but fundamentalists wish to stop this practice. *See* Raday, *supra* note 36, at 214.

241. *See* Strum, *supra* note 216, at 483.

However, these religious fundamentalist laws may themselves claim protection under these same human rights instruments as manifestations of religious belief. Thus, religious fundamentalism presents clearly an acute conflict between international human rights that promote equality and liberty for women and human rights that promote the freedom of religion or belief.[242]

This section analyzes religious fundamentalist laws under the United Nations Charter and the Universal Declaration.[243] The Charter is the foundational treaty of contemporary international law and prevails over all other international obligations.[244] It provides the overall legal framework for relations between states and constitutes the primary source for legal guidance with respect to the challenge posed by religious fundamentalism to women's rights. The Universal Declaration, as an authoritative interpretation of the human rights guaranteed in the Charter, provides further guidance. Thus a resolution to the challenge posed by religious fundamentalism as provided by the Charter and the Universal Declaration is suggested.

As with any international treaty, analysis must be based squarely on the text.[245] Where the text provides standards and guidance for resolving conflicts, it is inappropriate to resort prematurely to a balancing approach.[246] This is especially true with regard to the Charter and the major human rights instruments, where the parties have already identified and negotiated which factors are important, and agreed to a final text that reflects the balance acceptable to all parties. Focusing on the text is particularly important in areas of cultural sensitivity, where the parties have compromised in a specific way in order to resolve potential conflicts. Given the

---

242. It has been suggested that the conflict between women's rights and religious freedom sets "tenets of equality against values of liberty." Donna J. Sullivan, *Gender Equality and Religious Freedom: Toward a Framework for Conflict Resolution*, 24 N.Y.U. J. INT'L L. & POL. 795 (1992). However, this implies that women's equality is the only right at stake in this conflict, whereas women's liberty is also at stake. Women's submissive status and inability to move beyond the realms of male authority impact on their liberty rights of freedom of association and of political and religious belief. *See infra* notes 343–66 and accompanying text.

243. *See* supra notes 1, 2.

244. U.N. Charter art. 103 ("In the event of conflict between obligations of Members . . . under the . . . Charter and their obligations under any other international agreement, their obligations under the . . . Charter shall prevail.").

245. Vienna Convention on the Law of Treaties, *opened for signature* 23 May 1969, art. 31, 1155 U.N.T.S. 331, 341, U.N. Doc. A/Conf. 39/27 (1969) (*entered into force* 27 Jan. 1980). This and many other articles of the Vienna Convention are generally agreed to represent customary law. *See* MALCOLM N. SHAW, INTERNATIONAL LAW 561 (3d ed. 1991).

246. A balancing approach attempts to identify factors of importance related to the text but not necessarily in the text, that are then weighed, in a process that is not itself guided by the text, to determine an outcome. *See, e.g.,* Sullivan, *supra* note 242, at 821–23; Donna J. Sullivan, *Advancing the Freedom of Religion or Belief Through the UN Declaration on the Elimination of Religious Intolerance and Discrimination*, 82 AM. J. INT'L L. 487, 510 (1988). Balancing approaches may be helpful in contexts where there is no great diversity among the disputants because there is greater chance of agreement in identifying which factors are important. Although a balancing procedure is often used in the context of U.S. Constitutional law, there is no equivalent in international law and limited authority for introducing a balancing approach into international law.

diversity of cultures of the state parties to the Charter, cultural sensitivity requires an acknowledgment that the agreed language in the documents already represents the balance that states desired to strike among themselves to harmonize their potentially conflicting cultures and religions.

Analysis under the Charter requires an evaluation of the substantive content of human rights covered by the Charter, which itself offers guidance as to how its broad language may be given more specific content. The Universal Declaration also provides an interpretive framework for discerning the substantive content of the human rights implicated under the Charter. Analysis of the Universal Declaration raises further issues such as the extent to which it is a legal obligation at all, what substantive rights it protects, and which states are bound by this determination.

This section will discuss the human rights standards under the Charter and the Universal Declaration; evaluate religious fundamentalist laws under these instruments; address state accountability in order to ascertain whether religious laws or the activities of nonstate religious actors may be attributed to the state; argue that reservations made to human rights treaties on the basis of religious fundamentalist principles are themselves violations of the Charter; and, suggest the appropriate consequences for states in violation of the Charter.

The United Nations Charter and the Universal Declaration

Almost all states are members of the United Nations and are thus bound by the minimum standards set by the Charter.[247] The promotion of women's liberty and equality appears in the preamble of the Charter, alongside the promotion of peace, security, and tolerance among nations.[248] The preamble makes no reference to religion. Rather, the underlying premise is that the dignity of each human being and equal rights among humans (and specifically between men and women) are of paramount importance.

The Charter affirms the broader purposes of the United Nations in article 1(3), including ''promoting and encouraging respect for human rights and for fundamental freedoms for all without distinction as to race, sex, language, or religion. . . .''[249] Furthermore, in article 56, all members ''pledge themselves to take joint and separate action in cooperation with the Organization for the achievement of the purposes

---

247. As of December 31, 1995, 184 states were parties to the U.N. Charter. *See* Multilateral Treaties Deposited with the Secretary-General: Status as of 31 December 1995, at 3–10, U.N. Doc. ST/LEG/SER.E/14, U.N. Sales No. E.96.V.5 (1996) [hereinafter Multilateral Treaties]. Basic Charter norms are also considered applicable to nonmember states because these norms have entered into customary law. *See infra* notes 281, 282, 292 and accompanying text.

248. The preamble ''reaffirm[s] faith in fundamental rights, in the dignity and worth of the human person, in the equal rights of men and women and of nations large and small. . . .'' U.N. Charter 1.0.

249. U.N. Charter art. 1(3). This is the first mention of religion. U.N. Charter article 76(c) provides parallel objectives to article 1(3) by its encouragement of respect for human rights and fundamental freedoms in the context of the international trusteeship system. The Charter also requires studies to produce recommendations in order to promote the realization of human rights and fundamental freedoms without distinction. U.N. Charter art.13(1)(b).

set forth in article 55,''[250] specifically, the promotion of "universal respect for, and observance of, human rights and fundamental freedoms for all without distinction as to race, sex, language, or religion" as guaranteed by article 55(c).[251]

Implications of the Language of the Charter

This language of articles 55(c) and 56 carries several important implications. First, under article 56 member states have a two-fold legal duty with respect to article 55(c).[252] The article 56 pledge constitutes an affirmative obligation to cooperate with the work of the United Nations in observing and promoting human rights.[253] Moreover, "[a]n undertaking to cooperate in the promotion of human rights certainly does not leave a State free to suppress or even to remain indifferent to those rights."[254] Member states must not put themselves in the position of being incapable of cooperating as this would undermine the object and purpose of the Charter.[255] The language of these articles is at once binding and aspirational, and both qualities demand that member states take no action to prevent or undermine the development and understanding of human rights in accordance with the Charter. This two-fold duty—the duty of cooperation and the obligation not to undermine—exists for each U.N. member state, regardless of whether it is a party to any other human rights treaty.

---

250. U.N. Charter art. 56.

251. U.N. Charter art. 55(c).

252. Although a few scholars argued that the human rights provisions of the Charter, particularly article 56, do not impose legal obligations, see, e.g., Manley O. Hudson, *Integrity of International Instruments*, 42 Am. J. Int'l L. 105, 105–08 (1948), this view is now generally discredited and article 56 is understood to impose a legal duty which members cannot disregard and violate. See Oscar Schachter, *International Law Implications of U.S. Human Rights Policies*, 24 N.Y.L. Sch. L. Rev. 63, 67–69 (1978); Egon Schwelb, *The International Court of Justice and the Human Rights Clause of the Charter*, 66 Am. J. Int'l. L. 337, 350 (1972); Hersch Lauterpacht, International Law and Human Rights 147–49 (Garland Publishing Inc. 1973) (1950); Georges Scelle, Summary Records and Documents of the First Session Including the Report of the Commission to the General Assembly (23rd Mtg.), [1949] 1 Y.B. Int'l L. Comm'n 163, ¶76, at 169, U.N. Doc. A/CN.4/Ser.A/1949; F. Blaine Sloan, *Human Rights, The United Nations and International Law*, 20 Nordisk Tidsskrift for International Ret, Acta Scandinavica juris gentium 30–31 (1950). The International Court of Justice (ICJ) has also accepted this interpretation. See infra note 256; Schwelb, *supra*, at 349 (noting that ICJ adopted this approach in case of *Legal Consequences for States of the Continued Presence of South Africa in Namibia (South West Africa) Notwithstanding Security Council Resolution 276*, 1971 I.C.J. 16, ¶131, at 57 (June 21)). Although article 56 is understood as imposing a legal obligation on members, scholarly opinion is not uniform with respect to the scope of the legal obligation. See infra notes 265–93 and accompanying text.

253. See supra note 250.

254. Sloan, *supra* note 252, at 31.

255. Vienna Convention on the Law of Treaties, *opened for signature* 23 May 1969, art. 31(1), 1155 U.N.T.S. 331, 341, U.N. Doc. A/Conf. 39/27 (1969) (*entered into force* 27 Jan. 1980). Even a state that has signed a treaty but not yet ratified it must not undermine its object and purpose. *Id.* at art. 18. *A fortiori,* a member of the United Nations must not do so. See also Louis B. Sohn, *John A. Sibley Lecture: The Shaping of International Law*, 8 Ga. J. Int'l & Comp. L. 1, 18–19 (1978) [hereinafter Sohn, *John S. Sibley Lecture*] (noting that article 56 language of "pledge" has "the force of positive international law and creates basic duties which all members must fulfill in good faith.").

The duty of each state to cooperate and not to undermine now arguably extends to a direct obligation of the state to promote and observe human rights, including with respect to the state's internal affairs. The United Nations has already acted extensively in the area of human rights by setting standards for promotion and observance of human rights and by establishing goals for the achievement of respect for human rights. This activity is of such breadth and depth that the affirmative obligations of states to cooperate and not to undermine may only be understood to mean that states have an individual affirmative duty to promote and observe human rights. Thus, the nature of a member state's affirmative obligation, as delineated under article 55(c), is to observe the rules of human rights and fundamental freedoms and to promote their observance.[256]

Second, the language of the Charter makes clear that human rights under the Charter are not dependent upon religion, nor is any particular religion their source.[257] The Charter contains provisions in favor of religion, but these are simply one manifestation of the principle of nondistinction.[258] The Charter establishes the principle of nondistinction by explicitly listing those characteristics of human beings that may not be used as a basis for denying human rights and fundamental freedoms. These characteristics—race, sex, language, and religion—are listed as separate and independent characteristics. Religion is not privileged in protection over any other characteristic, and moreover, the prohibition of distinction based on religion means that no religion is privileged over any other religion. By direct implication, the language of the nondistinction provision establishes that the entitlement to human rights and fundamental freedoms under the Charter is not to be determined or evaluated by any religious law.[259]

---

256. The ICJ has indicated that the language of "pledging" in article 56 is a substantive legal obligation with respect to article 55(c) rights. Although the ICJ was dealing with South Africa's Mandate under the trusteeship system (U.N. Charter articles 75–85), the language that it used with respect to human rights—"pledged itself to observe and respect"—is found in articles 55(c) and 56 rather than in article 76(c). The ICJ stated that: "Under the Charter of the United Nations, the former Mandatory [South Africa] had *pledged itself to observe and respect* . . . human rights and fundamental freedoms for all without distinction as to race. To establish instead, and to enforce, distinctions, exclusions, restrictions and limitations exclusively based on grounds of race . . . which constitute a denial of fundamental human rights is a flagrant violation of the purposes and principles of the Charter." Legal Consequences for States of the Continued Presence of South Africa in Namibia (South West Africa) Notwithstanding Security Council Resolution 276 (1970), 1971 I.C.J. 16, ¶131, at 57 (June 21) (emphasis supplied). The ICJ's references to a denial of fundamental human rights and a violation of the purposes and principles of the Charter clearly indicate that the Court was referring to direct obligations of a state under the Charter and not merely those deriving from South Africa's Charter obligations as a trustee. *See infra* note 261; Schwelb, *supra* note 252, at 348–49.

257. *See also* David Little, *Religion—Catalyst or Impediment to International Law? The Case of Hugo Grotius*, 87 Am. Soc'y Int'l L. Proc. 322, 323 (1993) (discussing religious freedom rights in context of language of Universal Declaration).

258. *See also* Little, *supra* note 257, at 323 ("In short, the secularity of human rights [in the Universal Declaration], carefully specified in this way, appears to be a corollary of the principle of nondiscrimination, which is fundamental to the whole idea of human rights.").

259. There is nothing to prevent religious laws providing inspiration for international legal standards, and various religions have influenced the formation of international law. *See* The Influence of Religion on the Development of International Law (Mark W. Janis ed., 1991). Moreover, international law

A third important implication of this Charter language is that it recognizes and anticipates the potential for denying human rights and fundamental freedoms on the basis of the specified characteristics. Moreover, it is clear that groups of the very types that article 55 protects may be the source of unlawful distinctions against other such groups. For example, the prohibited distinctions made on the basis of race will generally be made by another race, and the prohibited distinctions on the basis of religion will generally be those made by a different religion. The Charter language presupposes that restrictions may need to be imposed on the very groups that article 55 protects. Therefore, with the protections of human rights and fundamental freedoms based on a particular group identity come corollary duties of these same groups to respect the liberty and the equal protections afforded to the other protected groups.

Fourth, the Charter's command that human rights and fundamental freedoms are to be enjoyed "without distinction,"[260] sets a minimum standard of conduct

---

does not require that states be secular or that church and state be separated. A religious state, with its own municipal religious laws, merely needs to conform to international human rights standards. *See infra* notes 424–25 and accompanying text (discussing that municipal law is no defense to state's violation of international treaty obligations). States and U.N. studies have acknowledged a danger in a state recognizing a single, particular religion in that the mere recognition discriminates against other religions. *See, e.g.,* UNITED NATIONS GENERAL ASSEMBLY, DRAFT DECLARATION ON THE ELIMINATION OF ALL FORMS OF RELIGIOUS INTOLERANCE: REPORT OF THE SECRETARY-GENERAL 17, 31 U.N. Doc. A/9134 (1973) (statements of Finland and Sweden); ARCOT KRISHNASWAMI, STUDY OF DISCRIMINATION IN THE MATTER OF RELIGIOUS RIGHTS AND PRACTICES, at 47, U.N. Doc. E/CN.4/Sub. 2/200/Rev. 1, U.N. Sales No. E.60.XIV.2 (1960). Nonetheless, the existence of a state religion is not *per se* a violation of international law as long as there is "no discrimination against persons practicing other religions." *Summary Records of the 328th Meeting* (1981–82), [1989] 1 Y.B. HUM. RTS. COMM. ¶39, at 241, U.N. Doc. CCPR/C/10/Add. 2 (discussing Morocco's report under the International Covenant on Civil and Political Rights, Dec. 16, 1966, 999 U.N.T.S. 171 [hereinafter ICCPR]). For this reason, it is particularly important at the international level that no one religion be preferred over any other and that no one religion is determinative of human rights. For an example of a religious state specifically stating its intentions to abide by international law in the event of a conflict with municipal religious law, *see infra* note 427 (discussing Tunisia).

260. Later human rights treaties generally use the term "discrimination" rather than "distinction." However, "without distinction" appears in article 2(1) of the ICCPR. The ICCPR elsewhere specifically prohibits "discrimination," and drafting debates make clear that there was no attempt to distinguish these two terms. *See* B. G. Ramcharan, *Equality and Nondiscrimination, in* THE INTERNATIONAL BILL OF RIGHTS: THE COVENANT ON CIVIL AND POLITICAL RIGHTS 246, 259 (Louis Henkin ed., 1981). Human Rights Committee interpretations of these provisions also make clear that the terms are used interchangeably. *See* Human Rights Committee, General Comments adopted by the Human Rights Committee Under Article 40, ¶4 of the International Covenant on Civil and Political Rights, Addendum: General Comment 18 [37] (nondiscrimination) *(adopted* 21 Nov. 1989), U.N. GAOR , 45th Sess., Supp. No. 40, at 173, ¶1, at 173, U.N. Doc. A/45/40, CCPR/C/21/Rev.1/Add.1 (1990)[hereinafter Human Rights Committee, General Comment Non-Discrimination]. "Discrimination" is the principal concept also used in such human rights treaties as The International Covenant on Economic, Social and Cultural Rights, *see* Dec. 16, 1966, 993 U.N.T.S. 3, and The Convention on the Elimination of All Forms of Discrimination Against Women, G.A. Res. 34/180, U.N. GAOR, 34th Sess., Supp. No. 46, at 193, art. 1, U.N. Doc. A/34/46 (1979); 19 I.L.M. 33 (1980) [hereinafter CEAFDAW]. (The abbreviation "CEAFDAW" is used instead of "Women's Convention" because the latter term suggests that this treaty serves only to benefit women, whereas all society is richer economically, socially, and ethically if all members are capable of full participation, and free to the "full development of the human personality." *See* Universal Declaration art. 26(2)). For example, CEAFDAW article 1 defines "discrim-

required of all members. Thus, the International Court of Justice (ICJ) has held that "without distinction" certainly prohibited South Africa's establishing and enforcing "distinctions, exclusions, restrictions and limitations exclusively based on grounds of race . . . which constitute a denial of fundamental human rights . . . a flagrant violation of the purposes and principles of the Charter."[261] Thus, provisions that on their face either impose unequal burdens, or grant unequal favors, are obvious barriers to equal enjoyment of human rights and fundamental freedoms.

Fifth, the "without distinction" language establishes the principle that the distinctions are themselves of equal importance. There is no notion of any hierarchy among these distinctions that might privilege one prohibited distinction over another. The explicit language of article 55 does not differentiate between distinctions on the basis of race, distinctions on the basis of sex, and distinctions on the basis of religion. Thus, not only are these distinctions equally prohibited, but the standard for evaluating whether there is a violation of the "without distinction" language must be the same.

Sixth, in addition to the right to be free from illegal distinctions, the Charter protects substantive "human rights and fundamental freedoms."[262] Scholars differ as to the meaning of "human rights and fundamental freedoms."[263] Nonetheless, merely because the international community is unable to agree exactly which human rights and fundamental freedoms are covered by article 55 does not transform it into a "procedural" statute such that if there are rights, then article 55 prohibits certain distinctions, but if there are no rights, then article 55 does not supply them. The preamble of the Charter particularly reaffirms a faith in fundamental rights and the dignity and worth of the person.[264] The Charter thus presumes the existence

---

ination against women" as meaning "any distinction, exclusion or restriction made on the basis of sex which has the effect or purpose of impairing or nullifying the recognition . . . of equality of men and women. . . ."

261. Legal Consequences for States of the Continued Presence of South Africa in Namibia (South West Africa) Notwithstanding Security Council Resolution 276 (1970), 1971 I.C.J. 16, ¶131, at 57 (June 21). The fact that the ICJ was dealing with South Africa's actions in "a territory having an international status" does not imply that South Africa could therefore impose apartheid elsewhere. A state's duty under the Charter applies uniformly and universally. *See* Schwelb, *supra* note 252, at 348–49.

262. Charter art. 55(c).

263. *See infra* notes 265–93 and accompanying text.

264. *See supra* note 248 and accompanying text. The Charter uses the terms "fundamental human rights" in the preamble, and "human rights and fundamental freedoms" in the articles 1(3), 13(b), 55(c), 62(2) and 76(c). There is no indication that a substantive difference between "fundamental human rights" and mere "human rights" was intended. If such a difference were intended, then the Charter, although recognizing "fundamental" human rights in the preamble, proceeds to extend protection to all (not just "fundamental") human rights in the substantive articles. At the same time, it extends protection to "fundamental" freedoms but not other freedoms. This interpretation results in a disjointed, haphazard understanding of the Charter, and makes the preamble seem at odds with the substantive articles. Whereas, if the terms are read to be interchangeable, then the preamble and subsequent articles appear as an intelligible and comprehensive whole. Thus, there is no hierarchy in the Charter between fundamental human rights and human rights. *See also* Theodor Meron, *On a Hierarchy of International Human Rights*, 80 Am. J. Int'l .L. 1, 5 (1986).

of fundamental rights and freedoms and article 55 reaffirms this presumption along with the substantive prohibition of distinction.

The Human Rights and Fundamental Freedoms Protected Directly by the Charter

There are several approaches for determining which human rights and fundamental freedoms the Charter substantively protects. Starting with the narrowest interpretation of article 55, it refers, at a minimum, to those fundamental rights and freedoms that are *jus cogens*.[265] However, if the "human rights and fundamental freedoms" of article 55 include only *jus cogens* norms, article 55 would appear to be superfluous, because all states are bound by *jus cogens* even in absence of the Charter. A possible response is that article 55 is merely declarative of what all states agreed as *jus cogens*. But under this interpretation the nondistinction principle of article 55 becomes redundant.[266] Thus, this narrow interpretation of article 55 is quite strained, and the article should be read as indicating that there are additional human rights and fundamental freedoms that may not be denied on a discriminatory basis.

The second argument is that article 55, in addition to incorporating *jus cogens* norms, incorporates or parallels customary international law of human rights and fundamental freedoms, including those not necessarily at the level of *jus cogens*.[267] This suggests a reciprocal effect: article 55 helps to determine what is customary

---

265. *Jus cogens*, or peremptory norms, are a subset of international customary law, *see infra* notes 267–73 and accompanying text, and are those norms accepted and recognized by the international community from which no derogation is permissible and which may only be modified by subsequent norms of the same fundamental character. States may not contract out of these norms. *See* Vienna Convention on the Law of Treaties, 23 May 1969, 1155 U.N.T.S. 331, U.N. Doc. A/CONF 39/27 (1969), 8 I.L.M. 679 (1969) (*entered into force* 27 Jan. 1980); IAN BROWNLIE, PRINCIPLES OF PUBLIC INTERNATIONAL LAW 512–25 (4th ed. 1990). These peremptory norms address, for the most part, actions that shock the conscience of the international community, and suggest the need for universal jurisdiction and international criminal liability. *See* OPPENHEIM'S INTERNATIONAL LAW 7–8, §2 (R.Y. Jennings & A. Watts eds., 9th ed. 1992). Peremptory norms are considered to prohibit: genocide; slavery; the murder or causing disappearance of individuals; torture or other cruel, inhuman, or degrading treatment or punishment; prolonged arbitrary detention; and systematic racial discrimination such as apartheid. AMERICAN LAW INSTITUTE, RESTATEMENT OF THE LAW THIRD: THE FOREIGN RELATIONS LAW OF THE UNITED STATES (VOL. 2), § 702, at 161, § 702, Comment n, at 167 (1987) [hereinafter RESTATEMENT]; THEODOR MERON, HUMAN RIGHTS AND HUMANITARIAN NORMS AS CUSTOMARY LAW 23, 94–98 (1989); *see* BROWNLIE, *supra*, at 512–25.

266. Thus, killing half the members of a racial group violates the *jus cogens* prohibition of genocide whether the victims are chosen without sexual distinction, or are all women, or all men.

267. There is a tendency to find human rights principles as customary law only if they meet the higher burden of proof of being *jus cogens*. This confers the benefit of not allowing states to agree to violate human rights norms among themselves. However, it is undesirable to prevent human rights norms becoming part of customary law because they do not meet the higher standard of *jus cogens*. A human rights norm that is part of international customary law is nonetheless binding on states. For example, the prohibition of hate speech is arguably at least a local customary law of Europe, but is not at the level of being *jus cogens*. This does not prevent European states, and possibly new neighbors, being bound by the law.

law and customary law helps to flesh out what article 55 means. This reciprocal effect must be explored in the context of the process of development of customary international law. A new rule of customary international law is recognized where there is first, evidence of sufficient state practice, and second, a determination that states conceive themselves as acting under a legal obligation (*opinio juris*).[268] State practice requires substantial "uniformity" and "generality" of practice by the states whose interests are affected.[269] The recognition of a rule of customary law does not require absolute or universal practice. It is "sufficient that the conduct of States should, in general, be consistent with such rules, and that instances of State conduct inconsistent with a given rule, should generally have been treated as breaches of that rule, not as indications of the recognition of a new rule."[270] Evidence of state practice and *opinio juris* is found in, *inter alia*, the decisions of international tribunals, the actions and opinions of organs and representatives of international organizations, particularly the United Nations, the actions and expressed views of states, including the decisions of national tribunals, and scholarly writings.[271]

International and national courts and commentators have identified a minimum list of customary international human rights that substantially overlaps with *jus cogens* norms.[272] However, the list is somewhat greater, and it is acknowledged that the general principles of equality and nondiscrimination form part of customary law.[273] Prohibition of systematic discrimination on the basis of race is considered

---

268. Statute of the International Court of Justice, art. 38(1)(b); *see* Colombian-Peruvian Asylum Case, 1950 I.C.J. 266 (Nov. 20).

269. North Sea Continental Shelf Cases (Germ. v. Den.; Germ. v. Neth.), 1969 I.C.J. 3.

270. Military and Paramilitary Activities in and against Nicaragua (Nicar. v. U.S.), 1986 I.C.J. 14, 98 (June 27).

271. *See* Military and Paramilitary Activities in and against Nicaragua (Nicar. v. U.S.), 1986 I.C.J. 14, 98 (June 27); MERON, *supra* note 265, at 113; *see also* Filartiga v. Pena-Irala, 630 F.2d 876 (2d. Cir. 1980) (reviewing U.N. declarations and actions as evidence of *opinio juris* intertwined with state practice); Anne F. Bayefsky, *General Approaches to the Domestic Application of Women's International Human Rights Law, in* HUMAN RIGHTS OF WOMEN, *supra* note 128, at 351, 361 [hereinafter Bayefsky, *General Approaches*] (discussing necessary evidence for *opinio juris* and state practice regarding norms of customary law affecting women).

272. This minimum list of human rights norms as customary international law includes the following prohibitions: genocide; slavery or the slave trade; the murder or causing the disappearance of individuals; torture or other cruel, inhuman, or degrading treatment or punishment; prolonged arbitrary detention; systematic racial discrimination; and consistent patterns of gross violations of internationally recognized human rights. *See* RESTATEMENT, *supra* note 265, at §702, at 161; Bayefsky, *General Approaches, supra* note 271, at 361 (adding freedom from loss of consortium to list); *see also* Barcelona Traction, Light and Power Co., Ltd. (Belg. v. Spain) (New Application), 1970 I.C. J. 3, ¶¶33, 34, at 32 (Feb. 5) (finding prohibition against racial discrimination is customary norm). The Restatement states that the list of norms "is not closed," RESTATEMENT, *supra* note 265, at §702, Comment a, at 162, and "[m]any other rights will be added in the course of time." MERON, *supra* note 265, at 95, 99.

273. BROWNLIE, *supra* note 265, at 598 & n.3; Ramcharan, *supra* note 260, at 249; *see also* Anne F. Bayefsky, *The Principle of Equality or Non-Discrimination in International Law*, 11 HUM. RTS. L. J. 1, 19 (1990)[hereinafter Bayefsky, *Equality*].

customary law, and also meets the burden of proof of being *jus cogens*.[274] Commentators, although absolute and insistent about the status of systematic racial discrimination under customary law, have been surprisingly less emphatic in their declarations concerning the status of systematic sex discrimination.[275] Some, nonetheless, are willing to acknowledge that the prohibition of state sex discrimination "may already be a principle of customary international law."[276] This acknowledgment is supported by *opinio juris* and state practice; ample evidence exists over the last twenty-five years of pronouncements of the international community at United Nations conferences,[277] of member states reaffirming their commitment to women's equality in numerous human rights treaties,[278] and of national legislatures and courts enforcing equality for women.[279] The fact that some states still practice discrimination and distinction on the basis of sex should be treated as noncompliance with the norm rather than as evidence of a new rule.[280]

---

274. RESTATEMENT, *supra* note 265, §702, Comment i, at 165; *see* BROWNLIE, *supra* note 265, at 598–99 (noting that prohibition against race discrimination is principle based in part on articles 55 and 56 of Charter, Universal Declaration, and other international Covenants). It is unclear whether non-systematic racial discrimination violates customary international law. *Compare* RESTATEMENT, *supra* note 265, §702, Comment i, at 165 (limiting racial nondiscrimination norm to systematic discrimination) *with* Barcelona Traction, Light and Power Co., Ltd. (Belg. v. Spain) (New Application), 1970 I.C. J. 3, ¶¶33, 34, at 32 (Feb. 5) (finding racial nondiscrimination is norm of customary law).

275. The Restatement acknowledges that religion and race are treated alike under the Charter such that there is a "strong case that systematic discrimination on the grounds of religion as a matter of state policy is also a violation of customary law." *See* RESTATEMENT, *supra* note 265, §702, Comment j, at 165. But it fails to note that sex too is treated alike with race and religion. *See* RESTATEMENT, *supra* note 265, at §702, Comment l, at 165.

276. RESTATEMENT, *supra* note 265, §702, Comment l, at 166; *see* BROWNLIE, *supra* note 265, at 599; *see also* Myres S. McDougal et al., *Human Rights for Women and World Public Order: The Outlawing of Sex-Based Discrimination*, 69 AM. J. INT'L L. 497, 509–31 (1975) (finding that prohibition of sex-discrimination is becoming fairly accepted norm).

277. The most recent pronouncement of equality being at the United Nations Fourth World Conference on Women held in Beijing in 1995. *See* Beijing DECLARATION AND PLATFORM FOR ACTION, Preamble ¶¶3, 8, 9, 13, 15, 32 (1995).

278. *See* Bayefsky, *Equality*, *supra* note 273, at 20–23, 21 n.100 (listing such treaties); Bayefsky, *General Approaches*, *supra* note 271, at 369 n.1 (listing such treaties); *see also* BROWNLIE, *supra* note 265, at 598–99 (noting that prohibition against sex discrimination is based on same set of multilateral instruments as prohibition against race discrimination).

279. *See, e.g.*, Dow v. Attorney General, Civ. App. No. 4/91, Law Rep. of the Commonwealth 1992, at 623 (Court of Appeal Botswana, July 3, 1992) (holding that sex discriminatory nationality laws violated international principles of women's equality); Case of Abdulaziz, Cabales & Balkandali, 94 Eur. Ct. H. R.(Ser. A) 8, ¶78, at 38 (28 May 1985) (Judgment) ("it can be said that the advancement of the equality of the sexes is today a major goal in the member States of the Council of Europe"); Reed v. Reed, 404 U.S. 71 (1971) (finding that sex discrimination is subject to scrutiny under U.S. Constitution); *see also* McDougal, *supra* note 276, at 509–31.

280. *See* Military and Paramilitary Activities in and against Nicaragua (Nicar. v. U.S.), 1986 I.C.J. 14, 98 (June 27). Shame, however, has not prevented states arguing that their denials of equality to women under conventional law is because of different concepts of equality. For example, Egypt has declared that its interpretation of Islamic law gives an equivalency of rights and duties to ensure the "complementary which guarantees true equality between the spouses." MULTILATERAL TREATIES, *supra* note 247, at 169. It nonetheless had to admit that its religious concept of "equivalency" diverged from the concept

These customary norms of nondiscrimination that have developed since the Charter help to elucidate the Charter, and in this manner, articles 55 and 56 incorporate customary international law, and subsequent state practice and *opinio juris* help set the standards with regard to human rights and fundamental freedoms. But customary norms must also be interpreted in conformity with the Charter. The Charter is more than just a treaty, "it prevails expressly over all other treaties, and implicitly over all laws, anywhere in the world."[281]

Because the Charter requires that the standards for "without distinction" are the same for race, sex, and religion, then the customary norm of the prohibition against systematic race discrimination sets the standard for prohibition of discrimination with respect to sex and religion. The Charter's principle of equality between nondistinctions controls in this setting. Thus, if states develop and uphold a standard with respect to the prohibition of systematic racial discrimination regarding fundamental rights, states must apply the same standard with respect to sex and religious discrimination. For example, if states conclude that it is impermissible to disallow voting on the basis of race, then it is equally impermissible to disallow voting on the basis of sex or religion. Systematic discrimination on the basis of sex or religion must be a violation of customary international law as long as discrimination on the basis of race is treated as such. Moreover, the standards set in one area may not be used to shift the balance already set between the prohibited distinctions

of equality during marriage and at divorce under the treaty. *See Report of the Committee on the Elimination of Discrimination Against Women*, U.N. GAOR, 39th Sess., Vol. II (Third Sess.), Supp. No. 45, at 29, U.N. Doc. A/39/45 (1984). However, states presenting a religious fundamentalist viewpoint, such as Sudan, *see infra* notes 423, 425, seem to be claiming that they are setting forth a new rule by their activities to replace the human rights concepts under international law. Thus, the Sudan representative to the Human Rights Committee stated that "the Covenant should be adapted to the Islamization movement, which was recent, and the wording of the Covenant's provisions, which dated from a bygone era, should be amended." U.N. HUMAN RIGHTS COMMITTEE, SUMMARY RECORD OF THE CONSIDERATION OF THE INITIAL REPORT OF THE SUDAN, CONTINUED, 42d Sess., 1067th mtg., ¶74, at 18, U.N. Doc. CCPR/C/SR.1067 (1991). This argument must be rejected. First, it is not a sufficient defense to treaty violations. *See infra* notes 424–25 and accompanying text. Second, the Islamization movement is based on an interpretation of Islam that is 14 centuries old, *see* Hélie-Lucas, *supra* note 6, at 54, and thus represents a retreat from the Charter, subverting it in violation of the pledge in articles 55 and 56. *See supra* notes 250–56 and accompanying text. Third, it also violates articles 55 and 56 of the Charter, which prevent any particular religion being privileged over others or of being determinative of human rights standards. *See supra* notes 257–59 and accompanying text. Fourth, such a declaration cannot be considered as *opinio juris* with respect to creation of a customary norm regarding sex discrimination because such a declaration violates the Charter and obviously *opinio juris* may not attach to anything that would be a Charter violation.

281. Louis B. Sohn, *The New International Law: Protection of the Rights of Individuals Rather than States*, 32 AM. U. L. REV. 1, 13 (1982) [hereinafter Sohn, *The New International Law*] ("The Charter was not meant to be a temporary document, to be easily and perpetually amended, but, rather, to be a lasting expression of the needs of humanity as a whole."). Virtually all states in the world are bound by the Charter. *See* U.N. Charter art. 103. The Charter itself has been taken as evidence of *opinio juris* and state practice, and even as having become part of customary law. *See* Military and Paramilitary Activities in and against Nicaragua (Nicar. v. U.S.), 1986 I.C.J. 4, 98 (June 27) (holding that certain articles of Charter are norms of customary law); ROSALYN HIGGINS, PROBLEMS AND PROCESS: INTERNATIONAL LAW AND HOW WE USE IT 30–32 (1994); Sohn, *The New International Law, supra*, at 13–14 (arguing that Charter is customary international law and *jus cogens*).

under the Charter. The Charter disallows a hierarchy in the prohibitions of discriminations that would elevate the prohibition of one distinction as more important than the prohibition of another. For example, the very recognition of a customary norm of nondiscrimination based on religion, but not on sex, shifts the delicate balance of human rights between competing interests that the Charter achieves. It would open up the possibility of privileging religious rights of freedom at the expense of women's equality and liberty rights and allowing for exactly the odious distinctions that article 55 forbids. Thus, the Charter disallows an imbalance to be created in the development of customary law, and a customary norm in conflict with the Charter cannot exist.

If articles 55 and 56 are understood to cover, in addition to the *jus cogens* norms, these additional customary norms of nondiscrimination, then these customary norms appear to add little to the Charter's explicit language of nondistinction. In fact, it would appear that the reciprocal effect of the Charter determining customary law is more evident in this instance than that of customary norms illuminating the Charter.[282] These customary norms prohibit discriminating about underlying rights and freedoms, but their standards give us little clear guidance as to the nature of the underlying human rights and fundamental freedoms. The Charter itself, on the other hand, does give such guidance. The ICJ, for example, found that South Africa's racial systematic discrimination violated the Charter, and the Court made specific reference to the underlying rights and freedoms that were being denied on this basis.[283] Thus, the implication of article 55 is that there are underlying rights and freedoms that article 55 also protects, in addition to the right to be free from discrimination.

It should now be clear that the Charter must cover a range of substantive rights and freedoms in order for articles 55 and 56 to make comprehensive sense when read in light of its object and purpose.[284] Many commentators have argued that the Universal Declaration[285] provides the obvious answer as to what rights and freedoms

---

282. *See supra* pp. 333–37. If the nondiscrimination principles are part of customary law then they bind all states, including non-members of the United Nations. John P. Humphrey, *The Implementation of International Human Rights Law*, 24 N.Y.L. Sch. L. Rev. 31, 32 (1978–79).

283. Legal Consequences for States of the Continued Presence of South Africa in Namibia (South West Africa) Notwithstanding Security Council Resolution 276 (1970), 1971 I.C.J. 16, ¶131, at 57 (June 21). The fact that the ICJ was dealing with South Africa's imposition of apartheid in the territory of Namibia did not limit the ICJ's determination that systematic racial discrimination violated the Charter to only such situations. South Africa's systematic racial discrimination was a violation whether imposed on a territory or elsewhere. *See supra* notes 256, 261.

284. The general rule is that a treaty ''shall be interpreted in good faith in accordance with the ordinary meaning to be given to the terms of the treaty in their context and in the light of its object and purpose.'' Vienna Convention on the Law of Treaties, *opened for signature* 23 May 1969, art. 31 (1), 1155 U.N.T.S. 331, U.N. Doc. A/CONF 39/27 (1969) (*entered into force* 27 Jan. 1980).

285. The Universal Declaration was adopted by the General Assembly, consisting of all the original members save eight abstainers, within three and half years of the Charter. G.A. Res. 217A (III), U.N. GAOR, 3rd Sess., pt. 1, at 71, U.N. Doc. A/180, at 71 (1948). It was adopted on December 10, 1948, with 48 states voting in favor, none against, and 8 abstaining (Byelorussian S.S.R., Czechoslovakia, Poland, Saudi Arabia, Ukrainian S.S.R, U.S.S.R., Union of South Africa, and Yugoslavia). The commu-

are covered in the Charter. The argument that the Universal Declaration explicates articles 55 and 56 in the Charter takes various forms, with some arguments interweaving with others. Some commentators argue that although declarations by the General Assembly are not technically binding,[286] they nonetheless have legal effect as evidence of customary law.[287] Others agree that the Universal Declaration has such legal effect, but attribute this effect to the General Assembly having quasi-legislative status.[288] Another group of commentators finds that the Universal Declaration is an "authoritative interpretation" of the human rights referred to in the Charter, and that the derivation from the binding authority of the Charter gives obligatory force to the Universal Declaration,[289] such that "[t]he Declaration, as an authoritative listing of human rights, has become a basic component of international

---

nist states of Europe that had initially abstained later expressly accepted the Universal Declaration in the Final Act of the Conference on Security and Cooperation in Europe (Helsinki 1975).

286. Some commentators have argued that because General Assembly Declarations are not legally binding, they therefore have no legal effect. *See* Stephen M. Schwebel, *The Effect of Resolutions of the UN General Assembly on Customary International Law* AM. SOC'Y INT'L L. PROC. 301, 301–02 (1979); Gerald Fitzmaurice, *The Future of Public International Law and of the International Legal System in the Circumstances of Today: Special Report, in* INSTITUT DE DROIT INTERNATIONAL, LIVRE DU CENTENAIRE 270–74 (1973). According to this argument, the Universal Declaration would not even impose a legal obligation on members who voted for it, and certainly does not bind members who have not approved it. At the time of its adoption, the U.S. representative declared that the Universal Declaration was not a treaty and imposed no legal obligation. 19 Dep't State Bull. 751 (1948); *see* Bayefsky, *General Approaches, supra* note 271, at 362 (stating that General Assembly resolutions, like Universal Declaration, do not alone constitute international legal obligation); *see also* LAUTERPACHT, *supra* note 252, at 408–17.

287. *See* HIGGINS, *supra* note 281, 22–38 (arguing that General Assembly resolutions, although not binding, have legal effect). Falk similarly argues that although General Assembly resolutions are not *per se* binding, they are nonetheless indications of general customary law and serve as a source of evidence. *See* Richard Falk, *On the Quasi-Legislative Competence of the General Assembly*, 60 AM. J. INT'L L. 782, 785 (1966).

288. *See* MYRES MCDOUGAL ET AL., HUMAN RIGHTS AND WORLD PUBLIC ORDER 272–74 (1980). With respect to General Assembly declarations, Falk argues that the General Assembly has quasi-legislative capacity and thus makes "norm-positing" resolutions. *See* Falk, *supra* note 287, at 791. However, others reject viewing the General Assembly as a quasi-legislative body. *See, e.g.*, Gaetano Arangio-Ruiz, *The Normative Role of the General Assembly of the United Nations and the Declaration of Principles of Friendly Relations*, RECUEIL DES COURS 431, 729–30 (III, 1972).

289. *See* Sohn, *The New International Law, supra* note 281, at 16–17; Sohn, *John A. Sibley Lecture, supra* note 255, at 18–19; *see also* Schwelb, *supra* note 252, at 337. The Universal Declaration has been subsequently affirmed "as an obligation for the members of the international community" in the Proclamation of Teheran, *see* Final Act of the International Conference on Human Rights 3, ¶2 , at 4, U.N. GAOR, 23rd Sess., Supp. No. 41, at 1, U.N. Doc. A/CONF. 32/41 (1968); U.N. Sales No. E.68.XIV.2, which itself was subsequently affirmed by the General Assembly "as a reaffirmation of the principles embodied in the Universal Declaration of Human Rights." G.A. Res. 2442 (XXIII), 19 Dec. 1968; U.N. GAOR, 23rd Sess., Supp. No. 18 (A/7218), at 49, U.N. Doc. A/7218 (1968); *see also Montreal Statement of the Assembly for Human Rights, reprinted in* 9 J. INT'L COMM'N JURISTS 94, 94–95 (1968). For a discussion of the legal status and effect of the Universal Declaration, particularly in light of these subsequent affirmations, see LOUIS B. SOHN & THOMAS BUERGENTHAL, INTERNATIONAL PROTECTION OF HUMAN RIGHTS 518–19, 522 (1973). Furthermore, member states recently reaffirmed their commitment to the Universal Declaration by the General Assembly adopting a resolution "Strengthening of the rule of law," declaring "that, by adopting the Universal Declaration of Human

customary law, binding on all states, not only on members of the United Nations.''[290] Thus, ''[m]embers can no longer contend that they do not know what human rights they promised in the Charter to promote,''[291] and nonmembers as well are bound by the human rights Charter provisions as explicated by the Universal Declaration because these provisions have entered into customary international law.[292] The Universal Declaration thus gives shape to articles 55 and 56 of the

---

Rights, member states have pledged themselves to achieve, in cooperation with the United Nations, the promotion of universal respect for and observance of human rights and fundamental freedoms. . . .'' G.A. Res. 50/179, U.N. Report: A/50/635/Add. 2, 22 Dec. 1995, in Resolutions adopted on the reports of the Third Committee 400 (1996).

290. Sohn, *The New International Law, supra* note 281, at 17; *see* McDougal, *supra* note 288, at 274; John P. Humphrey, Human Rights & the United Nations: A Great Adventure 64, 65, 75–76 (1984)[hereinafter Humphrey, Human Rights]; Humphrey, *supra* note 282, at 32–33 (''Universal Declaration of Human Rights . . . is now part of customary law of nations not because it was adopted as a resolution of the General Assembly but because of juridical consensus from its invocation as law on countless occasions); Louis B. Sohn, *Protection of Human Rights Through International Legislation*, 1 René Cassin, Amicorum Discipulorumque Liber 325 (1969). For an analysis which accepts ''Professor Sohn's method [as] perfectly legitimate,'' *see* Meron, *supra* note 265, at 82–99. The argument that the Universal Declaration is part of customary law is that declarations adopted by an overwhelming majority of the General Assembly demonstrate consensus and constitute *opinio juris* that the provisions are generally acceptable to the international community, and subsequent practice of a reasonable number of states and acquiescence by others show states' willingness to abide by the principles. *See* Louis B. Sohn, *''Generally Accepted'' International Rules*, 61 Wash. L. Rev. 1073, 1077–79, 1078 n.3 (1986); *see also* Antonio Cassese, *The Geneva Protocols of 1977 on the Humanitarian Law of Armed Conflict and Customary International Law*, 3 U.C.L.A. Pac. Basin L.J. 55, 58–68, 113–17 (1984) (arguing that birth of certain customary international norms may occur from previous state practice combined with consensus at treaty conference). Implicit recognition by non-member states of the binding nature of the human rights obligations of the Charter with respect to non-member states constitutes acquiescence and thus the non-member is bound by these obligations. *See* Schachter, *supra* note 252, at 69. *Opinio juris* and state practice make clear the customary law status of the Universal Declaration. For example, the ICJ has relied upon the obligatory nature of the principles of the Universal Declaration and the Charter. *See* Case Concerning United States Diplomatic and Consular Staff in Tehran (U. S. v. Iran), 1980 I.C.J. 3, 42 (May 24); *see also* Humphrey, Human Rights, *supra*, at 75–76. The obligatory status of these principles has also been recognized in U.N. reports and declarations, *see supra* note 289; Meron, *supra* note 265, at 83 n.9, 87 n.18 (listing such numerous U.N. reports and statements), and by governments, *see, e.g.*, J.O. Débats parlementaires, Conseil de la République 418 (1957) (representative of France), *quote reprinted in* Meron, *supra* note 265, at 82 (''Although these conventions cannot be invoked [against Saudi Arabia and Yemen, which] abstained or were absent when the United Nations General Assembly adopted the Universal Declaration of Human Rights in 1948, it nevertheless remains that slavery is prohibited under the general principles of the Charter relating to fundamental human rights.''). It has also been recognized by national courts. *See, e.g.*, Filartiga v. Pena-Irala, 630 F.2d 876, 883 (2d. Cir. 1980) (holding that Universal Declaration was authoritative statement of international community and prohibition on torture is customary norm of international law). For a further discussion of arguments concerning customary international law, *see* Meron, *supra* note 265, at 79–135.

291. Louis B. Sohn, Supplementary Paper, *A Short History of United Nations Documents on Human Rights, in* The United Nations and Human Rights, 18th Report of the Commission 39, 71–72 (Commission to Study the Organization of Peace ed., 1968).

292. *See supra* notes 281, 282 and accompanying text; Sohn, *The New International Law, supra* note 281, at 17.

Charter. Like the Charter, the Universal Declaration also has aspirational goals, and members are expected to work towards those goals in accordance with article 56.[293]

The Human Rights and Fundamental Freedoms Protected by the Universal Declaration Under the Charter

The Universal Declaration provides that all persons are entitled to the rights and freedoms in the Universal Declaration without discrimination of any kind, including that based on race, sex, or religion.[294] As with the Charter's nondistinction language, the implication of this nondiscrimination language is that no particular religious law is the source for human rights nor may be determinative of international human rights standards.[295]

If there is any doubt concerning this implication of the nondiscrimination language, the preparatory work of the Universal Declaration makes clear that no particular religion was to be deemed the foundation for human rights.[296] For example, in drafting the Universal Declaration the issue was raised as to whether to include some reference to a deity in the preamble and in article 1, such that article 1 would read that "human beings are created in the image of God . . . . [and] are endowed by nature with reason and conscience."[297] The drafters deliberately rejected any references to a deity or to the immortal destiny of human beings so as not to impose the philosophical concepts of natural law (which derives from one particular religion) on countries to which it was alien and also not to impose it on nonbelievers.[298] This refusal to introduce particular religious reference supports interpretation of the nondiscrimination language of the Universal Declaration as rejecting any particular religion as a preferred foundation of international human rights.[299]

---

293. *See supra* notes 249-56 and accompanying text. Members must not act contrary to the object and purpose of the Charter. *Id.*

294. Universal Declaration art. 2.

295. *See supra* notes 257–59 and accompanying text.

296. Article 32 of the Vienna Convention on the Law of Treaties allows recourse to supplementary means of interpretation including preparatory work in cases of ambiguity or obscurity in the meaning of treaty language. Vienna Convention on the Law of Treaties, *opened for signature* 23 May 1969, art. 32, 1155 U.N.T.S. 331, 341, U.N. Doc. A/Conf. 39/27 (1969) (*entered into force* 27 Jan. 1980). Although the Universal Declaration is not a treaty, it is reasonable to apply the same procedures because of its status as a law-creating instrument.

297. Summary Records of Meetings of the Third Committee Sept. 21–Dec. 8, 1948, Official Records of the Third Session of the General Assembly, Part I, at 55, U.N. Doc. (A/C.3/SR.) 84–180 (1948); *see* HUMPHREY, HUMAN RIGHTS, *supra* note 290, at 67. These suggestions were made by Christians: the Brazilian delegation and Father Beaufort of the Netherlands. HUMPHREY, HUMAN RIGHTS, *supra* note 290, at 67; *see also* U.N Doc. A/C.3/215.

298. *See* HUMPHREY, HUMAN RIGHTS, *supra* note 290, at 67; Summary Records of Meetings of the Third Committee Sept. 21–Dec. 8, 1948, Official Records of the Third Session of the General Assembly, Part I, at 108–25, U.N. Doc. (A/C.3/SR.) 84–180 (1948).

299. *See* Little, *supra* note 257, at 323.

Moreover, article 18, which protects the right to freedom of thought, conscience, and religion,[300] was the subject of much discussion because it was considered to include the right to change one's religion or belief.[301] Saudi Arabia opposed the right to change one's religion because the right conflicted with Saudi Arabia's interpretation of the Qur'an, and also might favor proselytizing missionaries.[302] Afghanistan, Iraq, Pakistan, and Syria joined Saudi Arabia's rejection of this right during Committee discussions.[303] However, the right was adopted by the Committee, and later the Pakistani representative prepared a speech arguing that the right was not inconsistent with the Qur'an.[304] All Muslim member states except Saudi Arabia voted for the Universal Declaration after being on notice as to the meaning of article 18 and of the intentional rejection of making any particular religion the determinative source for human rights.[305] Therefore, the Universal Declaration must be seen as the agreed balance that member states fairly struck between their different religions and cultures, and thus the introduction of subsequent factors to that balance should be avoided.[306]

Article 18 also guarantees the right to freedom of thought, conscience, and religion and the manifestation of religion or belief in practices and observance.[307] The right to nonreligious beliefs is of equal status with the right to religious beliefs, and different religious beliefs are of equal status with each other. The Universal Declaration also guarantees the right to education, whose aim is the full development of the individual and the promotion of tolerance and friendship among all nations, and racial and religious groups.[308]

With respect to discrimination on the basis of sex, the Universal Declaration states that men and women "are entitled to equal rights as to marriage, during

---

300. For a full discussion of article 18, see *infra* notes 351–57 and accompanying text.

301. *See* HUMPHREY, HUMAN RIGHTS, *supra* note 290, at 67–68.

302. *See id.* at 68.

303. *See id.*

304. *See id.* at 73.

305. *See id.* For example, Iraq has subsequently relied on the legal principles of the Charter and the Universal Declaration to denounce South Africa's apartheid policy as "a massive and ruthless denial of human rights" such that South Africa should be expelled from the U.N. *See* U.N., Security Council Official Records, 29th Year, 1808th Mtg., Oct. 30, 1974, U.N. Doc. S/PV.1808, ¶146, at 17; U.N., Security Council Official Records, 29th Year, 1807th Mtg., Oct. 30, 1974, U.N. Doc. S/PV.1807, ¶31, at 5. Saudi Arabia apparently abstained from the vote because of its objection to article 18 including the right to change one's religion although it made no public explanation of this. Thus, at the most, Saudi Arabia could be seen as a persistent objector to the customary law of the right to change religion, but even this stretches the definition of persistent objector because "[e]vidence of objection must be clear and there is probably a presumption of acceptance which is to be rebutted." BROWNLIE, *supra* note 265, at 10. Certainly, its abstention cannot insulate it from being bound by other norms of customary international law deriving from the Universal Declaration. *See supra* note 290 (French representative noting that Saudi Arabia was bound by prohibition of slavery in Universal Declaration and Charter).

306. *See supra* notes 245–246 and accompanying text.

307. Universal Declaration art. 18.

308. Universal Declaration art. 26.

marriage and at its dissolution.''[309] Analyses of equality in international law do not require identical treatment in every case.[310] Nonetheless, only distinctions that are reasonable or just, based on objective criteria, and proportionate to the justification are allowed.[311] A finding of unjust or unreasonable discrimination may be made without regard to intention or motive, "whether the motive be bona fide or mala fide.''[312]

Given that there is great potential for conflict between these various rights and freedoms, the Universal Declaration allows for certain limitations on them. The methodology suggested by the language of the Universal Declaration is as follows: first, there needs to be a determination of whether a particular law or act attributable to the state fails to safeguard a substantive right in the Universal Declaration.[313] If so, there needs also to be a corresponding determination of whether the law or act itself represents the exercise of a protected freedom or right. If it does, then there is a clear case of conflict between rights, and the question is whether the law or act constitutes a permissible limitation under article 29.

Article 29 deals with the permissible limitations allowed for all rights under the Universal Declaration. Such limitations are to be "solely for the purpose of securing due recognition and respect for the rights and freedoms of others and of meeting the just requirements of morality, public order and the general welfare of a democratic society.''[314] This suggests a two-prong approach to discerning whether

---

309. Universal Declaration art. 16(1).

310. For example, according to the Human Rights Committee, identical treatment is not required under the ICCPR and not every differentiation will amount to discrimination. *See* Human Rights Committee, General Comment Non-Discrimination, *supra* note 260, ¶8, at 174.

311. *See* South West Africa Cases (Second Phase) (Eth. v. S. Afr.; Liber. v. S. Afr.), 1966 I.C.J. 6, 306–16 (July 18) (dissenting opinion of Judge Tanaka); *see also* Human Rights Committee, General Comment Non-Discrimination, *supra* note 260, at ¶13, at 175. For a general discussion of the standards to be employed in sex discrimination, see Bayefsky, *Equality*, *supra* note 273, at 12.

312. South West Africa Cases (Second Phase) (Eth. v. S. Afr.; Liber. v. S. Afr.), 1966 I.C.J. 6, 306, 309, 314 (July 18) (dissenting opinion of Judge Tanaka) (finding that "the practice of apartheid is fundamentally unreasonable and unjust. The unreasonableness and injustice do not depend upon the intention or motive."). Moreover, some analyses of equality impose the further requirement that a distinction which otherwise meets the requirements of an allowable distinction must also be invoked for a legitimate purpose. *See* Human Rights Committee, General Comment Non-Discrimination, *supra* note 260, ¶13, at 175 (stating that differentiation will be justified only if such "criteria for such differentiation are reasonable and objective and if the aim is to achieve a purpose which is legitimate under the Covenant."). The Human Rights Committee has justified affirmative action on this basis. *Id.* ¶10.

313. The article 29 approach applies to all acts attributable to a state, not just "laws." For a discussion of acts attributable to a state, see *infra* subsection entitled "The Accountability of States for Religious Fundamentalist Laws."

314. Universal Declaration art. 29(2). Article 29(2) uses the connector "and" rather than "or" which implies that limitations are permissible only if other individuals' rights are not recognized and society's interests are not met. In other human rights treaties, however, the "and" has become an "or." *See, e.g.*, ICCPR art. 18(3). It might be argued that the "and" in article 29(2) should therefore be understood as an "or" as if the clause is providing separate paragraphical alternatives, but this interpretation creates

limitations are allowable. The "due recognition" standard allows that if the exercise of a right by one individual results in failure to acknowledge a right that is clearly owed to another individual, then the former right may be limited. The "just requirements" standard allows a society to limit rights to the extent necessary to maintain a democratic form of government.[315] The terms "morality" and "public order" are thus limited to meaning public order and morality in the context of democratic principles. These terms of article 29(2) should also be read in light of the requirement of article 29(3) that "rights and freedoms may not be exercised contrary to the purposes and principles of the United Nations."[316] Democratic principles, therefore, may not be interpreted in such a way as to subvert the rights and freedoms recognized by the Charter, and which the United Nations promotes under article 55.

The "due recognition" and "just requirements" standards are standards determined by international law. Thus, national law or religious law may not be the source for either of these standards.[317] Furthermore, article 29 requires the same treatment for all rights, and thus corresponding situations must be treated symmetrically. For example, if a state enacts a law protecting religion to the detriment of women, a determination must be made as to whether such limitations on the rights of women are necessary for the due recognition of the religion and the just requirements of a democratic society. This must be symmetric to the case of a state that enacts a law protecting women against religious pressures and a determination must

---

an ellipsis. Because there is some ambiguity with respect to this term, for the purpose of argument, an interpretation which favors religious fundamentalism throughout is used. That is, it demands an "and" interpretation to justify any constraint on religion, but accepts an "or" interpretation as justifying a limitation on women's rights. These interpretations are made in the context of an article 29 analysis as applied to religious fundamentalist laws. *See infra* notes 367–410 and accompanying text. A further requirement is that limitations must be determined by law. Universal Declaration art. 29. At the very least, this means that they may not be imposed arbitrarily, but under a law that gives clear notice as to the consequences of any proscribed action. *See* Olsson v. Sweden, 130 Eur. Ct. H.R. (ser. A) at 30 (1988) (discussing comparable limitations clause in article 8 of European Convention for the Protection of Human Rights and Fundamental Freedoms, Nov. 4, 1950, 213 U.N.T.S. 221). Religious fundamentalist laws generally give ample notice of the consequences of violation, and thus this requirement is not normally at issue except for laws that operate extra-legally. *See supra* notes 189–190 and accompanying text and *infra* notes 322–325 accompanying text (discussing laws absolving husband's who kill their wives for moral disobedience).

315. *See generally* Alexandre Charles Kiss, *Permissible Limitations on Rights, in* THE INTERNATIONAL BILL OF RIGHTS: THE COVENANT ON CIVIL AND POLITICAL RIGHTS, *supra* note 260, at 290, 305–08 (discussing meaning of democracy in context of ICCPR limitations).

316. Universal Declaration art. 29(3).

317. So, for example, in the case of a religious law that discriminates against a particular race, the importance to the religion of the right to discriminate is not a factor to be considered because this would subvert the "due recognition" standard being based on international law. It has been argued, in the context of a balancing approach to women's rights and religious freedom, that a factor to consider is "the importance of the religious law or practice to the right of religious freedom . . . . [and] [a]ssessments of the significance of a religious practice should proceed from the significance accorded that practice by the religion or belief itself." Sullivan, *supra* note 242, at 822 (footnote omitted). This factor is impermissible under international law, and moreover, is unworkable on a practical basis.

be made as to whether the limitation on religion is necessary for the due recognition of the rights of women and the just requirements of a democratic society. The determination of "due recognition" in each case needs to establish the same level of respect between the rights of women and religion in both cases. Thus, by symmetry, "due recognition" of religion cannot be determined in isolation from concerns of "due recognition" of the rights of women or other groups. This implies that "due recognition" requires at a minimum a respecting of the basic norms of human dignity and freedom.[318] This approach treats the two different discriminations (on the basis of sex and religion) equally and according to the methodology suggested by the language itself.

Finally, article 30 allows a state to impose limitations on rights or freedoms if "any states, groups or person . . . engage in any activity or to perform any act aimed at the destruction of any of the rights and freedoms set forth herein."[319] Article 30 is thus concerned with not only the actions of states but the actions of private individuals as well.[320]

Religious Fundamentalism Evaluated Under International Standards

This subsection first analyzes religious fundamentalist laws[321] directly under the Charter according to the minimal standards applicable to all states without taking

318. For a discussion of how the international standard of due recognition has been worked out in the context of racial discrimination and religious rights, see *infra* notes 362–334, 372–408 and accompanying text.

319. Universal Declaration art. 30. This is very similar to the wording in article 5(1) of the ICCPR, which has been understood to mean that, even when individuals engage in the destruction of the rights guaranteed, the individuals "do not lose all rights, but only those that directly promote the destructive activities." Thomas Buergenthal, *To Respect and Ensure: State Obligations and Permissible Derogations, in* THE INTERNATIONAL BILL OF RIGHTS: THE COVENANT ON CIVIL AND POLITICAL RIGHTS, *supra* note 260, at 72, 89.

320. A state is permitted to limit the actions of such groups within the guidelines of article 30. *See supra* note 319 and accompanying text. However, it may also be argued that a state *must* limit such groups. Article 30 was originally "designed to enable the state to protect itself against individuals relying on the human rights guarantees to promote activities seeking to establish totalitarian regimes." Buergenthal, *supra* note 319, at 86–87 (footnote omitted). Because article 30 denies to private actors the right to destroy other rights in the Declaration, it is arguable that article 30 grants to everyone the corresponding right to be free from the intimidating actions of any such individuals or groups who are attempting to destroy rights. For example, a group may act toward an individual in a threatening and intimidating way that does not yet invade a right under another article of the Universal Declaration, but nonetheless results in the silencing and coercing of the individual into foregoing rights for fear of reprisal. Such groups may create an atmosphere of fear such that others are too frightened to exercise their rights. If the state fails to act against such destructive and terrorist groups under article 30, then the right to be free of the actions of these groups is empty and also threatens to undermine individuals' other rights under the Universal Declaration. Article 30 might therefore be understood to impose an affirmative obligation on a state to ensure that nonstate actors do not engage in activities aimed at destroying the rights of others.

321. "Religious fundamentalist laws" in this subject means all religious fundamentalist laws and acts discussed in the section entitled "Religious Fundamentalist Laws Requiring Obedience of Women" that are attributable to a state. *See supra* note 313.

the Universal Declaration into account. Second, the Section analyzes religious fundamentalist laws under the Universal Declaration.

Religious Fundamentalist Laws Analyzed Directly Under the Charter

Assuming that articles 55 and 56 cover only *jus cogens* norms, it is nonetheless clear that some religious fundamentalist laws violate these norms. For example, a *jus cogens* norm prohibits state murders as arbitrary and extra-legal.[322] These murders are "defined as killings committed outside the judicial process by, or with the consent of, public officials, other than necessary measures of law enforcement to protect life or as acts of armed conflict."[323] If a state explicitly delegates to a husband the right to kill his wife for adultery,[324] it has consented to his acting as prosecutor, judge, and summary executioner. The result is arbitrary deprivation of life by extra-legal killing in violation of the *jus cogens* norm. Thus, a state's passage of this type of law violates its Charter duty under articles 55 and 56.[325]

The second suggested minimum standard under the Charter is that articles 55 and 56 are informed by at least the customary law of nondiscrimination in addition to *jus cogens* norms. As discussed, these customary norms must develop in conformity with the Charter's principle of equality in the treatment of prohibited distinctions.[326] The best guidance is offered by the ICJ in its Advisory Opinion in the *Namibia* case, which sets forth the standards for racial nondiscrimination that would be applicable to all prohibited distinctions under the Charter and that implicitly rejects any religious justification of systematic racial discrimination and apartheid.[327] The apartheid system in South Africa (and consequently Namibia) was founded on the Afrikaners' Old Testament Christianity of Calvinist origin.[328] Afrikaners believed that they were the chosen people with a divine mission to rule over all others, and from this followed their belief in white supremacy and a policy of

---

322. *See supra* note 265.

323. NIGEL S. RODLEY, THE TREATMENT OF PRISONERS UNDER INTERNATIONAL LAW 148 (1987).

324. *See supra* notes 189–190 and accompanying text (discussing Iraq's and Kurdistan's laws).

325. This same analysis applies to the state flogging women for breaking modesty code laws. There is strong evidence that flogging is a violation of the *jus cogens* prohibition against torture and ill-treatment. *See* RODLEY, *supra* note 323, at 254.

326. *See supra* text between notes 256 and 260.

327. *See* Legal Consequences for States of the Continued Presence of South Africa in Namibia (South West Africa) Notwithstanding Security Council Resolution 276 (1970), 1971 I.C.J. 16, ¶131, at 57 (June 21). "Apartheid" is based on the separation of each culture requiring geographical segregation based on race such that blacks were only permitted in "white areas" if they were performing an essential economic service for whites. GEORGE M. FREDRICKSON, WHITE SUPREMACY: A COMPARATIVE STUDY IN AMERICAN AND SOUTH AFRICAN HISTORY 175, 240–41 (1981). Under apartheid, Africans of color were denied most civil and political rights, employment rights, and property rights. *See infra* notes 389–403, 438, and accompanying text; Legal Consequences for States of the Continued Presence of South Africa in Namibia (South West Africa) Notwithstanding Security Council Resolution 276 (1970), 1971 I.C.J. ¶130, at 57.

328. *See infra* notes 391–400 and accompanying text.

racial segregation and discrimination.[329] The ICJ refused to allow South Africa to present factual evidence to prove both South Africa's "good faith" concerning apartheid and its intention to promote the well-being and progress of the inhabitants.[330] Instead the ICJ found as a matter of law that the government's intent and motives concerning its systematic discrimination were irrelevant and that it was not necessary to determine the effects of apartheid.[331] Thus, it would not have been relevant if South Africa had argued any of the following: that its intent concerning apartheid was in "good faith" because it was protecting the (Afrikaner) populace's right to religious freedom; that its good intent was clear because it was fulfilling the divine plan for Afrikaners; that Afrikaners' freedom of religious belief would be deeply infringed if they were not able to assert their divinely ordained supremacy over Africans; or that the divine plan was clear about the natural role for whites and blacks and this was reflected in the policy of apartheid. The Court found that no motive or intent, whatever the source, could justify such systematic discrimination and denial of human rights under the Charter. Furthermore, evidence that the apartheid system worked well—such as testimony by Africans that the system of apartheid promoted their well-being and progress—was also irrelevant. By refusing to hear evidence on either intent or the beneficial quality of apartheid the Court was essentially finding systematic discrimination *per se* illegal and without any possible justification under the Charter.

Although South Africa did not raise the religious arguments, the ICJ must have been aware of them. The Court specifically noted that the policy of apartheid, and its related laws and decrees, were a matter of public record of which the Court was cognizant.[332] Thus, the Court did not need to be informed of the Afrikaners' religious beliefs because those beliefs were evidenced in all the past laws and decrees as a matter of public record from the early *Voortrekker* republics to contemporary South Africa and Namibia.[333] Such knowledge did not persuade the Court that religious beliefs could justify apartheid policy or be evidence of "good faith" with respect to the policy.

These arguments justifying systematic racial discrimination and apartheid on the basis of religious belief are superfluous now. There is no chance that the international community would accept that religious belief justifies systematic racial

---

329. *See infra* notes 391–400 and accompanying text.

330. *See* Legal Consequences for States of the Continued Presence of South Africa in Namibia (South West Africa) Notwithstanding Security Council Resolution 276 (1970), 1971 I.C.J. ¶¶128–29, at 56–57.

331. *See* Legal Consequences for States of the Continued Presence of South Africa in Namibia (South West Africa) Notwithstanding Security Council Resolution 276 (1970), 1971 I.C.J. ¶129, at 57. This accords with Judge Tanaka's earlier dissenting opinion where he found that apartheid was fundamentally unreasonable and unjust without regard to motive or purpose, whether the intent was oppressive or benevolent. South West Africa Cases (Second Phase) (Eth. v. S. Afr.; Liber. v. S. Afr.), 1966 I.C.J. 6, 306–16 (July 18) (dissenting opinion of Judge Tanaka); *see supra* note 312 and accompanying text.

332. *See* Legal Consequences for States of the Continued Presence of South Africa in Namibia (South West Africa) Notwithstanding Security Council Resolution 276 (1970), 1971 I.C.J. ¶¶129, 130, at 57.

333. *See infra* notes 390–400 and accompanying text.

discrimination. Thus, even to the extent that the Court did not have the religious justification arguments in mind in the opinion, it is clear that international law would not now accept the freedom of religious belief as justification for systematic racial discrimination. In this context of racial discrimination, the ICJ established the standard for nondiscrimination under the Charter: the Charter prohibits establishing and enforcing distinctions, exclusions, restrictions, and limitations exclusively on the ground of race.[334]

As discussed, the "without distinction" language of the Charter does not distinguish between the prohibited distinctions, and thus this standard for nondiscrimination in the context of race discrimination and religious freedom is applicable to the context of sex discrimination and religious freedom.[335] The systematic discrimination on the basis of sex under religious fundamentalist laws is not permissible as a manifestation of the freedom of religious belief under the Charter any more than South Africa's system of apartheid was permissible. Both violate the Charter.

Religious Fundamentalist Laws Analyzed Under the Universal Declaration

Assuming that the Universal Declaration is an authoritative interpretation of the human rights in the Charter or is itself customary international law, then it becomes clear that a number of religious fundamentalist laws conflict with guarantees under the Universal Declaration. As we have seen, many religious fundamentalist systems of marriage and divorce require women to submit to their husbands, and even to obey their husbands. These laws conflict with two areas of protection in the Universal Declaration: liberty rights and equality rights. Evaluation of liberty rights first requires an inquiry into what articles of the Universal Declaration are apparently violated by the laws. Then, if there are apparent violations and thus a conflict between women's rights and the right to freedom of religion, the analysis proceeds to consider whether these laws constitute permissible limitations on women's rights in accordance with the methodology of article 29.[336] Evaluation of equality rights first requires an inquiry as to whether the laws differentiate between men and women, and if so, then whether the differentiation constitutes discrimination under international legal standards. If the laws discriminate, then there is a conflict between women's rights and the right to freedom of religion, and the issue becomes whether the laws are permissible limitations on women's rights under the methodology of article 29. Thus, the equality analysis requires an extra step to

---

334. *See* Legal Consequences for States of the Continued Presence of South Africa in Namibia (South West Africa) Notwithstanding Security Council Resolution 276 (1970), 1971 I.C.J. ¶131, at 57 ("To establish . . . [such] distinctions . . . exclusively based on grounds of race . . . which constitute a denial of fundamental human rights is a flagrant violation of the purposes and principles of the Charter"); *see supra* notes 253–60 and accompanying text and *infra* notes 372–410 and accompanying text.

335. *See supra* text between notes 259 and 260 and *infra* notes 438–40 and accompanying text (discussing similarity of the denial of rights to Africans of color under apartheid to the denial of rights of women under religious fundamentalist laws).

336. *See supra* notes 313–18 and accompanying text.

determine if the differentiations are discriminatory *before* turning to article 29, at which point the analysis proceeds exactly as it does for the liberty issues.

It is important to note that the Universal Declaration mandates that article 29 is the sole method for dealing with a conflict between rights. Thus, it is only at the article 29 stage of analysis that the primary religious fundamentalist justification for these laws—that they constitute the exercise or manifestation of religious belief—may be considered.[337] The religious-belief justification may not be presented at an earlier stage of the analysis because it would subvert and avoid the Universal Declaration's standard for how conflicts between rights must be resolved. The earlier stages of both the equality and liberty analyses are for the purpose of determining whether women's rights are impinged upon and limited by religious fundamentalist laws such that a conflict is presented between women's rights and the right to religious freedom. The earlier stages of both analyses do not consider the argument that these laws are based on religious freedom because that claim is, and must be, dealt with by the analysis under article 29. This subsection therefore first discusses the equality and discrimination analysis, then the liberty issues, and finally evaluates both under the article 29 methodology.

Equality Analysis

The first stage in the equality analysis—whether there is differentiation—is straightforward. Religious fundamentalist laws differentiate on their face with respect to marriage, divorce, and modesty. The differentiation places obvious burdens on women: submissive status, physical abuse, economic dependence, limitations on travel in their own community and abroad, and limitations on their ability to work and seek education. The laws place women in an inferior position to men and demand that women have less power than men, granting men the final say in all matters as the head of the family.

The second stage in the equality analysis is to determine whether the distinctions amount to what would be discrimination against women under international standards if there were no issues of exercise or manifestation of religious belief to be considered (these issues are, of course, considered under the article 29 analysis.) Although international standards do not require identical treatment of men and women similarly situated, they nonetheless do require the distinctions to be reasonable or just, based on objective criteria, and to be proportionate to the justification.[338]

---

337. The justification normally offered for such laws is that they constitute the exercise of religious belief and freedom protected under the Universal Declaration. For example, Iran stated in its report to the Human Rights Committee that its strict dress code for women was intended to ensure respect for the country's religious beliefs and was not intended to repress or penalize women. *See* U.N. HUMAN RIGHTS COMMITTEE, 46TH SESS., SUMMARY RECORD OF THE 1195TH MTG.: SECOND PERIODIC REPORT OF THE ISLAMIC REPUBLIC OF IRAN, U.N. Doc. CCPR/C/SR.1195, ¶21, at 7 (1992).

338. *See* South West Africa Cases (Second Phase) (Eth. v. S. Afr.; Liber. v. S. Afr.), 1966 I.C.J. 6, 306–16 (July 18) (dissenting opinion of Judge Tanaka); *see also* Human Rights Committee, General Comment Non-Discrimination, *supra* note 260, at ¶13, at 175. The Human Rights Committee imposes the further requirement that any distinction must be for a legitimate purpose. However, the distinctions that religious fundamentalism imposes on women fail to satisfy the requirements of being reasonable

The justifications that religious fundamentalist groups give, explicitly or implicitly, are generally that women are inferior, that women's sexuality needs external controls (as provided for in these laws), that women should be economically dependent upon men, and that the man is the proper head of the household and the family.[339] Religious fundamentalists may base these justifications on religious norms or on stereotypes. Religious norms are considered below under the article 29 methodology dealing with the conflict between religious belief and women's rights. For the present stage of the analysis, it should be recalled that the language of the Charter and the Universal Declaration disallows any religious norms to determine international standards of equality and human rights, so that no religious norm may determine the definition of what constitutes discrimination against women under the Charter and the Universal Declaration.[340] Moreover, stereotypes are not considered reasonable justifications for the systematic denial of equality in general, nor for the specific discriminatory treatment under the marriage and divorce laws.[341] Consequently, the justifications given by religious fundamentalists do not satisfy the requirements of being reasonable or just, and based on objective criteria. Finally, even if it is alleged that the laws do not intend to discriminate, lack of intent is irrelevant under international standards.[342] Thus, under international standards of nondiscrimination, the systematic quality of the sex discrimination of religious fundamentalist laws violates article 16(1) (dealing specifically with marriage and divorce) and the general prohibition of nondiscrimination under article 2. A clear conflict is thus presented between women's equality rights and religious freedom, which must be analyzed under article 29.

Liberty Analysis

The obedience and modesty laws impinge on the liberty rights of women, particularly those relating to security of the person, participation in a democratic society, and religious freedom and belief. Article 3 guarantees everyone the right

---

or just, and based on objective criteria, *see infra* notes 341–42 and accompanying text, and so there is no need to consider legitimacy of purpose in determining whether discrimination exists.

339. *See supra* notes 48–54, 56–59 (Buddhism), 75–87, 92, 95–99 (Christianity), 112–13, 119–24, 129–32, 149 (Hinduism), 159–69, 173, 179 (Islam), 207–08, 210–12, 224–30 (Judaism) and accompanying text.

340. *See supra* notes 257–59 and accompanying text.

341. For example, in the context of the ICCPR, see S.W.M. Broeks v. the Netherlands (*adopted* 9 April 1987, 29th Sess.), Communication No. 172/1984, Report of the Human Rights Committee, U.N. GAOR, 42d Sess., Supp. No. 40, 139, ¶ 8.2, at 145, ¶8.4, at 147, ¶¶14,15, at 150, U.N. Doc. A/42/40, at 139 (1987) (rejecting notion that a prevailing view in the society's culture that men are naturally "breadwinners" justifies differential treatment).

342. Even if fundamentalists allege that the obedience and modesty laws are not intended to make women unequal, lack of intent is irrelevant to laws discriminatory on their face. *See supra* notes 312, 331 and accompanying text. For example, in the context of the ICCPR, see S.W.M. Broeks v. the Netherlands (*adopted* 9 April 1987, 29th Sess.), Communication No. 172/1984, Report of the Human Rights Committee, U.N. GAOR, 42d Sess., Supp. No. 40, 139, ¶¶14,15, 16, at 150, U.N. Doc. A/42/40, at 139 (1987) (finding that lack of intent is irrelevant to laws that are discriminatory on their face).

to life, liberty, and the security of the person.[343] Explicitly or implicitly authorizing husbands to discipline their wives results in the physical abuse of women and violates their article 3 right to security of the person.[344] Moreover, article 8 guarantees everyone the right to an effective judicial remedy for violations of human rights guaranteed under law.[345] Thus, the state's failure to provide a woman with effective remedies for assault and battery by her husband violates a woman's article 8 right to effective remedies.

Requiring wives to be obedient to their husbands also interferes directly with their liberty rights associated with participation in a democratic society, thus violating articles 18–21. These rights include the right to freedom of thought and conscience (article 18),[346] the right to freedom of opinion and expression (article 19),[347] the right to freedom of assembly (article 20),[348] and the right to take part in government, including the right to vote (article 21).[349] There are no limitations on what the husband may require under the obedience rule, and for this reason, the need for his permission is a direct interference with a woman's rights under these articles.[350]

The article 18 guarantee of the freedom of thought encompasses political thought. The right to political belief is also bolstered by article 19, which guarantees

---

343. Universal Declaration art. 3.

344. For example, in the context of the ICCPR's guarantee of the security of the person, the Human Rights Committee has declared that "[i]t cannot be the case that, as a matter of law, States can ignore known threats to the life of persons under their jurisdiction, just because he or she is not arrested or otherwise detained. States parties are under an obligation to take reasonable and appropriate measures to protect them." *See* W. Delgado Páez v. Columbia, Communication No. 195/1985 (*adopted* 12 July 1990, 39th Sess.), Report of the Human Rights Committee, Vol. II, Comm. No. 195/1985, U.N. GAOR, 45th Sess., Supp. No. 40, at 43, ¶5.5, at 47, U.N. Doc. A/45/40 (1990) (holding that anonymous threats and attack on state school teacher, following harassment by ecclesiastical and educational authorities, constituted violation of article 9 of the ICCPR which guarantees security of the person); *see infra* notes 418–19 and accompanying text (discussing relevance of *Delgado* to issue of state accountability for violative actions by nonstate actors). The Committee specifically rejected that the right to security of the person found in the first sentence of ICCPR article 9(1) was in any way limited to the circumstances of the second sentence of article 9(1) referring to arrest and detention. *See* Delgado Páez v. Columbia, ¶5.5, at 147. Article 3 in the Universal Declaration has no such potentially limiting provision in any event.

345. Universal Declaration art. 8.

346. Universal Declaration art. 18.

347. Universal Declaration art. 19.

348. Article 20 gives everyone the right to freedom of peaceful assembly. Universal Declaration art. 20(1).

349. Article 21 gives everyone the right to take part in government, directly or through freely chosen representatives, the right of equal access to public service, and the right to vote in periodic elections. Universal Declaration art. 21.

350. The only exception is that, in some cases, a husband may not demand that his wife do something that would violate other strong norms of the religion. *See* MAUDUDI, THE MEANING OF THE QUR'AN (VOL. II), *supra* note 164, at 325 n.58. There are no strong fundamentalist norms that require women to vote or to be involved in political matters, so nothing within the religion prevents the husband from limiting his wife's action with respect to all political matters.

everyone the right to freedom of opinion and expression, and "this right includes freedom to hold opinions without interference and to seek, receive and impart information and ideas through any media and regardless of frontiers."[351] The obedience rule and modesty rules directly impinge on these rights because a woman may not seek, receive, or impart information without her husband's permission. In some cases, she is not supposed to leave her own house unless absolutely necessary and with her husband's permission, and she is not allowed to leave the country without his permission. The result is that she has no public place to express her political opinion and belief and no forum in which to exchange ideas. Thus, she is subjected to interference in her freedom to hold opinions and her ability to receive information on which to base her opinions.

Even if a woman is confined to her home, she continues to have rights under articles 18 and 19. Her expression of these rights within her home can be little more than an expression of opposition to the requirement of obedience. Thus, her acts of civil protest must take place within her home. Acts of disobedience may be interpreted as reflecting her general political belief in the equality of women or a more specific political belief that women should not be in submission to their husbands. In any event, it is quite clear that her political belief does not have to amount to a comprehensive political theory in order to qualify as an article 18 or 19 right. In the contexts of political asylum and refugee applications,[352] courts are recognizing that a woman's opposition to the subservient role imposed on her by her husband and societal norms is the expression of political belief, and that mandating her to conform to those roles is repression of her political belief.[353] Feminism

---

351. Universal Declaration art. 19.

352. Canada and the United States define "refugee" consistently with the 1967 Protocol Relating to the Status of Refugees, 31 Jan. 1967, 19 U.S.T. 6223, 606 U.N.T.S. 267, thus conforming their national law to their international obligations. *See, e.g.,* I.N.S. v. Cardozo-Fonseca, 480 U.S. 421, 436–37 (1987). The recognition of gender-related asylum, formalized through administrative guidelines in Canada and the United States, has been developing in other national courts and through pronouncements of international organizations. For example, the United Nations High Commission on Refugees concluded that states "are free to adopt the interpretation that women asylum-seekers who face harsh and inhumane treatment due to their having transgressed the social mores of the society in which they live may be considered as a 'particular social group' within the meaning of . . . the United Nations Refugee Convention." U.N. Doc. HRC/IP/2/Rev. 1986, at Conclusion No. 39, (XXXVI), ¶(k) (8 July 1985); *see generally* A. Johnson, *The International Protection of Women Refugees: a Summary of Principal Problems and Issues,* 1 INT'L J. REFUGEE L. 221 (1989). Thus, in these contexts, there is increasing awareness that gender-based persecution may take the form of reprisals against women for contravening their society's norms. I would like to thank Minty Chung for her help and advice with regard to the law and practice of political asylum and refugee cases.

353. *See, e.g.,* In the Matter of A and Z: In Deportation Proceedings (A 72–190–893; A 72–793–219) (Exec. Office for Immigration Review, Arlington, Va., U.S.A.) (Dec. 20, 1994) 14 (unpublished opinion), *reported in* 72 INTERPRETER RELEASES 521 (Apr. 17, 1995) (holding that Jordanian woman and son were entitled to asylum in U.S. due to persecution by husband "for their political belief in the importance of individual freedom . . . for women and children."); In the Matter of M.K.: In Deportation Proceedings (A 72–374–558) (Exec. Office for Immigration Review, Arlington, Va., U.S.A.), 19 (Aug. 9, 1995) (unpublished opinion) (" 'Political opinion' includes not only a woman's attitude about her government, but also includes her opinion relating to the treatment and status of women generally within her country

itself has been recognized as political opinion and is entitled to the same protection as other political opinions.[354] Furthermore, courts are recognizing that the physical abuse a woman receives from her husband may serve as a reprisal for her political views and for her failure to conform to a subservient role. For example, an Immigration Judge granted political asylum in the United States to a Jordanian woman who had suffered severe, sustained abuse by her husband for years, finding a direct nexus between her expression of political opinion and the abuse she received.[355] In cases where the state authorizes the husband to be the head of the family or fails to protect women who suffer abuse at the hands of their husbands,[356] courts have found that domestic abuse may serve as the means by which a state persecutes a woman for her political beliefs and thus she may properly be regarded as a victim of state political repression.[357]

---

or culture, or within her social, religious, or ethnic group. . . . 'Political opinion' includes . . . her refusal to conform to religious or cultural norms or the roles assigned women within her country or culture.''); Decision of the Federal Office for the Recognition of Foreign Refugees 439–26428–86 (Federal Republic of Germany) (24 Nov. 1988) (granting refugee status to Iranian woman and holding that ''the ideologically based power of men over women results in a general political repression of women in defiance of their individual liberties and human rights.'').

354. *See* Fatin v. INS, 12 F.3d 1233, 1242 (3rd Cir. 1993) (''feminism qualifies as a political opinion'').

355. The Judge stated:

> She is not content to be a slave. . . . The emancipation of women is one of the most important world-wide political and social movements of this century. Precisely because of its importance, the freedom and equality of women is dangerous and threatening politics to her husband, his society, and his government. . . . [Her] husband has beaten and abused [her] . . . for three decades, but [she] . . . remains unbowed . . . and seek[s] protection . . . for . . . political belief in the importance of individual freedom.

In the Matter of A and Z: In Deportation Proceedings (A 72–190–893; A 72–793–219), at 14 (Exec. Office for Immigration Review, Arlington, Va., U.S.A.) (Dec. 20, 1994) (unpublished opinion), *reported in* 72 INTERPRETER RELEASES 521 (Apr. 17, 1995). *See also* Rhonda Copelon, *Intimate Terror: Understanding Domestic Violence as Torture, in* HUMAN RIGHTS OF WOMEN, *supra* note 128, at 116, 120–21 (discussing that wife-battering is related to and triggered by women's expressions of capacity and power, and by their ''rebellions'' small and large).

356. In the asylum context, actions of nonstate actors may be attributed to the state from the state's unwillingness to control the actors. *See* U.S. DEPARTMENT OF JUSTICE: IMMIGRATION AND NATURALIZATION SERVICE INTERNATIONAL DIVISION, MEMORANDUM: CONSIDERATIONS FOR ASYLUM OFFICERS ADJUDICATING ASYLUM CLAIMS FROM WOMEN 16 (May 26, 1995). Thus, courts have found states complicit in the reprisals women suffer at the hands of their husbands, nonstate actors, because of states' failure to provide a remedy, even if the failure is due to state cultural and religious norms. *See* Convention Refugee Determination Decision, 1993 C.R. D.D. No. 307 (No. T93–08296) (Immig. and Refugee Board of Canada, Convention Refugee Determination Div.) (Toronto, Ontario, Canada) (Sept. 29, 1993) (holding that Argentinean woman subjected to years of violence from ''machismo'' husband met refugee status and that state did not have impetus to provide effective remedy in part because of Roman Catholic norms that limited women to domestic sphere and mandated men as heads of family); *see also supra* note 353 and accompanying text. Systematic failure to provide a remedy may also be grounds in international human rights law for attributing nonstate third party acts to the state. The issue of state accountability for acts of nonstate actors under general international human rights law is discussed *infra. See infra* notes 412–20 and accompanying text; *see generally* Celina Romany, *State Responsibility Goes Private: A Feminist Critique of the Public/Private Distinction in International Human Rights Law, in* HUMAN RIGHTS OF WOMEN, *supra* note 128, at 85, 100.

357. *See, e.g.,* In the Matter of M.K.: In Deportation Proceedings (A 72–374–558) (Exec. Office for

Article 20 provides the right to freedom of peaceful assembly and association. Obedience rules and modesty codes directly impinge on this political right because a woman may not join any assembly without her husband's permission, and may also be subject to modesty code penalties if she joins a public assembly. Article 21 gives everyone the right to vote, to take part in the conduct of public affairs, or to be elected to government.[358] Plainly, religious fundamentalist laws of modesty and obedience that restrict women's voting rights are a direct infringement of article 21 rights.[359] In addition, obedience rules operate as restrictions on rights in that they entitle a husband to require his wife to vote a certain way, and to forbid her to run for election or even obtain information about political parties. Even if a wife obtains her husband's permission to run for election, the modesty code prohibitions on her appearing and speaking in public may make this impossible in practice.[360] The requirements of obedience and modesty codes thus are a direct infringement of a woman's article 21 rights.

Furthermore, the combination of modesty codes and the obedience rules foreclose a woman's participation in the democratic process of society because she has no opportunity to lobby or work for the change of the very laws that repress her political rights. It is fair to conclude that these religious fundamentalist laws do not reflect the result of democratic process because there is no evidence that women have had any opportunity to participate in the passage of these laws that subject them to a submissive status backed up by sanctions.[361] Thus, these obedience and modesty laws, enforced by physical violence, repress a woman's political beliefs and their expression.

The obedience and modesty laws also conflict with a woman's freedom of religious belief guaranteed under article 18. A wife's disobedient act may well arise out of a religious belief concerning appropriate behavior that differs from her husband's belief. Even a wife who remains obedient for fear of reprisal may nonetheless believe that her religious duty should not be to submit to her husband's authority. In either case, the result is suppression of her religious belief and its manifestation. Thus, obedience rules and modesty codes clearly impinge on the

---

Immigration Review, Arlington, Va., U.S.A.) 13–15 (Aug. 9, 1995) (unpublished opinion)(holding that spouse abuse was attributable to the state and that wife was "persecuted by being punished with spousal abuse for attempting to assert her individual autonomy and resisting mandated female subservience."); In the Matter of A and Z: In Deportation Proceedings (A 72–190–893; A 72–793–219) (Exec. Office for Immigration Review, Arlington, Va., U.S.A.) 18 (Dec. 20, 1994) (unpublished opinion), *reported in* 72 INTERPRETER RELEASES 521 (Apr. 17, 1995); *see also supra* note 351.

358. Universal Declaration art. 21.

359. *See supra* note 201 (discussing limits on women's right to vote in Kuwait and Algeria).

360. *See, e.g.*, IQBAL, *supra* note 36, at 115–19 (arguing that under Islamic law women are prohibited from running for public office under modesty codes).

361. Women who claim that they support laws of obedience and modesty codes call into question the reliability of their own position. There is no way that an outside observer can evaluate whether or not this political position is her own because she is subject to obedience rules and corresponding coercive violent sanctions. The very existence of the rules undermines the credibility of a woman who supports such rules while subject to them.

religious beliefs of women who believe that obedience and submission are not required. The groups of religious women fighting fundamentalism in many different countries represent such women.[362] This is particularly true of those women who have had to go into exile for their religious and political beliefs because their society has become unsafe for them due to incitement of hatred for their beliefs.[363] The obedience and modesty laws conflict with these women's rights to freedom of religious belief and its manifestation.[364]

Furthermore, religious fundamentalist state laws that require a husband's permission for his wife to work impinge on the rights guaranteed under both articles 19 (right to freedom of association) and 23 (right to work).[365] The legal requirement that a wife needs her husband's permission to travel also conflicts with the article 13 guarantee of freedom of movement within one's own state and the right to leave one's own state.[366] Finally, the obedience and modesty laws will in many cases interfere with the right to education under article 26(1) and the right to full development of the personality under article 26(2).

It is clear that the obedience and modesty laws conflict with a multitude of the articles of the Universal Declaration, involving both equality and fundamental liberties, and constitute a substantial and systematic invasion of women's rights. At this stage, it is necessary to acknowledge that the obedience and modesty laws also are manifestations of religious belief (of at least part of the citizenry of a state). Thus, there is a conflict in rights and an analysis under article 29 is necessary.

Article 29 Analysis

The methodology for application of article 29 requires a determination as to whether the obedience laws and modesty codes, as manifestations of religious fundamentalist belief, operate as permissible limitations on the international legal rights of women. Such an invasion of women's rights is allowable only for the purpose of securing "due recognition" of the right to religious belief or the "just

---

362. *See supra* notes 4–6, 23 and accompanying text.

363. *See supra* notes 6, 23 and accompanying text.

364. As a U.S. circuit court declared in a political asylum case concerning an Iranian woman who had been harassed by Iranian authorities for "some strands of hair outside her veil or 'chador,' which the Iranian regime requires all women to wear," it is "clear that being forced to conform to, or being sanctioned for failing to comply with, a conception of Islam that fundamentally is at odds with one's own also can rise to the level of persecution. . . . Indeed, when a member of a religion is forced to comply with an interpretation of her faith with which she disagrees, . . . the individual may suffer not only the general 'torture' of conscience . . ., but also the additional consequence of having imposed upon her a particular conception of the dictates of her own religion." Fisher v. I.N.S., 37 F.3d 1371, 1381 (9th Cir. 1994) (remanding to Immigration Board for consideration of Iranian woman's claim of well-founded fear of persecution on account of her religious beliefs).

365. Universal Declaration art. 23; *see supra* notes 172, 182, and accompanying text (discussing codes requiring wife to have her husband's permission to work).

366. Universal Declaration art. 13.

requirements" of a democratic society.[367] The standard of "due recognition" is an international standard and has been developed in international law.[368] First, the standard may not depend upon the tenets of a particular religion and may not be determined by any particular religion, no matter how passionate its desire to discriminate as part of religious belief.[369] Second, the international community accepts certain activities as core and integral to the right of religious belief and manifestation of religious belief.[370] These activities include the right to worship, to maintain places of worship, and to choose religious leaders.[371] It has not been suggested that the obedience laws and modesty codes fall within the core activities of religion. Arguably it follows from this that religion can make no claim for due recognition of obedience laws and modesty codes, and that consequently international law tolerates no intrusion by these codes into the rights guaranteed to women. Even if this is not entirely accepted, it nonetheless remains the case that all religious activities, core or otherwise, are subject to the due recognition standard of article 29. The implementation of this standard is best explored in the context of the conflict between the manifestation of religious belief and the prohibition of racial discrimination, as discussed next.

Third, international jurisprudence has worked out the limits beyond which recognition of a religion is not due, in the context of racial discrimination. The major jurisprudential developments have taken place in the international approaches to slavery and apartheid.[372] In these contexts, gross and systematic discrimination was not accepted for the sake of giving due recognition to religion. As discussed, this demonstrates that the standard of due recognition for religion may not be interpreted without consideration of the due recognition of minimum basic norms of human dignity and freedom of other protected groups.[373]

---

367. See supra notes 314–18 and accompanying text.

368. See supra notes 295, 317 and accompanying text.

369. See supra notes 257–59, 295, 317 and accompanying text.

370. For example, the activities recognized as core to the manifestation of religious belief in article 6 of the U.N. Declaration on the Elimination of Religious Intolerance and Discrimination include the freedom, inter alia: to worship, and to maintain places of worship; to maintain charitable institutions; to make and use necessary articles related to the rites and customs of a religion; to issue and disseminate publications concerning the religion; to teach a religion in a place suitable for this purpose; to solicit financial support; to train leaders; to observe religious holidays; to have communications at the national and international level with other members of the religion. See U.N. Declaration on the Elimination of Religious Intolerance and Discrimination, G.A. Res. 36/55, 36 U.N. GAOR, 36th Sess., Supp. 51, at 171, U.N. Doc. A/36/51 (1981). The Human Rights Committee has recognized a similar list, focusing on acts that are integral and close to the basic affairs of religion. Human Rights Committee, General Comments Adopted under Article 40, Paragraph 4, of the ICCPR: General Comment No. 22 (48) (art. 18), U.N. GAOR, 48th Sess., Supp. 40., U.N. Doc. A/48/40 (Pt. I) (1993). The Committee recognizes the right to wear distinctive dress, and does not deal with mandatory modesty dress codes.

371. See supra note 370.

372. See also Sullivan, supra note 242, at 811.

373. See supra note 318 and accompanying text.

The major religions historically supported and justified slavery, with the three religions that rely on the Old Testament finding justification within it.[374] Religious justification supported the Christian and Islamic role in the North Atlantic slave trade and slavery in the New World.[375] The New World Christian doctrine preached to slaves was that: slaves should accept their servile position as part of the divine plan; they were spiritually equal even if not equal in the world; their religious duty was one of obedience to their master; they should feel happy and content with their position; and they should accept discipline and correction because it was for their sins, and in any event their reward for bearing their punishments patiently was to be in heaven.[376] Moreover, "Christianizing" slaves was regarded as good practice because it would increase the likelihood of their being obedient to their masters.[377]

---

374. Slavery was justified under traditional Buddhism and was considered legitimate under Hindu law. *See* DEV RAJ CHANANA, SLAVERY IN ANCIENT INDIA, AS DEPICTED IN PALI AND SANSKRIT TEXTS 2–3, 26–30, 39–63, 87 (1960). With respect to Christianity, Islam, and Judaism, *see* DAVID B. DAVIS, SLAVERY AND HUMAN PROGRESS 86–90 (1984)[hereinafter DAVIS, SLAVERY AND HUMAN PROGRESS]; FREDRICKSON, *supra* note 327, at 10. These religions relied on Genesis 9:24–25 where Noah awakens from his drunkenness and curses Ham, his youngest son, that Canaan (Ham's son) be a "servant of servants" of his brethren, and Leviticus 25:44–46 where God tells Moses that Hebrews should not sell their own brethren but should buy their slaves "of the nations that are around you." *See* DAVIS, SLAVERY AND HUMAN PROGRESS, *supra*, at 86–90. By the Middle Ages, Jewish, Muslim, and Christian writers all separately identified the curse of Noah on Canaan as referring specifically to the "black children of Ham" understood to be black Africans, *id.* at 87, although they justified the institution in general and did not limit it to black Africans. Christianity and Islam also justified taking infidels and captives of war as slaves, and consequently each enslaved prisoners of war taken from the other, a practice that continued for six centuries including through the Crusades and Jihads in the eleventh, twelfth and thirteenth centuries. *See* DAVID B. DAVIS, THE PROBLEM OF SLAVERY IN WESTERN CULTURE 41 (1966)[hereinafter DAVIS, PROBLEM OF SLAVERY]. I would like to thank Robert J. Cottrol for his help and advice with regard to the institution and history of slavery.

375. With respect to Christianity, see DAVIS, PROBLEM OF SLAVERY, *supra* note 374, at 101–02. By the middle of the eighteenth century, Christian doctrine and institutions in general played an important part in the procedures of slave control and enforcement of slave codes in the New World. *See* LESTER B. SCHERER, SLAVERY AND THE CHURCHES IN EARLY AMERICA 1619–1819, 15–16, 66–68 (1975); DAVIS, PROBLEM OF SLAVERY, *supra* note 374, at 88, 95–96; *see also* FREDRICKSON, *supra* note 327, at 141 (discussing Christian doctrine of spiritual equality which still, conveniently, allowed for hierarchical orders on earth). Canon law endorsed slavery to the extent that a bishop was not allowed to manumit a slave belonging to the RCC unless he made up the loss from his own property. DAVIS, PROBLEM OF SLAVERY, *supra* note 374, at 95. With respect to Islam, see Nehemia Levtzion, *Slavery and Islamization in Africa: A Comparative Study, in* SLAVES AND SLAVERY IN MUSLIM AFRICA: VOL. I ISLAM AND THE IDEOLOGY OF ENSLAVEMENT 182, 187, 188–95 (John R. Willis ed.,1985); *see generally* John R. Willis, *Preface, in* SLAVES AND SLAVERY IN MUSLIM AFRICA: VOL. I ISLAM AND THE IDEOLOGY OF ENSLAVEMENT, *supra*, at viii (noting that Islam justified slavery not only on the basis of the Old Testament, but also on the Sunnah (the model of the prophet Muhammed) "who was at once a slaveholder and a practitioner of polygamy and concubinage."); John R. Willis, *Introduction: The Ideology of Enslavement in Islam, in* SLAVES AND SLAVERY IN MUSLIM AFRICA: VOL. I ISLAM AND THE IDEOLOGY OF ENSLAVEMENT, *supra*, at 1, 4 [hereinafter Willis, *Introduction*]; ROBERT W. JULY, A HISTORY OF THE AFRICAN PEOPLE 97–99, 148–156, 165, 217–23 (1970).

376. SCHERER, *supra* note 375, at 76–78, 98–100; *see also* FREDRICKSON, *supra* note 327, at 185, 201–02 (discussing doctrine that found that some men were incapable of governing themselves and therefore were better off in slavery, particularly as they benefited by being under the care of Christians).

377. *See* FREDRICKSON, *supra* note 327, at 84; SCHERER, *supra* note 375, at 95–100; DAVIS, PROBLEM OF SLAVERY, *supra* note 374, at 203–05.

Despite some Christian sects' change in the nineteenth century to a new theological position mandating the abolition of slavery, other Christians continued to justify slavery on the basis of the Old Testament and fought its abolition.[378] Moreover, the underlying doctrine that Christianity was good for black African heathens served to feed ideologies of racial inferiority that justified institutionalizing racial discrimination into law long after slavery was abolished in the New World, and indeed such ideologies survive to the present day.[379]

The international community gradually became opposed to slavery. By 1919 the Allies had signed conventions which contained, *inter alia*, a brief clause committing them to the suppression of slavery, and the covenant of the League of Nations had also determined that slavery and the slave trade should be suppressed.[380] Nevertheless, slavery was not outlawed until 1962 in Saudi Arabia and 1970 in Oman.[381] Furthermore, certain Christian sects still justify the institution of slavery,[382] and Muslim religious fundamentalists still argue that enslavement of infidels is justified.[383] Regardless of religious doctrine in Christianity and Islam, international mores and law did not, and do not, hold that "due recognition" requires that these religious sects be allowed to determine the issue of slavery for themselves or to practice slavery. Slavery, particularly slavery based on belonging to a particular racial group, constitutes gross systematic discrimination and fails to give "due recognition" to the rights and freedoms of the group suffering discrimination. It is in this fashion that international law has rendered the standard of "due recognition" for religious rights consistent with the standard of "due recognition" for the rights of a racial group.[384]

---

378. *See* FREDRICKSON, *supra* note 327, at 172; DAVIS, SLAVERY AND HUMAN PROGRESS, *supra* note 374, at 111–12, 234, 260–61; *see generally* THOMAS V. PETERSON, HAM AND JAPETH: THE MYTHIC WORLD OF WHITES IN THE ANTEBELLUM SOUTH (1978).

379. *See* DAVIS, PROBLEM OF SLAVERY, *supra* note 374, at 473–74; SCHERER, *supra* note 375, at 142–44; *see, e.g., infra* note 382; *see also* FREDRICKSON, *supra* note 327, at 150–62.

380. *See* DAVIS, SLAVERY AND HUMAN PROGRESS, *supra* note 374, at 309–10; *see generally* United Nations Economic and Social Council, The Work of the League of Nations for the Suppression of Slavery, U.N. Doc. E/AC.33/2, at 2–3 (23 Jan. 1950), LNP, C.426.M157.1925.VI, 71–74.

381. *See* DAVIS, SLAVERY AND HUMAN PROGRESS, *supra* note 374, at 314, 319.

382. U.S. southern state senators may still be heard to defend slavery publicly on the basis of the Christian Bible. An Alabama senator recently defended flying the Confederate flag by quoting biblical passages on slavery, by arguing the benefits of southern farmers converting slaves to Christianity, and by arguing that those bitter about slavery "are obviously bitter and hateful against God and his word, because they reject what God says and embrace what mere humans say concerning slavery." *Alabama House Candidate Quits After Slavery Defense*, WASH. POST, May 12, 1996, at A11.

383. *See, e.g.,* IQBAL, *supra* note 36, at 158–63 (discussing that Islamic law allows for slavery of prisoners of war and that men are free to have "sexual relations" with their female slaves and to sell them); MAUDUDI, PURDAH, *supra* note 158, at 21 n.1 (arguing that if enemy refuses to give compensation for slaves or to release Muslim prisoners then it is lawful under Islam to keep a slave); *see also* ABDULAHI AHMED AN-NA'M, TOWARD AN ISLAMIC REFORMATION: CIVIL LIBERTIES, HUMAN RIGHTS, AND INTERNATIONAL LAW 175 (1990)("Muslim tribesmen of southwestern Sudan feel justified in capturing non-Muslims from southern Sudan and keeping them in secret slavery.").

384. *See supra* notes 317–18 and accompanying text.

Given the equal treatment of race and sex discrimination under the Charter and Universal Declaration,[385] the international standard of "due recognition" of religious rights would thus not require that religious fundamentalist groups be allowed to determine the issue of the equality of women for themselves and to practice systematic sex discrimination. Comparison may be drawn between slavery on the basis of race as it has been justified under religious rhetoric and women's inferior position as it is currently justified under religious fundamentalist rhetoric.[386] Both rhetorics regard the roles of women and slaves as part of a divine plan, where spiritual equality may be neatly separated from earthly hierarchies.[387] Contemporary religious fundamentalism (of all religions) promotes doctrine to women very similar to Christian doctrine preached to slaves: wives should accept their servile position as part of the divine plan; they are spiritually equal even if not equal in the world; their religious duty is one of obedience to their husband; they should feel happy and content with their position; and they should accept discipline and correction because it is for their sins, and in any event their reward for bearing their punishments patiently is in heaven or in rebirth.[388]

The second example of international consensus demonstrating that "due recognition" for religion nevertheless allows suppression of a religious manifestation is in the case of systematic racial discrimination and apartheid in South Africa and territories under South Africa's control. The Dutch settlers (Boers or Afrikaners) of South Africa practiced slavery and justified it on similar religious grounds to those used in the New World.[389] After Britain took over South Africa in the early 1800s and enacted laws liberating Africans from many restrictions, the Boers reacted in a mass organized migration away from British rule.[390] The participants in this migration, the *Voortrekkers*, took their inspiration from Old Testament Christianity of Calvinist origin.[391] With the Bible as their guide, they asserted their dominance over nonwhites as based on Ham's curse, and regarded them as "not

---

385. *See supra* text between notes 256 and 260 and 281 and 282, and text accompanying notes 294, 295.

386. A comparison between the ideology of slavery and the ideology of women's subordination is not only apt, but is so complete that some sects themselves have compared slavery to the servile state of women in simultaneous justification of both systems of domination. For example, Muslim ideology has explicitly compared the condition of the slave to the servile status of a wife to her husband: "a comparison is drawn between the dominion imposed by the husband through which his wife is caused to surrender her sexual self, and the sovereignty established by the master whereby the slave is compelled to alienate his right to dispose.... [T]he master buys his slave, whereas in marriage, the husband purchases his wife's productive part. For the security of dower, the woman's sexual self is enslaved—for the protection of his lord, the slave's person is secured." Willis, *Introduction, supra* note 375, at 1. In contemporary religious fundamentalism, see IQBAL, *supra* note 36, at 158–63 (making comparison of female slaves to wives).

387. *See supra* note 376 and accompanying text.

388. *See supra* note 376 and accompanying text.

389. *See* FREDRICKSON, *supra* note 327, at 18, 37, 65, 73.

390. FREDRICKSON, *supra* note 327, at 42, 48, 147–48, 163–72; T. DUNBAR MOODIE, THE RISE OF AFRIKANERDOM: POWER, APARTHEID, AND THE AFRIKANER CIVIL RELIGION 3–4, 19 (1975).

391 FREDRICKSON, *supra* note 327, at 37, 170; *see* MOODIE, *supra* note 390, at ix, 22–26.

actually human.''[392] The crucial event of the Great Trek was the Afrikaners' victory over the Zulu in the battle of Blood River in 1838 in which they not only won territories, but, crucially, were reassured in their belief that God had chosen them for the divine mission of preserving the rule of the Afrikaner white race.[393] In 1848 further British territorial annexations pressed the *Voortrekkers* to trek again to establish new republics that would protect their religious theory and practice of white supremacy.[394] They established the Orange Free State and Transvaal (South African Republic) as Christian societies whose laws explicitly prohibited ''equality between coloured people and the white inhabitants of the country either in Church or state.''[395] But the British annexed Transvaal in 1877, and under Paul Kruger Afrikaners' resistance to British rule culminated in the Anglo-Boer wars.[396] Kruger's nationalism was based on the Calvinism of the Afrikaner churches and the sacred history of the Great Trek and Blood River.[397] His Calvinist mission is the foundation for the Afrikaner nationalist apartheid policies a half-century later.[398] By 1948, the Afrikaner Nationalist Party was elected on a platform of apartheid, a policy that was regarded as a requirement of ''Divine Will'' because ''Blood River was, after all, a proof that God favored white civilization, or at least white Afrikaners.''[399] The *Voortrekkers'* belief in being the chosen people with a calling

---

392. FREDRICKSON, *supra* note 327, at 171 (quoting local official's report on treatment of servants by settlers; Landdrost Albert to Gov. Janssens, as quoted in MARAIS, MAYNIER 73); *see* MOODIE, *supra* note 390, at 29; *see also supra* note 374 (discussing Ham's curse). One participant in the Great Trek explained the necessity of migration because of ''our slaves . . . being placed on an equal footing with Christians, contrary to the laws of God and the natural distinctions of race and religion.'' FREDRICKSON, *supra* note 327, at 171 (*quoting* from W. M. MACMILLAN, THE CAPE COLOUR QUESTION: A HISTORICAL SURVEY 81 (1927)).

393. FREDRICKSON, *supra* note 327, at 174–75; MOODIE, *supra* note 390, at 6, 15, 199–200, 245. A visiting missionary described the Boers in the independent Boer republics, *see infra* note 395 and accompanying text, as having ''persuaded themselves . . . that they are God's chosen people, and that the blacks are wicked and condemned Canaanites over whose head the divine anger lowers continually.'' JOHN MACKENZIE, TEN YEARS NORTH OF THE ORANGE RIVER, 1859–1869 (London, 1971) (1871). They found it obvious that heathens and black Africans could not be members of their divinely chosen select group. MOODIE, *supra* note 390, at 28–29. The survivors of the battle covenanted to God to celebrate the victory every year thereafter, and accordingly the Day of the Covenant remains an important national holiday of Afrikaners. MOODIE, *supra* note 390, at 20–21.

394. FREDRICKSON, *supra* note 327, at 176; *see* MOODIE, *supra* note 390, at 7.

395. FREDRICKSON, *supra* note 327, at 177 (*quoting* Constitution of South African Republic); *see* MOODIE, *supra* note 390, at 7.

396. FREDRICKSON, *supra* note 327, at 191; *see* MOODIE, *supra* note 390, at 7–11, 26–38.

397. *See* MOODIE, *supra* note 390, at 7–11, 26–38; *see also* FREDRICKSON, *supra* note 327, at 193 (*quoting* President of Transvaal, Paul Kruger, in 1882).

398. FREDRICKSON, *supra* note 327, at 193; *see* JULY, *supra* note 375, at 493 (noting Kruger's religious view of the Boers as God's chosen people as genesis of apartheid and nationalism); *see* MOODIE, *supra* note 390, at 7–11, 26–38, 79, 104, 178, 199–200, 215. At the centenary celebration of the Day of the Covenant, a reenactment of the Great Trek galvanized thousands of Afrikaners into forming an association dedicated to promoting the Afrikaner race and culture and preserving the rule of the white race. *See* MOODIE, *supra* note 390, at 178–89, 199–200.

399. MOODIE, *supra* note 390, at 247, 248. When South Africa emerged as a selfgoverning union, the

to protect and defend their white civilization was fully expressed when South Africa became an independent republic in 1961.[400] Afrikaners had finally managed to merge completely their religious beliefs with their own political state, thereby creating the ideal religious fundamentalist state.

Despite the religious underpinnings of apartheid, international opinion had turned against it by the early 1970s.[401] The international community did not consider manifestation of religious belief as taking precedence over freedom from systematic racial discrimination and thereby constituting a defense of apartheid.[402] Indeed, the international community did not even take seriously the idea that a certain Christian sect's ideology could determine the standards for discrimination or practice it. It was self-evident that systematic racial discrimination was a gross violation of the Charter and the Universal Declaration,[403] and that "due recognition" of the right to religious freedom did not require the allowance of systematic discrimination as a manifestation of religious belief.

As previously discussed, under the language of the Charter and the Universal Declaration, these standards of the prohibition of discrimination apply equally to sex discrimination, and no religious sect may set these standards for international law.[404] Article 29 of the Universal Declaration does not require under international legal standards that recognition is "due" for white supremacy and male supremacy simply because these are manifestations of religious belief. Thus, according to these standards, manifestations of religious beliefs in the form of systematic sex discrimination, affecting most, if not all, of women's civil and political rights should not be accorded "due recognition." This does not amount to a destruction of religious rights. But if "due recognition" were understood to allow religious fundamentalist laws as permissible limitations on women's rights, the result would be the wholesale destruction of women's equality and liberty rights. In this context, parallel recognition of a basic minimum of women's equality and liberty rights is due.[405]

---

white supremacy laws of segregation, traceable back to the earlier Boer republics and slaveholding mentalities, were established. *See* FREDRICKSON, *supra* note 327, at 238, 239–40, 249.

400. *See* MOODIE, *supra* note 390, at 260–61, 265–66, 269–70, 280–85. Despite a small group of Dutch Reformed theologians (the "enlightened ones") questioning apartheid in 1961, they were still a minority in Afrikanerdom in the mid-1970s. *Id.* at 292.

401. *See infra* notes 436–43 and accompanying text (discussing potential expelling of South Africa from the United Nations); *see generally* JOHN DUGARD, THE SOUTH WEST AFRICA/NAMIBIA DISPUTE: DOCUMENTS AND SCHOLARLY WRITINGS ON THE CONTROVERSY BETWEEN SOUTH AFRICA AND THE UNITED NATIONS (1973).

402. *See supra* notes 327–35 and accompanying text (discussing *Legal Consequences for States of the Continued Presence of South Africa in Namibia (South West Africa) Notwithstanding Security Council Resolution 276 (1970)*, 1971 I.C.J. Rep. 16, ¶131, at 57 (June 21); *infra* notes 436–43 and accompanying text.

403. *See supra* notes 327–35.

404. *See supra* notes 257–59, 295–306, 317 and accompanying text.

405. *See supra* notes 317–18, 384 and accompanying text.

Article 29 also requires a second inquiry as to whether the obedience laws and modesty codes are permissible limitations on women's rights because they are needed to advance the "just requirements" of a democratic society.[406] As already discussed, the contrary is clearly the case. The marital submission and modesty laws for women grossly interfere with women's involvement in the creation and maintenance of a democratic society. Religious fundamentalist laws of marriage, divorce, and modesty present a system that is intrinsically repressive of divergent political views.[407] Thus, these religious fundamentalist laws are not necessary to advance the "just requirements" of a democratic society; indeed they positively undermine the democratic process by limiting the participation of half the population in democratic government.[408]

Therefore, under article 29, religious fundamentalist laws of obedience and modesty do not constitute permissible limitations on women's rights as they are not for the sole purpose of securing "due recognition" of the right to religious belief or for the just requirements of a democratic society. These laws, if attributable to the state, are thus in violation of the Universal Declaration.

Finally, article 30 permits a state to restrict groups or individuals that aim to destroy the rights of others. Religious fundamentalists would appear to be exactly the type of destructive group that article 30 contemplates: a group that aims to destroy the rights and freedoms of women. Religious fundamentalists' destructive tendencies are evidenced by their discriminatory legal systems, their political activity that targets women's rights, and their reservations to treaties that particularly implicate women's rights.[409] Restrictions on religious fundamentalist laws are warranted to the extent the laws destroy the rights of women.[410]

The Accountability of States for Religious Fundamentalist Laws

This subsection evaluates state accountability for religious fundamentalist laws that conflict with guarantees under the Charter and the Universal Declaration. It

---

406. *See supra* notes 315–17 and accompanying text.

407. Even without considering the negative impact of religious fundamentalist movements on women, fundamentalist movements promote an intolerance of other religions through elevation of their own religion over all others. The religious intolerance manifested by religious fundamentalists to those in their own religion and to outsider religions is contrary to democratic principles and to the object and purpose of the Universal Declaration.

408. *See supra* notes 346–61 and accompanying text.

409. For example, many states have submitted reservations to CEAFDAW that are contrary to the very aim of the treaty itself. A large number of the explicit and all-encompassing reservations resulted from religious fundamentalist influence. *See* UN-NGO GROUP ON WOMEN AND DEVELOPMENT, WOMEN AND HUMAN RIGHTS 116–120 (prepared by Katarina Tomasevki, 1993).

410. As has been argued, *see supra* note 319–20, article 30 may be interpreted to impose an affirmative duty on states concerning religious fundamentalist laws. Thus, in order to protect citizens' right to be free of the intimidating and silencing threat of such groups, a state is obliged to stop the destructive activities of such groups.

has already been determined that religious fundamentalist laws of obedience and modesty conflict with the guarantees of articles 55 and 56 of the Charter and numerous articles of the Universal Declaration. There is, however, no violation of these instruments unless states are accountable for the religious fundamentalist legal systems in question. A state is accountable in three kinds of situations: first, when the state acts directly by enacting state laws and by enforcing laws administratively and judicially; second, when the state enforces laws in a discriminatory fashion such that the state is complicit in the violations of private actors; and third, under certain circumstances, when the state is complicit in violations by private individuals by failing in its duty to provide any effective remedy for the violations.[411]

The first type of state accountability is generally manifest in practice: a state is accountable for laws it has enacted or enforced, and if the laws deny guarantees under the Charter and Universal Declaration then the state is therefore in violation of these instruments.[412] This means that religious fundamentalist states that have enacted and enforced laws that discriminate against women—such as Algeria, Bangladesh, Iran, Iraq, Pakistan, and Sudan[413]—are contravening the Charter and the Universal Declaration. Israel[414] and India[415] also directly contravene the Charter and the Universal Declaration by their enforcement of discriminatory religious laws

---

411. *See* Kenneth Roth, *Domestic Violence as an International Human Rights Issue, in* HUMAN RIGHTS OF WOMEN, *supra* note 128, at 326, 329–35; Dorothy Q. Thomas & Michele E. Beasley, *Domestic Violence as a Human Rights Issue,* 58 ALB. L. REV. 1119, 1121–34 (1995); Rebecca J. Cook, *State Responsibility for Violations of Women's Rights,* 7 HARV. HUM. RTS. J. 125, 151 (1994). The ICJ distinguished the first and third situations of accountability in *Case Concerning United States Diplomatic and Consular Staff in Tehran (U.S. v. Iran),* 1980 I.C.J. 3, 29 (May 24). The "militants" who first attacked the U.S. embassy in Tehran were not official agents of Tehran, and thus the state was not accountable for the attack. Once the state authorities approved the occupation and adopted a state policy to continue it, the attack was attributable to Iran. *Id.* at 35–36. This constitutes the first situation of accountability where the state is directly involved. The third type of situation was demonstrated by Iran's failure to protect the embassy from attack by the militants, contrary to its duty to do so under the Vienna Convention on Diplomatic Relations. *Id.* at 30–32.

412. A state is also accountable under customary law for state policy. *See* RESTATEMENT, *supra* note 265, at §702, Comment b, at 162. The Restatement takes the position that a state is not responsible for private acts in violation of customary law unless the state "required, encouraged, or condoned such private violations, but mere failure to enact laws prohibiting private violations of human rights would not ordinarily constitute encouragement or condonation." *Id.*

413. *See supra* note 176.

414. *See supra* note 236 and accompanying text. The recent elections in Israel increased the power of the religious fundamentalist parties, who seek to broaden the jurisdiction of the religious courts. This is likely to worsen the problem of discriminatory religious law.

415. India enforces discriminatory laws through its delegation to Christian and Muslim religious courts of jurisdiction in these matters, and has bowed under Muslim religious fundamentalist pressure to limit further women's rights under Muslim family laws. *See supra* notes 93, 152; Singh, *supra* note 128, at 384–85 (discussing passage of Muslim Women's Act due to Muslim fundamentalist pressure which overruled Supreme Court decision in *Shah Bano* and denied Muslim women maintenance on divorce beyond period of *iddat*). With respect to Hinduism, the recent elections in India enlarged the representation of the BJP which advocates implementation of discriminatory Hindu laws relating to marriage, divorce, and *sati* and may put India in further violation of its international responsibilities.

through their jurisdictional delegation to religious courts. The enactment and enforcement of these laws violates international obligations under the Charter, and states should vigilantly resist the temptation to enact such laws despite the often intense religious fundamentalist pressure to do so.

The second type of state accountability is found where the state has facially nondiscriminatory laws, but enforces them on a discriminatory basis. This involves state action in that, as a matter of state policy (explicit or otherwise) state police or prosecutors ignore certain crimes. Thus, even a state that has not enacted religious fundamentalist laws would be complicit if it enforced law on a discriminatory basis, thereby violating its international obligations. For example, the state might criminalize general physical assault but defer to societal norms of religious fundamentalism that permit a husband to discipline his wife. If, in consequence, the state fails to prosecute battering husbands under this general law, it is discriminating on the basis of sex in enforcement of the law.[416] Such discrimination in enforcement may be prevalent in society as a whole when religious fundamentalist pressure is strong, or may be applied particularly within religious fundamentalist communities that are separate from the main society.

The third type of state accountability applies when a state systematically fails to provide an effective remedy for violations of human rights or fundamental freedoms. Article 8 of the Universal Declaration specifically guarantees everyone the right of an effective judicial remedy for such violations.[417] It applies to all states, including those whose laws are nondiscriminatory both facially and in application, and thus imposes an affirmative obligation on states to provide effective remedies. This affirmative obligation requires the state to restrict nonstate actors from violative acts.

State accountability for private actions is particularly applicable with regard to violations of the right to security of the person in article 3 of the Universal Declaration. In the parallel context of the ICCPR's guarantee of the security of the person, the Human Rights Committee, in *Delgado Páez v. Columbia*, found that the state's failure to protect Delgado from anonymous threats and an attack by an unknown person violated his right to security of the person.[418] It was not sufficient protective

---

416. *See* Roth, *supra* note 411, at 333–35. The state is discriminating against women victims of assault crimes by failure to prosecute men.

417. *See supra* note 345 and accompanying text.

418. W. Delgado Páez v. Columbia, Communication No. 195/1985 (*adopted* 12 July 1990, 39th Sess.), Report of the Human Rights Committee, Vol. II, Comm. No. 195/1985, U.N. GAOR, 45th Sess., Supp. No. 40, at 43, ¶5.5, at 47, U.N. Doc. A/45/40 (1990) (holding that anonymous threats and attack on state school teacher, following harassment by ecclesiastical and educational authorities, constituted violation of article 9 of ICCPR). The Committee specifically rejected that the right to security of the person found in the first sentence of article 9(1) was in any way limited to the circumstances of the second sentence of article 9(1) referring to arrest and detention. *See* Delgado Páez v. Columbia, ¶5.5, at 47. Roth raises this issue of limitation regarding article 9, *see* Roth, *supra* note 411, at 335, but *Delgado* explicitly rejects it. Because the threats and attacks were by unknown persons, Delgado did not allege state action. Delgado Páez v. Columbia, ¶2.8, at 44, ¶2.9, at 45; *see also* Michael Singer, *Jurisdictional Immunity of International Organizations: Human Rights and Functional Necessity Con-*

state action that Delgado could use the Colombian court system or could report the threats and attack to the police; the state should have done more.[419]

The most compelling case of a state's accountability for failing to prevent or punish private acts is in the battering and murder of women that occur systematically under religious fundamentalist laws. Thus, a state's failure to act in these types of abuse cases makes the state complicit not only because the enforcement may be discriminatory as discussed above but because the state has failed to provide an effective remedy for the systematic violation of human rights. States that have not enacted religious fundamentalist laws still have an affirmative obligation to provide effective protection and effective remedies to women who are abused under the obedience laws of the fundamentalist communities. The state's affirmative duty to provide effective legal remedies may require more than providing a legal remedy for physical assault. Mere provision of legal remedies may not be sufficient in the religious fundamentalist context because women are often limited in their contact with outside sources of information and thus may not even be aware that such remedies exist. Thus, the affirmative duty of the state may require it to inform women about legal remedies, and to do so in such a way as to insure that women are not subject to reprisals by men in the community.

States' affirmative duty may also oblige them to take additional action, particularly in light of the systematic and wide-ranging violations of civil and political rights by religious fundamentalist discriminatory laws.[420] A state would be permitted, and indeed may have a duty, to outlaw religious practices that are systematically

---

cerns, 36 VA. J. INT'L L. 53, 148–49 (1995) (discussing state accountability for private action under *Delgado* as encompassing liability for actions of international organizations). *Delgado* also rejects Roth's notion that security of the person protects only against violence just short of murder. *Cf.* Roth, *supra* note 411, at 335.

419. Delgado Páez v. Columbia, ¶5.6, at 48, ¶6 at 49.

420. India and Egypt have taken this approach over many years. India has attempted to deal with Hindu fundamentalism by enacting civil laws of marriage and divorce that do not discriminate (or discriminate much less than do traditional and fundamentalist Hindu norms) and legislation specifically banning certain discriminatory Hindu religious practices such as *sati*, dowry deaths and the prohibition of widow remarriage. *See supra* notes 128, 135, 140, 147; *infra* note 421. Egypt's new educational initiative attempts to reclaim classrooms from fundamentalists, particularly The Muslim Brotherhood. *See* David Gardner, *Investing in the future*, FIN. TIMES, May 20, 1996, at VIII (Supp. Egypt). This new literacy crusade (52% of all Egyptians, but 70% of Egyptian women, are illiterate) emphasizes skills, agility, and innovation in order to encourage independence of mind in place of rote and passive learning. *Id.* It also incorporates a ban on *hejab* dress or the veil from girls' primary schools, *id.*, raising a question whether this violates the girls' right to religious freedom. A law banning religious dress in general would clearly violate rights to religious freedom concerning a basic manifestation of religious belief. However, there is no way of knowing whether the desire of a young child in the religious fundamentalist context to wear *hejab* dress is her own belief or merely the manifestation of obedience to her father. *See supra* note 361. Thus, banning the veil for primary school in order to eliminate the discriminatory effect of such modesty laws and to discourage submissive and passive behavior in the child as part of the learning experience is an important educational imperative of the state. It may be concluded therefore that banning particular dress in state schools is permissible because of the strong needs of the state to prepare citizens for full participation in state democratic affairs.

violative of women's liberty and equal rights.[421] Under this approach, it is arguable that states with strong religious fundamentalist movements, including, for example, Japan, Italy, Sri Lanka, and the United States, may have a duty to pass laws prohibiting the practice of requiring wives to be obedient.[422] Such laws would reach religious fundamentalist communities and also send a broader message to society that submission of women is unacceptable. However, determining the parameters of such a law to meet international law concerns is worthy of an article in itself.

Religious Fundamentalist Reservations to Treaties also Violate the Charter

This subsection considers state actions with respect to reservations to human rights treaties on the basis of religious fundamentalist laws, and argues that these reservations themselves constitute violations of the Charter.

Religious fundamentalism is premised on the notion that religious law takes precedence over all other law and defines, *inter alia*, relations between different religions and between men and women. Thus, some states have argued, in the context of human rights treaties, that religious law takes precedence over international human rights law even when the state has not entered reservations to the treaty on this basis.[423] A state that justifies its violation of a treaty on the basis that

---

421. For example, India reported to the Human Rights Committee that it passed laws making dowry deaths a recognizable offense and making the harassment of a woman for property an illegal act of cruelty for which her husband may be prosecuted. *See* Human Rights Committee, Summary Record of the 1041st Meeting: Second Periodic Report of India, ¶¶ 49–52, CCPR/C/SR.1041; *see* Indian Penal Code 304B (criminalizing dowry deaths), 498B (criminalizing cruelty to a woman by husband or relative of husband). The Committee regarded these laws as part of India's positive duty under the ICCPR, and the only question was whether India had done enough, especially in enforcing the laws and in educating the populace to a perspective which would improve women's status. *See* Human Rights Committee, Summary Record of the 1041st Meeting: Second Periodic Report of India, ¶ 52. For a discussion of the Indian government's failure to enforce these laws, see Singh, *supra* note 128, at 375, 388–93. The Committee did not find that the civil marriage laws (which attempt to provide equality between the sexes by outlawing religious practices), the laws criminalizing dowry deaths, and the aiding and abetting of *sati* were violations of the right to religious freedom. In fact, the issue was not even raised.

422. The approach is similar to that of India in enacting a law that outlawed the Hindu prohibition on widow remarriage. *See supra* note 146.

423. Since the Iranian Revolution, Iran has repeatedly made the claim that Islamic law takes precedence over international law. *See, e.g.,* U.N. GAOR 3d Comm., 36th Sess., 29th mtg. at 4–5, 6, U.N. Doc. A/C.3/36/SR.29 (1981); U.N. GAOR Hum. Rts. Comm., 37th Sess., Supp. No. 40, ¶300, at 66, U.N. Doc. A/37/40 (1982); U.N. GAOR Hum. Rts. Comm., 37th Sess., 56th mtg., ¶¶53–55, at 16, U.N. Doc. A/C.3/37/SR.56 (1982); U.N. ECOSOC Comm'n on Human Rts., 44th Sess., Provisional Agenda, Annex II, Agenda Item 12, U.N. Doc. E/CN.4/1988/12 (1988); Subcomm'n on Prevention of Discrimination and Protection of Minorities, 39th Sess., Agenda Item 6, ¶¶1–10, at 6–8, U.N. Doc. E/CN.4//Sub.2/1987/35 (1988); *see* Theodor Meron, *Iran's Challenge to the International Law of Human Rights*, 13 Hum. Rts. Internet Rep. 9 (1989). Sudan has also asserted this position in the context of the ICCPR. *See* U.N. Human Rights Committee, Summary Record of the Consideration of the Initial Report of the Sudan, Continued, 42d Sess., 1067th mtg. ¶2, at 2, ¶13, at 5, ¶74, at 18, U.N. Doc. CCPR/C/

its particular religious law preempts international law is obviously in violation of the core principle of international law that a state may not use municipal law to justify its failure to comply with international legal obligations.[424] This principle applies to religious municipal law just as it applies to secular municipal law.[425]

Other states have asserted that religious law takes precedence over international law human rights standards when they have entered reservations to treaties on that basis.[426] For example, Egypt's reservation to article 16 of CEAFDAW (concerning equality of men and women in all matters relating to family life) states that the "Islamic Sharia's provisions whereby women are accorded rights equivalent to those of their spouses . . . *may not be called in question.*"[427] In response, other states have argued that the reservations are in bad faith because they undermine the object and purpose of a particular treaty, while others have argued that the reservations are invalid or must be construed narrowly.[428]

SR.1067 (1991). Saudi Arabia has generally avoided signing any human rights treaty, but it does make general comments about religious law taking precedence over international law. *See* U.N. GAOR 3d Comm., 3d Sess., 124th mtg. at 363–65, U.N. Doc. A/C.3/SR.124 (1948); U.N. GAOR 3d Comm., 3d Sess., 125th mtg. at 367–70, U.N. Doc. A/C.3/SR.125 (1948) (opposing international guarantees of women's rights in marriage and inheritance).

424. *See* Vienna Convention on the Law of Treaties, *opened for signature* 23 May 1969, art. 27, 1155 U.N.T.S. 331, 341, U.N. Doc. A/Conf. 39/27 (1969) (*entered into force* 27 Jan. 1980).

425. Report of the Committee of Experts on the Application of Conventions and Recommendations, International Labour Conference, 71st Sess., Report III, Pt. 4A, at 290 (1985) (rejecting Iran's assertion of primacy of religious law over international human rights law); U.N. HUMAN RIGHTS COMMITTEE, SUMMARY RECORD OF THE CONSIDERATION OF THE INITIAL REPORT OF THE SUDAN, CONTINUED, 42d Sess., 1067th mtg ¶25, at 8, ¶30, at 9, ¶36–37, at 10–11, ¶39, at 11, ¶46, at 13, U.N. Doc. CCPR/C/SR.1067 (1991) (statements by members of Human Rights Committee that Sudan could not assert Islamic law as justification for failure to comply with ICCPR); *see* Sullivan, *supra* note 242, at 832–34; Meron, *supra* note 423, at 8. These claims must be resolutely rejected because if this "argument is raised to the level of theoretical discourse, there is a serious danger that many other states following fundamental religions, or groups (e.g., the Israeli fun[d]amentalist/extremist Gush Emunim . . .) will raise similar arguments to defeat the primacy of international law and divert attempts of the international community to bring about compliance with international law." Meron, *supra* note 423, at 8.

426. For example, other states have made similar broad reservations. *See* U.N. Doc. CEDAW/SP/1992/2, 1 Nov. 1991, at 11, 15, 16 (reservations of Egypt, Iraq, and Libya); MULTILATERAL TREATIES, *supra* note 247, at 169 (Egypt), 171 (Iraq), 172 (Libya). Israel has also made a reservation to the ICCPR on the basis of religious laws governing personal status. MULTILATERAL TREATIES, *supra* note 247, at 125.

427. MULTILATERAL TREATIES, *supra* note 247, at 169 (emphasis supplied). Contrast Tunisia, which regards Islamic law as a source of law and social progress, but has acknowledged that in the event of a conflict between Tunisia's law and the ICCPR the Shari'ah could not supplant the positive law of the ICCPR. *See Report of the Human Rights Committee*, U.N. GAOR, 42d Sess., Supp. No. 40, ¶108, at 26, U.N. Doc. A/42/40 (1987).

428. For example, Sweden objected to the reservations entered by the Government of Iraq on the ground that the reservations are incompatible with the object and purpose of the Convention and "would inevitably result in discrimination against women on the basis of sex, which is contrary to everything the Convention stands for," MULTILATERAL TREATIES, *supra* note 247, at 173, and other states, such as Finland, Federal Republic of Germany, Mexico, the Netherlands, Norway, and Sweden have also objected to Libya's reservation to CEAFDAW. *See* MULTILATERAL TREATIES, *supra* note 247, at 171 (Germany), 172 (Mexico, The Netherlands, Norway, Sweden); Sullivan, *supra* note 242, at 807. For

However, these assertions of a religious fundamentalist position in both declarations in response to accusations of a treaty violation and reservations to treaties should not be viewed merely in the context of the particular treaty in question. Rather, these assertions should be considered in light of the state's two-fold obligation under articles 55 and 56 of the Charter to cooperate with the United Nations in promoting equal rights for women and men and not to undermine the object and purpose of the Charter by putting themselves in a position of incapacity to cooperate with such promotion.[429] States also have a general duty to perform their obligations under the Charter in good faith according to the principle of *pacta sunt servanda*.[430]

A state's act of making a reservation is a public international act equivalent to the issuance of *opinio juris*. States that assert the supremacy of a particular religious law in determining issues of sex distinction (by the very act of claiming not to be bound on the basis of that particular religious law) are taking a position in direct conflict with articles 55 and 56.[431] The Charter specifically eschews religious law as the source for human rights, and, thus, any particular religious law may not determine the standards for the "without distinction" language.[432] Furthermore, these assertions conflict with article 55's requirement of equality between the prohibitions of distinctions and threaten to upset the delicate balance that the Charter achieves between these different types of distinctions. Thus, these declarative statements and reservations represent the state taking a public position that is contrary to the Charter. Public statements contrary to the Charter demonstrate bad faith and violate the state's two-fold duty to cooperate and not to undermine. Thus, these states by making these assertions are in violation of their legal obligations under articles 55 and 56.[433]

---

commentators' arguments, see Belinda Clark, *The Vienna Convention Reservations Regime and the Convention on Discrimination Against Women*, 85 AM. J. INT'L L. 281 (1991); Rebecca Cook, *Reservations to the Convention on the Elimination of All Forms of Discrimination Against Women*, 30 VA. J. INT'L L. 643 (1990).

429. *See supra* notes 249–56 and accompanying text.

430. *See* Vienna Convention on the Law of Treaties, *opened for signature* 23 May 1969, art. 26, 1155 U.N.T.S. 331, 341, U.N. Doc. A/Conf. 39/27 (1969) (*entered into force* 7 Jan. 1980).

431. *See supra* notes 257–59 and accompanying text.

432. *See supra* notes 257–59 and accompanying text. A number of these states (Afghanistan, Egypt, Iran, Iraq, Israel, Pakistan, Syria) voted for the Universal Declaration with the full knowledge that the Universal Declaration did not endorse any particular religion as its source of rights, *see supra* notes 285, 303–06 and accompanying text, in accordance with the Charter. Other states with strong fundamentalist movements also voted for the Universal Declaration; these include Chile, Columbia, India, Thailand, and the United States.

433. Some of these states have long been U.N. members and have benefited from their membership. Their relatively recent assertions of the absolute priority of religious law are due to domestic pressure from religious fundamentalists. Human rights and fundamental freedoms are fragile and constantly under assault from a variety of sources. The challenge to protect human rights will always be great and changes in municipal government are not an excuse to violate international law. As other countries begin to feel the pressure of religious fundamentalism, this problem of states violating the Charter will only increase.

The Consequences for Violation of the Charter

In previous subsections, it was determined that states which protect religious fundamentalist norms over international human rights norms are in violation of the Charter and the Universal Declaration.[434] These violations take the form of gross and systematic sex discrimination. The international community has already dealt with systematic discrimination as a Charter violation in the context of racial discrimination as a manifestation of religious belief and the same standards and compliance mechanisms must apply to sex discrimination.[435]

The international community expressed condemnation of South Africa's system of racial discrimination through various enforcement techniques, mainly relating to South African membership in the United Nations and other international organizations. Under the Charter, the Security Council may suspend a state's membership in the United Nations,[436] or the General Assembly, upon recommendation of the Security Council, may expel the state for consistent violation of the principles of the Charter.[437] In the early 1970s the United Nations gave serious consideration to expelling South Africa because its systematic racial discrimination violated the Charter. Those arguing for expulsion in the Security Council emphasized that under apartheid there were classifications of citizens solely on the basis of race with the result that blacks had highly unequal property rights, and suffered barriers to free movement, denial of the right to assemble freely, denial of voting rights, unequal educational opportunities, and cruel and degrading treatment by the state authorities.[438] The argument was that these practices violated the U.N. Charter as well as the Universal Declaration.[439] These limits on rights are directly parallel to the limits that women experience under religious fundamentalist laws: classification on the basis of sex resulting in denial of employment opportunities and property rights; denial of free voting; denial of the right of assembly; denial of free movement;

---

434. Earlier it was established that religious fundamentalist norms (laws and acts which are attributable to the state) of marriage, divorce, and modesty requiring that wives submit to their husbands and obey them violate the Charter and the Universal Declaration. In addition, some states are in violation of the Charter for their declarations and reservations to treaties to the effect that their particular religious law is supreme over international law and determinative of the interpretation of the prohibition of sex discrimination.

435. *See supra* notes 327–35, 372–405 and accompanying text.

436. U.N. Charter art. 5.

437. U.N. Charter art. 6.

438. For the debates, see U.N. SCOR, 29th Sess., 1796th mtg. U.N.Doc S/PV. 1796 (1974); U.N. SCOR, 29th Sess., 1800th mtg., U.N. Doc. S/PV. 1800 (1974); U.N. SCOR, 29th Sess., 1807th mtg., U.N. Doc. S/PV. 1807 (1974); U.N. SCOR, 29th Sess., 1808th mtg., U.N. Doc. S/PV.1808 (1974).

439. *See, e.g.*, U.N. SCOR, 29th Sess., 1796th mtg., ¶¶ 8–18, at 2–4, ¶35, at 5; ¶41, at 6, ¶47, at 7, ¶56, at 8, U.N. Doc. S/PV. 1796 (1974); U.N. SCOR, 29th Sess., 1800th mtg., ¶17, at 3, ¶31–33, at 5, ¶46, at 6, U.N. Doc. S/PV. 1800 (1974); U.N. SCOR, 29th Sess., 1807th mtg., at ¶3, at 1, ¶11, at 2, ¶19, at 3, U.N. Doc. S/PV. 1807 (1974); U.N. SCOR, 29th Sess., 1808th mtg., at ¶3, at 1, ¶5, at 2, ¶26, at 4, ¶¶33–34, at 5, ¶45, at 6, ¶51, at 6, ¶87, at 11, ¶113, at 13, ¶126, at 15, ¶129, at 15, U.N. Doc. S/PV. 1808 (1974).

unequal educational opportunities; cruel and degrading treatment by authorities in their act of enforcing obedience and modesty codes; and physical abuse by their husbands in which the state is complicit through its failure to provide effective remedies.[440]

On October 30, 1974, France, the United Kingdom, and the United States vetoed a proposed resolution in the Security Council to expel South Africa, primarily on the basis that expelling South Africa would reduce any influence the United Nations might have over changing South Africa's policies. [441] The General Assembly then took the matter into its own hands and refused to accept the credentials of the South African delegation, noting that South Africa's policy of apartheid was a constant violation of the principles of the Charter and the Universal Declaration.[442] The General Assembly's rejection of the credentials of South Africa was a use of the credentials process to question the legitimacy of the government of South Africa and, in practical effect, to suspend South Africa's membership in the United Nations.[443]

This same procedural process of rejecting credentials should be used with respect to states enforcing religious fundamentalist laws that establish a system of sex discrimination. This procedure is preferable to outright expulsion for two reasons. First, as a practical matter, the Security Council would not expel any member because of some states' belief that expulsion will limit international influence on a pariah state. Second, the procedural process of rejecting credentials has a strong coercive effect by shaming the state before the international community while at the same time allowing for the state to regain membership if it reforms. Other enforcement actions that should be taken against these states—again, parallel to the case of South Africa—include suspension and expulsion from various international

---

440. These limits on rights within each religion and their legal consequences are discussed *supra*.

441. *See* U.N. SCOR, 29th Sess., 1808th mtg., at ¶¶48–111, at 6–13, ¶154, at 17–18, U.N. Doc. S/PV. 1808 (1974).

442. *See U.N. Secretariat Summary of U.N. Credentials Practice Through 1973*, 1973 U.N. JURID. Y.B. 139, 140–41 (1973). For the debate of the General Assembly's final rejection of South Africa's credentials in 1974, see U.N. GAOR, 29th Sess., 2281st. plen. mtg., at 840–41, 854–55 (Nov. 12, 1974). The presenting of credentials by governments to the Secretary General before the opening of a new session of the General Assembly is normally a routine procedure. Rule 27 of the General Assembly's Rules of Procedure deals with the submission of credentials. *See* U.N. Doc. A/520/Rev. 15 (1985); *see also* 1985 U.N. JURID. Y.B. 128 (1985).

443. U.N. legal counsel expressed the opinion that the General Assembly could not suspend membership without following articles 5 and 6 of the Charter, which require action by the Security Council. The conclusion was that suspension of membership through the credentials process would be contrary to the Charter, particularly because there were no rival claimants to represent South Africa in the United Nations. *See* U.N. Legal Counsel, *Opinion on Rejection of Credentials*, 1970 U.N. JURID. Y.B. 169–70 (1970). Nonetheless, the General Assembly did exactly this with the result that South Africa could not participate, and by so doing, set a precedent. A subsequent initiative by some Arab states to take the same approach to Israel's credentials in the early 1980s was not successful because there was no broad-based support for the move.

organizations, particularly specialized U.N. organizations.[444] Censure by international organizations can also be particularly effective.[445]

These various measures to enforce the prohibition of systematic discrimination and subsequent denial of human rights are excellent precedents for the appropriate treatment of states that engage in systematic sex discrimination through religious fundamentalist legal systems. All enforcement mechanisms at the community's disposal should be used to coerce these pariah states to cease violating articles 55 and 56. It is time for the international community to live up to the standards of the Charter and the Universal Declaration.

---

444. For example, the International Labour Organization, Food and Agriculture Organization, United Nations Educational, Scientific and Cultural Organization, World Health Organization, International Civil Aviation Organization, Universal Postal Union, International Telecommunication Union, Intergovernmental Maritime Consultative Organization (since 1982 named International Maritime Organization, *see* 1982 U.N. JURID. Y.B. 126 (1982), U.N. Doc. ST/LEG/SER.C.20), and World Meteorological Organization all took measures to try to deny membership or certain privileges of membership to South Africa because of its policy of racial discrimination. Some were more successful than others. *See, e.g.,* World Meteorological Organization Resolution Suspending South African Rights and Privileges, WMO Congress, May 1975, Res. 38 (Cg. VII), Seventh World Meteorological Congress, Abridged Rep. with Res. 136; Universal Postal Union, Resolution C 6, 1979, Compendium of Congress Decisions (Paris 1947–Hamburg 1984), at 30 (1985)(expelling South Africa).

445. For example, the World Bank, in linking economic reforms to "good governance," refused to make new loans to Malawi until progress had been made on "basic freedoms and human rights" by its one-party "life president." World Bank Press Release, Paris, May 13, 1992; *Donors withdraw support until Malawi ends human-rights abuses*, Afr. Business, June 1992, at 5.

WOMEN AND CULTURE

Christina M. Cerna and Jennifer C. Wallace

INTRODUCTION

No discussion of the rights of women is complete without an analysis of the influence of culture. Culture, the source of our identity, provides the context that defines acceptable behavior in a society. Special bonds of community form between persons sharing a common cultural heritage. These ties can be very beneficial, especially to women, as they find a support system and share burdens within their particular cultural community. Cultural traditions can serve as devices designed to protect those at risk in society, including women, minorities, the elderly, the disabled, and children. Unfortunately, many practices originally intended to protect women (and the girl–child) instead become an obstacle to their empowerment and, in the most extreme cases, threaten their health and even survival. As one feminist scholar states: "No social group has suffered greater violation of its human rights in the name of culture than women. Regardless of the particular forms it takes in different societies, the concept of culture in the modern state circumscribes women's lives in deeply symbolic as well as immediately real ways."[1]

Although the status of women has greatly improved in some countries, as the United Nations recently reported, "in no society today do women enjoy the same opportunities as men."[2] Women are the subjects of discrimination in the public sphere regarding access to education, employment, health care, property ownership, inheritance practices, court testimony, and custody of children.[3] Women suffer additionally from discriminatory practices in the private sphere. Some of these practices, identified by the U.N., are female genital mutilation, child marriage, the various taboos or practices that prevent women from controlling their own fertility, nutritional taboos and traditional birth practices, female infanticide, adolescent pregnancy, and dowry price.[4] Many of these practices are a result of the greater

---

1. Arati Rao, *The Politics of Gender and Culture in International Human Rights Discourse,* in WOMEN'S RIGHTS, HUMAN RIGHTS: INTERNATIONAL FEMINIST PERSPECTIVES 167, 169 (Julie Peters & Andrea Wolper eds., 1995).

2. UNITED NATIONS DEVELOPMENT PROGRAMME, HUMAN DEVELOPMENT REPORT 1995 29 (1996).

3. U.S. Department of State, 104th Cong., 2d Sess., COUNTRY REPORTS ON HUMAN RIGHTS PRACTICES FOR 1995 xvi–xvii (1996).

4. Harmful Traditional Practices Affecting the Health of Women and Children, United Nations Fact Sheet #23, at 3 [hereinafter, Harmful Traditional Practices]. Although cultural practices contribute to the problems of domestic violence, this issue will not be discussed in this chapter. Domestic violence

value attributed to males, sometimes called "son preference." Despite many international legal instruments designed to eliminate discrimination against females, most cultures continue practices that are detrimental to the well-being of girls and women.

Frequently, women have no power to change harmful practices because of their lack of status in society. Lack of knowledge is also a problem as many of these women may not know that their rights have been violated or that they have rights at all. Even through logical reasoning and education it is difficult to overcome customs, which are frequently subconsciously motivated or the result of religious indoctrination. The norms of a culture become part of the identity of its members from infancy, providing deeply rooted convictions about what is right and wrong and what is "normal." Additionally, the practitioners of these customs view international norms as alien and illegitimate. Therefore, addressing abuses that are the result of cultural tradition is problematic at best. Dealing with these complicated issues requires sensitivity to the identity of others. As well, it is imperative that we avoid the mistake of allowing culture to be an excuse for harmful practices.

This chapter explores the issues surrounding the abuse of women's rights under the guise of cultural tradition. The first section offers a brief overview of the concept of culture and its role in creating the identity of individuals. The following section examines cultural rights and gives a brief overview of the universalist/cultural relativist argument. The third section extends the universalist/relativist debate by looking at the legitimacy of international human rights norms. In the fourth section various cultural traditions and their impact on women will be examined. Following, the chapter will give a brief overview of existing international protections for women. Finally, the last sections examine the impediments to changing traditional practices and offer a possible plan of action.

CULTURE

Culture is the context within which society functions. Beyond merely setting the boundaries for acceptable behavior, culture defines our identity and determines who we are. As one author notes, "the impact of culture on human behavior is often underestimated precisely because it is so powerful and deeply embedded in our self-identity and consciousness."[5] Although the dynamic and ambiguous nature of culture makes definition difficult, for the purposes of this chapter, culture is "the totality of the knowledge and practices, both intellectual and material," of a society.[6] This includes values, customs, norms, beliefs, practices, educational forms, behavioral patterns, and material goods. In other words:

---

occurs in almost every society in the world and is far too large a topic to address in a chapter devoted exclusively to cultural practices.

5. Abdullahi Ahmed An-Na'im, *Toward a cross-cultural approach to defining international standards of human rights, in* HUMAN RIGHTS IN CROSS-CULTURAL PERSPECTIVES: A QUEST FOR CONSENSUS 1, 23 (An-Na'im ed., 1991).

6. Lyndell V. Prott, *Cultural Rights as People's Rights in International Law, in* THE RIGHTS OF PEOPLES 93, 94 (James Crawford ed., 1988).

Culture is the source of the individual and communal world view: it provides both the individual and the community with the values and interests to be pursued in life as well as the legitimate means for pursuing them. It stipulates the norms and values that contribute to people's perception of their self-interest and the goals and methods of individual and collective struggles for power within a society and between societies. As such, culture is a primary force in the socialization of individuals and a major determinant of the consciousness and experience of the community.[7]

Our particular cultural tradition influences everything that we do, from the way we interpret history to the ways in which we communicate and the rules that govern our interactions.

The inevitable nature of culture does not suggest that its influence is easily identified. Rather, the subtle sway of culture informs our personality and governs our actions and reactions at a subconscious as well as a conscious level. This does not mean that we are prisoners of our particular culture; it is important to remember that culture is a social construction in constant flux. In addition, cultural influence is not a linear concept. Whereas culture influences individual perceptions and actions, those same actions, over the long run, can influence cultural change.

CULTURAL RIGHTS

Cultural Identity

Given the all-encompassing nature of culture, defining what should and should not be protected under cultural rights is a complex and contentious topic in the international arena. During the formulation of the Universal Declaration of Human Rights (UDHR), there was discussion about adding provisions for cultural groups. Whereas some states wanted to include specific protections for these groups (largely minority cultures), others felt that this was unnecessary.[8] As no consensus was ever reached, the rights related to culture contained within the UDHR are broad and amorphous. The cultural rights that the UDHR does include are the right to education (art. 26); the right of parents to choose the kind of education given to their children (art. 26(3)); the right of every person to participate in the cultural life of the community (art. 27); and the right to protection of artistic, literary, and scientific works (art. 27).[9] The UDHR does not define the "community" or "cultural life," leaving these notions open to interpretation. As well, these rights are essentially individual rather than group rights.

Many states saw the cultural rights provisions within the UDHR as inadequate and weak. Therefore, they extended these rights, at least theoretically, within the

---

7.   An-Na'im, *supra* note 5, at 23.

8.   Specifically, the Chair of the Commission, Eleanor Roosevelt, objected to their inclusion. *See* Rodolfo Stavenhagen, *Cultural Rights and Universal Human Rights, in* ECONOMIC, SOCIAL AND CULTURAL RIGHTS 63, 73 (Asbjørn Eide, Catarina Krause & Allan Rosas eds., 1995).

9.   These rights can also be found in the International Covenant on Economic, Social and Cultural Rights, A/RES/2200 A (XXI), 16 December 1966, arts. 13(I), 13(3), 15(I)(a), and 15(I)(c) respectively.

UNESCO declaration that declared a "right to develop a culture."[10] Cultural rights were more specifically addressed by the Algiers Declaration of 1976 and the Banjul Charter of 1981.[11] The rights contained in these regional documents are known as "people's rights" or the "right to cultural identity" and differ significantly from the individual rights established in the UDHR. In fact, the differences within these two distinct groups of rights represent the conflict between "Western" individualistic rights and communitarian values.

Communitarians insist that, within the current state system, minority cultures are threatened. Advocates for a right to cultural identity are concerned that minority cultures surrounded by a majority culture (such as indigenous groups within a state) will lose their distinctiveness and be assimilated into the dominant culture. These concerns have led to many international forums that attempted to extend cultural rights for indigenous groups.

One of the more interesting aspects of the individual versus group rights debate is that theorists on both sides of the argument acknowledge the importance of certain individual rights. For example, Lyndel Prott, in her examination of cultural rights for peoples, states: "[f]reedom to express one's view, to adhere to one's religion, to associate with others for peaceful purposes, are all essential to the maintenance and development of any culture. . . . [T]heir existence is a necessary prerequisite for the protection of culture, especially for the culture of minorities."[12] While individualists assert that these and other rights contained in the UDHR and related documents are sufficient for the protection of cultural identity, proponents of group rights insist that, without special protections for cultural identity, many cultures are at risk of being overrun.[13] These basic rights guarantee a level of openness or "political space" necessary for the protection of any group that is discriminated against, including women.

Universalism/Cultural Relativism

Related to the notion of a right to cultural identity is the belief that all cultures are equally valid. This world view, known as cultural relativism, contends that

---

10. *See* UNESCO Declaration of the Principles of International Cultural Co-operation, 1966, art. I(2). UNESCO's view of cultural rights was further clarified in the "Recommendation on participation by the people at large in cultural life and their contribution to it, 1976." *See* Prott, *supra* note 6, at 97.

11. The rights included in these documents are the right to preserve and develop a culture, the right to respect of cultural identity, the right of minority peoples to respect for identity, traditions, language, and cultural heritage, the right of a people to its own artistic, historical, and cultural wealth, the right of a people not to have an alien culture imposed on it, and the right to the equal enjoyment of a common heritage. For more detailed information, *see* Prott, *supra* note 6, at 97.

12. Prott, *id.* at 95.

13. *See* JACK DONNELLY, UNIVERSAL HUMAN RIGHTS IN THEORY AND PRACTICE 158–60 (1989); and Prott, *supra* note 6, at 103–06.

different cultures have different notions of human rights. For example, to a communitarian, human dignity is preserved through membership in a group or community.[14] In this view, international human rights law (which seeks to establish a universal minimum standard of decency) is, at best, meaningless, and at worst, cultural imperialism. Relativists argue that the principles enshrined in the Universal Declaration reflect Western values and not their own, and they complain that the West is interfering in their internal affairs when it imposes its own definition of human rights upon them.[15] They maintain that, despite desires of international human rights activists to regulate customs within a country, the continuation of these cultural practices is vital to their particular way of life. They contend that the validity of any practice must be determined by the specific culture where it occurs. Therefore, culture is the primary determinative factor in deciding whether or not a practice is acceptable.[16]

In preparation for the U.N. World Conference on Human Rights, held in Vienna in 1993, three regional meetings were held. At the end of each of these meetings—held in Africa, the Latin American and Caribbean region, and Asia—a "Final Declaration" was adopted that referred to the particular concerns and cultures of these regions and stated, for example, that while recognizing that human rights are universal in nature, "they must be considered in the context of a dynamic and evolving process of international norm-setting, bearing in mind the significance of national and regional particularities and various historical, cultural and religious backgrounds."[17]

This notion of cultural relativity is in direct conflict with the idea of an international system of human rights. Prior to World War II, international law was limited to the regulation of relations between states. Individuals were subjects of their own states, afforded no protection within the boundaries of those states by the international system. Some protections existed for aliens within a foreign state or during war, although these protections had to be invoked by the state of which the alien was a national vis-á-vis the foreign state. Treatment of a state's own citizens was considered beyond the purview of international law. States could convey benefits upon their citizens but this did not imply an obligation within the international system.

---

14. Nancy Kim, *Toward a Feminist Theory of Human Rights: Straddling the Fence Between Western Imperialism and Uncritical Absolutism,* 25 COLUM. HUM. RTS. L. REV. 49, 58 (1993).

15. Christina M. Cerna, *Universality of Human Rights and Cultural Diversity: Implementation of Human Rights in Different Socio-Cultural Contexts,* 16 HUM. RTS. Q. 740, 740 (1994).

16. Donnelly examines attitudes toward the validation of a cultural practice on a continuum. On one end of the continuum, a "radical" universalist would hold that culture has *no* weight in deciding the relevance of human rights whereas a "radical" cultural relativist would assert that culture is the *only* relevant factor. Further, a "strong" cultural relativist determines culture to be the "principal" source of the validity of human rights whereas, for a "weak" relativist, culture may be "important" but universalism is the first presumption. Strong and weak relativists serve as checks against the extremes of radical universalism and relativism. However, most theorists fall somewhere in the middle, acknowledging that culture is one factor among many. DONNELLY, *supra* note 13, at 109–10.

17. *See* Cerna, *supra* note 15, at 743.

Notions of human rights in international law changed significantly as a result of World War II. As the magnitude of the atrocities committed by the Nazis became clear, the Allies determined that any post-war agreement must include a commitment to protecting human rights.[18] As such:

> No longer should a state be able to argue that the way in which it treated its own citizens was simply a matter of exclusive domestic concern, but the treatment of those individuals should, where appropriate national protection of rights was deficient, become the concern of the international community.[19]

These norms were established as a secular basis of morality whereby the fundamental freedoms of all humanity would be protected regardless of distinctions of race, sex, language, or religion.[20]

LEGITIMACY OF NORMS

Much of the literature relating to human rights and cultural tradition revolves around the question of the universal legitimacy of international human rights norms.[21] The conflict over the legitimacy of international human rights standards began early in the development of the international human rights system. The Vienna Declaration, adopted at the 1993 U.N. World Conference, stated that all human rights—civil and political, as well as economic, social, and cultural—should be implemented simultaneously, and that neither set of rights should take precedence over the other. All states are willing to accept the universality of a certain core group of rights that are listed in the human rights treaties as "nonderogable" rights or are considered *jus cogens*. Examples of such nonderogable rights include the right to be free from racial discrimination, the rights not to be tortured or enslaved, and the right to be free from crimes against humanity and genocide.[22]

In further attempting to define the catalogue of rights that have achieved universal legitimacy, it is useful to consult the positions of individuals who have been most critical of Western conceptions of human rights. For example, Mr. Kishore Mahbubani, Deputy Secretary of the Ministry of Foreign Affairs of the Republic of Singapore, states:

---

18. SCOTT DAVIDSON, HUMAN RIGHTS 28–31 (1996).

19. *Id.* at 12.

20. CHARTER OF THE UNITED NATIONS, art. 1 ¶3, June 26, 1945.

21. For example, *see* An-Na'im, *State Responsibility Under International Human Rights Law to Change Religious and Customary Laws, in* HUMAN RIGHTS OF WOMEN (Rebecca J. Cook ed., 1994); DONNELLY, *supra* note 13; Isabelle R. Gunning, *Arrogant Perception, World-Traveling and Multicultural Feminism: The Case of Female Genital Surgeries*, 23 (2) COLUM. HUM. RTS. L. REV. 190 (1992); RHODA E. HOWARD, HUMAN RIGHTS AND THE SEARCH FOR COMMUNITY (1995); Adamantia Pollis & Peter Schwab, *Human Rights: A Western Construct with Limited Applicability, in* HUMAN RIGHTS: CULTURAL AND IDEOLOGICAL PERSPECTIVES 1, 4 (A. Pollis & P. Schwab eds., 1979).

22. *See* Cerna, *supra* note 15, at 744–45.

[B]oth Asians and Westerners are human beings. They can agree on minimal standards of civilized behavior that both would like to live under. For example, there should be no torture, no slavery, no arbitrary killings, no disappearances in the middle of the night, no shooting down of innocent demonstrators, no imprisonment without careful review. These rights should be upheld not only for moral reasons. Any society which is at odds with its best and brightest and shoots them down when they demonstrate peacefully, as Myanmar did, is headed for trouble. Most Asian societies do not want to be in the position that Myanmar is in today, a nation at odds with itself.[23]

Some publicists of international law argue that all the rights set forth in the Universal Declaration of Human Rights have become customary international law and, as such, have achieved universal acceptance as legally binding obligations on states. These civil, political, economic, social, and cultural rights have been most widely recognized in constitutions around the world. Although the rights set forth in the UDHR have been incorporated into many constitutions in the world, other publicists do not consider the entire UDHR to have become custom and legally binding. They argue that the entire document failed to crystallize into custom because, since 1948, certain provisions have not been universally accepted. These provisions regard private rights that relate to the private sphere or personal life of the individual[24]—rights that have traditionally been covered by religious law and, in many countries, still are.[25]

This private sphere, which deals with issues such as religion, culture, the status of women, the right to marry and divorce and to remarry, the protection of children, the question of choice as regards family planning, and the like, is a domain in which the most serious challenges to the universality of human rights arise.[26] Certain societies are unwilling to assume international human rights obligations in this private sphere; their own code of conduct, which is informed by their religious or traditional law, already covers this terrain. This tension between the universality of norms in the private sphere and the competing religious/traditional law renders those international human rights norms, which have not become part of *jus cogens*, suspect.

International human rights law has, in some sense, become the substitute for religion in secular societies. It aims to establish a minimum standard of decency or treatment, a common denominator of what is morally acceptable behavior in a civilized society. For this reason, regional human rights arrangements have been more successful in securing compliance with international human rights norms; there is a shared history, geography, and, in some cases, language and religion, as well as a commonality of values.

---

23. Kishore Mahbubani, *An Asian Perspective on Human Rights and Freedom of the Press,* U.N. Doc. A/Conf.157/PC/63/Add.28 (May 4, 1993).

24. *See* Cerna, *supra* note 15, at 746.

25. *See generally* Courtney W. Howland, *The Challenge of Religious Fundamentalism to the Liberty and Equality Rights of Women: An Analysis under the United Nations Charter,* 35 COLUM. J. TRANSNAT'L L. 271 (1997).

26. *See* Cerna, *supra* note 15, at 746 *et seq.*

Within the relativist argument of the illegitimacy of human rights norms is the implied assumption of the legitimacy of cultural practices. However, given the male bias of most cultures and using the logic of the cultural relativist argument, women may challenge the validity of cultural practices based on their inability to participate in the creation of these cultural norms in that many cultural practices are a reflection of the male-dominated structure. Often, women have little or no power to challenge cultural tradition. For example, if a woman's survival is dependent upon marriage and no man will marry her unless she is circumcised, the woman must comply with the cultural tradition in order to survive. Although one illegitimacy does not legitimate the other, this does demonstrate the problem of trying to determine the cultural legitimacy of any norm.

As previously mentioned, women have few opportunities to challenge their own cultural norms. Therefore, whether or not a culture sees international norms as illegitimate, they are necessarily invoked for whatever protections they can provide women at the national level. In addition, assumptions that civil and political rights did not require government intervention failed to address the issue of culture. Violations of civil and political rights are not limited to expressions of government oppression. It is possible for individuals or groups of individuals (including religions) to violate these rights. Because of the relative strength of cultural traditions, protection of women's rights requires a more affirmative program of government intervention even as regards civil and political rights. A later section of this chapter will address the obstacles to changing traditional practices, including the problems associated with government attempts to alter these practices.

HARMFUL TRADITIONAL PRACTICES

Many of the practices examined in this section could be attributed to son preference (the added value attached to males in a society to the detriment of females). As well, many of the traditions negatively affect the health of women. However, some organization or separation of the issues is attempted in order to adequately define each custom and examine its relevance to women. It should be noted that most of these customs are a result of the perceived inferior status and, at times, supposed worthlessness of women.

Son Preference and Its Effect on Women and Girl-Children

The following depicts a common situation facing many young women today:

> She knows that [her] parents are not happy at the birth of a girl and she should not complain about [her] parents not sending her to school as she is not expected to take up a job. She is taught to be patient, sacrificing, obedient and ready to take a secondary position as compared to men.[27]

One of the most disturbing and damaging cultural traditions is that of son preference. This belief that boys are inherently more valuable than girls not only

---

27. Fauzia Rafiq, *Growing up in Pakistan,* 13 CAN. WOMEN'S STUD.1 (Fall 1992).

negatively affects the girl–child's health, education, and psychological well-being, but also commonly results in her death. Although son preference is more prevalent in Asian cultures, it is a transcultural phenomenon rooted in patriarchical and patrilineal systems.[28] In a patrilineal system, daughters take the name of their husband. Inheritance of name and wealth passes from father to son. In these societies, boys are joyfully welcomed while the birth of a girl is marked by indifference, or, even worse, mourned as a tragedy. In some instances, giving birth to a daughter shames the family and decreases the value of the mother. Whereas girls are seen as a liability, sons are desired to "continue the patrilineage, serve as heirs, perform important funeral rituals for parents, and to provide security in old age."[29] Male children are needed to carry on the family name and to avoid insulting ancestors by allowing a name to end. In some societies, it is believed that parents cannot enter the afterlife if there is no son to perform the proper burial procedure. Additionally, sons add to the family coffers while daughters are an economic drain. Daughters will be unlikely to ever contribute to the family income (in many instances, women are forbidden to work). On the contrary, the family must pay a large sum—dowry—to obtain a husband for their daughter. While sons represent the future of the family, "bringing up girls is like watering the neighbour's garden."[30]

Psychological Factors

Although the liberation of women is largely dependent on action from the women within a culture, women from cultures that heavily favor males are unable to question, let alone try to change, their roles. Son preference can demoralize women to such an extreme level that they are essentially powerless. Women who transcend the bounds of acceptable behavior are severely punished. In one case in Saudi Arabia, a young Islamic girl fell in love with a foreigner of another faith. As punishment, she was confined for life to the "women's room."[31] This consisted of solitary confinement in a small dark room with only a small opening in the floor for removal of fecal matter and a slot in the door through which she received food. This particular woman suffered her imprisonment for fifteen years before finally dying. Stories such as this deter many women from taking any action on their own behalf. Many lose the will to fight at a young age and resign themselves to their fate, convinced of their own insignificance. In a recent article, a Pakistani woman recalls her feelings of worthlessness as a child growing up in a society where women are appreciated only for their physical appearance:

---

28. Harmful Traditional Practices, *supra* note 4, at 12.

29. Linda Stone & Caroline James, *Dowry, Bride-Burning, and Female Power in India,* 18 (2) WOMEN'S STUD. INT'L F. 131 (1995).

30. Asian Proverb—*see* Harmful Traditional Practices, *supra* note 4, at 12.

31. JEAN P. SASSON, PRINCESS: A TRUE STORY OF LIFE BEHIND THE VEIL IN SAUDI ARABIA (1992). This story is taken from a Saudi Arabian princess' diaries, which were smuggled out of the country. While the subjects are from the royal family and thus not applicable to greater Saudi society, the book offers an insightful look at the condition of women in Saudi Arabia from the perspective of one of their most privileged females.

I could not understand . . . why my body was so sacred that I was prohibited from revealing any part of it to anyone, while men were grabbing at it . . . on the roads, in the buses, in the bazaars, in my house. I also could not understand why I was born so lacking. . . . But when I connected with other young women at school . . . I realized that most of us were born lacking. The majority were not even close to the standard of beauty set for women by men. Most of us were made to feel helpless and ashamed of being born with "physical deficiencies." I could not understand why no one listened to me even when I had something sensible and important to say. . . . I could not understand why I had to be married before I was eighteen. I did not understand any of it because I was not supposed to. My only option was to contain my feelings of anger, outrage, powerlessness, and unhappiness and do what was asked of me.[32]

Female Infanticide and Selective Abortion

This preference for sons results in many dire consequences for putative daughters. The unacceptability of daughters has led to extremely high rates of selective abortion and female infanticide. A recent study of a community in south Asia revealed that 51 percent of the families had killed a baby girl after birth;[33] a study from India reported that 7,997 of 8,000 aborted fetuses were female.[34] Economic factors are the most common reasons for these practices. If a family cannot afford to raise many children, they will kill the girls so they can afford a boy(s). Additionally, the costs of raising a girl can be prohibitive in cultures that practice dowry. Abortions are more common among the middle class who can afford amniocentesis procedures to determine the sex of the child before birth. The upper classes who are wealthy enough to provide for their children generally do not resort to female infanticide or foeticide. However, among the rural poor, infanticide results in the death of over 16 million girl babies per year in India alone.[35] Because poor families cannot afford the tests to determine the sex of the child before birth, baby girls are killed immediately after birth, either by family members or the midwife. One midwife in the Chambal Valley, India, reported:

When the mother finally delivers the child, in case of a female, the baby is not even cleaned. She is laid out on the floor. The [senior woman of the house] stuffs her mouth with tobacco leading to the instant death of the child. [She] then declares that the mother delivered a still born female baby. Everybody in the family understands and the body of the baby is disposed of quietly.[36]

Access to Food

Where son preference is especially strong as in India, Pakistan, Afghanistan, and China, girls who live past birth are then subject to many other discriminations:

---

32. Rafiq, *supra* note 27.

33. *See* http://www.oneworld.org/guides/women/facts.html.

34. Indira Jaising, *Violence Against Women: The Indian Perspective, in* WOMEN'S RIGHTS, HUMAN RIGHTS: INTERNATIONAL FEMINIST PERSPECTIVES 51 (Julie Peters & Andrea Wolper eds., 1994).

35. *India Killing Girls*, THE LONDON TIMES (U.K.), Mar. 12, 1997, at http://www.gte.net/marydiaz/india.htm.

36. Sharmila Banerjee, *India: For Girl Child, Prejudice is Fatal*, at www.womensnet.org/wfs/stories.html.

"A baby girl born in southern Asia has a one in ten chance of dying before her first birthday and a one in five chance of dying before her fifth."[37] Malnutrition is one reason for high girl child mortality rates. Many countries report higher female rates of malnutrition and/or morbidity.[38] When food is scarce, boys are fed first to the detriment of girls. Some high protein foods, such as meat, eggs, fish, and milk are considered taboo for girls.[39] In one Pakistani case involving twins, the boy was breast-fed while the girl was given a bottle and eventually died.[40] Girls are often undersize and underweight because of malnutrition.

Access to Education

Statistics demonstrate that "[o]f the 960 million illiterate people in the world, two-thirds are women."[41] In some countries such as Afghanistan, Burkina Faso, Nepal, and Yemen, the female illiteracy rates are 80 percent or greater.[42] Higher female illiteracy rates are frequently related to son preference. Boys must be sent to school in order to provide for their parents later in life. Girls, on the other hand, will eventually leave the family to live with their husband's family. Therefore, if the family cannot afford to educate all of its children, boys are chosen first. Even in cases where education is provided free, costs of supplies and clothing can be prohibitive. In rural areas, girls are needed for household and agricultural chores. In Nepal and Indonesia, girls work an average of three hours more per day than do boys.[43] Many families are opposed to female education even when funds are sufficient. Additionally, some families believe that school will provide too much freedom for girls and possibly compromise their virginity.

Abnormal Sex Ratios

According to the United Nations Children's Fund (UNICEF), of 15 million girls born in India each year, one-third die before the age of fifteen.[44] Results of son preference are evident in other countries as well. Although average world populations show 106 females per 100 males, in India the ratio drops to 93 women per

---

37. *Women's Rights, the Facts,* available at http://www.oneworld.org/guides/women/facts.html (taken from 1995 World Health Report).

38. These countries include Bangladesh, India, Nepal, Pakistan, the Philippines, Algeria, Egypt, Iran, Jordan, the Libyan Arab Jamahiriya, Morocco, Saudi Arabia, the Syrian Arab Republic, Tunisia, Turkey, Cameroon, Liberia, Madagascar, Nigeria, Senegal, Bolivia, Columbia, Ecuador, Mexico, Peru, and Uruguay. Many other countries do not record death rates. *See* Harmful Traditional Practices, *supra* note 4, at 14.

39. Harmful Traditional Practices, *id.* at 20.

40. UNITED NATIONS, WOMEN CHALLENGES TO THE YEAR 2000 23 (1991).

41. *Women's Rights, the Facts, supra* note 37, at 2.

42. NAOMI NEFT & ANN D. LEVINE, WHERE WOMEN STAND: AN INTERNATIONAL REPORT ON THE STATUS OF WOMEN IN 140 COUNTRIES 30 (1997).

43. UNITED NATIONS, WOMEN: LOOKING BEYOND 2000 (1995).

44. Banerjee, *India: For Girl Child, supra* note 36.

100 men. These ratios are biased in favor of males in Bangladesh, Afghanistan, and China, as well as in several other countries.[45] In China, it is estimated that, by the end of the century, there will be 90 million more men than women.[46]

Marriage

> If something goes wrong with her marriage she is expected to take the blame. If any one of her children does not succeed in life, she is expected to be the main cause of their failure and in the rare circumstances she seeks a divorce her chances of a second marriage are very slim because Pakistani culture believes in putting all the blame on one partner, namely the weaker half.[47]

Marriage in one form or another exists in every society. The laws governing marriage and divorce were established by religious and customary traditions. Within Christianity, the Roman Catholic Church has played a significant role in prohibiting divorce. Confucianism gives fathers custody of any children in the event of a divorce and rights of inheritance favor sons over daughters. Within Islam, polygamy is permitted and in many cases women are denied rights of inheritance and child custody. Similarly, Hinduism supports the traditions of arranged marriage and dowry.[48] In all forms of marriage there is an attempt to control and define appropriate sexual interactions between members of the society. Most marriage practices place women in a position of subservience. The idea that marriage is a union between two equal individuals has emerged only in recent years. Following are some examples of marriage practices throughout the world and the effect of these practices on women.

Bride Price and Dowry

Bride price refers to an amount paid by the husband to the bride's family. The "pay" may consist of livestock, food, clothing, money, or other valuable objects. Bride price accomplishes two things: first, it provides compensation to the bride's family for the loss of their daughter and second, bride price gives the new husband all rights over his new bride including rights to her sexuality, labor, and any future children.[49] It is essentially a system whereby the father sells his daughter to her future husband, in contrast to dowry, where the father pays money to have his daughter married. In general, bride price is practiced in countries in Africa and the Middle East, whereas dowry is practiced in Asia. Both are deeply entrenched cultural practices that treat women and girls as chattel.

Dowry is essentially the opposite of bride price, and sometimes occurs simultaneously. This practice refers to the property or wealth that the bride brings into her

---

45. *India Killing Girls, supra* note 35, at 2.

46. *Female Infanticide Will Lead to Army of Bachelors*, LONDON TELEGRAPH REPORTS, April 4, 1997.

47. Rafiq, *supra* note 27.

48. NEFT & LEVINE, *supra* note 42, at 83.

49. *Id.* at 96.

future family to help pay the living expenses of the wife and her future children. Originally the payment of dowry was a gift (of expensive clothing, jewels, etc.) given to the daughter of the family to compensate for the fact that she would not inherit the family wealth.[50] The daughter would then give control of these gifts to her husband. It was hoped that the dowry would guarantee the wife good treatment within her new family. Unfortunately, the current practice of dowry frequently results in the harassment of the wife's family, in threats to her well-being, and sometimes in her death.

In recent years, dowry deaths have attracted the attention of the international human rights community. Officials in India estimate that over 7,000 women die every year over dowry disputes.[51] In India, dowry deaths are a relatively new phenomenon that reflects a transformation within Indian society. With the conversion to a cash economy, traditional dowries of livestock or handmade household objects became less acceptable. Expectations have risen and families of the groom are now demanding a cash dowry or expensive items such as televisions and refrigerators.

Because marriage is the only acceptable choice for females in India, their families are placed in a subordinate position in relation to the groom's family. The bride's family must find someone willing to marry her, and many times this can only be done with the promise of a large dowry. Many families begin saving for their daughter's dowry upon her birth and still remain indebted long after the daughter has been married. Despite ever-increasing dowries, the husband's family is frequently unsatisfied. Dowry deaths have emerged as a method for the husband's family to rid themselves of the first wife and then obtain a new wife and another dowry. In addition, before a family resorts to murdering the young bride, it frequently attempts to extort more dowry from her family through threats to her safety. As the father of one such bride reported:

> [A]s soon as we agreed on the marriage they started troubling us. First they told us to buy diamond rings instead of mere gold ones. . . . Then they insisted on a sofa bed for fifteen thousand rupees, but I could only afford one that cost seven thousand. Whatever was in my means I did, but they were always displeased. . . . [T]hey demanded a stereo and tape-cassette system, and then they asked for saris for the boy's sisters . . . and then for a gas stove. I gave them . . . [because] I had read that there were so many tortures and murders of young women over dowry and I was afraid of what might happen to [my daughter]. I told them I would pay whatever I could. . . . But they didn't even wait for the money to come. They probably realized they had gotten all they could from us. A few days later [my daughter] was dead. . . . There has never been an investigation. . . . Now they can marry their son to another girl and get another dowry.[52]

---

50. *Id.*

51. *Id.*

52. Stone & James, *supra* note 29, at 128.

Dowry murders are increasing in India despite a 1961 law prohibiting the giving or receiving of dowry. This is due to not only the increased consumerism of the society, but also to the diminishing value of women and children. Previously women were considered valuable because they were necessary for the production of children. However, with a move toward urbanization and mechanization, the labor of children is no longer necessary. Therefore, although children (mostly sons) are still desired for cultural reasons, they are not an economic necessity. Consequently, the value of women and the power they once held through reproduction is diminishing.[53] Additionally, enforcement of the dowry prohibition is difficult. Dowry deaths are usually blamed on kitchen accidents—a fire or a burst stove—and the silence of the police can be easily purchased.

Child Marriage

The practice of child marriage is intimately related to dowry and bride price customs. If the perceived value of a woman is high, the family can either expect more money in bride price or pay less dowry for her marriage. A woman's value is directly related to her virginity, beauty, and status. A plain woman from a wealthy family may still marry well because of the desire to form an association with her family. Likewise, a woman of great beauty may marry well despite the poverty of her family. However, the greatest determining factor is the bride's virginity. Parents of a non-virgin may find it difficult, if not impossible, to arrange a marriage for their daughter. This desire for female virginity leads many families to arrange marriages for their daughters as soon as they reach puberty. It is easier to guarantee the virginity of a twelve-year-old than that of a twenty-year-old. A virgin will fetch a much higher bride price for the family or allow them to pay less of a dowry.

In Turkey and elsewhere, forced virginity exams may be performed. Female genital mutilation (FGM), in which the genitalia may be sewn together to prevent intercourse, is practiced in some cultures to ensure a girl's virginity or to control a woman's sexuality. Complications arising from child marriage and issues surrounding FGM will be discussed in more detail *infra*.

Levirate

Widow inheritance, or levirate, is a tradition found most commonly in a few African societies as well as in Israel and other portions of the Middle East. Originally designed to provide for the economic viability of a woman upon her husband's death, the modern equivalent is instead harmful. Under a system of widow inheritance, when a woman's husband dies, the deceased's brother or closest relative inherits the rights to the woman or becomes her new husband. Originally, the man would merely financially provide for his deceased brother's wife. In most situations conjugal relations did not occur. However, in more recent years the practice has changed and the woman is required to have sexual relations with her husband's relative.

---

53. *Id.* at 132.

In Africa this practice has led to dire consequences for all of the parties involved. In cases where the husband died of an infectious disease such as AIDS, the disease is then passed on to the man who inherits the wife. This problem is demonstrated in a case from Kenya, where a woman named Auma faced decisions after her husband's death:

> Her husband had just succumbed to AIDS. She knew he had infected her. Now her in-laws clamored for her to allow one of her husband's brothers to make her his responsibility, as tradition here has long dictated. Auma, then 28, could scorn tradition, be driven from her community and face starvation with her three children. Or she could marry a brother-in-law, feed her offspring, protect her property—and pass on the virus. She chose the brother-in-law. He died of AIDS two years later, but not before infecting two other women. Then they both died. Another man has since inherited Auma, and when she was recently interviewed, she was nine months pregnant with his child.[54]

In many countries such as Kenya, basic protection from venereal diseases, such as condoms, are simply not available or affordable to the average person.

Women's Health

Many women's health problems are directly related to cultural practices. Although most countries have recognized a right to health, many cultural practices are not linked to health problems in the communities where they are practiced. Even education is sometimes ineffective in convincing members of a society that their particular cultural tradition contributes to health problems in women.

Female Genital Mutilation

Female genital mutilation (FGM), sometimes called female circumcision or female genital surgeries, refers to the practice of cutting away portions of the female genitals. This highly controversial practice can result in serious health problems for women. There are several types of FGM. One type, sunna, is limited to the removal of the tip of the clitoris. This limited form of FGM occurs with less frequency than the other, more invasive types. The most drastic form of FGM, called infibulation, involves the removal of the clitoris, the labia minora, and the labia majora followed by the fusing of the two sides to leave only a tiny opening. Some cultures have modified the practice of infibulation so that there are now intermediate forms of FGM.[55] Health consequences from FGM generally depend on several factors, including the severity of the procedure performed.

The most immediate health problem resulting from FGM is infection. Many times this procedure occurs in a non-sterile environment and is performed on several girls consecutively. The instruments may not be cleaned before the procedure or between girls. After the procedure, the wound is typically packed with

---

54. Stephen Buckley, *Wife Inheritance Spurs AIDS Rise in Kenya*, WASH. POST, Occasional Series, African Lives, Nov. 8, 1997.

55. Gunning, *supra* note 21, at 194.

herbs, mud, or even animal feces to promote healing and stop bleeding. In some instances, trained health officials now perform these surgeries in an effort to prevent complications associated with infection. Bleeding can also be a problem when subjects hemorrhage during the process.

Other harmful effects from FGM may occur during childbirth. Obstruction of the vaginal opening can lead to tearing during birth. Sometimes the tearing enlarges the anal opening, which leads to permanent incontinence. Labor is generally longer as a result of infibulation and, at times, rupture of the uterus may occur. Further problems that may result from these surgeries are painful intercourse, menstruation difficulties, and urinary tract infections, in addition to the immediate pain and trauma associated with the practice.[56]

A primary reason given for the continuation of FGM is the need to protect the virginity of the girl/woman. Uncircumcised women are thought to be promiscuous and unmarriageable. In societies that practice the custom of bride price, an uncircumcised woman is essentially worthless. Fathers know that unless their daughters are circumcised, no man will be willing to purchase them for marriage. As a former Kenyan president stated, "no proper Gikuyu would dream of marrying a girl who has not been circumcised."[57] In some Islamic societies it is believed that the practice is a religious requirement; however, Mohammed, the Prophet of the Islamic faith, gave no instructions on female circumcision.

While FGM is abhorred by some women in these societies, it is supported by others. FGM is a deeply ingrained cultural practice, and is often accompanied by a village celebration and ceremony. Thus, until it is recognized by women as destructive and an obstacle to equality, women will not support its termination. As a Saudi princess noted:

> The women of my mother's generation were uneducated, and had little knowledge other than what their men told them to be true; as a tragic result, such traditions as circumcision were kept alive by the very people who had themselves suffered under the cruel knife of barbarism. . . . [S]he could imagine no other path for her daughters than the one she herself had trod, for fear that any shift from tradition would harm their marriage chances.[58]

In order to cease or modify the more invasive forms of FGM, not only must gender-based stereotypes be redressed, but a way must be found to continue the important cultural ceremonial traditions without the harmful cultural practices.

Early Adolescent Pregnancy

The desire to wed virgins has encouraged men to marry girls as young as 11, 12, or 13, who often become pregnant shortly thereafter. Often these girls give

---

56. K.L. Savell, *Wrestling With Contradictions,* 41(4) McGILL L. J. 804 (1996).

57. *Id.* at 793.

58. SASSON, *supra* note 31, at 138.

birth before they are fully developed themselves and have many problems during labor. Some girls are too small and their bones too weak to withstand the birth process. Obstructed channels and hemorrhaging are not unusual.[59] Additionally, a girl's immature body cannot supply the necessary nutrition for her own, and her fetus', growth. Babies born to mothers younger than eighteen-years-old are more likely to die within the first year. Societies that practice child marriage subsequently suffer higher infant and maternal mortality rates.

Eating Disorders

Although eating disorders differ from many other cultural practices in that they do not involve overt force, the cultural forces and subtle coercion involved must be acknowledged. The number of women and girls who suffer from eating disorders in the northern hemisphere is significant and increasing: "In the United States one in every 200–250 women between 13 and 22 years old suffers from anorexia nervosa and between 20% to 33% of college women control their weight through vomiting, diuretics, and laxatives."[60] Although previously these difficulties were attributed to individual and familial disorder, newer research attributes this phenomenon to cultural pressures. "There is substantial evidence from popular culture that the ideal woman's figure has become more slender in recent decades. As a result, women, already the target of society's pressures to look slim, are following an even more dangerously low ideal weight."[61] In the United States, the "thinness" industry is booming, as evidenced by the popularity of health spas, exercise gyms, and products "guaranteed" to take off pounds. Surgical procedures such as liposuction are also increasingly common. Women try to conform to the standard for beauty in any culture in order to be accepted. Personal attractiveness (whatever the ideal) is a great asset in the marriage market. Additionally, some researchers believe that attractive women advance faster in their careers.

Health problems from women's attempts to maintain the "perfect" body are numerous. Anorexia nervosa is a disease of excessive dieting whereby women deny themselves often to the point of starvation. A person with bulimia consumes large amounts of food and then purges by inducing vomiting. Laxatives and diuretics are also used to purge the body of unwanted calories. Women and girls with eating disorders suffer from loss of bone mass that leads to osteoporosis and injuries later in life. Furthermore, hormonal and reproductive disorders are common among girls with eating disorders. Those afflicted with eating disorders are predominantly young girls and teens who have not finished growing. Many experience stunted development because of malnutrition. Left untreated, these disorders can have dire, even fatal, consequences.

---

59.   Harmful Traditional Practices, *supra* note 4, at 19.

60.   Sharlene Hesse-Biber, *Women, Weight and Eating Disorders: A Socio-Cultural and Political-Economic Analysis* 14 (3) WOMEN'S STUD. INT'L F. 173 (1991).

61.   *Id.* at 176.

Recently, in the United States, another health issue has developed as a result of the desire for thinness. Many were excited when the Food and Drug Administration (FDA) approved the new diet drugs. The first of these, REDUX, served to block the body's desire to eat. The drug's popularity grew at an incredible rate until it was found to destroy nerve tissue and possibly cause brain tumors. PhenFen (Phentermine/Fenfluramine) was also an overnight success until women who took it began developing heart valve problems.

Although there is no physical force involved in eating disorders or taking diet drugs, it can be argued that these practices are an outgrowth of the inordinate societal pressure placed on women to be thin. Even though these practices are not results of direct action, that fact does not reduce the relevance of the role of culture. Until this connection is acknowledged and redressed, the numbers of those who suffer from these disorders will continue to increase.

Rape and Judicial Inequality

Sexual violence against women is nothing new. Rape occurs in every country with deviating frequency. Responses to rape, however, vary depending on the particular culture. For example, in Haiti, rape is considered an "assault on morals," which reflects the perception that rape damages the victim's moral integrity.[62] There is more concern for the "destroyed" honor of the victim or her family than for the survivor's personal well-being. In Haiti, as in many other countries, rape is considered to be an act that shames the victim rather than the victimizer.

The situation in Somalia is even worse for a survivor of sexual violence. A woman there who has been raped is ostracized by her husband and family. The act of rape carries such a social stigma that most Somali men would never accept their wife after she has been raped.[63] Because of the severe shame attached to rape, women rarely report the incident and often avoid medical or other treatment.

In addition to social stigmas, many countries have laws regarding rape that make prosecution difficult or even dangerous. In Pakistan, the Zina Ordinance of the Hudood Ordinance states that, if there are not four male witnesses to "prove" that a rape occurred, there can be no conviction. Even more disturbing, if a rape case is filed and disproved, the woman can be jailed for adultery or fornication.[64]

Although many cultural practices appear to be isolated, holding a woman responsible for the crime of rape committed against her is a widespread, virtually universal, phenomenon. In the United States, rape victims are harassed in court and accused that they "led on" their rapist by their actions or dress. Ending this

---

62. Human Rights Watch, *Rape as a Weapon of War and a Tool of Political Repression, in* THE HUMAN RIGHTS WATCH GLOBAL REPORT ON WOMEN'S HUMAN RIGHTS 51 (1995).

63. *Id.* at 133.

64. Radhika Coomaraswamy, *To Bellow Like a Cow: Women, Ethnicity, and the Discourse of Rights, in* HUMAN RIGHTS OF WOMEN (Rebecca J. Cook ed., 1994).

type of violence against women will require a wide variety of internal actions, and considerable national and international efforts and support.

INTERNATIONAL INSTRUMENTS

Many existing international documents address the abuses of women's rights. Some of these specifically refer to cultural practices. Although these documents are important, they are only the beginning of an attempt to overcome harmful cultural and traditional practices.

Universal Declaration of Human Rights

The UDHR has sustained a significant amount of criticism that the rights enshrined in this document are gender biased. In fact, the addition of the category of sex to article 2 was a direct result of lobbying by women's rights groups. Although no specific rights for women are introduced in the UDHR, there are several articles that offer ''general'' protections for women, including the following: all human beings are born free and equal (art. 1); everyone is entitled to the rights in the UDHR without distinction of any kind, such as race, color, or sex (art. 2); everyone has the right to life, liberty, and security of person (art. 3); all are equal before the law and are entitled without any discrimination to equal protection of the law (art. 7).[65] Despite these fundamental principles, extensive discrimination against women continues to occur unabated.

Convention on Elimination of Discrimination Against Women

Concern over the disparaging treatment of women[66] led the General Assembly to adopt the Convention on the Elimination of all forms of Discrimination against Women (Women's Convention) in 1979. This convention, which entered into force in September 1981, represents an enormous leap forward for women's rights. The Women's Convention is the first comprehensive document exclusively focused on the human rights of women under international law. The Women's Convention specifically addresses cultural traditions in article 5, which declares:

> States Parties shall take all appropriate measures to modify the social and cultural patterns of conduct of men and women, with a view to achieving the elimination of prejudices and customary and all other practices which are based on the idea of the inferiority or the superiority of either of the sexes or on stereotyped roles for men and women.[67]

This clause confronts state responsibility and problems caused by public/private distinctions. Additionally, article 16 deals with rights of women within the family:

---

65. Universal Declaration of Human Rights, A/RES/217 A (III), Dec. 10, 1948.

66. This concern was largely generated by women's activist groups and NGOs working for standards of equality for women.

67. Convention on the Elimination of All Forms of Discrimination Against Women, U.N. Doc. A/RES/34/180, Dec. 18, 1979, at art. 5a [hereinafter Women's Convention].

"States parties shall take all appropriate measures to eliminate discrimination against women in all matters relating to marriage and family relations."[68] Subarticles under article 16 specifically address issues relating to marriage (consent prior to and equality within), reproduction, custody of children, and property rights.[69]

Convention on the Rights of the Child

The Convention on the Rights of the Child (Child's Convention), which entered into force in September 1990, offers protections for the girl-child.[70] Many harmful practices have a significant impact on girls, including child marriage, FGM, and infanticide. Ratified by most states, the Child's Convention is potentially a strong weapon against harmful traditional and cultural practices.[71]

Reservations to Conventions

In order to encourage ratification, states are often permitted to sign "with reservations." However, article 28(2) of the Women's Convention states that "a reservation incompatible with the object and purpose of the present convention shall not be permitted." The Child's Convention contains a similar article. These provisions are in conformity with article 19 of the Vienna Convention on the Law of Treaties, which notes that states may not enter a reservation to a treaty that is "incompatible with the object and purpose of the treaty."[72]

However, many signatories have entered reservations that are incompatible with the purposes of the Women's Convention and the Child's Convention. For example, upon signing and ratifying the Child's Convention, the Islamic Republic of Iran reserved a right of nonapplication of this convention in any instances that conflict with Islamic law and internal Iranian law. The states of Kuwait, Saudi Arabia, and the Syrian Arab Republic entered similar reservations.[73] These unlimited, undefined reservations leave all aspects of the convention in question. Other governments entered more specific reservations against particular articles. Some of these reservations, such as the Republic of Indonesia's objection to articles 1, 14, 16, 17, 21, 22, and 29 of the Child's Convention, effectively abrogate the purpose of the convention.

The Women's Convention experienced similar problems on a larger scale. In addition to states that objected to the fundamental guideline of the convention

---

68. *Id.*

69. *Id.*

70. Convention on the Rights of the Child, G.A. Res. 44/25, of Nov. 20, 1989 [hereinafter Child's Convention].

71. *See* Multilateral Treaties Deposited with the Secretary-General, United Nations, New York (ST/LEG/SER.E), as available on http://www.un.org/Depts/Treaty.

72. Vienna Convention on the Law of Treaties, U.N. Doc. A/CONF. 39/27, of May 23, 1969.

73. Report from the Committee on the Rights of the Child, "Reservations, Declarations and Objections Relating to the Convention on the Rights of the Child" at 1–27; U.N. Doc. CRC/C/2/Rev.5.

(article 2 on the elimination of discrimination),[74] several states entered reservations to articles 5 and 16, which specifically address cultural issues. India and Malaysia objected to both articles, while Algeria, Bangladesh, Egypt, Jordan, Korea, Kuwait, Morocco, Singapore, Thailand, Tunisia, and Turkey entered reservations only to article 16. India's reservation is quite interesting in that it agrees to "abide by and ensure these provisions (articles 5a and 16(1)) in conformity with its policy of non-interference in the personal affairs of any Community without its initiative and consent."

Presumably, states believe these provisions eliminate the government's obligation to stop violations from cultural practices or at the community level, where the vast majority of abuses against women occur. Through these reservations, states are able to give the appearance of compliance (by signing and ratifying the document) without conforming to the obligations of implementation. It is thus unclear, in instances in which a reservation goes against the object or purpose of the convention, whether the reservations are invalid, whether the ratification is nullified, or whether some other status is attributed.

Convention of Belém Do Pará

A regional convention addressing violence against women was adopted in the Inter-American system in 1994. The Inter-American Convention on the Prevention, Punishment and Eradication of Violence Against Women, also known as the Convention of Belém Do Pará, was adopted in June 1994 and entered into force the following March.[75] Twenty-six of the thirty-five states in the Inter-American system are currently parties to this regional treaty. Article 1 of the convention specifically addresses the public/private dichotomy, stating: "violence against women shall be understood as any act or conduct, based on gender, which causes death or physical, sexual or psychological harm or suffering to women, whether in the public or the private sphere."[76]

African Charter on Human and People's Rights

This regional agreement from the Organization of African Unity (OAU) stipulates protections for women and has been ratified by fifty African countries. Article 18(3) of this document states: "The state shall ensure the elimination of every discrimination against women and also ensure the protection of the rights of the

---

74. These states include the Bahamas, Bangladesh, Egypt, Iraq, Kuwait, Libya, Maldives, Morocco, and Singapore.

75. Inter-American Convention on the Prevention, Punishment and Eradication of Violence Against Women, *adopted by* acclamation of the twenty-fourth regular session of the General Assembly of the Organization of American States, June 9, 1994.

76. Basic Documents Pertaining to Human Rights in the Inter-American System, OEA/Ser.L.V/II.92 doc. 31 rev. 3 (May 3, 1996), at 110.

woman and the child as stipulated in international declarations and conventions.''[77] Additionally, article 16 requires that "every individual shall have the right to enjoy the best attainable state of physical and mental health.''[78] Considering the health implications of many harmful cultural practices, countries sanctioning or failing to prevent these practices can increasingly be held accountable for violations of this charter.

African Charter on the Rights and Welfare of the Child

This OAU document protects against detrimental cultural practices. Article 21, Protection against Harmful Social and Cultural Practices, provides:

1. States Parties to the present Charter shall take all appropriate measures to eliminate harmful social and cultural practices affecting the welfare, dignity, normal growth and development of the child and in particular:

   (a) those customs and practices prejudicial to the health or life of the child; and

   (b) those customs and practices discriminatory to the child on the grounds of sex or other status.

2. Child marriage and the betrothal of girls and boys shall be prohibited and effective action, including legislation, shall be taken to specify the minimum age of marriage to be 18 years and make registration of all marriages in an official registry compulsory.[79]

This instrument can also be used for protection of the girl-child in Africa.

Although each of the aforecited instruments represent a significant move forward and is a valuable tool in the protection and promotion of the human rights of women, there are limitations to these documents, including some inherent weaknesses within the implementation process. Even efforts to hold states responsible for fulfilling the obligations they assume under international law cannot remove all obstacles to eliminating harmful cultural practices. In some instances, these practices continue despite governmental efforts to stop them.

IMPEDIMENTS TO CHANGE

Obstacles to changing cultural practices that harm women include, but are certainly not limited to, ideological barriers, power struggles, and years of negative gender-based stereotypes. More practical impediments involve problems of compliance, enforcement, and implementation.

---

77. African Charter on Human and Peoples' Rights, OAU Doc. CAB/LEG/67/3/Rev. 5, 21 I.L.M. 59, at art. 18(3). *Entered into force* Oct. 21, 1986.

78. *Id.* at art. 16(1).

79. African Charter on the Rights and Welfare of the Child, OAU Doc. CAB/LEG/24.9/49 (1990), at art. 21.

Redressing and resolving harmful cultural practices requires confronting the lack of education. Frequently, women are unaware that their rights are being violated or even that they have rights at all. For example, a majority of the women interviewed in a recent study in Sri Lanka stated that their religion did not have practices that subordinate women.[80] However, another study of religious cultures (Buddhism, Christianity, Hinduism, Islam, and Judaism) demonstrates convincingly that religions have traditionally promoted or even required differentiated roles for men and women, which results in the subordination and disempowerment of women.[81]

In the case of Buddhism, monks (men) are elevated above nuns (women).[82] The subordination of women is more blatant within the Hindu culture. It is written in the Laws of Manu[83] that ''in childhood a female must be subjected to her father, in youth to her husband, when her lord is dead to her sons, a woman must never be independent.''[84] Although the subordination of women in Christianity is more subtle, it does exist. With some exceptions (depending on sect), women are not allowed to be priests, ministers, or other chief leaders in the church. The reasoning for this is that the priest represents Christ who is the son of God (also assumed to be male). Within the Bible are several references to the subordination of women, one of which is, ''women should keep silent in the churches, for they are not allowed to speak, but should be subordinate, as even the law says.''[85]

Many practices are promulgated by the very women that they harm. Women, as the main caretakers of children, are also the guardians and teachers of culture. For example, often it is the women of the family who insist that their girl children be circumcised. Frequently, this comes from either the belief that their particular religion demands it or the fear that, without circumcision, their daughters will not be able to find husbands. As one woman notes:

> It is necessary to understand that girls are socialized from the very beginning to accept their situation and the ideology of male supremacy which makes them prey to a whole range of discriminatory practices. This means that not only are girls and women socially and ideologically unequipped to retaliate against (or even question) the implicit and explicit injustices to which they are subjected, but that, in the absence of alternative models of role and conduct, they actually espouse and propagate the dominant social and cultural values that militate against their gender group.[86]

In addition, even when women are educated about their rights, they are often powerless to prevent or stop the practices. Women may face the unenviable choice

---

80. Thalatha Seneviratne & Jan Currie, *Religion and Feminism: A Consideration of Cultural Constraints on Sri Lankan Women*, 17 (6) WOMEN'S STUD. INT'L F. 601 (1994).

81. *See* Howland, *supra* note 25, at 273.

82. Seneviratne & Currie, *Religion and Feminism, supra* note 80, at 596.

83. Code of Hindu law governing ceremonies, rituals, and moral and social instruction.

84. Seneviratne & Currie, *Religion and Feminism, supra* note 80, at 598.

85. 1 Corinthians 14:34, THE NEW AMERICAN BIBLE.

86. KATARINA TOMASEVSKI, WOMEN AND HUMAN RIGHTS 28 (1993).

of either enduring harmful practices or abandoning all they know and leaving their particular culture. Women may even be unable to flee, because of financial constraints, actual detention, physical limitations, the need to protect children, or discriminatory immigration standards. Further, some women (for instance, in Egypt) are legally prevented from leaving a country without their husband's or father's approval.

An ideological barrier to eliminating harmful practices is the fact that some cultural relativists consider universal human rights norms to be of both Western and feminist origin. Therefore, once women within a culture are activated to fight a harmful cultural practice, they are frequently labeled "Westernized" feminists, which undermines their legitimacy. For example, if a woman in Iran takes a job outside the home, she is accused of neglecting her "natural" role as a wife and mother. According to one author, a working woman in Iran is likely to suffer "Westoxication," which means, "She could be accused of failing to safeguard the honour of the family and the cultural heritage of the country. A woman's failure to conform to the traditional norms could be labelled as renunciation of indigenous values and loss of cultural identity."[87] Women, as the "guardians of culture," are doubly damned because any deviance from the traditional path is seen as a subversion of their own role and damaging to the country as a whole.

Women activists from outside the culture can actually make the situation worse as they are labeled "Western imperialists" by those who support the cultural tradition. Negative feelings about colonialism can sometimes lead to the legitimization of practices that otherwise might be overthrown. For this reason, many theorists admonish women's rights activists against the tendency to impose cultural values on others.

Legal systems based on traditional liberal philosophy also make it difficult to stop these harmful practices. A defining feature of liberal systems is their protection of individual privacy and freedom from state intrusion. International human rights law conforms to this pattern by acknowledging a division between the public and private spheres. Traditionally, human rights law applies to the state and agents of the state; individuals are not held accountable for their actions under international law. This results in a public/private dichotomy, in which liberal political tradition provides for spheres of autonomy within the state. This tradition embodies respect for the privacy of the individual and freedom from intrusion by the state into family life. Therefore, in practice, actions that occur in the private or family sphere are not monitored. Practices that affect women regularly fall within the private sphere, which leaves them with few protections under traditional international law. States have used this distinction to the disadvantage of women by asserting that certain harmful practices are cultural traditions, and thus outside of the realm of human rights law.

---

87. Nayereh Tohidi, *Modernity, Islamization and Women in Iran*, *in* GENDER AND NATIONAL IDENTITY 110, 127 (Valentine M. Moghadam ed., 1994).

In response to the problem of the public/private dichotomy, some theorists have made compelling arguments for state responsibility for cultural practices. For example, An-Na'im suggests that "every state has the responsibility to remove any inconsistency between international human rights law binding on it, on the one hand, and religious and customary laws operating within the territory of that state, on the other."[88] This notion of state accountability puts the onus on governments to overcome harmful cultural practices within their own borders.

Holding a state responsible for fulfilling its legal obligations under international law is an important step. However, in cases of cultural tradition, accountability by the state is rarely sufficient. Harmful practices may continue even when governments try to force compliance. For example, despite Egypt's regulations against female genital mutilation, this practice continues, albeit at a reduced rate. Considering the impediments to change, new approaches that deal with women's rights in a cultural context are needed.

POSSIBLE ACTIONS/RESPONSES

There are clearly many impediments to women's rights. As mentioned previously, any attempt by women to change their own circumstances is typically met with hostility within their own culture. Therefore, arguments that all cultural changes should originate internally ignores the plight of women within a culture. However, it is evident from examining some of the obstacles that to rely solely on established international norms or external support is insufficient as well. A superior approach would focus on the dual need to address cultural differences and respect international norms. As Richard Falk argues:

> [W]ithout mediating international human rights through the web of cultural circumstances, it will be impossible for human rights norms and practice to take deep hold in non-Western societies except to the partial, and often distorting, degree that these societies—or, more likely, their governing elites—have been to some extent Westernized. At the same time, without cultural practices and traditions being tested against the norms of international human rights, there will be a regressive disposition toward the retention of cruel, brutal, and exploitative aspects of religious and cultural tradition.[89]

With this in mind, An-Na'im offers a cross-cultural dialogue model that attempts to legitimate international norms within cultures.

As previously asserted, maintaining freedoms of speech and expression will be essential to this process. Through An-Na'im's model, transformation will begin internally and find its support externally. This two-part model includes an internal discourse on women's rights augmented by support from women's rights activists

---

88. *See* An-Na'im, *State Responsibility Under International Human Rights Law, supra* note 21, at 167. For a similar argument, *see also* Rebecca Cook, *Women's International Human Rights Law: The Way Forward, in* HUMAN RIGHTS OF WOMEN 1, 21–2 (Rebecca Cook ed., 1994).

89. Richard Falk, *Cultural Foundations for Protection of Human Rights, in* HUMAN RIGHTS IN CROSS-CULTURAL PERSPECTIVES: A QUEST FOR CONSENSUS 44, 46 (An-Na'im ed., 1991).

outside the culture. Although both factors are equally important, An-Na'im emphasizes that any external support and influence must avoid even the appearance of
cultural imperialism. They must provide external support in ways that enhance,
rather than undermine, the integrity and efficacy of the internal discourse.

An-Na'im argues that the existence of subcultures augments the process of
internal discourse. Although the dominant culture maintains that a practice is sacrosanct, this may reflect only one available view within that culture. Through intellectual and scholarly debate, artistic and literary expression, and political and social
action, activists from within the culture can focus attention on human rights issues.
A cross-cultural dialogue should then augment this internal discourse. This model
accesses already existing avenues of cross-cultural exchange to enhance the internal
discourse on rights.[90]

Although this model may seem somewhat simplistic, it illustrates one of the
more recent changes in the effort to overcome harmful practices. Previously, many
women's activists were sent reeling from the reaction to their rather overbearing
activism. Motivated by their sense of horror at traditions such as female genital
mutilation, some women's rights activists denounced those acts as "barbaric" and
offended many women within the culture. Feminists within these cultures counseled
their Western counterparts to alter their offensive methods. In relation to the movement to overcome FGM, one African feminist stated, "one quickly discovers that
it is necessary to slow down a bit the ardor to eliminate [this practice] in order to
be more effective."[91] In response to this problem, An-Na'im offers a more sensitive
approach that avoids the problem of cultural imperialism. He states: "the prospects
for practical implementation of a given regime of human rights as a normative
system are related to the degree of its legitimacy in the context of the culture(s)
where it is supposed to be interpreted and implemented in practice."[92] Acknowledging the necessity for cultural legitimacy is the first step in the fight to eliminate
these practices.

The women's rights community has already taken many steps to increase
the cultural legitimacy of international norms and to overcome harmful practices.
These actions include, for example, information campaigns, training traditional
birth attendants and health practitioners, training native women activists, holding
educational seminars, providing medical services, and aiding in the development
of policy guidelines. Following are a few cases where these actions have had a
positive effect.

Tamunie Hegisso is a traditional midwife in a small village in Tula, Ethiopia.
Tamunie is a graduate of a government-sponsored program that trains health professionals. In this program Tamunie learned how to deliver babies safely (and hygieni-
cally) and how to give advice on proper nutrition for pregnant mothers and

---

90.   An-Na'im, *Toward a cross-cultural approach to defining international standards of human rights,
supra* note 5.

91.   Gunning, *supra* note 21, at 225.

92.   An-Na'im, *State Responsibility Under International Human Rights Law, supra* note 21, at 171.

newborns. In addition, she received the necessary equipment for her work.[93] The Ethiopian government has doubled its spending on health care in recent years and has increased efforts to educate girls. These efforts have reduced infant mortality rates from 250 per one thousand live births to 160.[94] The education of women like Tamunie has significantly aided this process. By educating respected members of a culture, new information can be introduced in an acceptable fashion.

Another case involves a woman from Bangladesh named Rubiya. Desperate to provide for her family of three children after a divorce, Rubiya joined the Rural Maintenance Program (RMP). Sponsored by Cooperative for American Relief Everywhere (CARE), the RMP was designed as a welfare program for rural women. These women join a crew that repairs roads within Bangladesh in exchange for a salary. The repaired roads also offer improved access to the market. Rubiya is just one of many women who has profited from this program. In a society where women are supposed to depend on men for their sustenance, and where working women are considered to be "bad" Muslims, many women have improved their stature. Not only is Rubiya now financially secure, she has become a respected member of her society.[95]

The case of Zainabe demonstrates how local action can be most effective. Zainabe is a nurse who is involved in the education and training of the midwives of Touil, Mauritania. In a speech to these midwives, Zainabe broached the custom of female genital mutilation. Rather than attacking the practice, Zainabe responded that she believed the Islamic religion requires this practice. Yet, she emphasized the manner in which the surgeries are done, stating, "one-third of the clitoris should be cut off and two-thirds left intact. Someone who practically attacks a girl with a knife, cutting off everything . . . is, in any case, going directly against the words of the Prophet."[96] The reaction from the midwives was significant. None of them had ever heard this statement. Zainabe, as a Muslim and a circumcised woman herself, was able to challenge a long standing cultural tradition. The women were willing to listen and learn from her, whereas a foreigner would probably have been ignored. Cases such as these demonstrate the importance of working for change at the local level. Of course, not all such efforts are successful.

The Indian government recently began a program to protect baby girls in Tamil Nadu, a region where the practice of female infanticide is most prevalent. Authorities installed cradles in public places where unwanted children could be placed. Rescued children would then be placed in orphanages. However, many women said "they would rather kill a female child than create an orphan with no caste and

---

93. Buckley, *supra* note 54, at 2.

94. *Id.*

95. Angela Mackay, *Bangladesh: On the Road to Dreams*, Women's Feature Service (WFS, a news feature service on the web.) Available at http://www.womensnet.org//wfs/index.html.

96. Savell, *supra* note 56, at 807.

identity, who they feared could one day dishonour the family or return to seek vengeance.''[97]

The U.N. working group on harmful traditional practices has compiled an extensive analysis of current activities at the international, national, and local levels. Fact sheet number 23, Harmful Traditional Practices Affecting the Health of Women and Children, contains an outline of some of these harmful practices as well as an outline of current action. Working group papers of the same name have more detailed and updated information. These documents include input from representatives within the cultures where these practices occur and are a valuable resource.

Many activist groups are working specifically for the ratification and implementation of the Women's Convention. This treaty provides the guidelines by which women can begin defining their rights within their own cultures. In this manner, even without full implementation, it can be used as an influential tool.

CONCLUSION

During the years of colonialization, cultures that differed from the "Western" norm were considered barbaric or uncivilized. Today, the world community is belatedly acknowledging the value of different cultural influences. Condemnation and accusations of barbarism are not always productive ways to address harmful cultural practices. As was wisely asserted:

> [I]t is unacceptable that the international community remain passive in the name of a distorted vision of multiculturalism. Human behaviours and cultural values, however senseless or destructive they may appear from the personal and cultural standpoint of others, have meaning and fulfill a function for those who practise them. However, culture is not static but it is in constant flux, adapting and reforming. People will change their behaviour when they understand the hazards and indignity of harmful practices and when they realize that it is possible to give up harmful practices without giving up meaningful aspects of their culture.[98]

While the tolerance for difference is a positive change, it is important nonetheless to continue looking critically at all cultural practices throughout the world and to assess their impact on women and men. Positive practices should be encouraged and continued, and destructive or harmful practices discontinued, modified, or replaced.

---

97. *India Killing Girls, supra* note 35, at 2.

98. World Health Organizations, *Female Genital Mutilation: A Joint WHO/UNICEF/UNFPA Statement,* 1996.

WOMEN AND TRADITIONAL PRACTICES: FEMALE GENITAL SURGERY

Isabelle R. Gunning

"Female genital surgeries" (FGS), also known as "female circumcision" or "female genital mutilation" (FGM),[1] refers to a range of physical or surgical excisions performed on the female genitalia. The surgeries have a long history and have been performed in a variety of both First and Third World[2] cultures and countries around the globe. They are practiced in over forty countries around the world, and estimates put the number of women currently subjected to some form of the practice in excess of 100 million.[3] Although FGS are defended within their various cultures for a number of reasons, including health, religion, and aesthetics, these surgeries function to control female sexuality and physicality and to underscore socially constructed binary gender differences.

---

1. For a brief explanation on the ramifications of the uses of the different terminologies, *see* Isabelle R. Gunning, *Arrogant Perception, World-Travelling and Multicultural Feminism: the Case of Female Genital Surgeries,* 23 COL. HUM. RTS. L. REV. 189, 193 n.15; Hope Lewis, *Between Irua and "Female Genital Mutilation": Feminist Human Rights Discourse and the Cultural Divide,* 8 HARV. HUM. RTS. J. 1, 4–9 (1995). Many authors prefer the term "female genital mutilation" (coined by Fran Hosken). These authors usually believe this term more accurately reflects the nature of the practice and removes it from comparison with the less invasive form of male circumcision. FRAN HOSKEN, FEMALE SEXUAL MUTILATIONS: THE FACTS AND PROPOSALS FOR ACTION 20 (1980); Layli Miller Bashir, *Female Genital Mutilation in the United States: An Examination of Criminal and Asylum Law,* 4 AM. U. J. GENDER & L. 415 n. a (1996); Lori Ann Larson, *Female Genital Mutilation in the United States: Child Abuse or Constitutional Freedom?,* 17 WOMEN'S RTS. L. REP. 237 n. 2. (1996) Other authors prefer the term "circumcision" because it is the term traditionally used in the cultures which practice it and because the term "mutilation" may connote a derogatory value judgement upon those practicing the tradition. HANNY K. LIGHTFOOT-KLEIN, PRISONERS OF RITUAL: AN ODYSSEY INTO FEMALE GENITAL CIRCUMCISION IN AFRICA (1989) [hereinafter LIGHTFOOT-KLEIN]; ASMA EL DAREER, WOMAN WHY DO YOU WEEP: CIRCUMCISION AND ITS CONSEQUENCES (1982). This author uses the term female genital surgeries in an effort to both respect the Third World cultures where the surgeries are performed and to avoid minimizing the physical effects of the more extreme forms of the surgeries, excision and infibulation. In addition, the term "surgeries" underscores the fact that many of the forms of these surgeries are analogizable to other cuttings and carvings of the female body that occur in First World countries but are falsely elevated above Third World practices by being associated with the more scientific term "surgery."

2. The author uses the terms First and Third Worlds reluctantly, but finds it preferable to Eurocentric terminology of Western and *non*-Western, which privileges Western or First World cultures by making all other cultures into the "other."

3. Catherine L. Annas, *Irreversible Error: The Power and Prejudice of Female Genital Mutilation,* 12 J. CONTEMP. HEALTH L. & POL'Y 325, 327–28 (1996); Larson, *Female Genital Mutilation in the United States, supra* note 1, at 237; Melissa A. Morgan, *Female Genital Mutilation: An Issue on the Doorstep of the American Medical Community,* 18 J. LEGAL MED. 93, 94 (1997).

TYPES OF SURGERIES

FGS encompass a range of surgeries involving varying degrees of invasiveness. There are generally three to four types of operations.[4] The "sunna" is the mildest and rarest form and is the closest to being a true "circumcision." It involves the cutting, or burning away, of the tip of the prepuce or hood of the clitoris. The "intermediate" form involves the removal of the clitoris and some or all of the labia minora. This form is sometimes also referred to as "excision." The intermediate form can involve not only the removal of the clitoris and labia minora, but also some slices of the labia majora. "Infibulation," or the pharonic[5] form, is the most severe and most prevalent form, and involves the removal of the clitoris and all of the labia minora and labia majora.[6]

The Surgeries

The surgeries are by and large performed by older women of the village.[7] Traditionally, the circumciser uses special knives or razor blades to perform the cutting, although other objects such as scissors, broken glass, or sharp stones may also be used.[8] The young woman or child is restrained and her legs held apart by other women involved in the ceremony (often the mother and aunts) and typically anesthesia is not used. Adhesives like sugar, egg, cigarette paper, or thorns are used to bind the wound together.

In the most extreme, but most common, forms of the surgeries, complete closure of the vaginal region is prevented by "inserting a splinter of wood, or a match stick, which preserves a small orifice through which urine and menstrual fluid can

---

4. Although most authors cite three forms, one author has delineated six different categories of surgeries. *See* Robbie D. Steele, *Silencing the Deadly Ritual: Efforts to End Female Genital Mutilation*, 9 GEO. IMMIGR. L. J. 105, 116–17 (1995).

5. Kaplan asserts that the practice began in Egypt during the times of the Pharaohs. *See* Roger Kaplan, *Prisoners of Ritual*, 25 FREEDOM REV. 25, 26 (1992). However, Brooks states that the practice "seems to have originated in Stone Age central Africa and travelled north, down the Nile, into ancient Egypt. It wasn't until Arab-Muslim armies conquered Egypt in the eighth century that the practices spread out of Africa in a systematic way, parallel to the dissemination of Islam, reaching as far as Pakistan and Indonesia. . . ." Geraldine Brooks, *Against the Verses*, GUARDIAN, Mar. 11, 1995, at T12.

6. *See* EL DAREER, *supra* note 1, at 1–5; MINORITY RIGHTS GROUP INTERNATIONAL, FEMALE GENITAL MUTILATION: PROPOSALS FOR CHANGE 7 (1992) [hereinafter MINORITY RIGHTS GROUP]; Nahid Toubia, *Female Circumcision as a Public Health Issue*, 331 NEW ENG. J. MED. 712 (1994); Morgan, *supra* note 3, at 94.

7. For example, in Somalia, the surgeries would be performed by a *Gedda*, and in Egypt and the Sudan a traditional birth attendant called *Daya* would perform the operation. In Mali and Senegal women of the blacksmith's caste who are knowledgeable of the occult traditionally serve as circumcisers. *See* MINORITY RIGHTS GROUP, *supra* note 6, at 7.

8. Barrett Breitung, *Interpretation and Eradication: National and International Responses to Female Circumcision*, 10 EMORY INT'L L REV. 657, 663 (1996); Larson, *supra* note 1, at 239.

pass.''[9] The legs are bound together for up to forty days,[10] and a healing liquid such as warm oil, acacia tar, tea, water, or a local liquor is poured in the wound to prevent infection and promote healing.[11] In recent years, certified nurses and doctors have performed a limited number of the surgeries;[12] in some cases, the surgeries are performed in hospitals.[13] Anesthesia is often used in the modern version. The healing period ranges from at least one month—following a "traditional" proce-dure—to approximately one week if a modernized surgery is performed.

The surgeries are performed on girls ranging in age from babies (days or months old) to adolescents (teenagers), depending upon the area and culture in which they occur. The Jewish Falasha in Ethiopia and the nomads of the Sudan, for example, have the surgeries performed on babies only days old. Ethnic groups in Egypt and many countries in central Africa have the operations performed when the girl is about seven years old. Among the Ibo of Nigeria, the excision takes place during the teen years, shortly before marriage.[14]

A wide range of both short- and long-term complications can beset the circum-cised girl or woman.[15] The existence and severity of any of these complications is generally related to the type of surgery performed, the eyesight and skill of the circumciser, the hygienic conditions employed, and the degree to which the child or young woman struggles during the operation. Short–term complications oc-curring at the time of the surgeries may include hemorrhaging, infections,[16] tetanus,

9.   Larson, *id.* at 238. *See also* Robyn C. Smith, *Female Circumcision: Bringing Women's Perspectives into the International Debate*, 65 S. CAL. L. REV. 2449, 2450 (1992).

10.   Robin M. Maher, *Female Genital Mutilation: The Struggle to Eradicate This Rite of Passage*, 23 HUM. RTS. 12, 13 (1996).

11.   Gunning, *Arrogant Perception*, *supra* note 1, at 194–195. In some cultures, bleeding is stopped with dirt or ashes, FRAN HOSKEN, THE HOSKEN REPORT-GENITAL AND SEXUAL FEMALES 37 (2d ed. 1979), or with pulverized animal feces. Maher, *supra* note 10, at 13.

12.   There is a debate about this. Some suggest that if the surgeries must be performed, it is best to have professionals perform the surgeries; others argue that medical personnel should lose their medical licenses or certifications if they do perform the surgeries.

13.   MINORITY RIGHTS GROUP, *supra* note 6, at 7. Nurses and doctors have been reported to perform the surgeries in studies in Egypt, the Sudan, and Somalia. The report on the surgeries occurring in urban hospitals comes from Mali. *See also* HOSKEN, THE HOSKEN REPORT, *supra* note 11, at 121–22.

14.   MINORITY RIGHTS GROUP, *supra* note 6, at 7.

15.   L. Amede Obiora, *Bridges and Barricades: Rethinking Polemics and Intransigence in the Cam-paign Against Female Circumcision*, 47 CASE W. RES. L. REV. 275 (1997) (page numbers not available), pg. 8 on Westlaw.

16.   FGS has been said to increase exposure to the AIDS virus. It is not only the use of an unsterile instrument which may have been previously used to cut other women which makes women susceptible to HIV/AIDS, but it is also the open wounds resulting from the procedure which put women at increased risk. Breitung, *supra* note 8, at 663. While the author is unaware of any scientific study that has confirmed that women have contracted the HIV virus as a result of the surgeries, it is a rational assumption that FGS, as does any surgery, results in bleeding, and the exposure of people to human blood likely increases the risk factor for the HIV infection. Consequently, it is essential that information regarding the possibility of severe health problems be relayed to people who would consider having the surgeries performed.

septicaemia, and shock. Death may occur unless blood transfusions and emergency resuscitation are available, which they rarely are, because neither circumcisers nor parents want health authorities informed.[17] A succession of girls may be subjected to the surgeries without intermittent cleansing of the blade or instrument, thereby increasing the risk of disease or infection.[18] The vaginal cavity sometimes retains blood or urine. Menstrual fluid blocked behind the tiny opening left can cause agonizing pain and an embarrassing odor. In some cases, the lack of a menstrual flow and the increased size of the abdomen causes the family to believe that the girl is pregnant. With the honor of the family thus at stake, the young woman may be punished or killed.[19] When there is a menstrual flow, it can be extremely painful (dysmenorrhea) and last for ten or more days. Urination, too, can be painful and lengthy, requiring from ten minutes to almost two hours to empty the bladder. If the vagina or uterus is ruptured, either through a mishandled cutting or through an obstructed labor, fistulas may form and cause incontinence later in life such that the woman constantly dribbles urine.

Chronic infections of the uterus and vagina are common long-term effects.[20] Mucous secretions and keloid scar tissue can form inside the vagina and grow to such sizes that walking is severely impaired.[21] The whole genital area can become permanently and unbearably sensitive to touch. Intercourse and childbirth can be both excruciating and difficult, either or both requiring some tearing or cutting of the scarred tissue.[22] Reproductive tract infections may cause infertility.[23] When some circumcised girls or women conceive, the birthing process can carry added dangers, such as hemorrhaging, tearing, and a prolapsed uterus. The infant, subject to a prolonged or difficult delivery, may be at risk of being stillborn, or may suffer brain damage because of lack of oxygen during the extended delivery.[24]

The surgeries may reduce or eliminate a woman's sexual sensation or pleasure. Some studies support the intuitive presumption that genital surgeries, especially the most severe forms which involve the removal of the entire clitoris, would rob

---

17.   The increased prohibitions of the practice make parents fearful of involving health authorities if something goes wrong.

18.   Larson, *supra* note 1, at 239.

19.   MINORITY RIGHTS GROUP, *supra* note 6, at 8.

20.   *See* Loretta M. Kopelman, *Female Circumcision/Genital Mutilation and Ethical Relativism*, 20 SECOND OPINION 55, 58–60 (1994).

21.   MINORITY RIGHTS GROUP, *supra* note 6, at 8.

22.   Gunning, *Arrogant Perception, supra* note 1, at 196; Doriane Lambelet Coleman, *Individualizing Justice Through Multiculturalism: The Liberals' Dilemma*, 96 COLUM. L. REV. 1093, 1112, *citing* H.R. Rep. No. 501, 103d Cong., 2d Sess. 66 (1994).

23.   Larson, *supra* note 1, at 239; Morgan, *supra* note 3, at 98; FRAN HOSKEN, THE HOSKEN REPORT: GENITAL AND SEXUAL MUTILATIONS OF FEMALES 37 (4th ed. 1993).

24.   Larson, *id.* at 239; Harvard Law Review Association, *What's Culture Got to Do With It?, Excising the Harmful Tradition of Female Circumcision*, 106 HARV. L. REV. 1944, 1948 (1993); Annas, *supra* note 3, at 331 ("The highest infant mortality rates in the world occur in areas where female genital mutilation is practiced.")

a woman of all sexual sensation or pleasure.[25] However, other studies suggest that equating the circumcision with automatic frigidity is incorrect.[26]

In the more common version, a woman is unsutured after marriage, generally either by her husband on their wedding night,[27] or by the mother and future mother-in-law before the wedding.[28] She may be subject to resuturing or reinfibulation (the vaginal area resewn, except for a tiny opening left for bodily fluids) after childbirth, divorce, when she becomes widowed, or during an extended separation from her husband.[29]

Some argue that female circumcision should be seen as distinct from male circumcision. Others argue that the two are similar. Physically, there is some difference. The more invasive forms of FGS—excision and infibulation—involve the actual removal of parts of the vulva, while male circumcision "involves the removal of the outer skin of the penis" without, arguably, damaging the organ itself.[30] In fact, the removal of the foreskin is justified in that the foreskin retains harmful germs or bacteria.[31] It is said that the physical equivalent of infibulation in men would be "if the penis were amputated"[32] or excised in whole or in part.[33] In contrast to male circumcision, FGS have no documented health benefits, and the more invasive forms may cause numerous physical and psychological harms.[34]

On the other hand, the two procedures have many similarities. Some argue that any cutting of the male genitalia, like any cutting of the female genitalia, should

25. *See* G. Zwang, Female Sexual Mutilation, Techniques and Results (1979) *cited in* Hanny K. Lightfoot-Klein, Prisoners of Ritual: An Odyssey into Female Genital Circumcision in Africa 81 (1989); Raqiya H.D. Abdalla, Sisters in Affliction—Circumcision and Infibulation of Women in Africa 26 (1982). Both report frigidity in circumcised women. *See also* Minority Rights Group, *supra* note 6, at 8 (citing a study indicating that circumcised women had no idea of what an orgasm was and that husbands with wives who were both circumcised and not preferred intercourse with non-excised or sunna-circumcised women). Annas states, however, that "[f]emale sexual pleasure occurs with stimulation. . . ." Annas, *supra* note 3, at 328–29; *see also* Obiora, *supra* note 15, at p. 17 Westlaw.

26. Lightfoot-Klein, *supra* note 1, at 80–91.

27. Annas, *supra* note 3, at 330, *citing A Traditional Practice That Threatens Health—Female Circumcision*, 40 WHO Chron. 31, 32 (1986).

28. Mary Ann French, *The Open Wound*, Wash. Post, Nov. 22, 1992, at F1.

29. Annas, *supra* note 3, at 330–31, *citing* A Traditional Practice That Threatens Health—Female Circumcision, 40 WHO Chron. 31, 32 (1986); Hosken, The Hosken Report, *supra* note 23, at 34; Alison T. Slack, *Female Circumcision: A Critical Appraisal*, 10 Hum. Rts Q. 437, 457 (1988).

30. Annas, *supra* note 3, at 327.

31. Sami A. Aldeeb Abu-Sahlieh, *To Mutilate in the Name of Jehovah or Allah: Legitimization of Male and Female Circumcision*, 13 Med. Law 575, 595 (1994). Women do not have this same foreskin.

32. Bashir, *supra* note 1, at 420; Annas, *supra* note 3, at n. 2, *citing* Phillipa Rispin, *It's Female Mutilation*, The Gazette (Montreal), Jun. 15, 1995, at B2.

33. Many advocates assert that male circumcision should also be condemned and halted. *See Unkindest Cut*, The Scotsman, Sept. 13, 1993, at 14.

34. Annas, *supra* note 3, at 327. *See also What's Culture Got to Do With It?*, *supra* note 24, at 1948; French, *The Open Wound*, *supra* note 28, at F1.

be considered mutilation. This perspective questions the purported health benefits of male circumcision,[35] and argues that male circumcisions can also cause physical and psychological harms.[36] This minority view, which analogizes male and female circumcision on cultural and symbolic levels, gets support from some medical evidence that suggests that FGS may historically have been a legitimate surgical response to certain diseases unique to Africa (e.g., genital filariasis), which attack both the male and female genitalia.[37] It is therefore possible to see male circumcision and FGS as cultural or symbolic equivalents. Both can be seen as unnecessary alterations of normal, healthy genitalia justified by questionable health benefits and bolstered by culturally, socially, or religiously defined notions of aesthetics and clearly delineated binary ideas of gender.[38]

THIRD WORLD SOCIOECONOMIC CONTEXTS

Currently, FGS are prevalent in over twenty African nations and in Oman, South Yemen, and the United Arab Emirates in the Arabian peninsula. It is also widespread in parts of Asia, particularly in certain Muslim populations of Indonesia, Malaysia, India, and Pakistan.[39] It is reportedly not practiced in Saudi Arabia, considered the preeminent Muslim state.[40]

The reason for the surgeries is explained in various ways. Preserving a woman's virginity or chastity is one rationale.[41] Some peoples use the surgeries as a form of

---

35.   See EDWARD WALLERSTEIN, CIRCUMCISION: AN AMERICAN FALLACY (1980); *Reconsidering Circumcision: North Dakota Woman Challenges Male Circumcision*, STAR TRIBUNE, May 19, 1997, at 7A [hereinafter *Reconsidering Circumcision*]. This article discusses the health arguments against male circumcision that were raised in a constitutional challenge to a North Dakota statute banning female circumcision. It notes that twenty-five years ago, the American Academy of Pediatrics declared that there were "no valid medical reasons" for routine male circumcision. In 1989, the Academy changed its stance to one of neutrality, not support, when some studies showed that male circumcision might reduce the rate of two rare health problems. *See generally* SEXUAL MUTILATIONS: A HUMAN TRAGEDY (George C. Deniston & Marilyn Fayre Milos eds., 1997). This book is a collection of essays which reflects an array of scholars' and health care professionals' opposition to both male and female mutilations on health, religious, and cultural grounds.

36.   *Reconsidering Circumcision, supra* note 35. The article notes that anti-circumcision activists argue that male circumcision deprives men of their most "sexually sensitive tissue."

37.   Presentation by Dr. Michael Scott, African Community Town Hall meeting: Completing the Circle of Understanding—Focus on Female Circumcision, June 20, 1997. This conference was sponsored by the African Community Resources Center, an African refugee and immigrant support center in Los Angeles in order to inform African refugees and immigrants of the new anti-FGM laws at the federal and state levels and to solicit the reactions and opinions of these community members to the bills. Dr. Scott, a medical doctor who, among other things, has performed reconstructive surgeries on circumcised women, discussed the historical roots of both male and female circumcisions in African cultures. (Videotape on file with the author.)

38.   *Reconsidering Circumcision, supra* note 35.

39.   MINORITY RIGHTS GROUP, *supra* note 6, at 9.

40.   Julie Dimauro, *Toward a More Effective Guarantee of Women's Human Rights: A Multicultural Dialogue in International Law*, 17 WOMEN'S RTS. L. REP. 333, 336 (1996), *citing* FEMALE CIRCUMCISION, EXCISION AND INFIBULATION 7 (Scilla McLean ed., 1980).

41.   *See* Morgan, *supra* note 3, at 95–96.

birth control,[42] while others, despite evidence to the contrary, believe that the surgeries enhance fertility.[43] Some groups believe that the surgeries are hygienic; an uncircumcised woman is seen as unclean.[44] Others believe that circumcision is required by Islamic law,[45] although most religious scholars say that no such requirement is actually in the Koran.[46] Among many peoples, the surgeries are a sign of womanhood, an initiation, and the cutting is accompanied by a public and joyous community celebration.[47] One author states:

> The rationale behind FG[S] is comprised of a matrix of superstitions, perceptions of gender roles, beliefs regarding health, and religious customs. According to four independent studies, the primary reasons for performing FG[S] include: meeting a religious requirement; preserving group identity; protecting virginity and family honor by preventing immorality; helping to maintain cleanliness and health; and furthering marriage goals, including greater sexual pleasure for men.[48]

The surgeries, like all cultural practices, have socially constructed justifications. But as with so many cultural practices that uniquely affect women, the surgeries are, in fact, part of a complex system of male domination of women. At the most fundamental level, FGS function to control women's sexuality and reproductive choices. In addition, some of the possible long-term consequences of the surgeries—incontinence, chronic pain, embarrassing body odor, constant infection, difficulty walking—also serve to severely circumscribe a woman's physical mobility and general ability to engage in various functions and levels of public activity. As is true in all cultures regarding all subordinating practices, women in countries and cultures where FGS are performed confront a range of socioeconomic pressures that encourage conformity. As is true for women around the world, women in cultures where genital surgeries are performed find that "their social status and economic security [derive] from their roles as wives and mothers."[49]

In Sudan, for example, a girl or woman would have few marriage prospects if she remained uncircumcised.[50] Marriage in these societies, in addition to satisfying

---

42. L.F. LOWENSTEIN, *Attitudes and Attitude Difference to Female Genital Mutilation in the Sudan: Is There A Change on the Horizon,* 12 Soc. Sci. & MED. 417 (1978).

43. LIGHTFOOT-KLEIN, *supra* note 1, at 40.

44. WORLD HEALTH ORGANIZATION/EASTERN MEDITERRANEAN REGIONAL OFFICE, TRADITIONAL PRACTICES AFFECTING THE HEALTH OF WOMEN AND CHILDREN: FEMALE CIRCUMCISION, CHILDHOOD MARRIAGE, NUTRITIONAL TABOOS, ETC., Technical Publication No.2, Reprint of a Seminar, Khartoum. 10–15 February 44 (1979) (presentation by Dr A. H. Taba) [hereinafter WHO Report].

45. *Id.* at 45; Hughes, *The Criminalization of Female Genital Mutilation in the United States,* 4 J. L & POL'Y 321, 330 (1995).

46. LIGHTFOOT-KLEIN, *supra* note 1, at 41; Hughes, *supra* note 45, at 331.

47. Ellen Gruenbaum, *Reproductive Ritual and Social Reproduction: Female Circumcision and the Subordination of Women in the Sudan, in* ECONOMY AND CLASS IN SUDAN 310 (Norman O'Neill & Jay O'Brien eds., 1988).

48. Bashir, *supra* note 1, at 424 [citations omitted].

49. Gruenbaum, *supra* note 47, at 311.

50. LIGHTFOOT-KLEIN, *supra* note 1, at 69.

emotional and psychological needs, is an essential career move. Even an educated woman is able to engage in only a handful of different types of economic activity outside the home.[51] In many societies, even a woman with a market-oriented job may be prohibited from owning property either through formal law or through customary practice.[52] In other societies, a woman who might otherwise be able to inherit and own money or property could not do so if she were uncircumcised; in more radical communities, offspring of an uncircumcised woman may be killed.[53]

As in most patriarchal societies, an unmarried girl or woman in a surgery-performing culture maintains her own reputation and marriageability as well as the reputation of her family members through her virginity. The purity of the "family" or male lineage is of great importance; thus, *female* sexuality must be controlled.[54] Rather than relying on "mere" moral persuasion to encourage chastity, the surgeries, arguably, physically ensure it.[55] Because chastity and marriage are essential components of economic survival in these patriarchal contexts, there is enormous pressure on women to be circumcised and to circumcise their daughters.[56] Indeed, Toubia states: "Female circumcision is the physical marking of the marriageability of women, because it symbolizes social control of their sexual pleasure (clitoridectomy) and their reproduction (infibulation)."[57] In addition, in some cultures, the practice confers another economic benefit in that it "ensures a virgin bride who will bring a high price to the family at the time of her marriage."[58]

Economic pressures are, of course, intertwined with social pressures. Preserving one's chastity and giving sexual pleasure to one's husband may stem from emotional needs to acquire and keep a husband and family. If a wife is not "properly" circumcised (and resutured after childbirth), she may risk losing her husband as he resorts to prostitutes, additional wives, or even divorce. The prospect of divorce can be particularly emotionally frightening in cultures where the divorced woman loses her children to their father and his family.[59] In addition to its emotional aspects, divorce typically has severe economic consequences, especially in societies

---

51. *Id.* at 65. *See also* Asim Z. Mustafa, *Female Circumcision and Infibulation in the Sudan*, 73 J. Obstetrics Gynaecology Brit. Cwlth. 302 (1966).

52. Lightfoot-Klein, *supra* note 1, at 69.

53. *Id.* at 39.

54. *Id.* at 39–40; Annas, *supra* note 3, at 331.

55. The term "arguably" is used here because while the Lightfoot-Klein study makes no attempt to guess the extent of pre- or extra-marital sex, Lightfoot-Klein did consult with at least one doctor who stated that some number of women could and did engage in pre-marital sex after circumcision and had themselves resutured, secretly, prior to their marriage in order to "preserve" their virginity on their wedding night. Lightfoot-Klein, *supra* note 1, at 152.

56. Coleman, *supra* note 22, at 1112.

57. Toubia, *supra* note 6, at 714.

58. Maher, *supra* note 10, at 13. In some regions, the circumciser provides a certificate that can be shown to prospective husbands. Abu-Sahlieh, *supra* note 31, at 588.

59. Lightfoot-Klein, *supra* note 1, at 68–69.

where women may not be afforded adequate access to education or career opportunities.

Aside from possible negative economic consequences that may befall an uncircumcised woman, she would likely also face severe social consequences. She would generally be considered by others within the community as immoral or unclean.[60] The woman or girl may be ridiculed and ostracized by family, friends, and the community, treated as a "social outcast, perceived as dirty, different, and even dangerous."[61] In some cultures, an uncircumcised woman is often equated with a prostitute.[62]

The complex array of social and economic rewards and punishments has encouraged many women in contemporary surgery-performing societies to support or submit to FGS. In the numerous societies where special women—midwives or circumcisers—perform the surgeries, the role of the circumciser is often one of honor and status. It can also be a source of some individual economic independence. For most FGS supporters—grandmothers, mothers, and daughters—the surgeries function as a complex symbol of the importance of women, within the dominant cultural framework, as unique and invaluable creators of life: "Circumcision as a symbolic act brings sharply into focus the fertility potential of women by dramatically de-emphasizing their inherent sexuality. By insisting on circumcision for their daughters, women assert their social indispensability, an importance that is not as the sexual partners of their husbands . . . but as the mothers of men."[63]

In spite of enormous pressures, there are women within surgery performing cultures, (often those who have had a better education and/or who have been exposed to different practices), who rigorously oppose FGS. Indeed:

> Research has demonstrated a direct correlation between the education of women and a decline of the practice. This may be because educated women see alternatives to the traditional roles of wife and mother, thus diminishing the importance of preserving a woman's status as a marriageable virgin. Educated women are also more likely to recognize the damaging physical and mental health aspects of the practice.[64]

There are individual heroines who have stood up to their families and communities and submitted to only a modified operation[65] or to a mock ceremony where the ritual and celebration were carried out but no actual cutting occured.[66] There are

---

60. *Id.* at 161.

61. Annas, *supra* note 3, at 332.

62. Coleman, *supra* note 22, at 1112; LIGHTFOOT-KLEIN, *supra* note 1.

63. Janice P. Boddy, *Womb as Oasis, The Symbolic Content of Pharonic Circumcision in Rural Northern Sudan*, 9 AMERICAN ETHNOLOGIST 682, 687 (1982). For a contrasting view, *see* Maher, *supra* note 10, at 13–14. For a fuller discussion of the perspectives of FGS supporters *see* Gunning, *Arrogant Perception*, *supra* note 1, at 218–223.

64. Maher, *supra* note 10, at 13.

65. LIGHTFOOT-KLEIN, *supra* note 1, at 256 app. I.

66. *Id.* at 127.

many African feminists who condemn FGS in all its forms and who have organized to denounce the practice through educational and other efforts.[67] These vocal and indigenous feminists, often at great emotional and personal risk, tend to complement their work at home by joining forces with health care professionals and activists in the international community to hold conferences exploring the ramifications of FGS and to create plans of action designed to eliminate the practice.

FIRST WORLD HISTORICAL AND CONTEMPORARY PRACTICE OF FGS

The countries and cultures that currently practice FGS are largely located in the Third World. It is important, however, to note two facts: 1) FGS have been practiced in First World countries, notably Britain and the United States, in the past; and 2) FGS are currently practiced in First World countries, in part because of migration, but also because of indigenous medical practices.

FGM or clitoridectomy, along with female castration, hysterectomies, and other surgical manipulations of the female genitalia, were created and thrived in the middle and late 1800s in the United States and several European countries. The best known article on this history is Ben Barker-Benfield's *Sexual Surgery in Late Nineteenth Century America,* which focuses on the historical and social contexts of FGM in the United States.[68] This article not only documents the existence of FGM and other related surgeries, but also unearths the same kinds of rationales that are currently expounded where FGM continues.

Barker-Benfield sets the stage for the rise of FGS in the United States by identifying some of the social concerns that confronted white men after the Civil War. First was an increasing patriarchal concern with the alleged propensity of women to fall into "hysteria" or "madness." This tendency was supposedly traced to their sexuality.[69] Second were "disorderly women," whom one doctor identified as "every woman," from women's rightists, bloomerwearers, to midwives.[70] Included too were lesbians, anyone suspected of lesbian inclinations, women with an "aversion to men,"[71] and women who, as described in 1871 by the American Medical Association president, "seek to rival men in manly sports and occupations."[72]

---

67. Some of the groups include the Somali Democratic Women's Organization, *Le Mouvement Femmes et Societe* (Senegal), Women's Group Against Sexual Mutilation (France), *Union Nationale des Femmes du Mali*, the Babiker Bedri Foundation for Women's Studies and Research (Sudan) and the Association of African Women in Research and Development.

68. Ben Barker-Benfield, *Sexual Surgery in Late Nineteenth Century America,* 5 INT'L J. OF HEALTH SERVICES 279 (1975).

69. *Id.* at 280.

70. *Id.*

71. John Money, *The Destroying Angel: Sex, Fitness and Food, in* THE LEGACY OF DEGENERACY THEORY, GRAHAM CRACKERS, KELLOGG'S CORNFLAKES AND AMERICAN HEALTH HISTORY 119, *cited in* Lightfoot-Klein, *supra* note 1, at 180.

72. Barker-Benfield, *supra* note 68, at 281.

Within this social context arose a new medical specialty, predominated by men, which was designed to cure women's conditions: gynecology. The new gynecologists attributed female mental disorders and discontent to their sexual organs. Female genital surgery was considered the logical answer, and it created a trend that Barker-Benfield describes as "characterized by flamboyant, drastic, risky and instant use of the knife."[73]

FGM was the first cure for female mental disorder.[74] The clitoridectomy of that day was invented by an English gynecologist, Dr. Isac Baker Brown, who was considered one of the ablest and most innovative surgeons in England. Brown's concern was to "solve" women's mental health problems: "[T]he main culprit was masturbation. . . . The treatment was clitoridectomy."[75] The market for the then-new North American genital surgeries was rich, or at least middle class, "disorderly" women.[76] These women, ironically the same class of women who actively supported the Suffrage Movement, developed "peculiar ills" such as "hypersexuality, hysteria and nervousness."[77] Lesbianism and aversion to men were also cause for the surgical treatment.[78] Masturbation was "cured" surgically, as were epilepsy, catalepsy, kleptomania, and melancholy.[79]

Brown's "cures" were repudiated as quackery by the British medical establishment in 1867, and he was expelled from the Obstetrical Society. Despite Brown's disgrace, the practice was adopted in the United States in the late 1860s and continued in some form until "at least 1937."[80] Barker-Benfield's article does not include a social history of FGM in European countries, but he does note that the operations were performed on women in England, France, and Germany.[81]

Currently, First World countries are experiencing an increase in FGS, an increase largely attributed to immigration. In a number of European and North American countries, migrants and refugees from surgery–performing countries have continued to practice FGS as one of the many aspects of their home culture.[82] Some families have their daughters sent to their home country at the required time to have the surgeries done. Other families combine resources to bring circumcisers to

---

73. *Id.* at 284.

74. *Id.* at 285.

75. EDWARD WALLERSTEIN, CIRCUMCISION: AN AMERICAN FALLACY 173 (1980), *cited in* LIGHTFOOT-KLEIN, *supra* note 1, at 179.

76. *Id.* at 288–89. For a brief discussion on the racial and class aspects of the creation of sexual surgeries in the United States, *see* Gunning, *Arrogant Perception, supra* note 1, at 207.

77. WALLERSTEIN, *supra* note 35, at 27.

78. Money, *supra* note 71, at 119.

79. LIGHTFOOT-KLEIN, *supra* note 1, at 180.

80. Barker-Benfield, *supra* note 68, at 285.

81. *Id.* at 286.

82. MINORITY RIGHTS GROUP, *supra* note 6, at 35.

their new country.[83] As discussed *infra*, a number of First World nations have passed or proposed legislation to prevent FGS performed by immigrant groups.[84]

Intersexed Persons in First World Nations

Developed nations, while generally opposed to traditional FGS practice, do not prevent genital mutilations that are "medically prescribed." About 4% of live births are babies with ambiguous genitalia: hermaphrodites or intersexed individuals.[85] These individuals, who have existed throughout documented history,[86] may exhibit both female and male genital characteristics.[87] A range of physical attributes marks the intersexed person. Some are born with penises that are significantly smaller than average; some are born with clitori that are significantly larger than average.[88] Another variant is an average-sized penis with the urethral opening along the underside or at the base of the penis rather than at the tip (hypospadias).[89] None of these particular physical attributes generally endangers the physical health of the individual.[90] However, parents, on the advice of doctors, often surgically manipulate their children's genitalia so that they conform to the social norm.[91] Girls with "extra

---

83. *Id.*

84. *See* Larson, *supra* note 1, at 252–57; Annas, *supra* note 3, at 332–52; Bashir, *supra* note 1, at 428–32; Breitung, *supra* note 8, at 664–84; Morgan, *supra* note 3, at 105–111.

85. Anne Fausto-Sterling, *The Five Sexes: Why Male and Female Are Not Enough,* 33 SCIENCES 20–26 (1993). Fausto-Sterling has done other studies that reduce that percentage to closer to 1%. Anne Fausto-Sterling, How Many Sexes Are There? (unpublished work) *in* M. Morgan Holmes, Medical Politics and Cultural Imperatives: Intersexual Identities Beyond Pathology and Erasure 3 (Sept. 1994) (unpublished master's thesis-on file with author).

86. Suzanne J. Kessler, *The Medical Construction of Gender: Case Management of Intersexed Infants,* 16 SIGNS 3 (1990).

87. This "true" intersexed individual with both ovarian and testicular tissue present is actually a rarity amongst intersexed individuals. More typically, the child has either ovaries or testicles but the external genitalia are ambiguous. *Id.* at 5.

88. The two main determinants for doctors in analyzing and distinguishing between these two medical "problems" are "1) the nature of the underlying defect that resulted in genital ambiguity and 2) the size of the phallus." Ellen Hyun-Ju Lee, Producing Sex: An Interdisciplinary Perspective on Sex Assignment Decisions for Intersexuals 43 (April 1994) (unpublished senior thesis on file with author). *See also* Kessler, *supra* note 86, at 11–12.

89. M. Morgan Holmes, *Queer Cut Bodies: Intersexuality and Homophobia in Medical Practice,* 9 (1995) (unpublished paper on file with author-available on internet).

90. Kessler, *supra* note 86, at 5. There are some physical configurations that can create physical health problems. For example, a child born without a vagina may have health problems at the onset of puberty if she is capable of menstruating; then some surgery will be required to allow for the release of the menstrual blood. And some infants whose condition is caused by "androgen insensitivity are in danger of malignant degeneration of the testes unless they are removed." *Id.* n.6.

91. Kessler's study was focused on doctors and their approach in assigning unequivocally the gender of the intersexed infant as soon as possible. She notes that there was little indication that parents had any input in this process. Indeed, part of the process of explaining to the parents' friends and neighbors the exact nature of the problem with the child involves using "medicalese" as a legitimating tool. *Id.* at 21–22. Doctors, though, did report that their responsibility to assign a gender early and unequivocally relates to the needs of parents. Parents need a clear gender assignment in order to know how to interact

long" clitori undergo FGM; part or all of the clitoris is cut off. Similarly, boys with "extra small" penises have their external genitals cut off and are surgically carved to be female.[92] These procedures are performed by certified doctors, so few health risks attend the procedures themselves. However, this genital mutilation, like the more widespread form, can rob the intersexed person of the capacity for sexual pleasure.[93] Typically, these surgeries are performed on babies or children who are not informed (or informable) of their exact nature. Their medical histories and difficulties may be shrouded in mystery and when, later in life, they learn of the circumstances of their physical health, there may be attendant psychological problems.[94] For males who have their urethral opening moved, long term health problems are likely. Infections inside the penis and other urinary problems, sometimes occasioning further genital operations, are not uncommon.[95]

While these surgeries are performed on a smaller segment of the population, some of their functions are similar to those of the more common forms of FGS. In both cases, the dominant patriarchal culture constructs certain ideals based upon the notion that people are "naturally" divided into only two distinct genders: there

---

with their child. Kessler quotes a geneticist who notes that "when parents change a diaper and see genitalia that don't mean much in terms of gender assignment, I think it prolongs the negative response to the baby. . ." *Id.* at 9.

92. *Id.* at 11–12.

93. Medical experts are concerned with "normal sexual functioning" of the surgically created genitalia. However, the focus is on the ability of the individuals to ". . . engage in genital [heterosexual] sex." *Id.* at 20. An assigned male needs to have a penis long enough to penetrate a vagina; hence the long time focus on the appropriate size of the penis including specific guidelines on the appropriate length published in 1942 and 1975. Lee, *supra* note 88, at 25–26. An assigned female needs a vagina large enough to receive a penis. Kessler, *supra* note 86, at 20. Consequently, little concern was given to the size and shape of the female clitoris outside of the individual aesthetic of the family and attending physician. No guidelines on the sizes of clitori were developed until the late 1980s and early 1990s. Lee, *supra* note 88, at 27. The role of an intact clitoris in female sexual pleasure seems to be of little concern.

There are few, if any, studies on the sexual lives and satisfaction of surgically altered intersexed individuals. Holmes' article reports on the members of the Intersexed Society of North America (ISNA) without specifying that actual number of people, and notes that ". . . only one person has reported being reliably responsive at the physical level of sexual activity and it is significant that her surgeries were performed after the onset of puberty." Holmes, *supra* note 89, at 10

94. The theory of management of intersexed infants designed by John Money relies upon three factors: 1) swift assignment of gender, i.e., when the individual is an infant; 2) gender appropriate hormones administered at puberty, and 3) keeping the intersexed child informed "about their situation." Kessler, *supra* note 86, at 7. However, the information the child and teenager gets about his/her situation may not be accurate. Doctors may hide information, unless other medical tests force them to make more accurate explanations, for "the greater good-keeping individual/concrete genders as clear and uncontaminated as the notions of female and male are in the abstract." Kessler, *id.* at 13. *See also,* Natalie Angier, *Intersexual Healing: An Anomaly Finds A Group,* N. Y. TIMES, Feb. 4, 1996, at E14. The members of ISNA suggest that there are far more psychological ramifications than the medical establishment will acknowledge.

95. Holmes, *supra* note 89, at 9. Some intersexed people in North America have organized to raise serious questions about these procedures, characterizing them as genital mutilation. Their group is called the Intersexed Society of North America (ISNA). Angier, *supra* note 94.

are only males and females, each with rigidly defined and contrasting physical features. In the more common form of FGS, the male as he is naturally formed or birthed, with external genitals, may be treated with a far less intrusive, painful, and debilitating form of circumcision. In contrast, the female may be extremely altered or mutilated, with some or all of her external genitals removed. Families are encouraged by the community at large, including some of its most respected members, to physically transform the female, even if that conformity exacts serious physical, sexual, and psychological tolls on the individual.

In this less common form of FGS, the medically proscribed form, a "norm" is defined for the physical appearance of males and females. The reason given is that individual genders should be distinct and contrasting; a male should have clearly projecting external genitalia and the female should have significantly less. For those individuals born with genitalia that do not fit these rigidly defined categories, surgery or mutilation is the recommended course of action. Families are again encouraged by the community at large, including its most respected members, to physically transform their child, even if conformity exacts serious physical, sexual and psychological tolls on the individuals. In both cases, this conformity and transformation caters to an ideal that ignores the range of physical variation in which healthy human beings are born. And this pressure to conform is significant enough, in both cases, that individual choice is largely precluded. Children are not confronted with the peer and social pressures of having genitalia unlike the societally prescribed ideal and then asked, at the age of majority, to decide whether, as adults, they feel that the health and sexuality costs and risks are worth social acceptance. In both cases, the parents decide that the cost of nonconformity for the child, for themselves, and for their families is too great, and decide for their children.

NATIONAL LEGISLATION AND EDUCATIONAL EFFORTS TO PROHIBIT FGS

Historical Efforts in Third World Countries

Campaigns against FGS have existed and continue today in both First and Third World countries. Some of these efforts involve research and educational campaigns spearheaded by local groups and individuals. Other efforts involve the introduction and passage of legislation prohibiting the surgeries.

In Africa, the earliest attempts to legislate against the surgeries were connected with colonial rule. The first such legal effort occurred in Kenya in 1906 at the insistence of the Church of Scotland.[96] Christian missionaries made similar efforts in Senegal, the Gambia, and Egypt.[97] The legal effort in Kenya was not supported by the population upon whom it was imposed. Indeed, under the post-colonial presidency of Jomo Kenyatta, the government expressed pride in and approval of the practice,[98] and Kenyatta himself suggested that "[t]he overwhelming majority

---

96. Allison Slack, *Female Circumcision: A Critical Appraisal*, 10 Hum. Rts. Q. 437,477 (1988).

97. *Id.* at 479.

98. *Id.* at 477.

of the [local people] believe that it is the secret aim of those who attack this country's old custom to disintegrate the social order and thereby hasten their Europeanization."[99]

Sudan passed a law in 1946 that outlawed the most popular and radical of the surgeries, infibulation, but still allowed for the removal of the "free and projecting part of the clitoris."[100] This effort, too, had colonial roots. British colonial authorities instituted midwifery training in Sudan in 1921 and, by 1948, "the midwifery school of the Wolff sisters had trained more than 500 midwives in different areas all over the country."[101] In 1943, the then governor-general had established a Medical Committee to study the problem of FGS, and created and disseminated a booklet and a press and radio campaign, with the support of religious leaders, to outlaw infibulation.[102] When this campaign failed, the 1946 legislation, which included fines and imprisonment for up to seven years for midwives who performed the surgeries, was enacted.[103] Because of traditional attitudes, Sudanese people were not supportive of this legislation. Parents rushed to have their daughters infibulated before the law took effect, thereby causing a higher rate of medical complications and deaths from the operations. When midwives were arrested, violent disturbances broke out and, consequently, few further arrests and prosecutions were made.[104]

Post-Colonial Efforts in Africa

Post-colonial efforts at legislation, resolutions, or proclamations have been few. Egypt has a history of some legal authority outlawing the surgeries, although the exact nature is not entirely clear. One article asserts that most educated people believe that the surgeries were outlawed; this belief is based either upon a decree passed by President Nasser in April of 1958, which prohibited the practice entirely and provided for penal sanctions for violators,[105] or upon a resolution signed by the Minister of Health in 1959, which recommended only partial clitoridectomy, required the consent of a physician, and provided for no penal sanctions.[106] However, in July 1996, Egypt's Health Minister, Ismail Sallam, banned all registered doctors, nurses, and health care workers from performing the surgeries and prohibited the performance of the surgeries in public hospitals.[107] Kenyan President Arap

---

99. KENYATTA, FACING MT. KENYA: THE TRIBAL LIFE OF THE KIKUYU 133 (1953).

100. Slack, *supra* note 96, at 477.

101. MINORITY RIGHTS GROUP, *supra* note 6, at 28.

102. *Id.*

103. *Id.*

104. *Id.*

105. Slack, *supra* note 96, at 478.

106. *Id. See also* MINORITY RIGHTS GROUP, *supra* note 6, at 11.

107. *Egyptian Doctor Held,* THE FINANCIAL TIMES, Aug. 27, 1995, at 1; XINHUA NEWS AGENCY, Aug. 27, 1996, *available in* LEXIS, Nexis Library. The fact that the health minister felt the need to issue some ban, after pressure from women's groups, suggests that the laws reportedly on the books were non-existent or reflective. *Girl Bleeds to Death During Circumcision Procedure,* The SUNDAY GAZETTE MAIL, Aug. 25, 1996, at 21A.

Moi called for the cessation of the surgeries in 1982.[108] His statements were followed by further efforts to ban FGS so that a circumciser discovered practicing the surgeries can be arrested under the Chiefs Act.[109] In addition, official declarations against FGS were made by the late Captain Thomas Sankara, the former head of state in Burkina Faso, and Abdou Diouf, the former head of state in Senegal.[110]

While Ethiopia, which has a high incidence of FGS, does not have any specific legislation outlawing the surgeries, the new Constitution (December 8, 1994) contains an article which states that "women have the right to protection by the State from harmful customs. Laws, customs and practices that oppress women or cause bodily or mental harm to them are prohibited."[111]

Research and educational efforts have been the more prevalent mode of anti-FGS campaigns, although some of these activities also aim for the introduction of legislation. In Egypt, research has focused on crafting plans that can warn both rural and urban women about the dangers of FGS.[112] In 1979, a ground-breaking seminar entitled *Bodily Mutilation of Young Females* was held in Cairo. This seminar brought together representatives from parts of the Egyptian and Sudanese governments, along with a range of United Nations organizations, nongovernmental organizations (NGOs), the Arab League, and medical and research faculties.[113] The resolutions passed by this seminar were implemented in a three-year project started in 1982 and funded by the Population Crisis Committee and the Cairo Family Planning Association. The results included interviews with circumcised women and the production of educational and training materials for health care professionals.[114] A twelve-member National Committee was formed to combat the surgeries, it has focused on public education through such means as family planning centers, secondary schools, and factories. A major aim of the National Committee is to obtain clear and specific legislation against FGS in all its farms.[115]

Sudan, Somalia, and Djibouti, all in northern Africa, are the countries with the highest concentration of infibulated women. Still, anti-FGS campaigns are active in all three countries. Midwifery schools in Sudan used to teach the sunna form of

---

108. Slack, *supra* note 96, at 477.

109. MINORITY RIGHTS GROUP, *supra* note 6, at 11.

110. *Id.*

111. *Alternative Approaches and Ways and Means Within the United Nations System for Improving the Effective Enjoyment of Human Rights and Fundamental Freedoms: Report of the Special Rapporteur on Violence Against Women, Its Causes and Consequences, Ms. Radhika Coomaraswamy, submitted in accordance with Commission on Human Rights resolution 1995/85*, Commission on Human Rights, U.N. ESCOR, 52d Sess., at 29, U.N. Doc. E/CN.4/1996/53 (1996) [hereinafter *Report of the Special Rapporteur—1996*].

112. *Id.* at 26–27. One of the noted researchers in this area is Marie Bassili Assaad, an Egyptian social scientist.

113. *Id.*

114. *Id.*

115. *Id.* at 28.

the surgeries and encourage the use of antiseptics until 1979, after which no techniques were taught and FGS were discouraged as a practice entirely.[116] The dean of the College of Nursing in Khartoum refers to the surgeries as "mutilations" as part of her ethics course.[117] In 1979, The Ahfad University College for Women sponsored a symposium, *The Changing Status of Women,* which denounced FGS, in all its forms, as part of its health-related recommendations. A voluntary association was formed as a result of this symposium, the Babiker Badri Scientific Association for Women's Studies, whose mission is to continue group discussions at the village level throughout Sudan on children's health and care, women's economic development, and the eradication of FGS.[118] In 1984, the Ministry of Health and Social Services established the Sudan National Committee on Traditional Practices as the national chapter of the Inter-African Committee on Traditional Practices Affecting the Health of Mothers and Children. Although this 1984 committee did not last, the Sudanese National Committee for the Eradication of Traditional Practices Affecting the Health of Women and Children, formed in 1988, has subsequently developed training and educational campaigns.[119]

In Somalia, when the Somali Women's Democratic Organization (SWDO) was first formed in 1977, the organization issued a call for the eradication of FGS. SWDO was instrumental in the establishment of the governmentally appointed Commission Concerned with the Abolishment of the Operations.[120] SWDO efforts have led to the prohibition of the surgeries in all government hospitals. This anti-FGS educational campaign is focused on health instead of sexuality. SWDO established a center for the anti-FGS campaign in its headquarters in 1987, to disseminate information packages and conduct training seminars. An international conference was held in Mogadishu in 1989, entitled *Female Circumcision: Strategies To Bring About Change,* which issued resolutions for change in the Somali government. This was supported by the then-ruling Somali Revolutionary Party. However, once the Somali Revolutionary Party was overthrown and the country plunged into civil disorder, much of SWDO's work was undermined.[121]

In Djibouti, the National Committee for the Fight Against Female Circumcision was established in 1987 and includes in its membership representatives from the Ministries of Health, Justice and Education, the Red Crescent Society, and the *Union Nationale des Femmes de Djibouti* (UNFD).[122] The Committee, which works

---

116. *See generally* Asma Mohamed Abdel Halim, *Rituals and Angels: Female Circumcision and the Case of Sudan, in* FROM BASIC NEEDS TO BASIC RIGHTS 249–65 (Margaret A. Schuler ed., 1995).

117. *Report of the Special Rapporteur—1996, supra* note 111, at 29.

118. *Id.* at 30.

119. *Id.*

120. *Id.*

121. *Id.* at 31.

122. *Study on Traditional Practices Affecting the Health of Women and Children: Final Report of Special Rapporteur, Mrs. Halima Embarek Warzazi,* Sub-Commission on Prevention of Discrimination and Protection of Minorities, Commission on Human Rights, U.N. ESCOR, 43d Sess., at 17, U.N. Doc. E/CN.4/Sub.2/1991/6 (1991) [hereinafter *Report of the Special Rapporteur—1991*].

under the umbrella of UNFD, conducts nationwide seminars and training sessions targeted at birth attendants, mothers, fathers, religious leaders, and policy makers.[123] While the UNFD supports the introduction of legislation against female circumcision, it has especially focused on the most extreme form of the surgeries, infibulation. Indeed, as an apparent interim measure, UNFD has run clinics designed to inform mothers not only about the dangers of circumcision but also to provide a place where girls can and do have less extreme circumcisions performed by traditional circumcisers under local anesthesia and sterile conditions.[124]

For eastern African nations, Kenya is the state in which there are reports of the most severe form of FGS, infibulation, and where there has been more anti-FGS activity. The National Council of Women of Kenya has worked to combat FGS. In 1979, this council identified as a primary goal the need for more local research on the extent of the practice, and sought international financial support for such work.[125] The University of Nairobi had already carried out some research on the matter, but the National Council determined that more systematic information was necessary. Their view was that education would be more effective than legislation, and they wanted to avoid using international materials and, rather, to create information based upon Kenyan women's experiences and perspectives.[126] The Women's Action Group on Excision and Infibulation of the Minority Rights Group supported these fund-raising efforts as early as 1982, although it was apparently the only international organization or agency to do so and, eventually, the National Council of Kenyan Women was dissolved by the government.[127] However, in 1990, the Kenyan National Committee on Traditional Practices was created in order to carry out local research and, on that basis, develop projects concerning traditional practices.[128]

In Nigeria, contemporary, formal opposition to the surgeries started when an outspoken woman journalist, Mrs. Esther Ogunmodede, spoke with circumcised women, like herself, and began to first question and then condemn FGS.[129] Ogunmodede believed that a campaign focused on the surgeries' medical and health problems would be effective but that this effort would need to be based upon

---

123. *Id.*

124. *Id.* at 19. The United Nations' sponsored team who visited such a clinic in 1991 noted that they were told that grandmothers often complained about the circumcisions the UNFD clinic performed as "not complete enough." *Id.*

125. *Id.* at 32. Mrs. Eddah Gachukia, a Kenyan parliament member, at the time was most instrumental in this work through the National Council. The Council appealed to the International Council of Women, UNICEF, the World Health Organization, and American anti-FGS activist Fran Hosken for grants to enable Kenyan women scholars to do this research in order to provide them with a solid statistical and information base with which to lobby for governmental opposition to the surgeries. The National Christian Council of Kenya also called for research.

126. *Id.*

127. *Id.*

128. *Id.*

129. *Id.*

extensive research on FGS in Nigeria proper; she hoped this research would be supported by international organizations such as the World Health Organization (WHO) in coordination with the Ministries of Health, Education and Information.[130] Ogunmodede published an article articulating her plan in the November 1977 issue of *Drum* magazine. *Drum* then conducted a survey which revealed that lay people and policy makers had strong feelings; the majority supported the abolition of the practice.[131] The Medical Women's Association of Nigeria undertook local research and issued its first report in 1983; the National Association of Nigerian Midwives conducted surveys in 1985 and 1986.[132] Also in 1985, the Nigerian National Committee on Traditional Practices was formed and has since engaged in a variety of educational programs for lay persons, professionals, and governmental representatives.[133]

In Burkina Faso, the Women's Federation of Upper Volta (later to become the Women's Federation of Burkina) began a radio campaign against excision (infibulation is not practiced in Burkina Faso) in 1975. However, the campaign was discontinued because of the hostile response to it.[134] Research conducted in Burkina between initiation of the campaign and 1983 prompted activists to determine that a medically oriented campaign would be the most effective. Anti-FGS activists received important support from the late Captain Thomas Sankara, the president of Burkina at the time, who made a radical statement opposing the surgeries and encouraging Burkina women not to wait for men to concede anything but to define their liberation for themselves.[135] President Sankara made his statement in 1983, but it was not until 1990 that action was taken with the creation, by decree, of the National Committee to Combat the Practice of Female Circumcision. This organization has supported the activities of Burkina feminists in conducting rural educational campaigns. In June of 1991, a draft constitution was voted upon in a referendum; that document both supports equality between men and women and prohibits FGS.[136]

In African countries, many feminists have found that an educational approach that focuses upon health concerns for mothers, babies, and children is more effective than legislation. Although legislative campaigns have been and continue to be made, legislation can sometimes still be tainted with the mark of imperialism from which the earlier legislative efforts arose. Health issues are often of greater moral strength

---

130. *Id.* at 32–33.

131. *Id.* at 34. The most compelling voice came from the principal of the School of Nursing in Ife, Mr. Olu Babajide, who described the medical problems and then condemned circumcision.

132. *Id.*

133. *Id.*

134. *Id.*

135. *Id.*

136. *Id.* WHO has supported the anti-FGS campaign in Burkina. In particular it created a film in 1991 depicting the life of a family doctor from Ouagadougou who visits his home village monthly and opposes circumcision.

in the face of custom and religious rationales. Moral persuasion is of great importance; in the past, when legislative or educational efforts lacked significant popular support, the surgeries did not decrease but rather were performed in hurried or secretive ways that only increased the attendant health risks to the children involved.[137] African activists have also been concerned about anti-FGS material that is not produced in the specific cultural context within which they battle; Eurocentric materials have been criticized as "alarmist" and for risking the provocation of "righteous indignation,"[138] because they are "highly coloured by prejudice . . . and based upon erroneous information."[139] African activists have a range of approaches rooted in the specific cultural, political, and economic contexts; First World financial support for these efforts is welcomed as long as the leadership of African women is accepted.

First World Efforts

Educational and legislative activity against FGS in First World countries began both because of the increasing awareness that FGS are being performed in developed countries by some immigrant groups,[140] and because persons from FGS-performing countries are seeking asylum in First World countries in order to flee from the practice.[141]

African women activists and health care workers have reported FGS-related concerns for the health of women and children in communities in Australia, Italy,

---

137. In some cases, African activists have also used religious persuasion when religious leaders were willing. But in some cases either the leaders were unavailable or because of the multiplicity of religious beliefs, activists have been concerned with contributing to the rise of religious tensions. *See* MINORITY RIGHTS GROUPS, *supra* note 6, at 27.

138. *Id.* at 31 (quoting Edna Ismail an experienced healthcare worker and anti-FGS activist in Somalia).

139. *Id.* at 32 (quoting Eddah Gachukia a Kenyan Parliament member and anti-FGS activist).

140. Barbara Crossette, *Female Genital Mutilation by Immigrants is Becoming Cause for Concern in U.S.*, NEW YORK TIMES, Dec. 10, 1995, at Y11; Larson, *supra* note 1, at 237–38; Coleman, *supra* note 22, at 1112, *citing* World Health Organization Office of Information, Press Release, *Female Genital Mutilation; World Health Assembly Calls for the Elimination of Harmful Traditional Practices*, May 12, 1993, at 1; Breitung, *supra* note 8, at 658–60.

141. For instance, a Malian woman, Aminata Diop, was denied political asylum in France, but because of the threat of FGS, was allowed to stay under a humanitarian exception. Bronwyn Winter, *Women, the Law, and Cultural Relativism in France: The Case of Excision*, 19 SIGNS 939 (1994). Fauziya Kassindja fled FGS in Togo and sought asylum in the U.S. Maher, *supra* note 10, at 12–13; Bashir, *supra* note 1, at 436–39; Kasigna, I. & N. Dec. No. 3278 (B.I.A. June 13, 1996) (interim decision). Kandra Hassan Farah, a Somali women, fled to Canada to prevent her daughter's circumcision. Clyde H. Farnsworth, *Canada Gives a Somali Mother Refugee Status*, NEW YORK TIMES (Late Ed.), July 21, 1994 (Lexis/Nexis News File); Breitung, *supra* note 8, at 671–72. Lydia Oluloro, a Nigerian woman, was allowed to stay in the U.S. to protect her daughters from circumcision. Patricia D. Rudloff, *In Re Oluloro: Risk of Female Genital Mutilation as "Extreme Hardship" in Immigration Proceedings*, 26 ST. MARY'S L. J. 877 (1995); *Female Genital Mutilation and Refugee Status in the United States: A Step in the Right Direction*, 19 B. C. INT'L & COMP. L. REV. 353 (1996); In re Olulora, No. A72-147-491, Exec. Office Immig. Rev., Mar. 23, 1994.

the Netherlands, Canada, the United States (U.S.), Belgium, Germany, Finland, Sweden, Norway, France, and the United Kingdom (U.K.).[142]

State Action in First World Countries

Some First World countries have taken action to prevent the practice. In Australia, after the Australian Family Law Council issued a report (June 1994), the government indicated a commitment to pursue uniform legislation making the practice of FGS an offense and providing educational programs for affected immigrant communities.[143] In Norway, an alert was issued to inform all hospitals of the practice (1985).[144] Belgium has a ban on the surgeries; Sweden passed a law specifically prohibiting excision, with or without consent (1982), which carries a two-year sentence.[145] In the U.S., several states have passed or introduced legislation prohibiting the surgeries,[146] and the federal government recently passed an anti-FGM law criminalizing the act.[147] The U.S. and Canada have also addressed the issue through the implementation of gender–based asylum and refugee guidelines which acknowledge that FGM, under some circumstances, can be the basis for refugee status.[148] While France does not have specific legislation outlawing FGS, it has used its penal

---

142. *Report of the Special Rapporteur—1991, supra* note 122, at 35.

143. *Report of the Special Rapporteur—1996, supra* note 111, at 28–29; *see also* Breitung, *supra* note 8, at 668–69.

144. *Report of the Special Rapporteur—1996, id.* at 11.

145. *Id.*

146. *Id. See also* Morgan, *supra* note 3, at 106–12; Breitung, *supra* note 8, passim; Bashir, *supra* note 1, at 346–450.

147. The Federal Prohibition of Female Genital Mutilation was first introduced in late 1993 by Representative Pat Schroeder. H.R. 7546, 103 Cong., 1st Sess. (1993). A companion bill was introduced in the US Senate. S. 2501, 103 Cong., 2nd Sess. (1994). Although no action was taken then, the bill was reintroduced in the next congress. H. R. 941, 104 Cong., 1st Sess. (1995). The bill was referred to the House Judiciary and Commerce Committees on February 28, 1996, and passed in September 1996.

148. *See* Immigration and Refugee Board, *Guidelines Issued By the Chairperson Pursuant to Section 65(3) of the Immigration Act,* (Ottawa, Canada, Immigration and Refugee Board, 9 March 1993) and Department of Justice, *Memorandum: Considerations For Asylum Officers Adjudicating Claims for Women,* 72 Interp. Rel. 781 (June 5, 1995).

In the United States, the first and, as of this writing, only case of asylum being granted on the basis of FGS involved a 19-year-old west African teenager, Fauziya Kasinga [also spelled Kassindja]. The Kasinga case made headlines in the U.S., because the teenager, who applied for asylum as soon as she arrived in the U.S. after fleeing Togo, was imprisoned for over one year pending her asylum hearing. The Board of Immigration Appeals in a narrowly crafted opinion determined that Kasinga met the well founded fear of persecution standard based upon her fear of suffering FGS. *See* Roberto Suro, *Woman Fleeing Tribal Rite Gains Asylum; Genital Mutilation is Ruled Persecution,* THE WASH. POST, June 14, 1996, at A06; Celia W. Dugger, *U.S. Grants Asylum to Woman Fleeing Genital Mutilation Rite,* The N.Y. TIMES, June 14, 1996, at A1. For a detailed discussion, *see* Arthur C. Helton & Alison Nicoll, *Female Genital Mutilation as Ground for Asylum in the United States: The Recent Case of In Re Fauziya Kasinga and Prospects for More Gender Sensitive Approaches,* 28 COLUM. HUM. RTS. L. REV. 375 (1997).

code, Article 312–3, to prosecute the surgeries as a criminal offense; prosecutions, primarily against circumcisers and mothers, have occurred.[149]

In the U.K., specific legislation against FGS came into effect in 1985 and carries a prison term of up to five years.[150] Subsequently, the Foundation for Women's Health and Development (FORWARD), an organization that grew out of a steering committee of African and Arabian women, held the first national conference on *Female Genital Mutilation: Unsettled Issues for Health and Social Workers in the UK* (1989) in order to move FGM from the margins of English health concerns, where it constituted an untouchable "quaint cultural practice," to the mainstream of combatable health matters.[151] The conference proposed treating FGS as a child physical abuse matter, and recommended the education and mobilization of social workers, health care professionals, police, lawyers, judges, and teachers—through the Department of Health and Social Security (now the Department of Health)—to identify at-risk children and to use child protective procedures to intervene.[152] The Department of Health accepted these recommendation and, in March 1991, issued guidelines to accompany the Children's Act of 1989 to provide interagency cooperation for the protection of children regarding FGS.[153] While no one has been criminally prosecuted under the U.K. statute, there have been at least seven legal interventions to stop the surgical alteration of children by their parents.[154]

Various Domestic and International Strategies and Conflicts

Educational and legislative campaigns at the state and local levels can address the abolition of FGS from a number of angles, including non-discrimination principles, the right to good health, the right to development,[155] and the right to be free from all forms of violence. Whether the approach focuses upon health, sexual freedom, women's equality, or violence will depend upon the circumstances in which the campaign is waged. However, even among anti-FGS activists, conflicts often arise about the appropriate approach.

---

149. MINORITY RIGHTS GROUP, *supra* note 6, at 11. A recent United Nations report on violence against women suggests that the gender bias apparent in the French prosecutions may be changing. *See Report of the Special Rapporteur—1996, supra* note 111, at 29. For a discussion of some of the prosecutions and the complex political ramifications of criminalization in Western countries, *see* Bronwyn Winter, *Women, the Law and Cultural Relativism in France: the Case of Excision,* 19 SIGNS 939 (Summer 1994).

150. MINORITY RIGHTS GROUP, *supra* note 6, at 11; Breitung, *supra* note 8, at 665–67.

151. MINORITY RIGHTS GROUP, *supra* note 6, at 37.

152. *Id.*

153. *Id.*

154. *Id.* at 11.

155. *Id.* at 16–17. *See also* Gunning, *Arrogant Perception, supra* note 1, at 231–238 (discussing the various international treaties and declarations which provide the basis for the articulation of a human rights norm prohibiting the surgeries); Slack, *supra* note 96, at 465; and Kay Bouleware-Miller, *Female Circumcision: Challenges to the Practice as a Human Rights Violation,* 8 HARV. WOMEN'S L.J. 155,166–75 (1985) (discussing possible human rights norms and possible conflicts between different norms).

First World nations and First World activists can combat FGS by financially supporting local initiatives spearheaded by African feminists.[156] Support for First World-based organizations, run by immigrant citizens and residents with connections to the minority communities within the First World nation who continue to practice the surgeries, is also largely unproblematic.

However, legislation in First World countries may lead to conflict. In France, for example, the criminalization of the surgeries has split the feminist and progressive communities. Some feminists, both black and white, support prosecutions as a way of stopping the practice and making a statement about the seriousness of the health of women. When other feminists see that circumcisers (women) and mothers are the main targets for such prosecutions, they question whether punishing women "for their own good"—in essence victimizing the victim—makes sense; these feminists focus on grassroots education that incorporates a complex understanding of the social, political, and economic isolation in which immigrant women often live their lives.[157]

Legislative efforts in First World countries too often invoke the kind of static, racist, and patriarchal representations of Africans and African women that African activists object to when determining whether to import First World materials. The ultimate goal of the legislation may be shared by anti-FGS activists, but the method used denigrates the voices, humanity, and complexities of the African women and cultures involved while it falsely elevates and aggrandizes First World cultures.[158]

In the U.S. immigration context, it is all too easy for the zealous advocate to defend the right of an immigrant African woman to stay in the U.S. by berating, *in toto*, the African culture from which the client comes and by suggesting that patriarchal violence is somehow unique to "barbaric" African countries and cultures. For example, in a highly publicized immigration case involving a Nigerian woman, Lydia Oluloro, who sought asylee status to spare her daughters the surgeries, Oluloro's lawyer used classic civilized/barbaric oppositional imagery to state her case. The lawyer described FGS as a "brutal, gruesome ritual that violates the

---

156. One such cooperative approach noted with approval by the Minority Rights Group was a joint project between the Somali Women Democratic Organization, the women's wing of the then ruling party, and the Italian Association for Women and Development. The Italians provided "technical and methodological support" while the Somalians "alone [were] responsible for the content and direction of the campaign." MINORITY RIGHTS GROUP, *supra* note 6, at 31.

157. *See* Winter, *supra* note 141, at 960–64.

158. This is a long-standing concern that has been heatedly expressed, recently by African feminists in the U.S. regarding allies on the issue (Alice Walker and Pratibha Parmar) for the reinvigoration of the old negative images of Africans in their widely acclaimed anti-FGS film, *Warrior Marks. See, e.g.* Seble Dawit & Salem Merkuria, *The West Just Doesn't Get It; Let Africans Fight Genital Mutilation,* N.Y. TIMES, Dec. 7, 1993, at A27; and Kagendo Murungi,*Get Away From My Genitals!: A Commentary on Warrior Marks,* 2 INTERSTICES 11 (Spring 1994). African-American feminists have recognized the problem in the past. *See, e.g.* ANGELA Y. DAVIS, *Women in Egypt: A Personal View, in* WOMEN, CULTURE & POLITICS 116, 124–34 (1989).

most fundamental notions of decency and civilization at the heart of this Republic,''[159] and catalogued the various ways in which Nigerian law and society deni-
grate women, e.g., by ''tolerat[ing] domestic violence'' as if such violence were
not the mark of all patriarchal societies throughout the world, including the U.S.[160]
This demeaning[161] exploitation of racist and imperial imagery may have proved
useful on a narrow basis (Oluloro was granted withholding of deportation and her
daughters were spared having to undergo the surgeries),[162] but on a more expansive
level, it may serve to undermine fundamental goals. It also cements ideas and
conceptions about Africans and African women that are not only false, but damaging to progress.

The way legislation is crafted can signal problems. In the U.S., some states
have developed new statutes that, like the federal bill, criminalize FGS specifically.[163] Unlike the federal bill, however, few of the state bills currently include
language that requires social service agencies to study the extent of the problem or
to provide educational and support services for the affected communities. The
absence of any outreach increases the likelihood that immmigrant women will
encounter anti-FGS information primarily through the criminal justice system.
Other statutes include FGM as a form of a pre-existing violation such as mayhem
or child abuse.[164] Some anti-FGS organizations, e.g., the Minority Rights Group,
recommend that First World countries should enact clear legislation characterizing
FGS as child abuse.[165] The advantage of such a characterization is that social service
intervention can be a part of such legislation.[166] This kind of legislation requires
community involvement so that governmental authorities choose parent education
and family support over arrest and imprisonment. The choice of one route or
another will be affected by the prevailing political climate: what is the current
attitude toward immigrants? Racialized conceptions of African cultures, or other

159. In The Matter of Lydia Omowunmi Oluloro, (File No. A72 147 491), Respondent's Summation
at Close of Hearing, U.S. Department of Justice, EOIR, at 1 (March 3, 1994) (on file with author).

160. *Id.* at 4.

161. Some lawyers would argue that Oluloro's lawyer, Tilman Hasche, did precisely what a zealous
advocate must do. But other immigration/refugee lawyers argue that no client would denounce so
entirely her own culture and that to articulate such an extreme position is a misrepresentation of the
client's voice and story that could backfire when the client's testimony is or appears inconsistent with
the lawyer's representations.

162. In the Matter of Lydia Omowunmi Oluloro, (File No. A72 147 491), U.S. Department of Justice,
EOIR, Oral Decision of the Immigration Judge (March 23, 1994) (on file with author).

163. Four states, as of this writing, have created new offenses in order to criminalize FGM: North
Dakota, Tennessee, Texas, and Wisconsin. *See* ND S.B. 2454, 54th Legis. Assembly. (North Dakota,
1995); TN S.B. 2394, 99th Gen. Assembly, 2nd Reg. Sess. (Tennessee, 1995); TX H.B. 2442, 74th Reg.
Sess. (Texas, 1995); WI A.B. 926, 92nd Legis. Sess. (Wisconsin, 1995).

164. California and Rhode Island both incorporate FGM as a form of felony mayhem. CA A.B. 2125,
Reg. Sess. (California, 1995) and RI H.B. 7769, Legis. Sess. (Rhode Island, 1996). Colorado defines
FGM as a form of child abuse. CO S.B. 31, 60th Gen. Assembly, 2nd Reg. Sess. (Colorado, 1996).

165. MINORITY RIGHTS GROUP, *supra* note 6, at 39.

166. This is the model used in the UK. *Id.* at 37–38.

Third World nations, as dramatically distinct and inferior to the First World also play a role; this conception conceives of "African FGM" as child abuse, but views "American FGM" as a "medical necessity."[167]

One extreme example of the kind of inappropriate and dangerous analogies made in U.S. statutes is the Illinois law that places FGS in a section on "ritual mutilation." Ritual mutilation is specifically not male circumcision. Rather, it is defined as a range of activities that approximate the practice of satan-worship, e.g., ingesting human or animal blood, urine, feces, or flesh and burying children alive with corpses.[168] Equating an African cultural practice with commonly understood savagery and bestiality evokes historical and racist imagery and beliefs about Blacks generally that have been a part of U.S. culture since its earliest years. The invocation of such imagery increases the chances that immigrants caught in the U.S. criminal justice system will experience the full weight of its punishment aspect rather than needed social services.

Another area of tension amongst anti-FGS activists involves clinicalization or medicalization. As mentioned previously, in Djibouti, the UNFD, the foremost anti-circumcision organization in the country, has used its clinics to not only educate against circumcision generally, but also to perform the less invasive and less physically harmful form of FGS under improved conditions. Although the organization promotes, in the long run, the abolition of FGS, in the short run it has engaged in accommodating a form of the surgeries. Similarly, in the Netherlands, the Ministry of Welfare, Health and Culture issued a report recommending that doctors be allowed to perform small incisions or ritual cuttings of the clitoris instead of infibulation.[169] The Ministry study of 500 Somali immigrant women found that immigrant women were intent upon assuaging some part of the alienation they felt in their new home by preserving various aspects of their original culture, including infibulation.

---

167. All of the U.S. statutes make exceptions for "medically necessary" surgeries, which presumably allow for the surgeries performed on intersexed children. The Texas bill does not require medical necessity; it allows for female genital mutilation as long as the circumciser is a physician licensed in the state.

Another example of this "civilized-savage" distinction between First and Third World cultures involves the British 1985 statute specifically outlawing FGS. Section one of the Act appears to outlaw female circumcision entirely, but section two makes exceptions when the operation "is necessary for the physical and mental health of the person on whom it is performed and is performed by a registered medical practitioner." This language apparently allows for First World women to have a cosmetic procedure known as "trimming" performed on their genitalia if its size or shape should cause them mental distress, but the section makes clear that mental distress on the part of Third World women is to be discounted when it states that in "determining whether an operation is necessary for the mental health of a person, no account shall be taken of the effect on that person of any belief on the part of that or any other person that the operation is required as a matter of custom or ritual." *See* Leslye Amede Obiora, *Bridges and Barricades: Rethinking Polemics and Intransigence in the Campaign Against Female Circumcision*, 47 Case W. Res. L.Rev. 275 (1997).

168. IL H.B. 3572, 89th Gen. Assembly, Reg. Sess. (Illinois, 1995–96).

169. *See* Obiora, *supra* note 15.

Because skillful and sanitary medical help in performing the surgeries was unavailable, many women performed the circumcision themselves and suffered severe health consequences.[170] The report thus recommended an accommodation. Nonetheless, the recommendation was overruled when political controversy erupted.[171]

The goals and policy of virtually all anti-FGS activists, NGOs, and state governments who have articulated a stance against circumcisions is the abolition of the surgeries. For example, the World Health Organization (WHO) condemns female circumcision and calls for its abolition; moreover, WHO specifically calls for the prohibition of medicalization.[172] However, activists have to confront the reality that many women continue to cherish the social, economic and symbolic meanings they accrue when circumcised—factors which are still prevalent. At least one feminist scholar has argued that if feminism is fundamentally about taking women's experiences and voices seriously, then the importance that many women attach to the surgeries cannot be dismissed as mere patriarchy-induced false consciousness; their complex perceptions and experiences, like European women's perspectives and experiences, must be taken seriously.[173] Others will argue that the very reasons these practices are so very important to the women and girls who insist on or submit to them are based upon male-oriented and patriarchal standards and submissions, and thus must be discounted.[174] However, at the sheer practical level, regardless of the reason, if women insist upon performing the surgeries or having them performed even under the worst of conditions, why not, as an interim measure, limit the extent of the physical damage and health complications by having trained health care practitioners perform some version of the surgeries? Educational campaigns against the surgeries, along with economic development plans targeting women and the countries and communities in which they live, can and should still be conducted; but during the "transition period," women's lives can be saved or improved.

Opponents of medicalization articulate several concerns. Medicalization would give a legitimacy to FGS that is contrary to the entire anti-FGS movement. Anti-FGS activists have raised concerns about the financial interests that drive, in part, the opposition of the traditional circumcisers (who are generally themselves circumcised women with few other economic options) to the anti-FGS movement.[175] In countries where modern health care professionals have participated in the performance of the surgeries, anti-FGS activists have complained that these health care

---

170. *Id.*; *see also* Henrietta Boas, *Problem of Female Circumcision in Holland,* JERUSALEM POST, May 10, 1992; and *Women: Dutch Government Ends Debate on Circumcision Proposal,* INT'L PRESS SERVICE, November 11, 1992.

171. Obiora, *supra* note 15 (page number unavailable).

172. *See Report of the Special Rapporteur—1991, supra* note 122, at 32.

173. *See generally* Obiora, *supra* note 15 (defending the clinicalization movement).

174. Larson, *supra* note 1, at 239–40 (women cannot assume equal personhood in a society which requires alteration of the female body's natural state in order for the woman to be accepted in society).

175. *See, e.g.,* Gunning, *Arrogant Perception, supra* note 1, at 222–23.

professionals were driven by greed to perpetuate the surgeries.[176] Medicalization merely substitutes modern, First World trained health care professionals for traditional circumcisers. Modern health care practitioners could become financially invested in the perpetuation of the surgeries and obstruct the long-term goals of the anti-FGS movement. Additionally, the transfer of authority to circumcise from traditional circumcisers to modern health care practitioners may also, in effect, become a transfer of the provision of health care from a more female-dominated model to a more male-dominated model; a transfer which, if First World history is any guide, could be detrimental to women's health overall.[177]

Efforts of International Organizations

The United Nations (U.N.) and other international NGOs and organizations have been involved with attempts to end FGS. The U.N. and its agencies could play the most important role in eradicating the practice, both because its leadership would indicate the support of a large number of nations and because it could coordinate the necessary international action.

---

176. *See Report of the United Nations Seminar on Traditional Practices Affecting the Health of Women and Children: Ouagadougou, Burkina Faso, 29 April–3 May 1991,* Sub-Commission on Prevention of Discrimination and Protection of Minorities, Commission on Human Rights, 43d Sess., at 4 & 7, U.N. Doc. E/CN.4/Sub.2/1991/48 (1991).

177. *See, e.g.,* Vanessa Merton, *The Exclusion of Pregnant, Pregnable and Once Pregnable People* (a.k.a. *Women) from Biomedical Research,* 19 Am. J. L. & Med. 369 (1993); Jonathan M. Eisenberg, *NIH Promulgates New Guidelines for the Inclusion of Women and Minorities in Medical Research,* 10 Berkeley Women's L.J. 183 (1995); Judith H. LaRosa & Vivian W. Pinn, *Gender Bias in Biomedical Research,* 48 JAMWA 145 (Sept/Oct 1993); Shari Roan, *Sex, Ethnic Bias in Medical Research Raises Questions,* L.A. Times, Aug. 3, 1990, at A1; and Janny Scott, *Aspirin Lowers Heart Attack Risk in Women,* L.A. Times, March 16, 1991, at A26. These all discuss bias against women (and people of color) in medical research, meaning that treatments and drugs widely marketed may have unknown effects on women and people of color who "test" them through actual and unsupervised use.

For an in-depth, though not recent, study of the negative impact of a male dominated medical profession on women's health, *see* Gena Corea, The Hidden Malpractice: How American Medicine Mistreats Women (1985). While Corea's study is over a decade old, more recent articles suggest that the problem continues. Increasing the number of women, who are still discriminated against in medical schools and the profession, is seen as the solution.

See, e.g., Shannon Brownlee & Elizabeth Pezzullo, *A Cure for Sexism: Women Doctors Herald a Kinder, Gentler Way to Practice Medicine,* U.S. News and World Report, March 23, 1992, at 86 (discussing the increase in numbers of female doctors since the first U.S. female was awarded a medical degree but also the continuing discrimination against women in medical schools); Leslie Lawrence, *Medical Gender Bias Hurts All Women, Not Just Doctors,* The Houston Chronicle, April 13, 1994, at 2 (describing how discrimination against women in medical schools means that research in areas of particular interest and concern to women is not done); Andrea Rock, *Women's Health is Our Modern Day Sufferage Movement: Interview with Dr. Bernardine Healey,* Ladies Home Journal, Oct. 1993, at 138 (discussing a range of issues with Healey, the first woman to ever head the National Institutes of Health, including the fact that more progress is being made in women's health because of more women in the medical profession, especially in decision making positions); and Abe Aamidor, *Medicine's Gender Gap: Although Treatment is Improving, Some Women Say They Still Can't Get Respect from a Male Medical Establishment,* The Indianapolis Star, Aug. 11, 1996, at J01.

The beginning of U.N. involvement came in 1958 when the Economic and Social Council (ECOSOC) asked WHO to examine the practice and plans for its eradication, and to communicate the results to the Commission on the Status of Women. But in 1959, WHO declined to do so because it regarded the matter as a cultural issue.[178] WHO was asked to study FGS in 1961 by ECOSOC and by the African participants in a U.N. seminar entitled *On the Participation of Women in Public Life.*[179] Again WHO refused and the U.N. did little for nearly twenty years.

Nonetheless, a number of initiatives taken by individuals and organizations were instrumental in maintaining the profile of and the fight against FGS, including: seminal articles in African publications starting in 1975; several research reports, including the *Hosken Report;* the publication of Awa Thiam's book on the situation of women in Africa, *La Parole aux Negresses;* and some important conferences held in 1979, in particular, the African symposium on *The World of Work and the Protection of the Child* sponsored by the International Institute for Labour Studies, and the second regional conference on *The Integration of Women in Development,* both of which condemned excision and infibulation.[180]

In February 1979, WHO finally organized a major conference on FGS. The conference, held in Khartoum, was entitled *Traditional Practices Affecting the Health of Women and Children.* Representatives from ten countries attended and recommended actions for governments to take in order to combat FGS, including the establishment of national commissions and the intensification of education for the general public and health care workers.[181] The implementation of these recommendations has been slow. One initial problem was that WHO focused its support on programs sanctioned by governments, not programs initiated by NGOs. However, in more recent years, WHO has collaborated closely with the NGO Group (NGO Sub-Committee on the Status of Women, Working Group on Female Circumcision) established by the Commission on Human Rights.[182] Another of WHO's special programs, the Women's Health and Development Programme, works closely with both NGOs and other U.N. agencies on FGS issues.[183] One of its most recent proposed programs involves conducting a multi-country study of the attitudes and practices among health care providers regarding FGS which will form the basis for educational materials.[184]

In March of 1980, WHO conducted a joint meeting with the United Nations Children's Fund (UNICEF), which constituted the first time UNICEF had taken

---

178. Katherine Brennan, *The Influence of Cultural Relativism on International Human Rights Law: Female Circumcision as a Case Study,* 7 L. & INEQUALITY 367, 378 (1989); *see also* MINORITY RIGHTS GROUP, *supra* note 6, at 17.

179. MINORITY RIGHTS GROUP, *supra* note 6, at 17.

180. *Id.* at 17–18.

181. *Id.* at 18.

182. *See Report of the Special Rapporteur—1991, supra* note 122, at 33.

183. *Id.*

184. *See Report of the Special Rapporteur—1996, supra* note 111, at 30.

any action on FGS. The agencies came up with a joint plan of action that focused on primary health care.[185] Although UNICEF has a history of taking little action, UNICEF and WHO did assist in the establishment of the Inter-African Committee on Traditional Practices (IAC). UNICEF supports and finances IAC workshops and meetings on FGS.[186] And in more recent years, UNICEF has increased its activity by instigating community education programs that work "directly with women's and community groups to educate women and in particular men to abandon the practice."[187]

The United Nations Educational, Scientific and Cultural Organization (UNESCO) holds conferences and sponsors research on cultural patterns, social change, education, and human rights. It has never made any statement about FGS or sponsored research in the area.[188]

During the United Nations Decade for Women, 1975–1985, FGS did emerge on the agenda. At the 1980 Copenhagen conference, FGS were mentioned once in the *Review and Evaluation of Progress Achieved in the Implementation of the (1975) World Plan of Action: Health* under "cultural practices affecting women" and again, obliquely, in the main policy document of the conference, *Programme of Action for the Second Half of the United Nations Decade for Women: Equality, Development and Peace.*[189] No African country took up the issue at the official governmental conference. However, at the NGO forum, the parallel gathering to the official conference, FGS were the subject of much debate.[190] When the Decade for Women ended with the Nairobi Conference in 1985, there were several workshops on FGS at the NGO forum in Nairobi, organized by the IAC[191] and the *Commission Internationale pour l'Abolition des Mutilations Sexuelles* (CAMS).[192]

---

185. *Id.*

186. *See Report of the Special Rapporteur—1991, supra* note 122, at 19.

187. *See Report of the Special Rapporteur—1996, supra* note 111, at 30.

188. *Id.*

189. *Id.*

190. *Id.* 18–19.

191. The IAC was established in 1984 by delegates to a conference on traditional practices organized by the U.N. NGO Working Group on Traditional Practices in Dakar, Senegal—this Working Group was formed in 1977 by members of NGOs with consultative status with ECOSOC which focuses on training and information around excision—and is currently headquartered in Geneva, Switzerland. It lobbies at the U.N. and has national chapters in a number of African countries. The IAC has a "softly, softly" approach to abolition and has a lot of support from officials and politicians in governments, U.N. agencies, and funding sources. *Id.* at 20–21.

In May 1984, the U.N. Secretary General created another Working Group pursuant to an ECOSOC resolution regarding slavery and nominated by the Sub-Commission for the Protection of Minorities and the Prevention of Discrimination with the purpose of *doing* a comprehensive study on traditional practices affecting women and children. This Working Group started meeting in 1985 and included FGS on its agenda. *Id. See also,* Brennan, *supra* note 178, at 380–93.

192. *Report of the Special Rapporteur—1996, supra* note 111, at 20. There were a number of other international conferences addressing the subject of FGS during the Decade on Women and afterwards. The Minority Rights Group report includes a list up until 1991. *Id.*

FGS were a major issue on the NGO platform at the 1993 World Conference on Human Rights held in Vienna and, by 1995, during the Fourth World Conference on Women held in Bejing, FGS were included in the official as well as the NGO discourse. Indeed, the Beijing Declaration and Platform for Action requests that governments enact and enforce legislation against perpetrators of violence against women and specifically names female genital mutilation as one example of such violence.[193]

The United Nations Commission on Human Rights has also done work in the area of FGS. By its 1988 resolution regarding traditional practices, it requested that the Sub-Commission on Prevention of Discrimination and Protection of Minorities (Sub-Commission) consider what measures needed to be taken both nationally and internationally to eradicate the surgeries. The Sub-Commission appointed one of its experts to study the matter. The study took several years, because, during the first mandated period of time, not enough governments responded to requests for information.[194] In connection with the Commission's work, the U.N. Centre for Human Rights was asked by the Commission in 1990 to conduct field missions and organize regional seminars. The Centre's research and discussion determined that FGS were not receiving the attention they deserved because of a "lack of political will of many states and the failure to inform and educate the public."[195]

The proposed regional conferences did occur. The first United Nations Seminar on Traditional Practices Affecting the Health of Women and Children took place from April 29 to May 3, 1991, in Ouagadougou, Burkina Faso.[196] The second United Nations regional seminar occurred on July 4–8, 1994, in Colombo, Sri Lanka.[197] Both seminars covered a range of practices—e.g., early marriages, son preference—that related to women's health. The Burkina Faso conference included a fairly extensive discussion on FGS. The result of the regional conferences was the creation of a Plan of Action to eliminate harmful traditional practices, which included a call to national governments for "a clear expression of political will" to put an end to all such practices, with a special mention of female circumcision.[198]

The Commission on Human Rights has continued its interest in FGS. In 1994, it appointed a Special Rapporteur on the causes and consequences of violence

---

193. *Report on the Fourth World Conference on Women, Beijing, 4–15 September 1995* A/CONF.177/20, para. 124.

194. *Id.*

195. *Id.*

196. *Report of the United Nations Seminar on Traditional Practices Affecting the Health of Women and Children, supra* note 176.

197. *Report of the Second United Nations Regional Seminar on Traditional Practices Affecting the Health of Women and Children,* Sub-Commission on Prevention of Discrimination and Protection of Minorities, Commission on Human Rights, U.N. ESCOR, 46th Sess. U.N. Doc. E/CN.4/Sub.2/1994/10 (1994).

198. *Plan of Action for the Elimination of Harmful Traditional Practices Affecting the Health of Women and Children,* Sub-Commission on Prevention of Discrimination and Protection of Minorities, Commission on Human Rights, U.N. ESCOR, 46th Sess. U.N. Doc E/CN.4/Sub.2/1994/10/Add.1 (1994).

against women to report, over a three-year period, to the Commission annually.[199] This Special Rapporteur, Ms. Radhika Coomaraswamy, has clearly included traditional practices affecting the health of women and children, including FGS, as a part of the global problem of violence against women. In a recent report to the Commission, she states that, while "not all customs and traditions are unprotective of women's rights . . . those practices that constitute definite forms of violence against women cannot be overlooked nor justified on grounds of tradition, culture or social conformity."[200] She cites to several of the major international human rights instruments that have defined the rights of women as human rights that governments must protect even in the face of custom and culture, including the Convention on the Elimination of All Forms of Discrimination Against Women, the Convention on the Rights of the Child, and the Declaration on the Elimination of Violence Against Women. The Special Rapporteur's section on FGM reports on the continuing global efforts to combat FGM by U.N.-related agencies, governments, NGOs, and activists. The report indicates that there is still a lot of work to be done before the surgeries will cease everywhere in the world. The fact that activity by dedicated and courageous individuals (in particular those women who themselves have had the surgeries and struggle so that no other women or girl will be altered) and monitoring of the issue by the international community continues are hopeful signs.

CONCLUSION

Not all agree that FGS should be debated in terms of a violation of human rights. Breitung argues that the Special Working Group on Traditional Practices established by the U.N. Sub-Commission for the Prevention of Discrimination and the Protection of Minorities has provided the best method of combating FGS by applying "a balancing process weighing the procedure's health consequences against its cultural function."[201] Obiora argues, among other things, that FGS "does not easily fall within the traditional definition of gender-specific human rights violation, nor does it seem completely analogous to violent coercion of women by men."[202] She also questions the practice among commentators of treating all forms of female genital surgeries alike, of referring to all methods uniformly as mutilations, and for calling for the eradication or criminalization of even the milder forms, when evidence has either not substantiated that the less invasive forms are harmful or has not proven that they outweigh their social value.[203]

Others argue that FGS are a violation of human rights and advocate the use of various international human rights instruments in the fight for eradication of FGS.[204]

199. *Report of the Special Rapporteur—1996, supra* note 111, at 3. Her three-year tenure has been extended another three-years.

200. *Id.* at 27.

201. Breitung, *supra* note 8, at 689–90.

202. Obiora, *supra* note 15, at p. 5 Westlaw.

203. Obiora, *id.* at p. 6 Westlaw.

204. Joan Fitzpatrick, *The Use of International Human Rights Norms to Combat Violence Against*

Fitzpatrick states that FGS "bears a powerful but complex relation to the principle of equality. The development and persistence of the practice of female genital mutilation seems deeply linked to the denigration of women as inferior beings and to a desire to subordinate women, especially to control their sexuality."[205] This would indicate a belief that even milder or less intrusive forms of the practice, if based on patriarchal notions of inferiority and control, should be prohibited by international human rights law.[206]

FGS have been practiced with varying degrees of severity for centuries in both First and Third World cultures. All cultures can work together and separately to combat the particularly harsh and invasive forms of the practice, particularly when performed on the girl-child or forced upon a woman without her informed consent. We must question and redefine notions of what makes a girl into a woman, not only in order to address FGS but also to address a range of cultural practices from bride-burning to cosmetic surgery. If this standard or rite of passage is based upon submission to discriminatory or harmful practices, then these—like all such standards, regardless of their cultural origins—must be rejected or modified in favor of practices that enrich the culture without degrading or harming persons within the society.

Women, in HUMAN RIGHTS OF WOMEN 540–43 (Rebecca Cook ed., 1994); Dimauro, *supra* note 40, at 341–44; Annas, *supra* note 3, at 347–51.

205. Fitzpatrick, *supra* note 204, at 541.

206. *See also* Isabelle R. Gunning, *Uneasy Alliances and Solid Sisterhood: A Response to Professor Obiora's Bridges and Barricades*, 47 CASE W. RES. L. REV. 445 (Winter 1997). This article appears in a colloquium edition of the Case Western Law Review entitled "Colloquium: Bridging Society, Culture and Law: The Issue of Female Circumcision." Most of the articles in this issue address some aspect of FGS.

WOMEN AND PROSTITUTION

Ann Lucas

INTRODUCTION

Speaking broadly, two sets of human rights issues arise in relation to women and prostitution: the right of women not to be forced to become prostitutes, and the right of women who *are* prostitutes (whether by choice[1] or force) to have their rights as human beings respected. These issues arise in all three kinds of legal regimes governing prostitution: *criminalization* (prostitution is legally prohibited, and violators are subject to criminal sanctions), *regulation* (some forms of prostitution are legal, subject to specific regulations governing matters such as solicitation and hygiene, and requiring, for example, licensing, registration, special taxation, health inspections, and fingerprinting; rule violations are subject to either civil or criminal penalties), and *decriminalization* (prostitution is considered a legitimate enterprise and subject only to generally applicable civil and criminal laws such as those prohibiting fraud and extortion, and to generally applicable business and professional regulations governing matters such as advertising, occupational safety and health, working conditions, social benefits, and taxation).

Regardless of the legal regime in effect, both the right not to be forced into prostitution and the right of prostitutes to have their human rights protected are equally central to a full and fair consideration of appropriate prostitution policy. In other words, the analyst must recognize that prostitutes can be both victims and agents,[2] and the human rights implications of each status. This chapter will discuss each of these issues in turn, and then consider whether advocating human rights for prostitutes implies advocating that women have the right to *be* prostitutes.[3] The chapter will conclude with some tentative proposals for reform.

---

1. The highly contentious issue of whether any prostitution is truly "voluntary" is discussed *infra*.

2. *Cf.* Christine Overall, *What's Wrong with Prostitution? Evaluating Sex Work,* 17 SIGNS: JOURNAL OF WOMEN IN CULTURE AND SOCIETY 705, 707 (1992) (discussing the split in feminist theories of sexuality between an emphasis on pleasure, freedom and women's agency and an emphasis on danger, degradation and the victimization of women); Carole S. Vance, *More Danger, More Pleasure: A Decade After the Barnard Sexuality Conference, in* PLEASURE AND DANGER: EXPLORING FEMALE SEXUALITY xvi, xvi (Carole S. Vance ed., 1992) (1984) (arguing that "women's relationships to sexuality will be diverse, not singular, and that any feminist program that requires uniformity in women's responses will be dishonest and oppressive" (hereinafter Pleasure and Danger)); Carole S. Vance, *Pleasure and Danger: Toward a Politics of Sexuality,* in Pleasure and Danger at 1 (expanding on same argument).

3. There are also male prostitutes, of course. Indeed, the fact of male prostitution is important to remember, especially in thinking about the role prostitution plays in enforcing women's subordination

Preliminarily, however, the matter of terminology should be addressed, which will also serve to introduce the controversies that commonly arise in treatments of prostitution. Some scholars and prostitutes' rights groups eschew the term "prostitute" because of its negative connotations: one common meaning of "to prostitute" is, of course, "to devote to corrupt or unworthy purposes (debase)."[4] Even in reference to the exchange of sexual services for money, the term "to prostitute" often implies the "indiscriminate" sale of sex,[5] an implication that many prostitutes and scholars claim is at odds with reality and ignores the possibility of prostitutes' autonomy and control in their work. Thus, many participants in this debate prefer the term "sex worker" to "prostitute," because the former avoids any necessary insinuation of debasement and at the same time emphasizes that, for its practitioners, prostitution is *work*, not simply (or not at all) degenerate sex.[6] In addition, the term "sex work" emphasizes prostitutes' connection with other workers in the sex industry, such as exotic dancers, adult-film actors, nude models, dominatrixes, sexual surrogates, etc.[7] Others wishing to focus on the problems and conditions unique to prostitution, but finding the term "prostitute" too prosaic, prefer the term "whore." Usually, this is an avowedly political decision to reclaim a term of derision and transform it into a term of pride.[8] In another camp are those who find the term "prostitution" too meek and mundane and prefer the phrase "sexual

---

and/or its potential as a site of resistance to gender-based subordination. However, the discussion here is confined to women.

4.   WEBSTER'S NINTH NEW COLLEGIATE DICTIONARY 946 (1985).

5.   *See, e.g., id.*

6.   *See* SHANNON BELL, READING, WRITING & REWRITING THE PROSTITUTE BODY 108 (quoting Veronica Vera); LAURIE SHRAGE, MORAL DILEMMAS OF FEMINISM: PROSTITUTION, ADULTERY, AND ABORTION 121–22 (1994); Lillian S. Robinson, *Subject/Position, in* "BAD GIRLS"/"GOOD GIRLS": WOMEN, SEX AND POWER IN THE NINETIES 177, 184 (Nan Bauer Maglin & Donna Perry eds., 1996).

7.   *See, e.g.,* SEX WORK: WRITINGS BY WOMEN IN THE SEX INDUSTRY (Frédérique Delacoste & Priscilla Alexander eds., 1987) [hereinafter SEX WORK] (emphasizing prostitution but containing pieces written by women from all arenas of the sex trade).

Some scholars even include surrogate mothering under the "sex work" label. *See, e.g.,* Heidi Tinsman, *Behind the Sexual Division of Labor: Connecting Sex to Capitalist Production,* 17 YALE J. INT'L L. 241, 241 (1992). This move is theoretically interesting and provocative on many levels, and may call into question the accepted view of prostitution. However, by expanding the category so radically, this move might also render the label, and its underlying quest for increased legitimacy for sex industry workers, meaningless.

8.   *See, e.g.,* Margo St. James, *The Reclamation of Whores, in* GOOD GIRLS/BAD GIRLS: FEMINISTS AND SEX TRADE WORKERS FACE TO FACE 81, 82 (Laurie Bell ed., 1987) [hereinafter GOOD/BAD]; NICKIE ROBERTS, WHORES IN HISTORY: PROSTITUTION IN WESTERN SOCIETY ix (1992); BELL, *supra* note 6, at 107–109; Gail Pheterson, *Not Repeating History, in* A VINDICATION OF THE RIGHTS OF WHORES 3, 4 (Gail Pheterson ed., 1989) [hereinafter VINDICATION]; Joan Nestle, *Lesbians and Prostitutes: A Historical Sisterhood, in* SEX WORK, *supra* note 7, at 231, 232; Marjan Sax, *The Pink Thread, in* SEX WORK, *supra* note 7, at 301, 301; International Committee for Prostitutes' Rights, *Draft Statements from the 2nd World Whores' Congress (1986), in* SEX WORK, *supra* note 7, at 307, 313.

The terms "sex worker" and "whore" are not, of course, diametrical opposites. Thus, it is not uncommon to see these overlapping terms used strategically in the same argument to emphasize different aspects of prostitution, or even used as approximate synonyms.

slavery.''[9] For these individuals, prostitution is never a freely chosen vocation; it is an institution and practice founded in male dominance which always leaves emotional and physical scars on its practitioners.[10] Thus, they use the term ''sexual slavery'' to emphasize the harms of prostitution and the elements of force that induce women to enter the trade.

This chapter uses the term ''prostitute,'' despite its limitations, because the alternatives appear even less satisfactory for a variety of reasons. As used here, ''prostitute'' refers to a person who provides sexual services for a fee, and ''prostitution'' refers to this practice/institution of commercial sex.[11] Although ''sex work'' has more positive (or at least neutral) connotations than does ''prostitute,'' the term is both over- and under-inclusive in regard to prostitution itself. ''Sex work'' is over-inclusive in the manner described above: the label includes those who perform for audiences rather than sell sexual services to other individuals (e.g., strippers and exotic dancers), those who have no contact with those who purchase the product of their labor (actors and models), and those who provide sexual services exclusively in a therapeutic setting (sexual surrogates). The label is under-inclusive in the sense that it is commonly used to refer to, and/or used by, upper- and middle-class workers in the sex industry, not to those coerced by force or by lack of alternatives into selling sex. As such, the term ''sex worker'' generally connotes an individual who has a certain degree of personal safety and security in her work, who made a conscious and relatively voluntary choice to enter this line of work, and who has a meaningful amount of choice as to where she will work, with whom she will work,

---

9.   *See, e.g.,* KATHLEEN BARRY, FEMALE SEXUAL SLAVERY (1979). Barry argues that ''[f]emale sexual slavery is present in ALL situations where women or girls cannot change the immediate conditions of their existence; where regardless of how they got into those conditions they cannot get out; and where they are subject to sexual violence and exploitation.'' *Id.* at 33. While this definition seems to allow for the coexistence of voluntary prostitution with forced prostitution, at other points in her work Barry disavows this possibility, arguing that slavery is *the* defining paradigm for prostitution world-wide. *See, e.g., id.* at 100–02, 114–17. In reference to WHISPER (Women Hurt in Systems of Prostitution Engaged in Revolt), an organization Barry supports, Barry has stated that ''by refusing to make a distinction between forced and voluntary prostitution . . . we refuse to recognize prostitution as a profession. . . . [We] recognize[] *all* commodification of women's bodies for sexual exchange as violations of human dignity and therefore of human rights.'' Kathleen Barry, *UNESCO Report Studies Prostitution,* WHIS-PER NEWSLETTER 1 (1986–87), *cited in* BELL, *supra* note 6, at 125 (emphasis added).

10.   *See, e.g.,* BARRY, *supra* note 9; Sarah Wynter, *Whisper: Women Hurt in Systems of Prostitution Engaged in Revolt, in* SEX WORK, *supra* note 7, at 266; ANDREA DWORKIN, INTERCOURSE 143 (1987).

11.   *See* Laurie Shrage, *Should Feminists Oppose Prostitution?,* 99 ETHICS 347, 348 (1989) (using these terms in a similar way). In her later work, Shrage sometimes avoids using ''prostitute'' and ''prostitution'' as descriptive terms, because ''to continue to use the term 'prostitution,' especially in reference to contemporary practices and institutions, involves a problematic ethnographic choice between competing representations of a particular activity.'' SHRAGE, *supra* note 6, at 121. As terms that are more neutral or connote both the business/trade aspect of prostitution and its proscribed/taboo behavior she uses ''sex lending,'' ''sex trafficking,'' and ''sex sharking.'' *Id.* at 123. While this author agrees with Shrage's motives for seeking alternatives to the standard term, her terminology remains problematic: ''sex lending'' risks de-emphasizing the commercial nature of prostitution, ''sex trafficking'' is likely to be confusing in a discussion such as this that distinguishes forced prostitution from voluntary prostitution, and ''sex sharking'' seems just as pejorative as ''prostitution.''

and what she will and will not do. This description fits many prostitutes—indeed, it fits the majority of them in certain countries—but it distorts the conditions under which many other prostitutes live and work. Indeed, if "sex work" is used to describe forced as well as voluntary prostitution, it can mask the truly slave-like conditions under which some women "work." For these reasons, this chapter does not use the term "sex work," despite its advantages.

Similarly, although the decision by some prostitutes to attempt to turn the term "whore" into one that demands respect is admirable, the word remains a charged one which, when used by outsiders, often connotes contempt rather than respect.[12] Finally, this chapter rejects the term "sexual slave" because it is based on a biased and often shallow view of the realities of prostitution. While it is undeniable that some prostitutes are literally enslaved, many others are not. Referring to all prostitutes as sexual slaves does injustice both to those who are not enslaved—by ignoring their realities, denying their ability to make rational choices, and, ultimately, denying their autonomy and humanity—and to those who *are* enslaved—by lumping their very dire and cruel circumstances with those of others who have much more control over their present circumstances and can enter and exit prostitution much more easily.[13]

FORCED AND CHILD PROSTITUTION[14]

Although nearly everyone agrees that forced prostitution is wrong, it remains a serious problem worldwide. To understand why this is so, one must consider global and regional economics and systems of exploitation. The most immediate culprit behind forced prostitution is the profit motive: significant amounts of money can be made procuring women and girls for prostitution, and in some cases the magnitude of profit available combined with disrespect for or denial of women's humanity creates the situation where women and girls are "procured" for prostitution by force and coercion.

---

12. *See, e.g., infra* text accompanying note 92.

13. An analogy may help clarify the distinction made here between "sex slaves" and prostitutes. Although farm workers in the United States often labor in appallingly harsh conditions, *see generally* DICK MEISTER & ANNE LOFTIS, A LONG TIME COMING: THE STRUGGLE TO UNIONIZE AMERICA'S FARM WORKERS (1977); TONY DUNBAR & LINDA KRAVITZ, HARD TRAVELING: MIGRANT FARM WORKERS IN AMERICA (1976), it would be wrong to suggest that their life circumstances are identical to those of African slaves in the plantations of the antebellum American South. Although the working and living conditions are in many ways similar, at the same time they are not identical. However terrible the working conditions of a modern-day farm worker or voluntary prostitute, the psychic toll of slavery and the minimal and risky opportunities for change (i.e., escape, rebellion, suicide) make enslavement a worse fate and justify the use of different terminology for these different conditions. *See also infra* note 174 and accompanying text. *Cf.* CLEO ODZER, PATPONG SISTERS: AN AMERICAN WOMAN'S VIEW OF THE BANGKOK SEX WORLD 96 (1994).

14. The subjects of forced prostitution and trafficking in women, sexual slavery, and child prostitution are treated in more detail in other chapters of this work. For that reason, this discussion simply provides an overview of these issues.

Scholars and rule-making bodies generally consider the issue of *child prostitution* under the rubric of forced prostitution, even when minors are not literally forced into becoming prostitutes. Child prostitution receives this treatment for good reason: regardless of what one thinks about the commodification of adult sexuality, most people agree that children's self-development (including the eventual development of healthy attitudes toward sex) requires protective measures. The reasons for this position are probably obvious, and can be summarized as follows: (1) children should not be forced through violence, coercion or circumstance to work—childhood should be protected as a time for growth, learning, socialization, play, maturation, etc., and these processes are halted or corrupted by child labor; (2) the sexual exploitation of children (whether in incest, pornography, prostitution, or any other way) often causes irreversible damage to the child and the adult she/he later becomes and violates children's human rights; and (3) the *combination* in juvenile prostitution of these malignant influences—child labor and sexual exploitation—generally has even worse consequences for childhood development.[15] Whether a child is literally forced into prostitution or turns to prostitution out of desperation or lack of information is irrelevant—both eventualities are intolerable. As a Nepali girl working in prostitution in India said about her situation, "Yes, I was poor. Yes, I wanted to come to Bombay. *But I was 9*. My father didn't tell me what I was getting into when he sent me off with the sirdar [gang leader]."[16] Thus, this chapter treats child prostitution under the rubric of forced prostitution and considers it an institution we must try seriously to eliminate.[17]

---

15. *See* KATHLEEN M. KURZ & CYNTHIA J. PRATHER, IMPROVING THE QUALITY OF LIFE OF GIRLS 25 (1995); Jon Henley, *World States Tackle Spiralling Child Sex Abuse,* THE GUARDIAN (London), Aug. 28, 1996, *available in* LEXIS, News Library, Majpap File; Marlise Simons, *The Littlest Prostitutes,* N.Y. TIMES, Jan 16, 1994, *available in* LEXIS, News Library, Majpap File.

16. *Children for Sale,* ASIAWEEK, Mar. 1, 1996, at 38 (italics added). *See also* Sudarsan Raghavan, *Growing Plague Grips Africa-Child Sex,* S.F. CHRONICLE, Aug. 31, 1996, at A1, A15 (discussing the "'survival sex' trade" in Africa).

17. Child prostitution occurs in Asia, the Americas, Africa, and Europe and, as such, is clearly a global problem. GERALDINE VAN BUEREN, THE INTERNATIONAL LAW ON THE RIGHTS OF THE CHILD 276 (1995) (citing UN Doc. E/CN.4/Sub.2/112/SR.7); Kevin Costelloe, *Global Talks on Halting Sex Exploitation of Children,* S.F. CHRONICLE, Aug. 28, 1996, at A10 (quoting executive director of UNICEF).

Reliable statistics of children involved in prostitution are difficult to obtain. UNICEF has estimated that one million children a year are commercially sexually exploited (referring to forced prostitution, sale of children for sexual purposes, and use of children in pornography). *Id.*; *Raghavan, supra* note 16, at A15. At the same time, social workers and government officials have estimated that more than a million children under age 17 are prostitutes in Asia, Nicholas D. Kristof, *Asian Childhoods Sacrificed to Prosperity's Lust,* N.Y. TIMES, Apr. 14, 1996, at A1, A8 (characterizing estimates as "wild guesses").

Christian Aid, a U.K. charity, and others estimate that there are 200,000 child prostitutes in Thailand, Patrick Quilligan, *International Community Acts to Combat Child Sex Exploitation Through Tough Legislation,* THE IRISH TIMES (Dublin), June 1, 1995, *available in* LEXIS, News Library, Majpap File; *Million Children in Sex Slavery,* THE HERALD (Glasgow, Scotland), June 14, 1994, *available in* LEXIS, News Library, Majpap File; *Asia's Sex Trade,* SACRAMENTO BEE, July 16, 1994, *available in* LEXIS, News Library, Majpap File; Henley, *supra* note 15, while UNESCO, the Children's Rights Protection Center, World Watch and others put that estimate at 800,000. Susan Jeanne Toepfer & Bryan Stuart Wells, *The Worldwide Market for Sex: A Review of International and Regional Legal Prohibitions*

   The issue of forced prostitution is both illuminated and complicated by a consideration of the larger social and economic context in which it occurs. Appreciating this backdrop improves our comprehension of the dynamics of forced prostitution—its scope and magnitude, the reasons it occurs, the identities of those who comprise the "supply" and create the demand, and the probable efficacy of proposed legal reforms—enabling us to think more intelligently about strategies to eliminate it. At the same time, understanding this context can also create despair and produce muddled thinking. That is, once it is recognized that extreme poverty and unequal distribution of resources, cultural devaluation of girls and women, greed, corruption, and an entrenched sex tourism industry are each centrally implicated in the continuing problem of forced prostitution, solutions can seem out of reach. In addition, appreciating the factors that create the conditions under which forced prostitution occurs can lead to the conclusion that all women's choices are constrained due to their social, legal, and economic inequality and thus that all prostitution is in some sense forced.

   On the surface this latter view may seem legitimate. Yet despite the constraints all women face, there is a *phenomenological* difference between being physically forced into prostitution and being "coerced by circumstance." A lack of welfare programs, free medical care, shelters, and the like may create a desperate need in poor people for money, which may result in a turn to prostitution as the most lucrative undertaking (especially for women). Or it may not: not all poor people or

---

Regarding Trafficking in Women, 2 MICH. J. GENDER & L. 83, 88 (1994); ODZER, *supra* note 13, at 2; *Saving Lost Childhoods,* CHRISTIAN SCIENCE MONITOR, Aug. 1, 1994, *available in* LEXIS, News Library, Majpap File; Michael S. Serrill, *Defiling the Children,* TIME (U.S. ed.), June 21, 1993, *available in* LEXIS, News Library, Mags File.

   Estimates of child prostitutes in India range from 100,000 to 500,000, the majority of them Nepali. Donna Bryson, *Child Sex Trade Thrives Despite Nations' Many Laws, Promises,* L.A. TIMES, Apr. 13, 1997, *available in* LEXIS, News Library, Majpap File (100,000 children); Glenda Cooper, *Men Turn to Children for Fear of AIDS,* THE INDEPENDENT (London), Aug. 21, 1996, *available in* LEXIS, News Library, Majpap File (100,000 Nepali girls); Quilligan, *supra* (200,000 Nepali girls); Tim McGirk, *Nepal's Lost Daughters, "India's Soiled Goods,"* TIME (Int'l Ed.), Jan. 27, 1997, *available in* LEXIS, News Library, Mags File [hereinafter McGirk, *Soiled*] (same); *Children for Sale, supra* note 16 (250,000 children); Tim McGirk, *Their Latest Holiday Destination,* THE INDEPENDENT (London), *available in* LEXIS, News Library, Majpap File [hereinafter McGirk, *Holiday*] (same); Rahul Bedi, *Fears Over Growth in Child Sex Tourism,* SOUTH CHINA MORNING POST (Hong Kong), Nov. 8, 1996, *available in* LEXIS, News Library, Majpap File (400,000 children); *Saving Lost Childhoods, supra* (same); Serrill, *supra* (same); *Million Children in Sex Slavery, supra* (400,000–500,000 children); Henley, *supra* note 15 (500,000 children).

   In the Philippines, child prostitutes were estimated at 20,000 in 1986, KURZ & PRATHER, *supra* note 15, at 26, and at 60,000 to 100,000 more recently, Quilligan, *supra* (60,000); *Saving Lost Childhoods, supra* (same); Serrill, *supra* (same); *Asia's Sex Trade, supra* (100,000). Brazil may have 250,000 to 500,000 child prostitutes, *Saving Lost Childhoods, supra;* estimates for China are similar, *Million Children in Sex Slavery, supra.*The U.S. is estimated to have 90,000 to 300,000 child prostitutes. Serrill, *supra.*

   Child prostitution in Africa differs from that in Asia, in that child prostitution is much less organized and is not controlled by crime syndicate leaders. Raghavan, *supra* note 16, at A15. However, the problem of child prostitution in Africa appears to be growing rapidly, probably because of the lack of legal prohibitions and law enforcement resources to curtail it. *Id.*

even poor women engage in prostitution, nor are poor women the only ones who enter prostitution. Thus, there is some modicum of choice involved in "coercion by circumstance" that is absent from truly forced prostitution.[18] Therefore, the problem with the conclusion that all prostitution is forced is less philosophical than practical: this conclusion leads to a loss of focus on those women and girls who are genuinely enslaved. In doing so it leads to solutions that, by virtue of the breadth they attempt, are not tailored to the specific issue of forced prostitution and create as many problems as they solve, doing little to eradicate forced prostitution in the short term. For these reasons, one must approach the global context of forced prostitution with some caution. A full understanding of the forces which have created this institution is essential, but so is retaining the focus on *unequivocally* forced prostitution rather than creating an ever-expanding definition of the problem.

Forced prostitution is often part-and-parcel of sex tourism; the magnitude of the problem is greatest in areas which are well-known as sex-tourism destinations.[19] For example, Nepali girls and women are trafficked in large numbers to brothels in India;[20] Burmese girls and women are trafficked to Thailand;[21] and Bangladeshi girls and women are trafficked to brothels in Pakistan and India.[22] For newly developed and developing countries, tourism/sex tourism can be extremely lucrative. Thailand provides an illustration: in 1986 it earned $1.5 billion from tourism, more foreign currency than it earned from any other industry, including rice export.[23] Tourism remains Thailand's primary draw for foreign currency, and is now estimated to earn $3 to $4.5 billion yearly, with sex tourism a major contributor to that total; the Thai tourism industry employs anywhere from 800,000 to 2,000,000 people.[24] Indeed, the connection between Thailand and tourism, especially sex tourism, is so strong that Thailand has been referred to as a "sex industry country"

---

18.   *Cf.* Chamlong Boonsong, *Ordeals of Hilltribe Girl Prostitutes,* THE NATION (Bangkok), Jan. 23, 1985, at 5, *cited in* ODZER, *supra* note 13, at 225 (reporting that 15 girls "rescued" from prostitution in Bangkok returned to the city and prostitution shortly thereafter, finding life in their home villages too harsh).

19.   Historically, military forces and policies were directly involved in the development of both sex tourism and forced prostitution. For discussions on the role of the military and forced prostitution during wartime, see, for example, TRUE STORIES OF THE KOREAN COMFORT WOMEN (Keith Howard ed. & Young Joo Lee trans., Cassell 1995) (1993); SAUNDRA POLLOCK STURDEVANT AND BRENDA STOLTZFUS, LET THE GOOD TIMES ROLL: PROSTITUTION AND THE U.S. MILITARY IN ASIA (1993); CYNTHIA ENLOE, BANANAS, BEACHES AND BASES: MAKING FEMINIST SENSE OF INTERNATIONAL POLITICS (1989); Nora V. Demleitner, *Forced Prostitution: Naming an International Offense,* 18 FORDHAM INT'L L.J. 163, 180–85 (1994). On forced prostitution during the war in Bosnia, *see, e.g.,* Roy Gutman, *Victims Recount Nights of Terror at Makeshift Bordello,* NEWSDAY, Aug. 23, 1992, at 37, *cited in* Toepfer & Wells, *supra* note 17, at 85 n.7; Catharine A. MacKinnon, *Turning Rape into Pornography: Postmodern Genocide,* Ms. MAGAZINE, Jul./Aug. 1993, at 24, 27, *cited in* Toepfer & Wells, *supra* note 17, at 86 n.10.

20.   HUMAN RIGHTS WATCH, THE HUMAN RIGHTS WATCH GLOBAL REPORT ON WOMEN'S HUMAN RIGHTS 230 (1995).

21.   *Id.* at 205.

22.   *Id.* at 197.

23.   ENLOE, *supra* note 19, at 37.

24.   HUMAN RIGHTS WATCH, *supra* note 20, at 207; Robinson, *supra* note 6, at 182; Paul Donovan,

rather than a "newly industrializing country."[25] Similarly, in the mid-1980s Philippines, 85% of tourists were men, and tourism—especially sex tourism—became essential to the survival of the Marcos regime.[26] Sex tourism and prostitution are also highly lucrative in India; a journalist has estimated that the red-light district in Bombay alone produces $400 million a year in revenue.[27] Finally, it is estimated that 70 to 80 percent of Japanese, American, Australian, and western European male tourists travel to Asia for purposes of sexual recreation,[28] supporting the claim that "[t]ourism-oriented prostitution has become an integral part of the economic base in several regions of South-east Asia."[29]

Sex tourism itself is of course not the same as forced prostitution; along with girls and women who have been kidnapped, coerced, and tricked into prostitution are women who entered the trade knowingly and purposefully. Nor is forced prostitution limited to sex-tourism destinations; it is, rather, a global problem. Nonetheless, the existence of sex tourism increases the incentive for traffickers to force females into prostitution, because it increases the demand for and the profits to be gained from prostitution.[30] Moreover, because sex tourism is so lucrative for cash-poor countries, officials tend to overlook violations of local law such as licensing requirements, age restrictions, and health standards. In a pre-existing climate of lax law enforcement and/or corruption, it becomes much easier for traffickers to violate laws against forced prostitution as well. More often than not, officials are complicit in prostitution trafficking, accepting bribes from procurers to look the other way or providing, for a fee, safe passage to a given destination and/or protection from arrest.[31] In fact, lack of legal sanctions or lax law enforcement appear to exert direct

---

Tourism: On Someone Else's Land, THE GUARDIAN (London), July 11, 1995, *available in* LEXIS, News Library, Majpap File; Quilligan, *supra* note 17.

25. Ann Usher, *The Dangerous Truth of "Foreign Bodies,"* THE NATION (Bangkok), Aug. 19, 1988, at 31, *cited in* ODZER, *supra* note 13, at 9. Indeed, one observer has claimed that "15 to 25 per cent of all Thai women between the ages of 15–30 are prostitutes." See also Mayuree Rattanawannatip, *Prostitution Plays on Rural Ignorance,* THE NATION (Bangkok), Feb. 18, 1988, at 16, *cited in* ODZER, *supra* note 13, at 9.

26. ENLOE, *supra* note 19, at 38. *See also* Martha O'Campo, *Pornography and Prostitution in the Philippines, in* GOOD/BAD, *supra* note 8, at 67, 70–73.

27. Robert I. Friedman, *India's Shame: Sexual Slavery and Political Corruption are Leading to an AIDS Catastrophe,* THE NATION (U.S.), Apr. 8, 1996, at 11, 19.

28. C. Michael Hall, *Sex Tourism in South-east Asia, in* TOURISM AND THE LESS DEVELOPED COUNTRIES 64, 64 (David Harrison ed., 1992), *cited in* Barbara Sullivan, Global Prostitution: Sex Tourism and Trafficking in Women 3 (July 1996) (paper presented at the Annual Meeting of the Law and Society Association, University of Strathclyde, Glasgow, Scotland, July 11–13, 1996) (on file with author).

29. Hall, *supra* note 28, at 74.

30. *See, e.g.,* HUMAN RIGHTS WATCH, *supra* note 20, at 197, 206; Lillian S. Robinson, *In the Penile Colony: Touring Thailand's Sex Industry,* THE NATION (U.S.), *available in* LEXIS, News Library, Mags File. In fact, U.N. rapporteur Jean Ferant has argued that trafficking in women (including forced marriage as well as forced prostitution) is more profitable even than drugs and arms smuggling. CAROLYN SLEIGHTHOLME & INDRANI SINHA, GUILTY WITHOUT TRIAL: WOMEN IN THE SEX TRADE IN CALCUTTA 49 (1996).

31. *See, e.g.,* HUMAN RIGHTS WATCH, *supra* note 20, at 209–10, 215–18 (Thailand); *id.* at 231–32, 244–45 (India); *id.* at 263 (Pakistan); *id.* at 196 (generally); Friedman, *supra* note 27, at 12 (India).

influence over international sex tourism patterns. Where Thailand, the Philippines, and Cambodia were once the primary destinations of choice for sex tourism, observers have recently noted a clear shift to India—particularly for sex tourists seeking children—where there are fewer legal prohibitions, less public outcry, and less law enforcement action against prostitution-related abuses.[32]

Sex tourism flourishes especially in areas in which other profitable undertakings are few, and in places in which law enforcement is desultory or corruption is common. It also flourishes by trading on stereotypical (and patriarchal) images of subservient women and "exotic" sexual practices. As Cynthia Enloe observes, "men from affluent societies . . . imagine certain women, usually women of color, to be more available and submissive than the women in their own countries,"[33] and advertisements capitalize on this idea.[34] However, that sex tourism is associated with the rise in forced prostitution is not to say that the primary exploiters of girls and women held captive in brothels are foreign men. The majority of customers seen by women in sex-tourism areas are locals, not foreigners.[35] Indeed, local men also often have stereotyped ideas about foreign women's passivity and/or sexual allure, creating a demand in local brothels for foreign women who are often imported by force.[36] Moreover, in both sending and receiving countries, procurers,

---

Even U.N. peacekeepers have been involved in forced and child prostitution. *See* Raghavan, *supra* note 16, at A15 (discussing trafficking, sexual exploitation, and sexual abuse of children by peacekeepers in Mozambique, Somalia, Rwanda, and West Africa).

32.   McGirk, *Holiday, supra* note 17; Bedi, *supra* note 17; *Children for Sale, supra* note 16; *Child Sex Tourism Under Pressure,* THE DOMINION (Wellington, NZ), Aug. 20, 1996, *available in* LEXIS, News Library, Majpap File. It also appears to be the case that prices are lower in India than in other sex-tourism areas, perhaps because the supply of prostitutes is so high. Bedi, *supra* note 17; *Children for Sale, supra* note 16.

33.   ENLOE, *supra* note 19, at 36.

34.   *Id.* at 37 (quoting West German travel brochure as stating: "Thailand is a world full of extremes and the possibilities are unlimited. Anything goes in this exotic country, especially when it comes to girls. [The traveler] can indulge in unknown pleasures [by] book[ing] a trip to Thailand with exotic pleasures included in the price"). *See also id.* at 38 (discussing the Marcos regime's use of "the reputed beauty and generosity of Filipino women as 'natural resources' to compete in the international tourism market"); Robinson, *supra* note 30 (noting Swiss tour operator's depiction of Thai women as "slim, sun-burnt and sweet . . . masters of the art of making love by nature," Dutch agency's reference to prostitutes as "little slaves who give real Thai warmth," and another brochure claiming that "Thai girls 'love the white man in an erotic and devoted way'").

35.   *See, e.g.,* HUMAN RIGHTS WATCH, *supra* note 20, at 233 n.70 (majority of customers of Nepali prostitutes in Indian brothels are Indian); *id.* at 207 (approximately 75 percent of Thai men have had sex with prostitutes); *id.* at 197 (in general, "local demand for prostitutes or wives is at least as important as tourism, if not more so" in promoting trafficking); Hnin Hnin Pyne, *AIDS and Gender Violence: The Enslavement of Burmese Women in the Thai Sex Industry, in* WOMEN'S RIGHTS, HUMAN RIGHTS: INTERNATIONAL FEMINIST PERSPECTIVES 215, 216, 219 (Julie Peters & Andrea Wolper eds., 1995) (clients of Burmese prostitutes enslaved in Thailand were mainly Thai, Chinese and Burmese); Aphaluck Bhatiasevi, *Thailand 'Fills Central Role on Sex Markets,'* BANGKOK POST, Sept. 2, 1995, at 6 (reporting that 4.6 million Thai men regularly patronize prostitutes, along with 500,000 foreign men); Bryson, *supra* note 17 (discussing customers of child prostitutes); Phil Pennington, *Breaking the International Trade in Innocents,* THE EVENING POST (Wellington, NZ), Oct. 1, 1996, *available in* LEXIS, News Library, Majpap File (same).

36.   *See, e.g.,* Bhatiasevi, *supra* note 35, at 6 (reporting that women from southern China, Burma,

agents, middlemen, police, and local government officials profit from the trafficking of females. Often implicated as well are families, neighbors, acquaintances, and innkeepers in the sending countries, and pimps, madams, brothel and bar owners, health inspectors, and vendors in receiving countries. Thus, while it is true that foreign tourists participate in the exploitation of captive prostitutes, it should not be imagined that eliminating international sex tourism would solve the problem of forced prostitution.

Sex tourism and its associated profits are only one factor contributing to the problem of forced prostitution. Equally important is the poverty and unemployment found in the sending regions. These conditions are often exacerbated by national and international lending practices which favor large and/or urban development projects over local, small-scale, and rural/agricultural projects which could enable families to support themselves without sending members to cities or resorts to find work that pays a living wage.[37] Extreme poverty enables traffickers to entice girls and women away from their homes with the promise of a good marriage or a well-paying job in a big city and deliver them instead to brothel slavery, or to persuade relatives to sell females into prostitution.[38] In many areas, traffickers time their visits to villages to coincide with periods of especially pronounced poverty, e.g., in the few months preceding harvests, when families and individuals are most vulnerable.[39]

In a context of severe poverty, and one in which women are valued only for their contribution to the family (if they are valued at all), families can rationalize the sacrifice of a daughter, niece, or sister to prostitution with the belief that it is the only way she can fulfill her duty to support her family,[40] and perhaps also with

---

Yugoslavia, and Latin America are trafficked to Thailand for prostitution); Pyne, *supra* note 35, at 217 (noting Thai men's preference for light-skinned females, such as women belonging to certain hill tribes); HUMAN RIGHTS WATCH, *supra* note 20, at 232–33 & n.70 (reporting that both local and foreign patrons of Indian brothels "seek out Nepali prostitutes for their 'golden' skin and their reputation for sexual compliance," but that most customers are Indian).

37. *See, e.g.,* Raghavan, *supra* note 16, at A15 (discussing role of World Bank "austerity measures" in cutting social welfare payments and increasing unemployment in Zambia, where children have turned to prostitution to help support their families); Robinson, *supra* note 6, at 180 (discussing role of World Bank and International Monetary Fund policies and national economic planning in contributing to child prostitution); Robinson, *supra* note 30 (same).

38. *See, e.g.,* HUMAN RIGHTS WATCH, *supra* note 20, at 196, 210, 238–44, 257–63 (discussing conditions promoting trafficking from Burma, Nepal, and Bangladesh to Thailand, India, and Pakistan, respectively); Pyne, *supra* note 35, at 216–19 (discussing factors contributing to trafficking of Burmese females to Thailand); Margot Hornblower, *The Skin Trade,* TIME (U.S. ed.), June 21, 1993, *available in* LEXIS, News Library, Mags File (discussing circumstances fostering both trafficking and voluntary prostitution in Eastern Europe and elsewhere).

39. *See, e.g.,* HUMAN RIGHTS WATCH, RAPE FOR PROFIT: TRAFFICKING OF NEPALI GIRLS AND WOMEN TO INDIA'S BROTHELS 21 (1995); HUMAN RIGHTS WATCH, *supra* note 20, at 196.

40. In reference to his sister's work as a prostitute in Bombay, India, one Nepali asked, "What is the harm? At least she can contribute to her family." *Children for Sale, supra* note 16. A Nepali father stated, "I had three daughters. I sent one off to a 'friend' in Bombay. Now with the money I get I can afford a TV." *Id.* Indeed, in the poverty-stricken Sindhupalchowk region of Nepal, "the conspicuous

the belief that her needs are better cared for in the brothel than they would have been at home.[41] However, the reality is usually the opposite: women held captive in brothels usually have to pay for their shelter, food, clothing, toiletries, and the like.[42] More important, the vast majority of women held captive in brothels are in "debt bondage," forced to work to pay off the fees paid for them by the brothel owner and agent to the procurer and the woman's family.[43] Brothel owners add "interest" to the debt of anywhere from 10 percent[44] to 100 percent[45] of the original amount, and will also add to the debt any outlays of cash made on the woman's behalf, including transportation fees.[46] The woman's "debt" may not be reported accurately to her, and she rarely handles her own "wages," making it difficult for her to know how much money is at issue, how much she has earned, how much she is supposed to earn, or precisely how long it will take her to purchase her freedom.[47] Thus, victims of forced prostitution usually suffer lengthy periods of confinement in dismal conditions.

An additional factor specific to the trafficking of girls has been the recent spread of HIV/AIDS in sex-tourism areas. Fear of AIDS has led brothel patrons to seek

---

presence of corrugated roofs, steel furniture, utensils, radios and tape recorders" in certain homes is said to indicate that these families had females working in Bombay. *Id. See also* VAN BUEREN, *supra* note 17, at 275; SLEIGHTHOLME & SINHA, *supra* note 30, at 3, 15–16, 21.

The same is true in Thailand: "[i]ndenturing a daughter to the sex-industry recruiters will enable an entire rural family to survive, and there are entire villages made up of such families."

Robinson, *supra* note 6, at 180. *See also* ODZER, *supra* note 13, at 79 (discussing Thai cultural expectation that children should support parents: "Thai culture decreed that Hoi support her father. That she did it by prostitution was less important than that she did it. It was the same for Jek, who supported his mother by pimping"); *id.* at 10.

Cultural norms which devalue girls—or value them only as property to be sold or exchanged—combine with "western-style consumerism" (the desire for consumer goods), and with the transformation of local economies into market- and cash-based systems, to exacerbate the problem of children being sold into prostitution. *See* Henley, *supra* note 15; Cameron W. Barr, *Asia's Traffickers Keep Girls in Sexual Servitude,* THE CHRISTIAN SCIENCE MONITOR, Aug. 22, 1996, *available in* LEXIS, News Library, Majpap File. *But see* Robinson, *supra* note 30 (arguing that sale of girls into prostitution is not just a result of "traditional sexism" which devalues females, but is also a product of the commodification of sexuality itself, which has led families to celebrate births of daughters because of their monetary value in sexual markets).

41. *Cf.* Kristof, *supra* note 17, at A8 (noting that customers sometimes justify child prostitution with the claim that at least the children earn lots of money to send home, and at the same time avoid even more demeaning, dangerous, and physically demanding work).

42. HUMAN RIGHTS WATCH, *supra* note 20, at 197, 212, 233; Friedman, *supra* note 27, at 12, 16; Hornblower, *supra* note 38.

43. HUMAN RIGHTS WATCH, *supra* note 20, at 197, 210–12, 231; Friedman, *supra* note 27, at 12, 16.

44. *See* HUMAN RIGHTS WATCH, *supra* note 20, at 239, 246 (India).

45. *Id.* at 211 (Thailand).

46. *See, e.g., id.* at 217 (Burmese trafficking victims working in Thai brothel were arrested by police and returned to brothel owner after the owner paid the women's fine; owner added the amount of the fine to their debts); *id.* at 233, 246 (Indian brothel owners added cost of medical care, protection money, and police payoffs to women's debts).

47. *See, e.g., id.* at 211–12, 234, 239, 241, 247.

younger females in the belief that young girls are less likely to transmit the AIDS virus.[48] Brothels charge patrons a high premium to see virgins, who are considered the safest of all.[49] Given these client preferences, not only can brothels command higher prices for younger prostitutes, but brokers, middlemen, and families can demand higher payments for young girls being sold into prostitution.[50]

In addition to coercion and debt bondage, forced prostitution subjects its victims to a variety of other injuries. The risk of injury is magnified by two factors: first, brothel prostitutes are generally not allowed to select and reject customers, but must submit to every customer who selects them, no matter how violent or unusual the sexual request;[51] second, foreign women held captive in brothels are especially isolated from help and support due to their limited mobility, inability to speak the local language, the social ostracism of prostitutes, and the corruption of local law enforcement.[52] Injuries suffered by captive prostitutes include physical and verbal

48. *See, e.g.,* Pyne, *supra* note 35, at 217; HUMAN RIGHTS WATCH, *supra* note 20, at 197, 225; KURZ & PRATHER, *supra* note 15, at 26; Demleitner, *supra* note 19, at 164; Friedman, *supra* note 27, at 12; Kristof, *supra* note 17, at A8; Costelloe, *supra* note 17, at A10; Simons, *supra* note 15; Cooper, *supra* note 17; Henley, *supra* note 15; Serrill, *supra* note 17; *Children for Sale, supra* note 16; George J. Bryjak, *The Children Condemned to Slavery,* SAN DIEGO UNION-TRIBUNE, Dec. 17, 1995, *available in* LEXIS, News Library, Majpap File. However, the physiology of most young girls makes them especially vulnerable to HIV infection. HUMAN RIGHTS WATCH, *supra* note 20, at 225 & n.54; KURZ & PRATHER, *supra* note 15, at 23 (*citing* UNITED NATIONS DEVELOPMENT PROGRAMME, YOUNG WOMEN: SILENCE, SUSCEPTIBILITY AND THE HIV EPIDEMIC (1993)); SLEIGHTHOLME & SINHA, *supra* note 30, at 85; Serrill, *supra* note 17. Indeed, Zambian girls between ages 15 and 19 are 17 times more likely to have AIDS than boys of the same ages. Raghavan, *supra* note 16, at A15.

49. Virgin children bring the highest price both because of their looks and innocence and because they are less likely to have HIV. Robinson, *supra* note 30; *Children for Sale, supra* note 16. *See also* Friedman, *supra* note 27, at 12. In areas of South and West Asia some people reportedly believe that virgin girls from Nepal can cure AIDS, McGirk, *Soiled, supra* note 17; *Children for Sale, supra* note 16; that virgins cure gonorrhea and syphilis, Friedman, *supra* note 27, at 12; Kristof, *supra* note 17, at A8; Serrill, *supra* note 17; McGirk, *Soiled, supra* note 17; that having sex with virgins increases virility, Pyne, *supra* note 35, at 217; Robinson, *supra* note 30; and/or that sex with virgins prolongs life or has related health benefits, Odzer, *supra* note 13, at 55; Simons, *supra* note 15; Kristof, *supra* note 17, at A8. A belief that sex with virgins or young girls can cure AIDS also apparently exists in some places in Africa. Raghavan, *supra* note 16, at A15.

Patrons who visit young prostitutes because of beliefs that virgins or young girls can cure disease are likely to be especially dangerous; the reasonable inference is that most such patrons are seeking to cure their own infections. Thus, young and/or virgin girls are especially vulnerable to HIV and other sexually transmitted diseases both for physiological reasons, *see supra* note 48, and because they are often favored by patrons already infected with such diseases.

50. Teenage Nepali girls reportedly are sold to Indian brothels for $1,000 or more. *Children for Sale, supra* note 16; Friedman, *supra* note 27, at 12.

51. *See, e.g.,* Pyne, *supra* note 35, at 219, 222; HUMAN RIGHTS WATCH, *supra* note 20, at 197, 214, 235.

52. *See, e.g.,* McGirk, *Soiled, supra* note 17 (discussing refusal of Nepali police to arrest trafficker identified by former prostitute). Debt-bonded prostitutes in Thailand and India are generally forbidden to leave the brothel or permitted to leave only with an escort in order to prevent escape; conversation with Nepali clients in India or Burmese patrons in Thailand may be forbidden; and communication with the outside world by telephone or correspondence is also forbidden or extremely limited. *See* HUMAN RIGHTS WATCH, *supra* note 20, at 212–13 (Thailand); *id.* at 248 (India). Moreover, "crackdowns" on

abuse, additional extortion, low self-esteem, depression, chronic malnutrition, hepatitis, tuberculosis, and, of course, venereal diseases and HIV.[53] AIDS, in particular, "can be a death sentence in more ways than one."[54] Women who are HIV-positive are often evicted from brothels,[55] yet may also be unable to return home because they will be shunned either for their AIDS[56] or because of their status as former prostitutes.[57] Some HIV-positive prostitutes have been killed, and their corpses mutilated to prevent identification, apparently by brothel-owners or their agents.[58]

Clearly, the existence of forced and child prostitution should be seen as outrages. Forced and child prostitution constitute denials of numerous human rights[59]—e.g., rights to liberty and security;[60] to be free from slavery and servitude;[61] to be free from torture and cruel, inhuman, and degrading treatment;[62] to be free from arbitrary detention;[63] to freedom of movement and residence;[64] to free choice of employment

---

forced and child prostitution may exempt brothel owners, pimps, and recruiters, focusing instead on the victims, who are arrested rather than rescued. *Id.* at 209, 216, 218–20 (discussing police crackdowns on Thai brothels in 1991, 1992, and 1993); *id.* at 256 (discussing police practices in India); *id.* at 260, 264–67 (discussing practices of Pakistani police); Friedman, *supra* note 27, at 16 (discussing India).

53. *See generally* HUMAN RIGHTS WATCH, *supra* note 20, at 196–273; Pyne, *supra* note 35, at 218; Simons, *supra* note 15; *Children for Sale, supra* note 16.

54. *Children for Sale, supra* note 16.

55. HUMAN RIGHTS WATCH, *supra* note 20, at 228; Friedman, *supra* note 27, at 20; Costelloe, *supra* note 17, at A10; McGirk, *Soiled, supra* note 17; *Children for Sale, supra* note 16.

56. HUMAN RIGHTS WATCH, *supra* note 20, at 229; McGirk, *Soiled, supra* note 17 (noting Nepali reference to AIDS as the "Bombay disease" and to HIV-positive prostitutes as "India's soiled goods").

57. *See, e.g.,* Pyne, *supra* note 35, at 223 (noting that loss of dignity and low self-esteem may increase women's vulnerability to HIV/AIDS, because women who felt they were ruined by prostitution and could not return home had no incentive to protect against infection); ODZER, *supra* note 13, at 10, 18 (discussing predominant Thai view that prostitute women are "loathsome"); Demleitner, *supra* note 19, at 195; Friedman, *supra* note 27, at 12; McGirk, *Soiled, supra* note 17.

58. *Children for Sale, supra* note 16. In addition, prostitutes with AIDS who were deported from Thailand to Burma reportedly were executed by the Burmese military government. *See, e.g.,* Serrill, *supra* note 17; *infra* note 74.

59. The list that follows is exemplary only; many other human rights protections and human rights documents could also be mentioned. In addition to the five human rights treaties cited *infra,* see also the international instruments drafted to address trafficking and forced prostitution, and those regarding forced labor and slavery. *See generally* HUMAN RIGHTS WATCH, *supra* note 20, at 206 & *passim* (listing violations).

60. *Universal Declaration of Human Rights,* G.A. Res. 217A, U.N. GAOR, 3d Sess., pt. 1, at 71, U.N. Doc. A/810, art. 3 (1948) [hereinafter "*UDHR*"]; International Covenant on Civil & Political Rights, Dec. 16, 1966, art. 9, 999 U.N.T.S. 171 [hereinafter "ICCPR"].

61. *UDHR, supra* note 60, art. 4; ICCPR, *supra* note 60, art. 8.

62. *UDHR, supra* note 60, art. 5; ICCPR, *supra* note 60, art. 7.

63. *UDHR, supra* note 60, art. 9; ICCPR, *supra* note 60, art. 9.

64. *UDHR, supra* note 60, art. 13; ICCPR, *supra* note 60, art. 12.

and just and favorable work conditions;[65] to an adequate standard of living; [66] to an education; [67] to physical and mental health;[68] to protection (for children) and freedom from exploitation.[69] Indeed, forced and child prostitution have even been tactics in campaigns of genocide.[70] Yet corrupt and uncaring politicians often see prostitutes as "an expendable commodity,"[71] ignoring the human rights and needs of both captive and voluntary prostitutes.

Although the next sections discuss problems associated with voluntary prostitution, they are relevant to forced prostitution as well. Appreciating the exploitation and abuse inherent in existing socio-legal regimes governing prostitution in general will help societies fashion better policies to address forced prostitution without further injuring *any* prostitute in the process.

VOLUNTARY PROSTITUTION: COMMON ABUSES OF PROSTITUTES

As many scholars and activists have pointed out, governmental regulation and/ or criminalization of prostitution usually worsens prostitutes' situations, both by creating or magnifying the stigma and marginalization associated with the profession, and by increasing prostitutes' risk of violence and other abuse.[72] Regardless of which prostitution control policy is in force, violence and abuse of prostitutes by police, customers, and pimps is common.

The Criminalization of Prostitution

Jurisdictions that criminalize prostitution tend to penalize the prostitute much more frequently and severely than they penalize the customer or the procurer (pimp, madam, etc.). For example, in the United States, only 10 percent or less of all arrests for prostitution are arrests of customers.[73] While in the U.S. the primary

---

65. *UDHR , supra* note 60, art. 23; International Covenant on Economic, Social and Cultural Rights, Dec. 16, 1966, arts. 6 & 7, 993 U.N.T.S. 3 [hereinafter "ICESCR"]; Convention on the Elimination of All Forms of Discrimination Against Women, Dec. 18, 1979, art. 11, 1249 U.N.T.S. 13, 19 I.L.M. 33 [hereinafter "Women's Convention"].

66. *UDHR, supra* note 60, art. 25; ICESCR, *supra* note 65, art. 11; Women's Convention, *supra* note 65, art. 15 (4).

67. *UDHR, supra* note 60, art. 26; ICESCR, *supra* note 65, art. 13; Women's Convention, *supra* note 65, art. 10.

68. ICESCR, *supra* note 65, art. 12.

69. For children's rights, see ICCPR, *supra* note 60, art. 24; ICESCR, *supra* note 65, art. 10 (3); Convention on the Rights of the Child, Nov. 20, 1989, arts. 19, 34, 35, 28 I.L.M. 1448. For women's rights, see Women's Convention, *supra* note 65, art. 6.

70. *See, e.g.,* Toepfer & Wells, *supra* note 17, at 88–89.

71. Friedman, *supra* note 27, at 12.

72. *See, e.g.,* Joan Fitzpatrick, *The Use of International Human Rights Norms to Combat Violence Against Women, in* HUMAN RIGHTS OF WOMEN: NATIONAL AND INTERNATIONAL PERSPECTIVES 532, 551 (Rebecca J. Cook ed., 1994).

73. *See* Priscilla Alexander, *Prostitution: A Difficult Issue for Feminists, in* SEX WORK, *supra* note 7,

penalty is a monetary fine and/or a short time in jail, in other places prostitutes are punished much more severely. Extreme examples are Burma and Iran, where prostitutes have been executed.[74] Even in the U.S., longer prison terms are possibilities (especially if the prostitute is charged with pandering),[75] and in many countries immigrant women who work in prostitution face the possibility of deportation if they are caught.[76] Migrant women who conceal their real identities in order to work as prostitutes sometimes have the opposite problem, being unable to return home.[77]

In jurisdictions that prohibit prostitution, prostitutes' lives are shaped in significant part by the criminalization of their livelihood. In the United States and many

---

at 184, 196 (10% of arrests are of customers, about 70% are female prostitutes, and the remaining 20% are male prostitutes); DOLORES FRENCH, WORKING: MY LIFE AS A PROSTITUTE 149 (1988) (same); DEBORAH L. RHODE, JUSTICE AND GENDER: SEX DISCRIMINATION AND THE LAW 261 (1989) (less than 10% of prostitution arrests are of male customers). *See also* ROSEMARIE TONG, WOMEN, SEX, AND THE LAW 55–56 (1984) (female prostitutes are disproportionately arrested in comparison to male prostitutes); RUTH ROSEN, THE LOST SISTERHOOD: PROSTITUTION IN AMERICA, 1900–1918, at 35, 176 (1982) (observing that unequal treatment of prostitutes and customers is a historical as well as contemporary practice in the U.S.); Frances P. Bernat, *New York State's Prostitution Statute: Case Study of the Discriminatory Application of a Gender Neutral Law, in* CRIMINAL JUSTICE POLITICS AND WOMEN: THE AFTERMATH OF LEGALLY MANDATED CHANGE 103, 103–120 (Claudine Schweber and Clarice Feinman eds., 1985) (data from case study); RONALD BARRI FLOWERS, WOMEN AND CRIMINALITY: THE WOMAN AS VICTIM, OFFENDER, AND PRACTITIONER 129 (1987) (stating that one customer is arrested for every four prostitutes arrested, despite the greater number of customers than prostitutes in the population, and noting that few men are arrested for procuring).

74. Fitzpatrick, *supra* note 72, at 552 (*citing* Laura Reanda, *Prostitution as a Human Rights Question: Problems and Prospects of United Nations Action,* 13 HUM. RTS. Q. 202, 203 (1991); Ralph Joseph, *Iran Hangs Five Women to Prove Its Islamic Zeal,* DAILY TELEGRAPH, Feb. 1, 1989, at 10; *AIDS-Infected Burmese Prostitutes Injected with Cyanide,* UPI, Apr. 2, 1992, *available in* LEXIS, Nexis Library, UPI File).

75. *See, e.g.,* NORMA JEAN ALMODOVAR, COP TO CALL GIRL 213, 288, 295 (1993) (California prostitute sentenced to 3 years in prison on one count of pandering). The law generally defines "pandering" as procuring, causing, inducing, persuading, or encouraging another person to engage in prostitution. *See, e.g.,* CAL. PENAL CODE § 266i (Deering 1996).

76. *See, e.g.,* [United States] Immigration and Nationality Act, § 241(a)(12), 8 U.S.C. 1251 (deportation); Immigration and Nationality Act § 212(a)(12), 8 U.S.C. 1182 (exclusion). Alien women who worked as prostitutes before coming to the United States can also be denied entry, even as tourists, or deported, even if they are legal immigrants. *See id.*; FRENCH, *supra* note 73, at 183, 286. *See also* Fitzpatrick, *supra* note 72, at 552 (*citing AIDS-Infected Burmese Prostitutes Injected with Cyanide,* UPI, Apr. 2, 1992, *available in* LEXIS, Nexis Library, UPI file) (prostitutes deported from Thailand to Burma, where they were executed); BARBARA MEIL HOBSON, UNEASY VIRTUE: THE POLITICS OF PROSTITUTION AND THE AMERICAN REFORM TRADITION 231 (1987) (discussing immigrant prostitutes' fear of deportation in the Netherlands); Carla Corso, *Migrant Prostitutes in Northeast Italy, in* VINDICATION, *supra* note 8, at 240, 241 (expulsion of Yugoslavian prostitutes from Italy). In Thailand, immigrants in the country illegally are required to pay for their transportation to the border for deportation. HUMAN RIGHTS WATCH, *supra* note 20, at 222–23 (*citing* Thailand Immigration Act of 1979, § 56). Thai women seem to have particular trouble obtaining travel visas, because of the assumption in foreign consulates that they will engage in prostitution abroad. ODZER, *supra* note 13, at 93. *See also* Licia Brussa, *Migrant Prostitutes in the Netherlands, in* VINDICATION, *supra* note 8, at 227, 231.

77. *See, e.g.,* Bhatiasevi, *supra* note 35, at 6 (reporting that Thai women who have taken false identities (e.g., by using Malaysian passports) in order to go abroad to work have been unable to return to Thailand because they have no proof of their real nationality). *See also supra* note 76.

other countries, this means that prostitutes may have to turn to pimps to post bail, hire an attorney, or arrange for child care when they are arrested,[78] will have to falsify their tax returns[79] (or not file at all), cannot receive compensation for work-related injuries and illnesses[80] nor earn other social benefits,[81] and may be forcibly tested for AIDS or venereal disease upon arrest or conviction for prostitution.

Laws prohibiting individuals from living off the earnings of a prostitute can also have significant negative effects. While such laws seem to be directed at pimps, brothel owners, and the like (i.e., they seem to be designed to prevent the proliferation of prostitution as a commercial enterprise), these laws generally are not narrowly worded, with the effect that adult children, lovers, spouses, and roommates who are supported by prostitutes are in violation of the law and are often punished for their relationships to prostitute women.[82] Similarly, prostitutes who work together or refer clients to one another can be arrested for pimping and pandering.[83] Related legal provisions may allow the property belonging to prostitutes or their children to be seized on the basis that it was purchased with the proceeds of criminal activity.[84]

---

78. Alexander, *supra* note 73, at 198.

79. *See, e.g.,* FRENCH, *supra* note 73, at 114 (reporting income accurately while listing occupation as "entertainer").

80. For examples of work-related injuries, see Barbara Goldsmith, *Women on the Edge,* THE NEW YORKER, Apr. 26, 1993, at 64, 64–66, 71, 74 (rape, battery by customers; HIV, gonorrhea, syphilis, herpes, hepatitis, and tuberculosis infections); Charles Gandee, *Portrait of a Lady of the Night,* VOGUE, Feb. 1993, at 238, 240 (dislocated jaw resulting from performing fellatio repeatedly). *See also infra* notes 102–03 and accompanying text.

81. *See, e.g.,* RHODE, *supra* note 73, at 259.

82. Alexander, *supra* note 73, at 209; *Human Rights: "Simple Human Respect," in* VINDICATION, *supra* note 8, at 52, 68 (comments of Grisélidis Réal regarding prostitution laws in France; *id.* at 74 (comments of Eva Rosta, England); *id.* at 76 (comments of Danny Cockerline, Canada); *id.* at 93 (Sweden).

Although minor children do not appear to be punished under pimping and pandering laws, prostitutes can lose custody of minor children upon suspicion of, or conviction for, prostitution. Alexander, *supra* note 73, at 184–85; FRENCH, *supra* note 73, at 286–87; *Human Rights: "Simple Human Respect," supra,* at 63 (comments of Brigitte Pavkovic, Austria); *id.* at 74 (comments of Eva Rosta, England); *id.* at 93 (Sweden). Losing custody is a serious threat for many prostitutes, as the majority of them in many countries are single mothers. ROBERTS, *supra* note 8, at 327–28.

As Alexander and French point out, the list of individuals and organizations that benefit from the illegal activity of prostitution should be much longer. *See* Alexander, *supra* note 73, at 198; FRENCH, *supra* note 73, at 184. For example, those who are paid from the proceeds of prostitution include cab drivers; publishers of some newspapers, magazines, and telephone directories; credit card companies; hotels, bars and cafes; travel agents, airlines, and tour guides promoting sex tours; attorneys; bail bondsmen; and myriad others.

83. *Human Rights: "Simple Human Respect," supra* note 82, at 78 (comments of Margo St. James, United States); *id.* at 74 (comments of Eva Rosta, England); *id.* at 93 (Sweden); Valerie Scott, *C-49: A New Wave of Repression, in* GOOD/BAD, *supra* note 8, at 100, 102 (Canada). *See also supra* note 75.

84. *Human Rights: "Simple Human Respect," supra* note 82, at 74 (comments of Eva Rosta, England); *id.* at 93 (Sweden).

However, many of the most serious abuses and problems prostitutes face are not the result of the criminal law, but rather of criminal status and its associated stigma. Especially where prostitution is illegal, prostitutes are generally reluctant to report crimes to the police. Not only may these prostitutes fear any contact with law enforcement because of the illegality of their vocation, but they also know that police often trivialize offenses against prostitutes as "the risks of the trade"[85] and/ or exploit prostitutes' vulnerability by demanding sexual or other favors in exchange for not arresting them.[86]

In other words, by criminalizing prostitution the law creates (or allows) abuses that exceed the intended effects of the law itself. For example, the legal definition of rape does not categorically exclude prostitutes as potential victims, but many (especially police) believe that prostitutes cannot be raped.[87] Thus when prostitutes report rapes they usually are not believed, and their attackers are either not arrested, not tried, or not convicted. Not surprisingly, then, most prostitutes do not bother to

---

85. *See generally* Glen Martin, *Arrest in Prostitute's Slaying,* S.F. CHRONICLE, May 15, 1996, at A14 (man arrested for murder of prostitute admitted assaulting and raping two other women also believed to be prostitutes; after first incident, in which a woman ran out of assailant's apartment nude and yelling that he had a gun, police interviewed assailant and, according to a witness, told assailant "he had better watch his step, . . . he couldn't go around doing things like that"; no arrest was made). *See also* NEIL MCKEGANEY & MARINA BARNARD, SEX WORK ON THE STREETS: PROSTITUTES AND THEIR CLIENTS 74, 80 (1996); *infra* notes 87–102 and accompanying text.

86. *See, e.g.,* Philip Matier & Andrew Ross, *The Matier & Ross Report,* S.F. CHRONICLE, Nov. 26, 1993, at A–21, A–22 (reporting that a "moonlighting cop . . . forc[ed] oral sex from five prostitutes by flashing his badge and threatening to arrest them"; note, however, that this assailant was tried and convicted by the City of San Francisco); Gabriela Silva Leite, *Women of the Life, We Must Speak, in* VINDICATION, *supra* note 8, at 288, 291 (discussing police abuse of prostitutes in Brazil).

87. Some police believe prostitutes cannot be raped because of prostitutes' criminal status: they have forfeited legal protection by engaging in a criminal act. In other words, they assume the risk of rape when they decide to become prostitutes. Others believe that prostitutes never say "no" to sexual encounters, and thus cannot be raped. *Cf. supra* text accompanying note 5 (prostitution defined as "indiscriminate" sale of sex). The belief appears to be either that a woman who has ever consented to commercial sex is legally incapable of withdrawing that consent, or that such a woman would always consent to sex if the price were right. People holding this belief think of rape involving prostitutes as "fraud," focusing not on the force, violence, and/or coercion, and lack of consent, involved in rapes of prostitutes, *see infra* note 88 (study showing rapes of prostitutes involve greater violence and more serious injuries than other rapes), but rather on the lack of payment, whether or not the prostitute was working at the time and whether or not the rapist approached her as a customer, *see infra* note 143 (judge analyzing rape of prostitute as "fraud"). In reality, nearly every prostitute *does* discriminate in choice of sexual partner, both paying customers and intimate lovers. *See generally* Carole, *Interview with Debra, in* SEX WORK, *supra* note 7, at 91, 94; Carole, *Interview with Barbara, in* SEX WORK, *supra* note 7, at 166, 171; ALMODOVAR, *supra* note 75, at 308; Roberts, *supra* note 8, at 335.

For discussions of police attitudes toward rape, see, for example, Carole, *Interview with Barbara, supra,* at 168, 169 (describing police attitude that rape is part of a prostitute's job, that she assumes the risk, and discussing case of twenty-one-year-old American prostitute who failed to report a rape because she assumed she had no rights); Carole, *Interview with Debra, supra,* at 95 (describing same police attitude); Gail Pheterson, *The Social Consequences of Unchastity, in* SEX WORK, *supra* note 7, at 215, 225 (describing Dutch study in which police ranked rape of street prostitutes as the least serious form of rape).

report rapes.[88] Even when they do, courts and police often minimize or dismiss the harm suffered. In one such case, when a seventeen-year-old prostitute in Fresno, California, was raped by a man with an ice pick, the police attempted to arrest *her* for assault on the rapist.[89] The police insisted that a prostitute, by definition, could not be raped and that the man was too drunk to have done anything.[90] The officers refused to take a police report when the woman sought to press charges for rape, and instead detained the rapist for three hours for public drunkenness.[91] Judicial attitudes often are no better than police attitudes. In a 1986 California case, a judge dismissed rape charges because the victim was a prostitute, stating ''a whore is a whore is a whore.''[92]

Murder is an equally chilling danger prostitutes face. Street prostitutes who are desperate for money, whose pimps force them to work, or whose judgment is clouded by chemical dependency are especially vulnerable.[93] Even absent these conditions, street prostitutes tend to be easy targets. First, because their work is illegal they necessarily seek to draw little attention to their comings and goings; few people know of their whereabouts at any given time. If there are witnesses to a prostitute's murder or abduction, they tend to be unreliable or uncooperative[94] for any number of reasons.[95] Second, because of the illegality and stigma of prostitution, many prostitutes are isolated from family and friends, so few people may notice or

---

88.   *See, e.g.,* Alexander, *supra* note 73, at 201 (noting that 70% of street prostitutes in one study had been raped on the job but that just 7% had sought assistance of any kind, and only 4% called the police); Carole, *Interview with Debra, supra* note 87, at 95; ROBERTS, *supra* note 8, at 303 (quoting British prostitutes with same expectations of police). For similar reasons (fear of police, avoidance of stigma and condescension) few prostitutes turn to rape crisis centers for help. *See* Carole, *Interview with Barbara, supra* note 87, at 174.

A University of Melbourne study of rapes of Australian prostitutes found that rapists of prostitutes used greater force than other rapists, including greater use of guns and knives, that prostitute victims suffered more serious injuries than other rape victims, but that rapists of prostitutes tended to receive much lesser sentences than other rapists and that prostitutes were less likely to report rapes. Michael Magazanik, *Australia: Sex and Violence—How the Court Got Them Confused,* THE AGE (Melbourne, Austl.), Jan. 7, 1992, *available in* LEXIS, Aust Library, Auspub File; Bob Drogin, *Rapes That are ''Not as Heinous,''* L.A. TIMES, Jan. 28, 1992, at A1.

89.   Karen, *The Right to Protection from Rape, in* SEX WORK, *supra* note 7, at 145, 145–46.

90.   *Id.*

91.   *Id.*

92.   Alexander, *supra* note 73, at 185 (describing 1986 case in Pasadena, California, as well as 1986 Fresno, California, case in which district attorney dropped 29 of 32 forcible sex charges against man accused of raping six women, because four were prostitutes).

93.   Mireya Navarro, *Prostitutes Defy Killer by Plying Their Trade,* N.Y. TIMES, Dec. 28, 1994, at A6.

94.   *Id.*

95.   For example, such reasons would include fear of the killer; the witness' own impaired state; fear of the police; the witness' criminal background or need to conceal involvement in criminal activity which was taking place when the witness saw the victim or assailant; and fear of shame and embarrassment if family and friends knew the witness was in an area frequented by prostitutes.

care if they disappear; their lives seem expendable.[96] Lacking any significant pressure to solve a case involving the murder of a prostitute, and often sharing prevailing attitudes about prostitutes' worthlessness,[97] police often will investigate prostitute deaths only superficially, if at all.[98]

For these reasons, prostitutes are at great, and perhaps disproportionate, risk for "garden-variety" murders. In addition, these facts may lead serial killers to target prostitutes for murder, or to "practice" on prostitutes before victimizing non-prostitute women.[99] Indeed, "prostitutes are 'the number one category of victims killed by serial killers'" according to a criminal justice scholar specializing in the study of serial killings.[100] A retired FBI agent with seven years' experience

---

96. Goldsmith, *supra* note 80, at 79; Navarro, *supra* note 93 (noting that missing persons reports have rarely been filed in cases where prostitutes are found dead). *Cf.* Elizabeth Fernandez, *Murder Stalks S.F. Prostitutes,* S.F. EXAMINER, Dec. 10, 1995, at A1.

97. Indeed, as Gail Pheterson points out, the killing of a prostitute is generally reported not as a generic "murder" but as a "prostitute murder," suggesting that by virtue of her profession the victim was an accomplice to her homicide. Pheterson, *supra* note 87, at 226.

In discussing the Yorkshire Ripper case in England, one prominent British official was quoted as saying that, of the victims, "some were prostitutes, but perhaps the saddest part of this case is that some were not." ROBERTS, *supra* note 8, at 303 (quoting British Attorney-General Sir Michael Havers). Another official, referring to non-prostitute victims, said "the Ripper is now killing innocent girls." *Id.* at 304 (quoting Jim Hobson, West Yorkshire Acting Assistant Police Chief Constable). *See also* McKEGANEY & BARNARD, *supra* note 85, at 80 (noting "qualitative shift in both the media coverage and the police investigation of the . . . Yorkshire Ripper" after he killed a woman who was not a prostitute). The man who confessed to the murders, Peter Sutcliffe, argued that his victims were "filth," so the murders simply "clean[ed] up the place a bit." ROBERTS, *supra* note 8, at 304 (quoting Peter Sutcliffe). *See also id.* at 305 (discussing New York police attitudes toward murders of prostitutes).

98. *See, e.g.,* Elizabeth Fernandez, *Tale of Love, Mystery and Murder,* S.F. EXAMINER, June 1, 1997, at A1 (murders of two prostitutes solved by victims' boyfriends after local law enforcement's failure to follow up on evidence).

In the 1980s case of the South Side Slayer, Los Angeles, California, police "waited until ten women were already dead before notifying the public that a serial murderer was operating, and fourteen women were murdered before they even formed a task force. . . ." Rachel West, *U.S. Prostitutes Collective, in* SEX WORK, *supra* note 7, at 279, 285. The killer murdered at least 17 women, all but three of them Black. *Id.*The police assumed the victims were prostitutes, initially referring to their task force as the "Prostitute Killer Task Force" and the murders as "prostitute slayings." *Id.* at 286. The victims' race and presumed vocation probably explains the lack of police attention to this case compared to other Los Angeles serial killings. *Id.* at 285–86. *See also* Navarro, *supra* note 93; ROBERTS, *supra* note 8, at 303 (noting that the Yorkshire Ripper, who was eventually arrested and confessed, was questioned by police seven times before confessing; a witness description matched the suspect perfectly but was discounted by police because the source was a Black prostitute they considered "stupid").

99. *See, e.g.,* Pheterson, *supra* note 87, at 226; West, *supra* note 98, at 285–87; Alexander, *supra* note 73, at 201; FRENCH, *supra* note 73, at 237; *Human Rights: "Simple Human Respect,"* *supra* note 82, at 60 (remarks of Roberta Perkins, Australia).

100. Navarro, *supra* note 93 (quoting James Alan Fox, dean of Northeastern University's College of Criminal Justice). In addition to the South Side Slayer, *see supra* note 98, known serial killings of prostitutes in the United States include the Green River murders in the state of Washington, where 49 women where killed, most last seen in areas of prostitution activity; the murders of 17 prostitutes in New York by Joel Rifkin; and the killing of at least 5 prostitutes in southwest Dade County, Florida. *Id.* The most notorious serial killer of prostitutes is, of course, Jack the Ripper, who killed five prostitutes

profiling serial killers agrees: "[P]rostitutes have been fair game."[101] Although serial killings are a relative rarity among all murders, the fact that prostitutes are primary targets for serial killings is still cause for concern.

The criminalization and stigmatization of prostitution thus results in a devaluation of prostitutes' lives. In addition to the murder, rape, and battery prostitutes face at the hands of customers and police,[102] prostitutes suffer a series of other indignities ranging from simple street harassment to severe exploitation. For example, customers may intentionally attempt to infect prostitutes with herpes, AIDS, and other diseases.[103] Even absent criminalization and stigmatization, prostitutes would face these risks to some (although a lesser) extent. However, criminalization magnifies these harms by making it effectively impossible for prostitutes to seek redress or compensation. Criminalization and its associated dangers also dramatically increase prostitutes' stress level, and the stigma of prostitution can have severe effects on self-esteem.[104] Discussing the intertwined effects of stigma and criminal status, one prostitute explains:

> If in fact we are those "poor, downtrodden women," it is because a prostitute can be evicted from her home for being a prostitute, because a dancer is arrested for doing her job, because our rights as human beings . . . are being taken away . . . because of our chosen employment. It's not so much that we're being exploited by our trades or by the individuals that are in our trades, namely, the agents in the dancing industry or even the pimps in prostitution. We are free individuals that do have a choice. It is society that stops us at every turn—from having bank accounts, from acquiring loans, from seeking other employment, from using the knowledge and the street expertise that we have obtained in our professions . . . for any other line of work or . . . way of life. That's where the *real* exploitation is.[105]

The Regulation of Prostitution

Jurisdictions that regulate prostitution also tend to subject prostitutes to significant levels of social control, such as requirements that they work in licensed brothels or specific districts,[106] and/or that they pay special taxes and submit to regular

---

in and around London in 1888. For an excellent analysis of "Jack the Ripper stories" and their social meaning, see JUDITH R. WALKOWITZ, CITY OF DREADFUL DELIGHT: NARRATIVES OF SEXUAL DANGER IN LATE-VICTORIAN LONDON (1992).

101. Navarro, *supra* note 93.

102. According to one study, 60% of the violence prostitutes experience comes from clients, 20% from police, and 20% from pimps. *Feminism: "Crunch Point," in* VINDICATION, *supra* note 8, at 144, 167 (*citing* Jennifer James, *A Formal Analysis of Prostitution,* Washington State Department of Social and Health Services (1972)). For a discussion of typical violence experienced by street prostitutes, see McKEGANEY & BARNARD, *supra* note 85, at 70–74.

103. *See, e.g.,* FRENCH, *supra* note 73, at 233–38 (recounting unsuccessful attempt by customer to get French drunk, hide his herpes lesions, distract her, and prevent her from using condom with him; when confronted by French, customer responded, "those are the risks of being in a business like yours").

104. ROBERTS, *supra* note 8, at 337.

105. *From the Floor, in* GOOD/BAD, *supra* note 8, at 114, 118 (comments of Mary Johnson) (emphasis in original).

106. *See, e.g.,* Fitzpatrick, *supra* note 72, at 552; Belinda Cooper, *Prostitution: A Feminist Analysis,* 11 WOMEN'S RTS. L. RPTR. 99, 110–12 (1989).

health inspections.[107] Under this form of regulation, prostitutes may be photographed, issued a work permit, and fingerprinted before being allowed to work.[108] In places where only brothel-prostitution is legal, such as New South Wales[109] and Nevada, brothel prostitutes' attire, hygiene, residence, and leisure time may be regulated.[110] For example, Nevada—the only state in the U.S. in which any form of prostitution is legal[111]—prohibits prostitutes from living in town centers and from entering bars and casinos.[112] Nevada law allows for even more restrictive regulations to be imposed by individual counties, such as additional residence restrictions, attire and health regulations, prohibitions on leaving the brothel during certain hours, rules against walking in certain areas at certain times or with men, and requirements that prostitutes immediately leave town when they are fired or quit their jobs.[113]

Although this system may seem safer for prostitutes than outright criminalization, the system is designed to protect the customer and the brothel-owner, not the prostitute. Thus it, too, creates the possibility of exploitation: brothel-keepers with the power to hire and fire may wield considerable control over prostitutes;[114] police (or other local officials) also may abuse power if they have discretion in granting and revoking work permits;[115] and customers may refuse to use condoms (with the

---

107. *See, e.g., Human Rights: "Simple Human Respect,"* supra note 82, at 62–63 (Austria); *id.* at 70–72 (Germany); *Health: "Our First Concern,"* in VINDICATION, *supra* note 8, at 109, 114–15; Fitzpatrick, *supra* note 72, at 552; Cooper, *supra* note 106, at 110–12; Jody Freeman, *The Feminist Debate Over Prostitution Reform: Prostitutes' Rights Groups, Radical Feminists, and the (Im)possibility of Consent,* 5 BERKELEY WOMEN'S L.J. 75, 78 (1989–90). Health inspections are mandatory in Germany, Austria, Turkey, and Nevada. They are also mandatory in Thailand, where prostitution is illegal but officially tolerated. In the Netherlands there are no mandatory medical tests, but the government strongly encourages regular inspections. Erin McCormick, *Giving Green Light to Red Light District,* S.F. EXAMINER, Dec. 5, 1993, at A1, A12.

108. *See, e.g.,* Freeman, *supra* note 107, at 78 (*citing* Pasqua Scibelli, *Empowering Prostitutes: A Proposal for International Reform,* 10 HARV. WOMEN'S L.J. 117, 145–46 (1987)).

109. In Australia, brothels are also legal in Victoria and the Australian Capital Territory, and escort services are licensed in the Northern Territory and Victoria. Some public solicitation is permitted in New South Wales. Sullivan, *supra* note 28, at 4.

110. Freeman, *supra* note 107, at 78–79; Cooper, *supra* note 106, at 111; ROBERTS, *supra* note 8, at 292. Brothel-prostitution is also legal and regulated in Turkey; prostitutes in brothels are registered and tested regularly for AIDS. McCormick, *supra* note 107, at A12.

111. In Nevada, counties with populations under 400,000 may legalize brothels (but not "independent" prostitution). NEV. REV. STAT. ANN. §§ 201.354, 244.345 (Michie 1995).

112. Freeman, *supra* note 107, at 79; ROBERTS, *supra* note 8, at 292; HOBSON, *supra* note 76, at 227–28.

113. Freeman, *supra* note 107, at 79; Cooper, *supra* note 106, at 111; HOBSON, *supra* note 76, at 227–28; McCormick, *supra* note 107, at A12 (quoting prostitute who states that in Nevada brothels women often must work 12- to 14–hour days, are prohibited from leaving the premises, and cannot refuse customers who seem drunk or unruly).

114. Freeman, *supra* note 107, at 79.

115. *Id.*

brothel owner's consent or acquiescence) because they know the women are regularly tested for sexually-transmitted diseases.[116] Given the evidence that men are much more likely to infect women with HIV than women are to transmit it to men,[117] this refusal to use condoms places prostitutes at a much greater risk than are their customers. Prostitutes working in these jurisdictions are not adequately protected if brothel-keepers make undue demands or cut corners in search of higher profits, because there is no legal alternative to the brothel. Finally, in addition to the possibility of abuse under this system is the actuality of severe state supervision of myriad aspects of prostitutes' lives, both on and off the job.

A variant of this approach is employed in some areas of Europe, such as Germany, where prostitution and solicitation (whether in brothels or not) are permitted only in certain areas—a zoning or "red-light district" approach to prostitution control.[118] This approach often appeals to policymakers, who see in it a way to tolerate prostitution but keep it relatively out of sight to protect public sensibilities, generate tax revenue, save money on law enforcement, and eliminate the worst abuses associated with commercial sex.[119] Critics of zoning approaches note that these policies tend to ghettoize prostitution and thereby marginalize prostitutes.[120] Moreover, zoning and its attendant regulations—health inspections, registration or work permits, fingerprinting, etc.—can create the familiar problems of exploitation,

---

116. See infra note 124 (discussing German men's reluctance to use condoms, for similar reasons).

117. GENA COREA, THE INVISIBLE EPIDEMIC: THE STORY OF WOMEN AND AIDS 85, 122 (1992) (according to Dr. Helen Rodriquez, medical director of the New York State AIDS Institute in 1988–1989, the risk of male-to-female AIDS transmission through intercourse is 10 times the risk of female-to-male AIDS transmission through intercourse); Ines Rieder & Patricia Ruppelt, AIDS Realities and Facts, in AIDS: THE WOMEN 14, 16 (Ines Rieder & Patricia Ruppelt eds., 1988) (reporting that 30% of women with AIDS in the U.S. were infected through heterosexual intercourse, compared to 2% of men with AIDS); HUMAN RIGHTS WATCH, supra note 20, at 229 (reporting that "male-to-female transmission is at least three times as efficient as female-to-male transmission," citing AIDS IN THE WORLD at App. 6.1A (Jonathan Mann et al., eds., 1992)); Zoe Leonard & Polly Thistletwaite, Prostitution and HIV Infection, in The ACT UP/NEW YORK WOMEN & AIDS BOOK GROUP, WOMEN, AIDS, & ACTIVISM 177, 179 (1990); GAIL PHETERSON, THE PROSTITUTION PRISM 34 (1996).

118. See Cooper, supra note 106, at 110–11. The Netherlands also has a zoning system, but it is unusual because state intervention is minimal. See, e.g., HOBSON, supra note 76, at 225–26; infra notes 137–142 and accompanying text.

119. See Cooper, supra note 106, at 110; McCormick, supra note 107; HOBSON, supra note 76, at 225–26. See also Ron Curran, The New Prohibition: Legal Lovin', S.F. BAY GUARDIAN, Oct. 5, 1994, at 29 (reporting the attractions of legalized brothel prostitution to local officials, but downplaying the abuses athat occur under the Nevada system).

As David Richards has pointed out, localities could pass zoning laws governing only solicitation, only the act of prostitution, or both, depending on the public harm sought to be prevented. David A.J. Richards, Commercial Sex and the Rights of the Person: A Moral Argument for the Decriminalization of Prostitution, 127 U. PA. L. REV. 1195, 1283 n.439 (1979). This author is unaware of any jurisdictions in which zoning applies only to solicitation and not to prostitution itself.

120. See, e.g., Human Rights: "Simple Human Respect," supra note 82, at 71 (comments of Flori, Germany); Cooper, supra note 106, at 117.

coercion, and stigma.[121] In addition, despite the legality of prostitution and the requirement that prostitutes pay taxes, under this regulatory approach prostitutes are usually denied employment benefits such as health insurance, unemployment insurance, workers' compensation, and pensions.[122] In Germany, although prostitution is legal, the prostitution transaction is treated as an immoral contract and contract enforcement is impossible: neither prostitute nor client can receive compensation if defrauded.[123] Thus, like the Nevada brothel system (although to a lesser extent), existing zoning approaches also seem designed for the public and the customer rather than for the prostitute.[124]

Other jurisdictions—notably Canada, Britain, Italy, and France—do not criminalize prostitution *per se,* but instead attempt to control it through penalizing soliciting, advertising, procuring, brothel-keeping, and living off the earnings of a prostitute.[125] These regulatory schemes may reflect a sincere intent to stop singling out prostitutes and instead direct the criminal law at others who profit from prostitution, or they may reflect a desire simply to make prostitution less visible. In either case, the problems such schemes create are just as serious as those associated with outright criminalization. As many have observed, the decriminalization or legalization of prostitution itself is little help to prostitutes if almost all of its components are prohibited; prostitution becomes "illegal in all but name."[126] That is, because these regulations make prostitution nearly impossible even if technically legal, prostitutes still work in the shadow of the law with the same potential for

---

121. *See* Cooper, *supra* note 106, at 117; ROBERTS, *supra* note 8, at 292–93 (discussing Germany's "eros centers").

122. *See Human Rights: "Simple Human Respect," supra* note 82, at 63 (comments of Frau Eva) (denial of social benefits in Austria); *id.* at 72 (comments of Flori) (same, Germany); Cooper, *supra* note 106, at 110 (same, Germany).

123. *Human Rights: "Simple Human Respect," supra* note 82, at 73; Cooper, *supra* note 106, at 110–11.

124. For example, the German system, which includes regular mandatory medical inspections of prostitutes, allows men to believe that they will not contract diseases from prostitutes and increases the frequency of customers' refusal to use condoms. *See Health: "Our First Concern," supra* note 107, at 116; Cooper, *supra* note 106, at 111 n.80.

This phenomenon also occurs in areas where prostitution is officially illegal but is de facto tolerated, such as Thailand and India. Prostitution is illegal in Thailand but flourishes in bars, massage parlors, and sex clubs in certain tourist areas such as Bangkok and Pattaya. Officials have forced women working in those places to take HIV tests. ENLOE, *supra* note 19, at 37; HUMAN RIGHTS WATCH, *supra* note 20, at 227. According to prostitutes, the use of condoms is rare. *See, e.g.,* Pyne, *supra* note 35, at 220–23; HUMAN RIGHTS WATCH, *supra* note 39, at 68–69; McGirk, *Soiled, supra* note 17; *Children for Sale, supra* note 16.

125. Fitzpatrick, *supra* note 72, at 552; Freeman, *supra* note 107, at 79–83 (describing Canadian system enacted following the Fraser Report of 1985); Cooper, *supra* note 106, at 101 n.8, 110 (describing British system enacted following the Wolfendon Report of 1957); ROBERTS, *supra* note 8, at 285–89 (describing French, Italian and British systems enacted following World War II); Friedman, *supra* note 27, at 14 (describing system in India).

126. MCKEGANEY & BARNARD, *supra* note 85, at 102 (discussing Britain). *See also* Cooper, *supra* note 106, at 101 n.8 (discussing England); Freeman, *supra* note 107, at 81 (discussing Canada); ROBERTS, *supra* note 8, at 285 (discussing France).

violence and police abuse,[127] the same risks to loved ones,[128] and the same inability to create safer working conditions[129] as exist in jurisdictions where prostitution is fully illegal. As Jody Freeman argues, "[this] approach enables the government to feel permissive while still treating prostitutes like criminals."[130]

The German system, which is mainly known for its zoning of prostitution into certain districts, is actually a hybrid. Like Canada and Britain, Germany also generally forbids advertising for prostitution, exploitation and procuring, exploitative pimping (a more narrow kind of "living off the earnings" provision), and brothel-keeping (on the grounds that brothels tend to be repressive of liberty and mobility).[131] The French and British systems, as well, contain aspects of regulation. French prostitutes are required by police to register and carry "health cards,"[132] so that even though prostitution is legal, French prostitutes are still subject to police harassment and can find it difficult to leave prostitution or take a different job because it is hard for them to get their names removed from the prostitution registry.[133] British women are labelled as "common prostitutes" after two police warnings for solicitation.[134] This label can be used as evidence in court even if the woman has never been *convicted* of a prostitution-related offense, and even if she no longer works as a prostitute.[135] Obviously this practice can doom a woman's

---

127. For example, Italian prostitutes can be banned from public areas and have their drivers' licenses confiscated. ROBERTS, *supra* note 8, at 287. Canadian prostitutes without criminal records are often photographed by police and thus branded as prostitutes; police tell prospective employers that these women have worked in prostitution. *From the Floor, supra* note 105, at 116. *See also* Leite, *supra* note 86, at 291 (discussing abuses in Brazil, where prostitution itself is not illegal but its companion activities are).

128. In these jurisdictions, police can use the prohibition against living off the avails of prostitution to arrest landlords, spouses, lovers, children, parents, other family, friends, or others who share living quarters with or are supported by a prostitute. *See* ROBERTS, *supra* note 8, at 287–89; Freeman, *supra* note 107, at 81–82; *Human Rights: "Simple Human Respect," supra* note 82, at 76 (comments of Danny Cockerline, Canada); CORP (Canadian Organization for the Rights of Prostitutes), *Realistic Feminists, in* GOOD/BAD, *supra* note 8, at 204, 216.

129. As Freeman observes in reference to Canada, this regulatory system "keeps prostitutes on the streets" by criminalizing brothel-keeping and "isolates prostitutes by criminalizing communication and living off the avails," so that, for example, prostitutes cannot warn each other (even by gesture) about potentially dangerous customers nor work together to provide some measure of safety and security. Freeman, *supra* note 107, at 81–82. *See also* Scott, *supra* note 83, at 100–03; MCKEGANEY & BARNARD, *supra* note 85, at 102.

130. Freeman, *supra* note 107, at 82.

131. Cooper, *supra* note 106, at 110.

132. ROBERTS, *supra* note 8, at 285. (A "health card" provides proof that a prostitute has completed mandatory periodic medical inspections/testing.)

133. *Id.* at 286. Austrian prostitutes experience similar problems due to the prostitution registry. *Human Rights: "Simple Human Respect," supra* note 82, at 62 (comments of Frau Eva).

134. ROBERTS, *supra* note 8, at 288.

135. *Id.*

chances of prevailing in court—whether she is charged with soliciting, or seeking to retain custody of her children, or is the prime witness in a rape case.[136]

The Netherlands has the reputation of being the most tolerant country on the issue of prostitution.[137] Prostitution and brothels are legal in certain areas, although "third-party involvement" is illegal and street prostitution is generally banned.[138] While there appears to have been a period of relatively peaceful coexistence between prostitutes and their neighbors,[139] in recent years conflicts have increased among prostitutes, pimps, other neighborhood residents, police and other officials, and individuals involved in drug dealing and organized crime.[140] Prostitution remains a regulated profession in the Netherlands, with the result that street prostitutes, in particular, are marginalized and harassed[141] and all prostitutes are denied the social benefits provided to other workers (e.g., health insurance and pensions).[142]

Indeed, although the stigmatization of prostitutes is usually more severe in places where prostitution is illegal, stigmatization also occurs under existing systems of regulation. The legal response to the rape of prostitutes in the U.S., Australia, and the Netherlands makes this clear. As discussed above, American prostitutes report not being believed by police or taken seriously by judges when they report rapes. Unfortunately, similar attitudes exist even in jurisdictions where prostitution is legal. For example, in Australia, the Supreme Court of Victoria claimed in 1992 that "[p]rostitutes suffer little or no sense of shame or defilement when raped" and sentenced a prostitute's rapist to 30 months in prison; the maximum possible sentence was 30 years.[143] And in a Netherland prostitute-rape case, the judge said that "given [the survivor's] profession, the sexual abuse could not have made a deep impression on her."[144] Given these attitudes on the part of state officials, it becomes clear that neither criminalization nor regulation necessarily do much to protect the welfare of women who are prostitutes.

---

136. *See id.*

137. *See, e.g.,* HOBSON, *supra* note 76, at viii, 225–26; ROBERTS, *supra* note 8, at 293.

138. ROBERTS, *supra* note 8, at 293–94; HOBSON, *supra* note 76, at 225–26, 229–33.

139. HOBSON, *supra* note 76, at 225–26.

140. HOBSON, *supra* note 76, at 229–31; ROBERTS, *supra* note 8, at 293–94.

141. ROBERTS, *supra* note 8, at 294.

142. HOBSON, *supra* note 76, at 231.

143. The Queen v. Hakopian, Sup. Ct. of Vict. (Austl.), Dec. 11, 1991 (unreported), quoting The Queen v. Harris, Sup. Ct. of Vict. (Austl.), Aug. 11, 1981 (unreported). *See* Magazanik, *supra* note 88; Michael Magazanik, *Australia: Court Upholds Prostitute Rape Ruling,* THE AGE (Melbourne, Austl.), Jan. 3, 1992, *available in* LEXIS, Aust Library, Auspub File; Drogin, *supra* note 88; McKEGANEY & BARNARD, *supra* note 85, at 80. Similarly, in 1990, a convicted rapist in Australia was sentenced to 18 months in prison for raping and assaulting a prostitute; focusing on the absence of payment as the central crime (fraud), rather than the use of force and the absence of consent, the judge reasoned that "the offense of rape on this occasion savored more of the offense of dishonesty than of a sexual offense." Magazanik, *supra* note 88; Drogin, *supra* note 88.

144. Pheterson, *supra* note 87, at 225 (citing Leidsch Dagblad, *Buitenlust, Officier: Verkrachting Doet Prostituee Minder,* Diemen, Oct. 9, 1985).

Both the "containment" approach (limiting legal prostitution to brothels or to red-light districts) and the criminalization of companion activities to prostitution, if implemented carefully, could be improvements over outright criminalization. However, the continued stigmatization and victimization of prostitutes in places where prostitution is regulated suggests that these approaches are not enough to improve prostitute welfare significantly. Moreover, these approaches remain paternalistic: prostitution is still treated as a social problem requiring special policies, and prostitutes are still people in need of protection and perhaps reform.[145]

THE RIGHT TO BE A PROSTITUTE?

Whether one views prostitution as respectable work or as a vocation inherently harmful to its practitioners and/or to women as a class, criminalization is the worst choice of possible social responses. Consider, first, the expense. In 1983, 30 percent of the Wandsworth, England, police spent their time enforcing prostitution laws.[146] In 1988, the city of Toronto, Ontario, Canada, spent $6.3 million fighting prostitution.[147] San Francisco, California, police make approximately 3,000 prostitution arrests per year.[148] The cost to San Francisco in criminal justice-related expenses of each individual arrest can be as high as $2,000,[149] resulting in an estimated toll of $3 to $7 million per year.[150] Such large commitments of monetary and human resources might seem disproportionate even if the criminal law were successful in controlling prostitution, but it is not. San Francisco police arrested the same prostitute 52 times in a three-month period during 1994—at a cost to the city of perhaps $100,000 or more.[151] Given the ineffectiveness (if not futility) of criminal sanctions, then, it is indisputable that these millions of dollars in public monies could be better spent.[152] In addition, "street sweeps" and other raids can have detrimental effects

---

145. Cooper, *supra* note 106, at 111 (discussing German attitudes toward prostitution, and recounting German court cases which have held that brothel owners are guilty of the crime of promoting prostitution if they provide overly-comfortable working conditions, because such conditions can encourage prostitutes to continue in prostitution). *See also infra* notes 215–226 and accompanying text.

146. ROBERTS, *supra* note 8, at 296 (citing English Collection of Prostitutes).

147. Freeman, *supra* note 107, at 82 (citing Wendy Dennis, *Street Fight*, TORONTO LIFE 85, 130 (Nov. 1988)).

148. Ron Curran, *The New Prohibition: Sex and Politics*, S.F. BAY GUARDIAN, Oct. 5, 1994, at 25.

149. *Id.* at 25 (*citing* Julie Pearl, *Note, The Highest Paying Customers: America's Cities and the Costs of Prostitution Control*, 38 HAST. L.J. 769 (1987)).

150. Curran, *supra* note 148, at 25; Martin Espinoza, *The New Prohibition: A Night of Vice*, S.F. BAY GUARDIAN, Oct. 5, 1994, at 22; Teri Goodson, *Why Legalizing Prostitution Makes Sense*, S.F. EXAMINER, Aug. 25, 1996, at B11.

151. Curran, *supra* note 148, at 25.

152. *See* Julie Pearl, *Note, The Highest Paying Customers: America's Cities and the Costs of Prostitution Control*, 38 HAST. L.J. 769, 784 (1987) (detailing costs of enforcing prostitution laws in 16 large American cities in terms of police, court and corrections administration, meager revenue (offset) generated by prostitution fines, and lost opportunities in fighting more serious and/or violent crime; noting that in at least two cities, increased police attention to prostitution was "accompanied by an increase

on local economies by withdrawing the money spent by prostitutes and customers in local hotels, bars, coffee shops, convenience stores, restaurants, parking lots, and the like.[153]

Criminalization is based on the idea that prostitution represents deviant female sexuality warranting punishment, and fails to recognize that men are participants in prostitution transactions and, often, victimizers of prostitutes. (Recall that women are the ones overwhelmingly punished for prostitution, and usually already marginalized women at that.)[154] Criminalization prevents safer and more responsible practices on the part of prostitutes by forcing the business underground, which makes sharing health and safety information difficult and establishing standards of conduct

---

in assaultive crimes or a decrease in their clearance-by-arrest rate, or both'').

> As Pearl argues,
> All factors considered, prostitution laws clearly represent lost opportunities for the protection of society against other crimes. An unacceptably large amount of assaultive crime goes undeterred and unpunished, and the criminal justice resources currently devoted to prostitution control are sufficiently significant to have an impact on law enforcement efforts against those other crimes.

Id. at 785. As a Memphis vice lieutenant commented to Pearl in regard to prostitution arrests, ''The girls are back on the street before we are. We get paid by the hour, so we don't mind much, but if this were a business, we'd be bankrupt.'' *Id.* at 781 (citation omitted).

153. ROBERTS, *supra* note 8, at 296 (quoting Bernard Cohen's research on street prostitution in New York in the 1970s).

The criminalization of prostitution has other serious collateral effects as well, many of them unintended. For example, the United States passed the White Slave Traffic Act (commonly known as the Mann Act) in 1910 in an attempt to repress a perceived epidemic in international forced prostitution (then called ''white slavery''). White-Slave Traffic (Mann) Act, ch. 395, 36 Stat. 825–27 (1910). The Act prohibited the interstate transportation of women and girls for immoral purposes. It was used not only to prosecute those involved in forced prostitution, but also to persecute myriad others, including African-American men who dated white women, and individuals ''who espoused unpopular political beliefs.'' DAVID J. LANGUM, CROSSING OVER THE LINE: LEGISLATING MORALITY AND THE MANN ACT 9 (1994). The Act has been modified over the years, but has never been repealed. *Id.* at 3.

Even as applied only to prostitutes, the criminal law is enforced unfairly. In the United States, street prostitutes are a minority of all prostitutes. Alexander, *supra* note 73, at 189; Cooper, *supra* note 106, at 100 (citing Alexander, *supra* note 73, and J. DECKER, PROSTITUTION: REGULATION AND CONTROL (1979)); Beth Bergman, *AIDS, Prostitution, and the Use of Historical Stereotypes to Legislate Sexuality,* 21 J. MARSHALL L. REV. 777, 783 n.29 (1988) (citing NATIONAL TASK FORCE ON PROSTITUTION, SUMMARY OF DATA ON PROSTITUTES AND AIDS (1987)); Lynn Hampton, *Hookers with AIDS—The Search, in* AIDS: THE WOMEN, *supra* note 117, at 162; FRENCH, *supra* note 73, at 149; RHODE, *supra* note 73, at 261; FLOWERS, *supra* note 73, at 126. Yet street prostitutes in the U.S. represent 90% of those arrested for prostitution. FRENCH, *supra* note 73, at 149; ROBERTS, *supra* note 8, at 295; RHODE, *supra* note 73, at 261; Alexander, *supra* note 73, at 196. Class bias in the United States is compounded by racial bias: observers estimate that women of color represent 40% of street prostitutes, 55% of arrests, and 85% of those sentenced to jail. RHODE, *supra* note 73, at 261; Alexander, *supra* note 73, at 197. *See also* ROBERTS, *supra* note 8, at 295–96; West, *supra* note 98, at 282–83; Carole, *Interview with Barbara, supra* note 87, at 171; Freeman, *supra* note 107, at 108; Curran, *supra* note 148, at 26.

154. Only about 10% of prostitution arrests in the U.S. involve men (whether prostitutes or clients). *See supra* note 73. Similar arrest patterns exist in other countries. *See, e.g.,* Barbara Sullivan, *Rethinking Prostitution, in* TRANSITIONS: NEW AUSTRALIAN FEMINISMS 184, 194 (B. Caine & R. Pringle eds., 1995) (women are vast majority of prostitution-related arrests and jailings in Australia). Arrest patterns for

impossible.[155] And, as discussed above, criminalization makes it easier for customers, police, and pimps to exploit prostitutes with impunity. These burdens are heaviest for women new to the business, and for women with little control over their working conditions (street workers and poor women, chemically-dependent prostitutes, and women working in prostitution because of threats and coercion).[156]

The remarkably similar abuse and exploitation experienced by prostitutes under a variety of legal regimes suggests that some underlying hostility toward prostitutes exists even in places with seemingly "progressive" policies; regulation of prostitution has not, to date, been much of an improvement over criminalization.[157] Regulation of prostitution appears to be based either on the idea that prostitutes need to be protected—that they are less able than other workers to take care of themselves—or on the idea that prostitution is detrimental to society and thus should not be allowed to flourish in a free market. However, the problems associated with regulation indicate that it protects neither the prostitute nor society adequately, because abuses continue to occur. Decriminalization is a better alternative than regulation because it gives prostitutes more choice and control in their work and reduces the problems of police and state abuse of discretion and violations of privacy. Consider state-sanctioned brothels, for example. The problems associated with brothels—ghettoization, stigma, and exploitation—would be considerably lessened if brothels were not the only legally-sanctioned arena for prostitution. If prostitutes had *legal* alternatives to working in brothels, many of the most serious problems would be ameliorated.[158] Studying the issue of prostitution, a special legislative committee in Canada stated:

> [I]t seems that those countries, the majority, which have ignored the importance of non-legal, social responses to prostitution have experienced less success in controlling prostitution than those, such as Sweden, Denmark and Holland, which have recognized the value of social strategies in changing attitudes and responding to the human problems associated with prostitution. . . . [T]here is no necessary correlation between the existence of harsh criminal law provisions and effective control of prostitution.[159]

For these reasons, the best alternative to criminalization is *de*criminalization, not legalization with its attendant state regulations.

---

prostitution in the United States demonstrate racial and class biases as well. *See supra* note 153.

    Of course, arresting more customers also can have detrimental effects on prostitutes, to the extent that arrests are publicized and drive away business for several weeks. Thus, while it is clearly unfair to place the burden and stigma of the criminal law solely on prostitutes themselves, to retain criminal prohibitions but focus enforcement on customers is only a minimal improvement from prostitutes' perspective.

155. Goodson, *supra* note 150, at B11.

156. *See id.*

157. *See* ROBERTS, *supra* note 8, at 295.

158. *See* Scarlot Harlot, *Whores Oppose Munipimp,* S.F. BAY GUARDIAN, Dec. 8, 1993, at 6; Richards, *supra* note 119, at 1284.

159. PORNOGRAPHY AND PROSTITUTION IN CANADA: REPORT OF THE SPECIAL COMMITTEE ON PORNOGRAPHY AND PROSTITUTION 507 (1985) (commonly known as the "Fraser Report"), *cited in* Freeman, *supra* note 107, at 81 n.34.

Prostitution may not be an ideal profession. Obviously, however, we do not live in an ideal world. The choices we make and the circumstances we face are constrained in many ways, as are the choices and circumstances of women who decide to enter prostitution.[160] Thus, if a woman decides that prostitution is her best choice for supporting herself,[161] feeding her family,[162] paying for expensive medical care,[163] enabling her to leave a bad relationship or family situation,[164] earning money to start a business[165] or pay for college,[166] for example, before condemning that choice we must seriously and realistically consider her alternatives, taking into account her social and geographic location, family history and present situation, educational and employment background and abilities, age, race, and other personal characteristics, and her subjective preferences.[167] In other words, we must respect her personhood and her exercise of her right to self-determination under nonideal conditions.[168] The Netherlands has taken just this position in a statement to the Economic and Social Council of the United Nations: "It follows from the right of self-determination . . . that [men and women are] at liberty to decide to act as a prostitute and allow another person to profit from his or her earnings."[169]

---

160. *See* CORP, *supra* note 128, at 207; Overall, *supra* note 2, at 712–13; *but see id.* at 711–12 (discussing the concept of "coercive offers" in the context of evaluating prostitution in the real world).

161. *See, e.g., Feminism: "Crunch Point," supra* note 102, at 161 (comments of Frau Eva); Carole, *Interview with Debra, supra* note 87, at 93, 95; McCormick, *supra* note 107, at A12.

162. *See, e.g.,* ROBERTS, *supra* note 8, at 327–28 (recounting women's stated motivations for entering prostitution, and noting that majority of prostitutes in western countries are mothers); Paola Tabet, *I'm the Meat, I'm the Knife: Sexual Service, Migration, and Repression in Some African Societies, in* VINDICATION, *supra* note 8, at 204, 217; Tracy Lea Landis, *When Colleen Needed a Job, in* SEX WORK, *supra* note 7, at 150, 150–51; Carole, *Interview with Barbara, supra* note 87, at 171.

163. *See, e.g.,* Sunny Carter, *A Most Useful Tool, in* SEX WORK, *supra* note 7, at 159 (author entered prostitution to pay for treatments for son's cystic fibrosis); McKEGANEY & BARNARD, *supra* note 85, at 24 (British woman entered prostitution to earn money to pay for an abortion).

164. *See* ODZER, *supra* note 13, at 302–03; Tabet, *supra* note 162, at 205, 208, 218.

165. *See, e.g.,* Tabet, *supra* note 162, at 218–19.

166. *See, e.g., Feminism: "Crunch Point," supra* note 102, at 168 (comments of Pieke Biermann, Germany); McCormick, *supra* note 107, at A12.

167. Pong, a Thai woman who had worked in rice fields and in the sex industry, told Cleo Odzer why she preferred sex work: "Rice boring. . . . Make love take three minute. Make rice take eleven hour in sun. Skin turn black; body have pain." ODZER, *supra* note 13, at 225.

Some might argue that Pong's preferences would be different if she had more information about the risk of disease or injury, or if she were better educated about the role of sexism and the sex industry in oppressing women. However, it is equally possible that with more information Pong would make the same choice, albeit more "knowingly," as other women have done. Certainly we should strive to be sure that *all* women have the information they need to make informed choices about the options they have. But at the same time we must respect the subjectivity and humanity of all women, which implies respecting their informed choices (in a highly imperfect world) even if we disagree with them.

168. *See* Overall, *supra* note 2, at 713.

169. U.N. Doc. E/1990/33 ¶ 20 (1990), *cited in* Fitzpatrick, *supra* note 72, at 569 n.177. *See also* U.N. Doc. E/1990/33 ¶¶ 18–60; Johannes C.J. Boutellier, *Prostitution, Criminal Law, and Morality in the Netherlands,* 15 CRIME, LAW & SOC. CHANGE 201 (1991), *cited in* Fitzpatrick, *supra* note 72, at 569 n.177.

Critics argue that this position amounts merely to an endorsement of liberal notions of individual free choice and privacy, and ignores the oppressive institutions, practices, expectations, and belief systems which shape and distort all women's "choices."[170] Contrary to such critics' assertions, however, the social, economic, and legal context figures prominently in many analyses leading to the conclusion that prostitution can be a rational choice under nonideal conditions. The structures and demands of global capitalism form or shape the conditions under which *all* people (and thus *all* women) work, as do relations of gender.[171] Women in *all* trades and occupations are exploited, specifically on account of their gender.[172] Those who distinguish between "voluntary" and "forced" prostitution are not suggesting that the choice to enter prostitution is made in a vacuum—quite the opposite. Economic and gender-based factors are extremely salient, both on the individual and the social level. Certainly the social, legal, and economic situation conditions whatever choice is made, and may extensively limit the range of options. But similarly situated individuals also *respond* to that situation in a variety of ways, some very self-consciously taking economic and gendered factors into account. As a means of earning a livelihood, "voluntary" prostitution is no more or less "forced" than other vocations—no one fully escapes her social environment, but no one is wholly determined by it.[173] Nor is prostitution necessarily exceptionally degrading, compared to the non-sex work that many women perform. As Heidi Tinsman explains:

> Women workers who make baseballs in Haiti have a two-year work-expectancy due to the crippling effects of their sewing activities. Garment workers in Mexico are paid below-subsistence wages that leave them unable to provide appropriate nutrition or healthcare for themselves and their families. Grape-pickers in Chile regularly give

---

Although space constraints prevent a full examination of this issue, it should be noted that the right of self-determination necessarily includes the right of sexual self-determination. Properly understood, the right of sexual self-determination includes not only freedom of choice regarding sexual practices and partners, but also a right to be free from discrimination, stigma, and other penalties based on those choices. As such, adult prostitutes' need for state recognition of the right of sexual self-determination is as great as it is for lesbians, gay men, bisexuals, transgendered people, and other sexual minorities. Recognition of a right to sexual self-determination for prostitutes would be best secured by decriminalization. The author thanks Mark Harris for bringing this issue to her attention.

170. This statement by Ninotchka Rosca is representative:

> "Voluntary" and "forced" . . . [are] . . . terms . . . which spring from a wilful isolation of prostitution from the rest of the economy, reducing it to an individual decision by an individual woman and then announcing that the most terrible thing about it is stigmatization. . . . As far as the [sex] industry goes, "voluntary" and "forced" are distinctions without meaning, labels without content.

Ninotchka Rosca, *Participant Observer,* WOMEN'S REVIEW OF BOOKS, Mar. 1995, at 17 (reviewing CLEO ODZER, PATPONG SISTERS (1994)). *See also* Wynter, *supra* note 10, at 266, 269; BARRY, *supra* note 9; DWORKIN, *supra* note 10, at 143, 181.

171. *See* Tinsman, *supra* note 7, at 242; Sullivan, *supra* note 154, at 193.

172. Tinsman, *supra* note 7, at 242, 247; Ann M. Lucas, The Dis(-)ease of Being a Woman: Rethinking Prostitution and Subordination (1997) (unpublished manuscript on file with author).

173. *Cf. supra* note 2 and accompanying text.

birth to deformed or dead babies as a result of exposure to high amounts of pesticides that have been used in the fields. Yet advocates for these women believe that the state and organized labor must act to improve work conditions, raise wages, and give workers greater power within decision-making processes. They do not call for the abolition of these specific types of employment. Why do they do so in the case of sex-work?[174]

In sum, then, the claim here is not that "voluntary prostitution" represents liberal (unconstrained) "free choice," but rather that it can represent *informed* and *rational* choice in a nonideal (constrained) world.[175] The choice is not necessarily an easy one—the work is still *work*, which can be tiring and dangerous, especially for women working on the streets—but it is still a choice.[176]

Even if prostitution can be voluntarily chosen, it may still be a bad choice. Critics charge that prostitution advocates are either deluding themselves about the reality of prostitution (the "false consciousness" line of argument),[177] or that they are insufficiently attentive to and concerned about the "macro" effects of prostitution on women as a class.[178] While these arguments overlap significantly, basically the first argues that prostitution is degrading to prostitutes themselves: whatever

---

174. Tinsman, *supra* note 7, at 243.

175. *See* ROBERTS, *supra* note 8, at 332; Sullivan, *supra* note 28, at 13 (discussing the work of Alison Murray).

176. *See* ROBERTS, *supra* note 8, at 332.

177. *See, e.g.,* Wynter, *supra* note 10, at 266–70; BARRY, *supra* note 9, at 102, 114–17; BELL, *supra* note 6, at 123–31 (describing position of the group WHISPER); ROBERTS, *supra* note 8, at 341 (describing position of American feminist Kate Millett).

178. *See, e.g.,* Freeman, *supra* note 107, at 104; Shrage, *supra* note 11, at 357. Shrage's objection is representative:

> According to [Margo] St. James [a prostitutes' rights activist and former prostitute], while the commercial sex provider may be unconventional in her sexual behavior, her work may be performed with honesty and dignity. However, this defense is implausible since it ignores the possible adverse impact of her behavior on herself and others, and the fact that, by participating in prostitution, her behavior does little to subvert the cultural principles that make her work harmful.

Id. Although it is beyond the scope of this discussion to explore these charges in depth, Shrage appears to misunderstand St. James' argument. Rather than *ignore* the possible adverse effects of prostitution or its larger social significance, St. James and many other prostitutes' rights activists *deny* that these outcomes must occur: they argue that prostitution can indeed subvert rigid gender norms and thus that prostitutes' behavior can benefit themselves and others. *See* St. James, *supra* note 8, at 81, 82, 84. *See also* Lucas, *supra* note 172; Alexander, *supra* note 73, at 184; Tabet, *supra* note 162, at 219–20, 222.

Unlike many other scholars, however, Shrage does recognize that alternatives to her interpretation are at least theoretically possible:

> [T]he political alternatives of reformation and abolition are not mutually exclusive: if prostitution were sufficiently transformed to make it completely nonoppressive to women, though commercial transactions involving sex might still exist, prostitution as we know it would not.

Shrage, *supra* note 11, at 359.

their subjective experience tells them, prostitutes are in reality involved in a system of degradation and sexual slavery. By implication, this system is also harmful to non-prostitute women, because no woman is truly free if other women are enslaved—societies that tolerate or promote sexual slavery and degradation do not respect women's personhood and result in social orders in which women are second-class citizens (at best), subject to discrimination, harassment, denials of human rights, and other forms of oppression in all walks of life—but the focus of this argument is on the harm of prostitution to prostitutes themselves.

The second argument does not necessarily claim that prostitutes are uniquely oppressed; the emphasis here is on the harm to women as a whole that occurs when some women's sexuality is commodified. In this line of argument, the fact that some women sell sex creates a climate in which commodified sexuality is normalized, with the result that all women may be seen as commodified sexual objects, not persons,[179] or even that all *human* sexuality is cheapened, robbed of its potential to play a meaningful role in human actualization and self-development.[180] Obviously, the problems created by commodification apply to prostitutes as well as to others, and the problems may be even worse for prostitutes since the association between sex and monetary exchange is most socially prominent in their case, but this argument focuses mainly on the social effects of prostitution, not its individual effects.

The problem with the false consciousness argument[181] is not simply that it posits an outsider's evaluation as superior to that of some of the affected individuals, or even that it insists on a universal ("essentialist") position on a given issue rather than a relativistic one. Although these moves can be problematic, they are not always wrong. (If they were, we could not take a moral position for or against anything unless those involved agreed with us.) Rather, what is wrong with the false consciousness argument in this case is that it is a superficial conclusion based on partial (biased) information. For the reasons discussed briefly above, given what we know about the variety of constraints facing women from *all* walks of life, given the variety of viewpoints of women in the sex industry, and given what we can imagine as alternatives to the current situations of prostitutes, the false consciousness argument is a morally and intellectually inferior one. As Christine Overall says,

---

179. *See* CAROLE PATEMAN, THE SEXUAL CONTRACT (1988). *See also* UNESCO & COALITION AGAINST TRAFFICKING IN WOMEN, THE PENN STATE REPORT: REPORT OF AN INTERNATIONAL MEETING OF EXPERTS ON SEXUAL EXPLOITATION, VIOLENCE AND PROSTITUTION 7 (1992), *cited in* Fitzpatrick, *supra* note 72, at 553 & n.175; Committee on the Elimination of Discrimination Against Women, *General Recommendation No. 19,* U.N. Doc. CEDAW/C/1992/L.1/Add.15 at ¶ 19, Note 3 (1992), *cited in* Fitzpatrick, *supra* note 72, at 569 n.176.

180. *See, e.g.,* Margaret Jane Radin, *Market-Inalienability,* 100 HARV. L. REV. 1849 (1987). Note that Radin might see the use of "cheapened" and "robbed" to explain the results of commodification as a good example of how our thinking about sexuality is affected when sex is for sale on the market.

181. Also called "the brainwash theory," *see* Overall, *supra* note 2, at 713 (citing Gayle Rubin).

[S]ome credence must be given to women when they speak from their own experience, . . . women who say they choose to engage in activities that I personally find bizarre or repugnant cannot merely be dismissed as having "false consciousness." I am not willing to assume a more privileged view of their circumstances and motivation, not willing to claim that they are all deluded. Some sex workers (perhaps most) appear to have little or no choice about their work; but some do have alternatives, are explicitly conscious of them, and deliberately choose prostitution.[182]

Moreover, rejecting the false consciousness argument need not lead to a pro-prostitution position; rather, objections to the practice and the institution simply must be based on more sound grounds (e.g., material and/or symbolic harm to women as a class, or the commodification of human sexuality).[183]

Prostitutes' rights groups argue that prostitution can be dignified, respectable employment, and that the problems associated with prostitution are the result of harsh legal provisions, overly moralistic social attitudes toward non-marital and commercial sex, and the concomitant stigmatization of "sexual deviance." In other words, these advocates insist that there is nothing *inherently* wrong with prostitution: what is wrong with it is a direct result of social attitudes and punitive policies. Danger, abuse, coercion, injury, and lack of control are not necessary components of prostitution, nor are they problems unique to prostitution (or even to paid work, as many women also suffer these harms at home).[184] Moreover, although prostitutes are usually stigmatized in their own communities, the profession may nonetheless enable them to escape repressive cultural norms governing gender, and gain autonomy in their lives and independence in thought and action.[185]

Analyses of prostitution in settings radically different from our own, but nonetheless patriarchal and capitalist, enable us to envision these possibilities more

---

182. Overall, *supra* note 2, at 713. *See also* SHRAGE, *supra* note 6, at 78–79 (noting that feminist criticism of minority sexual practices such as sado-masochism, cross-generational sex, bathhouse sex, prostitution, and pornography use often "perpetuate the stigmatization of social minorities such as gays and lesbians, women of color, and working class women" due to insufficient social analysis).

183. Laurie Shrage apparently takes this latter position: she argues that although commercialized sex is not necessarily or inherently degrading to women, in the present social and cultural context it represents and reinforces beliefs, values, and practices that further women's oppression and in this way is harmful both to prostitutes themselves and to all other women. *See* Shrage, *supra* note 11, at 349, 351–52.

184. *See, e.g.,* Overall, *supra* note 2, at 711, 714, 716; Tinsman, *supra* note 7, at 243 (quoted *supra* text accompanying note 174).

185. Sukanya Hantrakul, *Prostitution in Thailand,* paper presented at the Women in Asia Workshop, Monash University, Melbourne, Australia, July 22–24, 1983, *cited in* ODZER, *supra* note 13, at 133; Lucas, *supra* note 172. *See also* ODZER, *supra* note 13, at 18, 66, 70, 78, 273, 302–03, 309.

The arguments of prostitutes' rights groups should be understood to apply to voluntary, adult prostitution, and not to forced or child prostitution. *See, e.g.,* International Committee for Prostitutes' Rights, *World Charter for Prostitutes' Rights, February 1985, in* VINDICATION, *supra* note 8, at 40, 40–42 [hereinafter *World Charter*]; International Committee for Prostitutes' Rights, *Statement on Prostitution and Human Rights, in* VINDICATION, *supra* note 8, at 103, 103–08; International Committee for Prostitutes' Rights, *Statement on Prostitution and Feminism, in* VINDICATION, *supra* note 8, at 192, 192–97.

clearly and thus buttress some of the claims of prostitutes' rights advocates. For example, Luise White's work on prostitution in colonial Nairobi shows that, in Laurie Shrage's words, "the commercialization of sex here did not create a distinct, especially harsh and socially stigmatizing form of labor exploitation."[186] Instead, according to White and Shrage, prostitution served as a (proscribed) substitute for marriage for working class, migrant male laborers who could not afford to maintain families and households in the city and so purchased sex, companionship, cooking, and cleaning on a more temporary basis from prostitutes. In this colonial context, prostitution did not impose a particular stigma on women. As there were no pimps, women earned money through relatively stable relationships with migrant workers, and often used that money to purchase property, support family farms, or acquire livestock. These women often legally married former clients—additional evidence of the relative lack of stigma.

The problem with the second ("macro") critique of prostitution is that it tends to over-emphasize the coherence of prostitution as an oppressive institution, thereby overlooking or discounting instances, practices, and settings within the institution that contain the potential to transform its social meaning. In addition, an over-emphasis on the social and "macro" effects of prostitution can "underline[ ] the general perception that prostitutes are to be considered in terms of their impact on others," rather than as human beings with valid needs and interests of their own.[187]

The relevance of these views is not just intellectual or philosophical but practical. For example, those who oppose prostitution as a practice and an institution but favor decriminalization as an immediate strategy to alleviate certain problems are likely to propose solutions that have unwanted consequences for prostitutes. The legal reforms in Canada discussed above demonstrate this outcome: although one prominent motivation for the reforms decriminalizing prostitution was to improve the lives of prostitutes, discomfort with prostitution itself led to other "reforms" intended to prevent the proliferation and entrenchment of the sex industry, such as the bans on soliciting, advertising, and living off the avails, which made it nearly impossible for prostitutes legally to engage in prostitution.[188] Similarly, the view that prostitution involves the sale of self—that is, that prostitution is or is like sexual slavery—contributes to the abuse and stigmatization of prostitutes.[189] For

---

186. SHRAGE, *supra* note 6, at 109 (discussing LUISE WHITE, THE COMFORTS OF HOME: PROSTITUTION IN COLONIAL NAIROBI (1990)).

187. MCKEGANEY & BARNARD, *supra* note 85, at 99 (observing that their research with prostitutes probably would not have been funded were there no concern about the role of prostitution in spreading HIV).

188. *See supra* notes 125–130 and accompanying text. *See also* Sullivan, *supra* note 154, at 188 (describing tension in feminist approaches to prostitution that favor decriminalization but simultaneously see prostitution as exploitative and thus as a practice which the state should not endorse by, for example, licensing brothels or permitting advertising).

189. Sullivan, *supra* note 154, at 189–90; ROBERTS, *supra* note 8, at 342–43. In reality, prostitution sometimes functions in the opposite way. African "women . . . sometimes buy their freedom [from husbands] by repaying the brideprice which ties them to marriage with the money earned as prostitutes." Tabet, *supra* note 162, at 213 (citations omitted).

these reasons, the debates about the social and individual significance of prostitution cannot simply be put to one side: decisions must be reached about the desired role and status of prostitution in society in order to develop social policies regarding prostitution, even ''short-term'' policies, that have any chance of being effective. As Barbara Sullivan insightfully observes, ''[f]eminist efforts to intervene in and change the present practice of prostitution could place their emphasis on contesting dominant cultural meanings of prostitution (as 'sale of self') and bringing marginalised discourse, about prostitutes as rebels and empowered women, into the mainstream.''[190]

Finally, in deciding which policy approach toward prostitution is most appropriate for achieving any social goal, the broader context in which prostitution occurs must be kept in the foreground. That is, whether one favors the eventual ''withering away'' of the institution of prostitution or favors institutional reform that succeeds in creating ''sound'' prostitution, the factors that contribute to the supply of and demand for prostitution should be central in one's analysis. With few exceptions worldwide, prostitution is one of the most (if not *the* most) lucrative professions open to women, especially women of lower socio-economic standing.[191] As such, prostitution is one of the few means for many women to gain economic and social independence.[192] As Cynthia Enloe has said in regard to the Philippines:

> [T]he lack of the substantial resources it takes to offer prostitutes realistic job alternatives has been frustrating. Learning handicrafts may provide a woman working in [prostitution] with a new sense of confidence or self-worth, but it doesn't pay the rent or support a child. 'When it comes to income-generating alternatives, we don't think we offer anything because we are up against so much. Economically we cannot give them anything.'[193]

Thus, if the goal is the withering away of prostitution, society must address the factors that make it an attractive option for many women; prostitution is the symptom of the problem, not the root of it.[194] As such, for the most part reforms should

---

190. Sullivan, *supra* note 154, at 190.

191. *See, e.g.,* Demleitner, *supra* note 19, at 187; Sullivan, *supra* note 28, at 15; Aihwa Ong, *Industrialization and Prostitution in Southeast Asia,* SOUTHEAST ASIA CHRONICLE, Jan. 1985, at 96, *cited in* Odzer, *supra* note 13, at 159; ODZER, *supra* note 13, at 273; Robinson, *supra* note 6, at 180, 184; ROBERTS, *supra* note 8, at 326–29; PATEMAN, *supra* note 179, at 194–95.

192. *See* Cooper, *supra* note 106, at 109; ODZER, *supra* note 13, at 273; ROBERTS, *supra* note 8, at 342.

193. ENLOE, *supra* note 19, at 39 (quoting Liza Maza & Cath Jackson, *When the Revolution Came,* 14 TROUBLE & STRIFE 19, 19–22 (Autumn 1988)).

194. The eventual withering away of prostitution, if it is to occur at all, will occur only when prostitution is no longer an attractive option to women. The use of the law, criminal or civil, to further this outcome by making prostitution less attractive to women has not succeeded and will not succeed in the future in eliminating voluntary prostitution. Nor, by itself, will it succeed in eliminating forced and child prostitution. Rather, efforts should be focused on improving all women's social, cultural, and economic standing and on bringing prostitution above ground, so that its real benefits and/or harms to communities and individuals can be more fully understood.

be directed away from the practice of prostitution itself and more toward its anteced-ents. However, because such reforms will take significant time to become effective, more immediately there should also be legal reforms designed to improve the lives of the human beings who work in prostitution.

If the goal is the creation of sound prostitution, these same legal and social reforms would be sufficient in themselves. In undertaking this task, the opinions of those currently working in the sex industry must be taken seriously.[195] Many prostitutes' rights groups argue that prostitution should be decriminalized, and prostitutes allowed to work, organize, advertise, and receive employment benefits.[196] The European Parliament also favors decriminalization and equal rights for prosti-tutes.[197]

If decriminalization and not legalization is the best approach, as it appears to be, then there must be a "right" of sorts to be a prostitute. This right would be a qualified one, limited to adults voluntarily choosing the profession. Individuals should not be penalized for voluntarily exercising this right or for having exercised it in the past; nor should their other civil liberties, civil rights, and human rights be abrogated because of their decision to engage in prostitution. In other words, then, prostitutes' equal rights to police protection, to recourse for harassment and/ or discrimination, and to universal social benefits should not be denied on account of their status. The decision to leave prostitution should be as unconstrained as the decision to enter prostitution, with no penalties or disincentives imposed on leav-ing.[198] "Maximising the information and resources available to workers in the sex

---

195. Like other advocacy groups, prostitutes' rights groups may differ as to the best policy approach. Thus, for example, while the majority of prostitutes' rights groups appear to favor decriminalization as the best strategy, a few favor legalization (i.e., some form of state regulation) in order better to secure social welfare benefits. In cases such as this, the ultimate decision should be based on a fair assessment of local working conditions, problems, and needs; political will and leadership; public support; feasibil-ity; and ease of reform if the chosen policy does not work as intended.

196. *See, e.g., World Charter, supra* note 185; *COYOTE/National Task Force on Prostitution, in* SEX WORK, *supra* note 7, at 290, 290; International Committee for Prostitutes' Rights, *supra* note 8, at 308–21; Freeman, *supra* note 107, at 83–84; McCormick, *supra* note 107, at A12.

197. In 1986, the European Parliament included the following language in a resolution aimed at eliminat-ing violence against women:

In view of the existence of prostitution the European Parliament calls on the national authori-ties in the Member States to take the necessary legal steps:

a)   to decriminalize the exercise of this profession;

b)   to guarantee prostitutes the rights enjoyed by other citizens;

c)   to protect the independence, health and safety of those exercising this profession;

d)   to reinforce measures which may be taken against those responsible for duress or violence towards prostitutes . . .;

e)   to support prostitutes' self-help groups and to require police and judicial authorities to provide better protection for prostitutes who wish to lodge complaints.

International Committee for Prostitutes' Rights, *International Committee for Prostitutes' Rights World Charter and World Whores' Congress Statements, in* SEX WORK, *supra* note 7, at 305, 317.

198. *See supra* notes 127, 133, 134 and accompanying text.

industry will tend to enhance their agency and contractual capacity. This is, however, a very different and more limited sort of agency than that which is claimed by the autonomous, liberal individual.''[199] In other words, while dignifying the decisions of those women who choose prostitution, the right to be a prostitute is no substitute for concurrently offering women *more, better, and different* choices.

CONCLUSION: STRATEGIES FOR THE FUTURE

For the reasons stated above, the best approach to prostitution policy in the future should be a combination of immediate legal reforms with longer-term legal and social reform. These short and longer-term goals can be conceptualized as a strategy of "harm minimization," in which the present-day life circumstances of prostitutes are improved through decriminalization and respect for civil and human rights, along with a sustained attempt to provide all women with more resources, choices, and information.

The immediate goal should be the decriminalization of prostitution. Decriminalization would not mean that prostitutes could practice their profession recklessly or irresponsibly; like everyone else, prostitutes could still be held liable in appropriate cases for violating criminal laws regarding fraud, nuisance, indecency, disorderly conduct, and disturbing the peace.[200] With decriminalization, prostitute abuse by pimps,[201] customers, and police would likely decrease, because there would be less reason for prostitutes to fear calling the police and a legal environment less conducive to police abuse: police would no longer have the threat of arrest with which to exploit or harass prostitutes, and prostitutes' ability to seek redress for police abuses would improve. Customer misconduct also could be adequately controlled by enforcing existing criminal laws such as those against fraud, assault, battery, rape, and robbery.[202] And although progress is likely to be slow at this level, decriminalization might gradually work to reduce the automatic association of prostitution with deviance. Especially in combination with other social and attitudinal changes, prostitutes might begin to be recognized by some members of the public as workers with special knowledge and expertise.[203]

---

199. Sullivan, *supra* note 28, at 14.

200. Freeman, *supra* note 107, at 107; Cooper, *supra* note 106, at 117; Richards, *supra* note 119, at 1281.

201. As Nickie Roberts points out, much abuse of prostitutes by pimps should properly be characterized as domestic violence, rather than marked out as a separate kind of woman-battering by a specific kind of man against a specific kind of woman. ROBERTS, *supra* note 8, at 301. Labeling a relationship as pimp-prostitute marks it as economic, exploitative, and criminal regardless of its observable characteristics. When such a relationship involves violence it can be seen as worse than other violence against women because pimps are seen as exceptionally low forms of men, *id.*, or as less serious because prostitutes are seen as criminal and deviant women. Yet neither bias (against "pimps" or against "prostitutes") should affect the social and legal response to battery.

202. Cooper, *supra* note 106, at 117.

203. E.g., in the strengths and limitations of various "safer sex" practices. Sullivan, *supra* note 154, at 192. *See also* ROBERTS, *supra* note 8, at 356; Shrage, *supra* note 11, at 358.

As for longer-term reform, our goals should be twofold: increasing access to information so that choices can be more informed, and reducing or eliminating the constraints on choice such as poverty and discrimination.[204] Money currently used to enforce criminal laws or civil regulations regarding prostitution could instead be used to protect prostitutes' rights, to offer training, education, support, and/or information to prostitutes desiring to leave the profession, and to provide education and information to women and girls about the realities of prostitution (both positive and negative) and the alternatives available.[205]

Unions would be of great assistance to prostitutes in a regime of decriminalization, because such organizations would help prostitutes overcome the isolation that has been so much a part of their work in the past and enable them to work together to resist abuses by customers, pimps, and police.[206] Properly designed, unions should serve to empower prostitutes, equipping them to achieve many of the reforms they seek from within their own working structures rather than from without. Unionization is also very likely to further the perception of prostitution as *work*, which could both promote the drive for social benefits for prostitutes[207] and help improve prostitutes' public profile.

In regard to health and safety issues, decriminalization obviously would benefit both prostitutes and customers: with the individual prostitution contract no longer illegal, each party would be better able to ensure the other takes the necessary precautions, and would have some recourse if he or she did not.[208] In terms of public health concerns about sexually transmitted diseases, rather than single out prostitutes for mandatory medical testing, a better system of voluntary, free, and confidential treatment of sexually transmitted diseases should be put in place.[209]

---

204. Sullivan, *supra* note 28, at 13. Sound development programs, increasing the minimum wage, improving girls' education, and supporting women-owned and women-operated enterprises would help address women's poverty. *See, e.g.,* Freeman, *supra* note 107, at 108; *infra* notes 238–40 and accompanying text. Enforcing legal prohibitions against sex bias and developing programs to overcome social biases against women would help address the problem of discrimination. *See infra* notes 236–40 and accompanying text.

205. *Cf.* Freeman, *supra* note 107, at 108.

206. *See* Richards, *supra* note 119, at 1282. *Cf.* Torri Minton, *S.F. Sex Club Workers Vote on Union,* S.F. CHRONICLE, Aug. 31, 1996, at A17, A19 (for "exotic dancers," benefits of unionization could include regular work schedules, higher starting wages, grievance procedures, paid sick leave, an end to favoritism and bias in salary increases, and an end to one-way windows that enable customers to videotape dancers without dancers' consent).

207. *Cf.* Minton, *supra* note 206, at A19.

208. Of course, as prostitutes presently suffer the major brunt of criminal law enforcement, *see supra* notes 73, 154, the greatest benefit of decriminalization would be theirs, increasing their negotiating power and legal recourse *vis-à-vis* clients.

209. *See, e.g.,* HUMAN RIGHTS WATCH, A MODERN FORM OF SLAVERY: TRAFFICKING OF BURMESE WOMEN AND GIRLS INTO BROTHELS IN THAILAND 134 (1993) (noting consensus among public health experts that mandatory HIV testing is not effective in slowing the spread of the disease, *citing* UNITED NATIONS CENTER FOR HUMAN RIGHTS & WORLD HEALTH ORGANIZATION, REPORT OF AN INTERNATIONAL CONSULTATION ON AIDS AND HUMAN RIGHTS 15 (1991)); RANDY SHILTS, AND THE BAND PLAYED ON: POLITICS,

This treatment should be available to everyone on the same terms. Not only would this avoid the stigmatization of prostitutes as disease-carriers, but it would actually better serve the public health goals of disease containment and treatment by reaching more people in need. (Prostitutes are not the only nor even the majority of individuals with sexually transmitted diseases.) Obviously, police involvement would be unnecessary and counterproductive.

As argued earlier, in addition to improving the working conditions for women in prostitution, societies must simultaneously address the conditions under which women enter and remain in prostitution. Thus, there must be meaningful help and opportunities to leave the profession, with some protection from the stigma of past employment. Improved educational opportunities for girls would go far in improving their life circumstances, future earning potential, self-esteem, and ability to resist being pressured or coerced into prostitution. Indeed, "[e]fforts to increase girls' education may have the effect in many communities of raising girls' social status,"[210] making them less "expendable" to families and communities.

While improving the social status and life conditions of girls and women will contribute to a reduction in forced prostitution, more direct measures are also required. Some advocacy groups fighting forced prostitution in sex tourism have been promoting the concept of extraterritorial prosecution. Under such a scheme, the affluent countries from which most sex tourists originate pass laws criminalizing pedophilia or sexual exploitation[211] by their nationals no matter where such exploitation occurs. If some form of sexual abuse is reported and the nation in which the violation occurs cannot or will not prosecute, the offender's own government agrees to do so. Such laws have been passed in several countries,[212] and have met with some success.[213] However, these laws are not the full solution to forced prostitution in sex tourism. First, it can be exceptionally difficult to prosecute an individual for

PEOPLE, AND THE AIDS EPIDEMIC 587, 592 (1987) (recounting U.S. Surgeon General Everett Koop's conclusion that mandatory testing frightens away those most needing screening); International Committee for Prostitutes' Rights, *Statement on Prostitution and Health, in* VINDICATION, *supra* note 8, at 141, 142. *Cf.* Richards, *supra* note 119, at 1281 & n.429 (1979) (noting that treatment of venereal disease in England is voluntary, free, confidential, open to all, and lacks police involvement).

210. KURZ & PRATHER, *supra* note 15, at 60.

211. "Sexual exploitation" here refers to sexual activity between patrons and people the patron knows or should know are being held against their will, are being forced to have sex with strangers for money, are incapable of consenting to sexual activity due to age or other condition (mental impairment, judgment affected by drug or alcohol consumption, etc.), and the like. The actual wording of extraterritorial legislation differs from jurisdiction to jurisdiction.

212. These include Australia, Belgium, Denmark, Finland, France, Germany, Iceland, Norway, New Zealand, Sweden, Switzerland, and the United States. *See, e.g.,* Joy Copley, *Promoters of Child Sex Tours Could Face Prison,* THE DAILY TELEGRAPH (U.K.), Dec. 5, 1995, at 12.

213. *Activists Applaud Jailing of Germans for Sex Exploitation of Thai Children,* AGENCE FRANCE PRESSE, Nov. 28, 1996, *available in* LEXIS, News Library, Non-US File (eleven people have been arrested in Germany, Australia and Sweden under extraterritorial legislation covering child sex offenses; of these eleven, five were convicted, one was acquitted, and five cases were still pending in late 1996). Australia's law is reportedly the toughest, providing for up to 17 years' imprisonment, and the most actively enforced. Henley, *supra* note 15.

a crime committed abroad, particularly for evidentiary reasons (e.g., the difficulty and expense involved in obtaining reliable evidence and witness testimony, taking depositions, finding competent translators, and protecting the rights of both the accused and the victim).[214] Second, as mentioned above, the majority of patrons of prostitutes in sex-tourist areas are *not* foreign tourists, so prosecuting tourists in their home countries will not deter the majority of patrons from exploiting prostitutes. For these reasons, extraterritorial prosecution is more useful in drawing attention to the problem of forced prostitution, thereby creating publicity and pressure on all the governments involved to act, than it is in curbing the problem directly.

Scholars generally agree that existing international instruments addressing forced and child prostitution are inadequate and ineffective, for reasons of content and procedure as well as lack of government will.[215] One nongovernmental organization, the Coalition Against Trafficking in Women, hopes to secure international adoption of a Convention Against Sexual Exploitation, which it believes will cure many of the internal problems of existing international agreements and improve government accountability.[216] The draft convention states that "trafficking in women is sex discrimination" and "recognizes that all forms of discrimination against women are connected to women's sexual subordination [and] that prostitution is . . . a human rights violation."[217]

Despite the Coalition's beliefs, however, implementation of the Convention Against Sexual Exploitation and/or improved enforcement of the 1949 Convention for the Suppression of the Traffic in Persons and of the Exploitation of the Prostitution of Others[218] are the wrong approaches to the problem of forced and child

---

214. The accused, for example, may have the right to examine evidence and confront his/her accuser(s), rights that may be jeopardized by the logistics of extraterritorial prosecution. The defendant's right against self-incrimination or to assistance of counsel may not have been recognized by the jurisdiction in which the offense took place, complicating his/her own nation's prosecution of him/her for the offense.

The victim is often young, confused, and distraught, making the protection of his or her welfare difficult while proceeding with a sex crimes trial, given the need to ask personal and perhaps embarrassing questions and to subject the victim to cross-examination. Victims with conflicting loyalties, who fear dishonoring their families, or who are vulnerable to psychological or financial manipulation, may be especially reluctant to testify. The same factors may apply to witnesses. Even when victims are willing to testify, their testimony and demeanor may not seem credible because of cultural differences, embarrassment, shame, or conflicted feelings, making successful prosecution difficult. Finally, where victims or witnesses are homeless, it can be difficult for prosecutors to locate them (only the accused can be held pending trial). For a discussion of this last point, *see* Cameron W. Barr, *Thais Target World Trade in Child Sex,* THE CHRISTIAN SCIENCE MONITOR, Apr. 17, 1995, *available in* LEXIS, News Library, Majpap File.

215. *See, e.g.,* Demleitner, *supra* note 19; Toepfer & Wells, *supra* note 17; Sullivan, *supra* note 28, at 10, 17; KATHLEEN BARRY, THE PROSTITUTION OF SEXUALITY (1995).

216. *See* Sullivan, *supra* note 28, at 5; Toepfer & Wells, *supra* note 17, at 102–03. The Coalition was founded by Kathleen Barry, author of *Female Sexual Slavery, supra* note 9, and *The Prostitution of Sexuality, supra* note 215.

217. Toepfer & Wells, *supra* note 17, at 103. According to the Coalition, "'[l]egalized prostitution . . . 'is an open door for traffickers.'" Hornblower, *supra* note 38 (quoting Janice Raymond).

218. Dec. 2, 1949, *opened for signature* Mar. 21, 1950, 96 U.N.T.S. 272 (entered into force Jul. 25, 1951) [hereinafter 1949 Convention].

prostitution. Both documents define all prostitution, voluntary or involuntary, as a human rights violation. If prostitution violates human rights, the profession is necessarily illegitimate.[219] Regardless of drafters' intentions, in the real world it has always been a short step from treating prostitution as illegitimate to treating prostitutes as criminal and continuing to incarcerate them. Moreover, even if the conventions define all prostitutes as victims,[220] it is quite possible that prostitutes will continue to be arrested and jailed for their "protection."[221] Defining all prostitutes as victims in effect treats all prostitutes as persons unable to make informed decisions on their own behalf. In addition, defining prostitutes as victims also creates the possibility they will be subjected to social control mechanisms aimed at their "rehabilitation."[222] Rehabilitation provisions, in turn, can work a transformation in the status of the prostitute, as rehabilitation is usually provided to offenders, not victims.[223] Thus, in defining all prostitution as a human rights violation, these broadbrush approaches to forced and child prostitution risk perpetuating the marginalization and penalization of prostitutes themselves.[224] While it may seem possible for one to be both anti-prostitution and pro-prostitute, the association between prostitution and prostitutes is so acute that condemning one eventually results in general social condemnation of the other as well.[225] Thus, many activist groups

---

219. It has been argued that the 1949 Convention does not mandate the prohibition of prostitution. *See, e.g.,* Toepfer & Wells, *supra* note 17, at 96. However, the Convention seeks the "prevention" of prostitution (art. 16), penalizes prostitute-manager partnerships, even with the prostitute's consent (arts. 1, 2), and penalizes the "[e]xploit[ation of] the prostitution of another person, even with the consent of that person" (art. 1). This latter provision has been interpreted as prohibiting the "consumption" of prostitution. Toepfer & Wells, *supra* note 17, at 96. Prostitution cannot occur if there are no consumers (customers); thus, while the Convention does not seek to criminalize the *status* of prostitute, it does seem to seek the prohibition of prostitution itself. *But see* Demleitner, *supra* note 19, at 172, 176 n.76 (implying that the "exploitation of prostitution" can be understood to refer only to forced prostitution). Even if the Convention does not *require* the prohibition of prostitution, it does define prostitution as "incompatible with the dignity and worth of the human person," clearly *suggesting* that its elimination would be beneficial to human society. *See also supra* note 217 (Coalition Against Trafficking in Women's view of legalized prostitution).

220. The 1949 Convention is quite explicit in this regard, obliging states parties to take steps "for the prevention of prostitution and for the rehabilitation and social adjustment of the victims of prostitution." 1949 Convention, *supra* note 218, art. 16, 96 U.N.T.S. at 280. The draft Convention Against Sexual Exploitation also defines prostitutes as victims. Sullivan, *supra* note 28, at 5.

221. *See* HOBSON, *supra* note 76, at 222 (observing that "[s]ince policy makers continue to justify incarcerating juveniles and prostitutes as a measure for their protection, there is implicit danger in portraying prostitution as sexual slavery").

222. *Cf.* 1949 Convention, *supra* note 218, art. 16 (quoted *supra* note 220).

223. Demleitner, *supra* note 19, at 195.

224. There are other dangers inherent in these broad approaches as well. As Barbara Sullivan points out, the draft Convention requires that states parties not support development programs which "institutionalise sexual exploitation"; this requirement might prevent states from contributing to or accepting international aid programs developed to slow the spread of HIV/AIDS or assist people with AIDS. Sullivan, *supra* note 28, at 6.

225. *See* Sullivan, *supra* note 154, at 194–95; Sullivan, *supra* note 28, at 14 n.5 (arguing that the attempt to be anti-prostitution and pro-prostitute is "incoherent and politically unsustainable"); Demleitner, *supra* note 19, at 195; *supra* notes 57, 188–90 and accompanying text.

have opposed the introduction of the Convention Against Sexual Exploitation as it is currently envisioned.[226] Narrower and better focused undertakings are more appropriate and more likely to succeed without unintended side effects or counter-measures.

To begin to address the problem of forced and child prostitution, both immediate and long-term efforts are required. Respect for the human rights of all prostitutes, forced and voluntary, is paramount. As detailed above, respect for the dignity and humanity of prostitutes will lessen their marginalization, providing them with more effective measures to resist victimization, improve their working conditions, and/ or enable them to leave the profession, should they choose to do so. Better treatment of all prostitutes could, in combination with other measures, improve the life cir-cumstances of those in forced prostitution by improving the likelihood that officials will take their complaints seriously, that citizens will be concerned about their plight, and that effective legal recourse will be provided to address civil and human rights violations.

To respond to forced and child prostitution further, strict enforcement of laws against trafficking is required. This would involve monitoring borders, including inspections of vehicles as well as people.[227] In monitoring borders, however, care must be taken to ensure that border guards are properly trained and understand that the goal is not to prevent the *migration* of women, but rather to prevent the *traffick-ing* of women (i.e., migration involving force, coercion, or deception).[228] Local police in both sending and receiving areas should develop ways to track "fronts," such as employment centers, for prostitution trafficking and recruiting.[229] Officials involved in trafficking must be identified and prosecuted.[230] Abuses associated with forced prostitution, such as coerced marriage, debt bondage, rape, and illegal con-finement must also be prosecuted consistently.[231] Enforcement of statutory rape laws against brothels and customers would help address the problem of child prosti-tution.[232] Maintenance of a registry of missing persons in sending countries would

226. Examples include the Global Alliance Against Traffic in Women, the Network of Sex Work Projects (an international NGO funded by the World Health Organization), and the Scarlet Alliance (an Australian sex workers' lobby), among others. Sullivan, *supra* note 28, at 7–8.

227. *See, e.g.,* HUMAN RIGHTS WATCH, *supra* note 20, at 270; Demleitner, *supra* note 19, at 174.

228. Sullivan, *supra* note 28, at 7.

229. *See, e.g.,* HUMAN RIGHTS WATCH, *supra* note 20, at 270; Demleitner, *supra* note 19, at 174.

230. HUMAN RIGHTS WATCH, *supra* note 20, at 270–71.

231. *Id.* at 271–72.

232. *Id.* at 214, 218. Enforcement of laws against statutory rape and forced marriage would likely also contribute to decreasing the cultural tolerance of adult-child sexual liaisons; this cultural tolerance at present makes it more difficult to get police, government officials, and the general public to see child prostitution as a social problem. *See* Barr, *supra* note 214. Local tolerance of commercial sex involving children also contributes to the problem of international sex tourists' "geographic morality" ("the willingness to do something in a foreign land one wouldn't do at home"), *Saving Lost Childhoods, supra* note 17. *See also* Simons, *supra* note 15. Thus, a change in local attitudes should help make child prostitution less attractive to foreign tourists, by removing the convenient "cultural relativism" excuse for behavior. *See* Robinson, *supra* note 30.

help identify victims of trafficking, particularly if they are detained at border crossings or deported for immigration violations.[233] Finally, no penalties, direct or indirect, should be imposed on the victims of forced prostitution. Trafficking victims should not be arrested or prosecuted for engaging in offenses such as prostitution or illegal immigration, as their participation in these acts was obtained by force, fraud, or coercion. Indeed, the threat of arrest and imprisonment is used by traffickers to force victims to provide sexual services to customers; obviously, the state should not participate in, or even indirectly facilitate, such coercion.[234] Safe repatriation procedures should be provided to all victims of international trafficking who desire it. Those who prefer not to return to their countries of origin should be provided with alternatives such as refugee status, where appropriate, or some form of safe haven or legal residence.[235]

At the same time there must be more structural reforms to ameliorate the conditions under which forced and child prostitution flourish. For example, serious national and international programs are needed to eliminate as much police and governmental corruption as possible. Individuals and families at risk of becoming involved with traffickers should be provided information about the dangers of trafficking, about how to recognize traffickers, about women's and children's human rights to be free from torture, abuse, and involuntary servitude or imprisonment, and about forms of redress available to abducted individuals, whether abroad or at home.[236] Such information needs to be provided using media appropriate for the target population, taking into account its literacy rate and its access to different forms of information, such as workshops, street theater, posters, radio, or television.[237] On the national and international level, resources should be committed to identifying sound development practices that raise the standard of living and do not drive men or women away from their villages, nor force them to rely on their children as their sole source of income.[238] Finally, changes in cultural beliefs and practices that devalue females are essential. While this is a daunting task, inroads can be made by increasing girls' rate of education, which improves their self-esteem and leadership potential, raising their social status in the eyes of their communities.[239] For example, in one province of Thailand, a local organization identifies "at-risk" girls and sponsors them to attend school, while also working

---

233. *See, e.g.,* HUMAN RIGHTS WATCH, *supra* note 20, at 272.

234. *See, e.g., id.* at 259 (discussing Pakistani pimps' use of threats to force Bangladeshi trafficking victims to engage in prostitution; threats include reporting women as illegal immigrants or denouncing them under *Hudood* laws which prohibit non-marital sex and which carry penalties including long prison terms and extreme corporal punishment (stoning, flogging, and amputation, among others)).

235. Demleitner, *supra* note 19, at 179.

236. *See, e.g.,* HUMAN RIGHTS WATCH, *supra* note 20, at 270–71; Demleitner, *supra* note 19, at 174; *Children for Sale, supra* note 16.

237. *See, e.g.,* KURZ & PRATHER, *supra* note 15, at 62; HUMAN RIGHTS WATCH, *supra* note 20, at 270.

238. *See* Barr, *supra* note 40; *Children for Sale, supra* note 16.

239. KURZ & PRATHER, *supra* note 15, at 60. *See also* Barr, *supra* note 214; *Children for Sale, supra* note 16.

with parents and villages to overcome established patterns of village girls entering the sex industry.[240] International cooperation in emphasizing programs that improve women's status and autonomy can also assist the effort to effect cultural change.

Returning to the life circumstances of *all* prostitutes, a final point is in order: the decriminalization of prostitution and an improvement of prostitutes' social status would not benefit only prostitutes. Rather, these reforms would inure to the benefit of all women. Social or governmental tolerance of violence against prostitutes promotes the idea that some women deserve mistreatment because of their morality; from there, it is a small step to the view that because of their inherent potential to sin *all* women must be kept in line through force, or that all women's humanity is suspect and less deserving of protection. All women can be labelled as "whores" or "sluts" regardless of their (in)experience in prostitution; ending the division of women into "madonna" and "whore" categories benefits all women by reducing the coercion to be "good" or the punishment inflicted if one is "bad."[241]

---

240. Kurz & Prather, *supra* note 15, at 56; Barr, *supra* note 40.

241. Roberts, *supra* note 8, at 357–58; Pheterson, *supra* note 87; Lucas, *supra* note 172.

INDEX

Private sector factor, 128
Right of women to participate in decision making, 127
Universality vs cultural relativity, 130
Women's diversity, 129
BIODIVERSITY, 476
BUDDHISM, 645
Meiji Civil Code, 546
Political activity and, 546
Religious fundamentalism, 543–546
Religious-legal doctrine, 544–546

CAME (Conference of Inter-Allied Ministers of Education), 404
CBO (Community-based organizations), 484
CEDAW (Committee on the Elimination of Discrimination Against Women, xix, xxv, 120, 182, 275–277
Culture and, 641
Education and, 420, 423, 424
Employment,367, 382, 383, 401
Trafficking in women and, 348–350
Women's Convention, 641
CESCR (Committee on Economic, Social and Cultural Rights), 420CHR (UN Commission on Human Rights), 405
Education and, 418 *et seq*
CHR (Committee on Human Rights),421
CHRISTIANITY, 645
Falwell, Jerry and, 547, 551
Political activity and, 551, 552
Religious fundamentalism and, 547–552
Religious-legal doctrine, 548–551
CIM (Inter-American Commission for Women), 252
CIVIL RIGHTS ACT (1964), 260 *et seq.*
COMMON ABUSES AGAINST WOMEN, 139–176
Conclusion, 175, 176
Gender discrimination and , 162–171
See also GENDER DISCRIMINATION AND SEXUAL HARASSMENT
Introduction, 139–141
Prostitution, 171–175
See also PROSTITUTION
Violence against women, 141–162, 177–217
See also VIOLENCE AGAINST WOMEN
Violence in the workplace, 257–285
See also WORKPLACE, VIOLENCE IN

CONVENTION ON THE ELIMINATION OF ALL FORMS OF DISCRIMINATION AGAINST WOMEN
Emergence of women's rights and, 4
Environment and, 470–472
CONVENTION O THE RIGHTS OF THE CHILD, 351, 352, 642
Children's Convention, 351
CRC (Committee on the Rights of the Child), 352
Education and, 420 *et seq.*
CSD (Commission on Sustainable Development), 476
CSW (Commission on the Status of Women), xxv, 249, 405
Education and, 418
CULTURE, 623–650
Bride price and dowry, 634–636
Cross-cultural dialogue necessary, 647
Cultural identity, 625, 626
Cultural rights, 625–628
Eating disorders
Anorexia, 639
In U.S. thinness is a virtue, 639
Education, access to, 633
Female infanticide and selective abortion, 632
Freedom of expression, necessity of, 647
Genital mutilation, 637, 638
Harmful traditional practices, 630–641
Cases overcoming, 648–650
Health, 637
Impediments to change, 644–647
Acceptance of male culture, 645
Lack of acknowledgment of prejudicial practices, 645
Legal systems a problem, 646, 647
Western culture, bias against, 646
Inheritance or levirate, 636, 637
International instruments, 641–644
See also specific topics
Introduction, 623, 624
Legitimacy of norms, 628—630
Marriage, male preferences in, 634
Child marriage, 636
Pregnancy, early adolescent, 638, 639
Psychological factors, 631, 632
Rape and judicial inequality, 640
Son preference, 630, 631